HANDBOOK OF AUTOMATED REASONING

VOLUME II

HANDBOOK OF AUTOMATED REASONING

VOLUME II

Editors

Alan Robinson

and

Andrei Voronkov

ELSEVIER
AMSTERDAM · LONDON · NEW YORK
OXFORD · PARIS · SHANNON · TOKYO

THE MIT PRESS
CAMBRIDGE, MASSACHUSETTS

ELSEVIER B.V.
Radarweg 29
P.O. Box 211, 1000 AE
Amsterdam, The Netherlands

ELSEVIER Inc.
525 B Street
Suite 1900, San Diego
CA 92101-4495, USA

ELSEVIER Ltd
The Boulevard
Langford Lane, Kidlington,
Oxford OX5 1GB, UK

ELSEVIER Ltd
84 Theobalds Road
London WC1X 8RR
UK

First edition 2001
Reprinted 2006

British Library Cataloguing in Publication Data
A catalogue record is available from the British Library.

Library of Congress Control Number 2001090840

ISBN: 0-444-50812-0 (Volume II)
ISBN: 0-444-50813-9 (Set of Vols I and II)

∞ The paper used in this publication meets the requirements of ANSI/NISO Z39.48-1992 (Permanence of Paper).
Transferred to digital print 2007

Preface

Automated reasoning has matured into one of the most advanced areas of computer science. During the half-century since the pioneering publications of the 1950s, significant progress has been achieved both in its theory and practice, culminating in a completely automatic solution of the Robbins Problem by the theorem prover EQP implemented by Bill McCune. This problem in algebra had remained open for over 50 years despite repeated attempts of mathematicians to solve it.

Several theoretical results, ideas, and techniques contributed to the Robbins Problem solution. We mention only a few: equational unification, and in particular AC-unification (Chapter 8 of this Handbook), completion procedures and notions of redundancy (Chapters 2 and 7), the basic strategy (Chapter 7), and term indexing (Chapter 26).

This Handbook presents overviews of the fundamental notions, techniques, ideas, and methods developed and used in automated reasoning and its applications, which are used in many areas of computer science, including software and hardware verification, logic and functional programming, formal methods, knowledge representation, deductive databases, and artificial intelligence..

The idea of making this Handbook originated during a visit by the first editor to the Computing Science Department of Uppsala University in 1996, where the second editor was working at the time. The idea was then presented at the Dagstuhl workshop on Deduction in 1997, after which the work began. It has taken four years to put together all the papers in their current form. Over 2000 email messages were exchanged between the editors and the authors.

The material included in the Handbook is intended to cover most of the areas in automated deduction, from theory to implementation. Nearly every chapter can be used as a basis for an undergraduate or a postgraduate course. In fact, some of them have already been so used. The chapters contain both basic and advanced material. It was deliberately decided also to include material that bridges the gap between the traditional automated reasoning (as presented at the CADE conferences) and related areas. Examples are model checking (Chapter 24), nonmonotonic reasoning (Chapter 19), numerical constraints (Chapter 12), description logics (Chapter 23), and implementation of declarative programming languages (Chapter 26).

To help the reader navigate through a large amount of material in the Handbook, the global concept index is provided at the end. It contains references to the pages containing the main notions and concepts introduced in different chapters.

The structure of the book is as follows.

Part I consists of a single chapter: an overview of the *early history* of automated deduction by Martin Davis.

Part II presents reasoning methods in *first-order logic*. Two most popular methods: *resolution* and *semantic tableaux* are discussed in Chapters 2 by Leo Bachmair and Harald Ganzinger and 3 by Reiner Hähnle. Nearly all existing implementations of first-order theorem provers are based on variants of one of these methods. The *inverse method*, both for classical and nonclassical logics, is introduced in Chapter 4 by Anatoli Degtyarev and Andrei Voronkov. Systems implementing first-order logic usually transform the goal formula into a clausal normal form. Chapters 5 by Matthias Baaz, Uwe Egly, and Alexander Leitsch, and 6 by Andreas Nonnengart and Christoph Weidenbach, discuss *short normal forms*, both from the theoretical and practical viewpoints.

Part III is dedicated to *equality and other built-in theories*. The first four chapters of this part discuss reasoning with equality and related subjects: Chapter 7 by Robert Nieuwenhuis and Albert Rubio deals with *paramodulation-based reasoning*, Chapter 8 by Franz Baader and Wayne Snyder presents *unification theory*, Chapter 9 by Nachum Dershowitz and David A. Plaisted overviews *rewriting*, and Chapter 10 by Anatoli Degtyarev and Andrei Voronkov discusses *equality reasoning in tableau-based and sequent-based calculi*. The next two chapters treat other important theories: Chapter 11 by Shang-Ching Chou and Xiao-Shan Gao presents *theorem proving in geometry*, while Chapter 12 by Alexander Bockmayr and Volker Weispfenning overviews methods of *solving numerical constraints*.

Part IV discusses methods of automated reasoning using *induction*. Chapter 13 by Alan Bundy gives a general introduction to induction, then Chapter 14 by Hubert Comon presents the so-called *"inductionless induction"* where induction is implemented using equational reasoning.

Part V discusses higher-order logic, which is used in a number of automatic and interactive proof-development systems. This part begins with two fundamental Chapters 15 by Peter Andrews and 16 by Gilles Dowek introducing, respectively, *classical type theory* and *higher-order unification*. The next two Chapters 17 by Frank Pfenning, and 18 by Henk Barendregt and Herman Geuvers discuss variants of higher-order logic used in two kinds of interactive systems: *logical frameworks* and *proof-assistants* using dependent type systems.

Part VI presents automated reasoning in *nonclassical logics*. Chapter 19 by Jürgen Dix, Ulrich Furbach, and Ilkka Niemelä is devoted to *nonmonotonic reasoning*, while Chapter 20 by Matthias Baaz, Christian G. Fermüller, and Gernot Salzer to reasoning in *many-valued logics*. The next two Chapters 21 by Hans Jürgen Ohlbach, Andreas Nonnengart, Maarten de Rijke, and Dov M. Gabbay, and 22 by Arild Waaler discuss reasoning methods for a wide range of logics whose semantics is characterized by the possible worlds semantics, for example, intuitionistic and modal logics. They discuss *translation into first-order classical logic* and the *connection method*,

respectively. Also highly relevant to reasoning in nonclassical logics are Chapters 4
and 23 put in other Parts of this Handbook.

Part VII deals with *decidable classes and model building.* The first two chapters
concern two areas that have only recently emerged and which are now used in a
number of applications: Chapter 24 by Edmund M. Clarke and Bernd-Holger Schlingloff gives an overview of *model checking,* Chapter 23 by Diego Calvanese, Giuseppe
De Giacomo, Maurizio Lenzerini, and Daniele Nardi discusses reasoning in expressive *description logics.* In Chapter 25 Christian G. Fermüller, Alexander Leitsch,
Ullrich Hustadt, and Tanel Tammet present *resolution-based decision procedures* for
various classes of first-order formulas.

Part VIII deals with *implementation-related* questions. In Chapter 26 R. Sekar,
I.V. Ramakrishnan, and Andrei Voronkov give an overview of *term indexing* used in
implementing not only first-order theorem provers but also logic and functional programming languages. The next two Chapters 27 by Christoph Weidenbach and 28 by
Reinhold Letz and Gernot Stenz discuss implementation of, respectively, *resolution-
based* and *model elimination-based theorem provers.*

The Web page

> http://www.cs.man.ac.uk/~voronkov/handbook-ar/index.html

contains further material related to this book. All comments and corrections should
be sent to the second editor by email voronkov@cs.man.ac.uk or v@ronkov.com.

Alan Robinson, Andrei Voronkov
Greenfield and Manchester, 14 February 2001.

Contents

Volume 1

Part I History

Part II Classical Logic

Part III   Equality and other theories

Part IV   Induction

Concept Index   963

Volume 2

Part V Higher-order logic and logical frameworks

Part VI   Nonclassical logics

CHAPTER 19. NONMONOTONIC REASONING: TOWARDS EFFICIENT
CALCULI AND IMPLEMENTATIONS   1241
Jürgen Dix, Ulrich Furbach, and Ilkka Niemelä

CHAPTER 20. AUTOMATED DEDUCTION FOR MANY-VALUED LOGICS   1355
Matthias Baaz, Christian G. Fermüller, and Gernot Salzer

CHAPTER 21. ENCODING TWO-VALUED NONCLASSICAL LOGICS
IN CLASSICAL LOGIC   1403
*Hans Jürgen Ohlbach, Andreas Nonnengart, Maarten de Rijke, and
Dov M. Gabbay*

CHAPTER 22. CONNECTIONS IN NONCLASSICAL LOGICS   1487
Arild Waaler

Part VII   Decidable classes and model building

CHAPTER 23. REASONING IN EXPRESSIVE DESCRIPTION LOGICS   1581
Diego Calvanese, Giuseppe De Giacomo, Maurizio Lenzerini, and
Daniele Nardi

CHAPTER 24. MODEL CHECKING   1635
Edmund M. Clarke and Bernd-Holger Schlingloff

CHAPTER 25. RESOLUTION DECISION PROCEDURES   1791
Christian G. Fermüller, Alexander Leitsch, Ullrich Hustadt, and
Tanel Tammet

Part VIII   Implementation

CHAPTER 26. TERM INDEXING   1853
R. Sekar, I.V. Ramakrishnan, and Andrei Voronkov

List of contributors

This list contains the contributors of this Handbook with the corresponding chapter numbers.

List of second readers

This list contains the second readers of this Handbook with the corresponding chapter numbers.

Part V

Higher-order logic and logical frameworks

CHAPTER 15

Classical Type Theory

Peter B. Andrews

SECOND READERS: John Harrison and Michael Kohlhase.

Contents

HANDBOOK OF AUTOMATED REASONING
Edited by Alan Robinson and Andrei Voronkov
© 2001 Elsevier Science Publishers B.V. All rights reserved

Preface

Type theory, otherwise known as higher-order logic, is an extension of first-order logic which has significant advantages over first-order logic for formalizing certain domains, such as parts of mathematics and specifications for hardware and software. A number of versions of type theory have been developed. Constructive type theory is discussed in [Barendregt and Geuvers 2001] (Chapter 18 of this Handbook). In this chapter we provide an introduction to classical type theory, and discuss methods for automatically proving theorems of classical type theory.[1]

Of course, one can also construct computer-checked proofs in a mode which is primarily interactive. Since for certain applications (such as those noted in [Gordon 1986]) it is very important to obtain computer-checked proofs, and not currently practical to obtain them automatically, this is a very important activity. Interactive theorem proving can be partially automated through the use of *tactics*. We refer the interested reader to [Barendregt and Geuvers 2001, Pfenning 2001] (Chapters 18 of and 17 of this Handbook).

1. Introduction to type theory

We start with a brief introduction to type theory. Additional information may be obtained from sources such as [Andrews 1986, Hindley 1997, Leivant 1994, van Benthem and Doets 1983, Shapiro 1991, Wolfram 1993], and references cited therein.

1.1. Early versions of type theory

Type theory is a language for formalizing mathematics which was invented by Bertrand Russell [Russell 1908]. In [Whitehead and Russell 1910–1913], he and Alfred North Whitehead demonstrated that various fundamental parts of mathematics could indeed be formalized in this system. Russell was concerned with providing secure foundations for mathematics, and wished to enforce the *vicious-circle principle* that no totality can contain members defined in terms of itself. He therefore originally advocated using what is now called *ramified* type theory,[2] which is still important in various proof-theoretic studies (such as [Feferman 1964]) of the consistency of restricted portions of mathematics. However, ramified type theory did not prove adequate for formalizing mathematics in general, and we shall devote our attention to a simplified version of it which is known as *simple* type theory.

Type theory includes first-order logic, so type theory is also known as higher-order logic. In order to explain the features which distinguish higher-order logic from first-order logic, we shall first present a system $\mathcal{F}^\omega$ of type theory which is similar to Russell's simple type theory and is an obvious extension of first-order logic, and then present a modern system of type theory incorporating λ-notation.

---

[1] Substantial portions of this chapter are taken from cited references, particularly [Andrews 1986, Andrews 1989, Andrews, Bishop, Issar, Nesmith, Pfenning and Xi 1996].

[2] See [Hazen 1983] or [Church 1956, p. 347] for more details.

Each entity is regarded as being of some *type*, such as the type of natural numbers or the type of sets of vertices in a graph. We use *type symbols* to denote types. We let α, β, γ, etc. (but not o or $\imath$), stand for arbitrary type symbols.

The *type symbols* of $\mathcal{F}^\omega$ and their *orders* are defined inductively as follows:

(a) $\imath$ is a type symbol (denoting the type of individuals) of order 0.

(b) o is a type symbol (denoting the type of truth values) of order 1.

(c) If $\tau_1, \ldots, \tau_n$ are type symbols (with $n \geq 1$), then $(\tau_1 \ldots \tau_n)$ is a type symbol (denoting the type of n-ary relations with arguments of types $\tau_1, \ldots, \tau_n$, respectively), and its order is $1+$ the maximum of the orders of $\tau_1, \ldots, \tau_n$.

The primitive symbols of $\mathcal{F}^\omega$ are the improper symbols $[,]$, $\sim$, $\vee$, and $\forall$, a denumerable list of variables of each type, and (optionally) constants of certain types. Variables of type o are called *propositional variables*, and variables of type ι are called *individual variables*. Type symbols are attached to variables and constants as subscripts to indicate their types. However, these type symbols are often omitted when it is clear from the context what they must be; one often indicates the type of a variable only at its first occurrence in a formula or a paragraph.

The *wffs* of $\mathcal{F}^\omega$ are defined inductively as follows:

(a) Every propositional variable or constant is a wff.

(b) If $\mathbf{u}_{\tau_1 \ldots \tau_n}, \mathbf{v}^1_{\tau_1}, \ldots, \mathbf{v}^n_{\tau_n}$ are variables or constants of the types indicated by their subscripts, then $\mathbf{u}_{(\tau_1 \ldots \tau_n)} \mathbf{v}^1_{\tau_1} \cdots \mathbf{v}^n_{\tau_n}$ is a wff.

(c) If $\mathbf{A}$ and $\mathbf{B}$ are wffs and $\mathbf{u}$ is a variable of any type, then $\sim \mathbf{A}$, $[\mathbf{A} \vee \mathbf{B}]$, and $\forall \mathbf{u}\, \mathbf{A}$ are wffs.

The *order* of a variable or constant is the order of its type symbol. For any positive integer m, the wffs of $2m$th-order logic are the wffs in which no variable or constant of order greater than m occurs, and the wffs of $(2m - 1)$th-order logic are the wffs of $2m$th-order logic in which no variable of order m is quantified. The formulation of first-order logic given here differs from other well known formulations in only trivial ways, except that many popular formulations of first-order logic also have function symbols.

Other connectives and quantifiers are defined in familiar ways, and equality can also be defined:

$[\mathbf{A} \wedge \mathbf{B}]$	stands for	$\sim [\sim \mathbf{A} \vee \sim \mathbf{B}]$
$[\mathbf{A} \supset \mathbf{B}]$	stands for	$[\sim \mathbf{A} \vee \mathbf{B}]$
$[\mathbf{A} \equiv \mathbf{B}]$	stands for	$[[\mathbf{A} \supset \mathbf{B}] \wedge [\mathbf{B} \supset \mathbf{A}]]$
$[\exists \mathbf{x}\, \mathbf{B}]$	stands for	$\sim \forall \mathbf{x} \sim \mathbf{B}$
$[\mathbf{x}_\tau = \mathbf{y}_\tau]$	stands for	$\forall z_{(\tau)} [z_{(\tau)} \mathbf{x}_\tau \supset z_{(\tau)} \mathbf{y}_\tau]$,

where $z_{(\tau)}$ is a variable of type (τ).

This is called the Leibniz definition of equality; it asserts that two entities are the same if every property of one is also a property of the other.

Throughout this chapter, we use Church's convention that a dot in a wff stands for a left bracket whose mate is as far to the right as is consistent with the pairing of brackets already present and with the formula being well-formed. Also, $\wedge$ binds more tightly than $\lor$, and $\lor$ binds more tightly than $\supset$, so $\mathbf{A} \supset \mathbf{B} \lor \mathbf{C} \land \mathbf{D}$ is an abbreviation for $[\mathbf{A} \supset [\mathbf{B} \lor [\mathbf{C} \land \mathbf{D}]]]$. Otherwise, brackets and parentheses are to be restored using the convention of association to the left. Brackets (and parentheses in type symbols) may be omitted when no ambiguity is thereby introduced. Boldface letters stand for arbitrary wffs or variables of the indicated type.

We also use Church's notations for substitutions: $S_{\mathbf{A}}^{\mathbf{x}} \mathbf{B}$ denotes the result of substituting $\mathbf{A}$ for $\mathbf{x}$ at *all* occurrences of $\mathbf{x}$ in $\mathbf{B}$, and $S_{.\mathbf{A}}^{\mathbf{x}} \mathbf{B}$ denotes the result of substituting $\mathbf{A}$ for $\mathbf{x}$ at all *free* occurrences of $\mathbf{x}$ in $\mathbf{B}$. Similarly, $S_{.\mathbf{A}^1...\mathbf{A}^n}^{\mathbf{x}^1...\mathbf{x}^n} \mathbf{B}$ denotes the result of simultaneously substituting $\mathbf{A}^i$ for $\mathbf{x}^i$ at all free occurrences of $\mathbf{x}^i$ in $\mathbf{B}$ for $1 \leq i \leq n$. (Terms such as *free* and *free for* are defined in [Andrews 1986].)

The rules of inference of $\mathcal{F}^\omega$ are:

(1) **Modus Ponens.** From $\mathbf{A}$ and $\mathbf{A} \supset \mathbf{B}$ to infer $\mathbf{B}$.

(2) **Generalization.** From $\mathbf{A}$ to infer $\forall \mathbf{x}\, \mathbf{A}$, where $\mathbf{x}$ is a variable of any type.

The axiom schemata of $\mathcal{F}^\omega$ are:

(1) $\mathbf{A} \lor \mathbf{A} \supset \mathbf{A}$

(2) $\mathbf{A} \supset .\, \mathbf{A} \lor \mathbf{B}$

(3) $\mathbf{A} \lor \mathbf{B} \supset .\, \mathbf{B} \lor \mathbf{A}$

(4) $\mathbf{A} \supset \mathbf{B} \supset .\, \mathbf{C} \lor \mathbf{A} \supset \mathbf{C} \lor \mathbf{B}$

(5) $\forall \mathbf{x}_\tau \mathbf{A} \supset S_{\mathbf{y}_\tau}^{\mathbf{x}_\tau} \mathbf{A}$, where $\mathbf{y}_\tau$ is a variable or constant of the same type as the variable $\mathbf{x}_\tau$, and $\mathbf{y}_\tau$ is free for $\mathbf{x}_\tau$ in $\mathbf{A}$.

(6) $\forall \mathbf{x}\, [\mathbf{A} \lor \mathbf{B}] \supset .\, \mathbf{A} \lor \forall \mathbf{x}\, \mathbf{B}$, where $\mathbf{x}$ is any variable not free in $\mathbf{A}$.

(7) **Comprehension Axioms:**

$\exists \mathbf{u}_o\, [\mathbf{u}_o \equiv \mathbf{A}]$, where $\mathbf{u}_o$ does not occur free in $\mathbf{A}$.

$\exists \mathbf{u}_{(\tau_1...\tau_n)} \forall \mathbf{v}_{\tau_1}^1 \ldots \forall \mathbf{v}_{\tau_n}^n\, [\mathbf{u}_{(\tau_1...\tau_n)} \mathbf{v}_{\tau_1}^1 \ldots \mathbf{v}_{\tau_n}^n \equiv \mathbf{A}]$, where $\mathbf{u}_{(\tau_1...\tau_n)}$ does not occur free in $\mathbf{A}$, and $\mathbf{v}_{\tau_1}^1, \ldots, \mathbf{v}_{\tau_n}^n$ are distinct variables.

(8) **Axioms of Extensionality:**

$[x_o \equiv y_o] \supset x_o = y_o$

$\forall w_{\tau_1}^1 \ldots \forall w_{\tau_n}^n\, [x_{(\tau_1...\tau_n)} w_{\tau_1}^1 \ldots w_{\tau_n}^n \equiv y_{(\tau_1...\tau_n)} w_{\tau_1}^1 \ldots w_{\tau_n}^n]$
$\qquad \supset x_{(\tau_1...\tau_n)} = y_{(\tau_1...\tau_n)}$

Note the principal features which are added to first-order logic in order to obtain this formulation of higher-order logic:

1. Variables of arbitrarily high orders.

2. Quantification on variables of all types.

3. Comprehension Axioms.

4. Axioms of Extensionality.

Of course, the Comprehension Axioms and Axioms of Extensionality cannot even be stated in pure first-order logic.

1.2. Type theory with λ-notation

While the system $\mathcal{F}^\omega$ defined in the preceding section can in principle express virtually all mathematical ideas, a richer formulation of type theory was introduced by

Church [1940]. This system, which is commonly referred to as *Church's type theory*, has notations much closer to those actually used by mathematicians, and in the practical sense it is a more useful language for expressing the ideas of mathematics and related disciplines. This richer formulation is obtained by adding the following features to the language:

1. Functions from objects of any type to any other type are permitted as primitive objects.

2. There is a simple notation for functions, sets, and relations defined by expressions of the language.

We shall present a system $\mathcal{C}$ of type theory which is essentially that introduced by Church, but without the Axioms of Infinity or Choice, and with a strong Axiom of Extensionality. We start with an informal discussion of the features which distinguish $\mathcal{C}$ from $\mathcal{F}^\omega$.

For all types α and β, there is a type $(\alpha\beta)$ of functions from elements of type β to elements of type α. (Of course, we are now giving the type symbol $(\alpha\beta)$ a different meaning from that used for the system $\mathcal{F}^\omega$.) Some authors write $(\beta \to \alpha)$ instead of $(\alpha\beta)$. It is easy to remember the meaning of the notation $(\beta \to \alpha)$, but when it is used in long wffs with many variables, the numerous arrows provide useless visual clutter, so we shall normally use Church's original $(\alpha\beta)$ notation, and occasionally use $(\beta \to \alpha)$ as an abbreviation for $(\alpha\beta)$.

Since values of functions can themselves be functions, there is no need to make special provision for functions of more than one argument. For example, consider the function $+$ which carries any pair of natural numbers to their sum. We may denote this function by $+_{((\sigma\sigma)\sigma)}$, where σ is the type of natural numbers. The result $\left[+_{((\sigma\sigma)\sigma)}x\right]$ of applying this function to a number x is the function which, when applied to any number y, gives the value $\left[\left[+_{((\sigma\sigma)\sigma)}x\right]y\right]$, which is ordinarily written as $x + y$.

A set or property can be represented by a function which maps elements to truth values, so that an element is in the set, or has the property, in question iff the function representing the set or property maps that element to truth. o is used again as the type of truth values, so any function of type $(o\alpha)$ may be regarded as a *set* of elements of type α. A function of type $((o\alpha)\beta)$ may be regarded as a binary relation between elements of type β and elements of type α.

Expressions of $\mathcal{C}$ which denote elements of type α are called *wffs* of type α. Thus, statements are wffs of type o.

The Comprehension Principle is still needed; for any wff $\mathbf{A}_o$ of type o in which $\mathbf{u}_{o\beta}$ does not occur free, $\exists \mathbf{u}_{o\beta} \forall \mathbf{v}_\beta [\mathbf{u}_{o\beta}\mathbf{v}_\beta \equiv \mathbf{A}_o]$ must be a theorem. Indeed, it is natural to extend the principle to assert the existence of functions as well as sets, and state it as follows: $\exists \mathbf{u}_{\alpha\beta} \forall \mathbf{v}_\beta [\mathbf{u}_{\alpha\beta}\mathbf{v}_\beta = \mathbf{A}_\alpha]$ for any wff $\mathbf{A}_\alpha$ of type α in which $\mathbf{u}_{\alpha\beta}$ is not free, where α and β are any type symbols.

The function $\mathbf{u}_{\alpha\beta}$ whose existence is thus asserted is denoted by $[\lambda \mathbf{v}_\beta \mathbf{A}_\alpha]$. Thus, $\lambda \mathbf{v}_\beta$ is a new variable-binder, like $\forall \mathbf{v}_\beta$ or $\exists \mathbf{v}_\beta$ (but with a quite different meaning, of course); λ is known as an *abstraction operator*. $[\lambda \mathbf{v}_\beta \mathbf{A}_\alpha]$ denotes the function whose value on any argument $\mathbf{v}_\beta$ is $\mathbf{A}_\alpha$, where $\mathbf{v}_\beta$ may occur free in $\mathbf{A}_\alpha$. For example,

$[\lambda n_\sigma . n_\sigma^2 + 3]$ denotes the function whose value on any natural number n is $n^2 + 3$. Hence when we apply this function to the number 5 we obtain $[\lambda n_\sigma . n_\sigma^2 + 3]\, 5 = 5^2 + 3 = 28$.

When written in terms of λ-notation, the Comprehension Principle becomes $\forall \mathbf{v}_\beta . [\lambda \mathbf{v}_\beta \mathbf{A}_\alpha]\, \mathbf{v}_\beta = \mathbf{A}_\alpha$. From this by universal instantiation we obtain

$[\lambda \mathbf{v}_\beta \mathbf{A}_\alpha]\, \mathbf{B}_\beta = \underset{\cdot \mathbf{B}_\beta}{S}{}^{\mathbf{v}_\beta} \mathbf{A}_\alpha$ (provided $\mathbf{B}_\beta$ is free for $\mathbf{v}_\beta$ in $\mathbf{A}_\alpha$), i.e., the result of applying the function $[\lambda \mathbf{v}_\beta \mathbf{A}_\alpha]$ to the argument $\mathbf{B}_\beta$ is $\underset{\cdot \mathbf{B}_\beta}{S}{}^{\mathbf{v}_\beta} \mathbf{A}_\alpha$. The process of replacing $[\lambda \mathbf{v}_\beta \mathbf{A}_\alpha]\, \mathbf{B}_\beta$ by $\underset{\cdot \mathbf{B}_\beta}{S}{}^{\mathbf{v}_\beta} \mathbf{A}_\alpha$ (or vice-versa) is known as λ-*conversion* . Of course, when $\mathbf{A}_o$ is a wff of type o, $[\lambda \mathbf{v}_\beta \mathbf{A}_o]$ denotes the set of all elements $\mathbf{v}_\beta$ (of type β) of which $\mathbf{A}_o$ is true; this set may also be denoted by $\{\mathbf{v}_\beta \mid \mathbf{A}_o\}$. In familiar set-theoretic notation, $[\lambda \mathbf{v}_\beta \mathbf{A}_o]\, \mathbf{B}_\beta = \underset{\cdot \mathbf{B}_\beta}{S}{}^{\mathbf{v}_\beta} \mathbf{A}_o$ would be written $\mathbf{B}_\beta \in \{\mathbf{v}_\beta \mid \mathbf{A}_o\} \equiv \underset{\cdot \mathbf{B}_\beta}{S}{}^{\mathbf{v}_\beta} \mathbf{A}_o$. (By the Axiom of Extensionality for truth values, when $\mathbf{C}_o$ and $\mathbf{D}_o$ are of type o, $\mathbf{C}_o \equiv \mathbf{D}_o$ is equivalent to $\mathbf{C}_o = \mathbf{D}_o$.)

Connectives and quantifiers need no longer be regarded as improper symbols, but can be assigned types and denoted by constants of these types. Negation has type (oo), since it maps truth values to truth values. Similarly, disjunction and conjunction (etc.) are binary functions from truth values to truth values, so they have type $((oo)o)$.

The statement $\forall \mathbf{x}_\alpha \mathbf{A}_o$ is true iff the set $[\lambda \mathbf{x}_\alpha \mathbf{A}_o]$ contains all elements of type α. A constant $\Pi_{o(o\alpha)}$ is introduced to denote that property of sets such that a set $s_{o\alpha}$ has the property $\Pi_{o(o\alpha)}$ iff $s_{o\alpha}$ contains all elements of type α. Thus, $\forall \mathbf{x}_\alpha \mathbf{A}_o$ can be defined to be an abbreviation for $\Pi_{o(o\alpha)} [\lambda \mathbf{x}_\alpha \mathbf{A}_o]$, so λ is the only variable-binder that is needed.

Now we can define the system $\mathcal{C}$.

The type symbols of $\mathcal{C}$ are defined inductively as follows:

1. ι is a type symbol (denoting the type of individuals).
2. o is a type symbol (denoting the type of truth values).
3. $(\alpha\beta)$ is a type symbol (denoting the type of functions from elements of type β to elements of type α).

The *primitive symbols* of $\mathcal{C}$ are the following:

1. *Improper symbols*: [ ] λ
2. For each type symbol α, a denumerable list of *variables* of type α:

$$f_\alpha \ g_\alpha \ h_\alpha \ \cdots \ x_\alpha \ y_\alpha \ z_\alpha \ f_\alpha^1 \ g_\alpha^1 \ \cdots \ z_\alpha^1 \ f_\alpha^2 \ \cdots$$

We shall write *variable$_\alpha$* as an abbreviation for *variable of type α*. We shall let $\mathbf{f}_\alpha, \mathbf{g}_\alpha, \cdots, \mathbf{x}_\alpha, \mathbf{y}_\alpha, \mathbf{z}_\alpha$, etc., stand for arbitrary variables$_\alpha$.

3. *Logical constants*: $\sim_{(oo)} \ \vee_{((oo)o)} \ \Pi_{(o(o\alpha))} \ \iota_{(\iota(o\iota))}$
4. In addition there may be other constants of various types, which we call *nonlogical constants* or *parameters*.

We write *wff$_\alpha$* as an abbreviation for *wff of type$_\alpha$*, and let $\mathbf{A}_\alpha$, $\mathbf{B}_\alpha$, $\mathbf{C}_\alpha$, etc., stand for arbitrary wffs$_\alpha$; these are defined inductively as follows:

1. A primitive variable or constant of type α is a wff$_\alpha$.
2. $[\mathbf{A}_{\alpha\beta}\mathbf{B}_\beta]$ is a wff$_\alpha$.
3. $[\lambda\mathbf{x}_\beta\mathbf{A}_\alpha]$ is a wff$_{(\alpha\beta)}$.

$[\mathbf{A}_{\alpha\beta}\mathbf{B}_\beta]$ denotes the value of the function denoted by $\mathbf{A}_{\alpha\beta}$ at the argument denoted by $\mathbf{B}_\beta$.

An occurrence of $\mathbf{x}_\alpha$ is *bound (free)* in $\mathbf{B}_\beta$ iff it is (is not) in a well-formed part of $\mathbf{B}_\beta$ of the form $[\lambda\mathbf{x}_\alpha\mathbf{C}_\delta]$. A wff is *closed* iff no variable occurs free in it. A *sentence* is a closed wff$_o$. $\mathbf{A}_\alpha$ is *free for* $\mathbf{x}_\alpha$ *in* $\mathbf{B}_\beta$ iff no free occurrence of $\mathbf{x}_\alpha$ in $\mathbf{B}_\beta$ is in a well-formed part of $\mathbf{B}_\beta$ of the form $[\lambda\mathbf{y}_\gamma\mathbf{C}_\delta]$ such that $\mathbf{y}_\gamma$ is a free variable of $\mathbf{A}_\alpha$.

Definitions and abbreviations:

1. $[\mathbf{A}_o \vee \mathbf{B}_o]$ stands for $[[\vee_{((oo)o)}\mathbf{A}_o]\mathbf{B}_o]$.
2. $[\mathbf{A}_o \supset \mathbf{B}_o]$ stands for $[[\sim_{oo}\mathbf{A}_o]\vee\mathbf{B}_o]$.
3. $[\forall\mathbf{x}_\alpha\mathbf{A}_o]$ stands for $[\Pi_{(o(o\alpha))}[\lambda\mathbf{x}_\alpha\mathbf{A}_o]]$.
4. Other propositional connectives, and the existential quantifier, are defined in familiar ways.
5. $\mathcal{Q}_{o\alpha\alpha}$ stands for $[\lambda x_\alpha \lambda y_\alpha \forall f_{o\alpha} \cdot f_{o\alpha}x_\alpha \supset f_{o\alpha}y_\alpha]$.
6. $[\mathbf{A}_\alpha = \mathbf{B}_\alpha]$ stands for $\mathcal{Q}_{o\alpha\alpha}\mathbf{A}_\alpha\mathbf{B}_\alpha$.
7. $\exists_1\mathbf{x}_\alpha\mathbf{A}_o$ stands for $[\lambda p_{o\alpha} \cdot \exists y_\alpha \cdot p_{o\alpha}y_\alpha \wedge \forall z_\alpha \cdot p_{o\alpha}z_\alpha \supset z_\alpha = y_\alpha][\lambda\mathbf{x}_\alpha\mathbf{A}_o]$.

Rules of inference of C:

1. *Alphabetic change of bound variables* (α-*conversion*). To replace any well-formed part $[\lambda\mathbf{x}_\beta\mathbf{A}_\alpha]$ of a wff by $\left[\lambda\mathbf{y}_\beta S_{\mathbf{y}_\beta}^{\mathbf{x}_\beta}\mathbf{A}_\alpha\right]$, provided that $\mathbf{y}_\beta$ does not occur in $\mathbf{A}_\alpha$ and $\mathbf{x}_\beta$ is not bound in $\mathbf{A}_\alpha$.
2. β-*contraction*. To replace any well-formed part $[[\lambda\mathbf{x}_\alpha\mathbf{B}_\beta]\mathbf{A}_\alpha]$ of a wff by $S_{\mathbf{A}_\alpha}^{\mathbf{x}_\alpha}\mathbf{B}_\beta$, provided that the bound variables of $\mathbf{B}_\beta$ are distinct both from $\mathbf{x}_\alpha$ and from the free variables of $\mathbf{A}_\alpha$.
3. β-*expansion*. To infer $\mathbf{C}$ from $\mathbf{D}$ if $\mathbf{D}$ can be inferred from $\mathbf{C}$ by a single application of β-contraction.
4. *Substitution.* From $\mathbf{F}_{o\alpha}\mathbf{x}_\alpha$, to infer $\mathbf{F}_{o\alpha}\mathbf{A}_\alpha$, provided that $\mathbf{x}_\alpha$ is not a free variable of $\mathbf{F}_{o\alpha}$.
5. *Modus Ponens.* From $[\mathbf{A}_o \supset \mathbf{B}_o]$ and $\mathbf{A}_o$, to infer $\mathbf{B}_o$.
6. *Generalization.* From $\mathbf{F}_{o\alpha}\mathbf{x}_\alpha$ to infer $\Pi_{o(o\alpha)}\mathbf{F}_{o\alpha}$, provided that $\mathbf{x}_\alpha$ is not a free variable of $\mathbf{F}_{o\alpha}$.

Remark. It can be proved that $\Pi_{o(o\alpha)}\mathbf{F}_{o\alpha}$ is equivalent to $\forall\mathbf{x}_\alpha\mathbf{F}_{o\alpha}\mathbf{x}_\alpha$ if $\mathbf{x}_\alpha$ is not free in $\mathbf{F}_{o\alpha}$.

Axioms of C:

(1) $p_o \vee p_o \supset p_o$
(2) $p_o \supset p_o \vee q_o$
(3) $p_o \vee q_o \supset q_o \vee p_o$
(4) $p_o \supset q_o \supset [r_o \vee p_o \supset r_o \vee q_o]$
(5^α) $\Pi_{o(o\alpha)}f_{o\alpha} \supset f_{o\alpha}x_\alpha$
(6^α) $\forall x_\alpha[p_o \vee f_{o\alpha}x_\alpha] \supset .p_o \vee \Pi_{o(o\alpha)}f_{o\alpha}$

(7) **Axioms of Extensionality:**

(7°) $[x_o \equiv y_o] \supset x_o = y_o$

$(7^{\alpha\beta})$ $\forall x_\beta [f_{\alpha\beta} x_\beta = g_{\alpha\beta} x_\beta] \supset f_{\alpha\beta} = g_{\alpha\beta}$

(8) **Axiom of Descriptions:**

$$\exists_1 y_\alpha p_{o\alpha} y_\alpha \supset p_{o\alpha} [\iota_{\alpha(o\alpha)} p_{o\alpha}]$$

The Axiom of Descriptions is needed to prove such theorems as

$\sim [x_\iota = y_\iota] \supset \exists f_{\iota\iota}.fx = a_\iota \wedge fy = b_\iota$

Rules of inference 1, 2, and 3 of C are called rules of λ-conversion. Wffs which can be converted to each other by a sequence of applications of these rules are said to be λ-*convertible* to each other. A wff is in β-*normal form* if no β-contractions can be performed on any wff obtained from it by zero or more α-conversions. λ-convertibility is an equivalence relation. From each equivalence class we choose a wff $\downarrow$ **A** in β-normal form which we designate as *the* β-*normal form* of any wff **A** in the equivalence class. We may sometimes speak of λ-normalizing a wff; this generally means the same thing as β-normalizing, but in some contexts λ-normalization also involves η-reductions; see [Dowek 2001] (Chapter 16 of this Handbook) for information about this.

We shall refer to the subsystem of C which is obtained by deleting Axioms (7°), $(7^{\alpha\beta})$, and (8) as $\mathcal{T}$. This subsystem may also be called *elementary type theory*, since $\mathcal{T}$ simply embodies the logic of propositional connectives, quantifiers, and λ-conversion in the context of type theory. Much of the work which has been done on automatic proof search in classical type theory thus far has actually been concerned with proving theorems of $\mathcal{T}$ rather than C.

The Comprehension Principle is easily derivable in $\mathcal{T}$, so it is not needed as an axiom.

An alternative formulation of Church's type theory, called $\mathcal{Q}_0$ in [Andrews 1986], takes the equality symbols $\mathcal{Q}_{o\alpha\alpha}$ as logical constants and defines $\sim_{(oo)}$, $\vee_{((oo)o)}$, and $\Pi_{(o(o\alpha))}$ in terms of these.

1.3. The Axiom of Choice and Skolemization

The Axiom of Choice says (in one formulation) that there is a function which chooses from each nonempty set a member of that set. In type theory this takes the form of an axiom schema, since the choice function must have a particular type. For each type symbol α, let AC^α be the wff

$$\exists j_{\alpha(o\alpha)} \forall p_{o\alpha} .\exists x_\alpha p_{o\alpha} x_\alpha \supset p_{o\alpha} \cdot j_{\alpha(o\alpha)} p_{o\alpha}$$

The set of all wffs AC^α is called the Axiom Schema of Choice. A slight variation of AC^α is

$$\forall p_{o\alpha} .\exists x_\alpha p_{o\alpha} x_\alpha \supset p_{o\alpha} \cdot \iota_{\alpha(o\alpha)} p_{o\alpha}$$

which we shall call ACD^α. Here we have introduced a constant $\iota_{\alpha(o\alpha)}$ to denote a choice function for type α. This extends the role of the description operator $\iota_{(\iota(o\iota))}$

so that it becomes a choice function. It is easy to see that ACD^ι implies the Axiom of Descriptions.

The Axiom of Choice is widely believed to be true in all standard models[3] of type theory, and it plays an essential role in many parts of mathematics, but traditionally it is not regarded as part of the underlying logic, but as an extra logical principle whose use deserves special note. There are many different formulations of the Axiom of Choice [Rubin and Rubin 1985], and the equivalences between these formulations provide nice challenges for higher-order theorem proving systems.

Thus, for certain purposes it is desirable to avoid building the Axiom of Choice, or some of its consequences, into the basic procedures used to prove theorems. In first-order logic there is no danger of doing this, since the Axiom of Choice cannot even be stated in pure first-order logic. However, in higher-order logic, casual treatment of Skolemization can permit derivation of the Axiom of Choice or some of its consequences.

If one is working in a refutational mode and wishes to Skolemize $\forall x_\alpha \exists y_\beta r_{o\beta\alpha} xy$, it is natural to choose a new function symbol $f_{\beta\alpha}$ and replace the above wff by $\forall x_\alpha r_{o\beta\alpha} x.f_{\beta\alpha} x$. However, if suitable precautions are not taken, $f_{\beta\alpha}$ may play the role of a choice function. Indeed, it is a theorem of $\mathcal{T}$ that

$$\forall r_{o\beta(o\beta)}[\forall x_{o\beta} \exists y_\beta rxy \supset \exists f_{\beta(o\beta)} \forall x.rx.fx] \supset AC^\beta$$

(Figure 3 contains a proof of this theorem, which we call X5310. We discuss it further in section 3.1.)

If one is not concerned about avoiding the Axiom of Choice, a very simple method of Skolemization is to introduce a new constant $c_{\beta(o\beta)}$ for each type symbol β, and let the Skolemized form of $\sim \Pi_{o(o\beta)} P_{o\beta}$ be $\sim P_{o\beta} [c_{\beta(o\beta)} P_{o\beta}]$. The Skolem term $[c_{\beta(o\beta)} P_{o\beta}]$ has the same free variables as $P_{o\beta}$. Thus, $\exists y_\beta R_{o\beta\alpha} x_\alpha y_\beta$, which is actually $\sim \Pi_{o(o\beta)} [\lambda y_\beta \sim R_{o\beta\alpha} x_\alpha y_\beta]$, has Skolemized form

$$\sim [\lambda y_\beta \sim R_{o\beta\alpha} x_\alpha y_\beta] [c_{\beta(o\beta)}.\lambda y_\beta \sim R_{o\beta\alpha} x_\alpha y_\beta],$$

which λ-converts to

$$\sim\sim R_{o\beta\alpha} x_\alpha [c_{\beta(o\beta)}.\lambda y_\beta \sim R_{o\beta\alpha} x_\alpha y_\beta].$$

Note that if $R_{o\beta\alpha}$ is a constant, the Skolem term $[c_{\beta(o\beta)}.\lambda y_\beta \sim R_{o\beta\alpha} x_\alpha y_\beta]$ which replaces y_β has x_α as its sole free variable.

It can be seen that this naive method of Skolemization permits the derivation of AC^α in the system $\mathcal{R}$ of [Andrews 1971, pp. 427–428]. The crucial step involves substituting $[\lambda p_{o\alpha}.c_{\alpha(o\alpha)}.\lambda x_\alpha. \sim p_{o\alpha} x_\alpha]$ for $j_{\alpha(o\alpha)}$ at the appropriate point.

To see how Skolemization should be done so that Skolem functions do not serve as choice functions, let us recall the basic idea underlying Skolemization. To make this discussion more concrete, the reader may imagine that we are working in refutational mode and Skolemizing

---

[3]See [Henkin 1950] or [Andrews 1986] for the definition. A minor error in [Henkin 1950] which requires modifying the definition of general model given there is noted in [Andrews 1972].

$$\forall x^1 \ldots \forall x^n \exists y R x^1 \ldots x^n y.$$

There are certain variables $x^1, \ldots, x^n$ in a wff $R x^1 \ldots x^n y$ which are in principle replaced by wffs $T^1, \ldots, T^n$ of the corresponding types, and then a new parameter y is chosen. Since for different choices of instantiation terms $T^1, \ldots, T^n$, different choices of y should be made, we may write y as $y_{T^1 \ldots T^n}$. We may wish to postpone the choices of the actual instantiation terms, write y as $y_{x^1 \ldots x^n}$, and substitute the T^i's for the x^i's later. It is notationally convenient to write y as a function symbol Y, so that $y_{x^1 \ldots x^n}$ is written as the Skolem term $Y x^1 \ldots x^n$.

In first-order logic this can be done freely, but in type theory certain restrictions on the use of these Skolem constants Y must be observed:

1. Each Skolem constant Y has an *arity* n associated with it. Every occurrence of Y in a wff must be in a context $Y T^1 \ldots T^n$, where the T^i's are wffs of appropriate types called *necessary arguments* of Y. (Of course, Y may occur in a context where it has more than n arguments if $Y T^1 \ldots T^n$ is itself a wff with a function type.)

2. If $Y T^1 \ldots T^n$ occurs in a wff W and there is a free occurrence of a variable z in one of the necessary arguments T^i, then this occurrence of z must not be bound in W.

An alternative to Skolemization based on the *dependency* relation is discussed in section 2.2. For additional discussion of these matters see [Miller 1987].

1.4. The expressiveness of type theory

It has been found [Hanna and Daeche 1985, Hanna and Daeche 1986, Gordon 1986] that type theory is particularly well suited for specifying and verifying hardware and software. From this has grown an active field of research which is reflected in conferences such as [von Wright, Grundy and Harrison 1996, Gunter and Felty 1997, Grundy and Newey 1998].

Although it is a consequence of the Completeness Theorem that every theorem of first-order logic has a first-order proof, some theorems of first-order logic can be proved most efficiently by using concepts which can be expressed only in higher-order logic. An example may be found in [Andrews and Bishop 1996]. Statman proved (Proposition 6.3.5 of [Statman 1978]) that the minimal length of a proof in first-order logic of a wff of first-order logic may be extraordinarily longer than the minimal length of a proof of the same wff in second-order logic. Gödel asserted in [Gödel 1936] that "passing to the logic of the next higher order has the effect, not only of making provable certain propositions that were not provable before, but also of making it possible to shorten, by an extraordinary amount, infinitely many of the proofs already available". A complete proof of this may be found in [Buss 1994]. Further discussion of this topic may be found in [Leivant 1994].

In a computerized system for proving theorems of type theory, one will generally have some facility for handling abbreviations. An *abbreviation* will consist of a constant of a specified type, a wff of that type called its *definition*, for which it serves as a name or label, and a rewrite rule or axiom which justifies interchanging the abbreviation with its definition. We say that we *instantiate* an occurrence of an abbreviation when we replace it with its definition and β-normalize the resulting expression.[4]

For example, suppose we want to express the theorem that the transitive closure of any relation (between entities of type α) is transitive. Let us use $\mathbf{A} :: \mathbf{B}$ to mean that $\mathbf{A}$ is an abbreviation whose definition is $\mathbf{B}$, and introduce the following definitions:

$$\subseteq_{o(o\alpha)(o\alpha)} :: \lambda r_{o\alpha\alpha}\lambda p_{o\alpha\alpha}\forall x_\alpha\forall y_\alpha.rxy \supset pxy$$

$\subseteq_{o(o\alpha)(o\alpha)} r_{o\alpha\alpha}p_{o\alpha\alpha}$ means that r is a subrelation of p, i.e., p includes r. Binary operators such as $\subseteq$ are often written in infix position, so this can be written as $r_{o\alpha\alpha} \subseteq p_{o\alpha\alpha}$.

$\text{TRANSITIVE}_{o(o\alpha)} :: \lambda r_{o\alpha\alpha}\forall a_\alpha\forall b_\alpha\forall c_\alpha.rab \wedge rbc \supset rac$

$\text{TRANSITIVE-CLOSURE}_{o\alpha\alpha(o\alpha\alpha)} ::$

$$\lambda r_{o\alpha\alpha}\lambda x_\alpha\lambda y_\alpha\forall p_{o\alpha\alpha} \cdot r \subseteq p \wedge \text{TRANSITIVE } p \supset pxy$$

The transitive closure of r is defined to be the relation which relates x to y whenever x is related to y by every transitive relation p which includes r. With these definitions, the theorem can be expressed simply by the wff

$$\forall r_{o\alpha\alpha}\text{TRANSITIVE }.\text{TRANSITIVE-CLOSURE } r$$

Recursive definitions can easily be expressed in type theory. For example, if $\mathbb{0}_\sigma$ denotes zero and $\mathbb{S}_{\sigma\sigma}$ denotes the successor function, the set $\mathbb{N}_{o\sigma}$ of natural numbers can be defined by the wff

$$\lambda n_\sigma\forall p_{o\sigma}.p\mathbb{0}_\sigma \wedge \forall x_\sigma[px \supset p.\mathbb{S}_{\sigma\sigma}x] \supset pn,$$

which says that n is a natural number iff it is in every set which contains $\mathbb{0}_\sigma$ and is closed under $\mathbb{S}_{\sigma\sigma}$. With this definition it is easy to prove that $\mathbb{N}_{o\sigma}$ contains $\mathbb{0}_\sigma$, is closed under $\mathbb{S}_{\sigma\sigma}$, and satisfies the Principle of Mathematical Induction. One can define an explicit wff $F_{\alpha\sigma}$ (where α is any type symbol, possibly the type σ of natural numbers) containing no free variables except g_α and $h_{\alpha\alpha\sigma}$ such that

$$F_{\alpha\sigma} \mathbb{0}_\sigma = g_\alpha \wedge \forall n_\sigma.\mathbb{N}_{o\sigma} n \supset F[\mathbb{S}_{\sigma\sigma}n] = h_{\alpha\alpha\sigma} n.Fn$$

is derivable from an Axiom of Infinity. With appropriate substitutions for g_α and $h_{\alpha\alpha\sigma}$ one thus obtains many functions defined by primitive recursion. Details and additional examples may be found in [Andrews 1986].

1.5. Set theory as an alternative to type theory

Axiomatic set theory provides a vehicle for formalizing mathematical disciplines which could be used as an alternative to type theory. We shall not discuss this

---

[4]A discussion of selective instantiation of abbreviations in the context of automatic proof search may be found in [Bishop and Andrews 1998].

complex subject extensively, but we briefly mention the relative advantages of each approach in the context of automatic theorem proving.

Advantages of using set theory are:

(s1) Axiomatic set theory is formalized in first-order logic, which lacks some of the complexities of type theory.

(s2) Certain concepts, such as those involving sets whose members are not all of the same type, can be expressed easily in set theory, but not in type theory.

Advantages of using Church's type theory are:

(t1) When one writes out statements about functions and relations in the primitive notation of the formal language, these statements are often considerably simpler in type theory than in set theory. This can significantly affect the difficulty of proving these statements.

(t2) The types which are attached to wffs of type theory provide syntactic clues which help to limit the search involved in finding a proof.

(t3) Higher-order unification provides an important theorem-proving tool which is well worth the price of its relative complexity. This will be illustrated in section 2.4.1.

(t4) In type theory any wff of the appropriate type can be used to define a set, relation, or function, but in set theory the existence of such entities must be justified directly or indirectly by the axioms of set theory. See [Andrews and Bishop 1996] for an example related to this point.

Some papers relevant to this topic are [Bailin 1988, Bailin and Barker-Plummer 1993, Belinfante 1996, Boyer, Lusk, McCune, Overbeek, Stickel and Wos 1986, Gordon 1996, Quaife 1992].

2. Metatheoretical foundations

2.1. The Unifying Principle

The completeness of most proof procedures for first-order logic ultimately rests on Herbrand's Theorem [Herbrand 1971, Dreben, Andrews and Aanderaa 1963, Dreben and Denton 1966][5] or the closely related Hauptsatz (Cut-elimination Theorem) of Gentzen [1935]. These metatheorems allow one to drastically reduce the space one might otherwise search without loss of completeness.

Cut-elimination for type theory (known as Takeuti's Conjecture [Takeuti 1953]) was established independently by Takahashi [1967] and Prawitz [1968] for a system of type theory based on predicates rather than functions.[6] The ideas in Takahashi's proof were used in [Andrews 1971] to establish cut-elimination for $\mathcal{T}$ and to extend Smullyan's Unifying Principle [Smullyan 1963, Smullyan 1995] to $\mathcal{T}$. This Unifying Principle for $\mathcal{T}$ provides a basic tool for establishing completeness proofs for type theory such as those in [Huet 1973, Kohlhase 1995, Miller 1983]. We now state this principle.

---

[5] See [Andrews 1986] or [Gallier 1986] for very readable treatments.

[6] A general exposition may be found in [Takeuti 1987].

Definition. A property Γ of finite sets of wffs$_o$ is an *abstract consistency property* iff for all finite sets S of wffs$_o$, the following properties hold (for all wffs **A, B**):

1. If $\Gamma(S)$, then there is no atom **A** such that $\mathbf{A} \in S$ and $[\sim \mathbf{A}] \in S$.
2. If $\Gamma(S \cup \{\mathbf{A}\})$, then $\Gamma(S \cup \{\downarrow \mathbf{A}\})$.
3. If $\Gamma(S \cup \{\sim\sim \mathbf{A}\})$, then $\Gamma(S \cup \{\mathbf{A}\})$.
4. If $\Gamma(S \cup \{[\mathbf{A} \vee \mathbf{B}]\})$, then $\Gamma(S \cup \{\mathbf{A}\})$ or $\Gamma(S \cup \{\mathbf{B}\})$.
5. If $\Gamma(S \cup \{\sim [\mathbf{A} \vee \mathbf{B}]\})$, then $\Gamma(S \cup \{\sim \mathbf{A}, \sim \mathbf{B}\})$.
6. If $\Gamma\left(S \cup \{\Pi_{o(o\alpha)}\mathbf{A}_{o\alpha}\}\right)$, then for each wff $\mathbf{B}_\alpha$, $\Gamma\left(S \cup \{\Pi_{o(o\alpha)}\mathbf{A}_{o\alpha}, \mathbf{A}_{o\alpha}\mathbf{B}_\alpha\}\right)$.
7. If $\Gamma\left(S \cup \{\sim \Pi_{o(o\alpha)}\mathbf{A}_{o\alpha}\}\right)$, then $\Gamma\left(S \cup \{\sim \mathbf{A}_{o\alpha}\mathbf{c}_\alpha\}\right)$ for any variable or parameter $\mathbf{c}_\alpha$ which does not occur free in $\mathbf{A}_{o\alpha}$ or any wff in S.

REMARK. *Consistency* is an abstract consistency property.

2.1. THEOREM (Smullyan's Unifying Principle for $\mathcal{T}$ [Andrews 1971]). *If Γ is an abstract consistency property and $\Gamma(S)$, then S is consistent in $\mathcal{T}$.*

Here is a typical application of the Unifying Principle. Suppose there is a procedure $\mathcal{M}$ which can be used to refute sets of sentences, and we wish to show it is complete for $\mathcal{T}$. For any set S of sentences, let $\Gamma(S)$ mean that S is not refutable by $\mathcal{M}$, and show that Γ is an abstract consistency property. Now suppose that **A** is a theorem of $\mathcal{T}$. Then $\{\sim \mathbf{A}\}$ is inconsistent in $\mathcal{T}$, so by the Unifying Principle not $\Gamma(\{\sim \mathbf{A}\})$, so $\{\sim \mathbf{A}\}$ is refutable by $\mathcal{M}$.

Takahashi [1968, 1970] extended his cut-elimination result to systems with extensionality, and Kohlhase [1993] extended the Unifying Principle to systems with extensionality. This extended principle was used in [Benzmüller and Kohlhase 1998 a] to obtain a completeness proof for a system of extensional higher-order resolution which we shall discuss in section 3.3. This extended principle also appears in [Kohlhase 1998], where it is used to obtain a completeness proof for an extensional higher-order tableau calculus, which has been implemented under the name HOT [Konrad 1998].

2.2. Expansion proofs

A fundamental concept in higher-order theorem proving is that of an *expansion tree proof*, otherwise known as an *expansion proof*. This concept, which grew out of ideas in [Andrews, Miller, Cohen and Pfenning 1984], was developed by Dale Miller in his thesis [1983], and the details of the definition can also be found in [Miller 1987]. An expansion proof is a generalization of the notion of a Herbrand expansion of a theorem of first-order logic; it provides a very elegant, concise, and nonredundant representation of the relationship between the theorem and a tautology which can be obtained from it by appropriate instantiations of quantifiers and which underlies various proofs of the theorem.

A closely related concept is that of a *dual expansion proof*, which represents in a similar way the relationship between a refutable wff and the contradiction buried within it.

We refer the reader to the references cited for a precise definition of an expansion proof, and here provide an informal description of this concept and an example (displayed in Figure 1) which should convey the main ideas involved in it. A familiar way of representing a wff of first-order logic is to regard it as a tree (i.e., a connected graph with no cycles) growing downward from a topmost node which is called its root. With each node of the tree is associated a propositional connective, quantifier, or atom, and if the node is not associated with an atom, there are subtrees below the node which represent the scopes of the connective or quantifier. Starting from this idea, let us enrich it to obtain what Miller calls an *expansion tree* for a wff of first- or higher-order logic.

Let us call the wff represented by a tree Q as described above the *shallow formula* Sh(Q) of the tree (and of the node which is its root). With each expansion tree Q is also associated a *deep formula* Dp(Q) which represents the result of instantiating the quantifier-occurrences in Q with terms which are attached as labels to the arcs descending from their nodes.

Let us call a node of a tree an *expansion node* if it corresponds to an essentially existential[7] quantifier, and a *selection node* if it corresponds to an essentially universal quantifier. (In dual expansion trees, the roles of universal and existential quantifiers are interchanged.) Let finitely many arcs labeled with terms descend from each expansion node, so that if the expansion node has shallow formula $\exists x$ **B**, and if **t** is the term labeling an arc descending from that node, then the type of **t** is the same as that of **x**, and the node at the lower end of that arc has as shallow formula the β-normal form of $[[\lambda x\ B]\ t]$, i.e., the result of instantiating the quantifier with the term **t**. The term **t** is called an *expansion term*, and **x** is called an *expansion variable*. Selection nodes satisfy a similar condition, except that only one arc may descend from a selection node, and the term labeling it must be a suitably chosen parameter (which is not free in Sh(Q)) called a *selected parameter*.

In an expansion tree, if Q is an expansion node and $Q_1, \ldots Q_n$ are the nodes immediately below Q, then Dp(Q) is $[Dp(Q_1) \lor \ldots \lor Dp(Q_n)]$. (In a dual expansion tree, however, Dp(Q) is $[Dp(Q_1) \land \ldots \land Dp(Q_n)]$.) The deep formula of a leaf of such a tree is the same as the shallow formula.

In order to deal effectively with definitions, it is useful to add one more condition to the inductive definition of an expansion tree which is implicitly described above. If Q is a node whose shallow formula contains an abbreviation, then one may call Q a *definition node* and create a node Q' below Q whose shallow formula is the result of instantiating the abbreviation. Q' and Q have the same deep formulas.

The *dependency* relation between occurrences of expansion terms in an expansion tree is the transitive closure < of the relation $<^0$ such that $t <^0 s$ iff there is a parameter **u** which is selected for a node below the occurrence of **t** such that **u** occurs free in **s**.

---

[7]See [Andrews 1986, p. 123]

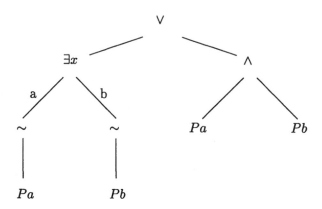

Figure 1: A simple expansion tree

An expansion tree is an *expansion proof* for its shallow formula iff it satisfies these conditions:

1. The deep formula is a tautology.
2. The dependency relation is irreflexive (acyclic).

The second condition, which we shall call the dependency condition, is discussed in [Miller 1987] and is similar to one in [Bibel 1987, pp. 169-176]. This condition will be satisfied if one generates the expansion tree in a step-by-step process starting from the formula to be proved, choosing a new parameter which occurs nowhere in the tree each time a selection is made.

A *dual expansion proof* (which might also be called an *expansion refutation*) is a dual expansion tree which satisfies the dependency condition and has a contradiction for its deep formula.

We give an example. Consider the wff

$$\forall x Px \supset Pa \wedge Pb \tag{2.1}$$

We shall temporarily regard $\sim$, $\wedge$, $\vee$, $\forall$ and $\exists$ as primitive, and write 2.1 as

$$\exists x \sim Px \vee [Pa \wedge Pb] \tag{2.2}$$

An expansion tree (indeed, an expansion proof) for 2.2 is shown in Figure 1. The deep formula for this expansion tree is

$$[\sim Pa \vee \sim Pb] \vee [Pa \wedge Pb] \tag{2.3}$$

which is a tautology from which the wff 2.2 can readily be derived.

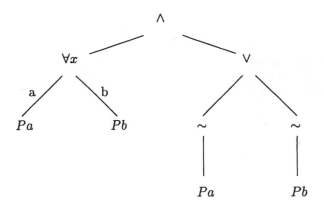

Figure 2: The dual expansion tree

Of course, an alternative way to establish 2.1 is to derive a contradiction from the wff

$$\forall x Px \wedge [\sim Pa \vee \sim Pb] \tag{2.4}$$

which is equivalent to the negation of 2.1. A dual expansion tree (indeed, an expansion refutation) for 2.4 is in Figure 2. Its deep formula is

$$[Pa \wedge Pb] \wedge [\sim Pa \vee \sim Pb] \tag{2.5}$$

which is a contradiction.

In an expansion tree, which represents a proof which works its way up from the bottom of the tree to the top node, expansion corresponds to inverse existential generalization, whereas in a dual tree, which represents a refutation which starts at the top node and works down to a contradiction, expansion corresponds to universal instantiation.

2.2. THEOREM (Miller's Expansion Proof Theorem [Miller 1987]). $\vdash_\mathcal{T} \mathbf{A}$ *if and only if* $\mathbf{A}$ *has an expansion proof.*

This may be regarded as an extension of Herbrand's Theorem to type theory.

When one searches for an expansion proof, it is generally not known just what expansion terms should be used, so it is natural to introduce expansion terms containing free variables for which substitutions can be made later. When such a substitution is applied, it must be applied uniformly to all occurrences of these variables throughout the expansion tree in such a way that the dependency condition is not violated. Just as in first-order logic, this can be done by introducing Skolem terms in place of the selected parameters. Skolemization for expansion trees in higher-order logic is discussed in [Miller 1987]. Of course, in higher-order logic new quantifiers may be introduced in the expansion terms, so the Skolemization cannot all be done in a preprocessing stage.

Skolem terms may get awkwardly long, and in some search procedures complex questions may arise about identifying Skolem terms whose arguments are logically equivalent. In such contexts it may be best to avoid Skolemization, and integrate the dependency relation into the unification algorithm so that only substitutions which do not violate the dependency condition are produced. This is discussed for first-order logic in [Bibel 1987, p. 185].

2.3. Proof translations

An expansion proof is a conceptual tool which may or may not be represented explicitly by various proof procedures. Nevertheless, a proof in virtually any format can generally be used to generate an expansion proof. (One may need to eliminate cuts from the proof in this process.) This expansion proof can then be translated into a readable format such as a proof in natural deduction [Gentzen 1935, Prawitz 1965, Quine 1950] style. An example of such a proof (presented in the fashion used in [Andrews 1986]) may be seen in Figure 3. Each line of the proof consists of a number in parentheses which serves as a label for that line and for the wff asserted in it, a list (possibly empty) of numbers of wffs which are assumed as hypotheses for that line, the assertion sign ⊢, the wff asserted in that line, and a justification. ⊥ denotes falsehood.

Translating an expansion proof into a natural deduction proof has a number of advantages:

1. The proofs are highly readable by those who understand the notation of symbolic logic.

2. Even if the process which found the proof produced a very awkward or redundant proof, redundancies can be eliminated from the expansion proof corresponding to it by a process called *merging*, and (if the translation process is good), the final proof in natural deduction style which is presented to the reader can be very elegant. Indeed, if one also has facilities for translating natural deduction proofs to expansion proofs, one may be able to improve the form of a natural deduction proof by translating back and forth.

3. Presenting the proof in natural deduction style often provides an extra check of its correctness.

4. Even if one can prove some theorems automatically, as a practical matter it will often be necessary to use a mixture of automatic and interactive procedures to prove hard theorems. One way to organize such a *semi-automatic* mode of operation is to have the user prepare an outline of the proof interactively (or semi-interactively) in natural deduction style, and then fill the gaps in this proof automatically. Filling in a gap involves proving that a certain line **B** of the proof follows from other specified lines $\mathbf{A}_1, \ldots, \mathbf{A}_n$; this can be accomplished

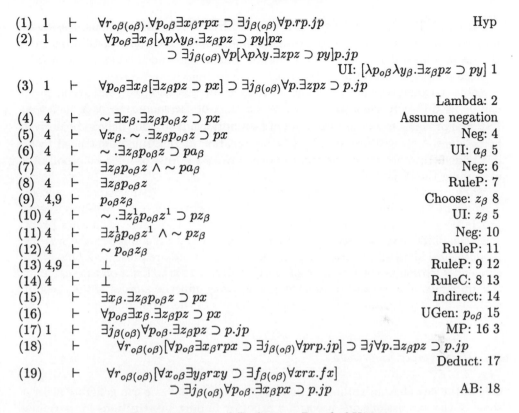

(1)	1	⊢	$\forall r_{o\beta(o\beta)}.\forall p_{o\beta}\exists x_\beta rpx \supset \exists j_{\beta(o\beta)}\forall p.rp.jp$	Hyp
(2)	1	⊢	$\forall p_{o\beta}\exists x_\beta[\lambda p\lambda y_\beta.\exists z_\beta pz \supset py]px$	
			$\supset \exists j_{\beta(o\beta)}\forall p[\lambda p\lambda y.\exists zpz \supset py]p.jp$	
				UI: $[\lambda p_{o\beta}\lambda y_\beta.\exists z_\beta pz \supset py]$ 1
(3)	1	⊢	$\forall p_{o\beta}\exists x_\beta[\exists z_\beta pz \supset px] \supset \exists j_{\beta(o\beta)}\forall p.\exists zpz \supset p.jp$	
				Lambda: 2
(4)	4	⊢	$\sim \exists x_\beta.\exists z_\beta p_{o\beta}z \supset px$	Assume negation
(5)	4	⊢	$\forall x_\beta. \sim .\exists z_\beta p_{o\beta}z \supset px$	Neg: 4
(6)	4	⊢	$\sim .\exists z_\beta p_{o\beta}z \supset pa_\beta$	UI: a_β 5
(7)	4	⊢	$\exists z_\beta p_{o\beta}z \wedge \sim pa_\beta$	Neg: 6
(8)	4	⊢	$\exists z_\beta p_{o\beta}z$	RuleP: 7
(9)	4,9	⊢	$p_{o\beta}z_\beta$	Choose: z_β 8
(10)	4	⊢	$\sim .\exists z_\beta^1 p_{o\beta}z^1 \supset pz_\beta$	UI: z_β 5
(11)	4	⊢	$\exists z_\beta^1 p_{o\beta}z^1 \wedge \sim pz_\beta$	Neg: 10
(12)	4	⊢	$\sim p_{o\beta}z_\beta$	RuleP: 11
(13)	4,9	⊢	$\perp$	RuleP: 9 12
(14)	4	⊢	$\perp$	RuleC: 8 13
(15)		⊢	$\exists x_\beta.\exists z_\beta p_{o\beta}z \supset px$	Indirect: 14
(16)		⊢	$\forall p_{o\beta}\exists x_\beta.\exists z_\beta pz \supset px$	UGen: $p_{o\beta}$ 15
(17)	1	⊢	$\exists j_{\beta(o\beta)}\forall p_{o\beta}.\exists z_\beta pz \supset p.jp$	MP: 16 3
(18)		⊢	$\forall r_{o\beta(o\beta)}[\forall p_{o\beta}\exists x_\beta rpx \supset \exists j_{\beta(o\beta)}\forall prp.jp] \supset \exists j\forall p.\exists z_\beta pz \supset p.jp$	
				Deduct: 17
(19)		⊢	$\forall r_{o\beta(o\beta)}[\forall x_{o\beta}\exists y_\beta rxy \supset \exists f_{\beta(o\beta)}\forall xrx.fx]$	
			$\supset \exists j_{\beta(o\beta)}\forall p_{o\beta}.\exists x_\beta px \supset p.jp$	AB: 18

Figure 3: Natural Deduction Proof of X5310

by proving $[\forall x^1 \ldots \forall x^k[A_1 \wedge \ldots \wedge A_n] \supset B]$, where the x^i are not free in the relevant hypotheses.

Miller showed [Miller 1983, Miller 1984, Miller 1987] that once an expansion proof has been found, it can be converted without further search into a natural deduction proof. This extended related work for first-order logic in [Andrews 1980] and [Bibel 1982]. Then Pfenning [1987] developed an improved translation method, which was further enhanced in [Pfenning and Nesmith 1990] with a method for generating more elegant natural deduction proofs. The ideas in [Felty 1986] are closely related to those developed by Pfenning.

Pfenning's translation procedure is based on the use of *tactics* [Gordon, Milner and Wadsworth 1979], which apply rules of inference to construct natural deduction proofs. A tactic examines a given goal situation (the problem of deriving a conclusion from a set of assumptions) and reduces it to the problem of solving a number of subgoals. This is done by applying rules of inference (forward or backwards) to derive new proof lines or to justify certain lines of the proof while introducing other lines which may still require justification. The tactics consult the expansion proof for useful information about how to apply the rules of inference.

For example, when proving a goal $[A \lor B]$ from some assumptions, the tactic may consult the expansion proof to determine if A by itself already follows from the assumptions. If so, it applies the relevant rule of inference (working backwards) and reduces the problem to deriving A.

Another example is a goal of the form $\exists x A$. In this case, the expansion proof can be used to determine whether there is a wff t of the same type as x such that $S_t^x A$ is provable from the current set of assumptions. If so, the goal can be derived by existential generalization; otherwise, application of this rule might need to be postponed. In some cases, the tactics might invoke the rule of indirect proof after examining the expansion proof.

Many proofs in a variety of formats may correspond to the same expansion proof. This produces an important equivalence relation between proofs. We may regard proofs as *essentially the same* if they correspond to the same expansion proof, since the differences between them are essentially trivial differences in the way the fundamental ideas and relationships underlying the proof are presented. One of the challenges in designing efficient proof-search procedures is to focus on the search for the fundamental ideas and relationships which may underlie a proof of the theorem without becoming entangled in superficial aspects of the problem.

2.4. Higher-order unification

One of the key ideas in automatic theorem proving is that one can generate at least some of the expressions one needs in a proof by finding substitutions for variables which cause certain expressions to become identical. In the context of type theory, it is most fruitful to combine the operation of substituting an expression for a variable with that of reducing the result to λ-normal form.

Definition A *higher-order unifier* for a pair $< t, u >$ of wffs is a substitution θ for free occurrences of variables such that θt and θu have the same λ-normal form. A higher-order unifier for a set of pairs of wffs is a unifier for each of the pairs in the set.

Higher-order unification is so important and rich a topic that an entire chapter of this handbook [Dowek 2001] (Chapter 16) is devoted to it. Here we provide only a brief introduction to this topic. Some additional information about it will be found in section 3.3.

2.4.1. An example

We now show how higher-order unification can be used to generate a proof of Cantor's Theorem that every set has more subsets than members.[8] We let α be the type of the elements of the set in question, and express the theorem by the assertion that there is no function g mapping elements of type α to sets of such elements (i.e., to elements of type $(o\alpha)$) such that every element f of type $(o\alpha)$ is

---

[8] This classic example of the power of higher-order unification is essentially due to Huet [1973].

in the range of g. Thus, Cantor's Theorem can be expressed by the wff

$$\sim \exists g_{o\alpha\alpha} \forall f_{o\alpha} \exists j_\alpha . gj = f$$

We start generating the proof with some straightforward preprocessing. We instantiate the definition of $=$, using the Leibniz definition, to obtain this wff to prove:

$$\sim \exists g_{o\alpha\alpha} \forall f_{o\alpha} \exists j_\alpha \forall q_{o(o\alpha)} . q[gj] \supset qf$$

We negate this and Skolemize to obtain:

$$\forall f_{o\alpha} \forall q_{o(o\alpha)} . q[G_{o\alpha\alpha} . J_{\alpha(o\alpha)} f] \supset qf$$

There is little hope of deriving a contradiction from this wff by instantiating its quantifiers unless it is expanded, so we duplicate the quantifier $\forall q_{o(o\alpha)}$ to obtain:

$$\forall f_{o\alpha} . \forall q^1_{o(o\alpha)} [q^1 [G_{o\alpha\alpha} . J_{\alpha(o\alpha)} f] \supset q^1 f] \wedge$$
$$\forall q^2_{o(o\alpha)} . q^2 [G.Jf] \supset q^2 f$$

We delete the quantifiers and put the wff into negation normal form:

$$[\sim q^1_{o(o\alpha)} [G_{o\alpha\alpha} . J_{\alpha(o\alpha)} f_{o\alpha}] \vee q^1 f] \wedge$$
$$. \sim q^2_{o(o\alpha)} [G.Jf] \vee q^2 f$$

Up to this point, the procedure has been quite straightforward except for the choice of the quantifier to duplicate. Actually, duplicating $\forall f_{o\alpha}$ instead of, or in addition to, $\forall q_{o(o\alpha)}$ would give results similar to, but a little messier than, those we give here. We must now make appropriate substitutions for the variables so that this wff reduces to a contradiction. The wff has the form

$$[A \vee B] \wedge$$
$$. C \vee D$$

We shall see that it can be reduced to the form

$$[E \vee E] \wedge$$
$$. \sim E \vee \sim E$$

Clearly, this simply involves solving a unification problem. Comparison of the wffs $\sim q^1_{o(o\alpha)} [G_{o\alpha\alpha} . J_{\alpha(o\alpha)} f_{o\alpha}]$ and $q^1_{o(o\alpha)} f_{o\alpha}$ might tempt one to conclude that they cannot be unified, but we shall show that they can be unified.

We substitute $[\lambda u_{o\alpha} . u . J_{\alpha(o\alpha)} f_{o\alpha}]$ for $q^1_{o(o\alpha)}$ and $[\lambda u_{o\alpha} . \sim u . J_{\alpha(o\alpha)} f_{o\alpha}]$ for $q^2_{o(o\alpha)}$ to obtain:

$$[\sim [\lambda u_{o\alpha} . u . J_{\alpha(o\alpha)} f_{o\alpha}] [G_{o\alpha\alpha} . Jf] \vee [\lambda u . u . Jf] f] \wedge$$
$$. \sim [\lambda u . \sim u . Jf] [G.Jf] \vee [\lambda u . \sim u . Jf] f$$

β-normalize:

$$[\sim G_{o\alpha\alpha}[J_{\alpha(o\alpha)}f_{o\alpha}][Jf] \vee f.Jf] \wedge$$
$$. \sim\sim G[Jf][Jf]\vee \sim f.Jf$$

Now we substitute $[\lambda w_\alpha. \sim G_{o\alpha\alpha}ww]$ for $f_{o\alpha}$, and write J^* as an abbreviation for the Skolem term $[J_{\alpha(o\alpha)}.\lambda w_\alpha. \sim Gww]$ to obtain:

$$[\sim G_{o\alpha\alpha}J^*J^* \vee [\lambda w. \sim Gww]J^*] \wedge$$
$$. \sim\sim GJ^*J^*\vee \sim [\lambda w. \sim Gww]J^*$$

β-normalize:

$$[\sim G_{o\alpha\alpha}J^*J^*\vee \sim GJ^*J^*] \wedge$$
$$. \sim\sim GJ^*J^*\vee \sim\sim GJ^*J^*$$

This completes the unification process. The contradiction thus obtained has been derived from the negation of Cantor's Theorem, so the theorem is proved. Note that the crucial substitution for $f_{o\alpha}$ can be written in conventional set-theoretic notation as $\{w|w \notin Gw\}$ and represents the diagonal set of the traditional ingenious proof of this theorem. This proof can be found completely automatically. Further discussion of this example may be found in [Andrews et al. 1984].

2.4.2. Properties of higher-order unification

Higher-order unification differs from first-order unification in a number of important respects. In particular:

1. Even when a unifier for a pair of wffs exists, there may be no most general unifier [Gould 1966].
2. Higher-order unification is undecidable [Huet 1973b], even in the "second-order" case [Goldfarb 1981].

Nevertheless, an algorithm has been devised [Huet 1975, Jensen and Pietrzykowski 1976] which will find a unifier for a set of pairs of wffs if one exists. The algorithm generates a search tree, certain branches of which may not terminate.

2.5. The need for arbitrarily high types

The terms which are used to instantiate quantifiers on higher-order variables may themselves contain quantified variables. Normally, one assumes that the types of these variables will not be significantly more complex than the types of variables occurring in the theorem being proved, but one cannot expect that this will always be the case. This is a vexing source of complexity in higher-order theorem proving.

2.3. THEOREM. *No bound on the orders of the types of the variables which may occur in the proof of a theorem of higher-order logic can be determined from the orders of the types of the variables in the theorem.*

We shall not give a detailed proof (or even a precise statement) of this theorem, since it is a quite general theorem which applies to a wide variety of formulations of higher-order logic, and the details will depend on the particular formal system. However, we sketch the main ideas of the proof.

Let *Infin* be an axiom of infinity, such as $\exists r_{o\iota\iota} \forall x_\iota \forall y_\iota \forall z_\iota . \exists w_\iota r x w \wedge \sim r x x \wedge . r x y \supset .ryz \supset rxz$. Let the system obtained by adding *Infin* to the axioms of nth-order logic be called *nth-order arithmetic*. Even with n quite small, one can define the natural numbers and derive Peano's Postulates in nth-order arithmetic.[9] As shown by Tarski [1956], one can prove in arithmetic of order (perhaps approximately) $n + 2$ a statement Cn which expresses the consistency of nth-order arithmetic. The consistency statement is purely syntactic, and can be expressed in an arithmetic of low order regardless of what n is, but the consistency proof cannot be carried out in nth-order arithmetic, since this would contradict Gödel's Second Theorem. Thus, $[Infin \supset C10], [Infin \supset C12], [Infin \supset C14], \ldots$ is a sequence of sentences of some low-order logic which are all provable in type theory, but their proofs require types of unboundedly high orders.

The reader who wishes to work out the details of this argument as it applies to $\mathcal{T}$ may find some of the ideas in [Andrews 1965, Andrews 1974, Buss 1994] helpful.

Of course, it is a consequence of Gödel's Completeness Theorem that every first-order theorem has a first-order proof.

3. Proof search

We now turn our attention to the basic problems of searching for proofs in classical type theory.

Since type theory includes first-order logic, a program which can prove theorems of type theory will also be able to prove theorems of first-order logic, and the methods used will be extensions of methods adequate for first-order logic. It seems likely that most automatic proof procedures for first-order logic can be extended to prove theorems of higher-order logic. Methods for proving theorems of classical type theory automatically which have been proposed thus far may be roughly classified as follows:

- resolution [Andrews 1971, Benzmüller and Kohlhase 1998a, Benzmüller and Kohlhase 1998b, Henschen 1972, Huet 1972, Huet 1973, Jensen and Pietrzykowski 1976, Kohlhase 1994b, Pietrzykowski 1973, Wolfram 1993]
- matings (connections) [Andrews 1989, Andrews et al. 1996]
- semantic tableaux [Kohlhase 1995, Kohlhase 1998, Konrad 1998, Robinson 1969]
- semantic partitions [Robinson 1969]
- reducing typed λ-calculus to first-order logic by using combinatory logic [Robinson 1970]
- proof planning [Richardson, Smaill and Green 1998]

---

[9]The details may be found in [Andrews 1986].

Implementations of these methods are TPS [Andrews et al. 1996], LEO [Benzmüller and Kohlhase 1998b], HOT [Konrad 1998], and $\lambda Clam$ [Richardson et al. 1998].[10] TPS also has an implementation of Pfenning's method of translating expansion proofs into natural deduction proofs. LEO is a subsystem of ΩMEGA [Benzmüller, Cheikhrouhou, Fehrer, Fiedler, Huang, Kerber, Kohlhase, Konrad, Melis, Meier, Schaarschmidt, Siekmann and Sorge 1997], which contains facilities for translating proofs into natural language.

Since proof procedures for type theory are also proof procedures for first-order logic, and each proof procedure for first-order logic is itself a major topic worthy of a whole chapter of this handbook, we shall not attempt to give complete descriptions of proof procedures for type theory. Instead, we shall concentrate our attention on the key ingredients involved in extending ideas and techniques for automatic theorem proving from first-order logic to type theory. Two crucial considerations which must be added to those relevant to proof search in first-order logic are:

1. the nature of higher-order unification;
2. the problem of instantiating higher-order quantifiers.

Methods of dealing with these problems depend to some extent on the methods of proof search which provide the contexts in which they are applied. We discuss several methods of proof search in sections 3.1 - 3.4.

3.1. Searching for expansion proofs

One of the vexing problems which distinguishes higher-order logic from first-order logic is the need to instantiate certain quantifiers with terms which cannot be generated by unification of subformulas of the theorem being proved. An example is provided by lines (1) and (2) of Figure 3, where the quantifier $\forall r_{o\beta(o\beta)}$ is instantiated with the wff $[\lambda p_{o\beta} \lambda y_\beta . \exists z_\beta p z \supset p y]$. Such wffs occur as expansion terms in expansion proofs, and often embody the key concepts of the proofs in which they occur.

One way to deal with this problem is to generate by methods other than unification partially specified expansion terms in the preprocessing stage (or later), and let the search process complete the specification of the forms of these terms. This can be done by having the expansion terms contain free variables, which we call *auxiliary* variables, for which substitutions can be made later. *Primitive substitutions* [Andrews 1989], which introduce single connectives and quantifiers in a general way, provide examples of such partially specified expansion terms. Examples of primitive substitutions for certain variables may be seen in Figures 4 and 5, where the terms to be substituted for the indicated variables are given. Note that they are determined by the types of these variables. In certain contexts, projections (such as the first substitution term in Figure 4) are also needed.[11]

A substitution term for a predicate variable has the form $\lambda x^1 ... \lambda x^n B_o$; we shall refer to the wff B_o as its *body*. In some contexts it is useful to introduce substitution

---

[10] Recall that in this chapter we do not attempt to discuss theorem proving which is interactive, tactic-based, or founded on nonclassical type theory.

[11] For an example, see the discussion of THM104 in [Andrews 1989].

$$\lambda w_{o\alpha} . w . q^0_{\alpha(o\alpha)} w$$
$$\lambda w_{o\alpha} . \sim q^0_{o(o\alpha)} w$$
$$\lambda w_{o\alpha} . q^1_{o(o\alpha)} w \wedge q^2_{o(o\alpha)} w$$
$$\lambda w_{o\alpha} . q^1_{o(o\alpha)} w \vee q^2_{o(o\alpha)} w$$
$$\lambda w_{o\alpha} . \exists w^1_\alpha\, q_{o\alpha(o\alpha)} w w^1$$
$$\lambda w_{o\alpha} . \forall w^1_\alpha\, q_{o\alpha(o\alpha)} w w^1$$

Figure 4: Primitive projection and primitive substitutions for $q_{o(o\alpha)}$

$$\lambda w^1_{o\beta} \lambda w^2_\beta . w^1 . r^0_{\beta\beta(o\beta)} w^1 w^2$$
$$\lambda w^1_{o\beta} \lambda w^2_\beta . \sim r^1_{o\beta(o\beta)} w^1 w^2$$
$$\lambda w^1_{o\beta} \lambda w^2_\beta . r^2_{o\beta(o\beta)} w^1 w^2 \wedge r^3_{o\beta(o\beta)} w^1 w^2$$
$$\lambda w^1_{o\beta} \lambda w^2_\beta . r^4_{o\beta(o\beta)} w^1 w^2 \vee r^5_{o\beta(o\beta)} w^1 w^2$$
$$\lambda w^1_{o\beta} \lambda w^2_\beta . \exists w^3_\beta r^7_{o\beta\beta(o\beta)} w^1 w^2 w^3$$
$$\lambda w^1_{o\beta} \lambda w^2_\beta . \forall w^3_\beta r^8_{o\beta\beta(o\beta)} w^1 w^2 w^3$$
$$\lambda w^1_{o\beta} \lambda w^2_\beta . \exists w^4_{o\beta} r^9_{o(o\beta)\beta(o\beta)} w^1 w^2 w^4$$
$$\lambda w^1_{o\beta} \lambda w^2_\beta . \forall w^4_{o\beta} r^{10}_{o(o\beta)\beta(o\beta)} w^1 w^2 w^4$$

Figure 5: Primitive projection and primitive substitutions for $r_{o\beta(o\beta)}$

terms whose bodies have more logical structure, or whose structure is more closely related to that of the theorem being proved. If more connectives and quantifiers are introduced in a single substitution term, the number of possible forms for the body may quickly become unmanageable. If the variables to which these substitutions will be applied occur in contexts such that equivalent bodies for the substitution terms will yield equivalent results when the substitutions are applied, this problem can be alleviated somewhat by using normal forms, such as prenex normal form with matrix in conjunctive or disjunctive normal form. Such substitutions are called *gensubs* (general substitutions). Some examples may be seen in Figure 6. Primitive substitutions are special cases of gensubs. One may often assume that negations have been pushed in to have minimal scope, and that the search process which determines the substitutions to be made for the auxiliary variables will determine where the negations must be, so substitutions which introduce negations (such as the second one in Figure 4) may not be needed when setting up the original expansion tree. Below we shall show how a gensub in prenex normal form can be used in finding the proof of X5310 in Figure 3 even though the desired instantiation term is not in prenex normal form.

It may also be useful to introduce into the substitution terms abbreviations which occur in the statement of the theorem being proved, or which heuristics suggest may be relevant the proof. A few simple examples may be seen in Figure 7.

We shall refer to a pair consisting of an expansion node and a wff of the cor-

$$\lambda w_{o\beta}^1 \lambda w_{\beta}^2 \exists w_{\beta}^5 . r_{o\beta\beta(o\beta)}^{11} w^1 w^2 w^5 \vee r_{o\beta\beta(o\beta)}^{12} w^1 w^2 w^5$$
$$\lambda w_{o\beta}^1 \lambda w_{\beta}^2 \exists w_{\beta}^5 . r_{o\beta\beta(o\beta)}^{13} w^1 w^2 w^5 \wedge r_{o\beta\beta(o\beta)}^{14} w^1 w^2 w^5$$
$$\lambda w_{o\beta}^1 \lambda w_{\beta}^2 \forall w_{\beta}^5 . r_{o\beta\beta(o\beta)}^{15} w^1 w^2 w^5 \vee r_{o\beta\beta(o\beta)}^{16} w^1 w^2 w^5$$
$$\lambda w_{o\beta}^1 \lambda w_{\beta}^2 \forall w_{\beta}^5 . r_{o\beta\beta(o\beta)}^{17} w^1 w^2 w^5 \wedge r_{o\beta\beta(o\beta)}^{18} w^1 w^2 w^5$$
$$\lambda w_{o\beta}^1 \lambda w_{\beta}^2 \exists w_{o\beta}^6 . r_{o(o\beta)\beta(o\beta)}^{19} w^1 w^2 w^6 \vee r_{o(o\beta)\beta(o\beta)}^{20} w^1 w^2 w^6$$
$$\lambda w_{o\beta}^1 \lambda w_{\beta}^2 \exists w_{o\beta}^6 . r_{o(o\beta)\beta(o\beta)}^{21} w^1 w^2 w^6 \wedge r_{o(o\beta)\beta(o\beta)}^{22} w^1 w^2 w^6$$
$$\lambda w_{o\beta}^1 \lambda w_{\beta}^2 \forall w_{o\beta}^6 . r_{o(o\beta)\beta(o\beta)}^{23} w^1 w^2 w^6 \vee r_{o(o\beta)\beta(o\beta)}^{24} w^1 w^2 w^6$$
$$\lambda w_{o\beta}^1 \lambda w_{\beta}^2 \forall w_{o\beta}^6 . r_{o(o\beta)\beta(o\beta)}^{25} w^1 w^2 w^6 \wedge r_{o(o\beta)\beta(o\beta)}^{26} w^1 w^2 w^6$$

Figure 6: Gensubs for $r_{o\beta(o\beta)}$

$$\lambda w_\alpha^1 \lambda w_\alpha^2 . \text{TRANSITIVE } [p_{o\alpha\alpha\alpha}^3 w^2 w^1] \wedge p_{o\alpha\alpha}^4 w^2 w^1$$
$$\lambda w_\alpha^1 \lambda w_\alpha^2 . \text{TRANSITIVE } [p_{o\alpha\alpha\alpha\alpha}^7 w^2 w^1] \vee p_{o\alpha\alpha}^8 w^2 w^1$$

Figure 7: General substitutions for a theorem involving transitivity

responding type as an *expansion option* for an expansion tree, and say that an expansion option is *applied* when a branch labeled with the wff and descending from the node is added to the tree. Once one has chosen a way to generate expansion terms for various nodes of the initial expansion tree representing the theorem to be proved, one can envision a master expansion tree to which all of these options have been applied. (Of course, some options may be associated with nodes which must first be created by application of other options.) How the master expansion tree is represented will depend on the implementation, but in general one will try to avoid explicit representation of those parts of it which are not yet needed.

One can then choose (by heuristics or exhaustive search) a subtree of the master tree of manageable size, and try to find substitutions for its free variables which make its deep formula a tautology (or a contradiction, if one is using a dual expansion tree). (Of course, replication of expansion variables must be allowed for in the generation of the subtree or the subsequent search process.) This part of the process resembles first-order proof search, except that higher-order unification must be used. A variety of first-order methods could be adapted to this task. One can also envision various ways of intertwining the process of applying expansion options with that of finding substitutions for variables which create a tautology.

An explicit example of a way to search for expansion proofs is provided by TPS [Andrews et al. 1996]. After a subtree of the master expansion tree has been chosen, a search for an *acceptable mating* [Andrews 1981] (*spanning set of connections* [Bibel 1987]) of the literals of the deep formula is conducted. The system starts with an empty mating and progressively adds connections between literals to span the paths through the wff. It replicates variables as it would in a first-order proof search, using the methods of Issar [1990] where appropriate. It uses Huet's [1975] higher-order unification algorithm to check the compatibility of the connections in the partial mating. A unification tree is associated with the partial mating, and when a new connection is added to the mating, the associated disagreement pair is added to all the leaves of the unification tree, and some work is done processing the unification tree. When incompatibilities are encountered, the process backtracks. Since higher-order unification may not terminate, the growth of the unification tree is arbitrarily limited by flags which are set by the user. Similar bounds limit the time which can be spent on any particular subtree of the master expansion tree.

Let us illustrate certain aspects of this process more concretely by discussing how it can be used to automatically find a proof of theorem X5310 like that in Figure 3. The crucial expansion variable for this proof is $r_{o\beta(o\beta)}$, which occurs at the beginning of line (1) of the proof. After trying various other expansion options (including those in Figure 5) and failing to find expansion proofs in the allocated time, the system will consider the third expansion option in Figure 6:

$$\lambda w^1_{o\beta} \lambda w^2_\beta \forall w^5_\beta . r^{15}_{o\beta\beta(o\beta)} w^1 w^2 w^5 \vee r^{16}_{o\beta\beta(o\beta)} w^1 w^2 w^5 \tag{3.1}$$

The system generates the deep formula which is obtained by using this expansion option and by using variables as expansion terms at other expansion nodes. It finds an acceptable mating of the literals in this formula, and an associated substitution which can be applied to the deep formula to render it tautological. To make the wff 3.1 easier to read we make alphabetical changes of bound variables and write it as

$$\lambda p_{o\beta} \lambda y_\beta \forall z_\beta . r^{15}_{o\beta\beta(o\beta)} pyz \vee r^{16}_{o\beta\beta(o\beta)} pyz \tag{3.2}$$

The substitution associated with the mating substitutes $\lambda p_{o\beta} \lambda y_\beta \lambda z_\beta . \sim pz$ for $r^{15}_{o\beta\beta(o\beta)}$ and $\lambda p_{o\beta} \lambda y_\beta \lambda z_\beta . py$ for $r^{16}_{o\beta\beta(o\beta)}$. Application of this substitution to these auxiliary variables in 3.2 produces

$$\lambda p_{o\beta} \lambda y_\beta \forall z_\beta . [\lambda p \lambda y \lambda z . \sim pz] pyz \vee [\lambda p \lambda y \lambda z . py] pyz \tag{3.3}$$

which λ-reduces to

$$\lambda p_{o\beta} \lambda y_\beta \forall z_\beta . \sim pz \vee py \tag{3.4}$$

This wff can be put into miniscope form, obtaining:

$$[\lambda p_{o\beta} \lambda y_\beta . \exists z_\beta pz \supset py] \tag{3.5}$$

At this point, a new expansion proof using this expansion term can easily be constructed, and the tactics which translate it to a natural deduction proof readily reduce the problem to deriving line (17) of Figure 3 from line (1). The expansion term for $r_{o\beta(o\beta)}$ in the expansion proof is used by the tactics to produce lines (2) - (3) of the proof. The antecedent of line (3) is easily provable by first-order methods (as shown in lines (4) - (16) of Figure 3), and the consequent of line (3) is line (17).

A powerful alternative procedure for finding expansion proofs which is also implemented in TPS is described in [Bishop 1999b, Bishop 1999a]. Called *component search*, it is an essentially breadth-first mating search procedure in which matings are constructed by taking unions from a fixed list of smaller matings. The unions are chosen with little effort by using a criterion which is satisfied by minimal complete matings, and the procedure looks for unspanned paths (a relatively expensive task) only rarely. The unifiers for each connection are computed within the constraints of the unification search bounds, and stored as a directed acyclic graph. Unifiers for sets of connections are quickly computed by merging sets of these directed acyclic graphs in an obvious way. We refer the reader to the cited publications for more details.

3.2. Constrained resolution

Since resolution plays such a significant role in first-order theorem proving, it is natural that a number of proposals [Andrews 1971, Benzmüller and Kohlhase 1998a, Benzmüller and Kohlhase 1998b, Henschen 1972, Huet 1972, Huet 1973, Jensen and Pietrzykowski 1976, Kohlhase 1994b, Pietrzykowski 1973, Wolfram 1993] for extending resolution to higher-order logic have been made, with varying degrees of detail. In this section we briefly describe one of the most notable of these, Huet's Constrained Resolution [1972, 1973].

We shall use the method of Skolemization discussed in section 1.3 whereby the Skolemized form of $\sim \Pi_{o(o\alpha)} P_{o\alpha}$ is $\sim P_{o\alpha} \left[c_{\alpha(o\alpha)} P_{o\alpha} \right]$. The fact that this method of Skolemization will permit the derivation of certain consequences of the Axiom of Choice does not concern us here.

As noted previously, there are two features of higher-order logic which complicate the task of extending first-order proof procedures to higher-order logic:

1. Most general unifiers need not exist, and higher-order unification is undecidable.
2. Not all necessary substitution terms can be generated by unification of formulas already present.

With regard to the first complication, suppose we have two clauses $\mathbf{N} \vee \mathcal{L}_1$ and $\sim \mathbf{M} \vee \mathcal{L}_2$ of first-order logic, and we wish to resolve on the literals $\mathbf{N}$ and $\sim \mathbf{M}$. (Here $\mathcal{L}_1$ and $\mathcal{L}_2$ are disjunctions of literals, possibly empty. Of course, a disjunction of literals may be represented as a multiset of literal-occurrences, but for the moment we regard that as an implementation detail and concentrate on the essential logic of the situation.) We may assume that these clauses have no variables in common. If $\mathbf{N}$ and $\mathbf{M}$ are unifiable, in first-order logic there is an essentially unique most general unifier (mgu) θ of $\mathbf{N}$ and $\mathbf{M}$, and the resolvent of these clauses is $\theta \mathcal{L}_1 \vee \theta \mathcal{L}_2$.

However, if these are clauses of higher-order logic, $\mathbf{N}$ and $\mathbf{M}$ may have no most general unifier even if they are unifiable, so many essentially different resolvents may be obtained by resolving these clauses on the specified literals. Moreover, since the unification search tree may be infinite, no matter how long one searches for unifiers, there is the possibility that additional unifiers (and hence additional resolvents) could be found with additional search. Of course, in general one does not know which resolvents will be needed to prove the theorem in question.

The solution to this problem proposed by Huet is to postpone computing unifiers whenever mgu's do not exist, and to attach to each clause a set of *constraints* on the variables in the clause. When one finally derives the empty clause, any unifier which satisfies its constraints will suffice.

This leads to the following definitions for higher-order resolution:

- A *constraint* is a set of wffs of the same type.
- A substitution θ *satisfies a constraint* C iff $\{\theta A \mid A \in C\}$ is a unit set.
- A substitution θ *satisfies a set* S *of constraints* iff it simultaneously satisfies all the constraints in S.
- A *clause* is a disjunction of literals; clauses are identified if they can be transformed into each other by applying λ-conversions and the laws of associativity and commutativity of disjunction (applied to disjunctions which are not buried in the arguments of predicate variables or constraints).
- A *constrained clause* $\mathcal{L} \mid S$ is a pair consisting of a clause $\mathcal{L}$ and a set S of constraints. Constrained clauses are identified if they can be obtained from each other by renaming of variables; of course, all the variables in the literals and the constraints must be renamed simultaneously.

To prove a sentence A of type theory, one transforms its negation into a set of constrained clauses in which the sets of constraints are empty. The procedure is generally like that used for first-order logic. One then uses the rules below to derive a constrained clause $\square \mid S$, where $\square$ is the empty clause, and S is a satisfiable set of constraints.

Constrained Resolution Rule:

- From $N \vee \mathcal{L}_1 \mid S_1$ and $\sim M \vee \mathcal{L}_2 \mid S_2$ infer
  $\mathcal{L}_1 \vee \mathcal{L}_2 \mid S_1 \cup S_2 \cup \{\{N, M\}\}$,
  where the given constrained clauses have no common variables, and N and $\sim M$ are literals.

Constrained Factoring Rule:

- From $N \vee M \vee \mathcal{L} \mid S$ infer
  $N \vee \mathcal{L} \mid S \cup \{\{N, M\}\}$,
  where N and M are literals.

In order to deal with the second complication mentioned above, there are additional rules called *splitting rules*, which are stated below. In each rule, P is an atom whose head predicate is a variable $p_{o\alpha_1\ldots\alpha_n}$. In essence, we unify P with a wff which has at its head a connective or quantifier, and reduce the result to one or more constrained clauses. In each of the rules as specified below, the variables q_o, r_o, $q_{o\alpha}$, and r_α must be new (i.e., not occur in P or in $\mathcal{L}$ or in the constraints in S).

- From $P \vee \mathcal{L} \mid S$ infer
  $\sim q_o \vee \mathcal{L} \mid S \cup \{\{P, \sim q_o\}\}$.
- From $P \vee \mathcal{L} \mid S$ infer
  $q_o \vee r_o \vee \mathcal{L} \mid S \cup \{\{P, q_o \vee r_o\}\}$.
- From $P \vee \mathcal{L} \mid S$ infer
  $q_{o\alpha} r_\alpha \vee \mathcal{L} \mid S \cup \{\{P, \Pi_{o(o\alpha)} q_{o\alpha}\}\}$.
- From $\sim P \vee \mathcal{L} \mid S$ infer
  $q_o \vee \mathcal{L} \mid S \cup \{\{P, \sim q_o\}\}$.

- From $\sim \mathbf{P} \vee \mathcal{L} \, / \, \mathcal{S}$ infer
  $\sim \mathbf{q}_o \vee \mathcal{L} \, / \, \mathcal{S} \cup \{\{\mathbf{P}, \, \mathbf{q}_o \vee \mathbf{r}_o\}\}$ and
  $\sim \mathbf{r}_o \vee \mathcal{L} \, / \, \mathcal{S} \cup \{\{\mathbf{P}, \, \mathbf{q}_o \vee \mathbf{r}_o\}\}$.
- From $\sim \mathbf{P} \vee \mathcal{L} \, / \, \mathcal{S}$ infer
  $\sim \mathbf{q}_{o\alpha} \left[c_{\alpha(o\alpha)} \mathbf{q}_{o\alpha} \right] \vee \mathcal{L} \, / \, \mathcal{S} \cup \{\{\mathbf{P}, \, \Pi_{o(o\alpha)} \mathbf{q}_{o\alpha}\}\}$.

Huet [1972] proved that every theorem of $\mathcal{T}$ can be established using these rules.

Of course, in addition to applying these rules, a system implementing constrained resolution would process the constraints in various ways, such as the following:

1. A constrained clause with an unsatisfiable set of constraints should be deleted as promptly as possible.
2. If some wff occurs in two constraints in a set of constraints, those constraints should be merged (i.e., replaced by their union) in that set.
3. If a general set of unifiers which satisfies some constraint is not too large, each of those substitutions can be applied to generate a new constrained clause; the constraint in question will reduce to a singleton in each of the new clauses, and can be deleted.

In addition, ways must be found to control the enormous proliferation of clauses which can be generated by these rules.

3.3. Extensional resolution

The ideas we have discussed so far have been directed toward proving theorems of the system $\mathcal{T}$ of elementary type theory, which lacks the axioms of Extensionality and Descriptions of the full system $\mathcal{C}$ of classical type theory. Of course, to prove a theorem $\mathbf{A}_o$ of $\mathcal{C}$, one can in principle prove $[\mathbf{H}_o \supset \mathbf{A}_o]$ in $\mathcal{T}$, where $\mathbf{H}_o$ is an appropriate conjunction of axioms of Extensionality and Descriptions, but this is often far from satisfactory in the practical sense.

An extension of constrained resolution to incorporate extensionality, and an implementation of these ideas in a system called LEO, are described in [Benzmüller and Kohlhase 1998a, Benzmüller and Kohlhase 1998b, Benzmüller 1999a]. The representation of constrained clauses is a little different from that discussed in section 3.2. Literals are represented as atoms with superscripts T or F to indicate whether they are positive or negative, and constraints are represented by negative equalities which are simply disjoined to the rest of the clause. Thus, the constrained clause

$$\sim \mathbf{q}^1_{o(o\alpha)}[\mathbf{G}_{o\alpha\alpha}.\mathbf{J}_{\alpha(o\alpha)} f_{o\alpha}] \vee \mathbf{q}^1 f \, / \, \{\{[\lambda u_{o\alpha}.u.\mathbf{J}_{\alpha(o\alpha)} f_{o\alpha}], \mathbf{q}^1_{o(o\alpha)}\}\}$$

is represented as

$$[\mathbf{q}^1_{o(o\alpha)}[\mathbf{G}_{o\alpha\alpha}.\mathbf{J}_{\alpha(o\alpha)} f_{o\alpha}]]^F \vee [\mathbf{q}^1 f]^T \vee [[\lambda u_{o\alpha}.u.\mathbf{J}_{\alpha(o\alpha)} f_{o\alpha}] = \mathbf{q}^1_{o(o\alpha)}]^F,$$

which is logically equivalent to

$$[[\lambda u_{o\alpha}.u.\mathbf{J}_{\alpha(o\alpha)} f_{o\alpha}] = \mathbf{q}^1_{o(o\alpha)}] \supset .[\mathbf{q}^1_{o(o\alpha)}[\mathbf{G}_{o\alpha\alpha}.\mathbf{J}_{\alpha(o\alpha)} f_{o\alpha}]]^F \vee [\mathbf{q}^1 f]^T.$$

Similarly,

$$\mathcal{L} \vee [\mathbf{A}^1 = \mathbf{A}^2]^F \vee [\mathbf{B}^1 = \mathbf{B}^2]^F \vee [\mathbf{C}^1 = \mathbf{C}^2]^F$$

is logically equivalent to

$$[[\mathbf{A}^1 = \mathbf{A}^2] \wedge [\mathbf{B}^1 = \mathbf{B}^2] \wedge [\mathbf{C}^1 = \mathbf{C}^2]] \supset \mathcal{L}.$$

The rules of inference of extensional resolution can be applied to all the literals of a clause, including those which represent constraints; indeed, higher-order unification is simply represented by additional rules of inference for processing clauses. We state the rules of inference of extensional resolution below. For the sake of brevity, we shall be somewhat informal, and tacitly assume that the rules are interpreted so that equality is commutative, variable conflicts are avoided, etc. For certain technical details the reader should consult the cited references.

We first introduce some notations. $\mathrm{CNF}(\mathbf{P})$ denotes the set of clauses obtained from $\mathbf{P}$ by Skolemizing, λ-normalizing, and putting the result into conjunctive normal form. A *Skolem term* for a clause with free variables $\mathbf{x}^1_{\alpha^1}, \cdots, \mathbf{x}^n_{\alpha^n}$ is a term of the form $\mathbf{f}^n_{\alpha^n \cdots \alpha^1} \mathbf{x}^1_{\alpha^1} \cdots \mathbf{x}^n_{\alpha^n}$, where $\mathbf{f}$ is a new constant and n specifies the number of necessary arguments[12] for $\mathbf{f}$. We shall sometimes use s_α as an abbreviation for such a term.

We now state the rules of inference. First, there are six rules for handling the unification constraints:

- (α) From $\mathcal{L} \vee [(\lambda \mathbf{x}_\alpha \mathbf{A}) = (\lambda \mathbf{y}_\alpha \mathbf{B})]^F$ infer
  $\mathcal{L} \vee [\; \mathsf{S}^{\mathbf{x}}_s \mathbf{A} = \; \mathsf{S}^{\mathbf{y}}_s \mathbf{B}]^F$,
  where s_α is a Skolem term for the given clause.
- (η) From $\mathcal{L} \vee [(\lambda \mathbf{x}_\alpha \mathbf{A}) = \mathbf{B}]^F$ infer
  $\mathcal{L} \vee [\; \mathsf{S}^{\mathbf{x}}_s \mathbf{A} = (\mathbf{B}s)]^F$,
  where s_α is a Skolem term for the given clause.
- (**Decompose**) From $\mathcal{L} \vee [\mathbf{c}\mathbf{U}^1 \cdots \mathbf{U}^n = \mathbf{c}\mathbf{V}^1 \cdots \mathbf{V}^n]^F$ infer
  $\mathcal{L} \vee [\mathbf{U}^1 = \mathbf{V}^1]^F \vee \ldots \vee [\mathbf{U}^n = \mathbf{V}^n]^F$,
  where $\mathbf{c}$ is a constant.
- (**Triv**) From $\mathcal{L} \vee [\mathbf{A} = \mathbf{A}]^F$ infer
  $\mathcal{L}$
- (**Subst**) From $\mathcal{L} \vee [\mathbf{x}^1 = \mathbf{N}^1]^F \vee \ldots \vee [\mathbf{x}^n = \mathbf{N}^n]^F$ infer
  $\mathrm{CNF}\left(\mathsf{S}^{\mathbf{x}^1 \cdots \mathbf{x}^n}_{\mathbf{N}^1 \cdots \mathbf{N}^n} \mathcal{L} \right)$,
  where $\mathbf{x}^1, \ldots, \mathbf{x}^n$ are distinct variables such that $\mathbf{x}^i$ does not occur free in $\mathbf{N}^j$ for $i, j \leq n$.
- (**Flex** $-$ **Rigid**) From $\mathcal{L} \vee [\mathbf{f}_\gamma \mathbf{U}^1 \cdots \mathbf{U}^n = \mathbf{c}\mathbf{V}^1 \cdots \mathbf{V}^m]^F$ infer
  $\mathcal{L} \vee [\mathbf{f} = \mathbf{G}]^F \vee [\mathbf{f}_\gamma \mathbf{U}^1 \cdots \mathbf{U}^n = \mathbf{c}\mathbf{V}^1 \cdots \mathbf{V}^m]^F$,
  where $\mathbf{f}_\gamma$ is a variable, $\mathbf{c}$ is a constant, $\mathbf{G}$ is a wff of type γ having the form $\lambda \mathbf{x}^1 \cdots \lambda \mathbf{x}^n . \mathbf{v}[\mathbf{h}^1 \mathbf{x}^1 \cdots \mathbf{x}^n] \cdots [\mathbf{h}^r \mathbf{x}^1 \cdots \mathbf{x}^n]$, the $\mathbf{h}^i$ are new variables, and $\mathbf{v}$ is one of the $\mathbf{x}^i$ (in which case $\mathbf{G}$ is called a *projection*), or $\mathbf{v}$ is $\mathbf{c}$ (in which case $\mathbf{G}$ is called an *imitation of* $\mathbf{c}$).

---

[12]See section 1.3.

Next are rules which correspond to the rules for constrained resolution listed in section 3.2.

- **(Resolve)** From $[\mathbf{N}]^\alpha \vee \mathcal{L}_1$ and $[\mathbf{M}]^\beta \vee \mathcal{L}_2$ infer
$\mathcal{L}_1 \vee \mathcal{L}_2 \vee [\mathbf{N} = \mathbf{M}]^F$,
where $\alpha \neq \beta$, and $\alpha, \beta \in \{T, F\}$.

- **(Factor)** From $[\mathbf{N}]^\alpha \vee [\mathbf{M}]^\alpha \vee \mathcal{L}$ infer
$[\mathbf{N}]^\alpha \vee \mathcal{L} \vee [\mathbf{N} = \mathbf{M}]^F$,
where $\alpha \in \{T, F\}$.

- **(Prim)** From $[\mathbf{p}_\gamma \mathbf{U}^1 \cdots \mathbf{U}^k]^\alpha \vee \mathcal{L}$ infer
$[\mathbf{p}_\gamma \mathbf{U}^1 \cdots \mathbf{U}^k]^\alpha \vee \mathcal{L} \vee [\mathbf{p}_\gamma = \mathbf{P}]^F$,
where $\mathbf{p}_\gamma$ is a variable and $\mathbf{P}$ is a primitive substitution term (such as may be found in Figure 4 or 5) of type γ.

Finally, there are three rules which, in conjunction with those above, provide for extensionality:

- **(Equiv)** From $\mathcal{L} \vee [\mathbf{M}_o = \mathbf{N}_o]^F$ infer
$\mathrm{CNF}(\mathcal{L} \vee [\mathbf{M}_o \equiv \mathbf{N}_o]^F)$.

- **(Leib)** From $\mathcal{L} \vee [\mathbf{M}_\alpha = \mathbf{N}_\alpha]^F$ infer
$\mathrm{CNF}(\mathcal{L} \vee [\forall \mathbf{p}_{o\alpha}.\mathbf{p}\mathbf{M} \supset \mathbf{p}\mathbf{N}]^F)$,
where $\alpha \in \{o, \iota\}$ and the variable $\mathbf{p}$ is not free in $\mathbf{M}$ or $\mathbf{N}$.

- **(Func)** From $\mathcal{L} \vee [\mathbf{M}_{\beta\alpha} = \mathbf{N}_{\beta\alpha}]^F$ infer
$\mathcal{L} \vee [\mathbf{M}s = \mathbf{N}s]^F$,
where s_α is a Skolem term for this clause.

Much experimentation with extensional resolution is still needed, but it is reported in [Benzmüller and Kohlhase 1998b] that LEO outperforms well known first-order theorem provers on many theorems involving set theory. Additional discussion of this topic may be found in [Benzmüller 1999b].

3.4. Other higher-order instantiation methods

The basic problems of instantiating higher-order quantifiers arise in a variety of contexts in addition to proving theorems of type theory, and ideas which have been developed for use in those contexts may also be adapted to type theory.

Z-match [Bailin and Barker-Plummer 1993] is an inference rule for incrementally elaborating set instantiations while searching for proofs in a sequent-calculus [Gentzen 1935] formulation of Zermelo Set Theory. However, the ideas can easily be reformulated to apply to a sequent-calculus formulation of type theory, where they become somewhat simpler since there is no need to guarantee (by means of the Axiom of Subsets of Zermelo Set Theory) that formulas for set instantiations denote subsets of existing sets.

Since we are only concerned with presenting essential ideas here, we shall simply write meta-variables denoting yet-to-be-specified expressions as variables, omitting explicit mention of the variables on which they depend. Also, since (as noted by Schütte) a sequent $\mathbf{A}_1, \ldots, \mathbf{A}_n \to \mathbf{B}_1, \ldots, \mathbf{B}_m$ can be represented as the disjunction

$\sim \mathbf{A}_1 \vee \ldots \vee \sim \mathbf{A}_n \vee \mathbf{B}_1 \vee \ldots \vee \mathbf{B}_n$, we shall regard sequents as disjunctions of wffs. We let Δ denote an arbitrary disjunction of wffs (possibly empty), and use the associativity and commutativity of disjunction implicitly. The axioms of the system are of the form $\sim \mathbf{P} \vee \mathbf{P} \vee \Delta$. When searching for a proof, one works backwards from the theorem to be proved according to the inverses of the rules of the sequent calculus. One of these rules (applied backwards) replaces $\mathbf{D}$ by $[\mathbf{D} \vee \mathbf{D}]$, essentially duplicating whatever quantifiers may occur in $\mathbf{D}$. When one applies inverse existential generalization, one replaces $\exists \mathbf{x}_\alpha \mathbf{B}_{o\alpha} \mathbf{x}_\alpha$ by $\mathbf{B}_{o\alpha} \mathbf{f}_\alpha$, where $\mathbf{f}_\alpha$ is a variable for which one can make appropriate substitutions later. In particular, α may have a form such as $(o\beta)$, in which case $\mathbf{f}_{o\beta}$ is a set variable. The essential problem is to make substitutions for such variables so that each of the leaves of the proof tree becomes an axiom.

The Z-match rule takes a variety of forms, depending on the sequent to which it is applied. In each case, it applies a substitution to a variable $\mathbf{f}_{o\beta}$ occurring in the sequent which reduces that sequent to one that is readily provable; the same substitution must be applied to all occurrences of $\mathbf{f}_{o\beta}$ in other sequents, and the term substituted for $\mathbf{f}_{o\beta}$ contains additional variables for which further substitutions can be applied in order to make other sequents provable. Thus, a sequence of applications of Z-match produces incremental elaboration of the wff needed to instantiate the original existentially quantified variable $\mathbf{x}_{o\beta}$.

If the sequent to be proved is convertible to the form

$$\sim \mathbf{f}_{o\beta} \mathbf{T}_\beta \vee \mathbf{P}_{o\beta} \mathbf{T}_\beta \vee \Delta,$$

where $\mathbf{f}_{o\beta}$ does not occur in $\mathbf{P}_{o\beta} \mathbf{T}_\beta$, the Z-match rule may be used to substitute for $\mathbf{f}_{o\beta}$ the wff $[\lambda \mathbf{y}_\beta . \mathbf{g}_{o\beta} \mathbf{y}_\beta \wedge \mathbf{P}_{o\beta} \mathbf{y}_\beta]$, where $\mathbf{g}_{o\beta}$ and $\mathbf{y}_\beta$ are new variables. The sequent becomes

$$\sim [\mathbf{g}_{o\beta} \mathbf{T}_\beta \wedge \mathbf{P}_{o\beta} \mathbf{T}_\beta] \vee \mathbf{P}_{o\beta} \mathbf{T}_\beta \vee \Delta',$$

which reduces to the axiom

$$\sim \mathbf{g}_{o\beta} \mathbf{T}_\beta \vee \sim \mathbf{P}_{o\beta} \mathbf{T}_\beta \vee \mathbf{P}_{o\beta} \mathbf{T}_\beta \vee \Delta'.$$

Additional substitutions can be made for $\mathbf{g}_{o\beta}$ to prove sequents on other branches of the proof tree.

If the sequent to be proved is convertible to the form

$$\mathbf{f}_{o\beta} \mathbf{T}_\beta \vee \mathbf{P}_{o\beta} \mathbf{T}_\beta \vee \Delta,$$

where $\mathbf{f}_{o\beta}$ does not occur in $\mathbf{P}_{o\beta} \mathbf{T}_\beta$, the Z-match rule may be used to substitute for $\mathbf{f}_{o\beta}$ the wff $[\lambda \mathbf{y}_\beta . [\mathbf{y}_\beta = \mathbf{T}_\beta \vee \mathbf{g}_{o\beta} \mathbf{y}_\beta] \wedge \sim \mathbf{P}_{o\beta} \mathbf{y}_\beta]$, where $\mathbf{g}_{o\beta}$ and $\mathbf{y}_\beta$ are new variables. The sequent becomes

$$[[\mathbf{T}_\beta = \mathbf{T}_\beta \vee \mathbf{g}_{o\beta} \mathbf{T}_\beta] \wedge \sim \mathbf{P}_{o\beta} \mathbf{T}_\beta] \vee \mathbf{P}_{o\beta} \mathbf{T}_\beta \vee \Delta',$$

which is readily proved.

Special cases of the Z-match rules above are those in which $\mathbf{P}_{o\beta}$ is λ-convertible to the form $[\lambda \mathbf{y}_\beta \mathbf{B}_o]$, where $\mathbf{y}_\beta$ is not free in $\mathbf{B}_o$. In these cases we have the rules of *simple* Z-match. The Z-match rules can be extended in various ways, such as by introducing quantifiers, conjunctions, and disjunctions into the term substituted for $\mathbf{f}_{o\beta}$ in appropriate circumstances. See [Bailin and Barker-Plummer 1993] for the details.

Additional methods of instantiating higher-order quantifiers were developed by Bledsoe, and later by Bledsoe and Feng, in order to prove certain theorems of analysis in second-order logic. These methods are based on the idea that it is often possible to construct expansion terms in a systematic way from expressions which are already present in the theorem to be proved. Specific basic rules and combining rules for doing this in certain contexts are given. A theorem prover using these rules is able to perform quite impressively on certain examples. See [Bledsoe 1977, Bledsoe 1979, Bledsoe 1983, Bledsoe and Feng 1993] for details.

3.5. Additional techniques

As noted in [Kohlhase 1994a], the introduction of sorts to first-order automated deduction has brought greater conciseness of representation and a considerable gain in efficiency by reducing the search space. It is therefore promising to treat sorts (subtypes) in higher-order theorem proving as well. Work related to this may be found in [Kohlhase 1994b] and (for the associated unification problem) [Johann and Kohlhase 1994, Nipkow and Qian 1994], and references cited therein.

Rippling is a technique developed for inductive theorem proving which uses syntactic differences between terms to guide the proof search. Annotations (colors) are attached to symbol occurrences to represent the relevant information. Coloring has been extended to type theory in [Hutter and Kohlhase 1997, Hutter and Kohlhase 2000].

4. Conclusion

Classical type theory is a rich language for expressing statements of mathematics and other disciplines. Proving theorems automatically or semi-automatically in this realm involves many complex problems, but can lead to many significant applications.

We list some areas of research where progress will facilitate the development of better theorem provers for classical type theory:

- Basic search mechanisms related to the first-order aspects of proof search.
- Methods of instantiating quantifiers on higher-order variables.
- Special methods for induction.
- Higher-order unification.
- Special methods for handling equality. While equality can be defined in type theory, simply relying on the definition does not generally suffice for proving

theorems involving equality efficiently. Much of the relevant work on this problem is concerned with higher-order equational unification (e-unification) and rewriting; references may be found in [Dowek 2001] (Chapter 16 of this Handbook).

- Rewriting.
- The treatment of extensionality in various contexts.
- Dealing with descriptions in an efficient way. Although description operators at higher types can be defined from those at lower types (see [Andrews 1986, section 53]), uniform techniques for handling descriptions efficiently at all types are needed.
- Developing libraries of definitions, theorems, and theories, and methods of using them.
- Subtypes.
- Improved methods of transforming proofs from one format to another, and improving the style of the proofs that are obtained.
- Precise definitions of search procedures, and completeness proofs for them.

Of course, solutions to problems in many of these areas have at least potential relationships to each other, and these need to be developed. Heuristics and metatheorems are needed to guide and restrict various search processes. Many ideas need to be extended from first-order logic to type theory.

Most methods for automatically proving theorems of first- or higher-order logic which have been developed so far trace their origins back to the methods of Herbrand, Gentzen, or Beth. In general, the proofs found automatically by these methods are essentially normal[13]. For example, such methods will find only first-order proofs for first-order theorems. Consideration of general mathematical practice makes it clear that there is also a need to develop quite different search procedures which may produce proofs which are not normal. For this, quite new ideas may be needed.

Acknowledgments

Work on this chapter was partially supported by the National Science Foundation of the United States under Grants CCR-9624683 and CCR-9732312.

Bibliography

ANDREWS P. B. [1965], *A Transfinite Type Theory with Type Variables*, North-Holland Studies in Logic and the Foundations of Mathematics.

ANDREWS P. B. [1971], 'Resolution in Type Theory', *Journal of Symbolic Logic* **36**, 414–432.

ANDREWS P. B. [1972], 'General Models and Extensionality', *Journal of Symbolic Logic* **37**, 395–397.

---

[13]See [Prawitz 1965] or [Prawitz 1971].

ANDREWS P. B. [1974], 'Resolution and the Consistency of Analysis', *Notre Dame Journal of Formal Logic* **15**(1), 73–84.

ANDREWS P. B. [1980], Transforming Matings into Natural Deduction Proofs, *in* W. Bibel and R. Kowalski, eds, 'Proceedings of the 5th International Conference on Automated Deduction', Vol. 87 of *Lecture Notes in Computer Science*, Springer-Verlag, Les Arcs, France, pp. 281–292.

ANDREWS P. B. [1981], 'Theorem Proving via General Matings', *Journal of the ACM* **28**, 193–214.

ANDREWS P. B. [1986], *An Introduction to Mathematical Logic and Type Theory: To Truth Through Proof*, Academic Press.

ANDREWS P. B. [1989], 'On Connections and Higher-Order Logic', *Journal of Automated Reasoning* **5**, 257–291.

ANDREWS P. B. AND BISHOP M. [1996], On Sets, Types, Fixed Points, and Checkerboards, *in* P. Miglioli, U. Moscato, D. Mundici and M. Ornaghi, eds, 'Theorem Proving with Analytic Tableaux and Related Methods. 5th International Workshop. (TABLEAUX '96)', Vol. 1071 of *Lecture Notes in Artificial Intelligence*, Springer-Verlag, Terrasini, Italy, pp. 1–15.

ANDREWS P. B., BISHOP M., ISSAR S., NESMITH D., PFENNING F. AND XI H. [1996], 'TPS: A Theorem Proving System for Classical Type Theory', *Journal of Automated Reasoning* **16**, 321–353.

ANDREWS P. B., MILLER D. A., COHEN E. L. AND PFENNING F. [1984], Automating Higher-Order Logic, *in* W. W. Bledsoe and D. W. Loveland, eds, 'Automated Theorem Proving: After 25 Years', Contemporary Mathematics series, vol. 29, American Mathematical Society, pp. 169–192.

BAILIN S. C. [1988], 'A λ-Unifiability Test for Set Theory', *Journal of Automated Reasoning* **4**, 269–286.

BAILIN S. C. AND BARKER-PLUMMER D. [1993], 'Z-match: An Inference Rule for Incrementally Elaborating Set Instantiations', *Journal of Automated Reasoning* **11**, 391–428. Errata: JAR 12 (1994), 411–412.

BARENDREGT H. AND GEUVERS H. [2001], Proof-Assistants Using Dependent Type Systems, *in* A. Robinson and A. Voronkov, eds, 'Handbook of Automated Reasoning', Vol. II, Elsevier Science, chapter 18, pp. 1149–1238.

BELINFANTE J. G. F. [1996], 'On a Modification of Gödel's Algorithm for Class Formation', *Association for Automated Reasoning Newsletter* **34**, 10–15.

BENZMÜLLER C. [1999a], Equality and Extensionality in Automated Higher-Order Theorem Proving, PhD thesis, Universität des Saarlandes.

BENZMÜLLER C. [1999b], Extensional Higher-Order Paramodulation and RUE-Resolution, *in* Ganzinger [1999], pp. 399–413.

BENZMÜLLER C., CHEIKHROUHOU L., FEHRER D., FIEDLER A., HUANG X., KERBER M., KOHLHASE M., KONRAD K., MELIS E., MEIER A., SCHAARSCHMIDT W., SIEKMANN J. AND SORGE V. [1997], ΩMEGA: Towards a Mathematical Assistant, *in* McCune [1997], pp. 252–255.

BENZMÜLLER C. AND KOHLHASE M. [1998a], Extensional Higher-Order Resolution, *in* Kirchner and Kirchner [1998], pp. 56–71.

BENZMÜLLER C. AND KOHLHASE M. [1998b], System Description: LEO — A Higher-Order Theorem Prover, *in* Kirchner and Kirchner [1998], pp. 139–143.

BIBEL W. [1982], *Automated Theorem Proving*, Vieweg, Braunschweig.

BIBEL W. [1987], *Automated Theorem Proving*, second edn, Vieweg, Braunschweig.

BISHOP M. [1999a], A Breadth-First Strategy for Mating Search, *in* Ganzinger [1999], pp. 359–373.

BISHOP M. [1999b], Mating Search Without Path Enumeration, PhD thesis, Department of Mathematical Sciences, Carnegie Mellon University. Department of Mathematical Sciences Research Report No. 99–223. Available at http://gtps.math.cmu.edu/tps.html.

BISHOP M. AND ANDREWS P. B. [1998], Selectively Instantiating Definitions, *in* Kirchner and Kirchner [1998], pp. 365–380.

BLEDSOE W. W. [1977], Set Variables, in 'Proceedings of the Fifth International Joint Conference on Artificial Intelligence', IJCAI, MIT, Cambridge, MA, pp. 501–510.

BLEDSOE W. W. [1979], A Maximal Method for Set Variables in Automatic Theorem Proving, in J. E. Hayes, D. Michie and L. I. Mikulich, eds, 'Machine Intelligence 9', Ellis Harwood Ltd., Chichester, and John Wiley & Sons, pp. 53–100.

BLEDSOE W. W. [1983], Using Examples to Generate Instantiations of Set Variables, in 'Proceedings of the Eighth International Joint Conference on Artificial Intelligence', IJCAI, Karlsruhe, Germany, pp. 892–901.

BLEDSOE W. W. AND FENG G. [1993], 'Set-Var', Journal of Automated Reasoning 11, 293–314.

BOYER R., LUSK E., MCCUNE W., OVERBEEK R., STICKEL M. AND WOS L. [1986], 'Set Theory in First-Order Logic: Clauses for Gödel's Axioms', Journal of Automated Reasoning 2, 287–327.

BUSS S. R. [1994], 'On Gödel's Theorem on Lengths of Proofs I: Number of Lines and Speedup for Arithmetic', Journal of Symbolic Logic 59, 737–756.

CHURCH A. [1940], 'A Formulation of the Simple Theory of Types', Journal of Symbolic Logic 5, 56–68.

CHURCH A. [1956], Introduction to Mathematical Logic, Princeton University Press, Princeton, N.J.

DOWEK G. [2001], Higher-Order Unification and Matching, in A. Robinson and A. Voronkov, eds, 'Handbook of Automated Reasoning', Vol. II, Elsevier Science, chapter 16, pp. 1009–1062.

DREBEN B., ANDREWS P. AND AANDERAA S. [1963], 'False Lemmas in Herbrand', Bulletin of the American Mathematical Society 69, 699–706.

DREBEN B. AND DENTON J. [1966], 'A Supplement to Herbrand', Journal of Symbolic Logic 31, 393–398.

FEFERMAN S. [1964], 'Systems of Predicative Analysis', Journal of Symbolic Logic 29, 1–30.

FELTY A. P. [1986], Using Extended Tactics to Do Proof Transformations, Technical Report MS-CIS-86-89, Department of Computer and Information Science, University of Pennsylvania.

GALLIER J. H. [1986], Logic for Computer Science. Foundations of Automatic Theorem Proving, Harper & Row.

GANZINGER, H., ED. [1999], Proceedings of the 16th International Conference on Automated Deduction, Vol. 1632 of Lecture Notes in Artificial Intelligence, Springer-Verlag, Trento, Italy.

GENTZEN G. [1969], Investigations into Logical Deductions, in M. E. Szabo, ed., 'The Collected Papers of Gerhard Gentzen', North-Holland Publishing Co., Amsterdam, pp. 68–131.

GÖDEL K. [1936], 'Über die Länge von Beweisen', Ergebnisse eines Mathematischen Kolloquiums 7, 23–24. Translated in [Gödel 1986], pp. 396–399.

GÖDEL K. [1986], Collected Works, Volume I, Oxford University Press.

GOLDFARB W. D. [1981], 'The Undecidability of the Second-Order Unification Problem', Theoretical Computer Science 13, 225–230.

GORDON M. [1986], Why higher-order logic is a good formalism for specifying and verifying hardware, in G. J. Milne and P. A. Subrahmanyam, eds, 'Formal Aspects of VLSI Design', North-Holland, pp. 153–177.

GORDON M. [1996], Set Theory, Higher Order Logic or Both?, in von Wright et al. [1996], pp. 191–201.

GORDON M. J., MILNER A. J. AND WADSWORTH C. P. [1979], Edinburgh LCF. A Mechanised Logic of Computation, Vol. 78 of Lecture Notes in Computer Science, Springer-Verlag.

GOULD W. E. [1966], A Matching Procedure for ω-order Logic, PhD thesis, Princeton University.

GRUNDY, J. AND NEWEY, M., EDS [1998], Theorem Proving in Higher Order Logics. 11th International Conference, TPHOLs'98, Vol. 1479 of Lecture Notes in Computer Science, Springer-Verlag, Canberra, Australia.

GUNTER, E. L. AND FELTY, A., EDS [1997], Theorem Proving in Higher Order Logics. 10th International Conference, TPHOLs'97, Vol. 1275 of Lecture Notes in Computer Science, Springer-Verlag, Murray Hill, NJ, USA.

HANNA F. K. AND DAECHE N. [1985], Specification and Verification using Higher-Order Logic, in Koomen and Moto-oka, eds, 'Computer Hardware Description Languages and their Applications', North Holland, pp. 418–433.
URL: *http://www.cs.ukc.ac.uk/pubs/1985/416*

HANNA F. K. AND DAECHE N. [1986], Specification and Verification Using Higher-Order Logic: A Case Study, in G. J. Milne and P. A. Subrahmanyam, eds, 'Formal Aspects of VLSI Design', North-Holland, pp. 179–213.

HAZEN A. [1983], Ramified Type Theories, in D. Gabbay and F. Guenthner, eds, 'Handbook of Philosophical Logic', Vol. I, Reidel, Dordrecht.

HENKIN L. [1950], 'Completeness in the Theory of Types', *Journal of Symbolic Logic* 15, 81–91.

HENSCHEN L. J. [1972], N-Sorted Logic for Automated Theorem Proving in Higher-Order Logic, in 'Proceedings of the ACM Conference, Boston', pp. 71–81.

HERBRAND J. [1971], *Logical Writings*, Harvard University Press. Edited by Warren D. Goldfarb.

HINDLEY J. R. [1997], *Basic Simple Type Theory*, Cambridge University Press.

HUET G. P. [1972], Constrained Resolution: A Complete Method for Higher Order Logic, PhD thesis, Case Western Reserve University.

HUET G. P. [1973a], A Mechanization of Type Theory, in 'Proceedings of the Third International Joint Conference on Artificial Intelligence', IJCAI, Stanford University, California, USA, pp. 139–146.

HUET G. P. [1973b], 'The Undecidability of Unification in Third-order Logic', *Information and Control* 22, 257–267.

HUET G. P. [1975], 'A Unification Algorithm for Typed λ-Calculus', *Theoretical Computer Science* 1, 27–57.

HUTTER D. AND KOHLHASE M. [1997], A Coloured Version of the λ-Calculus, in McCune [1997], pp. 291–305.

HUTTER D. AND KOHLHASE M. [2000], 'Managing Structural Information by Higher-Order Colored Unification', *Journal of Automated Reasoning* 25, 123–164.

ISSAR S. [1990], Path-Focused Duplication: A Search Procedure for General Matings, in 'AAAI-90. Proceedings of the Eighth National Conference on Artificial Intelligence', Vol. 1, AAAI Press/The MIT Press, pp. 221–226.

JENSEN D. AND PIETRZYKOWSKI T. [1976], 'Mechanizing ω-Order Type Theory Through Unification', *Theoretical Computer Science* 3, 123–171.

JOHANN P. AND KOHLHASE M. [1994], Unification in an Extensional Lambda Calculus with Ordered Function Sorts and Constant Overloading, in A. Bundy, ed., 'Proceedings of the 12th International Conference on Automated Deduction', Vol. 814 of *Lecture Notes in Artificial Intelligence*, Springer-Verlag, Nancy, France, pp. 620–634.

KIRCHNER, C. AND KIRCHNER, H., EDS [1998], *Proceedings of the 15th International Conference on Automated Deduction*, Vol. 1421 of *Lecture Notes in Artificial Intelligence*, Springer-Verlag, Lindau, Germany.

KOHLHASE M. [1993], A Unifying Principle for Extensional Higher-Order Logic, Technical Report 93–153, Department of Mathematics, Carnegie Mellon University.

KOHLHASE M. [1994a], Higher-Order Order-Sorted Resolution, SEKI Report SR–94-01, Fachbereich Informatik, Universität des Saarlandes.

KOHLHASE M. [1994b], A Mechanization of Sorted Higher-Order Logic Based on the Resolution Principle, PhD thesis, Universität des Saarlandes.

KOHLHASE M. [1995], Higher-Order Tableaux, in P. Baumgartner, R. Hähnle and J. Posegga, eds, 'Theorem Proving with Analytic Tableaux and Related Methods. 4th International Workshop. (TABLEAUX '95)', Vol. 918 of *Lecture Notes in Artificial Intelligence*, Springer-Verlag, Schloß Rheinfels, St. Goar, Germany, pp. 294–309.

KOHLHASE M. [1998], Higher-Order Automated Theorem Proving, in W. Bibel and P. Schmitt, eds, 'Automated Deduction – A Basis for Applications', Vol. 1, Kluwer, pp. 431–462.

KONRAD K. [1998], HOT: A Concurrent Automated Theorem Prover Based on Higher-Order Tableaux, *in* Grundy and Newey [1998], pp. 245–261.

LEIVANT D. [1994], Higher Order Logic, *in* D. M. Gabbay, C. Hogger and J. Robinson, eds, 'Handbook of Logic in Artificial Intelligence and Logic Programming', Vol. 2, Oxford University Press, pp. 229–321.

MCCUNE, W., ED. [1997], *Proceedings of the 14th International Conference on Automated Deduction*, Vol. 1249 of *Lecture Notes in Artificial Intelligence*, Springer-Verlag, Townsville, North Queensland, Australia.

MILLER D. A. [1983], Proofs in Higher-Order Logic, PhD thesis, Carnegie Mellon University. 81 pp.

MILLER D. A. [1984], Expansion Tree Proofs and Their Conversion to Natural Deduction Proofs, *in* R. E. Shostak, ed., 'Proceedings of the 7th International Conference on Automated Deduction', Vol. 170 of *Lecture Notes in Computer Science*, Springer-Verlag, Napa, California, USA, pp. 375–393.

MILLER D. A. [1987], 'A Compact Representation of Proofs', *Studia Logica* **46**(4), 347–370.

NIPKOW T. AND QIAN Z. [1994], 'Reduction and Unification in Lambda Calculi with a General Notion of Subtype', *Journal of Automated Reasoning* **12**, 389–406.

PFENNING F. [1987], Proof Transformations in Higher-Order Logic, PhD thesis, Carnegie Mellon University. 156 pp.

PFENNING F. [2001], Logical Frameworks, *in* A. Robinson and A. Voronkov, eds, 'Handbook of Automated Reasoning', Vol. II, Elsevier Science, chapter 17, pp. 1063–1147.

PFENNING F. AND NESMITH D. [1990], Presenting Intuitive Deductions via Symmetric Simplification, *in* M. E. Stickel, ed., 'Proceedings of the 10th International Conference on Automated Deduction', Vol. 449 of *Lecture Notes in Artificial Intelligence*, Springer-Verlag, Kaiserslautern, Germany, pp. 336–350.

PIETRZYKOWSKI T. [1973], 'A Complete Mechanization of Second-Order Type Theory', *Journal of the ACM* **20**, 333–364.

PRAWITZ D. [1965], *Natural Deduction*, Almqvist & Wiksell.

PRAWITZ D. [1968], 'Hauptsatz for Higher Order Logic', *Journal of Symbolic Logic* **33**, 452–457.

PRAWITZ D. [1971], Ideas and Results in Proof Theory, *in* J. E. Fenstad, ed., 'Proceedings of the Second Scandinavian Logic Symposium', Studies in Logic and the Foundations of Mathematics 63, North-Holland, pp. 235–307.

QUAIFE A. [1992], 'Automated Deduction in von Neumann-Bernays-Gödel Set Theory', *Journal of Automated Reasoning* **8**, 91–147.

QUINE W. V. [1950], 'On Natural Deduction', *Journal of Symbolic Logic* **15**, 93–102.

RICHARDSON J., SMAILL A. AND GREEN I. [1998], System Description: Proof Planning in Higher-Order Logic with $\lambda - Clam$, *in* Kirchner and Kirchner [1998], pp. 129–133.

ROBINSON J. A. [1968], New Directions in Mechanical Theorem Proving, *in* 'Proceedings of the IFIP Congress', pp. 206–210.

ROBINSON J. A. [1969], Mechanizing Higher-Order Logic, *in* 'Machine Intelligence 4', Edinburgh University Press, pp. 151–170.

ROBINSON J. A. [1970], A Note on Mechanizing Higher Order Logic, *in* 'Machine Intelligence 5', Edinburgh University Press, pp. 121–135.

RUBIN H. AND RUBIN J. E. [1985], *Equivalents of the Axiom of Choice, II*, North-Holland.

RUSSELL B. [1908], 'Mathematical Logic as Based on the Theory of Types', *American Journal of Mathematics* **30**, 222–262. Reprinted in [van Heijenoort 1967], pp. 150–182.

SHAPIRO S. [1991], *Foundations without Foundationalism : A Case for Second-order Logic*, Clarendon Press, Oxford.

SMULLYAN R. M. [1963], 'A Unifying Principle in Quantification Theory', *Proceedings of the National Academy of Sciences, U.S.A.* **49**, 828–832.

SMULLYAN R. M. [1995], *First-Order Logic*, second corrected edn, Dover Publications, New York. First published in 1968 by Springer-Verlag.

STATMAN R. [1978], 'Bounds for Proof Search and Speed-up in the Predicate Calculus', *Annals of Mathematical Logic* **15**, 225–287.

TAKAHASHI M. [1967], 'A Proof of Cut-Elimination Theorem in Simple Type Theory', *Journal of the Mathematical Society of Japan* **19**, 399–410.

TAKAHASHI M. [1968], 'Cut-Elimination in Simple Type Theory with Extensionality', *Journal of the Mathematical Society of Japan* **19**.

TAKAHASHI M. [1970], 'A System of Simple Type Theory of Gentzen Style with Inference on Extensionality, and the Cut Elimination in it', *Commentarii Mathematici Universitatis Sancti Pauli* **18**, 129–147.

TAKEUTI G. [1953], 'On a Generalized Logic Calculus', *Japanese Journal of Mathematics* **23**, 39–96. Errata: ibid, vol. 24 (1954), 149–156.

TAKEUTI G. [1987], *Proof Theory*, Elsevier Science Publishers.

TARSKI A. [1956], The Concept of Truth in Formalized Languages, *in* J. H. Woodger, ed., 'Logic, Semantics, Metamathematics', Oxford University Press, Oxford, pp. 152–278.

VAN BENTHEM J. AND DOETS K. [1983], Higher-Order Logic, *in* D. M. Gabbay and F. Günthner, eds, 'Handbook of Philosophical Logic', Vol. I, Reidel, Dordrecht, pp. 275–329.

VAN HEIJENOORT J. [1967], *From Frege to Gödel*, Harvard University Press, Cambridge, Massachusetts.

VON WRIGHT, J., GRUNDY, J. AND HARRISON, J., EDS [1996], *Theorem Proving in Higher Order Logics. 9th International Conference, TPHOLs'96*, Vol. 1125 of *Lecture Notes in Computer Science*, Springer-Verlag, Turku, Finland.

WHITEHEAD A. N. AND RUSSELL B. [1910–1913], *Principia Mathematica*, Cambridge University Press, Cambridge, England. 3 volumes.

WOLFRAM D. A. [1993], *The Clausal Theory of Types*, Vol. 21 of *Cambridge Tracts in Theoretical Computer Science*, Cambridge University Press.

Index

Symbols

CHAPTER 16

Higher-Order Unification and Matching

Gilles Dowek

SECOND READERS: Jean Goubault-Larrecq and Gopalan Nadathur.

Contents

HANDBOOK OF AUTOMATED REASONING
Edited by Alan Robinson and Andrei Voronkov

1. Type Theory and Other Set Theories

After the discovery of reasonably efficient proof search methods for first-order logic in the middle of the sixties, a next step seemed to be the extension of these methods to higher-order logic (also called simple type theory), i.e. a logic allowing quantification over sets (i.e. predicates) and functions. Indeed, many problems require such a quantification for a natural expression. A strong advocate for the automatization of higher-order logic was J.A. Robinson who wrote in 1968 that "its adoption, in place of the restricted predicate calculus [i.e. first-order logic], as the basic formalism used in mechanical theorem proving systems, [was] an absolute necessary step if such system [were] ever going to be developed to the point of providing a genuinely useful mathematical service, or of helping to bring a deeper understanding of the process of mathematical thinking" [Robinson 1969].

Replying to Robinson, M. Davis recalled that higher-order logic was just one among several variants of set theory that all permit to reason about sets and functions, and that the choice of this particular variant could only be justified if it was more adequate for automatization than others: "Since higher-order logics are just notational variants of set theories formalized in first-order logic, the question of the use of higher-order formalisms in mechanical theorem-proving is simply a matter of whether or not such formalisms suggest useful algorithms" [Davis 1969].

As we shall see, it is indeed the case that higher-order logic is, so far, more adequate for automatization than other variants of set theory.

1.1. Naive Set Theory

Naive set theory permits the definition of sets *in comprehension*, i.e. by a characteristic property of their elements. For instance we can define the interval of numbers between 4 and 6 by the property $z \in \mathbb{R} \wedge 4 \leq z \wedge z \leq 6$. The *comprehension scheme* is thus stated

$$\forall x_1 \ ... \ \forall x_n \ \exists y \ \forall z \ ((z \in y) \Leftrightarrow P)$$

where P is an arbitrary proposition, z a variable, $x_1, ..., x_n$ the free variables of P except z and y a fresh variable, i.e. a variable different from z and not occurring in P.

For example, an instance of this scheme is

$$\exists y \ \forall z \ ((z \in y) \Leftrightarrow (z \in \mathbb{R} \wedge 4 \leq z \wedge z \leq 6))$$

Then, another axiom, the *extensionality axiom*, defines the equality of two sets: two sets are equal if they have the same elements

$$\forall x \ \forall y \ ((\forall z \ (z \in x \Leftrightarrow z \in y)) \Rightarrow x = y)$$

If we want a notation for the objects whose existence is asserted by the comprehension scheme, we skolemize it and introduce function symbols $f_{x_1,...,x_n,z,P}$. The skolemized comprehension scheme

$$\forall x_1 \; ... \; \forall x_n \; \forall z \; ((z \in f_{x_1,...,x_n,z,P}(x_1,...,x_n)) \Leftrightarrow P)$$

is then called *conversion scheme*. If we write the term $f_{x_1,...,x_n,z,P}(x_1,...,x_n)$ as $\{z \mid P\}$ (such a term is called an *abstraction*), the conversion scheme is written

$$\forall x_1 \; ... \; \forall x_n \; \forall z \; ((z \in \{z \mid P\}) \Leftrightarrow P)$$

With this convention, the proposition P in an abstraction $\{z \mid P\}$ cannot contain further abstractions (because the comprehension scheme is only stated for propositions containing no Skolem symbols). If we write $\{z \mid (t_1/x_1,...,t_n/x_n)P\}$ for the term $f_{x_1,...,x_n,z,P}(t_1,...,t_n)$, where the terms $t_1,...,t_n$ may contain abstractions, the propositions in abstractions may then contain further abstractions, but unlike the occurrences of z in the proposition P, the occurrences of z in the terms $t_1,...,t_n$ are not bound by the abstraction $\{z \mid (t_1/x_1,...,t_n/x_n)P\}$. In fact, it is easy to prove that the theory allowing nested abstractions binding all the variables is equivalent (see, for instance, [Henkin 1953, Dowek 1995]). Thus, we can consider the construction $\{z \mid P\}$ as a basic term construction, and state the conversion axiom

$$\forall x_1 \; ... \; \forall x_n \; \forall z \; ((z \in \{z \mid P\}) \Leftrightarrow P)$$

1.2. Plotkin-Andrews Quotient

Using a standard proof-search method with such a conversion scheme is rather inefficient. Indeed, if we want to prove, for instance, the proposition

$$2 \in \{x \mid x = 2 \lor x = 3\}$$

using the conversion scheme, we can transform it into the equivalent one

$$2 = 2 \lor 2 = 3$$

and conclude with the axioms of equality. But, going in the wrong direction, we may also transform this proposition into the equivalent one

$$2 \in \{x \mid x \in \{y \mid y = 2\} \lor x = 3\}$$

Thus, using the conversion axiom, a proof search algorithm could spend most of its time uselessly expanding and reducing propositions.

This remark reminds that of G. Plotkin, who noticed in 1972 that with the associativity axiom

$$\forall x \; \forall y \; \forall z \; ((x + y) + z = x + (y + z))$$

a proof search method could spend most of its time uselessly rearranging brackets [Plotkin 1972]. More generally, in any equational theory, a proof search method may spend too much time randomly replacing equals by equals.

The well-know solution proposed by Plotkin is to identify propositions equivalent modulo the congruence generated by the axioms. When there is a confluent and terminating rewrite system such that two propositions are equivalent if and only if they have the same normal forms, normal forms can be chosen as representatives of their equivalence classes in the quotient. For instance, with the associativity axiom, we identify propositions with their normal forms for the rewrite system

$$(x + y) + z \triangleright x + (y + z)$$

This way, the associativity axiom is equivalent to the proposition

$$\forall x \ \forall y \ \forall z \ (x + (y + z) = x + (y + z))$$

thus it is a simple consequence of the axioms of equality and it can be dropped. On the other hand, a unifier of two propositions is now a substitution making the propositions equal *modulo the equivalence* (such a problem is called *equational unification*). For instance the propositions

$$a = X + d \quad \text{and} \quad a = b + (c + d)$$

are unifiable (while they are not for the usual notion of unification) because substituting X by $b + c$ yields

$$a = (b + c) + d$$

which reduces to

$$a = b + (c + d)$$

In other words, the associativity axiom is now mixed with the unification algorithm.

A similar program: mixing the conversion axiom and unification algorithm was proposed in 1971 by P.B. Andrews, in the context of type theory: "[First-order resolution] is an elegant combination of substitution and cut [...]. An important open problem concerning resolution in type theory is to find an equally elegant way of combining [substitution], [conversion] and [cut]" [Andrews 1971].

To achieve this goal in naive set theory, we would consider the rewrite system

$$t \in \{z \mid P\} \triangleright (t/z)P$$

identify propositions with their normal forms and drop the conversion axiom. A unifier of two propositions would be a substitution making the propositions having the same normal form.

1.3. Type Theory

Unfortunately, naive set theory has several drawbacks: first, as is well-known, it is inconsistent, second: the above rewrite system is not terminating.

Inconsistency is given by Russell's paradox. The proposition "the set of sets that do not belong to themselves belongs to itself"

$$\{x \mid \neg x \in x\} \in \{x \mid \neg x \in x\}$$

is equivalent, by the conversion scheme, to its negation. Thus, both it and its negation are provable. This proposition is also a counter-example to termination, as it rewrites to its negation.

To avoid Russell's paradox, and to get a (hopefully) consistent theory of sets, we can restrict naive set theory in two ways. The first method is to restrict the comprehension scheme to some particular propositions (for instance Zermelo's set theory permits four constructions : pairs, unions, power sets and subsets), the other is to move to a many-sorted theory with a sort (called 0) for atoms a sort (called 1) for sets of atoms, a sort (called 2) for sets of sets of atoms, etc. and allow propositions of the form $t \in_n u$ only when t is of sort n and u of sort $n + 1$ (which permits to construct unions, power sets and subsets but disallows arbitrary pairs). The formalism obtained this way is called *higher-order logic* or *simple type theory*. The original formulation of A.N. Whitehead and B. Russell [Whitehead and Russell 1910-1913, 1925-1927] has been modified by L. Chwistek, F. Ramsey and finally by A. Church [Church 1940].

Although, as remarked by W.V.O. Quine [Quine 1969], the difference between these two methods is rather shallow (as a many-sorted theory can always be relativized as a single-sorted one, and introducing sorts is thus also a way to restrict the comprehension scheme to relativizations of sorted propositions), it is important for automatization.

- First, as some meaningless propositions such as $\mathbb{N} \in \mathbb{N}$ are forbidden by the syntax, they are systematically avoided by the proof search method.
- Then, the rewrite system terminates in higher-order logic and not set theory. Indeed, given a set A and a proposition P, set theory allows to define the set $\{z \in A \mid P\}$ of the members of A verifying the proposition P, and the rewrite rule associated to this restriction of the comprehension scheme

$$t \in \{z \in A \mid P\} \rhd t \in A \wedge (t/z)P$$

  does not terminate. A counter-example, which is an adaptation of Russell's paradox is Crabbé's proposition C

$$\{x \in A \mid \neg x \in x\} \in \{x \in A \mid \neg x \in x\}$$

This proposition rewrites to

$$\{x \in A \mid \neg x \in x\} \in A \wedge \neg\{x \in A \mid \neg x \in x\} \in \{x \in A \mid \neg x \in x\}$$

i.e. to $B \wedge \neg C$ where B is the proposition $\{x \in A \mid \neg x \in x\} \in A$.
Thus, the Plotkin-Andrews quotient cannot be applied, in a simple way, to set theory, while it can be applied to higher-order logic. Equational unification modulo conversion is called *higher-order unification* .

- At last, most proof-search method rely on cut elimination (sometimes taking the form of Herbrand's theorem). Both higher-order logic and set theory introduce more cuts than those already there in first-order logic with no axioms. These cuts can be eliminated in higher-order logic [Takahashi 1967, Prawitz

1968, Girard 1970, Girard 1972] but, Crabbé's counter-example shows that they cannot be eliminated in set theory. Indeed, Crabbé's proposition C rewrites to $B \wedge \neg C$. The proposition $\neg B$ has the following natural deduction proof

$$
\cfrac{
  \cfrac{
    \cfrac{\cfrac{\overline{B,C \vdash B \wedge \neg C}\ \text{axiom}}{B,C \vdash \neg C}\ \wedge\text{-elim} \quad \overline{B,C \vdash C}\ \text{axiom}}{B,C \vdash \bot}\ \neg\text{-elim}
  }{B \vdash \neg C}\ \neg\text{-intro}
  \quad
  \cfrac{
    \overline{B \vdash B}\ \text{axiom}
    \quad
    \cfrac{\cfrac{\cfrac{\overline{B,C \vdash B \wedge \neg C}\ \text{axiom}}{B,C \vdash \neg C}\ \wedge\text{-elim} \quad \overline{B,C \vdash C}\ \text{axiom}}{B,C \vdash \bot}\ \neg\text{-elim}}{B \vdash \neg C}\ \neg\text{-intro}
  }{B \vdash C}\ \wedge\text{-intro}
}{
  \cfrac{B \vdash \bot}{\vdash \neg B}\ \neg\text{-intro}
}\ \neg\text{-elim}
$$

that contains a cut (the negation is first introduces then eliminated). But it is easy to check that this proposition does not have a cut-free proof (notice that after eliminating twice a cut in the proof above we get back the same proof). See [Hallnäs 1983, Ekman 1994] for a more detailed explanation.

1.4. Church's Type Theory

Instead of considering only sets, Church's type theory considers also relations of an arbitrary number of arguments (unary relations are sets, zero-ary relations are naturally identified with propositions). Then, functions are primitive objects and are distinct from their graphs that are relations. Functions of several arguments are curried, for instance the function mapping two numbers n and m to $n + m + 2$ is identified with the function mapping n to the function mapping m to $n + m + 2$. Just as we have a membership symbol $\in$ to build a proposition from two terms in set theory, we have an application symbol α to build a term from two terms. The term $\alpha(t, u)$ is written $(t\ u)$. At last, relations are expressed as functions mapping their arguments to a zero-ary relation i.e. a proposition. For instance, the relation $\leq$ is expressed as the function mapping a and b to the proposition $a \leq b$. Thus, if A is a set (unary relation), the notation $x \in A$ is an abbreviation for $(A\ x)$, i.e. $\alpha(A, x)$.

The sorts of the system are called *simple types*, they contain two base types ι for atoms and o for zero-ary relations (propositions), and whenever T and U are two types, $T \to U$ is also a type (the type of functions mapping objects in T to objects in U).

As we have a comprehension scheme for sets and relations, we have a comprehension scheme for functions

$$\forall x_1\ \ldots\ \forall x_n\ \exists f\ \forall y_1\ \ldots\ \forall y_p\ ((f\ y_1\ \ldots\ y_p) = t)$$

and an extensionality axiom for functions

$$\forall f\ \forall g\ ((\forall x\ (f\ x) = (g\ x)) \Rightarrow f = g)$$

Skolemizing the comprehension scheme yields an explicit language for functions where the function mapping $y_1, ..., y_p$ to t is written $y_1, ..., y_p \mapsto t$. Again, although the skolemized comprehension scheme provides only such terms when t does not contain Skolem symbols, it is easy to prove that the theory allowing such nested abstractions is equivalent (see, for instance, [Henkin 1953, Dowek 1995]). Then, curried functions of p arguments can be written $y_1 \mapsto (...y_p \mapsto t...)$. Following Church's original notation, the term $x \mapsto t$ is written $\lambda x\ t$. The conversion axiom, called β-*conversion* axiom is then stated

$$\forall x\ \forall y_1\ ...\ \forall y_p\ ((\lambda x\ t)\ x) = t$$

Notice that the functional comprehension scheme, asserts the existence of very few functions. For instance, if the atoms are taken to be natural numbers and the language contains a symbol 0 of type ι and S of type $\iota \to \iota$, for functions of type $\iota \to \iota$ the conversion scheme only asserts the existence of the constant functions and the functions adding a constant to their argument. Similarly, these functions are the only ones that are explicitly definable by a term (e.g. $\lambda x\ S(S(0))$ and $\lambda x\ S(S(x))$). For instance, the comprehension scheme does not assert the existence of the function χ mapping 0 to 0 and the other natural numbers to 1. In contrast, the graph of this function (which is a binary relation, i.e. an object of type $\iota \to \iota \to o$) can easily be defined $G = \lambda x\ \lambda y\ ((x = 0 \wedge y = 0) \vee (\neg(x = 0) \wedge (y = 1)))$. This motivates the introduction of another axiom: *the descriptions axiom*

$$\exists D\ \forall x\ ((\exists_1 y\ (x\ y)) \Rightarrow (x\ (D\ x)))$$

where $\exists_1 y\ P(y)$ is a proposition expressing the existence and unicity of an object verifying the property P, i.e. the proposition

$$\exists y\ P(y) \wedge \forall y_1\ \forall y_2\ ((P(y_1) \wedge P(y_2)) \Rightarrow y_1 = y_2)$$

When skolemizing this axiom, we introduce a Skolem symbol called the *descriptions operator* and the axiom

$$\forall x\ (\exists_1 y\ (x\ y)) \Rightarrow (x\ (D\ x))$$

This descriptions operator, that picks the element in every one element set, can be extended to a *choice operator* (also called Hilbert's ε operator, or Bourbaki's τ operator) that picks an element in any nonempty set. In this case the axiom is rephrased

$$\forall x\ (\exists y\ (x\ y)) \Rightarrow (x\ (D\ x))$$

and it is a form of the axiom of choice.

The descriptions operator and axiom permit to relate the functional relations and the functions. The function χ above can be defined by the term $\lambda x\ (D\ (\lambda y\ (G\ x\ y)))$. Then we can prove, for instance that $\chi(2) = 1$. Notice however that this theorem is not a consequence of the conversion axiom alone, the descriptions axiom is also needed.

When searching for proofs in higher-order logic, we transform the β-conversion axiom in a rewrite rule called β-*reduction*

$$((\lambda x\ t)\ u) \rhd (u/x)t$$

and we also take another rewrite rule called *η-reduction* which is a consequence of the extensionality axiom

$$\lambda x \ (t \ x) \rhd t \text{ provided } x \text{ does not appear free in } t$$

The extensionality axiom itself and the descriptions axiom remain as axioms of the theory.

1.1. REMARK. In the presentation above, when we want to substitute the predicate $Q(.,.)$ for the variable P in the proposition $P(a) \wedge P(b)$ to get the proposition $Q(a, a) \wedge Q(b, b)$, we first construct a term $\lambda z \ Q(z, z)$, then we substitute it for the variable P yielding $(\lambda z \ Q(z, z))(a) \wedge (\lambda z \ Q(z, z))(b)$ and at last we prove that this term is equivalent to $Q(a, a) \wedge Q(b, b)$, or we reduce it to $Q(a, a) \wedge Q(b, b)$.

An alternative, frequently used in second-order logic [Church 1956, Goldfarb 1981, Farmer 1988, Krivine 1993], is to a define a substitution operation $(Q(x, x)/P(x))A$ in such a way that $(Q(x, x)/P(x))(P(a) \wedge P(b))$ is $Q(a, a) \wedge Q(b, b)$. This way the reduction is included in the definition of substitution.

1.5. Equational Higher-order Unification

Higher-order unification is equational unification modulo $\beta\eta$-equivalence. As remarked above, as the function χ is defined with the descriptions operator, the proposition $\chi(2) = 1$ needs the descriptions axiom to be proved and the term $\chi(2)$ does not reduce to the term 1. Thus, we may want to extend the rewrite system above, for instance with rules

$$\chi(0) \rhd 0$$

$$\chi(S(x)) \rhd S(0)$$

In the same way, we may want to add rewrite rules for addition (which is also defined using the descriptions operator)

$$(+ \ 0 \ y) \rhd y$$

$$(+ \ (S \ x) \ y) \rhd (S \ (+ \ x \ y))$$

A rather general extension is to consider rewrite rules for the recursor R (which is also defined using the descriptions operator [Andrews 1986])

$$(R \ x \ f \ 0) \rhd x$$

$$(R \ x \ f \ (S \ y)) \rhd (f \ y \ (R \ x \ y))$$

This rewrite system is called *Gödel system T* [Gödel 1958, Girard, Lafont and Taylor 1989].

Equational unification modulo a rewrite system containing β, η and other rules like the ones above is called *equational higher-order unification*.

1.6. Expectations and Achievements

Initiated in the sixties, the search for an automated theorem proving method for higher-order logic was motivated by big expectations. "Providing a genuinely useful mathematical service" is one of the goals mentioned in Robinson's quotation above (although this quotation is still moderated for the sixties). With the passing of time, we know that fully automated theorem proving methods have not, or very rarely, permitted to solve really difficult mathematical problems.

On the other hand, automated theorem proving methods have found other fields where they have provided genuinely useful services (logic programming, deductive data bases, etc.). The major applications of proof search in higher-order logic are higher-order logic programming and logical frameworks (λ-Prolog [Nadathur and Miller 1998], Elf [Pfenning 1991a], Isabelle [Paulson 1991], etc., see also [Pfenning 2001], Chapter 17 of this Handbook) and tools to prove easy but cumbersome lemmas in interactive proof construction systems, see [Barendregt and Geuvers 2001] (Chapter 18 of this Handbook).

Besides automated theorem proving, higher-order unification has also been used to design of type reconstruction algorithms for some programming languages [Pfenning 1988], in computational linguistics [Miller and Nadathur 1986, Dalrymple, Shieber and Pereira 1991], program transformation [Huet and Lang 1978, Hannan and Miller 1988, Hagiya 1990], higher-order rewriting [Nipkow 1991, Nipkow and Prehofer 1998, Mayr and Nipkow 1998], proof theory [Parikh 1973, Farmer 1991b], etc.

2. Simply Typed λ-calculus

In this section, we give the definitions and elementary properties of simply typed λ-calculus which is the term-language of higher-order logic. The proofs of these properties can be found in [Barendregt 1984, Hindley and Seldin 1986, Krivine 1993].

2.1. Types

We consider a finite set whose elements are called *atomic types*.

2.1. DEFINITION. (Types)
  Types are inductively defined by:
  • atomic types are types,
  • if T and U are types then $T \to U$ is a type.

Notation The expression $T_1 \to T_2 \to ... \to T_n \to U$ is a notation for the type $T_1 \to (T_2 \to ... \to (T_n \to U)...)$.

2.2. DEFINITION. (Size of a type)
  The size of a type is defined as follows
  - $|T| = 1$ if T is atomic,
  - $|T \to U| = |T| + |U|$.

2.3. DEFINITION. (Order of a type)
  If T is a type, the *order* of T is defined by:
  - $o(T) = 1$ if T is atomic,
  - $o(T_1 \to T_2) = max\{1 + o(T_1), o(T_2)\}$.

2.2. Terms

We consider a finite set of constants, to each constant is assigned a type. We assume that we have at least one constant in each atomic type. This assumption corresponds to the fact that we do not allow empty types.

For each type, we consider an infinite set of variables. Two different types have disjoint sets of variables.

2.4. DEFINITION. (λ-terms)
  λ-terms are inductively defined by:
  - constants are terms,
  - variables are terms,
  - if t and u are two terms then $(t\ u)$ (i.e. $\alpha(t, u)$) is a term,
  - if x is a variable and t a term then $\lambda x\ t$ is a term.

Notation The expression $(u\ v_1\ ...\ v_n)$ is a notation for the term $(...(u\ v_1)\ ...\ v_n)$.

2.5. DEFINITION. (Size of a term)
  The size of a term is defined as follows
  - $|x| = |c| = 1$,
  - $|(u\ v)| = |u| + |v|$,
  - $|\lambda x\ u| = |u|$.

2.6. DEFINITION. (Type of a term)
  A term t is said to have the type T if either:
  - t is a constant of type T,
  - t is a variable of type T,
  - $t = (u\ v)$ and u has type $U \to T$ and v has type U for some type U,
  - $t = \lambda x\ u$, the variable x has type U, the term u has type V and $T = U \to V$.

A term t is said to be *well-typed* if there exists a type T such that t has type T. In this case T is unique and is called *the type of* t.

2.7. REMARK. In this chapter, we use an *explicitly typed λ-calculus*. For instance, the term $\lambda x \ x$ has a single type $T \to T$ where T is the type of the variable x. We could alternatively have used a *type assignment system*, with a single class of variables and rules assigning types to terms, for instance any type of the form $T \to T$ to the term $\lambda x \ x$.

In the rest of this chapter we consider only well-typed terms.

2.3. Substitution

2.8. DEFINITION. (Variables, free variables)
Let t be a term, the set $Var(t)$ is the set of all variables occurring in t, it is defined by induction on the structure of t by:

- $Var(c) = \emptyset$,
- $Var(x) = \{x\}$,
- $Var((t \ u)) = Var(t) \cup Var(u)$,
- $Var(\lambda x \ t) = Var(t) \cup \{x\}$.

In contrast, the set $FVar(t)$ is the set of the variables occurring freely in t, it is defined by induction on the structure of t by:

- $FVar(c) = \emptyset$,
- $FVar(x) = \{x\}$,
- $FVar((t \ u)) = FVar(t) \cup FVar(u)$,
- $FVar(\lambda x \ t) = FVar(t) \setminus \{x\}$.

A term with no free variables is called a *closed term*.

2.9. EXAMPLE. The variable x occurs in the terms $\lambda x \ x$, $\lambda x \ y$ and $\lambda y \ x$, but it occurs freely only in the third of these terms.

2.10. DEFINITION. (Substitution)
A *substitution* is a finite set of pairs $\{\langle x_1, t_1 \rangle, ..., \langle x_n, t_n \rangle\}$ where for each i, x_i is a variable and t_i a term of the same type and such that if $\langle x, t \rangle$ and $\langle x, t' \rangle$ are both in this set then $t = t'$. Such a substitution is written $t_1/x_1, ..., t_n/x_n$.

We now want to define the operation of substituting the terms $t_1, ..., t_n$ for the variables $x_1, ..., x_n$ in a term u. A first attempt leads to the following definition.

2.11. DEFINITION. (Replacement in a term)
If $\theta = t_1/x_1, ..., t_n/x_n$ is a substitution and t a term, then the term $\langle \theta \rangle t$ is defined as follows

- $\langle \theta \rangle c = c$,
- $\langle \theta \rangle x_i = t_i$ and $\langle \theta \rangle x = x$, if x is a variable not among $x_1, ..., x_n$,
- $\langle \theta \rangle (t \ u) = (\langle \theta \rangle t \ \langle \theta \rangle u)$,
- $\langle \theta \rangle (\lambda x \ t) = \lambda x \ \langle \theta \rangle t$,

This notion of replacement has two drawbacks: first if we replace the variable x by the variable y in the term $\lambda x\ x$ we get the term $\lambda x\ y$, while the variable x is bound in the term $\lambda x\ x$, and thus we would rather expect the term $\lambda x\ x$. Then if we replace the variable x by the variable y in the term $\lambda y\ x$ we get the term $\lambda y\ y$ where the variable y has been captured, we would rather want to get the term $\lambda z\ y$.

Nevertheless, this notion of replacement is useful in some situations. For instance, it will be used in section 5.3 and it is also useful to define the notion of equivalence of two terms modulo bound variable renaming (α-equivalence).

2.12. DEFINITION. (α-equivalence)

The α-equivalence of two terms is inductively defined by:

- $c \equiv c$,
- $x \equiv x$,
- $(t\ u) \equiv (t'\ u')$ if $t \equiv t'$ and $u \equiv u'$,
- $\lambda x\ t \equiv \lambda y\ u$ if $\langle z/x \rangle t \equiv \langle z/y \rangle u$ for some variable z different from x and y and occurring neither in t nor in u.

2.13. EXAMPLE. The terms $\lambda x\ x$ and $\lambda y\ y$ are α-equivalent.

2.14. PROPOSITION. *α-equivalence is an equivalence relation. Moreover, the operations on terms (application and abstraction with respect to a variable) are compatible with this relation. Thus, they are defined on equivalence classes.*

In the following we shall identify α-equivalent terms, i.e. consider terms as representatives of their α-equivalence class.

Now, we can define the substitution operation. To avoid capture, when we substitute the variable y for the variable x in the term $\lambda y\ x$, we need to rename the bound variable y, and get for instance the term $\lambda z\ y$. The choice of the variable z is purely arbitrary, thus the substitution operation is in fact defined on terms modulo α-equivalence, i.e. on α-equivalence classes.

2.15. DEFINITION. (Substitution in a term)

If $\theta = t_1/x_1, ..., t_n/x_n$ is a substitution and t a term then the term θt is defined as follows

- $\theta c = c$,
- $\theta x_i = t_i$ and $\theta x = x$, if x is a variable not among $x_1, ..., x_n$,
- $\theta(t\ u) = (\theta t\ \theta u)$,
- $\theta(\lambda x\ u) = \lambda y\ \theta(y/x)u$, where y is a fresh variable, with the same type as x, i.e. a variable that does not occur in t nor in $t_1, ..., t_n$ and is different from $x_1, ..., x_n$.

2.16. PROPOSITION. *If t is a term of type T, x is a variable of type U and u a term of type U then the term $(u/x)t$ has type T.*

2.17. DEFINITION. (Composition of substitutions)

Let θ and θ' two substitutions and $x_1, ..., x_n$ be the variables bound by one substitution or the other. We let

$$\theta \circ \theta' = \theta\theta' x_1/x_1, ..., \theta\theta' x_n/x_n$$

2.18. DEFINITION. (More general)

A substitution θ_1 is said to be *more general* than a substitution θ_2 ($\theta_1 \leq \theta_2$) if there exists a substitution η such that $\theta_2 = \eta \circ \theta_1$.

2.19. DEFINITION. (Size of a substitution)

The size of a substitution $t_1/x_1, ..., t_n/x_n$ is defined as

$$|t_1/x_1, ..., t_n/x_n| = |t_1| + ... + |t_n|$$

2.4. Reduction

2.20. DEFINITION. ($\beta\eta$-reduction)

The $\beta\eta$-reduction (in one step), written $\triangleright$, is inductively defined by:

- β: $((\lambda x \, t) \, u) \triangleright (u/x)t$,
- η: $\lambda x \, (t \, x) \triangleright t$ if x is not free in t,
- μ: if $u \triangleright u'$ then $(t \, u) \triangleright (t \, u')$,
- ν: if $t \triangleright t'$ then $(t \, u) \triangleright (t' \, u)$,
- ξ: if $t \triangleright t'$ then $\lambda x \, t \triangleright \lambda x \, t'$.

The $\beta\eta$-reduction (in several steps), written $\triangleright^*$, is the reflexive-transitive closure of the relation $\triangleright$, it is inductively defined by:

- if $t \triangleright u$, then $t \triangleright^* u$,
- $t \triangleright^* t$,
- $t \triangleright^* u$ and $u \triangleright^* v$ then $t \triangleright^* v$.

2.21. PROPOSITION. *If a term t has type T and t reduces to u then u has type T.*

2.22. PROPOSITION. *Substitution and reduction commute, i.e. if $t \triangleright^* u$ then $(v/x)t \triangleright^* (v/x)u$.*

2.23. THEOREM. *The $\beta\eta$-reduction relation is strongly normalizable and confluent on typed terms, and thus each term has a unique $\beta\eta$-normal form modulo α-conversion.*

2.24. PROPOSITION. *Let t be a normal well-typed term of type $T_1 \to ... \to T_n \to U$ (U atomic), the term t has the form*

$$t = \lambda x_1 \, ... \, \lambda x_m \, (y \, u_1 \, ... \, u_p)$$

where $m \leq n$ and y is a constant or a variable.

The symbol y is called the head symbol *of the term.*

2.25. DEFINITION. (Long normal form) If $t = \lambda x_1 \ldots \lambda x_m \ (y \ u_1 \ldots u_p)$ is a normal term of type $T_1 \to \ldots \to T_n \to U$ (U atomic) ($m \le n$) then its long normal form is the term

$$t' = \lambda x_1 \ldots \lambda x_m \ \lambda x_{m+1} \ldots \lambda x_n \ (y \ u'_1 \ldots u'_p \ x'_{m+1} \ldots x'_n)$$

where u'_i is the long normal form of u_i and x'_i is the long normal form of x_i.

This definition is made by induction on a pair whose first component is the size of the term and the second the size of its type.

The long normal form of an arbitrary term is that of its normal form.

2.26. REMARK. The β-normal form of a term is its normal form for the following rewrite system which is also strongly normalizing and confluent.

- β: $((\lambda x \ t) \ u) \rhd_\beta (u/x)t$,
- μ: if $u \rhd_\beta u'$ then $(t \ u) \rhd_\beta (t \ u')$,
- ν: if $t \rhd_\beta t'$ then $(t \ u) \rhd_\beta (t' \ u)$,
- ξ: if $t \rhd_\beta t'$ then $\lambda x \ t \rhd_\beta \lambda x \ t'$.

Because η-reduction can be delayed with respect to β-reduction, the long normal form of a term is also that of its β-normal form. Thus to compute the long normal form of a term, we do not need to perform η-reductions.

2.27. REMARK. Two terms have the same long normal form if and only if they have the same genuine normal form. Thus, as representatives of classes of terms we can either chose the genuine short normal form or the long normal form. Choosing the long one simplifies many problems. So in the rest of this chapter, "normal form" will always mean "long normal form".

2.5. Unification

2.28. DEFINITION. (Unification problem, Unifier)

An *equation* is a pair of terms t, u. A *unification problem* is a finite set of equations. A *solution* or a *unifier* of such a problem is a substitution θ such that for each pair t, u of the problem, the terms θt and θu have the same normal form.

2.29. DEFINITION. (Minimal unifier, Most general unifier)

A unifier θ of a problem is said to be *minimal* if all the unifiers of the problem more general than θ are renamings of θ, i.e. substitutions of the form $\eta \circ \theta$ with $\eta = y_1/x_1, \ldots, y_n/x_n$.

A unifier of a problem is said to be the *smallest* or the *the most general unifier* if it is more general than all the unifiers.

3. Undecidability

3.1. Higher-order Unification

In this section, we show that higher-order unification is undecidable, i.e. there is no algorithm that takes as argument a unification problem and answers if it has a solution or not. To achieve this goal, we reduce another undecidable problem: Hilbert's tenth problem.

3.1. THEOREM. *(Matiyacevich-Robinson-Davis [Matiyacevich 1970, Davis 1973])*
Hilbert's tenth problem is undecidable, i.e. there is no algorithm that takes as arguments two polynomials $P(X_1, ..., X_n)$ and $Q(X_1, ..., X_n)$ whose coefficients are natural numbers and answers if there exists natural numbers $m_1, ..., m_n$ such that

$$P(m_1, ..., m_n) = Q(m_1, ..., m_n)$$

We have seen that very few functions can be expressed in simply typed λ-calculus alone. With Peano numbers (i.e. with a symbol 0 of type ι and S of type $\iota \to \iota$), we can only define the constant functions and the functions adding a constant to one of their arguments. The descriptions operator is needed to define addition and multiplication and thus polynomials. Nevertheless, we can use another definition of natural numbers: Church numbers.

3.2. DEFINITION. (Church numbers)
With each natural number n, we associate its *Church number*

$$\bar{n} = \lambda x \; \lambda f \; (f \; (...(f \; x)...))$$

with n occurrences of the symbol f. This term has type $\iota \to (\iota \to \iota) \to \iota$.

Moving from Peano numbers to Church numbers increases only slightly the set of functions that can be expressed in simply typed λ-calculus: as proved by H. Schwichtenberg [Schwichtenberg 1976], the expressible functions are the so-called *extended polynomials*, i.e. the polynomials extended by the characteristic functions of $\{0\}$ and $\mathbb{N} \setminus \{0\}$ (for instance the function mapping n to 2^n still needs the descriptions operator). But polynomials are precisely what are needed to reduce Hilbert's tenth problem.

3.3. PROPOSITION. *Consider the terms*

$$add = \lambda n \; \lambda m \; \lambda x \; \lambda f \; (n \; (m \; x \; f) \; f)$$

$$mult = \lambda n \; \lambda m \; \lambda x \; \lambda f \; (n \; x \; (\lambda z \; (m \; z \; f)))$$

The normal form of the term $(add \; \bar{n} \; \bar{m})$ *is* $\overline{n+m}$. *The normal form of the term* $(mult \; \bar{n} \; \bar{m})$ *is* $\overline{n \times m}$. *Thus for every polynomial P there exists a λ-term p such that the normal form of the term* $(p \; \overline{m_1} \; ... \; \overline{m_n})$ *is the term* $\overline{P(m_1, ..., m_n)}$.

Obviously, if the polynomial equation

$$P(X_1, ..., X_n) = Q(X_1, ..., X_n)$$

has a solution $m_1, ..., m_n$ then the substitution $\overline{m_1}/X_1, ..., \overline{m_n}/X_n$ is a solution to the unification problem

$$(p\ X_1\ ...\ X_n) = (q\ X_1\ ...\ X_n)$$

The converse of this proposition is not obvious, indeed, there are terms of type $\iota \to (\iota \to \iota) \to \iota$, for instance variables, that are not Church numbers.

Thus we shall add more equations to the problem to force the solutions to be Church numbers.

3.4. PROPOSITION. *A normal term t of type $\iota \to (\iota \to \iota) \to \iota$ is a Church number if and only if t/X is a solution of the equation*

$$\lambda z\ (X\ z\ (\lambda y\ y)) = \lambda z\ z$$

PROOF. By induction on the structure of t.   □

Thus we can conclude.

3.5. THEOREM. *There is no algorithm that takes as argument a unification problem and answers if it has a solution or not.*

PROOF. With each polynomial equation

$$P(X_1, ..., X_n) = Q(X_1, ..., X_n)$$

we associate the unification problem

$$(p\ X_1\ ...\ X_n) = (q\ X_1\ ...\ X_n)$$

$$\lambda z\ (X_1\ z\ (\lambda y\ y)) = \lambda z\ z$$

$$...$$

$$\lambda z\ (X_n\ z\ (\lambda y\ y)) = \lambda z\ z$$

where p is the term expressing the polynomial P and q the term expressing the polynomial Q.

If the polynomial equation has a solution $m_1, ..., m_n$ then the substitution $\overline{m_1}/X_1, ..., \overline{m_n}/X_n$ is a solution of the unification problem. Conversely, if the unification problem has a solution $c_1/X_1, ..., c_n/X_n$ then the normal form of each c_i is a Church number $c_i = \overline{m_i}$. The natural numbers $m_1, ..., m_n$ are a solution to the polynomial equation.   □

3.6. REMARK. This theorem has been proved independently in 1972 by G. Huet [Huet 1972, Huet 1973b] and C.L. Lucchesi [Lucchesi 1972]. The original proofs did not reduce Hilbert's tenth problem, but Post's correspondence problem.

The unification problems built when reducing Post's correspondence problem have the property that the variables free in the problem are applied only to terms that do not contain further variables free in the problem. Thus, reducing Post's correspondence problem permits to sharpen the theorem and prove that there is no algorithm that takes as argument a unification problem of this special form and answers if it has a solution or not. Such a sharpened undecidability theorem is useful, for instance to prove the undecidability of type reconstruction in the extension of simply typed λ-calculus with dependent types [Dowek 1993c].

3.2. Second-order Unification

But, reducing Hilbert's tenth problem, we can sharpen the result in another direction. The variables $X_1, ..., X_n$ above have the type $\iota \to (\iota \to \iota) \to \iota$. This is the type of functionals taking in arguments an atom of type ι and a function of type $\iota \to \iota$. Using the definition 2.3, this type has order 3. We may try to sharpen the result and allow only variables of order 2 or even 1. If we restrict the types of the free variables to be first-order, the problem is just a variant of first-order unification and thus it is decidable. If we restrict the types of the free variables to be at most second-order, we get *second-order unification*, which has been proved to be undecidable by W.D. Goldfarb [Goldfarb 1981].

Goldfarb's proof relies on a expression of numbers that is a degeneracy of Church's. Taking $\lambda x \ \lambda f \ (f \ (...(f \ x)...))$ leads to a third-order type, thus the idea is to drop the abstraction on f and to take $\lambda x \ (f \ (...(f \ x)...))$ where f is a constant of type $\iota \to \iota$. Thus numbers now have the second-order type $\iota \to \iota$. More precisely, Goldfarb number $\overline{n}$ is the term $\lambda x \ (g \ a \ (...(g \ a \ x)...))$ where a and g are constants of type ι and $\iota \to \iota \to \iota$.

Goldfarb numbers can still be characterized by a unification problem.

3.7. PROPOSITION. *A normal term t of type $\iota \to \iota$ is a Goldfarb number if and only if t/X is a solution to the equation*

$$(g \ a \ (X \ a)) = (X \ (g \ a \ a))$$

Addition can still be expressed by the term

$$add = \lambda n \ \lambda m \ \lambda x \ (n \ (m \ x))$$

but multiplication cannot be expressed this way. Thus, it will be expressed, not by a term, but by a unification problem.

3.8. PROPOSITION. *(Goldfarb's lemma) The unification problem*

$$(Y \ a \ b \ (g \ (g \ (X_3 \ a) \ (X_2 \ b)) \ a)) = (g \ (g \ a \ b) \ (Y \ (X_1 \ a) \ (g \ a \ b) \ a))$$

$$(Y\ b\ a\ (g\ (g\ (X_3\ b)\ (X_2\ a))\ a)) = (g\ (g\ b\ a)\ (Y\ (X_1\ b)\ (g\ a\ a)\ a))$$

has a solution $\overline{m_1}/X_1, \overline{m_2}/X_2, \overline{m_3}/X_3, u/Y$ if and only if $m_1 \times m_2 = m_3$.

3.9. THEOREM. *(Goldfarb) Second-order unification is undecidable.*

PROOF. By reduction of Hilbert's tenth problem. Every equation of the form

$$P(X_1, ..., X_n) = Q(X_1, ..., X_n)$$

can be decomposed into a system of equations of the form

$$X_i + X_j = X_k$$

$$X_i \times X_j = X_k$$

$$X_i = p$$

With such a system we associate a unification problem containing:
- for each variable X_i, an equation as in proposition 3.7,
- for each equation of the form $X_i + X_j = X_k$, the equation $(add\ X_i\ X_j) = X_k$,
- for each equation of the form $X_i \times X_j = X_k$, two equations as in proposition 3.8,
- for each equation of the form $X_i = p$, the equation $X_i = \overline{p}$.

$\square$

3.10. REMARK. Goldfarb's result has been sharpened by W.M. Farmer [Farmer 1991a], J. Levy and M. Veanes [Levy and Veanes 1998] who study the number of variables, the number of variable occurrences and the arity of the variables that are needed to get undecidability.

3.11. REMARK. Reducing Hilbert's tenth problem is a powerful tool, but as the proof of undecidability of Hilbert's tenth problem itself is rather complicated, one may want to find a simpler undecidability proof, i.e. one reducing a problem that is simpler to prove undecidable (the halting problem, the semi-Thue problem, Post's correspondence problem, etc.). We have seen that such reductions are possible for third-order unification.

A. Schubert [Schubert 1998] has given another undecidability proof for second-order unification, reducing the halting problem of a two-counter automaton. This proof permits also to sharpen the result proving that there is no algorithm that takes as argument a unification problem where the variables free in the problem are applied only to terms that do not contain further variables free in the problem and answers if it has a solution or not. This sharpened undecidability theorem is applied to prove the undecidability of type reconstruction in some extension of simply typed λ-calculus with polymorphic types [Schubert 1998].

4. Huet's Algorithm

Higher-order unification is undecidable, but it is semi-decidable, i.e. we can build an algorithm that takes a unification problem as argument, terminates and returns a solution when the problem has one, but may loop forever when it does not. Indeed, given a problem and a substitution, it is possible to decide whether the substitution is a solution of the problem or not: it suffices to apply the substitution to both members of each equation, normalize the terms and check that their normal forms are equal. Thus, a naive generate and test algorithm terminates if the problem has a solution.

Such a generate and test algorithm is, of course, of no practical use. But as we shall see, it can be gradually improved so that we reach an algorithm that finds a solution rather quickly when such a solution exists and reports failure in many cases where the equation has no solutions (of course, not all of them, since the problem is undecidable).

4.1. A "Generate and Test" Algorithm

4.1.1. Generating Long Normal Closed Terms

Recall that we have assumed in section 2.2 that we had a constant c_U in each atomic type U. Thus, in a type $T_1 \to ... \to T_p \to U$, we always have a closed term $\lambda y_1 ... \lambda y_p\, c_U$. Obviously, if a substitution $t_1/X_1, ..., t_n/X_n$ is a solution to a problem then the substitution obtained by substituting each free variable of $t_1, ..., t_n$ by the term $\lambda y_1 ... \lambda y_p\, c_U$ corresponding to its type is also a solution. Moreover, this solution is closed, i.e. all the terms substituted to the variables $X_1, ..., X_n$ are closed terms. Thus, if a problem has a solution, it has also a closed solution and instead of enumerating all the terms $t_1, ..., t_n$ to be substituted for the variables $X_1, ..., X_n$ we can restrict to the closed ones. Similarly, if a substitution $t_1/X_1, ..., t_n/X_n$ is a solution to a problem then the substitution obtained by taking the long normal form of the terms $t_1, ..., t_n$ is also a solution. Thus, we can restrict the enumeration the long normal closed terms.

Using definition 2.25 long normal closed terms of type $T_1 \to ... \to T_p \to U$, where U is an atomic type, have the shape

$$\lambda y_1 ... \lambda y_p\, (h\ u_1\ ...\ u_r)$$

where $y_1, ..., y_p$ are variables of type $T_1, ..., T_p$, the head symbol h is either one of the variables $y_1, ..., y_p$ or a constant, and $u_1, ..., u_r$ are terms whose number and type depend on the type of the symbol h.

Thus a method to enumerate all the normal terms of a given type is to proceed step by step, enumerating all the possible head symbols of the term and then using recursively the same method to enumerate the terms $u_1, ..., u_r$.

A first, but naive, idea would be to use variables $H_1, ..., H_r$ to hold for the terms $u_1, ..., u_r$, i.e. to consider the term

$$\lambda y_1 ... \lambda y_p\, (h\ H_1\ ...\ H_r)$$

and then to enumerate the terms to be substituted for the variables $H_1, ..., H_r$. Unfortunately, such an idea does not work, because the variables $y_1, ..., y_p$ may occur in the terms $u_1, ..., u_r$, substituting such terms to the variables $H_1, ..., H_r$ would introduce captures, and substitution renames bound variables to avoid such captures. Thus, for instance, such a method would not generate the term $\lambda x \, \lambda f \, (f \, x)$ of type $\iota \rightarrow (\iota \rightarrow \iota) \rightarrow \iota$: a first step would consider the term $\lambda x \, \lambda f \, (f \, H)$ but then substituting the term x to the variable H would yield the term $\lambda y \, \lambda f \, (f \, x)$ and not $\lambda x \, \lambda f \, (f \, x)$.

A solution to this problem is to express functionally the dependence of the terms $u_1, ..., u_r$ with respect to the variables $y_1, ..., y_p$, considering the term

$$\lambda y_1 \, ... \, \lambda y_p \, (h \, (H_1 \, y_1 \, ... \, y_p) \, ... \, (H_r \, y_1 \, ... \, y_p))$$

Then the term $\lambda x \, \lambda f \, (f \, x)$ is generated in two steps: first, we generate the term $\lambda x \, \lambda f \, (f \, (H \, x \, f))$ then we substitute the term $\lambda x \, \lambda f \, x$ for the variable H.

A substitution of the form

$$\lambda y_1 \, ... \, \lambda y_p \, (h \, (H_1 \, y_1 \, ... \, y_p) \, ... \, (H_r \, y_1 \, ... \, y_p))/X$$

is called an *elementary substitution*.

4.1. DEFINITION. We consider the following inference system

$$\frac{t}{(\lambda y_1 \, ... \, \lambda y_p \, (h \, (H_1 \, y_1 \, ... \, y_p) \, ... \, (H_r \, y_1 \, ... \, y_p))/X)t}$$

where the terms are normal (i.e. $(\lambda y_1 \, ... \, \lambda y_p \, (h \, (H_1 \, y_1 \, ... \, y_p) \, ... \, (H_r \, y_1 \, ... \, y_p))/X)t$ actually stands for the long normal form of this term), X is a free variable of t of type $T_1 \rightarrow ... \rightarrow T_p \rightarrow U$ (U atomic), h is one of the variables $y_1, ..., y_p$ or a constant, the target type of h is U and the variables $H_1, ..., H_r$ are fresh variables of the appropriate type.

4.2. PROPOSITION. *All the long normal closed terms of type T are produced from a variable of type T by the inference system above.*

PROOF. By induction on the size of t. $\qquad\qquad\qquad\qquad\qquad\qquad\qquad\qquad$ □

4.3. REMARK. The inference system above has two forms of non-determinism: first the choice of the variable X of the term t to be substituted, then the choice of the head symbol h in the substituted term. The choice of the variable X is a *don't care* non-determinism, the choice of the head symbol h is a *don't know* non-determinism.

This *don't know* non-determinism can be handled by building a search tree as follows. Nodes are labeled by terms and leaves by closed terms. In each internal node, we chose a variable and we draw an edge corresponding to each possible head symbol.

Another solution is to consider an inference system defined on finite sets of terms, deriving from $A \cup \{t\}$, the set $A \cup \{\sigma_1 t, ..., \sigma_n t\}$ where $\sigma_1, ..., \sigma_n$ are the elementary substitutions corresponding to the different possible head symbols.

4.1.2. A Unification Algorithm

4.4. DEFINITION. (Generate and test algorithm)

We consider the inference system

$$\frac{E}{(\lambda y_1 \ ... \ \lambda y_p \ (h \ (H_1 \ y_1 \ ... \ y_p) \ ... \ (H_r \ y_1 \ ... \ y_p))/X)E}$$

where E is a unification problem (i.e. a finite set of equations), X is a free variable of E of type $T_1 \to ... \to T_p \to U$ (U atomic) and h is one of the variables $y_1, ..., y_p$ or a constant and the variables $H_1, ..., H_r$ are fresh variables of the appropriate type.

4.5. PROPOSITION. *The above algorithm is sound and complete, i.e. a problem has a solution if and only if a trivial problem (i.e. a problem where each equation relates identical terms) can be derived from it.*

PROOF. The soundness property is an obvious induction on the length of the derivation. The completeness property is proved by induction on the size of a long normal closed solution.   □

4.2. Huet's Algorithm

In the generate and test algorithm, the unification problem is completely passive, it is only used to test if a given substitution is a solution or not. In Huet's algorithm it is used in a much more active way to restrict the search space.

For instance, consider the problem $0 = S(X)$, whatever closed term we may substitute for X, we will get two terms which have a different head symbol and thus are different. Similarly the problem $S(u) = S(v)$ can be simplified into the problem $u = v$ that has the same solutions. Such a term where the head symbol is a constant or a bound variable and thus cannot be changed by a substitution is called *rigid*.

4.6. DEFINITION. (Rigid, flexible term)

A term is said to be *rigid* if its head symbol is a constant or a bound variable, it is said to be *flexible* if its head symbol is a free variable.

4.2.1. Rigid-rigid Equations

A first improvement that can be made to the generate and test algorithm is to simplify problems using the rules

$$\frac{E \cup \{\lambda x_1 \ ... \ \lambda x_n \ (f \ u_1 \ ... \ u_p) = \lambda x_1 \ ... \ \lambda x_n \ (g \ v_1 \ ... \ v_q)\}}{\bot} \ Fail$$

$$\frac{E \cup \{\lambda x_1 \ ... \ \lambda x_n \ u_1 = \lambda x_1 \ ... \ \lambda x_n \ v_1, ..., \lambda x_1 \ ... \ \lambda x_n \ u_p = \lambda x_1 \ ... \ \lambda x_n \ v_p\}}{E \cup \{\lambda x_1 \ ... \ \lambda x_n \ (f \ u_1 \ ... \ u_p) = \lambda x_1 \ ... \ \lambda x_n \ (f \ v_1 \ ... \ v_p)\}} \ Simplify$$

where the simplified equation relates two rigid terms (i.e. the symbols f and g are either constants or among $x_1, ..., x_n$) the head symbols of these terms are different for the rule *Fail* and identical for the rule *Simplify*.

Notice that these rules derive unification problems, i.e. finite set of equations, and that we have conventionally added an "unsolvable problem" $\bot$.

4.7. PROPOSITION. *If a problem E' is derived from a problem E by the rule* Fail *or the rule* Simplify, *then E and E' have the same solutions.*

4.8. PROPOSITION. *The application of the rules* Fail *and* Simplify *terminates and produces a problem that does not contain rigid-rigid equations.*

4.2.2. Flexible-rigid Equations

When the problem has an equation relating a flexible term and a rigid one $\lambda x_1 \ ... \ \lambda x_n \ (X \ u_1 \ ... \ u_p) = \lambda x_1 \ ... \ \lambda x_n \ (f \ v_1 \ ... \ v_q)$ we can decide to generate the substitutions to be substituted for the variable X. As in the generate and test algorithm, we try all the substitutions of the form $\lambda y_1 \ ... \ \lambda y_p \ (h \ (H_1 \ y_1 \ ... \ y_p) \ ... \ (H_r \ y_1 \ ... \ y_p))$ where h is a constant or among the variables $y_1, ..., y_p$.

In this case, if h is a constant different from the head f of the rigid term, this substitution leads to an unsolvable rigid-rigid equation. Thus such an enumeration can be avoided and we can restrict the symbol h to be among $y_1, ..., y_p$ (such a substitution is called a *projection*) or the symbol f, if this symbol is a constant (such a substitution is called an *imitation*).

$$\frac{E}{(\lambda y_1 \ ... \ \lambda y_p \ (h \ (H_1 \ y_1 \ ... \ y_p) \ ... \ (H_r \ y_1 \ ... \ y_p))/X)E} \ Generate$$

where E contains an equation of the form

$$\lambda x_1 \ ... \ \lambda x_n \ (X \ u_1 \ ... \ u_p) = \lambda x_1 \ ... \ \lambda x_n \ (f \ v_1 \ ... \ v_q)$$

or

$$\lambda x_1 \ ... \ \lambda x_n \ (f \ v_1 \ ... \ v_q) = \lambda x_1 \ ... \ \lambda x_n \ (X \ u_1 \ ... \ u_p)$$

and h is among $y_1, ..., y_p, f$ when f is a constant and among $y_1, ..., y_p$ otherwise.

4.2.3. Flexible-flexible Equations

Thus, while in a problem E we have a rigid-rigid equation, a flexible-rigid one or a rigid-flexible one, we do not need to use the blind generation of the potential solutions, but we can restrict to the rules *Fail*, *Simplify* and *Generate*. When all the equations are flexible-flexible, it seems that we have no way to restrict the blind enumeration anymore.

However, Huet's lemma shows that flexible-flexible equations always have solutions and thus, that if we are not interested in all the unifiers, but simply in the *existence* of such unifiers, we do not need to solve flexible-flexible equations.

4.9. DEFINITION. (Solved problem)

If all the equations of a problem E relate flexible terms, then the problem E is said to be *solved*.

4.10. PROPOSITION. *(Huet) Any solved problem has a solution.*

PROOF. For each atomic U type consider a constant c_U. Let θ the substitution that binds every variable X of type $T_1 \to \ldots \to T_p \to U$ of E to the term $\lambda y_1 \ldots \lambda y_p \, c_U$. The substitution θ is a solution of E, indeed applying θ to an equation of the form $\lambda x_1 \ldots \lambda x_n \, (X \, u_1 \ldots u_p) = \lambda x_1 \ldots \lambda x_n \, (Y \, v_1 \ldots v_q)$ yields $\lambda x_1 \ldots \lambda x_n \, c_U = \lambda x_1 \ldots \lambda x_n \, c_U$. □

In higher-order logic, testing unifiability is much simpler than enumerating unifiers. This motivates the design of proof-search methods, such as *constrained resolution* [Huet 1972, Huet 1973a], that require only the testing of unifiability and not the enumeration of solutions, see [Andrews 2001] (Chapter 15 of this Handbook).

4.2.4. Correctness

We want to prove the soundness and completeness of the inference system *Fail*, *Simplify* and *Generate*.

4.11. PROPOSITION. *(Soundness) If from a problem E we can infer a solved problem E' with the rules* Fail, Simplify *and* Generate, *then the problem E has a solution.*

PROOF. By induction on the length of the derivation.

If the derivation is empty, we conclude with the proposition 4.10.

If the first rule is *Fail* or *Simplify*, we conclude with the induction hypothesis and the proposition 4.7.

If the first rule is *Generate*, deriving the problem E' from the problem E, then by induction hypothesis the problem E' has a solution θ' and the substitution $\theta = \theta' \circ (\lambda y_1 \ldots \lambda y_p \, (h \, (H_1 \, y_1 \ldots y_p) \ldots (H_r \, y_1 \ldots y_p))/X)$ is a solution of E. □

4.12. PROPOSITION. *(Completeness) If the problem E has a solution θ, then from a problem E we can derive a solved problem E' with the rules* Fail, Simplify *and* Generate.

PROOF. By induction on the size of the substitution θ. First, we apply the rules *Fail* and *Simplify* to the problem E. By proposition 4.8 this process terminates and returns a problem E' that does not contain rigid-rigid equations and by proposition 4.7, the substitution θ is a solution of the problem E'. If the problem E' is solved, we have a derivation from E to a solved problem.

Otherwise, the problem E' contains a flexible-rigid equation (or a rigid-flexible one) $\lambda x_1 \ldots \lambda x_n \, (X \, u_1 \ldots u_p) = \lambda x_1 \ldots \lambda x_n \, (f \, v_1 \ldots v_q)$. Let $\lambda y_1 \ldots \lambda y_p \, (h \, w_1 \ldots w_r)$ be the term θX. The symbol h is among $y_1, \ldots, y_p, f$ if the symbol f is a constant, and among $y_1, \ldots, y_p$ otherwise.

By the rule *Generate* we derive the problem

$$E'' = (\lambda y_1 \ ... \ \lambda y_p \ (h \ (H_1 \ x_1 \ ... \ x_p) \ ... \ (H_r \ x_1 \ ... \ x_p))/X)E'$$

A solution to this problem is the substitution

$$\theta' = \theta - \{\theta X/X\} \cup \{\lambda y_1 \ ... \ \lambda y_p w_1/H_1, ..., \lambda y_1 \ ... \ \lambda y_p w_r/H_r\}$$

This substitution is smaller than the substitution θ and thus, by induction hypothesis, we can derive a solved problem from the problem E''. Thus, we can derive a solved problem from the problem E.   □

4.2.5. Non-determinism

The proof of the completeness lemma gives a complete strategy for applying these rules. While a problem contains rigid-rigid equations, the rules *Fail* and *Simplify* can be applied. The choice of applying these rules and the choice of the equation is *don't care*, i.e. we never need to backtrack to try another rule or another equation.

The *Generate* rule can be applied only to simplified problems, i.e. problems containing no rigid-rigid equation. The choice of the flexible-rigid equation is *don't care*, but the choice of the head-variable is *don't know* and may lead to backtrack.

Again, this *don't know* non-determinism can be handled by building a search tree called *unification tree*. Nodes are labeled by simplified problems. Leaves are solved problems and the unsolvable problem ($\perp$). In each internal node, we chose an equation and we draw an edge corresponding to each possible head symbol.

Another solution is to consider an inference system on finite set of unification problems, deriving from $A \cup \{E\}$ the set $A \cup \{\sigma_1 E, ..., \sigma_n E\}$ where $\sigma_1, ..., \sigma_n$ are the elementary substitutions corresponding to the different possible head symbols.

In some presentations, an equation is considered as an atomic proposition in a *unification logic*. A unification problem (finite set of equations) is then the conjunction of the atomic propositions corresponding to the equations. Sets of unification problems are then considered as disjunctions.

4.2.6. Empty Types

Above we have used the fact that we had a constant in each atomic type and thus that every type was inhabited and that the existence of a solution to a unification problem was equivalent to the existence of a closed solution.

If we allow empty types, finding a closed solution to a unification problem is more difficult that finding a (possibly open) solution. For instance, if we have a variable X of type T, the empty unification problem with respect to this variable (or, if we prefer, the problem $X = X$) has a trivial open solution, but has a closed solution only if the type T is inhabited.

When we have empty types, flexible-flexible equations do not always have closed solutions, for instance $X = X$ does not if the type of X is empty (the existence of a such a solution is even undecidable [Miller 1992]). Thus we cannot avoid solving flexible-flexible equations.

Notice that any type inhabitation problem can be expressed as a unification problem, taking a variable of type T and searching for a solution to the empty problem (or to the problem $X = X$).

4.2.7. Unification Modulo the Rule β Alone

A long normal term of type $T_1 \to ... \to T_p \to U$ (U atomic) has the form $\lambda x_1 ... \lambda x_p$ ($h\ u_1\ ...\ u_r$) where the number of abstractions is p, i.e. the arity of its type.

To define the long normal form, we need to have the rule η, which is a consequence of the extensionality axiom. If we drop the extensionality axiom, we have to unify terms modulo the rule β alone.

A β-normal term of type $T_1 \to ... \to T_p \to U$ is now of the form $\lambda x_1 ... \lambda x_q$ ($h\ u_1\ ...\ u_r$) with $q \leq p$. Thus we must consider more elementary substitutions where the number of abstractions ranges from 0 to n. Such an algorithm is described in [Huet 1975, Huet 1976].

For instance with the rules β and η, the problem

$$(X\ a) = (f\ a)$$

has the two solutions $\lambda x\ (f\ a)/X$ and $\lambda x\ (f\ x)/X$. But, with the rule β alone, it has also a third one f/X which is not equivalent to $\lambda x\ (f\ x)/X$ anymore.

4.3. Regular Trees, Regular Solutions

We have seen (proposition 3.4) that the solutions of the problem

$$\lambda z\ (X\ z\ (\lambda y\ y)) = \lambda z\ z$$

where X is a variable of type $\iota \to (\iota \to \iota) \to \iota$, are all the substitutions of the form t/X where t is a Church number.

When we apply the elementary substitution $\lambda x\ \lambda f\ x/X$ to this problem and simplify it, we get the empty problem that is solved. And when we apply the elementary substitution $\lambda x\ \lambda f\ (f\ (Y\ f\ x))/X$ we get the problem

$$\lambda z\ (Y\ z\ (\lambda y\ y)) = \lambda z\ z$$

which is a renaming of the initial problem. Thus, only a finite number of problems (in this case, two) can be generated. In other words, the unification tree is regular and can be represented by a finite skeleton.

M. Zaionc [Zaionc 1987] has remarked that when the number of problems we can generate from a given problem is finite (in other words when the problem has a regular unification tree) we can compute this set of problems (or the skeleton of the unification tree). If this finite set does not contain a solved problem, then we know that the problem is unsolvable. This way he has sharpened Huet's algorithm and proposed an algorithm that reports failures more often that Huet's. For instance, for the problem

$$(X \ a) = (f \ (X \ a))$$

Huet's algorithm constructs an infinite tree with no solved problem, while after an imitation step $\lambda x \ (f \ (H \ x))/X$ yielding after simplification to the problem

$$(H \ a) = (f \ (H \ a))$$

Zaionc's algorithm reports a failure.

Moreover, when the number of problems generated by a given problem is finite and the problem has solutions, the set of minimal unifiers may be infinite, but it can be described by a grammar. For instance, for the problem

$$\lambda z \ (X \ z \ (\lambda y \ y)) = \lambda z \ z$$

calling σ the elementary substitution $\lambda x \ \lambda f \ x/X$ and τ the elementary substitution $\lambda x \ \lambda f \ (f \ (X \ f \ x))/X$, all the solutions have the form $\tau \circ \tau \circ \ldots \circ \tau \circ \sigma$. Such a substitution can be represented by the word $\tau\tau\ldots\tau\sigma$ and the set of words corresponding to the minimal unifiers is produced by the grammar

$$s \to \sigma$$

$$s \to \tau s$$

4.4. Equational Higher-order Unification

Several extensions of Huet's algorithm have been proposed to higher-order equational unification (see section 1.5). Some aim at giving a general algorithm for an arbitrary higher-order equational theory (see, for instance, [Avenhaus and Loría-Sáenz 1994, Müller and Weber 1994, Prehofer 1994b, Prehofer 1995, Qian 1994, Qian and Wang 1992, Snyder 1990]). Others consider special theories (see, for instance, [Curien 1995, Qian and Wang 1994, Saïdi 1994, Boudet and Contejean 1997]).

5. Scopes Management

The idea, underlying Huet's algorithm is to build the terms substituted for the variables step by step and to transform the equations at each step substituting the part of the solution constructed so far. This is a rather general approach in equational unification. As compared to first-order equational unification methods, higher-order unification presents the particularity of a rather subtle management of scopes. For instance, as already mentioned, we cannot take the elementary substitution $\lambda y_1 \ \ldots \ \lambda y_p \ (f \ H_1 \ \ldots \ H_r)/X$ but we must express the dependence of the arguments of f with respect to the variables $y_1, \ldots, y_p$ in a functional way, taking the substitution $\lambda y_1 \ \ldots \ \lambda y_p \ (f \ (H_1 \ y_1 \ \ldots \ y_p) \ \ldots \ (H_r \ y_1 \ \ldots \ y_p))/X$. This is due to the fact that substitution in λ-calculus renames bound variables to avoid captures.

We might want to build the solutions with smaller steps, for instance substituting a variable of a functional type $T \rightarrow U$ by a term of the form $\lambda y \ H/X$ and then substitute H. But this is not possible as expressing functionally the dependence in such a substitution would yield $\lambda y \ (H \ y)/X$. i.e. H/X and thus the inductive argument in the completeness proof would not go through. (Because of the functional encoding of scopes we have to take $|\lambda x \ t| = |t|$ and not $|\lambda x \ t| = |t| + 1$, thus instantiating a variable by an abstraction does not let the problem progress).

In the same way, we might want to simplify an equation of the form $\lambda x \ u = \lambda x \ v$ into $u = v$, but such a simplification rule is unsound. For instance the equation $\lambda x \ Y = \lambda x \ (f \ x \ x)$ has no solution (as the substitution $(f \ x \ x)/Y$ would rename the bound variable to avoid the capture), while the equation $Y = (f \ x \ x)$ has the solution $(f \ x \ x)/Y$.

All these particularities of higher-order unification come from the particularities of the substitution in λ-calculus, and this particularities come from the fact that λ-calculus contains a binding operator λ.

5.1. Mixed Prefixes

To have the simplification rule

$$\frac{E \cup \{\lambda x \ t = \lambda x \ u\}}{E \cup \{t = u\}}$$

we must add to the simplified problem an *occurrence constraint* forbidding the variable x to appear in the term substituted for the variables free in t and u. This way both problems

$$\lambda x \ Y = \lambda x \ (f \ x \ x)$$

and

$$Y = (f \ x \ x), \ x \text{ not available to } Y$$

have no solution, and more generally the simplification of abstractions is sound. Such occurrence constraints can be elegantly expressed in a unification logic.

In a unification logic, unification problems are expressed as propositions and unification rules as deduction rules in such a way that a proposition P is provable if and only if it expresses a unifiable problem. An equation t, u is expressed as an atomic proposition $t = u$ introducing a predicate symbol $=$. A unification problem (i.e. a finite set of equations) is represented as the conjunction of the atomic propositions corresponding to equations. The variables occurring in the problem are then existentially quantified at the head of the problem and the constants can be considered as universally quantified variables.

For instance the problem

$$\lambda x \ Y = \lambda x \ (f \ x \ x)$$

is expressed as the proposition

$$\forall f \ \exists Y \ (\lambda x \ Y = \lambda x \ (f \ x \ x))$$

Unification problems are thus usually expressed as propositions of the form $\forall\exists$. D. Miller [Miller 1992] has proposed to consider propositions with a more complex alternation of quantifiers (*mixed prefixes*), in particular propositions of the form $\forall\exists\forall$. Then the problem

$$\forall f \; \exists Y \; (\lambda x \; Y = \lambda x \; (f \; x \; x))$$

can be simplified into

$$\forall f \; \exists Y \; \forall x \; (Y = (f \; x \; x))$$

in which the usual scoping rules for quantifiers manipulation express that the variable x is not available to Y and forbid the substitution $(f \; x \; x)/Y$. This way, he has been able to give more natural simplification rules. The study of quantifier permutation in such problems has also permitted to identify a decidable subcase of higher-order unification (see section 6.2).

Thus, mixed prefixes permit to give more natural simplification rules, but not to give more natural generation rules.

5.2. Combinators

Recall that higher-order logic is just one among several variants of set theory [Davis 1969]. Like other variants of set theory, it can be expressed in first-order logic.

When we express higher-order logic as a first-order theory, the term language is a first-order term language and thus, as opposed to λ-calculus it contains no binding operator. Thus, the substitution does not need to avoid captures and scope management is simpler. Expressing this way higher-order logic as a first-order theory permits also to use standard technique for proof search and in particular standard first-order equational unification algorithms for higher-order unification.

When we express higher-order logic as a (many-sorted) first-order theory, we need to distinguish zero-ary relations that are expressed by terms of sort o and propositions. We introduce a unary predicate symbol ε of rank (o) and if t is a term of type o, the corresponding proposition is written $\varepsilon(t)$. For each pair of type, we introduce also a function symbol $\alpha_{T,U}$ of rank $(T \to U, T, U)$ and the term $(t \; u)$ is a notation for $\alpha_{T,U}(t, u)$. We may also introduce symbols $=_T$ of type $T \to T \to o$ for equality.

As seen in section 1 we state the comprehension schemes

$$\forall x_1 \; ... \; \forall x_n \; \exists f \; \forall y_1 \; ... \; \forall y_p \; (\varepsilon(f \; y_1 \; ... \; y_p) \Leftrightarrow P))$$

$$\forall x_1 \; ... \; \forall x_n \; \exists f \; \forall y_1 \; ... \; \forall y_p \; \varepsilon((f \; y_1 \; ... \; y_p) = t)$$

These schemes are equivalent to the closed schemes

$$\exists f \; \forall y_1 \; ... \; \forall y_p \; (\varepsilon(f \; y_1 \; ... \; y_p) \Leftrightarrow P))$$

$$\exists f \; \forall y_1 \; ... \; \forall y_p \; \varepsilon((f \; y_1 \; ... \; y_p) = t)$$

where all the free variables of t and P are required to be among $y_1, ..., y_p$.

As seen in section 1, to have a language for the relations and functions we skolemize these axioms and introduce symbols that we may write $\lambda y_1 ... \lambda y_p \; t$ and $\lambda y_1 ... \lambda y_p \; P$ if we want, but we must recall that (1) in such expressions, the free variables of P and t must be among $y_1, ..., y_p$, (2) the proposition P and the term t do not contain further abstractions and (3) such terms are individual symbols. These symbols are called *combinators* [Curry 1942, Curry and Feys 1958, Hindley and Seldin 1986].

We can also chose to restrict the comprehension schemes to a finite number of instances that are equivalent to the full scheme. This way we have a finite number of combinators (e.g. $S, K, \Rightarrow, \wedge, \vee, \neg, \forall, \exists$).

We have said in section 1 that this language was equivalent to λ-calculus, but moving from this language to the more convenient notation of λ-calculus introduces the binding operator λ and thus the notion of substitution with renaming. An alternative is to keep this language and to perform unification modulo the combinators conversion axioms.

The use of combinators, instead of λ-calculus, was already investigated by J.A. Robinson in 1970 [Robinson 1970] (but, apparently, without stressing the relation to Davis' remark that higher-order logic could be expressed as a first-order theory). This approach has been pursued in [Dougherty 1993]. Using combinators instead of λ-calculus permits to use standard first-order equational unification algorithms to perform unification modulo the conversion axioms.

The translations from λ-calculus to combinators [Curry 1942, Curry and Feys 1958, Hindley and Seldin 1986, Hughes 1982, Johnsson 1985, Dowek 1995], such as λ-lifting, are correct if the extensionality axiom is taken, but not when this axiom is dropped: the theory of the conversion axiom alone are not equivalent in λ-calculus and in the theory of combinators. In other words, some proofs, for instance that of the proposition

$$((\lambda x \; \lambda y \; \lambda z \; x) \; w \; w) = ((\lambda x \; \lambda y \; \lambda z \; y) \; w \; w)$$

do not require the use of the extensionality axiom in λ-calculus and requires it with combinators.

If unification is seen as a part of resolution, then resolution in the λ-calculus presentation of higher-order logic is equivalent to resolution in the combinators presentation of higher-order logic, i.e. a proposition is provable in one system if and only if its translation is provable in the other (although the proofs may be different in the two systems, in particular one may need to use the extensionality axiom, while the other does not).

If unification is seen as an independent problem then combinator unification is weaker than higher-order unification, i.e. it is not the case that a problem has a solution in λ-calculus if and only if its translation has one in combinators, but combinator unification may be adapted to get the same power as higher-order unification, using a glimpse of extensionality [Dougherty 1993]. This algorithm is, however, more redundant than Huet's.

Notice, at last, that the higher-order unification algorithm itself uses part of the translation of λ-calculus to combinators. In particular the functional encoding of scopes is reminiscent of λ-lifting.

5.3. Explicit Substitutions

To avoid the problems with extensionality introduced by the use of combinators, another solution is to keep λ-calculus, but to avoid the difficulties of scopes management with the use the *replacement*, allowing capture (see definition 2.11) instead of substitution. In other words, when we have an equation $a = b$ we do not look for a substitution θ such that $\theta a = \theta b$ but for a substitution θ such that $\langle \theta \rangle a = \langle \theta \rangle b$.

Using such a notion of replacement permits to decompose the simplification rules into a rule simplifying equations of the form $\lambda x \ u = \lambda x \ v$ into $u = v$ an other one simplifying equations of the form $(f \ u_1 \ ... \ u_p) = (f \ v_1 \ ... \ v_p)$ into $u_1 = v_1, ..., u_p = v_p$ and $(f \ u_1 \ ... \ u_p) = (g \ v_1 \ ... \ v_q)$ into $\bot$ when f and g are different. The generation rule can also be simplified: if X is a variable of type $T \to U$ we can replace it by a term $\lambda x \ Y$ where Y is a variable of type U, and when X has an atomic type, we replace it by the term $(h \ H_1 \ ... \ H_r)$.

But, this notion of replacement raises two new difficulties. First replacement does not commute with reduction and thus it cannot be defined on the quotient of terms modulo reduction. For instance, the term $((\lambda x \ Y) \ a)$ reduces to Y, but replacing x for Y yields $((\lambda x \ x) \ a)$ that reduces to a and not to x. To avoid this difficulty, a solution is to delay the substitution of a for x in Y until Y is replaced and we know whether it contains an occurrence of x or not (when using substitution with renaming such a delay is not needed (proposition 2.22) because a term containing the variable x cannot be substituted for the variable Y).

Delaying this way the substitutions initiated by β-reduction requires an extension of λ-calculus with *explicit substitutions* [Abadi, Cardelli, Curien and Lévy 1991, Curien, Hardin and Lévy 1996, Nadathur and Wilson 1998]. Besides constants, variables, applications and abstractions, the calculus of explicit substitutions introduces another construction the *closure* $[\sigma]t$ where σ is a substitution and t a term. The β-reduction rule is replaced by the rule

$$((\lambda x \ t) \ u) \rhd [u/x]t$$

and more reduction rules permit to propagate the explicit substitution u/x in the term t. The simplest rules permits to distribute a substitution on an application

$$[\sigma](t \ u) \rhd ([\sigma]t \ [\sigma]u)$$

When such a substitution $[u/x]$ reaches the variable x the term $[u/x]x$ reduces to the term u, when it reaches another variable y the term $[u/x]y$ reduces to y, but when it reaches a *metavariable* Y the term $[u/x]Y$ cannot be reduced and thus the substitution is delayed until the metavariable Y is replaced. Thus, when we express a higher-order unification problem in the calculus of explicit substitutions free variables are expressed as metavariables and bound variables as ordinary variables.

The second difficulty is that some problems have solutions for replacement while they have none for substitution. This is the case for instance for the problem $\lambda x\; Y = \lambda x\; (f\; x\; x)$. If we use replacement, $(f\; x\; x)/Y$ is a solution, while the problem has no solution if we use substitution. This problem is solved again by the use of explicit substitutions. In this system, there are explicit renaming operators and thus we can use such an operator to protect the metavariable Y from being replaced by a term containing the variable x.

Thus we can define a translation from λ-calculus to λ-calculus with explicit substitutions such that a unification problem has a solution for substitution if and only if its translation has one for replacement. In other words, the substitution of λ-calculus is decomposed into an (explicit) renaming and a replacement.

This approach has been investigated in [Dowek, Hardin and Kirchner 1995, Borovanský 1995, Nadathur 1998, Nadathur and Mitchell 1999].

5.4. De Bruijn Indices

Like combinators, the calculus of explicit substitutions permits to avoid the subtle scope management of higher-order unification and it avoids also the use of extensionality. But, so far, it does not permit to use the standard first-order equational unification techniques because λ-calculus (with explicit substitutions or not) is still not a first-order language.

In fact, independently of combinators, N.G. de Bruijn [de Bruijn 1972] has proposed another notation for λ-calculus that happened to be also a first-order language.

The idea of de Bruijn notation, is that the name of bound variables is only used to indicate the binder they depend on. This dependency may also be indicated by the height of this binder above the variable. For instance, the term $\lambda x\; \lambda y\; (x\; \lambda z\; (x\; z))$ may be written $\lambda\lambda(2\; \lambda(3\; 1))$ because the first occurrence of the variable x refers to the second λ above it, the second occurrence of the variable x refers to the third λ above it and the occurrence of the variable z refers to the first λ above it.

In de Bruijn notation, the operator λ is not a binding operator anymore and thus λ-calculus can be represented as a first-order term language with a unary function symbol λ, a binary function symbol α and an infinite number of constant symbol 1, 2, etc.

Because of the presence of the substitution in the β-reduction rule, the reduction system in this language is not a first-order rewrite system, but the reduction system in λ-calculus with de Bruijn indices and explicit substitutions is first-order. In fact, the standard presentation of the calculus of explicit substitutions uses de Bruijn indices and not named variables. The metavariables of the calculus of explicit substitutions are the variables of the free algebra built on this language.

With de Bruijn indices and explicit substitutions, we can use first-order techniques to perform unification, we do not have scopes management problems nor those created by the use extensionality in translating λ-calculus to combinators [Dowek et al. 1995].

These investigations have also lead to another first-order presentation of higher-order logic based on de Bruijn indices and explicit substitutions that is extensionally equivalent to the presentation using λ-calculus [Dowek, Hardin and Kirchner 2001].

Presenting this way λ-calculus as a first-order language and higher-order unification as first-order equational unification modulo an equational theory T_1 permits to consider also equational higher-order unification modulo an equational theory T_2 as equational first-order unification modulo $T_1 \cup T_2$ [Dougherty and Johann 1992, Goubault 1994, Kirchner and Ringeissen 1997].

6. Decidable Subcases

As usual when a problem is undecidable, besides building a semi-decision algorithm, we are also interested in identifying decidable subcases. In this section, we present a few decidable subcases of higher-order unification. These subcases are obtained by restricting the order, the arity or the number of occurrences of variables, or by taking terms of a special form. For some subcases, Huet's algorithm terminates, for others it does not and we must design another algorithm to prove decidability.

The main conjectures in this area are the decidability of pattern-matching, i.e. the subcase of unification where variables occur only in a single side of equations and the decidability of context unification.

6.1. First-order Unification

The first decidable subcase of higher-order unification is obviously first-order unification. When all the variables of a problem have first-order, i.e. atomic, types (see definition 2.3), all the constants have at most second-order types and the terms in the equations have first-order types, then the problem is just a rephrasing of a first-order unification problem. Notice however that Huet's algorithm does not always terminate on such problems. For instance the problem

$$X = f(X)$$

leads to an infinite search. In other words, Huet's algorithm does not detect failure by occur-check. However, it can be sharpened, adding a rule called *rigid paths occur-check* [Huet 1975, Huet 1976] that forces failure in more cases and in particular for all the first-order unsolvable unification problems.

6.2. Patterns

When we define a function by an equation, for instance,

$$\forall x \; \forall y \; ((F \; x \; y) = x + y + x \times y)$$

we actually mean

$$F = \lambda x \; \lambda y \; (x + y + x \times y)$$

But the first definition can also be used because the equation has a single solution $\lambda x \, \lambda y \, (x + y + x \times y)$. In contrast, the definitions

$$\forall x \, ((F \, x \, x) = x + x + x \times x)$$

or

$$\forall x \, ((F \, 0 \, x) = x)$$

are incorrect because the equations have more than one solution.

This remark motivates the study of unification problems where the higher-order free variables can only be applied to distinct bound variables.

A *pattern* [Miller 1991] is a term t such that for every subterm of the form $(F \, u_1 \, ... \, u_n)$ where F is a free variable, the terms $u_1, ..., u_n$ are distinct variables bound in t. Unification of patterns is decidable and when a unification problem has a unifier, it has a most general unifier [Miller 1991].

For instance the problem

$$\lambda x \, \lambda y \, \lambda z \, (F \, x \, z) = (f \, (\lambda x \, \lambda y \, (G \, y \, x)) \, (\lambda x \, \lambda y \, (F \, x \, y)))$$

is a patterns unification problem.

Patterns unification extends first-order unification. It has the same properties (polynomial time decidability and most general unifier) and the algorithms have some similarities (in particular, the occur-check plays an essential role in both cases). The correspondence between first-order unification and patterns unification is better understood when we study quantifier permutation in mixed prefixes (see section 5.1) as patterns unification problems can be obtained by permuting quantifiers in first-order problems [Miller 1992]. This is also the way patterns unification was discovered.

Patterns unification is used in higher-order logic programming [Nadathur and Miller 1998, Pfenning 1991a].

Patterns unification with explicit substitutions is studied in [Dowek, Hardin, Kirchner and Pfenning 1996], the decidability and unicity of solution rely there on invertibility properties of explicit substitutions.

This subcase of unification called *patterns unification* must not be confused with *pattern matching* discussed in section 6.6.

6.3. Monadic Second-order Unification

Goldfarb's undecidability proof requires a language with a binary constant g. Thus, a natural problem to investigate is unification in second-order languages containing only unary constants, i.e. constants with a single argument. This problem, called *unary or monadic second-order unification* has been proved decidable by Farmer [Farmer 1988].

Farmer's proofs relies on the fact that a closed term of an atomic type in such a language has the form $(f_1 \, (f_2 \, ... \, (f_n \, c)...))$ and thus can be represented by the word $f_1 f_2 ... f_n$. Thus, a unification problem in such a language can be reduced to word unification problem, and such problems are known to be decidable.

In this case, the set of minimal unifiers may be infinite. For instance the unification problem

$$\lambda z \ (f \ (X \ z)) = \lambda z \ (X \ (f \ z))$$

which is equivalent to the word problem $fX = Xf$ has an infinite number of minimal solutions where the terms $\lambda x \ x$, $\lambda x \ (f \ x)$, $\lambda x \ (f \ (f \ x))$, $\lambda x \ (f \ (f \ (f \ x)))$, $\lambda x \ (f \ (f \ (f \ (f \ x))))$, etc. are substituted for the variable X, corresponding to the solutions of the word problem ε, f, ff, fff, etc. Farmer proposes to describe minimal unifiers using so called *parametric terms*, reminding of Zaionc's description by a grammar. For instance the parametric term $\lambda x \ (f^n \ x)$ (corresponding to the parametric word f^n) is the most general unifier of the problem above.

6.4. Context Unification

Context unification is a variant of second order unification with the extra condition that terms substituted to second order variables have to be *contexts*, i.e. normal terms of the form $\lambda x_1 \ ... \ \lambda x_n \ t$ where the variables $x_1, ..., x_n$ occur once in t. Such terms can be seen as first-order terms with holes. This problem is related to unification in linear lambda-calculus [Pfenning and Cervesato 1997].

The decidability of this problem is open, [Comon 1998, Schmidt-Schauß 1994, Levy 1996, Niehren, Pinkal and Ruhrberg 1997, Schmidt-Schauß and Schulz 1999, Schmidt-Schauß 1999, Levy and Villaret 2000, Niehren, Tison and Treinen 2000] give partial results.

6.5. Second-order Unification with Linear Occurrences of Second-order Variables

In second-order unification, when we have an equation

$$\lambda x_1 \ ... \ \lambda x_n \ (X \ a_1 \ ... \ a_p) = \lambda x_1 \ ... \ \lambda x_n \ (f \ b_1 \ ... \ b_q)$$

and we perform a projection, we replace a variable X by a closed term $\lambda x_1 ... \lambda x_n \ x_i$, thus the number of variables in the problem decreases. When we perform an imitation and simplify the problem, we get the equations

$$\lambda x_1 \ .. \ \lambda x_n \ (H_1 \ a_1 \ ... \ a_p) = \lambda x_1 \ ... \ \lambda x_n \ b_1$$

$$...$$

$$\lambda x_1 \ ... \ \lambda x_n \ (H_q \ a_1 \ ... \ a_p) = \lambda x_1 \ ... \ \lambda x_n \ b_q$$

which seem to be smaller than the equation we started with. Hence, it seems that Huet's algorithm should terminate, in contradiction with Goldfarb's undecidability result.

Actually, the variable X may have occurrences in the terms $a_1, ..., a_p, b_1, ..., b_q$ and in fact we get the equations

$$\lambda x_1 \ ... \ \lambda x_n \ (H_1 \ a_1' \ ... \ a_p') = \lambda x_1 \ ... \ \lambda x_n \ b_1'$$

$$...$$

$$\lambda x_1 \ ... \ \lambda x_n \ (H_q \ a_1' \ ... \ a_p') = \lambda x_1 \ ... \ \lambda x_n \ b_q'$$

where the variable X has been substituted everywhere. These equation need not be smaller than the equation we started with and thus the algorithm does not always terminate.

However this argument can be used to prove that second-order unification with linear occurrences of second-order variables is decidable, i.e. that there is an algorithm that decides unifiability of second-order problems where each second-order variable has a single occurrence (see, for instance, [Dowek 1993d]). In fact, to ensure that linearity is preserved by imitation we must first transform equations into *superficial* equations, i.e. equations where the second-order variables can occur only at the head of the members of the equations.

This algorithm has been extended by Ch. Prehofer [Prehofer 1994a, Prehofer 1995] mixing linearity conditions and patterns conditions.

G. Amiot [Amiot 1990] had used a similar transformation to prove that superficial second-order unification is undecidable.

Besides linear unification, a similar argument using the number of variables and the size of equations will be used in section 6.6.1 to prove the decidability of second-order matching.

6.6. Pattern Matching

A higher-order matching equation is an equation whose right hand side does not contain free variables. A higher-order matching problem is a finite set of matching equations. The decidability of higher-order matching, Huet's conjecture [Huet 1976], has been an open problem for more than twenty years.

6.6.1. Second-order Matching

The first positive result is the decidability of second-order matching.

6.1. PROPOSITION. *(Huet [Huet 1976, Huet and Lang 1978]) Second-order matching is decidable, i.e. there is an algorithm that takes in argument a matching problem whose free variables are at most second-order (in the sense of definition 2.3) and whose bound variables and constants are at most third-order and answers if it has a solution or not.*

PROOF. For second-order matching problems, Huet's algorithm terminates. Indeed, the pair (n, p) where n is the sum of the sizes of the right hand sides of equations and p the number of variables in the problem decreases at each step (i.e. each application of the *Generate* rules followed by a simplification) for the lexicographic order.

Imitations are always followed by a simplification, and thus the sum of the sizes of the right hand sides of equations decreases in such a step. Projections have the form $\lambda x_1 \ldots \lambda x_n \; x_i$ thus they do not introduce new variables $H_1, \ldots, H_r$ and the number of variables in the problem decreases in such a step and the closed right hand sides are never substituted, thus the sum of their sizes never increases. □

6.2. REMARK. In a matching problem there is no flexible-flexible equations. Thus the only solved problem is the empty problem and a second-order matching problem has a finite set of minimal solutions.

6.3. REMARK. L.D. Baxter has proved that the second order matching problem is NP-complete [Baxter 1977].

6.4. REMARK. The condition that bound variables and constants are at most third-order can be weakened (see, for instance, [Dowek 1991c]), but patterns-like terms need to be used in the algorithm.

6.6.2. Infinite Set of Solutions and Pumping

As soon as we have a third-order variable, Huet's algorithm may fail to terminate and may produce an infinite number of minimal solutions. For instance, as seen above (proposition 3.4) the problem

$$\lambda z \; (X \; z \; (\lambda y \; y)) = \lambda z \; z$$

has an infinite number of solutions of the form t/X where t is any Church number $\lambda x \, \lambda f \; (f \ldots (f \; x)\ldots)$.

Thus if we look for a terminating algorithm, we cannot use Huet's algorithm, and we cannot use any other algorithm enumerating all the minimal solutions. Thus, all the algorithms proposed so far (for restricted cases) all reduce the search space, dropping some solutions, but hopefully keeping at least one if the problem has solutions.

As an illustration we can use such a method to prove the decidability, in the domain of natural numbers, of polynomial equations with a constant right hand side (whereas Matiyacevich-Robinson-Davis [Matiyacevich 1970, Davis 1973] theorem proves the undecidability of polynomial equations in general). Notice that in this case also, a problem may have an infinite number of solutions (consider for instance the equation $XY + 4 = 4$).

6.5. PROPOSITION. *There is an algorithm that takes as arguments a polynomial P whose coefficients are natural numbers and a natural number b and answers if the equation $P(X_1, \ldots, X_n) = b$ has a solution or not in the domain of natural numbers.*

PROOF. If this equation has a solution $a_1, \ldots, a_n$ then it has a solution $a'_1, \ldots, a'_n$ such that $a'_1 \leq b$. Indeed either $Q(X) = P(X, a_2, \ldots, a_n)$ is not a constant polynomial and for all n, $Q(n) \geq n$, so $a_1 \leq b$, or the polynomial Q is identically equal to b and $\langle 0, a_2, ..., a_n \rangle$ is also a solution. A simple induction on n proves that if the equation has a solution then it also has a solution in $\{0, ..., b\}^n$ and an enumeration of this set gives a decision algorithm. $\square$

For instance, for the equation $XY + 4 = 4$, starting with the solution $\langle 1000, 0 \rangle$ we get the solution $\langle 0, 0 \rangle$. The method that transforms the solution $\langle 1000, 0 \rangle$ into $\langle 0, 0 \rangle$ is called *pumping*. It permits to know whether a solution exists in an infinite domain just by looking into a finite part of the domain, because this finite part mirrors all the domain.

6.6.3. Finite Models

Such an idea has been investigated by R. Statman using model theoretic techniques. H. Friedman's completeness theorem [Friedman 1975] is that if we interpret the atomic types by infinite sets and types of the form $A \to B$ by the set of all functions from the interpretation of A to the interpretation of B, then two terms have the same denotation if and only if they are $\beta\eta$-convertible.

Obviously, this theorem cannot be generalized to the case where the interpretation of atomic types are finite. Indeed, if the interpretation of the type ι is finite, that of the type $\iota \to (\iota \to \iota) \to \iota$ also and thus at least two different Church numbers have the same denotation, while they are not convertible.

However Statman's finite completeness theorem [Statman 1979, Statman and Dowek 1992] shows that for each λ-term b, there is a natural number n such that, in the finite model built from a base sets of cardinal n, the terms that have the same denotation as b are those convertible to b.

Thus, if a matching problem $(a\ X_1\ ...\ X_n) = b$ (b closed) has a solution, the corresponding equation in the model has a solution too, and as the denotation of each type in the model is finite, we can enumerate all the potential solutions and test one after another. Unfortunately, when we find a solution in the model this solution corresponds to a solution in λ-calculus only if the element of the model is the denotation of some λ-term. Thus the higher-order matching conjecture was reduced this way to the λ-definability decidability conjecture (Plotkin-Statman conjecture) [Statman 1979, Statman and Dowek 1992].

Another formulation, that strengthen the link to the pumping method is that assuming that we can decide whether an element is λ-definable or not we can compute a number n such that all the definable elements of the model of a given type are defined by a term of size lower than n. Thus, if the problem has a solution, then it has also a solution of size lower than n and to decide whether a problem has a solution, we only need to enumerate the terms of size lower to that bound. After this bound, the terms are redundant, i.e. their denotation is also a denotation of smaller terms and if they are solutions to the matching problem smaller terms also.

Unfortunately the λ-definability decidability conjecture has been refuted by R. Loader [Loader 1994].

However, V. Padovani has shown that λ-definability was decidable in other models: the *minimal models* where the interpretation of the type $A \to B$ contains only the λ-definable functions and from this result, he has deduced the decidability of the atomic higher-order matching problem (i.e. the higher-order matching problem where the right hand side is a constant) [Padovani 1996a, Padovani 1996b].

6.6.4. Third and Fourth-order Matching

A similar approach has permitted to prove the decidability of third-order and fourth-order matching problems i.e. matching problems whose free variables are at most third or fourth order (in the sense of definition 2.3).

Consider a variable X of type $\iota \to (\iota \to \iota) \to \iota$, the equation

$$(X \ c \ (\lambda y \ (g \ (h \ y)))) = c$$

and the potential normal solution $t = \lambda x \ \lambda f \ u$ for X. The term $(t \ c \ \lambda y \ (g \ (h \ y)))$ reduces to the normal form of $(c/x, \lambda y \ (g \ (h \ y))/f)u$ and, a simple induction on the depth of the structure of u shows that this term has a depth greater than or equal to that of u. For instance, taking $t = \lambda x \ \lambda f \ (f \ (f \ (f \ x)))$ and applying it to c and $\lambda y \ (g \ (h \ y))$ yields $(g \ (h \ (g \ (h \ (g \ (h \ c))))))$ where each f has been replaced by a g and a h. Thus, if such a term is to be a solution of the above problem u must be smaller than c. Thus, enumerating the terms smaller than c gives an algorithm to find all the solutions of this problem. In fact, the only solutions are $\lambda x \ \lambda f \ c$ and $\lambda x \ \lambda f \ x$.

But such a reasoning does not work for all the problems, for instance

$$(X \ c \ (\lambda y \ y)) = c$$

$$(X \ d \ (\lambda y \ e)) = e$$

has solutions of an arbitrary depth: all nonzero Church numbers

$$\lambda x \ \lambda f \ (f \ (...(f \ x)...)).$$

This can only happen when all the second arguments of X are either of the form $\lambda x_1 \ ... \ \lambda x_n \ x_i$ (e.g. $\lambda y \ y$) or an irrelevant term i.e. a term where a bound variable does not occur in the body (e.g. $\lambda y \ e$). In this case any sequence of f has the same effect as a single f thus, any solution of the form $\lambda x \ \lambda f \ (f \ (...(f \ x)...))$ is redundant with the smaller solution $\lambda x \ \lambda f \ (f \ x)$.

Erasing, this way, all the useless occurrences of variables permits to get smaller solutions whose depth can be bounded by a function in the depth of b. Thus, we can compute a bound such that if the problem has a solution, then it has also a solution whose depth is lower than that bound and hence achieve decidability.

The simpler case for which such a method works is the third-order interpolation problems.

6.6. DEFINITION. (Interpolation problem)

An *interpolation problem* is a finite set of equations of the form $(X \ a_1 \ ... \ a_n) = b$ where the terms $a_1, ..., a_n, b$ are closed.

Using the pumping method described above, we can prove the decidability of third-order interpolation problems. Then, the bound on the depth of solutions can be lifted to arbitrary third-order matching problems and this proves the decidability of third-order matching problems [Dowek 1994].

A. Schubert [Schubert 1997] has proved that the decidability of higher-order interpolation problems implies that of higher-order matching problems, unfortunately his transformation does not preserve the order of the variables.

V. Padovani [Padovani 1995] has proved that the decidability of the dual interpolation problem implies that of higher-order matching and his transformation preserves the order of the variables thus the decidability of the dual interpolation problem of order n implies that of the matching of order n (a dual interpolation problem is a pair (E, F) of interpolation problems and a solution to such a problem is a substitution that is solution to the equation of E but not to that of F).

Using this result, Padovani has proved the decidability of the fourth-order matching problem [Padovani 1994, Padovani 1996b].

6.6.5. Automata

All these proofs are rather technical (in particular the decidability of fourth-order matching is a real technical *tour de force*) because they all proceed by transforming potential solutions into smaller ones cutting and pasting term pieces. H. Comon and Y. Jurski [Comon and Jurski 1997] have proposed to reformulate these ideas in a much simpler way.

Instead of transforming a potential solution into a smaller one. Comon and Jurski propose, in a similar way as Zaionc (see section 4.3) and Farmer (see section 6.3) to build an automaton that recognizes the solutions of a given problem.

For instance, in the problem

$$(X \ c \ (\lambda y \ y)) = c$$

$$(X \ d \ (\lambda y \ e)) = e$$

the fact that any sequence of f has the same effect as a single f and thus that any solution of the form $\lambda x \ \lambda f \ (f \ (...(f \ x)...))$ is redundant with the smaller solution $\lambda x \ \lambda f \ (f \ x)$ is expressed as the fact that the automaton stays in the same state recognizing the sequence of f in the solution $\lambda x \ \lambda f \ (f \ (...(f \ x)...))$. This way a finite state automaton can recognize the infinite set of solutions and decidability is a consequence of the decidability of the nonemptiness of a set of terms recognized by an automaton.

This way they have given simpler decidability proofs for third-order and fourth-order matching. They have also proved that third order matching was NP-complete, hence that is not more complex than second-order matching.

6.6.6. Wolfram's Algorithm

A last approach has been investigated by D. Wolfram [Wolfram 1989]. Wolfram has proposed a pruning of the search tree for the full higher-order matching that produces a finite search tree. Thus, Wolfram's algorithm always terminates, but its completeness is still a conjecture.

7. Unification in λ-calculus with Dependent Types

To conclude this chapter we shall review unification algorithms in extensions of simply typed λ-calculus. We have already seen in section 1.5 and 4.4 that more reduction rules could be added, we can also consider richer type structure such as dependent types and polymorphism.

7.1. λ-calculus with Dependent Types

7.1.1. Types Parametrized by Terms
The λ-calculus with dependent types is an extension of simply typed λ-calculus where types contain more information on terms than their functional degree. For instance in simply typed λ-calculus, we may consider lists (i.e. finite sequences) of natural numbers as atoms and thus have an atomic type *list* and two symbols ε of type *list* for the empty list and . of type *list* → *nat* → *list*) to add an element at the end of a list. For instance the list $1, 1, 2, 3, 5$ is expressed by the term $(. (. (. (. (. \varepsilon 1) 1) 2) 3) 5)$.

But we may want to enrich the type system in such a way that the length of the list is a part of its type, i.e. we want to have a family of types $(list\ 0)$, $(list\ 1)$, $(list\ 2)$, etc. parametrized by a term of type *nat*.

The type of a function taking as argument a natural number n and returning a list of length n, cannot be written *nat* → $(list\ n)$ but we must express the information that the variable n refers to the argument of the function, thus we write such a type $\Pi n_{nat}\ (list\ n)$. When we apply such a function to, for instance, the term 4 we get a term of type $(list\ 4)$, i.e. a list of four elements. From now on, the notation $A \rightarrow B$ is just an abbreviation for $\Pi x_A\ B$ where x does not occur in B. The symbol *list* is not a type but it has type *nat* → *Type* where *Type* is a new base type.

As types contain terms, the type of a variable may be changed by a substitution, for instance if x is a variable of type $(list\ n)$ the term $\lambda x\ x$ has type $(list\ n) \rightarrow (list\ n)$, but substituting n by 4 changes the type of x to $(list\ 4)$ and the type of $\lambda x\ x$ to $(list\ 4) \rightarrow (list\ 4)$. In such a system, we usually indicate the type of each variable by a subscript at its binding occurrence, writing, for instance $\lambda x_{(list\ n)}\ x$.

7.1.2. Types Parametrized by Types
In the same way, we may want to parametrize the type *list* by the type of the elements of the list, in order to construct lists of natural numbers, lists of sets of natural numbers, lists of lists of natural numbers, etc. i.e. we want to have a family of type $(list\ nat)$, $(list\ (nat \rightarrow o))$, $(list\ (list\ nat))$, etc. parametrized by a type. When we have such types parametrized by types we need also to parametrize terms by types, i.e. to have terms taking a type as argument, for instance the symbol

ε must be parametrized by a type in such a way that (ε *nat*) be a term of type (*list nat*), (ε (*nat* → *o*)) a term of type (*list* (*nat* → *o*)), etc.

Taking none, one or several of the three features: types parametrized by terms (dependent types), types parametrized by types (type constructors), terms parametrized by types (polymorphic types), we get $2^3 = 8$ calculi ($\lambda\Pi$-calculus [Harper, Honsell and Plotkin 1993], systems F and F_ω [Girard 1970, Girard 1972], the Calculus of constructions [Coquand 1985, Coquand and Huet 1988], etc.) that are usually represented as the vertices of a cube [Barendregt 1992].

7.1.3. Proofs as Objects

These extensions of simply typed λ-calculus are needed when we consider extensions of higher-order logic where proofs are objects. In higher-order logic, the number 2 is expressed by a term, the set E of even numbers too, the proposition (E 2) that 2 is even also, but the proof that this proposition holds is not a term. *Intuitionistic type theory* [Martin-Löf 1984] and the *Calculus of Constructions* [Coquand 1985, Coquand and Huet 1988] are extensions of higher-order logic where such proofs are terms of the formalism too.

These formalisms use Brouwer-Heyting-Kolmogorov notion of proof : proofs of atomic propositions are atoms, proofs of propositions of the form $A \Rightarrow B$ are functions mapping proofs of A to proofs of B (for instance, the term $\lambda x_{P'} \lambda y_{Q'} x$ is a proof of $P \Rightarrow Q \Rightarrow P$) and proofs of propositions of the form $\forall x_T P$ are functions mapping every object a of the type T to a proof of (a/x)P.

As remarked by H.B. Curry [Curry and Feys 1958], N.G. de Bruijn [de Bruijn 1980] and W. Howard [Howard 1980], the type of such a term is isomorphic to the proposition itself, i.e. proofs of propositions of the form $A \Rightarrow B$ have type $A' \to B'$ where A' is the type of proofs of A and B' the type of proofs of B. Proofs of propositions of the form $\forall x_T P$ have type $\Pi x_T P'$ where P' the type of the proofs of P.

As usual, we identify isomorphic objects and thus identify $A \Rightarrow B$ and $A \to B$, $\forall x_T P$ and $\Pi x_T P$,

7.2. Unification in λ-calculus with Dependent Types

7.2.1. $\lambda\Pi$-calculus

The first unification algorithm for such an extension of simply typed λ-calculus has been proposed by C.M. Elliott [Elliott 1989, Elliott 1990] and D. Pym [Pym 1990] for $\lambda\Pi$-calculus i.e. a calculus where types may be parametrized by terms, but not by types and terms cannot be parametrized by types either. The main idea in this algorithm is still the same: simplify rigid-rigid equations, construct solutions to flexible-rigid equations incrementally with elementary substitutions, substituting variables by terms of the form $\lambda y_1 {}_{T_1} \ldots \lambda y_p {}_{T_p} (h (H_1 y_1 \ldots y_p) \ldots (H_r y_1 \ldots y_p))$ where h is either a bound variable or the head variable of the rigid term, and avoid solving flexible-flexible equations that always have solutions.

The main difference concerns the typing of substitutions. In simply typed λ-calculus, if we have a variable X of type $T \to U \to T$ and an equation $(X\ a\ b) = a$ then the potential elementary substitutions substitute the terms $\lambda x\ \lambda y\ x$, $\lambda x\ \lambda y\ y$, $\lambda x\ \lambda y\ a$ for the variable X. But the second term has type $T \to U \to U$ and thus cannot be substituted to X (see definition 4.1). We select this way the elementary substitutions that are well-typed, i.e. replace a variable by a term of the same type.

In $\lambda\Pi$-calculus a type may contain variables and thus a type may be changed by a substitution. Thus, when applying a substitution t/X we must not check that the type of X and t are the same, but we must unify them, or add an equation relating their types to the problem.

For instance, if the variable X has type $(list\ 0) \to (list\ Y) \to (list\ 0)$ and we have the problem $(X\ \varepsilon\ b) = \varepsilon$, although the elementary substitution $\lambda x_{(list\ 0)} \lambda y_{(list\ Y)}\ y/X$ is not well typed (the variable has type $(list\ 0) \to (list\ Y) \to (list\ 0)$ and the term $(list\ 0) \to (list\ Y) \to (list\ Y)$) we must not reject it. Indeed, this substitution will be well-typed when we substitute the term 0 for the variable Y leading to the solution $0/Y, \lambda x_{(list\ 0)} \lambda y_{(list\ 0)}\ y/X$. Thus we must consider all the potential elementary substitutions, well-typed or not, and when we perform such a substitution, we must add to the unification problem the *accounting equation* of this substitution, i.e. the equation relating the type of the variable and the type of the term.

In the example above the accounting equation is

$$(list\ 0) \to (list\ Y) \to (list\ Y) = (list\ 0) \to (list\ Y) \to (list\ 0)$$

and it simplifies to $Y = Y, Y = 0$.

As we consider ill-typed substitutions, we have to consider ill-typed, and thus potentially nonnormalizable, equations. In fact, Elliott and Pym have proved that, in $\lambda\Pi$-calculus, provided the simplification of the accounting equation succeeds, the equations, although ill-typed, always normalize [Elliott 1989, Elliott 1990, Pym 1990].

7.2.2. Polymorphism, Type Constructors, Inductive Types

When we consider also polymorphic types and types constructors, i.e. terms parametrized by types and types parametrized by types, we still need accounting equations, but new phenomena happen: the number of arguments of the head variable in an elementary substitution is not fixed by its type anymore, for instance if the variable h has type $\Pi x_{Type}\ x$ and we want to build a term of type A we can build the term

$$(h\ (\underbrace{A \to ... \to A}_{n\ \text{times}} \to A)\ \underbrace{a\ ...\ a}_{n\ \text{times}})$$

where the variable h has $n + 1$ arguments. Thus we need to consider elementary substitutions where the number of arguments of the head variable is arbitrary [Dowek 1993a, Dowek 1991a].

Another difference is that flexible-flexible equation do not always have solutions, for instance if the variable X has type $\Pi x_{Type}\ x$, the equation

$$(X\ (A \to B)\ a) = (X\ B)$$

has no solution [Dowek 1991a]. Thus we must enumerate the elementary substitutions for flexible-flexible equations too.

At last, we loose the normalization property for ill-typed equations but we can prove that in any situation there is always at least a variable that has a well-typed type and that we can instantiate.

Besides dependent types, polymorphic types and types constructors, we can also consider inductive types, i.e. reduction rules for recursor on some data types (see section 1.5 and 4.4) [Gödel 1958, Girard et al. 1989, Martin-Löf 1984, Paulin-Mohring 1993, Werner 1994] and extend the unification algorithm to these systems [Saïdi 1994, Cornes 1997].

7.3. Closed Solutions

In $\lambda\Pi$-calculus we cannot assume anymore that every atomic type is inhabited. For instance consider a type family $(even\ 0)$, $(even\ 1)$, $(even\ 2)$, etc. such that $(even\ n)$ is the type of proofs that n is even. When n is odd, for instance for $n = 1$, this type must be empty.

Thus, flexible-flexible equations do not always have closed solutions (see section 4.2.6). Like in simply typed λ-calculus, the existence of a closed solution to a flexible-flexible unification problem is undecidable. In $\lambda\Pi$-calculus type inhabitation is undecidable (see [Bezem and Springintveld 1996]) and thus even unification problems with no equations (or unification problems on the form $X = X$) are undecidable.

Thus, when looking for closed solutions in $\lambda\Pi$-calculus, we cannot avoid solving flexible-flexible equations.

7.4. Automated Theorem Proving as Unification

Using Curry-de Bruijn-Howard isomorphism, a provability problem in propositional minimal logic can be be expressed as a type inhabitation problem in simply typed λ-calculus and thus as an higher-order unification problem [Zaionc 1988]. In the same way a provability problem in first-order minimal logic can be expressed as a unification problem in $\lambda\Pi$-calculus [Hagiya 1991, Pfenning 1991a] and a provability problem in higher-order intuitionistic logic can be expressed as a unification problem in the Calculus of constructions [Dowek 1993a, Dowek 1991a].

Thus, in λ-calculi with dependent types, provided we search for closed solutions, unification is not a subroutine of automated theorem proving methods anymore, but automated theorem proving can be reduced to unification.

For instance, consider a context where we have

- a type symbol T, i.e. a symbol T of type $Type$,

- two symbols a and b of type T,
- a binary relation $\leq$, of type $T \to T \to Type$,
- an axiom h: $\forall x_T \forall y_T \forall z_T((x \leq y) \Rightarrow (y \leq z) \Rightarrow (x \leq z))$, i.e. a symbol h of type $\Pi x_T \Pi y_T \Pi z_T((x \leq y) \to (y \leq z) \to (x \leq z))$,
- two axioms v and w: $a \leq b$ and $b \leq c$, i.e. two symbols v and w of type $a \leq b$ and $b \leq c$.

We search a proof of the proposition $a \leq c$. We start with a variable X of type $a \leq c$ and no equation (or the equation $X = X$). As we have no equation, all the equations are flexible-flexible, thus we must try all the possible head variables for term substituted for X, among them we consider the substitution $(h\ Y_1\ Y_2\ Y_3\ Y_4\ Y_5)/X$ introducing variables Y_1, Y_2 and Y_3 of type T, Y_4 of type $Y_1 \leq Y_2$ and Y_5 of type $Y_2 \leq Y_3$. The accounting equation of this substitution is

$$(a \leq c) = (Y_1 \leq Y_3)$$

which simplifies to

$$a = Y_1$$
$$c = Y_3$$

These equations are flexible-rigid, the only possible elementary substitution for Y_1 is a/Y_1 and the only possible one for Y_3 is c/Y_3. The accounting equations of these substitution are trivial $(T = T)$, thus we get a problem with three variables (Y_2, Y_4, Y_5) and no equations.

Instantiating, for instance, the variable Y_5 we must try all the possible head variables, among them we consider the substitution w/Y_5 leading to the accounting equation

$$(Y_2 \leq c) = (b \leq c)$$

and it simplifies to

$$Y_2 = b$$

This equation is flexible-rigid, the only possible solution for Y_2 is b/Y_2. The accounting equation of this substitution is trivial $(T = T)$ and thus we get a problem with one variable (Y_4) and no equation.

Instantiating this variable, we must try all the possible head variables, among them we consider the substitution v/Y_4. The accounting equation of this substitution is trivial $((a \leq b) = (a \leq b))$ and thus, we get a problem with no variables and no equations. We are done. The term substituted for X, i.e. the proof of the proposition $a \leq c$ is $(h\ a\ b\ c\ v\ w)$.

Here, all the proof search has been performed by the unification algorithm. Notice that the elementary substitutions $(h\ Y_1\ Y_2\ Y_3\ Y_4\ Y_5)/X$, w/Y_5, v/Y_4 would be considered as resolution steps in more traditional approaches while the elementary substitutions a/Y_1, c/Y_3 and b/Y_2 would be considered as genuine unification steps.

Patterns unification is decidable in all the calculi with dependent types [Pfenning 1991b]. Pattern matching is undecidable in most of the calculi with dependent types [Dowek 1991b, Dowek 1993b, Dowek 1991a] but second-order matching is decidable

[Dowek 1991c, Dowek 1991a], and third-order matching is decidable in some systems [Springintveld 1995a, Springintveld 1995b, Springintveld 1995c].

With dependent types also, the unification steps can be decomposed using explicit substitutions [Magnusson 1994, Muñoz 1997].

Acknowledgments

I want to thank Gérard Huet who has initiated me into the theory of higher-order unification.

I also want to thank Peter Andrews, Jean Goubault-Larrecq, and Gopalan Nadathur for their comments on this chapter.

Bibliography

ABADI M., CARDELLI L., CURIEN P.-L. AND LÉVY J.-J. [1991], 'Explicit substitutions', *Journal of Functional Programming* 1(4), 375–416.

AMIOT G. [1990], 'The undecidability of the second order predicate unification problem', *Archive for mathematical logic* 30, 193–199.

ANDREWS P. [2001], Classical type theory, *in* A. Robinson and A. Voronkov, eds, 'Handbook of Automated Reasoning', Vol. II, Elsevier Science, chapter 15, pp. 965–1007.

ANDREWS P. B. [1971], 'Resolution in type theory', *The Journal of Symbolic Logic* 36(3), 414–432.

ANDREWS P. B. [1986], *An introduction to mathematical logic and type theory: to truth through proof*, Academic Press.

AVENHAUS J. AND LORÍA-SÁENZ C. A. [1994], Higher-order conditional rewriting and narrowing, *in* J.-P. Jouannaud, ed., 'International Conference on Constaints in Computational Logic', Vol. 845 of *Lecture Notes in Computer Science*, Springer-Verlag, pp. 269–284.

BARENDREGT H. AND GEUVERS H. [2001], Proof-assistants using dependent type systems, *in* A. Robinson and A. Voronkov, eds, 'Handbook of Automated Reasoning', Vol. II, Elsevier Science, chapter 18, pp. 1149–1238.

BARENDREGT H. P. [1984], *The Lambda-calculus, its syntax and semantics*, North Holland. Second edition.

BARENDREGT H. P. [1992], Lambda calculi with types, *in* S. Abramsky, D. M. Gabbay and T. S. E. Maibaum, eds, 'Handbook of logic in computer science', Vol. 2, Clarendon Press, pp. 118–309.

BAXTER L. D. [1977], The complexity of unification, PhD thesis, University of Waterloo.

BEZEM M. AND SPRINGINTVELD J. [1996], 'A simple proof of the undecidability of inhabitation in λP', *Journal of Functional Programming* 6(5), 757–761.

BOROVANSKÝ P. [1995], Implementation of higher-order unification based on calculus of explicit substitution, *in* M. Bartošek, J. Staudek and J. Wiedermann, eds, 'SOFSEM : Theory and Practice of Informatics', number 1012 *in* 'Lecture Notes in Computer Science', Springer-Verlag, pp. 363–368.

BOUDET A. AND CONTEJEAN E. [1997], AC-unification of higher-order patterns, *in* G. Smolka, ed., 'Principles and Practice of Constraint Programming', Vol. 1330 of *Lecture Notes in Computer Science*, Springer-Verlag, pp. 267–281.

CHURCH A. [1940], 'A formulation of the simple theory of types', *The Journal of Symbolic Logic* 5(1), 56–68.

CHURCH A. [1956], *Introduction to mathematical logic*, Princeton University Press.

COMON H. [1998], 'Completion of rewrite systems with membership constraints. Part II: Constraint solving', *Journal of Symbolic Computation* **25**, 421–453.

COMON H. AND JURSKI Y. [1997], Higher-order matching and tree automata, *in* M. Nielsen and W. Thomas, eds, 'Conference on Computer Science Logic', Vol. 1414 of *Lecture Notes in Computer Science*, Springer-Verlag, pp. 157–176.

COQUAND T. [1985], Une théorie des constructions. Thèse de troisième cycle, Université Paris VII.

COQUAND T. AND HUET G. [1988], 'The calculus of constructions', *Information and Computation* **76**, 95–120.

CORNES C. [1997], Conception d'un langage de haut niveau de représentation de preuves. récurrence par filtrage de motifs. unification en présence de types inductifs primitifs. synthèse de lemmes d'inversion. Thèse de Doctorat, Université de Paris VII.

CURIEN P.-L., HARDIN T. AND LÉVY J.-J. [1996], 'Confluence properties of weak and strong calculi of explicit substitutions', *Journal of the Association for Computing Machinery* **43**(2), 362–397.

CURIEN R. [1995], Outils pour la preuve par analogie. Thèse de Doctorat, Université Henri Poincaré - Nancy I.

CURRY H. B. [1942], 'The combinatory foundations of mathematical logic', *The Journal of Symbolic Logic* **7**(2), 49–64.

CURRY H. B. AND FEYS R. [1958], *Combinatory logic*, Vol. 1, North Holland.

DALRYMPLE M., SHIEBER S. AND PEREIRA F. [1991], 'Ellipsis and higher-order unification', *Linguistic and Philosophy* **14**, 399–452.

DAVIS M. [1969], Invited commentary of [Robinson 1969], *in* A. J. H. Morrell, ed., 'International Federation for Information Processing Congress, 1968', North Holland, pp. 67–68.

DAVIS M. [1973], 'Hilbert's tenth problem is unsolvable', *The American Mathematician Monthly* **80**(3), 233–269.

DE BRUIJN N. G. [1972], 'Lambda calculus notation with nameless dummies, a tool for automatic formula manipulation, with application to the Church-Rosser theorem', *Indagationes Mathematicae* **34**(5), 381–392.

DE BRUIJN N. G. [1980], A survey of the project automath, *in* J. R. Hindley and J. P. Seldin, eds, 'To H.B. Curry: Essays on combinatory logic, lambda calculus and formalism', Academic Press.

DOUGHERTY D. J. [1993], 'Higher-order unification via combinators', *Theoretical Computer Science* **114**, 273–298.

DOUGHERTY D. J. AND JOHANN P. [1992], A combinatory logic approach to higher-order E-unification, *in* D. Kapur, ed., 'Conference on Automated Deduction', Vol. 607 of *Lecture Notes in Artificial Intelligence*, Springer-Verlag, pp. 79–93.

DOWEK G. [1991a], Démonstration automatique dans le calcul des constructions. Thèse de Doctorat, Université de Paris VII.

DOWEK G. [1991b], 'L'indécidabilité du filtrage du troisième ordre dans les calculs avec types dépendants ou constructeurs de types (the undecidability of third order pattern matching in calculi with dependent types or type constructors)', *Comptes Rendus à l'Académie des Sciences* I, **312**(12), 951–956. Erratum, ibid. I, 318, 1994, p. 873.

DOWEK G. [1991c], A second-order pattern matching algorithm in the cube of typed λ-calculi, *in* A. Tarlecki, ed., 'Mathematical Foundation of Computer Science', Vol. 520 of *Lecture notes in computer science*, Springer-Verlag, pp. 151–160.

DOWEK G. [1993a], 'A complete proof synthesis method for the cube of type systems', *Journal of Logic and Computation* **3**(3), 287–315.

DOWEK G. [1993b], 'The undecidability of pattern matching in calculi where primitive recursive functions are representable', *Theoretical Computer Science* **107**, 349–356.

DOWEK G. [1993c], The undecidability of typability in the lambda-pi-calculus, *in* M. Bezem and J. F. Groote, eds, 'Typed Lambda Calculi and Applications', number 664 *in* 'Lecture Notes in Computer Science', Springer-Verlag, pp. 139–145.

DOWEK G. [1993d], A unification algorithm for second-order linear terms. Manuscript.

DOWEK G. [1994], 'Third order matching is decidable', *Annals of Pure and Applied Logic* **69**, 135–155.

DOWEK G. [1995], Lambda-calculus, combinators and the comprehension scheme, *in* M. Dezani-Ciancagliani and G. Plotkin, eds, 'Typed Lambda Calculi and Applications', number 902 *in* 'Lecture Notes in Computer Science', Springer-Verlag, pp. 154–170.

DOWEK G., HARDIN T. AND KIRCHNER C. [1995], Higher-order unification via explicit substitutions, *in* 'Logic in Computer Science', pp. 366–374.

DOWEK G., HARDIN T. AND KIRCHNER C. [2001], 'HOL-lambda-sigma: an intentional first-order expression of higher-order logic', *Mathematical Structures in Computer Science* **11**, 1–25.

DOWEK G., HARDIN T., KIRCHNER C. AND PFENNING F. [1996], Unification via explicit substitutions: the case of higher-order patterns, *in* M. Maher, ed., 'Joint International Conference and Symposium on Logic Programming', The MIT Press, pp. 259–273.

EKMAN J. [1994], Normal proofs in set theory. Doctoral thesis, Chalmers University and University of Göteborg.

ELLIOTT C. M. [1989], Higher-order unification with dependent function types, *in* N. Dershowitz, ed., 'Internatinal Conference on Rewriting Techniques and Applications', Vol. 355 of *Lecture Notes in Computer Science*, Springer-Verlag, pp. 121–136.

ELLIOTT C. M. [1990], Extensions and applications of higher-order unification, PhD thesis, Carnegie Mellon University.

FARMER W. M. [1988], 'A unification algorithm for second-order monadic terms', *Annals of Pure and applied Logic* **39**, 131–174.

FARMER W. M. [1991a], 'Simple second order languages for which unification is undecidable', *Theoretical Computer Science* **87**, 25–41.

FARMER W. M. [1991b], 'A unification theoretic method for investigating the k-provability problem', *Annals of Pure and Applied Logic* **51**, 173–214.

FRIEDMAN H. [1975], Equality between functionals, *in* R. Parikh, ed., 'Logic Colloquium', Vol. 453 of *Lecture Notes in Mathematics*, Springer-Verlag, pp. 23–37.

GIRARD J.-Y. [1970], Une extension de l'interprétation de Gödel à l'analyse et son application à l'élimination des coupures dans l'analyse et la théorie des types, *in* J. E. Fenstad, ed., 'Scandinavian Logic Symposium', North Holland.

GIRARD J.-Y. [1972], Interprétation fonctionnelle et élimination des coupures dans l'arithmétique d'ordre supérieur. Thèse d'État, Université de Paris VII.

GIRARD J.-Y., LAFONT Y. AND TAYLOR P. [1989], *Proofs and Types*, Cambridge University Press.

GÖDEL K. [1958], 'Über eine bisher noch nicht benützte Erweiterung des finiten Standpunktes', *Dialectica* **12**.

GOLDFARB W. D. [1981], 'The undecidability of the second-order unification problem', *Theoretical Computer Science* **13**, 225–230.

GOUBAULT J. [1994], Higher-order rigid E-unification, *in* F. Pfenning, ed., '5th International Conference on Logic Programming and Automated Reasoning', number 822 *in* 'Lecture Notes in Artificial Intelligence', Springer-Verlag, pp. 129–143.

HAGIYA M. [1990], Programming by example and proving by example using higher-order unification, *in* M. Stickel, ed., 'Conference on Automated Deduction', number 449 *in* 'Lecture Notes in Computer Science', Springer-Verlag, pp. 588–602.

HAGIYA M. [1991], Higher-order unification as a theorem proving procedure, *in* K. Furukawa, ed., 'International Conference on Logic Programming', MIT Press, pp. 270–284.

HALLNÄS L. [1983], On normalization of proofs in set theory. Doctoral thesis, University of Stockholm.

HANNAN J. AND MILLER D. [1988], Uses of higher-order unification for implementing programs transformers, in R. K. an K.A. Bowen, ed., 'International Conference and Symposium on Logic Programming', pp. 942–959.

HARPER R., HONSELL F. AND PLOTKIN G. [1993], 'A framework for defining logics', Journal of the Association for Computing Machinery 40(1), 143–184.

HENKIN L. [1953], 'Banishing the rule of substitution for functional variables', The Journal of Symbolic Logic 18(3), 201–208.

HINDLEY J. R. AND SELDIN J. P. [1986], Introduction to combinators and λ-calculus, Cambridge University Press.

HOWARD W. A. [1980], The formulæ-as-type notion of construction, in J. R. Hindley and J. P. Seldin, eds, 'To H.B. Curry: Essays on combinatory logic, lambda calculus and formalism', Academic Press.

HUET G. [1972], Constrained resolution: a complete method for higher order logic, PhD thesis, Case Western University.

HUET G. [1973a], A mechanization of type theory, in 'International Joint Conference on Artificial Intelligence', pp. 139–146.

HUET G. [1973b], 'The undecidability of unification in third order logic', Information and Control 22, 257–267.

HUET G. [1975], 'A unification algorithm for typed λ-calculus', Theoretical Computer Science 1, 27–57.

HUET G. [1976], Résolution d'équations dans les langages d'ordre 1,2, ..., ω. Thèse d'État, Université de Paris VII.

HUET G. AND LANG B. [1978], 'Proving and applying program transformations expressed with second order patterns', Acta Informatica 11, 31–55.

HUGHES R. [1982], Super-combinators, a new implementation method for applicative languages, in 'Lisp and Functional Programming', pp. 1–10.

JOHANN P. AND KOHLHASE M. [1994], Unification in an extensional lambda calculus with ordered function sorts and constant overloading, in A. Bundy, ed., 'Conference on Automated Deduction', number 814 in 'Lecture Notes in Artificial Intelligence', Springer-Verlag, pp. 620–634.

JOHNSSON T. [1985], Lambda lifting: transforming programs to recursive equations, in J.-P. Jouannaud, ed., 'Functional Programming Languages and Computer Architecture', number 201 in 'Lecture Notes in Computer Science', Springer-Verlag, pp. 190–203.

KIRCHNER C. AND RINGEISSEN C. [1997], Higher-order equational unification via explicit substitutions, in M. Hanus, J. Heering and K. Meinke, eds, 'Algebraic and Logic Programming, International Joint Conference ALP'97-HOA'97', Vol. 1298 of Lecture Notes in Computer Science, Springer-Verlag, pp. 61–75.

KRIVINE J.-L. [1993], Lambda calculus, types and models, Ellis Horwood series in computer and their applications.

LEVY J. [1996], Linear second order unification, in H. Ganzinger, ed., 'Rewriting Techniques and Applications', Vol. 1103 of Lecture Notes in Computer Science, Springer-Verlag, pp. 332–346.

LEVY J. AND VEANES M. [1998], On unification problems in restricted second-order languages. Manuscript.

LEVY J. AND VILLARET M. [2000], Linear second-order unification and context unification with tree-regular constraints, in 'Proceedings of the 11th Int. Conf. on Rewriting Techniques and Applications (RTA'00)', Vol. 1833 of Lecture Notes in Computer Science, Springer-Verlag, Norwich, UK, pp. 156–171.

LOADER R. [1994], The undecidability of λ-definability. To appear in Church memorial volume.

LUCCHESI C. L. [1972], The undecidability of the unification problem for third order languages, Technical Report CSRR 2060, Department of applied analysis and computer science, University of Waterloo.

MAGNUSSON L. [1994], The implementation of ALF, a proof editor based on Martin-Löf monomorphic type theory with explicit substitution. Doctoral thesis, Chalmers University and University of Göteborg.

MARTIN-LÖF P. [1984], *Intuitionistic type theory*, Bibliopolis.

MATIYACEVICH Y. [1970], 'Enumerable sets are diophantine', *Soviet Math. Doklady* 11, 354–357.

MAYR R. AND NIPKOW T. [1998], 'Higher-order rewrite systems and their confluence', *Theoretical Computer Science* (192), 3–29.

MILLER D. [1991], 'A logic programming language with lambda-abstraction, function variables, and simple unification', *Journal of Logic and Computation* 1(4), 497–536.

MILLER D. [1992], 'Unification under a mixed prefix', *Journal of Symbolic Computation* 14, 321–358.

MILLER D. AND NADATHUR G. [1986], Some uses of higher-order logic in computational linguistics, *in* 'Annual Meeting of the Association for Computational Linguistics', pp. 247–255.

MÜLLER O. AND WEBER F. [1994], Theory and practice of minimal modular higher-order E-unification, *in* A. Bundy, ed., 'Conference on Automated Deduction', number 814 *in* 'Lecture Notes in Artificial Intelligence', Springer-Verlag, pp. 650–664.

MUÑOZ C. [1997], Un calcul de substitutions explicites pour la représentation de preuves partielles en théorie des types. Thèse de Doctorat, Université de Paris VII.

NADATHUR G. [1998], An explicit substitution notation in a λprolog implementation, *in* 'First International Workshop on Explicit Substitutions'.

NADATHUR G. AND MILLER D. [1998], Higher-order logic programming, *in* D. M. Gabbay, C. J. Hogger and J. A. Robinson, eds, 'Handbook of logic in artificial intelligence and logic programming', Vol. 5, Clarendon Press, pp. 499–590.

NADATHUR G. AND MITCHELL D. [1999], System description : A compiler and abstract machine based implementation of λprolog, *in* 'Conference on Automated Deduction'.

NADATHUR G. AND WILSON D. [1998], 'A notation for lambda terms : A generalization of environments', *Theoretical Computer Science* 198(1-2), 49–98.

NIEHREN J., PINKAL M. AND RUHRBERG P. [1997], On equality up-to constraints over finite trees, context unification, and one-step rewriting, *in* 'Proceedings of the 14th Int. Conference on Automated Deduction (CADE-14)', Vol. 1249 of *Lecture Notes in Computer Science*, Springer-Verlag, Townsville, North Queensland, Australia, pp. 34–48.

NIEHREN J., TISON S. AND TREINEN R. [2000], 'On rewrite constraints and context unification', *Information Processing Letters* 74(1-2), 35–40.

NIPKOW T. [1991], Higher-order critical pairs, *in* 'Logic in Computer Science', pp. 342–349.

NIPKOW T. AND PREHOFER C. [1998], Higher-order rewriting and equational reasonning, *in* W. Bibel and P. Schmitt, eds, 'Automated Deduction - A Basis for Applications', Vol. 1, Kluwer, pp. 399–430.

NIPKOW T. AND QIAN Z. [1994], 'Reduction and unification in lambda calculi with a general notion of subtype', *Journal of Automated Reasoning* 12, 389–406.

PADOVANI V. [1994], Fourth-order matching is decidable. Manuscript.

PADOVANI V. [1995], On equivalence classes of interpolation equations, *in* M. Dezani-Ciancagliani and G. Plotkin, eds, 'Typed Lambda Calculi and Applications', number 902 *in* 'Lecture Notes in Computer Science', Springer-Verlag, pp. 335–349.

PADOVANI V. [1996a], Decidability of all minimal models, *in* S. Berardi and M. Coppo, eds, 'Types for Proof and Programs 1995', number 1158 *in* 'Lecture Notes in Computer Science', Springer-Verlag, pp. 201–215.

PADOVANI V. [1996b], Filtrage d'ordre supérieur. Thèse de Doctorat, Université de Paris VII.

PARIKH R. [1973], 'Some results on the length of proofs', *Transactions of the American Mathematical Society* 177, 29–36.

PAULIN-MOHRING C. [1993], Inductive definitions in the system Coq, rules and properties, *in* M. Bezem and J. F. Groote, eds, 'Typed Lambda Calculi and Applications', Vol. 664 of *Lecture Notes in Computer Science*, Springer-Verlag, pp. 328–345.

PAULSON L. C. [1991], Isabelle: The next 700 theorem provers, *in* P. Odifreddi, ed., 'Logic and computer science', Academic Press, pp. 361–385.

PFENNING F. [1988], Partial polymorphic type inference and higher-order unification, *in* 'Conference on Lisp and Functional Programming', pp. 153–163.

PFENNING F. [1991a], Logic programming in the LF logical framework, *in* G. Huet and G. Plotkin, eds, 'Logical frameworks', Cambridge University Press, pp. 149–181.

PFENNING F. [1991b], Unification and anti-unification in the calculus of constructions, *in* 'Logic in Computer Science', pp. 74–85.

PFENNING F. [2001], Logical frameworks, *in* A. Robinson and A. Voronkov, eds, 'Handbook of Automated Reasoning', Vol. II, Elsevier Science, chapter 17, pp. 1063–1147.

PFENNING F. AND CERVESATO I. [1997], Linear higher-order pre-unification, *in* 'Logic in Computer Science'.

PLOTKIN G. [1972], 'Building-in equational theories', *Machine Intelligence* 7, 73–90.

PRAWITZ D. [1968], 'Hauptsatz for higher order logic', *The Journal of Symbolic Logic* 33, 452–457.

PREHOFER C. [1994a], Decidable higher-order unification problems, *in* A. Bundy, ed., 'Conference on Automated Deduction', Vol. 814 of *Lecture Notes in Artificial Intelligence*, Springer-Verlag, pp. 635–649.

PREHOFER C. [1994b], Higher-order narrowing, *in* 'Logic in Computer Science', pp. 507–516.

PREHOFER C. [1995], Solving higher-order equations: from logic to programming. Doctoral thesis, Technische Universität München.

PYM D. [1990], Proof, search and computation in general logic. Doctoral thesis, University of Edinburgh.

QIAN Z. [1994], Higher-order equational logic programming, *in* 'Principle of Programming Languages', pp. 254–267.

QIAN Z. AND WANG K. [1992], Higher-order equational E-unification for arbitrary theories, *in* K. Apt, ed., 'Joint International Conference and Symposium on Logic Programming'.

QIAN Z. AND WANG K. [1994], Modular AC unification of higher-order patterns, *in* J.-P. Jouannaud, ed., 'International Conference on Constaints in Computational Logic', Vol. 845 of *Lecture Notes in Computer Science*, Springer-Verlag, pp. 105–120.

QUINE W. V. O. [1969], *Set theory and its logic*, Belknap Press.

ROBINSON J. A. [1969], New directions in mechanical theorem proving, *in* A. J. H. Morrell, ed., 'International Federation for Information Processing Congress, 1968', North Holland, pp. 63–67.

ROBINSON J. A. [1970], 'A note on mechanizing higher order logic', *Machine Intelligence* 5, 123–133.

SAÏDI H. [1994], Résolution d'équations dans le système *T* de Gödel. Mémoire de DEA, Université de Paris VII.

SCHMIDT-SCHAUSS M. [1994], Unification of stratified second-order terms, Technical Report 12, J.W.Goethe-Universität, Frankfurt.

SCHMIDT-SCHAUSS M. [1999], Decidability of bounded second order unification, Technical Report 11, J.W.Goethe-Universität, Frankfurt.

SCHMIDT-SCHAUSS M. AND SCHULZ K. [1999], Solvability of context equations with two context variables is decidable, *in* H. Ganzinger, ed., 'Conference on Automated Deduction', number 1632 *in* 'Lecture Notes in Artificial Intelligence', pp. 67–81.

SCHUBERT A. [1997], Linear interpolation for the higher order matching problem, *in* M. Bidoit and M. Dauchet, eds, 'Theory and Practice of Software Development', Vol. 1214 of *Lecture Notes in Computer science*, Springer-Verlag, pp. 441–452.

SCHUBERT A. [1998], Second-order unification and type inference for Church-style polymorphism, *in* 'Principle of Programming Languages', pp. 279–288.

SCHWICHTENBERG H. [1976], 'Definierbare Funktionen im λ-Kalkül mit Typen', *Archiv Logik Grundlagenforschung* 17, 113–114.

SNYDER W. [1990], Higher-order E-unification, *in* M. E. Stickel, ed., 'Conference on Automated Deduction', Vol. 449 of *Lecture Notes in Artificial Intelligence*, Springer-Verlag, pp. 573–587.

SNYDER W. AND GALLIER J. [1989], 'Higher order unification revisited: Complete sets of tranformations', *Journal of Symbolic Computation* 8(1 & 2), 101–140. Special issue on unification. Part two.

SPRINGINTVELD J. [1995a], Algorithms for type theory. Doctoral thesis, Utrecht University.

SPRINGINTVELD J. [1995b], Third-order matching in presence of type constructors, *in* M. Dezani-Ciancagliani and G. Plotkin, eds, 'Typed Lambda Calculi and Applications', Vol. 902 of *Lecture Notes in Computer Science*, Springer-Verlag, pp. 428–442.

SPRINGINTVELD J. [1995c], Third-order matching in the polymorphic lambda calculus, *in* G. Dowek, J. Heering, K. Meinke and B. Möller, eds, 'Higher-order Algebra, Logic and Term Rewriting', Vol. 1074 of *Lecture Notes in Computer Science*, Springer-Verlag, pp. 221–237.

STATMAN R. [1982], 'Completeness, invariance and λ-definability', *The Journal of Symbolic Logic* 47(1), 17–28.

STATMAN R. AND DOWEK G. [1992], On Statman's completeness theorem, Technical Report CMU-CS-92-152, Carnegie Mellon University.

TAKAHASHI M. O. [1967], 'A proof of cut-elimination in simple type theory', *Journal of the Mathematical Society of Japan* 19, 399–410.

WERNER B. [1994], Une théorie des constructions inductives. Thèse de Doctorat, Université de Paris VII.

WHITEHEAD A. N. AND RUSSELL B. [1910-1913, 1925-1927], *Principia mathematica*, Cambridge University Press.

WOLFRAM D. A. [1989], The clausal theory of types. Doctoral thesis, University of Cambridge.

ZAIONC M. [1987], 'The regular expression description of unifier set in the typed λ-calculus', *Fundementa Informaticae* X, 309–322.

ZAIONC M. [1988], 'Mechanical procedure for proof construction via closed terms in typed λ-calculus', *Journal of Automated Reasoning* 4, 173–190.

Index

CHAPTER 17

Logical Frameworks

Frank Pfenning

SECOND READERS: Robert Harper, Don Sannella, and Jan Smith.

Contents

HANDBOOK OF AUTOMATED REASONING
Edited by Alan Robinson and Andrei Voronkov

1. Introduction

Deductive systems, given via axioms and rules of inference, are a common conceptual tool in mathematical logic and computer science. They are used to specify many varieties of logics and logical theories as well as aspects of programming languages such as type systems or operational semantics. A *logical framework* is a meta-language for the specification of deductive systems. A number of different frameworks have been proposed and implemented for a variety of purposes. In addition, general reasoning systems have been used to study deductions as mathematical objects, without specific support for the domain of deductive systems.

In this chapter we highlight the major themes, concepts, and design choices for logical frameworks and provide pointers to the literature for further reading. We concentrate on systems designed specifically as frameworks and among them on those most immediately based on deduction: hereditary Harrop formulas (implemented in λProlog and Isabelle) and the LF type theory (implemented in Elf). We briefly mention other approaches below and discuss them in more detail in Section 8.

Logical frameworks are subject to the same general design principles as other specification and programming languages. They should be simple and uniform, providing concise means to express the concepts and methods of the intended application domains. Meaningless expressions should be detected statically and it should be possible to structure large specifications and verify that the components fit together. There are also concerns specific to logical frameworks. Perhaps most importantly, an implementation must be able to check deductions for validity with respect to the specification of a deductive system. Secondly, it should be feasible to prove (informally) that the representations of deductive systems in the framework are adequate so that we can trust formal derivations. We return to each of these points when we discuss different design choices for logical frameworks.

Historically, the first logical framework was Automath [de Bruijn 1968, de Bruijn 1980, Nederpelt, Geuvers and de Vrijer 1994] and its various languages, developed during the late sixties and early seventies. The goal of the Automath project was to provide a tool for the formalization of mathematics without foundational prejudice. Therefore, the logic underlying a particular mathematical development was an integral part of its formalization. Many of the ideas from the Automath language family have found their way into modern systems. The main experiment conducted within Automath was the formalization of Landau's *Foundations of Analysis* [Jutting 1977]. In the early eighties the importance of constructive type theories for computer science was recognized through the pioneering work of Martin-Löf [Martin-Löf 1980, Martin-Löf 1985a, Martin-Löf 1985b]. On the one hand, this led to a number of systems for constructive mathematics and the extraction of functional programs from constructive proofs (beginning with Petersson's implementation [Petersson 1982], followed by Nuprl [*Nuprl* 1999, Constable et al. 1986], Coq [*Coq* 1999, Dowek, Felty, Herbelin, Huet, Murthy, Parent, Paulin-Mohring and Werner 1993], PX [Hayashi and Nakano 1988], and LEGO [*LEGO* 1998, Luo and Pollack 1992, Pollack 1994]). On the other hand, it strongly influenced the design of LF [Harper, Honsell and Plotkin 1987, Harper, Honsell and Plotkin 1993], sometimes called the Edinburgh Logical Framework (ELF). Concurrent with the development of LF, frameworks based on higher-order logic and resolution were designed in the form of generic theorem provers [Paulson 1986, Paulson 1989, Nipkow and Paulson 1992] and logic programming languages [Nadathur and Miller 1988, Miller, Nadathur, Pfenning and Scedrov 1991]. The type-theoretic and logic programming approaches were later combined in the Elf language [Pfenning 1989, Pfenning 1991a]. At this point, there was a pause in the development of new frameworks, while the potential and limitations of existing systems were explored in numerous experiments (see Section 8.3). The mid-nineties saw renewed activity with implementations of frameworks based on inductive definitions such as FS_0 [Feferman 1988, Matthews, Smaill and Basin 1993, Basin and Matthews 1996] and ALF [Nordström 1993, Altenkirch, Gaspes, Nordström and von Sydow 1994], partial inductive definitions [Hallnäs 1991, Eriksson 1993a, Eriksson 1994], substructural frameworks [Schroeder-Heister 1991, Girard 1993, Miller 1994, Cervesato and Pfenning 1996, Cervesato 1996], rewriting logic [Martì-Oliet and Meseguer 1993, Borovanský, Kirchner, Kirchner, Moreau and Ringeissen 1998], and labelled deductive systems [Gabbay 1994, Basin, Matthews and Viganò 1998, Gabbay 1996]. A full discussion of these is beyond the scope of this chapter—the reader can find some brief remarks in Section 8.

Some researchers distinguish between logical frameworks and *meta-logical frameworks* [Basin and Constable 1993], where the latter is intended as a meta-language for reasoning *about* deductive systems rather than *within* them. Clearly, any meta-logical framework must also provide means for specifying deductive systems, though with different goals. We therefore consider them here and discuss issues related to meta-theoretic reasoning in Section 5. Systems not based on type theory are sometimes called *general logics*. We do not attempt to delineate precisely what characterizes general logics as a special case of logical frameworks, but we point out some methodological differences between approaches rooted in type theory and logic throughout this chapter. They are summarized in Section 8.

The remainder of this chapter follows the tasks which arise in a typical application of a logical framework: *specification, search,* and *meta-theory*. As an example we pick a fragment of predicate logic. In Section 2 we introduce techniques for the representation of formulas and other expressions of a given object logic. Section 3 treats the representation of judgments and legal deductions. These two sections therefore illustrate how logical frameworks support specification of deductive systems. Section 4 sketches generic principles underlying proof search and how they are realized in logical frameworks. It therefore covers reasoning *within* deductive systems. Section 5 discusses approaches for formal reasoning *about* the properties of logical systems. Sections 6 and 7 summarize the formal definitions underlying the frameworks under consideration in this chapter. We conclude with remarks about current lines of research and applications in Section 8.

2. Abstract syntax

The specification of a deductive system usually proceeds in two stages: first we define the syntax of an object language and then the axioms and rules of inference. In order to concentrate on the meanings of expressions we ignore issues of concrete syntax and parsing and concentrate on specifying abstract syntax. Different framework implementations provide different means for customizing the parser in order to embed the desired object-language syntax.

As an example throughout this chapter we consider formulations of intuitionistic and classical first-order logic. In order to keep this chapter to a manageable length, we restrict ourselves to the fragment containing implication, negation, and universal quantification. The reader is invited to test his or her understanding by extending the development to include a more complete set of connectives and quantifiers. Representations of first-order intuitionistic and classical logic in various logical frameworks can be found in the literature (see, for example, [Felty and Miller 1988, Paulson 1990, Harper et al. 1993, Pfenning 2001]).

Our fragment of first-order logic is constructed from individual variables, function symbols, and predicate symbols in the usual way. We assume each function and predicate symbol has a unique arity, indicated by a superscript, but generally omitted since it will be clear from the context. Individual constants are function symbols of arity 0 and propositional constants are predicate symbols of arity 0.

Function symbols	f^k	
Predicate symbols	p^k	
Variables	x	
Terms	t	$::= \quad x \mid f^k(t_1, \ldots, t_k)$
Atoms	P	$::= \quad p^k(t_1, \ldots, t_k)$
Formulas	A	$::= \quad P \mid A_1 \supset A_2 \mid \neg A \mid \forall x.\, A$

We assume that there is an infinite number of variables x. The set of function and predicate symbols is left unspecified in the general development of logic. We therefore view our specification as open-ended. A commitment, say, to arithmetic would fix the available function and predicate symbols. We write x and y for variables, t and s for terms, and A, B, and C for formulas. There are some important operations on terms and formulas required for the presentation of inference rules. Specifically, we need the notions of free and bound variable, the renaming of bound variables, and the operations of substitution $[t/x]s$ and $[t/x]A$, where the latter may need to rename variables bound in A in order to avoid variable capture. We assume that these operations are understood and do not define them formally. An assumption generally made in connection with variable names is the so-called *variable convention* [Barendregt 1980] (which goes back to Church and Rosser [Church and Rosser 1936]) which states that expressions differing only in the names of their bound variables are considered identical. We examine to which extent various frameworks support this convention.

2.1. Uni-typed representations

As the archetypical untyped representation language we choose first-order terms themselves. Actually, it is more appropriate to think of it as a *uni-typed* language, that is, a language with a single type of individuals. For each function symbol f we have a corresponding function symbol c_f of the same arity in the representation. Similarly, each predicate symbol p is represented by a constant c_p. The representation of variables is more complex, since there are infinitely many of them. For simplicity, we assume variables are enumerated and the nth variable x_n is represented by $\mathsf{var}(n)$, where the natural numbers n are either meta-language constants or constructed from constants for zero and successor. We write $\ulcorner - \urcorner$ for the representation function which maps expressions of an object language to objects in the meta-language. We use sans-serif font for constants in various logical frameworks we consider.

$$
\begin{aligned}
\ulcorner x_n \urcorner &= \mathsf{var}(n) \\
\ulcorner f^k(t_1,\ldots,t_k) \urcorner &= \mathsf{c}_f^k(\ulcorner t_1 \urcorner,\ldots,\ulcorner t_k \urcorner) \\
\ulcorner p^k(t_1,\ldots,t_k) \urcorner &= \mathsf{c}_p^k(\ulcorner t_1 \urcorner,\ldots,\ulcorner t_k \urcorner) \\
\ulcorner A \supset B \urcorner &= \mathsf{imp}(\ulcorner A \urcorner,\ulcorner B \urcorner) \\
\ulcorner \neg A \urcorner &= \mathsf{not}(\ulcorner A \urcorner) \\
\ulcorner \forall x.\, A \urcorner &= \mathsf{forall}(\ulcorner x \urcorner,\ulcorner A \urcorner)
\end{aligned}
$$

However, our task is not yet complete: we need to be able to check, for example, if a given meta-language term represents a formula. For this we use Horn clauses to axiomatize the atomic proposition $\mathsf{formula}(t)$ which expresses that the meta-language term t represents a formula of the object language. This requires several auxiliary predicates to recognize representations of variables and terms. The specification below is effective in the sense that it can be executed in pure Prolog to check if a given term represents a well-formed formula. For our purposes, we think of Horn clauses as generated by the following grammar.

$$
\text{Horn clauses} \quad D \quad ::= \quad P \mid \top \mid D_1 \wedge D_2 \mid P_1 \wedge \ldots \wedge P_n \supset P \mid \forall x.\, D
$$

where P stands for atomic propositions and $\top$ stands for the true proposition. We refer to a collection of closed Horn clauses as a *Horn theory* and write $T \vdash^H P$ if the Horn theory T entails P. Natural numbers are represented in unary form with z representing 0 and s representing the successor function.

$\mathsf{nat}(\mathsf{z})$
$\forall n.\, \mathsf{nat}(n) \supset \mathsf{nat}(\mathsf{s}(n))$

$\forall n.\, \mathsf{nat}(n) \supset \mathsf{variable}(\mathsf{var}(n))$

$\forall t.\, \mathsf{variable}(t) \supset \mathsf{term}(t)$

$\forall A.\, \forall B.\, \mathsf{formula}(A) \wedge \mathsf{formula}(B) \supset \mathsf{formula}(\mathsf{imp}(A,B))$
$\forall A.\, \mathsf{formula}(A) \supset \mathsf{formula}(\mathsf{not}(A))$
$\forall x.\, \forall A.\, \mathsf{variable}(x) \wedge \mathsf{formula}(A) \supset \mathsf{formula}(\mathsf{forall}(x,A))$

We have to add clauses for particular function and predicate symbols. For example, if an equality predicate eq^2 is available in the object logic, we add the clause

$$\forall x. \forall y. \, \mathsf{term}(x) \wedge \mathsf{term}(y) \supset \mathsf{formula}(\mathsf{eq}(x, y))$$

Arities of the function symbols and predicates are thus built into the representation. A drawback with this and related first-order, uni-typed methods is that we have to *prove* $\mathsf{formula}(t)$ to verify that t represents a formula of the object language; it is an *external* rather than an *internal* property of the representation. More precisely, if we denote the theory above by F, then we have the following representation theorem.

2.1. THEOREM (Adequacy).
  1. $F \vdash^{\mathit{H}} \mathsf{variable}(t')$ iff $t' = \ulcorner x_n \urcorner$ for a variable x_n.
  2. $F \vdash^{\mathit{H}} \mathsf{term}(t')$ iff $t' = \ulcorner t \urcorner$ for a term t.
  3. $F \vdash^{\mathit{H}} \mathsf{formula}(t')$ iff $t' = \ulcorner A \urcorner$ for a formula A.

PROOF. In one direction this follows by an easy induction on n and the structure of t and A.

In the other direction we need a deep semantic or proof-theoretic understanding of Horn logic. For example, we use the structure of the least Herbrand model, or we can take advantage of the fact that a Horn theory inductively defines its atomic predicates. □

Adequacy theorems play a critical role in logical frameworks. They guarantee that we can translate expressions from the object language to objects in the meta-language, compute with them, and then interpret the results back in the object language. This will be particularly important when we consider the adequacy of the encoding of inference rules (Theorem 3.1) and deductions (Theorem 3.2), because they ensure that formal reasoning in the logical framework is correct with respect to the object logic under consideration. Generally, we would like the representation function to be a bijection, but this is not always necessary as long as we can translate safely in both directions.

For the particular adequacy theorem above it is irrelevant whether the propositions of the meta-logic are interpreted classically or intuitionistically, since classical and intuitionistic provability coincide on Horn clauses. We can also view a fixed set of Horn clauses as an inductive definition of the atomic predicates involved. In our example, the predicates nat, variable, term, and formula are all inductively defined by the clauses given above. The fact that Horn clauses allow such diverse interpretations is one reason why they constitute a stable and frequently used basis for logical frameworks.

The first-order representation above does not support the variable convention: renaming of bound variables must be implemented explicitly. For example, the representations of $\forall x_1. p(x_1)$ and $\forall x_3. p(x_3)$ are not identified in the meta-language. Instead we can define a binary predicate id such that $\mathsf{id}(A_1, A_2)$ holds iff A_1 and A_2 represent formulas which differ only in the names of their bound variables. The technique of *de Bruijn indices* [de Bruijn 1972] eliminates this shortcoming without requiring a change in the expressive power of the meta-language. There, a variable is represented by a natural number n, which indicates that the variable is bound by the nth enclosing abstraction. For example, $\forall x_1. \forall x_5. p(x_5) \supset p(x_1)$ and all alphabetic variants of it would be represented as forall (forall (imp(p(var(1)), p(var(2))))). De Bruijn indices have been employed as the basic representation for many implementation and verification efforts for deductive systems (see, for example, [de Bruijn 1972, Shankar 1988]).

2.2. Simply-typed representation

A standard method for transforming an *external* validity condition (given here by a Horn theory) into an *internal* property of the representation is to introduce types. By designing the type system so that type checking is decidable, we turn a dynamic property into a static property. We begin with *simple types*. The idea is to introduce type constants i and o for object-level terms and formulas, respectively. Implication, for example, is then represented by a constant of type o $\rightarrow$ (o $\rightarrow$ o), that is, a formula constructor taking two formulas as arguments employing the standard technique of Currying. This idea can be directly applied to the representation in the previous section if we also introduce a type constant for variables. We can improve upon this by enriching the representation language to include higher-order terms, which leads us to the simply-typed λ-calculus, $\lambda^{\rightarrow}$. We briefly summarize it here; for more complete discussion, see Section 6.

$$
\begin{array}{llll}
\text{Types} & A & ::= & a \mid A_1 \rightarrow A_2 \\
\text{Objects} & M & ::= & c \mid x \mid \lambda x{:}A.\,M \mid M_1\,M_2
\end{array}
$$

We use a to range over type constants, c over object constants, and x over object variables. We follow the usual syntactic conventions: $\rightarrow$ associates to the right, and application to the left. Parentheses group subexpressions, and the scope of a λ-abstraction extends to the innermost enclosing parentheses or to the end of the expression. We allow tacit α-conversion (renaming of bound variables) and write $[M/x]N$ for capture-avoiding substitution of M for x in N. Constants and variables are declared and assigned types in a signature Σ and context Γ, respectively. Neither is permitted to declare constants or variables more than once.

Using the simply-typed λ-calculus $\lambda^{\rightarrow}$ as a representation language requires us to distinguish between arbitrary well-typed objects and *canonical forms*. Canonical forms directly represent object-language entities, while the meaning of arbitrary well-typed objects is computed by converting them to canonical form. This is similar to most programming languages where values represent data and the meaning of an expression is determined by evaluation. This point of view leads to the following principal judgments. They are parametrized by a signature Σ that declares type and object constants and a context Γ that declares the type of variables free in M

and M'.

$$\Gamma \vdash_\Sigma M : A \qquad\qquad M \text{ is an object of type } A$$

$$\Gamma \vdash_\Sigma M' \Uparrow A \qquad\qquad M' \text{ is a canonical object of type } A$$

$$\Gamma \vdash_\Sigma M \Uparrow M' : A \qquad\qquad M \text{ has canonical form } M' \text{ at type } A$$

The formal definition of the language and these judgments can be found in Section 6. The appropriate notion for canonical forms are long $\beta\eta$-normal forms, that is, β-reduced and η-expanded objects. Given a syntactic category in the object language and its representation type A, canonical forms of type A are in bijective correspondence with object-language expressions in the appropriate syntactic category (see Theorem 2.2 and the subsequent discussion). Since every valid object has a unique type and canonical form (see Theorem 6.1), the meaning of an arbitrary valid object is unambiguously determined.

Two objects are *definitionally equal* if they have the same canonical form.

$$\Gamma \vdash_\Sigma M \equiv N : A \qquad\qquad M \text{ is definitionally equal to } N \text{ at type } A.$$

This is equivalent to stipulating that two objects are definitionally equal if they can be transformed into each other by β- and η-conversion. Since canonical forms depend on types, definitional equality also depends on types, although we sometimes abbreviate it as $M \equiv N$. Formulations of typed λ-calculi as the foundation for functional programming normally do not include η-conversion, since it does not preserve observational equivalence under the usual operational semantics. For example, the Pure Type Systems reviewed in [Barendregt and Geuvers 2001] (Chapter 18 of this Handbook) typically do not include η-conversion.

Returning to the representation of first-order logic, we introduce two declarations

i : type
o : type

for the types of representations of terms and formulas, respectively. For every function symbol f of arity k, we add a corresponding declaration

$$f \ : \ \underbrace{i \to \cdots \to i \to i}_{k}.$$

One of the central ideas in using a λ-calculus for representation is to represent object-language variables by meta-language variables. Through λ-abstraction at the meta-level we can properly delineate the scopes of variables bound in the object language. For simplicity, we give corresponding variables the same name in the two languages.

$$\ulcorner x \urcorner \ = \ x$$
$$\ulcorner f(t_1, \ldots, t_k) \urcorner \ = \ f \ulcorner t_1 \urcorner \ldots \ulcorner t_k \urcorner$$

Predicate symbols are dealt with like function symbols. We add a declaration

$$p \; : \; \underbrace{i \to \cdots \to i}_{k} \to o$$

for every predicate symbol p of arity k. Here are the remaining cases of the representation function.

$$
\begin{aligned}
\ulcorner p(t_1, \ldots, t_k) \urcorner &= \mathsf{p} \ulcorner t_1 \urcorner \ldots \ulcorner t_k \urcorner \\
\ulcorner A_1 \supset A_2 \urcorner &= \mathsf{imp} \ulcorner A_1 \urcorner \ulcorner A_2 \urcorner & \mathsf{imp} &: o \to o \to o \\
\ulcorner \neg A \urcorner &= \mathsf{not} \ulcorner A \urcorner & \mathsf{not} &: o \to o \\
\ulcorner \forall x. A \urcorner &= \mathsf{forall} \, (\lambda x{:}i. \ulcorner A \urcorner) & \mathsf{forall} &: (i \to o) \to o
\end{aligned}
$$

The last case in the definition introduces the concept of *higher-order abstract syntax*. If we represent variables of the object language by variables in the meta-language, then variables bound by a construct in the object language must be bound in the representation as well. The simply-typed λ-calculus has a single binding operator λ, so all variable binding is mapped to binding by λ. This idea goes back to Church's formulation of classical type theory, see [Andrews 2001] (Chapter 15 of this Handbook), and Martin-Löf's system of arities [Nordström, Petersson and Smith 1990]. In programming environments this was proposed by Huet and Lang [1978] and developed further by Pfenning and Elliott [1988].

This leads to the first important representation principle of logical frameworks employing higher-order abstract syntax: *Bound variable renaming in the object language is modeled by α-conversion in the meta-language.* Since we follow the variable convention in the meta-language, the variable convention in the object language is automatically supported in a framework using the representation technique above. Consequently, it cannot be used directly for binding operators for which renaming is not valid such as occur, for example, in module systems of programming languages.

The variable binding constructor "$\forall$" of the object language is translated into a second-order constructor forall in the meta-language, since delineating the scope of x introduces a function $(\lambda x{:}i. \ulcorner A \urcorner)$ of type $i \to o$. What does it mean to apply this function? This question leads to the concept of *compositionality*, a crucial property of higher-order abstract syntax. First we note that

$$(\lambda x{:}i. \ulcorner A \urcorner) \ulcorner t \urcorner \equiv [\ulcorner t \urcorner / x] \ulcorner A \urcorner,$$

since β-conversion is an admissible rule for definitional equality. We can further prove (by a simple induction) that

$$[\ulcorner t \urcorner / x] \ulcorner A \urcorner = \ulcorner [t/x] A \urcorner.$$

Here, substitution (both at the object and meta-level) are defined to rename bound variables as necessary in order to avoid the capturing of variables free in t. Compositionality also plays a very important role in the representation of deductions in Section 3; we summarize it as: *Substitution in the object language is modeled by β-reduction in the meta-language.*

The declarations of the basic constants above are *open-ended* in the sense that we can always add further constants without destroying the validity of earlier representations. In logic programming, this is called the *open-world assumption*. However, the definition also has an inductive character in the sense that the validity judgment of the meta-language ($\lambda^\rightarrow$, in this case) is defined inductively by some axioms and rules of inference. Therefore we can state and prove that there is a *compositional bijection* between well-formed formulas and canonical objects of type o. Since a term or formula may have free individual variables, and they are represented by corresponding variables in the meta-language, we must take care to declare them with their proper types in the meta-language context. We refer to the particular signature with the declarations for term and formula constructors as F.

2.2. THEOREM (Adequacy).

1. *We have*

$$x_1{:}i, \ldots, x_n{:}i \vdash_F M \Uparrow i \quad iff \quad M = \ulcorner t \urcorner,$$

where the free variables of term t are among $x_1, \ldots, x_n$.

2. *We have*

$$x_1{:}i, \ldots, x_n{:}i \vdash_F M \Uparrow o \quad iff \quad M = \ulcorner A \urcorner,$$

where the free variables of formula A are among $x_1, \ldots, x_n$.

3. *The representation function $\ulcorner \cdot \urcorner$ is a compositional bijection in the sense that*

$$[\ulcorner t \urcorner / x] \ulcorner s \urcorner = \ulcorner [t/x]s \urcorner \quad and \quad [\ulcorner t \urcorner / x] \ulcorner A \urcorner = \ulcorner [t/x]A \urcorner$$

PROOF. In one direction we proceed by an easy induction on the structure of terms and formulas. Compositionality can also be established directly by an induction on the structure of s and A, respectively.

In the other direction we carry out an induction over the structure of the derivations of $M \Uparrow i$ and $M \Uparrow o$. To prove that the representation function is a bijection, we write down its inverse on canonical forms and prove that both compositions are identity functions.   □

An important aspect of this theorem is that it establishes a bijection between canonical forms of a given type (i and o) and the object-language entities we are trying to represent (terms and formulas, respectively). It is clear that not every well-typed object of type i or o lies in the image of the representation function. The next two examples show that canonical forms and not just β-normal forms are actually required. We assume we have one unary predicate p and a corresponding constant p:i $\rightarrow$ o.

$$\vdash \mathsf{forall}\ (\lambda x{:}i.\ ((\lambda q{:}o.\ q)\ (p\ x)))\ :\ o$$

$$\vdash \mathsf{forall}\ p\ :\ o$$

Both of these object have type o but are not in the image of the representation function $\ulcorner - \urcorner$. Their meaning can be determined by conversion to canonical form.

We calculate

$$\vdash \mathsf{forall}\,(\lambda x{:}\mathsf{i}.\,((\lambda q{:}\mathsf{o}.\,q)\,(\mathsf{p}\,x))) \Uparrow \mathsf{forall}\,(\lambda x{:}\mathsf{i}.\,\mathsf{p}\,x) : \mathsf{o}$$
$$\vdash \mathsf{forall}\,\mathsf{p} \Uparrow \mathsf{forall}\,(\lambda x{:}\mathsf{i}.\,\mathsf{p}\,x) : \mathsf{o}$$

and thus both objects represent $\forall x.\,P(x)$ (or an alphabetic variant, of course). Similar examples exist for the representation of derivations in Section 3. This shows that canonical forms play the role of *observable values* in a functional language, and conversion to canonical form the role of evaluation. A simple β-normal form would not be sufficient, as the second example illustrates.

We summarize the concepts and techniques introduced in this section. We noted the tension between *external* and *internal* validity of representations. The former arises if we write a general (logical) specification that allows us to prove that meta-language objects represent well-formed object-language expressions. The latter arises from a *typed* meta-language where well-typed meta-language objects correspond to well-formed expressions of the object language. Validity of internal representations are decidable by design, while this issue has to be reexamined in each case for external validity.

A central issue in the representation of syntax is the treatment of variables. An encoding where variables are represented by constants in the meta-language is awkward and requires a significant machinery to handle the frequently required operations of bound variable renaming and substitution. The more advanced technique of *de Bruijn indices* represents occurrences of bound variables by pointers to their binding occurrence, drastically simplifying many operations. Substitution must still be axiomatized explicitly. The technique of *higher-order abstract syntax* represents object language variables by meta-language variables. It requires λ-abstraction in the meta-language in order to properly delineate the scope of bound variables, which suggests the use of the simply-typed λ-calculus as a representation language. In this approach, variable renaming is modeled by α-conversion, and capture-avoiding substitution is modeled by β-reduction, both of which preserve definitional equality.

Languages such as the formulas of first-order logic are essentially *open-ended* in the sense that we may obtain specific theories by making a commitment to a particular set of function and predicate symbols. On the other hand they are also *inductive* in the sense that in order to prove a meta-theoretic property, we may need to proceed by induction over the structure of formulas, which is only possible if we know that we are considering all possible cases. The compositionality of the representation function is a simple example of such an inductive proof. This tension is reflected in the simply-typed λ-calculus as a representation language. On the one hand, it is open-ended in the sense that we can always declare new constants without invalidating any prior typing or equality judgments. On the other hand, the canonical objects constructed over a fixed signature are inductively defined, since the meta-language has an inductive definition. Some frameworks, such as FS_0 [Feferman 1988, Matthews et al. 1993] or ALF [Nordström 1993] make the inductive nature of these definitions explicit, at the price of giving up higher-order abstract syntax. On the other hand one can then reason internally about properties of deductive systems by induction. We will come back to inductive meta-reasoning in Section 5.

3. Judgments and deductions

After designing the representation of terms and formulas, the next step is to encode the axioms and inference rules of the logic under consideration. There are several styles of deductive systems which can be found in the literature. There is the *axiomatic style* (originated by Frege [1879] and in its modern form by Hilbert and Bernays [1934]) where a logical system is given by axioms and a minimal number of inference rules. Gentzen [1935] developed *natural deduction* in which the meaning of each logical symbol is explained by means of its introduction and elimination rules. Natural deductions were developed to model mathematical reasoning practices more closely than axiomatic derivations while still remaining completely formal. Gentzen also introduced *sequent calculi* in which certain properties of derivations (such as the subformula property) are explicit. Sequent calculi form the basis of many proof search procedures today. Yet another style of presentation is based on category theory [Lambek and Scott 1986].

Logical frameworks are typically designed to deal particularly well with some of these systems, while being less appropriate for others. The Automath languages were designed to reflect and promote good informal mathematical practice. It should thus be no surprise that they were particularly well-suited to systems of natural deduction. The same is true for hereditary Harrop formulas and the LF type theory, so we discuss the problem of representing natural deduction first. We return to axiomatic systems in Section 3.5. Other systems, including sequent calculi, can also be directly encoded [Pfenning 1995, Pfenning 2000].

3.1. Parametric and hypothetical judgments

First, we introduce some terminology used in the presentation of deductive systems introduced with their modern meaning by Martin-Löf [Martin-Löf 1985a]. We will generally interpret the notions as formal and syntactic, rather than semantic, since we would like to tie them closely to logical frameworks and their implementations. A *judgment* is defined by *inference rules*. An inference rule has zero or more premises and a conclusion; an axiom is an inference rule with no premises. A judgment is *evident* or *derivable* if it can be deduced using the given rules of inference. Most inference rules are *schematic* in that they contain meta-variables. We obtain *instances* of a schematic rule by replacing meta-variables with concrete expressions of the appropriate syntactic category. Each instance of an inference rule may be used in derivations. We write $\mathcal{D} :: J$ or

$$\frac{\mathcal{D}}{J}$$

when $\mathcal{D}$ is a derivation of judgment J. All derivations we consider must be finite. Natural deduction further employs *hypothetical judgments*. We write

$$\frac{\quad}{J_1}\, u$$
$$\vdots$$
$$J_2$$

to express that judgment J_2 is derivable under hypothesis J_1 labelled u, where the vertical dots may be filled by a *hypothetical derivation*. Hypotheses have scope, that is, they may be *discharged* so that they are not available outside a given sub-derivation. We annotate the discharging inference with the label of the hypothesis. The meaning of a hypothetical judgment can be explained by substitution: We can substitute an arbitrary deduction $\mathcal{E} :: J_1$ for each occurrence of a hypothesis J_1 labelled u in $\mathcal{D} :: J_2$ and obtain a derivation of J_2 that no longer depends on u. We write this substitution as $[\mathcal{E}/u]\mathcal{D} :: J_2$. For this to be meaningful we assume that multiple occurrences of a label annotate the same hypothesis, and that hypotheses satisfy the structural properties of *exchange* (the order in which hypotheses are made is irrelevant), *weakening* (a hypothesis need not be used) and *contraction* (a hypothesis may be used more than once).

An important related concept is that of a *parametric judgment*. Evidence for a judgment J that is parametric in a variable a is given by a derivation $\mathcal{D} :: J$ that may contain free occurrences of a. We refer to the variable a as a *parameter* and use a and b to range over parameters. We can substitute an arbitrary object O of the appropriate syntactic category for a throughout $\mathcal{D}$ to obtain a deduction $[O/a]\mathcal{D} :: [O/a]J$. Parameters also have scope and their discharge is indicated by a superscript as for hypothesis labels.

3.2. Natural deduction

Natural deduction is defined via a single judgment

$$\vdash^N A \qquad \text{formula } A \text{ is true}$$

and the mechanisms of hypothetical and parametric deductions explained in the previous section.

In natural deduction each logical symbol is characterized by its *introduction rule* or *rules* which specify how to infer a conjunction, disjunction, implication, universal quantification, etc. The *elimination rule* or *rules* for the connective then specify how we can use a conjunction, disjunction, etc. Underlying the formulation of the introduction and elimination rules is the principle of *orthogonality*: each connective should be characterized purely by its rules, and the rules should only use judgmental notions and not other logical connectives. Furthermore, the introduction and elimination rules for a logical connective cannot be chosen freely—as explained below, they should match up in order to form a coherent system. We call these conditions *local soundness* and *local completeness*.

Local soundness expresses that we should not be able to gain information by introducing a connective and immediately eliminating it. That is, if we introduce and then eliminate a connective we should be able to reach the same judgment without this detour. We show that this is possible by exhibiting a *local reduction* on derivations. The existence of a local reduction shows that the elimination rules are not too strong—they are locally sound.

Local completeness expresses that we should not lose information by introducing a connective. That is, given a judgment there is some way to eliminate its principal connective and then re-introduce it to arrive at the original judgment. We show that this is possible by exhibiting a *local expansion* on derivations. The existence of a local expansion shows that the elimination rules are not too weak—they are locally complete.

Under the Curry-Howard isomorphism between proofs and programs [Howard 1980], local reduction correspond to β-reduction and local expansion corresponds to η-expansion. We express local reductions and expansions via judgments which relate derivations of the same judgment.

$$
\begin{array}{ccll}
\mathcal{D} & & \mathcal{D}' & \\
\vdash^N A & \Longrightarrow_R & \vdash^N A & \quad \mathcal{D} \text{ locally reduces to } \mathcal{D}'
\end{array}
$$

$$
\begin{array}{ccll}
\mathcal{D} & & \mathcal{D}' & \\
\vdash^N A & \Longrightarrow_E & \vdash^N A & \quad \mathcal{D} \text{ locally expands to } \mathcal{D}'
\end{array}
$$

In the framework of *partial inductive definitions* [Hallnäs 1991] when used as a meta-logic [Hallnäs 1987, Schroeder-Heister 1991, Eriksson 1992, Eriksson 1993*b*, Eriksson 1993*a*, Eriksson 1994] the specification of introduction rules for a connective automatically leads to the proper elimination rules by virtue of general properties of the framework. We do not presuppose such a mechanism, but explicitly describe both introduction and elimination rules. In the spirit of orthogonality, we proceed connective by connective, discussing introduction and elimination rules and local reductions and expansions.

Implication. To derive $\vdash^N A \supset B$ we assume $\vdash^N A$ to derive $\vdash^N B$. Written as a hypothetical judgment:

$$
\cfrac{\cfrac{\overline{\vdash^N A}\ u}{\vdots \\ \vdash^N B}}{\vdash^N A \supset B}\supset I^u
$$

The hypothetical derivation describes a construction by which we can transform a derivation of $\vdash^N A$ into a derivation of $\vdash^N B$. This is accomplished by substituting the derivation of $\vdash^N A$ for every use of the hypothesis $\vdash^N A$ labelled u in the derivation of $\vdash^N B$. The elimination rule expresses just that: if we have a derivation of $\vdash^N A \supset B$ and also a derivation of $\vdash^N A$, then we can obtain a derivation of $\vdash^N B$.

$$\frac{\vdash^N A \supset B \qquad \vdash^N A}{\vdash^N B} \supset E$$

The local reduction carries out the substitution of derivations explained above.

$$\frac{\dfrac{\dfrac{\overline{\vdash^N A}\, u}{\begin{array}{c}\mathcal{D}\\ \vdash^N B\end{array}}}{\vdash^N A \supset B}\supset I^u \qquad \begin{array}{c}\mathcal{E}\\ \vdash^N A\end{array}}{\vdash^N B}\supset E \quad \Longrightarrow_R \quad \begin{array}{c}\dfrac{\mathcal{E}}{\vdash^N A}\,u\\ \mathcal{D}\\ \vdash^N B\end{array}$$

The derivation on the right depends on all the hypotheses of $\mathcal{E}$ and $\mathcal{D}$ except u, for which we have substituted $\mathcal{E}$. The reduction described above may significantly increase the overall size of the derivation, since the deduction $\mathcal{E}$ is substituted for each occurrence of the assumption labeled u in $\mathcal{D}$ and may therefore be replicated.

Local expansion is specified in a similar manner.

$$\begin{array}{c}\mathcal{D}\\ \vdash^N A \supset B\end{array} \quad \Longrightarrow_E \quad \frac{\dfrac{\dfrac{\begin{array}{c}\mathcal{D}\\ \vdash^N A \supset B\end{array} \qquad \overline{\vdash^N A}\,u}{\vdash^N B}\supset E}{\vdash^N A \supset B}\supset I^u}{}$$

Here, u must be a new label, that is, it cannot already be used in $\mathcal{D}$.

Negation. In order to derive $\vdash^N \neg A$ we assume $\vdash^N A$ and try to derive a contradiction. This is the usual formulation, but has the disadvantage that it requires falsehood ($\bot$) as a logical symbol, thereby violating the orthogonality principle. Thus, in intuitionistic logic, one ordinarily thinks of $\neg A$ as an abbreviation for $A \supset \bot$. An alternative rule sometimes proposed assumes $\vdash^N A$ and tries to derive $\vdash^N B$ and $\vdash^N \neg B$ for some B. This also breaks the usual pattern by requiring the logical symbol we are trying to define ($\neg$) in a premise of the introduction rule. However, there is another possibility to explain the meaning of negation without recourse to implication or falsehood. We specify that $\vdash^N \neg A$ should be derivable if we can conclude $\vdash^N p$ for any formula p from the assumption $\vdash^N A$. In other words, the deduction of the premise is hypothetical in the assumption $\vdash^N A$ and parametric in the formula p.

$$
\cfrac{\dfrac{\rule{2em}{0.4pt}}{\vdash^N A}u \\[1em] \vdots \\[0.5em] \vdash^N p}{\vdash^N \neg A}\neg I^{p,u}
\qquad\qquad
\cfrac{\vdash^N \neg A \qquad \vdash^N A}{\vdash^N C}\neg E
$$

According to our intuition, the parametric judgment should be derivable if we can substitute an arbitrary concrete formula C for the parameter p and obtain a valid derivation. Thus, p may not already occur in the conclusion $\neg A$, or in any undischarged hypothesis. The reduction rule for negation follows from this interpretation and is analogous to the reduction for implication.

$$
\cfrac{\cfrac{\dfrac{\dfrac{\rule{2em}{0.4pt}}{\vdash^N A}u}{\mathcal{D}} \\ \vdash^N p}{\vdash^N \neg A}\neg I^{p,u} \qquad \cfrac{\mathcal{E}}{\vdash^N A}}{\vdash^N C}\neg E
\qquad \Longrightarrow_R \qquad
\begin{array}{c} \dfrac{\mathcal{E}}{\vdash^N A}u \\[0.5em] [C/p]\mathcal{D} \\[0.5em] \vdash^N C \end{array}
$$

The local expansion is also similar to that for implication.

$$
\begin{array}{c}\mathcal{D} \\ \vdash^N \neg A\end{array}
\qquad \Longrightarrow_E \qquad
\cfrac{\cfrac{\dfrac{\mathcal{D}}{\vdash^N \neg A} \qquad \dfrac{\rule{2em}{0.4pt}}{\vdash^N A}u}{\vdash^N p}\neg E}{\vdash^N \neg A}\neg I^{p,u}
$$

Universal quantification. Under which circumstances should we be able to derive $\vdash^N \forall x.\, A$? This clearly depends on the domain of quantification. For example, if we know that x ranges over the natural numbers, then we can conclude $\vdash^N \forall x.\, A$ if we can derive $\vdash^N [0/x]A$, $\vdash^N [1/x]A$, etc. Such a rule is not effective, since it has infinitely many premises. Thus one usually uses induction principles as inference rules. However, in a general treatment of predicate logic we would like to prove statements which are true for *all* domains of quantification. Thus we can only say that $\vdash^N \forall x.\, A$ should be derivable if $\vdash^N [a/x]A$ is derivable for an arbitrary new parameter a. Conversely, if we know $\vdash^N \forall x.\, A$, we know that $\vdash^N [t/x]A$ for any term t.

$$
\cfrac{\vdash^N [a/x]A}{\vdash^N \forall x.\, A}\forall I^a
\qquad\qquad
\cfrac{\vdash^N \forall x.\, A}{\vdash^N [t/x]A}\forall E
$$

The superscript a is a reminder about the proviso for the introduction rule: the parameter a must be "new", that is, it may not occur in any undischarged hypothesis in the derivation of $[a/x]A$ or in $\forall x.\,A$ itself. In other words, the derivation of the premise is parametric in a. If we know that $\vdash^{\scriptscriptstyle N} [a/x]A$ is derivable for an arbitrary a, we can conclude that $\vdash^{\scriptscriptstyle N} [t/x]A$ should be derivable for any term t. Thus we have the reduction

$$
\cfrac{\cfrac{\mathcal{D}}{\vdash^{\scriptscriptstyle N} [a/x]A}}{\cfrac{\vdash^{\scriptscriptstyle N} \forall x.\,A}{\vdash^{\scriptscriptstyle N} [t/x]A}\;\forall E}\;\forall I^a
\qquad \Longrightarrow_R \qquad
\cfrac{[t/a]\mathcal{D}}{\vdash^{\scriptscriptstyle N} [t/x]A}
$$

Here, $[t/a]\mathcal{D}$ is our notation for the result of substituting t for the parameter a throughout the deduction $\mathcal{D}$. For this to be sensible, we must know that a does not already occur in A, because otherwise the conclusion of $[t/a]\mathcal{D}$ would be $[t/a][t/x]A$. Similarly, we would change the assumptions if a occurred free in any of the undischarged hypotheses. This might render a larger derivation incorrect. As an example, consider the judgment $\vdash^{\scriptscriptstyle N} \forall x.\,\forall y.\,p(x) \supset p(y)$ which should clearly not be derivable for an arbitrary predicate p. The following is *not* a deduction of this judgment.

$$
\cfrac{\cfrac{\cfrac{\cfrac{\cfrac{\cfrac{\cfrac{\overline{\vdash^{\scriptscriptstyle N} P(a)}\;u}{\vdash^{\scriptscriptstyle N} \forall x.\,P(x)}\;\forall I^a?}{\vdash^{\scriptscriptstyle N} P(b)}\;\forall E}{\vdash^{\scriptscriptstyle N} P(a) \supset P(b)}\;\supset I^u}{\vdash^{\scriptscriptstyle N} \forall y.\,P(a) \supset P(y)}\;\forall I^b}{\vdash^{\scriptscriptstyle N} \forall x.\,\forall y.\,P(x) \supset P(y)}\;\forall I^a}{}
$$

The flaw is at the inference marked with "?," where a is free in the assumption u. Applying a local proof reduction to the (incorrect) $\forall I$ inference followed by $\forall E$ leads to the assumption $[b/a]P(a)$ which is equal to $P(b)$. The resulting derivation

$$
\cfrac{\cfrac{\cfrac{\overline{\vdash^{\scriptscriptstyle N} P(b)}\;u}{\vdash^{\scriptscriptstyle N} P(a) \supset P(b)}\;\supset I^u}{\vdash^{\scriptscriptstyle N} \forall y.\,P(a) \supset P(y)}\;\forall I^b}{\vdash^{\scriptscriptstyle N} \forall x.\,\forall y.\,P(x) \supset P(y)}\;\forall I^a
$$

is once again incorrect since the hypothesis labelled u should be $P(a)$, not $P(b)$. The local expansion just introduces and immediately discharges the parameter.

$$
\cfrac{\mathcal{D}}{\vdash^{\scriptscriptstyle N} \forall x.\,A}
\qquad \Longrightarrow_E \qquad
\cfrac{\cfrac{\cfrac{\mathcal{D}}{\vdash^{\scriptscriptstyle N} \forall x.\,A}}{\vdash^{\scriptscriptstyle N} [a/x]A}\;\forall E}{\vdash^{\scriptscriptstyle N} \forall x.\,A}\;\forall I^a
$$

Classical logic. The inference rules so far only model intuitionistic logic, and some classically true formulas such as Peirce's law $((A \supset B) \supset A) \supset A$ (for arbitrary A and B) or double negation $(\neg\neg A) \supset A$ (for arbitrary A) are not derivable. There are a number of equivalent ways to extend the system to full classical logic, typically using negation (for example, the law of excluded middle, proof by contradiction, or double negation elimination). In the fragment without disjunction or falsehood, we might choose either a rule of double negation or proof by contradiction.

$$\cfrac{\vdash^N \neg\neg A}{\vdash^N A}\ \text{dbneg} \qquad\qquad \cfrac{\begin{array}{c}\cfrac{}{\vdash^N \neg A}\ u \\[2pt] \vdots \\[2pt] \vdash^N A\end{array}}{\vdash^N A}\ \text{contr}^u$$

The rule for classical logic (whichever we choose to adopt) breaks the pattern of introduction and elimination rules. One can still formulate some reductions for classical derivations, but natural deduction is at heart an intuitionistic calculus. The symmetries of classical logic are better exhibited in sequent calculi.

Here is a simple example of a natural deduction showing that $\vdash^N A \supset \neg\neg A$ is derivable in intuitionistic logic. We attempt to show the process by which such a deduction may have been generated, as well as the final deduction. The three vertical dots indicate a gap in the derivation we are trying to construct, with hypotheses shown above and the desired conclusion below the gap. A trace of this process when the search is carried out in a logical framework is given in Section 4.4.

$$\begin{array}{c}\vdots \\ \vdash^N A \supset \neg\neg A\end{array} \quad\rightsquigarrow\quad \cfrac{\begin{array}{c}\cfrac{}{\vdash^N A}\ u \\[2pt] \vdots \\[2pt] \vdash^N \neg\neg A\end{array}}{\vdash^N A \supset \neg\neg A}\ \supset I^u$$

$$\rightsquigarrow\quad \cfrac{\begin{array}{c}\cfrac{}{\vdash^N A}\ u \qquad \cfrac{}{\vdash^N \neg A}\ w \\[2pt] \vdots \\[2pt] \cfrac{\vdash^N p}{\vdash^N \neg\neg A}\ \neg I^{p,w}\end{array}}{\vdash^N A \supset \neg\neg A}\ \supset I^u \quad\rightsquigarrow\quad \cfrac{\cfrac{\cfrac{\cfrac{}{\vdash^N \neg A}\ w \qquad \cfrac{}{\vdash^N A}\ u}{\vdash^N p}\ \neg E}{\vdash^N \neg\neg A}\ \neg I^{p,w}}{\vdash^N A \supset \neg\neg A}\ \supset I^u$$

The symbol A in this deduction stand for an arbitrary formula; we can thus view the derivation above as parametric in A. In other words, every instance of this derivation (replacing A by an arbitrary formula) is a valid derivation.

Below is a summary of the rules of intuitionistic natural deduction. The use of hypotheses is implicit in this formulation, using our understanding of hypothetical judgments.

Introduction Rules   **Elimination Rules**

$$
\begin{array}{c}
\dfrac{}{\vdash^{\!N} A}\; u \\[2pt]
\vdots \\[2pt]
\dfrac{\vdash^{\!N} B}{\vdash^{\!N} A \supset B}\; \supset\! I^u
\end{array}
\qquad
\dfrac{\vdash^{\!N} A \supset B \qquad \vdash^{\!N} A}{\vdash^{\!N} B}\; \supset\! E
$$

$$
\begin{array}{c}
\dfrac{}{\vdash^{\!N} A}\; u \\[2pt]
\vdots \\[2pt]
\dfrac{\vdash^{\!N} p}{\vdash^{\!N} \neg A}\; \neg I^{p,u}
\end{array}
\qquad
\dfrac{\vdash^{\!N} \neg A \qquad \vdash^{\!N} A}{\vdash^{\!N} C}\; \neg E
$$

$$
\dfrac{\vdash^{\!N} [a/x]A}{\vdash^{\!N} \forall x.\, A}\; \forall I^a
\qquad
\dfrac{\vdash^{\!N} \forall x.\, A}{\vdash^{\!N} [t/x]A}\; \forall E
$$

3.3. Representing derivability

There are several approaches to the representation of natural deductions in logical frameworks. We can introduce a predicate nd such that nd($\ulcorner A \urcorner$) holds in the meta-logic if and only if $\vdash^{\!N} A$ has a derivation. This does not require an explicit representation of natural deductions as objects in the meta-language. Another possibility is to introduce an explicit representation for natural deductions and encode the property "$\mathcal{D}$ *is a deduction of* $\vdash^{\!N} A$".

We first consider the encoding of derivability via axioms in a meta-logic. In order to take advantage of higher-order abstract syntax in the representation, we need to go beyond Horn clauses as introduced in Section 2.1. An appropriate language is the language of *hereditary Harrop formulas* [Miller et al. 1991] which form the basis both of the logic programming language λProlog [*λProlog* 1997] and the generic theorem prover Isabelle [Paulson 1994]. Variations of this approach to encoding derivability have been devised by Paulson [1986] and Felty and Miller [1988, 1989]. Quantifiers in the meta-logic have type labels and range over simply-typed λ-terms. Since it is unnecessary for our purposes, we exclude quantification over formulas in the meta-logic and omit some logical connectives that are easily definable. The meta-variable A ranges here over simple types as in Section 6 and should not be confused with the formulas of first-order logic in the preceding section.

Hereditary Harrop formulas H $::=$ $P \mid \top \mid H_1 \wedge H_2 \mid H_1 \supset H_2 \mid \forall x{:}A.\,H$

There are two important differences to Horn logic: the addition of types so that quantifiers now range over simply-typed λ-terms, and the generalization which allows the body of clauses to contain implications and universal quantifications (so-called *embedded implication* and *embedded universal quantification*). On this fragment classical and intuitionistic logic diverge, so it is crucial that the meta-logic is intuitionistic. A theory T is a collection of closed hereditary Harrop formulas.

$T \vdash^{H\!H} H$ theory T intuitionistically entails proposition H

The extension to allow embedded implications also means that theories consisting of hereditary Harrop formulas no longer constitute inductive definitions the way Horn clauses do.

Derivability by natural deductions is represented by a predicate nd on representations of formulas, that is, meta-level terms of type o. The inference rules are then translated into meta-level axioms concerning the predicate nd. For example, the rule $\supset$E is implemented by

$\forall A{:}o.\,\forall B{:}o.\,(\mathsf{nd}\,(\mathsf{imp}\,A\,B) \wedge \mathsf{nd}\,A) \supset \mathsf{nd}\,B$

In order to represent hypothetical judgments we take advantage of embedded implication. This is correct only because the meta-logic is intuitionistic and a complete strategy for proving a formula $H_1 \supset H_2$ is to prove H_2 under assumption H_1. Using this fact, one can prove that the following axiom is an adequate representation of the $\supset$I rule.

$\forall A{:}o.\,\forall B{:}o.\,(\mathsf{nd}\,A \supset \mathsf{nd}\,B) \supset \mathsf{nd}\,(\mathsf{imp}\,A\,B)$

For parametric judgments we can use a similar encoding with embedded universal quantification. We state the remaining rules here for completeness; the same idea is employed in the type-theoretic treatment in Section 3.4 and explained there in detail.

$\forall A{:}o.\,(\forall p{:}o.\,\mathsf{nd}(A) \supset \mathsf{nd}(p)) \supset \mathsf{nd}(\neg A)$

$\forall A{:}o.\,\mathsf{nd}(\neg A) \supset \forall C{:}o.\,(\mathsf{nd}(A) \supset \mathsf{nd}(C))$

$\forall A{:}i \to o.\,(\forall x{:}i.\,\mathsf{nd}\,(A\,x)) \supset \mathsf{nd}\,(\mathsf{forall}\,(\lambda x{:}i.\,A\,x))$

$\forall A{:}i \to o.\,\mathsf{nd}\,(\mathsf{forall}\,(\lambda x{:}i.\,A\,x)) \supset (\forall x{:}i.\,\mathsf{nd}\,(A\,x))$

We summarize the representation principle in the phrase *judgments-as-propositions*: judgments of the object language (e.g., $\vdash^N A$) are represented by a proposition in the meta-logic (e.g., $\mathsf{nd}(\ulcorner A \urcorner)$). The adequacy theorem of this representation is rather direct. We refer to the theory consisting of the type declarations and the six axioms above as *ND*.

3.1. THEOREM (Adequacy).

$$ND \vdash^{HH} \mathsf{nd}(\ulcorner A \urcorner) \quad \textit{iff} \quad \vdash^{N} A$$

In order to prove this theorem, we need to generalize it to account for hypothetical judgments. One possible form employs meta-level implication.

$$ND \vdash^{HH} \mathsf{nd}(\ulcorner A_1 \urcorner) \supset \cdots \supset \mathsf{nd}(\ulcorner A_n \urcorner) \supset \mathsf{nd}(\ulcorner A \urcorner) \quad \text{iff} \quad \begin{array}{c} \overline{\vdash^{N} A_1}^{\, u_1} \quad \cdots \quad \overline{\vdash^{N} A_n}^{\, u_n} \\ \vdots \\ \vdash^{N} A \end{array}$$

Another form, given for the related type-theoretic interpretation in the next section, directly uses hypothetical reasoning in the meta-language.

3.4. Deductions as objects

If we have a general reasoning tool for hereditary Harrop formulas we can now reason in intuitionistic logic by using the axioms in the theory ND, and in classical logic if we assume an additional axiom modelling double negation elimination. Isabelle [Paulson 1994, Nipkow and Paulson 1992] is such a general tool. Proof search can be programmed externally by using a language of tactics and tacticals to construct derivations using these axioms and derived rules of inference. The meta-programming language in this case is ML, whose type system together with a correct implementation of hereditary Harrop formulas guarantees that only well-formed meta-derivations can be constructed. More on this style of reasoning with the aid of a logical framework implementation can be found in Section 4. As mentioned above, this is an implementation of *derivability* and explicit deductions need never be constructed. If they are maintained, they are only an internal data structure.

There are many circumstances where we are interested in deductions as explicit objects. For example, we may want to extract functional programs from constructive (or even classical) derivations. Or we may want to implement proof transformation and presentation tools in a theorem proving environment. If we do not trust a complex theorem prover, we may construct it so that it generates proof objects which can be independently verified. In the architecture of proof-carrying code [Necula 1997], deductions represented in LF are attached to mobile code to certify safety (see Section 8.2). Another class of applications is the implementation of the meta-theory of the deductive systems under consideration. For example, we may want to show that natural deductions and axiomatic derivations define the same theorems and exhibit translations between them (see Sections 5.2 and 5.4).

The simply-typed λ-calculus, which we used to represent the terms and formulas of first-order logic, is also a good starting point for the representation of natural deductions. As we will see below we need to refine it further in order to allow an internal validity condition for deductions. This leads us to λ^Π, the dependently typed λ-calculus underlying the LF logical framework [Harper et al. 1993].

We begin by introducing a new *type* nd of natural deductions instead of the predicate introduced in the previous section. An inference rule is a constant function from deductions of the premises to a deduction of the conclusion. For example,

impe : nd → nd → nd

might be used to represent implication elimination. A hypothetical deduction is represented as a function from a derivation of the hypothesis to a derivation of the conclusion.

impi : (nd → nd) → nd

One can clearly see that this representation requires an *external* validity condition since it does not carry the information about the conclusion of a derivation. For example, we have

$$\vdash \mathsf{impi}\,(\lambda u{:}\mathsf{nd}.\,\mathsf{impe}\,u\,u) \Uparrow \mathsf{nd}$$

but this term does not represent a valid natural deduction. An external validity predicate can be specified using hereditary Harrop formulas and is executable in λProlog [Felty and Miller 1988, Felty 1989]. However, it is dynamic (rather than static) and not *prima facie* decidable. Furthermore, during search external mechanisms must be put into place in order to prevent invalid deductions. This is related to the problem of *invalid tactics* in ML/LCF [Gordon, Milner and Wadsworth 1979]. Through data abstraction, tactics are guaranteed to generate only valid deductions, but the type system cannot enforce that they have the expected conclusion.

Fortunately, it is possible to refine the simply-typed λ-calculus so that validity of the representation of derivations becomes an *internal* property, without destroying the decidability of the type system. This is achieved by introducing *indexed types*. Consider the following encoding of the elimination rule for implication.

impe : nd (imp $A\,B$) → nd A → nd B

In this specification, nd (imp $A\,B$) is a *type*, the type representing derivations of $A \supset B$. Thus we speak of the *judgments-as-types* principle. The *type family* nd is indexed by objects of type o.

nd : o → type

We call o → type a *kind*. Secondly, we have to consider the status of the free variables A and B in the declaration. Intuitively, impe represents a whole family of constants, one for each choice of A and B. Schematic declarations like the one given above are desirable in practice, but they lead to an undecidable type checking problem [Dowek 1993]. We can recover decidability by viewing A and B as additional arguments in the representation of $\supset$E. Thus impe has four arguments representing A, B, a derivation of $A \supset B$ and a derivation of A. It returns a derivation of B. With the usual function type constructor we could only write

$$\mathsf{impe} \quad : \quad \mathsf{o} \to \mathsf{o} \to \mathsf{nd}\,(\mathsf{imp}\,A\,B) \to \mathsf{nd}\,A \to \mathsf{nd}\,B.$$

This does not express the dependencies between the first two arguments and the types of the remaining arguments. Thus we name the first two arguments A and B, respectively, and write

$$\mathsf{impe} \quad : \quad \Pi A{:}\mathsf{o}.\,\Pi B{:}\mathsf{o}.\,\mathsf{nd}\,(\mathsf{imp}\,A\,B) \to \mathsf{nd}\,A \to \mathsf{nd}\,B.$$

This is a closed type, since the *dependent function type* constructor Π binds the following variable. From the consideration above we can see that the typing rule for application of a function with dependent type should be

$$\frac{\Gamma \vdash_\Sigma M : \Pi x{:}A.\,B \qquad \Gamma \vdash_\Sigma N : A}{\Gamma \vdash_\Sigma M\,N : [N/x]B}\;\mathsf{app}$$

For example, given a variable $p{:}\mathsf{o}$ we have

$$p{:}\mathsf{o} \vdash_\Sigma \mathsf{impe}\,(\mathsf{not}\,p)\,p : \mathsf{nd}\,(\mathsf{imp}\,(\mathsf{not}\,p)\,p) \to \mathsf{nd}\,(\mathsf{not}\,p) \to \mathsf{nd}\,p$$

where the signature Σ contains the declarations for formulas and inferences rules developed above. The counterexample $\mathsf{impi}\,(\lambda u{:}\mathsf{nd}\,A.\,\mathsf{impe}\,u\,u)$ from above is now no longer well-typed: the instance of A would have to be of the form $A_1 \supset A_2$ (first occurrence of u) and simultaneously equal to A_1 (second occurrence of u). This is clearly impossible. The rule for λ-abstraction does not change much from the simply-typed calculus.

$$\frac{\Gamma \vdash_\Sigma A : \mathsf{type} \qquad \Gamma, x{:}A \vdash_\Sigma M : B}{\Gamma \vdash_\Sigma \lambda x{:}A.\,M : \Pi x{:}A.\,B}\;\mathsf{lam}$$

The variable x may now appear free in B, whereas without dependencies it could only occur free in M. From these two rules it can be seen that the rules for $\Pi x{:}A.\,B$ specialize to the rules for $A \to B$ if x does not occur in B. Thus $A \to B$ is generally considered a derived notation that stands for $\Pi x{:}A.\,B$ for a variable x not free in B.

Dependent types further create the need for a rule of *type conversion*. This is required, for example, in the representation of ∀I below. We take a brief excursion into the realm of functional programming to illustrate the nature of dependent types and the need for type conversion. Consider a type family vector indexed by a natural number representing its length. Then concatenation of vectors would have type

$$\mathsf{concat} \quad : \quad \Pi n{:}\mathsf{nat}.\,\Pi m{:}\mathsf{nat}.\,\mathsf{vector}\,n \to \mathsf{vector}\,m \to \mathsf{vector}\,(n + m).$$

Using the inference rules for application we find

$$\mathsf{concat}\,2\,3\,[1, 2]\,[1, 3, 5] \quad : \quad \mathsf{vector}(2 + 3),\ \text{and}$$
$$\mathsf{concat}\,3\,2\,[1, 2, 1]\,[3, 5] \quad : \quad \mathsf{vector}(3 + 2).$$

Since both expressions compute to the same value, namely

$$[1, 2, 1, 3, 5] \quad : \quad \mathsf{vector}(5),$$

we would expect that in a sensible type system all three expressions would have the same type. Evidently they do not, unless we identify the types $\mathsf{vector}(2 + 3)$, $\mathsf{vector}(3 + 2)$, and $\mathsf{vector}(5)$. All of them represent the type of vectors of length 5, so identifying them makes sense intuitively. In general, we add a rule of type conversion that allows us to apply definitional equalities in a type.

$$\frac{\Gamma \vdash_\Sigma M : A \qquad \Gamma \vdash_\Sigma A \equiv B : \mathsf{type}}{\Gamma \vdash_\Sigma M : B} \ \mathsf{conv}$$

The example above also shows that adding dependent types to a functional language can quickly lead to an undecidable type checking problem, since we need to compare expressions in the program language for equality (which is undecidable in general). The LF type theory contains no recursion at the level of objects and type-checking remains decidable since definitional equality remains decidable. This is an important illustration of the design principle that the framework should be as weak as possible. Adding recursion, while it may occasionally seem desirable, can easily destroy decidability of definitional equality and therefore typing. In an undecidable type system, validity of the representations for deductions then would no longer be a static, internal property.

A full complement of rules for the λ^Π type theory is given in Section 7. A version with a weaker notion of definitional equality is given in [Barendregt and Geuvers 2001] (Chapter 18 of this Handbook)

With dependent function types, we can now give a representation for natural deductions with an internal validity condition. This is summarized in Theorem 3.2 below. We first introduce a type family nd that is indexed by a formula. The LF type nd $\ulcorner A \urcorner$ is intended to represent the type of natural deductions of the formula A.

$$\mathsf{nd} : \mathsf{o} \to \mathsf{type}$$

Each inference rule is represented by an LF constant which can be thought of as a function from a derivation of the premises of the rule to a derivation of the conclusion. The constant further depends on the schematic variables that occur in the specification of the inference rule.

Implication. The introduction rule for implication employs a hypothetical judgment. The derivation of the hypothetical judgment in the premise is represented as a function which, when applied to a derivation of A, yields a derivation of B.

$$\cfrac{\begin{array}{c} \overline{\vdash^N A}\ u \\ \mathcal{D} \\ \vdash^N B \end{array}}{\vdash^N A \supset B}\supset\! I^u \quad = \mathsf{impi}\ \ulcorner A \urcorner \ulcorner B \urcorner\ (\lambda u{:}\mathsf{nd}\ \ulcorner A \urcorner.\ \ulcorner \mathcal{D} \urcorner)$$

The assumption A labelled by u which may be used in the derivation $\mathcal{D}$ is represented by the LF variable u which ranges over derivations of A.

$$\left\lceil \frac{}{\vdash^{\!N} A} u \right\rceil = u$$

From this we can deduce the type of the impi constant.

$$\text{impi} \quad : \quad \Pi A{:}o.\, \Pi B{:}o.\, (\text{nd}\, A \to \text{nd}\, B) \to \text{nd}\, (\text{imp}\, A\, B)$$

The elimination rule is simpler, since it does not involve a hypothetical judgment. The representation of a derivation ending in the elimination rule is defined by

$$\left\lceil \frac{\begin{array}{cc} \mathcal{D} & \mathcal{E} \\ \vdash^{\!N} A \supset B & \vdash^{\!N} A \end{array}}{\vdash^{\!N} B} \supset E \right\rceil = \text{impe}\, \ulcorner A \urcorner\, \ulcorner B \urcorner\, \ulcorner \mathcal{D} \urcorner\, \ulcorner \mathcal{E} \urcorner$$

where

$$\text{impe} \quad : \quad \Pi A{:}o.\, \Pi B{:}o.\, \text{nd}\, (\text{imp}\, A\, B) \to \text{nd}\, A \to \text{nd}\, B.$$

As an example we consider a derivation of $A \supset (B \supset A)$.

$$\frac{\dfrac{\dfrac{}{\vdash^{\!N} A} u}{\vdash^{\!N} B \supset A} \supset I^w}{\vdash^{\!N} A \supset (B \supset A)} \supset I^u$$

Note that the assumption $\vdash^{\!N} B$ labelled w is not used and therefore does not appear in the derivation. This derivation is represented by the LF object

$$\text{impi}\, \ulcorner A \urcorner\, (\text{imp}\, \ulcorner B \urcorner\, \ulcorner A \urcorner)\, (\lambda u{:}\text{nd}\, \ulcorner A \urcorner.\, \text{impi}\, \ulcorner B \urcorner\, \ulcorner A \urcorner\, (\lambda w{:}\text{nd}\, \ulcorner B \urcorner.\, u))$$

which has type

$$\text{nd}\, (\text{imp}\, \ulcorner A \urcorner\, (\text{imp}\, \ulcorner B \urcorner\, \ulcorner A \urcorner)).$$

This example shows clearly some redundancies in the representation of the deduction (there are many occurrence of $\ulcorner A \urcorner$ and $\ulcorner B \urcorner$). Fortunately, it is possible to analyze the types of constructors and eliminate much of this redundancy through term reconstruction [Pfenning 1991a, Necula and Lee 1998b]. Section 8.2 has some additional brief remarks on this issue.

Negation. The introduction and elimination rules for negation and their representation follow the pattern of the rules for implication.

$$
\begin{array}{c}
\ulcorner \quad \overline{\vdash^N A}\, u \quad \urcorner \\
\mathcal{D} \\
\vdash^N p \\
\overline{\vdash^N \neg A}\ \neg I^{p,u}
\end{array}
\quad = \text{noti } \ulcorner A \urcorner\, (\lambda p{:}o.\ \lambda u{:}\text{nd}\ulcorner A \urcorner.\ulcorner \mathcal{D} \urcorner)
$$

The judgment of the premise is parametric in p and hypothetical in u. It is thus represented as a function of two arguments, accepting both a formula p and a deduction of A.

> noti : $\Pi A{:}o.\,(\Pi p{:}o.\ \text{nd } A \to \text{nd } p) \to \text{nd (not } A)$

The representation of negation elimination

$$
\begin{array}{c}
\ulcorner \qquad\qquad\qquad \urcorner \\
\begin{array}{cc}
\mathcal{D} & \mathcal{E} \\
\vdash^N \neg A & \vdash^N A
\end{array} \\
\hline
\vdash^N C
\end{array}\ \neg E
\quad = \text{note } \ulcorner A \urcorner \ulcorner \mathcal{D} \urcorner \ulcorner C \urcorner \ulcorner \mathcal{E} \urcorner
$$

leads to the following declaration

> note : $\Pi A{:}o.\ \text{nd (not } A) \to \Pi C{:}o.\ \text{nd } A \to \text{nd } C$

This type just inverts the second argument and result of the noti constant, which is the reason for the chosen argument order. Clearly,

> note′ : $\Pi A{:}o.\ \Pi C{:}o.\ \text{nd (not } A) \to \text{nd } A \to \text{nd } C$

is an equivalent declaration.

Universal quantification. Recall that $\ulcorner \forall x.\, A \urcorner = \text{forall } (\lambda x{:}i.\,\ulcorner A \urcorner)$ and that the premise of the introduction rule is parametric in a.

$$
\begin{array}{c}
\ulcorner \qquad\qquad \urcorner \\
\mathcal{D} \\
\vdash^N [a/x]A \\
\overline{\vdash^N \forall x.\, A}\ \forall I^a
\end{array}
\quad = \text{foralli } (\lambda x{:}i.\,\ulcorner A \urcorner)\, (\lambda a{:}i.\,\ulcorner \mathcal{D} \urcorner)
$$

Note that $\ulcorner A \urcorner$, the representation of A, has a free variable x which must be bound in the meta-language, so that the representing object does not have a free variable x. Similarly, the parameter a is bound at this inference and must be correspondingly bound in the meta-language. The representation determines the type of the constant foralli.

foralli : $\Pi A{:}i \to o.\,(\Pi a{:}i.\,\mathsf{nd}\,(A\,a)) \to \mathsf{nd}\,(\mathsf{forall}\,A)$

In an application of this constant, the argument labelled A will be $\lambda x{:}i.\,\ulcorner A\urcorner$ and $(A\,a)$ will be $(\lambda x{:}i.\,\ulcorner A\urcorner)\,a$ which is equivalent to $[a/x]\ulcorner A\urcorner$ which in turn is equivalent to $\ulcorner [a/x]A\urcorner$ by the compositionality of the representation.

The elimination rule does not employ a hypothetical judgment.

$$
\begin{array}{c}
\ulcorner \\
\mathcal{D} \\
\vdash^{\!N} \forall x.\,A \\
\hline
\vdash^{\!N} [t/x]A
\end{array}\;\;\urcorner
\;\forall\mathrm{E}\quad = \mathsf{foralle}\,(\lambda x{:}i.\,\ulcorner A\urcorner)\,\ulcorner\mathcal{D}\urcorner\,\ulcorner t\urcorner
$$

The substitution of t for x in A is representation by the application of the function $(\lambda x{:}i.\,\ulcorner A\urcorner)$ (the first argument to foralle) to $\ulcorner t\urcorner$.

foralle : $\Pi A{:}i \to o.\,\mathsf{nd}\,(\mathsf{forall}\,A) \to \Pi t{:}i.\,\mathsf{nd}\,(A\,t)$

We now check that

$$
\begin{array}{c}
\ulcorner \\
\mathcal{D} \\
\vdash^{\!N} \forall x.\,A \\
\hline
\vdash^{\!N} [t/x]A
\end{array}\;\;\urcorner
\;\forall\mathrm{E}\quad : \mathsf{nd}\,\ulcorner [t/x]A\urcorner,
$$

assuming that $\ulcorner\mathcal{D}\urcorner : \mathsf{nd}\,\ulcorner\forall x.\,A\urcorner$. This is a part in the proof of adequacy of this representation of natural deductions. At each step we verify that the arguments have the expected type and compute the type of the application.

$$
\begin{array}{rcl}
\mathsf{foralle} & : & \Pi A{:}i \to o.\,\mathsf{nd}\,(\mathsf{forall}\,A) \to \Pi t{:}i.\,\mathsf{nd}\,(A\,t) \\
\mathsf{foralle}\,(\lambda x{:}i.\,\ulcorner A\urcorner) & : & \mathsf{nd}\,(\mathsf{forall}\,(\lambda x{:}i.\,\ulcorner A\urcorner)) \to \Pi t{:}i.\,\mathsf{nd}\,((\lambda x{:}i.\,\ulcorner A\urcorner)\,t) \\
\mathsf{foralle}\,(\lambda x{:}i.\,\ulcorner A\urcorner)\,\ulcorner\mathcal{D}\urcorner & : & \Pi t{:}i.\,\mathsf{nd}\,((\lambda x{:}i.\,\ulcorner A\urcorner)\,t) \\
\mathsf{foralle}\,(\lambda x{:}i.\,\ulcorner A\urcorner)\,\ulcorner\mathcal{D}\urcorner\,\ulcorner t\urcorner & : & \mathsf{nd}\,((\lambda x{:}i.\,\ulcorner A\urcorner)\,\ulcorner t\urcorner) \\
\mathsf{foralle}\,(\lambda x{:}i.\,\ulcorner A\urcorner)\,\ulcorner\mathcal{D}\urcorner\,\ulcorner t\urcorner & : & \mathsf{nd}\,([\ulcorner t\urcorner/x]\ulcorner A\urcorner)
\end{array}
$$

The last step follows by type conversion, noting that

$$(\lambda x{:}i.\,\ulcorner A\urcorner)\,\ulcorner t\urcorner \equiv [\ulcorner t\urcorner/x]\ulcorner A\urcorner.$$

Furthermore, by the compositionality of the representation we have

$$[\ulcorner t\urcorner/x]\ulcorner A\urcorner = \ulcorner [t/x]A\urcorner$$

which yields the desired

$$\mathsf{foralle}\,(\lambda x{:}i.\,\ulcorner A\urcorner)\,\ulcorner\mathcal{D}\urcorner\,\ulcorner t\urcorner : \mathsf{nd}\,(\ulcorner [t/x]A\urcorner).$$

The representation theorem relates canonical objects constructed in certain contexts to natural deductions. The restriction to canonical objects is once again crucial, as are the restrictions on the form of the context. We call the signature consisting of the declarations for first-order terms, formulas, and natural deductions ND.

3.2. THEOREM (Adequacy).

1. *If $\mathcal{D}$ is a derivation of A from hypotheses $\vdash^N A_1, \ldots, \vdash^N A_n$ labelled $u_1, \ldots, u_n$, respectively, with all free individual parameters among $a_1, \ldots, a_m$ and propositional parameters among $p_1, \ldots, p_k$ then*

$$a_1{:}\mathsf{i}, \ldots, a_m{:}\mathsf{i}, p_1{:}\mathsf{o}, \ldots, p_k{:}\mathsf{o}, u_1{:}\mathsf{nd}\ulcorner A_1 \urcorner, \ldots, u_n{:}\mathsf{nd}\ulcorner A_n \urcorner \vdash_{ND} \ulcorner \mathcal{D} \urcorner \Uparrow \mathsf{nd}\ulcorner A \urcorner$$

2. *If*

$$a_1{:}\mathsf{i}, \ldots, a_m{:}\mathsf{i}, p_1{:}\mathsf{o}, \ldots, p_k{:}\mathsf{o}, u_1{:}\mathsf{nd}\ulcorner A_1 \urcorner, \ldots, u_n{:}\mathsf{nd}\ulcorner A_n \urcorner \vdash_{ND} M \Uparrow \mathsf{nd}\ulcorner A \urcorner$$

then $M = \ulcorner \mathcal{D} \urcorner$ for a derivation $\mathcal{D}$ as in part 1.

3. *The representation function is a bijection, and is compositional in the sense that the following equalities hold.*

$$\begin{aligned}
\ulcorner [t/a]\mathcal{D} \urcorner &= [\ulcorner t \urcorner / a]\ulcorner \mathcal{D} \urcorner \\
\ulcorner [C/p]\mathcal{D} \urcorner &= [\ulcorner C \urcorner / p]\ulcorner \mathcal{D} \urcorner \\
\ulcorner [\mathcal{E}/u]\mathcal{D} \urcorner &= [\ulcorner \mathcal{E} \urcorner / u]\ulcorner \mathcal{D} \urcorner
\end{aligned}$$

PROOF. The proof proceeds by induction on the structure of natural deductions one direction and on the definition of canonical forms in the other direction. □

Each of the rules that may be added to obtain classical logic can be easily represented with the techniques from above. They are left as an exercise to the reader.

We summarize the LF encoding of natural deductions. We make a few cosmetic changes which reflect common practice in the use of logical frameworks. The first is the use of infix and prefix notation for logical connectives. According to our conventions, implication is right associative, and negation is a prefix operator binding more tightly than implication.

```
i : type.
o : type.
imp : o → o → o.
not : o → o.
forall : (i → o) → o.
```

The second simplification in the concrete presentation is to omit some Π-quantifiers. Free variables in a declaration are then interpreted as a schematic variables whose quantifiers remain implicit. The types of such free variables must be determined from the context in which they appear. In practical implementations such as Twelf [Pfenning and Schürmann 1998*b*, Pfenning and Schürmann 1998*c*], type reconstruction will issue an error message if the type of free variables is ambiguous.

```
nd : o → type.
impi : (nd A → nd B) → nd (A imp B).
impe : nd (A imp B) → nd A → nd B.
noti : (Πp:o. nd A → nd p) → nd (not A).
note : nd (not A) → (ΠC:o. nd A → nd C).
```

foralli : (Πa:i. nd $(A\ a)$) $\to$ nd (forall A).
foralle : nd (forall A) $\to$ (ΠT:i. nd $(A\ T)$).

When constants with implicitly quantified types are used, arguments corresponding to the omitted quantifiers are also left implicit. Again, in practical implementations these arguments are inferred from context. For example, the constant impi now appears to take only two arguments (of type nd A and nd B for some A and B) rather than four, like the fully explicit declaration

impi : ΠA:o. ΠB:o. (nd A $\to$ nd B) $\to$ nd $(A\ \mathsf{imp}\ B)$.

The derivation of $A \supset (B \supset A)$ from above has this very concise representation:
impi (λu:nd A. impi (λv:nd B. u)) : nd $(A\ \mathsf{imp}\ (B\ \mathsf{imp}\ A))$.

In summary, the basic representation principle underlying LF is the representation of judgments as types. A deduction of a judgment J is represented as a canonical object M whose type is the representation of J. This basic scheme is extended to represent hypothetical judgments as simple function types and parametric judgments as dependent function types. This encoding reduces the question of validity for a derivation to the question of well-typedness for its representation. Since type-checking in the LF type theory is decidable, the validity of derivations has been internalized as a decidable property in the logical framework.

3.5. An axiomatic formulation

A second important style of deductive system is *axiomatic*: rather than explaining the meaning of quantifiers and connectives by inference rules, we use mostly axiom schemas and as few inference rules as possible. The following is the system H_1-**IQC** [Troelstra and van Dalen 1988]. It consists of the following axiom schemas, and the two rules of inference below.

$$\vdash A \supset (B \supset A) \qquad\qquad\qquad\qquad\qquad (K)$$
$$\vdash (A \supset (B \supset C)) \supset ((A \supset B) \supset (A \supset C)) \quad (S)$$

$$\vdash (A \supset \neg B) \supset ((A \supset B) \supset \neg A) \qquad\qquad (N_1)$$
$$\vdash \neg A \supset (A \supset B) \qquad\qquad\qquad\qquad\qquad (N_2)$$

$$\vdash (\forall x.\ A) \supset [t/x]A \qquad\qquad\qquad\qquad\qquad (F_1)$$
$$\vdash (\forall x.\ (B \supset A)) \supset (B \supset \forall x.\ A) \qquad\qquad (F_2)^*$$

with the proviso that x must not be free in B in the rule (F_2). The two rules of inference are modus ponens MP and universal generalization UG.

$$\frac{\vdash A \supset B \qquad \vdash A}{\vdash B}\ MP \qquad\qquad \frac{\vdash [a/x]A}{\vdash \forall x.\ A}\ UG^a$$

The universal generalization rule carries the proviso that a must be a new parameter, that is, may not already occur in A. The representation of the propositional axioms and modus ponens is straightforward, following the ideas in the representation of natural deduction. We introduce a type family hil for axiomatic deductions, indexed by the conclusion of the derivation. In order to improve readability, we use infix notation for implication. Also, we have chosen constant names in lower case so that the presentation of the translations in Section 5.2 will be easier to read.

hil : o → type.
k : hil $(A$ imp B imp $A)$.
s : hil $((A$ imp B imp $C)$ imp $(A$ imp $B)$ imp A imp $C)$.
n_1 : hil $((A$ imp not $B)$ imp $(A$ imp $B)$ imp not $A)$.
n_2 : hil (not A imp A imp $B)$.

For rule (F_1) we need to implement substitution, which is done as usual in higher-order abstract syntax by application, here of A to T.

f_1 : ΠT:i. hil (forall $(\lambda x$:i. A $x)$ imp A $T)$.

For the rule (F_2) we must capture the side-condition that x is not free in the antecedent of the implication. The following achieves this directly.

f_2 : hil (forall $(\lambda x$:i. B imp A $x)$ imp B imp forall $(\lambda x$:i. A $x))$.

Since substitution in the meta-language will rename bound variables to avoid variable capture, we cannot instantiate B in this declaration with an object that contains a free occurrence of x (x would be renamed). Thus, using higher-order abstract syntax, one can concisely represent simple variable occurrence conditions. The rules of inference are isomorphic to ones we have seen for natural deduction.

mp : hil $(A$ imp $B)$ → hil A → hil B.
ug : $(\Pi a$:i. hil $(A$ $a))$ → hil (forall $(\lambda x$:i. A $x))$.

The adequacy theorem for axiomatic derivations is straightforward and left to the reader.

3.6. Higher-level judgments

Next we turn to the local reduction judgment for natural deductions introduced in Section 3.2.

$$\begin{array}{ccc} \mathcal{D} & & \mathcal{D}' \\ \vdash^N A & \Longrightarrow_R & \vdash^N A \end{array}$$

Recall that this judgment witnesses the local soundness of the elimination rules with respect to the introduction rules. We refer to this as a *higher-level judgment* since it relates derivations. The representation techniques underlying LF support this directly, since deductions are represented as objects which can in turn index type families representing higher-level judgments.

In this particular example, reduction is defined only by axioms, one each for implication, negation, and universal quantification. The representing type family in LF must be indexed by the representation of two deductions $\mathcal{D}$ and $\mathcal{D}'$, and consequently also by the representation of A. This shows that there may be dependencies between indices to a type family so that we need a dependent constructor Π for kinds in order to represent judgments relating derivations.

$\Longrightarrow_R$: $\Pi A{:}\mathsf{o}.\ \mathsf{nd}\ A \to \mathsf{nd}\ A \to \mathsf{type}.$

As in the representation of inference rules in Sections 3.4 and 3.5, we omit the explicit quantifier on A and determine A from context.

$\Longrightarrow_R$: $\mathsf{nd}\ A \to \mathsf{nd}\ A \to \mathsf{type}.$

We show the representation of the reduction rules for each connective in turn, writing $\Longrightarrow_R$ as an infix constant.

Implication. This reduction involves a substitution of a derivation for an assumption.

$$
\dfrac{\dfrac{\dfrac{\dfrac{\overline{\vdash^{\!N} A}\ u}{\begin{array}{c}\mathcal{D}\\ \vdash^{\!N} B\end{array}}}{\vdash^{\!N} A \supset B}\supset\!\mathrm{I}^u \qquad \dfrac{\mathcal{E}}{\vdash^{\!N} A}}{\vdash^{\!N} B}\supset\!\mathrm{E}} \qquad \Longrightarrow_R \qquad \dfrac{\dfrac{\mathcal{E}}{\vdash^{\!N} A}\ u}{\begin{array}{c}\mathcal{D}\\ \vdash^{\!N} B\end{array}}
$$

The representation of the left-hand side is

$\quad$ impe (impi ($\lambda u{:}\mathsf{nd}\ A$. $D\ u$)) E

where $E = \ulcorner\mathcal{E}\urcorner$: $\mathsf{nd}\ A$ and $D = (\lambda u{:}\mathsf{nd}\ \ulcorner A\urcorner.\ \ulcorner\mathcal{D}\urcorner)$: $\mathsf{nd}\ A \to \mathsf{nd}\ B$. The derivation on the right-hand side can be written more succinctly as $[\mathcal{E}/u]\mathcal{D}$. Compositionality of the representation (Theorem 3.2, part 3) and β-conversion in LF yield

$$
\ulcorner[\mathcal{E}/u]\mathcal{D}\urcorner = [\ulcorner\mathcal{E}\urcorner/u]\ulcorner\mathcal{D}\urcorner \equiv (\lambda u{:}\mathsf{nd}\ \ulcorner A\urcorner.\ \ulcorner\mathcal{D}\urcorner)\ \ulcorner\mathcal{E}\urcorner.
$$

Thus the representation of the right-hand side will be definitionally equal to $D\ E$ and we can formulate the rule concisely as

$\quad$ redl_imp : impe (impi ($\lambda u{:}\mathsf{nd}\ A$. $D\ u$)) $E \Longrightarrow_R D\ E.$

Negation. This is similar to implication. The required substitution of C for p in $\mathcal{D}$ is implemented by application and β-reduction at the meta-level.

$$
\dfrac{\dfrac{\dfrac{\dfrac{\overline{\vdash^{\!N} A}\ u}{\begin{array}{c}\mathcal{D}\\ \vdash^{\!N} p\end{array}}}{\vdash^{\!N} \neg A}\neg\mathrm{I}^{p,u} \qquad \dfrac{\mathcal{E}}{\vdash^{\!N} A}}{\vdash^{\!N} C}\neg\mathrm{E}} \qquad \Longrightarrow_R \qquad \dfrac{\dfrac{\mathcal{E}}{\vdash^{\!N} A}\ u}{\begin{array}{c}[C/p]\mathcal{D}\\ \vdash^{\!N} C\end{array}}
$$

redl_not : note (noti ($\lambda p{:}\mathsf{o}$. $\lambda u{:}\mathsf{nd}\ A$. $D\ p\ u$)) $C\ E \Longrightarrow_R D\ C\ E.$

Universal quantification. The universal introduction rule involves a parametric judgment. Consequently, the substitution to be carried out during reduction replaces a parameter by a term.

$$\dfrac{\dfrac{\mathcal{D}}{\vdash^{\scriptscriptstyle N} [a/x]A}}{\dfrac{\vdash^{\scriptscriptstyle N} \forall x.\,A}{\vdash^{\scriptscriptstyle N} [t/x]A} \,\forall E} \,\forall I^a \qquad \Longrightarrow_R \qquad \dfrac{[t/a]\mathcal{D}}{\vdash^{\scriptscriptstyle N} [t/x]A}$$

In the representation we once again exploit the compositionality.

$$\ulcorner [t/a]\mathcal{D}\urcorner = [\ulcorner t\urcorner/a]\ulcorner\mathcal{D}\urcorner \equiv (\lambda a{:}i.\,\ulcorner\mathcal{D}\urcorner)\,\ulcorner t\urcorner$$

This gives rise to the declaration

    redl_forall : foralle (foralli ($\lambda a{:}i.\ D\ a$)) $T \Longrightarrow_R D\ T$.

The adequacy theorem states that canonical LF objects of type $\ulcorner\mathcal{D}\urcorner \Longrightarrow_R \ulcorner\mathcal{D}'\urcorner$ constructed over the appropriate signature and in an appropriate parameter context are in bijective correspondence with derivations of $\mathcal{D} \Longrightarrow_R \mathcal{D}'$. We leave the precise formulation and simple proof to the diligent reader.

The encoding of the local expansions employs the same techniques. We summarize it below without going into further detail.

    $\Longrightarrow_E$: nd $A \to$ nd $A \to$ type.

    expl_imp : $\Pi D{:}$nd $(A$ imp $B).D \Longrightarrow_E$ impi ($\lambda u{:}$nd $A.$impe $D\ u$).

    expl_not : $\Pi D{:}$nd $(\text{not }A).D \Longrightarrow_E$ noti ($\lambda p{:}o.\lambda u{:}$nd $A.$note $D\ p\ u$).

    expl_forall : $\Pi D{:}$nd (forall ($\lambda x{:}i.A\ x$)).$D \Longrightarrow_E$ foralli ($\lambda a{:}i.$foralle $D\ a$).

In summary, the representation of higher-level judgments continues to follow the *judgments-as-types* technique. The expressions related by higher-level judgments are now deductions and therefore dependently typed in the representation. Substitution at the level of deductions is implemented by β-reduction at the meta-level, taking advantage of the compositionality of the representation. Further examples of higher-level judgments can be found in Section 5.

4. Meta-programming and proof search

An important motivation underlying the development of logical frameworks is to factor the effort required to build a theorem proving environment for specific logics. The idea is to build one generic environment for deriving judgments in the logical framework and use this for particular logical systems whose judgments are specified in the framework. Each logic is still likely to require a significant amount of development, but the goal is to reduce this effort as much as possible. Furthermore, by offering a high-level notation for the judgments of an object logic, one can increase the confidence in the correctness of an implementation, especially if the framework offers a notation for derivations independent of proof search. The practical evidence gathered through many experiments with Isabelle in a variety of logics indicates that this is indeed feasible and fruitful.

This raises two related questions: which are the common concepts in theorem proving shared among different logics, and how do we perform search in the logical framework? We concentrate on the latter question in the hope that the almost universal applicability of the ideas becomes apparent.

4.1. Sequent calculus

Many forms of proof search are based on sequent calculi. A *sequent* generally has the form $\mathcal{J} \implies J$ where $\mathcal{J}$ is a context of available labelled hypotheses $u_1 ::$ $J_1, \ldots, u_n :: J_n$ and J is the judgment we are trying to derive. This is just a less cumbersome notation for hypothetical judgments as introduced in Section 3.1. We refer to each J_i as an *antecedent* and J as the *succedent* of the sequent.

Fully automatic theorem proving for practically interesting logics is rarely feasible, so framework implementations such as Isabelle are based on partially automated search. In this case, it is most intuitive to think of the construction of a derivation as proceeding bottom-up, where a sequent $\mathcal{J} \implies J$ represents the goal of deriving J from $\mathcal{J}$. We describe the possible goal reductions in the form of inference rules for the sequent judgment. Since this view of search is a shared feature between many different logics, it is natural to base the generic search in the logical framework on the same principle, thereby directly supporting this view for a variety of object logics. The use of sequents for the top-down construction of derivations is the basis of the inverse method discussed in [Degtyarev and Voronkov 2001b] (Chapter 4 of this Handbook).

We describe here a sequent calculus for LF. A substantially similar and slightly simpler presentation can be given for hereditary Harrop formulas and related logical frameworks. The formulation below is based on work by Pym and Wallen [1990, 1991]. The presentation of LF motivated in Section 3.4 and summarized in Section 7 is highly economical in that the simple function type $A \to B$ is considered an abbreviation for a dependent function type $\Pi x{:}A.\, B$ where x does not occur in B. During search, however, these two are treated differently: $A \to B$ behaves like an implication, while $\Pi x{:}A.\, B$ behaves like a universal quantifier. Already in the description of our representation technique we have informally distinguished between them: $A \to B$ corresponded to a hypothetical judgment while $\Pi x{:}A.\, B$ corresponded to a parametric judgment. Our sequents have the form

$$\Gamma \stackrel{LF}{\Longrightarrow} M : A$$

where Γ is a context of parameter declarations and hypotheses and M is a proof term for A. During search we think of Γ and A as given, while M is filled in when a proof succeeds. We fix a signature Σ which encodes the expressions and inference rules of the object language under consideration and omit it from the judgment since it never changes. We maintain the following invariants:

1. $\vdash \Gamma$ *Ctx*
2. $\Gamma \vdash A$: type
3. $\Gamma \vdash M : A$

We use h to range over either a constant c declared in Σ or variable declared in Γ. We have initial sequents and so-called *right* and *left* rules for each type constructor ($\rightarrow$ and Π).

Initial sequents. We have solved a goal if a hypothesis matches the succedent, modulo definitional equality.

$$\frac{h{:}A' \text{ in } \Sigma \text{ or } \Gamma \qquad \Gamma \vdash A' \equiv A : \text{type}}{\Gamma \overset{LF}{\Longrightarrow} h : A} \text{ init}$$

Hypothetical judgments. To derive the representation $A \rightarrow B$ of a hypothetical judgment, we simply introduce a hypothesis A with a new label u.

$$\frac{\Gamma, u{:}A \overset{LF}{\Longrightarrow} M : B}{\Gamma \overset{LF}{\Longrightarrow} \lambda u{:}A.\, M : A \rightarrow B} \rightarrow R^u$$

If we have an assumption $A \rightarrow B$ we are allowed to assume B if we can derive A. The conclusion C does not change in this rule.

$$\frac{h{:}A \rightarrow B \text{ in } \Sigma \text{ or } \Gamma \qquad \Gamma \overset{LF}{\Longrightarrow} M : A \qquad \Gamma, u{:}B \overset{LF}{\Longrightarrow} N : C}{\Gamma \overset{LF}{\Longrightarrow} [(h\,M)/u]N : C} \rightarrow L^u$$

Parametric judgments. To derive the representation $\Pi x{:}A.\, B$ of a parametric judgment, we simply introduce a new parameter (for convenience also called x).

$$\frac{\Gamma, x{:}A \overset{LF}{\Longrightarrow} M : B}{\Gamma \overset{LF}{\Longrightarrow} \lambda x{:}A.\, M : \Pi x{:}A.\, B} \Pi R^x$$

To use a parametric assumption $\Pi x{:}A.\, B$ we instantiate x with an object of the correct type.

$$\frac{h{:}\Pi x{:}A.\, B \text{ in } \Sigma \text{ or } \Gamma \qquad \Gamma \vdash M \Uparrow A \qquad \Gamma, u{:}[M/x]B \overset{LF}{\Longrightarrow} N : C}{\Gamma \overset{LF}{\Longrightarrow} [(h\,M)/u]N : C} \Pi L^u$$

Note that we fall back on the ordinary typing judgment for LF to check that the substitution term M is well-typed in the appropriate context. The calculus shown above is sound and complete, as shown by Pym and Wallen [1991]. As usual, we assume a fixed valid signature Σ and that Γ is valid in Σ.

4.1. THEOREM (Properties of LF sequent calculus).

1. *If* $\Gamma \overset{LF}{\Longrightarrow} M : A$ *then* $\Gamma \vdash M : A$.

2. *If* $\Gamma \vdash M \Uparrow A$ *then* $\Gamma \overset{LF}{\Longrightarrow} M : A$.

PROOF. The first property is easy to see by induction on the sequent derivation. The second can be proved by induction on the definition of canonical forms, after appropriate generalization for atomic forms (defined in Section 7). ☐

We can sharpen this theorem if we restrict initial sequents to atomic types P. In that case $\Gamma \overset{LF}{\Longrightarrow} M : A$ implies that $\Gamma \vdash M \Uparrow A$ (see [Pinto and Dyckhoff 1998]). The additional rule of Cut which is sometimes allowed in sequent calculi plays a special role. It corresponds to the introduction of a lemma during proof search, which is very difficult to automate. Its discussion is left to Section 4.5.

When constructing a sequent derivation upwards from the conclusion, one is confronted with a variety of choices. In particular, we have to decide which rule to apply and, for the left rules, which hypothesis to use. Usually one takes advantage of additional properties of the logic to eliminate some of the choices. For example, in the sequent calculus for LF the conclusion of $\rightarrow R$ is derivable if and only if the premise is derivable. Therefore it is always safe to apply this rule when the succedent has the form $A \rightarrow B$. Implementations of logical frameworks take advantage of such inversion properties to eliminate non-determinism in search. However, some choices clearly will always remain—they have to be addressed either via user interaction or some form of meta-programming. This is the topic of the next section.

4.2. Tactics and tacticals

In this section we address the question which choices arise during search within a sequent calculus, and how the non-determinism inherent in these choices can be resolved. We assume a meta-level control structure of so-called *tactics* and *tacticals*. As a first approximation, a tactic transforms a partial proof structure with some unproven leaf sequents to another, while a tactical is a (higher-order) function to combine tactics to form more complex tactics. At the top level, the user can choose which tactic to apply, and which unproven sequent to apply it to. We analyze the structure of tactics and tacticals in more detail when discussing the kind of choices they have to resolve.

Tactics and tacticals arose out of the LCF theorem proving effort [Gordon et al. 1979, Paulson 1983] and are used in such diverse systems as HOL [Gordon and Melham 1993], Nuprl [*Nuprl* 1999, Constable et al. 1986], Coq [*Coq* 1999, Paulin-Mohring 1993], Isabelle [Paulson 1994, Paulson 1994], and λProlog [λ*Prolog* 1997, Nadathur and Miller 1988, Felty 1993]. In all but λProlog, they are programmed in ML which was originally developed to support theorem proving for LCF. Correctness for tactics is ensured dynamically through *data abstraction*. The basic idea is that at the core of the implementation is an abstract type of Theorem with constructors which implement and check the correct application of the primitive rules of inference for a judgment. Since the type is abstract, only the given rules can be used, thereby reducing the correctness problem for a complex theorem proving environment to the correctness of the implementation of the basic inference rules.

In a logical framework with dependent types the correctness of deductions may instead be enforced by type-checking alone, as we have seen in Section 3.4. We therefore skip more detailed discussion of the validation of tactics and consider how they deal with choices that arise during search in a sequent calculus. In the ELAN logical framework [*ELAN* 1998, Borovanský et al. 1998] the strategy language has independent status, rather than being embedded in a general-purpose functional language such as ML. Besides individual tactic combinators to address various aspects of search, tactic languages provide general mechanisms for composition of tactics and iteration or recursion.

Conjunctive choice. A conjunctive choice arises when a sequent rule has several premises. Each of these premises must be derived to derive the conclusion. The $\rightarrow L^u$ rule has this character: to derive the judgment C we derive A, and also C under the additional hypothesis B. A tactic can choose any unproven leaf from a partial proof structure to work on, usually the leftmost pending sequent. Tactic languages provide a tactical MAP such that MAP t is a tactic which applies t to all pending sequents in turn. In an interactive setting the user can navigate between unproven sequents.

Disjunctive choice. A disjunctive choice arises when there are several rules which could be applied, or several different ways in which a particular rule might be applied. For example, in the $\rightarrow L^u$ rule we have to pick a hypothesis $h{:}A \rightarrow B$ from Σ or Γ when there may be several such assumptions. When tactics are employed for proof search, this is handled by *backtracking*. A tactic may apply sequent rules (from the bottom up) to reduce an unproven sequent, or it might *fail*. Failure for a tactic to apply signals that an alternative should be tried for an earlier choice. In the language of tacticals this is expressed with the ORELSE combinator. The tactic t_1 ORELSE t_2 tries to apply t_1 and returns its result if successful. If t_1 fails it tries to apply t_2 instead and returns its result. In particular, if t_2 also fails, then t_1 ORELSE t_2 fails. We refer to this as *shallow backtracking* because when t_1 succeeds the alternative t_2 will never be reconsidered. We discuss *deep backtracking* below, when we examine the interaction between disjunctive choice and meta-variables.

Universal choice. This arises, for example, in the ΠR^a rule where we have to choose a new parameter a. Since the only relevant criterion is that a is new, this does not lead to any undesirable non-determinism: any new a suffices.

Existential choice. This arises when we have to pick a term as, for example, the object M in the rule ΠL. Early implementations of tactics typically either guessed a plausible term or required the user to supply it. Since there often are an infinite number of choices, more recent implementations usually postpone a commitment until further search uncovers information about which terms might lead to a successful derivation. We achieve this postponement by using a place-holder X for M, called a *meta-variable* or *logical variable*. In order to guarantee soundness when meta-variables are instantiated we record its type A_X and the context Γ_X which contains the parameters which are allowed to occur in the instantiation term for X. The latter constraint on X replaces Skolemization as used in classical first-order theorem proving, which does not work for all object logics and would therefore be a poor choice in a logical framework.

Postponed existential choices are resolved when initial sequents are reached. Rather than check if a hypothesis matches the succedent modulo definitional equality, we have to decide if there is a way to instantiate the meta-variables in a hypothesis and the succedent so that the resulting judgments are definitionally equal. This problem is called *unification* and discussed in the Section 4.3 and in more detail in [Dowek 2001] (Chapter 16 of this Handbook). The introduction of meta-variables into search also interacts strongly with conjunctive and disjunctive choices, which we now revisit.

Conjunctive choice with meta-variables. Meta-variables may be shared among several unproven leaf sequents. Since unification instantiates these variables globally in a partial proof structure, the order in which unproven sequents are reduced is no longer irrelevant. Tactics have to be aware of this interaction, although there are no simple and general recipes.

Disjunctive choice with meta-variables. Deriving an unproven sequent often requires a commitment to a particular instantiation for meta-variables as determined by unification at the leaves. This commitment could make it impossible to derive another sequent which shares some of the meta-variables. This means that even after successfully deriving a particular sequent, we might have to reexamine the choices made during this derivation in case another sequent turns out to be unprovable. This leads to *deep backtracking* which revisits disjunctive choices even though an alternative had previously been successful.

Under the simplified functional model for tactics introduced above, a tactic returns either no result (it fails) or a single result (the new partial proof structure). Deep backtracking requires that a tactic can return a potentially unbounded number of alternatives, where zero alternatives indicate failure. This can be done by using a lazily computed sequence of alternatives which can be incrementally expanded as necessary during backtracking. The Isabelle logical framework implementation uses this technique, since its meta-programming language ML is functional. In ELAN the operator dk (for *don't know choose*) achieves this behavior.

The λProlog and Elf implementations provide an alternative by using a logic programming interpretation of the logical framework to program search. Since logic programming inherently supports logical variables, unification, and deep backtracking, significantly less machinery is needed to implement tactics (see [Felty 1993]). On the other hand, don't-care non-determinism requires additional programming or extra-logical constructs such as the cut operator "!", since the operational interpretation of logic programs is based on don't-know non-determinism. We come back to this in Section 4.4.

We use t_1 THEN t_2 to denote the sequential composition of tactics and REPEAT t for the iterator which applies t until it fails and then returns the last result. REPEAT t is an example of an *unfailing* tactic which always succeeds, though subgoals may of course remain. The interaction of possibly failing and unfailing tactics is one of the difficulties in tactic programming.

As a simple example, assume we have basic tactics Init, ArrowR, and PiR which apply the rules init, $\to R$ and ΠR, respectively. Then the tactic

Right* = REPEAT (ArrowR ORELSE PiR ORELSE Init)

repeatedly applies the right rules to a sequent until the succedent is atomic. The atomic goal is solved if it unifies with a hypothesis; otherwise it remains as a subgoal. This tactic is *safe*, that is, if the original sequent is derivable, the resulting sequent will still be derivable. Right* is safe, despite the fact that we use a committed choice tactical ORELSE, since the right rules of the sequent calculus for λ^Π are *invertible*: the premise is derivable if and only if the conclusion is derivable. The interaction of safe and unsafe tactics is another complicated aspect of tactic programming.

4.3. Unification and constraint simplification

As sketched above, unification is a central and indispensable mechanism in traditional first-order theorem provers and logic programming languages. It allows the search algorithm to postpone existential choices until more information becomes available about which instances may be useful. Most logical frameworks go beyond first-order terms in two ways: they employ types and they employ λ-abstraction. Consequently, first-order unification is insufficient. In this section we briefly review the aspects of higher-order unification most relevant to the practice of logical frameworks. For more information see [Dowek 2001] (Chapter 16 of this Handbook).

One can identify the simply-typed λ-calculus ($\lambda^\to$) as motivated in Section 2.2 as an important base language. Fortunately, definitional equality ($\beta\eta$-conversion) is decidable. On the other hand, the general unification problem is undecidable [Huet 1973] even for the second-order fragment [Goldfarb 1981], and most general unifiers may not exist. To appreciate some of the problems of higher-order unification, consider the equation

$$(\lambda x{:}i.\, F\,(s\,x)) = (\lambda x{:}i.\, s\,(F\,x))$$

where $s{:}i \to i$ is a constant, and F is a meta-variable we are trying to solve for. Note that F itself may not contain free occurrences of x according to the definition of capture avoiding substitution. There are infinitely many different solutions for F, namely

$$(\lambda y{:}i.\, s \ldots (s\,y))$$

for any number of applications of s, including zero.

Despite the undecidability, Huet [1975] devised a practical algorithm for *higher-order pre-unification*, a form of unification which postpones certain solvable equations instead of enumerating their solutions. The resulting semi-decision procedure is non-deterministically complete, that is, if there is a unifier a less committed pre-unifier can in principle always be found. Moreover, when used to compute multiple solutions, it is guaranteed to enumerate non-redundant pre-unifiers to a given set of equations. With the addition of a modified version of the occurs-check, it coincides with first-order unification when called on first-order terms. Huet's algorithm has been used extensively in λProlog and Isabelle and generally seems to have good computational properties. Both languages must therefore manage constraints during search or execution of programs [Kirchner, Kirchner and Vittek 1993].

The practical success of Huet's algorithm seemed to be in part due to the fact that difficult, higher-order unification problems rarely arise in practice. An analysis of this observation led Miller [1991] to discover *higher-order patterns*, a sublanguage of the simply-typed λ-calculus with restricted variable occurrences. For this fragment, most general unifiers exist. In fact, the theoretical complexity of this problem is linear [Qian 1993], just as for first-order unification. Miller proposed it as the basis for a lower-level language L_λ similar to λProlog, but one where unification does not branch since only higher-order patterns are permitted as terms. An empirical study of this restriction by Michaylov and Pfenning [1992, 1993] showed that most dynamically arising unification problems lie within this fragment, while a static restriction rules out some useful programming idioms.

The Elf language therefore makes no syntactic restriction to higher-order patterns, nor does it use Huet's algorithm for higher-order unification as generalized to λ^Π (discovered independently by Elliott [1989, 1990] and Pym [1990, 1992]). Instead, it employs a constraint solving algorithm [Pfenning 1991a, Pfenning 1991b, Dowek, Hardin, Kirchner and Pfenning 1996] where unification problems within the decidable fragment proposed by Miller are solved directly, while all others (solvable or not) are postponed as constraints. This can drastically reduce backtracking compared to higher-order pre-unification and imposes no restrictions on variable occurrences. On the other hand, unsolvable constraints may remain until the end of the computation, in which case the answer is conditional: Each solution to the remaining constraints gives rise to a solution of the original equations, and each solution to the original equations will be an instance of the remaining constraints. In most practical applications, these somewhat weaker soundness and completeness theorems are sufficient.

4.4. Logic programming

Logic programming offers a different approach to meta-programming in a logical framework than ML or a separate strategy language. Rather than meta-programming in a language in which the logical framework itself is implemented (typically ML), we endow the logical framework with an operational interpretation in the spirit of Prolog. It should be clear that a specification of a logic under this approach does not automatically give rise to a theorem prover, but that theorem provers may be programmed in the meta-language. Two frameworks to date have pursued this approach: λProlog [λ*Prolog* 1997, Nadathur and Miller 1988], which gives an operational interpretation of hereditary Harrop formulas, and Elf [Pfenning and Schürmann 1998*b*, Pfenning 1994*a*], which gives an operational interpretation to λ^Π.

In logic programming the basic computational mechanism is proof search following a specific search strategy. Since the search strategy is fixed, the computational behavior of a program can be predicted and exploited by the programmer. This predictability comes at the price of completeness: programs may never terminate even if there is a proof. On the other hand, we are careful to preserve at least weak completeness, which means that if search fails then no proof can exist. Thus we can rely on success due to soundness and failure due to weak completeness, while we have no information if the program does not terminate. This summarizes some essential differences between logic programming and general theorem proving.

The idea of logical framework implementations such as λProlog and Elf is to use the operational reading of specifications to implement algorithms for proof search and related problems. In many cases, the original specification itself can be used algorithmically. For example, a natural semantics specification of Mini-ML [Hannan 1991, Michaylov and Pfenning 1991] can be used directly for evaluation or type-checking, one of the original motivations for natural semantics [Kahn 1987, Hannan 1993].

We base our operational understanding of logic programming on the sequent calculus. The operational interpretation of a logical specification is based on two principles: goal-directed search [Miller et al. 1991] and focusing [Andreoli 1992]. Goal-directed search expresses that we always first apply the right rules bottom-up to derive a given sequent until the succedent is atomic. An atomic succedent should now result in an analogue to procedure call. This is achieved by focusing on a particular hypothesis and applying a succession of left rules until it is atomic. If it then happens to unify with the atomic succedent we next attempt to derive the pending premises of the left rules; otherwise we fail and backtrack. In a slight abuse of terminology we refer to derivations which are both goal-directed and focused as *uniform*. If every derivable judgment has a uniform derivation we claim to have an *abstract logic programming language* because search following this operational specification will be sound and weakly complete.

We now specify uniform derivations more concretely, in the form of two mutually recursive judgments for LF.

$$\Gamma \stackrel{uni}{\Longrightarrow} M : A \qquad\qquad A \text{ is uniformly derivable}$$
$$\Gamma \stackrel{uni}{\Longrightarrow} u{:}A \gg N : P \qquad\qquad A \text{ immediately entails } P$$

In these judgments, M and N are proof terms for A and P, respectively. In the immediate entailment judgment, A is the hypothesis we have focused on and u its label. When viewed operationally, we think of Γ, A and P as given, while M and N are computed together with the derivation. We presuppose and maintain the following invariants:

1. $\vdash \Gamma$ *Ctx* in both judgments;
2. $\Gamma \vdash A :$ type and
3. $\Gamma \vdash M : A$ for uniform derivability, and
4. $\Gamma \vdash P :$ type and
5. $\Gamma, u{:}A \vdash N : P$ for immediate entailment.

Actually, the restricted form of search guarantees a stronger invariant, namely that M is always canonical and N always atomic.

Atomic judgments.

$$\frac{\Gamma \vdash Q \equiv P : \text{type}}{\Gamma \overset{uni}{\Longrightarrow} u{:}Q \gg u : P} \text{ init}$$

$$\frac{h{:}A \text{ in } \Sigma \text{ or } \Gamma \qquad \Gamma \overset{uni}{\Longrightarrow} u{:}A \gg N : P}{\Gamma \overset{uni}{\Longrightarrow} [h/u]N : P} \text{call}^u$$

Hypothetical judgments.

$$\frac{\Gamma, u{:}A \overset{uni}{\Longrightarrow} M : B}{\Gamma \overset{uni}{\Longrightarrow} \lambda u{:}A.\, M : A \to B} \to R^u$$

$$\frac{\Gamma \overset{uni}{\Longrightarrow} u{:}B \gg N : C \qquad \Gamma \overset{uni}{\Longrightarrow} M : A}{\Gamma \overset{uni}{\Longrightarrow} w{:}A \to B \gg [(w\,M)/u]N : C} \to L^u$$

Parametric judgments.

$$\frac{\Gamma, x{:}A \overset{uni}{\Longrightarrow} M : B}{\Gamma \overset{uni}{\Longrightarrow} \lambda x{:}A.\, M : \Pi x{:}A.\, B} \Pi R^x$$

$$\frac{\Gamma \vdash M \Uparrow A \qquad \Gamma \overset{uni}{\Longrightarrow} u{:}[M/x]B \gg N : C}{\Gamma \overset{uni}{\Longrightarrow} w{:}\Pi x{:}A.\, B \gg [(w\,M)/u]N : C} \Pi L^u$$

Uniform derivations are sound and complete with respect to sequent derivations. In fact, we can prove a stronger theorem that there is a bijection between canonical objects M of a given type A and the objects such that $\overset{uni}{\Longrightarrow} M : A$ is derivable [Pfenning 1991a, Dyckhoff and Pinto 1994, Pfenning 2001, Pinto and Dyckhoff 1998].

4.2. THEOREM (Properties of LF uniform derivations).

1. *If $\Gamma \overset{uni}{\Longrightarrow} M : A$ then $\Gamma \vdash M \Uparrow A$.*

2. *If $\Gamma \vdash M \Uparrow A$ then $\Gamma \overset{uni}{\Longrightarrow} M : A$.*

PROOF. The first property is easy to see by induction on the uniform derivation. The second can be proved by induction on the definition of canonical forms, after appropriate generalization for atomic forms (see [Pfenning 2001]). An alternative proof examines the permutability of inference rules in the sequent calculus for LF from Section 4.1. □

We now revisit the remaining non-deterministic choices we examined in the discussion of tactics in Section 4.2.

Conjunctive choice. We always solve the subderivations in the multiple premise rule $\rightarrow L$ from left to right. This means that when a hypothesis $u{:}A \rightarrow (B \rightarrow C)$ is used to derive C, the first subgoal to be solved is B and the second A. If we rewrite the same declaration with the arrows reversed, we obtain $u : (C \leftarrow B) \leftarrow A$ which lends itself to a natural reading as a labelled program clause in logic programming. Using the convention that "$\leftarrow$" is left-associative, we can write this even more concisely as $u : C \leftarrow B \leftarrow A$. It is important to derive the premises of $\rightarrow L$ in this order since we do not want to solve subgoals until we know if the target type (C in the example) matches the atomic goal. In Prolog terminology conjunctive choice is called *subgoal selection.*

Disjunctive choice. We employ deep backtracking as indicated in Section 4.2. Since only one inference rule applies to any sequent, disjunctive choices arise only in two circumstances: we have to decide which constant or hypothesis to use for one of the call rules, and unification may allow more than one possibility (see the notes on existential choice below). We first try constants from first to last in the fixed signature Σ, then the parameters and hypotheses from Γ from right to left (the most recently introduced hypothesis is tried first).

Universal choice. Just as before, we simply introduce new parameters or hypothesis labels.

Existential choice. In the ΠL rule we introduce a fresh meta-variable X, record Γ and A and proceed. When we try to complete a branch of the derivation with the init rule, we use unification instead of equality. λProlog employs Huet's unification algorithms to enumerate pre-unifiers, while Elf uses constraint simplification based on patterns [Dowek et al. 1996].

To illustrate uniform derivations we reconsider the example at the end of Section 3.2 with its encoding in LF from Section 3.4. We omit the proof terms for the sake of brevity.

$\cdot \overset{uni}{\Longrightarrow} \Pi A{:}\mathrm{o.\ nd}(A \text{ imp not not } A)$

ΠR^A which leaves

$A{:}\mathrm{o} \overset{uni}{\Longrightarrow} \mathrm{nd}(A \text{ imp not not } A)$

   call   with impi which leaves

$A{:}\mathrm{o} \overset{uni}{\Longrightarrow} (\Pi A{:}\mathrm{o.}\ \Pi B{:}\mathrm{o.}\ (\mathrm{nd}(A) \to \mathrm{nd}(B)) \to \mathrm{nd}(A \text{ imp } B)) \gg \mathrm{nd}(A \text{ imp not not } A)$

   ΠL with A which leaves

$A{:}\mathrm{o} \overset{uni}{\Longrightarrow} (\Pi B{:}\mathrm{o.}\ (\mathrm{nd}(A) \to \mathrm{nd}(B)) \to \mathrm{nd}(A \text{ imp } B)) \gg \mathrm{nd}(A \text{ imp not not } A)$

   ΠL with not not A which leaves

$A{:}\mathrm{o} \overset{uni}{\Longrightarrow} ((\mathrm{nd}(A) \to \mathrm{nd}(\text{not not } A)) \to \mathrm{nd}(A \text{ imp not not } A)) \gg \mathrm{nd}(A \text{ imp not not } A)$

   $\to L$ which leaves two subgoals

$A{:}\mathrm{o} \overset{uni}{\Longrightarrow} \mathrm{nd}(A \text{ imp not not } A) \gg \mathrm{nd}(A \text{ imp not not } A)$

   init   which is solved, leaving one subgoal

$A{:}\mathrm{o} \overset{uni}{\Longrightarrow} \mathrm{nd}(A) \to \mathrm{nd}(\text{not not } A)$

In the remainder we omit the immediate entailment steps.

$A{:}\mathrm{o} \overset{uni}{\Longrightarrow} \mathrm{nd}(A) \to \mathrm{nd}(\text{not not } A)$ $\to R^u$

$A{:}\mathrm{o}, u{:}\mathrm{nd}(A) \overset{uni}{\Longrightarrow} \mathrm{nd}(\text{not not } A)$ call   with noti

$A{:}\mathrm{o}, u{:}\mathrm{nd}(A) \overset{uni}{\Longrightarrow} \Pi p{:}\mathrm{o.}\ (\mathrm{nd}(\text{not } A) \to \mathrm{nd}(p))$ ΠR^p

$A{:}\mathrm{o}, u{:}\mathrm{nd}(A), p{:}\mathrm{o} \overset{uni}{\Longrightarrow} (\mathrm{nd}(\text{not } A) \to \mathrm{nd}(p))$ $\to R^w$

$A{:}\mathrm{o}, u{:}\mathrm{nd}(A), p{:}\mathrm{o}, w{:}\mathrm{nd}(\text{not } A) \overset{uni}{\Longrightarrow} \mathrm{nd}(p)$ call   with note, leaving subgoals

$A{:}\mathrm{o}, u{:}\mathrm{nd}(A), p{:}\mathrm{o}, w{:}\mathrm{nd}(\text{not } A) \overset{uni}{\Longrightarrow} \mathrm{nd}(\text{not } A)$ call   with w, solved, and

$A{:}\mathrm{o}, u{:}\mathrm{nd}(A), p{:}\mathrm{o}, w{:}\mathrm{nd}(\text{not } A) \overset{uni}{\Longrightarrow} \mathrm{nd}(A)$ call   with u, solved

To compute the proof term we proceed through the sequents, assigning proof terms at each step. At the root, this yields the sequent

$A{:}\mathrm{o} \overset{uni}{\Longrightarrow} (\mathrm{impi}\ (\lambda u{:}\mathrm{nd}\ A.\ \mathrm{noti}\ (\lambda p{:}\mathrm{o.}\ \lambda w{:}\mathrm{nd}\ (\text{not } A).\ \mathrm{note}\ w\ p\ u)))$
$: \mathrm{nd}\ (A \text{ imp not not } A).$

There are some advantages and some disadvantages to the logic programming approach to meta-programming. Perhaps the most important advantage is uniformity of language for specification and implementation. Specific algorithms such a evaluation, type inference, or certain theorem proving strategies can easily be implemented at a very high level. On the other hand, the logic programming paradigm does not lend itself very well to interactive theorem proving since the state of the search and user commands are inherently imperative in nature. In λProlog this is addressed with extra-logical constructs which augment the logical foundation, just as Prolog extends Horn logic in numerous ways. Furthermore, the current state of the art in implementation of λProlog is such that complex tactics or decision procedures can be much faster in a functional meta-language. An ongoing effort in compiler design and implementation might change this situation in the near future [Nadathur and Mitchell 1999].

Elf remains pure and is therefore difficult to use for interactive theorem proving. However the purity of the language has an important benefit, namely that we can express proofs of meta-theorems to a certain extent. In particular, we can write meta-programs in Elf which translate traces of a search algorithm written in Elf to deductions as specified in LF. We will see an example for this kind of application in the Section 5.

4.5. Theory development

In practical applications one is usually interested in more than just proving one theorem, but in the development of a whole theory consisting of declarations, definitions, lemmas, and theorems. Moreover, theories are often organized into subtheories related in a variety of ways.

At the most fundamental level, the logical framework calculus LF can be extended by global definitions of the form $c{:}A = M$ or by local definitions in the form **let** $x{:}A = M$ **in** N. These can be viewed as either introducing syntactic abbreviations (if the type A represents a syntactic category) or introducing a derived rule A with derivation M (if the type A represents a judgment). One can either view such an extension as semantically completely transparent so that the **let** above is treated as syntactic sugar for $(\lambda x{:}A.\, N)\, M$, or one can introduce a new typing rule

$$\frac{\Gamma \vdash M : A \qquad \Gamma, x{:}A \vdash N : C}{\Gamma \vdash \text{let } x{:}A = M \text{ in } N : C} \; \text{let}$$

and a new rule of definitional equality

$$\text{let } x{:}A = M \text{ in } N \equiv [M/x]N.$$

The canonical form theorem and decidability of type-checking continue to hold, but the search operations underlying both tactics and logic programming are complicated. The problem is that expansion of all definitions is rarely feasible, while not expanding them jeopardizes weak completeness. A solution of this problem for LF based on a simple form of strictness analysis is proposed in [Pfenning and Schürmann 1998a].

In the sequent calculus, the introduction of a lemma into the derivation during search corresponds to an application of the cut rule.

$$\frac{\Gamma \overset{LF}{\Longrightarrow} M : A \qquad \Gamma, u : A \overset{LF}{\Longrightarrow} N : C}{\Gamma \overset{LF}{\Longrightarrow} \text{let } u{:}A = M \text{ in } N : C} \; \text{Cut}^u$$

One could also choose the proof term $[M/u]N$ in the conclusion in order to avoid a language extension. The cut rule for LF is *admissible*, which means that any instance of this rule can be eliminated from a derivation.

For further discussion of modularity mechanisms in logical frameworks, see Section 8.1.

5. Representing meta-theory

Logical frameworks are designed to admit a direct and natural representation of deductive systems at a very high level of abstraction. In Section 3 we showed that checking the validity of a derivation can be reduced to type-checking in the framework which is decidable. In Section 4 we indicated how generic ideas for proof search in a logical framework can support theorem proving in particular logics, and how a logic programming interpretation of a framework can be used for the implementation of specific algorithms related to deductive systems.

This leaves the question if we can take advantage of the conciseness and elegance of the encodings to also mechanize the meta-theory of deductive systems. For example, we might want to prove that the natural deduction formulation of intuitionistic logic in Section 3.2 and the axiomatic formulation in Section 3.5 have the same theorems. Other examples from the area of logic include admissibility of inference rules such as cut in a sequent system, or the correctness of logical interpretations. In the area of programming languages we think of properties such as type preservation, correctness of type inference algorithms, or compiler correctness.

The answer is a qualified *"yes"*. Some frameworks such as FS_0 are specifically designed for meta-theoretic reasoning, but they give up techniques such as static proof checking, higher-order abstract syntax, or hypothetical judgments as functions. As we explain below, there are some difficulties with encodings utilizing higher-order abstract syntax with a number of possible solutions. In many ways the potential of logical frameworks for meta-theoretic reasoning has not yet been fully explored.

Just as we isolated the notions of variable binding, parametric, and hypothetical judgments as central in the presentation of deductive systems, we should analyze the proof techniques used to carry out the meta-theory of deductive systems and then consider how a framework might support them. By far the most common proof technique is induction, both over the structure of expressions and derivations. Thus one naturally looks towards frameworks that permit inductive definitions of judgments and allow the corresponding induction principles. Unfortunately, there is a conflict between induction and the representation techniques of higher-order abstract syntax and functional representation of hypothetical judgments. The issue is complicated further by dependent types, so we consider first the implicational fragment of the simply-typed representation of deductions.

```
nd    :  type
impi  :  (nd → nd) → nd
impe  :  nd → nd → nd
```

Even if we considered the above signature as complete (rather than open-ended), the type nd would not be inductively defined in the usual sense, because of the negative occurrence of nd in the type of impi. Straightforward attempts to formulate a valid induction principle for the type nd fail. Informally, at least one difficulty is clear: when we try to prove a theorem about natural deductions, we invariably have to generalize over all possible collection of hypotheses. Since they are not represented explicitly in our technique, we cannot directly formulate the required induction proofs. We consider an example below.

There is a further difficulty with induction in the framework which stems from the essential open-endedness of representations. For example, assume we declare constants z for zero and s for successor in the formulation of first-order logic, but we do not assume an induction principle for natural numbers in our object logic. If the framework permitted an induction principle over the representation type i, we would no longer have an adequate encoding of first-order logic with two uninterpreted function constants. The encoding of the universal introduction rule,

foralli : $\Pi A{:}i \to o.\,(\Pi a{:}i.\,\text{nd}\,(A\ a)) \to \text{nd}\,(\text{forall}\ A)$

now represents an ω-rule, since objects of type $\Pi a{:}i.\,\text{nd}\,(A\ a)$ allow case analysis on a and are therefore no longer necessarily parametric in a. Depending on the strength of the induction principle in the meta-language we would be able to derive various propositions in the object language that are not actually derivable in pure first-order logic and the adequacy of the representation is destroyed. A similar problem already arises at the level of syntax if we permit primitive recursion into the logical framework.

Several options have been explored to escape this dilemma. The first is to reject the notion of higher-order abstract syntax and use inductive representations directly (see, for example, [Matthews et al. 1993, Basin and Constable 1993, Feferman 1988, Magnusson and Nordström 1994]). This engenders a complication of the encoding and consequently of the meta-theory, which now has to deal with many lemmas regarding variable naming. This can be alleviated by using de Bruijn indices [de Bruijn 1972], yet formalizations are still substantially more complex than informal proofs. There are many examples of formal developments along these lines.

A second possibility is to relax the conditions on inductive definitions, which leads to *partial inductive definitions* [Hallnäs 1991]. They allow inversion principles but not a direct generalization of proofs by induction. Partial inductive definitions have been used as the basis for a logical framework [Hallnäs 1987, Eriksson 1993a], implemented in the Pi derivation editor [Eriksson 1994]. Their potential for formalizing meta-theory is currently being explored by McDowell and Miller [1997] (see also [McDowell 1997]); more on their approach below.

A third option is to employ reflection with some restrictions to ensure soundness. In [Despeyroux, Pfenning and Schürmann 1997] this was achieved by a modal type operator satisfying the laws of S4. However, the practicality of these and some related proposals [Despeyroux and Hirschowitz 1994, Despeyroux, Felty and Hirschowitz 1995, Leleu 1998] has never been demonstrated. Different reflection mechanisms have been employed in the Calculus of Construction [Rueß 1996, Rueß 1997] and Nuprl [Allen, Constable, Howe and Aitken 1990]. These last two do not use higher-order abstract syntax.

A fourth option is to externalize the induction. This leads to a three-level architecture: the object logic, the logical framework in which it is specified, and a meta-logic for reasoning about the logical framework. Variations of this are currently pursued by McDowell and Miller [1997] and Schürmann and Pfenning [1995, 1998]. In principle, any meta-logic could be used for reasoning about the logical framework, but the effort required to develop the theory of the framework and then apply it to individual signatures would be prohibitive unless the meta-logic was specifically designed for meta-theoretic reasoning. Briefly, the logic of McDowell and Miller is based on definitional reflection [Schroeder-Heister 1993] and natural number induction, while that of Schürmann and Pfenning admits only $\forall\exists$ formulas where the quantifiers range over closed LF objects and uses explicit termination orderings [Rohwedder and Pfenning 1996]. Recently, this approach has been generalized by Schürmann [2000].

A more detailed discussion of such meta-logical frameworks is beyond the scope of this chapter. In the next section we present another approach where the meta-theory is only partially verified, but where the computational contents of the meta-theoretic proofs is directly available for execution.

5.1. Relational meta-theory

As alluded to above, it is difficult to soundly extend the logical framework to include induction. However, it is possible to encode the computational contents of proofs of meta-theoretic properties in Elf and thereby partially verify them. Moreover, they can be executed for a number of different purposes. The technique employs higher-level judgments as introduced in Section 3.6.

As an example we consider the equivalence between natural deduction and axiomatic formulations of the fragment of first-order logic introduced in Sections 3.2 and 3.5. In one direction this is expressed simply as:

If $\vdash^A A$ then $\vdash^N A$.

Recall that formulas A are represented as objects of type o, while derivations of $\vdash^A A$ are represented by objects of type hil $\ulcorner A \urcorner$ and derivations of $\vdash^N A$ as objects of type nd $\ulcorner A \urcorner$. Expressed in a meta-logic for LF, we can use adequacy of the encodings to reformulate the theorem.

For any LF objects A : o and H : hil A there exists an LF object D : nd A.

If we ignore the issues of parameters for the moment, the quantifiers range over closed objects with respect to the signature that encodes natural and axiomatic formulations of intuitionistic logic. From a constructive proof of this proposition we can extract a function which maps a formula A and a derivation of $\vdash^A A$ to a deduction of $\vdash^N A$. If this function were representable in the logical framework, it would have type

$$\Pi A{:}\text{o. hil}\,A \to \text{nd}\,A.$$

Since the proof proceeds by induction over the structure of the axiomatic derivation $\mathcal{H}$ of $\vdash^{\!A} A$, such a function would be defined by induction over its second argument—something the framework does not allow. However, we can specify this function as a higher-level judgment relating $\mathcal{H}$ and the natural deduction $\mathcal{D}$. This higher-level judgment is declared as a type family hilnd.

$$\mathsf{hilnd} : \Pi A{:}\mathsf{o}.\, \mathsf{hil}\, A \to \mathsf{nd}\, A \to \mathsf{type}$$

This relation can be specified in LF and executed as a logic program in Elf. Queries have the form hilnd $A\, H\, \mathbf{D}$, where A and H are given closed objects of appropriate type, while $\mathbf{D}$ is a free variable which will be computed during logic programming search.

It is important to realize, however, that type-checking the signature declaring hilnd does not guarantee the validity of the meta-theorem we were trying to prove. For this, some additional conditions have to be satisfied: *mode correctness* which expresses that the logic programming interpretation of hilnd respects the desired input/output interpretation, *termination* which guarantees that each call of hilnd of the form above terminates, and *coverage* which guarantees that for each possible combination of input values a case in the definition of hilnd will be applicable. Some aspects of this check are discussed in [Pfenning and Rohwedder 1992, Rohwedder and Pfenning 1996].

A similar idea in the area of functional programming without the notion of higher-order abstract syntax has been explored in the ALF system [Magnusson 1995, Magnusson and Nordström 1994, Coquand and Smith 1993, Coquand, Nordström, Smith and von Sydow 1994] and the Foetus system [Abel 1999]. The empirical evidence suggests that this shortens developments considerably and allows the formulations of functions in a manner which is closer to functional programming practice [Coquand 1992, Gaspes and Smith 1992, Magnusson 1993]. In these systems, termination and coverage has also been externalized, rather than forcing adherence to an inflexible schema of primitive recursion.

5.2. Translating axiomatic derivations to natural deductions

In this section we illustrate the relational representation of proofs by relating derivations in the axiomatic system to natural deductions. As a first step we prove that every axiomatic deduction may be transformed into a natural deduction.

5.1. THEOREM. *If* $\vdash^{\!A} A$ *then* $\vdash^{\!N} A$.

PROOF. The proof proceeds by a simple structural induction over the derivation $\mathcal{H} :: \ \vdash^{\!A} A$. In each case we exhibit the corresponding natural deduction. Our representation of this proof introduces a new judgment relating, for any formula A, the Hilbert derivations of A to the natural deductions of A. This judgment is represented by the type family

$$\mathsf{hilnd} \quad : \quad \mathsf{hil}\, A \to \mathsf{nd}\, A \to \mathsf{type}$$

where we have left a quantifier over A implicit as explained in Section 3.4. As explained in the preceding section, this relation implements a total function $\Pi A{:}o.\,\mathsf{hil}\,A \to \mathsf{nd}\,A$ which is not directly expressible in the framework.

Each case in the induction argument turns into a declaration of a corresponding higher-level judgment.

Case:

$$\mathcal{H} = \dfrac{}{\vdash^{\!\!A} A \supset (B \supset A)}\,K$$

In this case we have to supply a natural deduction of $\vdash^{\!\!N} A \supset (B \supset A)$, which we have already seen at the end of Section 3.4. Recall that k implements the axiom K.

    hnd_k : hilnd k (impi ($\lambda u{:}$nd A. impi ($\lambda v{:}$nd B. u))).

Case:

$$\mathcal{H} = \dfrac{}{\vdash^{\!\!A} (A \supset (B \supset C)) \supset ((A \supset B) \supset (A \supset C))}\,S$$

A natural deduction of the conclusion is

$$\dfrac{\dfrac{\dfrac{\overline{\vdash^{\!\!N} A \supset (B \supset C)}\;u \quad \overline{\vdash^{\!\!N} A}\;w}{\vdash^{\!\!N} B \supset C}\,{\supset}E \quad \dfrac{\overline{\vdash^{\!\!N} A \supset B}\;v \quad \overline{\vdash^{\!\!N} A}\;w}{\vdash^{\!\!N} B}\,{\supset}E}{\dfrac{\dfrac{\vdash^{\!\!N} C}{\vdash^{\!\!N} A \supset C}\,{\supset}I^w}{\dfrac{\vdash^{\!\!N} (A \supset B) \supset (A \supset C)}{\vdash^{\!\!N} (A \supset (B \supset C)) \supset ((A \supset B) \supset (A \supset C))}\,{\supset}I^u}\,{\supset}I^v}}{}\,{\supset}E$$

This deduction can now be represented in LF by the usual method.

    hnd_s :
        hilnd s
            (impi ($\lambda u{:}$nd (A imp B imp C).
                impi ($\lambda v{:}$nd (A imp B).
                      impi ($\lambda w{:}$nd A. impe (impe u w) (impe v w))))).

Case:

$$\mathcal{H} = \dfrac{}{\vdash^{\!\!A} (A \supset \neg B) \supset ((A \supset B) \supset (\neg A))}\,N_1$$

This is similar to the previous case.

$$
\dfrac{
\dfrac{\dfrac{\rule{2.2em}{0.4pt}}{\vdash^N A \supset \neg B}\,u \quad \dfrac{\rule{1.5em}{0.4pt}}{\vdash^N A}\,w}{\vdash^N \neg B}\,\supset\!E
\qquad
\dfrac{\dfrac{\rule{2.2em}{0.4pt}}{\vdash^N A \supset B}\,v \quad \dfrac{\rule{1.5em}{0.4pt}}{\vdash^N A}\,w}{\vdash^N B}\,\supset\!E
}{
\dfrac{\dfrac{\vdash^N p}{\vdash^N \neg A}\,\neg I^{p,w}}{\dfrac{\vdash^N (A \supset B) \supset \neg A}{\vdash^N (A \supset \neg B) \supset ((A \supset B) \supset \neg A)}\,\supset I^u}\,\supset I^v
}\,\neg E
$$

In the formalization, the propositional parameter p appears as a bound variable.

```
hnd_n₁ :
    hilnd n₁
        (impi (λu:nd (A imp not B).
                impi (λv:nd (A imp B).
            noti (λp:o. λw:nd A. note (impe u w) p (impe v w))))).
```

The remaining axioms are easy to prove, and we only show their encodings

```
hnd_n₂ :
    hilnd n₂ (impi (λu:nd (not A). impi (λv:nd A. note u B v))).
hnd_f₁ :
    hilnd (f₁ T) (impi (λu:nd (forall (λx:i. A x)). foralle u T)).
hnd_f₂ :
    hilnd f₂
        (impi (λu:nd (forall (λx:i. B imp A x)).
                impi (λv:nd B. foralli (λa:i. impe (foralle u a) v)))).
```

Case:

$$
\mathcal{H} = \dfrac{\overset{\mathcal{H}_1}{\vdash^A A \supset B} \qquad \overset{\mathcal{H}_2}{\vdash^A A}}{\vdash^A B}\,MP
$$

By induction hypothesis on $\mathcal{H}_1$ and $\mathcal{H}_2$ there exist natural deductions $\mathcal{D}_1 :: \ \vdash^N A \supset B$ and $\mathcal{D}_2 :: \ \vdash^N A$, respectively. Using the rule of implication elimination $\supset E$, we obtain

$$
\mathcal{D} = \dfrac{\overset{\mathcal{D}_1}{\vdash^N A \supset B} \qquad \overset{\mathcal{D}_2}{\vdash^N A}}{\vdash^N B}\,\supset E
$$

In the representation we emphasize the operational reading of the implementation by using the arrow that points to the left. It associates to the left, and therefore $A_3 \leftarrow A_2 \leftarrow A_1$ is equivalent to $A_1 \rightarrow A_2 \rightarrow A_3$.

hnd_mp : hilnd (mp H_1 H_2) (impe D_1 D_2)
     ← hilnd H_1 D_1
     ← hilnd H_2 D_2.

Note that hilnd H_1 D_1 will be the first subgoal to be solved, and hilnd H_2 D_2 the second, according to the operational semantics sketched in Section 4.4.

Case:

$$\mathcal{H} = \frac{\begin{array}{c}\mathcal{H}_1 \\ \vdash^A [a/x]A\end{array}}{\vdash^A \forall x.\, A}\, UG^a$$

This case corresponds directly to universal introduction ($\forall$I) in natural deduction. By induction hypothesis on $\mathcal{H}_1$ there exists a natural deduction $\mathcal{D}_1 :: \; \vdash^N [a/x]A$. Since the deduction $\mathcal{D}_1$ is not hypothetical, the side condition on UG that a not appear in A is sufficient to guarantee the corresponding side condition on $\forall$I and we can form

$$\mathcal{D} = \frac{\begin{array}{c}\mathcal{D}_1 \\ \vdash^N [a/x]A\end{array}}{\vdash^N \forall x.\, A}\, \forall I^a$$

In the representation, $\mathcal{H}_1$ is a function from a to a deduction of $[a/x]A$. Thus the higher-level judgment relating $\mathcal{H}_1$ to $\mathcal{D}_1$ is parametric in a. Parametric judgments are represented by functions as usual, so a dependent function type will appear in the premise.

     hnd_ug : hilnd (ug H_1) (foralli D_1) ← ($\Pi a{:}i.$ hilnd (H_1 a) (D_1 a)).

Operationally in Elf, solving the subgoal introduces a new parameter a and substitutes it for the variable bound in H_1. The resulting deduction is translated to a natural deduction that may contain a. Matching this against the pattern (D_1 a) creates the correct functional representation of the judgment that is hypothetical in a, and which is the premise of $\forall$I and thus the argument to foralli.   □

The proof above describes a method for translating axiomatic derivations to natural deductions. Under the Curry-Howard isomorphism [Howard 1980], this corresponds to a translation from typed combinators (based on S and K and others) to typed λ-terms. As a sample execution of this program, consider the query

     hilnd (mp (mp s k) k) **D**

where **D** is a free variable of type nd $(A \, \text{imp} \, A)$. This will compute the following instantiation for **D**, which is an indirect way of deriving $\vdash^N A \supset A$.

```
impe
    (impe
        (impi
            (λu:nd (A imp (B imp A) imp A).
                impi
                    (λv:nd (A imp B imp A).
                        impi (λw:nd A. impe (impe u w)
                                            (impe v w)))))
            (impi (λu:nd A. impi (λv:nd (B imp A). u))))
    (impi (λu:nd A. impi (λv:nd B. u))).
```

5.3. The deduction theorem

One crucial step in proving the other direction (natural deductions can be translated to axiomatic derivations) is the *deduction theorem*. In its simplest form it concerns a hypothetical derivation: if we can prove B assuming A (written as $A \vdash^A B$), then we can derive $\vdash^A A \supset B$. This is not quite enough for our application, since during a natural deduction many hypotheses may arise. So we let Δ range over collections of hypotheses $A_1, \ldots, A_n$ and write $\Delta \vdash^A B$. An implementation of a proof of the deduction theorem using FS_0 is described in [Basin and Matthews 1996] and may be compared to the relational implementation below.

5.2. THEOREM (Deduction Theorem). *If* $\Delta, A \vdash^A B$ *then* $\Delta \vdash^A A \supset B$.

PROOF. The proof proceeds by induction on the structure of the derivation $\mathcal{H} ::$ $\Delta, A \vdash^A B$. In the implementation of the proof the extraneous hypotheses Δ will be represented by hypotheses in LF and can therefore be left implicit in the main judgment. Thus the proof is implemented as a higher-level judgment, relating the representation of the hypothetical derivation of $A \vdash^A B$ to the derivation of $\vdash^A$ $A \supset B$. Recall that a hypothetical derivation is represented as an LF function from derivations of the hypothesis to derivations of the conclusion. Thus we arrive at the type family

ded : (hil $A \to$ hil B) $\to$ hil $(A$ imp B) $\to$ type

where A and B are implicitly quantified.

Case: $\mathcal{H} = \Delta, A \vdash^A A$, that is, $\mathcal{H}$ consists of a use of the hypothesis A. Then we need to show that $\Delta \vdash^A A \supset A$. This follows by two applications of Modus Ponens from (S) and (K). Written in linear form instead of the more awkward tree we have

1	$(A \supset ((B \supset A) \supset A)) \supset ((A \supset (B \supset A)) \supset (A \supset A))$	S
2	$(A \supset ((B \supset A) \supset A))$	K
3	$(A \supset (B \supset A)) \supset (A \supset A)$	$MP\,1\,2$
4	$A \supset (B \supset A)$	K
5	$A \supset A$	$MP\,3\,4$

As an LF term, this is represented succinctly by mp (mp s k) k, a term already familiar from the sample query at the end of the previous section. The LF function $\lambda u{:}\mathsf{hil}\ A.\ u$ represents the immediate use of the hypothesis $\vdash^{\!\mathcal{A}} A$, labelled internally by u. Thus we have

> ded_id : ded $(\lambda u{:}\mathsf{hil}\ A.\ u)$ (mp (mp s k) k).

Case: $\mathcal{H} = \Delta, A \vdash^{\!\mathcal{A}} A_i$, where A_i occurs in Δ. In this case we have to give a derivation of $\Delta \vdash^{\!\mathcal{A}} A \supset A_i$. But this follows from an application of Modus Ponens and K.

$$
\begin{array}{cll}
1 & \Delta \vdash^{\!\mathcal{A}} A_i \supset (A \supset A_i) & K \\
2 & \Delta \vdash^{\!\mathcal{A}} A_i & (hyp) \\
3 & \Delta \vdash^{\!\mathcal{A}} A \supset A_i & MP\,1\,2
\end{array}
$$

There is no corresponding case in the implementation of the type family ded. Instead, we need to make the assumption that the deduction theorem applied to a new hypothesis labelled w yields mp k w wherever w is introduced. This technique will be illustrated in the next section.

Case:

$$
\mathcal{H} = \cfrac{}{\Delta, A \vdash^{\!\mathcal{A}} B_1 \supset (B_2 \supset B_1)}\ K
$$

Then we proceed as follows:

$$
\begin{array}{cll}
1 & \Delta \vdash^{\!\mathcal{A}} (B_1 \supset (B_2 \supset B_1)) \supset (A \supset (B_1 \supset (B_2 \supset B_1))) & K \\
2 & \Delta \vdash^{\!\mathcal{A}} B_1 \supset (B_2 \supset B_1) & K \\
3 & \Delta \vdash^{\!\mathcal{A}} A \supset (B_1 \supset (B_2 \supset B_1)) & MP\,1\,2
\end{array}
$$

> ded_k : ded $(\lambda u{:}\mathsf{hil}\ A.\ k)$ (mp k k).

Cases: All remaining axioms (S, N_1, N_2, F_1, F_2) are handled as in the previous case. We only show their implementations.

> ded_n_1 : ded $(\lambda u{:}\mathsf{hil}\ A.\ n_1)$ (mp k n_1).
> ded_n_2 : ded $(\lambda u{:}\mathsf{hil}\ A.\ n_2)$ (mp k n_2).
> ded_f_1 : ded $(\lambda u{:}\mathsf{hil}\ A.\ f_1\ T)$ (mp k ($f_1\ T$)).
> ded_f_2 : ded $(\lambda u{:}\mathsf{hil}\ A.\ f_2)$ (mp k f_2).

Case:

$$
\mathcal{H} = \cfrac{\overset{\mathcal{H}_1}{\Delta, A \vdash^{\!\mathcal{A}} B_1 \supset B_2} \qquad \overset{\mathcal{H}_2}{\Delta, A \vdash^{\!\mathcal{A}} B_1}}{\Delta, A \vdash^{\!\mathcal{A}} B_2}\ MP
$$

1   $\Delta \vdash^{A} A \supset (B_1 \supset B_2)$ Ind. hyp. on $\mathcal{H}_1$

2   $\Delta \vdash^{A} (A \supset (B_1 \supset B_2)) \supset ((A \supset B_1) \supset (A \supset B_2))$ S

3   $\Delta \vdash^{A} (A \supset B_1) \supset (A \supset B_2)$ $MP\,2\,1$

4   $\Delta \vdash^{A} A \supset B_1$ Ind. hyp. on $\mathcal{H}_2$

5   $\Delta \vdash^{A} A \supset B_2$ $MP\,3\,4$

Appeals to induction hypotheses are implemented in the premises of the higher level judgment, generating H_1' and H_2', respectively. Note how the premises $\mathcal{H}_1$ and $\mathcal{H}_2$ of $\mathcal{H}$ are once again hypothetical, that is, they may depend on the assumption A. This is implemented as $(H_1\ u)$ and $(H_2\ u)$ in the declaration below.

```
ded_mp :
    ded (λu:hil A. mp (H₁ u) (H₂ u)) (mp (mp s H₁') H₂')
      ← ded H₁ H₁'
      ← ded H₂ H₂'.
```

Case:

$$\mathcal{H} = \dfrac{\begin{array}{c}\mathcal{H}_1\\[2pt]\Delta, A \vdash^{A} [a/x]B_1\end{array}}{\Delta, A \vdash^{A} \forall x.\,B_1}\ UG^a$$

1   $\Delta \vdash^{A} A \supset [a/x]B_1$ Ind. hyp. on $\mathcal{H}_1$

2   $\Delta \vdash^{A} \forall x.\,(A \supset B_1)$ $UG^a\,1$

3   $\Delta \vdash^{A} (\forall x.\,(A \supset B_1)) \supset (A \supset \forall x.\,B_1)$ F_2

4   $\Delta \vdash^{A} A \supset \forall x.\,B_1$ $MP\,3\,2$

The side conditions on UG^a and F_2 are satisfied by virtue of the proviso that a not occur in Δ, A, or $\forall x.\,B_1$, that is, that $\mathcal{H}_1$ be parametric in a. In the implementation we simply create a new parameter a.

```
ded_ug :
    ded (λu:hil A. ug (H₁ u)) (mp f₂ (ug H₁'))
      ← (Πa:i. ded (λu:hil A. H₁ u a) (H₁' a)).
```

$\square$

The declarations for the higher-level judgment ded can be executed as a logic program, thus capturing the computational contents of the deduction theorem. This corresponds to the algorithm for *bracket abstraction* in combinatory logic [Curry and Feys 1958].

5.4. Translating natural deductions to axiomatic derivations

Obtaining a translation from natural deductions to axiomatic derivations is now straightforward. Note that we must allow for hypotheses, since the $\supset$I rule introduces them (if viewed from the bottom up).

5.3. THEOREM. *If $\vdash^{\!\!N} A$ follows from hypotheses $\vdash^{\!\!N} A_1, \ldots, \vdash^{\!\!N} A_n$, then there exists a hypothetical axiomatic derivation of $A_1, \ldots, A_n \vdash^{\!\!A} A$.*

PROOF. By induction on $\mathcal{D} :: \; \vdash^{\!\!N} A$. We abbreviate $A_1, \ldots, A_n$ by Δ. In the implementation we deal with each hypothesis as it is introduced, rather than globally. Thus the type family that implements the meta-proof just relates a natural deduction to a Hilbert derivation.

     ndhil : ΠA:o. nd $A \to$ hil $A \to$ type.

Case:

$$\mathcal{D} = \frac{}{\vdash^{\!\!N} A_i} \, u_i$$

This constitutes application of a hypothesis. Then $\mathcal{H}$ is a one-step derivation using the corresponding the hypothesis. It is implemented wherever hypotheses are introduced, which are the cases for $\supset$I and $\neg$I.

Case:

$$\mathcal{D} = \frac{\begin{array}{c} \dfrac{}{\vdash^{\!\!N} A_1} \, u \\[4pt] \mathcal{D}_1 \\[2pt] \vdash^{\!\!N} A_2 \end{array}}{\vdash^{\!\!N} A_1 \supset A_2} \, {\supset}\mathrm{I}^u$$

By induction hypothesis on $\mathcal{D}_1$, there exists a derivation $\mathcal{H}_1$ of $\Delta, A_1 \vdash^{\!\!A} A_2$. Hence, by the deduction theorem, there exists a derivation $\mathcal{H}_1'$ of $\Delta \vdash^{\!\!A} A_1 \supset A_2$, which is what we needed to show. The implementation combines this and the previous case by introducing hypotheses u:nd A_1 and v:hil A_1 and assuming that the translation of u should be v. Since this rule introduces a new hypothesis $\vdash^{\!\!A} A_1$, we must also indicate how the deduction theorem behaves on the new assumption. This may be gleaned from the second case in the proof of the deduction theorem.

```
    ndh_impi :
      ndhil (impi D₁) H₁'
        ← (Πu:nd A₁. Πv:hil A₁.
            (ΠC:o. ded (λw:hil C. v) (mp k v))
              → ndhil u v
              → ndhil (D₁ u) (H₁ v))
        ← ded H₁ H₁'.
```

Case:

$$\mathcal{D} = \dfrac{\begin{array}{c} \mathcal{D}_1 \\ \vdash^{\!\!N} \forall x.\, A_1 \end{array}}{\vdash^{\!\!N} [t/x]A_1} \; \forall\mathrm{E}$$

By induction hypothesis on $\mathcal{D}_1$ there exists a derivation $\mathcal{H}_1$ of $\Delta \vdash^{\!\!A} \forall x.\, A_1$. By modus ponens from an instance of axiom schema F_1 and $\mathcal{H}_1$ we can then construct a derivation $\mathcal{H}$ of $\Delta \vdash^{\!\!A} [t/x]A_1$.

    ndh_foralle : ndhil (foralle D_1 T) (mp (f$_1$ T) H_1) $\leftarrow$ ndhil D_1 H_1.

Cases: We omit the remaining cases which are similar to the two given above. It is an instructive exercise to reconstruct the informal argument from the implementation given below.

    ndh_impe : ndhil (impe D_1 D_2) (mp H_1 H_2)
            $\leftarrow$ ndhil D_1 H_1
            $\leftarrow$ ndhil D_2 H_2.
    ndh_noti :
      ndhil (noti D_1) (mp (mp n$_1$ $H_1{}'$) $H_1{}''$)
        $\leftarrow$ ($\Pi p{:}\mathrm{o}.\;\Pi u{:}\mathrm{nd}\;A_1.\;\Pi v{:}\mathrm{hil}\;A_1.$
            ($\Pi C{:}\mathrm{o}.\;\mathrm{ded}\;(\lambda w{:}\mathrm{hil}\;C.\;v)\;(\mathrm{mp}\;\mathrm{k}\;v))$
              $\rightarrow$ ndhil u v
              $\rightarrow$ ndhil (D_1 p u) (H_1 p v))
        $\leftarrow$ ded (H_1 (not A)) $H_1{}'$
        $\leftarrow$ ded (H_1 A) $H_1{}''$.
    ndh_note : ndhil (note D_1 C D_2) (mp (mp n$_2$ H_1) H_2)
             $\leftarrow$ ndhil D_1 H_1
             $\leftarrow$ ndhil D_2 H_2.
    ndh_foralli : ndhil (foralli D_1) (ug H_1)
             $\leftarrow$ ($\Pi a{:}\mathrm{i}.\;\mathrm{ndhil}\;(D_1\;a)\;(H_1\;a)$).

$\hfill\square$

In summary, we can represent some aspects of constructive meta-theoretic proofs as higher-level judgments in LF. These higher-level judgments can be executed in Elf with the operational semantics from Section 4.4 to translate derivations between deductive systems. While the result of each individual computation of this form is guaranteed to be correct, the higher-level judgment is only partially verified since termination and coverage of all possible cases are properties outside the scope of the type-checker.

6. Appendix: the simply-typed λ-calculus

For the representation of the abstract syntax of a language, the simply-typed λ-calculus ($\lambda^{\rightarrow}$) is usually adequate. When we tackle the task of representing inference rules, we will have to refine the type system by adding dependent types. The reader should bear in mind that $\lambda^{\rightarrow}$ should *not* be considered as a functional programming language, but as a representation language. In particular, the absence of recursion will be crucial in order to guarantee adequacy of representations. Our formulation of the simply-typed λ-calculus has two levels: the level of *types* and the level of *objects*, where types classify objects. Furthermore, we have *signatures* which declare type and object constants, and *contexts* which assign types to variables. The presentation is in the style of Church: Every valid object has a unique type. This requires that types appear in the syntax of objects to resolve the inherent ambiguity of certain functions such as the identity function. We let a range over type constants, c over object constants, x over variables.

$$
\begin{array}{llll}
\text{Types} & A & ::= & a \mid A_1 \rightarrow A_2 \\
\text{Objects} & M & ::= & c \mid x \mid \lambda x{:}A.\, M \mid M_1\, M_2 \\[4pt]
\text{Signatures} & \Sigma & ::= & \cdot \mid \Sigma, a{:}\text{type} \mid \Sigma, c{:}A \\
\text{Contexts} & \Gamma & ::= & \cdot \mid \Gamma, x{:}A
\end{array}
$$

We make the general restriction that constants and variables can occur at most once in a signature or context, respectively. We use A and B to range over types, and M and N to range over objects. We refer to type constants a as *atomic types* and types of the form $A \rightarrow B$ as *function types*. We also consider terms that differ only in the names of their bound variables as identical and use the variable convention as for first-order logic in Section 2.

The judgments defining $\lambda^{\rightarrow}$ are

$\vdash_\Sigma A : \text{type}$	A is a valid type
$\Gamma \vdash_\Sigma M : A$	M is a valid object of type A in context Γ
$\vdash_\Sigma \Gamma \; Ctx$	Γ is a valid context
$\vdash \Sigma \; Sig$	Σ is a valid signature

Note that the first three of these judgments depend on a signature Σ which we presuppose to be valid. Similarly, we assume that Γ is always valid in the judgment $\Gamma \vdash_\Sigma M : A$. The judgments are defined via the following inference rules.

Valid objects

$$
\frac{c{:}A \text{ in } \Sigma}{\Gamma \vdash_\Sigma c : A}\ \text{con} \qquad\qquad \frac{x{:}A \text{ in } \Gamma}{\Gamma \vdash_\Sigma x : A}\ \text{var}
$$

$$
\frac{\vdash_\Sigma A : \text{type} \qquad \Gamma, x{:}A \vdash_\Sigma M : B}{\Gamma \vdash_\Sigma \lambda x{:}A.\, M : A \rightarrow B}\ \text{lam}
$$

$$
\frac{\Gamma \vdash_\Sigma M : A \rightarrow B \qquad \Gamma \vdash_\Sigma N : A}{\Gamma \vdash_\Sigma M\, N : B}\ \text{app}
$$

Valid types

$$\frac{a\text{:type in } \Sigma}{\vdash_\Sigma a : \text{type}} \text{ con} \qquad \frac{\vdash_\Sigma A : \text{type} \qquad \vdash_\Sigma B : \text{type}}{\vdash_\Sigma A \to B : \text{type}} \text{ arrow}$$

Valid signatures

$$\frac{}{\vdash \cdot \; Sig} \text{ sigemp} \qquad \frac{\vdash \Sigma \; Sig}{\vdash \Sigma, a\text{:type} \; Sig} \text{ sigtyp}$$

$$\frac{\vdash \Sigma \; Sig \qquad \vdash_\Sigma A : \text{type}}{\vdash \Sigma, c\text{:}A \; Sig} \text{ sigobj}$$

Valid contexts

$$\frac{}{\vdash_\Sigma \cdot \; Ctx} \text{ ctxemp} \qquad \frac{\vdash_\Sigma \Gamma \; Ctx \qquad \vdash_\Sigma A : \text{type}}{\vdash_\Sigma \Gamma, x\text{:}A \; Ctx} \text{ ctxobj}$$

The rules for valid objects are somewhat non-standard in that they contain no check whether the signature Σ or the context Γ are valid, which we presuppose. Furthermore, the rules guarantee that if we have a derivation $\mathcal{D}$ of $\Gamma \vdash_\Sigma M : A$ and Γ is valid, then every context appearing in $\mathcal{D}$ is also valid. This is because the type A in the lam rule is checked for validity as it is added to the context.

Our formulation of the simply-typed λ-calculus above is parametrized by a signature in which new constants can be declared; only variables, λ-abstraction, and application are built into the language itself. The analogue of *observable values* in functional programming languages is the notion of *canonical form*, since they are in one-one correspondence with the data we are trying to represent. Unlike in functional languages, every well-typed object will have an equivalent canonical form which can be calculated with a simple algorithm. For the definition of canonical forms as a deductive system we need two mutually recursive judgments: canonical and atomic forms. For the sake of brevity, we elide the fixed signature Σ from this judgment.

$$\Gamma \vdash M \Uparrow A \qquad \text{object } M \text{ is canonical of type } A$$
$$\Gamma \vdash M \Downarrow A \qquad \text{object } M \text{ is atomic of type } A$$

An atomic form is a variable or constant applied to some number of arguments, each of which is in canonical form. A canonical form of functional type must be a λ-abstraction; a canonical form of atomic type a must itself be atomic. This is captured with the following inference rules.

$$\frac{\Gamma, x{:}A \vdash M \Uparrow B}{\Gamma \vdash \lambda x{:}A.\, M \Uparrow A \to B} \text{ arrow} \qquad \frac{\Gamma \vdash M \downarrow a}{\Gamma \vdash M \Uparrow a} \text{ coerce}$$

$$\frac{x{:}A \text{ in } \Gamma}{\Gamma \vdash x \downarrow A} \text{ var} \qquad \frac{c{:}A \text{ in } \Sigma}{\Gamma \vdash c \downarrow A} \text{ con}$$

$$\frac{\Gamma \vdash M \downarrow B \to A \qquad \Gamma \vdash N \Uparrow B}{\Gamma \vdash M N \downarrow A} \text{ app}$$

The algorithm for conversion to canonical and atomic forms introduces λ-abstractions if the object is of functional type, essentially applying η-expansion. At base type we check if the object has the form of a variable or constant applied to some arguments. If so, we convert the arguments to canonical form. If not, we repeatedly apply weak head reduction until the other case applies. This method of definition of a typed λ-calculus corresponds to an operational semantics for a functional language and is very much in the spirit of the method of algorithmic definition for type theories [de Bruijn 1993]. Related systems have been described in [Felty and Miller 1990, Coquand 1991]. The algorithm is given as a deductive system consisting of three judgments which may be interpreted as a logic program.

$$M \xrightarrow{whr} M' \qquad M \text{ weak head reduces to } M'$$
$$\Gamma \vdash M \Uparrow M' : A \qquad M \text{ converts to canonical form } M' \text{ at type } A$$
$$\Gamma \vdash M \downarrow M' : A \qquad M \text{ converts to atomic form } M' \text{ at type } A$$

First, the rules for weak head reduction. We write $[N/x]M$ for the result of substituting N for x in M, possibly renaming bound variables to avoid variable capture.

$$\frac{}{(\lambda x{:}A.\, M)\, N \xrightarrow{whr} [N/x]M} \text{ whr\_beta} \qquad \frac{M \xrightarrow{whr} M'}{M N \xrightarrow{whr} M' N} \text{ whr\_app}$$

The rules for conversion to canonical and atomic form mutually depend on each other. Note how the rules for canonical form are type-directed, while the rules for atomic form are object-directed.

$$\frac{\Gamma, x{:}A \vdash M\, x \Uparrow M' : B}{\Gamma \vdash M \Uparrow (\lambda x{:}A.\, M') : A \to B} \text{ arrow}$$

$$\frac{M \xrightarrow{whr} M' \qquad \Gamma \vdash M' \Uparrow M'' : a}{\Gamma \vdash M \Uparrow M'' : a} \text{ whr}$$

$$\frac{\Gamma \vdash M \downarrow M' : a}{\Gamma \vdash M \Uparrow M' : a} \text{ coerce} \qquad \frac{x{:}A \text{ in } \Gamma}{\Gamma \vdash x \downarrow x : A} \text{ var} \qquad \frac{c{:}A \text{ in } \Sigma}{\Gamma \vdash c \downarrow c : A} \text{ con}$$

$$\frac{\Gamma \vdash M \downarrow M' : A \to B \qquad \Gamma \vdash N \Uparrow N' : A}{\Gamma \vdash M\,N \downarrow M'\,N' : B} \text{ app}$$

The following properties of the simply-typed λ-calculus follow easily from known results for more conventional representations. The last is the most difficult and can be established rather elegantly using logical relations [Pfenning 2001].

6.1. THEOREM (Properties of $\lambda^{\to}$).
1. *If $\Gamma \vdash M \Uparrow A$ then $\Gamma \vdash M : A$.*
2. *If $\Gamma \vdash M \downarrow A$ then $\Gamma \vdash M : A$.*
3. *If $\Gamma \vdash M \Uparrow M' : A$ then $\Gamma \vdash M' \Uparrow A$.*
4. *If $\Gamma \vdash M \downarrow M' : A$ then $\Gamma \vdash M' \downarrow A$.*
5. *If $\Gamma \vdash M : A$ then there exists a unique N such that $\Gamma \vdash M \Uparrow N : A$.*

Two objects M and M' are definitionally equal at type A (written as $\Gamma \vdash M \equiv M' : A$) if they have the same canonical form at type A. This coincides with a notion of definitional equality based on β- and η-conversions. In particular, β- and η-conversion are admissible rules of inference to determine definitional equality of objects. We may omit the context, signature, and type and just write $M \equiv M'$. Systems are often defined based on a notion of conversion, in which case the system above could be considered as specifying an algorithm for deciding equality. The next section provides an example of this kind.

7. Appendix: the dependently typed λ-calculus

The typing rules for LF can be found under the name λP in [Barendregt and Geuvers 2001] (Chapter 18 of this Handbook), except that the rule of type conversion for LF is based on $\beta\eta$-conversion rather than just β-conversion. Because $\beta\eta$-conversion is not confluent on ill-typed terms, the standard approach to proving theoretical properties does not work in the context of LF, even though it may be adapted with some effort [Geuvers 1992, Ghani 1997, Goguen 1999].

We prefer a formulation with typed equality judgments in the style of Martin-Löf [Harper 1988] as presented in a slightly richer framework [Coquand 1991]. We call the resulting type theory λ^Π. First we define its basic judgments, which include typing and definitional equality. Coquand [1991] proves the correctness of an untyped algorithm for conversion which demonstrates decidability of the judgments defining LF. From this one can conclude easily that canonical (that is, long $\beta\eta$-normal) forms exist and are unique, which is critical for the adequacy theorems throughout this chapter. An alternative proof using an erasure interpretation for dependencies is given by Harper and Pfenning [2000]. We give an inductive definition of canonical forms which can be used directly in adequacy proofs to establish a compositional bijection between canonical objects of λ^Π and expressions or deductions in an object logic. This part is analogous to the development for the simply-typed λ-calculus in the preceding section. We also have eliminated the non-dependent function type $A \to B$ since we can think of it as an abbreviation for $\Pi x{:}A.\,B$ where x does not occur in B.

λ^Π is predicative calculus with three levels: kinds, families, and objects. We also define signatures and contexts as they are needed for the judgments.

Kinds	K	$::=$	$\mathbf{type} \mid \Pi x{:}A.\,K$
Families	A	$::=$	$a \mid A\,M \mid \Pi x{:}A_1.\,A_2$
Objects	M	$::=$	$c \mid x \mid \lambda x{:}A.\,M \mid M_1\,M_2$
Signatures	Σ	$::=$	$\cdot \mid \Sigma, a{:}K \mid \Sigma, c{:}A$
Contexts	Γ	$::=$	$\cdot \mid \Gamma, x{:}A$

Besides the typed notion of equality, this language differs from the one given by Harper et al. [1993] in that we do not allow families to be formed by explicit abstraction. Since such families never occur in canonical forms, this does not lead to any loss in expressive power. Unlike in $\lambda^\to$, we can no longer introduce typing independently of definitional equality, because of the rule of type conversion motivated in Section 3.4.

$\Gamma \vdash_\Sigma M : A$	M has type A
$\Gamma \vdash_\Sigma M \equiv M' : A$	M is definitionally equal to M' at type A
$\Gamma \vdash_\Sigma A : K$	A has kind K
$\Gamma \vdash_\Sigma A \equiv A' : K$	A is definitionally equal to A' at kind K
$\Gamma \vdash_\Sigma K : \mathsf{kind}$	K is a valid kind
$\Gamma \vdash_\Sigma K \equiv K' : \mathsf{kind}$	K is definitionally equal to K'
$\vdash \Sigma\ Sig$	Σ is a valid signature
$\vdash_\Sigma \Gamma\ Ctx$	Γ is a valid context

These judgment are defined by the rules given below. For the typing and equality judgments we presuppose that the signature Σ and the context Γ are valid, so we do not check this in the rules for variables and constants. Furthermore, we do not have an explicit rule for η-conversion, since it, together with a congruence rule for λ-abstraction, is equivalent to the extensionality rule eq_lam for functional equality.

Valid objects

$$\frac{\Gamma \vdash_\Sigma A : \mathsf{type} \qquad \Gamma, x{:}A \vdash_\Sigma M : B}{\Gamma \vdash_\Sigma \lambda x{:}A.\, M : \Pi x{:}A.\, B} \; \mathsf{lam}$$

$$\frac{\Gamma \vdash_\Sigma A : \mathsf{type} \qquad \Gamma, x{:}A \vdash_\Sigma M\, x \equiv M'\, x : B}{\Gamma \vdash_\Sigma M \equiv M' : \Pi x{:}A.\, B} \; \mathsf{eq\_lam}$$

$$\frac{c{:}A \text{ in } \Sigma}{\Gamma \vdash_\Sigma c : A} \; \mathsf{con} \qquad \frac{x{:}A \text{ in } \Gamma}{\Gamma \vdash_\Sigma x : A} \; \mathsf{var}$$

$$\frac{\Gamma \vdash_\Sigma M : \Pi x{:}A.\, B \qquad \Gamma \vdash_\Sigma N : A}{\Gamma \vdash_\Sigma M\, N : [N/x]B} \; \mathsf{app}$$

$$\frac{\Gamma \vdash_\Sigma M \equiv M' : \Pi x{:}A.\, B \qquad \Gamma \vdash_\Sigma N \equiv N' : A}{\Gamma \vdash_\Sigma M\, N \equiv M'\, N' : [N/x]B} \; \mathsf{eq\_app}$$

$$\frac{\Gamma, x{:}A \vdash_\Sigma M : B \qquad \Gamma \vdash_\Sigma N : A}{\Gamma \vdash_\Sigma (\lambda x{:}A.\, M)\, N \equiv [N/x]M : [N/x]B} \; \mathsf{beta}$$

Valid types

$$\frac{\Gamma \vdash_\Sigma A : \mathsf{type} \qquad \Gamma, x{:}A \vdash_\Sigma B : \mathsf{type}}{\Gamma \vdash_\Sigma \Pi x{:}A.\, B : \mathsf{type}} \; \mathsf{pi}$$

$$\frac{\Gamma \vdash_\Sigma A \equiv A' : \mathsf{type} \qquad \Gamma, x{:}A \vdash_\Sigma B \equiv B' : \mathsf{type}}{\Gamma \vdash_\Sigma \Pi x{:}A.\, B \equiv \Pi x{:}A'.\, B' : \mathsf{type}} \; \mathsf{eq\_pi}$$

$$\frac{a{:}K \text{ in } \Sigma}{\Gamma \vdash_\Sigma a : K} \; \mathsf{con}$$

$$\frac{\Gamma \vdash_\Sigma A : \Pi x{:}B.\, K \qquad \Gamma \vdash_\Sigma M : B}{\Gamma \vdash_\Sigma A\, M : [M/x]K} \; \mathsf{app}$$

$$\frac{\Gamma \vdash_\Sigma A \equiv A' : \Pi x{:}B.\, K \qquad \Gamma \vdash_\Sigma M \equiv M' : B}{\Gamma \vdash_\Sigma A\, M \equiv A'\, M' : [M/x]K} \; \mathsf{eq\_app}$$

Valid kinds

$$\frac{}{\Gamma \vdash_\Sigma \mathsf{type} : \mathsf{kind}} \text{ type}$$

$$\frac{\Gamma \vdash_\Sigma A : \mathsf{type} \qquad \Gamma, x{:}A \vdash_\Sigma K : \mathsf{kind}}{\Gamma \vdash_\Sigma \Pi x{:}A.\,K : \mathsf{kind}} \text{ pi}$$

$$\frac{\Gamma \vdash_\Sigma A \equiv A' : \mathsf{type} \qquad \Gamma, x{:}A \vdash_\Sigma K \equiv K' : \mathsf{kind}}{\Gamma \vdash_\Sigma \Pi x{:}A.\,K \equiv \Pi x{:}A'.\,K' : \mathsf{kind}} \text{ eq\_pi}$$

Equality rules. We present the equality rules for all three levels in abbreviated form, where U, V, and W range over objects, types, kinds, or the symbol kind as appropriate for the equality judgments shown above.

$$\frac{\Gamma \vdash_\Sigma U : V}{\Gamma \vdash_\Sigma U \equiv U : V} \text{ refl} \qquad \frac{\Gamma \vdash_\Sigma U_1 \equiv U_2 : V}{\Gamma \vdash_\Sigma U_2 \equiv U_1 : V} \text{ sym}$$

$$\frac{\Gamma \vdash_\Sigma U_1 \equiv U_2 : V \qquad \Gamma \vdash_\Sigma U_2 \equiv U_3 : V}{\Gamma \vdash_\Sigma U_1 \equiv U_3 : V} \text{ trans}$$

$$\frac{\Gamma \vdash_\Sigma U : V \qquad \Gamma \vdash_\Sigma V \equiv V' : W}{\Gamma \vdash_\Sigma U : V'} \text{ conv}$$

$$\frac{\Gamma \vdash_\Sigma U_1 \equiv U_2 : V \qquad \Gamma \vdash_\Sigma V \equiv V' : W}{\Gamma \vdash_\Sigma U_1 \equiv U_2 : V'} \text{ eq\_conv}$$

Valid signatures

$$\frac{}{\vdash \cdot \; Sig} \text{ sigemp} \qquad \frac{\vdash \Sigma \; Sig \qquad \vdash_\Sigma K : \mathsf{kind}}{\vdash \Sigma, a{:}K \; Sig} \text{ sigfam}$$

$$\frac{\vdash \Sigma \; Sig \qquad \vdash_\Sigma A : \mathsf{type}}{\vdash \Sigma, c{:}A \; Sig} \text{ sigobj}$$

Valid contexts

$$\frac{}{\vdash_\Sigma \cdot \; Ctx} \text{ ctxemp} \qquad \frac{\vdash_\Sigma \Gamma \; Ctx \qquad \Gamma \vdash_\Sigma A : \mathsf{type}}{\vdash_\Sigma \Gamma, x{:}A \; Ctx} \text{ ctxobj}$$

We can obtain the decidability of the judgments constituting this formulation of LF via a sequence of lemmas culminating in an argument via Kripke-logical relations and an untyped algorithm for testing equality as given by Coquand [1991]. The version of this theorem for β-conversion only (where the eq_lam rule is replaced by a congruence rule for λ-abstraction) is due to Harper et al. [1993].

7.1. THEOREM (Properties of LF).

1. If $\Gamma_1, x{:}A, y{:}B, \Gamma_2 \vdash_\Sigma M : C$ and $\Gamma_1 \vdash_\Sigma B :$ type then $\Gamma_1, y{:}B, x{:}A, \Gamma_2 \vdash_\Sigma M : C$.

2. If $\Gamma \vdash_\Sigma M : C$ and $\Gamma \vdash_\Sigma A :$ type then $\Gamma, x{:}A \vdash_\Sigma M : C$.

3. If $\Gamma_1, x{:}A, \Gamma_2 \vdash_\Sigma M : C$ and $\Gamma_1 \vdash_\Sigma N : A$
   then $\Gamma_1, [N/x]\Gamma_2 \vdash_\Sigma [N/x]M : [N/x]C$.

4. All judgments defining the λ^Π type theory are decidable.

We single out the properties of exchange, weakening, and substitution, since they are at the core of the judgments-as-types representation technique. Note that contraction is a simple consequence of substitution in our formulation. Parametric and hypothetical judgments can be implemented as functions in λ^Π because these properties match the properties of hypotheses. Logics such as linear logic in which assumptions do not satisfy these properties must be represented with different techniques. This has led, for example, to the development of the linear logical framework [Cervesato and Pfenning 1996] which provides more control over properties of assumptions.

We continue by presenting the notions of canonical and atomic form as a judgment, generalizing the analogous judgments from the simply-typed λ-calculus in Section 6.

$\Gamma \vdash_\Sigma M \Uparrow A$	M is canonical of type A
$\Gamma \vdash_\Sigma M \downarrow A$	M is atomic of type A
$\Gamma \vdash_\Sigma A \Uparrow K$	A is canonical of kind K
$\Gamma \vdash_\Sigma A \downarrow K$	A is atomic of kind K

These judgments are defined via the following inference rules. We use P for a *base type*, that is, one which has the form $a\,M_1 \ldots M_n$ rather than $\Pi x{:}A.\,B$.

Canonical objects

$$\frac{\Gamma \vdash_\Sigma A \Uparrow \text{type} \qquad \Gamma, x{:}A \vdash_\Sigma M \Uparrow B \qquad \Gamma \vdash_\Sigma A \equiv A' : \text{type}}{\Gamma \vdash_\Sigma \lambda x{:}A.\,M \Uparrow \Pi x{:}A'.\,B} \; \text{pi}$$

$$\frac{\Gamma \vdash_\Sigma M \downarrow P \qquad \Gamma \vdash_\Sigma P \equiv P' : \text{type}}{\Gamma \vdash_\Sigma M \Uparrow P'} \; \text{coerce}$$

Atomic objects

$$\frac{c{:}A \text{ in } \Sigma}{\Gamma \vdash_\Sigma c \downarrow A} \text{ con} \qquad \frac{x{:}A \text{ in } \Gamma}{\Gamma \vdash_\Sigma x \downarrow A} \text{ var}$$

$$\frac{\Gamma \vdash_\Sigma M \downarrow \Pi x{:}A.\, B \qquad \Gamma \vdash_\Sigma N \Uparrow A}{\Gamma \vdash_\Sigma M\, N \downarrow [N/x]B} \text{ atmapp}$$

Canonical types

$$\frac{\Gamma \vdash_\Sigma A \Uparrow \text{type} \qquad \Gamma, x{:}A \vdash_\Sigma B \Uparrow \text{type}}{\Gamma \vdash_\Sigma \Pi x{:}A.\, B \Uparrow \text{type}} \text{ pi}$$

$$\frac{\Gamma \vdash_\Sigma P \downarrow \text{type}}{\Gamma \vdash_\Sigma P \Uparrow \text{type}} \text{ coerce}$$

Atomic types

$$\frac{a{:}K \text{ in } \Sigma}{\Gamma \vdash_\Sigma a \downarrow K} \text{ con}$$

$$\frac{\Gamma \vdash_\Sigma A \downarrow \Pi x{:}B.\, K \qquad \Gamma \vdash_\Sigma M \Uparrow B}{\Gamma \vdash_\Sigma A\, M \downarrow [M/x]K} \text{ app}$$

It is easy to see that canonical forms are well-typed.

7.2. THEOREM (Properties of canonical forms).
1. *If* $\Gamma \vdash_\Sigma M \Uparrow A$ *then* $\Gamma \vdash_\Sigma M : A$.
2. *If* $\Gamma \vdash_\Sigma M \downarrow A$ *then* $\Gamma \vdash_\Sigma M : A$.
3. *If* $\Gamma \vdash_\Sigma A \Uparrow K$ *then* $\Gamma \vdash_\Sigma A : K$.
4. *If* $\Gamma \vdash_\Sigma A \downarrow K$ *then* $\Gamma \vdash_\Sigma A : K$.

PROOF. By straightforward induction on the structure of the canonical and atomic forms. □

Finally we come to algorithms for conversion to canonical form. They are designed so that two terms are definitionally equal if they have the same canonical form.

$$M \xrightarrow{whr} M' \qquad\qquad M \text{ weak head reduces to } M'$$

$$\Gamma \vdash_\Sigma M \Uparrow M' : A \qquad M \text{ has canonical form } M' \text{ at type } A$$

$$\Gamma \vdash_\Sigma M \downarrow M' : A' \qquad M \text{ has atomic form } M' \text{ at type } A'$$

$$\Gamma \vdash_\Sigma A \Uparrow A' : K \qquad A \text{ has canonical form } A' \text{ at kind } K$$

$$\Gamma \vdash_\Sigma A \downarrow A' : K' \qquad A \text{ has atomic form } A' \text{ at kind } K'$$

To read these judgments as algorithms we apply the logic programming interpretation of these rules for the bottom-up construction of a derivation. In weak head reduction we assume that M is given and M' is constructed. In the judgments for conversion to canonical form we assume that Σ, Γ, M, A, and K are given while we construct M' and A'. In the judgments for atomic forms we assume Σ, Γ, M, and A to be given and construct M', A' and K'.

Weak head reduction

$$\frac{}{(\lambda x{:}A.\, M)\, N \overset{whr}{\longrightarrow} [N/x]M} \; \text{whr\_beta}$$

$$\frac{M \overset{whr}{\longrightarrow} M'}{M\, N \overset{whr}{\longrightarrow} M'\, N} \; \text{whr\_app}$$

Conversion to canonical objects

$$\frac{\Gamma \vdash_\Sigma A \Uparrow A' : \text{type} \qquad \Gamma, x{:}A' \vdash_\Sigma M\, x \Uparrow M' : B}{\Gamma \vdash_\Sigma M \Uparrow \lambda x{:}A'.\, M' : \Pi x{:}A.\, B} \; \text{pi}$$

$$\frac{\Gamma \vdash_\Sigma M \downarrow M' : P \qquad \Gamma \vdash_\Sigma P \equiv P'}{\Gamma \vdash_\Sigma M \Uparrow M' : P'} \; \text{atm}$$

$$\frac{M \overset{whr}{\longrightarrow} M' \qquad \Gamma \vdash_\Sigma M' \Uparrow M'' : P}{\Gamma \vdash_\Sigma M \Uparrow M'' : P} \; \text{whr}$$

Conversion to atomic objects

$$\frac{c{:}A \text{ in } \Sigma}{\Gamma \vdash_\Sigma c \downarrow c : A} \; \text{con} \qquad \frac{x{:}A \text{ in } \Gamma}{\Gamma \vdash_\Sigma x \downarrow x : A} \; \text{var}$$

$$\frac{\Gamma \vdash_\Sigma M \downarrow M' : \Pi x{:}A.\, B \qquad \Gamma \vdash_\Sigma N \Uparrow N' : A}{\Gamma \vdash_\Sigma M\, N \downarrow M'\, N' : [M'/x]B} \; \text{app}$$

Conversion to canonical types

$$\frac{\Gamma \vdash_\Sigma A \Uparrow A' : \text{type} \qquad \Gamma, x{:}A' \vdash_\Sigma B \Uparrow B' : \text{type}}{\Gamma \vdash_\Sigma \Pi x{:}A.\, B \Uparrow \Pi x{:}A'.\, B' : \text{type}} \; \text{pi}$$

$$\frac{\Gamma \vdash_\Sigma P \downarrow P' : \text{type}}{\Gamma \vdash_\Sigma P \Uparrow P' : \text{type}} \; \text{atm}$$

Conversion to atomic types

$$\frac{a{:}K \text{ in } \Sigma}{\Gamma \vdash_\Sigma a \downarrow a : K} \text{ con}$$

$$\frac{\Gamma \vdash_\Sigma A \downarrow A' : \Pi x{:}B.\, K \qquad \Gamma \vdash_\Sigma M \Uparrow M' : B}{\Gamma \vdash_\Sigma A\, M \downarrow A'\, M' : [M'/x]K} \text{ app}$$

We show only the relevant properties for canonical forms on objects—atomic forms, types, and kinds satisfy similar properties.

7.3. THEOREM (Convertibility).

1. *If* $\Gamma \vdash_\Sigma M \Uparrow M' : A$ *then* $\Gamma \vdash_\Sigma M' \Uparrow A$.
2. *If* $\Gamma \vdash_\Sigma M \Uparrow M' : A$ *then* $\Gamma \vdash_\Sigma M \equiv M' : A$.
3. *If* $\Gamma \vdash_\Sigma M : A$ *then there is a unique* M' *such that* $\Gamma \vdash_\Sigma M \Uparrow M' : A$.
4. $\Gamma \vdash_\Sigma M \equiv M' : A$ *iff* $\Gamma \vdash_\Sigma M \Uparrow N : A$ *and* $\Gamma \vdash_\Sigma M' \Uparrow N : A$ *for some* N.

PROOF. The first two properties follow by simple structural inductions. The last two follow from Coquand's algorithm [Coquand 1991] by additional η-expansions. Related proofs are given by Harper and Pfenning [2000] and Virga [1999].   □

8. Conclusion

We have provided an introduction to the techniques of logical frameworks with an emphasis on LF which is based on the dependently typed λ-calculus λ^Π. We now summarize the basic choices that arise in the design of logical frameworks.

Equational vs. deductive encodings. Logical frameworks based on rewriting logic [Martì-Oliet and Meseguer 1993] (variations of which are implemented in Maude [*Maude* 1999] and ELAN [*ELAN* 1998, Kirchner et al. 1993, Haberstrau 1994, Borovanský et al. 1998]) are based on equational reasoning, rewriting, and constraints, while others discussed in this chapter (LF, hereditary Harrop formulas, FS_0, ALF) are based on deductive reasoning. It is clear that each approach can be simulated in the other, but usually with some loss of clarity, efficiency and elegance for certain classes of applications. Rewriting logic, for example, deals particularly well with concurrency, while it does not seem well suited for situations where deductions themselves need to be reified in the meta-language. First steps for combining ideas from these classes of frameworks are the rewriting mechanisms in Isabelle [Nipkow 1989] and the study of term rewriting in higher-order languages with dependent types [Virga 1996, Virga 1999]. For more on rewriting logic and its use as a logical framework, see [Meseguer 1998, Kirchner and Kirchner 1998]. The semantic origin of this work is *institutions* [Goguen and Burstall 1992]; a connection is made by Meseguer [1987].

Strong vs. weak frameworks. De Bruijn, the founder of the field of logical frameworks, argues in [de Bruijn 1991a] that logical frameworks should be foundationally uncommitted and as weak as possible. This allows simple proofs of adequacy for encodings, efficient checking of the correctness of derivations, and allows effective algorithms for unification and proof search in the framework which are otherwise difficult to design (for example, in the presence of iterated inductive definitions). This is also important if we use explicit proofs as a means to increase confidence in the results of a theorem prover: the simpler the logical framework, the more trusted its implementation is likely to be. While most frameworks are based on weak fragments of intuitionistic logic or type theory, *labelled deductive systems* as proposed by Gabbay [1994, 1996] are a notable exception. They are based essentially on classical, first-order logic where deductions are restricted through the use of labels endowed with an equational theory. Proof search can proceed, for example, by classical resolution techniques. For more on this approach, see [Ohlbach et al. 2001] (Chapter 21 of this Handbook). This encoding is well-suited for modal logics, but it appears less immediately applicable to other deductive systems, especially those arising in the theory of programming languages.

Inductive representations vs. higher-order abstract syntax. This is related to the previous question. Inductive representations of logics are supported in FS_0 [Feferman 1988] and ALF [Magnusson and Nordström 1994] and many logics not explicitly designed as logical frameworks such as Nuprl [Basin and Constable 1993], LEGO [Pollack 1994], Coq [Dowek, Felty, Herbelin, Huet, Murthy, Parent, Paulin-Mohring and Werner 1993], and Isabelle/HOL [Paulson 1993]. They allow a formal development of the meta-theory of the deductive system in question, but the encodings are less direct than for frameworks employing higher-order abstract syntax and functional representations of hypothetical derivations. These are the foundation of LF (underlying Elf) and hereditary Harrop formulas (underlying λProlog and Isabelle). Present work on combining advantages of both either employ reflection [Despeyroux et al. 1997, Leleu 1998] or formal meta-reasoning about the logical framework itself [McDowell and Miller 1997, Schürmann and Pfenning 1998, Schürmann 2000].

Logical vs. type-theoretic meta-languages. A logical meta-language such as one based on hereditary Harrop formulas encodes judgments as propositions. Search for a derivation in an object logic is reduced to proof search in the meta-logic. In addition, type-theoretical meta-languages such as LF offer a representation for derivations as objects. Checking the correctness of a derivation is reduced to type-checking in the meta-language. This is a decidable property that enables the use of a logical framework for applications such as proof-carrying code, where an explicit representation for deductions is required (see Section 8.2).

Functional vs. logical meta-programming. ML has originally been designed as a meta-language to program theorem provers for complex logics. It is still used in this capacity in many theorem proving environments and logical frameworks, including Isabelle. The strategy language of ELAN is similar, but has rich primitives for non-deterministic search which have to be programmed in ML, a sequential language. The functional meta-language approach has the disadvantage that the programmer must deal with many languages: the object logic, the logical framework, and the implementation language of the logical framework. A more uniform approach is to directly give an operational semantics to the logical framework in the spirit of abstract logic programming [Miller et al. 1991]. This makes it quite easy to program algorithms, but this approach has some drawbacks when it comes to user interaction.

8.1. Framework extensions

Logical framework languages are judged along many dimensions, as the discussions above indicate. Three of the most important concerns are how directly object languages may be encoded, how easy it is to prove the adequacies of these encodings, and how simple the proof checker for a logical framework can be. A great deal of practical experience has been accumulated, for example, through the use of λProlog, Isabelle, and Elf. These experiments have also identified certain shortcomings in the logical frameworks, some of them have even led to explicit negative results [Gardner 1992]. We briefly summarize some of the current research on refining or extending logical frameworks. Any proposed extension must carefully weigh the benefits for classes of applications against the complications it introduces into the meta-theory.

Substructural extensions. Frameworks such as hereditary Harrop formulas or LF can encode linear and other substructural logics [Girard 1987], but their encodings are not as direct as one might hope. The reason is that linear assumptions (each of which must be used exactly once) can not be modeled as hypotheses in the meta-language (which satisfy weakening and contraction). For similar reasons, the store in the encoding of an imperative programming language cannot be modeled via hypotheses on the values of the cells in the store. The linear frameworks Forum and linear LF have been designed to overcome these limitations. Forum [Miller 1994] is based on classical linear logic and extends hereditary Harrop formulas. Chirimar [1995] shows how to apply Forum to the theory of imperative programming languages. Linear LF [Cervesato and Pfenning 1997] is a conservative extension of LF with linear hypotheses. The desirable properties of LF are retained when the new connectives are restricted to linear implication, additive conjunction, and additive truth. Unlike Forum, the connectives are interpreted intuitionistically, which allows proof terms with decidable equality and type-checking relations to reify linear deductions and imperative computations. Applications to imperative programming can be found in [Cervesato 1996], applications to cut-elimination in both classical and intuitionistic sequent calculi are given in [Pfenning 1994b].

Subtyping. In many cases an object language or logic exhibits natural subtyping relationships. For example, deductions in normal form may be considered a subtype of arbitrary natural deductions. In the absence of subtyping, these can be coded either as explicit higher-level judgments or via explicit coercions, in both cases often significantly complicating the representation. In [Pfenning 1993], we have proposed an extension of LF to permit a simple and decidable subtyping judgment. Despite its relative simplicity it complicates unification and proof search [Kohlhase and Pfenning 1993] and the pragmatic consequences are unclear at present. Other approaches for general type theories have also been proposed recently [Aspinall and Compagnoni 1996], but their practicality in the context of logical frameworks is untested.

Polymorphism. Both Isabelle and λProlog allow polymorphism in the presentation of logics; in the case of Isabelle this includes sort restrictions on type variables. Like subtyping, polymorphism significantly complicates unification and proof search. Adequacy of encodings using higher-order abstract syntax is also more difficult to prove, since the notion of η-long form is more complex [Dowek, Huet and Werner 1993, Ghani 1997] and not preserved under substitution for type variables. On the other hand, polymorphism avoids code duplication—a similar effect might be achieved with module systems instead.

Module languages. The modular presentation of logical systems has always been considered important. For Automath, de Bruijn has proposed the notion of telescope [de Bruijn 1991*b*] as a modularity mechanism. For pure type systems [Barendregt 1992] (which include λ^{Π} as a subcalculus) Courant [1997, 1999] has described a general module calculus. The modular presentation of logics has been investigated in [Harper, Sannella and Tarlecki 1989*a*, Harper, Sannella and Tarlecki 1989*b*, Harper, Sannella and Tarlecki 1994] and cast in a concrete module language for Elf in [Harper and Pfenning 1998] following the ideas of signatures and functors in ML. Rewriting logic also explicitly supports logic morphisms within a flexible module language based on [Meseguer 1987]. The notion of theory in Isabelle provides another structuring mechanism [Nipkow 1993]. The module language for λProlog is more concerned with the operational semantics and search spaces while remaining based on solid logical foundations [Miller 1986, Miller 1989, Nadathur and Tong 1999].

8.2. Proof-carrying code

An important recent application of logical frameworks is the notion of *proof-carrying code* (PCC) [Necula 1997] and certifying compilation [Necula 1998, Necula and Lee 1998*a*]. Proof-carrying code is a safety infrastructure for mobile code and operating system extension. A code producer supplies not only a binary executable but also a proof of its safety according to some predetermined safety policy. This proof is expressed as an object in the LF logical framework, although other type-theoretic frameworks could be used as well. The code consumer downloads the binary and proof object and checks the safety proof against the binary. This is accomplished by generating a verification condition A from the binary in a single, linear sweep and then checking the proof object M against the verification condition by simple LF type-checking, $M : A$.

A safety policy is expressed by a verification condition generator and an LF signature which encodes the proof rules for verification conditions. Examples of such safety policies are type safety and memory safety, guaranteeing that a program will not access memory outside its address space [Necula 1998]. Another example is resource bounds in operating systems extensions such as packet filters [Necula and Lee 1996].

Since both the verification condition generator and the LF type-checker are relatively small (compared to compilers or theorem provers), the trusted computing base of this architecture is quite small. The use of a logical framework where deductions are reified as objects allows one single implementation to support multiple safety policies and proof rules, increasing trust in the reliability of the architecture, especially since the properties of LF are well understood and thoroughly investigated.

The realization of proof-carrying code raised some interesting directions for the development of logical frameworks. Here we consider two: how do we generate proof objects and how can we eliminate redundancy from LF objects to achieve compact encodings of proofs?

The generation of proof objects is the task of a *certifying compiler* which takes advantage of properties of the source language to generate annotations on the assembly code. In case of the Touchstone compiler [Necula 1998], this is a safe subset of C. The annotations guarantee that a specialized theorem prover has enough information to derive the verification condition for the binary. The specialized theorem prover maintains enough information to generate LF proof objects with respect to the axioms and inference rules available for the given safety policy. For type and memory safety, this has been shown to be practical, including a proof-generating version of the simplex algorithm described in [Necula 1998]. Thus, the theorem prover as a whole does not need to be trusted, since it generates derivations which can be verified independently.

The second question concerns the elimination of redundancy in the LF representation of derivations. A first proposal in this direction for the Elf logic programming language was made in [Michaylov and Pfenning 1992]. In PCC, the representation can be further optimized [Necula and Lee 1998b] since the main operation we are concerned with is type-checking, while Elf has to support unification and proof search. The principle, however is the same and goes back to the notion of strictness in functional languages. This has been analyzed by Pfenning and Schürmann [1998a].

8.3. Further reading

There have been numerous case studies and applications carried out with the aid of logical frameworks or generic theorem provers, too many to survey them here. The principal application areas lie in the theory of programming languages and logics, reasoning about specifications, programs, and protocols, and the formalization of mathematics. We refer the interested reader to [Pfenning 1996] for some further information on applications of logical frameworks. A survey with deeper coverage of modal logics and inductive definitions can be found in [Basin and Matthews 2000]. The textbook [Pfenning 2001] provides a gentler and more thorough introduction to the pragmatics of the LF logical framework and its use for the study of programming languages. The author also maintains a home page on logical frameworks [*Logical Frameworks* 1994] at http://www.cs.cmu.edu/~fp/lfs.html which is periodically updated, and which contains a more extensive bibliography and pointers to implementations, mailing lists, and related material.

Bibliography

ABEL A. [1999], A semantic analysis of structural recursion, Master's thesis, Ludwig-Maximilians-Universität München.

ALLEN S. F., CONSTABLE R. L., HOWE D. J. AND AITKEN W. E. [1990], The semantics of reflected proof, *in* 'Proceedings of the Fifth Annual Symposium on Logic in Computer Science (LICS'90)', IEEE Computer Society Press, pp. 95–105.

ALTENKIRCH T., GASPES V., NORDSTRÖM B. AND VON SYDOW B. [1994], *A User's Guide to ALF*, Chalmers University of Technology, Sweden.

ANDREOLI J.-M. [1992], 'Logic programming with focusing proofs in linear logic', *Journal of Logic and Computation* 2(3), 297–347.

ANDREWS P. [2001], Classical type theory, *in* A. Robinson and A. Voronkov, eds, 'Handbook of Automated Reasoning', Vol. II, Elsevier Science, chapter 15, pp. 965–1007.

ASPINALL D. AND COMPAGNONI A. [1996], Subtyping dependent types, *in* E. Clarke, ed., 'Proceedings of the 11th Annual Symposium on Logic in Computer Science', IEEE Computer Society Press, New Brunswick, New Jersey, pp. 86–97.

BARENDREGT H. AND GEUVERS H. [2001], Proof-assistants using dependent type systems, *in* A. Robinson and A. Voronkov, eds, 'Handbook of Automated Reasoning', Vol. II, Elsevier Science, chapter 18, pp. 1149–1238.

BARENDREGT H. P. [1980], *The Lambda-Calculus: Its Syntax and Semantics*, North-Holland.

BARENDREGT H. P. [1992], Lambda calculi with types, *in* S. Abramsky, D. Gabbay and T. Maibaum, eds, 'Handbook of Logic in Computer Science', Vol. 2, Oxford University Press, chapter 2, pp. 117–309.

BASIN D. A. AND CONSTABLE R. L. [1993], Metalogical frameworks, *in* G. Huet and G. Plotkin, eds, 'Logical Environments', Cambridge University Press, pp. 1–29.

BASIN D. AND MATTHEWS S. [1996], Structuring metatheory on inductive definitions, *in* M. McRobbie and J. Slaney, eds, 'Proceedings of the 13th International Conference on Automated Deduction (CADE-13)', Springer-Verlag LNAI 1104, New Brunswick, New Jersey, pp. 171–185.

BASIN D. AND MATTHEWS S. [2000], Logical frameworks, *in* D. Gabbay and F. Guenthner, eds, 'Handbook of Philosophical Logic', 2nd edn, Kluwer Academic Publishers. In preparation.

Basin D., Matthews S. and Viganò L. [1998], A modular presentation of modal logics in a logical framework, in 'The Tbilisi Symposium on Language, Logic and Computation: Selected Papers', CSLI Publications.

Borovanský P., Kirchner C., Kirchner H., Moreau P.-E. and Ringeissen C. [1998], An overview of ELAN, in C. Kirchner and H. Kirchner, eds, 'Proceedings of the International Workshop on Rewriting Logic and its Applications', Vol. 15 of *Electronic Notes in Theoretical Computer Science*, Elsevier Science, Pont-à-Mousson, France.
URL: *http://www.elsevier.com/locate/entcs/volume15.html*

Cervesato I. [1996], A Linear Logical Framework, PhD thesis, Dipartimento di Informatica, Università di Torino.

Cervesato I. and Pfenning F. [1996], A linear logical framework, in E. Clarke, ed., 'Proceedings of the Eleventh Annual Symposium on Logic in Computer Science', IEEE Computer Society Press, New Brunswick, New Jersey, pp. 264–275.

Cervesato I. and Pfenning F. [1997], Linear higher-order pre-unification, in G. Winskel, ed., 'Proceedings of the Twelfth Annual Sumposium on Logic in Computer Science (LICS'97)', IEEE Computer Society Press, Warsaw, Poland, pp. 422–433.

Chirimar J. L. [1995], Proof Theoretic Approach to Specification Languages, PhD thesis, University of Pennsylvania.

Church A. and Rosser J. [1936], 'Some properties of conversion', *Transactions of the American Mathematical Society* 39(3), 472–482.

Constable R. L. et al. [1986], *Implementing Mathematics with the Nuprl Proof Development System*, Prentice-Hall, Englewood Cliffs, New Jersey.

Coq [1999], Project home page. Version 6.2.3.
URL: *http://pauillac.inria.fr/coq/*

Coquand C. [1992], A proof of normalization for simply typed lambda calculus written in ALF, in 'Proceedings of the Workshop on Types for Proofs and Programs', Båstad, Sweden, pp. 85–92.

Coquand T. [1991], An algorithm for testing conversion in type theory, in G. Huet and G. Plotkin, eds, 'Logical Frameworks', Cambridge University Press, pp. 255–279.

Coquand T., Nordström B., Smith J. M. and von Sydow B. [1994], 'Type theory and programming', *Bulletin of the European Association for Theoretical Computer Science* 52, 203–228.

Coquand T. and Smith J. M. [1993], What is the status of pattern matching in type theory?, in 'Proceedings of the Workshop on Types for Proofs and Programs', Nijmegen, The Netherlands, pp. 91–94.

Courant J. [1997], A module calculus for pure type systems, in P. de Groote and R. Hindley, eds, 'Proceedings of the Third International Conference on Typed Lambda Calculus and Applications (TLCA'97)', Springer-Verlag LNCS, Nancy, France, pp. 112–128.

Courant J. [1999], MC: a modular calculus for Pure Type Systems, Rapport de Recherche 1217, CNRS Université Paris Sud.

Curry H. B. and Feys R. [1958], *Combinatory Logic*, North-Holland, Amsterdam.

de Bruijn N. [1968], The mathematical language AUTOMATH, its usage, and some of its extensions, in M. Laudet, ed., 'Proceedings of the Symposium on Automatic Demonstration', Springer-Verlag LNM 125, Versailles, France, pp. 29–61.

de Bruijn N. [1972], 'Lambda-calculus notation with nameless dummies: a tool for automatic formula manipulation with application to the Church-Rosser theorem', *Indag. Math.* 34(5), 381–392.

de Bruijn N. [1980], A survey of the project AUTOMATH, in J. Seldin and J. Hindley, eds, 'To H.B. Curry: Essays in Combinatory Logic, Lambda Calculus and Formalism', Academic Press, pp. 579–606.

de Bruijn N. [1991a], A plea for weaker frameworks, in G. Huet and G. Plotkin, eds, 'Logical Frameworks', Cambridge University Press, pp. 40–67.

DE BRUIJN N. [1991b], 'Telescopic mappings in typed lambda calculus', *Information and Computation* **91**(2), 189–204.

DE BRUIJN N. [1993], Algorithmic definition of lambda-typed lambda calculus, *in* G. Huet and G. Plotkin, eds, 'Logical Environment', Cambridge University Press, pp. 131–145.

DEGTYAREV A. AND VORONKOV A. [2001], The inverse method, *in* A. Robinson and A. Voronkov, eds, 'Handbook of Automated Reasoning', Vol. I, Elsevier Science, chapter 4, pp. 179–272.

DESPEYROUX J., FELTY A. AND HIRSCHOWITZ A. [1995], Higher-order abstract syntax in Coq, *in* M. Dezani-Ciancaglini and G. Plotkin, eds, 'Proceedings of the International Conference on Typed Lambda Calculi and Applications', Springer-Verlag LNCS 902, Edinburgh, Scotland, pp. 124–138.

DESPEYROUX J. AND HIRSCHOWITZ A. [1994], Higher-order abstract syntax with induction in Coq, *in* F. Pfenning, ed., 'Proceedings of the 5th International Conference on Logic Programming and Automated Reasoning', Springer-Verlag LNAI 822, Kiev, Ukraine, pp. 159–173.

DESPEYROUX J., PFENNING F. AND SCHÜRMANN C. [1997], Primitive recursion for higher-order abstract syntax, *in* R. Hindley, ed., 'Proceedings of the Third International Conference on Typed Lambda Calculus and Applications (TLCA'97)', Springer-Verlag LNCS 1210, Nancy, France, pp. 147–163. An extended version is available as Technical Report CMU-CS-96-172, Carnegie Mellon University.

DOWEK G. [1993], The undecidability of typability in the lambda-pi-calculus, *in* M. Bezem and J. Groote, eds, 'Proceedings of the International Conference on Typed Lambda Calculi and Applications', Springer-Verlag LNCS 664, Utrecht, The Netherlands, pp. 139–145.

DOWEK G. [2001], Higher-order unification and matching, *in* A. Robinson and A. Voronkov, eds, 'Handbook of Automated Reasoning', Vol. II, Elsevier Science, chapter 16, pp. 1009–1062.

DOWEK G., FELTY A., HERBELIN H., HUET G., MURTHY C., PARENT C., PAULIN-MOHRING C. AND WERNER B. [1993], The Coq proof assistant user's guide, Rapport Techniques 154, INRIA, Rocquencourt, France. Version 5.8.

DOWEK G., HARDIN T., KIRCHNER C. AND PFENNING F. [1996], Unification via explicit substitutions: The case of higher-order patterns, *in* M. Maher, ed., 'Proceedings of the Joint International Conference and Symposium on Logic Programming', MIT Press, Bonn, Germany, pp. 259–273.

DOWEK G., HUET G. AND WERNER B. [1993], On the definition of the eta-long normal form in type systems of the cube, *in* H. Geuvers, ed., 'Informal Proceedings of the Workshop on Types for Proofs and Programs', Nijmegen, The Netherlands.

DYCKHOFF R. AND PINTO L. [1994], Uniform proofs and natural deduction, *in* D. Galmiche and L. Wallen, eds, 'Proceedings of the Workshop on Proof Search in Type-Theoretic Languages', Nancy, France, pp. 17–23.

ELAN [1998], System home page. Version 3.3.
  URL: *http://www.loria.fr/ELAN*

ELLIOTT C. [1989], Higher-order unification with dependent types, *in* N. Dershowitz, ed., 'Rewriting Techniques and Applications', Springer-Verlag LNCS 355, Chapel Hill, North Carolina, pp. 121–136.

ELLIOTT C. M. [1990], Extensions and Applications of Higher-Order Unification, PhD thesis, School of Computer Science, Carnegie Mellon University. Available as Technical Report CMU-CS-90-134.

ERIKSSON L.-H. [1992], A finitary version of the calculus of partial inductive definitions, *in* L.-H. Eriksson, L. Hallnäs and P. Schroeder-Heister, eds, 'Proceedings of the Second International Workshop on Extensions of Logic Programming', Springer-Verlag LNAI 596, Stockholm, Sweden, pp. 89–134.

ERIKSSON L.-H. [1993a], Finitary Partial Inductive Definitions and General Logic, PhD thesis, Department of Computer and System Sciences, Royal Institute of Technology, Stockholm.

ERIKSSON L.-H. [1993b], Finitary partial inductive definitions as a general logic, *in* R. Dyckhoff, ed., 'Proceedings of the 4th International Workshop on Extensions of Logic Programming', Springer-Verlag LNAI 798.

ERIKSSON L.-H. [1994], Pi: An interactive derivation editor for the calculus of partial inductive definitions, *in* A. Bundy, ed., 'Proceedings of the 12th International Conference on Automated Deduction', Springer Verlag LNAI 814, Nancy, France, pp. 821–825.

FEFERMAN S. [1988], Finitary inductive systems, *in* R. Ferro, ed., 'Proceedings of Logic Colloquium '88', North-Holland, Padova, Italy, pp. 191–220.

FELTY A. [1989], Specifying and Implementing Theorem Provers in a Higher-Order Logic Programming Language, PhD thesis, University of Pennsylvania. Available as Technical Report MS-CIS-89-53.

FELTY A. [1993], 'Implementing tactics and tacticals in a higher-order logic programming language', *Journal of Automated Reasoning* **11**(1), 43–81.

FELTY A. AND MILLER D. [1988], Specifying theorem provers in a higher-order logic programming language, *in* E. Lusk and R. Overbeek, eds, 'Proceedings of the Ninth International Conference on Automated Deduction', Springer-Verlag LNCS 310, Argonne, Illinois, pp. 61–80.

FELTY A. AND MILLER D. [1990], Encoding a dependent-type λ-calculus in a logic programming language, *in* M. Stickel, ed., '10th International Conference on Automated Deduction', Springer-Verlag LNCS 449, Kaiserslautern, Germany, pp. 221–235.

FREGE G. [1879], *Begriffsschrift, eine der arithmetischen nachgebildete Formelsprache des reinen Denkens*, Verlag von Louis Nebert. English translation *Begriffsschrift, a formula language, modeled upon that of arithmatic, for pure thought* in J. van Heijenoort, editor, *From Frege to Gödel; A Source Book in Mathematical Logic, 1879–1931*, pp. 1–82, Harvard University Press, 1967.

GABBAY D. M. [1994], Classical vs non-classical logic, *in* D. Gabbay, C. Hogger and J. Robinson, eds, 'Handbook of Logic in Artificial Intelligence and Logic Programming', Vol. 2, Oxford University Press, chapter 2.6.

GABBAY D. M. [1996], *Labelled Deductive Systems*, Vol. 1, Oxford University Press.

GARDNER P. [1992], Representing Logics in Type Theory, PhD thesis, University of Edinburgh. Available as Technical Report CST-93-92.

GASPES V. AND SMITH J. M. [1992], Machine checked normalization proofs for typed combinator calculi, *in* 'Proceedings of the Workshop on Types for Proofs and Programs', Båstad, Sweden, pp. 177–192.

GENTZEN G. [1935], 'Untersuchungen über das logische Schließen', *Mathematische Zeitschrift* **39**, 176–210, 405–431. English translation *Investigations into logical deductions* in M. E. Szabo, editor, *The Collected Papers of Gerhard Gentzen*, pp. 68–131, North-Holland Publishing Co., 1969.

GEUVERS H. [1992], The Church-Rosser property for βη-reduction in typed λ-calculi, *in* A. Scedrov, ed., 'Seventh Annual IEEE Symposium on Logic in Computer Science', Santa Cruz, California, pp. 453–460.

GHANI N. [1997], Eta-expansions in dependent type theory — the calculus of constructions, *in* P. de Groote and J. Hindley, eds, 'Proceedings of the Third International Conference on Typed Lambda Calculus and Applications (TLCA'97)', Springer-Verlag LNCS 1210, Nancy, France, pp. 164–180.

GIRARD J.-Y. [1987], 'Linear logic', *Theoretical Computer Science* **50**, 1–102.

GIRARD J.-Y. [1993], 'On the unity of logic', *Annals of Pure and Applied Logic* **59**, 201–217.

GOGUEN H. [1999], Soundness of the logical framework for its typed operational semantics, *in* J.-Y. Girard, ed., 'Proceedings of the 4th International Conference on Typed Lambda Calculi and Applications (TLCA'99)', Springer-Verlag LNCS 1581, L'Aquila, Italy, pp. 177–197.

GOGUEN J. A. AND BURSTALL R. M. [1992], 'Institutions: Abstract model theory for specification and programming', *Journal of the ACM* **39**(1), 95–146.

GOLDFARB W. D. [1981], 'The undecidability of the second-order unification problem', *Theoretical Computer Science* **13**, 225–230.

GORDON M. J., MILNER R. AND WADSWORTH C. P. [1979], *Edinburgh LCF*, Springer-Verlag LNCS 78.

GORDON M. AND MELHAM T. [1993], *Introduction to HOL: A Theorem Proving Environment for Higher Order Logic*, Cambridge University Press.

HABERSTRAU M. [1994], ECOLOG: An environment for constraint logics, *in* J.-P. Jouannaud, ed., 'Proceedings of the First International Conference on Constraints in Computational Logics', Springer-Verlag LNCS 845, Munich, Germany, pp. 237–252.

HALLNÄS L. [1987], A note on the logic of a logic program, *in* 'Proceedings of the Workshop on Programming Logic', University of Göteborg and Chalmers University of Technology, Report PMG-R37.

HALLNÄS L. [1991], 'Partial inductive definitions', *Theoretical Computer Science* **87**(1), 115–142.

HANNAN J. [1993], 'Extended natural semantics', *Journal of Functional Programming* **3**(2), 123–152.

HANNAN J. J. [1991], Investigating a Proof-Theoretic Meta-Language for Functional Programs, PhD thesis, University of Pennsylvania. Available as Technical Report MS-CIS-91-09.

HARPER R. [1988], An equational formulation of LF, Technical Report ECS-LFCS-88-67, University of Edinburgh.

HARPER R., HONSELL F. AND PLOTKIN G. [1987], A framework for defining logics, *in* 'Symposium on Logic in Computer Science', IEEE Computer Society Press, pp. 194–204.

HARPER R., HONSELL F. AND PLOTKIN G. [1993], 'A framework for defining logics', *Journal of the Association for Computing Machinery* **40**(1), 143–184.

HARPER R. AND PFENNING F. [1998], 'A module system for a programming language based on the LF logical framework', *Journal of Logic and Computation* **8**(1), 5–31.

HARPER R. AND PFENNING F. [2000], On equivalence and canonical forms in the LF type theory, Technical Report CMU-CS-00-148, Department of Computer Science, Carnegie Mellon University.

HARPER R., SANNELLA D. AND TARLECKI A. [1989a], Logic representation, *in* D. Pitt, D. Rydeheard, P. Dybjer, A. Pitts and A. Poigneé, eds, 'Proceedings of the Workshop on Category Theory and Computer Science', Springer-Verlag LNCS 389, Manchester, UK, pp. 250–272.

HARPER R., SANNELLA D. AND TARLECKI A. [1989b], Structure and representation in LF, *in* 'Fourth Annual Symposium on Logic in Computer Science', IEEE Computer Society Press, Pacific Grove, California, pp. 226–237.

HARPER R., SANNELLA D. AND TARLECKI A. [1994], 'Structured presentations and logic representations', *Annals of Pure and Applied Logic* **67**, 113–160.

HAYASHI S. AND NAKANO H. [1988], *PX: A Computational Logic*, Foundations of Computing Series, MIT Press.

HILBERT D. AND BERNAYS P. [1934], *Grundlagen der Mathematik*, Springer-Verlag, Berlin.

HOWARD W. A. [1980], The formulae-as-types notion of construction, *in* J. P. Seldin and J. R. Hindley, eds, 'To H. B. Curry: Essays on Combinatory Logic, Lambda Calculus and Formalism', Academic Press, pp. 479–490. Hitherto unpublished note of 1969.

HUET G. [1973], 'The undecidability of unification in third order logic', *Information and Control* **22**(3), 257–267.

HUET G. [1975], 'A unification algorithm for typed λ-calculus', *Theoretical Computer Science* **1**, 27–57.

HUET G. AND LANG B. [1978], 'Proving and applying program transformations expressed with second-order patterns', *Acta Informatica* **11**, 31–55.

Isabelle [1998], System home page. Version 98-1.
   URL: *http://www.cl.cam.ac.uk/Research/HVG/Isabelle/*

JUTTING L. [1977], Checking Landau's "Grundlagen" in the AUTOMATH System, PhD thesis, Eindhoven University of Technology.

KAHN G. [1987], Natural semantics, *in* 'Proceedings of the Symposium on Theoretical Aspects of Computer Science', Springer-Verlag LNCS 247, pp. 22–39.

KIRCHNER, C. AND KIRCHNER, H., EDS [1998], *Proceedings of the International Workshop on Rewriting Logic and its Applications*, Vol. 15 of *Electronic Notes in Theoretical Computer Science*, Elsevier Science, Pont-à-Mousson, France.
  URL: *http://www.elsevier.com/locate/entcs/volume15.html*

KIRCHNER C., KIRCHNER H. AND VITTEK M. [1993], Implementing computational systems with constraints, *in* P. van Hentenryck and V. Saraswat, eds, 'Proceedings of the First Workshop on Principles and Practice of Constraints Programming', MIT Press, Newport, Rhode Island.

KOHLHASE M. AND PFENNING F. [1993], Unification in a λ-calculus with intersection types, *in* D. Miller, ed., 'Proceedings of the International Logic Programming Symposium', MIT Press, Vancouver, Canada, pp. 488–505.

LAMBEK J. AND SCOTT P. [1986], *Introduction to Higher-Order Categorical Logic*, Cambridge University Press.

LEGO [1998], System home page. Version 1.3.1.
  URL: *http://www.dcs.ed.ac.uk/home/lego*

LELEU P. [1998], Induction et Syntaxe Abstraite d'Ordre Supérieur dans les Théories Typées, PhD thesis, Ecole Nationale des Ponts et Chaussees, Marne-la-Vallee, France.

Logical Frameworks [1994], Home page. Includes bibliography and pointers to implementations. Last updated June 1997.
  URL: *http://www.cs.cmu.edu/˜fp/lfs.html*

LUO Z. AND POLLACK R. [1992], The LEGO proof development system: A user's manual, Technical Report ECS-LFCS-92-211, University of Edinburgh.

MAGNUSSON L. [1993], Refinement and local undo in the interactive proof editor ALF, *in* 'Proceedings of the Workshop on Types for Proofs and Programs', Nijmegen, The Netherlands, pp. 191–208.

MAGNUSSON L. [1995], The Implementation of ALF—A Proof Editor Based on Martin-Löf's Monomorphic Type Theory with Explicit Substitution, PhD thesis, Chalmers University of Technology and Göteborg University.

MAGNUSSON L. AND NORDSTRÖM B. [1994], The ALF proof editor and its proof engine, *in* H. Barendregt and T. Nipkow, eds, 'Types for Proofs and Programs', Springer-Verlag LNCS 806, pp. 213–237.

MARTÌ-OLIET N. AND MESEGUER J. [1993], Rewriting logic as a logical and semantical framework, Technical Report SRI-CSL-93-05, SRI International.

MARTIN-LÖF P. [1980], Constructive mathematics and computer programming, *in* 'Logic, Methodology and Philosophy of Science VI', North-Holland, pp. 153–175.

MARTIN-LÖF P. [1985a], On the meanings of the logical constants and the justifications of the logical laws, Technical Report 2, Scuola di Specializzazione in Logica Matematica, Dipartimento di Matematica, Università di Siena. Reprinted in the *Nordic Journal of Philosophical Logic*, 1(1), 11-60, 1996.

MARTIN-LÖF P. [1985b], Truth of a proposition, evidence of a judgement, validity of a proof. Notes to a talk given at the workshop *Theory of Meaning*, Centro Fiorentino di Storia e Filosofia della Scienza.

MATTHEWS S., SMAILL A. AND BASIN D. [1993], Experience with FS_0 as a framework theory, *in* G. Huet and G. Plotkin, eds, 'Logical Environments', Cambridge University Press, pp. 61–82.

Maude [1999], System home page. Version 1.00.
  URL: *http://maude.csl.sri.com*

MCDOWELL R. [1997], Reasoning in a Logic with Definitions and Induction, PhD thesis, University of Pennsylvania.

MCDOWELL R. AND MILLER D. [1997], A logic for reasoning with higher-order abstract syntax, *in* G. Winskel, ed., 'Proceedings of the Twelfth Annual Symposium on Logic in Computer Science', IEEE Computer Society Press, Warsaw, Poland, pp. 434–445.

MESEGUER J. [1987], General logics, *in* H.-D. Ebbinghaus, ed., 'Logic Colloquium '87', North-Holland, Granada, Spain, pp. 275–329.

MESEGUER, J., ED. [1998], *Proceedings of the First International Workshop on Rewriting Logic and its Applications*, Vol. 4 of *Electronic Notes in Theoretical Computer Science*, Elsevier Science, Pacific Grove, California.
URL: *http://www.elsevier.com/locate/entcs/volume4.html*

MICHAYLOV S. AND PFENNING F. [1991], Natural semantics and some of its meta-theory in Elf, *in* L.-H. Eriksson, L. Hallnäs and P. Schroeder-Heister, eds, 'Proceedings of the Second International Workshop on Extensions of Logic Programming', Springer-Verlag LNAI 596, Stockholm, Sweden, pp. 299–344.

MICHAYLOV S. AND PFENNING F. [1992], An empirical study of the runtime behavior of higher-order logic programs, *in* D. Miller, ed., 'Proceedings of the Workshop on λProlog Programming Language', University of Pennsylvania, Philadelphia, Pennsylvania, pp. 257–271. Available as Technical Report MS-CIS-92-86.

MICHAYLOV S. AND PFENNING F. [1993], Higher-order logic programming as constraint logic programming, *in* 'Position Papers for the First Workshop on Principles and Practice of Constraint Programming', Brown University, Newport, Rhode Island, pp. 221–229.

MILLER D. [1986], A theory of modules for logic programming, *in* R. M. Keller, ed., 'Third Annual IEEE Symposium on Logic Programming', Salt Lake City, Utah, pp. 106–114.

MILLER D. [1989], 'A logical analysis of modules in logic programming', *Journal of Logic Programming* 6(1-2), 79–108.

MILLER D. [1991], 'A logic programming language with lambda-abstraction, function variables, and simple unification', *Journal of Logic and Computation* 1(4), 497–536.

MILLER D. [1994], A multiple-conclusion meta-logic, *in* S. Abramsky, ed., 'Ninth Annual Symposium on Logic in Computer Science', IEEE Computer Society Press, Paris, France, pp. 272–281.

MILLER D., NADATHUR G., PFENNING F. AND SCEDROV A. [1991], 'Uniform proofs as a foundation for logic programming', *Annals of Pure and Applied Logic* 51, 125–157.

NADATHUR G. AND MILLER D. [1988], An overview of λProlog, *in* K. A. Bowen and R. A. Kowalski, eds, 'Fifth International Logic Programming Conference', MIT Press, Seattle, Washington, pp. 810–827.

NADATHUR G. AND MITCHELL D. J. [1999], System description: Teyjus—a compiler and abstract machine based implementation of lambda Prolog, *in* H. Ganzinger, ed., 'Proceedings of the 16th International Conference on Automated Deduction (CADE-16)', Springer-Verlag LNCS, Trento, Italy, pp. 287–291.

NADATHUR G. AND TONG G. [1999], 'Realizing modularity in lambdaProlog', *Journal of Functional and Logic Programming* 1999(9).

NECULA G. C. [1997], Proof-carrying code, *in* N. D. Jones, ed., 'Conference Record of the 24th Symposium on Principles of Programming Languages (POPL'97)', ACM Press, Paris, France, pp. 106–119.

NECULA G. C. [1998], Compiling with Proofs, PhD thesis, Carnegie Mellon University. Available as Technical Report CMU-CS-98-154.

NECULA G. C. AND LEE P. [1996], Safe kernel extensions without run-time checking, *in* 'Proceedings of the Second Symposium on Operating System Design and Implementation (OSDI'96)', Seattle, Washington, pp. 229–243.

NECULA G. C. AND LEE P. [1998a], The design and implementation of a certifying compiler, *in* K. D. Cooper, ed., 'Proceedings of the Conference on Programming Language Design and Implementation (PLDI'98)', ACM Press, Montreal, Canada, pp. 333–344.

NECULA G. C. AND LEE P. [1998b], Efficient representation and validation of logical proofs, *in* V. Pratt, ed., 'Proceedings of the 13th Annual Symposium on Logic in Computer Science (LICS'98)', IEEE Computer Society Press, Indianapolis, Indiana, pp. 93–104.

NEDERPELT, R., GEUVERS, J. AND DE VRIJER, R., EDS [1994], *Selected Papers on Automath*, Vol. 133 of *Studies in Logic and the Foundations of Mathematics*, North-Holland.

NIPKOW T. [1989], 'Equational reasoning in Isabelle', *Science of Computer Programming* **12**, 123–149.

NIPKOW T. [1993], Order-sorted polymorphism in Isabelle, *in* G. Huet and G. Plotkin, eds, 'Logical Environments', Cambridge University Press, pp. 164–188.

NIPKOW T. AND PAULSON L. C. [1992], Isabelle-91, *in* D. Kapur, ed., 'Proceedings of the 11th International Conference on Automated Deduction', Springer-Verlag LNAI 607, Saratoga Springs, NY, pp. 673–676. System abstract.

NORDSTRÖM B. [1993], The ALF proof editor, *in* 'Proceedings of the Workshop on Types for Proofs and Programs', Nijmegen, pp. 253–266.

NORDSTRÖM B., PETERSSON K. AND SMITH J. M. [1990], *Programming in Martin-Löf's Type Theory: An Introduction*, Oxford University Press.

Nuprl [1999], Project home page. Version 4.2.
   URL: *http://simon.cs.cornell.edu/Info/Projects/NuPrl/nuprl.html*

OHLBACH H., NONNENGART A., DE RIJKE M. AND GABBAY D. [2001], Encoding two-valued nonclassical logics in classical logic, *in* A. Robinson and A. Voronkov, eds, 'Handbook of Automated Reasoning', Vol. II, Elsevier Science, chapter 21, pp. 1403–1486.

PAULIN-MOHRING C. [1993], Inductive definitions in the system Coq: Rules and properties, *in* M. Bezem and J. Groote, eds, 'Proceedings of the International Conference on Typed Lambda Calculi and Applications', Springer-Verlag LNCS 664, Utrecht, The Netherlands, pp. 328–345.

PAULSON L. [1983], Tactics and tacticals in Cambridge LCF, Technical Report 39, University of Cambridge, Computer Laboratory.

PAULSON L. C. [1986], 'Natural deduction as higher-order resolution', *Journal of Logic Programming* **3**, 237–258.

PAULSON L. C. [1989], 'The foundation of a generic theorem prover', *Journal of Automated Reasoning* **5**(3), 363–397.

PAULSON L. C. [1990], Isabelle: The next 700 theorem provers, *in* P. Odifreddi, ed., 'Logic and Computer Science', Academic Press, pp. 361–386.

PAULSON L. C. [1993], Isabelle's object-logics, Technical Report 286, University of Cambridge, Computer Laboratory.

PAULSON L. C. [1994], *Isabelle: A Generic Theorem Prover*, Springer-Verlag LNCS 828.

PETERSSON K. [1982], A programming system for type theory, PMG Report 9, Chalmers University of Technology.

PFENNING F. [1989], Elf: A language for logic definition and verified meta-programming, *in* 'Fourth Annual Symposium on Logic in Computer Science', IEEE Computer Society Press, Pacific Grove, California, pp. 313–322.

PFENNING F. [1991*a*], Logic programming in the LF logical framework, *in* G. Huet and G. Plotkin, eds, 'Logical Frameworks', Cambridge University Press, pp. 149–181.

PFENNING F. [1991*b*], Unification and anti-unification in the Calculus of Constructions, *in* 'Sixth Annual IEEE Symposium on Logic in Computer Science', Amsterdam, The Netherlands, pp. 74–85.

PFENNING F. [1993], Refinement types for logical frameworks, *in* H. Geuvers, ed., 'Informal Proceedings of the Workshop on Types for Proofs and Programs', Nijmegen, The Netherlands, pp. 285–299.

PFENNING F. [1994*a*], Elf: A meta-language for deductive systems, *in* A. Bundy, ed., 'Proceedings of the 12th International Conference on Automated Deduction', Springer-Verlag LNAI 814, Nancy, France, pp. 811–815. System abstract.

PFENNING F. [1994*b*], Structural cut elimination in linear logic, Technical Report CMU-CS-94-222, Department of Computer Science, Carnegie Mellon University.

PFENNING F. [1995], Structural cut elimination, *in* D. Kozen, ed., 'Proceedings of the Tenth Annual Symposium on Logic in Computer Science', IEEE Computer Society Press, San Diego, California, pp. 156–166.

PFENNING F. [1996], The practice of logical frameworks, *in* H. Kirchner, ed., 'Proceedings of the Colloquium on Trees in Algebra and Programming', Springer-Verlag LNCS 1059, Linköping, Sweden, pp. 119–134. Invited talk.

PFENNING F. [2000], 'Structural cut elimination I. Intuitionistic and classical logic', *Information and Computation* **157**(1/2), 84–141.

PFENNING F. [2001], *Computation and Deduction*, Cambridge University Press. In preparation. Draft from April 1997 available electronically.
URL: *http://www.cs.cmu.edu/~twelf/notes/cd.ps*

PFENNING F. AND ELLIOTT C. [1988], Higher-order abstract syntax, *in* 'Proceedings of the ACM SIGPLAN '88 Symposium on Language Design and Implementation', Atlanta, Georgia, pp. 199–208.

PFENNING F. AND ROHWEDDER E. [1992], Implementing the meta-theory of deductive systems, *in* D. Kapur, ed., 'Proceedings of the 11th International Conference on Automated Deduction', Springer-Verlag LNAI 607, Saratoga Springs, New York, pp. 537–551.

PFENNING F. AND SCHÜRMANN C. [1998a], Algorithms for equality and unification in the presence of notational definitions, *in* T. Altenkirch, W. Naraschewski and B. Reus, eds, 'Types for Proofs and Programs', Springer-Verlag LNCS 1657, Kloster Irsee, Germany, pp. 179–193.

PFENNING F. AND SCHÜRMANN C. [1998b], 'Twelf', Project home page. Version 1.2.
URL: *http://www.cs.cmu.edu/~twelf*

PFENNING F. AND SCHÜRMANN C. [1998c], *Twelf User's Guide*, 1.2 edn. Available as Technical Report CMU-CS-98-173, Carnegie Mellon University.

PINTO L. AND DYCKHOFF R. [1998], Sequent calculi for the normal terms of the $\lambda\pi$- and $\lambda\pi\sigma$-calculi, *in* D. Galmiche, ed., 'Proceedings of the Workshop on Proof Search in Type-Theoretic Languages', Vol. 17 of *Electronic Notes in Theoretical Computer Science*, Elsevier Science, Lindau, Germany.
URL: *http://www.elsevier.com/locate/entcs/volume17.html*

POLLACK R. [1994], The Theory of LEGO: A Proof Checker for the Extended Calculus of Constructions, PhD thesis, University of Edinburgh.

λ*Prolog* [1997], Home page. Indexes lambda Prolog implementations.
URL: *http://www.cse.psu.edu/~dale/lProlog/*

PYM D. [1990], Proofs, Search and Computation in General Logic, PhD thesis, University of Edinburgh. Available as CST-69-90, also published as ECS-LFCS-90-125.

PYM D. [1992], 'A unification algorithm for the $\lambda\Pi$-calculus', *International Journal of Foundations of Computer Science* **3**(3), 333–378.

PYM D. AND WALLEN L. [1990], Investigations into proof-search in a system of first-order dependent function types, *in* M. Stickel, ed., 'Proceedings of the 10th International Conference on Automated Deduction', Springer-Verlag LNCS 449, Kaiserslautern, Germany, pp. 236–250.

PYM D. AND WALLEN L. A. [1991], Proof search in the $\lambda\Pi$-calculus, *in* G. Huet and G. Plotkin, eds, 'Logical Frameworks', Cambridge University Press, pp. 309–340.

QIAN Z. [1993], Linear unification of higher-order patterns, *in* M.-C. Gaudel and J.-P. Jouannaud, eds, 'Proceedings of the Colloquium on Trees in Algebra and Programming', Springer-Verlag LNCS 668, Orsay, France, pp. 391–405.

ROHWEDDER E. AND PFENNING F. [1996], Mode and termination checking for higher-order logic programs, *in* H. R. Nielson, ed., 'Proceedings of the European Symposium on Programming', Springer-Verlag LNCS 1058, Linköping, Sweden, pp. 296–310.

RUESS H. [1996], Reflection of formal tactics in a deductive reflection framework, *in* M. McRobbie and J. Slaney, eds, 'Proceedings of the 13th International Conference on Automated Deduction', Springer-Verlag LNAI 1104, New Brunswick, New Jersey, pp. 628–642.

RUESS H. [1997], Computational reflection in the calculus of constructions and its application to theorem proving, *in* P. de Groote and R. Hindley, eds, 'Proceedings fo the Third International Conference on Typed Lambda Calculus and Applications (TLCA'97)', Springer-Verlag LNCS, Nancy, France, pp. 319–335.

SCHROEDER-HEISTER P. [1991], Structural frameworks, substructural logics, and the role of elimination inferences, *in* G. Huet and G. Plotkin, eds, 'Logical Frameworks', Cambridge University Press, pp. 385–403.

SCHROEDER-HEISTER P. [1993], Rules of definitional reflection, *in* M. Vardi, ed., 'Proceedings of the Eighth Annual IEEE Symposium on Logic in Computer Science', Montreal, Canada, pp. 222–232.

SCHÜRMANN C. [1995], A computational meta logic for the Horn fragment of LF, Master's thesis, Carnegie Mellon University. Available as Technical Report CMU-CS-95-218.

SCHÜRMANN C. [2000], Automating the Meta Theory of Deductive Systems, PhD thesis, Department of Computer Science, Carnegie Mellon University. Available as Technical Report CMU-CS-00-146.

SCHÜRMANN C. AND PFENNING F. [1998], Automated theorem proving in a simple meta-logic for LF, *in* C. Kirchner and H. Kirchner, eds, 'Proceedings of the 15th International Conference on Automated Deduction (CADE-15)', Springer-Verlag LNCS 1421, Lindau, Germany, pp. 286–300.

SHANKAR N. [1988], 'A mechanical proof of the Church-Rosser theorem', *Journal of the Association for Computing Machinery* **35**(3), 475–522.

TROELSTRA A. S. AND VAN DALEN D. [1988], *Constructivism in Mathematics*, Vol. 121 of *Studies in Logic and the Foundations of Mathematics*, North-Holland, Amsterdam.

VIRGA R. [1996], Higher-order superposition for dependent types, *in* H. Ganzinger, ed., 'Proceedings of the 7th International Conference on Rewriting Techniques and Applications', Springer-Verlag LNCS 1103, New Brunswick, New Jersey, pp. 123–137. Extended version available as Technical Report CMU-CS-95-150, May 1995.

VIRGA R. [1999], Higher-Order Rewriting with Dependent Types, PhD thesis, Department of Mathematical Sciences, Carnegie Mellon University. Available as Technical Report CMU-CS-99-167.

Index

CHAPTER 18

Proof-Assistants Using Dependent Type Systems

Henk Barendregt

Herman Geuvers

Contents

HANDBOOK OF AUTOMATED REASONING
Edited by Alan Robinson and Andrei Voronkov

1. Proof checking

Proof checking consists of the automated verification of mathematical theories by first fully formalizing the underlying primitive notions, the definitions, the axioms and the proofs. Then the definitions are checked for their well-formedness and the proofs for their correctness, all this within a given logic. In this way mathematics is represented on a computer and also a high degree of reliability is obtained.

After a certain logic is chosen (e.g. classical logic or intuitionistic logic; first-, second- or higher-order logic) there are still several ways in which a theory can be developed. The Cantor-Hilbert-Bourbaki style is to use set-theory, say Zermelo-Fraenkel set-theory with the axiom of choice formalized in first-order classical logic (ZFC)[1]. Indeed, the great attraction of set-theory is the fact that *in principle* it can be used to formalize most mathematical notions. But set-theory has as essential problem that it cannot capture computations very well. Computations are needed for applications of theories and—as we will see later—also for providing proofs. In both cases we want, say for a function $f : \mathbb{N} \rightarrow \mathbb{N}$, that for numbers $n, m \in \mathbb{N}$ such that $f(n) = m$, we can find a formal proof of $\underline{f}(\underline{n}) = \underline{m}$, where the underlinings stand for representations in the theory. Although this is theoretically possible for set-theory, *in practice* this may not be feasible. This is because a computation has to be coded in set-theory as a sequence of sets being a formal description of a computation path (consecutive states) according to some computational model.

Type theory presents a powerful formal system that captures both the notion of *computation* (via the inclusion of functional programs written in typed λ-calculus) and of *proof* (via the so called 'propositions-as-types embedding', where types are viewed as propositions and terms as proofs). As a matter of fact there are various type theories, capturing various notions of computation (e.g. primitive recursion, recursion over higher types) and various logical systems (e.g. first order, higher order). In this article we will not attempt to describe all the different possible choices of type theories. Instead we want to discuss the main underlying ideas, with a special focus on the use of type theory as the formalism for the description of theories including proofs.

Once a theory is formalized, its correctness can be verified by a small program, the *proof checker*. But in order to make the formalization process feasible, an interactive *proof-development system* is needed. This is a proof environment that stands next to the proof-checker and helps the human to develop the proofs. The combination of a proof-development system and a proof checker is called a *proof-assistant*. Such a combination is different form a 'theorem prover'. This is a computer system that allows the user to check the validity of mathematical theorems by generating them automatically. Of course, for proof-assistants the end goal is also to prove theorems. But this is not done by implementing a number of smart algorithms (like resolution or binary decision diagrams), but by letting the user generate a *proof*, interactively with the system. So, the user of proof-assistants is very much in control: by means

---

[1] Or perhaps some stronger versions with large cardinals, e.g. for the formalization of category theory

of 'tactics' (that are input to the system) a so-called 'proof-term' is created that closely corresponds to a standard mathematical proof (in natural deduction style).

For machine assisted theorem proving (via automated theorem proving or via interactive proof generation or a combination of the two) the main goal is to increase the reliability of mathematical results[2]. Roughly there are two reasons why mathematical results may be difficult to verify. The first is *complexity*: the problem is very big, the number of cases to be distinguished being very large, etcetera. This is a situation that one often encounters in computer science, where, e.g. in a protocol one has to go through all possible states of a system. The second problem is *depth*: the problem is very deep, very complicated. This is a situation that is more often encountered in pure mathematics, e.g. Fermat's last theorem is an example. In case of *complexity*, we may expect help from an automated reasoning tool, e.g. to go through a huge number of cases that each by themselves is easily verified. In case of *depth*, an automated reasoning tool will be of little use, but we may expect some help from a proof assistant that does the bookkeeping and prevents us from overseeing details. In the latter case, we might also want to use the proof assistant as a tool for exploring new fields. At this moment however, there is not yet a user-friendly system that provides machine assistance for doing mathematical research. But the potential is there.

Proof assistants based on type theory present a general specification language to define mathematical notions and formulas. Moreover, it allows to construct algorithms and proofs as first class citizens. The advantages are that a user can define his or her own structures in a very flexible way, including the (executable) functions that are part of these structures. Furthermore—and this is what distinguishes the type theoretic approach to theorem proving from most of the other ones—presented in this style, theorem proving consists of the (interactive) construction of a proof-term, *which can be easily checked independently*. These issues will be discussed in more detail below. Again we want to point out that type theory presently does not provide a fast tool for automated theorem proving: there is (in general) not much automation and the fact that explicit proof-terms are constructed slows down the implementation. Also as a research tool proof-assistants are not yet mature. However, they provide a very high reliability, both because of the explicit proof-terms and their well-understood meta-theory. Another good point is their expressive flexibility. For further reading on these issues, beyond the scope of this Chapter, we advise [Luo 1994] or [Nordström, Petersson and Smith 1990].

Another possible (future) application of machine assisted theorem proving is the field of *computer mathematics*. Right now, computers are used in various parts of mathematics, notably for computer algebra and numerical methods. Each of such applications requires the formalization of a specific part of mathematics, covering the domain of the application. To have various systems interact with each other and with the user would require a formalization of substantial parts of mathematics.

---

[2]There are systems, like JAPE [1997], Mathpert [1997] and Hyperproof, see [Barwise and Etchemendy 1995], that have mainly an educational goal and are not geared towards proving large mathematical theorems. However these systems are comparable since they want to prevent their users from erroneous reasoning.

For example the language OpenMath [1998] is aiming at providing an intermediate level between such mathematical computer applications. Reaching even further is the idea, laid down the QED-manifesto (see [Bundy 1994]), of creating an electronic library of completely formalized and checked mathematical results, that one can refer to, browse through, use and extend. For this it is necessary that the proof-assistants become much more user-friendly. This would first of all require a very general and flexible mathematical vernacular by means of which ordinary mathematicians can do the work of formalizing and interact with the library. We believe that type theory can provide such a language. As it stands, only the Mizar project (see [Mizar 1989]) has created and maintains a large collection of mathematical results. There is, however, no obvious way of transferring a result from the Mizar theorem prover to another proof-assistant and also it is hard to find results in the Mizar library.

2. Type-theoretic notions for proof checking

The type systems that are used as a foundational theory are influenced by several people. We mention them here and name their important contribution. Brouwer and Heyting for intuitionistic logic; Russell for the notion of type and for the use of higher order quantification to define logical operations; Gentzen and Prawitz for natural deduction; Church and Curry for typed lambda terms; Howard for the propositions-as-types interpretation; de Bruijn for introducing dependent types and for type conversion for δ- and β-reduction; Scott for inductive types; Martin-Löf for the use of inductive types to define the logical operations, thereby completing the propositions-as-types interpretation, and for type conversion for iota-reduction; Girard for higher order type systems and their normalization; Coquand and Huet for building a type system that incorporates all the previous notions.

Besides this we mention the following people. McCarthy [1962] for his idea of proof checking, including symbolic computing. He did not, however, consider representing proofs in natural deduction form, nor did he have the use of higher types for making appropriate abstractions. De Bruijn for his vigorous plea for proof checking and revitalizing type systems for this purpose. Martin-Löf for his emphasis on reliability (by requiring a clear phenomenological semantics) and consequent proposal to restrict to predicative type systems.

2.1. Proof checking mathematical statements

Mathematics is usually presented in an informal but precise way. One speaks about 'informal rigor'. A typical result in mathematics is presented in the following form.

> In situation Γ we have A.
> Proof. p. ∎

Informal mathematics

Here Γ is an informally described set of assumptions and A is an informally given statement. Also the proof p is presented informally. In logic the statements Γ, A become formal objects and so does the notion of provability. Proofs still are presented in an informal way, but theoretically they can be formalized as a derivation-tree (following some precisely given set of rules).

$$\boxed{\begin{array}{l} \Gamma \vdash_L A \\ \text{Proof. } p. \; \blacksquare \end{array}}$$

Mathematics formalized in logic

It turns out that there are several natural ways to translate propositions as *types* (for the moment one may think of these as 'sets') and proofs as *terms inhabiting* ('elements of') these types. The intuitive difference between sets and types is that an object can be in several different sets, but only in one type. Moreover, a type is a rather 'simple' kind of set: whether a term is of a certain type is usually decidable, due to the fact that 'being of a type' is a syntactic criterion. In the context of type theory, membership of a term a to the type A is denoted by $a{:}A$ rather than $a{\in}A$. Writing the translation of proposition A as $[A]$ and of a proof p as $[p]$ one has

$$\vdash A \text{ using proof } p \;\Leftrightarrow\; \vdash [p] : [A],$$

and hence

$$A \text{ is provable } \;\Leftrightarrow\; [A] \text{ is inhabited.}$$

Therefore the formalization of mathematics in type theory becomes the following (we do not write the [ ] but identify a proposition or proof with its translation).

$$\boxed{\Gamma \vdash_T p : A}$$

Mathematics formalized in type theory

Now all of Γ, A and p are formalized linguistic objects. The statement $\Gamma \vdash_T p : A$ is equivalent to

$$\boxed{\text{Type}_\Gamma(p) = A}$$

Proof checking

Here, $\text{Type}_-(-)$ is a function that finds for p a type in the given context Γ. The decidability of type-checking follows from:

- $\text{Type}_\Gamma(p)$ generates a type of p in context Γ or returns 'false' (if p has no such type).
- The equality $=$ is decidable.

The story is a little bit more complicated. First there are several possible logics (e.g. first or second order logic; intuitionistic or classical logic). This will give rise to several type theories. Secondly the equality $=$ in the last statement depends on the type theory: it is a conversion relation generated from a specific set of elementary reductions.

In the practice of an interactive proof assistant based on type theory, the proof-terms are generated interactively between the user and the proof development system. The user types in so called *tactics*, guiding the proof development system to construct a proof-term. At the end, this term is type checked and the type is compared with the original goal. In connection to proof checking, decidability problems that we can distinguish.

$$\Gamma \vdash_T M : A? \quad \text{TCP,} \quad \text{Type Checking Problem;}$$
$$\Gamma \vdash_T M : ? \quad \text{TSP,} \quad \text{Type Synthesis Problem;}$$
$$\Gamma \vdash_T ? : A \quad \text{TIP,} \quad \text{Type Inhabitation Problem.}$$

If we think of A as a formula and M as its proof, then the TCP asks to verify *whether an alleged proof M indeed proves A*. TSP asks to verify *whether the alleged proof M is a proof at all*. TIP asks to verify *whether A is provable*. It will be clear that TIP is undecidable for any type theory that is of interest for formalizing mathematics (i.e. for any T in which enough first order predicate logic can be done). Whether TCP and TSP are decidable depends in general on the rules of the type theory and especially on how much type-information is added in the term M. In all of the systems that we discuss, both TCP and TSP are decidable. Decidability of TCP and TSP conforms with the intuition that, even though we may not be able to *find* a proof of a given formula ourselves, we can *recognize* a proof if presented to us.

Software (like our proof development system) is *a priori* not reliable, so why would one believe a system that says it has verified a proof? This is a good question. The pioneer of computer verified proofs, N.G. de Bruijn, has given a satisfactory answer. We should take care that the verifying program (the type checker) *is a very small program*; then this program can be verified by hand, giving the highest possible reliability to the proof checker. This is the so called *de Bruijn criterion.*

> A proof assistant satisfies the de Bruijn criterion if it generates 'proof-objects' (of some form) that can be checked by an 'easy' algorithm.

In the late sixties de Bruijn made an impressive start with the technology of proof checking. He designed formal systems for the efficient representation of proofs allowing a verifying algorithm that can be coded in 200 lines of imperative code. These systems were given the collective name Automath, see [Nederpelt, Geuvers and de Vrijer 1994] for an up to date survey. As to the point of reliability, de Bruijn has remarked that one cannot obtain absolute certainty. There always can be some kind of electronic failure that makes a proof-assistant accept a wrong proof (actually this is very unlikely; there is a bigger chance that a correct proof is not accepted). But formalized proofs provide results with the *highest possible reliability.* The reliability of machine checked proofs can be summarized as follows.

> Proof-objects may be large, possibly several Mb; but they are self-evident. This means that a small program can verify them; the program just follows whether locally the correct steps are being made.

We can summarize the type theoretic approach to interactive theorem proving as follows.

$$\begin{aligned}
\text{provability of formula } A &= \text{'inhabitation' of the type } A \\
\text{proof checking} &= \text{type checking} \\
\text{interactive theorem proving} &= \text{interactive construction of a term of} \\
&\quad\ \text{a given type.}
\end{aligned}$$

So the decidability of type checking is at the core of the type-theoretic approach to theorem proving.

2.2. Propositions as types

It is possible to represent proofs in a different and more efficient way as formal terms. The intuition behind this is inspired by intuitionistic (constructive) logic. In this philosophy a proof of an implication $A \supset B$ is a method that transforms a proof of A into a proof of B. A proof of $A \& B$ is a pair $\langle p, q \rangle$ such that p is a proof of A and q one of B. A proof of $A \vee B$ is a pair $\langle b, p \rangle$, where b is either 0 or 1 and if $b = 0$, then p is a proof of A; if $b = 1$ then p is a proof of B. There is no proof of $\bot$, the false proposition. A proof of $\forall x \in X.Ax$ is a method p that transforms every element $a \in A$ into a proof of Aa. Finally a proof of $\exists x \in X.Ax$ is a pair $\langle a, p \rangle$ such that $a \in A$ and p is a proof of Aa. Here, $\supset, \&, \vee, \bot, \forall$ and $\exists$ are the usual logical connectives and quantifiers. Negation is defined as $\neg A = A \supset \bot$.

The propositions as types interpretation intuitively can be defined as follows. A sentence A is interpreted as $[A]$, defined as the collection of proofs of A. Then, according to the intuitionistic interpretation of the logical connectives one has

$$\begin{aligned}
[A \supset B] &= [A] \to [B] \\
[A \& B] &= [A] \times [B] \\
[A \vee B] &= [A] \cup [B] \\
[\bot] &= \emptyset \\
[\forall x \in X.Ax] &= \Pi x{:}X.[Ax] \\
[\exists x \in X.Ax] &= \Sigma x{:}X.[Ax]
\end{aligned}$$

The operations $\to, \times$ and $\cup$ are respectively the formation of functions spaces, Cartesian products and disjoint unions. Intuitively this means the following.

$$\begin{aligned}
P \to Q &= \{f \mid \forall p{:}P.f(p) : Q\}; \\
P \times Q &= \{\langle p, q \rangle \mid p{:}P \text{ and } q{:}Q\}; \\
P \cup Q &= \{\langle 0, p \rangle \mid p{:}P\} \cup \{\langle 1, q \rangle \mid q{:}Q\}.
\end{aligned}$$

Furthermore, $\emptyset$ is the empty type. Finally, the (Cartesian) product and sum of a family $\{Px\}_{x:A}$ of types are intuitively defined as

$$\Pi x{:}A.Px \;=\; \{f{:}(A \to \cup_{x:A} Px) \mid \forall x{:}A \;(fx : Px)\}$$

$$\Sigma x{:}A.Px \;=\; \{(x,p) \mid x{:}A \text{ and } p{:}(Px)\}.$$

Now, a statement A is provable if $[A]$ is inhabited, i.e. if there is a p such that $p : A$ holds in type theory.

2.3. Examples of proofs as terms

To get an idea of what proof-objects really look like and how type checking works, we look at an example: we construct a proof-object and type-check it. This example should be understandable without any further knowledge of the typing rules: some basic 'programmers' intuition of types should suffice.

The first non-trivial example in predicate logic is the proposition that a binary antisymmetric relation is irreflexive.

Let X be a set and let R be a binary relation on X. Suppose

$$\forall x, y {\in} X.Rxy \supset \neg Ryx.$$

Then $\forall x {\in} X.\neg Rxx$.

We want to formalize this. In the type theory we have two *universes*, Set and Prop. The idea is that a term X of type Set, notation X:Set, is a type that represents a *domain* of the logic. (In logic one also speaks of *sorts* or just *sets*.) A term A:Prop, is a type that represents a *proposition* of the logic, the idea being that A is identified with the type of its proofs. So A is provable if we can find a term $p : A$.

Based on this idea, a predicate on $X(: \mathsf{Set})$ is represented by a term $P : X \to \mathsf{Prop}$. This can be understood as follows.

$t(:X)$ satisfies the predicate P iff the type Pt is inhabited,

i.e. there is a proof-term of type Pt. So the collection of predicates over X is represented as $X \to \mathsf{Prop}$ and similarly, the collection of binary relations over X is represented as $X \to (X \to \mathsf{Prop})$.

One of the basic operations of mathematics (even though it is not formally treated in ordinary logic!) is *defining*. This is formally captured in type theory via a kind of 'let' construction. Let us give some definitions.

$$\begin{aligned}
\mathsf{Rel} \;&:=\; \lambda X{:}\mathsf{Set}.X \to (X \to \mathsf{Prop}), \\
\mathsf{AntiSym} \;&:=\; \lambda X{:}\mathsf{Set}.\lambda R{:}(\mathsf{Rel}\,X).\forall x, y{:}X.(Rxy) \supset ((Ryx) \supset \bot), \\
\mathsf{Irrefl} \;&:=\; \lambda X{:}\mathsf{Set}.\lambda R{:}(\mathsf{Rel}\,X).\forall x{:}X.(Rxx) \supset \bot.
\end{aligned}$$

These definitions are *formal constructions* in type theory with a computational behavior, so-called δ-reduction, by which definitions are unfolded. Rel takes a domain

X and returns the domain of binary relations on X:

$$(\text{Rel}\,X) \quad \to_\delta \quad (\lambda X{:}\text{Set}.X{\to}(X{\to}\text{Prop}))X$$
$$\to_\beta \quad X{\to}(X{\to}\text{Prop}).$$

So by one definition unfolding and one β-step we find that $(\text{Rel}\,X) = X{\to}(X{\to}\text{Prop})$. Similarly, for $X : \text{Set}$ and $Q : X{\to}(X{\to}\text{Prop})$,

$$(\text{AntiSym}\,XQ) \;=\; \forall x,y{:}X.(Qxy) \supset ((Qyx) \supset \bot),$$
$$(\text{Irrefl}\,XQ) \;=\; \forall x{:}X.(Qxx) \supset \bot.$$

The type of AntiSym is $\Pi X{:}\text{Set}.(X{\to}(X{\to}\text{Prop})){\to}\text{Prop}$, the type of operators that, given a set X and a binary relation over this X, return a proposition. Here we encounter a *dependent type*, i.e. a type of functions f where the range-set depends on the input value. See the previous Section for a set-theoretic understanding. The formula $\forall x,y{:}X.(Qxy) \supset ((Qyx) \supset \bot)$ is translated as the dependent function type

$$\Pi x,y{:}X.(Qxy){\to}((Qyx){\to}\bot).$$

(For now, we take $\bot$ to be some fixed closed term of type Prop.) Given the (informal) explanation of the Π-type given before, we observe the following two rules for term-construction related to the dependent functions type.

- If $F : \Pi x{:}A.B$ and $N : A$, then $FN : B[N/x]$, (B with N substituted for x).
- If $M : B$ under the assumption $x : A$ (where x may possibly occur in M or B), then $\lambda x{:}A.M : \Pi x{:}A.B$

Let's now try to prove that anti-symmetry implies irreflexivity for binary relations R. So, we try to find a proof-term of type

$$\Pi X{:}\text{Set}.\Pi R{:}(\text{Rel}\,X)(\text{AntiSym}\,XR){\to}(\text{Irrefl}\,XR).$$

We claim that the term

$$\lambda X{:}\text{Set}.\lambda R{:}(\text{Rel}\,X).\lambda h{:}(\text{AntiSym}\,XR).\lambda x{:}X.\lambda q{:}(Rxx).hxxqq$$

is a term of this type. We have encountered a TCP; the verification of our claim is performed by the type-checking algorithm. Most type-checking algorithms work as follows:

1. First solve the TSP
   (compute a type C of the term
   $\lambda X{:}\text{Set}.\lambda R{:}(\text{Rel}\,X).\lambda h{:}(\text{AntiSym}\,XR).\lambda x{:}X.\lambda q{:}(Rxx).hxxqq$),
2. Then compare the computed type with the given type
   (check if $C =_{\beta\delta} \Pi X{:}\text{Set}.\Pi R{:}(\text{Rel}\,X)(\text{AntiSym}\,XR){\to}(\text{Irrefl}\,XR)$).

So a TCP is solved by solving a TSP and checking an equality. Note that this method is only complete if types are *unique up to equality*: if M has type A and type B, then $A =_{\beta\delta} B$. For the algorithm to terminate we must assure that TSP and equality checking are decidable.

For our example we solve the TSP step by step; there are two main steps

1. For a λ-abstraction $\lambda x{:}X.M$, we first compute the type of M, under the extra condition that x has type X. Say we find B as type for M. Then $\lambda x{:}X.M$ receives the type $\Pi x{:}X.B$.

2. For an application FN, we first compute the type of N. Say we find A as type for N. Then we compute the type of F, say C. Now we check whether C reduces to a term of the form $\Pi x{:}D.B$. If so, we check if $D =_{\beta\delta} C$. If this is the case, FN receives the type $B[N/x]$.

If a check fails, we return 'false', meaning that the term has no type.

For our example term $\lambda X{:}\mathsf{Set}.\lambda R{:}(\mathsf{Rel}\,X).\lambda h{:}(\mathsf{AntiSym}\,X R).\lambda x{:}X.\lambda q{:}(Rxx).hxxqq$, we compute the type

$$\Pi X{:}\mathsf{Set}.\Pi R{:}(\mathsf{Rel}\,X).\Pi h{:}(\mathsf{AntiSym}\,X R).\Pi x{:}X.\Pi q{:}(Rxx).C,$$

with C the type of $hxxqq$ under the conditions $X{:}\mathsf{Set}$, $R{:}(\mathsf{Rel}\,X)$, $h{:}(\mathsf{AntiSym}\,X R)$, $x{:}X$ and $q{:}(Rxx)$. Now, $h : (\mathsf{AntiSym}\,X R)$, which should be applied to x, of type X. We reduce $(\mathsf{AntiSym}\,X R)$ until we obtain $\Pi x,y{:}X.(Rxy){\to}((Ryx){\to}\perp)$. So, hx receives the type $\Pi y{:}X.(Rxy){\to}((Ryx){\to}\perp)$. The term hx has a Π-type with the right domain (X), so it can be applied to x, obtaining

$$hxx : (Rxx){\to}((Rxx){\to}\perp).$$

This again can be applied to q (twice), obtaining $hxxqq : \perp$, so TSP finds as type

$$\Pi X{:}\mathsf{Set}.\Pi R{:}(\mathsf{Rel}\,X).\Pi h{:}(\mathsf{AntiSym}\,X R).\Pi x{:}X.\Pi q{:}(Rxx).\perp.$$

We easily verify that this type is $\beta\delta$-convertible with the desired type and conclude that indeed

$$\lambda X{:}\mathsf{Set}.\lambda R{:}(\mathsf{Rel}\,X).\lambda h{:}(\mathsf{AntiSym}\,X R).\lambda x{:}X.\lambda q{:}(Rxx).hxxqq \ :$$
$$\Pi X{:}\mathsf{Set}.\Pi R{:}(\mathsf{Rel}\,X).(\mathsf{AntiSym}\,X R){\to}(\mathsf{Irrefl}\,X R).$$

By convention, $\forall$ and Π will often be used as synonymous, and similarly $\supset$ and $\to$.

¿From this example, one can get a rough idea of how type synthesis works: the structure of the term dictates the form of the type that is synthesized. For the type synthesis algorithm to terminate we need the convertibility $=_{\beta\delta}$ to be decidable. This is usually established by proving that $\beta\delta$-reduction is Normalizing (every term M $\beta\delta$-reduces to a normal form) and Confluent (if M $\beta\delta$-reduces to both P_1 and P_2, then there is a Q such that both P_1 and P_2 $\beta\delta$-reduce to Q). Then the question "$M=_{\beta\delta}N$?" can be decided by reducing both M and N to normal form and comparing these terms lexically. It should be pointed out here that comparing normal forms is often a very inefficient procedure for checking convertibility. (See [Coquand 1991] for a different approach to checking conversion in a dependent type theory.) Therefore, the convertibility checking algorithm will reduce only if necessary. (There is always a 'worst case' where we really have to go all the way to the normal forms.) In particular, this means that definitions are unfolded as little as possible: although the real complexity of $=_{\beta\delta}$ is in the β-reductions, the definitions 'hide' most of the β-redexes. This can be seen from the fact that proof-terms are almost always in β-normal form (but certainly not in δ-normal form). See [COQ 1999] and [van Benthem Jutting, McKinna and Pollack 1994] for more information on type-checking and checking convertibility in dependent type theories. In Section 3.2 we discuss in detail a type-checking algorithm for one specific type system.

2.4. Intermezzo: Logical frameworks

What has been described in the previous two Sections is sometimes called the *direct* encoding of logic in type theory. The logical constructions (connectives) each have a counterpart in the type theory, *implication*, for example, is mirrored by the *arrow type* in type theory. Moreover, the elimination and introduction rules for a connective also have their counterpart in type theory (λ-abstraction mirrors implication introduction and application mirrors implication elimination). In the rest of this paper we restrict ourselves to this direct encoding. There is, however, a second way of interpreting logic in type theory, which is called the *logical frameworks* encoding or also the *shallow* encoding. As the name already indicates, the type theory is then used as a *logical framework*, a meta system for encoding a specific logic one wants to work with. The encoding of a logic L is done by choosing an appropriate context Γ_L, in which the language of L (including the connectives) and the proof rules are declared. This context is usually called a *signature*. In the direct encoding, a context is used for declaring variables (e.g. declaring that the variable x is of domain A) or for making assumptions (by declaring $z : \varphi$, for φ a proposition, we *assume* φ). In logical frameworks, the context is used also to 'declare' the logic itself. One of the reasons that (even rather simple) type systems provide a very powerful logical framework is that type theory is very accurate in dealing with variables (binding, substitution, α-conversion). Hence, when encoding a logic, all issues dealing with variables can be left to the type theory: the logical framework is used as the underlying calculus for substitution and binding. How this works precisely is illustrated by three small examples. For further details on logical frameworks we refer to [Pfenning 2001] (Chapter 17 of this Handbook) or to [Harper, Honsell and Plotkin 1993, Pfenning 1991, de Bruijn 1980]. It should also be remarked here that, even though we do not treat the technical details of logical frameworks based on type theory and the encoding of logics in them, much of our discussions also apply to these type systems, notably the issue of type checking. We now recapitulate the main differences between the two encodings.

Direct encoding	Shallow encoding
One type system $\sim$ One logic	One type system $\sim$ Many logics
Logical rules $\sim$ type theoretic rules	Logical rules $\sim$ Context declarations

The encoding of logics in a logical framework based on type theory will be shown by giving three examples

1. The $\{\supset\}$-fragment of minimal propositional logic,
2. The $\{\supset, \forall\}$-fragment of minimal predicate logic,
3. The untyped λ-calculus.

Minimal propositional logic

The formulas are built up from atomic ones using implication ($\supset$) as only logical operator. In order to translate propositions as types, one postulates the 'signature':

$$\mathsf{prop : type} \tag{2.1}$$

$$\mathsf{imp : prop \to prop \to prop} \tag{2.2}$$

Now define the encoding of propositions $[-]$ as follows.

$$[A \supset B] = \mathsf{imp}[A][B].$$

Then one has for example $[A \supset A] = \mathsf{imp}[A][A]$ and $[A \supset A \supset B] = \mathsf{imp}[A](\mathsf{imp}[A][B])$. The type prop can be seen as the type of 'names' of propositions: a term of type prop is not a proposition itself, because it can not be inhabited (i.e. proved), as it is not a type. In order to state that e.g. $[A \supset A]$ is valid, one intoduces the following map:

$$\mathsf{T} \quad : \quad \mathsf{prop} \to \mathsf{type}. \tag{2.3}$$

The intended meaning of $\mathsf{T}p$ is 'the collection (type) of proofs of p', so T maps a 'name' of a proposition to the type of its proofs. Therefore it is natural to interpret 'p is valid' by '$\mathsf{T}p$ is inhabited'. In order to show now that tautologies like $A \supset A$ are valid in this sense (after translation), one postulates

$$\mathsf{imp\_intr} \quad : \quad \Pi p, q : \mathsf{prop}.(\mathsf{T}p \to \mathsf{T}q) \to \mathsf{T}(\mathsf{imp}\ p\ q), \tag{2.4}$$

$$\mathsf{imp\_el} \quad : \quad \Pi p, q : \mathsf{prop}.\mathsf{T}(\mathsf{imp}\ p\ q) \to \mathsf{T}p \to \mathsf{T}q. \tag{2.5}$$

Then indeed the translation of e.g. $A \supset A$, which is $\mathsf{imp}[A][A]$, becomes valid:

$$\mathsf{imp\_intr}[A][A](\lambda x{:}\mathsf{T}[A].x) : \mathsf{T}(\mathsf{imp}[A][A]),$$

since clearly $(\lambda x{:}\mathsf{T}[A].x) : (\mathsf{T}[A] \to \mathsf{T}[A])$. Similarly one can construct proofs for other tautologies (e.g. $(A \supset A \supset B) \supset A \supset B$. In fact one can show by an easy induction on derivations in the logic L that

$$\vdash_{\mathrm{PROP}} A \quad \Rightarrow \quad \Sigma_{\mathrm{PROP}}, a_1{:}\mathsf{prop}, \ldots, a_n{:}\mathsf{prop} \vdash p : \mathsf{T}[A], \text{ for some } p.$$

Here $\{a, \ldots, a_n\}$ is the set of basic proposition symbols in A and Σ_{PROP} is the *signature* of our minimal propositional logic PROP, i.e. the set of declarations (1-5). Property (6) is called *adequacy* or soundness of the encoding. The converse of it, *faithfulness* (or completeness), is also valid, but more involved to prove.

Minimal predicate logic

We consider the $\{\supset, \forall\}$-fragment of (one-sorted) predicate logic. Suppose we have a logical signature with one constant, one unary function and one binary relation. This amounts to the following (first part of the) type theoretic signature.

$$
\begin{array}{rcll}
\text{prop} & : & \text{type}, & (2.6)\\
\text{A} & : & \text{type}, & (2.7)\\
\text{c} & : & \text{A}, & (2.8)\\
\text{f} & : & \text{A}{\to}\text{A}, & (2.9)\\
\text{R} & : & \text{A}{\to}\text{A}{\to}\text{prop}, & (2.10)\\
\text{imp} & : & \text{prop}{\to}\text{prop}{\to}\text{prop}, & (2.11)\\
\text{imp\_intr} & : & \Pi p,q:\text{prop}.(\mathsf{T}p{\to}\mathsf{T}q){\to}\mathsf{T}(\text{imp } p\ q), & (2.12)\\
\text{imp\_el} & : & \Pi p,q:\text{prop}.\mathsf{T}(\text{imp } p\ q){\to}\mathsf{T}p{\to}\mathsf{T}q. & (2.13)
\end{array}
$$

This covers the language and the implicational part (copied from the logic PROP). Now one has to encode $\forall$, which is done by observing that $\forall$ takes a function from A to prop, $\forall : (\text{A}{\to}\text{prop}){\to}\text{prop}$. The introduction and elimination rules for $\forall$ are then remarkably straightforward.

$$
\begin{array}{rcll}
\text{forall} & : & (\text{A}{\to}\text{prop}){\to}\text{prop}, & (2.14)\\
\text{forall\_intr} & : & \Pi P{:}\text{A}{\to}\text{prop}.(\Pi x{:}\text{A}.\mathsf{T}(Px)){\to}\mathsf{T}(\text{forall}P), & (2.15)\\
\text{forall\_elim} & : & \Pi P{:}\text{A}{\to}\text{prop}.\mathsf{T}(\text{forall}P){\to}\Pi x{:}\text{A}.\mathsf{T}(Px). & (2.16)
\end{array}
$$

Now we translate universal quantification as follows.

$$[\forall x{:}A.Px] = \text{forall}(\lambda x{:}A.[Px]).$$

The proof of an implication like

$$\forall z{:}A(\forall x,y{:}A.Rxy) \supset Rzz$$

is now mirrored by the proof-term

$$\text{forall\_intr}[\_](\lambda z{:}A.\text{imp\_intr}[\_][\_](\lambda h{:}\mathsf{T}([\forall x,y{:}A.Rxy]).\text{forall\_elim}[\_](\text{forall\_elim}[\_]hz))),$$

where we have replaced – for readability – the instantiations of the Π-type by $[\_]$. This term is of type

$$\text{forall}(\lambda z{:}A.\text{imp}(\text{forall}(\lambda x{:}A.(\text{forall}(\lambda y{:}A.Rxy))))(Rzz)).$$

Again one can prove adequacy

$$\vdash_{\text{PRED}} \varphi \;\Rightarrow\; \Sigma_{\text{PRED}}, x_1{:}A,\ldots,x_n{:}A \vdash p : T[\varphi], \text{ for some } p,$$

where $\{x_1,\ldots,x_n\}$ is the set of free variables in φ and Σ_{PRED} is the signature consisting of the declarations (6–16). Faithfulness can be proved as well.

Untyped λ-calculus

Perhaps more unexpected is that untyped λ-calculus can be modeled in a rather simple type theory (the same as for PRED and PROP). The needed signature Σ_{lambda} now is

$$D \quad : \quad \text{type;} \tag{2.17}$$

$$\text{app} \quad : \quad D{\to}(D{\to}D); \tag{2.18}$$

$$\text{abs} \quad : \quad (D{\to}D){\to}D. \tag{2.19}$$

Now every variable x in the λ-calculus is represented by the variable $x : D$ in the type system. The translation of untyped λ-terms is defined as follows.

$$[x] \quad = \quad x;$$
$$[PQ] \quad = \quad \text{app } [P]\,[Q];$$
$$[\lambda x.P] \quad = \quad \text{abs } (\lambda x{:}D.[P]).$$

We now have to express that e.g. $(\lambda x.x)y = y$, and then we have to prove that this equality is valid. As to the statement of equalities, one declares a term

$$\text{eq}{:}D{\to}D{\to}\text{type.} \tag{2.20}$$

The λ-calculus equation $P = Q$ is now translated as the type eq $[P]\,[Q]$. The validity of this equation is by definition equivalent to the inhabitation of this type. In order to ensure this we need the following axioms.

$$\text{refl} \quad : \quad \Pi x{:}D.\text{eq } x\,x, \tag{2.21}$$

$$\text{sym} \quad : \quad \Pi x,y{:}D.\text{eq } x\,y{\to}\text{eq } y\,x, \tag{2.22}$$

$$\text{trans} \quad : \quad \Pi x,y,z{:}D.\text{eq } x\,y{\to}\text{eq } y\,z{\to}\text{eq } x\,z, \tag{2.23}$$

$$\text{mon} \quad : \quad \Pi x,x',z,z'{:}D.\text{eq}xx'{\to}\text{eq}zz'{\to}\text{eq}(\text{app } z\,x)(\text{app } z'\,x'), \tag{2.24}$$

$$\text{xi} \quad : \quad \Pi F,G{:}D{\to}D.(\Pi x{:}D.\text{eq}(Fx)(Gx)){\to}\text{eq}(\text{abs } F)(\text{abs } G), \tag{2.25}$$

$$\text{beta} \quad : \quad \Pi F{:}D{\to}D.\Pi x{:}D.\text{eq}(\text{app}(\text{abs } F)x)(Fx). \tag{2.26}$$

Now one can proof the adequacy

$$P =_\beta Q \;\Rightarrow\; \Sigma_{\text{lambda}}, x_1{:}D, \ldots, x_n{:}D \vdash p : \text{eq } [P]\,[Q], \text{ for some } p.$$

Here, $x_1, \ldots, x_n$ is the list of free variables in PQ and Σ_{lambda} is the signature for untyped λ-calculus, consisting of declarations (17–26). Again the opposite implication, faithfulness, also holds.

The three examples show that using type theories as logical framework is flexible, but somewhat tiresome. Everything has to be spelled out. Of course, in a concrete implementation this can be overcome by having some of the arguments inferred automatically. Note that for each formalization the faithfulness has to be proved separately.

2.5. Functions: algorithms versus graphs

In type theory there is a type of *functions* $A{\to}B$, for A and B types. Which functions there are depends on the derivation rules that tell us how to construct functions. Usually (certainly for the systems in this paper) we see three ways of constructing functions.

- Axiomatically declare $f : A{\to}B$ for a new symbol f.
- Given that $M : B$ in a context containing $x : A$ (and no other dependencies on x in the context), we construct, using the λ-rule,

$$\lambda x{:}A.M : A{\to}B.$$

- Via primitive recursion: given $b : B$ and $f : \mathsf{nat}{\to}B{\to}B$ we can construct

$$\mathsf{Rec}\ b\ f : \mathsf{nat}{\to}B.$$

These functions also *compute*: there are reduction rules associated to them, the β and ι rules:

$$(\lambda x{:}A.M)N \quad \to_\beta \quad M[N/x],$$
$$\mathsf{Rec}\ b\ f\ 0 \quad \to_\iota \quad b,$$
$$\mathsf{Rec}\ b\ f\ (\mathsf{S}^+ x) \quad \to_\iota \quad f\ x\ (\mathsf{Rec}\ b\ f\ x).$$

So, terms of type $A{\to}B$ denote *algorithms*, whose operational semantics is given by the reduction rules. In this view we can see a declaration $f : A{\to}B$ as an 'unknown' algorithm.

At the same time the set-theoretic concept of a *function as a graph* is also present in type theory. If $R : A{\to}B{\to}\mathsf{Prop}$ (R is a binary relation over A and B) and we have a proof-term of type $\forall x{:}A.\exists! y{:}B.Rxy$, then we can of course view this R as a function (graph) in the set-theoretic way. Note, however, that we have no way of really talking about the 'R-image' of a given $a : A$, because we can't give it a name (like $f(a)$). In terms of formal logic, the only way to use it is under an $\exists$-elimination, where we have given the y a name – locally – and we know it to be unique. So the set-theoretic concept of 'function' doesn't give us an algorithm that computes. To remedy this situation one can add a constant – Church [1940] uses the ι for this – that extracts a 'witness' from a predicate. In Church's higher order logic, if P is a predicate over A (i.e. $P : A{\to}\mathsf{Prop}$ in type-theoretical terms), then $\iota P : A$ and there is an axiom saying $\forall P{:}A{\to}\mathsf{Prop}(\exists! x{:}A.Px) \to P(\iota P)$. So, if there is a unique element for which P holds, then ιP denotes this element, otherwise ιP is an arbitrary unspecified element. Obviously, the latter aspect of the ι is not so nice, especially in a system with inductive types like nat, where we now will encounter closed terms of type nat (e.g. $\iota(\geq 0)$) that are not in constructor form, i.e. equal to $S^n 0$ for some $n{\in}\mathbb{N}$.

In constructive systems, there is a different way to obtain a 'witness' from a proof of an existential statement: if $\forall x{:}A\exists y{:}B.Rxy$ holds constructively, then there is a function (algorithm) that computes the y from the x. (This could almost be taken as a definition of what it means for a logic to be constructive.)

If p is a closed proof-term of type $\forall x{:}A\exists y{:}B.Rxy$, then p contains a term $f{:}A{\to}B$ and a proof-term of type $\forall x{:}A.Rx(fx)$.

Note that this is a *meta-theoretic* property of constructive systems: there is not (necessarily) a function *inside* the system that extracts the $f{:}A{\to}B$ from the proof-term p. In some systems, most notably the constructive type theories of Martin-Löf ([Martin-Löf 1984], [Nordström et al. 1990]), this property has been internalised by interpreting an existential fomula $\exists y{:}B.\varphi$ as a Σ-type $\Sigma y{:}B.\varphi$, consisting of pairs $\langle b, q\rangle$ with $b : B$ and $q : \varphi[b/x]$. So, the only way to construct a term of the Σ-type $\Sigma y{:}B.\varphi$ is by giving a $b : B$ for which $\varphi[b/x]$ holds. From a term $t : \Sigma y{:}B.\varphi$, one can extract the two components by projections: $\pi_1 t : B$ and $\pi_2 t : \varphi[\pi_1 t/x]$. These are the Σ-introduction and the Σ-elimination rules, respectively. This implies that from a proof-term $p : \forall x{:}A\exists y{:}B.Rxy$, we can immediately extract the *function* $f : A{\to}B$ defined by $\lambda x{:}A.\pi_1(px)$ and we can prove for this f that $\forall x{:}A.Rx(fx)$ holds. (The proof-term is $\lambda x{:}A.\pi_2(px)$.) The extracted function also has a proper computational behavior: a closed proof-term $p : \forall x{:}A\exists y{:}B.Rxy$ has the form $\lambda x{:}A.\langle t, q\rangle$; the function extracted from this p is (indeed) $\lambda x{:}A.t$.

The internalisation of the (constructive) existence property via a Σ-type may seem a neat way to solve the problem of 'functional-relations-not-being-functions'. However, every advantage has its disadvantage, in this case that we loose the immediate connection between type theory and logic. The reason is that with the Σ-type we can construct *objects that depend on proofs*, a feature alien to ordinary logic. The simplest example is where we have a proof p of $\Sigma x{:}\mathsf{nat}.A$, from which we get the object $\pi_1 p : \mathsf{nat}$. Ordinary logic is built up in *stages*, where

- in the first stage one defines what the domains and the terms of the domains are;
- in the second stage one defines the formulas (or one singles out the formulas from the collection of terms);
- in the third stage one defines what a proof is.

This built-up makes it impossible for objects to depend on proofs, for the simple reason that the objects were already there before we even thought about proofs. Note that Church' approach, using the ι operator, conforms with the conception of ordinary logic that we have just sketched: the object ιP does *not* depend on the proof of $\exists! y{:}A.Px$, but only on the object P. Choosing a type theory in which objects do not depend on proofs has some clear advantages if we want to explain and understand the system in terms of ordinary logic. We come back to this later in 2.9. Here we just remark that if a type theory is to be used as a basis for a theorem prover, a clear connection to some well-known standard logic is desirable.

We conclude that, if we look at functions in type theory, there is a clear distinction between algorithms ($f : A{\to}B$) and graphs ($R : A{\to}B{\to}\mathsf{Prop}$ such that $\forall x{:}A.\exists! y(Rxy)$ holds). Even if we allow to extract from a proof of $\forall x{:}A.\exists! y(Rxy)$ an $f : A{\to}B$, there is still a clear distinction: the proof is not the same as the function.

2.6. Subject Reduction

The property of Subject Reduction (SR) can be seen as the 'sine qua non' of type theory. It states that the set of typed terms of a given type A is closed under reduction. More formally: if $M : A$ and $M \twoheadrightarrow N$, then $N : A$. For A representing a data type, we can understand this as saying that A is closed under evaluation. The rules for evaluation are β, δ and ι that we have already encountered. We illustrate the use of reduction by an example.

Suppose we have as definition plus $:= \lambda x, y{:}\mathsf{nat}.\mathsf{Rec}\ x(\lambda z{:}\mathsf{nat}.\mathsf{S}^+)y$. Then the 'value' of the expression plus $1\,0$ is computed by first unfolding the plus (one δ-reduction step), then performing two β-steps and then one ι-step, to obtain 1. The Subject Reduction property says that all expressions in this computation are of type nat.

In a proof-term, reduction captures the well-known proof-theoretical notion of *cut-elimination*. A *cut* in a proof is a situation where an introduction rule (I) for a connective is immediately followed by an elimination rule (E) for that connective. It is then possible to make a 'shortcut', eliminating the consecutive application of the (I) rule and the (E) rule. (Note that this may not always make the proof literally shorter.) Suppose we have the proof-term $\lambda h{:}A{\rightarrow}A{\rightarrow}B.\lambda z{:}A.hzz :$ $(A{\rightarrow}A{\rightarrow}B){\rightarrow}(A{\rightarrow}B)$, corresponding to the standard natural deduction proof of this fact, ending with an introduction rule. Now, if we also have a proof $q : A{\rightarrow}A{\rightarrow}B$ we can eliminate the implication obtaining $(\lambda h{:}A{\rightarrow}A{\rightarrow}B.\lambda z{:}A.hzz)q : A{\rightarrow}B$. If we do one β-step we eliminate the cut obtaining the proof-term $\lambda z{:}A.qzz : A{\rightarrow}B$. So, for proof-terms,

> the Subject Reduction property states that *cut-elimination is correct* in the sense that if p is a proof of A and we obtain p' by eliminating some cuts from p, then also p' is a proof of A.

In practice, we seldom wish to perform β-reduction on proof-terms: once we have proved a result (i.e. we have constructed a term $p : A$), we are mainly interested in its statement (the type A) and the fact that there is *some* proof (inhabitant) of it. The proof is only inspected if we want to study its structure (e.g. to try to reuse it for proving similar statements). The actual situation is that once we have proved a lemma, say we have constructed $\lambda h{:}A{\rightarrow}A{\rightarrow}B.\lambda z{:}A.hzz : (A{\rightarrow}A{\rightarrow}B){\rightarrow}(A{\rightarrow}B)$ as above, we will *save* this lemma under a name, say lemma$_1$, and we will only refer to this 'name' lemma$_1$. In type theory, what happens is that we introduce a definition lemma$_1 := \lambda h{:}A{\rightarrow}A{\rightarrow}B.\lambda z{:}A.hzz$ and we use lemma$_1$ as a constant of type $(A{\rightarrow}A{\rightarrow}B){\rightarrow}(A{\rightarrow}B)$. It is a *defined* constant, but in implementations it will be *opaque*, meaning that it will never be unfolded by δ.

2.7. Conversion and Computation

We have already encountered three notions of computation: β-, ι- and δ-reduction. For most type theories these reduction relations together are confluent and normalizing, yielding a decidable *conversion* relation $=_{\beta\iota\delta}$ on the set of well-typed terms. This decidability also makes the type checking algorithm work, see Section 2.1. We will look more closely at the use of conversion.

Suppose again we have the definition of plus as given above and we want to prove $2 > 0$ from $p : \forall x, y, z{:}\mathsf{nat}.(x > (\mathsf{plus}\,yz)) \to (x > z)$ and $q : 2 > 1$. Now $p\,2\,1\,0 : (2 > (\mathsf{plus}\,1\,0)) \to (2 > 0)$ and we want to apply this proof to q to obtain the proof-term $p\,2\,1\,0\,q : (2 > 0)$. The application can only work if we first reduce the type $(2 > (\mathsf{plus}\,1\,0)) \to (2 > 0)$ to $(2 > 1) \to (2 > 0)$, which is done by one δ-reduction (unfolding the definition of plus), two β-steps and a ι-step. We can depict this in a deduction as follows.

$$
\cfrac{
\cfrac{
\cfrac{p : \forall x, y, z{:}\mathsf{nat}.(x > (\mathsf{plus}\,yz)) \to (x > z)}
{p\,2\,1\,0 : (2 > (\mathsf{plus}\,1\,0)) \to (2 > 0)}}
{p\,2\,1\,0 : (2 > 1) \to (2 > 0)}\ (\mathrm{conv})
\qquad q : (2 > 1)}
{p\,2\,1\,0\,q : (2 > 0)}
$$

Here we see an application of the conversion rule:

$$
(\mathrm{conv})\ \cfrac{M : \varphi \quad \psi : \mathsf{Prop}}{M : \psi}\ \text{if } \varphi =_{\beta\iota\delta} \psi
$$

In the example above, M is $p\,2\,1\,0$, φ is $(2 > (\mathsf{plus}\,1\,0)) \to (2 > 0)$ and ψ is $(2 > 1) \to (2 > 0)$. The proof-term M is left unchanged under the transition from φ to ψ. This poses no problem for the type checking algorithm, because the conversion $=_{\beta\iota\delta}$ is decidable. (So, if we are given a term M and we want to check whether M is of type ψ we only have to check whether M has a type and if so, verify whether it's convertible with ψ.) In case the equality in the side-condition to the conversion rule is not decidable (which is the situation in the type theory of Nuprl, [Constable et al. 1986]), the conversion from type φ to ψ would have to leave a 'trace' in the term M in order to make type checking decidable. (The trace could be the reduction sequence from φ to ψ.) One could also leave a trace of the conversion in order to help the type checking algorithm, but this is usually not done: it makes proof-terms unnecessarily complicated. Moreover we want to follow the so-called *Poincaré principle*, which can be stated intuitively as follows.

There is a distinction between *computations* and *proofs* and computations do not require a proof.

This implies, for example, that the equality of plus $1\,0$ and 1 does not require a proof: plus $1\,0$ and 1 are computationally equal, so plus $1\,0 = 1$ follows trivially (from the reflexivity of $=$). The power of the Poincaré principle depends on the expressivity of the type theory in terms of algorithms that can be written. Imagine the situation where we have a class of formulas that can be encoded syntactically in our type system. That is, we have a (inductive) type 'Class-of-Form' together with a 'decoding function' Dec : Class-of-Form$\to$Prop such that every formula T : Prop in our class has a syntactic representation t : Class-of-Form with $\text{Dec}\, t =_{\beta\iota\delta} T$. Suppose that we can write a decision algorithm in our type system, i.e. we have a term Check : Class-of-Form→Prop such that if $\text{Check}\, t =_{\beta\iota\delta} T$, then t encodes a provable formula from our class. ($\top$ is the proposition with one unique proof, true.) In more precise type-theoretic terms: suppose we have a proof-term ok with

$$\text{ok} : \forall t{:}\text{Class-of-Form}.(\text{Check}\, t) \to (\text{Dec}\, t).$$

Then, to prove that a formula T : Prop from our class is provable, we only have to find its encoding t : Class-of-Form and then

$$\text{ok}\, t\, \text{true} : T.$$

if T is indeed provable (inhabited), which can be verified by the type checker. In this example, the main task of the type checker is to execute the algorithm Check. This use of the Poincaré principle shows how automated theorem proving can be done (safely) *inside* type theory. This technique is usually called *reflection* (reflecting (part of) the language in itself). The origins date back to Howe [1988]. It has been used succesfully in the Coq system to write a tactic for deciding equality in ring-structures. See also [Barthe, Ruys and Barendregt 1996] – where it is called the 'two-level approach' – and [Oostdijk and Geuvers 2001]. To get really fast automated theorem proving, it is advisable to use a special purpose automated theorem prover, which has the extra adavantage that one doesn't have to program (and prove correct!) the decision procedures oneself. If one uses reflection (and the Poincaré principle) one obtains a medium fast descision procedure but very reliable proof-terms, which can be checked independently.

2.8. *Equality*

Note that we have not included η-reduction in the conversion rule, but just β, δ and ι. This may seem remarkable, because for the untyped λ-calculus, many nice results of β-reduction (like confluence) extend to $\beta\eta$. This is however not the case for typed λ-calculus. The snag lies in the fact that our typed terms have a type attached to the bound variable in the λ-abstraction $(\lambda x{:}\underline{A}.M)$. This information is crucial for the type checking algorithm (without it, type checking in dependent type theory is undecidable [Dowek 1993]), but it complicates the combination of β and η. For example consider $\lambda x{:}A.(\lambda y{:}B.y)x$,

$$\lambda x{:}A.(\lambda y{:}B.y)x \quad \to_\beta \quad \lambda x{:}A.x$$
$$\lambda x{:}A.(\lambda y{:}B.y)x \quad \to_\eta \quad \lambda y{:}B.y$$

The terms on the right hand side have a common reduct only if A and B do. This complication of η was already known to the Automath community [Nederpelt 1973]; Confluence and Normalization for types systems from the Automath family was proved by Daalen [1980]. For a study and proof of the general situation see

[Geuvers 1992], [Geuvers 1993]. For a study of type theory with λ-terms *without* types attached to the bound variables, see [Barthe and Sørensen 2000], where it is shown that the type checking (notably its undecidability) is not completely hopeless. In [Magnusson 1994], an implementation of a proof assistant based on such a type theory (without types attached to the bound variables) is described.

There are several other ways of extending the equality in the conversion rule. A prominent example is the *extensional equality* on functions. In mathematics, if $f, g : A{\rightarrow}B$, the f and g would be considered to be equal if they have the same graph, i.e. $f = g$ iff $\forall x{:}A(f\,x = g\,x)$. If we want to view the functions not so much as algorithms, but more abstractly as graphs, the inclusion of extensional equality in the convertibility (as side condition in the conversion rule) would be very natural. If we want to do this, it is required that we introduce an *equality judgment* of the form

$$\Gamma \vdash M = N : A.$$

Before discussing extensionality further, we first focus on the different notions of equality.

Equality as a judgment or as a type

As rules for deriving an equality judgment we would have β, δ and ι plus the normal rules for making it an equivalence relation (reflexivity, symmetry, transitivity) plus rules for making the equality compatible with the term-constructions. For example, we would have

$$(\beta) \quad \frac{\Gamma \vdash \lambda x{:}A.M : \Pi x{:}C.B \quad \Gamma \vdash N : C}{\Gamma \vdash (\lambda x{:}A.M)N = M[N/x] : B[N/x]}$$

$$(\delta) \quad \frac{\Gamma_1, c := M : A, \Gamma_2 \vdash c : B}{\Gamma \vdash c = M : B}$$

$$(\text{refl}) \quad \frac{\Gamma \vdash M : B}{\Gamma \vdash M = M : B}$$

$$(\text{trans}) \quad \frac{\Gamma \vdash M = N : B \quad \Gamma \vdash N = P : B}{\Gamma \vdash M = P : B}$$

$$(\text{app-comp}) \quad \frac{\Gamma \vdash M = N : \Pi x{:}A.B \quad \Gamma \vdash P = Q : A}{\Gamma \vdash MP = NQ : B[P/x]}$$

$$(\text{abs-comp}) \quad \frac{\Gamma, x{:}A \vdash M = N : B \quad \Gamma \vdash A = C : D}{\Gamma \vdash \lambda x{:}A.M = \lambda x{:}D.N : \Pi x{:}A.B}$$

The conversion rule then takes the following form

$$(\text{conv}) \quad \frac{\Gamma \vdash M : A \quad \Gamma \vdash A = B}{\Gamma \vdash M : B}$$

The addition of extensionality would amount to the rule

$$\text{(ext)} \; \frac{\Gamma \vdash M, N : A \to B \quad \Gamma \vdash p : \Pi x{:}A.(Mx = Nx)}{\Gamma \vdash M = N : A \to B}$$

In the (ext) rule, the equality in the premise $(=_B)$ is an equality that can be proved; we could call it a *logical equality*, but in type-theory it is usually called *book equality*, as it is thought of as the user-defined equality in 'the book'. (In Automath systems, the notion 'book' has a very precise formal meaning; it corresponds roughly to the user-defined context that represents some specific theory.) The equality in the conclusion of the (ext) rule is the 'internal equality' of the type system, usually called the *definitional equality*. This definitional equality can be represented by a judgment itself (as above), but often it is represented as a 'convertibility side condition', like in 2.7. In the latter case, the convertibility $A =_{\beta\delta\iota} B$ is understood as an equality on a set of 'pseudo terms', including the well-typed ones. Let us summarize the different equalities.

1. *Definitional equality.* The 'underlying equality' of the type system. Captures β, δ and, if present, also ι. Can be *judgemental* (i.e. built into the formal system) or a *convertibility side condition*.

2. *Book equality.* The 'equality provable' inside the type system. If $M =_A N$ is a book equality, then it is a type ($M =_A N$: Prop for $M, N : A$) and we can try to find a proof-term inhabiting it ($p : M =_A N$). Such an equality can be defined by the user.

Book equality comes in various flavours, depending not only on the user's choice, but also on the type theory, because most type theories (and certainly their implementations) have a 'built-in' or 'preferred' equality. We give a short overview of some options. First of all, we want the following from a book-equality.

- The equality should be an equivalence relation on the carrier type: for A : Set, $=_A: A \to (A \to \text{Prop})$ should be an equivalence relation.

- Substitution property. We want to replace 'equal terms in a proposition'. In type theoretical terminology, we want the following rule to be derivable (for some term construction $S(\_,\_)$).

$$\frac{\Gamma \vdash N : A(t) \quad \Gamma \vdash e : t =_A q}{\Gamma \vdash S(N, e) : A(q)}$$

To achieve this we distinguish the following three treatments of equality.

1. *Leibniz equality*, defined in higher order logic. We want to say (following Leibniz) that $t =_A q$ if for all predicates P over A, P holds for t iff P holds for q. In type theory:

$$t =_A q \; := \; \Pi P{:}A \to \text{Prop}(P\ t) \to (P\ q).$$

Note that this equality looks asymmetric; however, it can be shown that $=_A$ is symmetric.

2. *Inductively defined equality.* Equality $=_A$: $A{\to}(A{\to}\mathsf{Prop})$ is the 'smallest' reflexive relation on A, i.e. the 'smallest' relation R on A for which $\forall x{:}(R\ x\ x)$ holds. In type theoretic syntax this would look like

$$\mathsf{Inductive}\quad \mathsf{Eq}_A : A{\to}A{\to}\mathsf{Prop} :=$$
$$\mathsf{Refl} : \Pi x{:}A.(\mathsf{Eq}\ x\ x).$$

This specific form of definition, to be treated in more detail in Section 3.8, says that Refl is the only *constructor* for the inductively defined relation Eq. This is made precise by an *induction* principle that comes along with this definition.

3. *Special type with special rules*, roughly reflecting the inductivity of $=_A$, as in 2. In Martin-Löf's type theory (see [Martin-Löf 1984], [Nordström et al. 1990]), equality is taken as a basic type constructor:

$$\frac{\Gamma \vdash A : \mathsf{Set}}{\Gamma, x, y{:}A \vdash (\mathsf{Id}_A\ x\ y) : \mathsf{Set}} \qquad \frac{\Gamma \vdash M : A}{\Gamma \vdash (\mathsf{Refl}_A M) : (\mathsf{Id}_A\ M M)}$$

We don't give the full elimination (induction) principle, but only one of its instances:

$$\frac{\Gamma \vdash P : A{\to}\mathsf{Set} \quad \Gamma \vdash q : (Pa) \quad \Gamma \vdash e : (\mathsf{Id}_A\ ab)}{\Gamma \vdash (\mathsf{idrec}\ qe) : (Pb)}$$

Note that in the third approach, the identity type $(\mathsf{Id}_A\ ab)$ is of type Set, and not of type Prop. This is not a peculiar aspect of Martin-Löf's approach to equality, but a consequence of his approach to logic in general: there is no distinction between sets and propositions; both 'live' in the universe Set (and hence there is no universe Prop).

There are some clear differences, e.g. Leibniz equality requires impredicativity to be definable, while the inductively defined equality requires inductive types. However, each of these approaches to equality yields an equivalence relation for which the substitution property holds. Let us discuss one example where the different equalities diverge. Suppose we have defined (inductively) a map Fin : $\mathsf{nat}{\to}\mathsf{Set}$ such that $(\mathsf{Fin}\ n)$ represents the n-element type. Then one would like $(\mathsf{Fin}\ n)$ and $(\mathsf{Fin}\ m)$ to be isomorphic if n and m are equal. So we want (at least) the following to be derivable (for some some term construction $E(\_,\_)$).

$$\frac{\Gamma \vdash t : (\mathsf{Fin}\ n) \quad \Gamma \vdash e : n =_{\mathsf{nat}} m}{\Gamma \vdash E(t, e) : (\mathsf{Fin}\ m)}$$

For Leibniz equality ((1) above), we can not construct such a term $E(t, e)$, because it allows elimination 'over Prop' only. For the inductive equality, it depends on the elimination rules that are allowed in the type system (e.g. the type system of COQ [1999] does not allow it). For Martin-Löf's type theory, the above rule is obviously derivable, because Prop and Set are the same universe, and one can eliminate over it.

Extensionality versus intensionality

The definitional equality can be *intensional* or *extensional*. In the first case, we do not have a derivation rule (ext), and hence equality of functions is equality of algorithms. In the second case, we have a derivation rule (ext), and hence equality of functions is equality of graphs.

It follows from our discussion of TCP and TIP in 2.2 that the addition of the rule (ext) renders TCP undecidable. Viz. suppose $H : (A{\to}B){\to}\mathsf{Prop}$ and we know $x : (H\ f)$; then $x : (H\ g)$ iff there is a term of type $\Pi x{:}A.f\ x = g\ x$. So for this TCP to be solvable, we need to solve a TIP.

The first type systems by Martin-Löf (see [Martin-Löf 1984]) were extensional. Later he rejected extensionality, because of the implied undecidability of type checking. The interactive theorem prover Nuprl of Constable et al. [1986] is based on extensional type theory. It is clear that from a more classical view on mathematics (identifying functions with graphs in set-theoretic way), extensionality is very desirable. Recently, work has been done (mainly by Hofmann [1994]) showing how to encode (or explain) extensional equality in an intensional type theory. The idea is to translate an extensional type to a pair consisting of an intensional type and an equivalence relation on it. Here, the equivalence realtion is a user-defined (book) equality, built up according to the type constructions from basic equalities, which are the inductively defined one for inductive types and an axiomatically declared one for basic variable types.

Setoids

A pair $[A, =]$ with $A : \mathsf{Set}$, $= : A{\to}(A{\to}\mathsf{Prop})$ such that $=$ is an equivalence relation on A is called a *setoid*. In the translation of extensional types to setoids (in intensional type theory) one has to also translate compound types, like $A{\to}B$ and $\Pi x{:}A.B$, this amounts to defining the function space and the dependent function space between setoids. To give the idea we treat the function space here. Given two setoids $[A, =_A]$ and $[B, =_B]$, we define the *function space setoid* $[A\overset{s}{\to}B, =_{A\overset{s}{\to}B}]$ by

$$A\overset{s}{\to}B \quad := \quad \Sigma f{:}A{\to}B.(\Pi x,y{:}A.(x =_A y){\to}((f\ x) =_B\ (f\ y))),$$

$$f =_{A\overset{s}{\to}B} g \quad := \quad \Pi x{:}A.(\pi_1\ f\ x) =_B (\pi_1\ g\ x).$$

Note that, $f =_{A\overset{s}{\to}B} g$ is equivalent to $\Pi x,y{:}A.(x =_A y){\to}(\pi_1\ f\ x) =_B (\pi_1\ g\ x)$, because we require f and g to preserve $=_A$. Given A with equality $=_A$ and B with equality $=_B$, this is the 'canonical equality' on $A{\to}B$. Note that the carrier set $A\overset{s}{\to}B$ is not just $A{\to}B$, but the 'subset' of those $f : A{\to}B$ that respect the equalities R_A and $=_B$. Such an f is also called a *setoid function* from $[A, =_A]$ to $[B, =_B]$. In type theory, such a subset (of setoid functions) is represented by a Σ-type, consisting of pairs $\langle f,p, \rangle$ with (in this case) $f : A{\to}B$, $p : \Pi x,y{:}A.(x =_A y){\to}((f\ x) =_B (f\ y))$. The equivalence relation $=_{A\overset{s}{\to}B}$ ignores the proof-terms, so $\langle f,p\rangle =_{A\overset{s}{\to}B} \langle f,q\rangle$ holds for all elements of the carrier set $A\overset{s}{\to}B$.

The canonical equality on $A{\to}B$ is the extensional equality of functions. Therefore, the interpretation of extensional type theory in intensional type theory is sound. (Of course, the other type constructions still have to be verified; see [Hofmann 1994] for details.) It has been observed that setoids present a general and practical way of dealing with extensional equality and with mathematical constructions in general. If, in mathematics one speaks informally of a 'set', we encode this in type theory by a 'setoid'. To show the flexibility we show how a *quotient* and a *subset* can be represented using setoids.

Given a setoid $[A, =_A]$ and an equivalence relation Q over this setoid, we define the *quotient-setoid* $[A, =_A]/Q$. Note that the fact that Q is an equivalence relation over the setoid $[A, =_A]$ means that

- $Q : A \to (A \to \mathsf{Prop})$ is an equivalence relation,
- $=_A \subset Q$, i.e. $\forall x, y{:}A.(x =_A y) \to (Q\ x\ y)$.

We define the quotient setoid $[A, =_A]/Q$ simply as $[A, Q]$. It is an easy exercise to show how a setoid function f from $[A, =_A]$ to $[B, =_B]$ that respects Q (i.e. $\forall x, y{:}A.(Q\ x\ y) \to ((f\ x) =_B (f\ y)))$ induces a setoid function from $[A, =_A]/Q$ to $[B, =_B]$.

Given a setoid $[A, =_A]$ and a predicate P on A, we define the *sub-setoid* $[A, =_A]|P$ as the pair $[\Sigma x{:}A.(P\ x), =_A|P]$, where $=_A|P$ is $=_A$ restricted to P, i.e. for $q, r : \Sigma x{:}A.(P\ x)$,

$$q\ (=_A|P)\ r \quad := \quad (\pi_1\ q) =_A (\pi_1\ r).$$

In defining a subsetoid, we do not require the predicate P to respect the equality $=_A$. (That is, we do *not* require $\forall x, y{:}A(x = y \wedge Px) \to Py$ to hold.) So, in taking a subsetoid we may remove elements from the =-equivalence classes. This is natural, because we are not interested in the elements of A, but in the =-equivalence classes. Consider the following example where this appears rather naturally. Let $A := \mathsf{int} \times \mathsf{nat}$ be the type of pairs of an integer and a natural number. To represent the rationals we define, for $\langle x, p \rangle, \langle y, q \rangle{:}A$,

$$\langle x, p \rangle =_A \langle y, q \rangle \quad := \quad x(q+1) = y(p+1).$$

Now consider the predicate P on A defined by

$$P \langle x, p \rangle \quad := \quad \gcd(x, p+1) = 1.$$

The subsetoid $[A, =_A]|P$ is isomorphic to $[A, =_A]$ itself, but all equivalence classes have been reduced to a one element set.

Subtypes and coercions

When using setoids to formalize the notion of set, one encounters a typing problem. Suppose we have the setoid $[A, =_A]$. Now, $A : \mathsf{Set}$, but the setoid $[A, =_A]$ is not of type Set, but of type $\Sigma A{:}\mathsf{Set}.A \to (A \to \mathsf{Prop})$ Hence we can not declare a variable $x : [A, =_A]$ (because we can only declare a variable $x : B$ if $B : \mathsf{Set}$ or $B : \mathsf{Prop}$). Similarly, if $a : A$, then a is not of type $[A, =_A]$.

As a matter of fact, a setoid consists of a *triple*

$$[A, =_A, \mathsf{eq\_rel\_proof}] : \Sigma A{:}\mathsf{Set}.\Sigma R{:}A \to (A \to \mathsf{Prop}).(\mathsf{Is\_eq\_rel}\ A\ R),$$

where eq_rel_proof is a proof of (Is_eq_rel A R), stating that $=_A$ is an equivalence relation over A. If we formalize the type of equivalence relations over a fixed A as

$$\text{Eq\_Rel}_A := \Sigma R{:}A{\to}(A{\to}\text{Prop}).(\text{Is\_eq\_rel A R}),$$

then, if $R : \text{Eq\_Rel}_A$ and $a, a' : A$, one would like to write Raa', but this is not a proposition. (The R is really a *pair* consisting of a binary relation and a proof.)

If we look at the formalization of subsets as subsetoids, we encounter a similar problem. If $[A, =_A]|P$ is a subsetoid of $[A, =_A]$, then an 'element' of this subsetoid is given by a *pair* $\langle a, p \rangle$, where $a : A$ and $p : Pa$, but this is not an 'element' of $[A, =_A]$. Indeed, if $F : A{\to}B$ and $x : [A, =_A]|P$, we can not write Fx, as x itself is not of type A.

The problem lies in the fact that our terms are very explicit, whereas we would like to be more implicit. This situation is also encountered in mathematics, where one defines, for example a 'group' as a tuple $\mathcal{A} = \langle A, \circ, \text{inv}, e \rangle$, where A is a set, $\circ$ a binary operation, inv a unary operation and e an element of A, satisfying the group axioms. Then one speaks of 'elements of the group $\mathcal{A}$', where one really means 'elements of the (carrier) set A'. So, one (deliberately) mixes up the group $\mathcal{A}$ and its carrier set A. This is not sloppiness, but convenience: some of the details are deliberately omitted, knowing that one can fill them in if necessary. This is sometimes called 'informal rigor'.

As was first noted by Aczel, one would like to have a similar mechanism in type theory, for being able to use informal rigor. A way to do this is by creating a level on top of the type theory, where one can use more informal language, which is then translated to the formal level. This requires that the informal expressions are expanded in such a way that they become well-formed in the underlying formal type theory. It turns out that in this expansion, the type synthesis algorithm is very useful, as it generates the missing information. This can be made formally precise by introducing the notion of *coercion*.

Some of the problematic examples that we gave above can be seen as instances of the *sub-typing problem*. In type theory as we have discussed until now, there is no notion of subtype: we can not say that $A \subseteq B$, with as intended meaning that if $a : A$ then also $a : B$. It turns out that if one adds such a sub-typing relation, the decidability of type checking becomes rather problematic. Moreover, there are various ways in which the sub-typing relation can be lifted along the type constructions (like Π and $\to$). On the other hand, some of the problems discussed above can be solved using sub-typing:

If $\Sigma A{:}\text{Set}.A{\to}(A{\to}\text{Prop}) \subseteq \text{Set}$,   then $x : [A, =_A]$ can be declared,

If $\text{Eq\_Rel}_A \subseteq A{\to}(A{\to}\text{Prop})$,   then $R : \text{Eq\_Rel}_A, a, a' : A \vdash Raa' : \text{Prop}$,

If $[A, =_A]|P \subseteq [A, =_A]$,   then $F : A{\to}B, a : [A, =_A]|P \vdash Fa : B$.

Note, however that this does not solve all problems: if $a : A$, we can not write $a : [A, =_A]$ (the $\subseteq$ needs to be reversed). Furthermore, the meaning of $[A, =_A]|P \subseteq [A, =_A]$ is not so clear, as both are not themselves types.

A related but different solution can be found by making the inclusions $A \subseteq B$ explicit by a *coercion map*. Then we have e.g.

$$\pi_1 \quad : \quad \Sigma A{:}\mathsf{Set}.A{\to}(A{\to}\mathsf{Prop}) \subseteq \mathsf{Set},$$

$$\pi_1 \quad : \quad \mathsf{Eq\_Rel_A} \subseteq A{\to}(A{\to}\mathsf{Prop}).$$

We have no map from $[A, =_A]|P$ to $[A, =_A]$, as these are not types. The maps here are just definable terms and we can replace the $\subseteq$ by an $\to$. But then we are back to the original formulations where we have to give all terms explicitly everywhere. The idea is to declare the coercions as special maps, to be used by the type checker to type expressions. So the user does not have to insert these maps, but the type checker will do so to compute a type. Essentially, there are three ways in which a type checking algorithm can use a coercion map.

$\left.\begin{array}{l} c : A \subseteq \mathsf{Set} \\ (\text{or } c : A \subseteq \mathsf{Prop}) \end{array}\right\}$ the declaration $x : A$ is expanded to $x : (cA)$.

$\left.\begin{array}{l} G : D \\ c : D \subseteq A{\to}B \\ a : A \end{array}\right\}$ $G\,a$ is expanded to $c\,G\,a$ of type B.

$\left.\begin{array}{l} F : A{\to}B \\ c : D \subseteq A \\ a : D \end{array}\right\}$ $F\,a$ is expanded to $F\,(c\,a)$ of type B.

It should also be possible to use multiple coercion maps: if there are coercions $c_1 : A \subseteq B$ and $c_2 : B \subseteq C$, then there is a coercion $\lambda x{:}A.c_2(c_1 x) : A \subseteq C$. So the coercions are really just definable λ-terms that can be composed. Of course, there should be only one coercion between two types A and B and there should be no coercion from a type A to itself. This has to be checked by the system at the moment a coercion is declared: it should go through the 'coercion graph' to verify that it is still a tree. For more on coercions see [Barthe 1996] or [Luo 1999]. Another approach to subtypes is to treat them as real subsets: if $M : A$ and A is a subtype of B, then $M : B$ (without coercion). We will not discuss this possibility here; for a possible set of typing rules for subtypes we refer to [Zwanenburg 1999].

2.9. Connection between logic and type theory

When doing formal proofs with the help of some computer system, one may wonder what one is really proving. Or, to put it differently,

> what is the *semantics* of the formal objects that the system (and the user) is dealing with?

The systems that we are concerned with here are based on type theory, which moves the semantics-question from the level of the computer system to the level of the formal system:

what do the expressions of the type theory mean?

Note that this only gives a satisfactory answer in case the computer system is a faithful implementation of the type theory. The actual situation is as follows: the interactive proof development system (where the proof-terms are *created*) is not fully explained in terms of the type theory; however, the *proof checker* (which is executed after the proof-term has been completed) is completely faithful to the type theory.

So, we will confine ourselves to the question what the expressions of the type theory mean. This question can be dealt with in different ways. First we can look at some (preferred) model, $\mathcal{M}$, of a piece of mathematics and ask what the type theoretical expressions mean in $\mathcal{M}$. Second, we can look at some logic $\mathcal{L}$ and ask what the meaning of the type theoretical expressions in $\mathcal{L}$ is. This results in the following questions.

- What is the interpretation of the expressions in the model $\mathcal{M}$ and is there a soundness and/or completeness result? For $A : \mathsf{Prop}$,

$$\mathcal{M} \models A \text{ iff } \exists p (\vdash p : A)?$$

- What is the interpretation of the expressions in the logic $\mathcal{L}$ and, for $A : \mathsf{Prop}$, is A provable in $\mathcal{L}$ iff A is inhabited?

$$\vdash_{\mathcal{L}} A \text{ iff } \exists p (\vdash p : A)?$$

As type theory is generic, we are mainly interested in the second question. The connection with logic is even more relevant as type theory seeks to represent *proofs* as terms; these proof-terms then better have some relation to a proof in logic. Following the Curry-Howard-de Bruijn *propositions-as-types-embedding*, formulas of logic are interpreted as types, and at the same time, (natural deduction) derivations are interpreted as proof-terms. So, the answer to the question whether proof-terms in type theory represent proofs is affirmative: proof-terms represents natural deduction proofs. Of course, the situation is more complicated: there are a lot of logics and a lot of type theories. But if we choose, given our logic in natural deduction style $\mathcal{L}$, an appropriate type theory $S(\mathcal{L})$, we have the following

Soundness of the propositions-as-types embedding:
$$\vdash_{\mathcal{L}}^{\Sigma} \varphi \quad \Rightarrow \quad \Gamma \vdash_{S(\mathcal{L})} [\![\Sigma]\!] : \varphi,$$

where Σ denotes the deduction of φ in $\mathcal{L}$ and $[\![\Sigma]\!]$ its encoding as a term in $S(\mathcal{L})$. Γ is a context in which the relevant variables are declared. In Section 3.2, we describe the propositions-as-types embedding in more detail for higher order predicate logic and its corresponding type system.

The other way around, we may wonder whether, if φ is inhabited in $S(\mathcal{L})$, then φ is derivable in $\mathcal{L}$ (where φ : Prop).

Completeness of the propositions-as-types embedding:

$$\Gamma \vdash_{S(\mathcal{L})} M : \varphi \overset{?}{\Rightarrow} \vdash_{\mathcal{L}} \varphi,$$

where Γ is again a context in which the relevant variables are declared. If we take into account that a term $M : \varphi$ is intended to represent a natural deduction proof, we may strengthen our completeness by requiring an embedding [_] from proof-terms to deductions.

Strong Completeness of the propositions-as-types embedding:

$$\Gamma \vdash_{S(\mathcal{L})} M : \varphi \overset{?}{\Rightarrow} \vdash_{\mathcal{L}}^{[M]} \varphi.$$

Completeness is not in all cases so easy. Consider for example the Martin-Löf's type theories, where there is no distinction between 'sets' and 'propositions' – both are of type Set. We have already discussed this situation in Section 2.5, where we pointed out that in ordinary logic there is a sharp distinction between Prop and Set from the very start. It is just the way logic is defined, in *stages*, where one first defines the terms (including the domains), then the formulas and then the derivations. That means that for Martin-Löf's type theories, it is not so easy to define a mapping back to the logic (in this case first order intuitionistic logic). For example, look at the context

$$A{:}\mathsf{Set}, a{:}A, P{:}A{\rightarrow}\mathsf{Set}, h{:}(Pa), Q{:}(Pa){\rightarrow}\mathsf{Set}, f{:}(P\,a){\rightarrow}A.$$

If we try to interpret this in first order intuitionistic logic, we can view A as a domain, a as an element of A, P as a predicate on A and h as the assumption that $(P\,a)$ holds (h is an *assumed proof* of $(P\,a)$). But then Q can only be understood as a predicate on the set of proofs of $(P\,a)$[3], and f as a map from the proofs of $(P\,a)$ to the domain A. It will be clear that there are many types $X{:}\mathsf{Set}$ in the type theory that have no interpretation, neither as a 'domain' nor as a 'proposition', in first order intuitionistic logic. As a consequence, Strong Completeness fails for Martin-Löf's type theory. It has been shown – but the proof is really intricate, see [Swaen 1989] – that completeness (the weaker variant) holds. However, if we extend these type theories to higher order, we obtain either an inconsistent system (if we interpret the higher order $\exists$ as a Σ-type, see [Coquand 1986]), or (if we interpret the higher order $\exists$ impredicatively) a system for which completeness fails with respect to constructive higher order predicate logic; see [Berardi 1990], [Geuvers 1993].

Summarizing, we observe the following possible points of view: (1) first order predicate logic is incomplete, as it does not allow objects to depend on proofs, whereas both are just 'constructions'; (2) the idea of unifying the Prop and the Set universe into one (Set) is wrong, as it creates objects depending on proofs, a feature alien to ordinary logic. We tend to have the second view, although the situation is

---

[3] A – proof-theoretically – interesting predicate on proofs may be 'to be cut-free'. However, a predicate can not distinguish between β-equal terms, so this predicate can not be expressed.

not so easy, as can be seen from the two examples below, where we apply the idea of letting objects depend on proofs.

With respect to the interpretation of the constructive existential quantifier, there are also two possible positions: (I) interpret $\exists$ by the Σ-type, which does not work well for higher order logic, (but higher-order logic is often considered as non-constructive – because impredicative – anyway); (II) interpret it in a different way (e.g. using a higher order encoding or an inductive encoding) that avoids the projections of proofs to objects. Obviously, position (I) on the existential quantifier interpretation goes well with position (1) on the Prop-Set-issue above. Similarly (II) goes well with (2) above.

Concluding this discussion on the precise choice of the type theoretical rules to interpret the logic, we note the following. The build up of logic in *stages*, as described before, is very much related to a Platonist view of the world, where

> the objects are just *there* and logic is a means of deriving true properties about these objects.

So an object is not affected by our reasoning about it. In the constructive view,

> both objects and proofs are *constructions* and the only objects that exist are the ones that can be constructed.

Then a formula is identified with the set of its proofs and there is *a priori* no problem with constructing an element of one set (say the set nat) out of another set (say a formula A). So, if we take the constructive view as a starting point, the dependency of objects on proofs is no problem. Note that this still leaves a choice of really identifying the universe of sets and propositions (then A : Set for sets A and A : Set for formulas A) or keeping the distinction (then A : Set for sets A and A : Prop for formulas A). In this article we start from type systems where objects do not depend on proofs.

If one chooses a type theory that remains quite closely to the original constructive logic (in natural deduction style), it is not so difficult (although laborious) to prove Strong Completeness of the propositions-as-types embedding. See [Geuvers 1993] for some detailed proofs and examples.

Examples of objects depending on proofs

In the discussion above, we promoted the idea of not letting objects depend on proofs. Although this solves some of the completeness questions in a relatively easy way, this position is not so simple to be maintained. If one *really* starts formalizing mathematics in type systems, objects depending on proofs occur quite naturally.

Consider a A : Set that we want to show to be a field. That means that we have to define all kinds of objects $(0, 1)$ and functions $(\text{mult}, \ldots)$ on A and to prove that together they satisfy the field-axioms. Now what should the type of the reciprocal be, given that the reciprocal of 0 is not defined? An option is to let recip : $A \rightarrow A$ with the property that $\forall x{:}A.x \neq 0 \rightarrow \text{mult}\, x(\text{recip}\, x) = 1$. However, this is not very nice: recip0 should be undefined (whereas now it is an 'unspecified' element of A). In type theory there is a different solution to this: construct

$$\text{recip} : (\Sigma x{:}A.x \neq 0) \to A.$$

Then recip is only defined on the subset of elements that are non-zero: it receives a pair $\langle a, p \rangle$ with $a : A$ and $p : a \neq 0$ and returns $\text{recip}\langle a, p \rangle : A$. But how should one understand the dependency of this object (of type A) on the proof p in terms of ordinary mathematics?

A possible solution is provided by the setoids approach (see also the previous Section). We take as the carrier of a field a setoid $[A, =_A]$, so $A : \mathsf{Set}$ and $=_A$ is an equivalence relation on A. The operations on the field are now taken to be setoid functions, so e.g. mult has to preserve the equality: if $a =_A a'$ and $b =_A b'$, then $(\text{mult} ab) =_A (\text{mult} a'b')$. Similarly, all the properties of fields are now denoted using the setoid equality $=_A$ instead of the general equality $=$. For the reciprocal, this amounts to

$$\text{recip} : [A, =_A] | (\lambda x{:}A.x \neq_A 0) \to [A, =_A],$$

a setoid function from the subsetoid of non-zeros to $[A, =_A]$ itself. In this case, recip still takes a pair of an object and a proof $\langle a, p \rangle$, with $a : A$ and $p : a \neq_A 0$, and returns $\text{recip}\langle a, p \rangle : A$. The difference however is that recip now is a *setoid function*, which implies the following.

If $a, a' : A$ with $a =_A a', p : a \neq_A 0, q : a' \neq_A 0$, then $\text{recip}\langle a, p \rangle =_A \text{recip}\langle a', q \rangle$.

So, the value of $\text{recip}\langle a, p \rangle$ does not depend on the actual p; the only thing to ascertain is that such a term exists (i.e. that $a \neq_A 0$ is true).

We conjecture that if the objects that depend on proofs only occur in the context of setoids, as above, we can make sense of these objects in terms of standard mathematics. The general principle that for an object $t(p) : A$, where $p : \varphi$ denotes a sub-term of t,

$$t(p) = t(q) \text{ for all } p, q : \varphi$$

is called the *principle of Proof Irrelevance*. It states that the actual proof p of φ is irrelevant for the value of $t(p)$. The setoid equality discussed before obeys this principle, due to the way the setoid equality is promoted to subsetoids.

Another example of objects depending on proofs occurs for example in the definition of the absolute value in an ordered field. Suppose

$$p : \Pi x{:}F.(x \geq 0 \vee x \leq 0).$$

Then define the absolute value function abs as follows.

$$\text{abs} \quad := \quad \lambda x{:}F. \, \text{case } (px) \text{ of } \begin{array}{lcl} (\text{inl} \, \_) & \Rightarrow & x \\ (\text{inr} \, \_) & \Rightarrow & -x \end{array}$$

This function distinguishes cases according to the value of px. If it is of the form $\text{inl} \, r$ (with $r : x \geq 0$), we take x; if it is of the form $\text{inr} \, r$ (with $r : x \leq 0$), we take

$-x$. Now, for $a : F$, the term (abs a) contains a proof-term p. We want to prove that the values of abs do not depend on the actual value of p. In the context of setoids, this means that if we have two definitions of the absolute value function, abs_p and abs_q, one defined using the proof $p : \Pi x{:}F.x \geq 0 \vee x \leq 0$ and one using the proof q of the same type, we have to prove

$$\Pi x, x'{:}F.(x =_F x') \to (\mathsf{abs}_p x) =_F (\mathsf{abs}_q x').$$

Note that it may be the case that for some x, the value of $p\,x$ is inl_, while the value of $q\,x$ is inr_. Then $\mathsf{abs}_p x$ has value x and $\mathsf{abs}_q x$ has value $-x$. One then has to prove that in this overlapping case $x =_F -x$, which holds, as it only occurs if $x =_F 0$.

3. Type systems for proof checking

As we see it, there is not one 'right' type system. The widely used theorem provers that are based on type theory all have inductive types. But then still there are other important parameters: the choice of allowed quantification and the choice of reduction relations to be used in the type conversion rule. We have already mentioned the possibility of allowing impredicative quantification or not. Also, we mentioned the β, δ, ι and η rules as possible reduction rules. A very powerful extension of the reduction relation is obtained by adding a fixed-point-operator $\mathsf{Y}{:}\Pi A{:}\mathsf{Set}.(A{\to}A){\to}A$ satisfying

$$\mathsf{Y}f \to_\mathsf{Y} f(\mathsf{Y}f).$$

With this addition the reduction of the type system does not satisfy strong normalization and proof-objects are *potential* ones. It has been shown in [Geuvers, Poll and Zwanenburg 1999] that under mild conditions the Y-rules are conservative over the ones without a Y. A similar extension of type theory with fixed points is discussed in [Audebaud 1991], where the fixed points are used to define recursive data types.

It is outside the scope of this article to discuss the technical details of various different type systems. However, we do want to give some of the underlying theory, to show the sound theoretical base of type theoretical theorem provers and to make concrete some of the issues that were discussed in the previous Sections. Therefore we start off by considering one specific type system in detail. We define a type theory for higher order predicate logic, $\lambda\mathsf{HOL}$ and show how mathematical notions can be interpreted in it. To make the latter precise, we first look into higher order predicate logic itself. Then we study the formal interpretation from higher order predicate logic into $\lambda\mathsf{HOL}$, both as a motivation for the definition of $\lambda\mathsf{HOL}$ and as an illustration of how precisely mathematics is dealt with in type theory. Then we define a more general class of type systems. We discuss the essential properties and how type systems are used to create an interactive theorem prover. For $\lambda\mathsf{HOL}$ itself we give—in detail—the type checking algorithm, which is at the core of every type theoretical theorem prover.

By examples, we give some possible extensions of λHOL with other type constructions, like inductive types. The type systems that we discuss here all adhere to the principle that objects do not depend on proofs and that there is a distinction between sets and formulas. This is mainly done to keep the 'logical' explanation clear; see also the discussion in Section 2.9. We also give no formal treatment of definitions here (the δ-rule for unfolding definitions etc., see Section 2.8). Definitions are very prominent in a theorem prover and we believe that (hence) definitions are an important formal notion, but we want to restrict to the main issues here. See [Severi and Poll 1994] for the extension of type systems with a formal notion of definition.

3.1. Higher order predicate logic

If we want to do proof checking, we first have to make a choice for a logic. There are various possibilities: first order, second order, higher order. It is also possible to choose between either classical or intuitionistic logic, or between natural deduction and sequent calculus.

For checking formal proofs in a system based on type theory, it turns out that a calculus of intuitionistic natural deduction is the most adequate. Although it is not difficult to add classical reasoning, type theory is more tailored towards constructive reasoning. Furthermore, typed λ-terms are a faithful term representation of natural deductions. (In sequent calculus there is much more 'bureaucracy'.) The choice between first order, second order or higher order can be made by adapting the rules of the type system; we will come to that later. So, to set our logical system we choose constructive higher order predicate logic in natural deduction style.

3.1. DEFINITION. The language of **HOL** is defined as follows.
1. The set of *domains*, D is defined by

$$D ::= B \mid \Omega \mid D {\to} D,$$

where B represents a *basic domain* (we assume that there are countably many basic domains) and Ω represents the *domain of propositions*.
2. For every $\sigma {\in} D$, the set of *terms of type* σ, Term_σ is inductively defined as follows. (As usual we write $t : \sigma$ to denote that t is a term of type σ.)
   (a) the constants $c_1^\sigma, c_2^\sigma, \ldots$ are in Term_σ,
   (b) the variables $x_1^\sigma, x_2^\sigma, \ldots$ are in Term_σ,
   (c) if $\varphi : \Omega$ and x^σ is a variable, then $(\forall x^\sigma.\varphi) : \Omega$,
   (d) if $\varphi : \Omega$ and $\psi : \Omega$, then $(\varphi \Rightarrow \psi) : \Omega$,
   (e) if $M : \sigma{\to}\tau$ and $N : \sigma$, then $(MN) : \tau$,
   (f) if $M : \tau$ and x^σ is a variable, then $(\lambda x^\sigma.M) : \sigma{\to}\tau$.
3. The set of terms of **HOL**, Term, is defined by $\text{Term} := \cup_{\sigma \in D} \text{Term}_\sigma$.
4. The set of formulas of **HOL**, form, is defined by $\text{form} := \text{Term}_\Omega$.

We adapt the well-known notions of *free* and *bound* variable, substitution, β-reduction and β-conversion to the terms of this system.

There are no 'product' domains $(D \times D)$ in our logic. We present functions of higher arity by *Currying*: a binary function on D is represented as a term in the domain $D \rightarrow (D \rightarrow D)$. A predicate is represented as a function to Ω, following the idea (probably due to Church; it appears in [Church 1940]) that a predicate can be seen as a function that takes a value as input and returns a formula. So, a binary relation over D is represented as a term in the domain $D \rightarrow (D \rightarrow \Omega)$. (If $R : D \rightarrow (D \rightarrow \Omega)$ and $t, q : D$, then $((Rt)q) : \Omega$.) The logical connectives are just implication and universal quantification. Due to the fact that we have *higher order* universal quantification, we can express all other quantifiers using just $\Rightarrow$ and $\forall$. See 3.6 for more details.

3.2. NOTE. We fix the following notational conventions.
- Outside brackets are omitted.
- In the domains we omit the brackets by letting them associate to the right, so $D \rightarrow D \rightarrow \Omega$ denotes $D \rightarrow (D \rightarrow \Omega)$.
- In terms we omit brackets by associating them to the left, so Rtq denotes $(Rt)q$. Note that in ordinary mathematics, this is usually written as $R(t, q)$.
- If we write Rab, we *always* mean $((R \, a) \, b)$, so R applied to a, and then this applied to b. If we want to introduce a name (as an abbreviation), we will use the sans serif font, e.g. in writing trans as an abbreviation of the transitivity property.

3.3. EXAMPLE. Before giving the logical rules of **HOL**, we treat some examples of terms and formulas that can be written down in this language. Let the following be given: domains $\mathbb{N}$ and A, the relation-constant $>: \mathbb{N} \rightarrow \mathbb{N} \rightarrow \Omega$, the relation-variables $R, Q : A \rightarrow A \rightarrow \Omega$ and the function-constants $0 : \mathbb{N}$ and $S : \mathbb{N} \rightarrow \mathbb{N}$.
1. The predicate 'being larger than 0' is expressed by the term $\lambda x^{\mathbb{N}}.x > 0 : \mathbb{N} \rightarrow \Omega$.
2. Induction over $\mathbb{N}$ can be expressed by the (second order) formula ind defined as
$$\forall P^{\mathbb{N} \rightarrow \Omega}.(P0) \Rightarrow (\forall x^{\mathbb{N}}.(Px \Rightarrow P(Sx))) \Rightarrow \forall x^{\mathbb{N}}.Px.$$
3. The formula trans(R), defined as $\forall x^A y^A z^A (Rxy \Rightarrow Ryz \Rightarrow Rxz)$ denotes the fact that R is transitive. So, trans $: (A \rightarrow A \rightarrow \Omega) \rightarrow \Omega$. Note that we write $\forall x^A y^A z^A$ as a shorthand for $\forall x^A.\forall y^A.\forall z^A$.
4. The term $\subseteq: (A \rightarrow A \rightarrow \Omega) \rightarrow (A \rightarrow A \rightarrow \Omega) \rightarrow \Omega$ is defined by
$$R \subseteq Q := \forall x^A y^A.(Rxy \Rightarrow Qxy).$$
(We informally use the infix notation $R \subseteq Q$ to denote $\subseteq RQ$.)
5. The term $\lambda x^A y^A.(\forall Q^{A \rightarrow A \rightarrow \Omega}.(\text{trans}(Q) \Rightarrow (R \subseteq Q) \Rightarrow Qxy))$ is of type $A \rightarrow A \rightarrow \Omega$. It denotes the transitive closure of R. We use $\lambda x^A y^A$ as a shorthand for $\lambda x^A.\lambda y^A$.

The derivation rules of **HOL** are given in a natural deduction style.

(axiom)	$$\overline{\Gamma \vdash \varphi}$$	if $\varphi \in \Gamma$
($\Rightarrow$ -introduction)	$$\frac{\Gamma \cup \varphi \vdash \psi}{\Gamma \vdash \varphi \Rightarrow \psi}$$	
($\Rightarrow$ -elimination)	$$\frac{\Gamma \vdash \varphi \quad \Gamma \vdash \varphi \Rightarrow \psi}{\Gamma \vdash \psi}$$	
(∀-introduction)	$$\frac{\Gamma \vdash \varphi}{\Gamma \vdash \forall x^\sigma.\varphi}$$	if $x^\sigma \notin \mathrm{FV}(\Gamma)$
(∀-elimination)	$$\frac{\Gamma \vdash \forall x^\sigma.\varphi}{\Gamma \vdash \varphi[t/x^\sigma]}$$	if $t : \sigma$
(conversion)	$$\frac{\Gamma \vdash \varphi}{\Gamma \vdash \psi}$$	if $\varphi =_\beta \psi$

Figure 1: Deduction rules of **HOL**

3.4. DEFINITION. The notion of *provability*, $\Gamma \vdash \varphi$, for Γ a finite set of formulas (terms of type form) and φ a formula, is defined inductively by the rules in Fig. 1

3.5. REMARK. The rule (conversion) is an operationalization of the Poincaré principle discussed in Section 2.8. The rule says that we don't want to distinguish between β-equal propositions.

3.6. EXAMPLE. A well-known fact about this logic is that the connectives $\&, \vee, \perp, \neg$ and $\exists$ are definable in terms of $\Rightarrow$ and $\forall$. (This is due to [Russell 1903].) For $\varphi, \psi : \Omega$, define

$$\varphi \& \psi \quad := \quad \forall x^\Omega.(\varphi \Rightarrow \psi \Rightarrow x) \Rightarrow x,$$
$$\varphi \vee \psi \quad := \quad \forall x^\Omega.(\varphi \Rightarrow x) \Rightarrow (\psi \Rightarrow x) \Rightarrow x,$$
$$\perp \quad := \quad \forall x^\Omega.x,$$
$$\neg \varphi \quad := \quad \varphi \Rightarrow \perp,$$
$$\exists x^\sigma.\varphi \quad := \quad \forall z^\Omega.(\forall x^\sigma.(\varphi \Rightarrow z)) \Rightarrow z.$$

It's not difficult to check that the intuitionistic elimination and introduction rules for these connectives are sound.

Equality between terms of a fixed type σ is definable by saying that two terms are equal if they share the same properties. This equality is usually called *Leibniz equality* and is defined by

$$t =_A t' := \forall P^{A\to\Omega}.(Pt \Rightarrow Pt'), \text{ for } t,t' : A.$$

It is not difficult to see that this equality is reflexive and transitive. It is also symmetric: Let Q be a predicate variable over A (so $Q : A{\to}\Omega$). Take $\lambda y^A.Qy \Rightarrow Qt$ for P. The deduction is as follows. (At the left we apply the ($\forall$-elim) rule followed by the (conv) rule.)

$$\cfrac{\cfrac{\Gamma \vdash \forall P^{A\to\Omega}(Pt \Rightarrow Pt')}{\Gamma \vdash (Qt \Rightarrow Qt) \Rightarrow (Qt' \Rightarrow Qt)} \quad \cfrac{\Gamma, Qt \vdash Qt}{\Gamma \vdash Qt \Rightarrow Qt}}{\cfrac{\Gamma \vdash Qt' \Rightarrow Qt}{\Gamma \vdash \forall Q^{A\to\Omega}.(Qt' \Rightarrow Qt)}}$$

Impredicativity In the definition of the connectives (Example 3.6) and in the definition of equality, one makes use of *impredicativity*, that is

the possibility of constructing a term of a certain domain by abstracting over that same domain or over a domain of the same 'order'.

E.g. in Example 3.6 one constructs the *proposition* $\varphi\&\psi$ by abstracting (using the universal quantifier) over the collection of *all propositions*. Similarly in the definition of Leibniz equality one defines a binary *relation on A* by abstracting over the collection of all *predicates on A*. Both are domains of second order. (The basic domains are of first order.) The fact that this logic is higher order allows us to make these impredicative constructions.

The notion of order was first introduced by Russell (see [Whitehead and Russell 1910, 1927]) in his ramified type theory, to prevent the paradoxes arising from a naive conception of the notion of set. Later it was noted by Ramsey [1925] that the simple types suffice to avoid the syntactic paradoxes. The semantic paradoxes can be avoided by making a clear distinction between syntax (formal system) and semantics (models). In [Whitehead and Russell 1910, 1927] this distinction was not made and the ramification was used to prevent the semantical paradoxes.

Impredicativity is often seen as 'non-constructive': an impredicative definition can not really be understood as a *construction*, but only as a *description* of an object whose existence we assume on other grounds. For example, the definition of Leibniz equality *describes* a binary relation by quantifying over the collection of all predicates. This is not a *construction*, as that would require that the collection of all predicates had already been constructed, before we construct this binary relation. Therefore, impredicativity is seen as alien to constructive logic. We will still call our logic constructive, as it lacks the double negation law (and hence it is not classical). Moreover, the logic enjoys the *disjunction property* (if $\vdash \varphi\vee\psi$, then $\vdash \varphi$ or $\vdash \psi$) and the *existence property* (if $\vdash \exists x{:}A.\varphi$, then $\vdash \varphi[a/x]$ for some $a : A$) that we know from constructive logics. If we charachterize a logic as constructive if it satisfies the disjunction and the existence property, then our higher order predicate logic is constructive.

3.2. Higher order typed λ-calculus

In type theory, one interprets formulas and proofs via the well-known 'propositions-as-types' and 'proofs-as-terms' embedding, originally due to Curry, Howard and de Bruijn. (See [Howard 1980, de Bruijn 1970].) Under this interpretation, a formula is viewed as the type of its proofs. It turns out that one can define a typed λ-calculus λHOL that represents **HOL** in a very precise way. What *very precise* means will not be defined here, but see e.g. [Barendregt 1992] or [Geuvers 1993]. Here, we just define the system λHOL, using the intuitions of **HOL**. In order to get a better understanding we note a few things.

1. The language of **HOL** as presented in 3.1 is a typed language already. This language will be a part of λHOL

2. In λHOL, formulas like $\varphi \Rightarrow \psi$ and $\forall x^A.\varphi$ will become types. However, these 'propositional' types are not the same as the 'set' types like e.g. IN. Hence there will be two 'universes': Prop, containing the 'propositional' types, and Type, containing the 'set' types. Prop itself is a 'set' type.

3. The deductions are represented as typed λ-terms. The discharging of hypotheses is done by λ-*abstraction*. The modus ponens rule is interpreted via *application*.

The *derivable judgments* of λHOL are of the form

$$\Gamma \vdash M : A,$$

where Γ is a *context* and M and A are terms. A context is of the form $x_1{:}A_1, \ldots, x_n{:}A_n$, where $x_1, \ldots, x_n$ are variables and $A_1, \ldots, A_n$ are terms. The variables that occur in M and A are given a type in a context. If, in the judgment $\Gamma \vdash M : A$, the term A is a 'propositional type' (i.e. $\Gamma \vdash A : \mathsf{Prop}$), we view M as a *proof* of A. If the term A is a 'set type' (i.e. $\Gamma \vdash A : \mathsf{Type}$), we view M as an *element* of the set A.

3.7. DEFINITION. The typed λ-calculus λHOL, representing higher order predicate logic, is defined as follows. The set of *pseudo terms* $\mathcal{T}$ is defined by

$$\mathcal{T} ::= \mathsf{Prop} \mid \mathsf{Type} \mid \mathsf{Type}' \mid \mathcal{V} \mid (\Pi\mathcal{V}{:}\mathcal{T}.\mathcal{T}) \mid (\lambda\mathcal{V}{:}\mathcal{T}.\mathcal{T}) \mid \mathcal{T}\mathcal{T}.$$

Here, $\mathcal{V}$ is a set of variables. The set of *sorts*, $\mathcal{S}$ is $\{\mathsf{Prop}, \mathsf{Type}, \mathsf{Type}'\}$.

The typing rules, that select the *well-typed* terms from the pseudo terms, are given in Figure 2. Here, s ranges over the set of sorts $\mathcal{S}$.

In the rules (var) and (weak) it is always assumed that the newly declared variable is fresh, that is, it has not yet been declared in Γ. The equality in the conversion rule (conv) is the β-equality on the set of pseudo terms $\mathcal{T}$.

(axiom)	$\vdash$ Prop : Type	$\vdash$ Type : Type$'$

(var)	$$\dfrac{\Gamma \vdash A : s}{\Gamma, x{:}A \vdash x : A}$$

(weak)	$$\dfrac{\Gamma \vdash A : s \quad \Gamma \vdash M : C}{\Gamma, x{:}A \vdash M : C}$$

(Π)	$$\dfrac{\Gamma \vdash A : s_1 \quad \Gamma, x{:}A \vdash B : s_2}{\Gamma \vdash \Pi x{:}A.B : s_2}$$	if $(s_1, s_2) \in$ { (Type, Type), (Prop, Prop), (Type, Prop) }

(λ)	$$\dfrac{\Gamma, x{:}A \vdash M : B \quad \Gamma \vdash \Pi x{:}A.B : s}{\Gamma \vdash \lambda x{:}A.M : \Pi x{:}A.B}$$

(app)	$$\dfrac{\Gamma \vdash M : \Pi x{:}A.B \quad \Gamma \vdash N : A}{\Gamma \vdash MN : B[N/x]}$$

(conv)	$$\dfrac{\Gamma \vdash M : A \quad \Gamma \vdash B : s}{\Gamma \vdash M : B}$$	if $A =_\beta B$

Figure 2: Typing rules for λHOL

We see that there is no distinction between types and terms in the sense that the types are formed first and then the terms are formed using the types. A pseudo term A is *well-typed* if there is a context Γ and a pseudo term B such that $\Gamma \vdash A : B$ or $\Gamma \vdash B : A$ is derivable. The set of well-typed terms of λHOL is denoted by Term(λHOL). A context Γ is *well-formed* if it appears in some derivable statement, i.e. if there are some M and A such that $\Gamma \vdash M : A$ is derivable.

The only type-forming operator in this language is the Π, which comes in three flavors, depending on the type of the *domain* (the A in $\Pi x{:}A.B$) and the type of the *range* (the B in $\Pi x{:}A.B$). Intuitively, a Π-type should be read as a set of functions. If we depict the occurrences of x in B explicitly by writing $B(x)$, the intuition is:

$$\Pi x{:}A.B(x) \approx \prod_{a \in A} B(a) = \{f \mid \forall a \in A[f\ a \in B(a)]\}.$$

So, $\Pi x{:}A.B$ is the *dependent function type* of functions taking a term of type A as input and delivering a term of type B in which x is replaced by the input. We therefore immediately recover the ordinary function type as a special instance.

3.8. REMARK. In case $x \notin FV(B)$, we write $A{\to}B$ for $\Pi x{:}A.B$. We call this a *non-dependent* function type.

As examples we list all instances of the Π-type that can be encountered in λHOL.

3.9. EXAMPLE.
1. Using the combination (Type,Type), we can form the function type $A{\to}B$ for A, B:Type. This also comprises the types of unary predicates and binary relations: $A{\to}$Prop and $A{\to}A{\to}$Prop. Furthermore, it also extends to higher order predicate types like $(A{\to}A{\to}$Prop$){\to}$Prop.
   If $\Gamma \vdash A$: Type and $\Gamma, x{:}A \vdash B$: Type, then $x \notin FV(B)$ in λHOL, so all types formed by (Type,Type) are non-dependent function types.
2. Using (Prop,Prop), we can form the propositional type $\varphi{\to}\psi$ for φ, ψ:Prop. This is to be read as an *implicational formula*.
   If $\Gamma \vdash \varphi$: Prop and $\Gamma, x{:}\varphi \vdash \psi$: Prop, then $x \notin FV(\psi)$ in λHOL, so all types formed by (Prop,Prop) are non-dependent types.
3. Using (Type,Prop), we can form the dependent propositional type $\Pi x{:}A.\varphi$ for A:Type, φ:Prop. This is to be read as a *universally quantified formula*. This quantification can also range over higher order domains, like in $\Pi P{:}A{\to}A{\to}$Prop$.\varphi$.
   If $\Gamma \vdash A$: Type and $\Gamma, x{:}A \vdash \varphi$: Prop, then it *can* happen that $x{\in}FV(\varphi)$ in λHOL.

We do not define formal interpretations from **HOL** to λHOL and back. See e.g. [Barendregt 1992] for details. Instead, we motivate the interpretation by some (suggestive) examples. Then we discuss the main assets of the interpretation and motivate its completeness.

For a good reading of the examples below, we recall the notational conventions introduced in 3.2: Rab denotes $((R\ a)\ b)$, so R applied to a and that together applied to b. Moreover, application binds strong, so $Rab{\to}Rbc$ denotes $(Rab){\to}(Rbc)$ and $\lambda x{:}Rab.M$ denotes $\lambda x{:}(Rab).M$. As usual, arrow associate to the right, so $A{\to}A{\to}$Prop denotes $A{\to}(A{\to}$Prop$)$.

3.10. EXAMPLE.
1. $\mathbb{N}$:Type, $0{:}\mathbb{N}$, $>{:}\mathbb{N}{\to}\mathbb{N}{\to}$Prop $\vdash \lambda x{:}\mathbb{N}.x{>}0$: $\mathbb{N}{\to}$Prop. Here we see the use of λ-abstraction to define predicates.
2. $\mathbb{N}$:Type, $0{:}\mathbb{N}$, $S{:}\mathbb{N}{\to}\mathbb{N} \vdash \Pi P{:}\mathbb{N}{\to}$Prop$.(P0){\to}$
$$(\Pi x{:}\mathbb{N}.(Px{\to}P(Sx))){\to}\Pi x{:}\mathbb{N}.Px : \text{Prop}.$$
   This is the formula for induction written down in λHOL as a term of type Prop.
3. A:Type, $R{:}A{\to}A{\to}$Prop $\vdash \Pi x, y, z{:}A.Rxy{\to}Ryz{\to}Rxz$: Prop. (Transitivity of R)
4. A:Type $\vdash \lambda R, Q{:}A{\to}A{\to}$Prop$.\Pi x, y{:}A.Rxy{\to}Qxy$:
$(A{\to}A{\to}$Prop$){\to}(A{\to}A{\to}$Prop$){\to}$Prop. (Inclusion of relations)

5. $A{:}\mathsf{Type} \vdash \lambda x, y{:}A.\Pi P{:}A{\to}\mathsf{Prop}.(Px{\to}Py) : A{\to}A{\to}\mathsf{Prop}$.
   This is 'Leibniz equality' and is usually denoted by $=_A$, mentioning the domain type explicitly.

6. $A{:}\mathsf{Type}, x, y{:}A \vdash \lambda r{:}(x =_A y).\lambda P{:}A{\to}\mathsf{Prop}.r(\lambda z{:}A.Pz{\to}Px)(\lambda q{:}Px.q) :$
   $(x =_A y){\to}(y =_A x)$. The proof of the fact that Leibniz equality is symmetric.

Just as in **HOL**, it is possible to define the ordinary connectives &, $\vee$, $\perp$, $\neg$ and $\exists$ in λ**HOL**. For $\varphi, \psi{:}\mathsf{Prop}$, define

$$
\begin{aligned}
\varphi \& \psi &:= \Pi\alpha{:}\mathsf{Prop}.(\varphi{\to}\psi{\to}\alpha){\to}\alpha, \\
\varphi \vee \psi &:= \Pi\alpha{:}\mathsf{Prop}.(\varphi{\to}\alpha){\to}(\psi{\to}\alpha){\to}\alpha, \\
\perp &:= \Pi\alpha{:}\mathsf{Prop}.\alpha, \\
\neg\varphi &:= \varphi{\to}\perp, \\
\exists x{:}A.\varphi &:= \Pi\alpha{:}\mathsf{Prop}.(\Pi x{:}A.(\varphi{\to}\alpha)){\to}\alpha.
\end{aligned}
$$

To form these propositions (terms of type Prop), the rules $(\mathsf{Prop},\mathsf{Prop})$ (for all the arrows) and $(\mathsf{Type},\mathsf{Prop})$ (for all the Π-types) are used.

The logical rules for these connectives can be derived. For example, for $\varphi\&\psi$, we have terms $\pi_1 : (\varphi\&\psi){\to}\varphi$ and $\pi_2 : (\varphi\&\psi){\to}\psi$ (the projections) and a term $\langle-,-\rangle : \varphi{\to}\psi{\to}(\varphi\&\psi)$ (the pairing constructor). One can easily verify that if we take

$$
\begin{aligned}
\pi_1 &:= \lambda p{:}(\varphi\&\psi).p\varphi(\lambda x{:}\varphi.\lambda y{:}\psi.x), \\
\pi_2 &:= \lambda p{:}(\varphi\&\psi).p\psi(\lambda x{:}\varphi.\lambda y{:}\psi.y), \\
\langle-,-\rangle &:= \lambda x{:}\varphi.\lambda y{:}\psi.\lambda\alpha{:}\mathsf{Prop}.\lambda h{:}(\varphi{\to}\psi{\to}\alpha).hxy,
\end{aligned}
$$

then these terms are of the right type. Hence the introduction and elimination rules for the connective & are definable. They also have the correct reduction behavior, corresponding to cut-elimination in the logic:

$$
\begin{aligned}
\pi_1\langle t_1, t_2\rangle &\twoheadrightarrow_\beta t_1, \\
\pi_2\langle t_1, t_2\rangle &\twoheadrightarrow_\beta t_2.
\end{aligned}
$$

Similarly for the other connectives, the introduction and elimination rules can be defined.

Note that on the Type level, it is not possible to define data types, like the product type. A product type is equivalent to the conjunction (&), but the construction above for & can only be done at the Prop level.

Propositions-as-types for higher order predicate logic

The propositions-as-types interpretation from higher order predicate logic **HOL** into λ**HOL** maps a formula to a type and a proof (a derivation in natural deduction) of a formula φ to a term (i.e. a typed λ-term) of the type associated with φ:

$$\boxed{\begin{array}{c}\Sigma\\\\\psi\end{array}} \quad \mapsto \quad [\Sigma] : (\!(\psi)\!)$$

where $(\!(-)\!)$ denotes the interpretation of formulas as types and $[-]$ denotes the interpretation of derivations as λ-terms. In a derivation, we use expressions from the logical language (e.g. to instantiate the $\forall$), which may contain free variables, constants and domains (e.g. in $f(\lambda x{:}A.c)$). In type theory, in order to make sure that all terms are well-typed, the basic items (like variables and domains) have to be declared explicitly in the context. Also, a derivation will in general contain non-discharged assumptions $(\varphi_1,\ldots,\varphi_n)$ that will appear as variable declarations $(z_1 : \varphi_1,\ldots,z_n : \varphi_n)$ in the type theoretic context. So the general picture is this.

$$\begin{array}{c}\varphi_1\ldots\varphi_n\\\boxed{\Sigma}\\\psi\end{array} \quad \mapsto \quad \Gamma_\Sigma, z_1 : \varphi_1,\ldots,z_n : \varphi_n \vdash [\Sigma] : (\!(\psi)\!),$$

where Γ_Σ is the context that declares all domains, constants and free variables that occur in Σ.

As an example we treat the derivation of irreflexivity from anti-symmetry for a relation R. The derivation is as follows. (Γ denotes $\forall x^A y^A Rxy \Rightarrow Ryx \Rightarrow \bot$, Γ' denotes Γ, Rxx.)

$$\cfrac{\cfrac{\cfrac{\cfrac{\cfrac{\Gamma' \vdash \forall x^A y^A.Rxy \Rightarrow Ryx \Rightarrow \bot}{\Gamma' \vdash \forall y^A.Rxy \Rightarrow Ryx \Rightarrow \bot}}{\cfrac{\Gamma' \vdash Rxx \Rightarrow Rxx \Rightarrow \bot \qquad \Gamma' \vdash Rxx}{\Gamma' \vdash Rxx \Rightarrow \bot} \qquad \Gamma' \vdash Rxx}}{\Gamma' \vdash \bot}}{\Gamma \vdash Rxx \Rightarrow \bot}}{\Gamma \vdash \forall x^A.Rxx \Rightarrow \bot}$$

This derivation is mapped to the typed λ-term $\lambda x{:}A.\lambda q{:}(Rxx).zxxqq$. This term is well-typed in the context $A : \mathsf{Type}, R : A{\to}A{\to}\mathsf{Prop}, z : \Pi x,y{:}A.(Rxy{\to}Ryx{\to}\bot)$, yielding the following judgment, derivable in λHOL if we take for Γ the context $\Gamma = \{A{:}\mathsf{Type}, R{:}A{\to}A{\to}\mathsf{Prop}, z{:}\Pi x,y{:}A.(Rxy{\to}Ryx{\to}\bot)\}$.

$$\Gamma \vdash \lambda x{:}A\lambda q{:}(Rxx).zxxqq : (\Pi x{:}A.Rxx{\to}\bot).$$

The context Γ_Σ here consists of $A : \mathsf{Type}, R : (A{\to}A{\to}\mathsf{Prop})$.

Now one may wonder if the type system λHOL is really faithful to higher order predicate logic **HOL**. Put differently, one can ask the question of *completeness*: given a proposition of **HOL** such that $\Gamma_\varphi \vdash M : (\!\!(\varphi)\!\!)$ in λHOL, is φ derivable in **HOL**? It turns out that this is the case. Even though the number of rules of λHOL is limited (where one rule serves several different purposes, e.g. the (λ)-rule allows to form both functions, proofs of an implication and proofs of a universal quantification) and there seems to be hardly any distinction in treatment between the propositions (terms of type Prop) and the sets (terms of type Type), we can completely *disambiguate* the syntax. This is stated by the following Lemma.

3.11. LEMMA (Disambiguation Lemma). *Given a judgment $\Gamma \vdash M : A$ in λHOL, there is a λHOL-context $\Gamma_D, \Gamma_L, \Gamma_P$ such that*

1. *$\Gamma_D, \Gamma_L, \Gamma_P$ is a permutation of Γ,*
2. *$\Gamma_D, \Gamma_L, \Gamma_P \vdash M : A$*
3. *Γ_D consists only of declarations $A :$ Type,*
4. *Γ_L consists only of declarations $x : A$ with $\Gamma_D \vdash A :$ Type,*
5. *Γ_P consists only of declarations $z : \varphi$ with $\Gamma_D, \Gamma_L \vdash \varphi :$ Prop.*

Moreover the following are the case.

- *If $\Gamma \vdash A :$ Type, then $\Gamma_D \vdash A :$ Type and $A \equiv B_1 \to \cdots \to B_n$ $(n \geq 1)$ and $\Gamma_D \vdash B_i :$ Type for all i.*
- *If $\Gamma \vdash M : A$ where $\Gamma \vdash A :$ Type, then $\Gamma_D, \Gamma_L \vdash M : A$.*
- *If $\Gamma \vdash \Pi x{:}A.B :$ Prop where $\Gamma \vdash A :$ Prop, then $x \notin \mathrm{FV}(B)$ (and so $\Pi x{:}A.B \equiv A \to B$, representing a real implication).*

The Disambiguation Lemma really states that λHOL represents **HOL** very closely. Note that it says—among other things—that proof-terms (terms M with $M : \varphi$ for some $\varphi :$ Prop) do not occur in object-terms (terms $t : A$ with for some $A :$ Type). Using the Lemma, one can define a mapping back from λHOL to **HOL** that constructs a derivation out of a proof-term. Let a ψ with $\Gamma \vdash \psi :$ Prop be given.

$$\Gamma \vdash M : \psi \quad \mapsto \quad \dfrac{\begin{array}{c}\varphi_1 \ldots \varphi_n \\ [M]\end{array}}{\psi}$$

Here the $\varphi_1 \ldots \varphi_n$ are computed from Γ, using Lemma 3.11, in such a way that $\Gamma_P = z_1 : \varphi_1, \ldots, z_n : \varphi_n$.

The mapping back from λHOL to **HOL** proofs the completeness of the propositions-as-types interpretation: if $\Gamma \vdash M : \varphi$, then φ is derivable in **HOL** from the assumptions listed in Γ_P.

Type Checking

An important property of a type system is *computability of types*, i.e. given Γ and M compute an A for which $\Gamma \vdash M : A$ holds, and if there is no such A, return 'false'. This is usually called the *type synthesis problem, TSP* or the *type inference problem*. In this Section, a type synthesis algorithm for the system λHOL is given, which is quite reminiscent for type synthesis algorithms in general. Before discussing the details we briefly recapitulate some generalities on type synthesis and type checking. See also Sections 2.2, 2.3.

A problem related to type synthesis is *decidability of typing*, i.e. given Γ, M and A, decide whether $\Gamma \vdash M : A$ holds. This is usually called the *type checking problem, TCP*. Both problems are very much related, because in the process of type checking, one has to solve type synthesis problems as well: for example when *checking* whether $MN : C$, one has to *infer* a type for N, say A, and a type for M, say D, and then to check whether for some B, $D =_\beta \Pi x{:}A.B$ with $B[N/x] =_\beta C$. It should be clear from this case that type synthesis and type checking are closely entwined. (See Section 2.3 for an extended example.) The crucial algorithm to construct is an algorithm Type$_-(-)$, that takes a context Γ and a term M such that

$$\text{Type}_\Gamma(M) =_\beta A \;\Leftrightarrow\; \Gamma \vdash M : A.$$

Hence, one will need an algorithm for *β-equality checking* to decide typing.

There are two important properties that solve the decidability of β-equality checking: Confluence for β-reduction and Strong Normalization for β-reduction. (This is a well-known fact from rewriting: if a rewriting relation is confluent and strongly normalizing, then the induced equality relation is decidable: to determine $M =_\beta N$, one reduces M and N to normal form and compares these normal forms.)

3.12. PROPOSITION (Confluence). *On the set of pseudo terms $\mathcal{T}$, β-reduction is confluent i.e. for all $M, N_1, N_2 \in \mathcal{T}$, if $M \twoheadrightarrow_\beta N_1$ and $M \twoheadrightarrow_\beta N_2$, then there exists a $P \in \mathcal{T}$ such that $N_1 \twoheadrightarrow_\beta P$ and $N_2 \twoheadrightarrow_\beta P$.*

Confluence for β can be proved by following the well-known proofs for confluence for the untyped λ-calculus. Another important property of λHOL is Subject Reduction.

3.13. PROPOSITION (Subject Reduction). *The set of well-typed terms of a given type is closed under reduction. That is, for Γ a context and M, N, A in $\mathcal{T}$, if $\Gamma \vdash M : A$ and $M \twoheadrightarrow_\beta N$, then $\Gamma \vdash N : A$.*

See Section 2.6 for a discussion on Subject Reduction and Section 3.3 for a list of properties for λHOL (among which Subject Reduction). The following is a consequence of confluence on $\mathcal{T}$ and Subject Reduction.

3.14. COROLLARY (Confluence on well-typed terms). *On the set of well-typed terms of λHOL, β-reduction is confluent. That is, for M well-typed, if $M \twoheadrightarrow_\beta N_1$ and $M \twoheadrightarrow_\beta N_2$, then there exists a well-typed term P such that $N_1 \twoheadrightarrow_\beta P$ and $N_2 \twoheadrightarrow_\beta P$. Moreover, N_1 and N_2 are well-typed.*

3.15. PROPOSITION (Strong Normalization). *For any term M well-typed in λHOL, there are no infinite β-reduction paths starting from M. (Put differently: all reductions starting from a well-typed term terminate.)*

The proof of this Proposition is rather involved. See [Barendregt 1992] for references to proofs.

The *type synthesis algorithm* $\mathrm{Type}_-(-)$ attempts to apply the typing rules in the reverse direction. For example, computing $\mathrm{Type}_\Gamma(\lambda x{:}A.M)$ is done by computing $\mathrm{Type}_{\Gamma,x:A}(M)$, and if this yields B, computing $\mathrm{Type}_\Gamma(\Pi x{:}A.B)$. If this returns a $s \in \{\mathsf{Prop}, \mathsf{Type}\}$, then we return $\Pi x{:}A.B$ as result of $\mathrm{Type}_\Gamma(\lambda x{:}A.M)$. So, we read the ($\lambda$)-rule in the reverse direction.

There is a potential problem in this way of constructing the $\mathrm{Type}_-(-)$ algorithm by reversing the rules: a conclusion $\Gamma \vdash \lambda x{:}A.M : C$ need not have been obtained from the (λ)-rule. (It could also be a conclusion of the (weak)-rule or the (conv)-rule. This situation is usually referred to as the 'non-syntax-directedness' of the derivation rules. A set of derivation rules is called *syntax-directed* if, given a context Γ and a term M, *at most* one rule can have as conclusion $\Gamma \vdash M : C$ (for some C). See [Pollack 1995] and [van Benthem Jutting et al. 1994] for more on syntax-directed sets of rules for type systems and their advantages. We will treat the (potential) problem of non-syntax-directedness later when we discuss the soundness and completeness of the $\mathrm{Type}_-(-)$ algorithm.

Another part of the algorithm that needs some special attention is the variable case. The result of $\mathrm{Type}_\Gamma(x)$ should be A if $x{:}A$ occurs in Γ and 'false' otherwise. But, if Γ is not a well-formed context, we want to return 'false' as well! So we have to check the well-formedness of Γ. A type synthesis algorithm consists of two mutually dependent recursive functions: $\mathrm{Type}_-(-)$, the real type synthesis algorithm, and the *context checking algorithm* $\mathrm{Ok}(-)$. The latter takes as input a context and returns 'true' if and only if the context is well-formed (and 'false' otherwise).

3.16. DEFINITION. We define the algorithms $\mathrm{Ok}(-)$, taking a context and returning 'true' or 'false', and $\mathrm{Type}_-(-)$, taking a context and a term and returning a term or 'false', as follows. Here x denotes a variable.

$$\mathrm{Ok}(<>) \quad = \quad \text{'true' (the empty context)},$$

$$\mathrm{Ok}(\Gamma, x{:}A) \quad = \quad \mathrm{Type}_\Gamma(A) \in \{\mathsf{Prop}, \mathsf{Type}, \mathsf{Type}'\},$$

$$\mathrm{Type}_\Gamma(x) \quad = \quad \text{if } \mathrm{Ok}(\Gamma) \text{ and } x{:}A \in \Gamma \text{ then } A \text{ else 'false'},$$

$$\mathrm{Type}_\Gamma(\mathsf{Prop}) \quad = \quad \text{if } \mathrm{Ok}(\Gamma) \text{ then } \mathsf{Type} \text{ else 'false'},$$

$$\mathrm{Type}_\Gamma(\mathsf{Type}) \quad = \quad \text{if } \mathrm{Ok}(\Gamma) \text{ then } \mathsf{Type}' \text{ else 'false'},$$

$$\mathrm{Type}_\Gamma(\mathsf{Type}') \quad = \quad \text{'false'},$$

$$\mathrm{Type}_\Gamma(MN) \quad = \quad \text{if } \mathrm{Type}_\Gamma(M) = C \text{ and } \mathrm{Type}_\Gamma(N) = D$$
$$\qquad\qquad \text{then} \quad \text{if } C \twoheadrightarrow_\beta \Pi x{:}A.B \text{ and } A =_\beta D$$
$$\qquad\qquad\qquad\quad \text{then } B[N/x] \text{ else 'false'}$$
$$\qquad\qquad \text{else} \quad \text{'false'},$$

$$\text{Type}_\Gamma(\lambda x{:}A.M) \quad = \quad \text{if } \text{Type}_{\Gamma,x:A}(M) = B$$

$$\text{then} \qquad \text{if } \text{Type}_\Gamma(\Pi x{:}A.B) \in \{\text{Prop}, \text{Type}, \text{Type}'\}$$
$$\text{then } \Pi x{:}A.B \text{ else 'false'}$$
$$\text{else 'false'},$$

$$\text{Type}_\Gamma(\Pi x{:}A.B) \quad = \quad \text{if } \text{Type}_\Gamma(A) = s_1 \text{ and } \text{Type}_{\Gamma,x:A}(B) = s_2$$

$$\text{and } s_1, s_2 \in \{\text{Prop}, \text{Type}, \text{Type}'\}$$

$$\text{then} \qquad \text{if } (s_1, s_2) \in \{ (\text{Type}, \text{Type}), (\text{Prop}, \text{Prop}),$$
$$(\text{Type}, \text{Prop}) \}$$
$$\text{then } s_2 \text{ else 'false'}$$
$$\text{else 'false'},$$

The intuition behind the type synthesis algorithm being clear, we want to prove that it is sound and complete. This means proving the following.

3.17. DEFINITION. The type synthesis algorithm $\text{Type}_{-}(-)$ is *sound* if for all Γ and M,

$$\text{Type}_\Gamma(M) = A \; \Rightarrow \; \Gamma \vdash M : A.$$

The type synthesis algorithm $\text{Type}_{-}(-)$ is *complete* if for all Γ, M and A,

$$\Gamma \vdash M : A \; \Rightarrow \; \text{Type}_\Gamma(M) =_\beta A.$$

Note that completeness of $\text{Type}_{-}(-)$ implies that if $\text{Type}_\Gamma(M) = $ 'false', then M is not typable in Γ. The definition of completeness only makes sense if we have *uniqueness of types*:

$$\text{If } \Gamma \vdash M : A \text{ and } \Gamma \vdash M : B, \text{ then } A =_\beta B.$$

This property holds for λHOL. Without uniqueness of types, we would have to let $\text{Type}_{-}(-)$ generate a *set of possible types*, for otherwise it could happen that a valid type A for M in Γ is not computed (up to $=_\beta$) by $\text{Type}_\Gamma(M)$.

Besides soundness and completeness, we want to know that $\text{Type}_{-}(-)$ terminates on all inputs, i.e. it should be a *total* function. (A sound and complete algorithm may still not terminate on some non-typable term.) We will deal with soundness, termination and completeness now.

3.18. PROPOSITION (Soundness of $\text{Type}_{-}(-)$). *The type synthesis algorithm and the context checking algorithm, $\text{Type}_{-}(-)$ and $\text{Ok}(-)$, are sound, i.e. if $\text{Type}_\Gamma(M) = A$, then $\Gamma \vdash M : A$ and if $\text{Ok}(\Gamma) = $ 'true', then Γ is well-formed.*

The proof of soundness of $\text{Type}_{-}(-)$ and $\text{Ok}(-)$ is simultaneously, by induction on the number of evaluation-steps required for the algorithm to terminate. (Soundness states a property only for those inputs for which the algorithm terminates.) The only interesting case is $\text{Type}_\Gamma(MN)$, where one has to use the Subject Reduction property and Confluence.

The termination of $\text{Type}_-(-)$ and $\text{Ok}(-)$ should also be proved simultaneously, by devising a measure that decreases with every recursive call. We define the measure m for a context Γ or a pair of a context Γ and a term M as follows.

$$\text{m}(\Gamma) \quad := \quad \#\{\text{symbols in } \Gamma\},$$

$$\text{m}(\Gamma, M) \quad := \quad \#\{\text{symbols in } \Gamma, M\}.$$

Now, m decreases for every recursive call of $\text{Type}_-(-)$ or $\text{Ok}(-)$, except for the case of $\text{Type}_\Gamma(\lambda x{:}A.M)$, where $\text{m}(\Gamma, \Pi x{:}A.B)$ may be larger than $\text{m}(\Gamma, \lambda x{:}A.M)$ (if B is longer then M). So, the only problem with termination is in the side-condition of the (λ)-rule, where we have to verify whether $\Pi x{:}A.B$ is a well-typed type. This is a situation encountered very generally in type synthesis algorithms for dependent type theory. See [Pollack 1995] and [Severi 1998] for some general solutions to this problem and a discussion. In the case of λHOL, there is a rather easy way out: we can replace the side-condition $\Gamma \vdash \Pi x{:}A.B : s$ in the (λ)-rule by an equivalent but simpler one.

3.19. LEMMA. *Let $\Gamma, x{:}A$ be a context and B be a term. Suppose $\Gamma, x{:}A \vdash M : B$ for some M. Then the following holds.*

$$\Gamma \vdash \Pi x{:}A.B : s \quad \Leftrightarrow \quad \text{if } B \equiv C_0 \to \cdots \to C_n \text{ for some } n \in \mathbb{N} \text{ with}$$

$$(C_n \equiv \mathsf{Prop} \vee (C_n \equiv z \text{ for some } z \text{ with } (z{:}\mathsf{Type}) \in \Gamma))$$

$$\text{then} \quad \Gamma \vdash A : \mathsf{Type}$$

$$\text{else} \quad \text{if } B \not\equiv \mathsf{Type}, \mathsf{Type}' \text{ then } \Gamma \vdash A : \mathsf{Prop}$$

When applying the type synthesis algorithm to a λ-abstraction, we will replace the part ' if $\text{Type}_\Gamma(\Pi x{:}A.B) \in \{\mathsf{Prop}, \mathsf{Type}, \mathsf{Type}'\}$' by the equivalent condition given in the Lemma.

3.20. DEFINITION. The new *type synthesis algorithm* $\text{Type}_-(-)$ and the *context checking algorithm* $\text{Ok}(-)$ are defined by replacing in the case $\text{Type}_\Gamma(\lambda x{:}A.B)$ the part
if $\text{Type}_\Gamma(\Pi x{:}A.B) \in \{\mathsf{Prop}, \mathsf{Type}, \mathsf{Type}'\}$ by

$$\text{if} \quad B \equiv C_0 \to \cdots \to C_n \text{ for some } n \in \mathbb{N} \text{ with}$$

$$(C_n \equiv \mathsf{Prop} \vee (C_n \equiv z \text{ for some } z \text{ with } z{:}\mathsf{Type} \in \Gamma))$$

$$\text{then} \quad \text{Type}_\Gamma(A) = \mathsf{Type}$$

$$\text{else} \quad \text{if } B \not\equiv \mathsf{Type}, \mathsf{Type}' \text{then } \text{Type}_\Gamma(A) = \mathsf{Prop}$$

Note that the algorithm only verifies this condition when the premise in the Lemma is satisfied. The new condition may look rather complicated, but it is decidable and now all the recursive calls are done to inputs with a smallest measure. We remark that, this slight variation of the type synthesis algorithm is still sound.

To establish termination, we have to verify that all side conditions are decidable. Here the only work is in the application case: in computing $\text{Type}_\Gamma(MN)$, we have to check a β-equality and we have to check whether a term reduces to a Π-type. In general, checking β-equality on pseudo terms is *not decidable* because we have the full expressive power of the untyped λ-calculus. However, due to the soundness of the algorithm (Proposition 3.18), we know that the intermediate results in the computation of $\text{Type}_\Gamma(MN)$, C and D, are typable terms. Now, β-equality is decidable for typable terms, due to Strong Normalization and Confluence. Hence all side conditions are decidable. To make the algorithm fully deterministic we search the $\Pi x{:}A.B$ (in $C \twoheadrightarrow_\beta \Pi x{:}A.B$) by computing the *weak-head-normal-form* (which exists, due to Strong Normalization).

3.21. PROPOSITION. *The algorithms* $\text{Type\_}(-)$ *and* $\text{Ok}(-)$ *terminate on all inputs.*

Now we come to the completeness of the algorithms. Usually this is proved by defining a different set of derivation rules (1) that is equivalent to the original one (i.e. they have the same set of derivable statements $\Gamma \vdash M : A$), (2) for which the completeness of the algorithm are easy to prove. In order to achieve (2), we define a derivation system that is close to the type synthesis algorithm.

3.22. DEFINITION. The *modified derivation rules* of λHOL are to derive two forms of judgment: $\Gamma \vdash^{tc} M : A$ and $\Gamma \vdash^{tc} \text{ok}$. They are given by the original rules of λHOL, except that
- The rules (ax), (weak), (var) and (conv) are removed,
- The following rules are added.

$$
\begin{array}{ll}
\text{(empty)} & \langle\rangle \vdash^{tc} \text{ok} \\[2ex]
\text{(proj)} & \dfrac{\Gamma \vdash^{tc} \text{ok}}{\Gamma \vdash^{tc} x : A} \qquad \text{if } (x{:}A)\in\Gamma \\[3ex]
\text{(sort)} & \dfrac{\Gamma \vdash^{tc} \text{ok}}{\Gamma \vdash^{tc} \text{Prop} : \text{Type}} \qquad \dfrac{\Gamma \vdash^{tc} \text{ok}}{\Gamma \vdash^{tc} \text{Type} : \text{Type}'} \\[3ex]
\text{(context)} & \dfrac{\Gamma \vdash^{tc} A : s}{\Gamma, x{:}A \vdash^{tc} \text{ok}}
\end{array}
$$

- The (app) rule is replaced by

$$
\text{(app)} \quad \dfrac{\Gamma \vdash^{tc} M : C \quad \Gamma \vdash^{tc} N : D}{\Gamma \vdash^{tc} MN : B[N/x]} \qquad \text{if } C \twoheadrightarrow_\beta \Pi x{:}A.B \text{ and } D =_\beta A
$$

We state the following properties for the modified derivation rules.

3.23. PROPOSITION.   *1. Soundness of the modified rules*

$$\Gamma \vdash^{tc} M : A \Rightarrow \Gamma \vdash M : A$$

2. Completeness of the modified rules

$$\Gamma \vdash M : A \Rightarrow \exists A_0 [A_0 =_\beta A \,\&\, \Gamma \vdash M : A_0]$$

3. Completeness of the modified rules w.r.t $\text{Type}_{-}(-)$ *and* $\text{Ok}(-)$

$$\Gamma \vdash^{tc} M : A \quad \Rightarrow \quad \text{Type}_\Gamma(M) =_\beta A,$$

$$\Gamma \vdash^{tc} \text{ok} \quad \Rightarrow \quad \text{Ok}(\Gamma) = \text{'true'}.$$

All cases in the proof of this Proposition are by an easy induction.

3.3. Pure Type Systems

The system λHOL is just an instance of a general class of typed λ calculi, the so-called 'Pure Type Systems' or PTSs. These were first introduced by Berardi [1988] and Terlouw [1989], under different names and with slightly different definitions, as a generalization of the so called λ-*cube*, see [Barendregt 1992]. The reason for defining the class of PTSs is that many known systems are (or better: can be seen as) PTSs. This makes it fruitful to study the general properties of PTSs in order to obtain many specific results for specific systems as immediate instances. In what follows we will mention a number of these properties. Another advantage is that the PTSs can be used as a framework for comparing type systems and for defining translations between them.

Pure Type Systems are an immediate generalization of λHOL if we just note the following parameters in the definition of λHOL.

- The set of 'sorts' S can be varied. (In λHOL: Prop, Type, Type'.)
- The relation between the sorts can be varied. (In λHOL: { Type : Type', Prop : Type}.)
- The combinations of sorts for which we allow the construction of Π-types can be varied. (In λHOL: (Type, Type), (Prop, Prop), (Type, Prop).)

3.24. DEFINITION. For S a set (the set of sorts), $A \subset S \times S$ (the set of axioms) and $\mathcal{R} \subset S \times S \times S$ (the set of rules), the *Pure Type System* $\lambda(S, A, \mathcal{R})$ is the typed λ-calculus with the deduction rules given in Figure 3. If $s_2 \equiv s_3$ in a triple $(s_1, s_2, s_3) \in \mathcal{R}$, we write $(s_1, s_2) \in \mathcal{R}$. In the derivation rules, the expressions are taken from the set of *pseudo terms* $\mathcal{T}$ defined by

$$\mathcal{T} ::= S \,|\, \mathcal{V} \,|\, (\Pi \mathcal{V}{:}\mathcal{T}.\mathcal{T}) \,|\, (\lambda \mathcal{V}{:}\mathcal{T}.\mathcal{T}) \,|\, \mathcal{T}\mathcal{T}.$$

The pseudo term A is *well-typed* if there is a context Γ and a pseudo term B such that $\Gamma \vdash A : B$ or $\Gamma \vdash B : A$ is derivable. The set of well-typed terms of $\lambda(S, A, \mathcal{R})$ is denoted by $\text{Term}(\lambda(S, A, \mathcal{R}))$.

(sort)	$\vdash s_1 : s_2$	if $(s_1, s_2) \in \mathcal{A}$
(var)	$\dfrac{\Gamma \vdash A : s}{\Gamma, x{:}A \vdash x : A}$	if $x \notin \Gamma$
(weak)	$\dfrac{\Gamma \vdash A : s \quad \Gamma \vdash M : C}{\Gamma, x{:}A \vdash M : C}$	if $x \notin \Gamma$
(Π)	$\dfrac{\Gamma \vdash A : s_1 \quad \Gamma, x{:}A \vdash B : s_2}{\Gamma \vdash \Pi x{:}A.B : s_3}$	if $(s_1, s_2, s_3) \in \mathcal{R}$
(λ)	$\dfrac{\Gamma, x{:}A \vdash M : B \quad \Gamma \vdash \Pi x{:}A.B : s}{\Gamma \vdash \lambda x{:}A.M : \Pi x{:}A.B}$	
(app)	$\dfrac{\Gamma \vdash M : \Pi x{:}A.B \quad \Gamma \vdash N : A}{\Gamma \vdash MN : B[N/x]}$	
(conv)	$\dfrac{\Gamma \vdash M : A \quad \Gamma \vdash B : s}{\Gamma \vdash M : B}$	$A =_\beta B$

Figure 3: Typing rules for PTS

It is instructive to define some PTSs to see how flexible the notion is. In the following, we describe a PTS by just listing the sort, the axioms and the rules in a box. For λHOL this amounts to the following.

λHOL	
$\mathcal{S}$	Prop, Type, Type$'$
$\mathcal{A}$	Prop : Type, Type : Type$'$
$\mathcal{R}$	(Prop, Prop), (Type, Type), (Type, Prop)

To define first order predicate logic as a PTS, we have to make a syntactical distinction between 'first order domains' (over which one can quantify) and 'higher order domains' (over which quantification is not allowed). Therefore, a sort Set is introduced, the sort of first order domains, and associated with that a sort Type^s, the type of Set. The Pure Type System λPRED, representing first order predicate logic, is defined as follows.

λPRED	
$\mathcal{S}$	Set, Type^s, Prop, Type
$\mathcal{A}$	Set : Type^s, Prop : Type
$\mathcal{R}$	(Set, Set), (Set, Type), (Prop, Prop), (Set, Prop)

We briefly explain the rules. The rule (Prop, Prop) is the usual for forming the implication. With (Set, Type) one can form $A \rightarrow$ Prop : Type and $A \rightarrow A \rightarrow$ Prop : Type, the domains of unary predicates and binary relations. The rule (Set, Prop) allows the quantification over Set-types: one can form $\Pi x{:}A.\varphi$ (A : Set and φ : Prop, which is to be read as a universal quantification). Using (Set, Set) one can define function types like the type of binary functions: $A \rightarrow A \rightarrow A$, but also $(A \rightarrow A) \rightarrow A$, which is usually referred to as a 'higher order function type'. So note that λPRED is first order only in the *logical* sense, i.e. quantification over predicate domains (like $A \rightarrow A \rightarrow$ Prop) is not allowed.

The system λPRED, as described above, captures quite a lot of first order predicate logic. As a matter of fact it precisely captures *minimal* first order predicate logic with *higher order functions*. The minimality means that there are only two connectives: implication and first order universal quantification. As we are in a first order framework, the other connectives can not be defined. This makes the expressibility rather low, as one can not write down negative formulas. On the other hand, we do have higher order function types. It is possible to define a PTS that captures minimal first order predicate logic exactly (i.e. λPRED without higher order functions). See [Barendregt 1992] for details.

To regain all connectives, λPRED can be extended to the second order or higher order predicate logic (where all connectives are definable). We only treat the extension to higher order predicate logic (λPREDω) here and compare it with λHOL.

λPREDω	
$\mathcal{S}$	Set, Type^s, Prop, Type
$\mathcal{A}$	Set : Type^s, Prop : Type
$\mathcal{R}$	(Set, Set), (Set, Type), (Type, Type), (Prop, Prop),
	(Set, Prop), (Type, Prop)

The rule (Type, Prop) allows quantification over domains of type Type, which are $A \rightarrow$ Prop, $A \rightarrow A \rightarrow$ Prop etcetera. The addition of (Type, Type) implies that now also $(A \rightarrow$ Prop$) \rightarrow$ Prop : Type and $((A \rightarrow$ Prop$) \rightarrow$ Prop$) \rightarrow$ Prop : Type. Quantification is over Type, which covers all higher order domains.

Other well-known typed λ-calculi that can be described as a PTS are simple typed λ-calculus, polymorphic typed λ-calculus (also known as system F, [Girard 1972], [Girard, Lafont and Taylor 1989]), higher order typed λ-calculus (also known as Fω, [Girard 1972]). All these systems can be seen as subsystems of the Calculus of Constructions, [Coquand 1985], [Coquand and Huet 1988]. We define the Calculus of Constructions (CC) as the following PTS.

CC	
$\mathcal{S}$	$*, \square$
$\mathcal{A}$	$* : \square$
$\mathcal{R}$	$(*, *), (*, \square), (\square, *), (\square, \square)$

The aforementioned subsystems can be obtained from this specification by restricting the set of rules $\mathcal{R}$. This decomposition of the Calculus of Constructions is also known as the *cube of typed λ-calculi*, see [Barendregt 1992] for further details. In view of higher order predicate logic, one can understand CC as the system obtained by smashing the sorts Prop and Set into one, $*$. Hence, higher order predicate logic can be done inside the Calculus of Constructions. We describe the map from λPREDω to CC later in this Section in detail.

3.4. Properties of Pure Type Systems

As has already been mentioned, an important motivation for the definition of the general framework of Pure Type Systems is the fact that many important properties can be proved for all PTSs at once. Here, we list the most important properties and discuss them briefly. Proofs can be found in [Geuvers and Nederhof 1991] and [Barendregt 1992]. In the following, unless explicitly stated otherwise, $\vdash$ refers to derivability in an arbitrary PTS. As in λHOL, we define a context Γ to be *well-formed* if $\Gamma \vdash M : A$ for some M and A.

Two basic properties are Thinning, saying that typing judgments remain valid in an extended context, and Substitution, saying that typing judgments remain valid if we substitute well-typed terms.

3.25. PROPOSITION (Thinning). *For Γ a context, Γ' a well-formed context and M and A in $\mathcal{T}$, if $\Gamma \vdash M : A$ and $\Gamma \subseteq \Gamma'$, then $\Gamma' \vdash M : A$. Here, $\Gamma \subseteq \Gamma'$ denotes that all declarations that occur in Γ, also occur in Γ'.*

3.26. PROPOSITION (Substitution). *For $\Gamma_1, x{:}B, \Gamma_2$ a context, and M, N and A in $\mathcal{T}$, if $\Gamma_1, x{:}B, \Gamma_2 \vdash M : A$ and $\Gamma_1 \vdash N : B$, then $\Gamma_1, \Gamma_2[N/x] \vdash M[N/x] : A[N/x]$. Here, $M[N/x]$ denotes the substitution of N for x in M, which is straightforwardly extended to contexts by substituting in all types in the declarations.*

Two other properties we want to mention here are Strengthening, saying that variables that do not appear in the terms can be omitted from the context, and Subject Reduction, saying that typing is closed under reduction.

3.27. PROPOSITION (Strengthening). *For $\Gamma_1, x{:}B, \Gamma_2$ a context, and M, A in $\mathcal{T}$,*

$$\Gamma_1, x{:}B, \Gamma_2 \vdash M : A \quad \& \quad x \notin \mathrm{FV}(\Gamma_2, M, A) \; \Rightarrow \; \Gamma_1, \Gamma_2 \vdash M : A.$$

This property, though intuitively very plausible, is difficult to prove and requires a deep analysis of the typing judgment (see [van Benthem Jutting 1993]). (Note that Strengthening is not an immediate consequence of Substitution, because types may not be inhabited, i.e. there may not be an N such that $\Gamma_1 \vdash N : B$.)

3.28. PROPOSITION (Subject Reduction). *For Γ a context and M, N and A in $\mathcal{T}$, if $\Gamma \vdash M : A$ and $M \twoheadrightarrow_\beta N$, then $\Gamma \vdash N : A$.*

There are also many (interesting) properties that hold for specific PTSs or specific classes of PTSs. We mention some of these properties, but first we introduce a new notion.

3.29. DEFINITION. A PTS $\lambda(\mathcal{S}, \mathcal{A}, \mathcal{R})$ is *functional*, also called *singly sorted*, if the relations $\mathcal{A}$ and $\mathcal{R}$ are functions, i.e. if the following two properties hold

$$\forall s_1, s_2, s_2' \in \mathcal{S}(s_1, s_2), (s_1, s_2') \in \mathcal{A} \quad \Rightarrow \quad s_2 = s_2',$$
$$\forall s_1, s_2, s_3, s_3' \in \mathcal{S}(s_1, s_2, s_3), (s_1, s_2, s_3') \in \mathcal{R} \quad \Rightarrow \quad s_3 = s_3'$$

All the PTSs that we have encountered so far are functional. In general it is hard to find a 'natural' PTS that is not functional. Functional PTSs share the following nice property.

3.30. PROPOSITION (Uniqueness of Types). *This property holds for functional PTSs only. For Γ a context, M, A and B in $\mathcal{T}$, if $\Gamma \vdash M : A$ and $\Gamma \vdash M : B$, then $A =_\beta B$.*

One can sometimes relate results of two different systems by defining an embedding between them. There is one very simple class of embeddings between PTSs.

3.31. DEFINITION. For $T = \lambda(\mathcal{S}, \mathcal{A}, \mathcal{R})$ and $T' = \lambda(\mathcal{S}', \mathcal{A}', \mathcal{R}')$ PTSs, a *PTS-morphism from T to T'* is a mapping $f : \mathcal{S} \to \mathcal{S}'$ that preserves the axioms and rules. That is, for all $s_1, s_2 \in \mathcal{S}$, if $(s_1, s_2) \in \mathcal{A}$ then $(f(s_1), f(s_2)) \in \mathcal{A}'$ and if $(s_1, s_2, s_3) \in \mathcal{R}$ then $(f(s_1), f(s_2), f(s_3)) \in \mathcal{R}'$.

A PTS-morphism f from $\lambda(\mathcal{S}, \mathcal{A}, \mathcal{R})$ to $\lambda(\mathcal{S}', \mathcal{A}', \mathcal{R}')$ extends immediately to a mapping f on pseudo terms and contexts. Moreover, this mapping preserves reduction in a faithful way: $M \to_\beta N$ iff $f(M) \to_\beta f(N)$. We have the following property.

3.32. PROPOSITION. *For T and T' PTSs and f a PTS-morphism from T to T', if $\Gamma \vdash M : A$ in T, then $f(\Gamma) \vdash f(M) : f(A)$ in T'.*

Not all PTSs are Strongly Normalizing. We have the following well-known theorem.

3.33. THEOREM. *The Calculus of Constructions, CC, is Strongly Normalizing.*

The proof is rather involved and can be found in [Geuvers and Nederhof 1991, Coquand and Gallier 1990, Berardi 1990]. More general approaches to proving strong normalization for type systems with dependent types can be found in [Mellies and Werner 1998, Geuvers 1995].

As a consequence we find that many other PTSs are Strongly Normalizing as well. This comprises all the sub-systems of CC and also all systems T for which there is a PTS-morphism from T to CC. (Note that a PTS-morphism preserves infinite reduction paths.)

3.34. COROLLARY. *The following PTSs are all Strongly Normalizing. All subsystems of CC; λPRED; λPREDω.*

A well-known example of a PTS that is not Strongly Normalizing is $\lambda*$. This generalizes the Calculus of Constructions to the extent where $*$ and $\Box$ are unified, or put differently, the sort of types, $*$, is itself a type.

$\lambda*$	
$\mathcal{S}$	$*$
$\mathcal{A}$	$* : *$
$\mathcal{R}$	$(*, *)$

This PTS is also *inconsistent* in the sense that all types are inhabited (which means, if we view—following the propositions-as-types embedding—the type system as a logic, that all propositions are provable). The original proof of inconsistency of $\lambda*$ is in [Girard 1972]; a very clear exposition can be found in [Coquand 1986], while [Hurkens 1995] has improved and shortened the inconsistency proof considerably. From the inconsistency it easily follows that the system is not normalizing. The PTS $\lambda*$ is also the terminal object in the category of PTSs with PTS-morphisms as arrows.

As a matter of fact, we now have two formalizations of higher order predicate logic as a PTS: λHOL and λPREDω. We employ the notion of PTS-morphism to see that they are equivalent. ¿From λPREDω to λHOL, consider the PTS-morphism f given by

$$f(\text{Prop}) = \text{Prop},$$
$$f(\text{Set}) = \text{Type},$$
$$f(\text{Type}) = \text{Type},$$
$$f(\text{Type}^s) = \text{Type}'.$$

One verifies immediately that f preserves $\mathcal{A}$ and $\mathcal{R}$, hence we have

$$\Gamma \vdash_{\lambda\text{PRED}\omega} M : A \Rightarrow f(\Gamma) \vdash_{\lambda\text{HOL}} f(M) : f(A).$$

The inverse of f can almost be described as a PTS-morphism, but not quite. Define the PTS-morphism g from λPREDω to λHOL as follows.

$$g(\text{Prop}) = \text{Prop},$$

$$g(\mathsf{Type}) \;=\; \mathsf{Set},$$
$$g(\mathsf{Type}') \;=\; \mathsf{Type}^s$$

(In λHOL the sort Type' can not appear in a context nor in a term on the left side of the ':'.) We extend g to derivable judgments of λHOL in the following way.

$$g(\Gamma \vdash M : A) \;=\; g(\Gamma) \vdash g(M) : g(A), \text{ if } A \neq \mathsf{Type},$$
$$g(\Gamma \vdash M : \mathsf{Type}) \;=\; g(\Gamma) \vdash g(M) : \mathsf{Set}, \text{ if } M \equiv \cdots \to \alpha, (\alpha \text{ a variable}),$$
$$g(\Gamma \vdash M : \mathsf{Type}) \;=\; g(\Gamma) \vdash g(M) : \mathsf{Type}, \text{ if } M \equiv \cdots \to \mathsf{Prop}.$$

By easy induction one proves that g preserves derivations. Furthermore, $f(g(\Gamma \vdash M : A)) = \Gamma \vdash M : A$ and $g(f(\Gamma \vdash M : A)) = \Gamma \vdash M : A$. Hence, λPREDω and λHOL are equivalent systems. This equivalence implies that the system λHOL is Strongly Normalizing as well.

3.5. Extensions of Pure Type Systems

Several features are not present in PTSs. For example, it is possible to define data types (in a polymorphic sort, e.g. Prop in λHOL or $*$ in CC), but one does not get induction over these data types for free. (It is possible to define functions by recursion, but induction has to be assumed as an axiom.) Therefore, 'inductive types' an extra feature. The way we present them below, they were first defined in [Coquand and Paulin-Mohring 1990]. (See also [Paulin-Mohring 1994].) Inductive types are present in all widely used type-theoretic theorem provers, like [COQ 1999, LEGO 1998, Agda 2000].

Another feature that we will discuss is the notion of product and (strong) Σ-type. A Σ-type is a 'dependent product type' and therefore a generalisation of product type in the same way that a Π-type is a generalisation of arrow type: $\Sigma x{:}A.B$ represents the type of pairs (a, b) with $a : A$ and $b : B[a/x]$. (If $x \notin \mathrm{FV}(B)$, we just end up with $A \times B$.) Besides a pairing construction to create elements of a Σ-type, we have projections to take a pair apart: if $t : \Sigma x{:}A.B$, then $\pi_1 t : A$ and $\pi_2 t : B[\pi_1 t/x]$. Σ-types are very natural for doing abstraction over theories, as was first explained in [Luo 1989]. Products can be defined inside the system if one has polymorphism, but Σ-types cannot.

3.6. Products and Sums

We have already seen how to define conjunction and disjunction in λHOL. These are very close to product-types and sum-types. In Figure 4 the desired rules for a product-type are given. In presence of polymorphism, these constructions are all definable. For example in λHOL we have products in the sort Prop. Let $A_1, A_2 : \mathsf{Prop}$ and define

$$A_1 \times A_2 \;:=\; \Pi\alpha{:}\mathsf{Prop}.(A_1 \to A_2 \to \alpha) \to \alpha,$$

$$
\frac{\Gamma \vdash A_1 : s \quad \Gamma \vdash A_2 : s}{\Gamma \vdash A_1 \times A_2 : s} \quad \text{(products)}
$$

$$
\frac{\Gamma \vdash p : A_1 \times A_2}{\Gamma \vdash \pi_i p : A_i} \quad \text{(projection)}
$$

$$
\frac{\Gamma \vdash t_1 : A_1 \quad \Gamma \vdash t_2 : A_2}{\Gamma \vdash \langle t_1, t_2 \rangle : A_1 \times A_2} \quad \text{(pairing)}
$$

computation rule: $\quad \pi_i \langle t_1, t_2 \rangle \rightarrow t_i$

Figure 4: Rules for product types

$$
\begin{aligned}
\pi_1 &:= \lambda p{:}(A_1 \times A_2).pA_1(\lambda x{:}A_1.\lambda y{:}A_2.x), \\
\pi_2 &:= \lambda p{:}(A_1 \times A_2).pA_2(\lambda x{:}A_1.\lambda y{:}A_2.y), \\
\langle -, - \rangle &:= \lambda x{:}A_1.\lambda y{:}A_2.\lambda \alpha{:}\mathsf{Prop}.\lambda h{:}(A_1{\rightarrow}A_2{\rightarrow}\alpha).hxy,
\end{aligned}
$$

For sum-types one would like to have the rules of Figure 5. This can also be

$$
\frac{\Gamma \vdash A_1 : s \quad \Gamma \vdash A_2 : s}{\Gamma \vdash A_1 + A_2 : s} \quad \text{(sums)}
$$

$$
\frac{\Gamma \vdash p : A_i}{\Gamma \vdash \mathsf{in}_i \, p : A_1 + A_2} \quad \text{(injection)}
$$

$$
\frac{\Gamma \vdash f_1 : A_1{\rightarrow}C \quad \Gamma \vdash f_2 : A_2{\rightarrow}C}{\Gamma \vdash \mathsf{case}(f_1, f_2) : (A_1 + A_2){\rightarrow}C} \quad \text{(case)}
$$

computation rule: $\quad \mathsf{case}(f_1, f_2)(\mathsf{in}_i \, p) \rightarrow f_i p$

Figure 5: Rules for sum types

defined in a polymorphic sort (inspired by the $\vee$-construction). Let in λHOL, A_1, A_2 and C be of type Prop, $f_1 : A_1{\rightarrow}C$ and $f_2 : A_2{\rightarrow}C$.

$$
\begin{aligned}
A_1 + A_2 &:= \Pi \alpha{:}\mathsf{Prop}.(A_1{\rightarrow}\alpha){\rightarrow}(A_2{\rightarrow}\alpha){\rightarrow}\alpha, \\
\mathsf{in}_1 &:= \lambda p{:}A_1.\lambda \alpha{:}\mathsf{Prop}.\lambda h_1{:}(A_1{\rightarrow}\alpha).\lambda h_2{:}(A_2{\rightarrow}\alpha).h_1 p, \\
\mathsf{in}_2 &:= \lambda p{:}A_2.\lambda \alpha{:}\mathsf{Prop}.\lambda h_1{:}(A_1{\rightarrow}\alpha).\lambda h_2{:}(A_2{\rightarrow}\alpha).h_2 p,
\end{aligned}
$$

$$\mathsf{case}(f_1, f_2) \;\; := \;\; \lambda x{:}(A_1 + A_2).xC f_1 f_2.$$

3.7. Σ-types

In mathematics one wants to be able to reason about abstract notions, like the *theory of groups*. Therefore, in the formalization of mathematics in type theory, we have to be able to form something like the 'type of groups'. As an example, let us see what a group looks like in λHOL. Given A : Type, a *group over A* is a tuple consisting of the terms

$$\circ \;\; : \;\; A{\to}A{\to}A$$

$$e \;\; : \;\; A$$

$$\mathsf{inv} \;\; : \;\; A{\to}A$$

(the group-structure) such that the following types are inhabited (we use infix-notation for readability).

$$\Pi x, y, z{:}A.(x \circ y) \circ z \;\; = \;\; x \circ (y \circ z),$$

$$\Pi x{:}A.e \circ x \;\; = \;\; x,$$

$$\Pi x{:}A.(\mathsf{inv}\ x) \circ x \;\; = \;\; e.$$

For the type of the group-structure we can use the product: the *type of group-structures over A*, Group-Str(A), is $(A{\to}A{\to}A) \times (A \times (A{\to}A))$. If t : Group-Str(A), then $\pi_1 t$: $A{\to}A{\to}A$, $\pi_1(\pi_2 t)$: A, etcetera. However, this does not yet capture the axioms of group-theory. For this we can use the Σ-type: the *type of groups over A*, Group(A), is defined by

$$\begin{aligned}\mathsf{Group}(A) := \Sigma \circ{:}A{\to}A{\to}A.\Sigma e{:}A.\Sigma \mathsf{inv}{:}A{\to}A.\ &(\Pi x, y, z{:}A.(x \circ y) \circ z = x \circ (y \circ z))\wedge \\ &(\Pi x{:}A.e \circ x = x)\wedge \\ &(\Pi x{:}A.(\mathsf{inv}\ x) \circ x = e).\end{aligned}$$

Now, if t : Group(A), we can extract the elements of the group structure by projections as before: $\pi_1 t$: $A{\to}A{\to}A$, $\pi_1(\pi_2 t)$: A, etcetera. One can also extract proof-terms for the group-axioms by projection: $\pi_1(\pi_2(\pi_2(\pi_2 t)))$: $\Pi x, y, z{:}A.\pi_1 t(\pi_1 txy)z = \pi_1 tx(\pi_1 tyz)$, representing the associativity of the operation $\pi_1 t$.

Similarly, if f : $A{\to}A{\to}A$, a : A and h : $A{\to}A$ with p_1, p_2, p_3 and p_4 proof-terms of the associated group-axioms, then

$$\langle f, \langle a, \langle h, \langle p_1, \langle p_2, \langle p_3, p_4 \rangle\rangle\rangle\rangle\rangle\rangle : \mathsf{Group}(A).$$

The precise rules of the Σ-types in λHOL are as in Figure 6.

These rules allow the formation of the 'dependent tuples' we need for formalizing notions like Group and Ring. An even more general approach towards the theory

$$(\Sigma) \quad \frac{\Gamma \vdash A : \mathsf{Type} \quad \Gamma, x{:}A \vdash \varphi : \mathsf{Prop}}{\Gamma \vdash \Sigma x{:}A.\varphi : \mathsf{Type}}$$

$$(\langle -, - \rangle) \quad \frac{\Gamma \vdash a : A \quad \Gamma \vdash p : \varphi[a/x] \quad \Gamma \vdash \Sigma x{:}A.\varphi : \mathsf{Type}}{\Gamma \vdash \langle a, p \rangle : \Sigma x{:}A.\varphi}$$

$$(\pi_1) \quad \frac{\Gamma \vdash t : \Sigma x{:}A.\varphi}{\Gamma \vdash \pi_1 t : A}$$

$$(\pi_2) \quad \frac{\Gamma \vdash t : \Sigma x{:}A.\varphi}{\Gamma \vdash \pi_2 t : \varphi[\pi_1 t / x]}$$

computation rules: $\quad \pi_1 \langle a, p \rangle \to a$
$$\pi_2 \langle a, p \rangle \to p$$

Figure 6: Rules for Σ-types

of groups would be to also abstract over the carrier type, obtaining

$$\mathsf{Group} := \quad \Sigma A{:}\mathsf{Type}.\Sigma \circ {:}A{\to}A{\to}A.\Sigma e{:}A.\Sigma \mathrm{inv}{:}A{\to}A.$$
$$(\Pi x, y, z{:}A.(x \circ y) \circ z = x \circ (y \circ z)) \wedge$$
$$(\Pi x{:}A.e \circ x = x) \wedge$$
$$(\Pi x{:}A.(\mathrm{inv}\ x) \circ x = e).$$

This can be done by an easy extension of the rules, allowing to form $\Sigma x{:}A.B$ also for $A : \mathsf{Type}'$:

$$(\Sigma') \quad \frac{\Gamma \vdash A : \mathsf{Type}' \quad \Gamma, x{:}A \vdash B : \mathsf{Type}}{\Gamma \vdash \Sigma x{:}A.B : \mathsf{Type}}$$

However, if we want the system to remain consistent, it is not possible to allow $\Sigma x{:}\mathsf{Type}.B : \mathsf{Type}$. We must put $\Sigma x{:}\mathsf{Type}.B : \mathsf{Type}'$. This implies that $\mathsf{Group} : \mathsf{Type}'$, which may not be desirable.

We may observe that the Σ-type behaves very much like an *existential quantifier*. Apart from the fact that $\Sigma x{:}A.\varphi$ is not a proposition, but a type, we see that a (proof)term of type $\Sigma x{:}A.\varphi$ is constructed from a term a of type A for which $\varphi[a/x]$ holds. The other way around, from a (proof)term t of type $\Sigma x{:}A.\varphi$ one can construct the *witness* $\pi_1 t$ and the proof that for this witness φ holds. This very closely reflects the constructive interpretation of the existential quantifier ('if $\exists x{:}A.\varphi$ is derivable, then there exists a term a for which $\varphi[a/x]$ is derivable'). The use of Σ-types for the existential quantifier requires that $\Sigma x{:}A.\varphi : \mathsf{Prop}$ (not of type Type) in λHOL.

In order to achieve this we could modify the Σ-rule as follows.

$$(\Sigma) \quad \frac{\Gamma \vdash A : \mathsf{Type} \quad \Gamma, x{:}A \vdash \varphi : \mathsf{Prop}}{\Gamma \vdash \Sigma x{:}A.\varphi : \mathsf{Prop}}$$

However, the addition of this rule to λHOL makes the system inconsistent. In the case of λPREDω, it is possible to add a Σ-type that represents the existential quantifier, while remaining consistent, but only for $A : \mathsf{Set}$. On the other hand, one may wonder whether a Σ-type is the correct formalization of the constructive existential quantifier, because it creates set-terms that depend on proof-terms. For example, if we put $z : \Sigma x{:}A.\varphi$ in the context where $\Sigma x{:}A.\varphi$ is a proposition ($\Sigma x{:}A.\varphi : \mathsf{Prop}$), then $\pi_1 z : A$ ($A : \mathsf{Set}$). So we have an element-expression ($\pi_1 z$) that depends on a proof (z), a feature alien to ordinary predicate logic, where the expression-language is built up independently of the proofs.

3.8. Inductive Types

A basic notion in logic and set theory is induction: when a set is defined inductively, we understand it as being 'built up from the bottom' by a set of basic constructors. Elements of such a set can be decomposed in 'smaller elements' in a well-founded manner. This gives us the principles of 'proof by induction' and 'function definition by recursion'.

If we want to add inductive types to our type theory, we have to add a definition mechanism that allows us to introduce a new inductive type, by giving the name and the constructors of the inductive type. The theory should automatically generate a scheme for proof-by-induction and a scheme for primitive recursion. It turns out that this can be done very generally in type theory, including very many instances of induction. Here we shall use a variant of the inductive types that are present in the system COQ [1999] and that were first defined in Coquand and Paulin-Mohring [1990]. Another approach to inductive types is to encode them as 'well-ordering types', also called W-types. The W-type can be used to encode arbitrary inductive types, but only if we are in extensional type theory. As we are in an intensional framework, we do not pursue that thread; see e.g. [Goguen and Luo 1993] for details.

We illustrate the rules for inductive types in λHOL by first treating the (very basic) example of natural numbers nat. We would like the user to be able to write something like

$$\begin{aligned}
\mathsf{Inductive} \quad &\mathsf{nat} : \mathsf{Type} := \\
&0 : \mathsf{nat} \\
&\mid S : \mathsf{nat} {\rightarrow} \mathsf{nat}.
\end{aligned}$$

to obtain the following rules.

$$(\text{elim}_1) \quad \frac{\Gamma \vdash A : \text{Type} \quad \Gamma \vdash f_1 : A \quad \Gamma \vdash f_2 : \text{nat}\rightarrow A \rightarrow A}{\Gamma \vdash \text{Rec}_{\,\text{nat}} f_1 f_2 : \text{nat}\rightarrow A}$$

$$(\text{elim}_2) \quad \frac{\Gamma \vdash P : \text{nat}\rightarrow\text{Prop} \quad \Gamma \vdash f_1 : P0 \quad \Gamma \vdash f_2 : \Pi x{:}\text{nat}.Px\rightarrow P(Sx)}{\Gamma \vdash \text{Rec}_{\,\text{nat}} f_1 f_2 : \Pi x{:}\text{nat}.Px}$$

The rule (elim_1) allows the definition of functions by primitive recursion. The rule (elim_2) allows proofs by induction. To make sure that the functions defined by (elim_1) compute $\text{Rec}_{\,\text{nat}}$ has the following reduction rule.

$$\text{Rec}_{\,\text{nat}} f_1 f_2 0 \quad \rightarrow_\iota \quad f_1$$
$$\text{Rec}_{\,\text{nat}} f_1 f_2 (St) \quad \rightarrow_\iota \quad f_2 t(\text{Rec}_{\,\text{nat}} f_1 f_2 t)$$

It is understood that the additional ι-reduction is also included in the *conversion-rule* (conv), where we now have '$A =_{\beta\iota} B$' as a side-condition. The subscript in $\text{Rec}_{\,\text{nat}}$ will be omitted, when clear from the context.

An example of the use of (elim_1) is in the definition of the 'double' function d, which is defined by

$$d := \text{Rec}_{\,\text{nat}} 0(\lambda x{:}\text{nat}.\lambda y{:}\text{nat}.S(S(y))).$$

Now, $d0 \twoheadrightarrow_{\beta\iota} 0$ and $d(Sx) \twoheadrightarrow_{\beta\iota} S(S(dx))$. The predicate of 'being even', $\text{even}(-)$, can also be defined by using (elim_1):

$$\text{even}(-) := \text{Rec}_{\,\text{nat}}(\top)(\lambda x{:}\text{nat}.\lambda\alpha{:}\text{Prop}.\neg\alpha).$$

We obtain indeed that

$$\text{even}(0) \quad \twoheadrightarrow_{\beta\iota} \quad \top,$$
$$\text{even}(Sx) \quad \twoheadrightarrow_{\beta\iota} \quad \neg\text{even}(x)$$

An example of the use of (elim_2) is the proof of $\Pi x{:}\text{nat}.\text{even}(dx)$. Say that true is some canonical inhabitant of type $\top$. Using $\text{even}(d(Sx)) =_{\beta\iota} \neg\neg\text{even}(dx)$ we find that $\lambda x{:}\text{nat}.\lambda h{:}\text{even}(dx).\lambda z{:}\neg\text{even}(dx).zh$ is of type $\Pi x{:}\text{nat}.\text{even}(dx)\rightarrow\text{even}(d(Sx))$. So we conclude that

$$\vdash \text{Rec}_{\,\text{nat}} \text{true}(\lambda x{:}\text{nat}.\lambda h{:}\text{even}(dx).\lambda z{:}\neg\text{even}(dx).zh) : \Pi x{:}\text{nat}.\text{even}(dx).$$

Another well-known example is the type of lists over a domain D. It is defined as follows.

$$\text{Inductive} \quad \text{List} : \text{Type} :=$$
$$\text{Nil} : \text{List}$$
$$| \text{ Cons} : D\rightarrow\text{List}\rightarrow\text{List}$$

with the following rules.

$$(\text{elim}_1) \quad \frac{\Gamma \vdash A : \text{Type} \quad \Gamma \vdash f_1 : A \quad \Gamma \vdash f_2 : D \rightarrow \text{List} \rightarrow A \rightarrow A}{\Gamma \vdash \text{Rec}_{\text{List}} f_1 f_2 : \text{List} \rightarrow A}$$

$$(\text{elim}_2) \quad \frac{\Gamma \vdash P : \text{List} \rightarrow \text{Prop} \quad \Gamma \vdash f_1 : P\text{Nil} \quad \Gamma \vdash f_2 : \Pi d{:}D.\Pi x{:}\text{List}.Px \rightarrow P(\text{Cons } dx)}{\Gamma \vdash \text{Rec}_{\text{List}} f_1 f_2 : \Pi x{:}\text{List}.Px}$$

The rule (elim_1) allows the definition of functions by primitive recursion, while the rule (elim_2) allows proofs by induction. To make sure that the functions compute in the correct way, Rec_{List} has the following reduction rule.

$$\text{Rec}_{\text{List}} f_1 f_2 \text{Nil} \quad \rightarrow_\iota \quad f_1$$

$$\text{Rec}_{\text{List}} f_1 f_2 (\text{Cons } dt) \quad \rightarrow_\iota \quad f_2 dt (\text{Rec}_{\text{List}} f_1 f_2 t)$$

An example of the use of Rec_{List} is in the definition of the 'map' function that takes a function $f : D \rightarrow D$ and returns the function (of type $\text{List} \rightarrow \text{List}$) that applies f to all elements of the list. Define

$$\text{map} \quad := \quad \lambda f{:}D{\rightarrow}D.\lambda l{:}\text{List}.\text{Rec}_{\text{List}} \text{Nil}(\lambda d{:}D.\lambda k{:}\text{List}.\lambda h{:}\text{List}.\text{Cons } (fd)h)$$

$$: \quad (D{\rightarrow}D){\rightarrow}\text{List}{\rightarrow}\text{List}.$$

Then $\text{map } f(\text{Cons } dt) =_{\beta\iota} \text{Cons } (fd)\text{map } ft$.

Of course, there is a more general pattern behind these two examples. The extension of λHOL with inductive types is defined by adding the following scheme.

$$\text{Inductive} \quad \mu : \text{Type} :=$$
$$\text{constr}_1 : \sigma_1^1(\mu) \rightarrow \cdots \sigma_{m_1}^1(\mu) \rightarrow \mu$$
$$\vdots$$
$$| \text{ constr}_n : \sigma_1^n(\mu) \rightarrow \cdots \sigma_{m_n}^n(\mu) \rightarrow \mu$$

where the $\sigma_j^i(\mu)$ are all 'type schemes with a strictly positive occurrence of μ', i.e. each $\sigma_j^i(\mu)$ is of the form $A_1 \rightarrow \cdots A_n \rightarrow X$ with no occurrence of μ in the A_k and either $X \equiv \mu$ or μ not in X. This declaration of μ introduces μ as a defined type and it generates the constructors $\text{constr}_1, \ldots, \text{constr}_n$ plus the associated elimination rules and the reduction rules. For a general picture on inductive types we refer to [Paulin-Mohring 1994].

To illustrate the generality of inductive types, we give an example of an inductive type that is more complicated than nat and List. We want to define the type Tree of countably branching trees with labels in D. (So a term of type Tree represents a tree where the nodes and leaves are labelled with a term of type D and where at every node there are countably many subtrees.) The definition of Tree is as follows.

$$\text{Inductive} \quad \text{Tree} : \text{Type} :=$$
$$\text{Leaf} : D \rightarrow \text{Tree}$$
$$| \text{ Join} : D \rightarrow (\text{nat} \rightarrow \text{Tree}) \rightarrow \text{Tree}$$

Here, Leaf creates a tree consisting of just a leaf, labelled by a term of type D. The constructor Join takes a label (of type D) and an infinite (countable) list of trees to create a new tree. The (elim$_1$) rule is as follows.

$$(\text{elim}_1) \quad \frac{\Gamma \vdash A : \text{Type} \quad \Gamma \vdash f_1 : D{\to}A \quad \Gamma \vdash f_2 : D{\to}(\text{nat}{\to}\text{Tree}){\to}(\text{nat}{\to}A){\to}A}{\Gamma \vdash \text{Rec}_{\text{Tree}} f_1 f_2 : \text{Tree}{\to}A}$$

Rec$_{\text{Tree}}$ has the following reduction rule.

$$\text{Rec}_{\text{Tree}} f_1 f_2 (\text{Leaf} d) \quad \to_\iota \quad f_1 d$$

$$\text{Rec}_{\text{Tree}} f_1 f_2 (\text{Join} d\, t) \quad \to_\iota \quad f_2 d t (\lambda x{:}\text{nat}.\text{Rec}_{\text{Tree}} f_1 f_2 (tx))$$

It is an interesting exercise to define all kinds of standard functions on Tree, like the function that takes the nth subtree (if it exists and take Leaf$a$ otherwise) or the function that decides whether a tree is infinite (or just a single leaf).

For Tree, we have the following (elim$_2$) rule.

$$(\text{elim}_2) \quad \frac{\Gamma \vdash P : \text{Tree}{\to}\text{Prop} \qquad \Gamma \vdash f_1 : \Pi d{:}D.P(\text{Leaf} d)}{\Gamma \vdash f_2 : \Pi d{:}D.\Pi t{:}\text{nat}{\to}\text{Tree}.(\Pi n{:}\text{nat}.P(tn)){\to}P(\text{Join} d\, t)}{\Gamma \vdash \text{Rec}_{\text{Tree}} f_1 f_2 : \Pi x{:}\text{Tree}.Px}$$

Another interesting example of inductive types are inductively defined *propositions*. An example is the conjunction, which has one constructor (the pairing). Given φ and ψ of type Prop, it can be defined as follows.

$$\text{Inductive} \quad \varphi \wedge \psi : \text{Prop} :=$$
$$\text{Pair} : \varphi{\to}\psi{\to}(\varphi \wedge \psi)$$

As we do not have the (Prop, Type) rule in λHOL, we can only consider the second elimination rule, which will only appear in the case where P is a constant of type Prop. (So P : Prop instead of $P : \varphi \wedge \psi{\to}$Prop.) The elimination rule (elim$_2$) rule is then as follows.

$$(\text{elim}_2) \quad \frac{\Gamma \vdash P : \text{Prop} \quad \Gamma \vdash f_1 : \varphi{\to}\psi{\to}P}{\Gamma \vdash \text{Rec}_\wedge f_1 : (\varphi \wedge \psi){\to}P}$$

By taking φ (respectively ψ) for P and $\lambda x{:}\varphi.\lambda y{:}\psi.x$ (respectively $\lambda x{:}\varphi.\lambda y{:}\psi.y$) for f_1, one easily recovers the well-known projection from $\varphi \wedge \psi$ to φ (respectively ψ). The logical operators $\vee$ and $\exists$ can similarly be defined inductively.

More general inductive definitions

Above we have restricted ourselves to a specific class of inductive types. This class is very general, covering all the so called 'algebraic types', but it still can be extended. There are three main extensions that we discuss briefly by some motivating examples. They are

1. Parametric Inductive Types

2. Inductive Types with Dependent Constructors

3. Inductive Predicates

Many of these extensions occur together in more interesting examples.

Probably the most well-known situation of a 'parametric type' is the type of 'lists over a type D'. Here the type D is just a parameter: primitive recursive operations on lists do not depend on the specific choice for D. A possible way for defining the type of *parametric lists* would be the following.

$$
\begin{aligned}
\text{Inductive} \quad &\text{List} : \text{Type} \to \text{Type} := \\
&\text{Nil} : \Pi D{:}\text{Type}.(\text{List}D) \\
&| \text{ Cons} : \Pi D{:}\text{Type}.D \to (\text{List}D) \to (\text{List}D).
\end{aligned}
$$

Which would generate the following elimination rules and reduction rule.

$$
(\text{elim}_1) \quad \frac{\Gamma \vdash D : \text{Type} \quad \Gamma \vdash A : \text{Type} \quad \Gamma \vdash f_1 : A \quad \Gamma \vdash f_2 : D \to (\text{List}D) \to A \to A}{\Gamma \vdash \text{Rec}_{\text{List}} f_1 f_2 : (\text{List}D) \to A}
$$

$$
(\text{elim}_2) \quad \frac{\begin{array}{cc} \Gamma \vdash D : \text{Type} & \Gamma \vdash f_1 : P(\text{Nil}D) \\ \Gamma \vdash P : (\text{List}D) \to \text{Prop} & \Gamma \vdash f_2 : \Pi d{:}D.\Pi x{:}(\text{List}D).Px \to P(\text{Cons } Ddx) \end{array}}{\Gamma \vdash \text{Rec}_{\text{List}} f_1 f_2 : \Pi x{:}(\text{List}D).Px}
$$

$$
\begin{aligned}
\text{Rec}_{\text{List}} f_1 f_2 (\text{Nil}D) \quad &\to_\iota \quad f_1 \\
\text{Rec}_{\text{List}} f_1 f_2 (\text{Cons } Ddt) \quad &\to_\iota \quad f_2 dt(\text{Rec}_{\text{List}} f_1 f_2 t)
\end{aligned}
$$

To be able to write down the type of the constructors Nil and Cons, we need the rule $(\text{Type}', \text{Type})$ in λHOL, which makes the system inconsistent. Therefore, this extension works much better in a system like λPREDω, where we can consistently allow quantification over Set. We will not be concerned with these precise details here however.

In the example of parametric lists we have already seen constructors that have a dependent type. It turns out that this situation occurs more often. With respect to the general scheme, the extension to include dependent typed constructors is a straightforward one: all definitions carry through immediately. We treat an interesting example of an inductive type (the Σ-type), which is defined using a constructor that has a dependent type. Let $B : \text{Type}$ and $Q : A \to \text{Prop}$ and suppose we have added the rule $(\text{Prop}, \text{Type})$ to our system.

$$
\begin{aligned}
\text{Inductive} \quad &\mu : \text{Type} := \\
&\text{In} : \Pi z{:}B.(Qz) \to \mu.
\end{aligned}
$$

$$(\text{elim}_1) \quad \frac{\Gamma \vdash A : \text{Type} \quad \Gamma \vdash f_1 : \Pi z{:}B.(Qz){\to}A}{\Gamma \vdash \text{Rec}_{\mu} f_1 : \mu{\to}A}$$

$$(\text{elim}_2) \quad \frac{\Gamma \vdash P : \mu{\to}\text{Prop} \quad \Gamma \vdash f_1 : \Pi z{:}B.\Pi y{:}(Qz).P(\text{In} zy)}{\Gamma \vdash \text{Rec}_{\mu} f_1 : \Pi x{:}\mu.(Px)}$$

The ι-reduction rule is

$$\text{Rec}_{\mu} f_1(\text{In} bq) \quad \to_{\iota} \quad f_1 bq$$

Now, taking in (elim_1) B for A and $\lambda z{:}B.\lambda y{:}(Qz).z$ for f_1, we find that

$$\text{Rec}(\lambda z{:}B.\lambda y{:}(Qz).z)(\text{In} bq) \twoheadrightarrow b.$$

Hence, we define $\pi_1 := \text{Rec}(\lambda z{:}B.\lambda y{:}(Qz).z)$. Now, taking $\lambda x{:}\mu.Q(\pi_1 x)$ for P in (elim_2) and $\lambda z{:}B.\lambda y{:}(Qz).y$ for f_1, we find that $\text{Rec}(\lambda z{:}B.\lambda y{:}(Qz).y)$: $\Pi z{:}\mu.Q(\pi_1 z)$. Furthermore, $\text{Rec}(\lambda z{:}B.\lambda y{:}(Qz).y)(\text{In} bq) \twoheadrightarrow q$. Hence, we define $\pi_2 := \text{Rec}(\lambda z{:}B.\lambda y{:}(Qz).y)$ and we remark that μ together with In (as pairing constructor) and π_1 and π_2 (as projections) represents the Σ-type.

An example of an inductively defined predicate is the equality, which can be defined as follows.

$$\text{Inductive} \quad \text{Eq} : D{\to}D{\to}\text{Prop} :=$$
$$\text{Refl} : \Pi x{:}D.(\text{Eq} xx).$$

Just like in the example for the conjunction, we only have the second elimination rule for the non-dependent case (i.e. P only depends on $x, y{:}D$ but not on a proof of $\text{Eq} xy$). So we have

$$(\text{elim}_2) \quad \frac{\Gamma \vdash P : D{\to}D{\to}\text{Prop} \quad \Gamma \vdash f_1 : \Pi x{:}D.(Pxx)}{\Gamma \vdash \text{Rec}_{\text{Eq}} f_1 : \Pi x, y{:}D.(\text{Eq} xy){\to}(Pxy)}$$

The ι-reduction rule is

$$\text{Rec}_{\text{Eq}} xx f_1(\text{Refl} x) \quad \to_{\iota} \quad f_1 x$$

4. Proof-development in type systems

In this section we will show how a concrete proof-assistant works. First we show in what way the human has to interact with the system. Then a small proof-development is partially shown (most proof-objects are omitted). Finally it is shown how computations can be captured in formalized theories.

4.1. Tactics

In Section 2.1 and Section 4.3 examples will be given of an easy, and a more involved theorem with full proofs. Even before these examples are given, the reader will probably realize that constructing fully formalized proofs (the proof-objects) is relatively involved. Therefore tools have been developed—so-called *proof-assistants*— that make this task more easy. A proof assistant consists of a proof checker and an interactive proof-development system. We have depicted the situation graphically in Figure 7. In the proof-development system one chooses a context and formu-

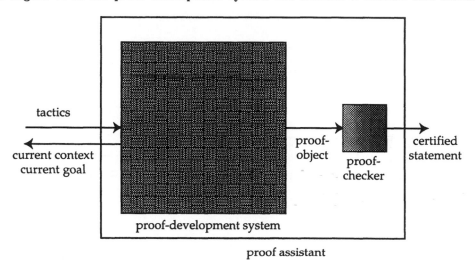

Figure 7: A proof-assistant and its components

lates a statement to be proved relative to that context. This statement is called the *goal*. Rather than constructing the required proof-object directly, one uses so-called *tactics* that give a hint to the machine as to what the proof-object looks like. For example, if one wants to prove

$$\forall x{:}A.(Px \Rightarrow Qx)$$

in context $A : \mathsf{Set}, P, Q : A{\to}\mathsf{Prop}$, then there is a tactic ('Intros') that changes the context by picking a fresh ('arbitrary') $x{:}A$ and assumes Px, the goal now becoming Qx. To be more precise, we give some extracts of Coq sessions. In Coq, the Π-abstraction and the λ-abstraction are represented by brackets: $(\mathtt{x}{:}\mathtt{A})\mathtt{B}$ denotes $\Pi x{:}A.B$ and $[\mathtt{x}{:}\mathtt{A}]\mathtt{M}$ denotes $\lambda x{:}A.M$. Furthermore, -> and abstraction bind stronger than application, so we have to put brackets around applications, writing $(\mathtt{x}{:}\mathtt{A})(\mathtt{P}\ \mathtt{x}){\text{->}}(\mathtt{Q}\ \mathtt{x})$ for $\Pi x{:}A.Px{\to}Qx$. In the following, $\mathtt{Unnamed\_thm} <$ and $\mathtt{Coq} <$ are the Coq prompts at which the user is expected to type some command: at $\mathtt{Coq} <$, the system is in 'declaration mode', where the user can extend the context with new declarations or definitions; at $\mathtt{Unnamed\_thm} <$, the system is in 'proof mode', where the user can type in tactics to solve the goal(s).

```
Coq < Variable A:Set; Variable P,Q:A->Prop.
A is assumed
P is assumed
Q is assumed

Coq <  Goal (x:A)(P x) -> (Q x).
1 subgoal

  ==============================
    (x:A)(P x)->(Q x)

Unnamed_thm < Intros.
1 subgoal

  x : A
  H : (P x)
  ==============================
   (Q x)
```

The H: (P x) means that we assume that H is a proof of (P x) (in order to construct a proof q of (Q x), thereby providing a proof of (P x) -> (Q x), namely [H:(P x)]q, and hence of (x:A)(P x) -> (Q x), namely [x:A][H:(P x)]q.

Another tactic is 'Apply'. If the current context contains a:A and p: (x:A)(P x) -> (Q x) and the current goal is (Q a), then the command Apply p will change the current goal into (P a). This is done by *matching* the type of p with the current goal where the universal variables (here just x) are the ones to be instantiated. So, the system matches (Q x) with (Q a), finding the instantiation of a for x. The proof-term that the system constructs is in this case p a ?, with ? the yet to be constructed proof of (P a).

```
Coq < Variable a:A; Variable p : (x:A) (P x) -> (Q x).
a is assumed
p is assumed

Coq < Goal (Q a).
1 subgoal

  ==============================
    (Q a)

Unnamed_thm < Apply p.
1 subgoal

  ==============================
    (P a)
```

Another essential tactic is concerned with inductive types. For example the type of natural numbers is defined by

```
Inductive nat := 0 :nat | S: nat -> nat.
```

This type comes together with an induction principle
nat_ind
    : (P:(nat->Prop))(P 0)->((n:nat)(P n)->(P (S n)))->(n:nat)(P n)
The way this can be used is as follows. If the (current) goal is (Q n) in context containing n : nat, then the tactic Elim n will produce the new goals (Q 0) and (n : nat)(Q n)-> (Q (n+1)). Indeed, if p is a proof of (Q 0) and q of (n:nat)(Q n)->(Q(n+1)), then (nat_ind Q p q n) will be a proof of (Q n).

Also this type nat comes with a recursor nat_rec satisfying

$$(\texttt{nat\_rec a b 0}) \;\; = \;\; \texttt{a};$$

$$(\texttt{nat\_rec a b (S n)}) \;\; = \;\; (\texttt{b n (nat\_rec a b n)}).$$

Indeed, going from left to right, these are ι-reductions that fall under the Poincaré principle.

As logical operators are defined inductively, we basically have all tools to develop mathematical proofs. The interactive session continues until all goals are solved. Then the system is satisfied and the proved result can be stored under a name that is chosen by the user.
Subtree proved!

```
Unnamed_thm < Save fst_lemma.
<tactics>
```

fst_lemma is defined
In the place of <tactics>, the system repeats the series of tactics that was typed in by the user to solve the goal. The system adds a definition fst_lemma := ... to the context, where ... is the proof term (a typed λ-term) that was interactively constructed. Then later the user can use the lemma by referring to fst_lemma, for example in the Apply tactic: Apply fst_lemma.

The set of tactics and its implementation together with the user interface will yield a large proof-development system. For example, several techniques of automated deduction may be incorporated as tactics. But even if the resulting proof-development system as subunit in general will be large, the reliability of the proof-assistant as such is still high, provided that the proof checker is small, i.e. satisfies the de Bruijn criterion.

4.2. Examples of Proof Development

Given a mathematical statement within a certain context, a *proof development* consists of a formalization of the context Γ and statement A and a construction of a proof-object for it, i.e. a term p such that

$$\Gamma \vdash p : A.$$

A substantial part of a proof development consists of a *theory development*, a name coined by Peter Aczel. This consists of a list of primitive and defined notions and axioms and provable theorems culminating in the goal A to be proved. In this section we will present such a theory development in the system Coq for the statement that every natural number greater than one has a prime divisor.[4]

Two aspects of the development are of interest. Whereas the logical operators $\rightarrow$ and $\forall$ are primitive notions of type theory (when translated as Π), the operators conjunction $\wedge$, disjunction $\vee$, false FF, negation $\tilde{\ }$ and existence $\exists$ are also definable using inductive types, see [Martin-Löf 1984]. For example

```
Inductive or [A:Prop; B:Prop] : Prop :=
       or_introl : A->(or A B)
     | or_intror : B->(or A B)
```

Here, the abstraction [A:Prop; B:Prop] says that A and B are parameters of the definition. Some pretty printing, a syntactic definition can be added, allowing to write A \/ B for (or A B). The inductive definition implies that A \/ B comes together with maps

```
or_introl  : (A,B:Prop)A->A\/B
or_intror  : (A,B:Prop)B->A\/B
```

We also need a map corresponding to the elimination principle for disjunction (for example to prove that A\/B -> B\/A):

```
or_ind     : (A,B,P:Prop)(A->P)->(B->P)->A\/B->P
```

It is also possible to define the operations $\wedge$, $\vee$, FF, $\tilde{\ }$ and $\exists$ without inductive types, using higher order quantification, as in [Russell 1903]. For example disjunction becomes

$$A \vee B \equiv \Pi C{:}\text{Prop}.(A{\rightarrow}C){\rightarrow}(B{\rightarrow}C){\rightarrow}A \vee B{\rightarrow}C.$$

In this way the elimination principle is the term

$$\lambda f{:}(A{\rightarrow}C)\lambda g{:}(B{\rightarrow}C)\lambda h{:}(A \vee B).hCfg.$$

The logical definitions defined this way turn out to be equivalent with the inductively defined ones. Following Martin-Löf we use the inductive definitions, because this way one can avoid impredicative notions like higher order quantification.

---

[4]From this statement Euclid's theorem that there are infinitely many primes is not far removed: consider a prime factor of $n! + 1$ and show that it is necessarily $> n$. Thus one obtains $\forall n \exists p > n.\text{prime } p$. A slightly different formalization is possible in type theory, where one can prove the statement $\forall n{:}\mathbb{N}\forall p_1, \ldots, p_n{:}\mathbb{N}[\text{prime } p_1 \wedge \ldots \wedge \text{prime } p_n \Rightarrow \exists x{:}\mathbb{N}[\text{prime } x \wedge x \neq p_1 \wedge \ldots \wedge x \neq p_n]]$. Note that it is impossible to even state this as a theorem in Peano Arithmetic, because of the use of n as a parameter denoting the length of the sequence $\vec{p}$ and the number of disjunctions $x \neq p_i$. In type theory it can be stated because of the rules for inductive types. In arithmetic one would have to go to second order logic to state (and prove) this theorem

Another point of interest is that inductive types are freely generated by their constructors. This has for example as consequence that for the type of natural numbers one can prove

```
(n : nat) ~( (S n) = 0 )
(n,m : nat) (S n) = (S m) -> n = m
```

Thus we see that within type theory with inductive types, Heyting arithmetic can be formalized, without assuming additional axioms or rules. To quote Randy Pollack: "Type theory with inductive types is intuitionistic: mathematical principles are wired in."

Now we will present a theory development in Coq (version 6.3), for the statement that every natural number has a prime divisor. The mathematics behind this is very elementary. Logic is introduced.[5] After the introduction of the natural numbers, plus and times are defined recursively. Then division and primality are defined. In order to prove our result the usual ordering $<$ is defined (first $\leq$) and course of value induction[6] is used. Text written between (* ... *) serves as a comment. In the following, the proofs are omitted but the definitions are given explicitly.

```
(*************** A simple proof-development ****************)

(****   Propositional connectives defined inductively.   ****)

Inductive and [A:Prop; B:Prop] :  Prop
                          := conj : A->B->(and A B).

Inductive TT :  Prop
            := trivial : TT.

Inductive FF : Prop
            :=.

Definition not : Prop->Prop
             := [A:Prop]A->FF.

Definition iff := [A,B:Prop](and (A->B)(B->A)).

(* For pretty printing syntactic definitions (not shown) are
   introduced that allow to use the following notations

     ~A   for (not A)
    A/\B  for (and A B)
    A\/B  for (or A B)
    A<->B for (iff A B)                                    *)


(* Introduction and elimination rules. *)
```

---

[5] In fact classical logic. An intuitionistic proof is much better, as it provides an algorithm to find the prime divisor. But this requires more work.

[6] If for every $n \in \mathbb{N}$ one has $(\forall m < n.Pm) \to Pn$, then $\forall n \in \mathbb{N}.Pn$.

```
Lemma  and_in :  (a,b:Prop)a->b->(and a b).
Lemma and_ell : (a,b:Prop)(and a b)->a.
Lemma and_elr : (a,b:Prop)(and a b)->b.

Lemma false_el : (a:Prop) FF->a.

Lemma or_inl : (a,b:Prop)a->(or a b).
Lemma or_inr : (a,b:Prop)b->(or a b).
Lemma  or_el : (a,b,c:Prop)(a->c)->(b->c)->(or a b)->c.

(* Lemmas combining connectives. *)

Lemma non_or : (a,b:Prop)~(or a b)->~a/\~b.
(* We show the proof-object (generated by the tactics):
   non_or =
   [a,b:Prop; p:(not (or a b))]
    (and_in (not a) (not b) [q:a](p (or_inl a b q))
      [q:b](p (or_inr a b q)))
        : (a,b:Prop)(not (or a b))->(and (not a) (not b))    *)

(* Some lemmas omitted *)

(****************** Predicate logic.  ****************** )

Inductive ex [A : Set; P : A->Prop] : Prop
                            := ex_intro : (x:A)(P x)->(ex A P).

(* A syntactic definition (not shown) is given that allows one
to write the usual

(EX x:A|(P x)) for ex A [x:A](P x)                          *)

Section Pred.

Variables A : Set; P : A->Prop; Q : A ->Prop.

Lemma all_el : (x:A)((y:A)(P y))->(P x).
Lemma  ex_in : (x:A)(P x)->(EX y:A|(P y)).

Lemma  non_ex : (~(EX x:A|(P x)))->(x:A)~(P x).
Lemma all_not : ((x:A)~(P x))->~(EX x:A|(P x)).
Lemma all_and : ((x:A)(P x)/\(Q x))->((x:A)(P x))/\((x:A)(Q x)).
Lemma   ex_or : (EX x:A|(P x)\/(Q x))
->(EX x:A|(P x))\/(EX x:A|(Q x)).

End Pred.

(* Classical logic. *)
```

```
Axiom DN : (a:Prop)(~~a->a).

Lemma dn_c : (a:Prop)~~a<->a.

Lemma (* Excluded middle: tertium non datur. *)
      tnd : (a:Prop)(a\/~a).


(* Some lemmas omitted *)

Section Pred_clas.

Variable A:Set; P:A->Prop.

Lemma non_all : (~(x:A)(P x))->(EX x:A|~(P x)).
Lemma     ex_c : (EX x:A|(P x))<->~(x:A)~(P x).

(* This lemma has the following proof-object. [Note the presence of DN]
   ex_c =
   (conj (EX x:A | (P x))->~((x:A)~(P x))
         ~((x:A)~(P x))->(EX x:A | (P x))
     [H:(EX x:A | (P x)); H0:((x:A)(P x)->FF)]
     (ex_ind A [x:A](P x) FF [x:A; H1:(P x)](H0 x H1) H)
     [H:(~((x:A)~(P x)))]
     (DN (EX x:A | (P x))
       [H0:((EX x:A | (P x))->FF)]
       (H [x:A; H1:(P x)](H0 (ex_intro A [x0:A](P x0) x H1)))))
     : (EX x:A | (P x))<->~((x:A)~(P x))                        *)

End Pred_clas.

(****************      Arithmetic    **********************)

Inductive eq [A:Set;x:A] :  A->Prop
                 := refl_equal : (eq A x x).

(* A syntactic definition (not shown) is introduced in order to use
   the abbreviation
             x = y  for  (eq A x y).
   In this syntactic definition, the type A can be used as an
   'implicit argument'. It is reconstructed by the type checking
   algorithm from the type of x                                 *)

Lemma    sym_eq : (A:Set)(x,y:A)(x = y)->(y = x).
Lemma     leib : (A:Set)(P:A->Prop)(x,y:A)(x = y)->(P x)->(P y).
Lemma eq_ind_r : (A:Set; x:A; P:(A->Prop))(P x)->(y:A)(y=x)->(P y).
Lemma f_equal : (A,B:Set; f:(A->B); x,y:A)(x=y) -> ((f x)=(f y)).

Inductive nat : Set := 0 : nat | S : nat->nat.
```

```
Definition   one : nat := (S O).
Definition   two : nat := (S one).


Definition Is_suc := [n:nat]
Cases n of
                    O     => FF
                 | (S p) => TT
           end.


Lemma no_conf : (n:nat)~(O= (S n)).


Inductive leseq [n:nat] :  nat->Prop :=
     leseq_n   : (leseq n n)
                    | leseq_suc : (m:nat)(leseq n m)->(leseq n (S m)).


Definition lthan := [n,m:nat](leseq (S n) m).


Lemma leseq_trans : (x,y,z:nat)(leseq x y)->(leseq y z)->(leseq x z).
Lemma lthan_leseq : (n,m:nat)((lthan n m)->(leseq n m)).
Lemma      non_lt0 : (n:nat)~(lthan n O).
Lemma   suc_leseq : (n,m:nat)(leseq (S n)(S m))->(leseq n m).
Lemma        lt01 : (x:nat)(x=O\/x=one\/(lthan one x)).
Lemma       nOn1lt : (n:nat)(~(n=O)->~(n=one)->(lthan one n)).


Definition before [n:nat; P:nat->Prop] := ((k:nat)(lthan k n)->(P k)).


Lemma (* Course of value induction *)
cv_ind : (P:nat->Prop)((n:nat)((before n P) -> (P n))-> (n:nat)(P n)).


Fixpoint plus [n:nat] :  nat -> nat := [m:nat]
Cases n of
                  O    => m
               | (S p) => (S (plus p m))
             end.


Lemma  plus_altsuc : (n,m:nat)(plus n (S m))=(S(plus n m)).
Lemma plus_altzero : (n:nat) (plus n O)=n.
Lemma     plus_ass : (n,m,k: nat)(n,m,k: nat)
                      (plus n (plus m k))=(plus(plus n m)k).
Lemma     plus_com : (n,m:nat)(plus n m)=(plus m n).


Fixpoint times [n:nat] :  nat -> nat := [m:nat]
Cases n of
               O    => O
            | (S p) => (plus (times p m) m)
              end.
```

```
Lemma           distr : (n,m,k: nat)(n,m,k: nat)
                        (times (plus n m) k)=(plus(times n k)(times m k)).
Lemma timesaltzero : (n:nat)(times n 0)=0.
Lemma   timesaltsuc : (n,m:nat)(times n (S m))=(plus(times n m) n).
Lemma      times_ass : (n,m,k:nat)(times n(times m k))=(times(times n m)k).


Definition        div : (nat->nat->Prop)
                        := [d,n:nat](EX x:nat|(times x d)=n).
Definition   propdiv : (nat->nat->Prop)
                        := [d,n:nat]((lthan one d)/\(lthan d n)/\(div d n)).
Definition      prime : nat -> Prop
                        := [n:nat]((lthan one n)/\~(EX d:nat|(propdiv d n))).
Definition primediv : nat->nat->Prop
                        := [p,n:nat](prime p)/\(div p n).


(* Some lemmas omitted *)


(* has prime divisor *)
Definition HPD  : nat->Prop := [n:nat](EX p:nat|(primediv p n)).


Theorem numbers_gt1_have_primediv : (n:nat)(lthan one n)->(HPD n).


(***********************************************************)
```

As stated before, from here one can prove Euclid's theorem that there are infinitely many primes. In order to do this one needs to know that if d divides both a and $a+b$, then it divides b (introduce cut-off subtraction for this and prove some lemmas about it).

4.3. Autarkic Computations

We have so far described how to formalize definitions, statements and proofs. Another important aspect of mathematics is *computing*. (In order to decide whether statements are true or simply because a numerical value is of interest). The following examples are taken from [Barendregt 1997]. These are examples of statements for which computations are needed.

(1) $\qquad [\sqrt{45}] = 6,$ $\qquad$ where $[r]$ is the integer part of a real

(2) $\qquad$ Prime(61)

(3) $\quad (x+1)(x+1) = x^2 + 2x + 1$

In principle computations can be done within an axiomatic framework, in particular within predicate logic with equality. But then proofs of these statements become rather long. E.g.

$$(x+1)^2 = (x+1) \cdot (x+1)$$

$$= (x+1) \cdot x + (x+1) \cdot 1$$
$$= x \cdot x + 1 \cdot x + x \cdot 1 + 1 \cdot 1$$
$$= x^2 + x + x + 1$$
$$= x^2 + 2 \cdot x + 1.$$

This is not even the whole story. Each use of '=' has to be justified by applying an axiom, substitutions and the fact that $+$ preserves equality[7].

A way to handle (1) is to use the Poincaré principle extended with the reduction relation $\twoheadrightarrow_\iota$ for primitive recursion on the natural numbers. Operations like $f(n) = [\sqrt{n}]$ are primitive recursive and hence are λ-definable (using $\twoheadrightarrow_{\beta\iota}$) by $\mathsf{Rec}_{\mathsf{nat}}$ introduced in Section 3.8. Then, writing $\ulcorner 0 \urcorner = 0, \ulcorner 1 \urcorner = \mathsf{S}\ 0, \ldots$, it follows from the Poincaré principle that the same is true for

$$F \ulcorner 45 \urcorner = \ulcorner 6 \urcorner,$$

since $\ulcorner 6 \urcorner = \ulcorner 6 \urcorner$ is formally derivable and we have $F \ulcorner 45 \urcorner \twoheadrightarrow_{\beta\iota} \ulcorner 6 \urcorner$. Usually, a proof obligation arises that F is adequately constructed. For example, in this case it could be

$$\forall n\ (F\,n)^2\ \leq\ n\ <\ ((F\,n)+1)^2.$$

Such a proof obligation needs to be formally proved, but only once; after that reductions like

$$F\ \ulcorner n \urcorner \twoheadrightarrow_{\beta\iota} \ulcorner f(n) \urcorner$$

can be used freely many times.

In a similar way, a statement like (2) can be formulated and proved by constructing a λ-defining term K_{Prime} for the characteristic function of the predicate Prime. This term should satisfy the following statement

$$\forall n\quad [(\mathsf{Prime}\,n\ \leftrightarrow\ K_{\mathsf{Prime}}\,n = \ulcorner 1 \urcorner)\ \&$$
$$(K_{\mathsf{Prime}}\,n = \ulcorner 0 \urcorner \ \vee\ K_{\mathsf{Prime}}\,n = \ulcorner 1 \urcorner)].$$

which is the proof obligation.

Statement (3) corresponds to a symbolic computation. This computation takes place on the syntactic level of formal terms. There is a function g acting on syntactic expressions satisfying

$$g((x+1)(x+1)) = x^2 + 2x + 1,$$

that we want to λ-define. While $x+1 : \mathsf{Nat}$ (in context $x{:}\mathsf{Nat}$), one has '$x + 1$' : $\mathsf{term}(\mathsf{Nat})$. Here $\mathsf{term}(\mathsf{Nat})$ is an inductively defined type consisting of the terms over the structure $\langle \mathsf{Nat}, +, \times, 0, 1 \rangle$. Using a reduction relation for primitive recursion over this data type, one can represent g, say by G, so that

$$G\ '(x+1)(x+1)'\ \twoheadrightarrow_{\beta\iota}\ 'x^2 + 2x + 1'.$$

---

[7]This is why some mathematicians may be turned off by logic. But these steps have to be done. Usually they are done within a fraction of a second and unconsciously by a mathematician.

Now in order to finish the proof of (3), one needs to construct a self-interpreter E, such that for all expressions $p : \mathsf{Nat}$ one has

$$\mathsf{E}\ \text{'}p\text{'} \twoheadrightarrow_{\beta\iota} p$$

and prove the proof obligation for G which is

$$\forall t{:}\mathsf{term}(\mathsf{Nat})\ \mathsf{E}(G\,t) = \mathsf{E}\,t.$$

It follows that
$$\mathsf{E}(G\,\text{'}(x+1)(x+1)\,\text{'}) = \mathsf{E}\,\text{'}(x+1)(x+1)\,\text{'}.$$

Now, since

$$
\begin{aligned}
\mathsf{E}(G\,\text{'}(x+1)(x+1)\,\text{'}) \quad &\twoheadrightarrow_{\beta\iota} \quad \mathsf{E}\,\text{'}x^2 + 2x + 1\,\text{'} \\
&\twoheadrightarrow_{\beta\iota} \quad x^2 + 2x + 1 \\
\mathsf{E}\,\text{'}(x+1)(x+1)\,\text{'} \quad &\twoheadrightarrow_{\beta\iota} \quad (x+1)(x+1),
\end{aligned}
$$

we have by the Poincaré principle

$$(x+1)(x+1) = x^2 + 2x + 1.$$

Bureaucratic details how to treat free variables under E are omitted.

The use of inductive types like Nat and $\mathsf{term}(\mathsf{Nat})$ and the corresponding reduction relations for primitive reduction was suggested by Scott [1970] and the extension of the Poincaré principle for the corresponding reduction relations of primitive recursion by Martin-Löf [1984]. Since such reductions are not too hard to program, the resulting proof checking still satisfies the de Bruijn criterion.

The general approach is as follows. In computer algebra systems algorithms are implemented by special purpose term rewriting. For example for polynomial expressions p one has for (formal) differentiation and simplification the following.

$$
\begin{array}{llll}
p & \to_{\mathtt{diff}} & \cdots & \to_{\mathtt{diff}} & p^{\mathtt{diff\text{-}nf}} & = p_1; \\
p & \to_{\mathtt{simpl}} & \cdots & \to_{\mathtt{simpl}} & p^{\mathtt{simpl\text{-}nf}} & = p_2.
\end{array}
$$

In this way the functions $f_{\mathtt{diff}}(p) = p_1$ and $f_{\mathtt{simpl}}(p) = p_2$ are computed. In type theory with inductive types and ι-reduction these computations can be captured as follows.

$$
\begin{array}{lll}
F_{\mathtt{diff}}\,p & \twoheadrightarrow_{\beta\delta\iota} & p_1; \\
F_{\mathtt{simpl}}\,p & \twoheadrightarrow_{\beta\delta\iota} & p_2.
\end{array}
$$

This is like replacing special purpose computers by the universal Turing-von Neumann computer with software.

In [Oostdijk and Geuvers 2001] a program is presented that, for every primitive recursive predicate P, constructs the lambda term K_P defining its characteristic function and the proof of the adequacy of K_P. That is, one proves $\forall n:\mathsf{Nat}.P(n) \leftrightarrow K_P(n) = 1$ (generically for all primitive recursive predicates P). In this way, proving $P(n)$ can be replaced by computing $K_P(n)$. The resulting computations for $P = \mathsf{Prime}$ are not efficient, because a straightforward (non-optimized) translation of primitive recursion is given and the numerals (represented numbers) used are in a unary (rather than n-ary) representation; but the method is promising. In [Caprotti and Oostdijk 2001], a more efficient ad hoc definition of the characteristic function of Prime is given, using Pocklington's criterion, based on Fermat's small theorem about primality. Also the required proof obligation is given. In this way it can be proved, formally in Coq, that a number like 1223334444555554444333221 is prime (but also bigger numbers, some of 44 digits!) So the statements in the beginning of this subsection can be obtained by computations.

Another use of reflection is to show that a function like

$$f(x) = e^{3x^2} + \sqrt{1 + \sin^2 x} + \cdots$$

is continuous. Rather than proving this by hand one can introduce a formal language L, such that a description of f is among them, and show that every expression $e : L$ denotes a continuous function.

5. Proof assistants

Proof assistants are interactive programs running on a computer that help the user to obtain verified statements (within a given mathematical context). This verification can be generated in two ways: automatically by a theorem prover, or provided by the user with a proof that is checked by the machine.

It is clear that proof checking is not automated deduction. The problem of deciding whether a putative proof is indeed a proof is decidable; on the other hand the problem whether a putative theorem is indeed a theorem is undecidable. Having said this, it is nevertheless good to remark that there is a spectrum ranging from on the one hand pure proof-checkers to on the other hand pure automated theorem provers. A pure proof-checker, to which one has to present an entire fully formalized proof, is impractical, because it is difficult to provide these proof-objects. On the other hand a pure automated theorem prover (that finds a proof if a statement A is provable and tells us that there is none otherwise) is impossible for theorems in theories as simple as predicate logic. Automated deduction is in general only possible as a partial algorithm (providing a proof if there is one, running forever otherwise).

For some special theories, like elementary geometry (which is decidable), a total algorithm may be possible (in the case of geometry there is the excellent theorem prover of Wu [1994]). In most cases an automated theorem prover requires that the user gives hints. Although this chapter is not about automated theorem provers, we would like to mention Otter [1998] for classical predicate logic, the system of Bibel and Schmitt [1998] for classical predicate logic with equality, Boyer and Moore's

[1997] theorem prover Nqthm, based upon primitive recursive arithmetic, and Wu's [1994] geometry theorem prover that was already mentioned.

At the other end of the spectrum a user-friendly proof-checker usually has some form of automated deduction in order to make it more easy for the user to provide proof-objects. Proof-assistants consists of a proof-development system together with a proof-checker.

5.1. Comparing proof-assistants

We will discuss several proof-assistants. All systems except Agda work with *proof scripts* that are a list of *tactics* needed to make the proof-assistant to verify the validity of the statement. The proof-assistants fall into two classes: those with *proof-objects* and those without proof-objects.

In the case of a proof-assistant with proof-objects the script generates and stores a term that is (isomorphic to) a proof that can be checked by a simple proof checker. This makes these systems highly reliable. In principle someone, who is doubtful whether a certain statement is valid, can download a proof-object via the internet and locally verify it using his or her own trusted proof checker of relatively small size.

Proof-assistants that have no proof-objects come in two classes. The first one consists of systems that in principle can translate the proof-script into a proof-object that can be verified by a small checker. In this case the proof-script can be considered as a *non-standard proof-object*. In order to make this translation these systems just need some system specific preprocessor after which a trustworthy check can be performed. The second class consists of proof-assistants for which there is not (yet) a way to provide a proof-object with high reliability. So for the correctness of theorems accepted by assistants in this class one has to trust these systems. The advantage of these kind of systems usually is their larger automated deduction facilities and (therefore) their larger user-friendliness.

We will discuss the following proof-assistants.

system	proof-objects
Coq, Lego, Agda	yes
Nuprl, HOL, Isabelle	non-standard
Mizar, PVS, ACL2	no

Coq, Lego and Agda

Of these three systems Coq is the most developed one. The systems Coq and Lego are based on versions of the calculus of constructions extended with inductive types. For the logical power of this formal system, see [Aczel 1999] and the references contained therein. An important difference between the proof-assistants is in their computational power. Both systems admit the Poincaré principle for $\beta\delta\iota$-conversion. This means that there are deduction steps like the following ones.

$$\frac{\text{Reflexive}(R)}{\forall x.Rxx}\,\delta \qquad \frac{A(\mathsf{I}x)}{A(x)}\,\beta\delta \quad \text{and} \quad \frac{A(\mathtt{fac}(4))}{A(24)}\,\iota\delta,$$

[Here one assumes to have defined $\text{Reflexive}(R) \equiv \forall x.Rxx$, $\mathsf{I} \equiv \lambda x.x$ and $\mathtt{fac}$ as the function representing the factorial.] One of the differences between Coq and Lego is that in Lego one can introduce other notions of reduction for which the Poincaré principle is assumed to hold (including non-terminating ones).

Both Coq and Lego create proof-objects from the proof-scripts and store them. These proof-objects are isomorphic to natural deduction proofs. The two systems allow impredicative arguments as used in actual mathematics, but argued to be potentially unreliable by Poincaré and Martin-Löf. The system Agda is similar to Coq and Lego, except that it is based on Martin-Löf type-theory in which impredicative quantifications are not allowed. The Poincaré principle can be assumed by the user for any notion of reduction that is proved to be strongly normalizing. Agda is not so much 'tactics based' as Coq and Lego. In Agda one edits a proof term by 'filling in the holes' in an open term. The system acts as a structure editor, providing support for term construction.

Nuprl, HOL and Isabelle

Constable et al.'s [1986] system Nuprl does have proof-objects, but a judgment

$$\vdash p : A,$$

indicating that p is a proof of A, is not decidable. The reason for this is that the Poincaré principle is assumed not only for $\beta\delta\iota$-conversion, (the intensional equality) but also for *extensional equality*. See Section 2.8. So there is a rule

$$\frac{p : A(t) \qquad q : (t = s)}{p : A(s)}$$

So, Nuprl is based on an extensional type system. This implies that type checking $p : A$? (TCP, see Section 2.1) is no longer decidable and therefore proofs cannot be checked. However, there are 'expanded' proof-objects d that can establish that $p : A$. In fact, the d takes into account the terms q for which $q : t = s$. So these d serve as the 'real' proof-objects.

The proof-assistant HOL [1998] is based on Church's [1940] simple type theory. This is a classical system of higher order logic. That HOL uses non-standard proof-objects has a different reason. HOL does not satisfy the Poincaré principle for any conversion relation. As a consequence computations involving recursion become quite lengthy when converted to a proof-object (for example establishing by a proof that $\vdash \mathtt{fac}\ c_n = c_{n!}$). Therefore the design decision was made that proof-objects are not stored, only the proof-scripts. Even if a proof of $\mathtt{fac}\ \mathbf{c}_n = \mathbf{c}_{n!}$ may be long, it is possible to give it a short description in the proof-script. Induction is done by defining an inductive predicate in a higher order way as the smallest set satisfying a closure property.

Also Isabelle is based on intuitionistic simple type theory. But this proof-assistant is fine-tuned towards using this logic as a meta-logic in which various logics (for example first-order predicate logic, the systems of the lambda cube or higher order logic) are described internally, in the Logical Framework style. This makes it having non-standard proof-objects. Again the system does not satisfy the Poincaré principle, but avoids the problem by not considering proof-objects. Both assistants HOL and Isabelle have pretty good rewrite engines, needed to run the non-standard proof-objects.

It should be emphasized that HOL and Isabelle did not fail to adept the Poincaré principle because it was forgotten, but because the problem of equational reasoning was solved in a different way, by the non-standard proof-objects in the form of the tactics. It makes formalizing more easy, but one cannot use proof-objects for example to see details of the proof or for program extraction. However, it is in principle not difficult to modify either HOL or Isabelle to create and store proof objects.

Mizar, ACL2, PVS

Mizar [1989] is based on a form of set theory (Tarski-Grothendieck, that is ZFC extended with an axiom expressing the existence arbitrary large cardinals). It does not work with proof-objects nor does it have the Poincaré principle. The system has some automated deduction and a user-friendly set of tactics. In fact a nice feature of the system is that the proof-script is close to an ordinary proof in mathematics (which are internally represented as proofs in set theory). An impressive collection of results is in the Mizar library. It seems that in principle it is possible that the Mizar scripts are translated into a proof-object.

ACL2 [2000] is an extension of the theorem prover of Boyer-Moore. It is based on classical primitive recursive arithmetic and it is used in industry. It is not possible for the user to construct inductive types, but there is a powerful built-in induction: a user can define his own well-founded recursive functions (up to ϵ_0 recursion) and let the system compute with them. (The functions are actually Lisp functions.)

PVS [1999] again is based on classical simple type theory. It is without proof-objects and exploits this by allowing all kind of rewriting, for numeric and symbolic equalities. The system is very user-friendly because of automated deduction that is built in. The system allows subtypes of the form

$$A = \{x : B \mid P(x)\}.$$

If the system has to check $a : A$ it will generate a proof-obligation for the reader: "prove $P(a)$". Up to our knowledge no effort has been made to provide PVS with proof-objects.

Comparison

The proof-assistants considered follow the following pattern:

Agda-Coq-Lego-Nuprl-HOL-Isabelle-Mizar-ACL2-PVS.

Agda, Coq and Lego are to the left, indicating reliability (Agda given the first place because it has only predicative logic; Coq coming second, since only strongly normalizing rewrite rules may be added). After that follow Nuprl, HOL and Isabelle, with their non-standard proof-objects (Nuprl coming first for the same reasons as Agda; Isabelle coming last, because the extra layer making things a bit harder to manage). Finally come Mizar, ACL2 and PVS, because they do not work with proof-objects. We put PVS last, because every now and then bugs are found in this system).

On the other hand, the order for internal automation is the opposite: ACL2 and PVS win and Agda loses. Of course eventually proof-assistants should be developed that are both reliable and user-friendly. The following judgments are based on some intuition and should not be taken too seriously.

Ass.	p.o.	reliab.	PP	logic	dep.t.	ind.t	autom.	#users
Agda	yes	+++	$\beta\delta\iota R_1$	int. pred.	yes	yes	none[8]	-
Coq	yes	++	$\beta\delta\iota R_2$	int.	yes	yes	+	++
Lego	yes	++	$\beta\delta\iota R_1$	int.	yes	yes	+	+
Nuprl	n.s.	++	$\beta\delta\iota R_3$	int.	yes	yes	+	++
HOL	n.s.	++	none	cl.	no	yes	++	++
Isabelle	n.s.	++	none	t.b.s.	no	no	++	++
Mizar	none	+	none	cl.	yes	no	+	++
ACL2	none	+	R_4	pra	no	yes[9]	+++	+++
PVS	none	−	none	cl.	no	no	+++	+++

---

[8] There is a little use of higher order unification

[9] Basically, there's only one inductive type in which the user 'codes' his induction

Legenda

Ass.	name of the Proof Assistant;
p.o.	proof-objects;
n.s.	non-standard;
reliab.	reliability;
PP	Poincaré principle;
dep.t.	dependent types;
ind.t.	inductive types;
autom.	degree of automation;
int.	intuitionistic logic preferred;
pred.	only predicative quantification;
cl.	classical logic;
pra	primitive recursive arithmetic (so no quantifiers);
t.b.s.	to be specified by the user;
R_1	arbitrary notion of reduction;
R_2	structurally well-founded recursion;
R_3	arbitrary provable equality;
R_4	ϵ_0-recursion.

There are very many other proof-assistants. See [Digimath 2000] for an impressive list.

5.2. Applications of proof-assistants

At present there are two approaches to the mechanical verification of complicated statements. The first one, that we may call the *pragmatic approach*, uses proof assistants with many complex tools to verify the correctness of statements. These tools include theorem provers and computer algebra systems, the correctness of which has not been verified (as a matter of fact, computer algebra systems are often not formally correct at all). Even if these systems may contain bugs the correctness of hardware systems and (relatively small but critical) software systems (like protocols) is dramatically increased, see [Rushby and Henke 1993] and [Ruess, Shankar and Srivas 1996]. Proof-assistants that are used include PVS, Nuprl, Isabelle and HOL.

The other approach, that we may call the *fundamental* one, aims at the highest degree of reliability. In this approach one only uses proof-assistants with a proof-checker that satisfies the de Bruijn criterion, i.e. have a small verifying program.

In this chapter we have focused our attention on the second approach. It should be remarked that even in this approach there is some spectrum of reliability. If the Poincaré principle is adopted for $\beta\delta\iota$-conversion, the verifying program is more complex than the one for just $\beta\delta$-conversion. This is natural and fair, since adopting the Poincaré principle for ι-conversion has as consequence that primitive recursive computations within a proof come without proof obligations. In fact the pragmatic proof-assistants can be viewed as a strong use of the computational power as provided by a form of the Poincaré principle.

Another parameter in a fundamental proof-assistant is the choice of strength of the underlying type system and hence the related logical system. For example, one may use first-order, second-order or higher-order logic. This parameter determines the *logical* strength of the proof system.

Rather than making a choice for the computational and logical strength one may think of a universal[10] system in which these two can be set according to the taste and application area of the user. It is hoped (and expected) that it is possible to construct a universal proof-assistant that is sufficiently efficient. Also there is a considerable foundational interest in the enterprise of constructing user-friendly proof-assistants. One has to realize which steps are obvious to the mathematician and provide suitable tools.

It is a (possibly long term) goal of the second approach to make the formalization of an informally known mathematical proof as easy as writing a mathematical paper say in LaTeX. At the same time the efficiency should be comparable to efficient systems for computer algebra.

Several notions in classical mathematics are not directly available in the constructive approach of type theory. Next to the failure of the excluded middle these include quotient sets, subsets defined by a property and partial functions. It is for good reasons that these constructions are not available. In the constructive type theoretic approach the notion $a : A$ should be decidable, a property that is lost in the presence of types representing undecidable sets.

In order to increase the ease of formalizing proofs several tools are being constructed that enhance the power of the fundamental approach. In this way eventually the power of the fundamental approach may be equal to that of the present day pragmatic one.

When the goal of easy formalization has been reached not only spin-off in system design, but also in the development of mathematics is expected. First of all there may emerge a different system of refereeing. People will only submit papers that are correct. The referee can focus on the judgment whether the paper is of interest and point out relations with other work. Then there will be an impact on teaching mathematics. The notion of proof can be taught by patient computers.

It is also to be expected that eventually proof-assistants will help the working mathematician. Arbitrary mathematical notions can be represented on a computer; not just the computable ones, as is presently the case in systems of computer algebra. The interaction between humans and computers may lead to fruitful new mathematics, where humans provide the intuition and machines take over part of

---

[10]Of course there cannot be a universal proof-assistant, due to Gödel's theorem. The word universal is used in the same way as ZFC is seen as a universal foundation: it captures large parts of mathematics

the craftsmanship.

Next to these theoretical aspects, there is a potential practical spin-off in the form of program extraction. In case a statement of the form

$$\forall x \exists y. A(x, y)$$

has been proved constructively, an algorithm finding the y in terms of the x can be extracted automatically. See [Mohring 1986, Paulin-Mohring and Werner 1993, Parent 1995].

For a discussion of issues related to (the future of) proof-assistants, see also the QED-manifesto in [Bundy 1994] (pp. 238–251).

Many (often smaller) proof-assistants we have not mentioned. For a (probably incomplete) but extended survey see [Digimath 2000].

Acknowledgments

We thank all people from the EC Working Group 'Types' and its predecessor 'Logical Frameworks' for the pleasant cooperation and the lively discussions over the years. In particular we want to thank Ana Bove, Thierry Coquand, Wolfgang Naraschewski, Randy Pollack, Dan Synek, Freek Wiedijk, Jan Zwanenburg and the readers for their very useful suggestions and comments.

Bibliography

ABRAMSKY, S., GABBAY, D. M. AND MAIBAUM, T., EDS [1992], *Handbook of Logic in Computer Science, Volume 2: Background: Computational Structures*, Oxford University Press.

ACL2 [2000], 'Applicative Common Lisp'. Architects: M. Kaufmann and J. Strother Moore.
    URL: *http://www.cs.utexas.edu/users/moore/acl2/acl2-doc.html*

ACZEL P. [1999], On relating type theories and set theories, *in* 'Altenkirch, Naraschewski and Reus [1999]'.

AGDA [2000], 'A system for incrementally developing proofs and programs'. Architect: C. Coquand.
    URL: *http://www.cs.chalmers.se/ catarina/agda/*

ALTENKIRCH, T., NARASCHEWSKI, W. AND REUS, B., EDS [1999], *International Workshop TYPES '98, Kloster Irsee, Germany, 1998: selected papers*, Vol. 1657, Springer-Verlag, Berlin.

AUDEBAUD P. [1991], Partial objects in the Calculus of Constructions, *in* 'Proceedings of the Symposium on Logic in Computing Science', IEEE, Amsterdam, NL, pp. 86–95.

BARENDREGT H. [1992], Lambda calculi with types, *in* 'Abramsky, Gabbay and Maibaum [1992]', Oxford University Press, pp. 117–309.

BARENDREGT H. [1997], 'The impact of the lambda calculus', *Bulletin of Symbolic Logic* **3**(2), 181–215.

BARENDREGT, H. AND NIPKOW, T., EDS [1994], *Types for proofs and programs: international workshop TYPES '93, Nijmegen, The Netherlands, 1993: selected papers*, Vol. 806 of *Lecture Notes in Computer Science*, Springer-Verlag, Berlin.

BARTHE G. [1996], Implicit coercions in type systems, *in* 'Berardi and Coppo [1996]', pp. 1–15.

BARTHE G., RUYS M. AND BARENDREGT H. [1996], A two-level approach towards lean proof-checking, *in* 'Berardi and Coppo [1996]', pp. 16–35.

BARTHE G. AND SØRENSEN M. [2000], 'Domain-free Pure Type Systems', *Journal of Functional Programming* **10**, 417–452. Preliminary version in S. Adian and A. Nerode, editors, Proceedings of LFCS'97, LNCS 1234, pp 9-20.

BARWISE J. AND ETCHEMENDY J. [1995], *Hyperproof*, Cambridge University Press.

BERARDI S. [1988], Towards a mathematical analysis of the Coquand-Huet Calculus of Constructions and the other systems in Barendregt's cube, Technical report, Dept. of Computer Science, Carnegie-Mellon University and Dipartimento Matematica, Universita di Torino.

BERARDI S. [1990], Type Dependence and Constructive Mathematics, PhD thesis, Dipartimento Matematica, Università di Torino.

BERARDI, S. AND COPPO, M., EDS [1996], *Types for proofs and programs: international workshop TYPES '95, Torino, Italy, 1995: selected papers*, Vol. 1158, Springer-Verlag, Berlin.

BEZEM, M. AND GROOTE, J., EDS [1993], *Typed Lambda Calculi and Applications, TLCA'93*, Vol. 664 of *Lecture Notes in Computer Science*, Springer, Berlin.

BIBEL, W. AND SCHMITT, P., EDS [1998], *Automated Deduction—A Basis for Applications*, Vol. I,II,III, Kluwer, Dordrecht.

BOYER R. AND MOORE J. [1997], *A Computational Logic Handbook*, second edn, Academic Press, London.

BUNDY, A., ED. [1994], *Automated deduction, CADE-12: 12th International Conference on Automated Deduction, Nancy, France, June 26–July 1, 1994: proceedings*, Vol. 814 of *Lecture Notes in Artificial Intelligence and Lecture Notes in Computer Science*, Springer-Verlag Inc.

CAPROTTI O. AND OOSTDIJK M. [2001], 'Formal and efficient primality proofs by use of computer algebra oracles', *Journal of Symbolic Computation* **to appear**. Special Issue on Computer Algebra and Mechanized Reasoning.

CHURCH A. [1940], 'A formulation of the simple theory of types', *Journal of Symbolic Logic* **5**, 56–68.

CONSTABLE ET AL. R. [1986], *Implementing Mathematics with the Nuprl Proof Development System*, Prentice-Hall, New Jersey.

COQ [1999], 'The Coq proof assistant version 6.9'. Architects: Chr. Paulin-Mohring et al.
  URL: *http://pauillac.inria.fr/coq/assis-eng.html*

COQUAND T. [1985], Une théorie des Constructions, PhD thesis, Université Paris VII, Thèse de troisième cycle.

COQUAND T. [1986], An analysis of Girard's paradox, *in* 'Proceedings of the Symposium on Logic in Computing Science', IEEE, Cambridge, Massachusetts.

COQUAND T. [1991], An algorithm for testing conversion in type theory, *in* 'Huet and Plotkin [1991]', Cambridge University Press.

COQUAND T. AND GALLIER J. [1990], A proof of strong normalization for the theory of Constructions using a Kripke-like interpretation, *in* G. Huet and G. Plotkin, eds, 'Preliminary Proceedings 1st Annual Workshop on Logical Frameworks, Antibes, France, 7–11 May 1990', pp. 479–497.
  URL: *ftp://ftp.inria.fr/INRIA/Projects/coq/types/Proceedings/book90.dvi*

COQUAND T. AND HUET G. [1988], 'The Calculus of Constructions', *Information and Computation* **76**, 95–120.

COQUAND T. AND PAULIN-MOHRING C. [1990], Inductively defined types, *in* 'Martin-Löf and Mints [1990]', Vol. 417 of *Lecture Notes in Computer Science*, Springer Verlag, Berlin.

DAALEN D. V. [1980], The Language Theory of Automath, PhD thesis, Eindhoven University of Technology, The Netherlands.

DE BRUIJN N. [1980], A survey of the project Automath, *in* 'Seldin and Hindley [1980]', Academic Press, pp. 579–606. Also in Nederpelt et al. [1994], pp 141–161.

DE BRUIJN N. G. [1970], The mathematical language AUTOMATH, its usage and some of its extensions, *in* M. Laudet, D. Lacombe and M. Schuetzenberger, eds, 'Symposium on Automatic Demonstration', Springer Verlag, Berlin, 1970, IRIA, Versailles, pp. 29–61. Lecture Notes in Mathematics **125**; also in Nederpelt et al. [1994].

DEZANI-CIANCAGLINI, M. AND PLOTKIN, G., EDS [1995], *Second International Conference on Typed Lambda Calculi and Applications, TLCA '95*, Vol. 902 of *Lecture Notes in Computer Science*, Springer, Berlin.

DIGIMATH [2000], 'A list of computer math systems'. F. Wiedijk.
   URL: *http://www.cs.kun.nl/ freek/digimath*

DOWEK G. [1993], The undecidability of typability in the $\lambda\pi$-calculus, *in* 'Bezem and Groote [1993]', pp. 139–145.

DYBJER, P., NORDSTRÖM, B. AND SMITH, J., EDS [1995], *Types for proofs and programs: international workshop TYPES '94, Båstad, Sweden, 1994: selected papers*, Vol. 996 of *Lecture Notes in Computer Science*, Springer-Verlag, Berlin.

GEUVERS H. [1992], The Church-Rosser property for $\beta\eta$-reduction in typed lambda calculi, *in* 'Proceedings of the seventh annual symposium on Logic in Computer Science, Santa Cruz, Cal.', IEEE, pp. 453–460.

GEUVERS H. [1993], Logics and Type Systems, PhD thesis, Catholic University of Nijmegen, The Netherlands.

GEUVERS H. [1995], A short and flexible proof of strong normalization for the Calculus of Constructions, *in* 'Dybjer, Nordström and Smith [1995]', pp. 14–38.

GEUVERS H. AND NEDERHOF M. [1991], 'A modular proof of strong normalization for the Calculus of Constructions', *Journal of Functional Programming* 1(2), 155–189.

GEUVERS H., POLL E. AND ZWANENBURG J. [1999], Safe proof checking in type theory with Y, *in* F. Flum and M. Rodriguez-Artalejo, eds, 'Computer Science Logic (CSL'99)', Vol. 1683 of *LNCS*, Spinger-Verlag, pp. 439–452.

GIMÉNEZ, E. AND PAULIN-MOHRING, C., EDS [1998], *International Workshop TYPES '96, Aussois, France, 1996: selected papers*, Vol. 1512 of *LNCS*, Springer-Verlag, Berlin.

GIRARD J.-Y. [1972], Interprétation fonctionelle et élimination des coupures de l'arithmétique d'ordre supérieur, PhD thesis, Thèse d'Etat, Université Paris VII.

GIRARD, J.-Y., ED. [1999], *Typed Lambda Calculus and Applications, TLCA '99*, Vol. 1581 of *Lecture Notes in Computer Science*, Springer, Berlin.

GIRARD J.-Y., LAFONT Y. AND TAYLOR P. [1989], *Proofs and Types*, Vol. 7 of *Cambridge Tracts in Theoretical Computer Science*, Cambridge University Press.

GOGUEN H. AND LUO Z. [1993], Inductive data types: Well-orderings revisited, *in* 'Huet and Plotkin [1993]', Cambridge University Press, pp. 198–218.

HARPER R., HONSELL F. AND PLOTKIN G. [1993], 'A framework for defining logics', *Journal of the ACM* 40(1), 143–184.

HOFMANN M. [1994], Elimination of extensionality and quotient types in Martin-Löf type theory, *in* 'Barendregt and Nipkow [1994]', pp. 166–190.

HOL [1998], 'Higher order logic theorem prover'. Architects: K. Slind et al.
   URL: *http://www.cl.cam.ac.uk/Research/HVG/HOL/*

HOWARD W. [1980], The formulas-as-types notion of construction, *in* 'Seldin and Hindley [1980]', Academic Press, pp. 479–490.

HOWE D. [1988], Computational metatheory in Nuprl, *in* E. Lusk and R. Overbeek, eds, 'Proceedings of the Ninth International Conference of Automated Deduction', number 310 *in* 'LNCS', Springer, Berlin, pp. 238–257.

HUET, G. AND PLOTKIN, G., EDS [1991], *Logical Frameworks*, Cambridge University Press.

HUET, G. AND PLOTKIN, G., EDS [1993], *Logical Environments*, Cambridge University Press.

HURKENS A. [1995], A simplification of Girard's paradox, *in* 'Dezani-Ciancaglini and Plotkin [1995]', pp. 266–278.

JAPE [1997], 'A framework for building interactive proof editors'. Architects: B. Sufrin and R. Bornat.
   URL: *http://users.comlab.ox.ac.uk/bernard.sufrin/jape.html*

LEGO [1998], 'The Lego proof assistant'. Architect: R. Pollack.
   URL: *http://www.dcs.ed.ac.uk/home/lego/*

Luo Z. [1989], ECC, the Extended Calculus of Constructions, *in* 'Logic in Computer Science', IEEE Computer Society Press.

Luo Z. [1994], *Computation and Reasoning: A Type Theory for Computer Science*, Vol. 11 of *Intl. Series of Monographs in Computer Science*, Clarendon Press.

Luo Z. [1999], 'Coercive subtyping', *Journal of Logic and Computation* **9**(1).

Magnusson L. [1994], The implementation of ALF: a proof-editor based on Martin-Löf's monomorphic type theory with explicit substitution, PhD thesis, Dept. of Comp. Science, Chalmers University, Sweden.

Martin-Löf P. [1984], *Intuitionistic Type Theory*, Studies in Proof Theory, Bibliopolis, Napoli.

Martin-Löf, P. and Mints, G., eds [1990], *COLOG-88: International conference on computer logic*, Vol. 417 of *Lecture Notes in Computer Science*, Springer Verlag, Berlin.

Mathpert [1997], 'Mathpert'. Architect: M. Beeson.
URL: *http://www.mathpert.com*

McCarthy J. [1962], Computer programs for checking mathematical proofs, *in* 'Proceedings of the Symposium in Pure Mathematics 5', American Mathematical Society.

Mellies P. and Werner B. [1998], A generic proof of strong normalisation for Pure Type Systems, *in* 'Giménez and Paulin-Mohring [1998]'.

Mizar [1989]. Architects: Andrzej Trybulec, Czeslaw Bylinski.
URL: *http://www.mizar.org*

Mohring C. [1986], Algorithm development in the Calculus of Constructions, *in* 'Proceedings of the First Symposium on Logic in Computer Science, Cambridge, Mass.', IEEE, Washington DC, pp. 84–91.

Nederpelt R. [1973], Strong normalisation in a lambda calculus with lambda structured types, PhD thesis, Eindhoven University of Technology, The Netherlands.

Nederpelt, R., Geuvers, H. and de Vrijer, R., eds [1994], *Selected Papers on Automath*, Studies in Logic and the Foundations of Mathematics **133**, North-Holland, Amsterdam.

Nordström B., Petersson K. and Smith J. [1990], *Programming in Martin-Löf's Type Theory*, Oxford University Press.

Oostdijk M. and Geuvers H. [2001], 'Proof by computation in the Coq system', *Theoretical Computer Sci.* **to appear**.

OpenMath [1998].
URL: *http://www.nag.co.uk/projects/openmath/omsoc*

Otter [1998]. Architect: William McCune.
URL: *http://www.mcs.anl.gov/AR/otter*

Parent C. [1995], Synthesizing proofs from programs in the Calculus of Inductive Constructions, *in* B. Möller, ed., 'Proceedings 3rd Intl. Conf. on Mathematics of Program Construction, MPC'95, Kloster Irsee, Germany, 1995', Vol. 947 of *Lecture Notes in Computer Science*, Springer-Verlag, Berlin, pp. 351–379.

Paulin-Mohring C. [1994], Inductive definitions in the system Coq; rules and properties, *in* 'Bezem and Groote [1993]', pp. 328–345.

Paulin-Mohring C. and Werner B. [1993], 'Synthesis of ML programs in the system Coq', *Journal of Symbolic Computation* **15**, 607–640.

Pfenning F. [1991], Logic programming in the LF logical framework, *in* 'Huet and Plotkin [1991]', Cambridge University Press, pp. 149–181.

Pfenning F. [2001], Logical frameworks, *in* A. Robinson and A. Voronkov, eds, 'Handbook of Automated Reasoning', Vol. II, Elsevier Science, chapter 17, pp. 1063–1147.

Pollack R. [1995], A verified type checker, *in* 'Dezani-Ciancaglini and Plotkin [1995]', pp. 365–380.

PVS [1999], 'Specification and verification system'. Architects: J. Rushby et al.
URL: *http://pvs.csl.sri.com/*

Ramsey F. [1925], 'The foundations of mathematics', *Proceedings of the London Mathematical Society* pp. 338–384.

RUESS H., SHANKAR N. AND SRIVAS M. [1996], Modular verification of SRT division, *in* 'Proceedings of the 8th International Conference on Computer Aided Verification, New Brunswick, NJ, USA, eds. R. Alur and T.A. Henzinger', Vol. 1102 of *Lecture Notes in Computer Science*, Springer, pp. 123–134.

RUSHBY J. AND HENKE F. V. [1993], 'Formal verification of algorithms for critical systems', *IEEE Transactions on Software Engineering* **19**(1), 13–23.

RUSSELL B. [1903], *The Principles of Mathematics*, Allen & Unwin, London.

SCOTT D. [1970], Constructive validity, *in* D. L. M. Laudet and M. Schuetzenberger, eds, 'Symposium on Automated Demonstration', Vol. 125 of *Lecture Notes in Mathematics*, Springer, Berlin, pp. 237–275.

SELDIN, J. AND HINDLEY, J., EDS [1980], *To H.B. Curry: Essays on Combinatory Logic, Lambda Calculus and Formalism*, Academic Press.

SEVERI P. [1998], 'Type inference for Pure Type Systems', *Information and Computation* **143**-1, 1–23.

SEVERI P. AND POLL E. [1994], Pure Type Systems with definitions, *in* A. Nerode and Y. Matiyasevich, eds, 'Proceedings of LFCS'94, St. Petersburg, Russia', number 813 *in* 'LNCS', Springer Verlag, Berlin, pp. 316–328.

SWAEN M. [1989], Weak and strong sum-elimination in intuitionistic type theory, PhD thesis, University of Amsterdam.

TERLOUW J. [1989], Een nadere bewijstheoretische analyse van GSTT's (Dutch), Technical report, Department of Computer Science, Catholic University of Nijmegen.

VAN BENTHEM JUTTING L. [1993], 'Typing in Pure Type Systems', *Information and Computation* **105**(1), 30–41.

VAN BENTHEM JUTTING L., MCKINNA J. AND POLLACK R. [1994], Checking algorithms for Pure Type Systems, *in* 'Barendregt and Nipkow [1994]', pp. 19–61.

WHITEHEAD A. AND RUSSELL B. [1910, 1927], *Principia Mathematica Vol 1 (1910) and 2 (1927)*, Cambridge University Press.

WU W. [1994], *Mechanical Theorem Proving in Geometries*, Texts and Monographs in Symbolic Computation, Springer.

ZWANENBURG J. [1999], Pure Type Systems with subtyping, *in* 'Girard [1999]', pp. 381–396.

Index

Symbols

A

B

C

D

E

F

G

H

I

Name index

Part VI

Nonclassical logics

Nonmonotonic Reasoning: Towards Efficient Calculi and Implementations

Jürgen Dix

Ulrich Furbach

Ilkka Niemelä

SECOND READERS: Gerd Brewka and Mirek Truszczyński.

Contents

HANDBOOK OF AUTOMATED REASONING
Edited by Alan Robinson and Andrei Voronkov
© 2001 Elsevier Science Publishers B.V. All rights reserved

Preface

Research in nonmonotonic reasoning has begun at the end of the seventies. One of the major motivations came from reasoning about actions and events. John McCarthy and Patrick Hayes had proposed their situation calculus as a means of representing changing environments in logic. The basic idea is to use an extra situation argument for each fact which describes the situation in which the fact holds. Situations, basically, are the results of performing sequences of actions. It soon turned out that the problem was not so much to represent what changes but *to represent what does not change* when an event occurs. This is the so-called *frame problem*. The idea was to handle the frame problem by using a default rule of the form

If a property P holds in situation S then P typically also holds in the situation obtained by performing action A in S.

Given such a rule it is only necessary to explicitly describe the changes induced by a particular action. All non-changes, for instance that the *real colour* of the kitchen wall does not change when the light is turned on, are handled implicitly. Although it turned out that a straightforward formulation of this rule in some of the most popular nonmonotonic formalisms may lead to unintended results, the frame problem was certainly the challenge motivating many people to join the field.

In the meantime a large number of different nonmonotonic logics have been proposed and we have many results that clarify the close relationship as well as the different aspects of such logics. There is quite an agreement in the field that now, after almost twenty years, the conceptual phase has ended and there is enough knowledge available to start implementing nonmonotonic reasoning systems and applying them to non-trivial problems.

Overall Organization

In this chapter we do not want to give a detailed overview of the various formalizations of nonmonotonic reasoning that have evolved (those can be found in [Brewka, Dix and Konolige 1997, Brewka 1996, Marek and Truszczyński 1993]), but we want to give an overview of the main computational techniques and methods leading to implementations of nonmonotonic reasoning. However, to make this chapter self-contained, we give compact overviews (parts of which are taken from [Brewka et al. 1997, Brewka and Dix 2001]) of the main nonmonotonic logics (in Section 1) and semantics of logic programs (in Section 4).

It turns out that logic programming techniques as well as methods that originated in automated reasoning, like *resolution* or *tableau calculi*, can be successfully applied. We can compare this with the programming language PROLOG, that proved to be successful because it is based on a subset of first-order predicate logic, so called *Horn-clauses*, or *definite logic programs*. Although already definite programs give rise to nonmonotonic semantics, full nonmonotonicity comes in when we extend definite programs by *negation* and/or *disjunction*. Consequently, we will distinguish in this chapter between general nonmonotonic logics and semantics of logic programs with negation and disjunction. The latter class is syntactically more restricted (no negation in the head) but has also features which makes it incomparable to general theories.

The chapter is organized as follows. In Section 1 we first introduce the main non-monotonic logics: *Default Logic, Circumscription* and *Autoepistemic Logic*. They form the basis of most nonmonotonic reasoning systems that are in use today. We also consider the abstract approach of Kraus, Lehmann and Magidor to associate with any reasoning system an *abstract consequence relation*. Abstract properties of these relations often help to better understand the overall behaviour of the reasoning system and irregularizes in the induced relations give sometimes rise to define new systems, like the *rational closure* $\mathcal{K}^{rat}$ of Lehmann and Magidor (which was motivated by shortcomings the *cumulative* and *preferential* system.

In Section 2 we investigate universal methods for computing in general nonmonotonic logics. We do this with a special eye on the underlying complexity and show how this lead to automated theorem proving in such logics.

Finding efficient computation mechanisms for the logics introduced in the former section is the aim of Section 3. There we consider techniques that originated from automated reasoning in first-order predicate calculus. We depict how these techniques can be applied for disjunctive logic programming with programs with variables but only limited use of negation. In particular, we handle GCWA as a basis for nonmonotonic negation therein.

Section 4 gives a declarative overview on nonmonotonicity in logic programming. We introduce (nonmonotonic) semantics of logic programs with negation and disjunction, notably the well-founded and the stable semantics and their extensions to programs containing disjunction— they constitute the most important semantics and are in close relation to the logics introduced in Section 1.

While in Section 3 we considered techniques that can be successfully applied for programs with variables and only limited use of negation, we treat in Section 5 propositional programs with full negation and disjunction. In particular, we provide implementations of D-WFS and D-STABLE in polynomial space.

We end with Section 6, where we treat the problem of finding good benchmarks to test and compare nonmonotonic systems against.

1. General Nonmonotonic Logics

Nonmonotonic reasoning as a form of reasoning contrasts with standard deductive reasoning in the following way. Suppose we know that all men are mortal and that Socrates is a man. Then it follows, by simple syllogistic reasoning, that Socrates is mortal. Further, nothing we can add to our knowledge will change that conclusion, given that we still hold the premises. Deductive reasoning within a theory is "local" in the sense that, having derived a conclusion from premises, we need not worry about any other sentences in the theory. To use the technical term, deductive reasoning is *monotonic*:

$$\text{If } S \vdash \varphi \text{ then } S \cup \{\psi\} \vdash \varphi, \tag{1.1}$$

where $S \vdash \varphi$ means that proposition φ follows from the propositions S.

Obviously, nonmonotonic reasoning does not share this property. Why would we ever want a logic that is nonmonotonic? Historically, the need for nonmonotonic reasoning was identified in the course of trying to solve knowledge representation problems in several application areas of Artificial Intelligence (AI). For more detailed discussions on the need of nonmonotonicity we refer to the literature ([Brewka et al. 1997, Brewka 1996, Marek and Truszczyński 1993]). Here it suffices as a first example to consider the *Closed World-Assumption* (CWA). It intuitively means that any information not mentioned in a database is taken to be false. More precisely, if a positive instance of a predicate is not contained in the database, its negation is assumed to hold. For example, if an airline flight database does not contain any information about a flight from Chicago to San Francisco on May 22, 1998, it is assumed that such a flight does not exist.

For a database that is a simple set of facts, the closed-world assumption can be implemented by a search of the database. If the database includes a deductive component, then the CWA can be phrased in terms of the models of the database. Generally the theories considered for the CWA are restricted to finite languages with only predicates and constant symbols. [Reiter 1978] defines the CWA as:

1.1. DEFINITION *(CWA)*.
The closed world assumption of a database T is the theory

$$\text{CWA}(T) = \text{Cn}(T \cup \{\neg p : T \nvdash p\}),$$

where p is a ground predicate instance.

That is, if a ground atom cannot be inferred from the database, its negation is added to the closure. The CWA is a strong nonmonotonic closure operation since any ground predicate not deduced from the database has its negation added to the closure. A problem with strong closures is that they risk being inconsistent for perfectly reasonable databases. For example, consider a database containing just the disjunctive statement $p \vee q$. Since neither p nor q is deduced, both $\neg p$ and $\neg q$ are in the closure, which is then inconsistent with the original database.

The CWA served us as one particular simple example of a nonmonotonic logic. There exist other systems and one usually can distinguish between four major types of such logics:

Section 1.2: Logics using nonstandard inference rules with an additional consistency check to represent default rules. Reiter's *Default Logic* and its variants are of this type.

Section 1.3: *Circumscription* and its variants. These approaches are based on a preference relation on models. A formula is a consequence *if and only if* it is true in all most preferred models of the premises. Syntactically, a second order formula is used to eliminate all non-preferred models.

Section 1.4: Nonmonotonic modal logics using a modal operator to represent consistency or (dis-) belief. These logics are nonmonotonic since conclusions may depend on disbelief. The most prominent example is Moore's autoepistemic logic.

Section 1.5: Conditional approaches which use a non truth-functional connective $\mid\sim$ to represent defaults. A particularly interesting way of using such conditionals was proposed by Kraus, Lehmann and Magidor. They consider φ as a default consequence of ψ *if and only if* the conditional $\psi\mid\sim\varphi$ is in the closure of a given conditional knowledge base under a collection of rules. Each of the rules directly corresponds to a desirable property of a nonmonotonic inference relation.

The various logics are intended to handle different intuitions about nonmonotonic reasoning in a most general way. On the other hand, the generality leads to problems, at least from the point of view of implementations and applications. In the first-order case the approaches are not even semi-decidable since an implicit consistency check is needed. In the propositional case we still have tremendous complexity problems. For instance, the complexity of determining whether a formula is contained in all extensions of a propositional default theory is on the second level of the polynomial hierarchy. As mentioned earlier we believe that logic programming techniques can help to overcome these difficulties (see Sections 4, 3).

Originally, nonmonotonic reasoning was intended to provide us with a *fast* but *unsound* approximation of classical reasoning in the presence of incomplete knowledge. Therefore one might ask whether the higher complexity of NMR-formalisms (compared to classical logic) is not a serious drawback of this aim?

The answer is that NMR-systems allow us to formulate a problem in a very *compact* way as a theory T. It turns out that there are theories T, where any equivalent formulation in classical logic (if possible at all) as a theory T' is much larger: the size of T' is exponential in the size of T! We refer to [Gogic, Papadimitriou, Selman and Kautz 1995] and [Cadoli, Donini and Schaerf 1996, Cadoli, Donini, Schaerf and Silvestri 1997, Cadoli, Donini, Liberatore and Schaerf 1995] where such problems are investigated.

1.1. Herbrand vs. General Models

The alert reader may have taken a second glance at the "ground term" phrase in the definition of CWA. In first-order logic, ground terms that are syntactically different can refer to the same individual, e.g., $a = b$ means that the individual referred to by a is the same as the one referred to by b. In deductive databases, one generally assumes that different terms refer to different individuals: the names are unique. For most database applications, this makes sense: *United* is a different airline than *Delta*, for example. The standard name schema is the Unique Names Assumption:

$$\text{UNA}: \quad \{t_i \neq t_j \mid t_i \text{ and } t_j \text{ are different ground terms}\} \qquad (1.2)$$

A second assumption is that the number of individuals is finite and that every individual has a name in the underlying language. Again, in the context of databases, this is justified because there exist only a finite number of airlines, cities, etc..

The assumption of a finite domain is formalized by assuming a finite set $\{t_i | 1 \leq i \leq n\}$ of ground terms and formulating the **Domain Closure Assumption**:

$$\text{DCA}: \quad \forall x\, (t_1 \doteq x \vee t_2 \doteq x \vee t_3 \doteq x \vee \cdots \vee t_n \doteq x) \qquad (1.3)$$

The schema UNA is a consequence of the CWA, and the schema DCA is consistent with it. We will consider the importance of these schemas when comparing the CWA to circumscription.

When function-symbols are available, then restricting to finite domains would be too restrictive in general. Therefore one often restricts the set of all models to *Herbrand* models. Herbrand models have as the underlying domain exactly the term-algebra generated by the underlying language. The domain closure assumption in this setting means that we restrict to those models $\mathcal{I}$ where for any element a in $\mathcal{I}$ there is a $\mathcal{L}$-term t that represents this element: $a = t^{\mathcal{I}}$.

The difference between Herbrand models and models satisfying UNA and DCA is that the interpretation of terms is uniquely determined in Herbrand models. It is required that a term "$f(t_1, \ldots, f_n)$" is interpreted in a Herbrand model $\mathcal{I}$ as "$f(t_1^{\mathcal{I}}, \ldots, t_n^{\mathcal{I}})$".

1.2. DEFINITION *(Herbrand Models).*

Given a theory T in a language $\mathcal{L}$, we define

Herbrand Universe U_T: it is the algebra consisting of all terms that can be built
  using the constants and function symbols from $\mathcal{L}$, and

Herbrand Base B_T: it is the set of all atomic formulae of the form $r(t_1, \ldots, t_n)$,
  where r is a relation symbol of $\mathcal{L}$ and $t_1, \ldots, t_n$ are ground terms from U_T.

It is well-known that restricting to Herbrand models (as opposed to truth in all models) is a much more complex task—namely Π_1^1-complete (while Π_1^0-complete, i.e. recursively enumerable, for all models). See also Section 2, Subsection 2.1.

1.2. Default Logic (DL)

Reiter's default logic [Reiter 1980] is one of the most prominent nonmonotonic logics. Default logic assumes knowledge to be represented in terms of a default theory. A default theory is a pair $(\mathcal{D}, W)$. W is a set of first-order formulas representing the facts which are known to be true with certainty. $\mathcal{D}$ is a set of defaults of the form

$$\frac{\varphi : \psi_1, \ldots, \psi_n}{\gamma}$$

where φ, ψ_i and γ are classical formulas. We will also frequently use the alternative, less space consuming notation $\varphi : \psi_1, \ldots, \psi_n / \gamma$ for this default. The default has the intuitive reading:

if φ is provable and, for all i ($1 \leq i \leq n$), $\neg \psi_i$ is not provable, then derive γ.

φ is called the *prerequisite*, ψ_i a *consistency condition* or *justification*, and γ the *consequent* of the default. For a default d we use pre(d), just(d), and cons(d) to denote the prerequisite, the set of justifications, and the consequent of d, respectively. Open defaults, i.e., defaults with free variables, are usually interpreted as schemata representing all of their closed instances.[1]

Default theories induce so-called *extensions* which represent acceptable belief sets a reasoner may adopt based on the available information. A formula φ is called a *sceptical* consequence of $(\mathcal{D}, W)$ *if and only if* φ is contained in all extensions of $(\mathcal{D}, W)$. φ is called a *credulous* consequence of $(\mathcal{D}, W)$ *if and only if* φ is contained in at least one extension of $(\mathcal{D}, W)$.

We will first present a definition of extensions which is slightly different from (but equivalent to) Reiter's original definition. We have found that this definition is somewhat easier to digest. The original definition will be presented later.

Intuitively, E is an extension of $(\mathcal{D}, W)$ *if and only if* E is a deductively closed (in the sense of classical logic) superset of W satisfying the following two properties

  1. all defaults that are "applicable" with respect to E have been applied,

  2. every formula in E has a "derivation" from W and applicable defaults.

To make the two requirements more precise we introduce the following notion:

1.3. Definition (*Default Proof, $Cn_{\mathrm{Mon}(\mathcal{D})}(W)$*).

Let $(\mathcal{D}, W)$ be a default theory, S a set of formulas, and φ a formula. A $(\mathcal{D}, W)$-default proof for φ is a finite sequence $\Delta = (d_1, \ldots, d_n)$ of defaults in $\mathcal{D}$ such that:

  1. $W \cup \{\mathrm{cons}(d_1), \ldots, \mathrm{cons}(d_{i-1})\} \vdash \mathrm{pre}(d_i)$, for $i \in \{1, \ldots, n\}$,

  2. $W \cup \{\mathrm{cons}(d_1), \ldots, \mathrm{cons}(d_n)\} \vdash \varphi$.

Δ is valid in S *if and only if* S does not contain the negation of a justification of a default in Δ.

A slightly different, but completely equivalent formulation is to associate to any set of defaults $\mathcal{D}$ a set $\mathrm{Mon}(\mathcal{D})$ of associated *monotonic* inference rules:

$$\mathrm{Mon}(\mathcal{D}) := \{ \frac{\mathrm{pre}(d)}{\mathrm{cons}(d)} : d \in \mathcal{D}\}.$$

Let us denote by $Cn_{\mathrm{Mon}(\mathcal{D})}(W)$ the closure of W with respect to classical derivability and the rules $\mathrm{Mon}(\mathcal{D})$. Then formulae having a $(\mathcal{D}, W)$-default proof are exactly those contained in $Cn_{\mathrm{Mon}(\mathcal{D})}(W)$. Valid proofs are those that also respect the justifications of the original defaults.

As usual $\vdash$ denotes classical provability. We now can state the definition of extensions formally:

1.4. Definition (*Extension 1*).

Let $(\mathcal{D}, W)$ be a default theory. E is an extension of $(\mathcal{D}, W)$ *if and only if* E is a deductively closed superset of W satisfying the conditions

---

[1]Reiter treats open defaults somewhat differently and uses a more complicated method to define extensions for them. We refer to [Kaminski 1995] for a detailed investigation.

1. if $\varphi{:}\psi_1,\ldots,\psi_n/\gamma \in \mathcal{D}$, $\varphi \in E$ and for all i $(1 \leq i \leq n)$ $\neg\psi_i \notin E$, then $\gamma \in E$, and

2. $\varphi \in E$ implies there is a $(\mathcal{D}, W)$-default proof for φ valid in E. This condition is also called *groundedness*.

Reiter's equivalent original definition is more compact. It defines extensions as fixed points of a certain operator.

1.5. DEFINITION *(Extension 2)*.
Let $(\mathcal{D}, W)$ be a default theory, S a set of formulas. Let $\Gamma(S)$ be the smallest set such that:

1. $W \subseteq \Gamma(S)$,
2. $\mathrm{Cn}(\Gamma(S)) = \Gamma(S)$,
3. if $\varphi{:}\psi_1,\ldots,\psi_n/\gamma \in \mathcal{D}$, $\varphi \in \Gamma(S)$, $\neg\psi_i \notin S$ $(1 \leq i \leq n)$, then $\gamma \in \Gamma(S)$.

E is an extension of $(\mathcal{D}, W)$ *if and only if* $E = \Gamma(E)$, that is, if E is a fixed point of Γ.

We finally give a third, quasi-inductive characterization of extensions, also due to Reiter. This version is often used in proofs about default logic and makes the way in which formulas have to be grounded in the premises more explicit. Let E be a set of formulas and define, for a given default theory $(\mathcal{D}, W)$, a sequence of sets of formulas as follows:

$E_0 = W$, and for $i \geq 0$

$E_{i+1} = \mathrm{Cn}(E_i) \cup \{\gamma \mid \varphi{:}\psi_1,\ldots,\psi_n/\gamma \in \mathcal{D}, \varphi \in E_i, \neg\psi_i \notin E\}$.

It can be shown that E is an extension of $(\mathcal{D}, W)$ *if and only if* $E = \bigcup_{i=0}^{\infty} E_i$. The appearance of E in the definition of E_{i+1} is what renders this alternative definition of extensions non-constructive.

Default theories may have an arbitrary number of extensions (including zero). Extensions are always consistent if W is and if there are no degenerate defaults without consistency conditions. If W is inconsistent then the single extension of $(\mathcal{D}, W)$ is the set of all formulas. Extensions are maximal in the following sense: if E is an extension then there is no extension E' such that $E' \subset E$.

Let us consider a few simple examples from the birds domain. Let

$\mathcal{D}_1 = \{bird(x){:}fly(x)/fly(x)\}$

$W_1 = \{bird(tw)\}$.

Since extensions are always deductively closed sets "generated" by W and some of the available default consequents, there are only two candidates to be tested here, namely $S_1 = \mathrm{Cn}(W_1)$ and $S_2 = \mathrm{Cn}(W_1 \cup \{fly(tw)\})$.[2] It is easy to see that $\Gamma(S_1)$ must contain $fly(tw)$. Since S_1 does not contain this formula, it is not a fixed point of Γ. S_2, on the other hand, is a fixed point, as can easily be verified.

Now let

$\mathcal{D}_2 = \mathcal{D}_1$

$W_2 = \{bird(tw), peng(tw), \forall x(peng(x) \leftarrow \neg fly(x))\}$.

---

[2]Other instances of the default rule need not be considered, since there is no way of deriving $bird(t)$ for any ground term t different from tw.

$\mathcal{D}$	W	Fixed Point(s)
$\frac{bird(x):fly(x)}{fly(x)}$	$bird(tw)$	$\mathrm{Cn}(W \cup \{fly(tw)\})$
$\frac{bird(x):fly(x)}{fly(x)}$	$bird(tw)$ $peng(tw)$ $\forall x(peng(x) \to \neg fly(x))$	$\mathrm{Cn}(W)$
$\frac{bird(x):fly(x)}{fly(x)}$ $\frac{peng(x):\neg fly(x)}{\neg fly(x)}$	$bird(tw)$ $peng(tw)$	$\mathrm{Cn}(W \cup \{fly(tw)\})$ $\mathrm{Cn}(W \cup \{\neg fly(tw)\})$
$\frac{bird(x):fly(x)\wedge\neg peng(x)}{fly(x)}$ $\frac{peng(x):\neg fly(x)}{\neg fly(x)}$	$bird(tw)$ $peng(tw)$	$\mathrm{Cn}(W \cup \{\neg fly(tw)\})$

Table 1: Some Default Theories and Their Extensions

Again there are two candidates, namely $S_1 = \mathrm{Cn}(W_2)$, $S_2 = \mathrm{Cn}(W_2 \cup \{fly(tw)\})$. This time, S_2, which is inconsistent, is not a fixed point of Γ since $\Gamma(S_2) = \mathrm{Cn}(W_2)$. The only fixed point is S_1.

Consider what happens if the universally quantified formula from W_2 is replaced by a corresponding default rule:

$\mathcal{D}_3 = \{bird(x):fly(x)/fly(x), peng(x):\neg fly(x)/\neg fly(x)\}$
$W_3 = \{bird(tw), peng(tw)\}$.

If instantiations of both defaults (with $x = tw$) are applied, an inconsistency is generated. $\mathrm{Cn}(W_3 \cup \{fly(tw), \neg fly(tw)\})$ cannot be an extension, since $\Gamma(S) = \mathrm{Cn}(W)$ whenever S is inconsistent. If a candidate contains neither $fly(tw)$ nor $\neg fly(tw)$, the operator Γ will produce the set of all formulas, and, again, the candidate is not a fixed point. However, if we apply one of the default instances, we obtain an extension. The two extensions are $\mathrm{Cn}(W_3 \cup \{fly(tw)\})$ and $\mathrm{Cn}(W_3 \cup \{\neg fly(tw)\})$.

Table 1 presents the simple default theories we just discussed together with their extensions.

1.3. Circumscription (CIRC)

Circumscription is a method of defining the closure of a theory by restricting its models to those that have minimal extensions of some of the predicates and functions. Since its first formulation by [McCarthy 1980], it has taken on several different forms, including domain circumscription [McCarthy 1979] (minimizing the elements in the universe of models) and the most popular and useful version, parallel predicate circumscription described in the papers [McCarthy 1980, McCarthy 1986, Lifschitz 1985]. We present this system and some of the major variants, along with a description of *abnormality theories*, a method for default reasoning using circumscription.

Although circumscription was originally presented as a schema for adding more

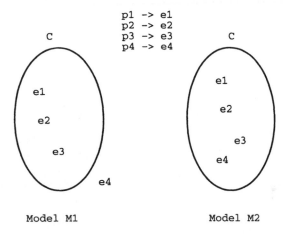

```
p1 -> e1
p2 -> e2
p3 -> e3
p4 -> e4
```

Figure 1: Two Models of a Theory with the Same Valuation.

formulas to a theory (just as Clark's completion does), here we describe it in terms of restricting the models of the theory. This view leads to the generalization of circumscription by model preference theories and is more useful analytically in relating circumscription to other nonmonotonic formalisms. More detailed references to circumscription can be found in Lifschitz's excellent survey article [Lifschitz 1994].

Parallel Predicate Circumscription

Choose a language $\mathcal{L}$ and let $\underline{p}$ be the set of predicate symbols that we are interested in minimizing and $\underline{z}$ another set of predicate symbols the interpretation of which we allow to vary across compared models. For example, if we wish to minimize the number of cannibals, we would let $\underline{p} = \{cannibal\}$ and $\underline{z}$ be all other predicate symbols (the importance of $\underline{z}$ will be indicated later). Suppose T is a theory containing the statements $cannibal(p_1)$, $cannibal(p_2)$, and $cannibal(p_3)$, but no other assertions using cannibal. Then every model of T will have at least the individuals referred to by p_1, p_2, and p_3 with property cannibal. Now consider two models with the same valuation function from terms to individuals, as in Figure 1. In model M_1, the extension of the predicate $cannibal()$ includes just the three individuals e_1, e_2, and e_3. In model M_2 there is a fourth individual, e_4, who is a cannibal. Circumscription would prefer M_1 to M_2, since the extension of $cannibal()$ in M_1 is a proper subset of its extension in M_2. Under appropriate assumptions (that these terms refer to different individuals), circumscription would yield the result $\neg cannibal(p_4)$, which is not present in the original theory. See Definition 2.10 where also *fixed* predicates are allowed.

Let $\psi(\underline{p}, \underline{z})$ be a first-order sentence containing the symbols $\underline{p}$ and $\underline{z}$. Circumscription prefers models of $\psi(\underline{p}, \underline{z})$ that are minimal in the predicates $\underline{p}$, assuming that these models have the same interpretation for all symbols not in $\underline{p}$ or $\underline{z}$: such predicates are called *fixed symbols*.

To state this more formally, let $\mathcal{M}_1$ and $\mathcal{M}_2$ be two models of $\psi(\underline{p}, \underline{z})$. $|\mathcal{M}|$ is the universe of model $\mathcal{M}$, and $\mathcal{M}[\![r]\!]$ is the interpretation of the predicate r in $\mathcal{M}$.

1.6. DEFINITION *(Minimal Models, Entailment $\models_{min}$)*.

$$\mathcal{M}_1 \leq^{\underline{p};\underline{z}} \mathcal{M}_2 \quad \Leftrightarrow \quad \begin{cases} 1. & |\mathcal{M}_1| = |\mathcal{M}_2|^3. \\ 2. & \mathcal{M}_1[\![r]\!] = \mathcal{M}_2[\![r]\!] \text{ for all } r \text{ not in } \underline{p}, \underline{z}. \\ 3. & \mathcal{M}_1[\![p_i]\!] \subseteq \mathcal{M}_2[\![p_i]\!] \text{ for all } p_i \in \underline{p}. \end{cases}$$

In many applications there are no fixed predicates and we are interested in minimizing all predicates while varying all predicates. In such applications we have $\underline{p} = \underline{z}$ and this is the set of all predicates. We write

$$T \models_{min} \phi$$

to denote that all minimal models of the set of formulae T also satisfy the sentence ϕ.

$\leq^{\underline{p};\underline{z}}$ is a preorder relation (reflexive and transitive) on models, but not necessarily a partial order since it is not antireflexive. We define the strict order $\mathcal{M}_1 <^{(\underline{p};\underline{z})} \mathcal{M}_2$ as $\mathcal{M}_1 \leq^{\underline{p};\underline{z}} \mathcal{M}_2$ and not $\mathcal{M}_2 \leq^{\underline{p};\underline{z}} \mathcal{M}_1$. The preferred models of $\psi(\underline{p}, \underline{z})$ are those that are minimal according to the strict ordering.

Second-order form
This form of circumscription is called *parallel predicate circumscription* because a set of predicates is minimized in parallel. It can be concisely written as a second-order formula, once we make the following definitions. Let u, v be predicates of the same arity.

$$\begin{array}{lll} u \leq v & \text{stands for} & \forall x \, (u(x) \rightarrow v(x)) \\ u < v & \text{stands for} & u \leq v \wedge v \not\leq u \\ u = v & \text{stands for} & u \leq v \wedge v \leq u \end{array}$$

These sentences express facts about the extensions of u and v: $u \leq v$ means that u's extension is a subset of v's, $u < v$ that it is a proper subset, and $u = v$ that they are coextensive. If u and v are tuples of predicates, then these formulas stand for the obvious conjunction of the operator applied to each pair of predicates. Now we define:

1.7. DEFINITION *(Parallel Predicate Circumscription)*.
The parallel predicate circumscription of a theory $\psi(\underline{p}, \underline{z})$ is defined as follows

$$\text{Circum}(\psi(\underline{p}, \underline{z}); \underline{p}; \underline{z}) = \psi(\underline{p}, \underline{z}) \, \wedge \, \neg \exists \underline{p}'\underline{z}' \, (\psi(\underline{p}', \underline{z}') \wedge \underline{p}' < \underline{p}) \, .$$

---

[3]We also assume that all *terms* get the same interpretation in both models.

[Lifschitz 1985] shows that this definition is equivalent to the minimal model semantics, that is, $\mathcal{M}$ is a model of $\text{Circum}(\psi(\underline{p}, \underline{z}); \underline{p}; \underline{z})$ *if and only if* it is a $\leq^{(\underline{p};\underline{z})}$-minimal model of ψ.

Note that circumscription allows comparison of models only if they have the same interpretations of terms and fixed predicates. In general, allowing more comparisons strengthens the results of circumscription since fewer minimal models are present. It is also possible to allow varying function symbols as well as predicates; this has important effects on equality results (see [Brewka et al. 1997]).

Abnormality Theories

[McCarthy 1986] originated the concept of an abnormality theory as a way to represent default reasoning in circumscription. Defaults are represented with an introduced abnormality predicate: for example, to say that normally birds fly, we would use:

$$\forall x \, (bird(x) \wedge \neg ab_1(x) \rightarrow fly(x)\,). \tag{1.4}$$

Here the meaning of $ab_1(x)$ is something like "x is abnormal with respect to flying birds." Note that there can be many different kinds of abnormality, and they are indexed according to kind. The circumscription would then minimize abnormalities, allowing relevant predicates to vary (e.g., fly). Let ψ stand for the conjunction of (1.4) and $bird(tweety)$. Using arguments about minimal models, we can show that

$$\text{Circum}(\psi; ab_1; fly, bird) \models fly(tweety)\,. \tag{1.5}$$

Abnormality theories can represent two important types of *defeating* arguments. One usually distinguishes between defeaters that contradict outright a default (Type I defeaters), and those where only the justification for a default is undermined, without contradicting its conclusion (Type II defeaters). Here is some illustrating example. If it is known that *tweety* doesn't fly (Type I defeat), we can add (to Example 1.4):

$$bird(tweety) \wedge \neg fly(tweety)\,. \tag{1.6}$$

Here the conclusion $ab_1(tweety)$ follows in all models. For Type II defeat, we simply assert that Tweety is abnormal, without asserting that he doesn't fly.

Abnormality theories are widely used in applications of circumscription. Some major examples are in logic-based diagnosis [Reiter 1987], inheritance theories [Etherington and Reiter 1983], and reasoning about time and action [Baker 1991, Kartha and Lifschitz 1995].

1.4. Autoepistemic Logic (AEL)

Modal logics are an extensively studied basis for formalizing nonmonotonic reasoning. The first proposal was made by McDermott and Doyle [McDermott and Doyle 1980]. In order to avoid some deficiencies of this logic Moore [Moore 1985] introduced autoepistemic logic as a reconstruction of McDermott and Doyle's logic.

The idea is to formalize nonmonotonic reasoning in terms of an ideally rational agent reasoning about its own beliefs. Hence, a modal language $\mathcal{L}_\mathbf{B}$ is employed which extends a classical first-order language with a new monadic operator $\mathbf{B}$. So, e.g., $\mathbf{B}(\varphi \wedge (\neg\mathbf{B}\psi \to \varphi))$ is a formula of $\mathcal{L}_\mathbf{B}$ where φ and ψ are classical formulae. For example, Chellas [Chellas 1980] and Hughes and Cresswell [Hughes and Cresswell 1984] are good sources on modal logics.

The intuitive reading of a formula $\mathbf{B}\varphi$ is that the agent believes φ. Nonmonotonicity is captured by the *negative introspection* capability of the agent which amounts to a rule

if φ is not believed, then $\neg\mathbf{B}\varphi$ is.

Such a rule is circular, i.e., beliefs are defined in terms of what is not believed, and a formalization of this principle leads to a fixed point equation. In autoepistemic reasoning it is assumed that an ideally rational agent has perfect introspection capabilities. This means that in addition to negative introspection the agent is capable of *positive introspection*:

if φ is believed, then $\mathbf{B}\varphi$ is believed.

Moore captures this notion of beliefs by defining the potential sets of beliefs of an ideally rational agent with full introspection capabilities when given a set of premises as the basis of the beliefs. The potential sets of beliefs are called *stable expansions* of the premises and they are defined by the following fixed point equation.

1.8. Definition *(Stable Expansion,Moore [Moore 1985])*.
Let $T \subseteq \mathcal{L}_\mathbf{B}$. A set of formulae S is a *stable expansion* of T *if and only if*

$$S = \{\phi \mid T \cup \mathbf{B}S \cup \neg\mathbf{B}\overline{S} \vdash \phi\} \tag{1.7}$$

where $\vdash$ is the classical consequence relation which treats $\mathbf{B}\phi$ formulae like atomic formulae and the following notations are used: $\mathbf{B}S = \{\mathbf{B}\phi \mid \phi \in S\}$, $\neg S = \{\neg\phi \mid \phi \in S\}$, and $\overline{S} = \mathcal{L}_\mathbf{B} \setminus S$. Hence, $\neg\mathbf{B}\overline{S} = \{\neg\mathbf{B}\phi \mid \phi \in \mathcal{L}_\mathbf{B} \setminus S\}$.

So a stable expansion S is the logical closure of the premises and the results of positive introspection $\mathbf{B}S$ and negative introspection $\neg\mathbf{B}S$ from S.

1.9. Example. A statement of the type "a bird typically flies" can be formalized in autoepistemic logic using a formula

$$b \wedge \neg\mathbf{B}\neg f \to f.$$

which states that if a bird is not believed not to fly, it flies. The set $\{b, b \wedge \neg\mathbf{B}\neg f \to f\}$ induces exactly one potential set of beliefs (stable expansion) which contains, e.g., $b, \mathbf{B}b, \neg\mathbf{B}\neg f, f, \mathbf{B}f, \mathbf{BB}f, \mathbf{BBB}f$.

This idea has also been used in [Przymusinski 1998] to define semantics for logic programs (see also [Brass, Dix and Przymusinski 1999]).

In first-order modal logics quantifying into the scope of a modal logic is problematic. Here we consider the case where quantifying-in is not allowed, e.g., formulae of the form $\forall x(\mathbf{B}\neg p(x) \to p(x))$ are not permitted. With this assumption formulae of the form $\mathbf{B}\varphi$ can be treated as new (ground) atoms as far as the underlying consequence relation ($\vdash$) is concerned. However, we allow formulae with free variables and they are interpreted as schemata representing all of the closed instances. We refer to [Konolige 1994] for a treatment of quantifying-in in autoepistemic logic. Konolige's [Konolige 1994] survey article provides a good source on autoepistemic logic.

The problem of McDermott and Doyle's [McDermott 1982] first attempt was that it missed positive introspection, i.e. they used equation (1.7) *without* the term $\mathbf{B}S$. Another way to adding positive introspection is by using appropriate modal axioms and the necessitation rule

$$\frac{\varphi}{\mathbf{B}\varphi}.$$

This observation leads to a scheme for defining a corresponding nonmonotonic modal logic for a given monotonic modal logic S, i.e., a notion of a potential set of beliefs (S-expansion) for each monotonic modal logic S specifying the choice of the positive introspection capabilities of the agent.

1.10. DEFINITION *(S-Expansion,McDermott and Doyle)*.
Let $T \subseteq \mathcal{L}_{\mathbf{B}}$. A set of formulae S is an *S-expansion* of T if and only if

$$S = \{\phi \mid T \cup \neg \mathbf{B}\overline{S} \vdash_S \phi\} \tag{1.8}$$

where $\vdash_S$ is the derivability relation of the logic S.

The work on this approach was initiated by McDermott [McDermott 1982] and continued first by Shvarts [Shvarts 1990] and then by Marek et al. [Marek, Schwarz and Truszczyński 1993]. A good source on nonmonotonic modal logics is the book [Marek and Truszczyński 1993]. Marek et al. [Marek et al. 1993] show that the structure of the space of nonmonotonic modal logics is simpler than that of monotonic modal logics. The underlying monotonic modal logic plays a secondary role in the definition of nonmonotonic reasoning based on the fixed point equation (1.8): several monotonic modal logics induce the same nonmonotonic system, i.e. expansions coincide for a range of underlying modal logics. For example, for every modal logic S between **5** and **KD45**, a S-expansion is a stable expansion. If the set of premises is taken from a restricted class of formulae, even larger ranges exist. For example, let T be strongly stratified [Marek et al. 1993]. Then for every modal logic S such that[4] $\mathbf{N} \subseteq S$ and $S \subseteq \mathbf{KD45}$ or $S \subseteq \mathbf{SW5}$, [Marek et al. 1993] proved:

S is an S-expansion *if and only if* S is the unique stable expansion of T.

---

[4]The modal logic **N** is an extension of the propositional calculus with no modal axioms but the rule of necessitation.

All nonmonotonic modal logics based on the fixed point equation (1.8) share a property that so called weakly grounded (or circular grounded) beliefs are not excluded from the expansions. For example, $\{\neg \mathbf{B} \neg \mathbf{B} p \to p\}$ has an N-expansion containing a circular grounded belief p. This property of N-expansions is immediately inherited by other McDermott and Doyle style nonmonotonic modal logics because of the following property of nonmonotonic modal logics:

- for any modal logics S_1, S_2 contained in **S5**, if S_1 is contained in S_2, then any S_1-expansion is an S_2-expansion [Marek et al. 1993].

We refer to [Niemelä 1991] for an approach for defining autoepistemic reasoning which avoids weakly grounded beliefs.

Autoepistemic logic is closely related to default logic and the main difference is groundedness. All McDermott and Doyle style logics allow weakly grounded beliefs whereas extensions in default logic are strongly grounded. This needs special attention when establishing translations between the two logics. However, a default theory can be translated into a set of autoepistemic formulae such that extensions coincide with expansions of the translated theory provided that a tightly enough grounded class of expansions is employed. Truszczyński [Truszczyński 1991] proposes the following quite natural translation of a default rule into an autoepistemic formula

$$\text{tr}_T(\frac{\varphi : \psi_1, \ldots, \psi_n}{\gamma}) \;=\; \mathbf{B}\varphi \wedge \mathbf{B}\neg\mathbf{B}\neg\psi_1 \wedge \cdots \wedge \mathbf{B}\neg\mathbf{B}\neg\psi_n \to \gamma \qquad (1.9)$$

and shows that for a wide range of modal logics, extensions and expansions coincide.

1.11. THEOREM ([Truszczyński 1991]).
*Let (D, W) be a default theory. For a modal logic S between **N** and **S4F** and a consistent set of formulae S, the set S is an extension of (D, W) if and only if S is the first-order part of an **S**-expansion of $W \cup \{\text{tr}_T(d) \mid d \in D\}$.*

The modal approach to nonmonotonic reasoning can be seen as a generalization of default logic because it can capture default extensions but also provides an expressive query language where distinctions can be made between whether a query is *true, believed, false* or *not believed*.

1.5. Rational Closure ($\mathcal{K}^{\text{rat}}$)

In the previous sections we have introduced some nonmonotonic reasoning systems. A natural question to ask is what the differences and similarities are and how much *nonmonotonicity* such logics contain? The idea to *abstract* from a particular representation and to ask for the properties a nonmonotonic consequence-relation ⊢should satisfy dates back to [Gabbay 1984] and was investigated in detail by [Kraus, Lehmann and Magidor 1990, Lehmann and Magidor 1992]. [Makinson 1994] is a nice overview article.

Obviously, any nonmonotonic system induces an entailment relation ⊢:

1.12. DEFINITION *(Induced Entailment Relation $\vdash\!\!\sim$).*
For default (resp. autoepistemic) logic, we can define a formula to be derivable if it is contained in all extensions (resp. expansions) of the theory in question. For Circumscription it is even simpler: a formula follows, if it is contained in the circumscribed theory. This approach (truth in all extensions) is often called *sceptical* as opposed to a *credulous* setting, where a formula is already declared to be entailed when it is true in at least one extension (resp. expansion) of the theory under consideration.

It turns out that there are abstract properties of an entailment relation $\vdash\!\!\sim$, that clearly distinguish between default logic and circumscription. While any circumscription logic is *cumulative* (a term to be explained below), default logic is not.

But we can use the $\vdash\!\!\sim$-setting also the other way around, by representing our theories using $\vdash\!\!\sim$. We consider the following set-up:

Default-base $\mathcal{K}$: A given situation is modeled by a (finite) set of *conditional assertions* of the form "$\alpha\vdash\!\!\sim\beta$", where α, β are expressions in propositional logic. This set forms the "default-knowledge-base" $\mathcal{K}$. An assertion "$\alpha\vdash\!\!\sim\beta$" may be read as "*normally (typically, in most cases, if there is no evidence to the contrary) α implies β*". We also allow *hard* knowledge, which is true in any case and not subject to later revision. We code such knowledge with a propositional theory T_{hard}.

Closure of $\mathcal{K}$: Starting from the default-base $\mathcal{K}$ one attempts to derive additional conditional assertions. The set $\mathcal{K}$ of elements of the form "$\alpha\vdash\!\!\sim\beta$" thus leads to a, usually bigger, set again made up of elements of the form "$\alpha\vdash\!\!\sim\beta$". The set of all conditional assertions derived from $\mathcal{K}$ is called the closure of $\mathcal{K}$. We will consider several different closure operators.

Query ?-$c\vdash\!\!\sim d$: Finally we can ask queries about $\mathcal{K}$. These are again of the form "$\gamma\vdash\!\!\sim\delta$" and will be answered by "yes" or "no", depending on whether "$\gamma\vdash\!\!\sim\delta$" is in the closure of $\mathcal{K}$ or not.

1.13. DEFINITION *(Cumulative Closure $\mathcal{K}^{cum}$).*
The cumulative closure $\mathcal{K}^{cum}$ of a knowledge base is defined by simply closing the given knowledge base by the following rules: Reflexivity, Left Logical Equivalence, Right Weakening, Cut and Cautious Monotonicity.

Let us define and discuss these inference rules.

$$\frac{}{\alpha\vdash\!\!\sim\alpha} \qquad (Reflexivity)$$

$$\frac{T_{hard} \vdash \alpha \Leftrightarrow \beta, \ \alpha\vdash\!\!\sim\gamma}{\beta\vdash\!\!\sim\gamma} \qquad (Left\ Logical\ Equivalence)$$

Left Logical Equivalence expresses the requirement that logically equivalent formulas should have the same nonmonotonic consequences. Here $\vdash$ denotes the classical logical consequence relation. Using the well-known completeness theorem for classical logic, we can also write "$T_{hard} \models \phi$". For ease of notation the reference to T_{hard} will be suppressed, unless it is absolutely crucial.

$$\frac{\vdash \alpha \to \beta, \ \gamma \vdash \alpha}{\gamma \vdash \beta} \qquad \text{(Right Weakening)}$$

Right Weakening may be paraphrased to say that any logical consequence of a nonmonotonic consequence is again a nonmonotonic consequence. *Reflexivity* and *Right Weakening* suffice to derive $\alpha \vdash \beta$ from $\alpha \vdash \beta$, i.e. the nonmonotonic consequence relation is an extension of the classical consequence relation.

$$\frac{\alpha \wedge \beta \vdash \gamma, \ \alpha \vdash \beta}{\alpha \vdash \gamma} \qquad \text{(Cut)}$$

Cut expresses the method of added hypothesis. When we try to prove γ from α, we adopt an additional hypothesis β, try to derive γ from $\alpha \wedge \beta$ and then try to get rid of the hypothesis again by proving that β follows from α.

$$\frac{\alpha \vdash \beta, \ \alpha \vdash \gamma}{\alpha \wedge \beta \vdash \gamma} \qquad \text{(Cautious Monotonicity)}$$

For a monotone consequence relation $\vdash$ the assertion $\alpha \wedge \beta \vdash \gamma$ could always be derived from $\alpha \vdash \gamma$. *Cautious Monotonicity* is a relaxation of this requirement in that monotony only applies, when we add assumptions that have already been proved. Thus cautious monotonicity may be thought of as sanctioning the use of lemmas in proofs.

1.14. DEFINITION *(Preferential Closure $\mathcal{K}^{\mathrm{pref}}$)*.
The preferential closure $\mathcal{K}^{\mathrm{pref}}$ of a knowledge base is defined by closing the given knowledge base by the rules: Reflexivity, Left Logical Equivalence, Right Weakening, Cut, Cautious Monotonicity and the following rule

$$\frac{\alpha \vdash \gamma, \ \beta \vdash \gamma}{\alpha \vee \beta \vdash \gamma} \qquad \text{(Or)}.$$

Obviously, $\mathcal{K}^{\mathrm{cum}} \subseteq \mathcal{K}^{\mathrm{pref}}$. But it turns out, that even the preferential closure is fairly weak [Dix and Schmitt 1993]. We illustrate this with the Nixon diamond:

1.15. EXAMPLE *(Weakness of $\mathcal{K}^{\mathrm{pref}}$)*.
We consider the knowledge base

$$\mathcal{K} := \{\ quaker \vdash pacifist, \ republican \vdash \neg pacifist \ \}.$$

Although "$quaker \wedge \neg republican \vdash pacifist$" and "$republican \wedge \neg quaker \vdash \neg pacifist$" are both expected to be contained in the preferential closure, they are not.

Often, one would like to derive even stronger statements. For example adding statements that are totally irrelevant with the situation at hand, should not affect it. For example, if Peter normally goes to a party, then learning that (say) Socrates was a Greek philosopher should not change that conclusion. The principle of *Rationality* states that any proposition that is not explicitly negated by a premise set can be added to that set without changing its conclusions:

$$\frac{\alpha \hspace{1pt}|\!\!\!\not\sim \neg\beta, \ \alpha \hspace{1pt}|\!\!\sim \gamma}{\alpha \wedge \beta \hspace{1pt}|\!\!\sim \gamma} \qquad (Rationality)$$

Consequently, Lehmann and Magidor defined a rational closure $\mathcal{K}^{\text{rat}}$, which is quite different from both $\mathcal{K}^{\text{cum}}$ and $\mathcal{K}^{\text{pref}}$:

$\mathcal{K} \rightsquigarrow \mathcal{K}^{\text{cum}}$: This closure operation, as well as $\mathcal{K} \rightsquigarrow \mathcal{K}^{\text{pref}}$ is *monotone*, i.e.

$$\mathcal{K} \subseteq \mathcal{K}' \implies \mathcal{K}^{\text{cum}} \subseteq (\mathcal{K}')^{\text{cum}}.$$

The reason for this is that both operations are defined by *inference rules* of the form:

"if $\alpha \hspace{1pt}|\!\!\sim \beta$ and $\gamma \hspace{1pt}|\!\!\sim \delta$ then $\zeta \hspace{1pt}|\!\!\sim \eta$".

$\mathcal{K}^{\text{cum}}$ and $\mathcal{K}^{\text{pref}}$ are the least sets containing $\mathcal{K}$ and closed under a set of inference rules of this form.

$\mathcal{K} \rightsquigarrow \mathcal{K}^{\text{rat}}$: This operation is *nonmonotonic* and not so easy to describe. But Lehmann and Magidor give in [Lehmann and Magidor 1992] a very effective and intuitive algorithm to compute $\mathcal{K}^{\text{rat}}$. We will restrict ourselves to the explanation of this algorithm.

Two important concepts have to be introduced before we can give the definition of the algorithm that computes $\mathcal{K}^{\text{rat}}$:

1. the notion of an *exceptional formula*,
2. the notion of *rank* for formulas.

1.16. DEFINITION *(Exceptional Formulas)*.
A formula α is called *exceptional* for $\mathcal{K}$, if $\mathsf{t} \hspace{1pt}|\!\!\sim \neg\alpha \in \mathcal{K}^{\text{pref}}$. A conditional assertion $\alpha \hspace{1pt}|\!\!\sim \beta$ is called *exceptional* for $\mathcal{K}$, if α is exceptional for $\mathcal{K}$.

Thus α is exceptional for $\mathcal{K}$ means that normally $\neg\alpha$ holds true (given $\mathcal{K}$). The set of all exceptional conditional assertions in $\mathcal{K}$ will be denoted by $E(\mathcal{K})$. Iterating the operator E leads to a sequence $\mathcal{C}_0, \mathcal{C}_1, \mathcal{C}_2, \ldots$

$$\mathcal{C}_0 := \mathcal{K}, \ \mathcal{C}_{i+1} := E(\mathcal{C}_i).$$

This is a decreasing sequence, i.e. $\mathcal{C}_{i+1} \subseteq \mathcal{C}_i$ is true for all i. Since $\mathcal{K}$ is finite there is an index n, such that

$$\mathcal{C}_1 \supset \mathcal{C}_2 \supset \ldots \supset \mathcal{C}_{n-1} \supset \mathcal{C}_n = \mathcal{C}_{n+1} = \ldots.$$

The rank of a formula α with respect to a knowledge base $\mathcal{K}$ is the number k such that $\alpha \in \mathcal{C}_k$ but $\alpha \notin \mathcal{C}_{k+1}$. If there is no such k, α is said to have no rank.

1.17. DEFINITION $(\mathcal{K}^{\mathrm{rat}})$.

Let $\mathcal{K}$ be a knowledge base. $\mathcal{K}^{\mathrm{rat}}$ consists of all conditional assertions $\alpha \hspace{-0.5mm}\mid\hspace{-2mm}\sim\hspace{-0.5mm} \beta$, such that either

1. the rank of α is strictly smaller than the rank of $\alpha \wedge \neg \beta$ (this includes the case that α has a rank and $\alpha \wedge \neg \beta$ does not) or
2. α has no rank.

Note that the definition of $\mathcal{K}^{\mathrm{rat}}$ depends essentially on $\mathcal{K}^{\mathrm{pref}}$. In fact, as shown in [Dix and Schmitt 1993], there exists a nice relation between these two closures:

$$\alpha \hspace{-0.5mm}\mid\hspace{-2mm}\sim\hspace{-0.5mm} \beta \ \in \mathcal{K}^{\mathrm{pref}} \quad \textit{if and only if} \quad \alpha \hspace{-0.5mm}\mid\hspace{-0.5mm}\mathbf{f} \ \in (\mathcal{K} \cup \{\alpha \hspace{-0.5mm}\mid\hspace{-2mm}\sim\hspace{-0.5mm} \neg \beta\})^{\mathrm{rat}}.$$

This means that once we have an efficient method for computing $\mathcal{K}^{\mathrm{rat}}$ we can use it for the computation of $\mathcal{K}^{\mathrm{pref}}$.

In [Dix and Schmitt 1993] many of the benchmark problems of [Lifschitz 1989] are discussed and it is investigated how they are handled by the various closures introduced above.

2. Automating General Nonmonotonic Logics

In this section we address the problem of automating general nonmonotonic logics and, in particular, default logic, autoepistemic logic and circumscription. We start the section by a brief survey of the complexity and decidability results on nonmonotonic logics. The idea is to provide an overview of the computational properties of nonmonotonic logics and discuss the implications of the properties on automated reasoning in these logics. Given this background we move towards automated theorem proving methods. The first issue is the problem of developing *finitary* characterizations of correct nonmonotonic reasoning. As we have seen in Section 1, when formalizing nonmonotonic logics such as default logic or circumscription the definitions are given in terms of infinite objects: fixed point equations over infinite sets of formulae in the case of default logic and autoepistemic logic or minimality over an infinite set of models in the case of circumscription. For developing computational treatments of the logics, it is necessary to find techniques for characterizing correct nonmonotonic reasoning using finitary means. These characterizations provide the basis for the decidability and complexity results as well as for the automated theorem proving methods. We present such characterizations and demonstrate how they lead to efficient decision methods.

This section is organized as follows. After a survey on general complexity results in Subsection 2.1, we turn to finitary characterizations of our nonmonotonic logics, which form the basis of the decision methods studied in the following Subsections 2.3, 2.4, 2.5 and 2.6. We give the most attention to default logic (Subsection 2.3) because it is perhaps the most popular general nonmonotonic logic which has close relationships to logic programs. In fact the method presented here for default logic provides the basis of our treatment of the stable model semantics of logic programs in Section 5. In Subsection 2.4 we show how the approach developed for default logic can be applied to autoepistemic logic. We discuss also the fundamental issues in automating circumscription (Subsection 2.5) and provide the basis for the treatment of circumscription presented in Section 3. We end with Subsection 2.6 by considering the automation of rational closure.

2.1. Decidability and Complexity

The fundamental decision problems for default logic and nonmonotonic modal logics are *sceptical reasoning* (i.e. determining sceptical consequences), *credulous reasoning* (i.e. determining credulous consequences) and the problem of deciding whether a set of premises has at least one extension/expansion (the *extension/expansion existence problem*). Circumscription can been seen as a form of sceptical reasoning because circumscriptive consequences are the formulae that are true in every minimal model of the premises.

First-Order Case

For first-order default logic these problems are not even semi-decidable [Reiter 1980]. This holds also for first-order autoepistemic logic even when quantifying into the scope of the modal operator is not allowed [Niemelä 1990]. If quantifying-in is allowed, the problems are highly undecidable [Konolige 1991]. General first-order circumscription is highly uncomputable, too [Schlipf 1986].

Propositional Case

Default logic For propositional default logic, extension existence problem and credulous reasoning are Σ_2^P-complete problems in the polynomial time hierarchy and sceptical default reasoning (the dual problem) is Π_2^P-complete [Gottlob 1992, Stillman 1992]. Balcázar et al. [Balcázar, Díaz and Gabarró 1988] and Garey and Johnson [Garey and Johnson 1979] provide good sources of basic definitions and results on the polynomial time hierarchy and related issues in complexity theory. Kautz and Selman [Kautz and Selman 1991], Stillman [Stillman 1990], and Ben-Eliyahu and Dechter [Ben-Eliyahu and Dechter 1991, Ben-Eliyahu and Dechter 1992] have obtained further complexity results on restricted subclasses of default theories.

Nonmonotonic modal logics Similar results as for default logic hold. For autoepistemic logic based on Moore style expansions and L-hierarchic expansions [Niemelä 1991] and for McDermott and Doyle style logics based on a number of modal logics *expansion existence problem* and *credulous reasoning* are Σ_2^P-complete problems and *sceptical reasoning* is Π_2^P-complete [Gottlob 1992, Niemelä 1990, Niemelä 1992, Schwarz and Truszczyński 1993]. [Marek and Truszczyński 1991a, Marek and Truszczyński 1991b] present complexity results on restricted subclasses of autoepistemic reasoning.

Circumscription The problem of deciding whether a propositional sentence is a circumscriptive consequence of a set of propositional sentences is also a Π_2^P-

complete problem [Eiter and Gottlob 1993, Eiter and Gottlob 1995a]. Cadoli and Lenzerini [Cadoli and Lenzerini 1990] establish complexity results on limited subclasses of circumscriptive reasoning including some tractability results.

Implications of the Results

The complexity results have interesting implications on theorem proving methods for nonmonotonic logics which we elaborate next. As mentioned above, the full first-order case is not even semi-decidable as is the case for classical first-order logic. Hence, theorem proving systems for first-order nonmonotonic logics cannot provide a similar level of completeness as classical theorem provers: a query can be a nonmonotonic consequence of the premises but no nonmonotonic theorem prover is able to establish this. This should be compared to first-order theorem proving where it can be guaranteed that for each valid formula a proof is eventually found.

If we consider the propositional case, the logics are decidable and the most important decision problems (sceptical and credulous consequence) are complete problems with respect to the second level of the polynomial time hierarchy. First, this implies that this kind of nonmonotonic reasoning can be implemented in *polynomial space*. Second, this indicates that nonmonotonic reasoning is strictly harder than classical reasoning unless the polynomial time hierarchy collapses which is regarded unlikely by the experts. This means that two orthogonal sources of complexity are involved in general nonmonotonic reasoning. One source originates from the classical reasoning on top of which nonmonotonic reasoning is built. The other source is related to the handling of the nonmonotonic constructs. These sources are independent of each other. In fact, even if we assume that we can use an oracle for classical reasoning, i.e., we are able to decide classical consequence in one computation step, solving a nonmonotonic reasoning problem remains on the difficulty level of an **NP/co-NP**-complete problem and no polynomial time algorithms are known even under the oracle assumption.

Hence, it is highly unlikely that general nonmonotonic reasoning can be implemented on top of a classical theorem proving method with only a polynomial overhead.

Tractable Subclasses

The complexity results provide important information when searching for tractable subclasses of nonmonotonic reasoning problems. In classical logics the standard approach to achieving tractability is to restrict the syntactic form of formulae, e.g., to consider only Horn clauses or clauses with only two literals. The complexity results indicate that this is not enough for nonmonotonic reasoning because only the complexity of the required classical reasoning is affected. The complexity related to the handling of the nonmonotonic constructs is orthogonal to this and can still lead to intractability. Hence, in order to achieve tractability both sources of complexity have to be addressed. A standard technique is to restrict the syntactic form of the premises (for guaranteeing the tractability of the required classical reasoning) and to limit the interaction of the nonmonotonic constructs.

The interaction can be controlled by syntactic restrictions such as stratification introduced in the logic programming setting [Chandra and Harel 1985, Apt, Blair and Walker 1988, Van Gelder 1988]. We refer to [Niemelä and Rintanen 1994] for a detailed investigation of the effects of stratification on the complexity of the nonmonotonic reasoning and for the associated decision methods and algorithms. Another approach to control the interaction is to use a weaker semantics. Examples of this approach are the well-founded semantics for logic programs [Van Gelder, Ross and Schlipf 1991] and the stationary semantics for default logic [Przymusinska and Przymusinski 1994, Gottlob 1995]. These kinds of restrictions cut the cost of implementing nonmonotonic reasoning but also limit the expressive power. This raises interesting questions about suitable trade-offs between expressive power and computational complexity because recent results show that general nonmonotonic reasoning techniques lead to very compact representation of knowledge and, e.g., exponentially more succinct representations than when using classical logic [Gogic et al. 1995, Cadoli et al. 1997].

2.2. Finitary Characterization

In this section we elaborate the definitions of default logic, autoepistemic logic and circumscription and present characterizations of reasoning in these logics with the aim of providing the basis for the automated theorem proving methods. We start by considering default logic and then proceed with autoepistemic logic and circumscription.

Default Logic

The key objects of interest in default logic are the extensions of a default theory. [Reiter 1980] made an important observation already in his original article: extensions can be captured in terms of the consequents of the default rules. Every extension of a default theory $(\mathcal{D}, W)$ can be represented as the logical closure of the classical formulas W and the consequents of a subset GD of the defaults $\mathcal{D}$ (the generating defaults).

2.1. THEOREM (Generating Defaults).

Let E be an extension of a default theory $(\mathcal{D}, W)$. Then there is a set $\text{GD} \subseteq \mathcal{D}$ such that $E = \text{Cn}(W \cup \{\text{cons}(d) \mid d \in \text{GD}, \text{pre}(d) \in E \text{ and for all } \psi \in \text{just}(d), \neg\psi \notin E\})$.

Hence, to find an extension we need to identify the generating defaults. We present two approaches to characterizing the generating defaults. We will use the notation $\text{Cn}_{\text{Mon}(\mathcal{D})}$ introduced in Section 1, Definition 1.3. $\text{Cn}_{\text{Mon}(\mathcal{D})}$ stands for the consequence relation induced by the monotonic versions of the default rules.

The first characterization is based on examining default rules directly. This approach has been presented in several papers [Marek and Truszczyński 1993, Risch and Schwind 1994, Baader and Hollunder 1995]. The idea is to project the conditions fulfilled by an extension to individual default rules. First, extensions are grounded (see Definition 1.4) which implies that the corresponding set of generating defaults must be grounded as well.

A set of defaults $\mathcal{D}$ is grounded in a set formulae W if and only if for all $d \in \mathcal{D}$, $\text{pre}(d) \in \text{Cn}_{\text{Mon}(\mathcal{D})}(W)$ where $\text{Mon}(\mathcal{D}) = \{\frac{\text{pre}(d)}{\text{cons}(d)} \mid d \in \mathcal{D}\}$. Second, extensions are closed under default rules, i.e. all applicable defaults are applied.

2.2. THEOREM (Extensions in Terms of Generating Defaults).
A set of formulae E is an extension of a default theory $(\mathcal{D}, W)$ if and only if $E = \text{Cn}(W \cup \{\text{cons}(d) \mid d \in \mathcal{D}'\})$ for a set of defaults $\mathcal{D}' \subseteq \mathcal{D}$ such that
  1. *$\mathcal{D}'$ is grounded in W and*
  2. *for all $d \in \mathcal{D}$:*

   $$d \in \mathcal{D}' \text{ if and only if } \text{pre}(d) \in \text{Cn}(W \cup \{\text{cons}(d) \mid d \in \mathcal{D}'\}) \text{ and}$$
   $$\text{for all } \psi \in \text{just}(d), \neg\psi \notin \text{Cn}(W \cup \{\text{cons}(d) \mid d \in \mathcal{D}'\}).$$

The second characterization is introduced in [Niemelä 1995b] and is based on focusing on justifications. Here the idea is that default rules are inference rules guarded with consistency conditions given by the justifications. Hence, it is the set of justifications that determines the extension and the rest is just monotonic derivation.

We denote by $\text{just}(\mathcal{D})$ the set of all justifications in the set of defaults $\mathcal{D}$ and for a set of formulae F, $\text{Mon}(\mathcal{D}, \text{F}) = \{\frac{\text{pre}(d)}{\text{cons}(d)} \mid d \in \mathcal{D}, \text{just}(d) \subseteq \text{F}\}$. A set of justifications corresponding to an extension is called *full* with respect to the default theory.

2.3. DEFINITION *(Full Sets).*
For a default theory $(\mathcal{D}, W)$, a set of justifications $\text{F} \subseteq \text{just}(\mathcal{D})$ is called $(\mathcal{D}, W)$-full if and only if the following condition holds:

$$\text{for all } \psi \in \text{just}(\mathcal{D}): \quad \psi \in \text{F} \iff \neg\psi \notin \text{Cn}_{\text{Mon}(\mathcal{D},\text{F})}(W)$$

For each full set there is a corresponding extension and for each extension a full set that induces it.

2.4. THEOREM (Extensions in Terms of Full Sets).
Let $(\mathcal{D}, W)$ a default theory.
  1. *If $\text{F} \subseteq \text{just}(\mathcal{D})$ is $(\mathcal{D}, W)$-full, then $\text{Cn}_{\text{Mon}(\mathcal{D},\text{F})}(W)$ is an extension of $(\mathcal{D}, W)$.*
  2. *If E is an extension of $(\mathcal{D}, W)$, then $\text{F} = \{B \in \text{just}(\mathcal{D}) \mid \neg B \notin E\}$ is $(\mathcal{D}, W)$-full and $E = \text{Cn}_{\text{Mon}(\mathcal{D},\text{F})}(W)$.*

2.5. EXAMPLE. Consider a default theory $(\mathcal{D}, W)$ where $\mathcal{D} = \{p:\neg s/r, q:\neg r/s\}$ and $W = \{q\}$. The $(\mathcal{D}, W)$-full sets are subsets of $\text{just}(\mathcal{D}) = \{\neg s, \neg r\}$. Consider $\text{F} = \{\neg r\}$. It is $(\mathcal{D}, W)$-full because $\text{Mon}(\mathcal{D}, \text{F}) = \{\frac{q}{s}\}$, $\neg\neg r \notin \text{Cn}_{\text{Mon}(\mathcal{D},\text{F})}(W)$ but $\neg\neg s \in \text{Cn}_{\text{Mon}(\mathcal{D},\text{F})}(W)$. Hence, $\text{Cn}_{\text{Mon}(\mathcal{D},\text{F})}(W) = \text{Cn}(W \cup \{s\})$ is an extension of $(\mathcal{D}, W)$. For instance, $\text{F}' = \{\neg s\}$ is not $(\mathcal{D}, W)$-full, because $\text{Mon}(\mathcal{D}, \text{F}') = \{\frac{p}{r}\}$ and, e.g., $\neg\neg r \notin \text{Cn}_{\text{Mon}(\mathcal{D},\text{F}')}(W)$ but $\neg r \notin \text{F}'$. It is easy to verify that F is the only $(\mathcal{D}, W)$-full set and, thus, $\text{Cn}_{\text{Mon}(\mathcal{D},\text{F})}(W)$ is the unique extension of $(\mathcal{D}, W)$.

Autoepistemic Logic

For autoepistemic expansions we present a characterization based on *full sets* [Niemelä 1990, Niemelä 1992]. A full set is constructed from the $\mathbf{B}\chi$ and $\neg\mathbf{B}\chi$ subformulae of the premises and it serves as the kernel of a stable expansion; it uniquely characterizes the expansion. An overview of other approaches to characterizing stable expansions can be found in [Niemelä 1992].

The characterization is based on the set of all subformulae of the form $\mathbf{B}\chi$ in a set of premises T. We denote this set by $\mathrm{Sf}_{\mathbf{B}}(T)$. Notice that in the characterization only the classical derivability relation $\vdash$ is used where $\mathbf{B}p$ formulae are treated as new atoms and no modal consequence relation is needed.

2.6. DEFINITION *(Full Sets)*.

For a set of sentences T, a set $\mathrm{F} \subseteq \mathrm{Sf}_{\mathbf{B}}(T) \cup \neg\mathrm{Sf}_{\mathbf{B}}(T)$ is T-full if and only if the following two conditions hold for every $\mathbf{B}\chi \in \mathrm{Sf}_{\mathbf{B}}(T)$:

1. $T \cup \mathrm{F} \vdash \chi$ if and only if $\mathbf{B}\chi \in \mathrm{F}$.
2. $T \cup \mathrm{F} \nvdash \chi$ if and only if $\neg\mathbf{B}\chi \in \mathrm{F}$.

In fact, for a T-full set F, the classical consequences of $T \cup \mathrm{F}$ provide the non-modal part of an expansion. It is known that this uniquely determines the expansion. The whole expansion including the modal formulae can be constructed from the non-modal part. First such construction was proposed by [Marek 1989]. Here we present an alternative construction presented in [Niemelä 1992] which is more suitable for automation. For this we employ a restricted notion of subformulae: $\mathrm{Sf}_{\mathbf{B}}^p(\varphi)$ is the set of *primary* subformulae of φ, i.e., all subformulae of the form $\mathbf{B}\chi$ of φ which are not in the scope of another $\mathbf{B}$ operator in φ. Hence, $\mathrm{Sf}_{\mathbf{B}}^p(\mathbf{B}(\neg\mathbf{B}p \rightarrow q) \wedge \mathbf{B}\neg q) = \{\mathbf{B}(\neg\mathbf{B}p \rightarrow q), \mathbf{B}\neg q\}$. The construction uses a simple consequence relation $\models_{\mathbf{B}}$ which is given recursively on top of the classical derivability relation $\vdash$. It turns out that this consequence relation corresponds exactly to membership in an expansion when given its characterizing full set.

2.7. DEFINITION *(B-consequence)*.

Given a set of sentences T and a sentence φ,

$$T \models_{\mathbf{B}} \varphi \text{ if and only if } T \cup \mathrm{SB}_T(\varphi) \vdash \varphi$$

where $\mathrm{SB}_T(\varphi) = \{\mathbf{B}\chi \in \mathrm{Sf}_{\mathbf{B}}^p(\varphi) \mid T \models_{\mathbf{B}} \chi\} \cup \{\neg\mathbf{B}\chi \in \neg\mathrm{Sf}_{\mathbf{B}}^p(\varphi) \mid T \nvDash_{\mathbf{B}} \chi\}$.

For an expansion S of T, there is a corresponding T-full set

$$\{\mathbf{B}\varphi \in S \mid \mathbf{B}\varphi \in \mathrm{Sf}_{\mathbf{B}}(T)\} \cup \{\neg\mathbf{B}\varphi \in S \mid \mathbf{B}\varphi \in \mathrm{Sf}_{\mathbf{B}}(T)\}$$

and for a T-full set F,

$$\{\varphi \in \mathcal{L}_{\mathbf{B}} \mid T \cup \mathrm{F} \models_{\mathbf{B}} \varphi\}$$

is a stable expansion of T. In fact it can be shown [Niemelä 1992] that there is a one-to-one correspondence between full sets and expansions.

2.8. THEOREM (Expansions in Terms of Full Sets).
Let T be a set of sentences of $\mathcal{L}_\mathbf{B}$. Then a function SE_T defined as

$$\mathrm{SE}_T(\mathrm{F}) = \{\varphi \in \mathcal{L}_\mathbf{B} \mid T \cup \mathrm{F} \models_\mathbf{B} \varphi\}$$

gives a bijective mapping from the set of T-full sets to the set of stable expansions of T and for a T-full set F, $\mathrm{SE}_T(\mathrm{F})$ is the unique stable expansion S of T such that $\mathrm{F} \subseteq \mathbf{B}S \cup \neg\mathbf{B}\overline{S}$.

2.9. EXAMPLE. The premise $T = \{\neg\mathbf{B}\neg\mathbf{B}p \to p\}$ has two T-full sets

$$\mathrm{F}_1 = \{\mathbf{B}\neg\mathbf{B}p, \neg\mathbf{B}p\} \quad \text{and} \quad \mathrm{F}_2 = \{\neg\mathbf{B}\neg\mathbf{B}p, \mathbf{B}p\}.$$

For example, F_1 is T-full as $T \cup \mathrm{F}_1 \vdash \neg\mathbf{B}p$ and $T \cup \mathrm{F}_1 \not\vdash p$. This implies that T has exactly two stable expansions $\mathrm{SE}_T(\mathrm{F}_1)$ and $\mathrm{SE}_T(\mathrm{F}_2)$. As $T \cup \mathrm{F}_1 \not\models_\mathbf{B} p$, $p \notin \mathrm{SE}_T(\mathrm{F}_1)$. However, $\neg\mathbf{B}\mathbf{B}p \in \mathrm{SE}_T(\mathrm{F}_1)$ as $T \cup \mathrm{F}_1 \models_\mathbf{B} \neg\mathbf{B}\mathbf{B}p$.

Circumscription
General circumscription is highly undecidable and computationally very hard to handle and we concentrate here on parallel predicate circumscription in the clausal case and with respect to Herbrand interpretations. In parallel predicate circumscription the predicates are partitioned into three disjoint sets:
 1. *minimized*, denoted by $\underline{p}$,
 2. *varying*, denoted by $\underline{f}$, and
 3. *fixed*, denoted usually by $\underline{z}$ (in this section we will simply omit it)
predicates. The key notion in circumscription is that of a minimal model introduced in Subsection 1.3, Definition 1.6. We present a characterization of minimal models where the minimality of a model can be determined independently of other models using a test for classical consequence. This characterization is proposed by [Niemelä 1996 a]. A similar characterization but for the propositional case has been used in [Eiter and Gottlob 1995 a] in the study of the computational complexity of propositional circumscription.

2.10. DEFINITION *(Grounded Models).*
  Let T be a set of clauses and let $\underline{p}$ and $\underline{f}$ be sets of predicates. A Herbrand interpretation M is said to be *grounded* in $\langle T, \underline{p}, \underline{f} \rangle$ if and only if for all ground atoms $p(\vec{t})$ such that $p \in \underline{p}$, $M \models p(\vec{t})$ implies $T \cup \mathrm{N}^{\langle \underline{p}, \underline{f} \rangle}(M) \models p(\vec{t})$ where

$$\mathrm{N}^{\langle \underline{p}, \underline{f} \rangle}(M) = \{\neg q(\vec{t}) \mid q(\vec{t}) \text{ is a ground atom}, q \in \underline{p} \cup \underline{f}, M \not\models q(\vec{t})\} \cup$$
$$\{q(\vec{t}) \mid q(\vec{t}) \text{ is a ground atom}, q \in \underline{f}, M \models q(\vec{t})\}$$

2.11. THEOREM (Minimal Models).
 Let $\underline{p}$ and $\underline{f}$ be the sets of minimized and fixed predicates, respectively. A Herbrand interpretation M is a minimal model of T if and only if M is a model of T and grounded in $\langle T, \underline{p}, \underline{f} \rangle$.

2.12. EXAMPLE. Let $T = \{p(x) \vee \neg q(x)\}$ and let the underlying language have only one ground term a. Then the Herbrand base is $\{p(a), q(a)\}$. Let the set of minimized predicates $\underline{p} = \{p\}$. If the set of fixed predicates $\underline{f} = \{q\}$, then the Herbrand interpretation $M = \{p(a), q(a)\}$, which is a model of T, is grounded in $\langle T, \underline{p}, \underline{f}\rangle$ because $N^{\langle \underline{p}, \underline{f}\rangle}(M) = \{q(a)\}$ and $T \cup N^{\langle \underline{p}, \underline{f}\rangle}(M) \models p(a)$ holds. Hence, M is a minimal model of T. If $F = \emptyset$, then M is not grounded in $\langle T, \underline{p}, \underline{f}\rangle$ because $N^{\langle \underline{p}, \underline{f}\rangle}(M) = \emptyset$ and $T \cup N^{\langle \underline{p}, \underline{f}\rangle}(M) \models p(a)$ does not hold. Thus, with no fixed predicates M is not a minimal model of T.

2.3. Algorithms for Default Logic

There are already quite a number of decision methods for default reasoning. Methods based on the characterization of extensions in terms of generating defaults (Theorem 2.1) can be found, e.g., in [Marek and Truszczyński 1993, Baader and Hollunder 1995, Risch and Schwind 1994]. There are approaches where default reasoning is reduced into another problem like a truth maintenance problem [Junker and Konolige 1990] or a constraint satisfaction problem [Ben-Eliyahu and Dechter 1991]. An interesting approach to provide proof theory for default reasoning based on sequent calculus is proposed by [Bonatti 1996, Bonatti and Olivetti 1997]. A novelty in this approach is that it includes an explicit proof theoretic treatment of non-validity needed in default reasoning.

The development in this section is based on the second characterization of extensions in terms of full sets and originates from the work in [Niemelä 1995b]. The aim is to develop a decision method for default reasoning by employing ideas similar those used in the Davis-Putnam procedure which is one of the most successful methods for deciding propositional satisfiability.

We start by presenting first a naive decision procedure for default logic and then show how to optimize it in a systematic way. Fig. 2 presents the naive decision procedure for both credulous and sceptical default reasoning. The idea is that when the procedure terminates, then for a default theory $(\mathcal{D}, W)$ and formula φ, the variable S-answer is set to Yes if and only if φ is a sceptical consequence of $(\mathcal{D}, W)$, i.e., in every extension of $(\mathcal{D}, W)$ and the variable C-answer is set to Yes if and only if φ is a credulous consequence of $(\mathcal{D}, W)$. Using Theorem 2.4 it is easy to show to be the case. Under what conditions is the procedure implementable, i.e., when are all subtasks decidable? It turns out that it is enough to require that (i) the default theory is finite and (ii) the first-order logic of W and the first-order formulae appearing in the defaults is decidable. Then there is a finite number of justifications and, thus, finitely many subsets of justifications. Hence, the main loop is iterated only a finite number of times. Decidability of the first-order logic implies the decidability of the membership in the closure $\mathrm{Cn}_{\mathrm{Mon}(\mathcal{D}, S)}(\cdot)$ and this implies the decidability of the fullness test. This means that each iteration of the main loop is computable. These two conditions imply the implementability of the optimized version of the decision procedure to be developed and they are assumed for the rest of the section.

S-answer:= Yes; C-answer:= No;
For every subset S of just($\mathcal{D}$) **do**
  If S is $(\mathcal{D}, W)$-full **then**
    If $\varphi \in \mathrm{Cn}_{\mathrm{Mon}(\mathcal{D},S)}(W)$ **then**
      C-answer:= Yes
    else
      S-answer:= No
    end if
  end if

Figure 2: A Naive Decision Procedure for Credulous and Sceptical DL

The naive decision procedure is not very efficient because for a default theory with n justifications, the main loop is iterated 2^n times and each iteration involves several calls to a classical theorem prover. We start optimizing the procedure using the following ideas which are similar to those found in the Davis-Putnam procedure for propositional satisfiability (see, e.g., [Fitting 1990]). (i) We employ a bottom-up backtracking search over candidate full sets, (ii) we prune the search space by making assumptions about the justifications one at a time and (iii) before making a new assumption, an *approximation* of the extensions agreeing with the current assumptions is computed and *conflicts* are detected. Fig. 3 presents the skeleton of the optimized decision procedure given as a function **extensions**. It employs four functions

- **expand** (for approximations),
- **conflict** (for conflict detection),
- **choose** (for search heuristics) and
- **test** (for testing extensions).

The first three functions identify the key subtasks of the procedure where optimizations are applied. By changing the **test** function, the procedure can be adapted to yield decision procedures for sceptical and credulous reasoning as well as for checking the existence of extensions. We will explain the role of the functions in more detail but first we discuss the representation of a full set in the procedure and its overall idea.

In the algorithm we need to represent a partially constructed full set and also explicate assumptions about which justifications are not included in the full set. Here we reverse the representation and describe a full set by speaking about the membership in the extension. With this representation it is easier to discuss the optimizations and the application of the method to logic programming semantics becomes more straightforward in Section 5.

As given in Definition 2.3, a full set F characterizing an extension E is a set of justifications such that for each justification ψ in the default theory, $\psi \in$ F if and only if $\neg \psi \notin E$. Our idea is to represent a partially constructed full set by using a set FS which is built from the *negations* of justifications and which explicates the

```
function extensions((D, W), FS, φ)
FS' := expand((D, W), FS);
if conflict((D, W), FS') returns Yes then return No
else if FS' covers the negation of each justification in D then
     return test((D, W), FS', φ)
else
     χ := choose((D, W), FS');
     if extensions((D, W), FS' ∪ {χ}, φ) returns Yes then return Yes
     else return extensions((D, W), FS' ∪ {compl(χ)}, φ)
     end if
end if
```

Figure 3: An optimized decision procedure for default logic

current assumptions about their membership in the extension under consideration. For representing the fact that a formula φ is not in the extension we employ what we call a not-formula which is just an expression of the form not(φ). So an expression not($\neg\chi$) in FS indicates that χ belongs to the full set to be constructed (and $\neg\chi$ does not belong to the corresponding extension). On the other hand, an formula $\neg\chi$ in FS indicates that χ does not belong to the full set under consideration (and $\neg\chi$ belongs to the corresponding extension).

Hence, a full set containing the justifications $\neg p, q$ but not containing the justifications $\neg r, s$ is represented as the set $\{\text{not}(\neg\neg p), \text{not}(\neg q), \neg\neg r, \neg s\}$. Note that for the corresponding extension E holds that, e.g., $\neg\neg p \notin E$ but $\neg s \in E$. On the other hand, when we speak about a full set represented in this way, we naturally mean the set of justifications which are the complements of formulae inside the not($\cdot$) operator. For instance, when we discuss the full set

$$\text{FS} = \{\text{not}(\neg\neg p), \text{not}(\neg q), \text{not}(\neg\neg r), \neg s\},$$

what is actually meant is the set $\text{F} = \{\neg p, q, \neg r\}$. Hence, we occasionally use a full set FS represented in this way instead of a set F represented in the original way. For instance, we write $\text{Mon}(D, \text{FS})$ which denotes the set

$$\{\frac{pre(d)}{cons(d)} \mid d \in D, \text{ for all } \psi \in \text{just}(d), \text{not}(\neg\psi) \in \text{FS}\}.$$

For discussing the procedure **extensions** we employ the following concepts:

- We say that a set of formulae S *agrees* with a set of formulae and not-formulae FS if for every ordinary formula $\varphi \in \text{FS}$, $\varphi \in S$ and for all not(φ) $\in$ FS, $\varphi \notin S$. For example, the set $\{a, b\}$ agrees with $\{a, \text{not}(c)\}$ but not with $\{a, \text{not}(b)\}$.
- A set of formulae and not-formulae FS *covers* a formula φ if either $\varphi \in \text{FS}$ or not(φ) $\in$ FS. For example, the set $\{\text{not}(a), b\}$ covers a. A set of formulae S is covered by FS if each formula in S is covered by FS.

- By $\text{compl}(\chi)$ we denote the not-complement of an expression: for an ordinary formula χ, $\text{compl}(\chi) = \text{not}(\chi)$ and $\text{compl}(\text{not}(\chi)) = \chi$.

The function **extensions** takes as input a default theory $(\mathcal{D}, W)$, and a set FS which determines the constraints on the extensions to be considered and a formula φ which is just passed as an argument to the function **test**. The function **extensions** performs *focused extension search*, i.e., given some conditions on the extensions of interest in terms of a set FS of ordinary formulae (to be included in the extension) and not-formulae (to be excluded from the extension), **extensions** focuses its search to these extensions to find one that passes the **test** function: For a default theory $(\mathcal{D}, W)$ and a formula φ, **extensions**$((\mathcal{D}, W), \text{FS}, \varphi)$ returns Yes if and only if there is an extension E agreeing with FS such that **test**$((\mathcal{D}, W), \text{FS}', \varphi)$ returns Yes where FS' is the full set of E. This is accomplished by constructing $(\mathcal{D}, W)$-full sets agreeing with FS until a full set FS' is found such that **test**$((\mathcal{D}, W), \text{FS}', \varphi)$ returns Yes in the following way.

The function **extensions** starts by expanding cautiously the set FS. The idea is that no extensions are lost in the expansion: every extension agreeing with the original FS agrees also with FS'. Then a conflict test is performed. If there are no conflicts and FS' covers the negations of justifications in $(\mathcal{D}, W)$, FS' is a full set for an extension agreeing with FS and **extensions** returns what **test**$((\mathcal{D}, W), \text{FS}', \varphi)$ returns. If there are negations of justifications in $(\mathcal{D}, W)$ not covered by FS', then **choose** selects one of them, say ψ, and returns either ψ or $\text{not}(\psi)$. For ψ there are two possibilities: either ψ belongs to the extension to be constructed or not. The two alternatives are covered by backtracking search. The decision in **choose** whether ψ or $\text{not}(\psi)$ is returned, determines in which order the alternatives are examined. Extensions containing ψ are covered by calling **extensions**$((\mathcal{D}, W), \text{FS}' \cup \{\psi\}, \varphi)$ and extensions not containing ψ are covered by calling **extensions**$((\mathcal{D}, W), \text{FS}' \cup \{\text{not}(\psi)\}, \varphi)$.

Soundness and completeness of the procedure can be guaranteed under quite weak assumptions about the three functions.

choose: **choose**$((\mathcal{D}, W), \text{FS})$ returns either $\neg\psi$ or $\text{not}(\neg\psi)$ for some justification ψ in $(\mathcal{D}, W)$ for which $\neg\psi$ is not covered by FS.

expand: **expand**$((\mathcal{D}, W), \text{FS})$ returns a set FS' of formulae and not-formulae which extends FS and with which every extension of $(\mathcal{D}, W)$ agreeing with FS agrees.

conflict: (i) If **conflict**$((\mathcal{D}, W), \text{FS})$ returns Yes, there is no extension agreeing with FS and (ii) if FS covers negations of every justification in $(\mathcal{D}, W)$, and for some $\text{not}(\chi) \in \text{FS}$, $\chi \in \text{Cn}_{\text{Mon}(\mathcal{D}, \text{FS})}(W)$ or for some $\chi \in \text{FS}$, $\chi \notin \text{Cn}_{\text{Mon}(\mathcal{D}, \text{FS})}(W)$, then **conflict**$((\mathcal{D}, W), \text{FS})$ returns Yes.

Under these assumptions we can establish the following theorem.

2.13. Theorem (Soundness and completeness).
Let $(\mathcal{D}, W)$ be a default theory and FS a set of formulae and not-formulae. Then the function **extensions**$((\mathcal{D}, W), \text{FS}, \varphi)$ *returns Yes if and only if there exists an extension of $(\mathcal{D}, W)$ agreeing with FS such that* **test**$((\mathcal{D}, W), \text{FS}', \varphi)$ *returns Yes where FS' is the corresponding full set.*

The theorem implies that decision procedures for the different reasoning tasks can be obtained by (i) taking the empty set as the common part of extensions to be constructed and (ii) choosing an appropriate **test** function as shown in the following corollary.

2.14. COROLLARY. *Let* $(\mathcal{D}, W)$ *be a default theory and* φ *a formula.*

1. *Let* **test**$((\mathcal{D}, W), \mathrm{FS}, \varphi)$ *return Yes for all* $(\mathcal{D}, W)$, FS, *and* φ.
   Then **extensions**$((\mathcal{D}, W), \emptyset, \varphi)$ *returns Yes if and only if* $(\mathcal{D}, W)$ *has an extension.*
2. *Let* **test**$((\mathcal{D}, W), \mathrm{FS}, \varphi)$ *return Yes if and only if* $\varphi \in \mathrm{Cn}_{\mathrm{Mon}(\mathcal{D}, \mathrm{FS})}(W)$.
   Then **extensions**$((\mathcal{D}, W), \emptyset, \varphi)$ *returns Yes if and only if there exists an extension of* $(\mathcal{D}, W)$ *containing* φ.
3. *Let* **test**$((\mathcal{D}, W), \mathrm{FS}, \varphi)$ *return Yes if and only if* $\varphi \notin \mathrm{Cn}_{\mathrm{Mon}(\mathcal{D}, \mathrm{FS})}(W)$.
   Then **extensions**$((\mathcal{D}, W), \emptyset, \varphi)$ *returns Yes if and only if there exists an extension of* $(\mathcal{D}, W)$ *not containing* φ *(i.e.,* **extensions**$((\mathcal{D}, W), \emptyset, \varphi)$ *returns No if and only if* φ *is contained in every extension of* $(\mathcal{D}, W)$*).*

In order to provide a systematic basis for developing implementations of **expand** and **conflict** we introduce two concepts: a lower bound and an upper bound of a set of extensions. The idea is that given a default theory $(\mathcal{D}, W)$ and some conditions FS on the extensions, all the extensions satisfying the conditions agree with the lower bound and are contained in the upper bound:

lower bound: LB$((\mathcal{D}, W), \mathrm{FS})$ is characterized with the property: every extension E of $(\mathcal{D}, W)$ agreeing with FS agrees with **LB**$((\mathcal{D}, W), \mathrm{FS})$ and

upper bound: UB$((\mathcal{D}, W), \mathrm{FS})$ satisfies the property: for every extension E of $(\mathcal{D}, W)$ which agrees with FS, $E \subseteq$ **UB**(P, FS).

Using these concepts we can implement the two functions in a unified way. In **expand** the idea is to extend the constraints FS by all negations of the justifications which are in the lower bound and by $\mathrm{not}(\neg\varphi)$ for all $\neg\varphi$ not in the upper bound. Of course, this can be iterated which leads to the following implementation:

expand$((\mathcal{D}, W), \mathrm{FS})$ returns the smallest set of formulae FS′ extending FS and closed under the following rules:

- if $\neg\varphi \in$ **LB**$((\mathcal{D}, W), \mathrm{FS}')$ for $\varphi \in \mathrm{just}(\mathcal{D})$, then include $\neg\varphi$ in FS′ and
- if $\neg\varphi \notin$ **UB**$((\mathcal{D}, W), \mathrm{FS}')$ for $\varphi \in \mathrm{just}(\mathcal{D})$, then include $\mathrm{not}(\neg\varphi)$ in FS′.

In **conflict** the idea is to check the requirements in FS against the lower and upper bounds:

conflict$((\mathcal{D}, W), \mathrm{FS})$ returns Yes if and only if for some formula φ,

$$\mathrm{not}(\varphi) \in \mathrm{FS} \text{ but } \varphi \notin \mathbf{UB}((\mathcal{D}, W), \mathrm{FS}) \text{ or}$$

$$\varphi \in \mathrm{FS} \text{ but } \varphi \notin \mathbf{LB}((\mathcal{D}, W), \mathrm{FS}).$$

It should be noted that the soundness and completeness of the decision procedure using the above implementations of the two functions is not guaranteed by the characterizing properties of the bounds. This is because the properties of the bounds do not imply the second soundness and completeness condition for **conflict**.

2.15. EXAMPLE. Consider the trivial bounds where $\mathbf{LB}((\mathcal{D}, W), \mathrm{FS})$ is the empty set and $\mathbf{UB}((\mathcal{D}, W), \mathrm{FS})$ is the whole language, a default theory $\mathcal{D} = \{:p/p\}$, $W = \{\neg p\}$ and a set $\mathrm{FS} = \{\mathrm{not}(\neg p)\}$. Clearly, the second condition for **conflict** does not hold: FS covers negations of every justification in $\mathcal{D}$, $\mathrm{not}(\neg p) \in \mathrm{FS}$ but $\neg p \in \mathrm{Cn}_{\mathrm{Mon}(\mathcal{D}, \mathrm{FS})}(W)$. However, given the trivial upper bound, $\mathbf{conflict}((\mathcal{D}, W), \mathrm{FS})$ does not return the answer Yes.

In order to have full freedom in developing lower and upper bounds, we assume that the implementation of **conflict** performs a *post-check*:

> when FS covers negations of every justification in $(\mathcal{D}, W)$, $\mathbf{conflict}((\mathcal{D}, W), \mathrm{FS})$ returns Yes if for some $\mathrm{not}(\chi) \in \mathrm{FS}$, $\chi \in \mathrm{Cn}_{\mathrm{Mon}(\mathcal{D}, \mathrm{FS})}(W)$ or for some $\chi \in \mathrm{FS}$, $\chi \notin \mathrm{Cn}_{\mathrm{Mon}(\mathcal{D}, \mathrm{FS})}(W)$.

and otherwise it functions as described above. With this addition the soundness and completeness of **extensions** is guaranteed for any upper and lower bound satisfying the respective characterizing properties.

2.16. EXAMPLE. We illustrate the idea of the decision procedure by a simple example using the trivial implementation, i.e., where **expand** and **conflict** are implemented using the trivial bounds. This actually is an implementation of the naive method in Fig. 2.

Consider a default theory $(\mathcal{D}, W)$ where

$$\mathcal{D} = \{\frac{:p}{\neg q}, \frac{:q}{\neg p}\}, W = \{\neg p \to r\}$$

and the tasks of deciding whether r is a sceptical consequence of $(\mathcal{D}, W)$. Hence, the function $\mathbf{test}((\mathcal{D}, W), \mathrm{FS}, \varphi)$ returns Yes if and only if $\varphi \notin \mathrm{Cn}_{\mathrm{Mon}(\mathcal{D}, \mathrm{FS})}(W)$ and the decision procedure is started by a call to $\mathbf{extensions}((\mathcal{D}, W), \emptyset, r)$. First $\mathrm{FS} = \emptyset$ is extended by $\mathbf{expand}((\mathcal{D}, W), \emptyset)$ but as the trivial bounds are used, nothing new is discovered and, similarly, no conflicts are detected. Hence, $\mathbf{choose}((\mathcal{D}, W), \emptyset)$ is called. Here the alternatives are in $\mathbf{just}((\mathcal{D}, W)) = \{p, q\}$. Assume that p is selected and $\mathrm{not}(\neg p)$ is returned by $\mathbf{choose}((\mathcal{D}, W), \emptyset)$. Then

$$\mathbf{extensions}((\mathcal{D}, W), \{\mathrm{not}(\neg p)\}, r)$$

is called and because of the trivial bounds the full set is not extended nor are conflicts detected. Hence $\mathbf{choose}((\mathcal{D}, W), \{\mathrm{not}(\neg p)\})$ is called. Assume it returns $\mathrm{not}(\neg q)$. Hence, $\mathbf{extensions}((\mathcal{D}, W), \{\mathrm{not}(\neg p), \mathrm{not}(\neg q)\}, r)$ is called. Now all the negations of the justifications in $(\mathcal{D}, W)$ are covered and the post-check is done. Here conflicts are found: $\{\neg p, \neg q\} \subseteq \mathrm{Cn}_{\mathrm{Mon}(\mathcal{D}, \mathrm{FS})}(W)$ where $\mathrm{FS} = \{\mathrm{not}(\neg p), \mathrm{not}(\neg q)\}$.

Hence, the procedure backtracks and $\mathbf{extensions}((\mathcal{D}, W), \{\mathrm{not}(\neg p), \neg q\}, r)$ is called. Now the post-check is passed and $\{\mathrm{not}(\neg p), \neg q\}$ covers the negations of justifications in $\mathcal{D}$. Thus, $\{\mathrm{not}(\neg p), \neg q\}$ is a $(\mathcal{D}, W)$-full set and

$$\mathbf{test}((\mathcal{D}, W), \{\mathrm{not}(\neg p), \neg q\}, r)$$

is called. It returns Yes which implies that $\mathbf{extensions}((\mathcal{D}, W), \emptyset, r)$ returns Yes. Hence, r is not a sceptical consequence of $(\mathcal{D}, W)$.

The efficiency of the decision procedure **extensions** is determined by the implementations of the three functions **expand**, **conflict**, and **choose**. The decision procedure performs search over extensions and the size of this search space has a crucial effect on the performance of the algorithm. The size depends on the implementations of **expand** and **conflict** as well as on the search heuristics (implemented by **choose**). The search heuristics can have a dramatic effect on the efficiency because the right choices can lead to the desired extension immediately. Even in the case where there are no extensions agreeing with the given requirements, the order in which the search space is examined can effect significantly the size of the space. We discuss the choice of a good search heuristics in more detail in Section 5 where we apply this method to logic programming semantics.

The role of the functions **expand** and **conflict** is to prune the search space by removing the choice points (**expand**) and cutting useless search when no solutions are left (**conflict**). Exponential savings can be achieved. For example, if **expand** extends the full set by one formula, this cuts the remaining search space by half. Similarly, detecting a conflict early in the search yields an exponential reduction on the size of the search space. Hence, good implementations of the functions can speed-up the decision procedure considerably. There is an interesting trade-off between the effort spent in the two functions and the size of the remaining search space. This leads to the question of deciding how much computation resources should be invested in the two pruning functions and how much in the actual search.

We have unified the development of the two functions by adopting the concepts of a lower and an upper bound. Hence, instead of discussing the implementations of the two functions separately, we can focus on finding good implementation techniques for the upper and lower bounds. Our approach to the trade-off between pruning efforts and search is to consider implementations of the bounds where a low polynomial number of calls to a decision procedure for classical monotonic derivation are needed. In the following we speak about these calls as theorem prover calls for short. Why is this a reasonable framework for developing the bounds? First, theorem prover calls are needed no matter how weak bounds are used because the soundness and completeness of the method requires the post-check where theorem prover calls are employed. Second, it seems unreasonable to use a high (e.g., exponential) number of classical theorem prover calls in the pruning functions because then the savings compared to performing the actual search are not clear.

Before we go into developing the bounds, let us consider the sources of complexity in the decision procedure and examine whether these are consistent with the complexity results. In the procedure there are two sources of complexity. One is the classical theorem proving task for implementing the upper and lower bounds and the other source is related to the search over the extensions. This is very consistent with the complexity results on default reasoning which indicate two independent sources of complexity. These sources are orthogonal to each other and hence, e.g., the implementation of the classical theorem proving task has little effect on the inherent complexity of the search.

Now we develop methods for implementing upper and lower bounds with the aim of obtaining tight bounds using a low number of theorem prover calls. Consider first the lower bound. For a default theory $(\mathcal{D}, W)$ and a set FS, it can safely contain the logical consequences of W but also those of the ordinary formulae in FS. We denote the set of the ordinary formulae in FS by FS^+. The lower bound can be made even tighter because the closure over the rules in $\mathcal{D}$ enabled by FS, $\text{Mon}(\mathcal{D}, FS) = \{\frac{\text{pre}(d)}{\text{cons}(d)} \mid d \in \mathcal{D}, \text{ for all } \psi \in \text{just}(\mathcal{D}), \text{not}(\neg\psi) \in FS\}$ can be added without compromising the characterizing property of the lower bound. These considerations lead to quite a tight lower bound:

$$\mathbf{LB}((\mathcal{D}, W), FS) = \text{Cn}_{\text{Mon}(\mathcal{D}, FS)}(W \cup FS^+) \qquad (2.1)$$

In order to obtain a tight upper bound one should remember that extensions are strongly grounded and everything in the extension is derived from W by classical derivations and the default rules $\mathcal{D}$. Hence, in the upper bound one should include the logical consequences of W but also cover the closure over the applicable rules. This means that one has to include all the possible ways of applying the *potentially applicable rules* in $\mathcal{D}$, i.e., rules that are not disabled by FS

$$\{d \in \mathcal{D} \mid \text{ for all } \psi \in \text{just}(\mathcal{D}), \neg\psi \notin FS\}.$$

One idea to find an upper approximation of the possible ways of applying the rules is to consider the consequents of the potentially applicable rules. This leads to an upper bound on extensions which is the logical consequences of W and the consequents of the potentially applicable rules. This can be made even tighter by restricting attention to the closure of the monotonic rules given by the potentially applicable ones. We denote this set of monotonic rules by

$$\mathcal{D}^{FS} = \{\frac{\text{pre}(d)}{\text{cons}(d)} \mid d \in \mathcal{D}, \text{ for all } \psi \in \text{just}(\mathcal{D}), \neg\psi \notin FS\}.$$

This development leads to a rather tight upper bound:

$$\mathbf{UB}((\mathcal{D}, W), FS) = \text{Cn}_{\mathcal{D}^{FS}}(W) \qquad (2.2)$$

The bounds given in equations (2.1) and (2.2) are so tight that the soundness and completeness of the decision methods is guaranteed without the post-check.

Notice that membership in the lower and upper bounds given in equations (2.1) and (2.2) can be determined by deciding membership in the closure over classical consequences and some monotonic rules. This problem is **co-NP**-complete [Gottlob 1995] and hence on the same level of complexity as deciding classical consequence.

The decision method **extensions** is essentially a bottom-up procedure for generating extensions but it includes ingredients with which a fair amount of goal-directedness can be built in, i.e., the computation can be made to concentrate on answering the given query. One technique is to design the search heuristics to focus on choices relevant to the query. Another one is to include the query into the constraints FS given as the initial input to the procedure. So when the task is to decide whether φ is a credulous consequence of a default theory, start the method with $FS = \{\varphi\}$ instead of $FS = \emptyset$ and when sceptical consequence needs to be decided, use FS $= \{\text{not}(\varphi)\}$. This has two effects. First, it can prune the search space considerably and, second, all extensions need not be generated fully in order to answer a query and sometimes answers can be given even without generating any of the extensions.

Notice that for general default reasoning it seems unfeasible to develop a fully goal-directed procedure, i.e., a procedure which would examine only those parts of the default theory which are somehow syntactically relevant to the query. This is because extensions are defined with a global condition on the whole theory requiring that each applicable default rule should be applied. Hence, there are theories with no extensions and in the worst case it is necessary to examine every default rule in order to guarantee the existence of an extension. For achieving a goal-directed decision method, one can consider a weaker notion of extensions or syntactically restricted subclasses of default theories such as normal defaults. See, e.g. [Schaub 1995, Schaub and Brüning 1996] for work in this direction.

2.4. Algorithms for Autoepistemic Logic

Now we turn to autoepistemic logic and show how the approach introduced for default reasoning leads to a decision procedure for autoepistemic reasoning. The development is based on the work in [Niemelä 1995a] where an overview of decision methods for autoepistemic logic can be found. In autoepistemic reasoning the full sets are constructed from $\mathbf{B}\varphi$ subformulae of the premises and their negations. The $\mathbf{B}$ operator provides the means to represent assumptions about the membership in expansions: $\mathbf{B}\chi$ in the full set says that χ belongs to the expansion and $\neg\mathbf{B}\chi$ in the full set asserts that χ is not contained in the expansion. For discussing the procedure we need the notions of *agreeing*, *covering* and *complement*. These remain essentially same as in the case of default logic.

- We say that a set of formulae S *agrees* with a set F of $\mathbf{B}\chi$ formulae and their complements if for every $\mathbf{B}\varphi \in$ F, $\varphi \in S$ and for each $\neg\mathbf{B}\varphi \in$ F, $\varphi \notin S$.
- A set F of $\mathbf{B}\chi$ formulae and their complements *covers* a formula $\mathbf{B}\varphi$ if either $\mathbf{B}\varphi \in$ F or $\neg\mathbf{B}\varphi \in$ F.
- The classical complement of χ is denoted by: $\text{compl}(\chi) = \neg\chi$ and $\text{compl}(\neg\chi) = \chi$.

We can still employ the function **extensions** in Fig. 3 which now takes as input (i) a set of autoepistemic formulae T (instead of a default theory $(\mathcal{D}, W)$), (ii) a set FS of $\mathbf{B}\varphi$ formulae and their complements which determines the common part of the expansions to be considered and (iii) an autoepistemic formula φ which is just passed as an argument to the function **test**. Furthermore, the covering test is rephrased as "**else if** FS$'$ covers all $\mathbf{B}\psi$ subformulae of T **then** ...."

Soundness and completeness of the procedure can be guaranteed under similar assumptions as in the case of default logic. The only difference is that autoepistemic expansions are more weakly grounded than default extensions. Hence, the conditions for the function **conflict** have to be adjusted. We use the notation $\text{AE-Cn}(T) = \{\varphi \in \mathcal{L}_{\mathbf{B}} \mid T \vdash \varphi\}$.

choose: choose(T, FS) returns either $\mathbf{B}\psi$ or $\neg\mathbf{B}\psi$ for a $\mathbf{B}\psi$ subformula of T not
   covered by FS.
expand: expand(T, FS) returns a set FS′ of $\mathbf{B}\psi$ formulae and their complements
   which extends FS and with which every expansion of T agreeing with FS agrees.
conflict: (i) If **conflict**(T, FS) returns Yes, there is no expansion agreeing with FS
   and (ii) if FS covers every $\mathbf{B}\psi$ subformula of T, and for some $\neg\mathbf{B}\chi \in \text{FS}$, $\chi \in$
   AE-Cn$(T\cup\text{FS})$ or for some $\mathbf{B}\chi \in \text{FS}$, $\chi \notin$ AE-Cn$(T\cup\text{FS})$ then **conflict**(T, FS)
   returns Yes.
Under these assumptions we can establish the following theorem.

2.17. THEOREM (Soundness and completeness).
*Let T be a set of autoepistemic formulae and FS a set of $\mathbf{B}\chi$ subformulae of T
and their complements. Then* **extensions**(T, FS, φ) *returns Yes if and only if there
exists an expansion of T agreeing with FS such that* **test**(T, FS', φ) *returns Yes
where the FS′ is the corresponding full set.*

In order to develop decision procedures for the different reasoning tasks the only
problem is to devise an appropriate **test** function. This can be done using the
consequence relation $\models_{\mathbf{B}}$ corresponding to membership in an expansion when given
its full set.

2.18. COROLLARY. *Let T be a set of autoepistemic formulae and φ an autoepistemic formula.*
1. *Let* **test**(T, FS, φ) *return Yes for all T, FS, and φ. Then* **extensions**$(T, \emptyset, \varphi)$
   returns Yes if and only if T has an expansion.
2. *Let* **test**(T, FS, φ) *return Yes if and only if $T \cup \text{FS} \models_{\mathbf{B}} \varphi$.*
   Then **extensions**$(T, \emptyset, \varphi)$ *returns Yes if and only if there exists an expansion
   of T containing φ.*
3. *Let* **test**(T, FS, φ) *return Yes if and only if $T \cup \text{FS} \not\models_{\mathbf{B}} \varphi$.*
   Then **extensions**$(T, \emptyset, \varphi)$ *returns Yes if and only if there exists an expansion
   of T not containing φ (i.e.,* **extensions**$(T, \emptyset, \varphi)$ *returns No if and only if φ is
   contained in every expansion of T).*

Now it remains to implement the lower and upper bounds. Consider first the
lower bound. Similar to the case of default logic the lower bound can safely include
the logical consequences of the premises and the assumptions, i.e., AE-Cn$(T\cup\text{FS})$.
This can be made tighter by allowing the necessitation rule

$$\frac{\varphi}{\mathbf{B}\varphi}.$$

We denote the closure of a set of autoepistemic formulae T under the classical
consequence $\vdash$ and the necessitation rule by AE-Cn$_{\mathbf{N}}(T)$.

$$\text{LB}(T, \text{FS}) = \text{AE-Cn}_{\mathbf{N}}(T \cup \text{FS}) \tag{2.3}$$

Obtaining a tight upper bound for autoepistemic expansions is not straightforward. Mainly this is because it is not easy to approximate autoepistemic derivations

using simple syntactic methods when arbitrary autoepistemic formulae are allowed. This should be compared to default logic where default rules have a very regular form leading to easy ways of devising upper bounds on the extensions in terms of the potentially applicable defaults. The situation changes somewhat if the autoepistemic formulae are assumed to be in some standard form. See [Niemelä 1995a] for a treatment of one such case.

2.5. Implementing Circumscription

Circumscription is somewhat different from default logic and autoepistemic logic as in circumscription the main objects of interest are minimal models whereas in the other two formalisms models play a secondary role and sets of formulae (extensions/expansions) are the key objects. However, surprisingly similar ideas are applicable for automating circumscription as, e.g., default logic. Here we discuss the basic problems in automating circumscription and provide the basis for methods described in Section 3.

A number of approaches have been proposed for implementing circumscriptive reasoning. In some cases circumscription can be replaced by equivalent first-order formulae (see, e.g., [Lifschitz 1985, Doherty, Lukaszewicz and Szalas 1995]). Przymusinski develops a resolution method (MILO resolution) for circumscriptive reasoning [Przymusinski 1989]. Ginsberg presents a technique employing assumption-based truth maintenance [Ginsberg 1989]. Nerode et al. devise a method for handling circumscriptive inference using integer programming techniques [Nerode, Ng and Subrahmanian 1995] and several methods are based on tableau techniques [Olivetti 1992, Inoue, Koshimura and Hasegawa 1992, Bry and Yahya 1996, Niemelä 1996b, Niemelä 1996a].

In circumscriptive reasoning we are interested in the question whether a formula φ is true in every minimal model of premises T. A straightforward way of implementing this is through enumerating counter-models, i.e., models where the premises are true but the query φ false. The feasibility of this approach builds on the availability of suitable model generating procedures. Fortunately, the idea of doing theorem proving by trying to find a counter-model for the query underlies much of the work in automated deduction. For example, in tableau-based methods the counter-models are quite explicitly represented. However, it is not straightforward to build a circumscriptive theorem prover on top of a classical theorem prover. The complexity results on circumscription (Π_2^P-completeness in the propositional case) indicate that it is highly unlikely that this can be done with only a polynomial overhead. Next we discuss the difficulties involved and present an approach to build a circumscriptive prover on top of a classical model generating procedure. In Section 3 we show how this approach can be integrated into an efficient tableau method.

In principle constructing a circumscriptive theorem prover on top of a classical model generating procedure seems straightforward: the procedure looks for counter-models, i.e., models where the premises T are true but the query φ false. All we need to do is to check for each counter-model whether it is a minimal model of T. If this is the case, then we know that φ is not a circumscriptive consequence of T. If no such model is found, φ is a circumscriptive consequence of T. The soundness and completeness of this method relies on the fact that we have a complete model generating procedure, i.e., it generates (at least) all the minimal models. This is very close to the idea introduced for sceptical default reasoning above, i.e., sceptical consequences are established by showing that no extension not containing the query exists.

A difficulty in this approach is the test for minimality. The naive approach (where minimality is established by searching through each smaller model and showing that this is no longer a model of the premises) seems unfeasible because of the potentially high number of smaller models. This is problematic specially in the presence of varying predicates. The characterization of minimal models given in Theorem 2.11 provides a solution to this problems because with it minimality of a model can be tested using a classical consequence test and without explicit comparisons to other models.

We demonstrate how this technique works in the propositional case. Now the models are sets of atomic propositions. Let $\underline{p}$ and $\underline{f}$ be sets of minimized and fixed atoms, respectively. By Theorem 2.11 a model M of a set of clauses T is a minimal model of T if and only if for each minimized atom p true in model M, $T \cup N^{\langle \underline{p}, \underline{f} \rangle}(M) \models p$ holds where

$$N^{\langle \underline{p}, \underline{f} \rangle}(M) \;=\; \{\neg q(\vec{t}) \mid q \in \underline{p} \cup \underline{f}, M \not\models q(\vec{t})\} \cup$$
$$\{q(\vec{t}) \mid q \in \underline{f}, M \models q(\vec{t})\}$$

This means that for establishing minimality of a model a single classical consequence test is enough: M is a minimal model of T if and only if

$$T \cup N^{\langle \underline{p}, \underline{f} \rangle}(M) \models p_1 \wedge \cdots \wedge p_n$$

where $p_1, \ldots, p_n$ are the minimized atoms true in M. Furthermore, the literals in $N^{\langle \underline{p}, \underline{f} \rangle}(M)$ often reduce the complexity of the classical consequence test.

2.19. EXAMPLE. Consider the case where we minimize every atom and the set T of clauses

$$a_1 \vee b_1$$
$$\vdots$$
$$a_n \vee b_n$$

The problem is to establish whether a model $M = \{a_1, \ldots, a_n\}$ of T is a minimal one. Using Theorem 2.11 this boils down to determining whether

$$T \cup \{\neg b_1, \ldots \neg b_n\} \models a_1 \wedge \cdots \wedge a_n$$

holds which is a trivial task for an efficient propositional theorem prover. This can be compared to the naive approach where the minimality can be established by testing that none of the subsets of M is a model of T in this case where there are no varying atoms.

2.6. Implementing Rational Closure

In Section 1, Definition 1.17 for $\mathcal{K}^{\text{rat}}$ was quite complicated. Also the very definition of $\mathcal{K}^{\text{pref}}$, closing a set of assertions under some inference rules, does not give any hints for an efficient computation. [Lehmann and Magidor 1992] give the following algorithm for computing $\mathcal{K}^{\text{rat}}$:

$\mathcal{K}$: Knowledge base,
?- $\alpha \hspace{-0.3em}\sim\hspace{-0.3em} \beta$: query to $\mathcal{K}$

C := $\mathcal{K}$;
while (α exceptional for C and E(C) $\neq$ C) **do**
   C := E(C) ;
if (α is exceptional for C)
   output "yes"   {α has a rank}
else
   if ($\alpha \wedge \neg\beta$ is exceptional for C)
    output "yes"
   else
    output "no";

This algorithm outputs *yes if and only if* $\alpha \hspace{-0.3em}\sim\hspace{-0.3em} \beta \in \mathcal{K}^{\text{rat}}$.

How can this algorithm be implemented? Fortunately, there is an efficient method which depends on a propositional theorem prover. Lehmann and Magidor defined:

2.20. DEFINITION $(\widetilde{\mathcal{K}})$.

Let $\widetilde{\mathcal{K}}$ be the set obtained from $\mathcal{K}$ by replacing all occurrences of $\hspace{-0.3em}\sim$ with the material implication $\rightarrow$. Thus $\widetilde{\mathcal{K}}$ is a set of ordinary propositional formulas.

The main notion for defining an equivalent formulation of $\mathcal{K}^{\text{rat}}$ is to reformulate the notion of exceptionality of a formula (see Definition 1.16). The following theorem gives us a simple test:

2.21. THEOREM (Testing Exceptionality).

Let $\mathcal{K}$ be a knowledge base. A formula α is exceptional for $\mathcal{K}$ if and only if $\widetilde{\mathcal{K}} \models \neg\alpha$.

A nice feature is that $\mathcal{K}^{\mathrm{rat}}$ can also be used to compute $\mathcal{K}^{\mathrm{pref}}$ quite efficiently, because the following relation holds [Dix and Schmitt 1993]:

$$\alpha \hspace{-0.3em}\mid\hspace{-0.6em}\sim \hspace{-0.3em}\beta \;\in\; \mathcal{K}^{\mathrm{pref}} \quad \text{iff} \quad \alpha \hspace{-0.3em}\mid\hspace{-0.6em}\sim \hspace{-0.3em}\mathbf{f} \;\in\; (\mathcal{K} \cup \{\alpha \hspace{-0.3em}\mid\hspace{-0.6em}\sim \hspace{-0.3em}\neg\beta\})^{\mathrm{rat}}$$

The above algorithm has been implemented using the *Protein Theorem Prover* developed and used in Koblenz. In fact, there are many more options available than mentioned above. For example, how should *hard knowledge*, i.e. knowledge which is certain, and not subject to any default information, be handled? We refer to [Dix and Schmitt 1993] where this is investigated in detail and where many examples are compared against. Our implementations handles all these options both for $\mathcal{K}^{\mathrm{rat}}$ and for $\mathcal{K}^{\mathrm{pref}}$. We refer the interested reader to http://www.uni-koblenz.de/ag-ki/Systems/NM/.

3. From Automated Reasoning to Disjunctive Logic Programming

In the previous sections we introduced various nonmonotonic logics and general methods for computing therein. We now focus on nonmonotonicity in logic programming. Instead of jumping directly into the issue of Horn clause-based logic programming, we will stay for this section within the general framework of first-order predicate logic, without restricting it to Horn clauses. The motivation for this is twofold:

Firstly, recent research in tableau-based deduction methods (for a comprehensive treatment see [Bibel and Schmitt 1998]) provides us with the insight, that SLD-resolution, as well as some of its nonmonotonic extensions are in fact specialised versions of proof procedures from automated deduction in full first-order predicate logic.

Secondly, there is a entire discipline, namely disjunctive logic programming which tries to directly use these unrestricted calculi for logic programming and database reasoning (the only textbook available is [Lobo, Minker and Rajasekar 1992]).

One of the important proof procedures for first-order clausal logic is model elimination which was introduced by Don Loveland already in [Loveland 1968] and in [Loveland 1969]. It was only recently that the presentation of the calculus as a tableaux calculus with special search pruning techniques became obvious. This generalised view of the calculus offers the opportunity of building in several refinements and defining variants thereof.

Nowadays there are two paradigms used as the basis of efficient general purpose theorem provers: *resolution* and *model elimination*. Indeed, the CADE System Competition (CASC) which is held every year, is won more or less alternating by a resolution and by a model elimination based theorem prover.

Disjunctive logic programming offers a programming application for those calculi. [Lobo et al. 1992] is a textbook dealing exclusively with the topic of disjunctive logic programming and its nonmonotonic extensions. The underlying language of this approach to programming and data bases is full first-order logic in clause normal form. In order to stress the procedural character of clauses they are written in this context as $A_1 \vee \cdots \vee A_m \leftarrow B_1 \wedge \cdots \wedge B_n$ instead of $A_1 \vee \cdots \vee A_m \vee \neg B_1 \vee \cdots \vee \neg B_n$. As an operational semantics of programs given by such rules, the authors of [Lobo et al. 1992] use SLI resolution, a calculus which was developed earlier in [Minker and Zanon 1982]. This tree like depicted calculus is in fact very similar to the model elimination calculus given by [Loveland 1968] and in particular to the modern presentations given in [Bibel and Schmitt 1998]. We will use below a variant of model elimination as an operational semantics for disjunctive logic programming, which is supporting the intended procedural reading of clauses. More details on the relation to SLI resolution are given in Section 3.4. The above mentioned calculi offer goal oriented procedures for the interpretation of logic programs.

We will start from theorem proving methods for first-order predicate logic and we demonstrate how to modify and extend these approaches in order to arrive at automated reasoning systems with nonmonotonic extensions. Note that we are discussing disjunctive logic programs *with variables*, while in the literature the non-monotonic aspects are often discussed with programs which are ground, hence without variables. However, the use of nonmonotonic negation will be rather limited in this section.

In a first step we present as a goal oriented calculus the model elimination and we show how to modify it, such that it can be used as an *interpreter* for positive disjunctive logic programming. We then extend this interpreter by *negation as failure-to-explain*. These variants of model elimination are studied in detail in [Baumgartner and Furbach 1994a, Baumgartner, Furbach and Stolzenburg 1997a, Baumgartner, Furbach and Stolzenburg 1997b, Hähnle and Pape 1997].

In a second approach, we introduce a bottom up proof procedure, the *hyper tableau calculus*, and we discuss how minimal model reasoning can be performed in this framework.

Hyper tableaux are introduced in [Baumgartner, Furbach and Niemelä 1996] as an extension and formalisation of the SATCHMO proof procedure. In the ground case hyper tableaux are similar to the model trees from [Fernandez and Minker 91]. In [Kühn 1997, Baumgartner 1998] this calculus is even more extended towards the use of resolution-like handling of variables.

There is a similar approach in [Rajasekar 1989]: SLO-resolution. This is a goal oriented calculus for positive disjunctive programs which is presented as an extension of SLD-resolution. If all literal signs from the program clauses and from the goal clause are complemented (which preserves satisfiability) our hyper tableaux calculus corresponds to SLO-resolution. It is exactly the case for ground derivations and for the non-ground case for positive disjunctive programs. The DISLOG implementation of the SLO-resolution was discussed in [Rajasekar and Yusuf 1995] along with completeness results. A detailed investigation of this topic can be found in [Baumgartner and Furbach 1997], where such bottom up calculi are shown to be a kind of fixpoint semantics for disjunctive logic programming and a theorem which relates this T_p-operator to the goal oriented restart model elimination is given.

Since the calculi used for disjunctive logic programming have their origin directly in the field of theorem proving and automated deduction, we have to put some additional effort into some data-structure-like formalities.

Literal Trees, Tableau and Branch Sets

We first state some basic definitions, which are used in this section. A *clause* is a multiset of literals, usually written as a disjunction $L_1 \vee \ldots \vee L_n$. Clauses can be alternatively represented with an arrow. $A_1 \vee \cdots \vee A_m \leftarrow B_1 \wedge \cdots \wedge B_n$ is a representation of the clause $A_1 \vee \cdots \vee A_m \vee \neg B_1 \vee \cdots \vee \neg B_n$, where the As and Bs are atoms. Clauses with $m \geq 1$ are called *program clauses* with *head literals* A_i and *body literals* B_i, if present. Clauses of the form $\leftarrow B_1 \wedge \cdots \wedge B_n$ are called *negative* clauses in the sequel. We assume a clause set to be transformed into Goal normal form by changing negative clauses $\leftarrow B_1 \wedge \cdots \wedge B_n$ into Goal $\leftarrow B_1 \wedge \cdots \wedge B_n$ and by adding the additional negative clause ¬Goal.

We consider *literal trees*, i.e. finite, ordered trees, all nodes of which, except the root, are labeled with a literal. The labeling function is denoted by λ. Such a literal tree is also called a *tableau* and it is represented as a set of branches, where a *branch (of length n)* is a sequence $[N_0 \cdot N_1 \cdot \ldots \cdot N_n]$ ($n \geq 0$, written as indicated) of nodes such that N_0 is the root of the tree, N_i is the immediate predecessor of N_{i+1} for $0 \leq i < n$, and N_n is a leaf; the functions First and Leaf return the first *labeled*, resp. last node of a branch, i.e. First($[N_0 \cdot N_1 \cdot \ldots \cdot N_n]$) = N_1 and Leaf($[N_0 \cdot N_1 \cdot \ldots \cdot N_n]$) = N_n.

Throughout this section, the letter N is used for nodes, L, K denote literals, and the symbols **p**, **q** are used for branches; like branches, branch-valued variables are also written with brackets, as in [**p**]. Branch sets are typically denoted by the letters $\mathcal{P}, \mathcal{Q}, \cdots$. We write $\mathcal{P}, \mathcal{Q}$ and mean $\mathcal{P} \cup \mathcal{Q}$ (multiset union is intended here). Similarly, [**p**], $\mathcal{Q}$ means $\{[\mathbf{p}]\}, \mathcal{Q}$. We write $N \in [\mathbf{p}]$ *if and only if* N occurs in [**p**]. A substitution σ is applied to a branch set $\mathcal{P}$, written as $\mathcal{P}\sigma$, by applying σ to all labels of all nodes in $\mathcal{P}$. We say that branch set $\mathcal{P}$ is *more general* than branch set $\mathcal{P}'$ *if and only if* $\mathcal{P}\delta = \mathcal{P}'$ for some substitution δ.

Now let [**p**] be a branch $[N_0 \cdot N_1 \cdot \ldots \cdot N_n]$. Any contiguous subsequence of [**p**] (possibly [**p**] itself) is called a *partial branch* (through [**p**]). The concatenation of partial branches [**p**] and [**q**] is denoted by [**p·q**]; similarly, [**p·N**] means the extension of [**p**] by the node N. We find it convenient to confuse a node with its label and write, for instance [**p** · L], where L is a literal, instead of "[**p** · N], where N is labeled with L"; the meaning of $L \in [\mathbf{p}]$ is obtained in the same way; also, we say "node L" instead of the "node labeled with L".

In order to memorize the fact that a branch contains a contradiction, we allow to label a branch with a "$\star$" as *closed*; we insist that if a branch is labeled as *closed* then its leaf is complementary to some of its ancestor nodes. Branches which are not labeled as closed are said to be *open*. A literal tree is *closed* if each of its branches is closed, otherwise it is *open*.

Equality on branch sets is defined wrt. the labels and the "closed" status. More precisely, suppose given branches [**p**] and [**p′**] stemming from (not necessarily different) branch sets $\mathcal{P}$ and $\mathcal{P}'$ with respective labeling functions λ and λ'; define $\lambda[N_0 \cdot N_1 \cdot \ldots \cdot N_n] = \langle \lambda(N_1), \cdots, \lambda(N_n) \rangle$, $[\mathbf{p}]\star =_{\lambda,\lambda'} [\mathbf{p}']\star$ *if and only if* $[\mathbf{p}] =_{\lambda,\lambda'} [\mathbf{p}']$, where $[\mathbf{p}] =_{\lambda,\lambda'} [\mathbf{p}']$ *if and only if* $\lambda[\mathbf{p}] = \lambda'[\mathbf{p}']$. Equality for branch sets, i.e. $\mathcal{P} = \mathcal{P}'$, is defined as the usual multiset extension of "$=_{\lambda,\lambda'}$".

3.1. Restart Model Elimination

By the previous definitions literal trees are introduced as static objects. We wish to construct such literal trees in a systematic way. This is accomplished by, for instance, the *restart model elimination calculus*.

3.1. DEFINITION *(Branch Extension, Connection).*
The *extension of a branch* $[\mathbf{p}]$ *with clause* C, written as $[\mathbf{p}] \circ C$, is the branch set $\{[\mathbf{p} \cdot L] \mid L \in C\}$. Equivalently, when viewed as a tree, this operation extends the branch $[\mathbf{p}]$ by $|C|$ new nodes which are labeled with the literals from C. A pair of literals (K, L) is a *connection with mgU* σ *if and only if* σ is a most general unifier for K and $\overline{L}$ (here $\overline{L}$ denotes the complement of L).

For the purpose of this section, we introduce restart model elimination in its strongest variant. For this we need the additional notion of a *head selection function*.

3.2. DEFINITION *(Head Selection Function).*
A *head selection function* ν is a function that maps a clause $A_1 \vee \cdots \vee A_n \leftarrow B_1 \wedge \cdots \wedge B_m$ with $n \geq 1$ to an atom $L \in \{A_1, \cdots, A_n\}$. L is called the *selected literal* of that clause by ν. The head selection function f is required to be *stable under lifting* which means that if ν selects $L\gamma$ in the instance of the clause $(A_1 \vee \cdots \vee A_n \leftarrow B_1 \wedge \cdots \wedge B_m)\gamma$ (for some substitution γ) then ν selects L in $A_1 \vee \cdots \vee A_n \leftarrow B_1 \wedge \cdots \wedge B_m$.

A head selection function will be used to distinguish one single head literal to be used as the only entry point during the whole derivation.

3.3. DEFINITION *(Restart Model Elimination (RME)).*
Given a clause set S in Goal normal form and a head selection function. The inference rules *extension step*, *reduction step* and *restart step* on branch sets are defined as in Figure 4. The branch $[\mathbf{p}]$ is called *selected branch* in all three inference rules. A restart step followed immediately by an extension step is also called a *restart extension step*.

Note that like in the usual tableau model elimination calculus (cf. [Letz, Mayr and Goller 1994]), an extension or a reduction step can be applicable to a negative leaf. To positive leaves, only restart step can be applied.

We need one more definition before turning towards derivations:

Restart Model Elimination (RME)

Extension Step:

$$\frac{[\mathbf{p}], \mathcal{P} \qquad A_1 \vee \cdots \vee A_m \leftarrow B_1 \wedge \cdots \wedge B_n}{([\mathbf{p} \cdot A_i]\star, [\mathbf{p}] \circ (A_1 \vee \cdots \vee A_{i-1} \vee A_{i+1} \vee \cdots \vee A_m \leftarrow B_1 \wedge \cdots \wedge B_n), \mathcal{P})\sigma}$$

if

1. $A_1 \vee \cdots \vee A_m \leftarrow B_1 \wedge \cdots \wedge B_n$ (with $m \geq 1$, $n \geq 0$ and $i \in \{1, \cdots, m\}$) is a new variant (called *extending clause*) of a clause in S, and
2. A_i is the selected literal, and
3. $(\text{Leaf}([\mathbf{p}]), A_i)$ is a connection with mgU σ. In this context A_i is called the *extension literal*.

Reduction Step:

$$\frac{[\mathbf{p}], \mathcal{P}}{([\mathbf{p}]\star, \mathcal{P})\sigma}$$

if

1. $\text{Leaf}([\mathbf{p}])$ is a positive literal, and
2. $(L, \text{Leaf}([\mathbf{p}]))$ is a connection with mgU σ, for some node $L \in [\mathbf{p}]$.

Restart Step:

$$\frac{[\mathbf{p}], \mathcal{P}}{[\mathbf{p}] \circ \text{First}([\mathbf{p}]), \mathcal{P}}$$

if $\text{Leaf}([\mathbf{p}])$ is a positive literal.

Figure 4: Inference rules for RME.

3.4. DEFINITION *(Computation Rule)*.

A *computation rule* is a total function κ which maps a tableau to one of its open branches. It is required that a computation rule is *stable under lifting*, which means that for any substitution σ, whenever $\kappa(\mathcal{Q}\sigma) = [\mathbf{q}]\sigma$ then $\kappa(\mathcal{Q}) = [\mathbf{q}]$.

The role of a computation rule is to determine in a derivation the selected branch for the next inference step:

3.5. DEFINITION *(Derivation)*.

Let S be a clause set in Goal normal form and κ be a computation rule. A *restart model elimination derivation (RME derivation) of branch set $\mathcal{P}_n$ with substitution $\sigma_1 \cdots \sigma_n$ via κ from S* consists of a sequence $((([\neg\text{Goal}] = \mathcal{P}_0), \mathcal{P}_1, \cdots, \mathcal{P}_n)$ of branch sets, where for $i = 1, \cdots, n$:

1. $\mathcal{P}_i$ is obtained from $\mathcal{P}_{i-1}$ by means of an extension step with an appropriate variant $\mathcal{C}$ of some clause from S and mgU σ_i, or
2. $\mathcal{P}_i$ is obtained from $\mathcal{P}_{i-1}$ by means of a reduction step and mgU σ_i, or
3. $\mathcal{P}_i$ is obtained from $\mathcal{P}_{i-1}$ by means of a restart step.

Any branch set which is derivable by some RME derivation is also called a *RME tableau*.

In each case the selected branch of the inference is determined by κ. Quite often we will omit the term "via κ" and mean that κ is some arbitrary, given computation rule.

Finally, a *RME refutation* is an RME derivation such that $\mathcal{P}_n$ is closed. The term "RME" is dropped if context allows.

Notice that due to the construction of the inference rules, $\mathcal{P}_1$ is obtained from $\mathcal{P}_0$ by an extension step with some clause Goal $\leftarrow B_1 \wedge \cdots \wedge B_n \in S$ and with empty substitution. This clause is called the *goal clause* of the derivation.

It is worth noting that in extension steps we can connect only with the head literals of input clauses. Since in general this restriction is too strong, because it destroys completeness, we have to "restart" the computation with a fresh copy of a negative clause. This is achieved by the restart rule, because refutations of clause sets in Goal normal form always start with First($[\mathbf{p}]$) $\equiv \neg\text{Goal}$, and thus only extension steps are possible to $\neg\text{Goal}$, which in turn introduce a new copy of a negative clause.

Figure 5 depicts the above introduced concepts with the following clause set $\{\neg p \vee \neg q, p \vee \neg q, \neg p \vee q, p \vee q\}$; the same clause set in rule notation is $\{\leftarrow p \wedge q, p \leftarrow q, q \leftarrow p, p \vee q \leftarrow\}$ The left hand side of the figure shows a model elimination derivation, where no restriction with respect to the use of extension literals or reduction steps is imposed. The inference rules for this calculus are not introduced formally in this paper, they simply consist of an extension rule as defined before, but without a selection rule and a reduction rule (indicated by dashed arrows in the tree). Note that all leaves in the tree are marked with a "$\star$" as *closed* and hence the tree corresponds to a refutation.

The right hand side of the figure shows a restart model elimination derivation as it is defined above. For this the clause set is transformed into the corresponding

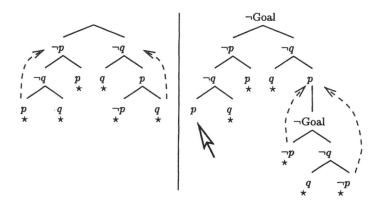

Figure 5: Model Elimination (left side) vs. Restart Model Elimination (right side).

goal normal form $\{\leftarrow \text{Goal}, \text{Goal} \leftarrow p \wedge q, p \leftarrow q, q \leftarrow p, p \vee q \leftarrow\}$. Note the open positive leaf, which is indicated by an arrow. In the present version of restart model elimination it is no more allowed to close the branch by application of a reduction step. This branch can only be extended by a further restart step as the rightmost branch of this tree. This would finally lead to a closed tree, hence a refutation.

3.6. Theorem (Correctness and Completeness).
Restart model elimination is correct and refutational complete

Correctness of the calculus can be derived very simply by writing the restart step as the introduction of an *atomic cut*, i.e. an extension of a branch with the tautology $\neg\text{Goal} \vee \text{Goal}$. In a subsequent step the branch containing Goal can be closed by a reduction step with the root node $\neg\text{Goal}$ and as a result we get the open branch with Goal, which would be the result of a restart step as well. A proof of the theorem can be found in [Baumgartner and Furbach 1994a]. A completeness result with respect to computed answers is given in [Baumgartner, Furbach and Stolzenburg 1997a].

3.2. Procedural Interpretation

We are claiming that RME, as it is introduced in the previous subsection can be used in a very natural way as an interpreter for positive disjunctive logic programs.

For the ease of notation we consider the non-Horn clause $A_1 \vee A_2 \leftarrow B$, for which we discuss a procedural interpretation:

- From the definition of the extension step we know that only one head literal, namely the one selected by the head selection function, can be used as the extension literal. Let this be A_1 in our example; i.e. there is exactly one *entry point* for the procedure $A_1 \vee A_2 \leftarrow B$, namely A_1. The clause never can be used for an extension step via A_2.

- Once the clause is used to extend a branch of the tableau, we can interpret the extension of the branch, as establishing the new subgoals from the body, in this case it is the *new goal B*.
- In addition, a new proof of the original goal has to be established with the original program, which, however, is augmented with a new fact $A_2 \leftarrow$. This additional proof is started via a subsequent restart step, which is the only applicable inference rule at the positive leaf A_2 of the tableau. Instead of adding the fact A_2 to the clause set for this additional proof, restart model elimination allows the closing of branch by reduction steps to the branch literal A_2 which obviously has the same effect.

It should be obvious, that restart model elimination is an extension of SLD-resolution[5]. When restricted to definite clauses, no restart step can occur and hence all inner nodes of a branch are negative. Since reduction steps can only occur at an open branch with a negative leaf, it is impossible to find a connection from such a literal and consequently reduction steps can never be applied.

This close relation to SLD-resolution can be used very elegantly for efficient implementation by using the PTTP-technique (Prolog Technology Theorem Proving) as introduced in [Stickel 1988]. This is a compilation technique which takes advantage of efficient commercial Prolog systems. The given set of non-Horn clauses is transformed in a preprocessing step into a Prolog-program, which contains code for the reduction steps and in the case of restart model elimination for the restart steps. The extension steps are performed by the SLD-resolution from the Prolog-system. The PROTEIN-system is a high performance prover which is based on this technique [Baumgartner and Furbach 1994b].

3.3. Negation as Failure-to-Explain

Having established a close relationship between SLD-resolution for definite programs and restart model elimination for positive disjunctive programs, we introduce a negation-as-failure rule, which has a close similarity to the negation-as-failure from Prolog.

[Aravindan 1996] introduces an abductive framework for positive disjunctive logic programs that captures minimal model reasoning. From now on we deal with disjunctive logic programs, which are clause sets consisting only of non-negative clauses.

Given a program P and an atom A, an abductive explanation $\mathcal{E}$ for A consists only of negative literals, s.t. $P \cup \mathcal{E} \models A$ and $P \cup \mathcal{E}$ is consistent. A set $\mathcal{E}$ of negative literals is referred to as a potential candidate for A if $P \cup \mathcal{E} \models A$.

3.7. DEFINITION *(Negation by failure-to-explain).*
Let P be a disjunctive logic program and A a be an atom. Then, the *negation by*

---

[5]This becomes very obvious, if one takes into account that SL-resolution [Kowalski and Kuehner 1971] is a variant of model elimination. Since this calculus is commonly accepted as an extension of SLD-resolution, the same holds for model elimination.

failure-to-explain inference rule is given as:

$$\frac{\text{there is no abductive explanation for } A \text{ wrt } P}{\neg A}$$

It is now natural to ask whether this negation by failure to explain is different from known and accepted semantics such as (E)GCWA.

For this the following theorem from [Aravindan 1996] is important. Note that this is very closely related to circumscription, where every predicate is minimized. We use the minimal entailment relation $\models_{min}$, as defined in Definition 1.6.

3.8. Theorem (Abductive Explanation).
Let P be a disjunctive logic program and A an atom. Then, there exists no abductive explanation for A wrt P if and only if $P \models_{min} \neg A$. *Also, the empty set $\emptyset$ is an abductive explanation for A wrt P* if and only if $P \models_{min} A$.

In other words, this theorem states, that negation-as-failure to explain captures exactly the minimal model reasoning as defined by the extended generalized world assumption [Lobo et al. 1992]. The negation by failure-to-explain can be seen as well as a special case of circumscription, by minimizing every atom (see section 1.3).

Let us investigate this rule with an example, where the program P consists of the following clauses:

$$P: \quad p \vee s \leftarrow t$$
$$p \vee r \leftarrow q$$
$$t \vee q \leftarrow$$

Given the atom p, the task is to generate potential candidates and to check if they are consistent with the given program. These candidates can be generated by obtaining the logical consequences K of $P \cup \{\neg p\}$, where K is a simple disjunction of ground atoms. Note that $\mathcal{E} = \{\neg A \mid A \in K\}$ is a potential candidate for p.

The key observation for the generation of potential candidates with the RME-calculus, is that those tableaux, which contain only open paths with positive literals represent such K. The literals from K are exactly the leaves from the open paths. If we start in our example with $\{\neg p\}$, we get with one extension the two paths $\{\neg t\}$ and $\{s\}$. A further extension step yields $\{q\}$ and $\{s\}$, and hence we have one potential candidate $K = \neg q \vee \neg s$.

At this point it is obvious that we have to weaken our calculus: If the head selection function would force us to use the first clause for an extension step only via the literal s, we can not derive this logical consequence. Hence for the purpose of negation as failure-to-explain, we have to use RME without head selection function. It is obvious, that this calculus is sound and complete as well.

In order to get a precise description, how RME computes negation as failure to explain, some further concepts are in order. First observe that one needs to generate only the minimal potential candidates: A potential candidate $\mathcal{E}$ for A wrt

P is *minimal* iff no proper subset of it is a potential candidate for A wrt P. The set of all minimal potential candidates for A wrt P is denoted by $\mathrm{MPOT}(A, P)$. In the same way we get the notion of an *minimal abductive explanation* and the set $\mathrm{ME}(A, P)$ and the following property.

3.9. PROPOSITION. *Let P be a disjunctive logic program and A an atom. Then,* $\mathrm{ME}(A, P) \subseteq \mathrm{MPOT}(A, P)$.

Thus generating MPOT and testing every member of it for consistency with the given program ensures that all minimal abductive explanations can be generated. Further, if all members of MPOT fail the consistency check then negation of the given sentence can be inferred according to the negation by failure to explain inference rule.

Generation of all minimal potential candidates may be costly and not necessary. It is possible to weaken this set, and for this we need the following notions.

3.10. DEFINITION *(Relevant Extension, $\mathcal{E}$ covers $\mathcal{E}'$).*
Let $\mathcal{E}$ and $\mathcal{E}'$ two potential candidates (not necessarily minimal) for A wrt P. Then $\mathcal{E}'$ is said to be a *relevant extension* of $\mathcal{E}$ iff $\mathcal{E} \subseteq \mathcal{E}'$ and for every literal $L \in \mathcal{E}' \backslash \mathcal{E}$, we have that $P \cup \mathcal{E} \models L$. $\mathcal{E}$ is said to *cover* $\mathcal{E}'$ if $\mathcal{E} \subseteq \mathcal{E}''$, where $\mathcal{E}''$ is a relevant extension of $\mathcal{E}'$.

Let us consider an example to clarify these notions: a program P with two clauses $p \vee q \vee r$ and $s \leftarrow r$. $\mathcal{E}_1 = \{\neg q, \neg r\}$ is a minimal potential candidate for p. It covers the other minimal potential candidate $\mathcal{E}_2 = \{\neg q, \neg s\}$ because it is contained in $\{\neg s, \neg q, \neg r\}$ which is a relevant extension of $\mathcal{E}_2$.

The essence of this discussion is that, given P and A, instead of generating $\mathrm{MPOT}(A, P)$ it is enough to generate a set of potential candidates so that every member of $\mathrm{MPOT}(A, P)$ is covered. We may not generate all minimal abductive explanations by this method, but we are assured that all of them are covered. Failing to find an abductive explanation from this set will ensure that $\neg A$ can be inferred.

Before we now turn towards a decision procedure for minimal model reasoning wrt negation as failure-to-explain, we introduce some notions for RME derivations.

In order to compute potential candidates we need the concept of a *saturated branch set* $\mathcal{P}$, which is a set of branches, i.e. a literal tree, where every leaf is a positive literal and the only inference rule, which can be applied is the restart rule. Suppose there exists a branch $[\mathbf{p}] \in \mathcal{P}$ s.t. Leaf($[\mathbf{p}]$) is not ground, then $\mathcal{P}$ is said to have *floundered*.

Another important concept is similar to loop checking in programming languages: it is called *blockwise regularity*. A branch in an RME derivation is said to be *blockwise regular* if every pair of identical negative leafs are separated by at least one restart and all positive literals in the branch are pairwise distinct. A literal tree is blockwise regular *if and only if* all branches in it are blockwise regular.

The following two theorems relate RME to abductive explanations. The first one states that every saturated branch set in an RME derivation constitutes a potential candidate; and the second one ensures that all minimal potential candidates are covered.

3.11. THEOREM (Computing Abductive Explanations).
Let P be a disjunctive logic program and A be a ground atom. Let $(\mathcal{P}_0, \cdots, \mathcal{P}_k, \cdots)$ be an RME derivation for $P \cup \{\neg A\}$, where $\mathcal{P}_k$ is saturated and non-floundered. Then, $\mathcal{E} = \{\neg \mathrm{Leaf}(\mathbf{p}) \mid \mathbf{p} \in \mathcal{P}_k\}$ is a potential candidate for explaining G. Further, if $P \cup \mathcal{E}$ is consistent, then $\mathcal{E}$ is an abductive explanation for A wrt P.

3.12. THEOREM (Covering Potential Candidates).
Let P be a disjunctive logic program and A an atom. Let $\mathcal{E}$ be a minimal potential candidate for explaining A wrt P. Then, there exists a saturated branch set in an RME derivation for A that constitutes a potential candidate $\mathcal{E}'$ that covers $\mathcal{E}$.

In Figure 3.3 the use of RME for computing negation-as-failure-to-explain in our small example from above is taken from [Aravindan 1996].

We start with the branch set $\{[\neg p]\}$. After two extension steps, we obtain a saturated the branch set with leafs q and s. This corresponds to a potential candidate $\{\neg q, \neg s\}$. Now a restart step can be applied to either of these paths, and let us say it is applied to q first. After an extension step and a reduction step, we get another saturated multiset and potential candidate $\{\neg r, \neg s\}$. Note that applying an extension step with the other clause $p \vee s \leftarrow t$ after restart, fails ultimately because of regularity check. By restarting at leaf s and continuing our derivation we arrive at two more candidates corresponding to $q \vee t \vee r$ and $r \vee t \vee r$. By employing some optimization techniques, this can be cut down to a single candidate $\{\neg t, \neg r\}$. As shown in the figure, further attempts to restart and continue the derivation are failed by regularity checks.

Thus, three potential candidates are generated: $\{\neg q, \neg s\}$, $\{\neg r, \neg s\}$, $\{\neg t, \neg r\}$. Consistency checks can be carried at any point, i.e. immediately after generating a candidate or delayed till further candidates are generated. In this case, all these candidates are consistent and correspond to three minimal abductive explanations. Note that p has explanations and $\emptyset$ is not an abductive explanation. Hence, if the query is "check if p is false", then the derivation can stop immediately after generating $\{\neg q, \neg s\}$ to answer negatively.

3.4. Relation to Other Work

In the textbook on disjunctive logic programming [Lobo et al. 1992] SLI resolution is used as a base for all proof theoretic aspects (several of the systems described in that book have been implemented by D. Seipel in his *DisLoG* system, see <URL:http://www-info1.informatik.uni-wuerzburg.de/database/DisLog>). SLI resolution was introduced originally in [Minker and Zanon 1982] as LUST resolution, *Linear Resolution with Unrestricted Selection function based on Trees*. This calculus is a variant of model elimination, as it was introduced before in

— Extension Step   - - Restart Step   ···· Reduction Step
★ Atom in the input clause upon which extension is carried out

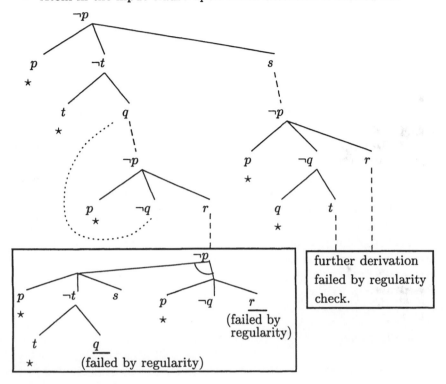

Figure 6: Abductive reasoning with modified restart model elimination calculus.

[Loveland 1968]. In this early reference, model elimination was even introduced in a tree-like manner. In so far SLI resolution is very well comparable with the presented approach via restart model elimination. The main difference, however, is that SLI resolution, like model elimination without the restart rule, needs all contrapositives of a program clause for being complete. As a consequence it does not allow for a procedural interpretation as it is mandatory for logic programming purposes. This disadvantage is removed in restart model elimination; clauses are used as expected in a programming system. Other calculi aiming at this important property are described by the family of near-Horn Prologs [Loveland 1991] or the Problem Reduction Format [Plaisted 1988].

The Failure-to-Explain rule which was introduced in the previous section established minimal model reasoning in an abductive framework. The main idea of this approach was to compute logical consequences to get explanations for a positive atom. A very similar idea is used by [Lobo et al. 1992], where the abductive explanations are given by the "support for negation", as they are called there. For the computation of these consequences SLI resolution is used. Both approaches, the one using abduction, as well as the SLI-based one, are very closely related to MILO resolution [Przymusinski 1989], where this idea was introduced for computing circumscription.

Model elimination can be seen as a natural extension of SLD resolution. This view can be used for efficient implementations of proof procedures based on model elimination by means of the PTTP-technique due to [Stickel 1988]. In a compilation phase a set of disjunctive program clauses is transformed into a Prolog-program, where those parts of the calculus, which are responsible for the non-Horn parts of the clauses are contained in the result of the compilation. The resulting Prolog program can be processed by efficient commercial Prolog systems. In [Baumgartner and Furbach 1994b] this technique is applied to implement PROTEIN, a theorem prover based on restart model elimination. In [Schaub and Brüning 1996] model elimination together with the PTTP-technique is used for query answering in default logics. In contrast to the algorithms, which are given in this article before, this approach incorporates default reasoning within an existing theorem prover. For this the compilation of the default rules is done in a way, that admissibility checks for the integration of default rules are handled in the resulting Prolog code. However, this works only in the semi-monotonic case, i.e. for normal default theories and not in the general case.

3.5. Hyper Tableau

In this section we discuss a bottom up calculus for positive disjunctive programs. This calculus can be seen as a model generation procedure and, hence, is very well suited for modification to enable minimal model reasoning.

In [Baumgartner et al. 1996] we introduced hyper tableaux as a variant of clausal normal form tableaux. They keep many desirable features of analytic tableaux (structure of proofs, reading off models in special cases) while taking advantage of central ideas from (positive) hyper resolution. In the ground case, hyper tableaux coincide with the well-known SATCHMO procedure of [Manthey and Bry 1988]; for the first-order case, hyper tableaux have significant advantages (see [Baumgartner et al. 1996]). For the purposes of this section, however, we use hyper tableaux in the ground case only.

As in the previous sections on model elimination, we introduce hyper tableaux, as a special kind of literal trees. In restart model elimination the generation of a tree started with a goal clause by extending always negative literals. In the hyper tableau calculus we go the other way round by starting with (possibly disjunctive) facts, which of course yields a tree which corresponds to partial models of the program. During a derivation the tree is extended such that in any step an open branch is a candidate for a partial model.

We assume a set of clauses S and a computation rule as defined in Section 3.1. In order to define hyper tableau as literal trees, we need the notion of an *initial tree*, which is a one-node literal tree, consisting of a root only, for which there is no label. Given a branch $[\mathbf{p}] = [N_0 \cdot N_1 \cdot \ldots \cdot N_n]$ the *literal set of* $\mathbf{p}$ is given as $lit(\mathbf{p}) = \{\lambda(N_1), \cdots, \lambda(N_n)\}$.

3.13. DEFINITION *(Hyper Tableau).*
Let S be a finite set of ground clauses and κ be a computation rule. *Hyper tableaux* are inductively defined as follows:

Initialisation Step: A tree, consisting of the root node only, is a hyper tableau for S. Its single branch is labeled as "open" (i.e. it is not labeled as "closed").

Hyper Extension Step: If

1. $[\mathbf{p}], \mathcal{P}$ is an open hyper tableau for S, i.e. $\mathbf{p}$ is the open branch selected by κ and

2. $\mathcal{C} = A_1 \vee \cdots \vee A_m \leftarrow B_1 \wedge \cdots \wedge B_n$ is a clause from S ($m \geq 0$, $n \geq 0$), called *extending clause* in this context, and

3. $\{B_1, \cdots, B_n\} \subseteq \mathbf{p}$ (referred to as *hyper condition*)

then the tree $\{[\mathbf{p} \cdot \neg B_1]\star, \cdots, [\mathbf{p} \cdot \neg B_n]\star\}, [\mathbf{p}] \circ (A_1 \vee \cdots \vee A_m), \mathcal{P}$ is a hyper tableau for S.

We will write the fact that a tree $\mathcal{T}'$ can be obtained from a tree $\mathcal{T}$ by a hyper extension step in the way defined as $\mathcal{T} \vdash_{\mathbf{p}, \mathcal{C}} \mathcal{T}'$, and say that $\mathcal{C}$ is *applicable* to $\mathbf{p}$ (or $\mathcal{T}$). Note that the head selection function κ does not appear explicitly in this relation; instead we prefer to let κ be given implicitly by the context.

The hyper condition of an extension expresses that *all* (possibly zero) body literals have to be satisfied by the branch to be extended. This similarity to hyper *resolution* coined the name "hyper tableau".

3.14. DEFINITION *(Hyper Tableau Derivation).*
Let κ be a selection function. A (possible infinite) sequence $\mathcal{T}_1, \cdots, \mathcal{T}_n, \cdots$ of hyper tableaux for S is called a *(hyper tableau) derivation from S if and only if* $\mathcal{T}_1$ is obtained by an initialisation step, and for $i > 1$, $\mathcal{T}_{i-1} \vdash_{\mathbf{p}_{i-1}, \mathcal{C}_{i-1}} \mathcal{T}_i$ for some clause $\mathcal{C}_{i-1} \in S$. This is also written as

$$\mathcal{T}_1 \vdash_{\mathbf{p}_1, \mathcal{C}_1} \mathcal{T}_2 \cdots \mathcal{T}_n \vdash_{\mathbf{p}_n, \mathcal{C}_n} \mathcal{T}_{n+1} \cdots$$

A derivation is called a *(hyper tableau) refutation* if it contains a closed tableau.

Note that extension steps are no longer applicable to a closed hyper tableau.

Figure 7 shows an example refutation. This example also demonstrates that hyper tableaux handle more than one negative clause. By this it is possible to have integrity constraints in the input clause set, and not just program clauses.

The ground version of the calculus as it is presented above resembles very much the proof procedure SATCHMO [Manthey and Bry 1988]. The reader is invited to study the first-order version of the hyper tableau calculus in [Baumgartner et al. 1996]. The main difference to SATCHMO only then becomes apparent: In principle SATCHMO works for ground clauses. This is necessary in order to avoid checking of substitutions for "splitted variables". Consider a clause $p(x) \vee q(x) \leftarrow b(a)$;

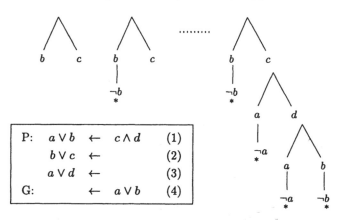

$$
\begin{array}{lll}
\text{P:} & a \vee b \;\leftarrow\; c \wedge d & (1) \\
& b \vee c \;\leftarrow & (2) \\
& a \vee d \;\leftarrow & (3) \\
\text{G:} & \;\leftarrow\; a \vee b & (4)
\end{array}
$$

Figure 7: A hyper tableau for P and G given in the figure. Notice that the formula G stands for the two clauses $\leftarrow a$ and $\leftarrow b$. For simplicity of presentation, negative leaf nodes stemming from program clauses are not drawn.

whenever this clause is used for an hyper extension step, the information that $p(x)$ in one branch and the $q(x)$ in the other branch stem from the same quantification $\forall x(p(x) \vee q(x) \leftarrow b(a))$ has to be memorized. This can be avoided by generating ground instances of clauses during the derivation, such that this splitting of the variable x cannot occur, because is instantiated by a ground term. SATCHMO achieves this by ground instantiating all variable occurrences dynamically during the proof. Hyper tableau maintains variables, only in those case where a splitting of variables can occur a ground instantiation of the corresponding occurrences is done. (In [Kühn 1997, Baumgartner 1998] this is even more liberalized.)

The central property of an open branch b is that it can be mapped to an interpretation in the usual way, i.e. by taking the positive literals of b as *true* and all others as *false*; for infinite derivations we take the chain limit of the increasing branches. Together with an appropriate *fairness* notion for derivations (roughly: at least one open branch has to be expanded as long as possible without violating regularity) a completeness result for the hyper tableau calculus can be proven (see again [Baumgartner et al. 1996]).

3.6. Minimal Model Reasoning

In this section we will introduce two methods for minimal model reasoning, which are closely related to model generation with hyper tableaux.

Tableaux with Groundedness Test
[Niemelä 1996b] presents a calculus for propositional minimal model reasoning. The basic idea is to generate models with a hyper tableau proof procedure and to

include an additional test for ruling out those branches in the tableau, which do not represent minimal models. This groundedness test is done *locally*, i.e. there is no need to compare a branch with other branches computed previously; hence there is no need to store models. The following definition of tableaux differs in two aspects from the hyper tableaux definition above. Firstly, the initialisation step introduces a kind of goal orientedness by introducing the atom, whose negation is to be proven and secondly, the extension rule performs the branching by the use of a cut rule.

3.15. DEFINITION *(Constructing Tableaux).*
Let S be a finite set of ground clauses, together with the problem of determining whether $S \vDash_{min} \neg A$ holds; and κ be a computation rule. Tableaux for $S \cup \{A\}$ are inductively defined as follows:

Initialisation Step: The tree, consisting of the root node labeled with A, is a tableau for $S \cup \{A\}$.

Extension Step 1: If
1. $[\mathbf{p}], \mathcal{P}$ is an open tableau for $S \cup \{A\}$, i.e. $\mathbf{p}$ is the open branch selected by κ and
2. $C = A_1 \vee \cdots \vee A_m \leftarrow B_1 \wedge \cdots \wedge B_n$ is a clause from S ($m \geq 0$, $n \geq 0$), and
3. $\{B_1, \cdots, B_n\} \subseteq \mathbf{p}$, and
4. $\{\neg A_1, \cdots, \neg A_{j-1}, \neg A_{j+1}, \cdots, \neg A_m\} \subseteq \mathbf{p}$

then the tree $([\mathbf{p}] \circ A_j, \mathcal{P})$ is a tableau for $S \cup \{A\}$.

Extension Step 2(Cut):
If
1. $[\mathbf{p}], \mathcal{P}$ is an open tableau for $S \cup \{A\}$, i.e. $\mathbf{p}$ is the open branch selected by κ and
2. $C = A_1 \vee \cdots \vee A_m \leftarrow B_1 \wedge \cdots \wedge B_n$ is a clause from S ($m \geq 0$, $n \geq 0$), and
3. $\{B_1, \cdots, B_n\} \subseteq \mathbf{p}$,

then the tree $(\{[\mathbf{p}] \circ A_j, [\mathbf{p}] \circ \neg A_j\}, \mathcal{P})$ is a tableau for $S \cup \{A\}$.

Note that in this definition there is no explicit labeling of branches with "open" or "closed", as it was in the definition of hyper tableaux. Here we assume a branch to be closed, whenever it contains two complementary literals.

In [Niemelä 1996b] this calculus is also given for deciding unsatisfiability of a clause set S and correctness and completeness is proven to this end as well. We introduced the calculus only for minimal model reasoning, i.e. together with a problem $S \vDash_{min} \neg A$.

Beside the closing due to complementary literals within a branch this calculus introduces a groundedness test.

3.16. DEFINITION *(Groundedness).*
A branch $[\mathbf{p}]$ is said to be ungrounded in S, when for some atom A in $[\mathbf{p}]$, $S \cup N_S([\mathbf{p}]) \models A$ does not hold, where

$$N_S([\mathbf{p}]) = \{\neg A \mid A \text{ occurs in the head of a } C \in S, \text{ but is not in } [\mathbf{p}]\}.$$

A branch is MM-closed w.r.t. S if it is closed or ungrounded in S.

Note that for checking $S \vdash_{min} \neg A$ we build the tableau for $S \cup \{A\}$, but for groundedness test, only S is used.

Consider as an example the set of clauses $S = \{a \vee b \vee c \leftarrow, a \vee c \leftarrow b\}$ and the problem of determining whether $S \vdash_{min} \neg b$ holds. We start with the initial tableau $[b]$. One extension with the cut-rule yields $\{[b \cdot \neg a], [b \cdot a]\}$. Further extension of the first branch with extension rule 1 gives $\{[b \cdot \neg a \cdot c], [b \cdot a]\}$. The first branch is ungrounded, because $N_S([b \cdot \neg a \cdot c]) = \{\neg a\}$ and b appears on the branch but $S \cup N_S([b \cdot \neg a \cdot c]) \models b$ does not hold. The second branch is ungrounded, because $N_S([b \cdot a]) = \{\neg c\}$ and b appears on the branch but $S \cup N_S([b \cdot a] \models b$ does not hold. Consequently, all branches are MM-closed w.r.t. S. Correctness of the calculus tells us that $S \vdash_{min} \neg b$ holds.

As in the case of hyper tableau, a fairness condition is needed in order to get a decision procedure (for the propositional case). This condition is called *finished* in [Niemelä 1996b] and it is the regularity condition introduced before. Together with this condition soundness and completeness of this calculus w.r.t. minimal model reasoning is proven. In [Niemelä 1996a] this approach is generalized for first-order circumscriptive reasoning. The aim is to handle parallel circumscription with fixed and varying predicates with respect to Herbrand models. This approach is proven to be correct and in case of absence of function symbols to be complete.

It is important to note, that in this approach the closing condition for branches is more complex than in the classical case; it involves not only a test on complementary literals, moreover it involves a test for classical consequence. This test can be realized by an additional call to a propositional theorem prover, which can be performed at any stage during the extension of a tableau. This seems to be in harmony with the complexity results, which tell us that propositional minimal model reasoning is a complete problem on the second level of the polynomial hierarchy. Hence minimal model reasoning is strictly harder than classical reasoning and it cannot be reduced to classical reasoning using a mapping computable in polynomial time.

MM-SATCHMO

MM-SATCHMO is described in [Bry and Yahya 1996] as an extension of the SATCHMO-proof procedure. As discussed before, the latter is similar to our ground version of hyper tableau. In order to compute minimal models, Bry and Yahya modify the generation of models in a way, that the first generated model is guaranteed to be a minimal one; while generating further models one always have to compare the current one with previously generated models. This comparison rules out the generation of non-minimal models.

In order to generate a first model, which is minimal, the extension step of a branch **p** with a clause $A_1 \vee \cdots \vee A_m \leftarrow B_1 \wedge \cdots \wedge B_n$ is modified, such that the leftmost open branch contains A_1 plus the additional literal $\neg A_2, \cdots, \neg A_m$. This is called complemented splitting, which is described elsewhere as factorization or folding up. Thus the first generated model is minimal and all other generation steps have to be constrained by the negation of the previously generated models.

In our small example $S = \{a \lor b \lor c \leftarrow, a \lor c \leftarrow b\}$ we can construct in a first step the $\{[a \cdot \neg b \cdot \neg c], [b], [c]\}$. The first branch cannot be expanded further with the second clause, because the hyper-condition is not fulfilled, hence we get a first minimal model $[a \cdot \neg b \cdot \neg c]$. Extension of the second branch $[b]$ gives us $[b \cdot a \cdot \neg c]$, which has to be identified as non-minimal by comparison with the previously generated model. The other branch $[b \cdot c]$ turns out to give non-minimal models in the next step.

Comparing MM-SATCHMO with the previous method by groundedness test, we (again) can study the tradeoff between time and space complexity. Whereas the groundedness method has to perform an extra call to a theorem prover to test groundedness of branches, the MM-SATCHMO procedure has to store generated models for further comparisons. The previously mentioned goal-orientedness of the groundedness-method is not available in MM-SATCHMO, here all minimal models have to be generated.

4. Nonmonotonic Semantics of Logic Programs

This section is devoted to logic programs. We assume some familiarity with the classical SLD-resolution for definite programs and will therefore just give a quick and compact description of the classical results in Subsection 4.1. A more detailed investigation is contained in [Brewka et al. 1997, Brewka and Dix 2001, Dix 1995c]. We also point to the LPNMR-series of conferences organized every other year ([Pereira and Nerode 1993, Marek, Nerode and Truszczyński 1995, Dix, Furbach and Nerode 1997]) and to the NMELP workshop series organized in conjunction with the international Logic Programming conferences ([Dix, Pereira and Przymusinski 1995, Dix, Pereira and Przymusinski 1997, Dix, Pereira and Przymusinski 1998]).

Instead, we will motivate (in Subsection 4.2) and investigate how positive programs can be extended by allowing *negation* in the bodies of rules (Subsection 4.3). This leads to the main competing approaches: the well-founded (WFS) and the stable (STABLE) semantics. In a second step, we will also allow disjunctions in the heads of rules. This leads for positive disjunctive programs to the generalized closed world assumption (GCWA) due to Minker (Subsection 4.4). In Subsection 4.5 we extend GCWA to programs with negation. This leads, like in the case of nondisjunctive programs, to an extension of WFS and one of STABLE.

Most of this section is written in a declarative style: the procedural aspect (already considered for positive programs in Section 3) will be considered in Section 5.

Let us fix some notation. A language $\mathcal{L}$ consists of a set of relation symbols and a set of function symbols (each symbol has an associated arity). Nullary functions are called constants. Terms and atoms are built from $\mathcal{L}$ in the usual way starting with variables, applying function symbols and relation-symbols.

Instead of considering arbitrary $\mathcal{L}$-formulae, our main object of interest is a program and we recall the definition introduced in the previous section:

4.1. DEFINITION *(Definite Logic Program)*.

A *definite* logic program consists of a finite number of *rules* of the form

$$A \leftarrow B_1, \ldots, B_m,$$

where $A, B_1, \ldots, B_m$ are positive atoms (containing possibly free variables). We call A the *head* of the rule and $B_1, \ldots, B_m$ its *body*. The comma represents conjunction $\wedge$.

We can think of a program as formalizing our knowledge about the world and how the world behaves. Of course, we also want to derive new information, i.e. we want to ask queries:

4.2. DEFINITION *(Query)*.

Given a definite program we usually have a definite query in mind that we want to be solved. A definite query Q is a conjunction of positive atoms $C_1 \wedge \ldots \wedge C_l$ which we denote by

$$?\text{-}\ C_1, \ldots, C_l.$$

These C_i may also contain variables. Asking a query Q to a program P means asking for all possible substitutions Θ of the variables in Q such that $Q\Theta$ follows from P. Often, Θ is also called an answer to Q. Note that $Q\Theta$ may still contain free variables.

4.1. Classical Results

Note that definite programs already contain some nonmonotonic component, which can be expressed in the following

4.3. PRINCIPLE *(Orientation)*.

If a ground atom A does not unify with some head of a program rule of P, then this atom is considered to be false. In this case we say that "*not A*" is derivable from P to distinguish it from classical $\neg A$.

The orientation principle is nothing but a weak form of *negation-by-failure*. Given an intermediate goal *not A*, we first try to prove A. But if A does not unify with any head, A fails and this is the reason to derive *not A*.

SLD-Resolution

SLD-Resolution[6] is a special form of Robinson's general Resolution rule. While Robinson's rule is complete for full first order logic, SLD is complete for definite

---

[6]**SL-resolution for Definite clauses. SL-resolution** stands for Linear resolution with Selection function.

logic programs (see Theorem 4.4). We do not give a complete definition of SLD-Resolution (see [Lloyd 1987]) but remind the reader the overall behaviour of SLD-resolution. We start with a query in the form $\leftarrow Q$. Sometimes the notation $\square \leftarrow Q$ is also used, where $\square$ denotes the falsum. In any round we have to select an atom where we have to resolve a clause against. Three different sorts of branches can occur, namely

1. *infinite* branches,
2. branches that *end up with the empty clause*, and
3. branches that *end in a deadlock ("Failure")*: no applicable rule is left.

Definite programs have the nice feature that the intersection of all Herbrand models exists and is again a Herbrand model of P. It is denoted by M_P and called the *least Herbrand model* of P. Note that our original aim was to find substitutions Θ such that $Q\Theta$ is derivable from the program P. This task as well as M_P is closely related to SLD:

4.4. THEOREM (Soundness and Completeness of SLD).
The following properties are equivalent:

- $P \models \forall\, Q\Theta$, *i.e.* $\forall\, Q\Theta$ *is true in all models of* P,
- $M_P \models \forall\, Q\Theta$,
- *SLD computes an answer* τ *that subsumes* Θ *wrt* Q
  (i.e. $\exists \sigma : Q\tau\sigma = Q\Theta$*).*

Note that not any correct answer is computed, only the most general one is (which of course subsumes all the correct ones).

The main feature of SLD-Resolution is its *Goal-Orientedness*. SLD automatically ensures (because it starts with the Query) that we consider only those rules that are relevant for the query to be answered. Rules that are not at all related are simply not considered in the course of the proof.

There is also an extension of SLD which can treat negative subgoals: SLDNF. Whenever a negative subgoal *not A* is reached, the procedure starts a negation-as-failure mode and tries to prove A. When this fails finitely, then the original subgoal *not A* succeeds. If, however, A succeeds, then *not A* fails and we have to backtrack. Complications arise when *not A* is called and it is not ground: the *floundering* problem. We refer to [Dix 1995c, Apt and Bol 1994, Apt and Doets 1994] for a more detailed discussion.

4.2. What Do we Want?

We now motivate the need for negative literals occurring in bodies of rules. When representing knowledge, we do not only want to formulate negative queries, we also want to express *default-statements* of the form

Normally, unless something abnormal holds, then ψ *implies* ϕ.

Such statements were the main motivation for nonmonotonic logics, like Default Logic or Circumscription (see Section 1, in particular Subsection 1.3). How can we formulate such a statement as a logic program? The most natural way is to use negation *"not"*

$$\phi \leftarrow \psi, \; not \; ab$$

where *ab* stands for *abnormality*. Obviously, this forces us to extend definite programs by negative atoms. Also the

Law of Inertia: Things normally tend to stay the same.

can be nicely captured with negation and abnormality predicates: abnormalities should be the exception rather than the rule.

4.5. DEFINITION *(Normal Logic Program).*
A *normal* logic program consists of a finite number of *rules* of the form

$$A \leftarrow B_1, \ldots, B_m, not \; C_1, \ldots, not \; C_n$$

where $A, B_1, \ldots, B_m, C_1, \ldots, C_n$ are positive atoms (containing possibly free variables). We call A the *head* of the rule, $B_1, \ldots, B_m$ its *positive body* and $C1, \ldots, C_n$ its *negative body*. The comma represents conjunction $\wedge$.

We now have two problems:
 1. to define a suitable semantics for programs with negation,
 2. to design efficient query-answering methods.
Is there only one possibility or do there exists various semantics, corresponding to different grades of nonmonotonicity? In fact, research in the last 10 years clarified this important question. Two main semantics evolved, the well-founded (WFS) and the stable semantics (STABLE) and led to various refinements and extensions. For detailed investigations and overview articles we refer the reader to [Apt and Bol 1994, Minker 1993, Minker 1996, Dix 1995c, Brewka et al. 1997, Brewka and Dix 2001].

We note that there is one nice feature of the classical bottom-up computation that is essential for our nonmonotonic semantics. In this framework of databases, rules of the form

$$A \leftarrow A$$

do not make any problems! They simply can not be applied or do not produce anything new. Whereas in the Top-Down approach, such rules give rise to infinite branches! Elimination of such rules will turn out to be an interesting property. We therefore formulate it as a principle:

4.6. PRINCIPLE *(Elimination of Tautologies).*
Suppose a program P has a rule which contains the same atom in its body as well as in its head (i.e. the head consists of exactly this atom). Then we can eliminate this rule without changing the semantics.

When we consider programs with negative literals, we need a slight extension of Principle 4.3:

4.7. PRINCIPLE *(Reduction)*.
Suppose we are given a program P with possibly default-atoms in its body. If a ground atom A does not unify with any head of the rules of P, then we can delete in every rule any occurrence of "*not A*" without changing the semantics.

Dually, if there is an instance of a rule of the form "$B \leftarrow$ " then we can delete all rules that contain "*not B*" in their bodies.

So far we have collected two principles, *Elimination of Tautologies* and *Reduction*. Are there more principles? How many? Let us consider a famous example:

4.8. EXAMPLE *(The Transitive Closure)*.
Assume we are given a graph consisting of nodes and edges between some of them. We want to know which nodes are reachable from a given one. A natural formalization of the property *reachable* would be

$$reachable(x) \leftarrow edge(x, y), reachable(y).$$

What happens if we are given the following facts

$$edge(a, b), \ edge(b, a), \ edge(c, d)$$

and *reachable(c)*? Of course, we expect that neither a nor b are reachable because there is no path from c to either a or b.

Also classical SLDNF-Resolution does not derive "*not reachable(a)*"!

Principle 4.6 does not help, because it simply does not apply. It turns out that we can augment our two principles by a third one, that constitutes together with them a very nice calculus handling the above example in the right way. This principle is related to *Partial Evaluation*, hence its name GPPE[7]. Here is some motivation. The query "*not reachable(a)*" leads to "*reachable(a) $\leftarrow$ edge(a, b), reachable(b)*" and "reachable(b)" leads to the rule "*reachable(b) $\leftarrow$ edge(b, a), reachable(a)*". Both rules can be seen as definitions for reachable(a) and reachable(b) respectively. So it should be possible to replace in these rules the body atoms of "reachable" by their definitions. Thus we obtain the two rules

$$reachable(a) \leftarrow edge(a, b), edge(b, a), reachable(a)$$
$$reachable(b) \leftarrow edge(b, a), edge(a, b), reachable(b)$$

that can both be eliminated by applying Principle 4.6. So we end up with a program that does neither contain *reachable(a)* nor *reachable(b)* in one of the heads. Therefore, according to Principle 4.3 both atoms should be considered false. The precise formulation of this principle is due to [Brass and Dix 1994] and, independently, to [Sakama and Seki 1994] for disjunctive programs and reads as follows:

---

[7]Generalized Principle of Partial Evaluation

4.9. PRINCIPLE *(Generalized Partial Evaluation, GPPE).*
We say that a semantics SEM satisfies GPPE, if the following transformation does not change the semantics. *Replace a rule* $A \leftarrow \mathcal{B}^+ \wedge \textit{not } \mathcal{B}^-$ *where* $\mathcal{B}^+$ *contains a distinguished atom* B *by the rules*

$$A \leftarrow (\mathcal{B}^+ \setminus \{B\}) \cup \mathcal{B}_i^+ \wedge \textit{not } (\mathcal{B}^- \cup \mathcal{B}_i^-) \ (i = 1, \ldots, n)$$

where $B \leftarrow \mathcal{B}_i^+ \wedge \textit{not } \mathcal{B}_i^-$ $(i = 1, \ldots, n)$ are all rules with head B.

Note that any semantics SEM satisfying GPPE and Elimination of Tautologies can be seen as extending SLD by doing some *Loop-checking*. We will call such semantics *NMR-semantics* in order to distinguish them from the classical *LP-semantics* which are based on SLDNF or variants of Clark's completion $comp(P)$:

- *NMR-Semantics = SLDNF + Loop-check.*

The last principle we need is the observation that a clause $A \leftarrow B, C, \textit{not } D, \textit{not } E$ is certainly subsumed by $A \leftarrow B, \textit{not } E$. We can get rid of non-minimal rules by simply deleting them.

4.10. PRINCIPLE *(Subsumption).*
In a program P we can delete a rule $A \leftarrow \mathcal{B}^+ \wedge \textit{not } \mathcal{B}^-$ whenever there is another rule $A \leftarrow \mathcal{B}'^+ \wedge \textit{not } \mathcal{B}'^-$ with

$$\mathcal{B}'^+ \subseteq \mathcal{B}^+ \text{ and } \mathcal{B}'^- \subseteq \mathcal{B}^-.$$

As a simple example, the rule $A \leftarrow B, C, \textit{not } D, \textit{not } E$ is subsumed by the 3 rules $A \leftarrow C, \textit{not } D, \textit{not } E$, $A \leftarrow B, C, \textit{not } E$ and by $A \leftarrow C, \textit{not } E$.

What is a Semantics?
Up to now, we have introduced four principles and we used the term *semantics of a program* in a loose, imprecise way. We end this section with a precise notion of what we understand by a semantics.

As a first attempt, we can view a semantics as a mapping that associates to any program a set of positive atoms and a set of default atoms. In the case of SLD-Resolution the positive atoms are the ground instances of all derivable atoms. But sometimes we also want to derive negative atoms (like in our two examples above). Our *Orientation*-Principle formalizes a minimal requirement for deriving such default-atoms.

Of course, we also want that a semantics SEM should *respect* the rules of P, i.e. whenever SEM makes the body of a rule true, then SEM should also make the head of the rule true. But it can (and will) happen that a semantics SEM does not always decide *all* atoms. Some atoms A are not derivable nor are their default-counterparts *not* A. This means that a semantics SEM can view the body of a rule as being *undefined*.

Suppose a semantics SEM treats the body of a program rule as undefined. What should we conclude about the head of this rule? We will only require that this head is not treated as false by SEM — it could be true or undefined as well. This means that we require a semantics to be compatible with the program *viewed as a 3-valued theory* — the three values being **t** ("true"), **f** ("false") and **u** ("undefined"). For the understanding it is not necessary to go deeper into 3-valued logic. We simply note that we interpret "←" as the Kleene-connective which is true for "**u** ← **u**" and false for "**f** ← **u**".

Our discussion shows that we can view a semantics SEM as a 3-valued model of a program. In classical logic, there is a different viewpoint. For a given theory T we consider there the set of all classical models MOD(T) as the semantics. The intersection of all these models is of course a 3-valued model of T, but MOD(T) contains more information. In order to formalize the notion of semantics as general as possible we define

4.11. DEFINITION *(SEM)*.

A semantics SEM is a mapping from the class of all programs into the powerset of the set of all 3-valued structures. SEM assigns to every program P a set of 3-valued models of P:

$$\text{SEM}(P) \subseteq \text{MOD}_{3-\text{val}}^{\mathcal{L}_P}(P).$$

This definition covers both the classical viewpoint (classical models are 2-valued and therefore special 3-valued models) as well as our first attempt in the beginning of this subsection. Later on, we will be really interested only in Herbrand models. It is also convenient to slightly abuse notation and view SEM(P) as a set consisting of atoms and default literals, namely those that are true in all intended models.

4.3. WFS and STABLE Semantics

The well-founded semantics, originally introduced in [Van Gelder, Ross and Schlipf 1988], is the *weakest* semantics satisfying our 4 principles (see [Brass and Dix 1999, Brass and Dix 1998, Dix 1995a]). We call a semantics

$$\text{SEM}_1 \text{ weaker than } \text{SEM}_2, \text{ written } \text{SEM}_1 \leq_k \text{SEM}_2,$$

if for all programs P and all atoms or default-atoms l the following holds: $\text{SEM}_1(P) \models l$ implies $\text{SEM}_2(P) \models l$. I.e. all atoms derivable from SEM_1 with respect to P are also derivable from SEM_2. The notion $\leq_k$ refers to the knowledge ordering in three-valued logic. Hence we have the following (due to [Brass and Dix 1999]):

4.12. THEOREM (Well-founded Semantics WFS).
There exists the weakest semantics satisfying our four principles Elimination of Tautologies, Reduction, Subsumption and GPPE. This semantics is called well-founded semantics WFS. WFS associates to every program P a unique 3-valued model of P.

This theorem gives a rather indirect, yet very interesting, explanation of WFS. But it can be shown, that all our transformations can be *applied* to really compute WFS.

4.13. Theorem (Confluent Calculus for WFS,[Brass and Dix 1998]).
The calculus consisting of our four transformations is confluent, i.e. whenever we arrive at an irreducible program, it is uniquely determined. The order of the transformations does not matter.

For finite propositional programs, it is also strongly terminating *for fair[8] sequences of transformations: any program P is therefore associated a unique normal form res(P). The well-founded semantics of P can be read off from res(P) as follows*

$$\mathrm{WFS}(P) = \{A: \ A \leftarrow \ \in res(P)\} \cup \{not\ A: \ A \ is \ in \ no \ head \ of \ res(P)\}$$

As an example let us consider the program

$$
\begin{aligned}
P: \quad p &\leftarrow q, not\ r \\
q &\leftarrow p, not\ r \\
r &\leftarrow not\ r \\
s &\leftarrow not\ p \\
t &\leftarrow q
\end{aligned}
$$

We can first apply GPPE to q in the first and the fifth rule to obtain P'. Then we can remove the first rule (tautology) and also the second and fifth, by 2 applications of GPPE to p (since there is no rule with p in the head, GPPE removes the whole rule). We get P''. Finally we can apply reduction (*not p* is true) and get the residual program $res(P)$.

$$
\begin{array}{llllll}
P': & p \leftarrow p, not\ r & \quad P'': & & \quad res(P): & \\
& q \leftarrow p, not\ r & & & & \\
& r \leftarrow not\ r & & r \leftarrow not\ r & & r \leftarrow not\ r \\
& s \leftarrow not\ p & & s \leftarrow not\ p & & s \leftarrow \\
& t \leftarrow p, not\ r & & & &
\end{array}
$$

Consequently, WFS(P) = {*not p, not q, s, not t*}.

We defined WFS as the weakest semantics satisfying our four principles. This already indicates that there are stronger semantics. One of the main competing approaches is the stable semantics STABLE. The stable semantics associates to any program P a set of 2-valued models, like classical predicate logic. STABLE satisfies the following property, in addition to those that have been already introduced:

4.14. Principle *(Elimination of Contradictions)*.
Suppose a program P has a rule which contains the same atom A and *not A* in its body. Then we can eliminate this rule without changing the semantics.

---

[8]This condition will be discussed in more detail in Section 5, in particular in Subsection 5.1.

This principle can be used, in conjunction with the others to define the stable semantics as shown by [Brass and Dix 1997].

4.15. THEOREM (STABLE).
There exists the weakest semantics satisfying our five principles Elimination of Tautologies, Reduction, Subsumption, GPPE and Elimination of Contradictions.

If a semantics SEM satisfies *Elimination of Contradictions* it is based on 2-valued models [Brass and Dix 1997]. The underlying idea of STABLE is that any atom in an intended model should have a definite reason to be true or false. This idea was made explicit by [Bidoit and Froidevaux 1991a, Bidoit and Froidevaux 1991b] and, independently, by [Gelfond and Lifschitz 1988]. We use the latter terminology and introduce the Gelfond-Lifschitz transformation: for a program P and a model $N \subseteq B_P$ we define

$$P^N := \{\text{rule}^N : \text{rule} \in P\}$$

where rule $:= A \leftarrow B_1, \ldots, B_n, not\ C_1, \ldots, not\ C_m$ is transformed as follows

$$(\text{rule})^N := \begin{cases} A \leftarrow B_1, \ldots, B_n, & \text{if } \forall j : C_j \notin N, \\ \mathbf{t}, & \text{otherwise.} \end{cases}$$

Note that P^N is always a *definite* program. We can therefore compute its least Herbrand model M_{P^N} and check whether it coincides with the model N with which we started:

4.16. DEFINITION *(STABLE).*
N is called a *stable* model[9] of P *if and only if* $M_{P^N} = N$. The stable semantics associates to every program P the set of stable models of P.

What is the relationship between STABLE and WFS? We have seen that they are based on rather identical principles.
- Stable models N extend WFS: $l \in$ WFS(P) implies $N \models l$.
- If WFS(P) is two-valued, then WFS(P) is the unique stable model.

But there are also differences. We consider the following example:

4.17. EXAMPLE *(Van Gelder's Example).*
Assume we are describing a two-players game like checkers. The two players alternately move a stone on a board. The moving player wins when his opponent has no more move to make. We can formalize that by
- $wins(x) \leftarrow move\_from\_to(x, y), not\ wins(y)$

meaning that
- the situation x is won (for the moving player A), if he can lead over[10] to a situation y that can never be won for B.

---

[9]Note that we only consider Herbrand models.
[10]With the help of a regular move, given by the relation $move\_from\_to/2$.

Assume the facts $move\_from\_to(a, b)$, $move\_from\_to(b, a)$ and $move\_from\_to(b, c)$. Our query to this program P_{game} is $?\text{-} wins(b)$. Here we have no problems with floundering, but using SLDNF we get an infinite sequence of oscillating SLD-trees (none of which finitely fails).

WFS derives the right results

$$\text{WFS}(P_{game}) = \{not\ wins(c), wins(b), not\ wins(a)\}$$

which matches completely with our intuitions. We get a different result when we consider the above clause $wins(x) \leftarrow move\_from\_to(x, y), not\ wins(y)$ together with the following facts: $move\_from\_to(a, b)$, $move\_from\_to(b, a)$, as well as $move\_from\_to(b, c)$, and $move\_from\_to(c, d)$. In this particular case we have two stable models: $\{wins(a), wins(c)\}$ and $\{wins(b), wins(c)\}$ and therefore

$$\text{WFS}(P) = \{wins(c), not\ wins(d)\} = \bigcap_{N \text{ a stable model of } P} N.$$

This means that the 3-valued well-founded model is exactly the set of all atoms or default-atoms true in all stable models. Again, there are examples where this is not always the case [Brewka and Dix 2001, Brewka et al. 1997].

The main differences between STABLE and WFS are

- STABLE is not always consistent,
- STABLE does not allow for a goal-oriented implementation.

The inconsistency comes from odd, negative cycles

$$\text{STABLE}(p \leftarrow not\ p) = \emptyset.$$

The idea to consider 2-valued models for a semantics necessarily implies its inconsistency [Brass and Dix 1997]. Note that the well-founded model exists: it is the empty 3-valued model. Sufficient criteria for the existence of stable models are contained in [Dung 1992, Fages 1993].

That STABLE does not allow for a Top-Down evaluation is a more serious drawback and has nothing to do with inconsistency.

4.18. EXAMPLE *(STABLE is not Goal-Oriented.)*.

$$
\begin{array}{llll}
P_{rel(a)}: & a \leftarrow not\ b & P: & a \leftarrow not\ b \\
& b \leftarrow not\ a & & b \leftarrow not\ a \\
& & & p \leftarrow not\ p \\
& & & p \leftarrow a
\end{array}
$$

$P_{rel(a)}$ is the subprogram of P that consists of all rules that are relevant to answer the query $?\text{-}\ a$. It has two stable models $\{a\}$ and $\{b\}$ — a is not true in all of them. But the program P has the unique stable model $\{p, a\}$, so a is true in all stable models of P.

The last example shows that the truth value of an atom a also depends on atoms that are totally unrelated with a! STABLE is not *relevant* or *modular* (see [Dix 1992a, Dix 1992b, Dix 1995a]). This is considered a drawback of STABLE by many people. Note that a straightforward modification of STABLE is not possible [Dix and Müller 1994a, Dix and Müller 1994b]. Other extensions of WFS based on confluent calculi have been considered in [Dix and Osorio 1999, Dix, Osorio and Zepeda 2001].

4.4. GCWA

What happens if we also allow disjunction in the head? It turns out that even for positive programs with disjunctions, we can express relations which belong to the second level of the polynomial hierarchy. Also, the complexity of deriving negative literals is at the second level. Therefore an extension of WFS to disjunctive programs can not have the same low complexity.

Concerning the right semantics for such programs, we are in the same situation as in the previous subsection — for positive programs there is general agreement while for disjunctive programs with default-negation there exist several competing approaches.

GCWA is defined for positive disjunctive programs consisting of rules of the form

$$A_1 \vee \ldots \vee A_n \leftarrow B_1, \ldots, B_m$$

by declaring all the minimal models to be the intended ones:

4.19. DEFINITION *(GCWA)*.
The generalized closed world assumption GCWA of P is the semantics given by the set of all classical (i.e. two-valued) minimal Herbrand models of P:

$$\text{GCWA}(P) := \text{MinMod}(P)$$

Originally, Minker denoted by GCWA(P) a set of negative atoms with the property that $P \cup \text{GCWA}(P) \models not\ A$ *if and only if* $\text{MinMod}(P) \models not\ A$ but we prefer here to denote by GCWA a semantics in the sense of Definition 4.11.

In Subsections 4.2 and 4.2 we have introduced the general notion of a semantics and various principles. Do they carry over to the disjunctive case? Fortunately, the answer is yes. In addition, GCWA not only satisfies all these properties, it is also uniquely characterized by them as the next theorem shows.

4.20. THEOREM (Characterization of GCWA, [Brass and Dix 1997]).
Let SEM be a semantics in the sense of Definition 4.11 satisfying GPPE and Elimination of Tautologies.
a) *Then: SEM(P)* $\subseteq$ *MinMod*$_{2-\text{val}}$*(P) for positive disj. programs P.*
   I.e. any such semantics is already based on 2-valued (as opposed to 3-valued) minimal models. In particular, GCWA is the weakest semantics with these properties.

b) *If SEM is non-trivial and satisfies in addition*[11] Isomorphy *and* Relevance, *then it coincides with GCWA on positive disjunctive programs.*

4.5. D-WFS and D-STABLE

Before we can state the definition of D-WFS we have to extend our principles to disjunctive programs with default-negation.

4.21. DEFINITION *(Disjunctive Logic Program).*
A *disjunctive* logic program consists of a finite number of *rules* of the form

$$A_1 \vee \ldots \vee A_k \leftarrow B_1, \ldots, B_m, not\ C_1, \ldots, not\ C_n$$

where $A_1, \ldots, A_k, B_1, \ldots, B_m, C_1, \ldots, C_n$ are positive atoms (containing possibly free variables). We call $A_1 \vee \ldots A_k$ the *head* of the rule, $B_1, \ldots, B_m$ its *positive body* and $C1, \ldots, C_n$ its *negative body*. The comma represents conjunction $\wedge$.
    We abbreviate these rules by

$$\mathcal{A} \leftarrow \mathcal{B}^+, not\ \mathcal{B}^-$$

where $\mathcal{A} := \{A_1, \ldots, A_k\}$, $\mathcal{B}^+ := \{B_1, \ldots, B_m\}$, $\mathcal{B}^- := \{C_1, \ldots, C_n\}$.

We also generalize our notion of a semantics slightly:

4.22. DEFINITION *(Operator* $\vdash\!\sim$, *Semantics* $\mathcal{S}_{\vdash\!\sim}$).
By a semantic operator $\vdash\!\sim$ we mean a binary relation between logic programs and pure disjunctions which satisfies the following three arguably obvious conditions:
  1. *Right Weakening:* If $P \vdash\!\sim \psi$ and $\psi \subseteq \psi'$[12], then $P \vdash\!\sim \psi'$.
  2. *Necessarily True:* If $\mathcal{A} \leftarrow \mathbf{t} \in P$ for a disjunction $\mathcal{A}$, then $P \vdash\!\sim \mathcal{A}$.
  3. *Necessarily False:* If $A \notin$ Head_atoms(P)[13] for a $\mathcal{L}$-ground atom A, then $P \vdash\!\sim not\ A$.

Given such an operator $\vdash\!\sim$ and a logic program P, by the semantics $\mathcal{S}_{\vdash\!\sim}(P)$ of P determined by $\vdash\!\sim$ we mean the set of all pure disjunctions derivable by $\vdash\!\sim$ from P, i.e., $\mathcal{S}_{\vdash\!\sim}(P) := \{\psi \mid P \vdash\!\sim \psi\}$.

In order to give a unified treatment in the sequel, we introduce the following notion:

4.23. DEFINITION *(Invariance of* $\vdash\!\sim$ *under a Transformation).*
Suppose that a program transformation *Trans* : $P \mapsto Trans(P)$ mapping logic programs into logic programs is given. We say that the operator $\vdash\!\sim$ is invariant under *Trans* (or that *Trans* is a $\vdash\!\sim$-equivalence transformation) *if and only if*

$$P \vdash\!\sim \psi \iff Trans(P) \vdash\!\sim \psi$$

---

[11] See [Brass and Dix 1997] for the precise definitions of Relevance and Isomorphy.
[12] I. e. ψ is a subdisjunction of ψ'.
[13] We denote by Head_atoms(P) the set of all (instantiations of) atoms occurring in some rule-head of P.

for any pure disjunction ψ and any program P.

All our principles introduced below can now be naturally extended.

4.24. DEFINITION *(Elimination of Tautologies, Non-Minimal Rules)*.
Semantics $S_{\vdash}$ satisfies **a)** the *Elimination of Tautologies*, resp. **b)** the *Elimination of Non-Minimal Rules if and only if* $\vdash$ is invariant under the following transformations:
a) Delete a rule $\mathcal{A} \leftarrow \mathcal{B}^+ \wedge not\ \mathcal{B}^-$ with $\mathcal{A} \cap \mathcal{B}^+ \neq \emptyset$.
b) Delete a rule $\mathcal{A} \leftarrow \mathcal{B}^+ \wedge not\ \mathcal{B}^-$ if there is another rule
$\mathcal{A}' \leftarrow \mathcal{B}^{+'} \wedge not\ \mathcal{B}^{-'}$ with $\mathcal{A}' \subseteq \mathcal{A}$, $\mathcal{B}^{+'} \subseteq \mathcal{B}^+$, and $\mathcal{B}^{-'} \subseteq \mathcal{B}^-$.

Our partial evaluation principle has now to take into account disjunctive heads. The following definition was introduced independently by [Brass and Dix 1994, Brass and Dix 1997, Sakama and Seki 1994]:

4.25. DEFINITION *(GPPE for Disjunctive Programs)*.
Semantics $S_{\vdash}$ satisfies GPPE *if and only if* it is invariant under the following transformation: *Replace a rule* $\mathcal{A} \leftarrow \mathcal{B}^+ \wedge not\ \mathcal{B}^-$ *where* $\mathcal{B}^+$ *contains a distinguished atom B by the rules*

$$\mathcal{A} \cup (\mathcal{A}_i \setminus \{B\}) \leftarrow (\mathcal{B}^+ \setminus \{B\}) \cup \mathcal{B}_i^+ \wedge not\ (\mathcal{B}^- \cup \mathcal{B}_i^-)\ (i = 1, \ldots, n)$$

where $\mathcal{A}_i \leftarrow \mathcal{B}_i^+ \wedge not\ \mathcal{B}_i^-\ (i = 1, \ldots, n)$ are all the rules with $B \in \mathcal{A}_i$.

Note that we are free to select a specific positive occurrence of an atom B and then perform the transformation. The new rules are obtained by replacing B by the bodies of all rules r with head literal B and adding the remaining head atoms of r to the head of the new rule.
Here is the analogue of Principle 4.7:

4.26. DEFINITION *(Positive and Negative Reduction)*.
Semantics $S_{\vdash}$ satisfies **a)** *Positive*, resp. **b)** *Negative* Reduction *if and only if* $\vdash$ is invariant under the following transformations:
a) Replace $\mathcal{A} \leftarrow \mathcal{B}^+ \wedge not\ \mathcal{B}^-$ by $\mathcal{A} \leftarrow \mathcal{B}^+ \wedge not\ (\mathcal{B}^- \cap \text{Head\_atoms}(P))$.
b) Delete $\mathcal{A} \leftarrow \mathcal{B}^+ \wedge not\ \mathcal{B}^-$ if there is a rule $\mathcal{A}' \leftarrow \mathbf{t}$ with $\mathcal{A}' \subseteq \mathcal{B}^-$.

Now the definition of a disjunctive counterpart of WFS is straightforward:

4.27. DEFINITION *(D-WFS)*.
There exists the weakest semantics satisfying positive and negative Reduction, GPPE, Elimination of Tautologies and non-minimal Rules. We call this semantics D-WFS.

As it was the case for WFS, our calculus of transformations is also confluent [Brass and Dix 1998].

4.28. THEOREM (Confluent Calculus for D-WFS).
The calculus consisting of our four transformations is confluent and strongly terminating for propositional programs and fair[14] sequences of transformations. I.e. we always arrive at an irreducible program, which is uniquely determined. The order of the transformations does not matter.

Therefore any program P is associated a unique normal form $res(P)$. The disjunctive well-founded semantics of P can be read off from $res(P)$ as follows

$$\psi \in D\text{-}WFS(P) \quad \Longleftrightarrow \quad \text{there is } \mathcal{A} \subseteq \psi \text{ with } \mathcal{A} \leftarrow \mathbf{t} \in res(P) \quad or$$
$$\text{there is not } A \in \psi \text{ and } A \notin \text{Head\_atoms}(res(P)).$$

Note that the original definition of WFS, or any of its equivalent characterizations, does not carry over to disjunctive programs in a natural way.

Two properties of D-WFS are worth noticing

- For positive disjunctive programs, D-WFS coincides with GCWA.
- For non-disjunctive programs with negation, D-WFS coincides with WFS.

Unlike the well-founded semantics, the original definition of stable models carries over to disjunctive programs quite easily:

4.29. DEFINITION *(D-STABLE).*
N *is called a stable* model[15] *of P if and only if $N \in \text{MinMod}(P^N)$. The disjunctive stable semantics associates to any disjunctive program P the set of stable models of P.*

In the last definition P^N is the positive disjunctive program obtained from P by applying the Gelfond/Lifschitz transformation (as introduced before Definition 4.16 — its generalization to disjunctive programs is obvious).

Analogously to D-WFS the following two properties of D-STABLE hold:

- For positive disjunctive programs, D-STABLE coincides with GCWA.
- For non-disjunctive programs with negation, D-STABLE coincides with STABLE.

What about our transformations introduced to define D-WFS? Do they hold for D-STABLE? Yes, they are indeed true. The most difficult proof is the one for GPPE. It was proved by [Brass and Dix 1994, Sakama and Seki 1994] independently that stable models are preserved under GPPE. Moreover, [Brass and Dix 1997] proved that STABLE can be almost uniquely determined by GPPE:

4.30. THEOREM (Characterization of D-STABLE).
Let SEM be a semantics satisfying GPPE, Elimination of Tautologies, and Elimination of Contradictions. Then: $SEM(P) \subseteq D\text{-}STABLE(P)$. Moreover, D-STABLE is the weakest semantics satisfying these properties.

---

[14]this condition will be discussed in more detail in Section 5, in particular in Subsection 5.1.
[15]Note that we only consider Herbrand models.

5. Implementing Nonmonotonic Semantics

In this section we present and discuss methods for implementing the two most popular nonmonotonic semantics for logic programs, the well-founded semantics and the stable model semantics. We study first normal programs (Subsections 5.1, 5.2) and then disjunctive programs (Subsections 5.3, 5.4). It turns out that the well-founded semantics is of *polynomial* complexity, in contrast to the stable semantics, which is located one level higher in the polynomial hierarchy. Therefore we only sketch a method for implementing the well-founded semantics and concentrate on efficient implementations of the stable semantics (Subsection 5.2).

We refer the interested reader to [Dix, Furbach and Nerode 1997], which contains a collection of nonmonotonic system descriptions and to the following webpage which is actively maintained and contains information on various logic programming systems that concentrate on nonmonotonic aspects (different kinds of negation, disjunction, abduction etc.): <URL:http://www.uni-koblenz.de/ag-ki/LP/>.

Before considering complexity results, we introduce an important notion which helps us to classify and to highlight different behaviour of certain classes of programs under some semantics.

5.1. DEFINITION *(Dependency Graph $\mathcal{G}_P$).*
For a general disjunctive program P with negation, the *dependency graph* $\mathcal{G}_P$ is a finite directed graph whose vertices are the predicate symbols from P. There is a *positive* (respectively *negative*) edge from p to p' *if and only if* there is a clause in P with

1. both p and p' occurring in the head, or
2. p in its head and p' occurring positively (respectively negative) in its body.

We also say

- p *depends on* p' if there is a path in $\mathcal{G}_P$ from p to p'.
  By definition, p depends on itself.
- p *depends positively* (resp. *negatively*) on p' if there is a path in $\mathcal{G}_P$ from p to p' containing only *positive* edges (resp. *at least one negative* edge).
  By definition p depends positively on itself.
- p *depends evenly* (resp. *oddly*) on p' if there is a path in $\mathcal{G}_P$ from p to p' containing an *even* (resp. *odd*) number of negative edges.
  By definition p depends evenly on itself.

The following properties of a program P turn out to be very important:
> *stratified:* no predicate depends negatively on itself[16],
> *strict:* there are no dependencies that are both even and odd,
> *call-consistent:* no predicate depends oddly on itself[17],
> *allowedness:* every variable occurring in a clause must occur in
> at least one positive atom of the body of that clause.

---

[16]or: there are no cycles containing at least one *negative* edge.
[17]or: there are no odd cycles.

For first-order programs an analogue of the dependency graph is easily constructed: the vertices of this infinite graph are exactly the *instantiated predicates* of the program. But note that for such programs the property of *being stratified* is not decidable [Cholak and Blair 1994].

The allowedness-condition (also called *range-restrictedness*) excludes constructs of the form $equal(x, x) \leftarrow$. This has the important effect that evaluating the truth of such a formula is to a large extent independent of the underlying domain (universe of discourse). It suffices to evaluate it on a *finite* subset of the underlying Herbrand domain. This ensures that in a bottom-up evaluation the underlying domains remain finite.

Let us consider some cases where restricting the class of programs has strong effects on the underlying semantics. For example, stratified programs always possess one unique stable model, which coincides with the well-founded model (which itself is therefore twovalued) and is denoted by M_P. Call-consistent programs also possess at least one stable model and for strict programs, the well-founded model is exactly the (3-valued) intersection of all stable models [Dung 1992].

We first collect some overall complexity results both for first-order as well as for propositional programs (we refer the reader to [Balcázar et al. 1988, Johnson 1990, Odifreddi 1989, Papadimitriou 1994, Eiter and Gottlob 1993, Gottlob 1992] for detailed investigations of complexity classes).

First-Order Programs

Tables 2 and 3 show that the full first-order versions are highly undecidable, if negation is allowed (Π_1^1-compl.[18] over $\mathbb{N}$). Also, there is no difference between WFS, STABLE and their disjunctive versions (all are Π_1^1-complete). Only for definite programs and positive disjunctive programs is the problem of deriving a positive atom recursively enumerable. But already deriving negative ground literals is Π_1^0-complete (for definite programs) and even Π_2^0-complete for positive disjunctive programs.

Although we did not introduce Clark's completion semantics COMP nor its 3-valued variant $COMP_3$ (but see Subsection 5.4), we mention in passing that both semantics are important because they constitute the *declarative* counterpart of SLDNF-resolution. This itself is too weak for our purposes (see the remark after Principle 4.9 in Section 4). More on Clark's completion can be found in [Brewka and Dix 2001, Clark 1978, Fitting 1985].

This shows that systems handling first-order programs must be necessarily incomplete. They can be only complete under additional assumptions on the underlying class of programs like

1. allowed programs without function symbols, also called *safe DATALOG*-programs, or

2. programs, where never a *negative literal with free variables* is selected (to resolve against), so called *non-floundering*-programs.

---

[18]To illustrate Π_1^1-completeness, we simply mention that such problems are of much higher complexity than the well-known halting problem of Turing-machines.

	Complexity	
	1. ord. prog. (with functions)	*prop. prog.* (no variables)
$\mathbf{M_P}$ (P is Horn)	A: Σ_1^0-compl. not A: Π_1^0-compl.	linear in $|P|$
$\mathbf{M_P^{supp}}$ (P is stratified)	arithm.-compl. (M_P^{supp} is Σ_n^0)	linear in $|P|$
COMP	Π_1^1-compl. over $\mathbb{N}$	co-NP-compl.
$\mathbf{COMP_3}$	Π_1^1-compl. over $\mathbb{N}$	linear in $|P|$
STABLE	Π_1^1-compl. over $\mathbb{N}$	co-NP-compl.
WFS	Π_1^1-compl. over $\mathbb{N}$	linear in $\#At \times |P|$

Table 2: Complexity of Non-Disjunctive Semantics

	Complexity	
	1. ord. prog. (with functions)	*prop. prog.* (no variables)
GCWA (P is positive)	A: Σ_1^0-compl. not A: Π_2^0-compl.	A: co-NP-compl. not A: Π_2^P-compl.
D-WFS	Π_1^1-compl. over $\mathbb{N}$	Π_2^P-compl.
D-STABLE	Π_1^1-compl. over $\mathbb{N}$	Π_2^P-compl.

Table 3: Complexity of Disjunctive Semantics

For propositional non-disjunctive programs we have a different situation (see Table 2). For non-disjunctive programs, WFS is at most quadratic, while STABLE is **co-NP**-complete. Thus for computing stable models, it makes sense to compute first the WFS (because this is cheap) and then use this result to reduce the program (by applying some of our transformations introduced in Section 4). Therefore an efficient computation of WFS also pays off for computing stable models.

For disjunctive propositional programs there is no difference in the complexity between D-WFS and D-STABLE: they are both Π_2^P-complete. Nevertheless, since D-STABLE is stronger than D-WFS, it makes sense to use an efficient computation of D-WFS first because many queries can be already decided (i.e. shown to be true or false) on this basis.

5.1. WFS for Normal Programs

One possibility to compute WFS is to just apply the confluent calculus of transformations described in Theorem 4.13. However, there are two details worth noticing. The first is the *fairness*-assumption mentioned in Theorem 4.13 and the second the complexity of the GPPE-transformation.

Fairness: Already the simple program consisting of just the loop "$p \leftarrow p$" shows a problem with termination. Applying GPPE leads to the same program, so GPPE can be applied infinitely often without leading to the residual program. There can also occur an oscillation:

$$P_{\text{loop}} : \quad p \; \leftarrow \; q$$
$$q \; \leftarrow \; p$$
$$r \; \leftarrow \; p, \neg r$$

If we apply GPPE_p to the third clause, this clause is replaced by $r \leftarrow q, \neg r$. We can now apply GPPE_q again to this clause and get the original program. So we have an oscillation

$$\text{GPPE}_q \circ \text{GPPE}_p(P_{\text{loop}}) = P_{\text{loop}}.$$

To get rid of these problems, we call a sequence of program transformations *fair*, if in the corresponding sequence of programs

1. every positive body-atom is eventually removed (either by removing the whole clause using a suitable transformation or by an application of GPPE), and
2. every tautology clause is eventually removed (either by applying *Elimination of Tautologies* or another suitable transformation).

With this fairness assumption, our calculus is strongly terminating.

Complexity: The second, and a much more important point is that the size of the residual program is in general *exponential* in the size of the original program! This is because rules of the form

$$p \; \leftarrow \; q$$
$$q \; \leftarrow \; r$$
$$r \; \leftarrow \; p$$

have to be fully evaluated by GPPE until the tautology transformation can be applied and all atoms classified as false. Recently it was shown by [Brass, Zukowski and Freitag 1997, Brass, Dix, Freitag and Zukowski 2001] how a small modification of the residual program, which still satisfies the nice characterization of computing WFS as given in Theorem 4.13, results in a *polynomial* computation. The idea is to replace the GPPE by another transformation, called *Loop-detection* that does not produce an exponential blow up. Note that all other transformations can be done in linear time.

To be more concrete, let us define the following two instances of GPPE ([Brass, Dix, Freitag and Zukowski 2001]).

5.2. DEFINITION *(Success and Failure).*
The success-transformation can be applied to a program P whenever there is a rule $A \leftarrow$ in P. Success then removes a positive occurrence of A in the body of another rule.

Dually, the failure-transformation can be applied to a program P whenever there is an atom A which does not occur in any head of a rule. Failure then removes a rule which contains A positively in its body.

If we forget about GPPE and the tautology rule we get the following interesting result:

5.3. THEOREM (Linear Complexity).
The calculus of rules consisting of success, failure and reduction (see Definition 4.7) is also confluent. In addition, it is strongly terminating and the normal form $nf(P)$ can be computed in linear time. The semantics according to the normal form coincides with the least fixpoint of the Fitting operator Φ_P and thus coincides with $comp_3$:

$$\mathrm{lfp}(\Phi_P) = \{A : A \leftarrow \; \in nf(P)\} \cup \{not \; A : A \text{ is in no head of } nf(P)\}$$

The last result is, from the complexity point of view quite promising. But it just computes a weak approximation of the WFS. What is missing is a loop detection rule:

5.4. DEFINITION *(Loop Detection).*
The Loop Detection transformation can be applied to a program P whenever there is a set $S_{\text{unfounded}}$ of ground atoms such that
- for each rule in $A \leftarrow \mathcal{B} \in P$, if $A \in S_{\text{unfounded}}$ then $\mathcal{B} \cap S_{\text{unfounded}} \neq \emptyset$.

Loop Detection then removes all rules of P which contain in their body a positive occurrence of an atom in $S_{\text{unfounded}}$.

Although checking for such a set $S_{\text{unfounded}}$ can be done in linear time, we may need various applications of it and therefore may reach an overall quadratic behaviour. A worst case estimate is the number of atoms $\#At$ occurring in P.

All the transformations above taken together, we get a calculus that also satisfies Theorem 4.13, i.e. it is confluent and the normal form (which is computable in quadratic time) determines the well-founded semantics.

But, as recently shown by [Berman, Schlipf and Franco 1995] WFS can be computed with *linear* complexity for a large class of programs. Rather than giving a detailed investigation, we just sketch a similar approach here. The method consists in three steps:
1. We first compute the *strongly connected components* of the program (as given by the dependency graph). As is well-known, this can be done in linear time (see eg. [Tarjan 1972, Berman et al. 1995]).

2. We start with working on the lowest component and propagate the values of atoms to the higher components.

3. In every connected component we iterate the following

   (a) apply *reduction* as well as *success* and *failure* until a fixpoint is reached. As mentioned in Theorem 5.3, this fixpoint corresponds exactly to the fixpoint of the Fitting operator Φ_P.

   (b) apply *loop-detection*, which amounts to computing the maximal unfounded set $S_{\text{unfounded}}$ [Van Gelder et al. 1988].

   If there are either *only* positive dependencies or *no* predicate defined in that component depends positively on itself, then no iteration of the two steps above are needed.

5.5. Theorem (Implementation of WFS).
The above described algorithm is provably better than the alternating fixpoint procedure of [Van Gelder 1989], which already works in $\#At \times |P|$, where $\#At$ is the number of atoms and $|P|$ the size of the program.

Moreover, the algorithm is linear for the class of all programs, where in each strongly connected component the following holds: either all the head-atoms defined in that component depend only *positively from each other* or *no predicate defined in that component depends positively on itself (also called* positive-acyclic*). Note that these two conditions can change from one connected component to the other.*

5.6. Example *(Algorithm for WFS using SCC's).*
We consider the following program, which contains both negative and positive dependencies.

$$
\begin{array}{llllll}
p_1 &\leftarrow q_1 & p_2 &\leftarrow not\ q_2 & q_3 &\leftarrow not\ w_3 \\
q_1 &\leftarrow r_1 & q_2 &\leftarrow not\ s_2 & w_3 &\leftarrow not\ z_3, x_3 \\
r_1 &\leftarrow q_1, z_3 & s_2 &\leftarrow t_2 & z_3 &\leftarrow \\
r_1 &\leftarrow p_2, not\ q_3 & t_2 &\leftarrow not\ q_3, t_2 & x_3 &\leftarrow not\ x_3 \\
\end{array}
$$

We have already split the program into strongly connected components and start with the lowest component, which is positive-acyclic. z_3 gets immediately true, while w_3 gets false and therefore q_3 becomes true and x_3 remains undefined. We propagate these values to the higher components. Note that the next component now also gets positive-acyclic, because $t_2 \leftarrow not\ q_3, t_2$ is removed due to propagation of the truth value of q_3. Consequently t_2, s_2 and p_2 are false while q_2 is true. The last component is purely positive, so we need the loop detection (linear) to determine that p_1, q_1, r_1 are all false.

XSB from Warren et. al.
The most advanced system (in terms of a full-fledged programming environment with various tools to support a programmer) has been implemented by David Warren and his group in Stony Brook: XSB is described by [Rao, Sagonas, Swift, Warren and Freire 1997, Sagonas, Swift and Warren 1994] and available by anonymous

ftp from `ftp.cs.sunysb.edu/pub/XSB/`. XSB is a full Prolog system which approximates the ISO standard. It can handle programs with negation and implements the well-founded semantics with respect to negation. The main contrast to a usual Prolog system is that XSB is not based on SLD-resolution, but on SLG-resolution (see [Chen and Warren 1993, Chen, Swift and Warren 1995, Chen and Warren 1996]), which allows to handle loops. Consequently, a modified WAM, the SLG-WAM, is the kernel of XSB. XSB is terminating for many programs where usual Prolog systems fall into an infinite loop.

The main feature of SLG is its use of *tabling*. For definite programs, SLG is similar to the OLDT-algorithm of [Tamaki and Sato 1986].

On an abstract level, the behaviour of SLG can be described by using the transformations *reduction*, *success*, *failure* and *loop detection* as used in Theorem 5.5. Of course, SLG works for rules containing variables, whereas our framework just treats propositional programs. In SLG, negative literals are delayed until they can be evaluated (i.e. their truth value can be computed). This is much the same as computing the modified normal form described above, where both negative literals and positive atoms are left in the body of rules. In fact our term *residual program* (but for disjunctive programs) was chosen according to the same term used in SLG.

In XSB one can use the residual program to compute stable models. Given a query and a program, the residual program with respect to that query is *almost ground*: this means that if variables are present in the residual program, they can be handled as *Skolem constants*. Then fast methods for computing stable models of propositional programs (see the next Subsection 5.2) can be used.

5.7. THEOREM (Completeness and Termination of XSB).
XSB is complete and terminating for non-floundering DATALOG (wrt WFS). It also works for general programs but termination is not guaranteed. If it terminates, the computed residual program is almost ground (and finite).

5.2. STABLE for Normal Programs

The stable model semantics for normal logic programs is closely related to Moore's autoepistemic logic and Reiter's default logic whose implementations have been discussed in Section 2. Our aim is to employ the techniques introduced there and show how they can be further developed to exploit the more limited structure of logic program. This is the approach used in a system called **smodels** [Niemelä and Simons 1996] which provides an implementation of the stable model semantics in C++. The system is publicly available (see `<http://www.tcs.hut.fi/Software/smodels/>`) and seems to outperform clearly other current approaches to implementing STABLE. We discuss first the propositional case, i.e., ground programs. In the end of the section we indicate how non-ground programs can be handled.

Several methods for computing stable models have already been proposed (see, e.g., [Baral and Gelfond 1994] for a survey). An interesting feature of the approach presented in this section is that for ground programs it enables *polyno-*

mial space implementation which is essential when working with larger programs. This is different from some recent advanced approaches [Bell, Nerode, Ng and Subrahmanian 1994, Subrahmanian, Nau and Vago 1995] which have exponential worst-case space requirements. The SLG system developed by Chen and Warren [Chen and Warren 1995] is closest to the method presented in this section and we compare the two approaches in the end of the section.

Normal logic programs can be seen as a special subclass of default theories where a logic program rule of the form

$$A \leftarrow B_1, \ldots, B_m, not\ C_1, \ldots, not\ C_n$$

corresponds to a default rule

$$\frac{B_1 \wedge \cdots \wedge B_m : \neg C_1, \ldots, \neg C_n}{A}$$

Under this mapping, the stable models of a logic program coincide with the extensions of the corresponding default theory [Gelfond and Lifschitz 1990]. Notice that the difference between logic programs and default rules is that in logic program rules the *not* operator speaks directly about membership in the extension whereas in default rules justifications state a consistency requirement (non-membership of the complement of the justification).

Our treatment of default logic in Section 2 is based on the notion of full sets (see Definition 2.3). When working with logic programs we use the representation of full sets introduced in Section 2.3 which employs the *not* operator and membership in extensions as the fundamental concepts. Hence, we can forget the "extra" negation in the justifications and work directly with the atoms appearing in the scope of the *not* operator. For a logic program P, we denote the set of atoms in the scope of the *not* operator by $NA(P)$. To illustrate the notation we show how to rewrite the definition of full sets using these concepts directly.

5.8. DEFINITION *(P-full Sets)*.
For a logic program P, a set $F \subseteq \{not\ A \mid A \in NA(P)\}$ is P-full if and only if

$$\text{for all } A \in NA(P),\ not\ A \in F \text{ if and only if } A \notin Cn_{\text{Mon}(P,F)}(\emptyset)$$

where

$$\text{Mon}(P, F) = \{A \leftarrow B_1, \ldots, B_m \mid A \leftarrow B_1, \ldots, B_m, not\ C_1, \ldots, not\ C_n \in P,$$
$$\{not\ C_1, \ldots, not\ C_n\} \subseteq F\}$$

and $Cn_{\text{Mon}(P,F)}(\emptyset)$ is the deductive closure of the rules $\text{Mon}(P, F)$.

The set of rules $\text{Mon}(P, F)$ can be seen as a set of definite clauses and their deductive closure is just the unique least model of the clauses. Now

1. for every P-full F, $Cn_{\text{Mon}(P,F)}(\emptyset)$ is a stable model of P and

```
function extensions(P, FS, φ)
FS' := expand(P, FS);
if conflict(P, FS') returns true then return false
else if FS' covers NA(P) then return test(P, FS', φ)
else
    χ := choose(P, FS');
    if extensions(P, FS' ∪ {χ}, φ) returns true then return true
    else return extensions(P, FS' ∪ {compl(χ)}, φ)
    end if
end if
```

Figure 8: A decision procedure for STABLE

2. for every stable model M, $F = \{not\ A \mid A \in NA(P) \setminus M\}$ is the unique corresponding full set such that $M = Cn_{Mon(P,F)}(\emptyset)$.

5.9. EXAMPLE. Consider the program P

$$p \leftarrow not\ q, r$$
$$q \leftarrow not\ p, r$$
$$r \leftarrow not\ q$$

Now $NA(P) = \{q, p\}$ and $F = \{not\ q\}$ is P-full as $Mon(P, F)$ has two rules $p \leftarrow r$ and $r \leftarrow$ and, hence, $Cn_{Mon(P,F)}(\emptyset) = \{p, r\}$. This is also a stable model of P. For instance, $F' = \{not\ p\}$ is not P-full since $Cn_{Mon(P,F')}(\emptyset) = \emptyset$ but $not\ q \notin F'$.

We exploit the connection between logic programming and default logic in order to develop an efficient implementation of the stable model semantics using the decision method for default logic presented in Section 2.3 (Fig. 3). In order to clarify the starting point we repeat the method in Fig. 8 with the modification that the input is a logic program P instead of a default theory and the current search assumptions FS is just a set of literals (formulae of the form A or $not\ A$ where A is atomic). The function **extensions** employs four subroutines. The function **test** is used for testing whether the extension (stable model) found by the procedure fulfills some given property, e.g., contains a given formula. The other three (**expand**, **conflict**, and **choose**) identify the key subtasks of the function **extensions** and we develop optimized implementations of these subroutines by exploiting the special properties of normal logic programs.

expand

In order to guarantee the soundness and completeness of the function **extensions**, the function **expand**(P, FS) should return a set of literals FS' which extends FS and with which every stable model of P agreeing with FS agrees. In Section 2.3 we introduced a technique for developing such functions by employing the notions of a lower and upper bound:

- For the lower bound $\mathbf{LB}(P, \text{FS})$ it holds that every stable model of P agreeing with FS, agrees with $\mathbf{LB}(P, \text{FS})$.
- For the upper bound $\mathbf{UB}(P, \text{FS})$ it holds that for every stable model M of P which agrees with FS, $M \subseteq \mathbf{UB}(P, \text{FS})$.

The implementation of **expand** is then based on the implementations of the bounds in the following way: $\textbf{expand}(P, \text{FS})$ returns the smallest set of literals FS' extending FS and closed under the following rules:

- if $\varphi \in \mathbf{LB}(P, \text{FS}')$, then include φ in FS' and
- if $A \notin \mathbf{UB}(P, \text{FS}')$ for $A \in \text{NA}(P)$, then include *not A* in FS'.

Hence, for implementing **expand**, it remains to devise the implementations of the bounds. In Section 2.3 we presented a technique for developing tight bounds for default logic. Here we show how even tighter bounds can be devised in the case of logic programs. First we generalize the notion of potentially applicable rules in a program P under a set of assumptions FS discussed in Section 2.3. We denote this set of rules by P/FS and require that a rule is potentially applicable only when the positive as well as negative body literals are not in conflict with FS.

$$P/\text{FS} = \{ \ A \leftarrow B_1, \ldots, B_m, not\ C_1, \ldots, not\ C_n \ | \\ \{not\ B_1, \ldots, not\ B_m, C_1, \ldots, C_n\} \cap \text{FS} = \emptyset\}$$

Consider the program P

$$
\begin{aligned}
p &\leftarrow q \\
q &\leftarrow p \\
p &\leftarrow s, not\ r \\
s &\leftarrow not\ t, not\ p \\
r &\leftarrow not\ t, not\ q \\
t &\leftarrow not\ r
\end{aligned}
\tag{5.1}
$$

For example, the program $P/\{not\ s, t\}$ consists of the first two and the last rule of P.

We define the lower bound $\mathbf{LB}(P, \text{FS})$ as the smallest set FS' including FS and closed under the rules

1. If for $A \leftarrow L_1, \ldots, L_n \in P/\text{FS}'$, $\{L_1, \ldots, L_n\} \subseteq \text{FS}'$, then $A \in \text{FS}'$
2. If an atom A is not a head of any rule in P/FS', then *not A* $\in \text{FS}'$.
3. If $A \in \text{FS}'$ is the head of only one rule $A \leftarrow L_1, \ldots, L_n$ in P/FS', then $\{L_1, \ldots, L_n\} \subseteq \text{FS}'$.
4. If *not A* $\in \text{FS}'$ and A is the head of a rule $A \leftarrow L_1, \ldots, L_n$ in P/FS' with $\{L_1, \ldots, L_{i-i}, L_{i+1}, \ldots, L_n\} \subseteq \text{FS}'$, then $compl(L_i) \in \text{FS}'$.

For the upper bound $\mathbf{UB}(P, \text{FS})$ we use the least model of the definite program obtained by removing all negative literals from P/FS.

5.10. EXAMPLE. Consider the program P defined in (5.1) and the execution of **expand**$(P, \{p\})$. First $\mathbf{LB}(P, \{p\}) = \{p, q, not\ s, not\ r, t\}$ where q is obtained by Rule (1), $not\ s$ and $not\ r$ by Rule (2) and finally t by Rule (1). Now $\mathbf{UB}(P, \{p, q, not\ s, not\ r, t\}) = \{t\}$. Hence, **expand** adds $not\ p, not\ q$ to the assumptions. No new assumptions are derivable and **expand**$(P, \{p\})$ returns $\{p, q, not\ s, not\ r, t, not\ p, not\ q\}$.

As another example, consider **expand**$(P, \{not\ s\})$. Now $\mathbf{LB}(P, \{not\ s\}) = \{not\ s\}$ but $\mathbf{UB}(P, \{not\ s\}) = \{s, r, t\}$. Thus, **expand** adds $not\ p, not\ q$ as new assumptions. Then $\mathbf{LB}(P, \{not\ s, not\ p, not\ q\}) = \{not\ s, not\ p, not\ q, t, not\ r\}$ where t is obtained by Rule (4) and $not\ r$ by Rule (3). No new assumptions are derivable. Hence, **expand**$(P, \{not\ s\})$ returns $\{not\ s, not\ p, not\ q, t, not\ r\}$.

Notice that Rules 1–2 for the lower bound correspond to the Fitting operator Φ_P, Rules 3–4 generalize the backward propagation of assumed truth values presented by [Chen and Warren 1995] and the upper bound rule generalizes loop detection discussed in the previous section to the case where assumptions are used. When employing the bounds given above the function **expand** computes a partial model which is closely related to the well-founded model of the program: if there are no initial assumptions, then **expand**$(P, \emptyset)$ computes the well-founded model of P but when assumptions are present the partial model computed by **expand** provides more information. For instance, as we demonstrated in the previous example for the program P from (5.1) **expand**$(P, \{p\})$ returns $\{p, q, not\ s, not\ r, t, not\ p, not\ q\}$ but the well-founded model of $P \cup \{p\}$ is $\{p, q, not\ s, not\ r, t\}$.

It turns out that the upper and lower bound are implementable in linear time using, e.g., data structures similar to those employed in a linear time algorithm for Horn clause satisfiability problem proposed in [Dowling and Gallier 1984]. This leads to quadratic time worst case performance for **expand**. The performance can be improved by exploiting the strongly connected components of the dependency graph of the program for computing the upper bound using, e.g., a similar technique as that proposed in the previous section for the well-founded model computation.

conflict

For soundness and completeness it is sufficient that

1. if **conflict**(P, FS) returns true, there is no stable model agreeing with FS and
2. if FS covers NA(P) and for some $not\ \chi \in \mathrm{FS}$, $\chi \in \mathrm{Cn}_{\mathrm{Mon}(P, \mathrm{FS})}(\emptyset)$ or for some $\chi \in \mathrm{FS}$, $\chi \notin \mathrm{Cn}_{\mathrm{Mon}(P, \mathrm{FS})}(\emptyset)$, then **conflict**$(P, \mathrm{FS})$ returns true.

These conditions are easy to fulfill because of the tightness of the bounds. As the conflict test is performed for a set of assumptions computed by **expand** it is sufficient to implement **conflict** as follows:

    conflict(P, FS) returns true if and only if there is some atom A such that $\{A, not\ A\} \subseteq \mathrm{FS}$.

choose

The function **choose** implements the search heuristics and **choose**(P, FS) should return either A or $not\ A$ for some atom $A \in \mathrm{NA}(P)$ which is not covered by FS.

The heuristics for choosing the next choice point has a strong influence on the performance of the decision method. For example, the following two approaches could be used.

- Start from the lowest strongly connected component in the dependency graph of the program.
  This kind of a heuristics has been proposed, e.g., in [Subrahmanian et al. 1995] and it is computationally inexpensive: a fixed order for atoms in $NA(P)$ can be computed once in linear time and this order can be used for selecting the next choice point. The disadvantage of the approach is that is it quite static and insensitive to the current search assumptions and can lead to a large search space.

- Maximum Occurrences in rules of Minimum size (Mom's) heuristics
  This approach is one of the most successful heuristics for the Davis-Putnam type procedure for propositional satisfiability. It can be adjusted to stable model computation and made quite dynamic, e.g., using the following approach employed in the **smodels** system [Niemelä and Simons 1996]. Given a set of current assumptions FS, select a negative literal from a body of a potentially applicable rule (i.e. included in P/FS) with the least number of negative literals not in FS. This heuristics is dynamic and needs to be re-evaluated each time the set of the assumptions FS changes. This re-evaluation can be done in linear time. Hence, the heuristics is more expensive than the previous static one but is more sensitive to the current search assumptions.

test
Notice that the use of the **test** function is not necessary when the queries are, e.g., literals. For such queries we can employ a function **test** which always returns true and implement the usual nonmonotonic reasoning tasks in the following way by employing the assumptions FS given as input for the function **extensions**.

- Finding a stable model:
  extensions$(P, \emptyset, \varphi)$ returns true *if and only if* there is an stable model of P.

- Credulous reasoning, i.e., deciding whether there is a stable model agreeing with a set of literals S:
  extensions(P, S, φ) returns true *if and only if* there is a stable model agreeing with S.

- Sceptical reasoning, i.e., deciding whether a literal L is in every stable model of P:
  extensions$(P, \{compl(L)\}, \varphi)$ returns false *if and only if* L is in every stable model of P.

For more complicated queries and reasoning tasks the **test** function provides the necessary flexibility.

5.11. Example. We illustrate the method with two examples. Consider the following program P.

$p \leftarrow not\ q, not\ u$

$q \leftarrow not\ p, not\ u$

$r \leftarrow p$

$s \leftarrow not\ q$

$s \leftarrow not\ r, q$

$t \leftarrow not\ s$

$s \leftarrow not\ t$

```
                                    1. not u                                    1. not s
                                      ↙↘                                        2. not u
                  2. not t          3. t                                        3. t
                  4. s              11. not s                                      ↙↘
                    ↙↘              12. q                  4. not p       5. p
   5. not r    6. r                 13. not p             6. q           9. r
   7. not p    9. p                 14. not r             7. r           10. not q
   8. q        10. not q            15. not q             8. not r       11. s
                                      ×                     ×              ×
```

First we discuss the problem of determining all of stable models of P. For finding one stable model, it is enough to let **test** return always true and start with an empty set of assumptions FS but the method can also compute all stable models by letting **test** return always false and recording full sets found.

We illustrate the execution of **extensions**$(P, \emptyset, \varphi)$ with the tableau like structure on the left-hand side which can be read as follows. Formula 1 is obtained in **expand** by Rule 1, then **choose** is called and it returns $not\ t$. Hence, the tableau splits in to two branches corresponding to the two recursive calls of **extensions**. Formula 4 is obtained in **expand** by Rule 1 etc. Thus, all formulae in the tableau are derived in **expand** (using the four rules for the lower bound and the upper bound rule) except those immediately after the splitting of the tableau which are provided by the function **choose**. When applying the rules, the current set of assumptions FS is given by the branch starting from the root of the tableau to the current leaf node. For example, consider how the formula 14 derived. The current set of assumptions (up to the formula 13) FS $= \{not\ u, t, not\ s, q, not\ p\}$ implies that the set of potentially application rules $P/$FS does not contain any rule for r and $not\ r$ is obtained by Rule 2. A branch ending with $\times$ contains a conflict, i.e., a pair $A, not\ A$ for some atom A.

The execution of **extensions** calls the **test** function for the first time after the formula 8 when

$$\mathrm{NA}(P) = \{p, q, u, r, s, t\}$$

is covered by the current assumptions FS $= \{not\ u, not\ t, s, not\ r, not\ p, q\}$ and no conflicts are detected. Hence, a stable model of P has been found. This can be obtained by computing the deductive closure $\mathrm{Cn}_{\mathrm{Mon}(P,\mathrm{FS})}(\emptyset)$ which in this case happens to coincide with the positive assumptions on the branch $\{s, q\}$.

If we were interested in finding one stable model, it would be enough to let **test** to return true. However, for finding all stable models of P we let **test** return false. Then **extensions** backtracks to the previous choice point and builds another branch. This does not contain any conflicts either and provides another stable model $\{s, r, p\}$. The function **test** returns false and **extensions** backtracks to the first choice point and builds the third branch which ends up with a conflict. No more backtracking is possible and **extensions** returns false. So P has two stable models $\{s, q\}$ and $\{s, r, p\}$ corresponding to the completed branches that contain no conflicts.

As another example, consider the problem of determining whether every stable model of P contains the atom s. Hence, we start with the initial assumptions FS = $\{not\ s\}$ and let **test** to return always true. The tableau on the right hand side illustrates the execution of **extensions**$(P, \{not\ s\}, \varphi)$. Two branches are built but both are not completed because a conflict is detected. Hence, **extensions**$(P, \{not\ s\}, \varphi)$ returns false implying that s is in every stable model of P. This example shows that it is not necessary to build any stable models in order to answer this kind of a sceptical query.

The approach presented here for implementing STABLE is quite similar to that used in the SLG system developed by Chen and Warren [Chen and Warren 1995]. The SLG system performs goal-directed query-evaluation and the well-founded semantics is employed for computing the residual program for a given query using SLG-resolution. The query can then be evaluated with respect to the well-founded semantics against the residual program. The SLG system evaluates the query with respect to the stable model semantics by computing the stable models of the ground residual program with an *assume-and-reduced* algorithm which assumes truth values of negative body literals and propagates these in order to prune the search space. However, the propagation is weaker than that in the function **expand**: assumed positive truth values are not propagated, backward propagation seems to be less dynamic and the upper bound is not employed. Hence, the assume-and-reduce algorithm prunes the search space less efficiently. This difference can also be observed experimentally when comparing the two approaches using larger ground programs [Niemelä and Simons 1996].

Notice that the SLG system can handle the stable model semantics also for nonground programs provided that the resulting residual program is finite. This seems to be a promising approach to implementing STABLE for non-ground programs: given a query, use an efficient implementation of SLG-resolution like XSB and compute the residual program and then use another method, like the one presented in this section, for evaluating the query with respect to STABLE on the basis of the residual program. However, the use of the residual program can led to unsound results: the stable models of the residual program are not necessarily stable models of the original program [Chen and Warren 1995]. For DATALOG programs which are allowed soundness can be guaranteed by employing a bottom-up method for computing a grounded version of a non-ground program such that the stable models are preserved. This approach has been employed, e.g., in the **smodels** system [Niemelä and Simons 1996].

5.3. D-WFS

Implementation of D-WFS is one of the main goals of the *DisLoP project*, undertaken by the Artificial Intelligence Research Group at the University of Koblenz and headed by J. Dix and U. Furbach [Aravindan, Dix and Niemelä 1997a, Aravindan, Dix and Niemelä 1997b], see also <http://www.uni-koblenz.de/ag-ki/DLP/>. It aims at extending the *restart model elimination* and *hyper tableau calculi*, for disjunctive logic programming (see also Section 3).

We have already seen in Section 4 that the very definition of D-WFS gives a method to compute it. The problem is the inherent complexity of applying the GPPE. We already mentioned in Subsection 5.1 the exponential behaviour of GPPE even for normal programs. So we need other techniques for efficient implementations. Currently, an extension of D-WFS first-order programs is on its way [Dix and Stolzenburg 1998, Sakama and Seki 1997]. In this framework constraint techniques are heavily used. As this approach is beyond the scope of this chapter, we consider in the following an implementation of D-WFS using an efficient *tableau-technique* as described in Section 3. The underlying theory of this implementation is studied by [Brass, Dix, Niemelä and Przymusinski 1998, Brass, Dix, Niemelä and Przymusinski 2001].

The main idea is to find an equivalent characterization of D-WFS which is related to circumscription. When considering disjunctive logic programs, it turns out that it makes sense to look at *minimal entailment* meaning that $not\ (\phi)$ atoms are fixed and all positive atoms are minimized.

But we have to strengthen the notion of *models* for a disjunctive logic program P by requiring that a model I (a set of atoms and formulae $not\ (\phi)$) of P has to be NAF-*consistent* for P, i.e., it must satisfy the following condition:

5.12. DEFINITION *(NAF-Consistency)*.
A model I for a disjunctive logic program P (viewed as a set of atoms and formulae $not\ (\phi)$) is called NAF-*consistent* if the following holds

$$\text{If } P \models A_1 \vee \cdots \vee A_n, \text{ then for some } i \in \{1, \ldots, n\}, not\ (A_i) \notin I.$$

Here $\models$ denotes the standard propositional consequence relation where the program is seen as a set of clauses and the $not\ (\phi)$ atoms as new atoms. Hence, e.g., $\{p \leftarrow not\ q, p \leftarrow q\} \models p$ does not hold.

For example, $\{p, r, not\ p, not\ q\}$ is not a NAF-consistent model of

$$P = \{p \vee q \leftarrow, r \leftarrow not\ p \wedge not\ q\}$$

but $\{p, r, not\ p\}$ is. However, the latter is not a minimal model of P.

In the following we will be interested in the consequence relation given by *truth in all* NAF-*consistent minimal models*. We denote this relation by $\models_{\min(N)}$:

$$P \models_{\min(N)} \neg A \text{ *if and only if* all NAF-consistent minimal models of } P \text{ satisfy } \neg A.$$

It turns out, that the following semantics SEM$_{\text{NAF}}$, defined by evaluating the truth of negative literals in NAF-*consistent* models coincides with D-WFS:

5.13. Definition *(SEM$_{\mathrm{NAF}}$)*.

Let P be a disjunctive logic program over $\mathcal{L}$. We define a set $\mathrm{Dis}_{\min}(P)$ of pure disjunctions as follows

$$\mathrm{Dis}_{\min}(P) := \mathrm{Dis}^+(P) \cup \mathrm{Dis}^-(P) \text{ where}$$

$$\begin{aligned}
\mathrm{Dis}^+(P) &:= \quad \{\quad A_1 \vee \ldots \vee A_k \quad : \quad P \models \quad\quad A_1 \vee \ldots \vee A_k \quad\} \\
\mathrm{Dis}^-(P) &:= \quad \{\quad \neg A \quad\quad\quad : \quad P \models_{\min(\mathrm{N})} \neg A \quad\quad\quad\quad\quad\}
\end{aligned}$$

Here, the series D_i defined by $D_0 := \emptyset$, $D_{n+1} := \mathrm{Dis}(P/D_n)$ grows monotonically and eventually gets constant. We define $\mathrm{SEM}_{\mathrm{NAF}}(P)$ to be the limit of this series.

It remains to explain the notion P/D_n. Intuitively, we mean the program obtained from *prog* by reducing it using disjunctions in D_n. More precisely, P/Dis is the program obtained by doing the following reductions on P for all *not C* and $C_1 \vee \ldots \vee C_k$:

- if $\neg C \in \mathrm{Dis}$, then remove all occurrences of *not C*,
- if $C_1 \vee \ldots \vee C_k \in \mathrm{Dis}$ then remove all rules that contain $\{not\ C_1, \ldots, not\ C_k\}$ in their bodies.

P/Dis is obviously a slight generalization of the Gelfond-Lifschitz transformation. Our P/Dis still contains negative literals in general.

5.14. Theorem. *D-WFS(P)* = $\mathrm{SEM}_{\mathrm{NAF}}(P)$.

Definition 5.13 can be employed to develop a novel implementation method for D-WFS which contrary to most other implementations of disjunctive semantics works in *polynomial space*. See `http://www.uni-koblenz.de/ag-ki/DLP` for an implementation of the method.

The idea is to exploit directly the new characterization of D-WFS in Theorem 5.14 and to implement D-WFS as an iterative reduction on disjunctive logic programs. The reduction starts with the original program P and leads to a reduced program P^* with the property that every query can be answered from this program with one call to a decision procedure of the minimal entailment $\models_{\min(\mathrm{N})}$. This can be seen as a compilation or (a partial evaluation) of the program leading to a smaller program from which all queries can be answered.

The reduced program is obtained as a fixed point of a reduction operator $\mathrm{R}_{\mathrm{D}}(\cdot)$ mirroring the operator in $\mathrm{SEM}_{\mathrm{NAF}}(P)$.

$$\begin{aligned}
\mathrm{R}_{\mathrm{D}}(P) = \quad &\{\mathcal{A} \leftarrow \mathcal{B}^+ \wedge not\ \mathcal{C}' \mid \mathcal{A} \leftarrow \mathcal{B}^+ \wedge not\ \mathcal{C} \in P, \\
&P/\mathrm{At}_{\mathcal{L}} \not\models C_1 \vee \cdots \vee C_n \text{ where} \\
&\mathcal{C} = \{C_1, \ldots, C_n\}, \\
&\mathcal{C}' = \{C \in \mathcal{C} \mid P \not\models_{\min(\mathrm{N})} \neg C\}\}
\end{aligned}$$

Now let P^* be the limit of the (monotonically decreasing) series of programs $P_0, P_1, \ldots$ where $P_0 = P$ and $P_{i+1} = \mathrm{R}_{\mathrm{D}}(P_i)$. Hence, the reduced program is obtained by

- removing each rule such that $C_1, \ldots, C_n$ are all the negative body literals and $C_1 \vee \cdots \vee C_n$ is a classical consequence of $P/\text{At}_{\mathcal{L}}$ and
- removing all *not* (C) from the bodies of the remaining rules for which $\neg C$ is minimally entailed by the remaining program

until no reduction is possible. It can be established that $P_i = P/D_i$ for all $i = 0, 1, \ldots$ Thus we have:

5.15. THEOREM. $D\text{-}WFS(P) = \text{SEM}_{\text{NAF}}(P) = \text{Dis}_{\min}(P^*)$.

Next we consider the problem of computing P^* within a polynomial space limit. Clearly, the required series of reductions can be implemented if decision procedures for classical entailment and minimal entailment $\models_{\min(\text{N})}$ are available. If the decision procedures work in polynomial space, then the whole series can be implemented within a polynomial space limit as the size of the program decreases after each step. Classical entailment can be implemented in polynomial space and this is also possible (see [Brass et al. 1998]) for $\models_{\min(\text{N})}$ by extending the tableau method for circumscription presented in [Niemelä 1996b, Niemelä 1996a].

5.16. THEOREM (Polynomial Space Complexity).
The entailment relation $\models_{\min(\text{N})}$, and therefore also D-WFS, can be implemented in polynomial space.

5.4. D-STABLE

D-STABLE is closely related to Reiter's default logic and methods presented in Section 2.3 can be employed to implement D-STABLE. In fact D-STABLE can be seen as a subclass of default logic, for example, using the following mapping from logic programs to default theories proposed by Sakama and Inoue [Sakama and Inoue 1993]. Given a disjunctive program P the corresponding default theory D_P contains the following default rules

1. for each rule $A_1 \vee \ldots \vee A_k \leftarrow B_1, \ldots, B_m, not\ C_1, \ldots, not\ C_n$ in P the default

$$\frac{: \neg C_1, \ldots, \neg C_n}{B_1 \wedge \cdots \wedge B_m \to A_1 \vee \ldots \vee A_k}$$

2. for each atom A appearing in P the default

$$\frac{: \neg A}{\neg A}$$

Then the atomic parts of the extensions of the corresponding default theory provide the stable models of the original program [Sakama and Inoue 1993], i.e.,

(i) each stable model of P is the set of atoms in some extension of D_P and

(ii) the set of atoms in an extension of D_P is a stable model of P.

In the following we describe an implementation of D-STABLE for allowed DATA-LOG programs due to [Brass and Dix 1995][19]. The main idea is to generalize a result of Fages and Ben-Eliyahu to the non-disjunctive case (see [Apt and Bol 1994]): if there are no positive loops, the stable models coincide with the supported models. This is certainly the case for residual programs because they have no positive body literals at all. Furthermore, supported models correspond to Clark's completion [Clark 1978, Bidoit and Hull 1986], which is a classical first-order theory. Stable models can then be determined by

1. computing the residual program $res(P)$,
2. computing Clark's completion $comp(res(P))$ as defined in Definition 1.6,
3. computing a theory $comp^*(res(P))$ by doing hyperresolution on comp(res(P)) (see Definition 5.19),
4. computing the minimal models of $comp^*(res(P))$, which are exactly the stable models of the original theory) by model-generation (Theorem 5.20).

We note that the main complexity lies in steps 1. and 3. The computation of the residual program is in general *exponential* in the size of P. Often, however, an exponential blow up does not actually occur (it is the worst case) and so the method works for small sized programs quite well. Computing comp* in the third step is also exponential, because it corresponds to doing hyperresolution. Obviously, more optimization techniques have to be considered to improve our method.

Fortunately, steps 2. and 4. are cheap. Computing comp is linear in res(P) and computing the minimal models of comp* by model generation is also not exponential. Here we can use the structure of comp* and do not need general minimal model reasoning to get the minimal models.

In order to define Clark's completion for disjunctive rules, we simply view a rule like $p \lor q \leftarrow not\ r$ as a shorthand for the two rules $p \leftarrow not\ q \land not\ r$ and $q \leftarrow not\ p \land not\ r$. This idea is made precise in

5.17. DEFINITION *(Completion of a Residual Program).*
Let res(P) be a program without positive body literals. Then we define the set $comp^+(res(P))$ to be

$$\{A_1 \lor \ldots \lor A_m \lor C_1 \lor \ldots \lor C_n \mid A_1 \lor \ldots \lor A_m \leftarrow not\ C_1, \ldots, not\ C_n \in res(P)\}$$

and $comp^-(res(P))$ to consist of the set

$$\{\neg A \lor \neg C_1 \lor \ldots \lor \neg C_n \mid \quad A \text{ is a ground atom}, C_i \in \mathcal{B}_i^- \cup (\mathcal{A}_i \setminus \{A\}),$$
$$\text{where } \mathcal{A}_i \leftarrow not\ \mathcal{B}_i^- \in res(P), i = 1, \ldots, n$$
$$\text{are all the conditional facts with } A \in \mathcal{A}_i\}.$$

Finally, we set

$$comp(res(P)) := comp^+(res(P)) \cup comp^-(res(P)).$$

---

[19] ftp://ftp.informatik.uni-hannover.de/software/index.html

For instance, consider the following residual program res(P) and the completed definitions for p and q in the standard "if and only if"-notation:

$$res(P): \quad p \vee q \leftarrow not\ r. \qquad\qquad comp(res(P)): \quad p \leftrightarrow (\neg q \wedge \neg r) \vee (\neg s \wedge \neg t).$$
$$p \leftarrow not\ s \wedge not\ t. \qquad\qquad\qquad\qquad q \leftrightarrow (\neg p \wedge \neg r).$$

The direction $\leftarrow$ corresponds to the logical information in the given program, and is represented by the positive disjunctions above. The negative disjunctions are the clausal ("multiplied out") form of the direction $\rightarrow$.

Now this completion of the residual program characterizes the stable models:

5.18. LEMMA. *A two-valued Herbrand interpretation I is a stable model of P if and only if $I \models comp(res(P))$, where res(P) is the residual program of P.*

So an answer θ to a query ψ is (sceptically) correct wrt the stable model semantics *if and only if $comp(res(P)) \vdash \psi\theta$.* Any theorem prover can be used to check that (or generate answers during the proof of ψ). It is also possible to use standard model generating algorithms on $comp(res(P))$ to construct the stable models of P.

However, we can also make use of the very special structure of $comp(res(P))$. By applying the "hyperresolution" [Chang and Lee 1973] technique, we can compute the set $comp^*(res(P))$ of all positive consequences of $comp(res(P))$.

5.19. DEFINITION *(Implied Positive Disjunctions).*
Hyperresolution with rules from $comp^-(res(P))$ is defined as follows:

$$H(\mathcal{D}) := \left\{ \bigcup_{i=1}^{m} (\mathcal{A}_i \setminus \{A_i\}) \;\middle|\; \mathcal{A}_i \in \mathcal{D},\ A_i \in \mathcal{A}_i,\ \neg A_1 \vee \ldots \vee \neg A_m \in comp^-(res(P)) \right\}.$$

I.e. for every purely negative clause $\neg A_1 \vee \ldots \vee \neg A_m$ of $comp^-(res(P))$, we look at all positive clauses $head_i \in \mathcal{D}$ that contain one of the A_i in their heads. Then we resolve these clauses by getting rid of all the A_i and putting the remaining parts $\mathcal{A}_i \setminus \{A_i\}$ of the together as one clause: the resolvent.

We start with $\mathcal{D}_0 := comp^+(res(P))$ and iterate $\mathcal{D}_i := H(\mathcal{D}_{i-1})$ until a fixpoint $\mathcal{D}_n$ is reached. Then let

$$comp^*(res(P)) := \{\mathcal{A} \in \mathcal{D}_n \mid \text{for all } \mathcal{A}' \subset \mathcal{A}: \mathcal{A}' \notin \mathcal{D}_n\}.$$

In the above computation the negative disjunctions $\neg A_1 \vee \wedge \cdots \wedge \vee \neg A_n$ are interpreted as rules $\leftarrow A_1 \wedge \cdots \wedge A_n$. The body atoms are matched with the positive disjunctions. The result of the rule application consists of the disjunctive contexts. Note that it is possible that the empty disjunction is computed, which is interpreted as logically false. This happens if the completion is inconsistent, e.g. for the program $p \leftarrow not\ p$.

Here is an example. Consider the following residual program $res(P)$ and its completion $comp(res(P))$ written as facts and rules:

$$res(P) : p \vee q. \qquad comp^+(res(P)): p \vee q. \qquad comp^-(res(P)): \leftarrow p \wedge q.$$
$$r \leftarrow not\ p. \qquad\qquad r \vee p. \qquad\qquad \leftarrow q \wedge p.$$
$$r \leftarrow not\ q. \qquad\qquad r \vee q. \qquad\qquad \leftarrow r \wedge p \wedge q.$$
$$s \leftarrow not\ r. \qquad\qquad s \vee r. \qquad\qquad \leftarrow s \wedge r.$$

The second and the third rule of $comp^-(res(P))$ are of course superfluous. We can derive r (with the first rule applied to the second and third disjunctive fact), and after deleting non-minimal disjunctions we get

$$comp^*(res(P)) = \{p \vee q,\ r\}.$$

This directly describes the two stable models $I_1 := \{p, r\}$ and $I_2 := \{q, r\}$. In general, we have the following:

5.20. Theorem (Reduction to **comp(res(P))**).
I is a stable model of P if and only if I is a minimal model of $comp^*(res(P))$.

We now consider the computation of the stable models themselves. In the special case that there is only a single stable model, $comp^*(res(P))$ is the set of atoms true in it, so no further computation is needed. If there are multiple models, we construct them by a case analysis. Note that any atom contained in a proper disjunction of $comp^*(res(P))$ can really be true or false (of course, the decision on different atoms is not independent). So we also need no further computation if we are only interested in credulous truth of ground literals. In the general case, we choose a truth value for a ground atom, and then compute the implied positive disjunctions which follow from this new information. We repeat this process until no proper disjunctions remain:

    procedure $model\_generation(comp^+(res(P)),\ comp^-(res(P)))$:

        compute $comp^*(res(P)))$;

        if $comp^*(res(P)))$ contains no proper disjunction **then**

            print $comp^*(res(P)))$;

        else

            let A be contained in a proper disjunction;

            $model\_generation(comp^+(res(P)) \cup \{A\},\ comp^-(res(P)))$;

            $model\_generation(comp^+(res(P)),\ comp^-(res(P)) \cup \{\neg A\})$;

Note that by the completeness of hyperresolution, we can be sure that if we choose A to be true or false, there is really a stable model in which A has this truth value. So our algorithm never runs into "dead ends". This is an important difference to the algorithm used in [Chen and Warren 1995] for propagating guessed truth values of atoms. For instance, the following residual program has only a single stable model (namely $\{p, \neg q, r\}$), but it is reduced in the sense of [Chen and Warren 1995], so their algorithm has to guess a truth value of some atom:

$$p \leftarrow not\ p.$$
$$p \leftarrow not\ q.$$
$$q \leftarrow not\ r.$$
$$r \leftarrow not\ q.$$

Of course, this example is quite pathological, and their reduction algorithm works well in the more usual simpler cases. In particular, their algorithm does not need to compute the residual program first. However, it is not clear how to generalize their method to the disjunctive case.

We end this section with pointing to a very recent approach relying on complexity-theoretic considerations. dlv [Eiter, Leone, Mateis, Pfeifer and Scarcello 1997, Eiter, Leone, Mateis, Pfeifer and Scarcello 1998] is a knowledge representation system, based on disjunctive logic programming, which offers front-ends to several advanced KR formalisms (developed since the end of 1996).

dlv is based on solid theoretical foundations [Leone, Rullo and Scarcello 1997], and recent comparisons [Eiter et al. 1998] are encouraging. Major emphasis has been put on advanced knowledge modelling features. The kernel language, which extends disjunctive logic programming by true negation and integrity constraints, allows for representing complex knowledge based problems in a highly declarative fashion [Eiter et al. 1998].

The computational kernel of dlv is an efficient engine for computing the stable models of a disjunctive logic program, based on algorithms presented in [Leone et al. 1997], together with various improvements by suitable optimization techniques.

The system runs in *polynomial space* and *single exponential time*, and is able to efficiently recognize and process syntactical subclasses of disjunctive logic programs which have lower computational complexity than the general case (like, e.g., programs with head-cycle free disjunction or stratified negation). Modular evaluation techniques are currently under development along with linguistic extensions to deal also with quantitative information [Buccafurri, Leone and Rullo 1997].

The three main modules of the dlv kernel are the

1. *Intelligent Grounding*,
2. the *Model Generator* and
3. the *Model Checker*.

All of these modules perform a modular evaluation of their input according to various dependency graphs as defined in [Leone et al. 1997, Eiter, Leone, Mateis, Pfeifer and Scarcello 1997] and try to detect and efficiently handle special (syntactic) subclasses, which in general yields a tremendous speedup.

The Intelligent Grounding takes an input program, whose facts can be stored also in the tables of external relational databases, and efficiently generates a subset of the program instantiation that has exactly the same stable models as the full program, but is much smaller in general. (For stratified programs, for example, the Grounding already computes the single stable model.)

Then the Model Generator is run on the (ground) output of the Intelligent Grounding. It generates one candidate for a stable model at a time and invokes the Model Checker to verify whether it is indeed a stable model.

The Model Generator first computes the least fixpoint $W_P^\infty(\emptyset)$ of a deterministic operator W_P [Leone et al. 1997], which extends to the disjunctive case the well-founded operator of Van Gelder, Ross and Schlipf. If $W_P^\infty(\emptyset)$ is a total interpretation, then it is the unique stable model [Leone et al. 1997], which can be returned to the user without any further check. Otherwise, $W_P^\infty(\emptyset)$ is contained in every stable model [Leone et al. 1997] and is therefore the deterministic basis for the computation of the stable semantics. To move beyond $W_P^\infty(\emptyset)$, a literal is then added to $W_P^\infty(\emptyset)$ and its deterministic consequences are computed; the process is repeated until (i) either a contradiction arises, or (ii) a total interpretation is reached (actually, a total interpretation is not extensionally generated; rather, a sufficient logical condition guarantees totality). A contradiction causes backtracking and removal of the last chosen literal; while reaching a total interpretation implies a call to the Model Checker which verifies whether the generated interpretation is a stable model or not. Thus, the Model Generator implements a backtracking algorithm that generates all possible "candidate" stable models. To improve the efficiency of the backtracking algorithm, dlv extends the concept of *possibly-true literals* [Leone et al. 1997, Leone and Rullo 1992, Leone, Romeo, Rullo and Saccà 1993, Buccafurri, Leone and Rullo 1996] to the disjunctive case.

Candidate stable models produced by the Model Generator are checked for stability by the Model Checker of dlv. Verifying the stability condition is a difficult task in general, as it is a well-known co-**NP**-hard problem (i.e., basically, as hard as computing the stable models of a non-disjunctive program). Instead of rewriting the program by the Gelfond-Lifschitz transformation and then checking the minimality of the candidate stable model on the rewritten program, the Model Checker verifies the stability directly, by checking whether the candidate stable model is unfounded-free (this condition is equivalent to stability checking [Leone et al. 1997]). This check is performed in polynomial time for head-cycle free programs (i.e., programs where recursion does not pass *through* disjunction), and for general programs the inefficient part of the computation is limited to only the components of the program that are not head-cycle free.

Thus, thanks to the efficient strategy implemented by the Model Checker, on a large and meaningful class of disjunctive programs dlv obtains basically the same performances that are obtainable on or-free programs (note that the semantics of programs with recursion through disjunction is often very hard to understand).

6. Benchmarks

In this section we address the problem of devising benchmarks for nonmonotonic reasoning techniques. We are especially interested in families of test cases with increasing size and complexity because they provide a systematic way for analyzing experimentally effects of different design decisions and for comparing the performance, scalability and limits of different implementations.

The problem of providing these kinds of families of benchmarks has been addressed only recently in the literature. In earlier papers benchmarks are usually examples illustrating important aspects of nonmonotonic reasoning (see, e.g., [Lifschitz 1989]). Typically these examples are quite small and directed to evaluating the correctness of an implementation rather than its performance. One of the first examples of a scalable collection of test cases is presented in [Subrahmanian et al. 1995] where Van Gelder's win-move example is used with randomly generated game graphs of increasing size.

In this section we discuss families of benchmarks arising from combinatorial graph problems, propositional satisfiability, planning, and diagnosis. Most of the benchmarks are given in terms of normal logic programs with the stable model semantics. However, the benchmarks can be employed as test cases for systems implementing other formalizations of nonmonotonic reasoning by representing the benchmark problems in the formalism of interest or by utilizing a direct translation from logic programs with the stable model semantics to the formalism of interest.

6.1. Graph Problems

The idea of producing benchmarks from graphs provides an interesting approach to generating families of test cases with similar structure but increasing size and complexity. Furthermore, a large variety of different types of test cases are available, and test cases can be grounded to realistic data by choosing interesting graphs representing real-life information.

This approach of building benchmarks from graphs forms the basis of the Theory Base system [Cholewiński, Marek, Mikitiuk and Truszczyński 1995] that generates test default theories and logic programs. The idea is to generate a default theory or a logic program from a given graph and a graph problem in such a way that the extensions of the default theory or the stable models of the program corresponds to the solutions of the original graph problem for the given graph. For example, given a graph and the 3-colorability problem a logic program is generate such that the stable models of the program provide the 3-colorings of the graph. This approach is employed also by [Niemelä and Simons 1996]. Further information about interesting classes of graphs, graph problems and mappings to nonmonotonic formalisms can be found in [Cholewiński et al. 1995, Niemelä and Simons 1996].

We illustrate the approach by presenting mappings from the 3-colorability and Hamiltonian circuit problems to normal logic programs with the stable model semantics. First, we consider the 3-colorability problem, i.e., the problem of assigning each vertex of a given graph one of three colors such that if two vertices are connected with an arc, they do not have the same color. Given a graph we construct a logic program as follows: (i) a set of atomic facts of the form $vertex(v)$ and $arc(v,u)$ corresponding to the vertices and arcs of the graph is taken and (ii) the following rules are included

$$color(V, blue) \leftarrow vertex(V), not\ color(V, green), not\ color(V, red)$$

$$color(V, green) \leftarrow vertex(V), not\ color(V, blue), not\ color(V, red)$$

$$color(V, red) \leftarrow vertex(V), not\ color(V, green), not\ color(V, blue)$$

$$noncoloring \leftarrow arc(V, U), color(V, C), color(U, C)$$

$$p \leftarrow not\ p, noncoloring$$

Now the program has a stable model if and only if there is a 3-coloring of the graph. In fact, the coloring can be read from the stable model directly by taking the facts of the form $color(v, c)$ true in the model. For systems supporting query-evaluation in the form of finding stable models where a given query holds, benchmarks are obtained by removing the last rule. Then there is a 3-coloring of the graph if and only if the resulting program has a stable model not containing *noncoloring*.

The 3-colorability problem does not seem to require the enhanced expressivity of nonmonotonic formalisms and can be mapped straightforwardly to, e.g., propositional satisfiability. As an example where the expressivity of nonmonotonic logics provides compact representation we consider the Hamiltonian circuit problem, i.e., the problem of finding a path that visits each vertex of a given graph exactly once and returns to the starting vertex. The corresponding logic program is constructed as follows: (i) a set of atomic facts of the form $vertex(v)$ and $arc(v, u)$ corresponding to the vertices and arcs is taken, (ii) the following rules are included

$$hcircuit(V_1, V_2) \leftarrow arc(V_1, V_2), not\ otherroute(V_1, V_2)$$

$$otherroute(V_1, V_2) \leftarrow arc(V_1, V_2), hcircuit(V_1, V_3), not\ (V_2 = V_3)$$

$$otherroute(V_1, V_2) \leftarrow arc(V_1, V_2), hcircuit(V_3, V_2), not\ (V_1 = V_3)$$

$$reached(V_2) \leftarrow hcircuit(V_1, V_2), reached(V_1)$$

$$reached(V_2) \leftarrow hcircuit(V_1, V_2), initialnode(V_1)$$

$$noncircuit \leftarrow vertex(V), not\ reached(V)$$

$$p \leftarrow not\ p, noncircuit$$

and (iii) one of the vertices v is taken as the starting vertex ($initialnode(v)$ is added). The resulting program has a stable model if and only if the graph has a Hamiltonian circuit. Again, a stable model of the program provides directly a Hamiltonian circuit by the facts of the form $hcircuit(v, u)$ true in the model. A benchmark for query-evaluation can be obtained by removing the last rule. Then the graph has a Hamiltonian circuit if and only if the resulting program has a stable model not containing *noncircuit*.

6.2. Propositional Satisfiability

Propositional satisfiability problems can be employed as benchmarks for nonmonotonic reasoning systems in a similar way as the graph problems, i.e., by mapping sets of propositional formulae to nonmonotonic theories. Although general nonmonotonic logics contain classical logic, propositional satisfiability problems can provide interesting benchmarks for the nonmonotonic aspects of the logics, too. The idea is that propositional satisfiability is captured using the nonmonotonic primitives of the formalism rather than directly in terms of classical logical operators that are included in the formalism. In this way very challenging test cases for evaluating the implementation of the nonmonotonic primitives are obtained. For example, hard random satisfiability problems from the phase transition region [Crawford and Auton 1996] could be employed and results compared with the best satisfiability checkers. This approach has been used in [Niemelä and Simons 1997].

Here we demonstrate the idea by presenting a mapping from propositional satisfiability to the problem of finding a stable model. The mapping is devised in a way that very little classical reasoning is required and propositional satisfiability is reduced to the problem of handling the nonmonotonic operator *not* .

For a set of clauses S, we build a logic program as follows:

1. we introduce for each atom a appearing in S two atoms a and $\hat{a}$ and include two rules

$$\hat{a} \leftarrow not\ a$$

$$a \leftarrow not\ \hat{a}$$

2. for each clause in S, we introduce a new atom c and include one rule for each literal l in the clause as follows: if l is a positive atom a, take the rule $c \leftarrow a$ and if l is the negation of an atom a, add $c \leftarrow \hat{a}$ and

3. finally we include the rules

$$satisfied \leftarrow c_1, \dots, c_n$$

$$p \leftarrow not\ p, not\ satisfied$$

where $c_1, \dots, c_n$ are all the atoms introduced for the clauses in S.

Then the set of clauses S has a model if and only if the resulting program has a stable model. The propositional model is obtained from the stable model by assigning true for atoms true in the stable model and assigning false to the rest of the atoms (for atoms a for which $\hat{a}$ is true in the stable model). For query-evaluation a benchmark is obtained by removing the last rule. Then the set of clauses S has a model if and only if the resulting program has a stable model containing the atom *satisfied*.

6.3. Planning

Planning provides particularly interesting benchmarks for nonmonotonic reasoning systems because this is a domain from which some of the main motivation for developing nonmonotonic formalisms originates. In planning difficult issues related to reasoning about action and change such as the frame problem have to be addressed and the expressivity of the nonmonotonic formalisms can be utilized to overcome some of the difficulties. However, a detailed account of using nonmonotonic formalisms in planning is beyond the scope of this article. Instead, we illustrate with an example of blocks world planning how planning problems can be mapped to nonmonotonic reasoning problems. For more detailed accounts, we refer the reader, e.g., to [Gelfond and Lifschitz 1993, Dimopoulos, Nebel and Koehler 1997].

In the blocks world we are given initial conditions of blocks on a table stating how they are stacked on top of each other, similar goal conditions and a robot that is able to move blocks. The aim is to generate a plan for the robot to move blocks from the initial configuration so that the goal conditions are satisfied. Families of benchmarks are obtained by increasing the number of blocks and the complexity of the initial and goal conditions.

Consider the following example. In the initial configuration we have three blocks a, b, c such that b and c are on the table and a is on top of b. The goal conditions are that c is on a and b is on c. A solution for this planning problem is a sequence of moves where a is moved on the table, c is moved on a and finally b is moved on c.

The idea is to map a planning problem to a logic program such that stable models correspond to valid plans. For formalizing blocks world planning we use situations where facts hold. We assume that we have situations $t_0, \ldots, t_n$ where t_0 is the initial situation and a predicate $nextstate$ specifying the order of the situations, i.e., for which $nextstate(t_{i+1}, t_i)$ for $i = 0, \ldots, n-1$ holds. We employ predicates $on(X, Y, T)$ (X is on Y in the situation T) and $moveop(X, Y, T)$ (X is moved on Y in the situation T) and assume that the available blocks are specified using facts of the form $block(b)$.

The initial conditions are straightforward to formalize. For instance, for the example above it is sufficient to include the facts

$$on(a, b, t_0)$$
$$on(b, table, t_0)$$
$$on(c, table, t_0)$$

In order to capture the goal conditions we employ a predicate $goal$ which holds in any situation where the goal conditions have been reached and in all subsequent situations. For the example above, the resulting rules are

$$goal(T) \leftarrow on(b, c, T), on(c, a, T), on(a, table, T)$$
$$goal(T_2) \leftarrow nextstate(T_2, T_1), goal(T_1)$$
$$goal \leftarrow goal(T)$$
$$p \leftarrow not\ p, not\ goal$$

In order to formalize the preconditions and effects of the move operator we use the following rules.

$$moveop(X, Y, T) \leftarrow moveable(X), block(Y), not\ (X = Y),$$
$$on\_something(X, T),$$
$$not\ covered(X, T), not\ covered(Y, T),$$
$$not\ blocked\_move(X, Y, T)$$

$$on(X, Y, T_2) \leftarrow nextstate(T_2, T_1), moveop(X, Y, T_1)$$
$$on\_something(X, T) \leftarrow on(X, Z, T)$$
$$covered(X, T) \leftarrow moveable(X), on(Z, X, T)$$
$$moveable(X) \leftarrow block(X), not\ (X = table)$$

It is enough to provide a frame axiom only for the predicate *on*.

$$on(X, Y, T_2) \leftarrow nextstate(T_2, T_1), on(X, Y, T_1), not\ moving(X, T_1)$$
$$moving(X, T) \leftarrow moveop(X, Y, T)$$

What remains to be stated are the blocking conditions for the moves. The first set of conditions covers the cases where the goal has been reached or the instance of the move operator has not been chosen.

$$blocked\_move(X, Y, T) \leftarrow moveable(X), block(Y), goal(T)$$
$$blocked\_move(X, Y, T) \leftarrow on\_something(X, T), block(Y), not\ moveop(X, Y, T)$$

The second set depends on whether concurrency is allowed, i.e., whether more than one operator can be applied in a situation. We allow this and block only the operator instances whose effects are in conflict.

$$blocked\_move(X, Y, T) \leftarrow moveable(X), block(Y),$$
$$moveop(X, Z, T), not\ (Y = Z)$$
$$blocked\_move(X, Y, T) \leftarrow moveable(X), moving(Y, T)$$
$$blocked\_move(X, Y, T) \leftarrow moveable(X), block(Y), not\ (Y = table),$$
$$moveop(Z, Y, T), not\ (X = Z)$$

For a program constructed like this it holds that the program has a stable model if and only if there is a sequence of moves from the initial configuration to a situation satisfying the goal conditions that can be executed concurrently in at most n steps. For query-evaluation a benchmark is obtained by removing the rule with p in the head. Then there is plan if and only if the resulting program has a stable model containing *goal*.

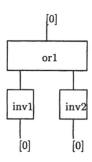

Figure 9: A Circuit

6.4. Diagnosis Problems

Model-based diagnosis of technical systems provides an interesting class of benchmark problems for two reasons. Firstly, the examples which stem from hardware design usually contain a large number of clauses, which have to be handled efficiently in order to solve realistic problems. Secondly, the diagnosis task involves minimal model reasoning by definition, and hence techniques from nonmonotonic reasoning have to be applied.

According to [Reiter 1987] a simulation model of the technical device under consideration is constructed and is used to predict its normal behavior. By comparing this prediction with the actual behavior it is possible to derive a diagnosis. This approach uses a logical description of the device, called the system description (SD), formalized by a set of first–order formulas. The system description consists of a set of axioms characterizing the behavior of system components of certain types. The topology is modeled separately by a set of facts. The diagnostic problem is described by system description SD, a set $COMP$ of components and a set OBS of observations (logical facts). With each component we associate a behavioral mode: $Mode(c, Ok)$ means that component c is behaving correctly, while $Mode(c, Ab)$ (abbreviated by $Ab(c)$) denotes that c is faulty.

A *Diagnosis* of $(SD, COMP, OBS)$ is a set $\Delta \subseteq COMP$, such that

$$SD \cup OBS \cup \{Mode(c, Ab)|c \in \Delta\} \cup \{\neg Mode(c, Ab)|c \in COMP - \Delta\}$$

is consistent. Δ is called a *Minimal Diagnosis, if and only if* it is the minimal set (wrt. $\subseteq$) with this property.

The set of all minimal diagnoses can be large for complex technical devices. Therefore, stronger criteria than minimality are often used to further discriminate among the minimal diagnoses.

These criteria are usually based on the probability or cardinality of diagnoses. In the remainder of this section we will use restrictions on the cardinality of diagnoses. We say that a diagnosis satisfies the *n-fault assumption if and only if* $|\Delta| \leq n$.

As an example consider the simple digital circuit in Figure 9 consisting of an or–gate (*or*1) and two inverters *inv*1 and *inv*2. The system description SD is given by the following propositional clauses:[20].

OR1: $ab(or1), high(or1, i1), high(or1, i2) \leftarrow high(or1, o)$
            $ab(or1), high(or1, o) \leftarrow high(or1, i1)$
            $ab(or1), high(or1, o) \leftarrow high(or1, i2)$

INV1: $ab(inv1) \leftarrow high(inv1, o), high(inv1, i)$
            $ab(inv1), high(inv1, i), high(inv1, o) \leftarrow$

INV2: $ab(inv2) \leftarrow high(inv2, o), high(inv2, i)$
            $ab(inv2), high(inv2, i), high(inv2, o) \leftarrow$

$high(or1, i1) \leftarrow high(inv1, o)$ $high(or1, i2) \leftarrow high(inv2, o)$
$high(inv1, o) \leftarrow high(or1, i1)$ $high(inv2, o) \leftarrow high(or1, i2)$

We observe that both inputs of the circuit have low voltage and the output also has low voltage, i.e. the clause set of OBS is given by $\{\leftarrow high(inv1, i), \leftarrow high(inv2, i), \leftarrow high(or1, o)\}$.

The expected behavior of the circuit given that both inputs are low would be high voltage at the outputs of both inverters and consequently high voltage at the output of the or–gate. This model of the correctly functioning device, namely

$$I_0 = \{high(inv1, o), high(inv2, o), high(or1, i1), high(or1, i2), high(or1, o)\},$$

can be computed very efficiently even for large devices by domain–specific tools, e.g. circuit simulators.

[Baumgartner, Fröhlich, Furbach and Nejdl 1997*a*] show how the diagnosis task can be efficiently solved by a general first-order theorem prover, based on model generation. The proof system used therein is based on the hyper tableau calculus presented above. In this approach a minimal diagnosis is a computed model of a clause set, as given in our example. However, it turned out, that for examples from the ISCAS-85 benchmarks [Isc 1985], which is a standard from the diagnosis literature, one needs additional domain dependent pruning techniques of the search space. This can be achieved by taking into account an initial model of a correctly functioning device I_0, as it is called in the above example. This set of atoms can be used in a compilation step to transform the given clause sets for the diagnosis task, such that only deviations from this initial model are computed. It is shown in [Baumgartner, Fröhlich, Furbach and Nejdl 1997*b*], that these deviations correspond to the minimal diagnosis. In Figure 10 some experiments from the benchmark suites are reported.

---

[20]These formulas can be obtained by instantiating a first-order description of the gate functions with the structural information. For instance, the clauses for the OR1 gate stem from the formula
$\forall OR\_gate : (\neg ab(OR\_gate) \rightarrow (high(OR\_gate, o) \leftrightarrow (high(OR\_gate, i1) \lor high(OR\_gate, i2))))$

Name	# Gates	# Clauses	# Diagnosis	Time (sec.)	# Steps	All?
C499	202	1685	2	5	3015	no
2-fault:			67	50	27323	yes
C880	383	2776	19	2	161	yes
C1355	546	3839	5	47	24699	no
2-fault:			5	2948	1284454	no
C2670	1193	8260	31	6	533	yes
C3540	1669	10658	3	10853	1473572	yes
C5315	2307	16122	5	13	3071	yes

Figure 10: ISCAS'85 Circuits and runtime results.

7. Conclusion

Reasoning in everyday life is quite different from the kind of reasoning considered in classical formal logic. While the latter has been investigated exhaustively in this century, the former has been brought to attention in the early research on artificial intelligence. In many areas (like planning or diagnosis) we are faced up with problems related to *uncertainty* about the current situation: we do not have complete knowledge, neither about the facts that are true nor about the rules describing how the world evolves. Many competing methods arose out of this problem: *fuzzy logic, probabilistic reasoning, case-based reasoning, qualitative reasoning, spatial reasoning* etc. Most, if not all of them, have an important nonmonotonic component. Recently there has been growing interest in *Multi-Agent Systems*. A particular system, based on logic programming and incorporating the above mentioned methods is described in [Subrahmanian, Bonatti, Dix, Eiter, Kraus, Özcan and Ross 2000] (see also [Dix, Subrahmanian and Pick 2000, Eiter and Subrahmanian 1999, Eiter, Subrahmanian and Pick 1999, Dix, Nanni and Subrahmanian 2000, Dix, Kraus and Subrahmanian 2001]).

We tried in this chapter to provide the reader with a concise yet understandable description of the state-of-the-art in nonmonotonic reasoning, with special attention to implementations. While we left out many of the numerous theoretical variants of classical frameworks, we hope not to have forgotten any of the implemented systems that are currently in use. We again refer to the following webpage which is and will be actively maintained and contains information on various logic programming systems that concentrate on non-monotonic aspects: <URL:http://www.uni-koblenz.de/ag-ki/LP/>.

The future of nonmonotonic reasoning (see [Dix 1995b, Dix 1998] will heavily depend on the applications such systems can successfully cope with. With applications, we mean *real-world* applications and not the well-known blocksworlds examples or the good old Tweety.

In our section on *Benchmarks* we tried to point to some interesting areas. They all seem to contain promising problems for nonmonotonic systems. Of course, much more applications are needed and future work will show if nonmonotonic reasoning can offer valuable tools to deal with them.

We end this article with giving some pointers to actively maintained web-pages providing the interested reader with more information about nonmonotonic reasoning and nonmonotonic aspects of logic programming (see also the recent [Dix and Lobo 1999]):

General Sites:

- **NMR:** <URL:http://www.medg.lcs.mit.edu/nm/,
- **LP:** <URL:http://www.cwi.nl/projects/alp/index.html,
- **LPNMR:** <URL:http://www.cs.engr.uky.edu/~lpnmr/,
- **CLN:** <URL:http://www.compulog.org/,
  <URL:http://www.cs.nmsu.edu/~complog/,

Conferences:

- **NMR 00:** <URL:http://www.cs.engr.uky.edu/nmr2000>,
- **ICLP 99:** <URL:http://www.cs.kuleuven.ac.be/~iclp99>,
- **LPNMR 99:** <URL:http://www.dbai.tuwien.ac.at/lpnmr99/>,
- **CL 00:** <URL:http://www.doc.ic.ac.uk/cl2000/>.

Acknowledgments

Many people contributed to this article. Most of them indirectly (via many coauthored papers or books) others more directly, by giving us suggestions on how to modify and strengthen this paper. We owe special thanks to Gerd Brewka and Mirek Truszczyński for a careful reading of drafts of this article. Nevertheless, all remaining typos and mistakes are under our sole responsibility.

Bibliography

APT K., BLAIR H. AND WALKER A. [1988], Towards a theory of declarative knowledge, *in* J. Minker, ed., 'Foundations of Deductive Databases and Logic Programming', Morgan Kaufmann Publishers, Los Altos, pp. 89–148.

APT K. R. AND BOL R. N. [1994], 'Logic Programming and Negation: A Survey', *Journal of Logic Programming* **19-20**, 9–71.

APT K. R. AND DOETS H. [1994], 'A new definition of SLDNF-resolution', *Journal of Logic Programming* **18**(2), 177–190.

ARAVINDAN C. [1996], An abductive framework for negation in disjunctive logic programming, *in* 'Proc. JELIA 96', number 1126 *in* 'LNAI', European Workshop on Logic in AI, Springer.

ARAVINDAN C., DIX J. AND NIEMELÄ I. [1997a], 'Dislop: A research project on disjunctive logic programming', *AI Communications* **10**(3/4), 151–165.

ARAVINDAN C., DIX J. AND NIEMELÄ I. [1997b], DisLoP: Towards a Disjunctive Logic Programming System, *in* J. Dix, U. Furbach and A. Nerode, eds, 'Logic Programming and Non-Monotonic Reasoning, Proceedings of the Fourth International Conference', LNAI 1265, Springer, Berlin, pp. 342–353.

BAADER F. AND HOLLUNDER B. [1995], 'Embedding defaults into terminological knowledge representation formalisms', *Journal of Automated Reasoning* **14**, 149–180.

BAKER A. B. [1991], 'Nonmonotonic reasoning in the framework of situation calculus', *Artificial Intelligence* **49**, 5–23.

BALCÁZAR J., DÍAZ I. AND GABARRÓ J. [1988], *Structural Complexity I*, Springer-Verlag, Berlin.

BARAL C. AND GELFOND M. [1994], 'Logic Programming and Knowlege Representation', *Journal of Logic Programming* **19-20**, 73–148.

BAUMGARTNER P. [1998], Hyper Tableaux — The Next Generation, *in* H. de Swaart, ed., 'Automated Reasoning with Analytic Tableaux and Related Methods', number 1397 *in* 'Lecture Notes in Artificial Intelligence', Springer.

BAUMGARTNER P., FRÖHLICH P., FURBACH U. AND NEJDL W. [1997a], Semantically Guided Theorem Proving for Diagnosis Applications, *in* '15th International Joint Conference on Artificial Intelligence (IJCAI 97)', pp. 460–465.

BAUMGARTNER P., FRÖHLICH P., FURBACH U. AND NEJDL W. [1997b], Semantically Guided Theorem Proving for Diagnosis Applications, *in* '15th International Joint Conference on Artificial Intelligence (IJCAI 97)', International Joint Conference on Artificial Intelligence, Nagoya, pp. 460–465.

BAUMGARTNER P. AND FURBACH U. [1994a], 'Model Elimination without Contrapositives and its Application to PTTP', *Journal of Automated Reasoning* **13**, 339–359. Short version in: Proceedings of CADE-12, Springer LNAI 814, 1994, pp 87–101.

BAUMGARTNER P. AND FURBACH U. [1994b], PROTEIN: A *PRO*ver with a *T*heory Extension *I*nterface, *in* A. Bundy, ed., 'Automated Deduction – CADE-12', Vol. 814 of *Lecture Notes in Artificial Intelligence*, Springer, pp. 769–773.

BAUMGARTNER P. AND FURBACH U. [1997], Calculi for Disjunctive Logic Programming, *in* J. Maluszynski, ed., 'Logic Programming - Proceedings of the 1997 International Symposium', The MIT Press, Port Jefferson, New York.
    URL: *http://www.uni-koblenz.de/ peter/Publications/ilps97-proceedings.ps.gz*

BAUMGARTNER P., FURBACH U. AND NIEMELÄ I. [1996], Hyper Tableaux, *in* 'Proc. JELIA 96', number 1126 *in* 'LNAI', European Workshop on Logic in AI, Springer. (Long version in: *Fachberichte Informatik*, 8–96, Universität Koblenz-Landau).

BAUMGARTNER P., FURBACH U. AND STOLZENBURG F. [1997a], 'Computing Answers with Model Elimination', *Artificial Intelligence* **90**(1-2), 135–176.

BAUMGARTNER P., FURBACH U. AND STOLZENBURG F. [1997b], Model Elimination, Logic Programming and Computing Answers, *in* '14th International Joint Conference on Artificial Intelligence (IJCAI 95)', Vol. 1, International Joint Conference on Artificial Intelligence, Montreal, pp. 335–340.

BELL C., NERODE A., NG R. AND SUBRAHMANIAN V. [1994], 'Mixed integer programming methods for computing nonmonotonic deductive databases', *Journal of the Association for Computing Machinery* **41**(6), 1178–1215.

BEN-ELIYAHU R. AND DECHTER R. [1991], Default logic, propositional logic and constraints, *in* 'Proceedings of the 9th National Conference on Artificial Intelligence', The MIT Press, pp. 370–385.

BEN-ELIYAHU R. AND DECHTER R. [1992], Propositional semantics for default logic, *in* 'Working Notes of the 4th International Workshop on Nonmonotonic Reasoning', Plymouth, Vermont, USA, pp. 13–27.

BERMAN K. A., SCHLIPF J. S. AND FRANCO J. V. [1995], Computing the Well-Founded Semantics Faster, in A. Nerode, W. Marek and M. Truszczyński, eds, 'Logic Programming and Non-Monotonic Reasoning, Proceedings of the Third International Conference', LNCS 928, Springer, Berlin, pp. 113–126.

BIBEL, W. AND SCHMITT, P. H., EDS [1998], *Automated Deduction — A Basis for Applications*, Kluwer Academic Publishers.

BIDOIT N. AND FROIDEVAUX C. [1991a], 'General logical Databases and Programs: Default Logic Semantics and Stratification', *Information and Computation* 91, 15–54.

BIDOIT N. AND FROIDEVAUX C. [1991b], 'Negation by Default and unstratifiable logic Programs', *Theoretical Computer Science* 78, 85–112.

BIDOIT N. AND HULL R. [1986], Positivism vs. minimalism in deductive databases, in 'Proc. of the 5th ACM Symp. on Principles of Database Systems (PODS'86)', pp. 123–132.

BONATTI P. [1996], Sequent calculi for default and autoepistemic logics, in 'Proceedings of the Fifth Workshop on Theorem Proving with Analytic Tableaux and Related Methods', Springer-Verlag, Terrasini, Italy, pp. 127–142. Lecture Notes in Artificial Intelligence 1071.

BONATTI P. AND OLIVETTI N. [1997], A sequent calculus for skeptical default logic, in 'Proceedings of the International Conference on Automated Reasoning with Analytic Tableaux and Related Methods', Springer-Verlag, Pont-à-Mousson, France, pp. 107–121. Lecture Notes in Artificial Intelligence 1227.

BRASS S. AND DIX J. [1994], A disjunctive semantics based on unfolding and bottom-up evaluation, in B. Wolfinger, ed., 'Innovationen bei Rechen- und Kommunikationssystemen, *(IFIP '94-Congress, Workshop FG2: Disjunctive Logic Programming and Disjunctive Databases)*', Springer, Berlin, pp. 83–91.

BRASS S. AND DIX J. [1995], A General Approach to Bottom-Up Computation of Disjunctive Semantics, in J. Dix, L. Pereira and T. Przymusinski, eds, 'Nonmonotonic Extensions of Logic Programming', LNAI 927, Springer, Berlin, pp. 127–155.

BRASS S. AND DIX J. [1997], 'Characterizations of the Disjunctive Stable Semantics by Partial Evaluation', *Journal of Logic Programming* 32(3), 207–228. (Extended abstract appeared in: Characterizations of the Stable Semantics by Partial Evaluation *LPNMR, Proceedings of the Third International Conference, Kentucky*, pages 85–98, 1995. LNCS 928, Springer.).

BRASS S. AND DIX J. [1998], 'Characterizations of the Disjunctive Well-founded Semantics: Confluent Calculi and Iterated GCWA', *Journal of Automated Reasoning* 20(1), 143–165. (Extended abstract appeared in: Characterizing D-WFS: Confluence and Iterated GCWA. *Logics in Artificial Intelligence, JELIA '96*, pages 268–283, 1996. Springer, LNCS 1126.).

BRASS S. AND DIX J. [1999], 'Semantics of (Disjunctive) Logic Programs Based on Partial Evaluation', *Journal of Logic Programming* 38(2), 167–213. (Extended abstract appeared in: Disjunctive Semantics Based upon Partial and Bottom-Up Evaluation, *Proceedings of the 12-th International Logic Programming Conference, Tokyo*, pages 199–213, 1995. MIT Press.).

BRASS S., DIX J., FREITAG B. AND ZUKOWSKI [2001], 'Transformation-based bottom-up computation of the well-founded model', *Theory and Practice of Logic Programming* to appear.

BRASS S., DIX J., NIEMELÄ I. AND PRZYMUSINSKI T. [2001], 'On the Equivalence of the Static and Disjunctive Well-Founded Semantics and its Computation', *Theoretical Computer Science* 256.

BRASS S., DIX J., NIEMELÄ I. AND PRZYMUSINSKI T. C. [1998], A Comparison of the Static and the Disjunctive Well-founded Semantics and its Implementation, in A. G. Cohn, L. K. Schubert and S. C. Shapiro, eds, 'Principles of Knowledge Representation and Reasoning: Proceedings of the Sixth International Conference (KR '98)', San Francisco, CA, Morgan Kaufmann, pp. 74–85. appeared also as TR 17/97, University of Koblenz.

BRASS S., DIX J. AND PRZYMUSINSKI T. [1999], 'Computation of the semantics of autoepistemic belief theories', *Artificial Intelligence* 112(1-2), 104–123.

BRASS S., ZUKOWSKI U. AND FREITAG B. [1997], Transformation Based Bottom-Up Computation of the Well-Founded Model, in J. Dix, L. Pereira and T. Przymusinski, eds, 'Nonmonotonic Extensions of Logic Programming', LNAI 1216, Springer, Berlin, pp. 171–201.

BREWKA G. [1996], *Principles of Knowledge Representation*, CSLI, Dikran.

BREWKA G. AND DIX J. [2001], Knowledge representation with extended logic programs, *in* D. Gabbay and F. Guenthner, eds, 'Handbook of Philosophical Logic, 2nd Edition, Volume 6, Methodologies', Reidel Publ., chapter 6.

BREWKA G., DIX J. AND KONOLIGE K. [1997], *Nonmonotonic Reasoning: An Overview*, CSLI Lecture Notes 73, CSLI Publications, Stanford, CA.

BRY F. AND YAHYA A. [1996], Minimal Model Generation with Positive Unit Hyper-Resolution Tableaux, *in* P. Miglioli, U. Moscato, D. Mundici and M. Ornaghi, eds, 'Theorem Proving with Analytic Tableaux and Related Methods', number 1071 *in* 'Lecture Notes in Artificial Intelligence', Springer, pp. 143–159.

BUCCAFURRI F., LEONE N. AND RULLO P. [1996], 'Stable models and their computation for logic programming with inheritance and true negation', *Journal of Logic Programming* 27(1), 5–43.

BUCCAFURRI F., LEONE N. AND RULLO P. [1997], Strong and Weak Constraints in Disjunctive Datalog, *in* 'Proceedings of the 4th International Conference on Logic Programming and Non-Monotonic Reasoning (LPNMR '97)', Dagstuhl, Germany, pp. 2–17.

CADOLI M., DONINI F. M., LIBERATORE P. AND SCHAERF M. [1995], The size of a revised knowledge base, *in* 'PODS '95', pp. 151–162.

CADOLI M., DONINI F. M. AND SCHAERF M. [1996], 'Is intractability of non-monotonic reasoning a real drawback?', *Artificial Intelligence Journal* 88, 215–251.

CADOLI M., DONINI F. M., SCHAERF M. AND SILVESTRI R. [1997], 'On compact representations of propositional circumscription', *Theoretical Computer Science* 182, 183–202. (Extended abstract appeared in: On Compact Representations of Propositional Circumscription. *STACS '95*, pages 205–216, 1995.).

CADOLI M. AND LENZERINI M. [1990], The complexity of closed world reasoning and circumscription, *in* 'AAAI-90 — Proceedings of the 9th AAAI National Conference on Artificial Intelligence', The MIT Press, Boston, MA, USA, pp. 550–555.

CERI S., GOTTLOB G. AND TANCA L. [1990], *Logic Programming and Databases*, Surveys in Computer Science, Springer.

CHANDRA A. AND HAREL D. [1985], 'Horn clause queries and generalizations', *Journal of Logic Programming* 2, 1–15.

CHANG C.-L. AND LEE R. C.-T. [1973], *Symbolic Logic and Mechanical Theorem Proving*, Academic Press, New York.

CHELLAS B. [1980], *Modal Logic: an Introduction*, Cambridge University Press, Cambridge.

CHEN W., SWIFT T. AND WARREN D. S. [1995], 'Efficient Top-Down Computation of Queries under the Well-Founded Semantics', *Journal of Logic Programming* 24(3), 219–245.

CHEN W. AND WARREN D. S. [1993], 'A Goal Oriented Approach to Computing The Well-founded Semantics', *Journal of Logic Programming* 17, 279–300.

CHEN W. AND WARREN D. S. [1995], 'Computing of Stable Models and its Integration with Logical Query Processing', *IEEE Transactions on Knowledge and Data Engineering* 17, 279–300.

CHEN W. AND WARREN D. S. [1996], 'Tabled Evaluation with Delaying for General Logic Programs', *Journal of the ACM* 43(1), 20–74.

CHOLAK P. AND BLAIR H. [1994], 'The Complexity of Local Stratification', *Fundamenta Informaticae* **XXI**(4), 333–344.

CHOLEWIŃSKI P., MAREK V., MIKITIUK A. AND TRUSZCZYŃSKI M. [1995], Experimenting with nonmonotonic reasoning, *in* 'Proceedings of the 12th International Conference on Logic Programming', Tokyo, pp. 267–281.

CLARK K. L. [1978], Negation as Failure, *in* H. Gallaire and J. Minker, eds, 'Logic and Data-Bases', Plenum, New York, pp. 293–322.

CRAWFORD J. AND AUTON L. [1996], 'Experimental results on the crossover point in random 3-SAT', *Artificial Intelligence* 81(1), 31–57.

DIMOPOULOS Y., NEBEL B. AND KOEHLER J. [1997], Encoding planning problems in non-monotonic logic programs, *in* 'Proceedings of the Fourth European Conference on Planning', Springer-Verlag, Toulouse, France. To appear.

DIX J. [1992a], A Framework for Representing and Characterizing Semantics of Logic Programs, *in* B. Nebel, C. Rich and W. Swartout, eds, 'Principles of Knowledge Representation and Reasoning: Proceedings of the Third International Conference (KR '92)', San Mateo, CA, Morgan Kaufmann, pp. 591–602.

DIX J. [1992b], Classifying Semantics of Disjunctive Logic Programs, *in* K. R. Apt, ed., 'LOGIC PROGRAMMING: Proceedings of the 1992 Joint International Conference and Symposium', MIT Press, Cambridge, Mass., pp. 798–812.

DIX J. [1995a], 'A Classification-Theory of Semantics of Normal Logic Programs: II. Weak Properties', *Fundamenta Informaticae* **XXII(3)**, 257–288.

DIX J. [1995b], 'Detailed Report on the First LP & NMR retreat', *AI Communications* **Vol. 8, No. 1**, 39–43. Also in Computational Logic, Vol. 2, 1995, pages 94–97.

DIX J. [1995c], Semantics of Logic Programs: Their Intuitions and Formal Properties. An Overview., *in* A. Fuhrmann and H. Rott, eds, 'Logic, Action and Information – Essays on Logic in Philosophy and Artificial Intelligence', DeGruyter, pp. 241–327.

DIX J. [1998], 'The Logic Programming Paradigm', *AI Communications* **Vol. 11, No. 3**, 39–43. Short version in Newsletter of ALP, Vol. 11(3), 1998, pages 10–14.

DIX, J., FURBACH, U. AND NERODE, A., EDS [1997], *Logic Programming and Nonmonotonic Reasoning*, LNAI 1265, Springer, Berlin.

DIX J., KRAUS S. AND SUBRAHMANIAN V. S. [2001], 'Temporal agent reasoning', *Artificial Intelligence* .

DIX J. AND LOBO J. [1999], 'Logic Programming and non-monotonic reasoning', *Special Issue of the Annals in Mathematics and Artificial Intelligence* **25(3–4)**.

DIX J. AND MÜLLER M. [1994a], Partial Evaluation and Relevance for Approximations of the Stable Semantics, *in* Z. Ras and M. Zemankova, eds, 'Proceedings of the 8th Int. Symp. on Methodologies for Intelligent Systems, Charlotte, NC, 1994', LNAI 869, Springer, Berlin, pp. 511–520.

DIX J. AND MÜLLER M. [1994b], The Stable Semantics and its Variants: A Comparison of Recent Approaches, *in* L. Dreschler-Fischer and B. Nebel, eds, 'Proceedings of the 18th German Annual Conference on Artificial Intelligence (KI '94), Saarbrücken, Germany', LNAI 861, Springer, Berlin, pp. 82–93.

DIX J., NANNI M. AND SUBRAHMANIAN V. [2000], 'Probabilistic Agent Programs', *ACM Transactions of Computational Logic* **I(2)**, 207–245.

DIX J. AND OSORIO M. [1999], 'Confluent rewriting systems in non-monotonic reasoning', *Computacion y Sistemas* **Volume II, No. 2-3**, 104–123.

DIX J., OSORIO M. AND ZEPEDA C. [2001], 'A General Theory of Confluent Rewriting Systems for Logic Programming and its Applications', *Annals of Pure and Applied Logic* to appear.

DIX, J., PEREIRA, L. AND PRZYMUSINSKI, T., EDS [1995], *Non-Monotonic Extensions of Logic Programming*, LNAI 927, Springer, Berlin.

DIX, J., PEREIRA, L. AND PRZYMUSINSKI, T., EDS [1997], *Non-Monotonic Extensions of Logic Programming*, LNAI 1216, Springer, Berlin.

DIX, J., PEREIRA, L. AND PRZYMUSINSKI, T., EDS [1998], *Logic Programming and Knowledge Representation*, LNAI 1471, Springer, Berlin.

DIX J. AND SCHMITT P. [1993], 'Nichtmonotones Schließen: Wieviel Nichtmonotonie ist nötig?', *Kognitionswissenschaft* **3**, 53–69.

DIX J. AND STOLZENBURG F. [1998], 'A Framework to incorporate Nonmonotonic Reasoning into Constraint Logic Programming', *Journal of Logic Programming* **37(1,2,3)**, 47—76. Special Issue on *Constraint Logic Programming*, Guest Editors: Kim Marriott and Peter Stuckey.

DIX J., SUBRAHMANIAN V. AND PICK G. [2000], 'Meta Agent Programs', *Journal of Logic Programming* **46(1–2)**, 1–60.

DOHERTY P., LUKASZEWICZ W. AND SZALAS A. [1995], Computing circumscription revisited: Preliminary report, *in* 'Proceedings of the 14th International Joint Conference on Artificial Intelligence', Morgan Kaufmann Publishers, Montreal, Canada, pp. 1502–1508.

DOWLING W. AND GALLIER J. [1984], 'Linear-time algorithms for testing the satisfiability of propositional Horn formulae', *Journal of Logic Programming* **3**, 267–284.

DUNG P. M. [1992], 'On the relations between stable and wellfounded semantics of logic programs', *Theoretical Computer Science* **105**, 7–25.

EITER T. AND GOTTLOB G. [1993], 'Propositional Circumscription and Extended Closed World Reasoning are Π_2^P-complete', *Theoretical Computer Science* **144**(2), 231–245, Addendum: vol. 118, p. 315, 1993.

EITER T. AND GOTTLOB G. [1995a], 'On the Computational Cost of Disjunctive Logic Programming: Propositional Case', *Annals of Mathematics and Artificial Intelligence* **15**(3/4), 289–323.

EITER T. AND GOTTLOB G. [1995b], 'The Complexity of Logic-Based Abduction', *Journal of the Association for Computing Machinery* **42**(1), 3–42.

EITER T. AND GOTTLOB G. [1996], 'Mächtigkeit von Logikprogrammierung über Datenbanken', *KI* **3**, 32–39.

EITER T., GOTTLOB G. AND MANNILA H. [1997], 'Disjunctive Datalog', *ACM Transactions on Database Systems* **22**(3), 364–417.

EITER T., LEONE N., MATEIS C., PFEIFER G. AND SCARCELLO F. [1997], A Deductive System for Nonmonotonic Reasoning, *in* J. Dix, U. Furbach and A. Nerode, eds, 'Proceedings of the 4th International Conference on Logic Programming and Nonmonotonic Reasoning (LPNMR '97)', number 1265 *in* 'Lecture Notes in AI (LNAI)', Springer, Berlin.

EITER T., LEONE N., MATEIS C., PFEIFER G. AND SCARCELLO F. [1998], The KR System dlv: Progress Report, Comparisons and Benchmarks., *in* 'Proceedings Sixth International Conference on Principles of Knowledge Representation and Reasoning (KR'98)', pp. 406–417.

EITER T., SUBRAHMANIAN V. AND PICK G. [1999], 'Heterogeneous Active Agents, I: Semantics', *Artificial Intelligence* **108**(1-2), 179–255.

EITER T. AND SUBRAHMANIAN V. S. [1999], 'Heterogeneous Active Agents, II: Algorithms and Complexity', *Artificial Intelligence* **108**(1-2), 257–307.

ETHERINGTON D. W. AND REITER R. [1983], On Inheritance Hierarchies with Exceptions, *in* 'Proceedings AAAI'.

FAGES F. [1993], 'Consistency of Clark's completion and existence of stable models', *Methods of Logic in Computer Science* **2**.

FERNANDEZ J. AND MINKER J. [91], Bottom-up evaluation of hierarchical disjunctive deductive databases, *in* K. Furukawa, ed., 'Proc. 8th International Conference on Logic Programming', pp. 660–675.

FITTING M. [1990], *First-Order Logic and Automated Theorem Proving*, Springer-Verlag, New York.

FITTING M. C. [1985], 'A Kripke-Kleene Semantics of logic Programs', *Journal of Logic Programming* **4**, 295–312.

GABBAY D. [1984], Theoretical Foundations for Non-Monotonic Reasoning in Expert- Systems, *in* K. R. Apt, ed., 'Logics and Models of Concurrent Systems', Springer, Berlin, pp. 439–458.

GAREY M. AND JOHNSON D. [1979], *Computers and Intractability*, W.H. Freeman and Company, San Francisco.

GELFOND M. AND LIFSCHITZ V. [1988], The Stable Model Semantics for Logic Programming, *in* R. Kowalski and K. Bowen, eds, '5th Conference on Logic Programming', MIT Press, pp. 1070–1080.

GELFOND M. AND LIFSCHITZ V. [1990], Logic Program with Classical Negation, *in* D. H. Warren and P. Szeredi, eds, 'Proceedings of the 7th Int. Conf. on Logic Programming', MIT, pp. 579–597.

GELFOND M. AND LIFSCHITZ V. [1993], 'Representing Actions and Change by Logic Programs', *Journal of Logic Programming* **17**, 301–322.

GINSBERG M. [1989], 'A circumscriptive theorem prover', *Artificial Intelligence* **39**, 209–230.

GOGIC G., PAPADIMITRIOU C., SELMAN B. AND KAUTZ H. [1995], The Comparative Linguistics of Knowledge Representation, *in* 'Proceedings of the 14th International Joint Conference on Artificial Intelligence', Morgan Kaufmann Publishers, Montreal, Canada, pp. 862–869.

GOTTLOB G. [1992], 'Complexity results for nonmonotonic logics', *Journal of Logic and Computation* **2**(3), 397–425.

GOTTLOB G. [1995], 'The complexity of default reasoning under the stationary fixed point semantics', *Information and Computation* **121**, 81–92.

HÄHNLE R. AND PAPE C. [1997], Ordered tableaux: Extensions and applications, *in* D. Galmiche, ed., 'Automated Reasoning with Tableaux and Related Methods', number 1227 *in* 'LNAI', Springer, pp. 173–187.

HUGHES G. AND CRESSWELL M. [1984], *A Companion to Modal Logic*, Methuen and Co., London.

INOUE K., KOSHIMURA M. AND HASEGAWA R. [1992], Embedding negation as failure into a model generation theorem prover, *in* 'The 11th International Conference on Automated Deduction', Springer-Verlag, Saratoga Springs, NY, USA, pp. 400–415.

ISC [1985], 'The ISCAS-85 Benchmarks', http://www.cbl.ncsu.edu/www/CBL_Docs/iscas85.html.

JOHNSON D. [1990], A catalog of complexity classes, *in* J. van Leeuwen, ed., 'Handbook of Theoretical Computer Science', Vol. A. Algorithms and Complexity, Elsevier, pp. 67–161.

JUNKER U. AND KONOLIGE K. [1990], Computing the extensions of autoepistemic and default logics with a truth maintenance system, *in* 'Proceedings of the 8th National Conference on Artificial Intelligence', MIT Press, Boston, MA, USA, pp. 278–283.

KAMINSKI M. [1995], 'A Comparative Study of Open Default Theories', *Artificial Intelligence* **77**, 285–319.

KARTHA G. N. AND LIFSCHITZ V. [1995], A Simple Formalization of Actions Using Circumsription, *in* C. S. Mellish, ed., '14th IJCAI', Vol. 2, Morgan Kaufmann, pp. 1970–1975.

KAUTZ H. AND SELMAN B. [1991], 'Hard problems for simple default logics', *Artificial Intelligence* **49**, 243–279.

KONOLIGE K. [1991], Quantification in autoepistemic logic, Technical Note 510, SRI International, Menlo Park, California, USA.

KONOLIGE K. [1994], Autoepistemic logic, *in* D. Gabbay, C. Hogger and J. Robinson, eds, 'Handbook of Logic and Artificial Intelligence and Logic Programming, Volume 3: Nonmonotonic Reasoning and Uncertain Reasoning', Oxford University Press, pp. 217–295.

KOWALSKI R. A. AND KUEHNER D. [1971], 'Linear resolution with selection function', *Artificial Intelligence* **2**, 227–260.

KRAUS S., LEHMANN D. AND MAGIDOR M. [1990], 'Nonmonotonic Reasoning, Preferential Models and Cumulative Logics', *Artificial Intelligence* **44**(1), 167–207.

KÜHN M. [1997], Rigid Hypertableaux, *in* G. Brewka, C. Habel and B. Nebel, eds, 'KI-97: Advances in Artificial Intelligence', number 1303 *in* 'LNAI', Springer, pp. 87–99.

LEHMANN D. AND MAGIDOR M. [1992], 'What does a conditional knowledge base entail?', *Artificial Intelligence* **55**, 1–60.

LEONE N., ROMEO M., RULLO P. AND SACCÀ D. [1993], Effective implementation of negation in database logic query languages, *in* 'LOGIDATA+: Deductive Database with Complex Objects', LNCS 701, pp. 159–175.

LEONE N. AND RULLO P. [1992], 'Safe computation of the well-founded semantics of datalog queries', *Information Systems* **17**(1), 17–31.

LEONE N., RULLO P. AND SCARCELLO F. [1997], 'Disjunctive stable models: Unfounded sets, fixpoint semantics and computation', *Information and Computation* **135**(2), 69–112.

LETZ R., MAYR K. AND GOLLER C. [1994], 'Controlled Integrations of the Cut Rule into Connection Tableau Calculi', *Journal of Automated Reasoning* **13**.

LIFSCHITZ V. [1985], Computing Circumscription, *in* 'Proceedings of the International Joint Conference on Artificial Intelligence, Los Angeles, California', pp. 121–127.

LIFSCHITZ V. [1989], Benchmark Problems for Formal NMR, Version 2.00, *in* Reinfrank, de Kleer, Ginsberg and Sandewall, eds, 'Non-Monotonic Reasoning', LNAI 346, Springer, Berlin, pp. 202–219.

LIFSCHITZ V. [1994], *Circumscription*, Clarendon, Oxford, pp. 297–353.

LLOYD J. W. [1987], *Foundations of Logic Programming*, Springer, Berlin. 2nd edition.

LOBO J., MINKER J. AND RAJASEKAR A. [1992], *Foundations of Disjunctive Logic Programming*, MIT Press.

LOVELAND D. [1968], 'Mechanical Theorem Proving by Model Elimination', *JACM* 15(2).

LOVELAND D. [1969], 'A Simplified Version for the Model Elimination Theorem Proving Procedure', *Journal of the Association for Computing Machinery* 16(3).

LOVELAND D. [1991], 'Near-Horn Prolog and Beyond', *Journal of Automated Reasoning* 7, 1–26.

MAKINSON D. [1994], General Patterns in Nonmonotonic Reasoning, *in* D. Gabbay, C. Hogger and J. Robinson, eds, 'Handbook of Logic in Artificial Intelligence and Logic Programming Vol. 3, Nonmonotonic and Uncertain Reasoning', Oxford University Press, chapter 3, pp. 35–110.

MANTHEY R. AND BRY F. [1988], SATCHMO: a theorem prover implemented in Prolog, *in* E. Lusk and R. Overbeek, eds, 'Proceedings of the 9th Conference on Automated Deduction, Argonne, Illinois, May 1988', Vol. 310 of *Lecture Notes in Computer Science*, Springer, pp. 415–434.

MAREK W. [1989], 'Stable theories in autoepistemic logic', *Fundamenta Informaticae* 12, 243–254.

MAREK, W., NERODE, A. AND TRUSZCZYŃSKI, M., EDS [1995], *Logic Programming and Non-monotonic Reasoning*, LNAI 928, Springer, Berlin.

MAREK W., SCHWARZ G. AND TRUSZCZYŃSKI M. [1993], 'Modal nonmonotonic logics: Ranges, characterization, computation', *Journal of the Association for Computing Machinery* 40(4), 963–990.

MAREK W. AND TRUSZCZYŃSKI M. [1991a], 'Autoepistemic logic', *Journal of the Association for Computing Machinery* 38, 588–619.

MAREK W. AND TRUSZCZYŃSKI M. [1991b], Computing intersection of autoepistemic expansions, *in* 'Proceedings of the 1st International Workshop on Logic Programming and Non-monotonic Reasoning', The MIT Press, Washington, D.C., USA, pp. 37–50.

MAREK W. AND TRUSZCZYŃSKI M. [1993], *Nonmonotonic Logics; Context-Dependent Reasoning*, 1st edn, Springer, Berlin.

McCARTHY J. [1979], First order theories of individual concepts and propositions, *in* B. Meltzer and D. Michie, eds, 'Machine Intelligence 9', Edinburgh University Press, Edinburgh, pp. 120–147.

McCARTHY J. [1980], 'Circumscription: A Form of Nonmonotonic Reasoning', *Artificial Intelligence* 13, 27–39.

McCARTHY J. [1986], 'Applications of Circumscription to formalizing Common-Sense Reasoning', *Artificial Intelligence* 28, 89–116.

McDERMOTT D. [1982], 'Non-monotonic logic II', *Journal of the Association for Computing Machinery* 29, 33–57.

McDERMOTT D. AND DOYLE J. [1980], 'Non-monotonic logic I', *Artificial Intelligence* 13, 41–72.

MINKER J. [1993], 'An Overview of Nonmonotonic Reasoning and Logic Programming', *Journal of Logic Programming, Special Issue* 17(2/3/4), 95–126.

MINKER J. [1996], Logic and databases: A 20 year retrospective, *in* D. Pedreschi and C. Zaniolo, eds, 'Proceedings of the International Workshop on Logic in Databases (LID)', LNCS 1154, Springer, Berlin, pp. 3–58.

MINKER J. AND ZANON G. [1982], 'An extension to linear resolution with selection function', *Information Processing Letters* 14(3), 191–194.

MOORE R. [1985], 'Semantical considerations on nonmonotonic logic', *Artificial Intelligence* **25**, 75–94.

NERODE A., NG R. AND SUBRAHMANIAN V. [1995], 'Computing circumscriptive databases: I. theory and algorithms', *Information and Computation* **116**, 58–80.

NIEMELÄ I. [1990], Towards automatic autoepistemic reasoning, *in* 'Proceedings of the European Workshop on Logics in Artificial Intelligence—JELIA'90', Springer-Verlag, Amsterdam, The Netherlands, pp. 428–443.

NIEMELÄ I. [1991], Constructive tightly grounded autoepistemic reasoning, *in* 'Proceedings of the 12th International Joint Conference on Artificial Intelligence', Morgan Kaufmann Publishers, Sydney, Australia, pp. 399–404.

NIEMELÄ I. [1992], 'On the decidability and complexity of autoepistemic reasoning', *Fundamenta Informaticae* **17**(1,2), 117–155.

NIEMELÄ I. [1995a], 'A decision method for nonmonotonic reasoning based on autoepistemic reasoning', *Journal of Automated Reasoning* **14**, 3–42.

NIEMELÄ I. [1995b], Towards efficient default reasoning, *in* 'Proceedings of the 14th International Joint Conference on Artificial Intelligence', Morgan Kaufmann Publishers, Montreal, Canada, pp. 312–318.

NIEMELÄ I. [1996a], Implementing circumscription using a tableau method, *in* W. Wahlster, ed., 'Proceedings of the European Conference on Artificial Intelligence', John Wiley, Budapest, Hungary, pp. 80–84.

NIEMELÄ I. [1996b], A tableau calculus for minimal model reasoning, *in* P. Miglioli, U. Moscato, D. Mundici and M. Ornaghi, eds, 'Proceedings of the Fifth Workshop on Theorem Proving with Analytic Tableaux and Related Methods', LNAI 1071, Springer-Verlag, Terrasini, Italy, pp. 278–294.

NIEMELÄ I. AND RINTANEN J. [1994], 'On the impact of stratification on the complexity of nonmonotonic reasoning', *Journal of Applied Non-Classical Logics* **4**(2), 141–179.

NIEMELÄ I. AND SIMONS P. [1996], Efficient Implementation of the Well-founded and Stable Model Semantics, *in* M. Maher, ed., 'Proceedings of the Joint International Conference and Symposium on Logic Programming', The MIT Press, Bonn, Germany, pp. 289–303.

NIEMELÄ I. AND SIMONS P. [1997], Smodels – an implementation of the stable model and well-founded semantics for normal logic programs, *in* 'Proceedings of the 4th International Conference on Logic Programming and Non-Monotonic Reasoning', Springer-Verlag, Dagstuhl, Germany.

ODIFREDDI P. [1989], *Classical Recursion Theory*, North-Holland.

OLIVETTI N. [1992], 'A tableaux and sequent calculus for minimal entailment', *Journal of Automated Reasoning* **9**, 99–139.

PAPADIMITRIOU C. [1994], *Computational Complexity*, Addison-Wesley.

PEREIRA, L. M. AND NERODE, A., EDS [1993], *Logic Programming and Non–monotonic Reasoning: Proceedings of the Second Int. Ws.*, MIT Press. Lisboa, Portugal.

PLAISTED D. [1988], 'Non-Horn Clause Logic Programming Without Contrapositives', *Journal of Automated Reasoning* **4**, 287–325.

PRZYMUSINSKA H. AND PRZYMUSINSKI T. [1994], 'Stationary default extensions', *Fund. Informat.* **21** (1,2), 67–87.

PRZYMUSINSKI T. C. [1989], 'An Algorithm to Compute Circumscription', *Artificial Intelligence* **38**, 49–73.

PRZYMUSINSKI T. C. [1998], 'Autoepistemic logic of knowledge and beliefs', *Artificial Intelligence* **95**, 115–154.

RAJASEKAR A. [1989], Semantics for Disjunctive Logic Programs, PhD thesis, University of Maryland.

RAJASEKAR A. AND YUSUF H. [1995], 'DWAM – A WAM model extension for disjunctive logic programs', *Annals of Mathematics and Artificial Intelligence* **14**(2-4), 275–308. Presented also at the Symposium on Logic in Databases, Knowledge Representation and Reasoning, College Park, Md., USA.

RAO P., SAGONAS K., SWIFT T., WARREN D. S. AND FREIRE J. [1997], XSB: A System for Efficiently Computing Well-Founded Semantics, *in* J. Dix, U. Furbach and A. Nerode, eds, 'Logic Programming and Non-Monotonic Reasoning, Proceedings of the Fourth International Conference', LNAI 1265, Springer, Berlin, pp. 430–440.

REITER R. [1978], On closed world data bases, *in* H. Gallaire and J. Minker, eds, 'Logic and Data Bases', Plenum, New York, pp. 55–76.

REITER R. [1980], 'A Logic for Default-Reasoning', *Artificial Intelligence* **13**, 81–132.

REITER R. [1987], 'A Theory of Diagnosis from First Principles', *Artificial Intelligence* **32**, 57–97.

RISCH V. AND SCHWIND C. [1994], 'Tableau-based characterization and theorem proving for default logic', *Journal of Automated Reasoning* **13**, 223–242.

SAGONAS K., SWIFT T. AND WARREN D. S. [1994], XSB as an Efficient Deductive Database Engine, *in* 'Proc. of the Thirteenth ACM SIGACT-SIGMOD-SIGART Symposium on Principles of Database Systems (PODS'94)', ACM Press, Minneapolis, Minnesota, pp. 442–453.

SAKAMA C. AND INOUE K. [1993], Relating disjunctive logic programs to default theories, *in* 'Proceedings of the 2nd International Conference on Logic Programming and Non-Monotonic Reasoning', MIT Press, pp. 266–282.

SAKAMA C. AND SEKI H. [1994], Partial Deduction of Disjunctive Logic Programs: A Declarative Approach, *in* 'Logic Program Synthesis and Transformation – Meta Programming in Logic', LNCS 883, Springer, Berlin, pp. 170–182.

SAKAMA C. AND SEKI H. [1997], 'Partial Deduction in Disjunctive Logic Programming', *Journal of Logic Programming* **32(3)**, 229–245.

SCHAUB T. [1995], 'A new methodology for query-answering in default logics via structure-oriented theorem proving', *Journal of Automated Reasoning* **15(1)**, 95–165.

SCHAUB T. AND BRÜNING S. [1996], Prolog technology for default reasoning, *in* 'Proceedings of the European Conference on Artificial Intelligence', John Wiley, Budapest, Hungary, pp. 105–109.

SCHLIPF J. [1986], How uncomputable is general circumscription?, *in* 'Symposium on Logic in Computer Science', IEEE Computer Society Press, Cambridge, USA, pp. 92–95.

SCHWARZ G. AND TRUSZCZYŃSKI M. [1993], Nonmonotonic reasoning is sometimes simpler, *in* 'Proceedings of the 3rd Kurt Gödel Colloquium on Computational Logic and Proof Theory', Springer, LNCS, Brno, Czech Republic, pp. 313–324.

SHVARTS G. [1990], Autoepistemic modal logics, *in* 'Proceedings of the 3rd Conference on Theoretical Aspects of Reasoning about Knowledge', Morgan Kaufmann Publishers, Pacific Grove, USA, pp. 97–109.

STICKEL M. [1988], 'A Prolog Technology Theorem Prover: Implementation by an Extended Prolog Compiler', *Journal of Automated Reasoning* **4**, 353–380.

STILLMAN J. [1990], It's not my default: the complexity of membership problems in restricted propositional default logics, *in* 'AAAI-90 — Proceedings of the 9th AAAI National Conference on Artificial Intelligence', The MIT Press, Boston, Massachusetts, USA, pp. 571–578.

STILLMAN J. [1992], The complexity of propositional default logics, *in* 'AAAI-92 — Proceedings of the AAAI National Conference on Artificial Intelligence', The MIT Press, San Jose, California, USA, pp. 794–800.

SUBRAHMANIAN V., BONATTI P., DIX J., EITER T., KRAUS S., ÖZCAN F. AND ROSS R. [2000], *Heterogenous Active Agents*, MIT-Press.

SUBRAHMANIAN V., NAU AND VAGO [1995], 'WFS + Branch and Bound = Stable Models', *IEEE Transactions on Knowledge and Data Engineering* **17(3)**, 362–377.

TAMAKI H. AND SATO T. [1986], OLD Resolution with Tabulation, *in* 'Proceedings of the Third International Conference on Logic Programming, London', LNAI, Springer, Berlin, pp. 84–98.

TARJAN R. [1972], 'Depth first search and linear graph algorithms', *SIAM Journal on Computing* **1**, 146–160.

TRUSZCZYŃSKI M. [1991], Embedding default logic into modal nonmonotonic logics, *in* 'Proceedings of the 1st International Workshop on Logic Programming and Non-monotonic Reasoning', The MIT Press, Washington, D.C., USA, pp. 151–165.

VAN GELDER A. [1988], Negation as failure using tight derivations for general logic programs, *in* J. Minker, ed., 'Foundations of Deductive Databases and Logic Programming', Morgan Kaufmann Publishers, Los Altos, pp. 149–176.

VAN GELDER A. [1989], The Alternating Fixpoint of Logic Programs with Negation, *in* 'Proc. of the Eight ACM SIGACT-SIGMOD-SIGART Symposium on Principles of Database Systems, Philadelphia, Pennsylvania', ACM Press, pp. 1–10.

VAN GELDER A., ROSS K. A. AND SCHLIPF J. S. [1988], Unfounded Sets and well-founded Semantics for general logic Programs, *in* 'Proceedings 7th Symposion on Principles of Database Systems', pp. 221–230.

VAN GELDER A., ROSS K. AND SCHLIPF J. [1991], 'The well-founded semantics for general logic programs', *Journal of the Association for Computing Machinery* **38**(3), 620–650.

Index

CHAPTER 20

Automated Deduction for Many-Valued Logics

Matthias Baaz   Christian G. Fermüller

Gernot Salzer

SECOND READERS: Viorica Sofronie.

Contents

HANDBOOK OF AUTOMATED REASONING
Edited by Alan Robinson and Andrei Voronkov

1. Introduction

Many-valuedness is one of the central topics in non-classical logics. It is also a classical theme in modern logic, dating back at least to [Łukasiewicz 1920], [1930], [Łukasiewicz and Tarski 1930], and [Post 1921]. Material on the history of many-valued logic can be found in many of the textbooks in this field, e.g. [Rescher 1969], [Rosser and Turquette 1952], and [Gottwald 1989], to give some references to classical literature. Many interesting philosophical, linguistic but also mathematical motivations for the investigation of many-valued logics have been offered. However, it has also been doubted whether the immense amount of papers and books in this field matches its significance. We refrain from contributing to this ongoing discussion, but point out that a number of different applications in computer science have emerged more recently. Some of the fields in which many-valued formalisms are important tools are: error correcting codes [Mundici 1990], reasoning with inconsistent and partial sets of data [Arieli and Avron 1998], [Murata, Subrahmanian and Wakayama 1991], [Lu, Henschen, Subrahmanian and da Costa 1991], hardware verification [Hayes 1986], [Hähnle and Kernig 1993], [Bryant and Seger 1991], multi agent systems [Nowana 1995], [Pfalzgraf, Sigmund and Stokkermans 1996], [Wooldridge and Jennings 1995], non-monotonic reasoning [Doherty 1991], [Bell et al. 1994] and logic programming [Lu and Rosenthal 1997], [Jaffar and Maher 1994], [Kunen 1987]. In addition to this impressive range of actual and potential applications we want to emphasize that the generalization from two to many truth values also provides a tool for investigating phenomena in classical logics, like aspects of the relation between proof theory and semantics [Baaz, Fermüller, Salzer and Zach 1998], [Baaz, Fermüller and Zach 1994] or classical and intuitionistic logic, [Baaz and Fermüller 1996a], [1996b].

A thorough survey of literature concerning automated deduction in many-valued logics has been attempted in [Hähnle 1994a] and, more recently, in [Hähnle and Escalada-Imaz 1997]. We refer to this work for an extensive enumeration of relevant books, papers and systems. As will be explained below we do not aim at an exhaustive survey of previous approaches, but rather want to provide a guideline in this lively growing field; we will present only one very general approach in detail. Section 2 demarcates the scope of this article and serves as a reference point for all other sections. This is followed by a systematic (as opposed to historic or application oriented) classification of approaches to deduction in many-valued logics in Section 3. In Section 4 signed logic – a framework for classical reasoning about all truth functional finitely-valued first-order logics – is presented. Section 5 is devoted to one of the most promising approaches to efficient deduction for finitely-valued first-order logics: signed resolution. In Section 6 we provide an example that illustrates several of the concepts defined in earlier sections. Section 7 deals with the important problem of computing small normal forms for finitely-valued connectives and quantifiers. We conclude with a few remarks on the still rather unexplored field of deduction for infinitely-valued logics in Section 8.

2. What is a many-valued logic?

The demarcation of the realm of logics we are to deal with in this chapter is a less simple task as it may seem at first glance. Traditionally, any logic characterized by a semantic based on more than two truth values is called "many-valued" or "multiple-valued"[1]. However, only ideological or historical reasons would drive us to exclude classical two-valued logic from the realm of all many-valued logics. Indeed, although historically particular many-valued logics have been presented as *alternatives* to classical logic, from the viewpoint of computer science it is often much more appropriate to study broad families of many-valued logics as *generalizations* of classical logic.

It is well known that some logics that have originally been represented in quite different semantic contexts (like the modal logic S5) have later been recognized to have "natural" many-valued semantics or to coincide extensionally with well-known many-valued logics (see, e.g. [Gottwald 1993]). This is particularly true if we consider infinitely many truth values. In fact, in a very abstract sense every logic can be viewed as a many-valued one: Just take the equivalence classes with respect to the corresponding notion of logical equivalence as truth values. Of course, this level of generality will hardly lead to any insights or applications of particular logics. More restricted definitions of "many-valuedness" have been suggested [e.g. Avron 1991b] but always depend on the intended context of investigation.

Here we are interested in (efficient) proof search methods for many-valued logics, and thus feel justified to take a pragmatical stand. Very little is known about theorem proving for infinitely-valued logics. In fact, most first-order logics of this kind are incomplete anyway. (I.e., the set of valid formulae and the consequence relations are not recursively enumerable.) We shall make some remarks on infinitely-valued logics in Section 8 and dedicate the main sections to finitely-valued logics. More exactly, we consider the class of all finitely-valued logics with arbitrary truth-functional connectives and arbitrary distribution quantifiers. This denotes a very broad family of first-order logics that contains all important particular logics, like classical (two-valued) logic, Kleene's three-valued logic [1938], or Belnap's four-valued one [1977]. But also all important *sequences* of finitely-valued logics, like the Post, Gödel, and Łukasiewicz logics, known from standard textbooks like [Rosser and Turquette 1952], [Rescher 1969], [Gottwald 1989], or [Bolc and Borowik 1992].

The following formal definitions fix the frame for the technical sections.

2.1. DEFINITION. The alphabet of an *object language* consists of an infinite supply of object variables; of infinitely many predicate and function symbols of arity n for each $n \geq 0$; of a finite number of logical connectives $\square_1, \ldots, \square_r$ of arity $n_1, \ldots, n_r$, respectively; and of a finite number of quantifiers $Q_1, \ldots Q_k$. Constants are considered as 0-place function symbols.

2.2. DEFINITION. Let Σ be an alphabet. An *atomic formula* or simply *atom* is an

---

[1]We have no particular preference for either of these terms which we take as synonymous. For sake of clarity, we stick to the first one throughout this chapter.

expression of the form $P(t_1, \ldots, t_n)$ where P is an n-place predicate symbol of Σ and $t_1, \ldots, t_n$ are terms built up from the variables and function symbols of Σ.

Formulae (of a language $\mathcal{L}_\Sigma$ corresponding to an alphabet Σ) are defined inductively as usual. Atoms are formulae. If $\Box_i$ is a logical connective and $F_1, \ldots, F_{n_i}$ are formulae then $\Box_i(F_1, \ldots, F_{n_i})$ is a formula, too. (For some binary connectives we will also use infix notation.) If F is a formula, x a variable and Q_i a quantifier then $(Q_i x)F$ is a formula, too.

Throughout the paper "W" denotes the set of truth values of a logic. The semantics for a language $\mathcal{L}_\Sigma$ is given as follows.

2.3. DEFINITION. With each logical connective $\Box_i$ and each quantifier Q_i we associate

- a *truth table* $\widetilde{\Box}_i : W^{n_i} \to W$, and
- a *truth function* $\widetilde{Q}_i : (2^W - \{\emptyset\}) \to W$, respectively.

2.4. EXAMPLE. The concept of a truth table hardly needs any illustration. But remember that whole *families* of logics can be compactly specified by referring to one or more ordering structures on the set of truth values. We exemplify this fact by describing the sequence $\mathbf{G}_n$ of Gödel logics [Gödel 1932] and the sequence $\mathbf{L}_n$ of Łukasiewicz logics [Łukasiewicz 1930], $n \geq 2$.

Let $W = \{v_0, v_1, \ldots, v_{n-1}\}$; to enhance readability we define $f = v_0$ and $t = v_{n-1}$. The truth tables for conjunction ($\wedge$) and disjunction ($\vee$) are identical for both sequences of logics:

$$\widetilde{\wedge}(v_i, v_j) = v_{\min(i,j)} \quad \text{and} \quad \widetilde{\vee}(v_i, v_j) = v_{\max(i,j)} \quad .$$

The semantics of negation and implication in Gödel logics is given by

$$\widetilde{\neg}(v_i) = \begin{cases} t & \text{if } v_i = f \\ f & \text{otherwise} \end{cases}$$

$$\widetilde{\supset}(v_i, v_j) = \begin{cases} t & \text{if } i \leq j \\ v_j & \text{otherwise} \end{cases}$$

whereas for the Łukasiewicz logics $\mathbf{L}_n$ we have

$$\widetilde{\neg}(v_i) = v_{(n-1)-i}$$

$$\widetilde{\supset}(v_i, v_j) = \begin{cases} t & \text{if } i \leq j \\ v_{(n-1)-(i-j)} & \text{otherwise} \end{cases} .$$

2.5. REMARK. Some authors prefer to identify the set W of truth values with a set of equidistant numbers from the rational or real interval $[0, 1]$. This notational convention certainly assists in visualizing the implicit total ordering used in the definition of truth tables for Gödel, Łukasiewicz and many other logics. It also suggests a certain relation of these logics to classical logic: 0 and 1 are intended to represent absolute falsity and truth, respectively; the other truth values are called *intermediate*. However, the reader should be aware of the fact that for many interesting logics, no "natural" total ordering on the set of truth values exists. Moreover, it does not always make sense to single out a truth value as representing absolute truth (or falsity). As an example consider Belnap's 4-valued logic [1977] for the representation of possibly incomplete and inconsistent sets of data, where the two classical truth values are augmented by the values "inconsistent" and "not determined". This logic received a lot of attention in recent years; most of the relevant material is summarized in [Arieli and Avron 1998].

A quantified formula $(Qx)F(x)$ is evaluated by first computing the distribution of $F(x)$ and then using the truth function $\widetilde{Q}$ to map the distribution to a single truth value. The *distribution* of $F(x)$ is the set of truth values obtained by evaluating $F(x)$ for all possible values of x in the domain under consideration (see below for a formal definition). Observe that there are $|W|^{2^{|W|}-1}$ different distribution quantifiers.

2.6. EXAMPLE. Suppose we have a three-valued logic with

$$W \;=\; \{t(rue), u(ndefined), f(alse)\}$$

and want to specify $\forall'$ as a kind of "strong and crisp universal quantifier". More precisely, we stipulate that the formula $(\forall'x)A(x)$ takes the truth value t iff for all objects d of the domain of the interpretation, $A(d)$ evaluates to t. For all other situations, $(\forall'x)A(x)$ is assigned the value f. Thus the truth function for $\forall'$ is defined as:

$$\widetilde{\forall'}(V) \;=\; \begin{cases} t & \text{if } V = \{t\} \\ f & \text{otherwise, i.e., if } u \in V \text{ or } f \in V \end{cases}$$

where $V \subseteq W$, but $V \neq \emptyset$.

2.7. EXAMPLE. All two-place connectives $\square$ which are associative, commutative and idempotent induce a quantifier $Q^\square$, to be understood as "generalized $\square$", by

$$\widetilde{Q^\square}(\{w\}) = w \quad \text{and} \quad \widetilde{Q^\square}(\{w_1, \ldots, w_k\}) = \widetilde{\square}(w_1, \widetilde{\square}(w_2, \ldots \widetilde{\square}(w_{k-1}, w_k) \ldots)) \;.$$

A quantifier Q can only be expressed as the generalization of a binary connective if it satisfies

$$\widetilde{Q}(\{w\}) = w \quad \text{and} \quad \widetilde{Q}(U \cup V) = \widetilde{Q}(U \cup \{\widetilde{Q}(V)\})$$

for all $U, V \neq \emptyset$ with $U \cup V \subseteq W$ and $U \cap V = \emptyset$. The inducing connective $\square$ is then given by

$$\widetilde{\square}(w_i, w_j) \;=\; \widetilde{Q}(\{w_i, w_j\}) \;.$$

In particular, universal and existential quantification for Gödel and Łukasiewicz logics, $\forall$ and $\exists$, can be defined as generalized $\wedge$ and $\vee$, respectively:

$$\widetilde{\forall}(V) = v_{\min V} \quad \text{and} \quad \widetilde{\exists}(V) = v_{\max V} \; ,$$

where $\min V = \min\{i \mid v_i \in V\}$ and $\max V = \max\{i \mid v_i \in V\}$.

2.8. DEFINITION. A *frame* for $\mathcal{L}_\Sigma$ and W is a pair $\langle D, \Phi \rangle$ where

- D is a non-empty set, the *domain of discourse*;
- Φ is a *signature interpretation*, i.e. a mapping assigning a function $D^n \to D$ to each n-place function symbol, and a function $D^n \to W$ to each n-place predicate symbol of the alphabet.

An *interpretation* I for $\mathcal{L}_\Sigma$ and W is a triple $\langle D, \Phi, \delta \rangle$ where $\langle D, \Phi \rangle$ is a frame and δ is a *variable assignment* $\delta: V \to D$; I is said to be *based on* the frame $\langle D, \Phi \rangle$.

Given an interpretation I we define an evaluation function val_I that assigns an element of the domain to each term and a truth value to each formula:

2.9. DEFINITION. Let $I = \langle D, \Phi, \delta \rangle$ be an interpretation for $\mathcal{L}_\Sigma$ and W then the corresponding *evaluation function* val_I is defined inductively as follows:

- $\mathrm{val}_I(x) = \delta(x)$ for all variables x in Σ.
- $\mathrm{val}_I(f(t_1, \ldots, t_n)) = \Phi(f)(\mathrm{val}_I(t_1), \ldots, \mathrm{val}_I(t_n))$ for all n-place function symbols f, $n \geq 0$.
- $\mathrm{val}_I(P(t_1, \ldots, t_n)) = \Phi(P)(\mathrm{val}_I(t_1), \ldots, \mathrm{val}_I(t_n))$ for all n-place predicate symbols P, $n \geq 0$.
- $\mathrm{val}_I(\square_i(F_1, \ldots, F_{n_i})) = \widetilde{\square}_i(\mathrm{val}_I(F_1), \ldots, \mathrm{val}_I(F_{n_i}))$ for all logical connectives $\square_i$ in Σ.
- $\mathrm{val}_I((Q_i x)F) = \widetilde{Q}_i(distr_{I,x}(F))$ for all quantifiers Q_i in Σ, where $distr_{I,x}(F) = \{\mathrm{val}_{I_d^x}(F) \mid d \in D\}$ is the distribution of F in I with respect to the variable x. (I_d^x is the interpretation identical to I except for setting $\delta(x) = d$.)

It is sometimes argued that, in order to define a logic, we also need to fix a set of *designated truth values* $W_t \subset W$ and distinguish the *valid* formulae as those F, for which $\mathrm{val}_I(F) \in W_t$ for all I. However, for most applications it is adequate to take the more general point of view of being interested in proofs or refutations of claims of form "$\mathrm{val}_I(F) \in V$ for all I" for *arbitrary* $V \subset W$. Similarly, we might ask for a notion of "logical consequence". Again, the answer is that all relevant questions about usual types of logical consequence (for finitely-valued logics) can be expressed in the signed logic described in Section 4 below.

3. Classification of proof systems for many-valued logics

There is an impressive body of literature dedicated to theorem proving for many-valued logics. We do not aim at a complete review of all different approaches to this topic. Rather, we are convinced that a systematic *classification* of existing proof systems is of greater value to the reader. The following attempt at such a classification should allow to assess the status of the various methods and recognize connections between them.[2]

All types of calculi (Hilbert-type, Gentzen-type, resolution, etc.) for almost any kind of many-valued logic abound in literature. Some proof-search systems attempt to find proofs of valid formulae (or consequence relations between given formulae) *within the language* of the logics in question. Some applications might indeed ask for proofs presented in the syntax and using the rules of special calculi for particular logics. However, in most situations we are interested in problems of the form "does the formula always evaluate to (one of) a certain (set of) truth value(s)?", possibly under the assumption that other formulae evaluate to certain truth values. This allows us to make full use of *classical* reasoning *about* the various logics, since the semantics of the logics are always available in ordinary, i.e. classical, mathematical language. We call proof systems of the first type – where the syntactic restrictions of particular logics are respected within the proofs – *internal*. Systems that formalize reasoning *about* the logics are called *external*.[3]

3.1. REMARK. Observe that even if we are interested in formal proofs presented within a specific calculus C_L for a logic L, external systems can be useful, if we know how to translate a proof of "provability in C_L" into a proof in C_L. On the other hand, it is often impossible to express a statement like "formula F of L never evaluates to truth value v" within the syntax of logic L. To prove such statements external systems are *needed*.

Most proof search systems make use of *normal forms*. Of course, the internal/external distinction carries over to normal forms. Whereas for instance external conjunctive (CNF) and disjunctive normal forms (DNF) of classical statements about truth value assignments to formulae are always available in the familiar form, internal counterparts of CNF or DNF might look quite different in each case or might even fail to exist.

As a consequence of the last observation, internal systems are generally bound to deal with particular logics or families of logics only. In fact, hardly any "internal" treatment of quantifiers has been worked out. The systems are restricted to propositional logics or formulae with free variables only. In contrast, external systems are characterized by a high level of generality. The whole class of all finitely-valued logics with distribution quantifiers (as defined in Section 2) can be given a uniform treatment.

---

[2] Chapter 8 of Reiner Hähnle's monograph [1994a] provides a rather detailed review of the literature up to 1993. Also [Hähnle and Escalada-Imaz 1997] surveys relevant literature.

[3] A similar distinction characterizes the two main paradigms of theorem proving for modal logics. There are systems that work within the syntax of modal operators like the non-prefix tableau methods of [Fitting 1983], and those that proceed by coding the possible worlds semantics into classical logic like the resolution concept of [Ohlbach 1993], or contain explicit references to the semantics like prefixed tableaux.

3.1. Internal proof systems

The most common examples of internal proof systems for many-valued logics are Frege/Hilbert-style calculi. Like in other areas of non-classical logics, most many-valued logics have originally been introduced by presenting Hilbert-style axiomatizations for them. The corresponding literature is nearly unsurmountably large. The classic text books of Rosser and Turquette [1952], Rescher [1969], and Gottwald [1993] provide Hilbert-style systems for a broad range of important many-valued logics. Unfortunately, proof search in Hilbert-style systems tends to be extremely inefficient and thus is hardly a promising paradigm for automated deduction.[4] A theorem prover that basically performs top down search for proofs of propositional formulae in any finitely-axiomatized Hilbert-style system is *AUTOLOGIC* of [Morgan 1985].

Of greater relevance for our topic are various resolution systems for particular finitely-valued logics or families of logic that can be found in the literature. In contrast to the resolution principle investigated in [Baaz and Fermüller 1995] and Section 5 below, the following calculi are based on *internal* normal forms and thus are classified as internal proof systems: Morgan's resolution calculus [1976]; Schmitt's resolution system for L_3 [1986]; Resolution in the style of Stachniak [1988], [1996] and [Stachniak and O'Hearn 1990], [1992]; and Orłowska's resolution for Post logics [1978]. As argued above, we consider external normal forms to be a much better suited basis for efficient proof search than internal ones. Therefore we refrain from describing these internal systems here. The interested reader can find descriptions of the above mentioned calculi in [Hähnle 1994a].

3.2. External proof systems

External proof systems for many-valued logics can be viewed as classical first-order systems for which the atomic formulae take the form "one of the truth values $v_1, \ldots, v_n$ is assigned to formula A" (of a certain many-valued logic), denoted by $\{v_1, \ldots, v_n\}$:A. The set $\{v_1, \ldots, v_n\}$ is called the *sign* of A.

Since we need it also for the presentation of transformation rules in Section 4 and many-valued resolution in Section 5, we formally define the logic of *signed formula expressions*. This formalism is also called *signed logic* (see [Hähnle 1994a] and [Lu, Murray and Rosenthal 1993]).

3.2. DEFINITION. Let $\mathcal{F}$ be the set of first-order formulae over some alphabet Σ, and let W be the set of truth values. The set of signed formula expressions over Σ and W is inductively defined as follows.

---

[4]Still, we should keep in mind that – due to the fact that modus ponens is a cut rule – the length of shortest Hilbert-type proofs may be vastly smaller than the length of proofs in analytic tableau calculi and certain types of resolution. In the first-order case the difference is even non-elementary (in the sense of Kalmár) and therefore not only holds for the length of proofs but also for proof search complexity; the latter can be reasonably assumed to be related to proof length by an elementary function. See [Baaz, Fermüller and Leitsch 1994].

- If $S \subseteq W$ and $\psi \in \mathcal{F}$, then $S{:}\psi$ is a *signed formula expression, called* (atomic) signed formula. S is called *sign*.
- $\perp$ and $\top$ are signed formula expressions.
- If ψ_1 and ψ_2 are signed formula expressions, then $\psi_1 \wedge \psi_2$, $\psi_1 \vee \psi_2$, $\psi_1 \supset \psi_2$, $\psi_1 \equiv \psi_2$ and $\neg\psi_1$ are signed formula expressions.
- If x is a variable and ψ is a signed formula expression, then $(\forall x)\psi$ and $(\exists x)\psi$ are signed formula expressions.

We use $\bigwedge_{i=1}^{n} \psi_i$ as an abbreviation for $\psi_1 \wedge \cdots \wedge \psi_n$, and $\bigvee_{i=1}^{n} \psi_i$ as an abbreviation for $\psi_1 \vee \cdots \vee \psi_n$. The empty conjunction equals $\top$ and the empty disjunction equals $\perp$.

For any signed formula $S{:}\psi$ we denote by $\overline{S}{:}\psi$ its *dual* signed formula $(W-S){:}\psi$.

3.3. DEFINITION. Let $I = \langle D, \Phi \rangle$ be an interpretation for Σ and W. The semantics of signed formula expressions is given by a valuation sval_I based on an evaluation function val_I for the underlying language of formulae as defined in Section 2:

- $\mathrm{sval}_I(S{:}\psi) = \mathbf{true}$ iff $\mathrm{val}_I(\psi) \in S$,
- $\mathrm{sval}_I(\top) = \mathbf{true}$ and $\mathrm{sval}_I(\perp) = \mathbf{false}$,
- $\mathrm{sval}_I(\psi_1 \wedge \psi_2) = \mathbf{true}$ iff $\mathrm{sval}_I(\psi_1) = \mathbf{true}$ and $\mathrm{sval}_I(\psi_2) = \mathbf{true}$,
  $\mathrm{sval}_I(\psi_1 \vee \psi_2) = \mathbf{false}$ iff $\mathrm{sval}_I(\psi_1) = \mathbf{false}$ and $\mathrm{sval}_I(\psi_2) = \mathbf{false}$,
  $\mathrm{sval}_I(\psi_1 \supset \psi_2) = \mathbf{false}$ iff $\mathrm{sval}_I(\psi_1) = \mathbf{true}$ and $\mathrm{sval}_I(\psi_2) = \mathbf{false}$,
  $\mathrm{sval}_I(\psi_1 \equiv \psi_2) = \mathbf{true}$ iff $\mathrm{sval}_I(\psi_1) = \mathrm{sval}_I(\psi_2)$,
  $\mathrm{sval}_I(\neg\psi) = \mathbf{true}$ iff $\mathrm{sval}_I(\psi) = \mathbf{false}$,
- $\mathrm{sval}_I((\forall x)\psi) = \mathbf{true}$ iff $\mathrm{sval}_{I_d^x}(\psi) = \mathbf{true}$ for all $d \in D$,
  $\mathrm{sval}_I((\exists x)\psi) = \mathbf{false}$ iff $\mathrm{sval}_{I_d^x}(\psi) = \mathbf{false}$ for all $d \in D$.
  (Remember that I_d^x is the interpretation identical to I except for setting $\delta(x) = d$.)

A signed formula expression ψ is *valid* iff $\mathrm{sval}_I(\psi) = \mathbf{true}$ for all I, it is *satisfiable* iff $\mathrm{sval}_I(\psi) = \mathbf{true}$ for some I, and *unsatisfiable* otherwise.

By definition all familiar laws of classical logic, like the distribution of $\exists$ over $\vee$, of $\forall$ over $\wedge$, de Morgan's laws etc. also hold for signed formulae. Additionally we have the following tautologies.

3.4. PROPOSITION. *The following equivalences are valid:*

- $\{\}{:}\psi \equiv \perp$, $W{:}\psi \equiv \top$
- $\neg(S{:}\psi) \equiv \overline{S}{:}\psi$
- $S_1{:}\psi \vee S_2{:}\psi \equiv (S_1 \cup S_2){:}\psi$, *in particular*
  $\{w_1\}{:}\psi \vee \cdots \vee \{w_n\}{:}\psi \equiv \{w_1, \ldots, w_n\}{:}\psi$
- $S_1{:}\psi \wedge S_2{:}\psi \equiv (S_1 \cap S_2){:}\psi$ *in particular*
  $(\{w_1\}{:}\psi \wedge \{w_2\}{:}\psi) \equiv \perp$ *for* $w_1 \neq w_2$.

The second equivalence shows that negations can be completely eliminated from signed formula expressions. The third allows to eliminate all non-singleton signs by introducing disjunctions. Clearly, the semantics of arbitrary connectives and distribution quantifiers can be expressed as signed formula expressions.

3.5. EXAMPLE. Remember from Example 2.4 that conjunction and disjunction for Gödel and Łukasiewicz logics (and in fact for many other important logics) are defined by

$$\tilde{\wedge}(v_i, v_j) = v_{\min(i,j)} \quad \text{and} \quad \tilde{\vee}(v_i, v_j) = v_{\max(i,j)}$$

where $W = \{v_0, \ldots, v_{n-1}\}$. This can be expressed in the language of signed formula expressions as

$$\{w_i\}{:}(\psi_1 \wedge \psi_2) \quad \equiv \quad \{w_j \mid j \geq i\}{:}\psi_1 \wedge \{w_j \mid j \geq i\}{:}\psi_2 \wedge (\{w_i\}{:}\psi_1 \vee \{w_i\}{:}\psi_2)$$

$$\{w_i\}{:}(\psi_1 \vee \psi_2) \quad \equiv \quad \{w_j \mid j \leq i\}{:}\psi_1 \wedge \{w_j \mid j \leq i\}{:}\psi_2 \wedge (\{w_i\}{:}\psi_1 \vee \{w_i\}{:}\psi_2) \;.$$

Concerning the "strong and crisp universal quantifier" $\forall'$ of Example 2.6 we obtain the following signed formula expression as specification of its semantics:

$$(\{t\}{:}\forall'\psi(x) \equiv (\mathbb{V}x)\{t\}{:}\psi(x)) \quad \wedge \quad (\{f\}{:}\forall'\psi(x) \equiv (\exists x)\{f, u\}{:}\psi(x)) \;.$$

Although there are different types of external proof systems for many-valued logics, all of them represent strategies of ordinary (classical) first-order reasoning in the theory that consists of the semantic definitions of connectives and quantifiers for some object logic written as signed formula expressions. We offer the following *criteria of classification* for such systems:

DNF versus CNF: Since classical reasoning systems usually are based on the existence of certain normal forms, the same holds true for external proof systems for many-valued logics. In particular, *analytic tableau calculi* can be viewed as methods for generating DNFs for arbitrary signed formulae. The tableau rule for analyzing a signed formula $S{:}\psi$ corresponds to a signed formula expression in DNF that specifies the semantics of the leading connective or quantifier, as in the example above. Applying the closure rules for a tableau amounts to checking the unsatisfiability of the DNF of the formula to be refuted. In *resolution systems* a CNF, called *clause form* is generated explicitly first. The resolution rule then serves to test the satisfiability of the original formula. (We describe many-valued resolution in detail in Section 5.)

Refutational versus validational: Most systems intended for automated deduction proceed indirectly: One tries to refute the negation of the statement which is claimed to be valid. In classical logic refutational and validational (direct) proof search are completely dual to each other. It is well known for instance that a closed classical tableau for a signed formula $\{\mathbf{false}\}{:}A$ can be interpreted as encoding a proof of the sequent "$\rightarrow A$" in Gentzen's sequent calculus **LK**. For logics with more than two truth values the dualism between "negative" and "positive" formulations gets less trivial. We refer to [Baaz, Fermüller and Zach 1992] for an investigation of aspects of this dualism.

At the first order level it is essential for efficient proof search that the systems make use of the unification principle. This implies that Skolemization steps are either explicitly carried out in the conversion to clause form, or appear as quantifier rules in free-variable tableau systems. Depending on whether the system is refutational or validational, either the positively occurring existential quantifiers (and negatively occurring universal quantifiers) of the signed formula expressions, or the negatively occurring existential quantifiers (and positively occurring universal quantifiers) are eliminated by Skolemization.

Types of signs: Many calculi consider only singleton sets as signs. In particular, the concept of *many-sided (or many-placed) sequents* [Schröter 1955], [Rousseau 1967], [Baaz, Fermüller and Zach 1994] corresponds to signed formula expressions by interpreting the place of a formula within a sequent (which corresponds to a truth value) as its sign. Reiner Hähnle [1991] has pointed out that, for purposes of automated deduction, it can be very advantageous to base a many-valued tableau or resolution system on other types of sets. In many important logics the set of truth values W is considered as a totally ordered set. For such logics so-called *up-sets* and *down-sets*, i.e. subsets of form $\{v \mid v \geq w\}$ or $\{v \mid v \leq w\}$ for $w \in W$, turn out to be useful. Generally speaking, taking into account the algebraic structure of the set of truth values (where applicable) leads to a choice of sets of truth values as signs that may result in an exponential speed-up for each application of a corresponding rule compared with the singleton sets as signs calculus. A general investigation of the relation between systems of signs and truth values can be found in [Baaz, Fermüller, Salzer and Zach 1998]. The computation of optimal derivation rules for a given logic is an important research topic in itself (see Section 7).

The presented criteria should allow the reader to classify most proof systems for finitely-valued logics that have been described in the literature. Although the motivations and syntactic formats of various calculi are often very different, their connection gets clear if we translate them into the language of signed formula expressions as presented here.

Historically, the oldest generic and analytic proof systems for the family of finitely-valued logics are *sequent calculi*, based on the concept of many-sided (or many-placed) sequents. This generalization of Gentzen's sequent calculus [1934-35] arises naturally by observing that a classical sequent $\Gamma \to \Delta$ is satisfied in an interpretation I iff I either evaluates one of the formulae in Γ to **false** or one of the formulae in Δ to **true**. Thus the two sides of the sequent correspond to the two truth values **false** and **true**. In moving from classical to n-valued logics, we have to replace the binary relation on sequences of formulae – represented by the sequent arrow – by an n-ary relation. More exactly, an n-placed sequent $\Gamma_1 \mid \Gamma_2 \mid \cdots \mid \Gamma_n$ corresponds to the signed formula expression

$$\bigvee_{\psi \in \Gamma_1} \{v_1\}{:}\psi \vee \bigvee_{\psi \in \Gamma_2} \{v_2\}{:}\psi \vee \cdots \vee \bigvee_{\psi \in \Gamma_n} \{v_n\}{:}\psi \ .$$

Introduction rules for arbitrary truth functional connectives and distribution quantifiers can easily be constructed from the truth tables of a logic (see Section 4). In fact, these rules correspond to signed formula expressions that specify the semantics of connectives and quantifiers just as in Example 3.5 above. Axiom sequents take the form $\psi \mid \psi \mid \cdots \mid \psi$ – expressing the fact that each formula ψ has to take at least one truth value.

Clearly, top-down proof search in the resulting sequent calculus should be classified as an *external, validational* proof system based on *DNFs* with *singleton sets of signs*. Observe that we can express the validity of a classical sequent $\Gamma \to \Delta$ also as follows: either one of the formulae in Δ is *not* **false** or one of the formulae in Γ is *not* **true**. This dual, negative reading leads to different calculi for logics with more than two truth values. Under the negative reading an n-placed sequent corresponds to the signed formula expression

$$\bigvee_{\psi \in \Gamma_1} \neg\{v_1\}{:}\psi \vee \bigvee_{\psi \in \Gamma_2} \neg\{v_2\}{:}\psi \vee \ldots \vee \bigvee_{\psi \in \Gamma_n} \neg\{v_n\}{:}\psi \ .$$

Since $W = \{v_1, \ldots, v_n\}$ and any formula has to take exactly one truth value this is equivalent to

$$\bigvee_{\psi \in \Gamma_1} \overline{\{v_1\}}{:}\psi \vee \bigvee_{\psi \in \Gamma_2} \overline{\{v_2\}}{:}\psi \vee \ldots \vee \bigvee_{\psi \in \Gamma_n} \overline{\{v_n\}}{:}\psi$$

(see Proposition 3.4).

Already in [Schröter 1955] many-placed sequent calculi based on the negative reading for propositional logics were introduced. Seemingly independently, Rousseau [1967] treated sequent calculi for first-order finitely-valued logics in full generality and also gave soundness and completeness proofs. Since then, negative and positive sequent calculi have been re-invented many times. (See [Zach 1993] for a systematic development of proof theory for finitely-valued logics.)

Of considerable importance for automated deduction are signed tableau calculi with sets of truth values as signs. Such calculi can be understood as *refutational*, *DNF*-based proof search systems for refuting statements $\{v_i\}{:}\psi$ by looking for a negative sequent calculus proof of $\overline{\{v_i\}}{:}\psi$ in a bottom-up manner. Tableau systems of this type for Łukasiewicz logics where given by Suchon [1974]. Later, Surma [1984] and Carnielli [1987] described signed tableau for the family of all finitely-valued logics with distribution quantifiers. Efficient tableau proof procedures based on more general sets of truth values as signs are presented in [Hähnle 1991], [1994a].

As mentioned in Section 3.1, *internal* resolution systems for particular logics have been described already in the 1970s. A much more general *external* resolution principle has been worked out in [Baaz and Fermüller 1992], [1995]. Related systems appear in [Murray and Rosenthal 1991], [1994] [Hähnle 1994c], and [Messing and Stackelberg 1995]. In Section 4 we describe this approach to automated deduction for finitely-valued first-order logics in detail.

3.3. Other proof systems

If we restrict our attention to propositional logics, several other methods for evaluating formulas exist that have aspects of both, internal and external proof systems. We first mention two approaches based on term rewriting.

Knuth-Bendix completion: There have been some attempts to reduce proving in non-classical logics to rewriting in the equational theories of their algebraic models. In the field of many-valued logics we refer for instance to [Bonacina 1991] (see also [Anantharaman and Bonacina 1991]) where several problems in Łukasiewicz logics have been solved automatically by using the Knuth-Bendix algorithm for Wajsberg algebras.

Polynomial translation and Gröbner bases: In [Chazarain, Riscos, Alonso and Briales 1991] the formulae of arbitrary finitely-valued logics are translated to polynomials by using the truth tables of the operators; unsatisfiability is then checked by computing the Gröbner basis of a certain ideal. (An extension to first-order finitely-valued logics or to infinitely-valued logics does not seem straightforward.)

The same idea was used in [Wu, Tan and Li 1998]: formulae are transformed to polynomials, and automated theorem proving is reduced to deciding whether a polynomial vanishes on an algebraic variety. This is done by using Wu's method.

A uniform framework for the study of critical-pair completion procedures is given in [Stokkermans 1995, Stokkermans 1999] where the theoretical results are in particular applied to many-valued resolution as presented in [Baaz and Fermüller 1995]. In [Ganzinger and Sofronie-Stokkermans 1999] it is shown that superposition for finitely-valued logics reduces to (an order-refinement of) the many-valued resolution procedure given in [Baaz and Fermüller 1995]. Recent work (in progress) indicates that "ordered chaining" can also be used for automated theorem proving in regular logics.

Another approach to finitely-valued propositional logics that leads to external proof systems without signed formula expressions is presented in [Konikowska, Morgan and Orłowska 1998]. There a "relational formalization" for arbitrary finitely-valued logics is described as instance of the general relational framework for non-classical logics.

In fact, as long as we are not interested in specific proof formats, but only in the truth value of a propositional formula with respect to finite truth tables, we have to solve a simple and well understood combinatorial task, to which methods from different areas of computer science apply. For example, the problem of deciding validity in many interesting logics can be efficiently translated into a mixed integer programming problem as shown in [Hähnle 1994b]; this method even works for infinitely-valued Łukasiewicz logic.

4. Signed logic: reasoning classically about finitely-valued logics

We investigate the use of signed formula expressions for describing the semantics of many-valued connectives and quantifiers, or, more generally, for manipulating assertions about many-valued formulae. We are mainly interested in finitely-valued logics; to some extent the main ideas carry over to infinitely-valued logics. We will see how finitely-valued logics can be completely characterized within classical first-order logic.

There are several advantages to this approach. First, finitely-valued logics can be given a uniform treatment: certain forms of signed formula expressions – existing for any finitely-valued logic – directly yield many-valued calculi, like sequent calculi (cf. the discussion in Section 3.2), tableaux, natural deduction systems, and clause formation rules. Completeness and correctness of these calculi immediately follow from the completeness and correctness of the two-valued characterization. Second, techniques developed for classical logic can be directly applied to the two-valued translation of many-valued formulae, like quantifier shifting and quantifier elimination, or resolution and its refinements. Furthermore, the language of signed formula expressions is a tool for stating and proving assertions about many-valued logics in a concise way; see e.g. the abbreviation of sub-formulae by new predicate symbols below.

4.1. Transformation rules

Signed formula expressions consist of three layers. The outermost layer is nothing but classical logic based on atomic formulae of type $S{:}\psi$ where S is a sign and ψ is a many-valued formula. Transformations on this level are governed by the usual Boolean and quantificational laws. The medium layer can be termed 'logic of signs'. The interaction of signs with the classical layer is characterized by a handful of equivalences stated in Proposition 3.4. Finally, at the core of signed formula expressions we have proper many-valued formulae. Their syntax and semantics are the only part depending on the many-valued logic under consideration. In the following we discuss transformation rules for signed formulae, which can be regarded as a formalization of many-valued semantics.

4.1. DEFINITION. A *transformation rule* (or rule for short) is a pair (σ, Σ), written as $\sigma \Rightarrow \Sigma$, where σ is a signed formula and Σ is a signed formula expression. The rule is *correct* iff $\sigma \equiv \Sigma$ is valid. A rule is *reducing* (or a *reduction rule*) iff every many-valued formula in Σ is a proper sub-formula of the many-valued formula in σ. A set of rules, R, is *complete* if for every signed formula $S{:}\psi$ there is a reduction rule in R that is applicable to the formula, unless ψ is atomic.

We do not want to give a formal definition of what it means to apply a rule to a signed formula expression. Intuitively, the atomic formulae in a rule serve as formula variables, i.e., as place-holders for arbitrary many-valued formulae. A rule is applicable if the formula variables can be instantiated such that the left-hand side of the rule becomes identical (modulo renaming of bound variables) to a signed formula occurring in the expression. Applying the rule consists of finding a proper instantiation and replacing the signed formula by the right-hand side of the rule.

Clearly, if R is a complete set of correct reduction rules then it can be used to transform any signed formula to an equivalent signed formula expression consisting of atomic signed formulae only. For instance, R is complete if it contains rules $S{:}\Box(A_1, \ldots, A_n) \Rightarrow \Sigma$ and $S{:}(Qx)A(x) \Rightarrow \Sigma$ for every n-ary connective $\Box$, every quantifier Q and every non-empty sign S. In fact, by Proposition 3.4 it suffices to consider singleton sets for achieving completeness.

4.2. EXAMPLE. Consider classical logic, $W = \{t, f\}$, with just the connectives $\wedge$ and $\neg$. A complete set of correct reduction rules is given by

$$\{t\}{:}(A \wedge B) \quad \Rightarrow \quad \{t\}{:}A \wedge \{t\}{:}B$$
$$\{f\}{:}(A \wedge B) \quad \Rightarrow \quad \{f\}{:}A \vee \{f\}{:}B$$
$$\{t\}{:}(\neg A) \quad \Rightarrow \quad \{f\}{:}A$$
$$\{f\}{:}(\neg A) \quad \Rightarrow \quad \{t\}{:}A$$

With these rules the expression $\{f\}{:}(A \wedge \neg(B \wedge \neg C))$ transforms in the following way:

$$\begin{aligned}
\{f\}{:}(A \wedge \neg(B \wedge \neg C)) \quad &\equiv \quad \{f\}{:}A \vee \{f\}{:}(\neg(B \wedge \neg C)) \\
&\equiv \quad \{f\}{:}A \vee \{t\}{:}(B \wedge \neg C) \\
&\equiv \quad \{f\}{:}A \vee (\{t\}{:}B \wedge \{t\}{:}\neg C) \\
&\equiv \quad \{f\}{:}A \vee (\{t\}{:}B \wedge \{f\}{:}C)
\end{aligned}$$

4.2. Connectives

We now show how transformation rules can be constructed systematically for arbitrary finitely-valued connectives. For an n-ary connective $\square$ and a sign S, let

$$DNF_\square(S) \quad \overset{\text{def}}{\equiv} \quad \bigvee_{\substack{w_1, \ldots, w_n \in W \\ \tilde{\square}(w_1, \ldots, w_n) \in S}} \quad \bigwedge_{i=1}^{n} \{w_i\}{:}A_i \quad .$$

The conjunction $\bigwedge \{w_i\}{:}A_i$ is a formula characteristic of the tuple $(w_1, \ldots, w_n)$: it evaluates to **true** if and only if for all i, A_i takes the value w_i. $DNF_\square(S)$ is the disjunction of all characteristic formulae for which $\tilde{\square}(w_1, \ldots, w_n)$ is in S, i.e., $DNF_\square(S)$ is **true** iff $S{:}\square(A_1, \ldots, A_n)$ is **true**. Therefore $S{:}\square(A_1, \ldots, A_n) \Rightarrow DNF_\square(S)$ is a correct reduction rule.

$DNF_\square(S)$ is maximal: every disjunctive normal form which is equivalent to $S{:}\square(A_1, \ldots, A_n)$ has at most as many disjuncts[5] as $DNF_\square(S)$; their number is bounded by $|W|^n$. As mentioned in Section 3.2, disjunctive or conjunctive normal forms can be used to construct sequent calculi, tableau systems etc. The number of disjuncts and conjuncts corresponds to the branching factor of the rules in the calculi, and thus influences search space as well as proof length. A natural question to ask is whether it is possible to find normal forms with a smaller number of disjuncts and conjuncts. In fact, there is a uniform method for all connectives which yields normal forms bounded by $|W|^{n-1}$. The idea is to treat tuples differing only

---

[5] Disregarding, of course, disjuncts which are equivalent to **false**.

in their last components by a single characteristic formula:

$$dnf_\square(S) \overset{\text{def}}{=} \bigvee_{w_1,\ldots,w_{n-1} \in W} \left(\bigwedge_{i=1}^{n-1} \{w_i\}{:}A_i \wedge \{w_n \mid \tilde{\square}(w_1,\ldots,w_n) \in S\}{:}A_n \right).$$

Further optimizations on the number of disjuncts are possible; see Section 7. However, $|W|^{n-1}$ is a tight upper-bound in the sense that there is a connective $\square$ for which $dnf_\square(S)$ is minimal [Zach 1993].

While $DNF_\square(S)$ and $dnf_\square(S)$ directly translate to tableau rules, they are less suited for transforming formulae to sets of clauses: the latter require conjunctive normal form. Of course, we may apply the law of distributivity, but this results in an exponential growth of formulae in general. A cheaper way is to start with the equivalent expressions[6] $\neg DNF_\square(\overline{S})$ or $\neg dnf_\square(\overline{S})$, to apply de Morgan's law, and to eliminate all negation signs. We obtain

$$CNF_\square(S) \overset{\text{def}}{=} \bigwedge_{\substack{w_1,\ldots,w_n \in W \\ \tilde{\square}(w_1,\ldots,w_n) \in \overline{S}}} \bigvee_{i=1}^{n} \overline{\{w_i\}}{:}A_i \quad,$$

$$cnf_\square(S) \overset{\text{def}}{=} \bigwedge_{w_1,\ldots,w_{n-1} \in W} \left(\bigvee_{i=1}^{n-1} \overline{\{w_i\}}{:}A_i \vee \{w_n \mid \tilde{\square}(w_1,\ldots,w_n) \in S\}{:}A_n \right).$$

4.3. PROPOSITION. *For every finitely-valued n-ary connective $\square$ and every sign S, the rule $S{:}\square(A_1,\ldots,A_n) \Rightarrow X$ is correct and reducing, where X is any of $DNF_\square(S)$, $dnf_\square(S)$, $CNF_\square(S)$, or $cnf_\square(S)$. The number of disjuncts and conjuncts, respectively, in $DNF_\square(S)$ and $CNF_\square(S)$ is bounded by $|W|^n$, in $dnf_\square(S)$ and $cnf_\square(S)$ by $|W|^{n-1}$.*

4.4. EXAMPLE. Consider the implication in three-valued Łukasiewicz logic, $W = \{f, p, t\}$, defined by

$\tilde{\supset}$	f	p	t
f	t	t	t
p	p	t	t
t	f	p	t

Using $cnf_\square(S)$ we obtain the following rules for Łukasiewicz implication:

$$\{f\}{:}(A_1 \supset A_2) \Rightarrow \{p,t\}{:}A_1 \wedge \{f,t\}{:}A_1 \wedge (\{f,p\}{:}A_1 \vee \{f\}{:}A_2)$$

$$\{p\}{:}(A_1 \supset A_2) \Rightarrow \{p,t\}{:}A_1 \wedge (\{f,t\}{:}A_1 \vee \{f\}{:}A_2) \wedge (\{f,p\}{:}A_1 \vee \{p\}{:}A_2)$$

$$\{t\}{:}(A_1 \supset A_2) \Rightarrow (\{f,t\}{:}A_1 \vee \{p,t\}{:}A_2) \wedge (\{f,p\}{:}A_1 \vee \{t\}{:}A_2)$$

The rules have already been simplified a bit: three literals of the form $\{\}{:}A_2$ and one disjunction containing $\{f,p,t\}{:}A_2$ were deleted. Further simplifications are possible.

---

[6]Equivalent by Proposition 3.4.

Section 7 shows how minimal conjunctive rules can be obtained. For Łukasiewicz implication they read:

$$\{f\}{:}(A_1 \supset A_2) \;\Rightarrow\; \{t\}{:}A_1 \wedge \{f\}{:}A_2$$

$$\{p\}{:}(A_1 \supset A_2) \;\Rightarrow\; \{p,t\}{:}A_1 \wedge (\{t\}{:}A_1 \vee \{f\}{:}A_2) \wedge (\{p\}{:}A_1 \vee \{p\}{:}A_2)$$

$$\{t\}{:}(A_1 \supset A_2) \;\Rightarrow\; (\{f\}{:}A_1 \vee \{p,t\}{:}A_2) \wedge (\{f,p\}{:}A_1 \vee \{t\}{:}A_2)$$

4.3. Quantifiers

For a distribution quantifier Q and a sign S, let

$$DNF_Q(S) \;\overset{\text{def}}{=}\; \bigvee_{\substack{\emptyset \subset V \subseteq W \\ \widetilde{Q}(V) \in S}} \left((\forall x)V{:}A(x) \wedge \bigwedge_{w\in V} (\exists x)\{w\}{:}A(x) \right) \;.$$

$DNF_Q(S)$ contains one characteristic formula for each distribution V satisfying the condition $\widetilde{Q}(V) \in S$. By definition, the distribution of $A(x)$ is the collection of all truth values that can be obtained by evaluating $A(x)$. In other words, V is the distribution of $A(x)$ if the value of $A(x)$ is in V for all x, i.e. $(\forall x)V{:}A(x)$, and if for every truth value $w \in V$ there is an x such that $A(x)$ evaluates to w, i.e. $(\exists x)\{w\}{:}A(x)$ for all $w \in V$.

The number of disjuncts in $DNF_Q(S)$ is bounded by $2^{|W|}$. This bound can be lowered to $2^{|W|-1}$ by observing that for an arbitrary truth value u, the characteristic formulae for V and $V \cup \{u\}$, $u \notin V$, can be merged into a single expression. We obtain

$$dnf_{Q,u}(S) \;\overset{\text{def}}{=}\; \bigvee_{V \subseteq (W-\{u\})} \left((\forall x)\alpha_S(V){:}A(x) \wedge \bigwedge_{w\in\beta_S(V)} (\exists x)\{w\}{:}A(x) \right),$$

where $\alpha_S(V)$ and $\beta_S(V)$ are given by the table

$\widetilde{Q}(V)$	$\widetilde{Q}(V \cup \{u\})$	$\alpha_S(V)$	$\beta_S(V)$
$\notin S$	$\notin S$	$\{\}$	$\{\}$
$\notin S$	$\in S$	$V \cup \{u\}$	$V \cup \{u\}$
$\in S$	$\notin S$	V	V
$\in S$	$\in S$	$V \cup \{u\}$	V

(we stipulate $\widetilde{Q}(\{\}) \notin S$ for all S). Further optimizations on the number of disjuncts are possible; see Section 7. However, $2^{|W|-1}$ is a tight upper-bound in the sense that there is a quantifier Q for which $dnf_{Q,u}(S)$ is minimal [Zach 1993].

As for connectives, we obtain conjunctive normal forms by applying de Morgan's law to $\neg DNF_Q(\overline{S})$ and $\neg dnf_{Q,u}(\overline{S})$ and then eliminating all negations:

$$CNF_Q(S) \overset{\text{def}}{=} \bigwedge_{\substack{\emptyset \subset V \subseteq W \\ \widetilde{Q}(V) \in \overline{S}}} \left((\exists x)\overline{V}{:}A(x) \vee \bigvee_{w \in V} (\forall x)\overline{\{w\}}{:}A(x) \right) \ ,$$

$$cnf_{Q,u}(S) \overset{\text{def}}{=} \bigwedge_{V \subseteq (W - \{u\})} \left((\exists x)\overline{\alpha_{\overline{S}}(V)}{:}A(x) \vee \bigvee_{w \in \beta_{\overline{S}}(V)} (\forall x)\overline{\{w\}}{:}A(x) \right) .$$

4.5. PROPOSITION. *For every finitely-valued distribution quantifier Q, every sign S, and every truth value u, the rule $S{:}(Qx)A(x) \Rightarrow X$ is correct and reducing, where X is any of $DNF_Q(S)$, $dnf_{Q,u}(S)$, $CNF_Q(S)$, or $cnf_{Q,u}(S)$. The number of disjuncts and conjuncts, respectively, in $DNF_Q(S)$ and $CNF_Q(S)$ is bounded by $2^{|W|}$, in $dnf_{Q,u}(S)$ and $cnf_{Q,u}(S)$ by $2^{|W|-1}$.*

4.6. EXAMPLE. Consider the universal quantifier $\forall$ of three-valued Łukasiewicz logic, defined by $\widetilde{\forall}(\{t\}) = t$, $\widetilde{\forall}(V) = f$ for $f \in V$, and $\widetilde{\forall}(V) = p$ otherwise. We construct $cnf_{\forall,p}(\{p\})$. We start by determining $\alpha_{\overline{\{p\}}} = \alpha_{\{f,t\}}$ and $\beta_{\overline{\{p\}}} = \beta_{\{f,t\}}$:

V	$\widetilde{\forall}(V)$	$\widetilde{\forall}(V \cup \{p\})$	$\alpha_{\{f,t\}}(V)$	$\beta_{\{f,t\}}(V)$
$\{\}$	—	p	$\{\}$	$\{\}$
$\{f\}$	f	f	$\{f,p\}$	$\{f\}$
$\{t\}$	t	p	$\{t\}$	$\{t\}$
$\{f,t\}$	f	f	$\{f,p,t\}$	$\{f,t\}$

Now the conjunctive normal form can be easily constructed:

$$
\begin{aligned}
cnf_{\forall,p}(\{p\}) \ = \quad & (\exists x)\overline{\{\}}{:}A(x) \\
\wedge \ & (\exists x)\overline{\{f,p\}}{:}A(x) \vee (\forall x)\overline{\{f\}}{:}A(x) \\
\wedge \ & (\exists x)\overline{\{t\}}{:}A(x) \vee (\forall x)\overline{\{t\}}{:}A(x) \\
\wedge \ & (\exists x)\overline{\{f,p,t\}}{:}A(x) \vee (\forall x)\overline{\{f\}}{:}A(x) \vee (\forall x)\overline{\{t\}}{:}A(x) \\
\equiv \quad & (\exists x)\{t\}{:}A(x) \vee (\forall x)\{p,t\}{:}A(x) \\
\wedge \ & (\exists x)\{f,p\}{:}A(x) \vee (\forall x)\{f,p\}{:}A(x) \\
\wedge \ & (\forall x)\{p,t\}{:}A(x) \vee (\forall x)\{f,p\}{:}A(x)
\end{aligned}
$$

After eliminating obviously redundant formulae we end up with three conjuncts. Further optimizations would lead us to the minimal, quite intuitive expression $(\exists x)\{p\}{:}A(x) \wedge (\forall x)\{p,t\}{:}A(x)$ with only two conjuncts.

4.4. Structure preserving transformations

The rules presented in the last two sections decompose many-valued formulae into their sub-formulae, with appropriate signs attached. The sub-formulae get duplicated in the course of the transformation, since in general $A(x)$ and the A_i appear several times on the right side of the rules. Moreover, the decomposition dissolves the original structure of the formula. This phenomenon – well-known from clause form transformations in classical logic – is not always desirable. As an alternative, we can apply structure preserving rules. The idea is to introduce new predicate symbols as an abbreviation for sub-formulae. This way it is possible to refer to a sub-formula by using its associated predicate symbol.

Formally, the introduction of predicate symbols is described by the rule

$$\text{(IP)} \qquad S{:}\psi[A(\vec{x})] \Rightarrow S{:}\psi[P(\vec{x})] \wedge \bigwedge_{w \in W} (\forall \vec{x})(\{w\}{:}A(\vec{x}) \equiv \{w\}{:}P(\vec{x})) \quad .$$

$\psi[A(\vec{x})]$ denotes a many-valued formula containing the sub-formula A in one or more positions; $\vec{x}$ is the vector of free variables in A. $\psi[P(\vec{x})]$ is obtained by replacing in ψ one or more occurrences of A (not necessarily all) by $P(\vec{x})$; P is a new predicate symbol occurring nowhere else. The equivalence $\{w\}{:}A(\vec{x}) \equiv \{w\}{:}P(\vec{x})$ ensures that $P(\vec{x})$ faithfully represents sub-formula $A(\vec{x})$: in every interpretation satisfying the equivalence, $P(\vec{x})$ and $A(\vec{x})$ evaluate to the same truth value for all x.

In clausal theorem proving equivalences are usually replaced by two implications. The equivalence of rule (IP) thus becomes

$$\bigwedge_{w \in W} (\forall \vec{x})(\{w\}{:}A(\vec{x}) \supset \{w\}{:}P(\vec{x})) \quad \wedge \quad \bigwedge_{w \in W} (\forall \vec{x})(\{w\}{:}P(\vec{x}) \supset \{w\}{:}A(\vec{x})) \quad .$$

Because of $W{:}A(\vec{x}) \equiv W{:}P(\vec{x}) \equiv \top$ the two conjuncts in the above formula are logically equivalent. Therefore we may drop one of them and obtain for instance

$$\text{(IP')} \qquad S{:}\psi[A(\vec{x})] \Rightarrow S{:}\psi[P(\vec{x})] \wedge \bigwedge_{w \in W} (\forall \vec{x})(\{w\}{:}A(\vec{x}) \supset \{w\}{:}P(\vec{x})) \quad .$$

The rules (IP) and (IP') are not correct in the strict sense: the right side contains a predicate symbol not occurring on the left. However, the two sides are equivalent with respect to satisfiability. Every interpretation satisfying the right side also satisfies the left one, and every interpretation satisfying the formula to the left can be extended to an interpretation satisfying the formula to the right by making P behave identical to A. This kind of equivalence suffices for resolution-style theorem proving which is concerned with the (un)satisfiability of formulae.

The rules are not reducing, either: $\psi[P(\vec{x})]$ is no sub-formula of $\psi[A(\vec{x})]$, and $\psi[A(\vec{x})]$ might occur also on the right side of the rule in the case that A is identical to ψ. To avoid infinite chains of 'reductions', we may for instance require that no occurrence of $P(\vec{x})$ or A on the right side may be the target of another application of this rule; it obviously does not make sense to introduce an abbreviation for an abbreviating predicate symbol or for an already abbreviated formula.

For the purpose of clause formation it is convenient to combine (IP') with a transformation rule that eliminates the top connective or top quantifier in $A(\vec{x})$. For connectives we get

$$S{:}\psi[\square(A_1, \ldots, A_n)] \quad \Rightarrow \quad S{:}\psi[P(\vec{x})] \wedge \bigwedge_{w \in W} (\forall \vec{x})(DNF_\square(\{w\}) \supset \{w\}{:}P(\vec{x}))$$

where $\vec{x}$ denotes the free variables in $\Box(A_1, \ldots, A_n)$. Some simplification steps lead to the required conjunctive normal form to the right of $\Rightarrow$:

$$S{:}\psi[P(\vec{x})] \wedge \bigwedge_{w_1,\ldots,w_n \in W} (\forall \vec{x})\left(\bigvee_{i=1}^{n} \overline{\{w_i\}}{:}A_i \vee \{\widetilde{\Box}(w_1,\ldots,w_n)\}{:}P(\vec{x}) \right).$$

Of course we are not bound to use $DNF_\Box(\{w\})$; other disjunctive forms would do as well.

In a completely analogous manner we obtain a combined rule for quantifiers:

$$S{:}\psi[(Qy)A(y)] \quad \Rightarrow$$
$$S{:}\psi[P(\vec{x})] \wedge \bigwedge_{\emptyset \subset V \subseteq W} (\forall \vec{x})\left((\exists y)\overline{V}{:}A(y) \vee \bigvee_{w \in V} (\forall y)\overline{\{w\}}{:}A(y) \vee \{\widetilde{Q}(V)\}{:}P(\vec{x}) \right)$$

where $\vec{x}$ denotes the free variables in $(Qy)A(y)$. The total number of conjuncts introduced by these combined rules is bounded by $|W|^n$ and $2^{|W|}$, respectively.

The combined rules are called *structure preserving*, since the structure of the original formula is encoded by the newly introduced predicate symbols. In contrast, the transformation rules of the last section are called *language preserving*, since no new symbols are added to the language of the original formula.

4.5. Translation to clause form

Suppose we want to show that the many-valued formula F always evaluates to some truth value in S, i.e., that $S{:}F$ is valid. For instance, to prove F we would choose for S the set of designated truth values. A proof of $S{:}F$ by signed resolution consists of two steps:

1. Transform $\neg S{:}F = \overline{S}{:}F$ into a set $\mathcal{C}$ of clauses.
2. Show that $\mathcal{C}$ is unsatisfiable by deriving a contradiction using many-valued resolution.

In this section we discuss the first step, while many-valued resolution will be the topic of the next section. We start by defining the notion of many-valued clauses.

In classical clause logic a clause is a disjunction of literals, i.e., of negated or unnegated atomic formulae. Since disjunction is associative, commutative and idempotent we can treat a clause as a finite set of literals. Interpreting the presence or absence of the negation sign as expressing the meta-linguistic statement that the atomic formula evaluates to **false** or **true**, we may view a literal as a pair consisting of an atomic formula and a truth value. This leads to the concept of many-valued resolution as described in [Baaz and Fermüller 1992], [1995]. For reasons of efficiency it is advantageous to allow not just single truth values but sets of truth values as sign of a literal.

4.7. DEFINITION. Let W be the set of truth values. For every atomic formula A and every subset $S \subseteq W$, the signed formula expression $S{:}A$ is called a *literal*. A *clause* is a finite set of literals. The *signed formula expression corresponding to a clause* C, denoted by $\forall C$, is the universally closed disjunction of all literals in C: $\forall C \overset{\text{def}}{=} \mathbf{\forall} \vec{x} \mathbf{\bigvee} C$, where $\vec{x}$ is the set of variables occurring in C. An interpretation I *satisfies* C if $\mathrm{sval}_I(\forall C) = \mathbf{true}$. A set of clauses, $\mathcal{C}$, is *satisfiable* if there is an interpretation I satisfying simultaneously all clauses in $\mathcal{C}$, i.e., $\mathrm{sval}_I(\mathbf{\bigwedge}_{C \in \mathcal{C}} \forall C) = \mathbf{true}$.

The transformation of $\overline{S}{:}F$ to clausal form proceeds in the following steps:

1. *Elimination of many-valued connectives and quantifiers.* Apply to $\overline{S}{:}F$ exhaustively the rules of a complete set of correct reduction rules (cf. Section 4.1).[7] The result is a classical first-order formula over atomic signed formulae, i.e., over literals.

2. *Elimination of existential quantifiers.* Replace all existentially quantified variables by Skolem terms.[8]

3. *Conjunctive normal form.* Apply distributivity until the formula is a conjunction of disjunctions of literals. Each conjunct corresponds to a clause.

The steps need not be applied in the given order. One could for instance eliminate existential quantifiers immediately when they are introduced by a reduction rule, and flatten the formula by distributivity after every application of a reduction rule. Moreover, at any time in the transformation process the formula can be simplified according to the laws of classical logic; in particular, we could strive to minimize the scope of classical quantifiers to obtain small Skolem terms. Finally, additional transformations can be applied as long as they preserve satisfiability. Most notably, some or all sub-formulae can be abbreviated by new predicate symbols (see Section 4.4).

In general the number of clauses derived by structure preserving rules will be much smaller than the number of clauses derived by language preserving rules, since in the first case distributivity is not needed. The clause form of a formula with m occurrences of at most n-ary connectives and l occurrences of quantifiers contains not more than

$$m|W|^n + l2^{|W|} + 1$$

clauses when using optimal structure preserving rules. In contrast, the following example shows that clause forms obtained by optimal language preserving rules may contain as many as $|W|^m$ clauses even if the formula contains only $m - 1$ binary and one unary connective.

4.8. EXAMPLE. Let $W = \{w_0, \ldots, w_{n-1}\}$, let $\oplus$ be the binary connective defined by

$$\widetilde{\oplus}(w_i, w_j) \quad = \quad w_{i+j \bmod n} \quad ,$$

---

[7] With regard to the third step the rules should be those derived from CNFs.

[8] In general distribution quantifiers cannot be eliminated within the many-valued logic itself. In our setting, however, only classical universal and existential quantifiers remain after replacing quantified formulae by signed formula expressions.

and let $\diamond$ be the unary operator defined by

$$\tilde{\diamond}(w_i) \;=\; \begin{cases} w_0 & \text{if } i = 0 \\ w_1 & \text{if } i \neq 0 \end{cases} \;.$$

We define the formulae G_k recursively as follows: G_0 is a predicate symbol of arity 0; $G_k = \oplus(G_{k-1}, G'_{k-1})$ for $k > 0$, where G'_k is identical to G_k except for renaming all predicate symbols such that G_k and G'_k do not share any predicate symbols. F_k is defined as $\diamond(G_k)$; it can be viewed as a fully balanced binary tree of depth k with an additional node attached below the root and pairwise distinct predicate symbols as leaf nodes. By definition F_k has the property that

$$\mathrm{val}_I(F_k) = w_1 \quad \text{iff} \quad (\Sigma_{1 \leq j \leq 2^k}\, \mathrm{val}_I(P_j)) \not\equiv 0 \bmod |W| \quad,$$

where the P_j are the 2^k different predicate symbols occurring in F_k. It can be shown that the clause form of $\{w_1\}{:}F_k$ contains at least $|W|^{2^k-1}$ clauses if we use language preserving transformation rules as described in Section 4.2. On the other hand, a structure preserving translation of $\{w_1\}{:}F_k$ will result in a clause form with at most $2^k|W|^2 + 1$ clauses.

In many cases a combination of structure and language preserving rules determines the most efficient translation strategy. This, of course, depends on the logic concerned and is a delicate matter if also the form of the particular formula to be translated is taken into consideration. (For the case of classical logic, see [Boy de la Tour 1992] for some results along this line.) The most important effect of the use of structure preserving translation calculi, however, may consist in the reduction of proof length: structure preserving translation rules are non-analytic and are able to encode certain types of non-atomic cuts. This may lead to a non-elementary reduction of proof length [Baaz, Fermüller and Leitsch 1994].

5. Signed resolution

Given the concept of clauses as presented in Definition 4.7, the classical resolution principle of [Robinson 1965] is straightforwardly generalized to many-valued logic. Different variants of many-valued resolution appear in the literature. Below, we describe a first-order version of "signed resolution" as defined, e.g., in [Hähnle 1994c].

5.1. Inference rules

The conclusion of the following inference rule:

$$\frac{\{S{:}P\} \cup C_1 \qquad \{R{:}Q\} \cup C_2}{(\{S \cap R{:}P\} \cup C_1 \cup C_2)\sigma} \quad \text{binary resolution}$$

is called a *binary resolvent* of the variable disjoint *parent clauses* $\{S{:}P\} \cup C_1$ and $\{R{:}Q\} \cup C_2$, if $S \neq R$ and σ is an mgu of the atoms P and Q.

Like in the classical case we need a *factorization rule* to obtain a refutationally complete calculus:

$$\frac{C}{C\sigma} \text{ factorization}$$

where σ is an mgu of a subset of C. $C\sigma$ is called a *factor* of C.

The combination of factorization and binary resolution does not yet guarantee that the empty clause can be derived from all unsatisfiable sets of clauses. We also have to remove literals with empty signs by the following *simplification rule*:[9]

$$\frac{C \cup \{\emptyset{:}P\}}{C} \text{ simplification}$$

C is called a *simplification* of C' if it results from C' by removing all literals with empty sign. (I.e., by applying the simplification rule to C' as often as possible.)

The *merging rule* unites literals that share the same atom. It is not needed for completeness but helps to reduce the search space and to simplify the completeness proof.[10]

$$\frac{\{S_1{:}P\} \cup \ldots \cup \{S_\ell{:}P\} \cup C}{\{S_1 \cup \ldots \cup S_\ell{:}P\} \cup C} \text{ merging}$$

C is called a *normal form* or *normalized* version of C' if it results from C' by applying the simplification rules and the merging rule to C' as often as possible. I.e., all literals with empty signs are removed and all different literals in C have different atoms.

One can combine factoring, simplification, merging, and binary resolution into a single resolution rule. This corresponds to a particular strategy for the application of these rules.

The following alternative version of signed resolution can be considered as a combination of a series of binary resolution and simplification steps into one "macro inference step".

$$\frac{\{S_1{:}P_1\} \cup C_1 \quad \ldots \quad \{S_k{:}P_k\} \cup C_k}{(C_1 \cup \ldots \cup C_k)\sigma} \text{ macro-resolution}$$

where $S_1 \cap \ldots \cap S_k = \emptyset$ and σ is the mgu of the atoms P_i $(1 \leq i \leq k)$. The conclusion is called *macro-resolvent*.

It is useful to consider resolution as a set operator (mapping sets of clauses into sets of clauses).

---

[9] Alternatively, we can dispose with the simplification rule by defining a clause to be empty if all literals have empty sets as signs.

[10] In [Hähnle 1994c] it is claimed that the merging rule is needed for completeness. However, this is only correct if clauses are not treated modulo idempotency of disjunction (e.g., as multi-sets as opposed to sets).

5.1. DEFINITION. For a set of clauses $\mathcal{C}$ let $\mathcal{R}_b(\mathcal{C})$ be the set of all binary resolvents of (variable renamed) normalized factors of clauses in $\mathcal{C}$. The transitive and reflexive closure of the set operator $\mathcal{R}_b$ is denoted by $\mathcal{R}_b^*$.

Similarly, we define $\mathcal{R}_m(\mathcal{C})$ as the set of all macro-resolvents of (variable renamed) normalized factors of clauses in $\mathcal{C}$. $\mathcal{R}_m^*$ denotes the transitive and reflexive closure of $\mathcal{R}_m$.

5.2. Correctness and completeness

A proof of correctness and refutational completeness for propositional signed "macro-resolution" can be found in [Hähnle 1994c]. The correctness and completeness of binary resolution follows directly from that of macro-resolution. Lifting to the first-order level is also rather straightforward. However, to keep this article self-contained and to provide the reader with machinery that is useful in many contexts (as witnessed by the following subsections) we present correctness and alternative completeness proofs for first-order signed resolution.

As usual in automated deduction we employ a semantic version of Herbrand's Theorem that allows to restrict the attention to so-called Herbrand interpretations (term models).

5.2. DEFINITION. The *Herbrand universe* $H(\mathcal{C})$ of a clause set $\mathcal{C}$ is the set of variable free terms that consist of constants and function symbols occurring in $\mathcal{C}$. If there are no constants occurring in $\mathcal{C}$ we introduce a special constant symbol to prevent $H(\mathcal{C})$ from being empty. The elements of $H(\mathcal{C})$ are called *ground terms*.

5.3. DEFINITION. A variable-free atom, literal or clause is called *ground*. A *ground instance* C' of a clause (or atom) C (with respect to a clause set $\mathcal{C}$) is a substitution instance of C where terms in $H(\mathcal{C})$ replace the variables of C.

5.4. DEFINITION. The *Herbrand base* $A(\mathcal{C})$ of $\mathcal{C}$ is the set of all ground instances of atoms that occur in clauses of $\mathcal{C}$.[11]

5.5. DEFINITION. An *assignment* associates truth values with atoms. A *complete assignment to a set of atoms* K is defined as a set of (singleton-as-sign) literals $\{\{\psi(P)\}{:}P \mid P \in K\}$, where ψ is a function from K into W. Any subset of a complete assignment to K is called *partial assignment* to K.

An *Herbrand interpretation (H-interpretation)* of a clause set $\mathcal{C}$ is a complete assignment to $A(\mathcal{C})$.

5.6. DEFINITION. For any set of atoms K the corresponding *literal set* $\Lambda(K)$ is the set $\{V{:}A \mid A \in K, V \subseteq W, V \neq \emptyset\}$.

---

[11]Sometimes the Herbrand base is defined as the set of all ground atoms over the signature of S. Since we never have to care about the interpretation of atoms that are not instances of atoms occurring in the clause set under consideration, we may safely ignore them.

To assist concise statements about the relation between arbitrary sets of literals we use the following notation:

5.7. DEFINITION. For a set of literals C let $\widehat{C}$ be the equivalent set that consists of singleton-as-sign literals only. More exactly, $\widehat{C} = \{\{v\}{:}A \mid S{:}A \in C, v \in S\}$. We say that C is *contained* in another set of literals D if $\widehat{C} \subseteq \widehat{D}$.

5.8. DEFINITION. An H-interpretation $\mathcal{M}$ *satisfies* a clause set $\mathcal{C}$ iff for all ground instances C' of each $C \in \mathcal{C}$: $\widehat{C'} \cap \mathcal{M} \neq \emptyset$. $\mathcal{M}$ is called an *H-model* of $\mathcal{C}$. $\mathcal{C}$ is *H-unsatisfiable* if there is no H-interpretation that satisfies $\mathcal{C}$.

Just like in classical logic we have the following important fact:

5.9. PROPOSITION. *A set of clauses $\mathcal{C}$ is unsatisfiable iff it is H-unsatisfiable.*

PROOF. (Sketch) Each H-interpretation of $\mathcal{C}$ can trivially be extended to an interpretation in the sense of Section 2. On the other hand, each ordinary interpretation I induces an H-interpretation $\mathcal{M}_I = \{\{w\}{:}P \mid \mathrm{val}_I(P) = w, P \in A(\mathcal{C})\}$. Clearly, $\mathcal{M}_I$ satisfies $\mathcal{C}$ iff I satisfies $\mathcal{C}$. $\qquad\square$

5.10. THEOREM. *For every satisfiable set of clauses $\mathcal{C}$, $\mathcal{R}_b(\mathcal{C})$ and $\mathcal{R}_m(\mathcal{C})$ are satisfiable, too.*

PROOF. An interpretation assigns a truth value to every atom. Therefore all ground instances of literals with the empty set as sign are always evaluated to **false** (in the meta-language; i.e. the theory of signed formula expressions). A clause corresponds to a (universally closed) disjunction. (See Definition 4.7.) It is therefore logically equivalent to its simplification.

The same holds for the merging rule. The corresponding signed formula expression forms of a clause C' and its normal form C are logically equivalent in the theory of signed formula expressions, which provides the semantics for clause logic.

A factor of clause C is an instance of C. Therefore the corresponding signed formula expression is implied by that of C.

Let I be an interpretation that satisfies the ground clauses $\{S{:}P\} \cup C_1$ and $\{R{:}P\} \cup C_2$. We show that I also satisfies the binary resolvent $D = \{S \cap R{:}P\} \cup C_1 \cup C_2$. Let W be the set of all truth values. I assigns some truth value v to P.

Case 1: $v \in W - S$. Then I satisfies some literal in C_1 and therefore also D.

Case 2: $v \in W - R$. Then I satisfies some literal in C_2 and therefore also D.

Case 3: $v \in S \cap R$. Then I satisfies the literal $S \cap R{:}P$ and therefore also D.

Lifting to the first-order level is as usual. (By Proposition 5.9 we may view every clause as the representation of the set of its ground instances.)

Since the operator $\mathcal{R}_b$ just combines factoring, simplification, merging, and binary resolution, we obtain that every interpretation that satisfies $\mathcal{C}$ also satisfies $\mathcal{R}_b(\mathcal{C})$.

As already remarked above, macro-resolution can be decomposed into a series of binary resolution steps, where the final resolvent is simplified. It thus follows that every interpretation satisfying $\mathcal{C}$ also satisfies $\mathcal{R}_m(\mathcal{C})$. $\qquad\square$

5.11. COROLLARY. *For every finite set of clauses* C, *if* $\{\} \in \mathcal{R}_b^*(C)$ *or* $\{\} \in \mathcal{R}_m^*(C)$ *then* C *is unsatisfiable.*

Our completeness proof is based on the concept of semantic trees. It differs from the proof in [Hähnle 1994c] but straightforwardly generalizes the completeness proof [Baaz and Fermüller 1995] for singletons-as-signs resolution. It also allows us to show the completeness of various refinements of resolution, deletion strategies as well as a many-valued version of Lee's theorem on "implicational" (in contrast to refutational) completeness of resolution (see Section 5.5 below).

As usual in automated theorem proving, we consider a tree as growing downwards; i.e. the *root* is the top node of a tree. A node or edge α *is above* a node or edge β if α is part of the path (considered as alternating sequence of nodes and edges) connecting β with the root. A *branch* of T is a path that starts with the root and either is infinite or else ends in a leaf node of T.

5.12. DEFINITION. Let W be a finite set of truth values and K be a set of ground atoms. For any subset Δ of the literal set $\Lambda(K)$ of K we say that Δ *omits* the assignment A_K to K if $\widehat{\Delta} \cap A_K = \emptyset$. A finitely branching tree T is a *semantic tree for* K if finite, non-empty subsets of $\Lambda(K)$ label the edges of T in the following way:
(1) The set of the sets of literals labeling all edges leaving one node is an H-unsatisfiable set of clauses.
(2) For each branch of T the union of the sets of literals labeling the edges of the branch omits exactly one complete assignment A_K to K. For short, we say that *the branch omits A_K* as well as any H-interpretation containing A_K.
(3) For each complete assignment A_K to K there is a branch of T such that this branch omits A_K.
The union of all sets of literals labeling the edges of the path from the root down to some node α of T forms the *refutation set* of α.

For a set of clauses C any semantic tree T for $A(C)$ represents an exhaustive survey of all possible H-interpretations. Each branch omits exactly one H-interpretation and each H-interpretation is omitted by at least one branch.

5.13. DEFINITION. A clause C *fails* at a node α of a semantic tree T if there is some ground instance C' of C such that C' is contained in the refutation set of that node. A node α is a *failure node* for a clause set C if some clause of C fails at α but no clause in C fails at a node above α. A node is called an *inference node* if all of its successor nodes are failure nodes. T is *closed* for C if there is a failure node for C on every branch of T.

5.14. THEOREM. *A set of clauses* C *is H-unsatisfiable iff there is a finite subset* $K \subseteq A(C)$ *such that every semantic tree for K is closed for C.*

PROOF. $\Rightarrow$: Let T be a semantic tree for $A(C)$, the Herbrand base of C. By definition of a semantic tree, any branch B of T omits exactly one complete assignment to

$A(\mathcal{C})$, which extends to an H-interpretation $\mathcal{M}$ of $\mathcal{C}$. If $\mathcal{C}$ is H-unsatisfiable then $\mathcal{M}$ does not satisfy all clauses in $\mathcal{C}$. This means that there is some ground instance C' of a clause C in $\mathcal{C}$ such that $\widehat{C'} \cap \mathcal{M} = \emptyset$. But since B omits only the literals of $\Lambda(A(\mathcal{C}))$ that are true in $\mathcal{M}$ this implies that the union of labels of the edges of B contains C'; i.e., C' is contained in the refutation set of some node of B. We have thus proved that every branch of T contains a failure node for some clause of $\mathcal{C}$. In other words, T is closed for $\mathcal{C}$. Moreover, by König's Lemma, the number of nodes in T that are situated above a failure node is finite. But this implies that for each unsatisfiable set of clauses $\mathcal{C}$ there is a finite unsatisfiable set C' of ground instances of clauses of $\mathcal{C}$. Since any semantic tree that is closed for C' is also closed for S it is sufficient to base the tree on a finite subset of $A(\mathcal{C})$: the set K of ground atoms occurring in C'. Observe that we have not imposed any restriction on the form of the tree. Thus every semantic tree for K is closed for $\mathcal{C}$.

$\Leftarrow$: Let T be a closed semantic tree for a finite $K \subseteq A(\mathcal{C})$. Suppose $\mathcal{M}$ is an H-model of $\mathcal{C}$; i.e. for all ground instances C' of $C \in \mathcal{C}$ we have $\mathcal{M} \cap \widehat{C'} \neq \emptyset$. By definition of a semantic tree, $\mathcal{M}$ is omitted by some branch B of T. Since T is closed, some clause $C \in \mathcal{C}$ fails at a node α of B. That means that some ground instance C' of C is contained in the refutation set of α. Therefore $\mathcal{M} \cap \widehat{C'} \neq \emptyset$ implies that $\mathcal{M}$ contains some literal that also occurs in some refutation set of a node on B. But this contradicts the assumption that B omits $\mathcal{M}$. Therefore $\mathcal{C}$ is H-unsatisfiable.   □

Theorem 5.14 can be used to prove the completeness of a great number of different versions and refinements of signed resolution. We present the completeness proof for binary resolution in some detail and provide sketches for some other completeness results.

5.15. Theorem (Refutational completeness of $\mathcal{R}_b$). *If a finite set of clauses $\mathcal{C}$ is unsatisfiable then* $\{\} \in \mathcal{R}_b^*(\mathcal{C})$.

Proof. By Theorem 5.14 we know that for any unsatisfiable $\mathcal{C}$ there is some $K \subseteq A(\mathcal{C})$ such that all semantic trees for K are closed for $\mathcal{C}$. We choose a binary tree T, the labels of which are of form $\{\{v\}{:}A\}$, i.e., sets consisting of a single singleton-as-sign literal. (The existence of such semantic trees is trivial.)

Suppose C_1 and C_2 are clauses in $\mathcal{C}$ that fail immediately below an inference node α of T. Let $\{\{v\}{:}A\}$ and $\{\{w\}{:}B\}$, be the sets labeling the edges leaving the inference node α. By condition (1) in the definition of a semantic tree we have $A = B$ and $v \neq w$. Since C_1 and C_2 only fail below α but not at α there is some ground substitution γ such that $\{\{v\}{:}A\}$ is contained in a literal $S{:}A$ of $C_1\gamma$ and $\{\{w\}{:}A\}$ is contained in a literal $R{:}A$ of $C_2\gamma$ (or vice versa). Observe that every clause fails at exactly the same nodes as its normal form. Therefore we may assume without loss of generality that $C_1\gamma$ and $C_2\gamma$ are normalized. Since $v \neq w$ there exists the binary resolvent $G = \{S \cap R{:}A\} \cup (C_1\gamma - \{S{:}A\}) \cup (C_2\gamma - \{R{:}A\})$. Since the parent clauses are normalized, $S \cap R{:}A$ is the only literal in G with atom A. Since neither v nor w is contained in $S \cap R$, G is contained in the refutation set of α.

In other words G fails at α. (Possibly also above α). By the Lifting Lemma 5.16 G contains an instance of a binary resolvent D of C_1' and C_2', where C_1' and C_2' are normalized factors of C_1 and C_2, respectively. Summarizing we have shown that

(C) for any two clauses C_1, C_2 which fail at different nodes immediately below an inference node of T there is a resolvent $D \in \mathcal{R}_b(\{C_1, C_2\})$ which fails at this inference node.

Since T is closed for C there must be at least one inference node for C in T. But then, as we have just seen, there exists a failure node for $C \cup \{D\}$ in T, where D is in $\mathcal{R}_b(C)$, that is situated above some failure nodes for C. That means that the number of nodes in T at which no clause fails strictly decreases when adding $\mathcal{R}_b(C)$ to C. By iteratively adding new generations of resolvents we eventually arrive at a clause set for which the root of T is a failure node. Since the only clause failing at the root of a semantic tree is $\{\}$ we conclude that $\{\} \in \mathcal{R}_b^*(C)$. $\qquad\square$

5.16. LEMMA (Lifting Lemma). *Let D_1 be an instance of clause C_1 and D_2 be an instance of clause C_2. If F is a binary resolvent of D_1 and D_2, then F contains an instance of a binary resolvent E of C_1' and C_2', where C_1' and C_2' are normalized factors of C_1 and C_2, respectively.*

PROOF. Analogous to the classical case. $\qquad\square$

5.17. REMARK. In fact, F *is* an instance of E if all clauses are considered to be in normal form. A similar Lifting Lemma holds for macro-resolution.

5.18. THEOREM (Refutational completeness of $\mathcal{R}_m$). *If a finite set of clauses C is unsatisfiable then $\{\} \in \mathcal{R}_m^*(C)$.*

PROOF. Again, we rely on Theorem 5.14. Let K be a finite subset of the Herbrand base such that every semantic tree based on K is closed for the unsatisfiable clause set C. Let $W = \{w_0, \ldots, w_{n-1}\}$ be the set of truth values. This time we choose an n-ary tree T; i.e., every internal node has a successor node for each truth value.

Let $\langle A_0, \ldots, A_m \rangle$ be some enumeration of K. The nodes of T are naturally partitioned into levels. The only node at level 0 is the root. If α is a node at level i ($0 \le i \le m$) there is an edge to a successor node α_j at level $i+1$ for each truth value w_j. The edge connecting α with α_j is labeled by $\{W - \{w_j\}:A_i\}$. It is easily checked that T is indeed a semantic tree.

According to the same argument as in the proof of Theorem 5.15 it remains to show the following:

(C') If $C_0, \ldots C_{n-1}$ are clauses failing at the successor nodes $\alpha_0, \ldots \alpha_{n-1}$, respectively, of some inference node α of T, then there exists a macro-resolvent $D \in \mathcal{R}_m(\{C_0, \ldots C_{n-1}\})$ which fails at α.

Observe that the clauses $C_0, \ldots C_{n-1}$ need not be distinct. In other words, strictly less than n clauses may be involved in the macro-resolution step. That n clauses suffice follows from the argument below.

For simplicity we only consider the ground case. (As usual, lifting to first-order requires factoring.) Let i be the level of α. For all $0 \le j \le n-1$: if C_j fails at node α_j but not at α it has to contain a literal $S_j{:}A_i$ where $w_j \notin S_j$. Obviously $\bigcap_{0 \leq j \leq n-1} S_j = \emptyset$. Without loss of generality, we may assume the clauses C_j to be in normal form. This implies that the macro-resolvent $D = (C_0 - \{S_0{:}A_i\}) \cup \dots \cup (C_{n-1} - \{S_{n-1}{:}A_i\})$ does not contain any literal with atom A_i. Since D is composed of subsets of the C_j it fails at node α, as required. $\qquad\square$

5.19. REMARK. It is quite obvious from the above proofs that only factors, where the unified literals are actually resolved upon, are needed for completeness.

5.3. A-ordering resolution

A very useful refinement of resolution that is well known for the classical case is based on substitution stable orderings of the Herbrand base called A-orderings. Since this concept only refers to atoms (not to literals) it can directly be applied to many-valued clauses, as well.

5.20. DEFINITION. An *A-ordering* $<_A$ is a binary relation on atoms such that
- $<_A$ is irreflexive,
- $<_A$ is transitive, and
- for all atoms A,B and all substitutions θ: $A <_A B$ implies $A\theta <_A B\theta$.

We refine the macro-resolution rule by requiring that the resolved atom is not smaller (with respect to $<_A$) than any literal in the macro-resolvent. More exactly, the inference rule is:

$$\frac{\{S_1{:}P_1\} \cup C_1 \quad \dots \quad \{S_k{:}P_k\} \cup C_k}{(C_1 \cup \dots \cup C_k)\sigma} \quad P_i\sigma \not<_A Q \text{ for all } R{:}Q \in C_i\sigma$$

where $S_1 \cap \dots \cap S_k = \emptyset$ and σ is the mgu of the atoms P_i $(1 \leq i \leq k)$. The conclusion of the rule is called $<_A$-*ordered macro-resolvent*.

5.21. DEFINITION. Let $<_A$ be an A-ordering of $A(\mathcal{C})$. $\mathcal{R}_{m,<_A}(\mathcal{C})$ is the set of all $<_A$-ordered macro-resolvents of (variable renamed) normalized factors of clauses in $\mathcal{C}$. $\mathcal{R}^*_{m,<_A}$ denotes the transitive and reflexive closure of $\mathcal{R}_{m,<_A}$.

Of course, we can apply an analogous restriction to refine binary resolution. The resulting operator is called $\mathcal{R}_{b,<_A}$. The correctness of A-ordered resolution follows directly from that of ordinary resolution. (Observe that $\mathcal{R}_{m,<_A}(\mathcal{C}) \subseteq \mathcal{R}_m(\mathcal{C})$ and $\mathcal{R}_{b,<_A}(\mathcal{C}) \subseteq \mathcal{R}_b(\mathcal{C})$.)

5.22. THEOREM. *If a finite set of clauses $\mathcal{C}$ is unsatisfiable then $\{\} \in \mathcal{R}^*_{m,<_A}(\mathcal{C})$ and $\{\} \in \mathcal{R}^*_{b,<_A}(\mathcal{C})$.*

PROOF. In the completeness proof for $\mathcal{R}_m$ (Theorem 5.18) we have based the semantic tree on an arbitrary enumeration $\langle A_0, \dots, A_m \rangle$ of the relevant subset K of the Herbrand base. To see that we may impose the ordering restriction on the resolvents without loosing completeness, let the enumeration respect the A-ordering in question. More exactly, we require that $j > i$ implies $A_j \not<_A A_i$ for all $0 \leq i, j \leq m$. This guarantees that the macro-resolvents failing at an inference node for C are in $\mathcal{R}_{m,<_A}(C)$. The rest of the completeness proof is the same as for unrefined resolution.

The argument for $\mathcal{R}_{b,<_A}$ is analogous. □

5.4. Deletion rules

The importance of removing redundant clauses from the search space is well known. Indeed, anyone who experiments with a resolution based theorem prover, learns that many interesting problems are only within the realm of automatically solvable problems (within reasonable bounds on time and space) if deletion rules like subsumption and tautology removal are used. This holds for many-valued clause logic just as well as for classical logic.

5.23. DEFINITION. A clause is called *tautology* if its normal form contains a literal of form $W{:}A$, where W is the set of all truth values.

5.24. DEFINITION. A clause C subsumes a clause D if D contains an instance of C; i.e., $\widehat{C\theta} \subseteq \widehat{D}$ for some substitution θ.

Obviously, tautologies are satisfied by every interpretation. Therefore we may remove tautologies from all sets of clauses before applying a resolution based prover to test for unsatisfiability. Similarly, a clause set C remains unsatisfiable if we remove from C any clause that is subsumed by another clause remaining in C. However, this does not answer the question whether we may delete tautologies and subsumed clauses when they occur during proof search.

Consider the following deletion rules. (Note that deletion rules operate on *sets* of clauses.)

$$\frac{\mathcal{C} \cup \{C\}}{\mathcal{C}} \text{ tautology removal}$$

if C is a tautology.

$$\frac{\mathcal{C} \cup \{C, D\}}{\mathcal{C} \cup \{C\}} \text{ subsumption}$$

if C subsumes D.

5.25. DEFINITION. A *reduction operator* red is a mapping from clause sets $\mathcal{C}$ into clause sets $\text{red}(\mathcal{C})$, where $\text{red}(\mathcal{C})$ results from $\mathcal{C}$ by applying an arbitrary number of tautology removal or subsumption steps to $\mathcal{C}$.

Let $\mathcal{R}$ be a resolution operator and red a reduction operator. We define $(\mathcal{R}^{\text{red}})^0(\mathcal{C}) = \text{red}(\mathcal{C})$ and $(\mathcal{R}^{\text{red}})^{i+1}(\mathcal{C}) = \text{red}((\mathcal{R}^{\text{red}})^i(\mathcal{C}) \cup \mathcal{R}((\mathcal{R}^{\text{red}})^i(\mathcal{C})))$, for $i > 0$.

5.26. THEOREM. *If C is an unsatisfiable set of clauses then there exists a $k \geq 0$ such that $\{\} \in (\mathcal{R}_b^{\text{red}})^k(C)$. The same holds for $\mathcal{R}_m$ and $\mathcal{R}_{m,<_A}$ in place of $\mathcal{R}_b$.*

PROOF. (Sketch.) We claim that the completeness proofs for binary and macro-resolution (Theorems 5.15 and 5.18) go through without change if we replace $\mathcal{R}_b$ and $\mathcal{R}_m$ by $\mathcal{R}_b^{\text{red}}$ and $\mathcal{R}_{m,<_A}^{\text{red}}$, respectively. To see this, observe that, by condition (2) of the definition of a semantic tree, tautologies cannot fail at any node of a semantic tree. Therefore tautology removal cannot affect completeness. For subsumption observe that, if C subsumes D then C fails at every node at which D fails. Therefore $\{\} \in (\mathcal{R}_b^{\text{red}})^k(C)$ for some k, whenever $\{\} \in \mathcal{R}_b^*(C)$ and likewise for $\mathcal{R}_m$.   □

5.27. REMARK. More general results on the compatibility of resolution refinements and deletion rules have been presented in [Fermüller 1996] for the classical case. These results can easily be transferred to many-valued resolution.

5.5. Implicational completeness

Resolution is usually employed in a refutational setting. To prove that a set of signed formula expressions $\{\psi_1, \ldots, \psi_n\}$ implies a signed formula ϕ, we try to derive the empty clause from a set of clauses corresponding to $(\bigwedge_{i=1}^n \psi_i) \wedge \neg\phi$. (Remember that questions about entailment of formulae of finitely-valued logics can easily be reduced to questions about the satisfiability of corresponding signed formula expressions.) For clause logic we define:

5.28. DEFINITION. A set of clauses C *implies* a clause C if for all interpretations I $\text{sval}_I(\bigwedge_{D \in C} \forall D) = \textbf{false}$ or $\text{sval}_I(\forall C) = \textbf{true}$.

An interesting property of classical resolution is the fact that it is not only refutationally complete, but that – modulo subsumption – all non-tautological clauses C that are implied by a clause set C can indeed be derived from C by resolution.

5.29. DEFINITION. A resolution operator $\mathcal{R}$ is called *implicationally complete* if, for all clause sets C and clauses C, either C is a tautology or C is subsumed by some $C' \in \mathcal{R}^*(C)$ whenever C implies C.

That unrefined Robinson-resolution is implicationally complete for *classical* clause logic is stated in [Lee 1967] and sometimes called Lee's Theorem. (A much more satisfying proof appears in [Leitsch 1997].) It does not receive much attention in the literature; probably, since most people in automated deduction think that it is of theoretical interest only. However, in Section 7 we apply a many-valued version of Lee's Theorem to the problem of computing optimal translation rules. The latter problem is certainly of central relevance to the practice of theorem proving.

Observe that macro-resolution does *not* enjoy implicational completeness. Consider, e.g., the propositional clauses

$$\{\{u,v\}{:}A\} \quad \text{and} \quad \{\{u,w\}{:}A\} \ ,$$

where u, v, w are pairwise different truth values. The macro-resolution rule is not applicable. However, the non-tautological clause $\{\{u\}:A\}$ is implied by $\{\{\{u,v\}:A\}, \{\{u,w\}:A\}\}$, without being subsumed by one of its members.

5.30. DEFINITION. For a clause $C = \{S_1:P_1, \dots S_n:P_n\}$ let

$$[\neg C] = \{\{\overline{S_1}:P_1\gamma\}, \dots \{\overline{S_n}:P_n\gamma\}\},$$

where γ is a substitution that replaces each variable in C by a new constant. (Remember that $\overline{S}$ denotes the sign dual to S, i.e., $\overline{S} = W - S$ where W is the set of all truth values.)

5.31. PROPOSITION. *For every clause C and interpretation*[12] *I : I is a model of $[\neg C]$ iff I does not satisfy C.*

PROOF. Follows from the definition of $[\neg C]$.   □

5.32. DEFINITION. A clause C *subsumes* a clause D if some instance of C is contained in D; more formally: if $\widehat{C\theta} \subseteq \widehat{D}$, for some substitution θ. A set of clauses $\mathcal{C}$ *implies* a clause C if all models of $\mathcal{C}$ satisfy C.

We state some simple facts about implication of clauses and subsumption.

5.33. PROPOSITION. *Let C and D be clauses. If C subsumes D then $\{C\}$ implies D.*

PROOF. Follows from the definitions of subsumption and implication.   □

Observe that the converse of Proposition 5.33 does not hold. E.g.,

$$\{\{u\}:P(x), \{v\}:P(f(x))\}$$

implies but does not subsume

$$\{\{u\}:P(x), \{v\}:P(f(f(x)))\}$$

if $u \neq v$. Whereas the problem to decide whether a clause C subsumes a clause D is NP-complete [see Garey and Johnson 1979], it is undecidable whether $\{C\}$ implies D, in general as proved in [Schmidt-Schauss 1988].

5.34. PROPOSITION. *Let $\mathcal{C}$ be a clause set and C be a non-tautological clause. $\mathcal{C}$ implies C iff $\mathcal{C} \cup [\neg C]$ is unsatisfiable.*

PROOF. Follows from Proposition 5.31 and the definition of implication.   □

5.35. LEMMA. *Let C and D be non-tautological clauses. C subsumes D iff there exists a ground substitution θ such that $\{C\theta\} \cup [\neg D]$ is unsatisfiable.*

---

[12] Of course, the Herbrand universe has to include also the new constants occurring in $[\neg C]$.

Proof. ⇒: Suppose $\widehat{C\sigma} \subseteq \widehat{D}$. Then also $\widehat{C\sigma\gamma} \subseteq \widehat{D\gamma}$, where γ is the substitution replacing every variable by a new constant in $[\neg D]$. This implies that for each literal $V{:}A \in C\sigma\gamma$, there is a clause of form $\{V'{:}A\} \in [\neg D]$ such that $V \cap V' = \emptyset$. This means that $\{C\sigma\gamma\} \cup [\neg D]$ is unsatisfiable.

⇐: Suppose $\{C\theta\} \cup [\neg D]$ is unsatisfiable, where $C\theta$ is ground. Since D is non-tautological, $[\neg D]$ is satisfiable. Therefore, for each literal $\{v\}{:}A \in \widehat{C\theta}$ there has to exist a clause $\{S{:}A\} \in [\neg D]$ such that $v \notin S$. This implies $\widehat{C\theta} \subseteq \widehat{D}$. In other words: C subsumes D. □

5.36. Theorem (Implicational completeness of $\mathcal{R}_b$). *If C is a non-tautological clause that is implied by a set of clauses $\mathcal{C}$ then there exists a $D \in \mathcal{R}_b^*(\mathcal{C})$ such that D subsumes C.*

Proof. By Propositon 5.34 $\mathcal{C} \cup [\neg C]$ is unsatisfiable. Hence, by Theorem 5.14 there is a finite subset K of $A(\mathcal{C} \cup [\neg C])$ such that every semantic tree for K is closed for $\mathcal{C} \cup [\neg C]$.

Let $[\neg C] = \{\{V_1{:}A_1\}, \ldots, \{V_m{:}A_m\}\}$ and W be the set of all truth values. Since C is non-tautological $\overline{V_i}$ is not empty. Without loss of generality we may assume C to be normalized; i.e., $A_i \neq A_j$ if $i \neq j$. We choose a semantic tree T for K that starts with the following subtree:

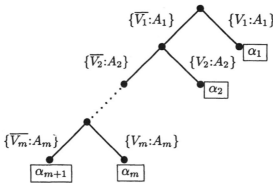

The subtrees of T rooted in the nodes $\alpha_1, \ldots, \alpha_m$, respectively, are arbitrary (since these nodes obviously are failure nodes).

For the construction of the subtree T_{m+1} of T rooted in α_{m+1} we have to take care that it does not contain a failure node for any clause in $[\neg C]$. This can be achieved as follows. Let $V_1^1, \ldots, V_1^k$ be the subsets of V_1 that contain all but one element of V_1. (If V_1 is a singleton simply skip this part of the construction of T.) Attach k successor nodes $\beta_1, \ldots, \beta_k$ to α_{m+1}, the edges to which are labeled by $\{V_1^1{:}A_1\}, \ldots, \{V_1^k{:}A_1\}$, respectively. Clearly, the refutation set of β_i $(1 \leq i \leq k)$ omits exactly one assignment to the atom A_1. By proceeding in the same way for $A_2, \ldots A_n$ we arrive at a partial semantic tree T_C, each branch of which omits exactly one assignment to the atoms occurring in $[\neg C]$. Thus no literals signing atoms of $[\neg C]$ will have to occur below T_C. Therefore we can assume that the only failure nodes in T of clauses in $[\neg C]$ are $\alpha_1, \ldots, \alpha_m$. In other words: all failure nodes in T_{m+1} are failure nodes for clauses in C.

The only restriction (in addition to the requirement that T is a semantic tree for K) that we pose on the structure of T below T_C is that the literals labeling edges directly connected to a common node all contain the same atom. This way the following statement is easily seen to follow from condition (1) of the definition of a semantic tree.

(R) Let α be an inference node in T. Let $C_1, \ldots C_\ell$ be the clauses failing at its successor nodes $\beta_1, \ldots \beta_\ell$, respectively. Then some resolvent $D \in \mathcal{R}_b^*(\{C_1, \ldots C_\ell\})$ fails at α.

Since T is closed for $C \cup [\neg C]$ it must contain at least one inference node. Therefore, by iteratively adding resolvents to $C \cup [\neg C]$ and applying **(R)**, we must eventually derive a clause D that fails at the node α_{m+1}. Since T_{m+1} contains no failure nodes for clauses in $[\neg C]$ we conclude that $D \in \mathcal{R}_b^*(C)$. By Theorem 5.14 it follows that $\{D\theta\} \cup [\neg C]$ is unsatisfiable, where θ is a ground substitution such that $D\theta$ is contained in the refutation set of node α_{m+1}. By Lemma 5.35 it follows that D subsumes C. $\qquad\square$

6. An example

Consider a two-valued logic $\mathcal{L}$ with operators $\neg, \wedge, \vee$, quantifiers $\forall, \exists$, and a modal operator $\square$. Let the semantics be defined via a Kripke structure with two worlds, α and β, where both worlds are reachable from α:

Thus, $\square F$ is true in α if F is true in both worlds, and it is true in β if F is at least true in β.

Equivalently, $\mathcal{L}$ can be defined by a many-valued semantics such that a formula is true in the Kripke-style semantics exactly when it is true in the many-valued one. As truth values we choose $W = \{\langle 0,0\rangle, \langle 0,1\rangle, \langle 1,0\rangle, \langle 1,1\rangle\}$, with the intended meaning that a formula F obtains the value $\langle u, v\rangle$ in the four-valued semantics iff F evaluates to u in world α and to v in world β. Negation and the box operator can be characterized by the tables

	$\tilde{\neg}$
$\langle 0,0\rangle$	$\langle 1,1\rangle$
$\langle 0,1\rangle$	$\langle 1,0\rangle$
$\langle 1,0\rangle$	$\langle 0,1\rangle$
$\langle 1,1\rangle$	$\langle 0,0\rangle$

	$\tilde{\square}$
$\langle 0,0\rangle$	$\langle 0,0\rangle$
$\langle 0,1\rangle$	$\langle 0,1\rangle$
$\langle 1,0\rangle$	$\langle 0,0\rangle$
$\langle 1,1\rangle$	$\langle 1,1\rangle$

Conjunction, disjunction and the quantifiers can be defined as the infimum and supremum with respect to the ordering $\leq$ on W, given by

$$\langle u_1, v_1 \rangle < \langle u_2, v_2 \rangle$$
$$\text{iff } u_1 < u_2 \text{ and } v_1 \le v_2$$
$$\text{or } u_1 \le u_2 \text{ and } v_1 < v_2$$

$$\langle 1,1 \rangle$$
$$\langle 1,0 \rangle \qquad \langle 0,1 \rangle$$
$$\langle 0,0 \rangle$$

i.e., for $u, v \in W$ we have $\tilde{\wedge}(u,v) = \inf_{\le}(u,v)$ and $\tilde{\vee}(u,v) = \sup_{\le}(u,v)$, and for $\emptyset \subset V \subseteq W$ we have $\tilde{\forall}(V) = \inf_{\le}(V)$ and $\tilde{\exists}(V) = \sup_{\le}(V)$.

We now present a set of reduction rules for the four-valued semantics of $\mathcal{L}$. In clausal theorem proving the purpose of rules is to reduce signed formulae of the form $\overline{S}{:}F$ to sets of clauses, where S is the set of designated truth values. In our example a formula F is true in the Kripke semantics if it is true in both worlds, i.e., if F evaluates to $\langle 1, 1 \rangle$ in the four-valued semantics; in other words, we have $S = \{\langle 1, 1 \rangle\}$. In principle it suffices to give four rules per connective and per quantifier, one for every singleton sign. However, this would mean that we had to apply three rules to $\overline{S}{:}F = \{\langle 0,0 \rangle, \langle 0,1 \rangle, \langle 1,0 \rangle\}{:}F = \langle 0,0 \rangle{:}F \vee \langle 0,1 \rangle{:}F \vee \langle 1,0 \rangle{:}F$ in order to eliminate the top symbol of F. Alternatively, with the aim of obtaining fewer clauses we could use a single rule to decompose $\overline{S}{:}F$ directly, at the price of needing also rules for non-singleton signs.

We choose the second approach. It turns out that we have to consider only eight out of 15 possible signs:

$$
\begin{array}{llll}
D_1 & = & \{\langle 0,0 \rangle\} & \qquad U_1 & = & \{\langle 1,1 \rangle\} \\
D_2 & = & \{\langle 0,0 \rangle, \langle 0,1 \rangle\} & \qquad U_2 & = & \{\langle 1,1 \rangle, \langle 1,0 \rangle\} \\
D_3 & = & \{\langle 0,0 \rangle, \langle 1,0 \rangle\} & \qquad U_3 & = & \{\langle 1,1 \rangle, \langle 0,1 \rangle\} \\
D_4 & = & \{\langle 0,0 \rangle, \langle 0,1 \rangle, \langle 1,0 \rangle\} & \qquad U_4 & = & \{\langle 1,1 \rangle, \langle 1,0 \rangle, \langle 0,1 \rangle\}
\end{array}
$$

Except for D_4 and U_4 the signs are exactly the non-trivial down- and up-sets with respect to $\le$. We obtain the optimized reduction rules listed in Figure 1. The set of signs is indeed closed under the reduction rules: all signs introduced by the rules are among the D_i and U_i. Note that the set of signs forms a *system of signs* [Baaz, Fermüller, Salzer and Zach 1998] since every singleton sign can be obtained as the intersection of some signs.

Consider the formula $F_1 = \forall x \Box \exists y (\neg A(x) \vee A(y))$, which is valid in $\mathcal{L}$. According to Section 4.5 we can prove F_1 by transforming $D_4{:}F_1$ to a set of clauses and then deriving a contradiction. As first step we apply the rules of Figure 1 and eliminate all many-valued connectives and quantifiers:

$$
\begin{aligned}
D_4{:}F_1 & = & D_4{:}\forall x \Box \exists y (\neg A(x) \vee A(y)) \\
& \equiv & \exists x\, D_4{:}\Box \exists y (\neg A(x) \vee A(y)) \\
& \equiv & \exists x\, D_4{:}\exists y (\neg A(x) \vee A(y)) \\
& \equiv & \exists x \left(\mathbb{\forall} y\, D_2{:}(\neg A(x) \vee A(y)) \vee\kern-0.5em\vee \mathbb{\forall} y\, D_3{:}(\neg A(x) \vee A(y)) \right) \\
& \equiv & \exists x \left(\mathbb{\forall} y\, (D_2{:}\neg A(x) \wedge D_2{:}A(y)) \vee\kern-0.5em\vee \mathbb{\forall} y\, (D_3{:}\neg A(x) \wedge D_3{:}A(y)) \right)
\end{aligned}
$$

$$D_i : \neg F \;\Rightarrow\; U_i : F \qquad\qquad U_i : \neg F \;\Rightarrow\; D_i : F$$

$$D_1 : \Box F \;\Rightarrow\; D_3 : F \qquad\qquad U_1 : \Box F \;\Rightarrow\; U_1 : F$$
$$D_2 : \Box F \;\Rightarrow\; D_4 : F \qquad\qquad U_2 : \Box F \;\Rightarrow\; U_1 : F$$
$$D_3 : \Box F \;\Rightarrow\; D_3 : F \qquad\qquad U_3 : \Box F \;\Rightarrow\; U_3 : F$$
$$D_4 : \Box F \;\Rightarrow\; D_4 : F \qquad\qquad U_4 : \Box F \;\Rightarrow\; U_3 : F$$

$$D_i : (F \wedge G) \;\Rightarrow\; D_i : F \vee D_i : G \qquad U_j : (F \wedge G) \;\Rightarrow\; U_j : F \wedge U_j : G$$
$$U_4 : (F \wedge G) \;\Rightarrow\; U_4 : F \wedge (U_3 : F \vee U_2 : G) \wedge (U_2 : F \vee U_3 : G) \wedge U_4 : G$$

$$D_j : (F \vee G) \;\Rightarrow\; D_j : F \wedge D_j : G \qquad U_i : (F \vee G) \;\Rightarrow\; U_i : F \vee U_i : G$$
$$D_4 : (F \vee G) \;\Rightarrow\; D_4 : F \wedge (D_3 : F \vee D_2 : G) \wedge (D_2 : F \vee D_3 : G) \wedge D_4 : G$$

$$D_i : (\forall x F(x)) \;\Rightarrow\; \exists x \, D_i : F(x) \qquad U_j : (\forall x F(x)) \;\Rightarrow\; \forall x \, U_j : F(x)$$
$$U_4 : (\forall x F(x)) \;\Rightarrow\; \forall x \, U_2 : F(x) \vee \forall x \, U_3 : F(x)$$

$$D_j : (\exists x F(x)) \;\Rightarrow\; \forall x \, D_j : F(x) \qquad U_i : (\exists x F(x)) \;\Rightarrow\; \exists x \, U_i : F(x)$$
$$D_4 : (\exists x F(x)) \;\Rightarrow\; \forall x \, D_2 : F(x) \vee \forall x \, D_3 : F(x)$$

Figure 1: Reduction rules for $\mathcal{L}$, where $1 \leq i \leq 4$ and $1 \leq j \leq 3$.

$$\equiv\; \exists x \left(\forall y \, (U_2 : A(x) \wedge D_2 : A(y)) \vee \forall y \, (U_3 : A(x) \wedge D_3 : A(y)) \right) \;.$$

Next we remove the existential quantifier – introducing a Skolem constant c – and shift the universal quantifiers in front of the formula:

$$\forall y \, \forall y' \left((U_2 : A(c) \wedge D_2 : A(y)) \vee (U_3 : A(c) \wedge D_3 : A(y')) \right)$$

Finally, we apply distributivity to obtain conjunctive normal form:

$$\forall y \, \forall y' \left((U_2 : A(c) \vee U_3 : A(c)) \wedge (U_2 : A(c) \vee D_3 : A(y')) \wedge \right.$$
$$\left. (D_2 : A(y) \vee U_3 : A(c)) \wedge (D_2 : A(y) \vee D_3 : A(y')) \right)$$

Observing $U_2 \cup U_3 = U_4$ this formula corresponds to the clause set

$$\{ \{U_4 : A(c)\}, \; \{U_2 : A(c), D_3 : A(y')\}, \; \{D_2 : A(y), U_3 : A(c)\}, \; \{D_2 : A(y), D_3 : A(y')\} \} \;.$$

Figure 2 gives a refutation of the clause set: from the first three clauses we derive the singleton $\{U_1 : A(c)\}$, which leads to the empty clause by resolving it with a factor of the fourth clause. By the correctness of many-valued resolution we may conclude that F_1 is valid.

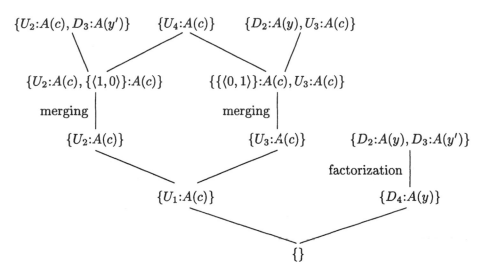

Figure 2: A refutation of the clause set corresponding to $D_4{:}F_1$

As another example, consider the formula $F_2 = \forall x \Box \forall y (\neg A(x) \lor A(y))$, which is *not* valid in $\mathcal{L}$. To see this we construct the clause set for $D_4{:}F_2$:

$$\{\,\{U_4{:}A(c)\},\ \{U_3{:}A(c), D_2{:}A(d)\},\ \{U_2{:}A(c), D_3{:}A(d)\},\ \{D_4{:}A(d)\}\,\}\ ,$$

where c and d denote Skolem constants. The only new clauses that can be derived by resolution are $\{U_4{:}A(c), D_1{:}A(d)\}$ and $\{U_1{:}A(c), D_4{:}A(d)\}$, having as parents the second and third clause. But obviously the new clauses are redundant since they are subsumed by the first and last clause, respectively. By the completeness of many-valued resolution with subsumption we may conclude that the clause set is satisfiable, i.e., that the original formula F_2 is falsifiable.

6.1. REMARK. Let $W = \{0,1\}^n$ be the truth values corresponding to a Kripke structure with n worlds, where n is finite. For $w \in W$, let w^i denote the i-th component of w. Furthermore, let $<$ be defined on W as: $u < v$ iff $u^i \leq v^i$ for all $1 \leq i \leq n$ and $u^i < v^i$ for at least one i.

Observe that though the number of truth values is exponential in n, the number of clauses generated by transformation rules for singleton signs is only linear in n. E.g., disjunctions decompose into $n + 2$ clauses at most:

$$\{v\}{:}(F \lor G) \Rightarrow \left(\bigvee_{u \leq v} \{u\}{:}F \right) \land \left(\bigvee_{u \leq v} \{u\}{:}G \right) \land \bigwedge_{1 \leq i \leq n} \left(\bigvee_{\substack{u \leq v \\ u^i = v^i}} \{u\}{:}F \lor \{u\}{:}G \right)$$

Conjunction and the quantifiers behave similar. Negation and the box operator generate just one clause, since both are unary connectives.

6.2. REMARK. In [Sofronie-Stokkermans 1997] (see also [1998] and [2000]) some situations are analyzed when there exists a link between the algebra of truth values of such logics and a suitably defined Kripke-style semantics. Such links can be established e.g. when the algebra of truth values is a distributive lattice with well-behaved operators. More specifically, it is shown that in this case only some of the sets of truth values are really needed as signs, namely only the filters generated by join-irreducible elements in the algebra of truth values and their complements; these sets of truth values correspond to the possible worlds of a Kripke-style model. We can obtain even shorter clause forms by a suitable structure-preserving translation.

In the example above it turns out that only the up-sets $\uparrow w_i$ and their complements are needed, where $w_i \in W$ corresponds to the singleton consisting of the possible world i; there are $2n$ such sets. The method is presented in detail in [Sofronie-Stokkermans 1999a]. These ideas are extended in [Sofronie-Stokkermans 1999b] to more general classes of logics, which are not necessarily finitely-valued, but sound and complete with respect to suitable classes of distributive lattices with well-behaved operators. The method is related to relational translation methods for modal logics and provides a common framework that subsumes both relational translation methods in modal logics and methods used for automated theorem proving in regular logics.

7. Optimization of transformation rules

Sections 4.2 and 4.3 showed how correct transformation rules can be systematically constructed for arbitrary connectives and distribution quantifiers. It was also mentioned that $cnf_\square(S)$ and $cnf_{Q,u}(S)$ are optimal in the sense that there are operators and quantifiers for which there is no normal form with fewer conjuncts. However, when axiomatizing "real-world" logics like Łukasiewicz', Gödel's, and Post's, we soon realize that the operators and quantifiers occurring there can be specified by CNFs which are much shorter than those produced by the general method (see also examples 4.4 and 4.6). In this section we sketch a method for minimizing the number of conjuncts.

The key idea is to anticipate resolution and subsumption steps between clauses that originate from the same rule application. Let X be a signed formula expression in conjunctive normal form as described in sections 4.2 and 4.3.

1. *Write X as a set C of clauses; treat formula variables as predicate symbols and replace existentially quantified variables by Skolem symbols.* Note that because of the particular structure of the normal forms, predicate symbols are at most unary and have as arguments just variables and Skolem constants.

2. *Saturate C under many-valued resolution, remove tautologies and subsumed clauses; call the resulting set C'.* Saturation terminates since C contains no function symbols except constants and no predicate symbols of arity greater than one. C' is logically equivalent to C, and it is minimal in the sense that none of its clauses is subsumed by any other clause in C'. Moreover, by implicational completeness of many-valued resolution, any clause that occurs in a minimal

clause set equivalent to C is subsumed by some clause in C'.

3. *Select a minimal subset C'' of C' such that every clause in C' is a logical consequence of C''.* The problem of selecting a minimal subset is equivalent to the "minimum cover" problem for sets, which is NP-complete. In the context of Boolean circuit minimization various heuristics and strategies have been devised to solve this problem efficiently [Sasao 1993, Hachtel and Somenzi 1996], which can be partly generalized to signed logics.

   It is also possible to use resolution for selecting a minimal subset. Pick indeterministically two clauses from C', saturate under resolution, and remove subsumed clauses. If the resulting set is not identical to C' up to variable renaming, add another clause from C' that is not already contained in the saturated set and repeat the procedure. As soon as the saturated set is equal to C', the clauses picked from C' form a candidate set, which is equivalent to C' and contains no redundant clauses. Among all candidate sets obtained this way select one with the smallest number of clauses.[13]

The clause set obtained in the last step can be translated back to a signed formula expression, by replacing constants again by existentially quantified variables. Note that the scope of quantifiers may now overlap, while in the original expression the scopes were disjoint.

Usually it is not possible to guess in advance the number of clauses or the form of signs generated by the procedure above. The situation changes, however, when considering only connectives and quantifiers defined as the infimum or supremum with respect to a lattice ordering on truth values. [Hähnle 1998, Salzer 1996, Salzer 2000, Sofronie-Stokkermans 2000] investigate small normal forms for several types of lattices and signs.

7.1. EXAMPLE. Consider the universal quantifier of the three-valued Łukasiewicz logic. In example 4.6 we computed for $\{p\}{:}(\forall x)A(x)$ the signed formula expression

$$((\exists x)\{t\}{:}A(x) \lor (\forall x)\{p,t\}{:}A(x))$$
$$\land \quad ((\exists x)\{f,p\}{:}A(x) \lor (\forall x)\{f,p\}{:}A(x))$$
$$\land \quad ((\forall x)\{p,t\}{:}A(x) \lor (\forall x)\{f,p\}{:}A(x)) \ .$$

To minimize it we first construct the corresponding clause set:

clause 1: $\{\{t\}{:}A(a), \{p,t\}{:}A(x)\}$

clause 2: $\{\{f,p\}{:}A(b), \{f,p\}{:}A(x)\}$

clause 3: $\{\{p,t\}{:}A(x'), \{f,p\}{:}A(x)\}$

Next we perform some resolution and factorization steps:

---

[13]If the candidate sets are generated in parallel, i.e., if we start with all pairs of clauses simultaneously then we may stop as soon as the first candidate set is found, since it has to be one with the fewest clauses.

clause 4:	$\{\{f,p\}{:}A(b)\}$	factor of clause 2
clause 5:	$\{\{p,t\}{:}A(x),\{p,t\}{:}A(x')\}$	resolvent of clauses 1&3
clause 6:	$\{\{p,t\}{:}A(x)\}$	factor of clause 5
clause 7:	$\{\{p\}{:}A(b)\}$	resolvent of clauses 4&6

Clause 6 subsumes clauses 1, 3, and 5, while clause 7 subsumes 2 and 4. Thus we are left with clauses 6 and 7, which admit no further resolvents or factors. Re-skolemizing the constant b we obtain the minimal expression

$$(\forall x)\{p,t\}{:}A(x) \wedge (\exists x)\{p\}{:}A(x) \quad .$$

8. Remarks on infinitely-valued logics

For obvious reasons we have to restrict ourselves to specific classes of many-valued logics: if we would talk about all substitutive logics, the statements would be so general that they become trivial in each special case. We therefore concentrate on ordered logics, without claiming that other logics are uninteresting: they are simply better dealt with in another context. In the following discussion we distinguish propositional logics from their first-order extensions and internal proof systems from external ones.

For internal propositional proof systems the most rewarding approaches to automated deduction are related to the application of the merging of formulae with subsequent deterministic simplifications, e.g. the non-clausal resolution introduced by Stachniak [Stachniak 1988, Stachniak 1996], or proof systems related to the Knuth-Bendix algorithm.

External proof systems can be seen from two different perspectives. The first variant is related to the extension of the sets-as-signs concept to infinite sets. In principle this is always possible, but to be feasible the sets-as-signs have to be represented by effectively manageable constraints, for example linear ones. [Hähnle 1994b] gives an efficient treatment of Łukasiewicz logic based on mixed integer programming; Gödel and Product logic can be treated similarly. These logics are the most prominent fundamental formalizations of fuzzy logic [Hajek 1998].

The second variant interprets (sub)formulae as algebraic functions, c.f. the concepts of literals developed for Łukasiewicz logic by Mundici and Aguzzoli. This more geometric approach is rewarding if the knowledge about the logic is sufficiently deep to prove relevant characterization theorems like McNaughton's theorem.

Proof-theoretic calculi like Avron's hypersequent calculus for infinitely-valued Gödel logic [Avron 1991a] should be considered as external proof systems, too, since they are related to adequate systems of constraints. Implementations of theorem provers for logics represented by analytic calculi are easily obtained by using the Maslov-Mints transformation, i.e. by encoding the possible derivation steps as clauses for two-valued resolution. Note however that little is known about the conditions under which logics admit analytic calculi.

In the first order case, relevant examples of internal proof systems use the Skolemization of prenex formulae followed by a calculation within the corresponding propositional proof systems [Stachniak 1996]. The limitations of this approach are obvious: most relevant first-order logics like first-order Łukasiewicz and first-order Product logic are incomplete, i.e., there is no finitary calculus for deriving all valid formulae [Scarpellini 1962], [Baaz, Hajek, Krajiecek and Svejda 1998]. This property extends to all logics whose semantic evaluations depend on arithmetic calculations.

Consequently, there are the following possibilities for future research. One alternative is to investigate partially complete proof systems as described in [Hajek 1998]. The advantage is the freedom of choice: among the infinitely many systems we may choose those which have exactly the adequate strength and the computational properties necessary for a successful implementation.

Otherwise, we may concentrate on complete logics, like infinitely-valued first-order Gödel logic [Horn 1969], [Takeuti and Titani 1984]. This logic has a smooth analytic representation: add the usual intuitionistic quantifier rules to Avron's propositional hypersequent calculus mentioned above. Therefore, there is a straightforward implementation in the Maslov-Mints style for this and related logics.

In the case of incomplete logics, there is still the possibility that the monadic fragment is axiomatizable or even decidable. Filtrations fail, but the development of adequate resolution systems might provide a positive answer using methods similar to resolution decision procedures for subclasses of two-valued first-order logic [Fermüller, Leitsch, Tammet and Zamov 1993].

Acknowledgments

The authors wish to thank Viorica Sofronie-Stokkermans for her detailed comments on an earlier version of this article which led to several improvements.

Bibliography

ANANTHARAMAN S. AND BONACINA M. [1991], An application of the theorem prover SBR3 to many-valued logic, in 'Proceedings of the Second International Workshop on Conditional and Typed Rewriting Systems (CTRS 90), LNCS 516', pp. 156–161.

ARIELI O. AND AVRON A. [1998], 'The value of four values', *Artificial Intelligence* 102, 97–141.

AVRON A. [1991a], 'Hypersequents, logical consequence and intermediate logics for concurrency', *Annals of Mathematics and Artificial Intelligence* 4, 225–248.

AVRON A. [1991b], 'Natural 3-valued logics—characterization and proof theory', *Journal of Symbolic Logic* 56(1), 276–294.

BAAZ M. AND FERMÜLLER C. G. [1992], Resolution for many-valued logics, in A. Voronkov, ed., 'Proc. Logic Programming and Automated Reasoning LPAR'92', LNAI 624, Springer-Verlag, pp. 107–118.

BAAZ M. AND FERMÜLLER C. G. [1995], 'Resolution-based theorem proving for many-valued logics', *Journal of Symbolic Computation* 19(4), 353–391.

BAAZ M. AND FERMÜLLER C. G. [1996a], Combining many-valued and intuitionistic tableaux, in P. Miglioli, U. Moscato, D. Mundici and M. Ornaghi, eds, 'Theorem Proving with Analytic

Tableaux and Related Methods, 5th Int. Workshop, TABLEAUX'96', Vol. 1071 of *LNCS*, Springer, Palermo, pp. 65–79.

BAAZ M. AND FERMÜLLER C. G. [1996*b*], Intuitionistic counterparts of finitely-valued logics, *in* 'Proc. 26th International Symposium on Multiple-valued Logic', IEEE Press, Los Alamitos, pp. 136–143.

BAAZ M., FERMÜLLER C. G. AND LEITSCH A. [1994], A non-elementary speed-up in proof length by structural clause form transformation, *in* 'Proc. Logic in Computer Science LICS', IEEE Press, Los Alamitos, pp. 213–219.

BAAZ M., FERMÜLLER C. G., SALZER G. AND ZACH R. [1998], 'Labeled calculi and finite-valued logics', *Studia Logica* **61**(1), 7–13.

BAAZ M., FERMÜLLER C. G. AND ZACH R. [1992], Dual systems of sequents and tableaux for many-valued logics, *in* 'Proc. 2nd Worshop on Theorem Proving with Tableaux and Related Methods, Marseille', Tech. Report, MPI Saarbrücken.

BAAZ M., FERMÜLLER C. G. AND ZACH R. [1994], 'Elimination of cuts in first-order finite-valued logics', *J. Inform. Process. Cybernet. (EIK)* **29**(6), 333–355.

BAAZ M., HAJEK P., KRAJIECEK J. AND SVEJDA D. [1998], 'Embedding logics into product logic', *Studia Logica* **61**, 35–47.

BELL C., NERODE A., NG R. AND SUBRAHMANIAN V. [1994], 'Mixed integer programming methods for computing nonmonotonic deductive databases', *Journal of the ACM* **41**(6), 1178–1215.

BELNAP JR. N. D. [1977], A useful four-valued logic, *in* J. M. Dunn and G. Epstein, eds, 'Modern uses of multiple-valued logic', Reidel, Dordrecht, pp. 8–37.

BOLC L. AND BOROWIK P. [1992], *Many-Valued Logics. 1: Theoretical Foundations*, Springer-Verlag.

BONACINA M. P. [1991], 'Problems in Łukasiewicz logic', Newsletter of the Association for Automated Reasoning, No. 18, June 1991.

BOY DE LA TOUR T. [1992], 'An optimality result for clause form translation', *Journal of Symbolic Computation* **14**, 283–301.

BRYANT R. E. AND SEGER C.-J. H. [1991], Formal verification of digital circuits using symbolic ternary system models, *in* E. M. Clarke and R. P. Kurshan, eds, 'Computer-Aided Verification: Proc. of the 2nd International Conference CAV'90', LNCS 531, Springer-Verlag, pp. 33–43.

CARNIELLI W. A. [1987], 'Systematization of finite many-valued logics through the method of tableaux', *Journal of Symbolic Logic* **52**(2), 473–493.

CHAZARAIN J., RISCOS A., ALONSO J. A. AND BRIALES E. [1991], 'Multi-valued logic and Gröbner bases with applications to modal logic', *Journal of Symbolic Computation* **11-12**, 181–191.

DOHERTY P. [1991], A constraint-based approach to proof procedures for multi-valued logics, *in* 'First World Conference on the Fundamentals of Artificial Intelligence WOCFAI-91, Paris'.

FERMÜLLER C. G. [1996], Semantic trees revisited: Some new completeness results, *in* M. McRobbie and J. Slaney, eds, 'Proc. 13th Conference on Automated Deduction, New Brunswick/NJ, USA', Vol. 1104 of *LNCS*, Springer-Verlag, pp. 568–582.

FERMÜLLER C. G., LEITSCH A., TAMMET T. AND ZAMOV N. [1993], *Resolution Methods as Decision Procedures*, Vol. 679 of *LNAI*, Springer-Verlag, Berlin.

FITTING M. C. [1983], *Proof Methods for Modal and Intuitionistic Logics*, D. Reidel Publishing Co., Dordrecht.

GANZINGER H. AND SOFRONIE-STOKKERMANS V. [1999], 'Chaining techniques for automated theorem proving in many-valued logic', In preparation.

GAREY M. AND JOHNSON D. [1979], *Computers and Intractability: A Guide to the Theory of NP-Completeness*, Freeman, San Francisco.

GENTZEN G. [1934-35], 'Untersuchungen über das logische Schließen I-II', *Mathematische Zeitschrift* **39**, 176–210 and 405–431.

GÖDEL K. [1932], 'Zum intuitionistischen Aussagenkalkül', *Anzeiger der Akademie der Wissenschaften in Wien* **69**, 65–66.

GOTTWALD S. [1989], *Mehrwertige Logik. Eine Einführung in Theorie und Anwendungen*, Akademie-Verlag Berlin.

GOTTWALD S. [1993], *Fuzzy Sets and Fuzzy Logic*, Vieweg, Braunschweig.

HACHTEL G. D. AND SOMENZI F. [1996], *Logic Synthesis and Verification Algorithms*, Kluwer Academic Publishers.

HÄHNLE R. [1991], Towards an efficient tableau proof procedure for multiple-valued logics, *in* E. Börger, H. Kleine Büning, M. M. Richter and W. Schönfeld, eds, 'Selected Papers from Computer Science Logic, CSL'90, Heidelberg, Germany', Vol. 533 of *LNCS*, Springer-Verlag, pp. 248–260.

HÄHNLE R. [1994a], *Automated Deduction in Multiple-Valued Logics*, Vol. 10 of *International Series of Monographs on Computer Science*, Oxford University Press.

HÄHNLE R. [1994b], 'Many-valued logic and mixed integer programming', *Annals of Mathematics and Artificial Intelligence* 12(3,4), 231–264.

HÄHNLE R. [1994c], 'Short conjunctive normal forms in finitely-valued logics', *Journal of Logic and Computation* 4(6), 905–927.

HÄHNLE R. [1998], 'Commodious axiomatization of quantifiers in multiple-valued logic', *Studia Logica* 61(1), 101–121.

HÄHNLE R. AND ESCALADA-IMAZ G. [1997], 'Deduction in many-valued logics: a survey', *Mathware & Soft Computing* IV(2), 69–97.

HÄHNLE R. AND KERNIG W. [1993], Verification of switch level designs with many-valued logic, *in* A. Voronkov, ed., 'Proc. LPAR'93, St. Petersburg, Russia', Vol. 698 of *LNCS*, Springer-Verlag, pp. 158–169.

HAJEK P. [1998], *Metamathematics of Fuzzy Logics*, Kluwer Academic Publishers.

HAYES J. P. [1986], 'Pseudo-Boolean logic circuits', *IEEE Transactions on Computers* C-35(7), 602–612.

HORN A. [1969], 'Logic with truth values in a linearly ordered Heyting algebra', *Journal of Symbolic Logic* 34(3), 395–401.

JAFFAR J. AND MAHER M. J. [1994], 'Constraint logic programming: A survey', *Journal of Logic Programming* 19 & 20, 503–582.

KLEENE S. [1938], 'On a notation for ordinal numbers', *Journal of Symbolic Logic* 3, 150–155.

KONIKOWSKA B., MORGAN C. AND ORŁOWSKA E. [1998], 'A relational formalization of arbitrary finite valued logics', *Logical Journal of the IGPL* 6(5), 755–774.

KUNEN K. [1987], 'Negation in logic programming', *Journal of Logic Programming* 4, 289–308.

LEE R. [1967], *A completeness theorem and a computer program for finding theorems derivable from given axioms*, Ph.D. Thesis, University of California, Berkely.

LEITSCH A. [1997], *The Resolution Calculus*, Texts in Theoretical Computer Science, Springer-Verlag.

LU J. J., HENSCHEN L. J., SUBRAHMANIAN V. S. AND DA COSTA N. C. A. [1991], Reasoning in paraconsistent logics, *in* R. Boyer, ed., 'Automated Reasoning: Essays in Honor of Woody Bledsoe', Kluwer, pp. 181–210.

LU J. J., MURRAY N. V. AND ROSENTHAL E. [1993], Signed formulas and annotated logics, *in* 'Proc. 23rd International Symposium on Multiple-Valued Logics', IEEE Press, Los Alamitos, pp. 48–53.

LU J. J. AND ROSENTHAL E. [1997], Logic-based deductive reasoning in AI systems, *in* A. B. Tucker, ed., 'The Computer Science And Engineering Handbook', CRC Press, chapter 29, pp. 654–657.

ŁUKASIEWICZ J. [1920], 'O logice trójwartościowej', *Ruch Filozoficzny* 5, 169–171.

ŁUKASIEWICZ J. [1930], 'Philosophische Bemerkungen zu mehrwertigen systemen des Aussagenkalküls', *Comptes rendus des séances de la Société des Sciences et des Lettres de Varsovie Cl. III* 23, 51–77.

ŁUKASIEWICZ J. AND TARSKI A. [1930], 'Untersuchungen über den Aussagenkalkül', *Comptes rendus des séances de la Société des Sciences et des Lettres de Varsovie Cl. III* 23, 30–50.

Messing B. and Stackelberg P. [1995], Regular signed resolution applied to annotated logic programs. Poster abstract, in J. Lloyd, ed., 'Proceedings of the International Logic Programming Conference, Portland/OR', MIT Press, p. 268.

Morgan C. G. [1976], 'A resolution principle for a class of many-valued logics', *Logique et Analyse* **19**(74–75–76), 311–339.

Morgan C. G. [1985], 'Autologic', *Logique et Analyse* **28**(110/111), 257–282.

Mundici D. [1990], The complexity of adaptive error-correcting codes, in 'Proceedings Workshop Computer Science Logic 90, Heidelberg', LNCS 533, Springer-Verlag, pp. 300–307.

Murata T., Subrahmanian V. S. and Wakayama T. [1991], 'A Petri net model for reasoning in the presence of inconsistency', *IEEE Transactions on Knowledge and Data Engineering* **3**(3), 281–292.

Murray N. V. and Rosenthal E. [1991], Resolution and path-dissolution in multiple-valued logics, in 'Proceedings International Symposium or Methodologies for Intelligent Systems, Charlotte', LNAI, Springer-Verlag.

Murray N. V. and Rosenthal E. [1994], 'Adapting classical inference techniques to multiple-valued logics using signed formulas', *Fundamenta Informaticae* **21**(3), 237–253.

Nowana H. [1995], 'Software agents: An overview', *Knowledge Engineering Review* **11**(2), 205–244.

O'Hearn P. and Stachniak Z. [1992], 'A resolution framework for finitely-valued first-order logics', *J. Symbolic Computation* **13**, 235–254.

Ohlbach H. J. [1993], 'Translation methods for non-classical logics – an overview', *Journal of the IGPL* **1**(1), 69–90.

Orłowska E. [1978], 'The resolution principle for ω^+-valued logic', *Fundamenta Informaticae* **II**(1), 1–15.

Pfalzgraf J., Sigmund U. C. and Stokkermans K. [1996], 'Towards a general approach for modeling actions and change in cooperating agents scenarios', *Journal of the Interest Group in Pure and Applied Logics* **4**(3), 445–472.

Post E. L. [1921], Introduction to a general theory of elementary propositions, in J. van Heijenoort, ed., 'From Frege to Gödel. A Source Book in Mathematical Logic, 1879–1931', Harvard University Press, Cambridge MA, pp. 264–283.

Rescher N. [1969], *Many-Valued Logic*, McGraw-Hill, New York.

Robinson J. A. [1965], 'A machine-oriented logic based on the resolution principle', *JACM* **12**(1), 23–41.

Rosser J. B. and Turquette A. R. [1952], *Many-Valued Logics*, North-Holland, Amsterdam.

Rousseau G. [1967], 'Sequents in many valued logic I', *Fundamenta Mathematicæ* **LX**, 23–33.

Salzer G. [1996], Optimal axiomatizations for multiple-valued operators and quantifiers based on semilattices, in M. McRobbie and J. Slaney, eds, 'Proc. 13th Conference on Automated Deduction, New Brunswick/NJ, USA', Vol. 1104 of *LNCS*, Springer-Verlag, pp. 688–702.

Salzer G. [2000], 'Optimal axiomatizations of finitely-valued logics', *Information and Computation* **162**(1/2), 185–205.

Sasao, T., ed. [1993], *Logic Synthesis and Optimization*, Kluwer Academic Publishers.

Scarpellini B. [1962], 'Die Nichtaxiomatisierbarkeit des unendlichwertigen Prädikatenkalküls von Lukasiewicz', *Journal of Symbolic Logic* **27**(2), 159–170.

Schmidt-Schauss M. [1988], 'Implication of clauses is undecidable', *Theoretical Computer Science* **59**, 287–296.

Schmitt P. H. [1986], Computational aspects of three-valued logic, in J. H. Siekmann, ed., 'Proc. 8th International Conference on Automated Deduction', LNCS, Springer-Verlag, pp. 190–198.

Schröter K. [1955], 'Methoden zur Axiomatisierung beliebiger Aussagen- und Prädikatenkalküle', *Zeitschrift für math. Logik und Grundlagen der Mathematik* **1**, 241–251.

Sofronie-Stokkermans V. [1997], Fibered Structures and Applications to Automated Theorem Proving in Certain Classes of Finitely-Valued Logics and to Modeling Interacting Systems, PhD thesis, RISC-Linz, J.Kepler University Linz, Austria.

SOFRONIE-STOKKERMANS V. [1998], On translation of finitely-valued logics to classical first-order logic, *in* H. Prade, ed., 'Proceedings of the 13th European Conference on Artificial Intelligence (ECAI 98)', John Wiley & Sons, Brighton, UK, pp. 410–411.

SOFRONIE-STOKKERMANS V. [1999a], 'Automated theorem proving by resolution for finitely-valued logics based on distributive lattices with operators', *Multiple-Valued Logic - An International Journal*. To appear.

SOFRONIE-STOKKERMANS V. [1999b], Representation theorems and automated theorem proving in non-classical logics, *in* 'Proceedings of the 29th IEEE International Symposium on Multiple-Valued Logic (ISMVL 99)', IEEE Computer Society, IEEE Computer Society Press, pp. 242–247.

SOFRONIE-STOKKERMANS V. [2000], Resolution-based theorem proving for SH_n-logics, *in* R. Caferra and G. Salzer, eds, 'Automated Deduction in Classical and Non-Classical Logics', LNCS 1761 (LNAI), Springer, pp. 268–282.

STACHNIAK Z. [1988], The resolution rule: An algebraic perspective, *in* 'Proc. of Algebraic Logic and Universal Algebra in Computer Science Conf.', Springer LNCS 425, Heidelberg, pp. 227–242.

STACHNIAK Z. [1996], *Resolution Proof Systems: an Algebraic Theory*, Kluwer, Dordecht.

STACHNIAK Z. AND O'HEARN P. [1990], 'Resolution in the domain of strongly finite logics', *Fundamenta Informaticae* 8, 333–351.

STOKKERMANS K. [1995], A Categorical Framework and Calculus for Critical-Pair Completion, PhD thesis, RISC-Linz, Johannes-Kepler-Universität, Linz.

STOKKERMANS K. [1999], 'A categorical critical-pair completion algorithm', *Journal of Symbolic Computation* 27(5), 435–477.

SUCHÓN W. [1974], 'La méthode de Smullyan de construire le calcul n-valent de Lukasiewicz avec implication et négation', *Reports on Mathematical Logic, Universities of Cracow and Katowice* 2, 37–42.

SURMA S. J. [1984], An algorithm for axiomatizing every finite logic, *in* D. C. Rine, ed., 'Computer Science and Multiple-Valued Logics', second edn, North-Holland, Amsterdam, pp. 143–149. Selected Papers from the International Symposium on Multiple-Valued Logics 1974.

TAKEUTI G. AND TITANI S. [1984], 'Intuitionistic fuzzy logic and intuitionistic fuzzy set theory', *Journal of Symbolic Logic* 49(3), 851–866.

WOOLDRIDGE M. AND JENNINGS N. R. [1995], 'Intelligent agents: Theory and practice', *Knowledge Engineering Review* 10(2), 115–152.

WU J., TAN H. AND LI Y. [1998], 'An algebraic method to decide the deduction problem in many-valued logics', *Journal of Applied Non-Classical Logics* 8(4), 353–360.

ZACH R. [1993], Proof theory of finite-valued logics, Master's thesis, Institut für Algebra und Diskrete Mathematik, TU Wien. Available as Technical Report TUW-E185.2-Z.1-93.

Index

CHAPTER 21

Encoding Two-Valued Nonclassical Logics in Classical Logic

Hans Jürgen Ohlbach

Andreas Nonnengart

Maarten de Rijke

Dov M. Gabbay

SECOND READERS: Nikolaj Bjorner.

Contents

HANDBOOK OF AUTOMATED REASONING
Edited by Alan Robinson and Andrei Voronkov

1. Introduction

Classical logic has been the principal logic used in applications for many years. One of its main application areas has been mathematics, simply because it is ideally suited for the formalization of mathematics. Its model theory and proof theory have had an enormous impact on the foundations of mathematics. Many logicians continue to hold the view that logic has four subareas: model theory, proof theory, recursion theory and set theory. In all these four areas classical logic reigns supreme.

But as soon as we try to apply logic to the more human-oriented applications arising in computer science, artificial intelligence, natural language processing and philosophy, we find that we need to depart from the basic features of classical logic. These departures come in several kinds:

1. extend the language of classical logic with additional operators, connectives, and quantifiers to service applications involving time, knowledge, belief, necessity, actions, etc.;

2. restrict the language to guarantee better computational or logical properties, such as (strong forms of) decidability and interpolation;

3. change the basic deductive structure of classical logic to create new logics (intuitionistic, relevance, linear, paraconsistent, many-valued, fuzzy, etc.) to obtain systems whose reasoning mechanisms are closer to the domain being modeled.

For many applications a combined system may need to be used, for example systems like intuitionistic many-valued logics, or a fuzzy modal logic, or relevance modal logic etc. At the same time, under pressure from application areas, the notion of a logic itself has changed; the basic datastructures and concepts of "logic" have evolved. A theory need no longer be a set of formulae, but it can be a list, or a list of lists, a tree, or a labeled datastructure in general. Inference mechanisms are defined on top of these structures. We witness a wide landscape of nonmonotonic logics (default logic, defeasible logic, circumscription, etc.) and inference mechanisms (negation as failure, abduction, defaults, etc.). Today, a logical system may be a combination of many of the above and may look very different from classical logic (see [Gabbay 1996]).

In this chapter we are concerned with the more traditional monotone two-valued nonclassical logics, and modal logic is the most prominent example of these logics. Despite this restriction, we are still faced with an overwhelming number of logics. Encoding these logics into other logics gives us a powerful tool for understanding them from both a logical, algorithmic, and computational point of view, as we will see below. Before we come to the main issues of the chapter, we will explain the main topics being discussed in the context of nonclassical logics; this will enable us to explain what this chapter is about, and what it is not about.

1.1. Expressive power

The two most important properties of a logic are its *expressive power* and the (decidability of) the *reasoning tasks* that can be performed in the logic, in particular theoremhood. In this subsection we focus on expressive power, leaving reasoning tasks to the next one.

The expressive power of a logic may be analyzed from a number of angles. First of all, how do we express things in a given logic, or put differently, what is the *syntax* of the logic? This may seem a trivial point, but a poor syntax may be an important barrier to using a given logic.

Second, *what* do we say in a given logic? That is, what is the *meaning* of our well formed formulae (wffs)? This is a non-trivial question, because it is application dependent and because it requires a thorough understanding of the intended application. For example, if one wants to develop a logic of *knowledge and belief* [Fagin, Halpern, Moses and Vardi 1995], one has to find a precise characterization of 'knowledge' and 'belief,' before one can start specifying the corresponding logic.

There are various ways of specifying the meaning of wffs. Usually, this is done either *proof theoretically*, *semantically* or by *embedding* the logic into an already established logic. All of these methods specify the meaning of formulae in a rather indirect way. A proof theoretic specification by means of a *Hilbert system*, for example, is a kind of grammar for generating *theorems*. The theorems are a distinguished subset of the well formed formulae, which are supposed to 'be true' a-priori, without any extra assumptions.

A *semantic* characterization of the meaning of a wff is a mapping of the syntactic elements to a mathematical domain. The latter are usually simple and well understood, for example sets equipped with functions and relations. Thus, the very idea of a semantic characterization is to explain a new logical system in terms of something old, simple and well understood.

This familiar system actually need not be a mathematical domain. It can also be a previously defined logic. If the wffs of the new logic are translated into the wffs of a given logic, we speak of *embedding* or *translating* the new logic into the given one. In this way we can use an old logic to explain the meaning and expressive power of the wffs of the new logic.

Third is the issue of *comparing* the relative expressive power of logics. As indicated at the start of this section, we often need to depart from a given logic to cater for the needs of new applications. As a concrete example, one can think of the area of *description logics* (see [Calvanese et al. 2001], Chapter 23 of this Handbook), where lots of logical languages have been explored with varying sets of admissible connectives and quantifiers. Some versions allow negation to occur only in front of predicate symbols, which makes them different from logics where negation is allowed to occur everywhere. Others impose restrictions on the arguments of some of the quantifiers. The resulting plethora of logics creates many theoretical challenges; two of the most interesting are

- identifying 'dangerous' and 'safe' constructs in syntax and semantics, which do or do not make the decision problem harder when present;

- developing tools for comparing the relative expressive power of logics, in terms of special semantic or algorithmic characteristics;

As we will see below, encoding logics into each other or in some 'big' background logic, often provides a powerful way of addressing the above challenges.

1.2. Reasoning tasks

In addition to its expressive power, the other important feature of a logic are its *reasoning tasks*, and the *methods* for performing these. Reasoning tasks that have traditionally been considered include consequence or theoremhood proving, counterexample generation, model checking, subsumption checking, and satisfiability checking, see [Clarke and Schlinghoff 2001, Calvanese et al. 2001] (Chapters 24 and 23 of this Handbook) for examples and details). To simplify our presentation, let us focus on the first of these.

A first issue to be addressed when studying the problem of consequence checking for a given logic is *decidability* of the problem; and if theoremhood is decidable, what is its complexity? This goes along with the development of decision or — if theoremhood is not decidable — semi-decision proof procedures.

An actual proof procedure has several layers. The lowest layer consists of the basic *calculus*, a set of non-deterministic inference rules. Soundness (the rules identify only theorems) and completeness (the rules reject any non-theorem) of the calculus ensures that it works as expected. Since the rules of the basic calculus are non-deterministic, they generate a *search space*. The overall efficiency of a proof procedure depends on how this search space is explored. The next layer in a proof procedure therefore consists of *search strategies*. Search strategies, for example ordering strategies or selection strategies in predicate logic, prune the search space by restricting the application of the rules; see [Bachmair and Ganzinger 2001] (Chapter 2 of this Handbook).

Since search strategies cut out large parts of the search space, additional completeness proofs are called for. The resulting system is still non-deterministic. Therefore, in a third layer *search heuristics* are employed to control the application of the inference rules.

Orthogonal to these three layers is another component of a good proof procedure: the ability to recognize and eliminate redundancies in the search space. Inference steps which obviously cannot contribute to the final solution should be avoided as far as possible. Tautology and subsumption deletion in predicate logic resolution systems provide typical examples; again, see [Bachmair and Ganzinger 2001] (Chapter 2 of this Handbook).

Most successful implementations of proof procedures do not only rely on the strength of the calculus, the strategies, heuristics and redundancy elimination in the system, but also on sophisticated technical optimizations on various levels. This ranges from good datastructures and strong indexing techniques for dealing with large sets of terms and formulae [Graf 1996] to parallel processing on computer networks.

Let us return to a theme introduced at the start of this section (page 1405). Applications of logic call for many new logics to be defined. Changing the specification

of a logic influences most of its key properties, in particular the decidability of theoremhood, the complexity of the decision problem, the structure of the proof procedures etc. More concretely, the following have proved to be the key concerns:
- identifying 'dangerous' constructs in syntax and semantics, which make the decision problem harder when present;
- understanding why certain modifications do not influence the complexity of the decision procedure;
- developing parametrized proof procedures, which work for a whole class of logics by changing the parameters;
- developing proof procedures for more general logics which automatically become efficient proof procedures for less general logics when faced with a problem in the less general logic.

As should be clear from the above discussion, proof procedures have many different aspects to them; and developing procedures for a given logic is a non-trivial task.

1.3. Why encode?

In the previous subsections we have discussed what we take to be the main aspects of logics, classical or nonclassical, viz. their expressive power and their reasoning tasks. With the advent of more and more special purpose logics, we are faced with the daunting task of having to analyze the expressive power and develop proof procedures for each of these logics. This is where we think that methods of encoding one logic (the *source logic*) into another logic (the *target logic*) may provide an invaluable tool — quite often they are the only options available.

In particular, methods for encoding a source logic into a target logic can be used to achieve the following:

1. To grasp the expressive power, both of the source logic and of the target logic.
2. To export any proof procedures and tools that we may have for the target logic to the source logic.
3. To grasp the computational costs of various reasoning tasks, again both for the source logic and for the target logic.
4. To combine two logics, sometimes the most natural solution is to translate both into the same target logic, and to work inside the target logic (see [Gabbay 1999]).

In the remainder of this chapter we elaborate on these ideas, especially the first two, and present numerous uses and applications.

The automated reasoning community is by no means the first to think of encoding one logic into another as a useful tool. In mathematical logic, the topic of *interpreting* one logic inside another one has a long history, and it has in fact been motivated by much the same motivation as we have given above (see, for instance, [Hájek and Pudlák 1991]). In a similar spirit, philosophers of science have long been interested in *reducing* systems — formal or informal — to each other with a view to understanding what claims scientific theories are actually making about real world phenomena [Quine 1953].

But let us return to automated reasoning matters. We want to raise an important issue concerning the encoding of logics that some people have found troubling. We will mostly be encoding 'small' decidable source logics into 'big' undecidable target logics, and we will perform reasoning tasks for the source logic within the target logic, thereby 'reducing' a decidable problem to an undecidable one. Surely, it must be much more effective to reason directly within the source logic, say with the techniques explained in [Calvanese et al. 2001] (Chapter 23 on description logics in this Handbook) or [Waaler 2001] (Chapter 22 on tableaux methods for nonclassical logics)? A number of replies are appropriate. For getting a really efficient system for a given source logic, one has to exploit the characteristics of its (translated) formulae as much as possible, and this usually requires special implementations of any tools that one may have for the target logic. At the time of writing all systematic comparisons between proof procedures working directly on the original formulae on the one hand, and proof procedures working at the translated predicate logic formulae on the other hand have been done using general purpose predicate logic theorem provers. Predicate logic theorem provers which are highly optimized for the particular fragment of predicate logic which is the target of the translation are not available. Nevertheless, it turned out that the general purpose theorem provers can compete well with highly optimized tableaux provers for the source logics [Hustadt 1999]. Since all these theorem provers are improving every day, the comparisons are only snapshots that may be outdated very rapidly; therefore it is not worth reporting details of the experiments in this chapter.

We think that encoding nonclassical logics into first-order logic is important, not just for understanding the expressive power and computational powers of the source logics, but also because it gives users of nonclassical logics access to the sophisticated, state-of-the-art tools that are available and that continue to be developed in the area of first-order theorem proving. At present, no purpose built theorem prover for nonclassical logic has the level of sophistication that first-order provers have. Admittedly, a pre-processing step or a very careful encoding is often needed to exploit the restricted expressive power of the source logic and to help a general purpose tool become an efficient system for a given source logic, but even without this, an encoding gives direct access to valuable tools.

1.4. What this chapter is about

This chapter is about methods for encoding (axiomatizing, translating, simulating) a nonclassical logic in predicate logic, in particular in first-order predicate logic. We will focus mainly on matters related to expressive power and reasoning tasks; specific questions that we will be concerned with are:

1. What are the different options for encoding the formulae in predicate logic?
2. Do particular translation methods work for a whole class of logics, and how do the differences manifest themselves in the encoding?
3. What is the fragment of predicate logic, into which the formulae of a given logic or a whole class of logics are translated with a particular translation method?

4. What kind of proof procedures are adequate for the translated formulae?

5. Can we exploit special features of the source logic to enhance the encoding?

6. Are there general purpose proof procedures for predicate logic, which work well enough for the translated formulae?

In general, the answers to these questions depend on the particular translation method being used, and we will see that many of the questions are still open.

In this chapter we take for granted that the enterprise of encoding nonclassical logics into classical logic has definite merits. We will concentrate on the fundamental ideas and results about encodings. The main ideas of the most important encoding techniques are presented in such a way that after studying the method, the reader should be able to find a suitable encoding for a given new logic herself.

More specifically, this chapter is organized as follows. Section 2 contains basic definitions and may be skipped on first reading. Section 3 explores the first of a number of ways of encoding a source logic into a target logic: syntactic encodings; we discuss the basic ideas and consider the merits of the approach from an automated reasoning point of view. In Section 4 we consider the standard relational translation; in this way of encoding we transcribe the semantics of the source logic in the target logic; we discuss the implications of this approach for our understanding of the expressive power of the source logic, and we discuss how the approach necessitates different ways of encoding if one is to do efficient automated reasoning for the source logic. Some of these alternatives are explored in Sections 5 and 6 where we consider the functional, the optimized functional, and the semi-functional translation. Further variations on and extensions of these ideas are discussed in Section 7. Finally, in Section 8 we formulate some conclusions and open questions.

2. Background

The purpose of this subsection is to set the scene for the remainder of the chapter, by introducing the basic syntactic and semantic prerequisites. We refer the reader to [Blackburn, de Rijke and Venema 2001] for further details.

2.1. Syntax

We will assume basic familiarity with first-order logic (FO). Throughout the chapter we consider a number of nonclassical logics; below we list most of them.

2.1. DEFINITION *(Modal Logic)*. Let $\mathcal{P}$ be a collection of proposition letters. The syntax of propositional *(uni-) modal logic* is given by the following rule

$$\text{ML} ::= \mathcal{P} \mid \neg\text{ML} \mid \text{ML} \wedge \text{ML} \mid \Diamond\text{ML} \mid \Box\text{ML}.$$

We freely use the usual boolean abbreviations. The $\Diamond$-operator is usually referred to as 'diamond,' and the $\Box$ as 'box.'

The language of *multi-modal logic* is just like the language of uni-modal logic except that in multi-modal logic we have a collection of diamonds $\langle a \rangle$ and boxes $[a]$, where a is taken from some index set. In the setting of description logics, multi-modal logic is sometimes referred to as $\mathcal{ALC}$; see [Calvanese et al. 2001] (Chapter 23 of this Handbook).

Propositional dynamic logic arises as a special case of multi-modal logic, where the diamonds and boxes are equipped with structure, corresponding to certain program forming operators: ; for sequential composition, $\cup$ for non-deterministic choice, * for finite iterations, and ? for testing. Let $\mathcal{A}$ be a collection of atomic programs; from these we define a collection of complex programs as follows:

$$\mathcal{R} ::= \mathcal{A} \mid \mathcal{R} ; \mathcal{R} \mid \mathcal{R} \cup \mathcal{R} \mid \mathcal{R}^* \mid \text{PDL?}$$

By mutual recursion, PDL formulae are defined by

$$\text{PDL} ::= \mathcal{P} \mid \neg\text{PDL} \mid \text{PDL} \wedge \text{PDL} \mid \langle\mathcal{R}\rangle\text{PDL} \mid [\mathcal{R}]\text{PDL}.$$

Here, $\langle\alpha\rangle A$ is read as 'there exists a terminating execution of the program α which leads to a state where A holds,' and $[\alpha]A$ means that all terminating executions of α lead to a state where A holds. Harel [1984] contains lots of background material on (propositional) dynamic logic. In the setting of description logics, propositional dynamic logic is sometimes referred to as $\mathcal{ALC}_{reg}$; again, see [Calvanese et al. 2001] (Chapter 23 of this Handbook).

Consider a multi-modal language with two diamonds, $\langle F \rangle$ and $\langle P \rangle$. Temporal logic arises when we assign very specific readings to $\langle F \rangle A$ and $\langle P \rangle A$: 'sometime in the future, A will be the case' and 'sometime in the past, A was the case.'

2.2. DEFINITION *(Temporal Logic)*. The language of *basic temporal logic* is given by the following rule

$$\text{BTL} ::= \mathcal{P} \mid \neg\text{BTL} \mid \text{BTL} \wedge \text{BTL} \mid \langle F \rangle\text{BTL} \mid [F]\text{BTL} \mid \langle P \rangle\text{BTL} \mid [P]\text{BTL}.$$

Here, $[F]$ ('it will always be the case that') and $[P]$ ('it has always been the case that') are dual operators for $\langle F \rangle$ and $\langle P \rangle$, respectively, just like $\square$ is the dual of $\lozenge$.

Linear time temporal logic (LTL) extends basic temporal logic by the addition of operators to talk about 'the next moment in time' and 'the previous moment in time,' and operators to express properties of intervals between two moments.

$$\text{LTL} ::= \mathcal{P} \mid \neg\text{LTL} \mid \text{LTL} \wedge \text{LTL} \mid \bigcirc\text{LTL} \mid \square\text{LTL} \mid U(\text{LTL}, \text{LTL}) \mid$$
$$\bullet\text{LTL} \mid \blacksquare\text{LTL} \mid S(\text{LTL}, \text{LTL}).$$

Here, $\bigcirc$ is the 'next time' operator, and $\bullet$ is the 'last time' operator; $\square A$ stands for 'always in the future A,' while $\blacksquare A$ stands for 'always in the past A;' and the until-operator $U(A, B)$ is meant to capture that A holds at some point in the future, and until then, B holds; the since-operator S is its 'backward' looking counterpart.

2.3. DEFINITION *(Intuitionistic and Relevance Logic)*. *Propositional intuitionistic logic* (IL) has the same connectives as classical propositional logic, but the implication is weaker than the classical implication.

$$\text{IL} ::= \mathcal{P} \mid \perp \mid \neg\text{IL} \mid \text{IL} \vee \text{IL} \mid \text{IL} \wedge \text{IL} \mid \text{IL} \rightarrow \text{IL}.$$

Relevance logic is essentially like intuitionistic logic, but with an even weaker implication. The idea is that $A \rightarrow B$ can only be a valid statement if A must actually be used to conclude B, i.e., A is *relevant* for B.

2.4. DEFINITION *(Quantified Modal Logic)*. Quantified modal logic is an extension of FO in the same way as propositional modal logic is an extension of propositional logic. Besides all the syntactic elements of FO, there are the two usual modal operators $\square$ and $\lozenge$.

We now turn to proof-theoretic matters. We first give some general definitions, and then present derivation systems for each of the logics we have just introduced.

2.5. DEFINITION. A *consequence relation* $\vdash$ is a relation between two sets (multisets, lists, trees or any other suitable datastructure) of formulae. $\phi \vdash \psi$ expresses that the set (multiset, list, ...) ψ of formulae is a consequence of the set (multiset, ...) of formulae ϕ. A specification of a logic by means of a consequence relation consists of a set of *axioms*

$$\phi_1 \vdash \psi_1, \phi_2 \vdash \psi_2, \ldots$$

and a set of *inference rules*

$$\frac{\phi_1 \vdash \psi_1, \phi_2 \vdash \psi_2, \ldots}{\phi \vdash \psi.}$$

The axioms are a kind of *a-priori* consequences. For many logics, finitely many axioms are sufficient, but nothing stops us from requiring infinitely many axioms. The inference rules allow us to derive new (*output*) consequences from a finite or infinite set of given (*input*) consequences. Again, there may be finitely many or infinitely many inference rules, but in most cases this number is very small. The inference rules may have side conditions restricting there applicability with extra requirements on the structure of the formulae involved.

More generally, the inference rules may require the non-derivability of some consequences. This means that some of the expressions $\phi_i \vdash \psi_i$ in the input part of the inference rule may actually occur in the form *not* $\phi_i \vdash \psi_i$. This gives the system a nonmonotonic behavior because adding *more* axioms may cause *fewer* derived consequences.

2.6. DEFINITION. The consequence relation $\vdash \psi$ of a *Hilbert system* (HS) has an empty set of premises and just a single formula as conclusion. $\vdash \psi$ means that ψ is a theorem.

$$\left\{ \begin{array}{l} \vdash A \to (B \to A) \\ \vdash (A \to (B \to C)) \to ((A \to B) \to (A \to C)) \\ \vdash ((A \to B) \to A) \to A \\ \vdash A \wedge B \to A \\ \vdash A \wedge B \to B \\ \vdash A \to (B \to A \wedge B) \\ \vdash A \to (A \vee B) \\ \vdash B \to (A \vee B) \\ \vdash (A \to C) \to ((B \to C) \to (A \vee B \to C)) \\ \vdash (A \to \neg B) \to (B \to \neg A) \\ \vdash \neg\neg A \to A \end{array} \right.$$

propositional part $\qquad$ (2.1)

K $\qquad \vdash \Box(A \to B) \to (\Box A \to \Box B)$ $\qquad$ (2.2)

modus ponens $\qquad \dfrac{\vdash A \qquad \vdash A \to B}{\vdash B}$ $\qquad$ (2.3)

necessitation rule $\qquad \dfrac{\vdash A}{\vdash \Box A}$ $\qquad$ (2.4)

Table 1: Axioms and rules for **K**

2.7. DEFINITION (**K**, **K**$_m$ *and* **PDL**). The *basic (uni-) modal logic* is called **K** (after Kripke), and it is axiomatized by the axioms and rules listed in Table 1.

The diamond operator $\Diamond$ is defined in terms of the box operator $\Box$ by $\Diamond p \leftrightarrow \neg\Box\neg p$.

The set of axioms for the *basic multi-modal logic* **K**$_m$ (where $m \in \mathbb{N}$) consists of (2.1), m copies of the K axiom (2.2) and the necessitation rule, one for each modal operator $[\alpha]$, and modus ponens (2.3).

An axiom system **PDL** for propositional dynamic logic is obtained by taking the **K** axioms and rules for all operators $[R]$ ($R \in \mathcal{R}$) and adding the following

(Comp) $\qquad \vdash [\alpha\,;\beta]A \leftrightarrow [\alpha][\beta]A$

(Alt) $\qquad \vdash [\alpha \cup \beta]A \leftrightarrow [\alpha]A \wedge [\beta]A$

(Mix) $\qquad \vdash [\alpha^*]A \to A \wedge [\alpha][\alpha^*]A$

(Ind) $\qquad \vdash [\alpha^*](A \to [\alpha]A) \to (A \to [\alpha^*]A)$

(Test) $\qquad \vdash [A?]B \leftrightarrow (A \to B)$

(Mix) and (Ind) are sometimes referred to as the *Segerberg axioms*; together they capture the fact that the program α^* is α iterated finitely often.

Extensions of **K** are obtained by adding further axioms and/or rules to **K**. For instance, the logic **S4** is obtained by adding the following axioms to **K**:

(T) $\vdash \Box A \to A$

(4) $\vdash \Box A \to \Box\Box A$

2.8. DEFINITION *(Classical Modal Systems)*. The so-called *classical* modal system [Chellas 1980] is a restriction of **K** in which the K axiom (2.2) and the necessitation rules (2.4) are replaced by:

$$(RE) \quad \frac{\vdash A \leftrightarrow B}{\vdash \Box A \leftrightarrow \Box B} \tag{2.5}$$

This rule ensures that the box operator is syntax independent in the sense that it does not distinguish equivalent formulae.

In a similar way as with extensions of the modal logic **K**, one can build logics as extensions of the system characterized by **RE**. Examples of other rules are:

$$(RM) \quad \frac{\vdash A \to B}{\vdash \Box A \to \Box B} \tag{2.6}$$

$$(RR) \quad \frac{\vdash (A \wedge B) \to C}{\vdash (\Box A \wedge \Box B) \to \Box C} \tag{2.7}$$

2.9. DEFINITION *(Axioms for Temporal Logic)*. The smallest *basic temporal logic* $\mathbf{K}_t$ consists of the **K**-axioms for each of $[F]$ and $[P]$, as well as the 4 axiom for both $[F]$ and $[P]$, and the following two axioms that are meant to express that the temporal operators explore the same flow of time, but in opposite directions.

(Conv1) $\vdash A \to [P]\langle F\rangle A$

(Conv2) $\vdash A \to [F]\langle P\rangle A$

The axioms for linear time temporal logic, **LTL**, consist of the **K** axioms for $\Box$, $\bigcirc$ and $\bullet$, the Segerberg axioms for $\Box$ and $\bigcirc$, and for $\blacksquare$ and $\bullet$, as well as axioms for functionality and U and S; see [Goldblatt 1992] or [Clarke and Schlingloff 2001] (Chapter 24 of this Handbook) for details.

2.10. DEFINITION *(Axioms for Intuitionistic Logic)*. An axiom system **IL** for intuitionistic logic is given by

$\vdash A \to (B \to A)$

$\vdash (A \to B) \to ((A \to (B \to C)) \to (A \to C))$

$\vdash A \to (B \to A \wedge B)$

$\vdash (A \wedge B) \to A$

$\vdash (A \wedge B) \to B$

$\vdash A \to (A \vee B)$

$\vdash B \to (A \vee B)$

$\vdash (A \to C) \to ((B \to C) \to (A \vee B \to C))$

$\vdash (A \to B) \to ((A \to \neg B) \to \neg A)$

$\vdash (A \to (\neg A \to B))$.

The only deduction rule is modus ponens (2.3).

2.2. Semantics

We will first give a general definition, and then instantiate it for particular logics.

Many two-valued nonclassical logics have a characterization in terms of a so-called *possible worlds semantics*.

2.11. DEFINITION *(Possible World Semantics)*. The basis for a possible world semantics is a *frame* $\mathcal{F} = (W, S)$ consisting of a non-empty set W of worlds or states and some structure S on these worlds. S may be just a binary relation between worlds (the *accessibility relation*) as in normal modal logics and in intuitionistic logic, or a binary relation satisfying special properties (such as the later-than relation in temporal logic), or a set of binary relations as in multi-modal logic, or a relation between worlds and sets of worlds (the *neighborhood relation*) as in classical modal logic, or a ternary relation between worlds as in relevance logic.

An *interpretation* (or *model*) $\mathfrak{I}$ based on a frame $\mathcal{F}$ associates a classical interpretation with each world, sometimes subject to some restrictions. In addition, an interpretation may contain an *actual world* and, if the logic has quantifiers, a variable assignment.

Let us now instantiate the general definition for some specific logics. We start with (uni-) modal logic.

2.12. DEFINITION *(Semantics of Modal Logic)*. A frame, or *Kripke frame*, for the (uni-) modal language with just $\Diamond$ and $\Box$ is a structure $\mathcal{F} = (W, R)$ consisting of a non-empty set of worlds W and a binary accessibility relation R on W.

An interpretation, or *Kripke model*, $\mathfrak{I} = (\mathcal{F}, P)$ consists of a frame $\mathcal{F}$, and a *valuation* or *predicate assignment* P which assigns to each proposition letter p the subset of worlds where p is interpreted as *true*. Each model induces a *satisfiability relation* $\models$ that determines the truth of a formula at a given *actual world* $w \in W$.

The *satisfiability relation* for the basic uni-modal language is given by the following clauses.

$$
\begin{aligned}
\mathfrak{I}, w &\models p & \text{iff} \quad & w \in P(p) \quad \text{in case } p \text{ is a predicate symbol} \\
\mathfrak{I}, w &\models \neg A & \text{iff} \quad & \text{not } \mathfrak{I}, w \models A \\
\mathfrak{I}, w &\models A \wedge B & \text{iff} \quad & \mathfrak{I}, w \models A \ \& \ \mathfrak{I}, w \models B \\
\mathfrak{I}, w &\models A \vee B & \text{iff} \quad & \mathfrak{I}, w \models A \text{ or } \mathfrak{I}, w \models B \\
\mathfrak{I}, w &\models \Box A & \text{iff} \quad & \forall v \, (R(w, v) \Rightarrow \mathfrak{I}, v \models A) \\
\mathfrak{I}, w &\models \Diamond A & \text{iff} \quad & \exists v \, (R(w, v) \ \& \ \mathfrak{I}, v \models A).
\end{aligned}
$$

A *frame* for a multi-modal language whose collection of modal operators is $\{\langle \alpha \rangle \mid \alpha \in \mathcal{R}\}$ is a tuple $\mathcal{F} = (W, \{R_\alpha \mid \alpha \in \mathcal{R}\})$. The satisfaction relation for multi-modal languages is defined just as for the uni-modal language, albeit that every modal operator $\langle \alpha \rangle$ is interpreted using its own relation R_α.

A *model* for the language of propositional dynamic logic is a structure $\mathfrak{I} = (W, \{R_\alpha \mid \alpha \in \mathcal{R}\}, P)$ just as for multi-modal logic, but the difference is that the relations R_α (for α non-atomic) are required to satisfy certain structural constraints:

$$R_{\alpha;\beta} \;=\; R_\alpha \circ R_\beta, \text{ the relational composition of } R_\alpha \text{ and } R_\beta$$

$$R_{\alpha \cup \beta} \;=\; R_\alpha \cup R_\beta$$

$$R_{\alpha^*} \;=\; \bigcup_n (R_\alpha)^n, \text{ where } (R_\alpha)^0 \text{ is the identity relation, and}$$

$$(R_\alpha)^{n+1} = (R_\alpha)^n \circ R_\alpha$$

$$R_{A?} \;=\; \{(w,w) \mid \Im, w \models A\}$$

A formula ϕ is a *semantic consequence* of a particular logic, characterized by a particular frame class, if and only if it is *true* for all such interpretations, i.e., for all frames in a given class, for all actual worlds and for all predicate assignments.

Particular logics are characterized by certain frame classes, or in more complex cases, by certain model classes. To be *characterized by a frame class* means that the set of semantic consequences of this logic consists of all formulae which are interpreted as *true* in all interpretations based on all frames of this class. For example, **K** is characterized by the class of frames (W, R) where R is an arbitrary binary relation between worlds. Further examples for axioms and the corresponding properties of the accessibility relation are given in Table 2. It is not always possible to characterize a logic just by a frame class [van Benthem 1983]. More complex logics may require special conditions on interpretations, too.

name	axiom	property of R
4	$\Box A \to \Box\Box A$	transitivity
5	$\Diamond A \to \Box\Diamond A$	euclidean[1]
T	$\Box A \to A$	reflexivity
B	$A \to \Box\Diamond A$	symmetry
D	$\Box A \to \Diamond A$	seriality

Table 2: Axioms and their frame properties

2.13. DEFINITION *(Semantics of Temporal Languages).* The semantics of the temporal languages considered in this chapter are defined as follows. A *temporal frame* is a structure $\mathcal{F} = (W, \leq)$ where W should now be thought of as a collection of points in time, and $\leq$ is a transitive binary relation on W representing the 'later-than' relation.

The key aspect of the truth definition is in the clauses for the modal operators:

$$\Im, w \models \langle F \rangle A \quad \text{iff} \quad \exists v \, (w \leq v \;\&\; \Im, v \models A)$$

$$\Im, w \models \langle P \rangle A \quad \text{iff} \quad \exists v \, (v \leq w \;\&\; \Im, v \models A).$$

---

[1]A relation R is called *euclidean* if it satisfies $\forall v, w, u \, (R(v, w) \wedge R(v, u) \to R(w, u))$.

Thus, $\langle F \rangle$ and $\langle P \rangle$ are interpreted using the same relation $\leq$.

Models for linear time temporal logic are structures $\Im = (W, <, P)$ where $(W, <)$ is an initial segment of the natural numbers $(\omega, <)$ with its natural ordering, and P is a valuation. The truth conditions for the temporal operators are as follows:

$$\Im, w \models \bigcirc A \quad \text{iff} \quad \Im, w + 1 \models A$$

$$\Im, w \models \Box A \quad \text{iff} \quad \forall v \, (w < v \Rightarrow \Im, v \models A)$$

$$\Im, w \models U(A, B) \quad \text{iff} \quad \exists v \, (w \leq v \,\&\, \Im, v \models A \,\&\, \forall u \, (w \leq u < v \Rightarrow \Im, u \models B))$$

$$\Im, w \models \bullet A \quad \text{iff} \quad w > 0 \,\&\, \Im, w - 1 \models A,$$

while $\blacksquare$ and S are simply backward looking versions of $\Box$ and U.

2.14. DEFINITION (*Semantics of Intuitionistic and Relevance Logic*). The semantics of intuitionistic logic can also be defined in terms of possible worlds, but we need to impose a restriction on assignments. An *intuitionistic frame* $\mathcal{F} = (W, R)$ consists of a non-empty set of worlds, together with a *reflexive* and *transitive* relation R. An interpretation $\Im = (\mathcal{F}, P)$ is similar to an interpretation for modal logic, but whenever P assigns *true* to some predicate symbol p at some world w then it must assign *true* to p at all w-accessible worlds.

The possible worlds semantics of relevance logic is more complex. It has a *ternary* accessibility relation R, a unary function $(\cdot)^*$ and a distinguished world 0. A *relevant frame* is therefore a 4-tuple $\mathcal{F} = (W, R, (\cdot)^*, 0)$ consisting of a non-empty set of worlds, a distinguished world $0 \in W$, a ternary accessibility relation R, and a unary function $(\cdot)^*$ satisfying the following conditions:

$$\forall x \, R(0, x, x)$$
$$\forall x, y, z \, (R(x, y, z) \rightarrow R(y, x, z))$$
$$\forall x, y, z, u \, (\exists v \, (R(x, y, v) \land R(v, z, u)) \rightarrow \exists v \, (R(x, v, u) \land R(y, z, v)))$$
$$\forall x \, R(x, x, x)$$
$$\forall x, y, z, x' \, (R(x, y, z) \land R(0, x', x) \rightarrow R(x', y, z))$$
$$\forall x \, x^{**} = x$$
$$\forall x, y, z \, (R(x, y, z) \rightarrow R(x, z^*, y^*)).$$

An *interpretation* consists of a frame and a predicate assignment P with a restriction which is similar to the restriction for intuitionistic logic: whenever P assigns *true* to some predicate symbol p at some world w then it must assign *true* to p at all worlds u with $R(0, w, u)$. The non-standard parts of the satisfiability relation are

$$\Im, w \models A \rightarrow B \quad \text{iff} \quad \forall u, v \, R(w, u, v) \Rightarrow \Im, u \models A \Rightarrow \Im, v \models B, \text{ and}$$
$$\Im, w \models \neg A \quad \text{iff} \quad \Im, w^* \not\models A$$

2.15. DEFINITION (*Semantics of Classical Modal Logic*). The axiom K is valid in all modal logics whose semantics are based on binary accessibility relations. If this axiom is undesirable for some reason, a different kind of semantics is necessary, *neighborhood semantics*, also called *minimal model semantics* [Chellas 1980]. In its weakest version, it just ensures that the modal operators cannot distinguish between equivalent formulae, or, in other words, if $A \leftrightarrow B$ is valid then $\Box A \leftrightarrow \Box B$ is valid, too.

A neighborhood frame $\mathcal{F} = (W, N)$ consists of a non-empty set of possible worlds and a *neighborhood relation* N between worlds and *sets of worlds*. The interpretation for the classical connectives is the same as for normal modal logics. Only the interpretation of the modal operators changes. For the weaker version of classical modal logics the interpretation is:

$$\Im, w \models \Box A \quad \text{iff} \quad \exists V \, (N(w, V) \,\&\, \forall v \, (v \in V \Leftrightarrow \Im, v \models A))$$
$$\Im, w \models \Diamond A \quad \text{iff} \quad \forall V \, (N(w, V) \Rightarrow \exists v \, (v \in V \Leftrightarrow \Im, v \models A)).$$

If the rule **RM** (2.6)

$$\frac{\vdash A \to B}{\vdash \Box A \to \Box B}$$

holds, then the following stronger semantics is to be used instead

$$\Im, w \models \Box A \quad \text{iff} \quad \exists V \, (N(w, V) \,\&\, \forall v \, (v \in V \Rightarrow \Im, v \models A))$$
$$\Im, w \models \Diamond A \quad \text{iff} \quad \forall V \, N((w, V) \Rightarrow \exists v \, (v \in V \,\&\, \Im, v \models A)).$$

The weak version of the minimal model semantics states that $\Box A$ is true in a world w iff the truth set of A is one of w's neighborhoods. Therefore, equivalent formulae are not distinguishable by the box operator. The stronger version of the semantics weakens this requirement: the truth set of A only needs to be a superset of one of w's neighborhoods.

2.16. Definition *(Quantified Modal Logic)*. The semantics of quantified modal logic has the same kind of frames $\mathcal{F} = (W, R)$ with a binary accessibility relation as normal propositional modal logic. An interpretation $\Im = (\mathcal{F}, P, V)$ consists of a frame $\mathcal{F}$, an assignment P associating with each world w a classical predicate logic interpretation $P(w)$, and a variable assignment V.

Each predicate logic interpretation $P(w)$ may associate a different meaning to the function and predicate symbols. *Rigid* symbols are function and predicate symbols whose interpretation does not change from world to world, otherwise they are called *flexible* symbols. $P(w)$ may even associate a different domain with each world (varying domain interpretation). Alternatively, the domain may remain the same for all worlds (constant domain) or increase (decrease) when moving from a world to an accessible world.

The interpretation $P(w)(p)$ of a function or predicate symbol p must be defined for all elements of all domains, not only for the domain associated with the world w, otherwise the following problem arises. For the formula $\exists x \, \Diamond p(x)$ the interpretation of the existential quantifier chooses an element a of the domain of the actual world

w as the assignment for the variable x. The $\Diamond$-operator guides us to another world v. We can only interpret $p(x)$ in v's domain if $P(v)(p)$ is also defined for objects in the other world's domains.

Let $\mathcal{D}(w)$ denote w's domain, let $\Im[x/a]$ be just like $\Im$, except that the variable x is mapped to a, and let $\Im(t,w)$ represent the interpretation of the term t in the world w. Then the satisfiability relation $\models$ is defined as

$$\Im, w \models q(t_1, \ldots, t_n) \quad \text{iff} \quad (\Im(t_1, w), \ldots, \Im(t_n, w)) \in P(q)$$
$$\text{in case } q \text{ is a predicate symbol}$$
$$\Im, w \models \forall x\, A \quad \text{iff} \quad \forall a\, (a \in \mathcal{D}(w) \Rightarrow \Im[x/a], w \models A)$$
$$\Im, w \models \exists x\, A \quad \text{iff} \quad \exists a\, (a \in \mathcal{D}(w) \,\&\, \Im[x/a], w \models A).$$

After this short summary of the semantics of the most prominent modal-like logics, we come to the core of this chapter: how to encode these logics into predicate logic.

3. Encoding consequence relations

If we want to encode a given source logic into a target logic, and if the source logic is given as a Hilbert system, we can try to use the target logic, $\mathbf{L_2}$, as a metalevel language for the source logic, $\mathbf{L_1}$. The well-formed formulae (wffs) of $\mathbf{L_1}$ become terms of $\mathbf{L_2}$ and the axioms and theorems of $\mathbf{L_1}$ become theorems of $\mathbf{L_2}$. Let us make this more precise.

A Hilbert system HS — with all predicate symbols implicitly universally quantified, and where the inference rules have only finitely many (positive) input formulae and no side conditions — can be encoded in first-order predicate logic (FO) in the following manner.

3.1. EXAMPLE. Take the source logic to be the uni-modal logic $\mathbf{K}$, and the target logic is simply FO. To cater for the operators present in the source logic, we take function symbols $f_\wedge$, $f_\vee$, $f_\rightarrow$, $f_\neg$, $f_\square$, $f_\Diamond$ in the vocabulary of the target logic. We form all terms out of constants $\{c_1, c_2, c_3, \ldots\}$ and variables $\{p_1, p_2, p_3, \ldots\}$. We define a translation $(\cdot)^*$ assigning to each modal wff A a FO-term A^*, as detailed in Table 3.

We can identify the axioms and theorems of the source logic $\mathbf{L_1}$ by defining a predicate $Th(x)$ (x is a *theorem*) on the terms obtained as translations of $\mathbf{L_1}$. More precisely, in the syntactic way of encoding a logic, formulae are represented as FO-terms; HS-predicate symbols become universally quantified FO-variables, while the HS-connectives become FO-function symbols, and the consequence relation $\vdash$ becomes a unary FO-predicate Th (for theoremhood). The axioms are encoded as unit clauses and the inference rules are encoded as Horn-formulae.

3.2. EXAMPLE. We build on Example 3.1 to encode a Hilbert system for the modal logic $\mathbf{S4}$. Recall that $\mathbf{S4}$ can be axiomatized by adding the following axioms on top of the axioms and rules given for $\mathbf{K}$ in Definition 2.7:

$$(c_n)^* = a_{c_n}, \text{ for the } n\text{th constant } c_n$$

$$(p_n)^* = x_{p_n}, \text{ for the } n\text{th variable } p_n$$

$$(A \wedge B)^* = f_\wedge(A^*, B^*)$$

$$(A \rightarrow B)^* = f_\rightarrow(A^*, B^*)$$

$$(A \vee B)^* = f_\vee(A^*, B^*)$$

$$(\neg A)^* = f_\neg(A^*)$$

$$(\Box A)^* = f_\Box(A^*)$$

$$(\Diamond A)^* = f_\Diamond(A^*).$$

Table 3: Syntactic encoding

(T) $\vdash \Box A \rightarrow A$

(4) $\vdash \Box A \rightarrow \Box\Box A$

Take the metalevel translation as specified in Example 3.1. We can identify the axioms and theorems of **S4** by defining a predicate $Th(x)$ (x is a *theorem*) in classical logic on the terms (wff) of **S4*** (the translation of **S4**).

As the theory τ_* of classical logic we take

(universal closure of) $Th(t^*)$

where t^* is a variable translation of any **S4** axiom, e.g., $t^* = f_\rightarrow(x, f_\rightarrow(y, x))$ as translation of $A \rightarrow (B \rightarrow A)$, plus the metalevel translation of modus ponens and the necessitation rule:

$$\forall x, y \ (Th(x) \wedge Th(f_\rightarrow(x,y)) \rightarrow Th(y)) \tag{3.1}$$

$$\forall x \ (Th(x) \rightarrow Th(f_\Box(x))). \tag{3.2}$$

Then it follows, for all modal formulae A, that

$$\mathbf{S4} \vdash A \quad \text{iff} \quad \tau_* \vdash Th(A^*).$$

How does a FO theorem prover behave when fed with the syntactic encoding of a Hilbert system? Observe first that a UR-resolution or a hyperresolution sequence with the FO encoding of a Hilbert system corresponds directly to a derivation in the system itself [McCune and Wos 1992]. Since the clause set obtained from an encoded Hilbert system is a Horn clause set, the (unique) Herbrand model represents the theorems of the Hilbert system. Now, the syntactic way of encoding a logic does not automatically provide a decision procedure for theoremhood within the source logic, even if this problem is decidable in principle. In particular, UR-resolution with a syntactically encoded Hilbert system just enumerates the — usually infinitely many — theorems of the logic. A non-theorem can therefore never be refuted this way.

Experiments with first-order theorem provers have shown that the search space for this kind of encoding is very large [McCune and Wos 1992], and therefore the theorem provers are very slow.

Ohlbach [1998b] has investigated a transformation which can eliminate self-resolving clauses like the condensed detachment clause (3.1) from a clause set in a satisfiability preserving way. Self-resolving clauses can be deleted from a clause set if sufficiently many other clauses, which are consequences of the self-resolving clauses and the other clauses, are added. For the transitivity clause, for example, it is sufficient to add for each positive literal in the other clauses one single resolvent with a selected negative literal of the transitivity clause. Afterwards, transitivity is not needed anymore. This transformation can also be applied to the condensed detachment clause.

Unfortunately, it turns out that infinitely many resolvents are to be added before one can delete a condensed detachment clause. The clauses to add are (for each positive literal) a resolvent with the first literal in each of the infinitely many clauses below, which are themselves self-resolvents between the first and third literal of condensed detachment.

$$\neg Th(f_\rightarrow(x,y)), \neg Th(x), Th(y)$$
$$\neg Th(f_\rightarrow(x, f_\rightarrow(z_1, z_2))), \neg Th(x), \neg Th(z_1), Th(z_2)$$

$\cdots$

$$\neg Th(f_\rightarrow(x, f_\rightarrow(z_1, f_\rightarrow(\ldots z_j)))), \neg Th(x) \neg Th(z_1), \ldots, \neg Th(z_{j-1}), Th(z_j)$$

$\cdots$

3.3. EXAMPLE. We illustrate this transformation with Łukasiewicz's single axiom axiomatization of the implicational fragment of propositional logic [Łukasiewicz 1970, p. 295]:

$$\vdash ((x \rightarrow y) \rightarrow z) \rightarrow ((z \rightarrow x) \rightarrow (u \rightarrow x)). \tag{3.3}$$

The transformation yields

$Th(f_\rightarrow(f_\rightarrow(f_\rightarrow(x,y),z), f_\rightarrow(f_\rightarrow(z,x), f_\rightarrow(u,x))))$
$Th(f_\rightarrow(f_\rightarrow(x,y),z) \rightarrow Th(f_\rightarrow(f_\rightarrow(z,x), f_\rightarrow(u,x)))$
$Th(f_\rightarrow(f_\rightarrow(x,y),z) \wedge Th(f_\rightarrow(z,x)) \rightarrow Th(f_\rightarrow(u,x))$
$Th(f_\rightarrow(f_\rightarrow(x,y),z) \wedge Th(f_\rightarrow(z,x)) \wedge Th(u) \rightarrow Th(x)$
$Th(f_\rightarrow(f_\rightarrow(f_\rightarrow(u_1,u_2),y),z) \wedge Th(f_\rightarrow(z, f_\rightarrow(u_1,u_2))) \wedge Th(u) \wedge$
$\quad Th(u_1) \rightarrow Th(u_2)$
$Th(f_\rightarrow(f_\rightarrow(f_\rightarrow(u_1, f_\rightarrow(u_2,u_3)),y),z) \wedge Th(f_\rightarrow(z, f_\rightarrow(u_1, f_\rightarrow(u_2,u_3)))) \wedge$
$\quad Th(u) \wedge Th(u_1) \wedge Th(u_2) \rightarrow Th(u_3)$

$\cdots$,

which is infinite, but with a very regular structure. With some standard and well-known tricks one can convert it into a finite clause set suitable as input to any resolution-based theorem prover. Longer subformulae are replaced with newly defined predicates $(q_1, \ldots, q_4)$ and the recursive structure of the infinitely many formulae above is turned into a 'generator clause' (the third but last clause below). The result is

$$Th(f_\to(f_\to(f_\to(x,y),z),f_\to(f_\to(z,x),f_\to(u,x)))))$$
$$Th(f_\to(f_\to(x,y),z) \to q_1(x,z)$$
$$q_1(x,z) \to Th(f_\to(f_\to(z,x),f_\to(u,x)))$$
$$q_1(x,z) \wedge Th(f_\to(z,x)) \to q_2(x)$$
$$q_2(x) \to Th(x)$$
$$q_2(x) \to q_3(x)$$
$$q_3(f_\to(u,v)) \wedge Th(u) \to q_4(v)$$
$$q_4(v) \to q_3(v)$$
$$q_4(v) \to Th(v).$$

Experiments have shown that proving theorems from this clause set instead of the original condensed detachment clause can speed up the theorem prover by a factor of 50 [Ohlbach 1998b]. But there is no guarantee. In other cases this transformation has slowed theorem provers down considerably.

To sum up, the direct syntactic encoding of Hilbert systems into FO is certainly not the optimal way of proving theorems in these logics. Nevertheless, for experimenting with new logics or for getting alternative formulations of a given logic, this encoding together with a fast FO theorem prover provides a very useful tool.

One possible obstacle for such experiments is that there is no general recipe for encoding side conditions of inference rules in FO. This is usually quite complicated because the side conditions may refer to the syntactic structure of a formula. Here is a particular example.

3.4. EXAMPLE. In modal logic one of the best-known inference rules with a side condition is Gabbay's *irreflexivity rule* [Gabbay 1981b]

$$\frac{\vdash \neg(\Box p \to p) \to A}{\vdash A} \quad \text{if } p \notin A$$

To encode the irreflexivity rule, we need a predicate $in(p, A)$ which checks whether p occurs in A. The FO-axiom for in would look like

$$in(p, A) \quad \leftrightarrow \quad p = A' \vee$$
$$(\exists B \ A = f_\neg(B) \wedge in(p, B)) \vee$$
$$(\exists A_1, A_2 \ A = f_\to(A_1, A_2) \wedge (in(p, A_1) \vee in(p, A_2))) \vee \dots$$

Adding this axiom, however, requires equational reasoning. Most FO theorem provers have serious difficulty with this formulation.

Binary consequence relations $\phi \vdash \psi$, where both ϕ and ψ are single formulae, can be encoded in a similar way as the unary consequence relation of Hilbert systems. Instead of the unary predicate $Th(x)$ ('x is a theorem'), we use the binary predicate $D(x, y)$ (y can be derived from x).

If ϕ and ψ are more complex datastructures, one has to axiomatize these datastructures. For instance, if the datastructure is a list (as in linear logic), a constant *empty* needs to be introduced as well as an associative function symbol *append* that takes the FO-encoded formulae as arguments. The axiom $X, A \vdash A$, for example, would be encoded as

$$\forall X, A\, D(append(X, A), append(A, empty)).$$

Unfortunately, automated reasoning based on these kinds of axioms, and either paramodulation or theory unification for the associativity property of *append*, becomes much more complicated and inefficient than in the Hilbert system case. Therefore, we think that it is not worthwhile to go into further details here.

The situation is even worse if some of the input consequences of a consequence relation are negated. *not* $\phi \vdash \psi$ means that the input condition is satisfied if $\phi \vdash \psi$ is *not* derivable. This cannot be encoded using the FO-negation, because it requires a proof that $\phi \vdash \psi$ is not a theorem. Another metalevel, which encodes the FO-derivability relation itself as a predicate, or some Prolog-like operational treatment (negation by failure) may help here.

To conclude, then, the syntactic encoding of logics is an easy and flexible way of encoding a nonclassical logic in FO, which imposes only a few conditions on the source logics being encoded. This flexibility proves to be an advantage as well as a disadvantage: only very little information about the source logic is actually encoded into the target logic by means of syntactic encodings.

4. The standard relational translation

If a given nonclassical logic comes with a possible worlds semantics of the kind described in Section 2.2, there is an alternative to the syntactic encoding that we have seen in Section 3: we can encode the semantics of the source logic by simply transcribing it inside the target logic.

Below we will introduce the idea using the uni-modal language, as well as a number of other ones. In most cases the semantics-based relational encoding is fairly simple and the reader should have no difficulties in doing something similar for other logics. After the examples, we will explore the implications of having this translation for understanding the expressive power of the source logics being encoded, and for the purposes of reasoning with the source logic. The latter will also form the motivation for refinements of the relational translation.

4.1. The basic case

The prototypical example for the standard or relational translation is propositional uni-modal logic. Recall the truth conditions for the modal operators:

$$\Im, w \models \Box A \quad \text{iff} \quad \forall v\, (R(w, v) \Rightarrow \Im, v \models A)$$
$$\Im, w \models \Diamond A \quad \text{iff} \quad \exists v\, (R(w, v) \,\&\, \Im, v \models A).$$

From these definitions we can derive the definition of the *standard* or *relational translation* $ST_m(w, A)$.

4.1. DEFINITION *(Standard Relational Translation)*. The source logic is uni-modal logic, and the target logic is FO; its vocabulary of the target logic consists of a binary predicate symbol R to represent the accessibility relation, and unary predicate symbols to represent proposition letters. Then, the recursive definition for the *standard relational translation* is

$$
\begin{aligned}
ST_m(w, p) &= p(w) \\
ST_m(w, \neg A) &= \neg ST_m(w, A) \\
ST_m(w, A \wedge B) &= ST_m(w, A) \wedge ST_m(w, B) \\
ST_m(w, A \vee B) &= ST_m(w, A) \vee ST_m(w, B) \\
ST_m(w, \Box A) &= \forall v\, (R(w, v) \rightarrow ST_m(v, A)) \qquad (4.1) \\
ST_m(w, \Diamond A) &= \exists v\, (R(w, v) \wedge ST_m(v, A)). \qquad (4.2)
\end{aligned}
$$

Now, on the semantic side, Kripke models have all the ingredients to serve as models for the first-order language that we have just defined: they have a binary relation for the binary predicate symbol, and they have valuations to cater for the unary predicate symbols.

4.2. THEOREM. *Let A be a modal formula. Then the following hold:*
1. *For any model $\mathfrak{I}$ and state w we have that $\mathfrak{I}, w \models A$ iff $\mathfrak{I} \models ST_m(w, A)$, where $\models$ on the left-hand side is the modal satisfiability relation, and $\models$ on the right-hand side denotes first-order satisfiability.*
2. $\models A$ *iff* $\models \forall x\, ST(x, A)$

Item 1 of the theorem says that when we interpret modal formulae on models we can view them as first-order formulae, while item 2 says that a modal formula is valid on all Kripke models iff the universal closure of its standard translation is valid on all FO models.

4.3. EXAMPLE. $ST_m(w, A)$ yields a first-order formula and can be submitted to a first-order theorem prover. As an example, in the modal logic **K**, the axiom $\Box(p \rightarrow q) \rightarrow (\Box p \rightarrow \Box q)$ is a theorem. Its standard translation $\forall w\, (\forall v\, R(w, v) \rightarrow (p(v) \rightarrow q(v))) \rightarrow ((\forall v\, R(w, v) \rightarrow p(v)) \rightarrow (\forall v\, R(w, v) \rightarrow q(v)))$ is therefore a FO theorem.

While the standard relational translation was implicit in much of the work in modal and temporal logic going on in the early 1970s, the first systematic study seems to be due to [van Benthem 1976].

Recall from Table 2 that many of the well-known modal logics are characterized by first-order definable frame classes. For such logics Theorem 4.2 may be specialized as follows.

4.4. THEOREM. *Let A be a uni-modal formula, and let $B_1, \ldots, B_n$ be characterized by first-order frame conditions $\tau_{B_1}, \ldots, \tau_{B_n}$, respectively. Then A is a semantic consequence of $\mathbf{K B}_1 \ldots \mathbf{B}_n$ iff $(\tau_{B_1} \wedge \cdots \wedge \tau_{B_n}) \to \forall x \, ST_m(x, A)$ is a theorem of first-order logic.*

4.5. EXAMPLE. **S4** is complete for several semantic interpretations. The one that we are interested in here is the usual Kripke semantics, where R is a reflexive and transitive accessibility relation, and $w \vDash \Box A$ iff $\forall u \, (wRu \Rightarrow u \vDash A)$. Let τ be the FO theory

$$\tau = \{\forall x \, R(x, x), \forall x, y, z \, (R(x, y) \wedge R(y, z) \to R(x, z))\}.$$

Then we have, for every modal formula A,

$$\mathbf{S4} \vDash A \text{ iff } \tau \vDash \forall x \, ST_m(x, A).$$

Before addressing the issue of reasoning with (translated) modal formulae in greater depth, we will look at uses of the standard relational translation for nonclassical logics other than uni-modal logic.

4.2. Further examples

The ideas underlying the standard translation are not restricted to the basic modal logic **K**. Below we list some examples.

4.6. EXAMPLE *(Multi-Modal Logic)*. Definition 4.1 can easily be extended to multi-modal logic; we simply make sure that the vocabulary of the target logic has 'enough' binary relation symbols R_a, R_b, $\ldots$: one for every diamond $\langle a \rangle$ and box $[a]$. Then, the key clause in the translation becomes

$$ST_m(w, [a]A) = \forall v \, (R_a(w, v) \to ST_m(v, A)).$$

So, the formula $\langle a \rangle [b] \langle a \rangle p$ is translated as

$$\exists v \, (R_a(w, v) \wedge \forall u \, (R_b(v, u) \to \exists t \, (R_a(u, t) \wedge (p(t))))).$$

We leave it to the reader to establish equivalences analogous to those in Theorem 4.2.

4.7. EXAMPLE *(Propositional Dynamic Logic)*. If we want to provide a relational translation for propositional dynamic logic (PDL), we have to change our target logic because of the presence of programs of the form α^*. Recall that a program α^* is interpreted using the reflexive, transitive closure of R_α. But the reflexive, transitive closure of a relation is not a first-order definable relation (see Definition 2.12).

What is a suitable target logic here? There are many options, but to motivate our choice recall the definition of the meaning of a PDL program α^*:

$$R_{\alpha^*} = \bigcup_n (R_\alpha)^n,$$

where R_α^n is defined by $R^0(x, y)$ iff $x = y$, and $R^{n+1}(x, y)$ iff $\exists z\, (R^n(x, z) \wedge R(z, y))$. If we are allowed to write infinitely long disjunctions, we see how to capture the meaning of an iterated program α^*:

$$(R_\alpha)^* xy \text{ iff } (x = y) \vee R_\alpha xy \vee \bigvee \exists z_1 \ldots z_n\, (R_\alpha x z_1 \wedge \cdots \wedge R_\alpha z_n y).$$

The infinitary predicate language allows us to write down such formulae. More precisely, in $\mathcal{L}_{\omega_1\omega}$ one is allowed to form formulae just as in first-order logic, but in addition countably infinite disjunctions and conjunctions are allowed.

Finally, then, the relational translation $ST_p(\cdot, \cdot)$ of PDL into $\mathcal{L}_{\omega_1\omega}$ has the following modal clauses:

$$ST_p(w, \langle \alpha \rangle A) = \exists v\, (ST_p(wv, \alpha) \wedge ST_p(v, A)),$$

where the translation $ST_p(wv, \alpha)$ of programs α requires two free variables:

$$
\begin{aligned}
ST_p(wv, a) &= R_a(w, v) \text{ (and similarly for other pairs of variables)} \\
ST_p(wv, \alpha \cup \beta) &= ST_p(wv, \alpha) \vee ST_p(wv, \beta) \\
ST_p(wv, \alpha\, ; \beta) &= \exists u\, (ST_p(wu, \alpha) \wedge ST_p(uv, \beta)) \\
ST_p(wv, \alpha^*) &= (w = v) \vee ST_p(wv, \alpha) \vee \\
&\quad \bigvee_{n \geq 1} \exists u_1 \ldots u_n\, (ST_p(wu_1, \alpha) \wedge \cdots \wedge ST_p(u_n v, \alpha)).
\end{aligned}
$$

It may be proved that every PDL-formula ϕ is equivalent to its relational translation on the class of PDL-models.

4.8. EXAMPLE *(Linear Temporal Logic)*. For (linear) temporal logic, too, a relational translation may be obtained by simply transcribing its truth definitions in a suitable target logic. Here we can simply take FO for the target logic, and its vocabulary should contain a binary relation symbol $\leq$ as well as the usual unary predicate symbols. Then, the relational translation simply becomes

$$
\begin{aligned}
ST_t(w, U(A, B)) &= \exists v\, (w \leq v \wedge ST_t(v, A) \wedge \\
&\quad \forall u\, (w \leq u \wedge u < v \rightarrow ST_t(u, B))).
\end{aligned}
$$

Observe that this translation needs 2 quantifiers (and three variables), whereas the translation for uni-modal logic only needs 1 quantifier (and 2 variables). We will come back to this issue in Subsection 4.3.

4.9. EXAMPLE *(Intuitionistic Logic)*. Recall from Definition 2.14 that the semantics of intuitionistic logic is based on a reflexive, transitive relation and that assignments need to satisfy the following restriction

$$\forall w, u\, (p(w) \wedge R(w, u) \rightarrow p(u)) \tag{4.3}$$

for each translated proposition letter p. The relational translation for all connectives except for the implication are as in the modal case. The intuitionistic semantics of the implication

$$\Im, w \models A \to B \quad \text{iff} \quad \forall v\, (R(w,v) \Rightarrow \Im, v \models A \Rightarrow (\Im, v \models B))$$
$$\Im, w \models \neg A \quad \text{iff} \quad \forall v\, (R(w,v) \Rightarrow \Im, v \not\models A)$$

yields the relational translation

$$ST_i(w, A \to B) \;=\; \forall v\, (R(w,v) \to (ST_i(v,A) \to ST_i(v,B))) \qquad (4.4)$$
$$ST_i(w, \neg A) \;=\; \forall v\, (R(w,v) \to \neg ST_i(v,A)). \qquad (4.5)$$

4.10. EXAMPLE *(Relevance Logic)*. The semantics of relevance logic was given in Definition 2.14. From the definition, the relational translation can be derived:

$$ST_r(w, A \to B) \;=\; \forall u, v\, (R(w,u,v) \to (ST_r(u,A) \to ST_r(v,B)))$$
$$ST_r(w, \neg A) \;=\; \neg ST_r(w^*, A).$$

A formula A is a theorem of relevance logic if it is valid in the distinguished world 0. To check this with a FO theorem prover, $ST_r(0, A)$ has to be proved from the axioms about R and $(\cdot)^*$ that were listed in Definition 2.14. Further, A *entails* B in relevance logic if and only if for all interpretations and worlds w, if $\Im, w \models A$ then $\Im, w \models B$ holds. This can be checked by using a FO-theorem prover to derive $\forall w\, (ST_r(w,A) \to ST_r(w,B))$ from the axioms.

4.11. EXAMPLE *(Classical Modal Logic)*. The key parts of the relational translation for classical modal logic are

$$ST_c(w, \Box A) \;=\; \exists V\, (N(w,V) \wedge \forall v\, (v \in V \leftrightarrow ST_c(v,A)))$$
$$ST_c(w, \Diamond A) \;=\; \forall V\, (N(w,V) \to \exists v\, (v \in V \leftrightarrow ST_c(v,A))) \qquad (4.6)$$

for the first version (weak semantics), and

$$ST'_c(w, \Box A) \;=\; \exists V\, (N(w,V) \wedge \forall v\, (v \in V \to ST'_c(v,A)))$$
$$ST'_c(w, \Diamond A) \;=\; \forall V\, (N(w,V) \to \exists v\, (v \in V \wedge ST'_c(v,A))) \qquad (4.7)$$

for the second version (stronger semantics).

Since the variable V is interpreted as a set and the membership predicate $\in$ has the usual special meaning, this is not yet a suitable first-order translation. It is, however, possible to eliminate the set variables and to replace the membership predicate $\in$ with an uninterpreted binary symbol in. Suppose ϕ is the result of one of the above relational translations of a modal formula. We can add the equivalence

$$\forall w, X\, (N(w,X) \leftrightarrow \exists u\, (N'(w,u) \wedge (\forall v\, in(u,v) \leftrightarrow v \in X))) \qquad (4.8)$$

to ϕ. Then, ϕ is satisfiable if and only if $\phi \wedge (4.8)$ is satisfiable. The non-trivial part is to construct a model $\mathfrak{I}'$ for $\phi \wedge (4.8)$ from a model $\mathfrak{I}$ for ϕ. The formulae in ϕ may contain translations of formulae $\Box A$ or $\Diamond A$ (since $\Diamond A \leftrightarrow \neg \Box \neg A$, this case can be reduced to the $\Box$-case).

Applying (4.8) as a rewrite rule to $ST_c(w, \Box A)$ yields:

$$
\begin{aligned}
&ST_c(w, \Box A) \\
&\quad = \quad \exists V \, (N(w, V) \wedge \forall v \, v \in V \leftrightarrow ST_c(v, A)) \\
&\quad \leftrightarrow \quad \exists V \, \exists u \, (N'(w, u) \wedge (\forall v \, in(u, v) \leftrightarrow v \in V) \wedge \forall v \, v \in V \leftrightarrow ST_c(v, A)) \\
&\quad \leftrightarrow \quad \exists V \, \exists u \, (N'(w, u) \wedge (\forall v \, in(u, v) \leftrightarrow v \in V) \wedge \forall v \, in(u, v) \leftrightarrow ST_c(v, A)) \\
&\quad \leftrightarrow \quad \exists u \, (N'(w, u) \wedge (\exists V \, \forall v \, in(u, v) \leftrightarrow v \in V) \wedge \forall v \, in(u, v) \leftrightarrow ST_c(v, A)) \\
&\quad \leftrightarrow \quad \exists u \, (N'(w, u) \wedge \forall v \, in(u, v) \leftrightarrow ST_c(v, A)).
\end{aligned}
$$

This way, all occurrences of N can be eliminated from ϕ, and subsequently (4.8) can also be eliminated in a satisfiability-preserving way. N' and in are now uninterpreted binary relations, just as ordinary accessibility relations in normal modal logics. For the logic with the stronger semantics (4.7) we get a similar translation

$$ST'_c(w, \Box A) \quad \leftrightarrow \quad \exists u \, (N'(w, u) \wedge \forall v \, (in(u, v) \rightarrow ST'_c(v, A)))$$

which is, in fact, equivalent to the relational translation of a normal bi-modal logic formula $\langle N' \rangle [in] A$ with two modalities corresponding to the two accessibility relations N' and in. This justifies a translation from classical modal logic (with strong neighborhood semantics) to normal bi-modal logic: $Tr(\Box A) = \langle N' \rangle [in] \, Tr(A)$ (cf. also [Gasquet and Herzig 1993]). Due to the equivalence sign at the right-hand side of (4.6) there is no such simple translation for classical modal logic with weak neighborhood semantics. Nevertheless, the trick with (4.8) yields a translation into FO. Unfortunately, the translation usually yields very large clause sets.

4.12. REMARK. The technique for eliminating the set variables and the membership relation is typical for a general technique to modify or improve existing transformations and translations. If A is the result of an existing translation, one adds a definition δ of some relation or function f, occurring in A, to ϕ. δ must define f in terms of some *new* relations or functions, and adding δ must be satisfiability preserving. Once this is proved, one can apply the definition of f to A and eliminate f completely from A. After this, one has to prove that deleting δ is also satisfiability preserving. The net effect is a transformation of A to some A', which, in most cases, can be defined as a single rewrite operation.

In [Baaz, Fermüller and Leitsch 1994] such transformations are called *structural* since they preserve much of the structure of the original input formula; see [Baaz et al. 2001] (Chapter 5 of this Handbook) for the use of abbreviations in the setting of normal form transformations. In Subsection 5.4 we briefly mention their use in decision procedures.

4.13. EXAMPLE *(Quantified Modal Logic)*. The standard relational translation for the quantified case can also be derived in a straightforward way. Each flexible function symbol gets an extra argument for the world variable. For a term t, $ST(w, t)$ inserts the variable w into these extra argument positions. For formulating the condition "a in w's domain" in the quantifiers we introduces a relation $in(w, a)$ and translate quantified formulae as

$$ST(w, \forall x\, A) \quad = \quad \forall x\, (in(w, x) \to ST(w, A)) \tag{4.9}$$

$$ST(w, \exists x\, A) \quad = \quad \exists x\, (in(w, x) \wedge ST(w, A)). \tag{4.10}$$

The translation rules for the other connectives and operators are as usual. As an example, take the translation of the well-known *Barcan formula*:

$$ST(w, \forall x \Box p(x) \to \Box \forall x\, p(x)) =$$
$$\forall x\, (in(w, x) \to \forall v\, (R(w, v) \to P(v, x))) \to$$
$$\forall v\, (R(w, v) \to \forall x\, (in(v, x) \to P(v, x)))$$

The *in* predicate can be omitted for logics with constant domain interpretation ($in(x, w)$ is always *true*). For increasing domain interpretations, however, the extra axiom $\forall x, w, v\, (in(w, x) \wedge R(w, v) \to in(v, x))$ is needed, and for decreasing domain interpretations we use the corresponding dual form.

We hope that these examples demonstrate that the standard relational translation can be derived in a straightforward way from the semantics of the connectives and quantifiers in the source logic. Since the translation is almost one-to-one, soundness and completeness proofs are usually straightforward.

Finally, we should point out that it is possible to give a possible worlds semantics for a very general class of logics, thus allowing the formulae of these logics to be translated into classical logic (see [Gabbay 1999, Chapter 2]).

4.3. Expressive power

Now that we have introduced the standard relational translation, which identifies modal languages as fragments of first-order or other predicate logics, let us take a closer look at what we have actually obtained. We will first consider matters related to expressive power, and then, in Section 4.4, focus on computing with translations of nonclassical formulae. In particular, we will first look at semantic characterizations of the modal fragment in terms of bisimulations; after that we consider several explanations for the good logical and computational behavior of the modal fragment.

By Theorem 4.2, a modal formula A of the basic modal language can be viewed as a unary FO formula $\alpha(x)$. How much of FO does this modal fragment cover? While this is essentially a *syntactic* question, the best way to answer it is using *semantic* means. The key tool here is provided by the notion of bisimulation.

4.14. DEFINITION. Let $\mathfrak{I}$, $\mathfrak{I}'$ be two interpretations for the basic modal language. A *bisimulation* between $\mathfrak{I}$ and $\mathfrak{I}'$ is a non-empty relation Z between the domain of $\mathfrak{I}$ and the domain of $\mathfrak{I}'$, respectively, that satisfies the following conditions:

1. Z-related states satisfy the same proposition letters;
2. if wZw' and $R(w,v)$ in $\mathfrak{I}$, then there exists $v' \in \mathfrak{I}'$ such that $R'(w',v')$ in $\mathfrak{I}'$ and vZv'; and
3. if wZw' and $R'(w',v')$ in $\mathfrak{I}$, then there exists $v \in \mathfrak{I}$ such that $R(w,v)$ in $\mathfrak{I}$ and vZv'.

The following figure illustrates items 2 and 3:

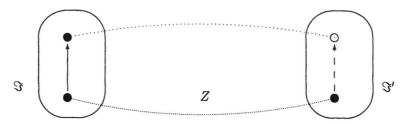

Here, the dotted lines indicate the bisimulation relation, the solid and dashed arrows indicates the binary relations R and R'.

If there exists a bisimulation linking two states w and w', then we say that w and w' are *bisimilar*; two models are called *bisimilar* if there exists a bisimulation between them.

4.15. EXAMPLE. Figure 1 contains two bisimilar interpretations $\mathfrak{I}$ and $\mathfrak{I}'$; the p's indicate that the proposition letter p is true at the state it decorates. We leave it to the reader to show that the dotted lines form bisimulation between $\mathfrak{I}$ and its unfolding $\mathfrak{I}'$.

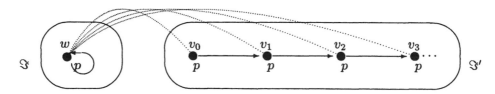

Figure 1: Bisimilar models

Our second example concerns two states w and w' in two interpretations $\mathfrak{J}$ and $\mathfrak{J}'$ such that there cannot be a bisimulation between w and w'. Consider Figure 2; here, each interpretation has a single branch of finite length, and, in addition, $\mathfrak{J}'$ has one branch of infinite length. Because of this infinite branch, there cannot be a bisimulation linking the roots w and w'. Observe that, despite this, w and w' do satisfy exactly the same modal formulae.

The following result explains why bisimulations matter for modal logic.

4.16. PROPOSITION. *Bisimilar models are modally equivalent. More precisely, let* $\mathfrak{S}$ *and* $\mathfrak{S}'$ *be two interpretations for the basic modal logic, and let* w *and* w' *be two states in* $\mathfrak{S}$ *and* $\mathfrak{S}'$, *respectively. Assume that* w *and* w' *are bisimilar. Then, for every modal formula* A *we have that* $\mathfrak{S}, w \models A$ *iff* $\mathfrak{S}, w' \models A$.

It follows from Proposition 4.16 that all FO formulae in the modal fragment (i.e., unary FO formulae that are in the range of the standard relational translation) are *preserved under bisimulations* in the sense that whenever two interpretations are bisimilar, then we cannot distinguish between them using formulae from the modal fragment. The following result states that this behavior is in fact characteristic of the modal fragment.

4.17. THEOREM. *Let* $\alpha(x)$ *be a unary first-order formula over a vocabulary with a single binary relation symbol and unary predicate symbols. Then* $\alpha(x)$ *is (equivalent to) the standard relational translation of a uni-modal formula iff it is preserved under bisimulations.*

PROOF. The 'only-if' direction is just a reformulation of Proposition 4.16. The 'if' direction requires some work. Given a unary FO formula $\alpha(x)$ with the stated property, we have to find a modal formula A such that $ST_m(x, A)$ is equivalent to $\alpha(x)$. The key steps in the proof are as follows.

Consider the set $MC(\alpha) := \{ST_m(x, A) \mid A \text{ is modal}, \alpha(x) \models ST_m(x, A)\}$. It suffices to show that $MC(\alpha) \models \alpha$. To do so, take an interpretation $\mathfrak{S}$ and state and w such that $\mathfrak{S}, w \models MC(\alpha)$; we need to show that $\mathfrak{S}, w \models \alpha$.

First, we use some general tricks from first-order logic to find an interpretation $\mathfrak{J}$ and state v such that $\mathfrak{J}, v \models MC(\alpha) \cup \{\alpha(x)\}$. Then, v (in $\mathfrak{J}$) and w (in $\mathfrak{S}$) satisfy the same modal formulae — but they need not be bisimilar. By some general tricks from first-order logic again, we can massage $\mathfrak{S}, w$ and $\mathfrak{J}, v$ into so-called ω-saturated interpretations $\mathfrak{S}^*, w^*$ and $\mathfrak{J}^*, v^*$, respectively, where it can be shown that the relation of satisfying the same modal formulae is indeed a bisimulation. To wrap up the proof, we chase α from $\mathfrak{J}, v$ to $\mathfrak{J}^*, v^*$ (by first-order logic) to $\mathfrak{S}^*, w^*$ (by preservation under bisimulations) to $\mathfrak{S}, w$ (by first-order logic) — and this is what we needed.   □

Theorem 4.17 is originally due to van Benthem [1976]. During the 1990s many differ-

Figure 2: Equivalent but not bisimilar

ent flavors of Theorem 4.17 were established: for the modal mu-calculus [Janin and Walukiewicz 1996], for finite models [Rosen 1997], for temporal logic [Kurtonina and de Rijke 1997], for certain fragments of knowledge representation languages [Kurtonina and de Rijke 1999], for CTL* [Moller and Rabinovich 1999], and for description logics [Areces and de Rijke 2000].

Now that Theorem 4.17 has given us a precise characterization of the modal fragment, let us take a closer look at some of its logical and computational properties. We will see that the fragment behaves very well in many respects, and our main concern will be to try and understand why this is so. To begin with, the modal fragment has the finite model property.

4.18. DEFINITION. A set of formulae X is said to have the *finite model property* if every satisfiable formula in X is satisfiable in a finite interpretation.

The modal fragment, or equivalently, the uni-modal language, has the finite model property in a very strong sense: a modal formula is A satisfiable iff it is satisfiable on an interpretation $\mathfrak{S}$ with at most $2^{|A|}$ states, where $|A|$ is the length of A. *Deciding* whether a modal formula is satisfiable at all is in fact 'easier' than the strong finite model property may lead one to believe: it is a PSPACE-complete problem [Ladner 1977].

What is probably more significant from an automated reasoning point of view is the fact that the modal fragment has the tree model property.

4.19. DEFINITION. A *tree model* for the basic modal language is an interpretation $\mathfrak{S} = (W, R, P)$ where (W, R) is a tree. A set of formulae X is said to have the *tree model property* if every satisfiable formula $A \in X$ is satisfiable at the root of a tree model.

Using the notion of bisimulation (Definition 4.14) it is easy to show that the modal fragment does indeed have the tree model property: let A be a satisfiable modal formula, and let $\mathfrak{S}, w$ be such that $\mathfrak{S}, w \models A$. Let $\mathfrak{J}, w'$ be the complete unfolding of $\mathfrak{S}$ (starting from w). Then, $\mathfrak{J}$ is a tree model, and $\mathfrak{J}$ and $\mathfrak{S}$ are bisimilar via a bisimulation that links w in $\mathfrak{S}$ to w' in $\mathfrak{J}$. Thus, A is satisfied at the root of a tree model, as desired.

What's the importance of the tree model property? First, it paves the way for the use of automata-theoretic tools and tableaux-based decision methods. Moreover, according to Vardi [1997] the tree model property is essential for explaining the *robust decidability* of the modal fragment. This is the phenomenon that the modal fragment is decidable itself, and of reasonably low complexity, and that these features are preserved when the fragment is extended by a variety of additional constructions, including counting, transitive closure, and least fixed points.

So far, we have seen a number of examples of the good logical and computational behavior of the modal fragment: the finite model property, the tree model property, robust decidability, but there are many more — see [de Rijke 1999]. *Why* does the modal fragment enjoy this behavior? Since the early 1980s several answers have been suggested. One of the first was due to Gabbay [1981a], who tried to give an explanation in terms of finite variable fragments; these are defined by restricting the number of variables (free or bound) that may be used.

4.20. DEFINITION *(Finite Variable Fragments)*. Let k be a natural number. We write FO^k to denote the restriction of first-order logic to formulae of a relational vocabulary (that is, without function symbols) that contain only the variables v_1, ..., v_k. Note that interesting sentences in FO^k are not in prenex normal form; on the contrary, one extensively re-uses variables.

4.21. EXAMPLE. To express that a graph $G = (V, E)$ contains a path of length 4, a sentence in prenex normal form needs 5 variables. By re-using variables, the property is expressible in FO^2, by a sentence of the form

$$\exists v_1 \exists v_2 \, (E(v_1, v_2) \wedge \exists v_1 \, (E(v_2, v_1) \wedge \exists v_2 \, (E(v_1, v_2) \wedge \exists v_1 \, (E(v_2, v_1))))).$$

Finite variable fragments have a long history. The earliest systematic study seems to be due to Henkin [1967] in the setting of algebraic logic; Gabbay [1981a] develops the modal connection, and Immerman and Kozen [1987] study the link with complexity and database theory. We refer the reader to [Otto 1997] for more on FO^k.

What do finite variable fragments have to do with modal logic and with the modal fragment? Gabbay [1981a] observed that we only need two variables to carry out the standard relational translation; see Table 4. By way of example, consider the formula $\Diamond\Box\Diamond p$ again; using only two variables, its translation becomes $ST_m(v_1, \Diamond\Box\Diamond p) = \exists v_2 \, (R(v_1, v_2) \wedge \forall v_1 \, (R(v_2, v_1) \rightarrow \exists v_2 \, (R(v_1, v_2) \wedge p(v_2))))$.

$$
\begin{aligned}
ST_m(v_1, p) &= p(v_1) \\
ST_m(v_1, \neg\phi) &= \neg ST_m(v_1, \phi) \\
ST_m(v_1, \phi \wedge \psi) &= ST_m(v_1, \phi) \wedge ST_m(v_1, \psi) \\
ST_m(v_1, \Diamond\phi) &= \exists v_2 \, (R(v_1, v_2) \wedge ST_m(v_2, \phi)) \\
ST_m(v_1, \Box\phi) &= \forall v_2 \, (R(v_1, v_2) \rightarrow ST_m(v_2, \phi)) \\
ST_m(v_2, p) &= p(v_2) \\
ST_m(v_2, \neg\phi) &= \neg ST_m(v_2, \phi) \\
ST_m(v_2, \phi \wedge \psi) &= ST_m(v_2, \phi) \wedge ST_m(v_2, \psi) \\
ST_m(v_2, \Diamond\phi) &= \exists v_1 \, (R(v_2, v_1) \wedge ST_m(v_1, \phi)) \\
ST_m(v_2, \Box\phi) &= \forall v_1 \, (R(v_2, v_1) \rightarrow ST_m(v_1, \phi))
\end{aligned}
$$

Table 4: Two variables suffice

It is easy to see that for all modal formulae A: $\mathfrak{I}, w \models A$ iff $\mathfrak{I}, w \models ST_m(w, A)$. Hence, the modal fragment is really part of FO^2. Does this embedding explain the good behavior of the modal fragment? The first decidability result for FO^2 was obtained by Scott [1962], who showed that the decision problem for FO^2 can be reduced to that of the Gödel class, i.e., the set of first-order formulae with quantifier prefix $\exists^*\forall\forall\exists^*$. Since the Gödel class without equality is decidable [Gödel 1932, Kalmár 1933, Schütte 1934], Scott's reduction yields the decidability of FO^2 without equality. Mortimer [1975] established decidability of FO^2 with equality. In contrast, for $k \geq 3$, FO^k is undecidable. Moreover, FO^k does not have the tree model property for any $k \geq 2$; to see this, simply observe that $\forall x, y\, R(x, y)$ is in FO^2. To make matters worse, FO^2 is not robustly decidable: adding any of counting, transitive closure, or least fixed points results in undecidable systems [Grädel, Otto and Rosen 1997b].

In conclusion, then, finite variable fragments don't seem to offer a satisfactory explanation for the good logical and computational properties of the modal fragment. An alternative proposal, launched in the late 1990s stresses the special nature of the quantifiers occurring in formulae in the modal fragment. Guarded logics [Andréka, van Benthem and Németi 1998] are defined by restricting quantification in first-order logic, second-order logic or fixed-point logic in such a way that, semantically speaking, subformulae can only refer to objects that are 'nearby' or 'guarded.' Syntactically, this means that all quantifiers must be relativized by 'guards.'

4.22. DEFINITION *((Loosely) Guarded Fragment)*. The *guarded fragment* (GF) is defined as follows

1. Every relational atomic formula $Rx_{i_1} \ldots R_{i_k}$ or $x_i = x_j$ is in GF;
2. GF is closed under boolean connectives
3. GF is closed under guarded quantification: if $\overline{x}$ and $\overline{y}$ are tuples of variables, $\alpha(\overline{x}, \overline{y})$ is an atomic formula, and $A(\overline{x}, \overline{y})$ is a formula in GF such that free$(A) \subseteq$ free$(\alpha) = \{\overline{x}, \overline{y}\}$, then the formulae

$$\exists \overline{x}\, (\alpha(\overline{x}, \overline{y}) \wedge A(\overline{x}, \overline{y})) \text{ and } \forall \overline{x}\, (\alpha(\overline{x}, \overline{y}) \rightarrow A(\overline{x}, \overline{y}))$$

are in GF as well. (Here, free(A) denotes the set of free variables in A.)
The formula $\alpha(\overline{x}, \overline{y})$ in item 3 is called a *guard*.

The *loosely guarded fragment* (LGF) is obtained by relaxing the third condition somewhat, to the following.

3'. LGF is closed under loosely guarded quantification: if $A(\overline{x}, \overline{y})$ is in LGF, and $\alpha(\overline{x}, \overline{y}) = \alpha_1 \wedge \cdots \wedge \alpha_m$ is a conjunction of atomic formulae, then

$$\exists \overline{x}\, (\alpha(\overline{x}, \overline{y}) \wedge A(\overline{x}, \overline{y})) \text{ and } \forall \overline{x}\, (\alpha(\overline{x}, \overline{y}) \rightarrow A(\overline{x}, \overline{y}))$$

belong to LGF provided that free$(A) \subseteq$ free$(\alpha) = \{\overline{x}, \overline{y}\}$ and for any two variables $z \in \overline{y}$ and $z' \in \{\overline{x}, \overline{y}\}$ there is at least one atom α_j that contains both z and z'.

Clearly, the modal fragment is part of GF. As a further example, the formula $\forall x \forall y\, (R(x, y) \rightarrow R(y, x))$ is in GF, but transitivity $(\forall x \forall y \forall z\, (R(x, y) \wedge R(y, z) \rightarrow$

$R(x, z)))$ is not in GF or in LGF. The formula $\exists y\, (R(x, y) \wedge Py \wedge \forall z\, (R(x, z) \wedge R(z, y) \to Qz))$ is in LGF, but not in GF.

The guarded fragment behaves much better — both logically and computationally — than finite variable fragments.

4.23. THEOREM ([Andréka et al. 1998]). *GF has the (strong) finite model property.*

4.24. THEOREM ([Grädel 2000]). *The satisfiability problem for GF is 2EXPTIME-complete. By imposing an upper bound on the arity of the predicates or on the number of variables this may be brought down to EXPTIME-completeness.*

In addition, we have practical decision methods for GF and LGF [de Nivelle 1998, de Nivelle and de Rijke to appear]. As to the *robust* decidability of GF, adding counting, transitivity or functionality statements destroys decidability [Grädel 2000]. Ganzinger, Meyer and Veanes [1999] consider the restriction of the guarded fragment to the two-variable case where, in addition, binary relations may be specified as transitive. This very restricted form of GF without equality is undecidable, but when allowing non-unary relations to occur only in guards, the logic becomes decidable; this latter class contains standard relational translations of modal logics such as **K4**, **S4**, and **S5**. Transitive closure and least fixed points can be added to GF or LGF at no additional computational costs [Grädel and Walukiewicz 1999].

All in all, the guarded fragment seems to offer a much better syntactic explanation for the good logical and computational behavior of the modal fragment than finite variable fragments. But GF is not perfect either: its coverage is too limited to explain the good behavior of, for instance, linear temporal logic (LTL) and systems such as **S4**. Now, LTL can be covered by the loosely guarded fragment LGF [van Benthem 1997], but **S4** is beyond its scope. However, de Nivelle [1999] devised an extended relational translation method, which introduces new relational symbols to translate systems like **S4** into monadic second-order logic; the scope of this method remains to be explored.

Capturing nonclassical logics in terms of guarded or guarded-like fragments continues to be an area of active research.

4.4. Reasoning tasks

We have now got a fairly good understanding of the expressive power of modal fragments. Let us try to exploit the connection between modal and first-order logic, and feed our modal reasoning problems to general first-order automated reasoning tools. Unfortunately, most first-order theorem provers, especially those working with resolution, simply do not constitute decision procedures for (translated) modal formulae. Given an unsatisfiable set of clauses $\mathcal{C}$, any complete resolution procedure will of course generate a contradiction, but the problem is that resolution need not terminate if $\mathcal{C}$ happens to be satisfiable, not even if $\mathcal{C}$ belongs to a decidable fragment (as in the modal case).

4.25. EXAMPLE. Consider the formula $\Box(p \rightarrow \Diamond p)$, which is clearly satisfiable. Proving this amounts to showing that the following set of clauses is satisfiable.

1. $\neg R(c, y) \vee \neg p(y) \vee R(y, f(y))$
2. $\neg R(c, y) \vee \neg p(y) \vee p(f(y))$

The clauses have two resolvents:

3. $\neg R(c, c) \vee \neg p(c) \vee \neg p(f(c)) \vee p(f^2(c))$
4. $\neg R(c, f(y)) \vee R(f(y), f^2(y)) \vee \neg R(c, y) \vee \neg p(y)$.

Clauses 2 and 4 resolve to produce

5. $\neg R(c, f^2(y)) \vee R(f^2(y), f^3(y)) \vee \neg R(c, f(y)) \vee \neg R(c, y) \vee \neg p(y)$.

Clauses 2 and 5 resolve again to produce an analogue of 5 with even higher term-complexity, and so on. None of the clauses is redundant and can be deleted. In the limit our input set has infinitely many resolvents, and this shows that standard 'plain' resolution does not terminate for relational translations of satisfiable modal formulae.

Even for unsatisfiable modal formulae, a 'plain' resolution method is not ideal: the performance may seriously lag behind procedures that have been purpose-built for modal reasoning. Table 5 illustrates the point with a brief comparison between a number of tools. The results in columns 2–4 are taken from [Giunchiglia, Giunchiglia and Tacchella 2000, Horrocks, Patel-Schneider and Sebastiani 2000]; they were obtained on a Pentium 350Mhz with a time out of 100 seconds; the results in column were obtained on a Sun ULTRA II 300MHz, with the same time out. The experiments were performed on 9 collections of tests; each collection consists of 21 provable (in **K**) and 21 unprovable (in **K**) formulae of increasing difficulty; provable formulae are indicated with the 'p' suffix, unprovable ones with the 'n' suffix. If a system could solve all 21 problems, Table 5 lists a $>$ in the relevant cell; the times indicated are times spent on solving the most difficult problems in each category.

The systems mentioned are *SAT 1.2 [Giunchiglia et al. 2000], DLP 3.2 [Patel-Schneider 1998], and TA 1.4 [Hustadt, Schmidt and Weidenbach 1998]. DLP out-performs the other systems on nearly all tests; it is a tableau-based system which implements intelligent backtracking. *SAT also implements intelligent backtracking, and is SAT-based. TA is a translation-based system that does not use the standard relational translation but the more sophisticated functional translation (as discussed in Section 5) on top of various resolution refinements. For comparison, the fifth column, labeled 'Bliksem 1.10a' contains figures obtained by feeding the relational translation to the general purpose FO theorem prover Bliksem [Bli 2000] in auto mode. The experiments, though superficial, seem to indicate that the relational translation combined with plain resolution is simply no match.

What's the cause for the poor performance of general purpose resolution-based tools compared to purpose-built tools? Plain resolution simply does not exploit the special nature of the original modal input formulae — we are 'reducing' a nicely decidable logic to an undecidable one, and, thus far, our reduction does not use, for instance, the finite model property or the tree model property of the modal input.

Roughly speaking, there are two responses to this issue: one which tries to stick to the standard relational translation as we have defined it in Definition 4.1 and

Test		*SAT 1.2		DLP3.2		TA 1.4		Bliksem 1.10a	
		Size	Time	Size	Time	Size	Time	Size	Time
branch	p	>	0.21	19	46.06	6	65.76	3	20.78
	n	12	94.49	13	53.63	6	65.33	3	32.03
d4	p	>	0.06	>	0.05	15	71.11	3	66.57
	n	>	2.87	>	1.12	14	44.06	1	1.65
dum	p	>	0.04	>	0.02	17	64.99	3	55.10
	n	>	0.12	>	0.02	16	65.82	1	4.78
grz	p	>	0.04	>	0.04	>	0.51	5	81.04
	n	>	0.01	>	0.05	>	0.33	0	0.00
lin	p	>	0.01	>	0.03	>	9.24	>	80.57
	n	>	47.80	>	0.13	>	80.01	4	19.86
path	p	>	0.72	>	0.32	5	25.03	4	26.32
	n	>	0.96	>	0.36	4	60.84	2	61.96
ph	p	8	48.54	7	10.23	6	43.16	5	11.33
	n	12	0.60	>	2.69	9	55.13	5	8.21
poly	p	>	1.73	>	0.11	5	53.48	5	70.46
	n	>	2.25	>	0.18	4	9.09	4	52.24
t4p	p	>	0.29	>	0.06	16	88.66	0	0.00
	n	>	1.28	>	0.13	9	87.72	0	0.00

Table 5: Comparison

refines the resolution procedure to combine it with some kind of preprocessing that exploits the special nature of the modal input; the other response is to abandon the translation and use one that somehow encodes more modal information. Sections 5 and 6 below are devoted to a number of alternative translations; the remainder of the present section is devoted to a brief discussion of the former response.

How can resolution be turned into a decision procedure for formulae that we get out of the relational translation? During the 1990s special resolution refinements became available that are aimed at doing just this. Some of this work has been collected in [Fermüller, Leitsch, Tammet and Zamov 1993], which includes a decision procedure for $\mathcal{ALC}$, the description logic counterpart of the modal logic **K** that uses orderings plus saturation. We refer the reader to [Fermüller et al. 2001] (Chapter 25 of this Handbook) for more details on resolution-based decision procedures relevant for the (relational) modal fragment.

De Nivelle [1998] has given a resolution decision procedure for GF without equality. In his procedure, a non-liftable ordering is employed, and, as a consequence, additional work is needed for proving refutational completeness; see [de Nivelle and de Rijke to appear] for further details. Ganzinger and de Nivelle [1999] describe a decision procedure for GF with equality which is based on resolution and superposition. More precisely, ordered paramodulation with selection is a decision procedure for GF with equality, and the worst-case time complexity of the decision procedure is doubly-exponential, which is optimal, given that the logic is 2EXPTIME-complete. The procedure can be extended to LGF with equality, but is much more involved there and needs hyper inferences which simultaneously resolve a set of 'guards.'

Instead of devising resolution decision procedures based on the relational translation, an alternative approach is to devise preprocessing techniques that enhance standard resolution by encoding information about the source logic. Areces, Gennari, Heguiabehere and de Rijke [2000] exploit a very strong form of the tree model property to complement the standard relational translation for **K** with additional semantic information. The key idea here is to encode the layering present in tree models into the syntax of modal formulae, by first translating them into an extended multi-modal language where each modal depth has its own modal operators and its own proposition letters, thus avoiding that clauses stemming from different levels will be resolved.

4.26. Example. Consider the satisfiable formula $\Box(p \to \Diamond p)$ from Example 4.25 again. By exploiting the tree model property of modal logic it is easy to see that $\Box(p \to \Diamond p)$ is satisfiable iff the following two clauses are:

1. $\neg R_1(c, y) \lor \neg p_1(y) \lor R_2(y, f(y))$
2. $\neg R_1(c, y) \lor \neg p_1(y) \lor p_2(f(y))$.

Here, a literal with subscript i corresponds to a modal operator or proposition letter occurring at modal depth i. Clearly, the set of clauses 1, 2 is saturated — a dramatic improvement over Example 4.25.

To make things precise, we need an intermediate multi-modal language, whose collection of modal operators is $\{\Diamond_i \mid i \geq 0\}$. Let A be a uni-modal formula, and let n be a natural number. The translation $Tr(A, n)$ of A into the intermediate language is defined by

$$
\begin{aligned}
Tr(p, n) &:= p_n \\
Tr(\neg B, n) &:= \neg Tr(B, n) \\
Tr(B \land C, n) &:= Tr(B, n) \land Tr(C, n) \\
Tr(\Diamond B, n) &:= \Diamond_{n+1} Tr(B, n+1).
\end{aligned}
$$

The *layered relational translation* $LT(A)$ is the composition of Tr and the relational translation ST_m: $LT(A) = ST_m(w, Tr(A, 0))$. The following result may be found in [Areces et al. 2000].

4.27. Proposition. *Let A be a uni-modal formula. Then A is satisfiable in* **K** *iff its layered relational translation $LT(A)$ is.*

To evaluate the net effects of the additional preprocessing step used in the layered relational translation, Areces et al. [2000] carry out tests running the resolution-based prover Bliksem with and without the extra layering on a number of test sets.

For a start, the tests in Table 5 were carried out for the layered translation, leading to significant improvements:

Test		Relational		Layered	
		Size	Time	Size	Time
branch	p	3	20.78	8	76.36
	n	3	32.03	8	70.25
d4	p	3	66.57	11	71.76
	n	1	1.65	6	56.36
dum	p	3	55.10	>	5.01
	n	1	4.78	>	6.45
grz	p	5	81.04	>	12.56
	n	0	0.00	>	53.79
lin	p	>	80.57	>	81.28
	n	4	19.86	5	73.75
path	p	4	26.32	7	50.25
	n	2	61.96	4	26.69
ph	p	5	11.33	5	11.17
	n	5	8.21	5	7.99
poly	p	5	70.46	13	75.76
	n	4	52.24	14	69.36
t4p	p	0	0.00	13	82.77
	n	0	0.00	6	55.94

In addition, test were carried out on problems generated by the modal QBF test set. The latter is the basic yardstick for the TANCS (Tableaux Nonclassical Systems Comparisons) competition on theorem proving and satisfiability testing for nonclassical logics [TAN 2000]. It is a random problem generator that has been designed for evaluating solvers of (un-) satisfiability problems for the modal logic **K**. The formulae of this benchmark are generated using quantified boolean formulae. For unsatisfiable formulae, the use of layering results in a reduction in computing time of up to four orders of magnitude, and an average reduction in the number of clauses generated by one order of magnitude. For satisfiable formulae, similar though less dramatic improvements may be observed.

The layered preprocessing step may be combined with any existing decision procedure. Alternatively, one can devise decision procedures that fully exploit the restricted syntactic nature of the range of the layered relational translation.

To conclude this section, we briefly list what little is known about reasoning with relational encodings of other nonclassical logics. Proving relevance logic theorems with a FO theorem prover using the standard translation is possible. The performance of FO theorem provers without extra strategies, however, is quite poor [Ohlbach and Wrightson 1984]. Moreover, the usual systems do not provide a decision procedure. Unfortunately, not much is known about special strategies for this

kind of translated relevance logic formulae, and the same holds true for intuitionistic logic and for classical modal logic. The guarded and loosely guarded fragment
provide general first-order fragments into which many nonclassical logics can be
embedded via the relational translation and this gives us at least a starting point
for computing with such logics. But, clearly, extensive experimental and theoretical
work is needed here.

5. The functional translation

In the late 1980s and early 1990s the functional translation approach appeared
simultaneously and independently in a number of publications; see [Ohlbach 1988a,
Fariñas del Cerro and Herzig 1988, Herzig 1989, Zamov 1989, Auffray and Enjalbert
1992]. The functional translation can provide a considerable improvement of the
behavior of FO theorem provers on translated nonclassical formulae. In this section
we first provide some background material; after that we discuss the expressive
power of the functional translation, as well as the notion of prefix stability, which
gives rise to an *optimized* functional translation, for which we discuss decidability
results in the final subsection.

5.1. Background

The *functional translation* is based on an alternative semantics of modal logic. The
fundamental idea is that each binary relation can be defined by a set of (partial or
total) functions.

5.1. PROPOSITION. *For any binary relation R on a non-empty set W there is a set
AF_R of accessibility functions, that is, a set of partial functions $\gamma : W \to W$, such
that*

$$\forall x, y \, (R(x,y) \leftrightarrow (\exists \gamma : AF_R \, \gamma(x) = y)). \qquad (5.1)$$

Consider the relation R_1 represented by the arrows in the tree below:

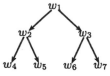

There are many different ways to decompose R_1 into sets of two functions $\{\gamma_1, \gamma_2\}$.
For example:

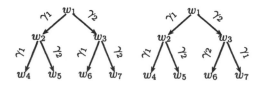

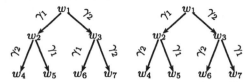

Since the relation is not serial, and there are dead ends, all these γ_1 and γ_2 are partial functions. With partial functions there are even more possible decompositions for a relation. The picture below shows an extreme case where the functions $\gamma_1, \ldots, \gamma_6$ are "as partial as possible".

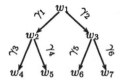

There is also the other extreme, where each accessibility function is *maximally defined*, i.e., whenever there is some y with $R(x, y)$ then $\gamma(x)$ must be defined. For total (serial) relations it is therefore always possible to decompose the relation into a set of *total* functions. For example, the relation R_2 displayed on the left-hand side can be decomposed into the relation on the right-hand side, where all the functions γ_i are total:

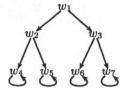 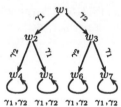

These observations can be exploited for a number of manipulations of formula sets containing a binary relation, and in particular for the relational translation of modal and intuitionistic logics.

Let us make things more formal. First, we need some notation. To avoid quantification over function symbols (in the first-order encoding) as in (5.1), we use a list notation in which any term $\gamma(x)$ is rewritten as $[x\gamma]$. Here, $[\cdot, \cdot]$ denotes the functional application operation which is defined to be a mapping from a domain W to the set of all partial functions over W. So complex terms of the form $\gamma_m(\ldots \gamma_2(\gamma_1(x))\ldots)$ become terms of the form $[[[[x\gamma_1]\gamma_2]\ldots]\gamma_m]$. We usually omit all brackets except the outermost ones, and write $[x\gamma_1\gamma_2 \ldots \gamma_m]$ instead of $[[[[x\gamma_1]\gamma_2]\ldots]\gamma_m]$.

Recall that a relation R is *serial* if it satisfies $\forall x \exists y\, R(x, y)$. For serial relations R it is always possible to define R in terms of a set of total functions. For the general case that R is not serial, there can be no set AF_R of *total* functions that 'captures' R. The problem is that the target logic for the functional translation cannot cater for partial functions: $[x\gamma]$ is a first-order term and will always have an interpretation. A standard solution is to adjoin a special element $\perp$ to the domain W of the model at hand, thus obtaining $W^{\perp}$, and to encode every partial function γ as a total function which maps the elements for which it is not defined to the new 'undefined' state $\perp$. Accordingly, any formula in which such an 'undefined' situation occurs, is translated into a conditional formula.

We introduce a special predicate de_R, called the *dead-end* predicate, which is defined by

$$\forall x \, (de_R(x) \leftrightarrow \forall \gamma \, (\gamma \in AF_R \rightarrow [x\gamma] = \perp)) \tag{5.2}$$

5.2. THEOREM. *Let R be a binary relation on a set W, and let $W^{\perp} = W \cup \{\perp\}$. Then, the following defines R in terms of a set AF_R of total functions $\gamma : W^{\perp} \rightarrow W^{\perp}$:*

$$\forall x, y : W \, (R(x,y) \leftrightarrow (\neg de_R(x) \land \exists \gamma \, (\gamma \in AF_R \land [x\gamma] = y))), \tag{5.3}$$

where de_R is defined as in (5.2).

The equivalence (5.3) defines any binary relation R in terms of a set AF_R of total functions and a special set de_R of states. The right-hand side of (5.3) says that if x is not a dead-end in R, then there is a total function γ which maps x to y. If R is serial, then de_R is the empty set, and (5.3) simplifies to (5.1).

We are ready to define the functional semantics for modal logic.

5.3. DEFINITION. A *functional frame* is a 4-tuple $\mathcal{F} = (W, de, AF, [\cdot, \cdot])$, where W is a non-empty set, de is a subset of W, AF is a set of *total* functions $\gamma : W \rightarrow W$, and $[\cdot, \cdot] : W \times AF \rightarrow W$ the functional application operation.

A *functional model* is a pair $\mathfrak{S} = (\mathcal{F}, P)$, where $\mathcal{F}$ is a functional frame, and P is a valuation. The new truth definition for the diamond operator is

$$\mathfrak{S}, w \models \Diamond A \text{ iff } w \notin de \text{ and } \exists \gamma : AF \, (\mathfrak{S}, [w\gamma] \models A),$$

and dually for the box operator.

It can be shown that any modal logic $\mathbf{K}\Sigma$ is complete with respect to a class of relational frames (or models) iff it is complete with respect to a class of functional frames (or models); see, for instance, [Schmidt 1997, Chapter 2].

5.4. DEFINITION (*Functional Translation*). First, we need to specify the target logic. Following [Schmidt 1997] we use a many-sorted logic with a sort hierarchy and set declarations for function symbols [Walther 1987]. In this logic, a sort symbol can be a viewed as a unary predicate and it denotes a subset of the domain.

For the functional translation we introduce the sorts W and AF. The variables $x, y, z, \ldots$, are assumed to be of sort W; the functional variables are denoted by $\gamma, \gamma_1, \gamma_2, \ldots$, and are or sort AF. The sort of the operator $[\cdot, \cdot]$ is $W \times AF \rightarrow W$. The *functional translation* $FT(t, A)$ is defined as follows:

$$FT(t, p) \; = \; p(t)$$

$$FT(t, \neg A) = \neg FT(t, A)$$

$$FT(t, A \vee B) = FT(t, A) \vee FT(t, B)$$

$$FT(t, A \wedge B) = FT(t, A) \wedge FT(t, B)$$

$$FT(t, \Diamond A) = \begin{cases} \exists \gamma : AF \, FT([t\gamma], A), & \text{if } \Diamond \text{ is serial} \\ \neg de(t) \wedge \exists \gamma : AF \, FT([t\gamma], A), & \text{otherwise.} \end{cases}$$

$$FT(t, \Box A) = \begin{cases} \forall \gamma : AF \, FT([t\gamma], A), & \text{if } \Box \text{ is serial} \\ \neg de(t) \rightarrow \forall \gamma : AF \, FT([t\gamma], A), & \text{otherwise.} \end{cases}$$

Here, γ is assumed to be a variable not occurring in t.

The functional translation can easily be extended to multi-modal logic. For each modality M one introduces an extra sort AF_M.

5.5. EXAMPLE. Take the McKinsey formula $\Box \Diamond p \rightarrow \Diamond \Box p$. Its functional translation is

$$\forall x \, (\neg de(x) \rightarrow \forall \gamma (\neg de([x\gamma]) \wedge \exists \delta \, p([x\gamma\delta])) \rightarrow (\neg de(x) \wedge \exists \gamma (\neg de[x\gamma] \rightarrow \forall \delta \, p([x\gamma\delta])))).$$

5.6. EXAMPLE *(Wise Men Puzzle)*. This example is a famous puzzle used to illustrate the application of modal logic in formalizing the notion of *knowledge*.

> A certain king wishes to determine which one of his three wise men is the wisest. He arranges them in a circle so that they can see and hear each other and tells them that he will put a white or black spot on each of their foreheads, but at least one spot will be white. (In fact all three spots are white.) He offers his favor to the one who first tells him the color of his own spot. After a while, the wisest announces that his spot is white. How does he know?

In our formalization we introduce constant symbols a, b, c to name the three wise men. They are rigid symbols, not depending on the worlds. Modal operators $[a]$, $[b]$ and $[c]$ are used to encode the notion "wise man a (b, c) *knows*." For a variable y, the operator $[y]$ means "wise man y knows." In addition, we use the standard $\Box$-operator to encode "everybody knows." The modality associated with this $\Box$ is of **S5**-type; it quantifies over all worlds. The predicate $WS(a)$ means "a has a white spot." WS is the only flexible symbol in this example. Let c be the wisest of the three men. The axioms relevant for solving this puzzle are:

- $a \neq b \wedge a \neq b \wedge b \neq c$ (All three wise men are different.)
- $\Box(WS(a) \vee WS(b) \vee WS(c))$ (Everybody knows that one of them has a white spot.)
- $\Box(\forall x, y \, x \neq y \rightarrow (\neg WS(x) \rightarrow [y] \neg WS(x)))$ (They can see each other. Therefore they know when any other one has no white spot.)
- $[c][b]\neg[a] \, WS(a)$ (c knows that b knows that a is not aware of his white spot.)
- $[c]\neg[b] \, WS(b)$ (c knows that b is not aware of his white spot.)

The theorem to prove is $[c] \, WS(c)$ (c knows the color of his own spot).

We use this example also to illustrate some optimizations of the functional translation. An optimized functional translation and clausification of the axioms and the *negated* theorem is:

(1)　$b \neq a$

(2)　$c \neq a$

(3)　$c \neq b$

(4)　$WS(w, a) \lor WS(w, b) \lor WS(w, c)^2$

(5)　$x = y \lor WS(w, x) \lor \neg WS([w\gamma_y], x)^3$

(6)　$\neg WS([w_0 \gamma_{1c} \gamma_{2b} d_a], a)^4$

(7)　$\neg WS([w_0 \gamma_{1c} d_b], b)$

(8)　$\neg WS([w d_c], c).^5$

A sequence of UR resolutions proves the theorem:

(9)　$[7, 5, 1]$　$\neg WS([w_0 \gamma_{1c} d_b \gamma_a], b)^6$　$([c]\langle b\rangle [a] \neg WS(b))^7$

(10)　$[9, 4, 6]$　$WS([w_0 \gamma_{1c} d_b d d_a], c)^8$　$([c]\langle b\rangle\langle a\rangle \, WS(c))^9$

(11)　$[10, 5, 2]$　$WS([w_0 \gamma_{1c}, d_b], c)$　$([c]\langle b\rangle \, WS(c))^{10}$

(12)　$[11, 5, 3]$　$WS([w_0 \gamma_{1c}], c)$　$([c] \, WS(c))$

(13)　$[12, 8]$　empty clause.

The derivations obviously represent nontrivial conclusions. A more intuitive and comprehensible explanation requires a lot more intermediate steps.

The following result states that the functional translation is sound and complete.

5.7. THEOREM. *Let* $\mathbf{K\Sigma}$ *be a modal logic that is complete with respect to a class of relational models. A modal formula* A *is a theorem of* $\mathbf{K\Sigma}$ *iff the conjunction of the following formulae is unsatisfiable*

1. $\forall \overline{p} \forall x \, FT(x, \Sigma)$

2. $\neg \forall x \, FT(x, A)$

3. $(5.3).$

---

[2]The variable w originates from the $\Box$-operator which in this case quantifies over all worlds. Therefore it is still a "world variable," not a accessibility function variable.

[3]The variable w again originates from the $\Box$-operator. The variable y ranges over the three wise men. The term γ_y denotes an accessibility function for the knowledge operator for wise man y.

[4]w_0 is a Skolem constant originating from the negated universal quantifier for the negated theorem. It denotes the world where the contradiction manifests itself if the unnegated theorem is in fact universally valid. The terms in the world path $\gamma_{1c} \gamma_{2b} d_a$ have to be written this way in order to match γ_y in the axiom above; γ_{1c} stems from $[c]$, γ_{1b} stems from $[b]$ and d_a is a Skolem constant that stems from $\neg[a]$.

[5](8) is the translated negated theorem. d_c is the Skolem constant stemming from the negated $[c]$-operator.

[6]The variable w in (5) ranges over all worlds. It can therefore be instantiated with whole world paths (this requires a theory unification procedure). The unifier for this step is actually $\{x \mapsto b, y \mapsto a, w \mapsto w_0 \gamma_{1c} d_b\}$.

[7]c knows that b considers that a knows that b does not know the color of his spot.

[8]The unifier for this step is $\{\gamma \mapsto b, w \mapsto w_0 \gamma_{1c}) d_b d_a\}$.

[9]c knows that b considers that a considers that c's spot is white.

[10]c knows that b considers that c's spot is white.

5.2. Frame properties

Many variants of modal logics and other nonclassical logics are characterized by properties of the accessibility relation. If these properties are first-order axiomatizable, the corresponding axioms can easily be added to the standard translation. For the functional translation, the axioms must be translated into the functional language. This is usually straightforward, but the translated axioms are in general equations. In some cases one can simplify the resulting equations again by pulling the existential quantifier over the universal quantifiers.

Let us have a look at some examples; consult Table 6 for a summary.

5.8. EXAMPLE. We use the "$[x\gamma]$" notation. The functional counterpart of *reflexivity* (the modal logic **T**) is:

$$\forall x \exists \gamma : AF\,[x\gamma] = x$$

In maximal functional frames one may pull the existential quantifier to the front:

$$\exists \gamma : AF \forall x\,[x\gamma] = x.$$

Skolemization then yields $\forall x\,[x\,id] = x$, where id is the identity function on worlds. The result is quite intuitive. It means that every world can be mapped to itself by an accessibility function, and this is reflexivity.

5.9. EXAMPLE. On serial frames, the functional version of the *symmetry* axiom $p \to \Box \Diamond p$ (modal logic **B**) is

$$\forall x \forall \gamma_1 \exists \gamma_2\,(x = [x\gamma_1\gamma_2])$$

(If γ_1 takes some world x to some world y then γ_2 takes y back to γ_1; γ_2 is some kind of inverse function to γ_1. In tree-like frames, it really is the inverse function.)

5.10. EXAMPLE. For the transitivity axiom $\Box p \to \Box \Box p$ (modal logic **K4**) we obtain

$$\forall x \forall \gamma_1, \gamma_2 \exists \gamma\,((\neg de(x) \wedge \neg de([x\gamma_1])) \to [x\gamma_1\gamma_2] = [x\gamma])$$

(In words: γ is the composition of γ_1 and γ_2. The equation states that the composition of accessibility functions is again an accessibility function, mapping worlds to accessible worlds.)

5.3. Prefix stability and the optimized functional translation

The clause form of functionally translated formulae may contain Skolem functions. These may cause complex terms to be built up during resolution. It can be shown that at least for the case of propositional modal logics, Skolem constants are sufficient. This means that functionally translated formulae in clausal form are function

name	axiom	functional property (without seriality)
D	$\Box A \to \Diamond A$	$\forall x \, \neg de(x)$
T	$\Box A \to A$	$\forall x \exists \gamma \, (\neg de(x) \wedge x = [x\gamma])$
B	$A \to \Box \Diamond A$	$\forall x \forall \gamma \exists \delta \, ((\neg de(x) \to \neg de([x\gamma])) \wedge (\neg de(x) \to x = [x\gamma\delta]))$
4	$\Box A \to \Box\Box A$	$\forall x \forall \gamma_1, \gamma_2 \exists \gamma \, ((\neg de(x) \wedge \neg de([x\gamma_1])) \to [x\gamma_1\gamma_2] = [x\gamma])$
5	$\Diamond A \to \Box \Diamond A$	$\forall x \forall \gamma \forall \delta \exists \epsilon \, ((\neg de(x) \to \neg de([x\delta])) \wedge (\neg de(x) \to [x\gamma] = [x\delta\epsilon]))$

Table 6: Axioms and their functional frame properties

free (if world paths are taken as sequences of variables and constants), and this simplifies the development of terminating resolution strategies. The present and the
next subsection are devoted to an explanation of the underlying machinery. The
first concept that we need to understand is *prefix stability*.

Skolem functions can be avoided if it is possible to pull existential quantifiers originating from $\Diamond$-operators over universal quantifiers originating from $\Box$-operators.
The following formula illustrates what this means.

$$FT(\Box \Diamond p) \;\; := \;\; \forall w \, FT(w, \Box \Diamond p) \;\; = \;\; \forall w \forall \gamma_1 \exists \gamma_2 \, p([w\gamma_1\gamma_2])$$
$$\Leftrightarrow \;\; \forall w \exists \gamma_2 \forall \gamma_1 \, p([w\gamma_1\gamma_2]).$$

From a predicate logic point of view, this equivalence does not hold. In general,
we are not allowed to pull existential quantifiers arbitrarily over universal quantifiers. Syntactic properties of functionally translated formulae and certain semantic
features of "functional frames," however, do indeed guarantee both directions of
the equivalence. The syntactic property is "prefix stability" [Ohlbach 1988a] (or
"unique prefix property" [Auffray and Enjalbert 1992]).

5.11. DEFINITION. Consider a term $t = [x\gamma_1\gamma_2 \ldots \gamma_i\gamma_{i+1} \ldots \gamma_m]$ in the target logic
of the functional translation. Any subterm x or $[x\gamma_1 \ldots \gamma_i]$ (for $1 \le i \le m$) is a *prefix
in the term t*. The *prefix of a variable* γ_{i+1} in the term t is the term $[x\gamma_1 \ldots \gamma_i]$.

Let T be a set of terms of the form t as above. T is said to be *prefix stable* if any
variable γ of type AF occurring in T has exactly one prefix. That is: for any γ, the
set $\{s \mid [s\gamma \ldots] \text{ occurs in } T\}$ is a singleton.

5.12. PROPOSITION. *Let A be a modal formula. The set of terms occurring in
$FT(w, A)$ is prefix stable.*

PROOF. Consider a term $[w\gamma_1 \ldots \gamma_n\gamma]$, occurring somewhere in a functionally translated modal formula; the prefix of γ is $[w\gamma_1 \ldots \gamma_n]$. Of course, γ originates from a
particular modal operator M, and $\gamma_1 \ldots \gamma_n$ originate from the nested sequence of
modal operators preceding M on the path in the formula tree leading to M. Hence
all other occurrences of γ have exactly the same prefix $w\gamma_1 \ldots \gamma_n$. $\qquad\square$

Because prefix stability of terms is such a fundamental concept, Schmidt [1997] gives an independent definition of a logic, called basic non-optimized path logic, that emphasizes the particular ordering of the variables occurring in a literal.

5.13. DEFINITION. The language of *basic non-optimized path logic* is that of monadic first-order logic extended with a non-associative binary operation $[\cdot, \cdot]$ and a designated constant $[]$ which plays the role of the initial world variable w in our functional translation. The sorts are W and AF. There are finitely many unary predicate symbols p, q, $\ldots$, and possibly also a special unary predicate de. The constant $[]$ has sort W, and the function $[\cdot, \cdot]$ maps pairs of world terms and functional terms to world terms. Terms are of the form

$$[[[[[]\gamma_1]\gamma_2]\ldots]\gamma_m] \text{ or in shorthand notation } [\gamma_1 \gamma_2 \ldots \gamma_m].$$

An atomic basic non-optimized path formula over an ordered set of variables $X_i = \{\gamma_1, \ldots, \gamma_i\}$ is a monadic literal with an argument, as in $p([\gamma_1 \ldots \gamma_i])$ or $\neg p([\gamma_1 \ldots \gamma_i])$. Complex formulae are defined by induction:

1. Any atomic basic non-optimized path formula over X_i is a basic non-optimized path formula over X_i.
2. $\exists \gamma_{i+1} A$ and $\forall \gamma_{i+1} A$ are basic non-optimized path formulae over X_i, whenever A is a basic non-optimized path formula over X_{i+1}.
3. Any boolean combination of basic non-optimized path formulae over X_i is a basic non-optimized path formula over X_i.

A sample basic non-optimized path formula over X_3 is the formula

$$\exists \gamma_1 \, (\forall \gamma_2 \exists \gamma_3 \, p([\gamma_1 \gamma_2 \gamma_3]) \wedge \forall \gamma_2 \gamma_3 \, \neg p([\gamma_1 \gamma_2 \gamma_3])).$$

5.14. PROPOSITION. *Let A be a basic non-optimized path formula. The set of terms occurring in A is prefix stable.*

5.15. PROPOSITION. *Let A be a modal formula. Then $FT(w, A)$ is equivalent to a basic non-optimized path formula.*

5.16. PROPOSITION. *Let A be a basic non-optimized path formula. Then there exists a modal formula B such that A is equivalent to $FT(w, B)$.*

The results above establish a direct correspondence between **KD**-formulae and basic non-optimized path formulae. What about non-serial logics? The modal logic **K** can be translated into the modal logic **KD** adjoined with a special propositional symbol de. The translation $(\cdot)^*$ from **K** to **KD** is defined by

$$
\begin{aligned}
p^* &= p \\
(\neg A)^* &= \neg A^* \\
(A \wedge B)^* &= A^* \wedge B^* \\
(\Diamond A)^* &= \neg de \wedge \Diamond A^*
\end{aligned}
$$

Informally, the new propositional symbol *de* has the same interpretation as the dead-end predicate of the functional translation: it denotes the set of states at which the accessibility relation is not defined.

5.17. PROPOSITION. *Let A be a modal formula. Then A is provable in* **K** *iff A* is provable in* **KD**.

The *optimized* functional translation of a modal formula A is obtained by a sequence of two transformations: (1) the functional translation FT as discussed in the preceding subsections, and (2) the quantifier exchange operator Υ, which swaps quantifiers according to the following principle:

$$\exists \gamma \forall \delta \, A \leftrightarrow \forall \delta \exists \gamma \, A. \tag{5.4}$$

The crucial argument which allows one to prove that existential quantifiers over accessibility functions can be pulled over universal quantifiers is of a semantic nature. There are in general many different ways to decompose a binary relation into sets of accessibility functions. We are interested in those functional frames which justify moving existential quantifiers over universal quantifiers. Let us illustrate the basic idea with an example.

Suppose a formula $\Box \Diamond p$ is true at the state w_1, i.e., $w_1 \models \Box \Diamond p$. This means that for every world w accessible from w_1 there is a world accessible from w where p is true. In terms of the relation symbol R this reads as $\forall w \, (R(w_1, w) \Rightarrow \exists v \, (R(w, v) \, \& \, v \models p))$. Consider the situation in the diagram on the left-hand side below. In this model the formula $\exists v \forall w \, (R(w_1, w) \Rightarrow R(w, v) \, \& \, v \models p)$ in which we have swapped the existential quantifier $\exists v$ with the universal quantifier $\forall w$ is false.

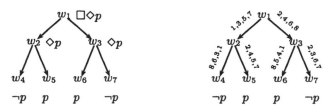

But now consider the functional frame in the diagram on the right-hand side. The numeric labels i denote the accessibility functions γ_i. In the functional language we can express the fact that $\Box \Diamond p$ is true at w_1 by $\forall \gamma \exists \delta \, \delta(\gamma(w_1)) \models p$. In this model we can swap the $\exists \delta$ quantifier and the $\forall \gamma$ quantifiers. $\exists \delta \forall \gamma \, \delta(\gamma(w_1)) \models p$ is true, because the function γ_4 (as well as the function γ_5) maps the worlds w_2 and w_3 to a world where p holds. Moreover, regardless of which one of the worlds w_4, w_5, w_6 or w_7 p is true, in this model there is always a function γ_i which maps w_2 and w_3 to the right worlds.

It can be shown that in functional frames which are *maximal*, i.e., which contain *all* maximally defined accessibility functions, moving the existential quantifiers in front of the universal quantifiers is always justified [Ohlbach and Schmidt 1997]. More precisely, define the *functional extension* of a serial interpretation $\Im =$

(W, R, P) to be the structure $\mathfrak{S}^* = (W, R, AF, [\cdot, \cdot], P)$, where AF is the *largest* set of all functions that define R.

5.18. THEOREM. *Let A be a modal formula true in a relational interpretation $\mathfrak{S}$. Let $\mathfrak{S}^*$ be its functional extension. For the functional translation B of A the following equivalence is true in $\mathfrak{S}^*$:*

$$\forall \gamma \exists \delta \, B([xt\gamma t' \delta t'']) \leftrightarrow \exists \delta \forall \gamma \, B([xt\gamma t' \delta t'']).$$

The so-called *quantifier exchange operator* Υ converts a non-optimal path formula into prenex normal form and moves *all* quantifiers of functional variables inward as far as possible according to the rule

$$\exists \gamma \forall \delta A \text{ becomes } \forall \delta \exists \gamma A.$$

For any modal formula A, $\Upsilon FT(w, A)$ has a quantifier prefix consisting of a universally quantified world variable followed by a sequence of universally quantified variables of sort AF, and a sequence of existentially quantified variables of sort AF. The quantifier prefix of the negation $\neg \Upsilon FT(w, A)$ is then a sequence of existential quantifiers followed by a sequence of universal quantifiers.

5.19. EXAMPLE. Consider the McKinsey formula $\Box \Diamond p \to \Diamond \Box p$. Recall that the D axiom $\Box p \to \Diamond p$ is a theorem of **K** plus the McKinsey formula. The functional translation is given by

$$\forall x \, (\forall \gamma \exists \delta \, p([x\gamma\delta]) \to \exists \gamma' \exists \delta' \, p([x\gamma'\delta'])).$$

The prefix normal form is

$$\forall x \exists \gamma \forall \delta \exists \gamma' \forall \delta' \, (p([x\gamma\delta]) \to p([x\gamma'\delta'])).$$

Applying Υ produces

$$\forall x \forall \delta \forall \delta' \exists \gamma \exists \gamma' \, (p([x\gamma\delta]) \to p([x\gamma'\delta'])).$$

And the negation $\neg \Upsilon \forall FT(x, \Box\Diamond p \to \Diamond\Box p)$ is given by

$$\exists x \exists \delta \exists \delta' \forall \gamma \forall \gamma' \, (p([x\gamma\delta]) \wedge p([x\gamma'\delta'])).$$

Applying Υ to a formula A results in a weaker formula A', since $A \to A'$, for in general $\exists x \forall y \, B$ implies $\forall y \exists y \, B$, but not conversely. The next result provides conditions under which working with the weaker form does suffice to prove A.

5.20. PROPOSITION. *Let $\mathbf{K(D)}\Sigma$ be a complete (or complete and first-order definable) modal logic. Then, for any modal formula A, A is a theorem of $\mathbf{K(D)}\Sigma$ iff $\forall x \, FT(x, \Sigma) \to \Upsilon \forall x \, FT(x, A)$ is a second-order (or first-order) theorem.*

5.21. PROPOSITION. *Let $K(D)\Sigma$ be a complete (or complete and first-order definable) modal logic with modus ponens and necessitation as its only proof rules. Then, for any modal formula A, A is a theorem of $K(D)\Sigma$ iff $\Upsilon \forall x \, FT(x, \Sigma) \to \Upsilon \forall x \, FT(x, A)$ is a second-order (or first-order) theorem.*

The functional language is more expressive than the relational language, and properties which are second-order in the relational language may become first-order in the functional language. We should stress that the above results only state that a formula A is a theorem of $K\Sigma$ iff a weaker theorem follows from weaker frame properties. The net effect of moving existential quantifiers over universal quantifiers in the functional translation of modal formulae is that complex Skolem terms are avoided; at most Skolem constants occur in the resulting clausal forms. In the following subsection we will reap the rewards of this fact. First, however, we will introduce *basic path logics*.

5.22. DEFINITION. *Path logics* are clausal logics. Clauses of basic path logic have the form $p([c\delta e]) \vee \neg q([c\kappa\lambda])$, and are built from constant symbols, like c, e, variables like δ, κ, λ, a special constant symbol $[]$ (denoting the empty path), a left associative operation $[\cdot, \cdot]$, and unary predicate symbols, like p, q, as well as $\vee$ and $\neg$.

The only Skolem terms in basic path clauses are constants. Terms, like $[c\delta e]$ and $[c\kappa\lambda]$, are called paths, and they are required to satisfy prefix stability for variables.

A *path formula* is a conjunction of basic path clauses. *Non-basic path logic* arises when we allow non-empty theories $\Upsilon \forall x \, FT(x, \Sigma)$.

Examples of non-basic path logics are provided by the theories associated with the modal logics T and $K4$; their Skolemized formulations are
(right identity) $[x \, id] = x$, where id is the identity function, and
(associativity) $[x(\gamma \circ \delta)] = [x\gamma\delta]$, where $\circ$ is functional composition.

5.23. PROPOSITION. *Let C be an operator on first-order formulae such that $C(A)$ is a clausal form of A. Let A be a modal formula. The set of clauses $C(\neg \Upsilon \forall x \, FT(x, A))$ is a well-formed expression in (basic) path logic, provided that the operation Υ moves all existential functional quantifiers inward over all universal quantifiers.*

5.4. Decidability of path logic

In this subsection we discuss decidability aspects of path logics, and hence, by Proposition 5.23, of modal logics. The core idea underlying a resolution-based decision proof for path logic goes back to Joyner Jr. [1976]: let S be a set of path clauses generated by saturation from a finite input set, and establish the existence of a *term depth bound* for terms in S and a bound on the *size* of any clause in S.

Inference for basic path logic may be performed using resolution with syntactic unification. Now, standard equational reasoning with equations such as (right identity) and (associativity) is not very efficient. Therefore, it is usually better to incorporate the equations into suitable theory unification algorithms for the world paths, and, hence, to do inference for non-basic path logics with theory resolution.

In [Ohlbach 1988b] unification algorithms for combinations of the above two properties have been presented and proved to be terminating, sound and complete. The proof relies heavily on the prefix stability of world-paths. The algorithm is presented in a Martelli-Montanari style as a number of transformation rules for sets of equations:

(Decomposition) $f(s_1, \ldots, s_n) = f(t_1, \ldots, t_n) \rightarrow s_1 = t_1 \,\&\, \ldots \,\&\, s_n = t_n$

(Separation) $s\,s = t\,t \rightarrow s = t \,\&\, s = t$

(Identity) $s\,w\,s' = t \rightarrow w = [] \,\&\, s\,s' = t$

(Inverse) $s\,s\,w\,s' = t \rightarrow w = s^{-1} \,\&\, s\,s' = t$

(Path-Separation) $w\,s = tt' \rightarrow w = t \,\&\, s = t'$

(Splitting) $w\,s\,s = t\,t\,v\,t' \rightarrow v = v_1\,v_2 \,\&\, w = t\,t\,v_1 \,\&\, s\,s = v_2\,t'.$

Boldface letters represent longer world-paths, whereas normal letters represent single terms. The "Decomposition" and "Separation" rules are sufficient for modal logics **K** and **KD**. The "Identity" rule encodes the reflexivity axiom. It instantiates a variable with an empty world path. The "Inverse" rule encodes the symmetry axiom. It goes together with a simplification rule: $xx^{-1} = []$ and exploits the fact that the prefix of variables w is always the same. Therefore, all occurrences of sw which are instantiated with $w \mapsto s^{-1}$ can be simplified to $[]$ in the same way. The last two rules, "Path-Separation" and "Splitting" encode the transitivity axiom. They are very similar to the corresponding unification rules for associative functions [Auer 1992]. But due to the prefix stability, the application of these rules terminates, in contrast to the rules for associative function symbols.

In the basic case of the modal logics **K** and **KD** there is at most one most general unifier for world-paths. In all other cases there are finitely but sometimes exponentially many most general unifiers. The application of the rules becomes nondeterministic, requiring a tree-like representation of the intermediate steps in the unification. The unification algorithm is no longer minimal, and the same solutions may be computed repeatedly. Schmidt [1998a] presents improved unification rules for transitivity, where the world paths are unified mainly from left to right, thus reducing the branching rate of the unification tree.

The optimized functional translation of propositional modal logic formulae yields clauses without function symbols in the world paths. Moreover, instantiation with unifiers computed using the above unification rules except "Path-Separation" and "Splitting" does not increase the length of world-paths. Hence, resolution and factorization do not increase the size of the literals. As a consequence, the number of condensed[11] and not subsumed clauses remains finite.

5.24. THEOREM ([Schmidt 1998]). *Any complete resolution procedure with condensing is a decision procedure for the satisfiability problem of a finite set of finite clauses of the basic path logic.*

---

[11] A clause is *condensed* iff it is not equivalent to one of its factors.

The proof of the above result uses the fact that, for basic path logic, there is no growth of terms, that the basic path logic is closed under resolution with condensing, and that there is no unbounded growth of the size of clauses.

The result can be formulated more generally, as follows.

5.25. THEOREM. *Any complete resolution procedure with condensing and possibly a normalization function is a decision procedure for the satisfiability problem of finite clauses in path logics, provided*

1. *a term depth bound exists,*
2. *unification is finitary, and*
3. *the normalization function is effective and returns basic path clauses.*

Although any input set is a set of basic path clauses without any non-constant occurrences of functional terms, the third condition in the above theorem is important as theory unification (needed to handle the theories built into non-basic path logic) may introduce non-constant functional terms.

The first condition in Theorem 5.25 can be interpreted in two ways. First, a term depth bound exists for the particular resolution procedure. Or, an a priori term depth bound exists for the particular path logic; the latter can, for instance, be extracted from the finite model property of the logic. The given term depth can then be used in a simple blocking mechanism to stop the proof procedure from generating clauses whose depth is larger than the given value.

Theorem 5.25 describes the class of path logics (in general, with a theory) for which unrestricted resolution plus condensing is guaranteed to terminate. In particular, the theorem provides a decidability result for the satisfiability problem for those modal logics that can be embedded in path logics such that the three conditions in Theorem 5.25 are met.

5.26. THEOREM. *Resolution and condensing (combined with any compatible refinement strategies) is a decision procedure for*

1. *basic path logic and for (the optimized functional translation of)* **K**, **KD**, **S5** *and the multi-modal versions of* **K** *and* **KD***;*
2. *(the optimized functional translation of)* **KT***, and*
3. **KD4** *and* **S4***.*

For practical purposes the solution of using an artificial term depth (as provided by e.g., the finite model property) is poor [Hustadt et al. 1998]. Hence, the search space is very large, even for small input formulae. Therefore, from an efficiency point of view, good search strategies are still badly needed. But due to the above results, any fair strategy is automatically complete.

5.5. Extensions and variations

The idea behind the functional translation is not restricted to logics with ordinary binary accessibility relations, and in this subsection we consider the functional translation of a number of logics other than uni-modal logic.

To begin with, what's the functional translation of quantified modal logic? Modal and intuitionistic formulae that have been translated with the relational translation have a particular structure which can be exploited to get rid of the introduced binary relations. For operators of "universal force" the standard translation yields formulae of the kind $\forall v\, (R(w,v) \to A(v))$ (cf. (4.1), (4.4), (4.5), (4.9)), whereas operators of existential force are turned into $\exists v\, (R(w,v) \wedge A(v))$ (cf. (4.2), (4.10)). If it is known that the relation R is serial, which is the case for the *in* relation introduced by the standard translation (4.9), (4.10) for quantifiers,[12] then Definition 5.4 can be applied to the translated operators of universal force, and translated operators of existential force can be modified in a similar way:

$$FT(w, f(t_1, \ldots, t_n)) \;=\; f(w, FT(w, t_1), \ldots, FT(w, t_n)) \qquad (5.5)$$

$$\text{if } f \text{ is a function or predicate symbol}$$

$$FT(w, \forall x\; A(x)) \;=\; \forall \delta : AF_{in}\; FT(w, A)[x \mapsto [w\delta]]^{13} \qquad (5.6)$$

$$FT(w, \exists x\; A(x)) \;=\; \exists \delta : AF_{in}\; FT(w, A)[x \mapsto [w\delta]]. \qquad (5.7)$$

5.27. EXAMPLE. An example for the functional translation of a quantified modal formula (assuming a serial accessibility relation, but arbitrary domains) is

$$FT(w, \Diamond\Diamond\,(\forall x\,(\Diamond p(x) \wedge \Box q(x)) \to \Diamond(\forall y\, p(y) \wedge \forall z\, q(z)))) =$$

$$\exists \gamma_1, \gamma_2 : AF_R
\begin{bmatrix}
\forall \delta_1 : AF_{in}
\begin{bmatrix}
\exists \gamma_3 : AF_R\, p([w\gamma_1\gamma_2\gamma_3], [w\gamma_1\gamma_2\delta_1]) \wedge \\
\forall \gamma_4 : AF_R\, q([w\gamma_1\gamma_2\gamma_4], [w\gamma_1\gamma_2\delta_1])
\end{bmatrix} \\
\to \exists \gamma_5 : AF_R
\begin{bmatrix}
\forall \delta_2 : AF_{in}\, p([w\gamma_1\gamma_2\gamma_5], [w\gamma_1\gamma_2\gamma_5\delta_2]) \wedge \\
\forall \delta_3 : AF_{in}\, q([w\gamma_1\gamma_2\gamma_5], [w\gamma_1\gamma_2\gamma_5\delta_3])
\end{bmatrix}
\end{bmatrix}$$

The term $[w\gamma_1\gamma_2\gamma_3]$ denotes the world accessible from w via γ_1, γ_2, γ_3 transitions; it corresponds to the first sequence of three nested $\Diamond$-operators. The variable is replaced by the term $[w\gamma_1\gamma_2\delta_1]$; the latter denotes an element in the domain of the world $[w\gamma_1\gamma_2]$. The function δ_1 maps this world to the domain element. The quantifier $\forall \delta_1 : AF_{in}$, which originated from the $\forall x$-quantifier, ensures that all domain elements are covered.

Unfortunately, the quantifier exchange operator Υ which helped us to turn the functional translation into the optimized functional translation, cannot be used in the setting of quantified modal logic. An example (due to Andreas Herzig) shows what can happen. The formula $\Box(\exists x\,(p(x) \wedge \Box\Diamond\neg p(x)))$ is true at the world w_1 of the following model.

---

[12] The interpretations for quantified modal logics are restricted to non-empty domains. Therefore $\forall w\; \exists x\; in(w, x)$ can always be assumed.

[13] $FT(w, A)[x \mapsto [w\delta]]$ means translating A and then replacing all occurrences of x with $[w\delta]$. The translation rules for the domain quantifiers eliminate the *in* predicate as well. This need not be done if one wants to keep the domain variables as they are.

For every world u accessible from w_1 (these are w_2 and w_3) and for some object x, $p(x)$ holds (for w_2, x is a and for w_3, x is b), and for every world v accessible from u (w_1) there is a world y accessible from v (w_2 and w_3 are the candidates) such that $\neg p(x)$ holds at y. Now we have to choose either w_2 or w_3 and check whether $\neg p(x)$ holds. However, x was determined in a previous world, in the case that $u = w_2$, x is a and in the case that $u = w_3$, x is b. Our choice depends on the path we took to get to $v = w_1$. This example shows that we must be careful where we apply the trick of moving existential quantifiers to the front. For quantified modal logic the trick does not work in general.

5.28. EXAMPLE. Next, we turn to intuitionistic logic. The "functional version" of the restriction on the assignment of predicates (4.3) that we find in intuitionistic logic is

$$\forall w \, \forall \gamma : AF_R \, (p(w) \to p([w\gamma])). \tag{5.8}$$

This axiom can easily be turned into a theory resolution rule.

$$\frac{p(s), C \qquad\qquad}{\neg p([s't]), D \quad \sigma \text{ unifies } s \text{ and } s'}{C\sigma, D\sigma}$$

5.29. EXAMPLE. Functional translations can always be tried when the binary relations occur in the typical guarded patterns $\forall y \, (R(x,y) \to \ldots)$ and $\exists y \, (R(x,y) \wedge \ldots)$. This is the case, for example, in (4.6), the standard translation for classical modal logics with neighborhood semantics. Here it is the neighborhood predicate N which can be replaced by functions AF_N, mapping worlds to their neighborhoods. Assuming seriality of N (each world has at least one neighborhood) one can define a functional translation FT as follows:

$$\begin{aligned} FT_c(w, \Box A) &= \exists \gamma : AF_N \, \forall v \, (in([w\gamma], v) \leftrightarrow FT_c(v, A)) \\ FT_c(w, \Diamond A) &= \forall \gamma : AF_N \, \exists v \, (in([w\gamma], v) \leftrightarrow FT_c(v, A)). \end{aligned}$$

It is possible, although it would not make much sense, to replace the in-predicate with functions AF_{in}; in does not occur in the typical modal pattern. Therefore, the translation introduces equations and in-equations requiring equation handling in the theorem prover.

The standard translation for classical modal logic with the stronger semantics is

$$\begin{aligned} ST_c'(w, \Box A) &= \exists V \, (N(w, V) \wedge \forall v \, (in(V, v) \to ST_c'(v, A))) \\ ST_c'(w, \Diamond A) &= \forall V \, (N(w, V) \to \exists v \, (in(V, v) \wedge ST_c'(v, A))). \end{aligned}$$

Now it does make sense to replace both relations, N and in, by accessibility functions. Assuming seriality of N and in, i.e., each world has a non-empty neighborhood, we get a much more compact functional translation:

$$FT'_c(w, \Box A) \;=\; \exists \gamma : AF_N \, \forall \delta \in AF_{in} \, FT'_c([w\gamma\delta], A)$$
$$FT'_c(w, \Diamond A) \;=\; \forall \gamma : AF_N \, \exists \delta : AF_{in} \, FT'_c([w\gamma\delta], A).$$

Intuitively, γ maps the world w to a neighborhood of w and δ maps this neighborhood back to a world.

5.30. EXAMPLE. It is instructive to see what happens if we try to prove the **K**-axiom $\Box(p \to q) \to (\Box p \to \Box q)$ using the above translation for classical modal logic. Since the **K**-axiom does not hold in classical modal logic, a resolution refutation should fail. The negation of the **K**-axiom is $\Box(p \to q) \wedge \Box p \wedge \Diamond \neg q$. The translation yields three clauses:

$\neg p([w_0 a \gamma]) \vee q([w_0 a \gamma])$	a is a Skolem constant
$p([w_0 b \gamma])$	b is a Skolem constant
$\neg q([w_0 \gamma c])$	c is a Skolem constant.

After one resolution between the first and last clause, giving $\neg p([w_0 a c])$, no further inference step is possible. The clause set cannot be refuted.

6. The semi-functional translation

The semi-functional translation combines the advantages of the relational and the functional translation while trying to avoid their respective disadvantages. One of the advantages of the relational translation is that the translation result is "natural" because it mirrors the Kripke-semantics of modal logics. The background theory to be added to the translation result is simple, and, in particular, does not introduce "unnecessary" new equations. Its disadvantage is that it produces large formulae which open huge search spaces for automated theorem provers. The functional translation, on the other hand, provides us with a very compact translation result. The price for this advantage is that we may have to cope with an additional equational theory. The introduction of theory-unification algorithms may simplify matters, though.

The semi-functional translation also produces a fairly compact translation result (although not as compact as the functional translation) and, like the relational translation, it does not introduce new equational theories. It even turns out that its syntactic peculiarities allow us to simplify background theories such that they can sometimes be reduced to simple unit clauses.

The semi-functional translation is called *semi-functional* because the operator $\Diamond$ is translated functionally whereas the $\Box$ is translated as in the relational approach. Just as with the functional translation its definition depends on whether we consider

$$
\begin{aligned}
SF(w, p) &= p(w) \\
SF(w, \neg A) &= \neg SF(w, A) \\
SF(w, A \wedge B) &= SF(w, A) \wedge SF(w, B) \\
SF(w, \Box A) &= \forall v : W \, (R(w, v) \rightarrow SF(v, A)) \\
SF(w, \Diamond A) &= \exists \gamma : AF_R \, SF([w\gamma], A)
\end{aligned}
$$

Table 7: The semi-functional translation

serial or non-serial accessibility relations. Here, we will focus on the serial case. For non-serial accessibility relations similar additions have to be made as for the functional approach (see Nonnengart [1992, 1993, 1995, 1996]).

6.1. DEFINITION. The *semi-functional translation* from modal logic into first-order logic is given by the clauses given in Table 7.

Obviously, the only difference between the functional and the semi-functional translation seems to be the treatment of $\Diamond$-formulae. However, this is not quite the only difference. We must ensure that $\Box$ and $\Diamond$ are dual operators, i.e., that for any formula A it holds that $\Box A \leftrightarrow \neg \Diamond \neg A$. In the functional translation this is obviously guaranteed. In the semi-functional translation the duality of the translations of $\Box$ and $\Diamond$ is not automatically given.

6.2. PROPOSITION (Nonnengart [1993, 1995, 1996]). *The duality principle* $\Box A \leftrightarrow \neg \Diamond \neg A$ *holds if and only if* $\forall w : W \, \forall \gamma : AF_R \, R(w, [w\gamma])$ *holds.*

In words: regardless of the serial modal logic that we are considering, its background theory must contain the above formula to ensure duality between the modal operators. This *minimal background theory* states that every world that is accessible via the accessibility functions is also accessible via the accessibility relation.

Recall that a formula is in *negation normal form* if it contains no implication or equivalence and all negations only occur immediately in front of atoms. Every formula can easily be transformed into an equivalent formula in negation normal form.

6.3. THEOREM ([Nonnengart 1995]). *Let* A *be a uni-modal formula in negation normal form. Then* A *is unsatisfiable (in the serial case) iff* $SF(x, A)$ *cannot be satisfied on any model which satisfies both* $\forall w : W \, \forall \gamma : AF_R \, R(w, [w\gamma])$ *and the properties induced by the specific axiom schemata for the modal logic under consideration.*

Therefore, the semi-functional translation behaves as desired. But what has been gained so far? Our aim was to define a translation that produces compact results and does not introduce new equations into the background theory of the modal logic under consideration. The latter is obviously fulfilled by the semi-functional translation as shown in Theorem 6.3. As for the former, it is easy to show that after transformation into clause normal form there is no difference in the number of clauses generated in the semi-functional and in the functional approach (in the semi-functional approach the clauses are bigger, though). However, there is a third invariant of this translation approach which turns out to be useful: given a formula A, the clause normal form of $SF(u, A)$ does not contain any positive R-literal. Thus, positive R-literals can occur only in the background theory of the modal logic under consideration. Below, we will take advantage of this fact.

6.1. Saturating background theories

The fact that no positive R-literals occur in semi-functional translation of modal formulae can be used by pre-computing everything that can possibly be derived from the background theory, i.e., this theory gets *saturated*. Such a saturation characterizes the modal logic and is thus independent of the theorem to be proved.

6.4. DEFINITION. We call a clause C *p-positive* (*p-negative*) if there is a positive (negative) occurrence of a p-literal in C. If, in addition, C is not p-negative (not p-positive) then we call C *pure-p-positive* (*pure-p-negative*).

6.5. DEFINITION ((*Partial*) Saturation). Let p be a designated predicate symbol and let C be a set of p-positive clauses. The *saturation* of C with respect to p is defined to be the set $\{C \mid C \vdash_{\text{res}} C$ and C is pure-p-positive$\}$, i.e., the set of clauses we obtain by resolution within C, and whose elements are pure-p-positive.

As an example, consider the clause set $\{p(a), \neg p(x) \lor p(f(x))\}$. The only clause which is pure-p-positive is $p(a)$. But it is possible to derive more pure-p-positive clauses by resolution, namely all atoms of the form $p(f^n(a))$, for $n \geq 0$.

Knowing about the saturation of a given clause set is often quite helpful.

6.6. LEMMA. *Let C be a clause set and let p be a designated predicate symbol. Let $C' \subseteq C$ be the subset of C whose elements are positive with respect to p. If C'' is the saturation of C' with respect to p then C is unsatisfiable iff $(C \setminus C') \cup C''$ is unsatisfiable.*

The problem with the above lemma is that saturations are usually infinite. However, if we are able to find a finite alternative clause set with exactly the same saturation we can use this one instead.

6.7. THEOREM. *Let C be a finite clause set, let p be a designated predicate symbol, and let $D \subseteq C$ contain the p-positive clauses of C. Moreover, let B be a finite set of p-positive clauses whose saturation with respect to p is identical to D's saturation with respect to p. Then C is unsatisfiable iff $(C \setminus D) \cup B$ is unsatisfiable.*

Thus, the idea is to extract $\mathcal{D}$ and to find a simpler clause set $\mathcal{B}$ with the same saturation.

6.8. EXAMPLE. Consider the simple background theory given by the clauses:

$$p(a)$$
$$p(f(a)) \tag{6.1}$$
$$\neg p(x) \vee \neg p(f(x)) \vee p(f(f(x)))$$

Its saturation is $\{p(f^n(a)) \mid n \geq 0\}$. One may prove this is as follows. First, each of these elements can indeed be derived. A simple induction on n will do. For the induction step assume that $p(f^k(a))$ is derivable for all $k < n$. So both $p(f^{n-2}(a))$ and $p(f^{n-1}(a))$ are derivable and therefore $p(f^n(a))$ can be obtained by two resolution steps with the third clause from the original clause set. Thus $\{p(f^n(a)) \mid n \geq 0\}$ is at least contained in the saturation we are looking for.

It remains to show that the saturation is contained in the derived clause set. To this end we show that any pure p-positive clause which is derivable from $\{p(f^n(a)) \mid n \geq 0\}$ and the p-positive clauses of the clause set under consideration is already of the form $p(f^n(a))$. Evidently, resolution steps between $p(f^k(a))$, $p(f^l(a))$ and $\neg p(x) \vee \neg p(f(x)) \vee p(f(f(x)))$ are possible only if $k = l + 1$ (or $l = k + 1$) and they result in $p(f^{l+2}(a))$ ($p(f^{k+2}(a))$ respectively). This derived unit clause does indeed belong to $\{p(f^n(a)) \mid n \geq 0\}$ and we are done.

Now consider the somewhat "simpler" clause set

$$p(a)$$
$$\neg p(x) \vee p(f(x)). \tag{6.2}$$

The saturation of this clause set is also $\{p(f^n(a)) \mid n \geq 0\}$ and therefore (Theorem 6.7) this new clause set may be used to replace the original background theory.

Observe that the two clause sets (6.1) and (6.2) are not equivalent. It is the mere fact that they form a background theory in the sense that they contain the only p-positive literals occurring anywhere in the clause set being considered which allows us to perform such a "simplification." Hence, what we use here is not just that the background theory is *something* we know about p but is indeed *all* we know about p.

For two well-known serial modal logics the saturation approach does not lead to anything new, namely **KD** and **KT**. However, the background theories for these modal logics are represented by one or two unit clauses anyway, and, thus, the proof search will not be influenced too heavily.[14]

6.9. EXAMPLE. Consider the logic **KDB**, which is axiomatized by the additional axiom schemata $\Box p \rightarrow \Diamond p$ and $p \rightarrow \Box \Diamond p$. These two schemata characterize seriality

---

[14]Note that for the logic **KD** we could incorporate this very unit clause directly in the translation description. Interestingly, this would result in exactly the same clause set we would get if we applied the functional translation approach.

and symmetry of the underlying accessibility relation; see Table 2. Therefore, the background theory for **KDB** is:

$$\forall w : W \, \forall \gamma : AF_R \, R(w, [w\gamma])$$
$$\forall u, v : W \, (R(u, v) \to R(v, u)). \tag{6.3}$$

The saturation of this background theory can easily be found, and we end up with

$$\forall w : W \, \forall \gamma \in AF_R \, R(w, [w\gamma])$$
$$\forall w : W \, \forall \gamma : AF_R \, R([w\gamma], w).$$

Hence, these two unit clauses are sufficient as the background theory for **KDB**. Although this only seems to be a minor improvement over (6.3), such a replacement at least avoids undesirable cycles in the search space.

6.10. EXAMPLE. Consider the modal logic **S4**, which is characterized by reflexivity and transitivity (see Table 2); the corresponding axiom schemata are $\Box p \to p$ and $\Box p \to \Box\Box p$. The background theory is given by

$$\forall w : W \, \forall \gamma : AF_R \, R(w, [w\gamma])$$
$$\forall w : W \, R(w, w) \tag{6.4}$$
$$\forall u, v, w : W \, (R(u, v) \wedge R(v, w) \to R(u, w)).$$

Again, we have to saturate this clause set bearing in mind that this is indeed all we know about R, for any formula to be proved unsatisfiable (in **S4**) will not contain R-positive clauses. Let us show now that the saturation consists of the (infinite) set of unit clauses of the form $\{R(w, [w\gamma_1 \ldots \gamma_n]) \mid n \geq 0\}$.

To this end we show that the purely positive R-clauses in the background theory (which are $R(w, [w\gamma])$ and $R(w, w)$) are contained in this set; this is trivial. Then we have to show that resolving upon two arbitrary elements of the candidate saturation of the transitivity clause does not produce anything new, and indeed, resolving $R(w, [w\gamma_1 \ldots \gamma_n])$ and $R(w, [w\delta_1 \ldots \delta_m])$ with the first two literals in $R(u, v) \wedge R(v, w) \to R(u, w)$ results in $R(w, [w\gamma_1 \ldots \gamma_n \delta_1 \ldots \delta_m])$ which is already contained in $\{R(w, [w\gamma_1 \ldots \gamma_n]) \mid n \geq 0\}$. Finally, we have to show that the candidate saturation is not too large, i.e., that each of its elements can in fact be derived and this follows by a simple induction on n.

At this stage we have found the saturation of the **S4** background theory. Next, we have to find an alternative clause set with the same saturation but which is somehow simpler than the original one. Finding such an alternative is still to be performed by a *good guess*; it is not yet known how this can be automated. For the present example it is not hard to find a suitable clause set, namely

$$\forall u : W \, R(u, u)$$
$$\forall u, v : W \, \forall \gamma : AF_R \, (R(u, v) \to R(u, [v\gamma])) \tag{6.5}$$

or, equally simple,

$$\forall u : W \, R(u, u)$$
$$\forall u, v : W \, \forall \gamma : AF_R \, (R([u\gamma], v) \to R(u, v)).$$

It is easy to show that the saturation of this clause set is identical to the saturation of the **S4** background theory, and what we have gained is that we may replace the background theory for **S4** by the two simpler clauses in (6.5). In particular, the deletion of the transitivity clause turns out to be of major importance.

Our next example illustrates the effect of the semi-functional translation together with saturation with a little example.

6.11. EXAMPLE. We want to prove the validity of the formula $\Diamond \Box p \leftrightarrow \Diamond \Box \Diamond \Box p$ in **S4**. After negating and translating semi-functionally we end up with the following clause set (where γ, a, b are Skolem constants, f, h, k are Skolem functions and all variables are assumed to be universally quantified):

$$\neg R([\gamma a], u) \vee \neg R([\gamma b], v) \vee \neg R([vf(v)], w) \vee p(u) \vee p(w)$$
$$\neg R(\gamma, u) \vee \neg p([u.g(u)]) \vee \neg R(\gamma, v) \vee \neg R([vh(v)], w) \vee \neg p([wk(w,v)])$$
$$R(u, u)$$
$$\neg R(u, v) \vee R(u, [v\gamma_1]).$$

This clause set is much smaller than what we would obtain from the relational translation; moreover, the search space has been reduced to such an extent that no standard FO theorem prover will have difficulties with it.

It should now be obvious how a logic like **KD4** has to be treated. Its background theory is described by

$$\forall u : W \, \forall \gamma : AF_R \, R(u, [u\gamma])$$
$$\forall u, v, w : W \, ((R(u, v) \wedge R(v, w)) \to R(u, w)),$$

and it can easily be shown that the saturation of this theory is

$$\{R(u, [u\gamma_1 \ldots \gamma_n]) \mid n \geq 1, \gamma_i : AF_R\},$$

i.e., it differs from the saturation of the **S4**-theory only in that it lacks the reflexivity clause $R(u, u)$. An alternative clause set for this background theory, with the same saturation, is easily found:

$$\forall u : W \, \forall \gamma \in AF_R \, R(u, [u\gamma])$$
$$\forall u, v : W \, \forall \gamma : AF_R \, (R(u, v) \to R(u, [v\gamma])).$$

So far only a few modal logics have been examined with respect to semi-functional translation and saturation of background theories. There is a property which allows us to broaden the scope of the method, viz. the so-called rootedness property of modal frames. Let us first have a look at the technique applied to the logic **S5**.

6.12. EXAMPLE. **S5** can be axiomatized by the schemata $\Box p \to p$, $\Box p \to \Box\Box p$, and $p \to \Box\Diamond p$ or, equivalently, by $\Box p \to p$ and $\Diamond p \to \Box\Diamond p$. The corresponding properties of the accessibility relation are reflexivity, transitivity and symmetry in the former and reflexivity and euclideanness in the latter axiomatization; the two are obviously equivalent. Now, the saturation of either background theory consists of all unit clauses of the form $\{R([u\gamma_1 \ldots \gamma_n], [u\delta_1 \ldots \delta_m]) \mid n, m \geq 0\}$. Also, it is easy to find an alternative clause set which is simpler than the original one, but generates the same saturation. The axioms are

$$\forall u : W\, R(u, u)$$
$$\forall u, v : W\, \forall \gamma : AF_R\, (R(u, v) \to R(u, [v\gamma]))$$
$$\forall u, v : W\, \forall \gamma : AF_R\, (R(u, v) \to R([u\gamma], v)),$$

which are still rather complicated. This background theory can be significantly simplified if we exploit the fact that we need only consider *rooted* frames as defined in [Segerberg 1971].

6.13. DEFINITION *(Rooted Frames)*. A frame $\mathcal{F} = (W, R)$ is called *rooted* if there exists a world w in W such that for every world v in W it holds that $R^*(w, v)$, where R^* denotes the reflexive and transitive closure of R.

Hence, in a rooted frame any world can be reached from an initial world by zero or more R-steps and it is thus impossible to have two unconnected "islands" of worlds.

6.14. DEFINITION *(Generated Frames)*. Given a frame $\mathcal{F} = (W, R)$ and an arbitrary world w in W we define $W' = \{v \in W \mid R^*(w, v)\}$ and $R' = R \cap (W' \times W')$. The frame (W', R') is called the frame *generated from* $\mathcal{F}$ (with initial world w).

Evidently, every generated frame is rooted. Modal logics are not able to distinguish between rooted and non-rooted frames and this is shown by the following result.

6.15. LEMMA (Segerberg). *Let $\mathcal{F}$ be a modal logic frame and let $\mathfrak{I} = (\mathcal{F}, P)$ be an arbitrary interpretation based on $\mathcal{F}$. Let $\mathfrak{I}' = (\mathcal{F}', P)$ where $\mathcal{F}'$ is the frame generated from $\mathcal{F}$. Then, for all worlds $v \in W'$ and for all modal formulae A,*

$$\mathfrak{I}, v \models A \text{ iff } \mathfrak{I}', v \models A.$$

PROOF. The identity relation is a bisimulation between $\mathfrak{I}$ and $\mathfrak{I}'$, as the reader can easily check. Hence, the lemma follows by Proposition 4.16. $\square$

As a consequence of the lemma, we may restrict our attention to rooted frames. What does rootedness actually mean in (semi-)functional frames?

6.16. LEMMA. *A frame (interpretation) is rooted (with initial world w) iff for every world u there exist some $\gamma_1, \ldots, \gamma_n \in AF_R$ ($n \geq 0$) such that $u = [w\gamma_1\gamma_2\gamma_3 \ldots \gamma_n]$.*

Proof. In rooted frames each world u can be reached from the initial world w by a finite sequence of R-transitions, i.e., there exist worlds $w_1, \ldots, w_{n-1}$ such that $R(w, w_1)$, $R(w_1, w_2)$, $\ldots$, $R(w_{n-1}, u)$. In the extended functional frames this is just $[w\gamma_1 \ldots \gamma_n]$ for suitable γ_i. $\square$

We may therefore assume that the property $\forall u \exists \gamma_1, \ldots, \gamma_n \; (u = [w_0\gamma_1 \ldots \gamma_n])$ holds, where w_0 is the initial world. This can be used for further optimizations of the semi-functional translation.

6.17. Example. Recall from Example 6.12 that the saturation of **S5** resulted in an infinite clause set consisting of unit clauses of the form $R([u\gamma_1 \ldots \gamma_n], [u\delta_1 \ldots \delta_m])$ with $n, m \geq 0$ (and universally quantified variables u, γ_i, δ_j). Now consider the subset we get after instantiating the variable u with w_0, the initial world. Then both arguments of the R-literals are of the form $w_0\gamma_1 \ldots \gamma_n$, where every γ_i is universally quantified, and therefore this term can represent any world. Thus, we know that (given the rootedness assumption) $R([w_0\gamma_1 \ldots \gamma_n], [w_0\delta_1 \ldots \delta_m])$ can be simplified to $R(v, w)$, i.e., the universal relation, which obviously subsumes all of the unit clauses described by $R([u\gamma_1 \ldots \gamma_n], [u\delta_1 \ldots \delta_m])$. More formally:

$$\forall u \, \exists \gamma_1, \ldots, \gamma_n \; (u = [w_0\gamma_1 \ldots \gamma_n]) \Rightarrow$$
$$\forall u, \gamma_i, \delta_j \; R([u\gamma_1 \ldots \gamma_n], [u\delta_1 \ldots \delta_m]) \leftrightarrow \forall v, w \; R(v, w).$$

Thus, instead of considering the still rather complicated background theory for **S5** as described above, we can simplify it.

6.18. Example. Consider **KD5** and **KD45**. These are axiomatized by the clause set

$$\forall u : W \; \forall \gamma : AF_R \; R(u, [u\gamma])$$
$$\forall u, v, w : W \; (R(u, v) \land R(u, w) \to R(v, w)) \qquad \textbf{(KD5)}$$

and

$$\forall u : W \; \forall \gamma : AF_R \; R(u, [u\gamma])$$
$$\forall u, v, w : W \; (R(u, v) \land R(v, w) \to R(u, w)) \qquad \textbf{(KD45)}$$
$$\forall u, v, w : W \; (R(u, v) \land R(u, w) \to R(v, w))$$

respectively, i.e. seriality and euclideanness (for **KD5**) and, additionally, transitivity (for **KD45**). Their saturations consist of the unit clause sets with all elements of the form $R([u\gamma_1 \ldots \gamma_n], [u\delta_1 \ldots \delta_m])$, where $m, n \geq 1$ for **KD5**, and $m \geq 1$ and $n \geq 0$ for **KD45**; in addition, the saturation of **KD5** also contains $R(u, [u\gamma])$. Both are quite similar to **S5**.

Unfortunately, since $m \geq 1$ (and $n \geq 1$ for **KD5**) these two arguments are not yet in the form that the rootedness assumption can be applied. However, since $m \geq 1$ we know that $m - 1 \geq 0$ and we therefore get for all $m \geq 1$ and $n \geq 0$, i.e., for **KD45**

$$\forall u \, \exists \gamma_1, \ldots, \gamma_k \; (u = [w_0\gamma_1 \ldots \gamma_k]) \Rightarrow$$
$$\forall u, \gamma_i, \delta_j \; R([u\gamma_1 \ldots \gamma_n], [u\delta_1 \ldots \delta_m]) \leftrightarrow \forall v, w, \gamma \; R(v, [w\gamma]) \qquad (6.6)$$

and for all $m \geq 1$ and $n \geq 1$, and so for **KD5**

$$\forall u \,\exists \gamma_1, \ldots, \gamma_k \,(u = w_0 \gamma_1 \ldots \gamma_k) \Rightarrow$$

$$\forall u, \gamma_i, \delta_j \, R([u\gamma_1 \ldots \gamma_n], [u\delta_1 \ldots \delta_m]) \leftrightarrow \forall v, w, \gamma, \delta \, R([v\gamma], [w\delta]). \quad (6.7)$$

The unit clause $R(v, [w\gamma])$ that we got for **KD45** subsumes the whole saturation and can therefore be used as the background theory for the logic **KD45**, whereas the unit clause $R([v\gamma], [w\delta])$ subsumes almost the whole saturation for **KD5**; the only clause which is not subsumed is $R(u, [u\gamma])$ and therefore the background theory for **KD5** can be described by the two unit clauses $R(u, [u\gamma])$ and $R([v\gamma], [w\delta])$.[15]

Table 8 summarizes the background theories for well-known serial modal logics in the setting of the semi-functional translation; all variables are universally quantified.

logic	background theory
KD	$R(u, [u\gamma])$
KT	$R(u, [u\gamma])$ and $R(u, u)$
KDB	$R(u, [u\gamma])$ and $R([u\gamma], u)$
KD4	$R(u, [u\gamma])$ and $(R(u, v) \rightarrow R(u, [v\gamma]))$
S4	$R(u, u)$ and $R(u, v) \rightarrow R(u, [v\gamma])$
KD5	$R(u, [u\gamma])$ and $R([u\gamma], [v\delta])$
KD45	$R(u, [v\gamma])$
S5	$R(u, v)$

Table 8: Logics and their background theories

How should these results, and in particular those for the logics **S5**, **KD45**, and **KD5**, be interpreted? Their simplicity and generality may be surprising. As Segerberg found out by examining the model theory for various modal logics [Segerberg 1971], the characteristic frames for **S5** are so-called *clusters*; that is, sets of worlds such that each world has access to any other world including itself. Thus we may assume that the accessibility relation for **S5** is the universal relation over $W \times W$.

The models for **KD45** are characterized by either a single cluster (as for **S5**) or a single world together with a cluster such that this particular world has access to each element of the cluster. The characteristic frames for **KD5** differ from those for **KD45** in that the single world does not necessarily have access to *all* elements in the cluster.

If we compare Segerberg's results with the saturated background theory we obtained for these logics, we see that for **S5** we do indeed find the universal accessibility relation; that for **KD45** every world does indeed have access to every other

---

[15] Actually, this can be even further simplified, for this first unit clause is subsumed for every instance but one, namely $\forall \gamma \, R(w_0, [w_0\gamma])$, where w_0 denotes the initial world. Hence, the two unit clauses $\forall \gamma \, R(w_0, [w_0\gamma])$ and $\forall v, w, \gamma, \delta \, R([v\gamma], [w\delta])$ would already suffice in case of **KD5**.

world which itself is somehow accessed; and that for **KD5** any two worlds can
indeed access each other provided both have predecessors. It is remarkable how
Segerberg's model-theoretic results are mirrored in the saturation approach and
that with essentially syntactic means; the extent of the correspondence remains to
be explored.

6.2. From saturations to inference rules

For many modal logics the semi-functional translation allows us to simplify the
background theory after saturation to a few unit clauses. There are exceptions,
however, for which the saturation is not that successful, although the simplifications
are still significant.

   The idea we will pursue in this section is to cast the whole saturation set into
a suitable inference rule instead of trying to find an alternative clause set for the
saturation found. We will illustrate how this can be done for **S4**. Recall that the
saturation for **S4** is

$$R(u, u)$$
$$R(u, [u\gamma])$$
$$\dots$$
$$R(u, [u\gamma_1 \dots \gamma_n])$$
$$\dots$$

Observe that each first argument of the respective R-literals is a variable and that
each second argument "starts" with the same variable. This observation guarantees
that — given an arbitrary unsatisfiable formula to be refuted — a corresponding
finite and unsatisfiable set of ground instances of clauses taken from this formula
contains negative R-literals only of the form $\neg R(s, [s\alpha_1 \dots \alpha_k])$. It suffices to unify
the first argument of such a negative R-literal with a *prefix* of its second argument
and thus to forget about the background theory or its saturation.

6.19. DEFINITION *(The **S4** Inference Rule)*. Let s and $t.\alpha_1 \dots \alpha_n$ be two world
terms and let C be a clause. Then the **S4** *inference rule* is the following rule

$$\frac{\neg R(s, [t\alpha_1 \dots \alpha_n]) \vee C}{\sigma C} \qquad n \geq 0,$$

where σ is the most general unifier of (s, t).

The above inference rule is the only inference mechanism that has to be added to
a clause-based theorem prover in order to obtain refutation completeness for **S4**.

6.20. DEFINITION *(The **S4** Inference System)*. The **S4** *inference system* consists
of the standard resolution and factorization rules together with the **S4** inference
rule.

6.21. THEOREM. *Let A be a uni-modal formula in negation normal form. Then A is **S4**-unsatisfiable iff the **S4** inference system refutes $\exists w\, SF(w, A)$.*

Similar inference systems can be defined for other (more complicated) modal and temporal logics; see Nonnengart [1993, 1995, 1996]. Since the functional translation for modal logics above **KD** require special unification algorithms, and the optimized semi-functional translation requires special inference rules, both require modifications of theorem provers. This has not yet been implemented, and therefore there are no systematic performance comparisons available.

7. Variations and alternatives

In this section we briefly discuss a number of alternative encodings of nonclassical logics into first-order logic and into other logics. We begin by mixing syntactic and semantic encodings. After that we discuss a number of internal, 'modal-to-modal' translations that will allow us to use FO tools to reason in non-first-order definable modal logics. We conclude the section with two flavors of encoding that escape the first-order realm but that have proved to be important for working with a large number of logics.

7.1. Mixing Hilbert-style and semantic reasoning

The translation approaches presented so far depend on the semantics of the logic under consideration, as the translation rules for the connectives and operators are derived from their semantics. In addition, first-order axiomatizations of the semantic structures are needed. If the semantics is not clear, or not first-order, the translation approaches cannot work in the usual way. But, as long as (parts of) the logic have a suitable Hilbert axiomatization, it is possible to combine Hilbert-style reasoning with the translation method [Ohlbach 1998a]. To this end the Hilbert system is encoded in first-order logic, not exactly as shown in Section 3, but similarly. Instead of the unary truth predicate T, we use a binary truth predicate $T(A, m)$. Intuitively it means "A is true in the model m."

7.1. DEFINITION *(T-Encoding).* A Hilbert axiom A with the predicate variables p_1, ..., p_n is *T-encoded* as

$$\forall p_1, \ldots, p_n\ \forall m\, T(A, m).$$

An inference rule "from $\vdash A_1, \ldots, \vdash A_k$ infer $\vdash A$" with the predicate variables $p_1, \ldots, p_n$ is *T-encoded* as

$$\forall p_1, \ldots, p_n\ (\forall m\, T(A_1, m) \wedge \cdots \wedge \forall m\, T(A_k, m) \rightarrow \forall m\, T(A, m)).$$

If A is a Hilbert axiom or rule then let $\tau(A)$ be its *T-encoding*.

The second argument of the T-predicate is completely redundant for the Hilbert system itself. It becomes important in combination with the second part of the specification, the "T-encoding" of the semantics of those operators for which a semantics is known. In the combined method it is not necessary to have a semantics and a translation rule for all operators. If, however, there is a suitable semantics for a given operator, it is encoded as a predicate logical equivalence which can be used immediately as a translation rule.

For example the semantics of the classical connective $\wedge$ (conjunction) is

$$m \models A \wedge B \text{ iff } m \models A \,\&\, m \models B.$$

Using a binary predicate $T(A, m)$ this can be expressed as a FO equivalence

$$\forall A, B \,\forall m \,(T(A \wedge B, m) \leftrightarrow (T(A, m) \wedge T(B, m))). \tag{7.1}$$

The semantics of the other classical connectives can be expressed in a similar way; observe that the symbols for the Boolean connectives are at the formula level and at the term level.

Examples for "T-encoded" semantics of nonclassical operators are:

$$\forall A \,\forall m \,(T(\Box A, m) \quad \leftrightarrow \quad \forall m' \; R(m, m') \to T(A, m')) \tag{7.2}$$

$$\forall A \,\forall m \,(T(\Diamond A, m) \quad \leftrightarrow \quad \exists m' \; R(m, m') \wedge T(A, m')) \tag{7.3}$$

$$\forall A \,\forall m \,(T(\Box A, m) \quad \leftrightarrow \quad \forall \gamma \; T(A, [m\gamma])) \tag{7.4}$$

$$\forall A \,\forall m \,(T(\Diamond A, m) \quad \leftrightarrow \quad \exists \gamma \; T(A, [m\gamma])) \tag{7.5}$$

$$\forall A \,\forall m \,(T(\bigcirc A, m) \quad \leftrightarrow \quad T(A, m + 1)) \tag{7.6}$$

$$\forall A, B \,\forall m \,(T(A \to B, m) \quad \leftrightarrow \quad \forall m' \; (R(m, m') \to T(A, m') \to T(B, m'))) \tag{7.7}$$

Equations (7.2) and (7.3) represent the standard possible worlds semantics for the modal operators $\Box$ and $\Diamond$ for modal logics above $\mathbf{K}$; (7.4) and (7.5) describe the corresponding "functional" semantics for modal logics above $\mathbf{KD}$. The γ are accessibility functions, (7.6) represents the semantics of the temporal *next* operator $\bigcirc$ in an integer-like time structure, and (7.7) is the semantics of intuitionistic implication.

The *T-encoded semantics* for the corresponding connectives and operators can be used to rewrite (translate) a term-encoded formula to the formula level of predicate logic. For example, $T(\Box(A \wedge B), m)$ can be rewritten to

$$\forall m' \,(R(m, m') \to T(A \wedge B, m'))$$

using (7.2) and then, using (7.1), further to

$$\forall m' \,(R(m, m') \to (T(A, m') \wedge T(B, m'))).$$

7.2. DEFINITION *(Semantic Normalizing)*. Given a set S of T-encoded semantics for some operators, let $\pi_S(T(A, m))$ be the formula obtained by applying the equivalences in S to $T(A, m)$ exhaustively from left to right. We call $\pi_S(T(A, m))$ the *semantically normalized* or *S-normalized* formula.

Semantic normalizing is an equivalence preserving transformation. In other words,

$$(S \wedge T(A, m)) \leftrightarrow (S \wedge \pi_S(T(A, m)))$$

holds universally. If S represents the semantics of *all* the connectives and operators occurring in some (ground) formula A, then $\forall m\ \pi_S(T(A, m))$ is essentially a FO-translated nonclassical formula. The only difference to the translation methods presented above is that in the final result of the translation, literals $T(p, m)$ are usually replaced with $p(m)$. Completeness of the semantics means that after the rewrite step the equivalences are not needed any more.

If p is a constant, there is no big difference between $T(p, m)$ and $p(m)$. If p, however, is a predicate variable, then there is a big difference between $T(p, m)$ and $p(m)$. The first literal is first-order, whereas the second literal is second-order. For clause sets of the first kind, the Herbrand Theorem applies. Whenever there is a refutation proof for some theorem, then there is also a ground refutation proof, where the variable p in $T(p, m)$ is instantiated with a term-encoded formula. This cannot be guaranteed for literals $p(m)$ with predicate variables p. Therefore, in this case $p(m)$ is stronger than $T(p, m)$. Since predicate variables implicitly quantify over formulae in a Hilbert calculus, the first-order version $T(p, m)$ is appropriate, but the second-order version $p(m)$ is not.

The set S need not contain T-encoded semantics for *all* the connectives. For example, if S only contains the semantics of the classical connectives, then

$$\pi_S(T(\square(p \wedge q) \vee r, m)) = T(\square(p \wedge q), m) \vee T(r, m).$$

The "$\wedge$" inside the $\square$ cannot be rewritten at this step, but it might be rewritten after some inference steps which bring the $\wedge$ to the top-level of the term.

Semantic normalizing can simplify T-encoded Hilbert axioms. For example the **K**-axiom "$\square A \wedge \square(A \to B) \to \square B$" for modal logic is T-encoded as

$$\forall A, B\ \forall m\ (T((\square A \wedge \square(A \to B)) \to \square B, m)) \tag{7.8}$$

and S-normalized without using a semantics of the $\square$-operator to

$$\forall A, B\ \forall m\ (T(\square A, m) \wedge T(\square(A \to B), m) \to T(\square B, m)). \tag{7.9}$$

The necessitation rule "from $\vdash A$ derive $\vdash \square A$" is T-encoded as

$$\forall A\ (\forall m\ T(A, m) \to \forall m\ T(\square A, m)). \tag{7.10}$$

7.3. DEFINITION *(Mixed Problem Specification)*. A mixed problem specification $(S, \tau_{\mathcal{F}}, C, \neg Th)$ consists of a set S of T-encoded semantics, a set $\tau_{\mathcal{F}}$ of axioms for restricting the semantic structures, a set C of T-encoded Hilbert axioms and rules and a *negated* T-encoded candidate theorem of the form $\exists \bar{p} \forall \bar{q} \exists m\ \neg T(A, m)$. It represents the problem of proving $\forall \bar{p} \exists \bar{q} \forall m\ T(A, m)$ in the logic specified by $S, \tau_{\mathcal{F}}$ and C.

The problem specification is *S-normalized* if all atoms $T(A, m)$ in $\tau_{\mathcal{F}}, C, \neg Th$ are S-normalized. The connectives with a semantics definition in S are the *defined connectives*. All other connectives are the *undefined* or *axiomatized* connectives.

The above schema is not the most general one. In some logics, for example in relevance logic, a theorem is supposed to hold only in some selected world 0. In this case one must refute the formula $\exists \bar{p} \forall \bar{q} \neg T(A, 0)$ instead of the formula with the $\exists m$ quantification. For most logics it is obvious how to adapt this schema.

Equations (7.1)–(7.7) are examples for S. (7.8) and (7.10) are examples for C. $\tau_{\mathcal{F}}$ may, for example, contain the reflexivity axiom for the accessibility relation R used in (7.2). It may also contain the restrictions on the assignment which is necessary for intuitionistic logic: for all propositional constants p: $\forall m, m'\ ((T(p, m) \wedge R(m, m')) \to T(p, m'))$. The formulae in $\tau_{\mathcal{F}}$ may actually be represented by theory unification algorithms, or by theory resolution or constraint rules; see [Nonnengart 1995].

A T-encoded mixed problem specification is first-order and can be given to any FO theorem prover. Let us illustrate the combination of S-normalizing and resolution with a simple example from modal logic.

7.4. EXAMPLE. Suppose we want to prove $\Box(A \wedge B) \to \Box A$ from the **K**-axiom and the necessitation rule, and we want to use only the semantics of the classical connectives. This means that the S-part of the mixed problem specification $(S, \tau_{\mathcal{F}}, C, \neg Th)$ consists of clauses for the booleans only; $\tau_{\mathcal{F}}$ is empty, and C contains the **K**-axiom. The S-normal form of the T-encoded K-axiom (7.8) is

$$\neg T(\Box A, w) \vee \neg T(\Box(A \to B), w) \vee T(\Box B, w). \tag{7.11}$$

The clause form of the necessitation rule (7.10) is

$$\neg T(A, f(A)) \vee T(\Box A, w) \tag{7.12}$$

where f is a Skolem function. The negation of the T-encoded theorem $\Box(A \wedge B) \to \Box A$ is rewritten to

$$T(\Box(a \wedge b), w_0) \tag{7.13}$$

$$\neg T(\Box a, w_0) \tag{7.14}$$

where a, b and w_0 are Skolem constants. Two resolution steps with (7.11), (7.13) and (7.14) yield

$$\neg T(\Box(a \wedge b \to a), w_0).$$

This is resolved with the T-encoded necessitation rule (7.12). The resolvent $\neg T(a \wedge b \to a, f(a \wedge b \to a))$ is rewritten to the following refutable set:

$$T(a, f(a \wedge b \to a))$$
$$T(b, f(a \wedge b \to a))$$
$$\neg T(a, f(a \wedge b \to a)).$$

T-encoded Hilbert axioms are particularly suited for logics with a semantics which is appropriate for translation into predicate logic, but where the class of semantic structures is not first-order axiomatizable. The second-order properties of the semantics usually correspond to particular Hilbert axioms.

With some key examples, we show that it is possible to use the basic semantics for translation, whereas the critical Hilbert axioms are just T-encoded, and not turned into conditions on the semantic structures, which may be second-order. This simplifies the proof procedures considerably. Moreover, we do not get the completeness problems related to the transition from implicit quantifiers over formulae in the Hilbert axiom to second-order quantifiers over predicates in the standard translation [Sahlqvist 1975].

7.5. EXAMPLE. We show that the McKinsey axiom (see Example 5.19) together with the transitivity of the accessibility relation implies $\Diamond(p \to \Box p)$ (atomicity). Van Benthem's semantic proof of this theorem uses the axiom of choice ("it is as serious as this" [van Benthem 1984]). We use the **KD4** possible-worlds semantics (with seriality and transitivity of the accessibility) for the modal operators instead, and leave the McKinsey axiom essentially as it is. To make the example small enough we make use of the functional semantics $S = \{(7.4),(7.5)\}$.

The T-encoded and S-normalized McKinsey axiom, using (7.4) and (7.5) for the modal operators, is

$$\forall p \forall w \, (\exists a \, \forall x \, \neg T(p, [wax]) \vee \exists b \, \forall y \, T(p, [wby])) \, ,$$

and so we obtain its clause form as $\neg T(p, [wa(w,p)x]) \vee T(p, [wb(w,p)y])$. The negated theorem $\Box(q \wedge \Diamond \neg q)$ is T-encoded and S-normalized to $T(q, [w_0 u])$ and $\neg T(q, [w_0 vc(v)])$. The empty clause is derivable in two resolution steps using the (transitive) unifier $\{p \mapsto q, w \mapsto w_0, u \mapsto a(w_0, q)x, v \mapsto b(w_0, q), y \mapsto c(b(w_0, q))\}$.

7.6. EXAMPLE. This example is from temporal logic. To make it more interesting, we choose an integer-like time structure such that an induction axiom holds:

$$p \wedge \Box(p \to \bigcirc p) \to \Box p. \tag{7.15}$$

Here, the $\Box$-operator means "always in the future" and the $\bigcirc$-operator means "at the next moment in time." The induction axiom (7.15) expresses: "if p holds now, and at all times t in the future, if p holds at time t then it holds at time $t+1$, then p will always hold in the future." The temporal semantics of the $\Box$- and $\bigcirc$-operators are functionally T-encoded as

$$\forall p \, \forall m \, (T(\Box p, m) \quad \leftrightarrow \quad \forall m' \, T(p, [mm'])) \tag{7.16}$$

$$\forall p \, \forall m \, (T(\bigcirc p, m) \quad \leftrightarrow \quad T(p, [m1])). \tag{7.17}$$

As an aside, the "functional" reading of an atom like $T(p, [mm_1 \ldots m_n])$ is that p holds at a time point determined by starting at time point m, applying the function m_1 to m to get to time point $m_1(m)$ and so on. The *next time* operator $\bigcirc$ generates a constant 1, which is to be interpreted as the successor function. For example $T(p, [ma1])$ expresses that p holds at time point $a(m) + 1$. Notice that $[m1a1]$ and $[ma11]$ as the second argument of the T-predicate denote different time points, because $a(m+1)+1$ may be different from $a(m)+1+1$. Terms like $[ma11]$ may be abbreviated as $[ma2]$.

The T-encoded induction axiom is

$$\forall p \, \forall m \, (T(p,m) \wedge \forall n \, (T(p,[mn]) \rightarrow T(p,[mn1])) \rightarrow \forall n \, T(p,[mn])) \qquad (7.18)$$

and so we get as its clause form

$$\neg T(p,m) \vee T(p,[mf(p)]) \vee T(p,[mn]) \qquad (7.19)$$
$$\neg T(p,m) \vee \neg T(p,[mf(p)1]) \vee T(p,[mn]) \qquad (7.20)$$

Suppose we want to prove the theorem $p \wedge \bigcirc p \wedge \square(p \rightarrow \bigcirc\bigcirc p) \rightarrow \square p$. After negation and translation:

(1) $T(a,m_0)$
(2) $T(a,[m_0 1])$
(3) $\neg T(a,[m_0 x]) \vee T(a,[m_0 x2])$
(4) $\neg T(a,[m_0 b])$

Here is a refutation:

(5)	$T(a \wedge \bigcirc a, m_0)$	(1), (2), (7.17), (7.1)[16]
(6)	$T(a \wedge \bigcirc a, [m_0 f(a \wedge \bigcirc a)]) \vee T(a \wedge \bigcirc a, [m_0 n])$	(5), (7.19)
(7)	$T(a, [m_0 f(a \wedge \bigcirc a)])$	(6) S-normalized, (4)[17]
(8)	$T(a, [m_0 f(a \wedge \bigcirc a)1])$	
(9)	$\neg T(a \wedge \bigcirc a, [m_0 f(a \wedge \bigcirc a)1]) \vee T(a \wedge \bigcirc a, [m_0 n])$	(5), (7.20)
(10)	$\neg T(a, [m_0 f(a \wedge \bigcirc a)1]) \vee \neg T(a, [m_0 f(a \wedge \bigcirc a)2])$	S-normalized, (4)
(11)	$\neg T(a, [m_0 f(a \wedge \bigcirc a)2])$	(10), (8)
(12)	$\neg T(a, [m_0 f(a \wedge \bigcirc a)])$	(11), (3).2
(13)	empty clause	(12), (7).

Together with T-encoded semantics definitions, T-encoded Hilbert systems yield first-order clause sets which can in principle be given to a FO theorem prover. A lot more efficiency, however, can be gained if extra mechanisms are integrated into the theorem prover [Ohlbach 1998a]. The interplay between inference steps and simplification steps using the equivalences as rewrite rules must be carefully controlled. T-encoded Hilbert axioms and rules can be quite naturally turned into theory resolution rules and even recursive applications of the theorem prover itself.

---

[16]This step actually consists of several steps. First of all, $T(a,[m_0 1])$ is turned into $T(\bigcirc a, m_0)$ using (7.17). Then $T(a,m_0)$ and $T(\bigcirc a, m_0)$ are comprised into $T(a \wedge \bigcirc a, m_0)$ using the T-encoded semantics of $\wedge$ (7.1). A heuristics for triggering these steps is that in the clauses (7.19) and (7.20) a predicate variable occurs in a Skolem function. This gives rise to the fact that a conjunction of instances of the second literal, for example $T(a,[mf(a)]) \wedge T(b,[mf(b)])$, is different to $T(a \wedge b, [mf(a \wedge b)])$. Therefore one should guide the application of clauses with predicate variables in Skolem functions such that conjunctions appear at the term level.

[17]The second literal, $T(a \wedge \bigcirc a, [m_0 n])$ is S-normalized to $T(a,[m_0 n])$ and $T(\bigcirc a,[m_0 n])$. $T(a,[m_0 n])$ is resolved against $\neg T(a,[m_0 b])$, which leaves the first literal of (6) to be S-normalized.

7.2. Indirect translations

We have already seen two examples of indirect translations of one modal logic into another one: the translation from classical modal logic to bi-modal logic given towards the end of Example 4.11, and the layered translation discussed on page 1438. The first results concerning simulations of modal logics in terms of other modal logics were results of Thomason [1974, 1975], where encodings are used to obtain substantial negative results. Thomason shows how one can encode multi-modal logics (and even second-order logic) in uni-modal logic, and obtains incompleteness results and failure of the finite model property. Kracht and Wolter [1999] define encodings of non-normal modal logics in terms of polymodal ones to obtain a series of positive results on axiomatic completeness for non-normal modal logics.

Below, we consider translations from one uni-modal logic into another uni-modal logic, with the aim of putting tools that are available for the latter to work for the former. In particular, we consider the translation from **S4** into **T** as proposed by Cerrito and Cialdea Mayer [1997]. In **S4**, the 4-axiom $\Box p \to \Box\Box p$ allows us to expand $\Box$-formulae to obtain arbitrarily long sequences of $\Box$-operators. With the help of the **T**-axiom $\Box p \to p$, on the other hand, we may delete $\Box$-operators at will.

The idea of the **S4** to **T** translation is to expand $\Box$-formulae sufficiently enough, such that during the proof search one can get the number of nested $\Box$-operators that are really needed by using the **T**-axiom to delete the superfluous $\Box$-operators. This technique must be modified somewhat for **K4**, for which the **T**-axiom is not available. In this case, all formulae $\Box A$ must be replaced by a conjunction $\Box A \wedge \Box\Box A \wedge \cdots \wedge \Box^n A$, which yields very large formulae.

The problem is to determine the maximum number of nested $\Box$-operators which will be needed in the proof, just by inspecting the formula. Cerrito and Cialdea Mayer [1997] found this number by analyzing how often the 4-axiom can be used in a tableaux refutation of a formula A in *negation normal form*. They found that $n \cdot (p+1)$ nested $\Box$-operators are sufficient, where p is the number of $\Box$-subformulae and n is the number of $\Diamond$-subformulae of A.

The precise definition of their translation $Tr_{\mathbf{S4,T}}(A, n)$ with a formula A and a natural number n as arguments is:

$$
\begin{aligned}
Tr_{\mathbf{S4,T}}(p, n) &= p \quad \text{if } p \text{ is a literal} \\
Tr_{\mathbf{S4,T}}(A \wedge B, n) &= Tr_{\mathbf{S4,T}}(A, n) \wedge Tr_{\mathbf{S4,T}}(B, n) \\
Tr_{\mathbf{S4,T}}(A \vee B, n) &= Tr_{\mathbf{S4,T}}(A, n) \vee Tr_{\mathbf{S4,T}}(B, n) \\
Tr_{\mathbf{S4,T}}(\Box A, n) &= \Box^n Tr_{\mathbf{S4,T}}(A, n) \\
Tr_{\mathbf{S4,T}}(\Diamond A, n) &= \Diamond Tr_{\mathbf{S4,T}}(A, n).
\end{aligned}
$$

The soundness and completeness theorem for this translation says that A is **S4**-satisfiable if and only if $Tr_{\mathbf{S4,T}}(A, n \cdot (p+1))$ is **T**-satisfiable. Cerrito and Cialdea Mayer's technique compiles the 4-axiom into the formula so that it will not be needed during proof search.

Demri and Goré [1998] have applied this idea to the provability logic **Grz** (for

$$Tr_{\text{Grz,S4}}(p, i) \;\; = \;\; p \;\; \text{if } p \text{ is a literal}$$

$$Tr_{\text{Grz,S4}}(\neg A, i) \;\; = \;\; \neg Tr_{\text{Grz,S4}}(A, 1 - i)$$

$$Tr_{\text{Grz,S4}}(A \wedge B, i) \;\; = \;\; Tr_{\text{Grz,S4}}(B, i) \wedge Tr_{\text{Grz,S4}}(B, i)$$

$$Tr_{\text{Grz,S4}}(A \rightarrow B, 1) \;\; = \;\; Tr_{\text{Grz,S4}}(A, 0) \rightarrow Tr_{\text{Grz,S4}}(B, 1)$$

$$Tr_{\text{Grz,S4}}(A \rightarrow B, 0) \;\; = \;\; Tr_{\text{Grz,S4}}(A, 1) \rightarrow Tr_{\text{Grz,S4}}(B, 0)$$

$$Tr_{\text{Grz,S4}}(\Box A, 1) \;\; = \;\; \Box(\Box(Tr_{\text{Grz,S4}}(A, 1) \rightarrow \Box Tr_{\text{Grz,S4}}(A, 0)) \rightarrow$$
$$Tr_{\text{Grz,S4}}(A, 1))$$

$$Tr_{\text{Grz,S4}}(\Box A, 0) \;\; = \;\; \Box Tr_{\text{Grz,S4}}(A, 0).$$

Table 9: $Tr_{\text{Grz,S4}}$

Grzegorczyk). **Grz** is an extension of **S4** with the Grz-axiom

(Grz) $\vdash \Box(\Box(A \rightarrow \Box A) \rightarrow A) \rightarrow \Box A.$

This axiom cannot be characterized by a first-order property (see [Blackburn et al. 2001, Chapter 3]). Therefore, the usual translations into FO are not applicable. Demri and Goré's translation function $Tr_{\text{Grz,S4}}(A, i)$ works for formulae A which need not be in negation normal form; see Table 9. The second argument i is merely used to record the polarity of the subformula.

Exploiting the properties of a cut-free Gentzen calculus for **Grz**, Demri and Goré could prove that a formula A is a **Grz**-theorem if and only if $Tr_{\text{Grz,S4}}(A, 1)$ is a **S4**-theorem.

The recursive nature of the translation rule for $\Box A$ can cause an exponential blow-up. This can be avoided using standard renaming techniques. Complex subformulae which might get duplicated repeatedly are replaced by new predicate symbols. Adding the definition of these predicate symbols to the original formula usually does not cause a more than polynomial blow-up. By combining the translations $Tr_{\text{Grz,S4}}$, $Tr_{\text{S4,T}}$ and ST_m, with suitable renamings of subformulae, Demri and Goré finally obtained a translation from **Grz** into FO such that the size of the translated formulae is $\mathcal{O}((n \log n)^3)$ times the size of the original formula.

Indirect translations like $Tr_{\text{Grz,S4}}$ and $Tr_{\text{S4,T}}$ depend very much on the proof theoretic properties of the logic. There is no simple recipe for developing indirect translations. The general idea is to compile Hilbert axioms into the translated formulae. Slight changes to the logic itself, however, may make the translation impossible. Nevertheless, as $Tr_{\text{Grz,S4}}$ has shown, this technique may help considerably in applying FO proof techniques to complex logics with higher-order features (cf. also [Herzig 1990] which contains a translation from the provability logic **G** into **K4**).

7.3. Translations into SnS

In the previous section we managed to reason with an essentially second-order logic such as **Grz** by first-order means. The techniques were very specific, however. The aim of this section is to explore a more general technique for translation-based reasoning with modal logics that escape the first-order realm: translating into the monadic second-order theory of n successor functions. The big advantage of the approach is the large expressive power of the target logic: it allows us to obtain decidability results and reasoning procedures for a large class of modal logics.

The set of monadic second-order logic (MSO) formulae includes all atomic formulae $s = t$, and $X(s)$, where s and t are terms and X is a unary set variable. MSO formulae are closed under the usual boolean connectives, first-order quantifiers over individual variables ($\exists x$, $\forall x$), and second-order quantifiers over the set variables ($\exists X$, $\forall X$). Let $\mathcal{T}_n$ denote the structure of n ($1 \leq n \leq \omega$) successor functions; it is the infinite, uniformly n-branching tree, where the i-th successor function leads to the i-th daughter of a node.

By SnS we denote the monadic second-order theory of n successor functions, and by WSnS we denote the *weak* monadic second-order theory of n successor functions, where the set variables are constrained to range over finite sets only. The decidability of WSnS is due to Thatcher and Wright [1968] and Doner [1970]. The decidability of SnS is known as *Rabin's Tree Theorem* [Rabin 1969]. The decidability of WSnS is based on a close correspondence between formulae in WSnS and finite automata. More precisely, any relation definable in WS2S can also be defined by a tree automaton that encodes the satisfying assignments to the formula in the labels on the nodes of the tree that it accepts. The coding is simple: assignment functions map first-order variables to nodes in $\mathcal{T}_2$ and second-order variables to sets of nodes in $\mathcal{T}_2$. The labeling functions on the trees accepted by the automaton do the opposite: they map nodes to the set of variables to which that is assigned.

When dealing with *weak* S2S, all sets are finite, so we can restrict ourselves to automata over finite trees; since efficient minimization techniques exists for finite trees, this opens the way to the development of automated reasoning tools, at least in principle. But there are some challenging difficulties. The correspondence between WS2S and automata is an inductive one, that follows the construction of formulae. Now, the negation construction on automata only works for deterministic automata, while the projection function (which implements quantification) yields *non*-deterministic automata. Using the subset construction, tree automata may be determinized, but at the cost of an exponential blow-up. Nevertheless, the logic-automata connection may be used successfully for a number of purposes.

For a start, it provides a powerful tool for establishing decidability results in nonclassical logic. Rabin's Tree Theorem was applied in modal logic almost immediately: Fine [1970] used it to prove decidability results in second-order modal logic (that is, modal logic in which it is possible to bind propositional variables), and Gabbay [1971a, 1971b, 1971c] applied it to a wide range of modal logics in many different languages. These papers are essential reading for readers interested in the method, though before tackling them, it's probably best to first see what Gabbay,

Hodkinson and Reynolds [1994] have to say on the subject.

Secondly, as indicated above, the decision procedure for WS2S is semantically based: it translates a WS2S formula A to an automaton $\mathcal{A}_A$ that recognizes valuations verifying A. The MONA system [Henriksen, Jensen, Jørgensen, Klarlund, Paige, Rauhe and Sandhol 1995] implements this decision procedure. Input to MONA is a script consisting of a sequence of definitions followed by a formula A to be proved. MONA computes $\mathcal{A}_A$ and, depending on the result, declares A to be valid or delivers a counter example. Despite the non-elementary worst-case complexity of WS2S, MONA works well in practice on a large range of problems; Basin and Klarlund [1998] offer empirical evidence and an analysis of why this is the case. At the time of writing there are no experimental results evaluating the performance of tools such as MONA on nonclassical logics such as propositional dynamic logic.

7.4. Translations into weak set theories

The final approach towards translation-based automated reasoning for modal logic that we want to mention here is due to Montanari, Policriti, and their colleagues and students. In [D'Agostino, Montanari and Policriti 1995] they propose a translation of modal logic into (weak) set theories that works for all normal complete finitely axiomatizable modal logics, not just for the ones that are complete with respect to a first-order definable class of structures. In particular, the method is also applicable if the modal logic at hand is specified with Hilbert axioms only.

The basic idea is to represent a Kripke frame as a set, with the accessibility relation modeled using the membership relation $\in$. For computational reasons the set theory that axiomatizes $\in$ should be a finitely (first-order) axiomatizable theory Ω. Given a modal formula $A(p_1, \ldots, p_n)$, its translation as a set-theoretic term with variables $x, x_1, \ldots, x_n$ is written as $A^*(x, x_1, \ldots, x_n)$. The latter represents the set of states in the frame x in which the formula A holds.

To make things precise, we start by specifying the theory Ω; its (first-order) language contains relation symbols $\in$, $\subseteq$, and function symbols $\cup$, $\setminus$, and Pow (the power set operation). The axioms are $x \in y \cup z \leftrightarrow x \in y \vee x \in z$; $x \in y \setminus z \leftrightarrow x \in y \wedge x \notin z$; $x \subseteq y \leftrightarrow \forall z\, (z \in x \rightarrow z \in y)$; and $x \in Pow(y) \leftrightarrow x \subseteq y$. Observe that this theory Ω lacks both the extensionality and foundation axioms found in traditional set theories; in fact, the authors prefer to work with set-theoretic universes satisfying the *anti*-foundation axiom AFA [Aczel 1988].

Now, the translation $(\cdot)^*$ is defined as follows:

$$
\begin{array}{llll}
p_i^* & := & x_i & \qquad (A \vee B)^* & := & A^* \cup B^* \\
(\neg A)^* & := & x \setminus A^* & \qquad (\Box A)^* & := & Pow(A^*),
\end{array}
\tag{$\dagger$}
$$

where x is a variable different from x_i $(i = 1, \ldots, n)$.

7.7. THEOREM. *For any finitely axiomatizable modal logic* $\mathbf{L} = \mathbf{K} + B(\alpha_1, \ldots, \alpha_m)$, *where* $B(\alpha_1, \ldots, \alpha_m)$ *is an axiom schema, the following are equivalent:*

1. $\vdash_{\mathbf{L}} A(p_1, \ldots, p_n)$

2. $\Omega \vdash \forall x\, (\textit{Trans}(x) \wedge \textit{Axiom}_{\mathbf{L}}(x) \to \forall x_1 \ldots \forall x_n\, (x \subseteq A^*(x, x_1, \ldots, x_n)))$.

Here, $\textit{Trans}(x)$ is short for $\forall y\, (y \in x \to y \subseteq x)$, and $\textit{Axiom}_{\mathbf{L}}(x)$ is short for $\forall y_1 \ldots \forall y_m\, (x \subseteq B^*(x, y_1, \ldots, y_m))$.

Instead of translating Hilbert axioms, one may use a semantics for **L** whenever it is available. Furthermore, the method is easily extended to poly-modal logics. As to actual reasoning with the set theories into which modal logics are translated, D'Agostino et al. [1995] consider the use of theory resolution; to this end, skolemized versions of Ω must be decidable [Policriti and Schwartz 1992]. At the time of writing, experimental results comparing the approach to other translation-based approaches to automated reasoning in modal logic are not available.

Van Benthem, D'Agostino, Montanari and Policriti [1997] extend the connection between modal logic and set theory outlined above to capture a larger part of the non r.e. notion of modal logical consequence. The notion of validity on so-called *general frames* [Blackburn et al. 2001, Chapter 5] — and hence modal derivability in its full strength — can be captured by modifying the translation (†) without changing the underlying set theory Ω. To deal with so-called *extended modal logics* [de Rijke 1993], there is a further proposal to enrich the underlying set theory Ω containing, essentially, the Gödel constructible functions that allows one to capture weak monadic second-order logic [van Benthem, D'Agostino, Montanari and Policriti 1998].

8. Conclusion

In this chapter we have discussed various ways of translating nonclassical logics into first-order predicate logic. We have tried to explain the basic ideas and principles to help the reader understand and apply the ideas to his or her own logic.

Nonclassical logics presented as Hilbert systems can be translated into FO by encoding the formulae as FO-terms. This is the easiest and most flexible way of encoding a nonclassical logic in FO. Unfortunately, FO theorem provers are extremely inefficient for this kind of encoding.

Many familiar nonclassical logics, however, enjoy a sound and complete possible worlds semantics. We have shown how to derive a relational translation directly from their semantics. The main purpose of the translation idea is to use the results, tools, and techniques from the target logic, in particular theorem provers, for proving translated theorems. Unfortunately, standard inference techniques for FO do not automatically provide decision procedures for the corresponding fragments. To overcome this we presented modifications of the translation method.

The layered relational translation encodes a very strong form of the tree model property; it can be used as a preprocessing technique for existing tools. Resolution (with factoring and condensing) refined by a very simple ordering may be used as a decision procedure for the resulting modal fragment.

Another, more dramatic, modification of the relational translation starts from the observation that binary relations can be decomposed into sets of functions. In the resulting functional translation, reasoning about accessible worlds is incorporated into the unification algorithm. Resolution becomes a decision procedure without any special strategies. Specifying frame classes in the functional style may introduce equations. This is an advantage if the equations can be turned into a theory unification algorithm, and the algorithm can actually be incorporated in a prover. Unfortunately, only the developer of a theorem prover is usually able to do this.

To overcome this problem we introduced the semi-functional translation. In the case of modal logic it translates the ◇-operator functionally and the □-operator relationally. The characteristic frame properties are specified relationally. Using saturation techniques one can simplify the characteristic frame axioms considerably. In the end we achieved the best of both kinds of translations: small translated formulae and the possibility to do a considerable part of the reasoning about accessible worlds within the (standard) unification algorithm, and an optimized treatment of the characteristic frame axioms without having to change the implementation of the unification algorithm.

Finally, we presented a few examples of indirect translations for modal logics where the Hilbert axioms are compiled into modal formulae. This way one can even translate logics with second-order properties into first-order logic. The techniques, however, are very specific to the logics, and require a detailed analysis of a Gentzen or sequent type proof system. More widely applicable solutions for logics with second-order properties are provided by translations into SnS, or into weak set theories.

In the course of this chapter we have touched on many open issues, ranging from examining the performance of provers on (translated) nonclassical logics other than familiar modal logics (page 1440), to the connection between Segerberg's cluster-based analysis of modal logics and saturating background theories in the semi-functional translation approach (page 1464).

The big issue that drives the field as a whole, however, is how we can encode, by syntactic means, the restricted nature of source logics inside the target logic. We have seen several proposals, formulated in terms of special fragments such as finite variable fragments or guarded fragments, or in terms of modified translations such as the layered, functional, and semi-functional translation. It is not the actual syntax that matters here. The satisfiability problem for the logics we consider is usually PSPACE-hard or worse [Ladner 1977, Fagin et al. 1995, Blackburn et al. 2001]. Therefore, the performance of satisfiability checkers depends more on the strategies and heuristics than on the actual syntax, whether it is the original or the translated one. Different syntactic presentations, however, may give more or less easy access to the information which is relevant for strategies and heuristics to guide the search. What really matters is the right combination of the syntactic presentation of the satisfiability problem and the corresponding search control mechanisms. For the time being there is no clear winner among the different approaches.

To conclude the chapter, we return to an issue raised in the introduction to this chapter: at the end of the day, what should one use: direct, purpose-built proof tools for nonclassical logics, or indirect, translation-based ones? The problem of finding efficient proof procedures for the translated formulae has not yet been solved satisfactorily. The main reason for this is that the original motivation for developing translation methods came from the desire to use existing predicate logic theorem provers for proving theorems in nonclassical logics *without* making any changes to the implementation of the theorem prover. This works, but only to a certain extent. Experience has shown that we need special, purpose-built refinements to complement our translations if we are going to keep up with dedicated tools, and more importantly, if we are going to get acceptable performance.

Acknowledgments

We would like to thank the editors for their patience. Maarten de Rijke was supported by the Spinoza project 'Logic in Action' and by a grant from the Netherlands Organization for Scientific Research (NWO), under project number 365-20-005.

Bibliography

ACZEL P. [1988], *Non-Well-Founded Sets*, CSLI Publications.

ANDRÉKA H., VAN BENTHEM J. AND NÉMETI I. [1998], 'Modal languages and bounded fragments of predicate logic', *Journal of Philosophical Logic* **27**, 217–274.

ANDREWS P. [2001], Classical type theory, *in* A. Robinson and A. Voronkov, eds, 'Handbook of Automated Reasoning', Vol. II, Elsevier Science, chapter 15, pp. 965–1007.

ARECES C. AND DE RIJKE M. [2000], Description and/or hybrid logic, *in* 'Proceedings AiML-ICTL 2000'.

ARECES C., GENNARI R., HEGUIABEHERE J. AND DE RIJKE M. [2000], Tree-based heuristics for modal theorem proving, *in* W. Horn, ed., 'Proceedings ECAI-2000', IOS Press.

AUER P. [1992], Unification with associative functions, PhD thesis, Technical University Vienna.

AUFFRAY Y. AND ENJALBERT P. [1992], 'Modal theorem proving: An equational viewpoint', *Journal of Logic and Computation* **2**(3), 247–297.

BAADER F. AND SNYDER W. [2001], Unification theory, *in* A. Robinson and A. Voronkov, eds, 'Handbook of Automated Reasoning', Vol. I, Elsevier Science, chapter 8, pp. 445–532.

BAAZ M., EGLY U. AND LEITSCH A. [2001], Normal form transformations, *in* A. Robinson and A. Voronkov, eds, 'Handbook of Automated Reasoning', Vol. I, Elsevier Science, chapter 5, pp. 273–333.

BAAZ M., FERMÜLLER C. AND LEITSCH A. [1994], A non-elementary speed up in proof length by structural clause transformation, *in* 'Proceedings LICS'94: Logic in Computer Science', IEEE Computer Society, pp. 213–219.

BAAZ M., FERMÜLLER C. AND SALZER G. [2001], Automated deduction for many-valued logics, *in* A. Robinson and A. Voronkov, eds, 'Handbook of Automated Reasoning', Vol. II, Elsevier Science, chapter 20, pp. 1355–1402.

BACHMAIR L. AND GANZINGER H. [2001], Resolution theorem proving, *in* A. Robinson and A. Voronkov, eds, 'Handbook of Automated Reasoning', Vol. I, Elsevier Science, chapter 2, pp. 19–99.

BARENDREGT H. AND GEUVERS H. [2001], Proof-assistants using dependent type systems, *in* A. Robinson and A. Voronkov, eds, 'Handbook of Automated Reasoning', Vol. II, Elsevier Science, chapter 18, pp. 1149–1238.

BASIN D. AND KLARLUND N. [1998], 'Automata based symbolic reasoning in hardware verification', *Journal of Formal Methods in Systems Design* **13**, 255–288.

BLACKBURN P., DE RIJKE M. AND VENEMA Y. [2001], *Modal Logic*, Cambridge University Press.

BLI [2000]. Bliksem Version 1.10B. URL: http://www.mpi-sb.mpg.de/~bliksem/. Accessed Jan. 16, 2000.

BOCKMAYR A. AND WEISPFENNING V. [2001], Solving numerical constraints, *in* A. Robinson and A. Voronkov, eds, 'Handbook of Automated Reasoning', Vol. I, Elsevier Science, chapter 12, pp. 749–842.

BUNDY A. [2001], The automation of proof by mathematical induction, *in* A. Robinson and A. Voronkov, eds, 'Handbook of Automated Reasoning', Vol. I, Elsevier Science, chapter 13, pp. 845–911.

CALVANESE D., GIACOMO G. D., LENZERINI M. AND NARDI D. [2001], Reasoning in expressive description logics, *in* A. Robinson and A. Voronkov, eds, 'Handbook of Automated Reasoning', Vol. II, Elsevier Science, chapter 23, pp. 1581–1634.

CERRITO S. AND CIALDEA MAYER M. [1997], 'A polynomial translation of **S4** into **T** and contraction-free tableaux for **S4**', *Logic Journal of the IGPL* **5**(2), 287–300.

CHELLAS B. F. [1980], *Modal Logic: An Introduction*, Cambridge University Press, Cambridge.

CHOU S. C. AND GAO X. S. [2001], Automated reasoning in geometry, *in* A. Robinson and A. Voronkov, eds, 'Handbook of Automated Reasoning', Vol. I, Elsevier Science, chapter 11, pp. 705–747.

CLARKE E. AND EMERSON E. [1982], 'Using branching time temporal logic to synthesize synchronization skeletons', *Science of Computer Programming* **2**, 241–266.

CLARKE E. AND SCHLINGLOFF H. [2001], Model checking, *in* A. Robinson and A. Voronkov, eds, 'Handbook of Automated Reasoning', Vol. II, Elsevier Science, chapter 24, pp. 1635–1790.

COMON H. [2001], Inductionless induction, *in* A. Robinson and A. Voronkov, eds, 'Handbook of Automated Reasoning', Vol. I, Elsevier Science, chapter 14, pp. 913–962.

D'AGOSTINO G., MONTANARI A. AND POLICRITI A. [1995], 'A set-theoretic translation method for polymodal logics', *Journal of Automated Reasoning* **15**, 317–337.

DAVIS M. [2001], The early history of automated deduction, *in* A. Robinson and A. Voronkov, eds, 'Handbook of Automated Reasoning', Vol. I, Elsevier Science, chapter 1, pp. 3–15.

DE NIVELLE H. [1998], A resolution decision procedure for the guarded fragment, *in* C. Kirchner and H. Kirchner, eds, 'Proceedings CADE-15: International Conference on Automated Deduction', Vol. 1421 of *LNAI*, Springer-Verlag, pp. 191–204.

DE NIVELLE H. [1999], A new translation method for **S4**. Manuscript.

DE NIVELLE H. AND DE RIJKE M. [to appear], 'Deciding the guarded fragments by resolution', *Journal of Symbolic Computation* .

DE RIJKE M. [1993], Extending Modal Logic, PhD thesis, ILLC, University of Amsterdam.

DE RIJKE M. [1999], Restricted description languages. Manuscript, ILLC, University of Amsterdam.

DEGTYAREV A. AND VORONKOV A. [2001*a*], Equality reasoning in sequent-based calculi, *in* A. Robinson and A. Voronkov, eds, 'Handbook of Automated Reasoning', Vol. I, Elsevier Science, chapter 10, pp. 609–704.

DEGTYAREV A. AND VORONKOV A. [2001*b*], The inverse method, *in* A. Robinson and A. Voronkov, eds, 'Handbook of Automated Reasoning', Vol. I, Elsevier Science, chapter 4, pp. 179–272.

DEMRI S. AND GORÉ R. [1998], An $\mathcal{O}((n \log n)^3)$-time transformation from *Grz* into decidable fragments of classical first-order logic, *in* 'Proceedings FTP'98: International Workshop on First-Order Theorem Proving', TU-Wien Technical Report E1852-GS-981, pp. 127–134.

DERSHOWITZ N. AND PLAISTED D. [2001], Rewriting, *in* A. Robinson and A. Voronkov, eds, 'Handbook of Automated Reasoning', Vol. I, Elsevier Science, chapter 9, pp. 533–608.

DIX J., FURBACH U. AND NIEMELÄ I. [2001], Nonmonotonic reasoning: Towards efficient calculi and implementations, *in* A. Robinson and A. Voronkov, eds, 'Handbook of Automated Reasoning', Vol. II, Elsevier Science, chapter 19, pp. 1241–1354.

DONER J. [1970], 'Tree acceptors and some of their applications', *Journal of Computer and System Sciences* **4**, 406–451.

DOWEK G. [2001], Higher-order unification and matching, *in* A. Robinson and A. Voronkov, eds, 'Handbook of Automated Reasoning', Vol. II, Elsevier Science, chapter 16, pp. 1009–1062.

EMERSON E. AND HALPERN J. [1985], 'Decision procedures and expressiveness in the temporal logic of brnaching time', *Journal of Computer and System Sciences* **30**, 1–24.

FAGIN R., HALPERN J., MOSES Y. AND VARDI M. [1995], *Reasoning About Knowledge*, The MIT Press.

FARIÑAS DEL CERRO L. AND HERZIG A. [1988], Linear modal deductions, *in* E. Lusk and R. Overbeek, eds, 'Proceedings CADE'88: International Conference on Automated Deduction', Springer.

FERMÜLLER C., LEITSCH A., HUSTADT U. AND TAMMET T. [2001], Resolution decision procedures, *in* A. Robinson and A. Voronkov, eds, 'Handbook of Automated Reasoning', Vol. II, Elsevier Science, chapter 25, pp. 1791–1849.

FERMÜLLER C., LEITSCH A., TAMMET T. AND ZAMOV N. [1993], *Resolution Methods for the Decision Problem*, Vol. 679 of *LNAI*, Springer.

FINE K. [1970], 'Propositional quantifiers in modal logic', *Theoria* **36**, 331–346.

GABBAY D. [1971*a*], 'Decidability results in non-classical logics', *Annals of Mathematical Logic* **10**, 237–285.

GABBAY D. [1971*b*], 'On decidable, finitely axiomatizable modal and tense logics without the finite model property I', *Israel Journal of Mathematics* **10**, 478–495.

GABBAY D. [1971*c*], 'On decidable, finitely axiomatizable modal and tense logics without the finite model property II', *Israel Journal of Mathematics* **10**, 496–503.

GABBAY D. [1981*a*], Expressive functional completeness in tense logic (preliminary report), *in* U. Mönnich, ed., 'Aspects of Philosophical Logic', Reidel, pp. 91–117.

GABBAY, D. AND GUENTHNER, F., EDS [1984], *Handbook of Philosophical Logic*, Vol. 2, Reidel, Dordrecht.

GABBAY D., HODKINSON I. AND REYNOLDS M. [1994], *Temporal Logic: Mathematical Foundations and Computational Aspects*, Oxford University Press.

GABBAY D. M. [1981*b*], An irreflexivity lemma with applications to axiomatizations of conditions on tense frames, *in* U. Monnich, ed., 'Aspects of Philosophical Logic', Reidel, pp. 67–89.

GABBAY D. M. [1996], *Labelled Deductive Systems; Principles and Applications. Vol 1: Introduction*, Vol. 126, Oxford University Press.

GABBAY D. M. [1999], *Fibring Logics*, Oxford University Press.

GANZINGER H. AND DE NIVELLE H. [1999], A superposition decision procedure for the guarded fragment with equality, *in* 'Proceedings LICS'99: Logic in Computer Science', IEEE Computer Society, pp. 295–304.

GANZINGER H., MEYER C. AND VEANES M. [1999], The two-variable guarded fragment with transitive relations, *in* 'Proceedings LICS'99: Logic in Computer Science', IEEE Computer Society, pp. 24–34.

GASQUET O. AND HERZIG A. [1993], Translating non-normal modal logics into normal modal logics, *in* I. J. Jones and M. Sergot, eds, 'Proceedings DEON-94: International Workshop on Deontic Logic in Computer Science', TANO, Oslo.

GIUNCHIGLIA E., GIUNCHIGLIA F. AND TACCHELLA A. [2000], 'SAT-based decision procedures for classical modal logics', pp. 403–426.

GÖDEL K. [1932], 'Ein Spezialfall des Entscheidungsproblem der theoretischen Logik', *Ergebn. math. Kolloq.* **2**, 113–115.

GOLDBLATT R. [1992], *Logics of Time and Computation*, CSLI Publications.

GRÄDEL E. [2000], 'On the restraining power of guards', *Journal of Symbolic Logic* . to appear.

GRÄDEL E., OTTO M. AND ROSEN E. [1997*a*], Two-variable logic with counting is decidable, *in* 'Proceedings LICS'97: Logic in Computer Science', IEEE Computer Society, pp. 306–317.

GRÄDEL E., OTTO M. AND ROSEN E. [1997b], Undecidability results on two-variable logics, in 'Proceedings STACS'97', Vol. 1200 of *LNCS*, Springer, pp. 249–260.

GRÄDEL E. AND WALUKIEWICZ I. [1999], Guarded fixed point logic, in 'Proceedings LICS'99: Logic in Computer Science', IEEE Computer Society, pp. 45–54.

GRAF P. [1996], *Term Indexing*, Vol. 1053 of *LNAI*, Springer.

HÄHNLE R. [2001], Tableaux and related methods, in A. Robinson and A. Voronkov, eds, 'Handbook of Automated Reasoning', Vol. I, Elsevier Science, chapter 3, pp. 100–178.

HÁJEK P. AND PUDLÁK P. [1991], *Metamathematics of First-Order Arithmetic*, Perspectives in Mathematical Logic, Springer.

HALPERN J. [1995], 'The effect of bounding the number of primitive propositions and the depth of nesting on the complexity of modal logic', *Artificial Intelligence* **75**, 361–372.

HAREL D. [1984], Dynamic logic, in Gabbay and Guenthner [1984], pp. 497–604.

HENKIN L. [1967], 'Logical systems containing only a finite number of symbols'. Séminiare de Mathématique Supérieures 21, Les Presses de l'Université de Montréal, Montréal.

HENRIKSEN J., JENSEN J., JØRGENSEN M., KLARLUND N., PAIGE R., RAUHE T. AND SANDHOL A. [1995], MONA: Monadic second-order logic in practice, in 'Proceedings TACAS'95', LNCS, Springer, pp. 479–506.

HERZIG A. [1989], Raisonnement Automatique en Logique Modale et Algorithmes d'unification., PhD thesis, Université Paul-Sabatier, Toulouse.

HERZIG A. [1990], 'A translation from propositional modal logic G into K4', Université Paul Sabatier, Toulouse.

HORROCKS I., PATEL-SCHNEIDER P. AND SEBASTIANI R. [2000], 'An analysis of emperical testing for modal decision procedures', *Logic Journal of the IGPL* **8**(3), 293–323.

HUSTADT U. [1999], Resolution-Based Decision Procedures for Subclasses of First-Order Logic, PhD thesis, Max-Planck Institute for Computer Science, Saarbrücken.

HUSTADT U., SCHMIDT R. AND WEIDENBACH C. [1998], Optimised functional translation and resolution, in 'Proceedings Tableaux'98', LNCS, Springer, pp. 36–37.

IMMERMAN N. AND KOZEN D. [1987], Definability with bounded number of bound variables, in 'Proceedings LICS'87: Logic in Computer Science', IEEE Computer Society, Washington, pp. 236–244.

JANIN D. AND WALUKIEWICZ I. [1996], On the expressive completeness of the propositional μ-calculus w.r.t. monadic second-order logic, in 'Proceedings CONCUR'96', pp. 263–277.

JOYNER JR. J. [1976], 'Resolution strategies as decision procedures', *Journal of the ACM* **23**, 398–417.

KALMÁR L. [1933], 'Über die Erfüllbarkeit derjenigen Zählausdrücke, welche in der Normalform zwei benachbarte Allzeichen enthalten', *Math. Annal.* **108**, 466–484.

KRACHT M. AND WOLTER F. [1999], 'Normal monomodal logics can simulate all others', *Journal of Symbolic Logic* **64**, 99–138.

KURTONINA N. AND DE RIJKE M. [1997], 'Bisimulations for temporal logic', *Journal of Logic, Language and Information* **6**, 403–425.

KURTONINA N. AND DE RIJKE M. [1999], 'Expressiveness of concept expressions in first-order description logics', *Artificial Intelligence* **107**, 303–333.

LADNER R. [1977], 'The computational complexity of provability in systems of modal logic', *SIAM Journal on Computing* **6**, 467–480.

LETZ R. AND STENZ G. [2001], Model elimination and connection tableau procedures, in A. Robinson and A. Voronkov, eds, 'Handbook of Automated Reasoning', Vol. II, Elsevier Science, chapter 28, pp. 2015–2114.

LUKASIEWICZ J. [1970], *Selected Works*, North Holland. Edited by L. Borkowski.

MCCUNE W. AND WOS L. [1992], Experiments in automated deduction with condensed detachment, in D. Kapur, ed., 'Proceedings CADE-11', Vol. 607 of *LNAI*, Springer Verlag, pp. 209–223.

MINTS G. [1989], 'Resolution calculi for modal logics', *Amer. Math. Soc. Transl.* **143**, 1–14.

MOLLER F. AND RABINOVICH A. [1999], On the expressive power of CTL*, *in* 'Proceedings LICS'99: Logic in Computer Science', IEEE Computer Society, pp. 360–369.

MORTIMER M. [1975], 'On languages with two variables', *Zeitschr. f. math. Logik u. Grundlagen d. Math.* **21**, 135–140.

NIEUWENHUIS R. AND RUBIO A. [2001], Paramodulation-based theorem proving, *in* A. Robinson and A. Voronkov, eds, 'Handbook of Automated Reasoning', Vol. I, Elsevier Science, chapter 7, pp. 371–443.

NONNENGART A. [1992], First-order modal logic theorem proving and standard PROLOG, Technical Report MPI-I-92-228, Max-Planck-Institute for Computer Science, Saarbrücken, Germany.

NONNENGART A. [1993], First-order modal logic theorem proving and functional simulation, *in* R. Bajcsy, ed., 'Proceedings IJCAI-13', Vol. 1, Morgan Kaufmann Publishers, pp. 80–85.

NONNENGART A. [1995], A Resolution-Based Calculus for Temporal Logics, PhD thesis, Universität des Saarlandes, Saarbrücken, Germany.

NONNENGART A. [1996], Resolution-based calculi for modal and temporal logics, *in* S. McRobbie, ed., 'Proceedings CADE-13: International Conference on Automated Deduction', Vol. 1104 of *LNAI*, Springer Verlag, pp. 598–612.

NONNENGART A. AND WEIDENBACH C. [2001], Computing small clause normal forms, *in* A. Robinson and A. Voronkov, eds, 'Handbook of Automated Reasoning', Vol. I, Elsevier Science, chapter 6, pp. 335–367.

OHLBACH H. J. [1988a], A resolution calculus for modal logics, *in* E. Lusk and R. Overbeek, eds, 'Proceedings CADE-88: International Conference on Automated Deduction', Vol. 310 of *LNCS*, Springer-Verlag, pp. 500–516.

OHLBACH H. J. [1988b], A resolution calculus for modal logics, SEKI Report SR-88-08, FB Informatik, Universität Kaiserslautern, Germany. PhD Thesis, short version appeared in [Ohlbach 1988a].

OHLBACH H. J. [1991], 'Semantics based translation methods for modal logics', *Journal of Logic and Computation* **1**(5), 691–746.

OHLBACH H. J. [1998a], Combining Hilbert-style and semantic reasoning in a resolution framework, *in* C. Kirchner and H. Kirchner, eds, 'Proceedings CADE-15: International Conference on Automated Deduction', Vol. 1421 of *LNAI*, Springer Verlag, pp. 205–219.

OHLBACH H. J. [1998b], 'Elimination of self-resolving clauses', *Journal of Automated Reasoning* **20**(3), 317–336.

OHLBACH H. J. AND SCHMIDT R. A. [1997], 'Functional translation and second-order frame properties of modal logics', *Journal of Logic and Computation* **7**(5), 581–603.

OHLBACH H. J. AND WRIGHTSON G. [1984], Solving a problem in relevance logic with an automated theorem prover, *in* R. E. Shostak, ed., 'Proceedings CADE-7: International Conference on Automated Deduction', Vol. 170 of *LNCS*, Springer Verlag, pp. 496–508.

OHLBACH H., NONNENGART A., DE RIJKE M. AND GABBAY D. [2001], Encoding two-valued nonclassical logics in classical logic, *in* A. Robinson and A. Voronkov, eds, 'Handbook of Automated Reasoning', Vol. II, Elsevier Science, chapter 21, pp. 1403–1486.

OTTO M. [1997], *Bounded Variable Logics and Counting — A Study in Finite Models*, Vol. 9 of *Lecture Notes in Logic*, Springer.

PATEL-SCHNEIDER P. [1998], DLP system description, *in* 'Proceedings DL'98', pp. 87–89. URL: http://suncite.informatik.rwth-aachen.de/Publications/CEUR-WS.

PAULSON L. C. [1994], *Isabelle: a Generic Theorem Prover*, Vol. 828 of *LNCS*, Springer Verlag, Berlin.

PFENNING F. [2001], Logical frameworks, *in* A. Robinson and A. Voronkov, eds, 'Handbook of Automated Reasoning', Vol. II, Elsevier Science, chapter 17, pp. 1063–1147.

POLICRITI A. AND SCHWARTZ J. [1992], T-theorem proving I, Research report 08/92, Università di Udine.

QUINE W. [1953], *From a Logical Point of View*, Harvard Umiversity Press.

RABIN M. [1969], 'Decidability of second-order theories and automata on infinite trees', *Transactions of the American Mathematical Society* **141**, 1–35.

RAMAKRISHNAN I., SEKAR R. AND VORONKOV A. [2001], Term indexing, *in* A. Robinson and A. Voronkov, eds, 'Handbook of Automated Reasoning', Vol. II, Elsevier Science, chapter 26, pp. 1853–1964.

ROSEN E. [1997], 'Modal logic over finite structures', *Journal of Logic, Language and Information* **6**, 427–439.

ROUNDS W. [1997], Feature logics, *in* van Benthem and ter Meulen [1997].

SAHLQVIST H. [1975], Completeness and correspondence in the first and second order semantics for modal logics, *in* S. Kanger, ed., 'Proceedings of the 3rd Scandinavian Logic Symposium, 1973', North Holland, Amsterdam, pp. 110–143.

SCHMIDT R. [1997], Optimised Modal Translation and Resolution, PhD thesis, Universität des Saarlandes.

SCHMIDT R. A. [1998a], E-unification for subsystems of **S4**, *in* 'Proceedings RTA'98: Term Rewriting and Applications', Vol. 1379 of *LNCS*, Springer, pp. 106–120.

SCHMIDT R. A. [1998b], Resolution is a decision procedure for many propositional modal logics, *in* M. Kracht, M. de Rijke, H. Wansing and M. Zakharyaschev, eds, 'Advances in Modal Logic, Vol. 1', CSLI Publications, pp. 189–208.

SCHÜTTE K. [1934], 'Untersuchungen zum Entscheidungsproblem der mathematischen Logik', *Math. Annal.* **109**, 572–603.

SCOTT D. [1962], 'A decision method for validity of sentences in two variables', *Journal of Symbolic Logic* **27**, 377.

SEGERBERG K. [1971], An essay in classical modal logic, Technical Report 13, University of Uppsala, Filosofiska Studier. Volume 1-3.

TAN [2000]. TANCS: Tableaux Non Classical Systems Comparison. URL: http://www.dis.uniroma1.it/~tancs/. Accessed Jan. 16, 2000.

THATCHER J. AND WRIGHT J. [1968], 'Generalized finite automata theory with an application to a decision problem of second-order logic', *Mathematical Systems Theory* **2**, 57–81.

THOMASON S. [1974], 'Reduction of tense logic to modal logic I', *Journal of Symbolic Logic* **39**, 549–551.

THOMASON S. [1975], 'Reduction of tense logic to modal logic II', *Theoria* **41**, 154–169.

VAN BENTHEM J. [1976], Modal Correspondence Theory, PhD thesis, Mathematisch Instituut & Instituut voor Grondslagenonderzoek, University of Amsterdam.

VAN BENTHEM J. [1983], *Modal Logic and Classical Logic*, Bibliopolis.

VAN BENTHEM J. [1984], Correspondence theory, *in* D. M. Gabbay and F. Guenthner, eds, 'Handbook of Philosophical Logic, Vol. II, Extensions of Classical Logic, Synthese Library Vol. 165', D. Reidel Publishing Company, Dordrecht, pp. 167–248.

VAN BENTHEM J. [1997], Dynamic bits and pieces, Technical Report LP-1997-01, ILLC, University of Amsterdam.

VAN BENTHEM J., D'AGOSTINO G., MONTANARI A. AND POLICRITI A. [1997], 'Modal deduction in second-order logic and set theory I', *Journal of Logic and Computation* **7**, 251–265.

VAN BENTHEM J., D'AGOSTINO G., MONTANARI A. AND POLICRITI A. [1998], 'Modal deduction in second-order logic and set theory II', *Studia Logica* **60**, 387–420.

VAN BENTHEM, J. AND TER MEULEN, A., EDS [1997], *Handbook of Logic and Language*, Elsevier Science.

VARDI M. [1997], Why is modal logic so robustly decidable?, *in* 'DIMACS Series in Discrete Mathematics and Theoretical Computer Science 31', AMS, pp. 149–184.

WAALER A. [2001], Connections in nonclassical logics, *in* A. Robinson and A. Voronkov, eds, 'Handbook of Automated Reasoning', Vol. II, Elsevier Science, chapter 22, pp. 1487–1578.

WALTHER C. [1987], *A Many-Sorted Calculus Based on Resolution and Paramodulation*, Pitman.

WEIDENBACH C. [2001], Combining superposition, sorts and splitting, *in* A. Robinson and A. Voronkov, eds, 'Handbook of Automated Reasoning', Vol. II, Elsevier Science, chapter 27, pp. 1965–2013.

ZAMOV N. [1989], 'Modal resolutions', *Soviet Math.* **33**, 22–29.

Index

CHAPTER 22

Connections in Nonclassical Logics

Arild Waaler

SECOND READERS: Hans de Nivelle, Christoph Kreiz, and Lincoln Wallen.

Contents

HANDBOOK OF AUTOMATED REASONING
Edited by Alan Robinson and Andrei Voronkov

1. Introduction

There has in the last decade been a renewed interest in the study of proof systems for nonclassical logics. This is partly due to the fact that nonclassical systems continue to find new applications in areas related to computation, some of which put high demands on the proof system. But the increased activity has to a large extent also been stimulated by new syntactical frameworks proposed entirely within the logical community itself like labelled deductive systems [Gabbay 1996], display logic [Belnap 1982] and systems of hypersequents [Avron 1991]. These frameworks have enabled researchers to design nonclassical systems which overcome some of the antinomies of the earlier, destructive systems.

The goal of this chapter is to give an exposition of nonclassical systems which admit connection–driven search. Systems of this kind belong to the family of labelled or prefixed systems. In section 2.1 I argue that connection–driven search relies on full permutability between inferences. The core systems presented in the chapter possess this property.

Scope. To keep the scope at a manageable level I have restricted the exposition to intuitionistic logic and some of the most basic modal systems. In the literature the freely permuting systems have either been presented as matrix systems or as systems of prefixed tableaux with free variables. Since they are best understood in relation to systems with ground prefixes, I have also included an exposition of systems in the latter category. Many of the systems are presented in an original way. I have also given new proofs of of some of the main results, even though the main ideas are well–known from the literature.

Perspective. I have tried to present a *method* for the design of a particular type of proof systems rather than giving a complete catalogue of nonclassical systems at their current level of sophistication. In particular, I have tried to clarify the logical foundation of the calculi. The dominant perspective has been to view the systems from the point of view of permutation. Much less will be said about particular search procedures and implementations; in fact we shall barely reach the point where discussion of efficient proof–search procedures can begin. The agenda for the chapter is to show the conditions under which standard search methods apply to nonclassical logics, at least to the degree they are independent of normal forms.

Systems. The sheer fact that many of the ideas and results in the field have been formulated within different logical settings makes a uniform presentation difficult. The direct use of connections in nonclassical logic has been limited to matrix characterizations. It can hardly be denied that the syntax of these systems is rather involved. A main objective for this work has been to present the idea underlying the matrix systems in a simpler way, and in a way which also accommodates the related activity within the tableau community. Since sequent calculi are particularly well suited for the study of permutation, I work predominantly with sequent calculus formulations. However, to do justice to the role of connections, I have established a relationship between matrices, tableaux and sequent calculi without using normal forms. This is spelled out for classical first–order logic in section 2 and explains the rather lengthy section on classical logic. Many of the main constructions used in the analysis of nonclassical systems are first presented for classical logic and then used extensively in later sections.

Guided trip. For an exposition at an informal level, the reader may be content with just reading the introductory paragraphs in sections 2 and 3. The main ideas are presented in these two sections. For a quick read at a technical level I invite the reader to a guided trip. I shall at the same time make three central remarks at points where the exposition deviates from main sources in the literature. Following the trip, be aware that you sometimes will have to figure out the meaning of concepts from the way they are used.

The purpose of section 2 is to introduce basic concepts, correspondences and methods in a way which generalizes to the nonclassical systems. The classical first–order system is a variant of the free variable tableaux with run–time skolemization and delayed instantiation, cnf. [Fitting 1996]. The system, given in figure 1 on page 1498, has free variable rules and no eigenparameter conditions. Skeletons are closed by unifiers. Look briefly at examples 2.4 and 2.6. The latter example uses the notions of variable–sharing and pure variable skeletons. A skeleton in the former class corresponds, roughly, to a matrix; a skeleton in the latter class is essentially a free variable tableau. Pure variable skeletons can be used to simulate derivations in ground tableaux with eigenparameter conditions. Hence a completeness argument for ground tableaux also shows the completeness of free variable tableaux. The first central remark is related to this point. It turns out that ground tableaux permit tight termination conditions, while it is far from obvious that these conditions can be used in matrix search. For most of the nonclassical systems I have used tableau methods in the completeness proof. I have therefore, strictly speaking, only given partial completeness proofs for the matrix procedures. This allows me to increase the degree of constructivity in the arguments. The soundness argument for the free variable system is more complex than the proof for ground tableaux (or Gentzen's LK); the main line of argument is surveyed in the 1–page discussion opening section 2.7.

Labels are addressed in section 3. Labels are finite strings of prefix variables (upper case letters) and prefix parameters (lower case letters) without repetition of symbols. Parameters function as constants. The section contains a detailed exposition of unification. By studying example 3.3 and the rules in table 1 the reader will see the general pattern of the unification algorithm.

Intuitionistic logic is addressed in sections 4 and 5. The propositional rules listed in figure 6 give a rendition of Wallen's matrix system [Wallen 1990] in the form of a sequent calculus. The system permits free variables in the labels. Free variables are assigned values by label substitutions, which map skeletons into derivations. Look at examples 4.1 and 4.5. Completeness is established nonconstructively via a ground single step system; the rules are listed in figure 7. The construction of countermodels to unprovable sequents is partially formalized. It should be possible to grasp the idea by reading examples 4.7 and 4.12.

The second central remark pertains to the nature of the completeness construction for PSPACE complete propositional systems. The search procedures used in this chapter generate a (possibly) exponential number of minimal derivations rather than one limit derivation with a massive amount of redundancy. I think this gives a better model of the search space. Moreover, I think search procedures should aim at constructing as small objects as possible to witness unprovability. A main intuition is that the label substitutions for the labelled systems can be viewed as projections into the space of minimal derivations.

Modal logics up to S4 are treated in the same way as intuitionistic logic. Examples 6.1, 6.2 and 6.3 illustrate the systems applied to some well–known modal principles. The S5–like systems are treated differently, using labels of length at most 1. Example 7.1 applies the system to a propositional sequent.

The nonclassical proof objects are generated by checking classical proof objects for a particular consistency property. The third central remark has to do with the formulation of this property for quantified systems. Wallen defines the consistency property in terms of the reduction ordering, which requires information about how a matrix has been generated. I have presented the property in a more explicit form by exploiting the labelled language. In the matrix setting the property pertains directly to the matrices which, in each particular example, give rise to a system of equations. Using these equations the consistency condition can be defined exactly as for the propositional systems. An interesting observation is that the constant domain logics require skolemization of prefix parameters (like in [Ohlbach 1988]), while the cumulative and varying domain logics can use a less complex language of labels. The Barcan formula and its converse are studied in cumulative and varying domain systems in example 6.9 and in the constant domain language in example 7.2. A well–known modal fallacy is refuted in the former class of systems in example 6.10 and in the constant domain systems in example 7.3.

2. Prelude: Connections in classical first–order logic

The purpose of section 2.1 is to identify properties which systems with efficient connection–driven proof procedures possess. The rest of section 2 introduces a family of systems and technical material related to soundness and the construction of countermodels. In section 2.9 we shall briefly view the systems from the perspective of proof–search.

2.1. Introduction: a sequent calculus perspective on classical matrices

The basic idea behind matrix methods is to represent a formula as a two–dimensional matrix and characterize provability in terms of properties of the matrix. The idea has a firm logical basis. In first–order classical logic the characterization can be taken as a reformulation of the Herbrand theorem. Characterizations of classical provability in terms of matrices date back to the Swedish logicians Kanger [1957] and Prawitz [1960]. Prawitz used unification to control the term universe; the technique, originally due to Herbrand, received a mature form in Robinson's important work [1965]. Using Robinson's unification theory, matrix characterizations were introduced for the automated deduction community independently by Andrews [1981] and Bibel [1981, 1982c]. From a computational point of view their contributions were significant improvements of the work of the Swedish logicians, mainly due to their identification of connection–driven search methods based on unification. For more historical comments on matrices the reader may consult [Bibel 1987].

Let us, as a point of departure, address the following propositional matrix, where the letters P and Q denote atomic formulae:

$$\begin{bmatrix} P^0 & R^1 & \begin{bmatrix} \overline{P}^2 & \overline{Q}^4 \\ Q^3 \\ \overline{P}^5 \end{bmatrix} \end{bmatrix}$$

The matrix represents the formula $(P^0 \vee R^1) \vee (((\neg P^2 \wedge Q^3) \vee \neg Q^4) \wedge \neg P^5)$; indices are given to distinguish different formula occurrences. Observe that the matrix is just an array presentation of the formula in which a horizontal arrangement corresponds to disjunction and a vertical arrangement corresponds to conjunction. To make the representation independent of the negation normal form I have used a meta–negation instead of the object language negation and replaced, e.g., $\neg P$ with $\overline{P}$. There are three *paths* in this matrix: $\{P^0, R^1, \overline{P}^2, \overline{Q}^4\}$, $\{P^0, R^1, Q^3, \overline{Q}^4\}$, and $\{P^0, R^1, \overline{P}^5\}$. If we draw a line between the formula occurrences in a path, the path will be seen as a horizontal bar through the matrix. A *connection* is a set of complementary literals. The matrix defines three connections: $\{P^0, \overline{P}^2\}$, $\{P^0, \overline{P}^5\}$, and $\{Q^3, \overline{Q}^4\}$. Since every path through the formula matrix is a superset of one of these connections, the set of connections *spans* the matrix. Since there is a spanning set of connections, the formula is *matrix provable*.

The matrix characterization is a relative to the cut–free fragments of Gentzen's sequent calculus LK [1934–35] and its tableaux variants [Smullyan 1968]. The relationship is particularly close for the propositional fragment. The rules of propositional LK consist of the axiom $\Gamma, A \vdash A, \Delta$ and the propositional rules of figure 1 on page 1491. Let us say that a *complete* propositional LK derivation is a derivation without instances of weakening whose leaves contain only atomic formulae. The following complete derivation is an LK proof of the formula at hand:

$$\cfrac{\cfrac{\cfrac{\cfrac{P^2, Q^4 \vdash P^0, R^1}{P^2 \vdash P^0, R^1, \neg Q^4}\,r_7}{\vdash P^0, R^1, \neg P^2, \neg Q^4}\,r_6 \quad \cfrac{Q^4 \vdash P^0, R^1, Q^3}{\vdash P^0, R^1, Q^3, \neg Q^4}\,r_8}{\cfrac{\vdash P^0, R^1, \neg P^2 \wedge Q^3, \neg Q^4}{\vdash P^0, R^1, (\neg P^2 \wedge Q^3) \vee \neg Q^4}\,r_4}\,r_5 \quad \cfrac{P^5 \vdash P^0, R^1}{\vdash P^0, R^1, \neg P^5}\,r_9}{\cfrac{\cfrac{\vdash P^0, R^1, (((\neg P^2 \wedge Q^3) \vee \neg Q^4) \wedge \neg P^5)}{\vdash P^0 \vee R^1, (((\neg P^2 \wedge Q^3) \vee \neg Q^4) \wedge \neg P^5)}\,r_2}{\vdash (P^0 \vee R^1) \vee (((\neg P^2 \wedge Q^3) \vee \neg Q^4) \wedge \neg P^5)}\,r_1}\,r_3$$

Each leaf in the derivation corresponds directly to a path in the matrix. The notational redundancy in the LK proof is significant compared to the matrix. One can partly compensate for this by writing only the principal formula and the side formulae, which is what we do in tableau proofs. Tableaux are essentially sequent calculus derivations displayed as directed acyclic graphs.

The matrix representation has two important consequences for the organization of the search space. First, it is possible to design search procedures which operate on a single formula structure. This is achieved by implementing the formula as a shared structure and construct derivations by way of pointers into this structure [Boyer and Moore 1972, Bibel 1982b]. Second, matrices facilitate the specification of connection–driven search procedures.

The first point eliminates the notational redundancy in the syntax of the LK rules. As to the second point, let me first explain the notion of connection–driven search. The basic idea is that connections can be identified in an initial step of the search algorithm and then be used to control further expansion of branches. This may cut off significant parts of the search space. Let us return to the matrix figure above and imagine that R is replaced by a massive formula, say C. This results in a two–dimensional arrangement which we shall call M. A matrix contains only atomic formulae, so M is not a matrix. However, an initial step of the search procedure may already at this point detect the connections $\{P^0, \overline{P}^2\}$, $\{P^0, \overline{P}^5\}$, and $\{Q^3, \overline{Q}^4\}$. M can be extended to a matrix, but regardless of the form of C every path through the resulting matrix must contain one of the three connections. If these connections are selected, one can hence prevent a massive expansion of C, simply by virtue of the three connections.

The formulation of connection–driven search procedures is significantly facilitated by the matrix syntax. In the LK setting connection–driven search means that expansion of a formula is made on account of its relation to other formulae in the sequent and the structure of the formula as a whole, and not merely by virtue of its outermost logical symbol. Observe that if we replace R with C in the LK proof above, the leaves are still axioms. Expansion of C is hence not necessary, and this is precisely what a connection–driven procedure can be used to detect ahead of the proof generation.

Let us take the matrix and the LK proof as a point of departure and reflect about the relationship between LK and the matrix characterization. One way to portray this relationship is to take the matrix as a compressed representation of the LK search space. Note incidentally that while checking an LK proof is of polynomial complexity, checking a matrix is NP–complete. Hence LK proofs are exponentially larger than matrices.

To pin down the exact relationship between matrices and LK we must invoke the concept of permutation. A permutation of the complete LK derivation above is obtained by interchanging inferences, e.g., r_2 and r_3. A succession of 0 or more permutation steps results in a *permutation variant* of the derivation. Since the structural rules of weakening and contraction are redundant in propositional LK, they are for the time being neglected; every propositional LK rule is then invertible. Hence all complete LK derivations of a formula are permutation variants, i.e. they are equivalent up to permutation. *The matrix characterization can be taken as an abstract presentation of this equivalence class of LK proofs.* It is essential that the notion of matrix provability be identified with an equivalence class of sequent calculus proofs and not merely with one proof in this class. This becomes clear once we draw some consequences of the permutation properties for propositional LK.

The permutation properties are in fact implicit in the *universal* statement which defines matrix provability: "every path contains a complementary connection". In terms of the sequent calculus this statement corresponds to the universal statement (1) "every complete derivation of the endsequent is a proof". The sequent calculus notion of provability is, however, the *existential* statement (2) "there is a proof of the endsequent". By virtue of the permutation properties these two statements are equivalent in propositional LK, i.e. (2) holds if and only if (1). The matrix characterization reflects this fact in that the matrix statement corresponding to (1) is taken as definition instead of the statement corresponding to (2). Moreover, since the rules of propositional LK permute, all complete derivations over a given sequent agree on the set of leaves. Since the leaves are independent of the way in which they are generated, they can be separated from the derivations. This is exactly what the matrix characterization presumes.

Even though we can treat the matrix characterization and propositional LK as essentially the same system, the view taken above in a sense gives conceptual priority to the sequent calculus: matrices are tools for the organization of the LK search space. The perspective is instructive in classical propositional logic, especially for the motivation of matrices. Classical propositional logic is, however, in a favoured position, since its sequent calculus rules are both natural and well–behaved wrt. permutation. As soon as we allow quantifiers this no longer holds. Even though one can give rules which always permute, they will not be as intuitive as their nonpermuting counterparts. This is even more the case intuitionistically, where one can argue that systems with full permutability are designed mainly in response to a technical challenge.

The perspective of this chapter is to take the sequent calculi as presentations of path generation rules over matrices. By hiding implementational details in the matrix structure sequent calculi reveal the logical structure in a particularly clear and simple way. They are for this reason well suited for the presentation of fundamental logical properties. In addition, the syntax of the sequent calculi provides structures which are useful in proofs of meta–results. The syntax of matrices, on the other hand, facilitates both the formulation and the implementation of efficient proof–search procedures.

Turning to classical first–order logic it is clear that first–order LK is not the sequent calculus presentation of a matrix system. Following Frege, Gentzen analyzed quantifiers in terms of eigenparameter conditions. These conditions constrain the development of derivations in that rules cannot be applied in any order. Order dependencies mean lack of permutability. Two simple figures illustrate the point:

$$\cfrac{\cfrac{Pa \vdash Pa \vee Q}{\forall x Px \vdash Pa \vee Q} \; L\forall}{\forall x Px \vdash \forall x (Px \vee Q)} \; R\forall \qquad \cfrac{\cfrac{Pa \vdash Pa \vee Q}{Pa \vdash \forall x (Px \vee Q)} \; R\forall}{\forall x Px \vdash \forall x (Px \vee Q)} \; L\forall$$

The parameter a introduced in the $R\forall$–inferences is an *eigenparameter* (often called an eigen*variable*; to prevent confusion I shall consistently use parameters in instantiations which require an arbitrary witnesses and variables as placeholders for particular terms in inferences which are not subjected to instantiation conditions). The Eigenparameter condition, which pertains to $R\forall$ and $L\exists$ inferences, states that the eigenparameter of the inference is not allowed to occur in the conclusion. The rightmost figure above violates this and hence fails to be an LK derivation. Since the figures are not interpermutable the symmetry in the sequent calculus is destroyed.

A first–order system in which all rules permute can be obtained by using what Prawitz and Kanger called "dummies". "Dummies" are variables standing for arbitrary parameters; being faithful to common practice I will refer to them as *free variables*. Free variables can be used to delay the quantifier instantiation of principal formulae in $L\forall$ and $R\exists$ inferences until we see clearer what the smart instantiations are. But we can make a much more powerful use of them than this. For the free variables allow us to drop the Eigenparameter condition entirely and replace it with a unification condition on the terms. Let us redo the examples:

$$\frac{\dfrac{Px \vdash Pa \vee Q}{\forall x Px \vdash Pa \vee Q}\ L\forall}{\forall x Px \vdash \forall x (Px \vee Q)}\ R\forall \qquad \frac{\dfrac{Px \vdash Pa \vee Q}{Px \vdash \forall x (Px \vee Q)}\ R\forall}{\forall x Px \vdash \forall x (Px \vee Q)}\ L\forall$$

Note initially that since there is no eigenparameter condition, the two figures permute. The a is now a 0–argument *Skolem function*. Trees constructed with the free variable rules are called *skeletons*. This is to reflect the fact that they do not necessarily carry logical force. The crucial point is that skeletons can be instantiated with substitutions and in this way be made logically sound. To illustrate the point, assume that we expand the right disjunctions in the leaves of the skeletons above; both leaves will then be of the form $Px \vdash Pa, Q$. We shall call the pair (Px, Pa) a *connection*. The substitution $\sigma = \{x/a\}$ unifies Px and Pa and yields the axiom $Pa \vdash Pa, Q$. Since σ turns every leaf into an axiom, the skeletons are *closed* by σ.

Observe that σ encodes a dependency between terms. The key point is that free variables eliminate rule dependencies at the cost of *term dependencies*. It is the unification problem which gives rise to the term dependencies. Since this problem is separated from the application of rules, we have full permutability and hence also a matrix representation. And by making the dependency constraints appear in the form of a unification problem derivations can be constructed undisturbed by constraints on the inference order. In particular the proof construction can be guided by connections.

Hence connection–driven search methods rely on full permutability between inferences. If we, on the contrary, try to implement connection–driven search for LK (without free variables), the Eigenparameter condition will cause problems. In addition to connections we must also keep track of quantifier dependencies, which is nontrivial. A procedure of this kind has up to my knowledge not been specified. The free variable rules, on the other hand, allow us to develop the skeleton in any order we like and afterwards check if the appropriate dependency constraints can be met.

Whereas contraction can be neglected in classical propositional logic this is not the case in first–order logic. The presence of contraction complicates the generalization of the propositional notion of matrix provability as a property of a matrix. Bibel identified the notion of a multiplicity for this purpose by exploiting the Herbrand theorem [Bibel 1982c]. A slight refinement of his solution is presented in section 2.5 along with the basic definitions used throughout the chapter.

2.2. Language and models

The set of *standard terms* (*terms* when context permits) is a denumerable set of finite strings inductively defined from a set of *quantifier variables* (denoted x, y, z, u, v, w) and a set of function symbols of every arity (denoted f, g) in the usual way. 0–argument function symbols are called *parameters*. Function symbols will be called *parameter functions* when it is necessary to distinguish them from other kinds of function symbols. A list $t_1 \ldots t_n$ of terms is denoted $\vec{t}$ whenever possible. A term is *ground* if it contains no variables. There is a dummy constant 0 which we assume is always available.

The set of *formulae* is inductively defined from the set of terms, predicate letters and logical symbols. Besides the logical symbols no restrictions are placed on the object language. *Atomic* formulae are formulae of the form $P(\vec{t})$, where P is a placeholder for a predicate symbol with arity n and $\vec{t}$ is a list of n terms. The variables in $\vec{t}$ occur *free* in $P(\vec{t})$. If A and B are formulae, the following are also formulae: $(A \wedge B)$, $(A \vee B)$, $(A \supset B)$, $\neg A$, $\forall x A$, and $\exists x A$. In the latter two cases the quantifiers *bind* the free occurrences of x in A, hence x is not free in the quantified formulae. There is no author of logical texts who is not sloppy with parentheses; I shall, e.g., write $P\vec{t}$ for $P(\vec{t})$ and $A \wedge B$ for $(A \wedge B)$. A formula without free variable occurrences is *closed*. A formula is *propositional* if it contains no variables (free or bound). The symbols P, Q, R are used for atomic propositional formulae. The *propositional fragment* of the language is simply the set of propositional formulae.

A *quantifier substitution* is a partial function from variables into terms. A substitution σ is given as a set of *bindings*: $x/t \in \sigma$ means $\sigma(x) = t$; $\mathrm{dom}(\sigma)$ denotes the domain of σ. $Z\sigma$ denotes the result of replacing every free Z–occurrence of x with $\sigma(x)$ for every x in $\mathrm{dom}(\sigma)$, possibly renaming bound variables in a way I shall explain below. σ *unifies* a nonempty set Γ if $\Gamma\sigma$ is singleton. It is *idempotent* if $Z\sigma = (Z\sigma)\sigma$ for any Z.

2.1. LEMMA. *Let σ be idempotent, y occur in $\sigma(x)$ and $y \in \mathrm{dom}(\sigma)$. Then $\sigma(y) = y$.*

As noted, $A\{x/t\}$ denotes the formula obtained from A by substituting the term t for every free occurrence of x. However, if an unconditioned substitution clashes with quantifier bindings, bound variables are renamed. The situation arises in $\forall x P x y \{y/x\}$, which yields, e.g., $\forall z P z x$. We shall use the same notation for substitution of arbitrary terms: $Z\{t_1/t_2\}$ denotes the object constructed from Z by replacing every occurrence of t_1 with t_2. Substitutions of this kind are, however, only permitted if all variables in t_1 are free in Z. As above, it is sometimes necessary to adjust the result by renaming.

A *sequent* is an object of the form $\Gamma \vdash \Delta$, where the *antecedent* Γ and the *succedent* Δ are finite multisets of formulae. A multiset is an unordered collection of objects in which different occurrences of the same object are distinguished. With this proviso, the usual set operations are defined on multisets. Γ, A is shorthand for $\Gamma \cup \{A\}$.

Formulae will not have any existence "on their own" in this text; they will always be part of larger syntactical objects like sequents and trees. When discussing properties of formulae, we shall hence always mean properties of specific formula *occurrences* in a given construction. Indices are used to distinguish different occurrences of the same formula when needed; the indices are not part of the formal language. Here is an example: $A^1, A^2 \vdash (A \wedge B)^3$. There are three formula occurrences in the sequent: two occurrences of A and one occurrence of $A \wedge B$.

The semantical structures used in this chapter are based on substitution. A *model* for classical logic is a pair $(\mathbf{D}, x)$, where the *domain* $\mathbf{D}$ is a nonempty set of ground terms and x is a set of atomic propositional formulae such that every ground term in x occurs in $\mathbf{D}$. A model can only be used to evaluate a set of formulae if every ground term which occurs in one of the formulae also occurs in $\mathbf{D}$. The satisfaction relation $\models$ is a relation between the set of all models over $\mathbf{D}$ and the set of closed formulae, inductively defined by

$$x \models P \quad \text{iff} \quad P \in x, \ P \text{ atomic},$$
$$x \models A \wedge B \quad \text{iff} \quad x \models A \text{ and } x \models B,$$
$$x \models A \vee B \quad \text{iff} \quad x \models A \text{ or } x \models B,$$
$$x \models \neg A \quad \text{iff} \quad x \not\models A,$$
$$x \models A \supset B \quad \text{iff} \quad x \not\models A \text{ or } x \models B,$$
$$x \models \forall y A \quad \text{iff} \quad x \models A\{y/c\} \text{ for each } c \in \mathbf{D},$$
$$x \models \exists y A \quad \text{iff} \quad x \models A\{y/c\} \text{ for a } c \in \mathbf{D}.$$

Observe that only closed formulae are evaluated. A formula A is *true in* the model x if $x \models A$, otherwise it is *false in* x. x is a *countermodel* to the sequent $\Gamma \vdash \Delta$ if every formula in Γ is true in x and every formula in Δ is false in x. A sequent is *valid* if it has no countermodels.

Proofs and models are duals and serve dual functions: validity is witnessed by a proof, invalidity is witnessed by a countermodel. Besides their part in the semantical consequence relation, models are important tools in the analysis of search procedures.

2.3. Free variable LK

A *rule* is a relation between a set of sequents, called *premisses*, and one sequent, the *conclusion*. A rule is taken as a scheme which quantifies over formulae of particular forms; the instances of these schemes are called *inferences*. A sequent calculus is

Structural rules:

$$\frac{\Gamma \vdash \Delta}{\Gamma, A \vdash \Delta} \ LW \qquad \frac{\Gamma \vdash \Delta}{\Gamma \vdash A, \Delta} \ RW \qquad \frac{\Gamma, A, A \vdash \Delta}{\Gamma, A \vdash \Delta} \ LC \qquad \frac{\Gamma \vdash A, A, \Delta}{\Gamma \vdash A, \Delta} \ RC$$

Logical rules:

$$\frac{\Gamma, A, B \vdash \Delta}{\Gamma, A \wedge B \vdash \Delta} \ L\wedge \qquad \frac{\Gamma, A \vdash \Delta \quad \Gamma, B \vdash \Delta}{\Gamma, A \vee B \vdash \Delta} \ L\vee \qquad \frac{\Gamma, A\{x/f\bar{y}\} \vdash \Delta}{\Gamma, \exists x A \vdash \Delta} \ L\exists$$

$$\frac{\Gamma \vdash A, \Delta \quad \Gamma \vdash B, \Delta}{\Gamma \vdash A \wedge B, \Delta} \ R\wedge \qquad \frac{\Gamma \vdash A, B, \Delta}{\Gamma \vdash A \vee B, \Delta} \ R\vee \qquad \frac{\Gamma \vdash A\{x/y\}, \Delta}{\Gamma \vdash \exists x A, \Delta} \ R\exists$$

$$\frac{\Gamma \vdash A, \Delta \quad \Gamma, B \vdash \Delta}{\Gamma, A \supset B \vdash \Delta} \ L\supset \qquad \frac{\Gamma \vdash A, \Delta}{\Gamma, \neg A \vdash \Delta} \ L\neg \qquad \frac{\Gamma, A\{x/y\} \vdash \Delta}{\Gamma, \forall x A \vdash \Delta} \ L\forall$$

$$\frac{\Gamma, A \vdash B, \Delta}{\Gamma \vdash A \supset B, \Delta} \ R\supset \qquad \frac{\Gamma, A \vdash \Delta}{\Gamma \vdash \neg A, \Delta} \ R\neg \qquad \frac{\Gamma \vdash A\{x/f\bar{y}\}, \Delta}{\Gamma \vdash \forall x A, \Delta} \ R\forall$$

In $R\forall$ and $L\exists$ $\bar{y}$ is a list of all free variables in the principal formula.

Figure 1: Structural and logical rules of free variable LK.

defined by its set of rules. The *structural* rules of *contraction* and *weakening*, shared by all sequent calculi in this chapter, are listed in figure 1. While contraction serves a key function in proof–search procedures, the destructive weakening rule is avoided. In certain cases, however, weakening is necessary for permutation.

The logical rules of free variable LK are given in figure 1. The *principal formula* of a logical rule is the formula in the conclusion with the logical symbol of the rule as the outermost; the *side formulae* are the premiss occurrences of the immediate subformulæ of the principal formula. All other formulæ are called *extra formulæ*. We shall also refer to the two premiss occurrences of the contraction formula as side formulae. The function symbol f occurring in the premisses of $L\exists$ and $R\forall$ is called a *Skolem function*; if r is an inference of this kind, r is said to *belong* to its Skolem function. Similarly is an inference of type $R\exists$ or $L\forall$ said to *belong* to its free variable.

A *skeleton* is a finitely branching tree. A skeleton is generated by the rules of the system and satisfies the Skeleton condition defined below. It is hence not necessarily finite. Finite skeletons have leaf sequents in every branch and can be inductively defined in a straightforward way. All formula occurrences in a skeleton are distinct.

In an upwards development of a skeleton there is an implicit copying of the extra formula occurrences in the conclusion of an inference. In a 1–premiss logical inference all extra formulae are copied into the premiss, while two copies are made in a branching inference like the following:

$$\frac{A^{11}, A^{21} \vdash \Delta \quad A^{12}, B^{22} \vdash \Delta}{A^1, A \vee B^2 \vdash \Delta}$$

A^{11} and A^{12} are two copies of the extra formula A^1. We shall say that A^1 is a *descendent* of A^{11} and A^{12}. This implicit copying must be distinguished from the explicit copying of the constituents of the principal formula into the side formulae. In the example above the side formulae A^{21} and B^{22} are explicit copies of the two disjuncts of the principal formula $A \vee B^2$. In a contraction

$$\frac{\Gamma, A^{31}, A^{32} \vdash \Delta}{\Gamma, A^3 \vdash \Delta}$$

the side formula occurrences A^{31} and A^{32} are explicit copies of the contraction formula A^3. We shall say that the principal formula occurrence is a descendent of all its side formula occurrences. The notion of a descendent is lifted from inferences to skeletons by transitive closure (in the obvious way). If a formula occurrence A is a descendent of B, B is an *ancestor* to A.

It is important for the connection to matrices to keep track of occurrences generated by implicit contraction. We shall achieve this by identifying the copied occurrences and the occurrence in the conclusion by means of an equivalence relation.

2.2. DEFINITION. The relation of *contextual equivalents* is defined on the formula occurrences in a skeleton as the least equivalence relation such that:

- in a 1–premiss inference an extra formula occurrence in the conclusion is contextually equivalent to its ancestor in the premiss,
- in a 2–premiss inference an extra formula occurrence in the conclusion is contextually equivalent to each of its ancestors in the premisses,
- in a contraction, the contraction formula in the conclusion is contextually equivalent to one of its ancestors in the premiss and not contextually equivalent to the other ancestor,
- assume in the following contractions that A^1 and A^2 are contextually equivalent.

$$\frac{\Gamma_i, A^{11}, A^{12} \vdash \Delta_i}{\Gamma_i, A^1 \vdash \Delta_i} \; r_i \qquad \qquad \frac{\Gamma_j, A^{21}, A^{22} \vdash \Delta_j}{\Gamma_j, A^2 \vdash \Delta_j} \; r_j$$

If A^1 is contextually equivalent to A^{11} and A^2 is contextually equivalent to A^{21}, then A^{12} is contextually equivalent to A^{22},
- let r_i and r_j be logical inferences of the same type whose principal formulae are contextual equivalents. Then the left side formula of r_i is contextually equivalent to the left side formula of r_j and the right side formula of r_i is contextually equivalent to the right side formula of r_j.

Two inferences are contextual equivalents if their principal formulae are contextually equivalent.

2.3. EXAMPLE. In this example I have marked contextually equivalent occurrences with the same number.

$$
\cfrac{
  \cfrac{
    \cfrac{
      \cfrac{Pf\!:\!5, Qg\!:\!6 \vdash Px\!:\!7}{Pf\!:\!5, \exists x Qx\!:\!4 \vdash Px\!:\!7}\,g
    }{\exists x Px\!:\!3, \exists x Qx\!:\!4 \vdash Px\!:\!7}\,f
    \qquad
    \cfrac{
      \cfrac{Pf\!:\!5, Qg\!:\!6 \vdash Qx\!:\!8}{Pf\!:\!5, \exists x Qx\!:\!4 \vdash Qx\!:\!8}\,g
    }{\exists x Px\!:\!3, \exists x Qx\!:\!4 \vdash Qx\!:\!8}\,f
  }{\exists x Px\!:\!3, \exists x Qx\!:\!4 \vdash Px \wedge Qx\!:\!2}
}{\exists x Px\!:\!3, \exists x Qx\!:\!4 \vdash \exists x(Px \wedge Qx)\!:\!1}
$$

Observe that if the Skolem function f is used in place of g, the substitution $\{x/f\}$ will make both leaves axiomatic. The possibility of doing this is ruled out by the Skeleton condition below. Note that the endsequent is invalid.

The *Skeleton condition* states: If two inferences belong to the same Skolem function, they are contextually equivalent. The condition can be weakened (and simplified) to: if two inferences belong to the same Skolem function, they are of the same type and their principal formulae are identical up to variable renaming. I have adopted the stronger (and more complex) definition in preparation for the matrix relationship and the presentation of nonclassical systems. The tableau δ^{++}–rule selects the same Skolem function in all inferences of the same type whose principal formulae are identical up to variable renaming [Beckert and Schmitt 1993, Baaz and Fernmüller 1995].

A sequent of the form $\Gamma, P\vec{s} \vdash P\vec{t}, \Delta$ is a σ–*axiom* provided that σ unifies $\{P\vec{s}, P\vec{t}\}$. I will adopt matrix terminology and call the pair $(P\vec{s}, P\vec{t})$ a *connection*. The connection is said to be σ–*complementary* if the unification condition holds. A branch is *closed* by σ if it contains a σ–axiom. A σ–*proof* is a finite skeleton δ in which every leaf is a σ–axiom. When this holds we will refer to $\delta\sigma$, the image of δ under σ, as a *proof* of the endsequent. Observe that there are cases where a skeleton is also a proof: this holds whenever the skeleton is a $\emptyset$–proof.

Since the substitutional part of the search is constrained by a set of connections, it can be posed as a problem of solving a set of simultaneous equations. The equations can then be effectively solved by unification algorithms. The point is illustrated in the two examples below. For ample information about unifiers and unification algorithms in first–order logic consult [Baader and Snyder 2001] (Chapter 8 of this Handbook).

2.4. EXAMPLE. A skeleton over a well–known unprovable sequent:

$$
\cfrac{
  \cfrac{
    \cfrac{
      \cfrac{
        \cfrac{Pxfx \vdash Pgyy}{Pxfx \vdash \forall x Pxy}
      }{Pxfx \vdash \exists y \forall x Pxy}
    }{\exists y Pxy \vdash \exists y \forall x Pxy}
  }{\forall x \exists y Pxy \vdash \exists y \forall x Pxy}
}{}
$$

The connection induces the equations $x = gy$ and $y = fx$, which can be reduced to $x = gfx$ and $y = fgy$. Even though these equations clearly have fixed point

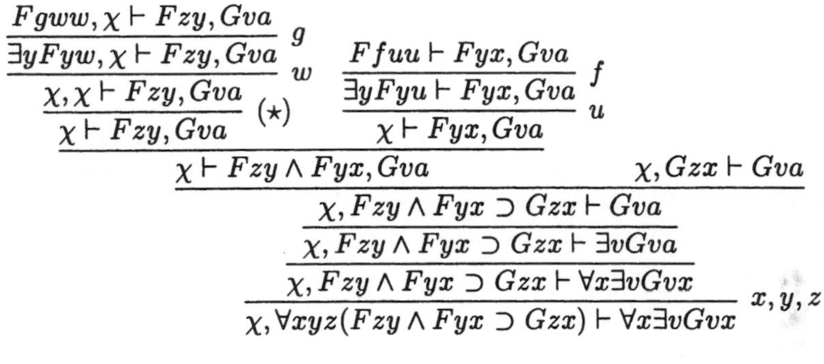

$$\frac{\dfrac{\dfrac{\dfrac{Fgww,\chi \vdash Fzy,Gva}{\exists yFyw,\chi \vdash Fzy,Gva}\ g}{\dfrac{\chi,\chi \vdash Fzy,Gva}{\chi \vdash Fzy,Gva}\ (\star)}\ w \qquad \dfrac{\dfrac{Ffuu \vdash Fyx,Gva}{\exists yFyu \vdash Fyx,Gva}\ f}{\chi \vdash Fyx,Gva}\ u}{\dfrac{\chi \vdash Fzy \wedge Fyx,Gva \qquad\qquad \chi,Gzx \vdash Gva}{\dfrac{\chi,Fzy \wedge Fyx \supset Gzx \vdash Gva}{\dfrac{\chi,Fzy \wedge Fyx \supset Gzx \vdash \exists vGva}{\dfrac{\chi,Fzy \wedge Fyx \supset Gzx \vdash \forall x\exists vGvx}{\chi,\forall xyz(Fzy \wedge Fyx \supset Gzx) \vdash \forall x\exists vGvx}\ x,y,z}}}}}$$

Figure 2: Proof wrt. the ground substitution $\{x/a, y/fa, z/gfa, u/a, v/gfa, w/fa\}$. χ is shorthand for $\forall u\exists yFyu$.

solutions, they have no *finite* solution. Observe that the fixed point solutions do not close the skeleton; the skeleton hence fails to be a proof. Since inadmissible fixed point solutions can be ruled out by a simple occurs check, unifiers can be effectively computed.

The notions in the next definition are used to single out two classes of skeletons. The classes are not disjoint. Since the notions are original, and since they serve an important function in this chapter, they are illustrated by a fairly rich example.

2.5. DEFINITION. A skeleton δ is *variable–pure* if, for each free variable in δ, there is a unique inference which belongs to it. It is *variable–sharing* provided any two inferences in δ belong to the same free variable if and only if their principal formulae are contextually equivalent.

2.6. EXAMPLE. In this example the intended interpretation of Fxy is "x is the father of y." The skeleton in figure 2 gives rise to the equations

$$x = a,\ x = u,\ y = w,\ y = fu,\ z = v,\ z = gw$$

with the finite solution $x = a$, $y = fa$, $z = gfa$, $u = a$, $v = gfa$, $w = fa$.

The skeleton can be both variable–sharing and variable–pure, it all depends on the relationship between the inferences r_w and r_u which belong to w and u. Observe that we have not specified which of the two occurrences of χ in the premiss of the contraction $(\star)$ is contextually equivalent to the conclusion occurrence and which is not. By definition, the principal formula of r_u is contextually equivalent to the principal formula of $(\star)$.

Option 1: the principal formula of r_w is not contextually equivalent to the principal formula of $(\star)$. It follows from definition that r_w and r_u are not contextually equivalent. In this case the skeleton is both variable–pure and variable–sharing.

Option 2: the principal formula of r_w is contextually equivalent to the principal formula of $(\star)$. Then r_w is contextually equivalent to r_u and r_g is contextually equivalent to r_f. Since two contextually equivalent inferences belong to different variables, the skeleton is variable–pure.

Observe finally that if the skeleton is variable–pure, $(\star)$ is redundant: the instance of χ in the leftmost axiom is generated by $(\star)$, but is not further expanded in the proof. If we, on the other hand, require sharing of variables, $(\star)$ is not redundant. To see this, observe that if the $(\star)$ contraction is removed, r_w is contextually equivalent to r_u and r_g is contextually equivalent to r_f. If we still want sharing of variables, w must be changed to u. But this results in an unsolvable set of equations: $x = a$, $x = u$, $y = u$, $y = fu$, $z = v$, $z = gu$.

The permutation properties of the skeletons are determined by the choices of both free variables and Skolem functions. *We shall assume that contextually equivalent inferences of type $R\forall$ or $L\exists$ belong to the same Skolem function in variable–sharing skeletons.* Under this assumption all contextually equivalent formula occurrences in a variable–sharing skeleton have the same form. The previous example indicates that sharing of variables gives rise to redundancy in the search space since the number of contractions is increased beyond necessity.

Contraction can be limited to antecedent occurrences of the form $\forall xB$ and succedent occurrences of the form $\exists xB$. The reason for this is that $L\forall$ and $R\exists$ are the only rules which generate free variables. In the general case we shall say that an occurrence is *generative* if it has the same form and occurs at the same side of the sequent symbol '$\vdash$' as one of the principal formulae in the variable–generating rules. *For all systems in this chapter we shall assume that contraction is limited to generative occurrences.*

2.4. Free variable tableaux

The rules of free variable LK can be read as inverted branch extension rules in a signed free variable tableau system. When shifting to tableau syntax we may work with signs T and F, informally taken as truth values. A *signed* formula is a pair consisting of a sign and a formula, written TA or FA. Let r be an inference in a sequent calculus. $P(r)$ is the principal formula of r signed with T if it occurs in the antecedent and F if it occurs in the succedent. $L(r)$ is the left side formula of r signed in the same way and $R(r)$ is the signed right side formula. The sequent calculus rules can be mapped into branch extension rules for tableaux by the transformations

$$\frac{S_1}{S_0}\, r \quad \rightsquigarrow \quad \frac{P(r)}{\substack{L(r) \\ R(r)}} \qquad\qquad \frac{S_1 \quad S_2}{S_0}\, r \quad \rightsquigarrow \quad \frac{P(r)}{L(r)|R(r)}$$

The principal formula (side formulæ) of an LK rule are mapped into *numerator (denominators)* of the tableau rule. A *tableau* over a set Γ of signed formulæ is a downwards growing tree inductively defined by:

1. A vertical arrangement of the formulae in Γ is a tableau over Γ.

2. If a branch in a tableau over Γ contains A, then the tree obtained by adding the denominators of the rule with numerator A to the branch is a tableau over Γ, possibly splitting the branch.

A tableau is *closed* by σ if σ closes every branch; a branch is closed by σ if it contains occurrences TA and FB such that σ unifies A and B.

Define the mapping ϕ from sequents into sets of signed formulae by $\phi(\Gamma \vdash \Delta) = \{TA \mid A \in \Gamma\} \cup \{FA \mid A \in \Delta\}$. Up to structural rules there is an obvious provability-preserving isomorphism between a skeleton and a tableau over its ϕ'd endsequent. In fact, a tableau *is* a sequent calculus skeleton; the only difference is the amount of redundancy. The reader may therefore convert every statement about skeletons into a statement about tableaux.

2.5. Matrices

A matrix is a two–dimensional arrangement of atomic formulae in which the relative positions of two formula occurrences have logical meaning. The dimensions are interpreted logically as conjunction and disjunction. Of course, the graphical display is just a visual aid; there is no need to change the underlying representation of the sequent (or formula) which comprises the matrix, although parts of this structure may sometimes have to be copied. Logical validity is determined by inspecting the paths through the matrix. Contrary to the display of a matrix, path generation is not just a matter of syntax; it is the heart of the proof–search operation. The role of the path generation rules corresponds to the role of logical rules in LK.

The generation of paths can be viewed as a systematic operation on the formation tree of a sequent (or formula). To formulate this smoothly we need some way of distinguishing the parts of the structure which have been processed from the parts which remain. We shall do this by simply letting the path generation rules introduce matrix syntax. More precisely, this means that parentheses are replaced by brackets and logical symbols are removed. We can then use a set of reduction rules to introduce both the notion of a matrix and the set of paths through the matrix.

The system of reduction rules takes a sequent as input and generates the matrix successively. If we want to test the validity of a formula A, we start off with the sequent $\vdash A$. If we want to show that A is inconsistent, we start off with $A \vdash$. There are two *structural* rules, i.e. rules which are not triggered by logical form. The first of them simply displays the initial sequent as a row vector:

$$A_1, \ldots, A_n \vdash B_1, \ldots, B_m \quad \rightsquigarrow \quad [\, \overline{A}_1 \ \ldots \ \overline{A}_n \ B_1 \ \ldots \ B_m \,].$$

There is only one path through the vector, namely $\{\overline{A}_1, \ldots, \overline{A}_n, B_1, \ldots, B_m\}$. The bar is a kind of meta–negation which corresponds to the T sign in semantic tableaux. In terms of the sequent calculus the bar is a sign for antecedent occurrence or, more precisely, a sign for a switch of side. A *signed* formula is a formula with or without a bar.

$$(A \wedge B) \rightsquigarrow \begin{bmatrix} A \\ B \end{bmatrix} \qquad (A \vee B) \rightsquigarrow \begin{bmatrix} A & B \end{bmatrix} \qquad (A \supset B) \rightsquigarrow \begin{bmatrix} \overline{A} & B \end{bmatrix}$$

$$(\overline{A \wedge B}) \rightsquigarrow \begin{bmatrix} \overline{A} & \overline{B} \end{bmatrix} \qquad (\overline{A \vee B}) \rightsquigarrow \begin{bmatrix} \overline{A} \\ \overline{B} \end{bmatrix} \qquad (\overline{A \supset B}) \rightsquigarrow \begin{bmatrix} A \\ \overline{B} \end{bmatrix}$$

$$\neg A \quad \rightsquigarrow \quad \overline{A} \qquad \forall x A \quad \rightsquigarrow \quad A\{x/f\vec{y}\} \qquad \exists x A \quad \rightsquigarrow \quad A\{x/y\}$$

$$\overline{\neg A} \quad \rightsquigarrow \quad A \qquad \overline{\forall x A} \quad \rightsquigarrow \quad \overline{A}\{x/y\} \qquad \overline{\exists x A} \quad \rightsquigarrow \quad \overline{A}\{x/f\vec{y}\}$$

Figure 3: Logical reduction rules: y and f are fresh symbols, $\vec{y}$ is a list of the free variables in the signed formula which triggers the rule.

The second structural rule is *contraction*. It operates on signed formulae of any form:

$$A^i \rightsquigarrow \begin{bmatrix} A^j & A^k \end{bmatrix},$$
$$\overline{A}^i \rightsquigarrow \begin{bmatrix} \overline{A}^j & \overline{A}^k \end{bmatrix}.$$

The superscripts are part of our meta–language, cnf. section 2.2. The *logical* reduction rules are listed in figure 3. Observe that the rules replace connectives with conjunctive force with a vertical arrangement and connectives with disjunctive force with a horizontal arrangement. Matrices are limit objects generated by the rules, as explained in the following.

Let S be a sequent and r' be the initial reduction which displays S as a row vector V. The set of *reduction sequences from* S is defined by:

- r' is a reduction sequence from S which leads to V,
- if ρ is a reduction sequence from S which leads to M, A^i occurs in M, and $r : A^i \rightsquigarrow N$ is an instance of a rule, then ρr is a reduction sequence from S which leads to $M\{A^i/N\}$.

Assume that ρ leads to M. The set of *paths through* M is inductively defined over the generation of M. If M is a row vector $[A_1 \;\; \ldots \;\; A_m]$, then $\{A_1, \ldots, A_m\}$ is a path through M. The paths through $M = M'\{A^i/N\}$ are given by two clauses:

- if p is a path through M' and $A^i \notin p$, then p is a path through M.
- if p is a path through M' and $A^i \in p$, let p' be $p \setminus \{A^i\}$. There are three cases.
  (i) N is $[B \; C]$. Then $p' \cup \{B, C\}$ is a path through M.
  (ii) N is column vector with B over C. Then both $p' \cup \{B\}$ and $p' \cup \{C\}$ are paths through M.
  (iii) N is a formula B. Then $p' \cup \{B\}$ is a path through M.

If ρ leads to M and every signed formula in M is atomic, ρ is *complete*. ρ *generates* a signed formula occurrence A if an initial sub–sequence of ρ leads to M and A occurs in M.

2.7. DEFINITION. M is a *matrix* if there is a complete reduction sequence ρ which leads to M.

2.8. EXAMPLE. Applied to the example at the beginning of section 2.1 the reduction rules define the matrix

$$\left[\left[\begin{array}{cc}\left[\begin{array}{cc}P^0 & R^1\end{array}\right] & \left[\left[\begin{array}{c}\left[\begin{array}{c}\overline{P}^2 \\ Q^3 \\ \hline \overline{P}^5\end{array}\right] & \overline{Q}^4\end{array}\right]\right]\end{array}\right]\right]$$

The matrix is generated by any complete reduction sequence which does not use contraction. The nicer layout of the matrix in section 2.1 is obtained from the above by the simplification rules $[[M]] \rightsquigarrow [M]$ and $[[M_1] [M_2]] \rightsquigarrow [M_1 \, M_2]$. The readers will have no difficulty in defining an appropriate set of simplification rules.

A formula occurrence in a reduction sequence is *generative* if it triggers a reduction rule introducing a <u>fresh</u> free variable. In the system at hand generative occurrences have the form $\overline{\forall x B}$ or $\exists x B$. Clearly, matrices are correlated to the number of contractions applied to these occurrences and we shall use a notion of multiplicity to record this information. However, Bibel's original notion, which is a property of a formula, is not sufficiently fine–grained for nonclausal formulae. What we need is a contraction property, i.e. a property at the level of derivations. To capture this I shall define the multiplicity in relation to a reduction sequence.

2.9. DEFINITION. Let ρ be a reduction sequence. Let us say that the *duplication set* of a formula occurrence is the smallest set such that

• a formula is in its own duplication set,
• in a contraction $A^i \rightsquigarrow \left[A^j \, A^k \right]$ (A a signed formula) the three occurrences of A have identical duplication set.

We shall refer to the cardinality of a duplication set as the *multiplicity* of the set. The multiplicity of ρ is a collection of multiplicities of the duplication sets which pertain to occurrences generated by ρ.

Observe that all occurrences in a duplication set have identical form. If we slightly abuse notation and use formulae to refer to duplication sets, a formula A can be used to denote the duplication set of A–occurrences. We may hence talk about the multiplicity of a *formula* A and mean the number of occurrences of A in the reduction sequence. This notation is ambiguous when there are different duplication sets with occurrences of the same form. Whenever we talk about the multiplicity of a formula we shall hence assume that this is not the case.

2.10. LEMMA. *Let S be a sequent. Then all complete reduction sequences from S which agree on multiplicity lead to the same matrix (up to free variables and Skolem functions).*

The result is established in section 2.6. In light of this result we can unambiguously talk about *the* matrix of a sequent S. Formally, M is *the matrix of S with multiplicity μ* if there is a reduction sequence from S with multiplicity μ which leads to M.

The matrix terminology exploits graphical metaphors. A *connection* is a set of atomic occurrences of the form $\{P\vec{s}, P\vec{t}\}$. It is *σ–complementary* if the quantifier substitution σ unifies $\{P\vec{s}, P\vec{t}\}$. A set of connections is *spanning* if every path through the matrix contains a connection from the set. S is *matrix provable* if there is a multiplicity μ and a quantifier substitution σ such that the matrix of S wrt. μ contains a spanning set of σ–complementary connections.

2.11. EXAMPLE. Figure 2 on page 1501 shows a variable–sharing skeleton over the sequent $\chi, \forall xyz(Fzy \wedge Fyx \supset Gzx) \vdash \forall x \exists v Gvx$, where χ is $\forall u \exists y Fyu$. Below is the matrix over the same sequent with multiplicity 2 for $\overline{\chi}$.

$$\left[\quad \overline{Fgww} \quad \overline{Ffuu} \quad \left[\begin{array}{c} Fzy \\ Fyx \\ \overline{Gzx} \end{array} \right] \quad Gva \quad \right]$$

There are three paths through the matrix, namely $\{\overline{Fgww}, \overline{Ffuu}, Fzy, Gva\}$, $\{\overline{Fgww}, \overline{Ffuu}, \overline{Gzx}, Gva\}$, and $\{\overline{Fgww}, \overline{Ffuu}, Fyx, Gva\}$. The three connections $\{\overline{Fgww}, Fzy\}$, $\{\overline{Gzx}, Gva\}$, and $\{\overline{Ffuu}, Fyx\}$ are spanning and complementary wrt. $\{x/a, y/fa, z/gfa, u/a, v/gfa, w/fa\}$.

2.12. EXAMPLE. Connections can reduce the search space significantly. Consider a simple matrix over the sequent $\forall x Px \vee \forall x \exists y Qxy \vdash$:

$$\left[\begin{array}{c} \overline{Pu} \\ \overline{Qxfx} \end{array} \right]$$

Since there are no connections, the sequent is trivially unprovable.

A reduction sequence can be encoded in the sequent calculus. The general pattern of the translation is illustrated with the sequent $\vdash \neg Q, \neg R, Q \wedge R$. The leftmost figure below shows the first step in the development of a matrix, the rightmost figure shows the initial part of the corresponding skeleton:

$$[\neg Q \quad \neg R \quad Q \wedge R] \qquad \vdash \neg Q, \neg R, Q \wedge R$$

Assume that we next expand the conjunction in both figures. This yields

$$\left[\neg Q \quad \neg R \quad \left[\begin{array}{c} Q \\ R \end{array} \right] \right] \qquad \frac{\vdash \neg Q, \neg R, Q \quad \vdash \neg Q, \neg R, R}{\vdash \neg Q, \neg R, Q \wedge R}$$

Expanding $\neg Q$ in the matrix arrangement corresponds to expansion of the succedent $\neg Q$ in *both* leaves of the skeleton, resulting in the following figures:

$$\left[\overline{Q} \;\; \neg R \;\; \left[\begin{matrix} Q \\ R \end{matrix} \right] \right]$$

$$\cfrac{\cfrac{Q \vdash \neg R, Q}{\vdash \neg Q, \neg R, Q} \qquad \cfrac{Q \vdash \neg R, R}{\vdash \neg Q, \neg R, R}}{\vdash \neg Q, \neg R, Q \wedge R}$$

Expansion of $\neg R$ gives the resulting matrix and the corresponding skeleton:

$$\left[\overline{Q} \;\; \overline{R} \;\; \left[\begin{matrix} Q \\ R \end{matrix} \right] \right]$$

$$\cfrac{\cfrac{\cfrac{Q, R \vdash Q}{Q \vdash \neg R, Q}}{\vdash \neg Q, \neg R, Q} \qquad \cfrac{\cfrac{Q, R \vdash R}{Q \vdash \neg R, R}}{\vdash \neg Q, \neg R, R}}{\vdash \neg Q, \neg R, Q \wedge R}$$

Observe that:

- a formula occurrence in the matrix corresponds to a set of contextual equivalents in the skeleton,
- a path through the matrix corresponds to a leaf in the skeleton,
- the reduction sequence corresponds to a variable–sharing skeleton.

Let us say that a variable–sharing skeleton is *balanced* if the following holds for all inferences (including contraction). Let r be an inference with principal formula A^i, the branch β contain a contextual equivalent to A^i. Then there is an inference r' in β which is contextually equivalent to r. A balanced skeleton is *complete* if all leaves contain only atomic formulae. Clearly, complete reduction sequences are mapped into complete skeletons.

2.13. EXAMPLE. A complete skeleton can be obtained from the skeleton in figure 2 by adding a contraction similar to $(\star)$ to the two rightmost branches or, alternatively, pushing the $(\star)$ below the lowermost branching inference. The leftmost leaf will then be unchanged. The leftmost branch does not satisfy the conditions as it stands, but it will if the following two inferences are added above the leaf:

$$\cfrac{\cfrac{Fgww, Ffuu \vdash Fzy, Gva}{Fgww, \exists y Fyu \vdash Fzy, Gva} \; f}{Fgww, \chi \vdash Fzy, Gva} \; u$$

Both the middle and the rightmost leaf will get a new copy of χ. They will then be $\chi, Ffuu \vdash Fyx, Gva$ and $\chi, \chi, Gzx \vdash Gva$. We must now expand the new copies of χ in a variable–sharing way, using the terms u, w, f and g. The resulting skeleton is balanced and complete.

Even though a reduction sequence corresponds to a balanced skeleton, it is not the case that every balanced skeleton corresponds to a reduction sequence. Balanced skeletons are closed under certain types of permutation, a fact which has consequences for the treatment of matrices. But first a word about permutation.

2.6. Permutation

Permutation is used to relate skeletons which differ only in the order of inferences. In order to restrict the space of skeletons to those which can possibly be generated by a feasible search strategy, we shall only use permutation schemes which avoid additional weakenings. Since contraction plays a prominent role in the analysis of proof–search, we shall assume that instances of contraction take part in permutations in the same way as 1–premiss logical inferences.

Different types of permutation fall into two general cases. If both inferences are 1–premiss, the situation is particularly simple. Example:

$$\frac{\dfrac{\Gamma, Ax \vdash Bf\bar{z}, \Delta}{\Gamma, Ax \vdash \forall y By, \Delta}}{\Gamma, \forall x Ax \vdash \forall y By, \Delta} \qquad \frac{\dfrac{\Gamma, Ax \vdash Bf\bar{z}, \Delta}{\Gamma, \forall x Ax \vdash Bf\bar{z}, \Delta}}{\Gamma, \forall x Ax \vdash \forall y By, \Delta}$$

The leftmost figure permutes to the rightmost figure and *vice versa*. The example shows the effect of the free variable rules. Due to the Eigenparameter condition, a $L\forall$ over a $R\forall$ presents an exception to permutation in Gentzen's LK.

The second general case arises when one of the inferences is branching. Example (extra formulae neglected):

$$\frac{\dfrac{A \vdash Bf\bar{z} \quad C \vdash Bf\bar{z}}{A \vdash \forall y By \quad C \vdash \forall y By}}{A \vee C \vdash \forall y By} \qquad \frac{\dfrac{A \vdash Bf\bar{z} \quad C \vdash Bf\bar{z}}{A \vee C \vdash Bf\bar{z}}}{A \vee C \vdash \forall y By}$$

The leftmost figure clearly permutes to the rightmost and conversely. But observe that the inferences in the figure to the left will not permute to the rightmost pattern if the two $R\forall$–inferences belong to different Skolem functions. The point can be made at a general level by considering the following inference pattern:

$$\frac{\dfrac{\text{premisses of } r_2}{\Gamma' \vdash \Delta'} r_2 \quad \dfrac{\text{premisses of } r_3}{\Gamma'' \vdash \Delta''} r_3}{\Gamma \vdash \Delta} r_1$$

We are interested in *symmetrical* permutations, i.e. permutations in which all three inferences are included. It is easy to see that the inferences in the figure above permute symmetrically whenever r_2 and r_3 are contextually equivalent and the skeleton is variable–sharing; this holds regardless of the type of r_2 and r_3.

The reader can easily work out a permutation example with two branching inferences. A *permutation variant* of a skeleton in this form is obtained by applying a sequence of 0 or more primitive permutation steps of the symmetrical kind introduced above.

2.14. LEMMA. *Let A be a nonatomic occurrence in the endsequent of a balanced variable–sharing skeleton. Assume that A is expanded by an inference in the skeleton. There is then a permutation variant of the skeleton in which A is the principal formula of the lowermost inference.*

PROOF. By assumption there is a class of contextually equivalent inferences in the skeleton whose principal formulae are contextually equivalent to the endsequent occurrence of A. All of these inferences occur in different branches. Select repeatedly an inference r which is furthest away from the root. If the inference immediately below is branching, the inference above the other premiss is contextually equivalent to r, otherwise either r is not furthest away from the root or the skeleton is not balanced. We can then apply the symmetrical permutation scheme and permute downwards.   □

By repeated application of this lemma one can show the following statement. *Let ρ_1 and ρ_2 be reduction sequences from a sequent S which agree on multiplicity, free variables and Skolem functions. Let δ_1 and δ_2 be the corresponding balanced skeletons. Then δ_1 and δ_2 are permutation variants.* It is immediate from definition that two permutation variants have the same leaves. Since there is a direct correspondence between leaves and paths, the statement above provides a proof of lemma 2.10.

More generally one can show that the class of balanced variable–sharing skeletons which agree on contractions, free variables and Skolem functions is closed under permutation. Complete skeletons hence differ only insignificantly by the order of inferences. We know that each complete skeleton δ has a number of permutation variants which correspond to complete reduction sequences and that all of these reduction sequences lead to the same matrix. The paths through this matrix are given by the leaves of δ. What this shows is that the matrix characterization is equivalent to the system of complete variable–sharing skeletons.

Moreover, from the point of view of proof length and complexity of the search space, it is not essential for the comparison that the variable–sharing skeletons are complete. To see this, let us return to the development of the matrix for the sequent $\vdash \neg Q, \neg R, Q \wedge R$ at the beginning of this section. Recall that we had to make *two* skeleton expansions for each of the last two reductions in the matrix development. The source of this lies in the redundancy in the sequent calculus. Now, if we have a variable–sharing skeleton δ' at hand and extend this to a balanced skeleton δ, we must add a number of redundant inferences to each branch. Assume that δ corresponds to a reduction ρ. Since all of the inferences added to a branch in δ' have already been made in other branches of δ', they are accounted for also in ρ. It is hence fair to say that ρ corresponds to δ' just as much as it corresponds to δ, the only difference is the amount of redundancy in the derivations.

From the point of view of this chapter the main observation is that the class of variable–sharing skeletons has the same fundamental logical properties as the matrix system. Fundamental results established in one setting hence carry directly over to the other. We shall use this fact extensively in this chapter.

There is in general not a strong correspondence between matrices and variable–pure skeletons. The correspondence with variable–sharing skeletons relies on the identical form of contextually equivalent occurrences, a property which also makes skeletons permute so nicely by symmetrical schemes. This is not always the case for pure variable skeletons, and permutation schemes for these skeletons reflect the asymmetry. Example:

$$\dfrac{\dfrac{A \vdash Bx \quad C \vdash By}{A \vdash \exists y By \quad C \vdash \exists y By}}{A \vee C \vdash \exists y By}$$

$$\dfrac{\dfrac{\dfrac{\dfrac{\dfrac{A \vdash Bx \qquad C \vdash By}{A \vdash Bx, By \quad C \vdash Bx, By}}{A \vee C \vdash Bx, By}}{A \vee C \vdash \exists y By, By}}{A \vee C \vdash \exists y By, \exists y By}}{A \vee C \vdash \exists y By}$$

The figure to the left permutes into the figure to the right. The rightmost figure contains a contraction to preserve the two different instances of the quantifier. The leaves are then adjusted by weakening. As we shall henceforth focus on variable–sharing skeletons generated without use of weakening, we may ignore schemes of this type. For further information about permutation consult [Kleene 1952] or the text by Schwichtenberg and Troelstra [1996].

2.7. Soundness

Soundness proofs for systems without free variables are in general quite simple. In, e.g., Gentzen's LK the Eigenparameter condition ensures that quantifier inferences preserve validity. Since this property holds also for propositional inferences soundness can be established by a routine induction over proofs. Free variable LK, on the other hand, requires a more elaborate argument than this. I shall in the following identify the source of the problem and try to motivate the technical steps in a proof–theoretical solution. This is all the more important for this chapter as similar steps will be used for all free variable systems.

Basically the problem is that a proof of a valid sequent in free variable LK may contain invalid sequents. Consider the following two trees.

$$\dfrac{\dfrac{\dfrac{Px \vdash Pa, Q}{Px \vdash Pa \vee Q}}{Px \vdash \forall x (Px \vee Q)} \; a}{\forall x Px \vdash \forall x (Px \vee Q)} \; x \qquad\qquad \dfrac{\dfrac{\dfrac{Pa \vdash Pa, Q}{Pa \vdash Pa \vee Q}}{Pa \vdash \forall x (Px \vee Q)}}{\forall x Px \vdash \forall x (Px \vee Q)}$$

The leftmost figure is a skeleton closed by the substitution $\{x/a\}$. The rightmost figure is the image of the skeleton under this substitution. Note that the third sequent from above, $Pa \vdash \forall x (Px \vee Q)$, is not classically valid.

The solution presented in this chapter exploits two basic properties. First, the closing substitutions induce a well–founded reduction ordering on the inferences in a proof. Second, proofs can be permuted into a form which reflects this ordering. For the two figures above the permutative transformation yields the trees

$$\dfrac{\dfrac{\dfrac{Px \vdash Pa, Q}{Px \vdash Pa \vee Q}}{\forall x Px \vdash Pa \vee Q} \; x}{\forall x Px \vdash \forall x (Px \vee Q)} \; a \qquad\qquad \dfrac{\dfrac{\dfrac{Pa \vdash Pa, Q}{Pa \vdash Pa \vee Q}}{\forall x Px \vdash Pa \vee Q}}{\forall x Px \vdash \forall x (Px \vee Q)}$$

As in the previous example the rightmost figure is the image of the leftmost figure under the mapping $\{x/a\}$. The leftmost skeleton conforms to the substitution in the sense that the inference which belongs to x occurs above the inference which belongs to a. Note that the permutations have the same effect as the Eigenparameter condition: all inferences in the proof preserve validity. With the permutative steps completed soundness can, as usual, be established by routine induction.

Technically, the most difficult step in the soundness argument is to show that the reduction ordering is well–founded. We shall first define the reduction ordering relation with some care and subsequently introduce some minor simplifications which will facilitate the formulation of the argument. The term 'reduction ordering' alludes to the reductions of formulae. In matrix terminology the relation is denoted $\lhd$. However, since we now state the results relative to the sequent calculus it is better to take skeletons as the main objects and view them from above. To accomplish this, we just shift the direction of the symbol to $\rhd$.

2.15. DEFINITION. Let σ be a quantifier substitution. We first introduce the two binary relations $\gg$ and $\sqsupset$ as the weakest relations such that

- if the principal formula of r_1 is an ancestor to a side formula of r_2, then $r_1 \gg r_2$,
- if r_1 belongs to x, r_2 belongs to $y \neq x$, and $\sigma(x) = y$, then $r_1 \sqsupset r_2$,
- if r_1 belongs to x, r_2 belongs to f, and $\sigma(x) = f(\cdot)$, then $r_1 \sqsupset r_2$.

The *reduction ordering induced by* σ, denoted $\rhd$. is defined as the transitive closure of $\gg \cup \sqsupset$. The skeleton *conforms to* $\rhd$ if there are no two inferences r and r' such that $r \rhd r'$ and r is below r'.

Let us say that a substitution σ is *homogeneous* over a structure if the following property holds. If $\sigma(x) = f\vec{t}$ and $f\vec{y}$ occurs in the structure, then $f\vec{t} = f\vec{y}\sigma$. To motivate this notion, recall from examples 2.4 and 2.6 that a closing substitution can be viewed as a solution to a set of equations. A Skolem function f which occurs in the equation set is of the form $f\vec{y}$; moreover, the arguments $\vec{y}$ are unique for f if the underlying skeleton is either variable–sharing or variable–pure. Given a skeleton of one of these forms, the most general solution to a set of equations is homogeneous over the equations. If the property holds for all free variables in a skeleton, the substitution is homogeneous over the skeleton. We then simply say that the substitution is *homogeneous*.

We shall in the soundness proof assume that the closing substitutions are homogeneous and ground. None of these conditions are necessary for the proof, but they allow us skip some technical details of less importance. If a skeleton can be closed, it can be closed by a ground, homogeneous substitution; I leave the proof of this for the reader.

2.16. LEMMA. *The reduction ordering $\rhd$ induced by a ground, homogeneous substitution is well–founded.*

PROOF. Assume that $\rhd$ induced by σ is not well–founded. There must then be a sequence of inferences $r_1, \ldots, r_n$ belonging to Skolem functions $f_1, \ldots, f_n$ and inferences $r'_1, \ldots, r'_n$ belonging to variables $x_1, \ldots, x_n$ such that

$$r_1 \gg r'_1, r'_1 \sqsupset r_2, \ \ldots \ , r_n \gg r'_n, r'_n \sqsupset r_1.$$

Let $\sigma(x_1) = f_2\vec{t_2}, \ldots, \sigma(x_n) = f_1\vec{t_1}$. Observe that x_i occurs as an argument to the Skolem function f_i; this follows by the quantifier rule which introduces f_i into the skeleton. Since σ is homogeneous this means that $f_2\vec{t_2}$ occurs in $\vec{t_1}$, $f_3\vec{t_3}$ occurs in $\vec{t_2}$, etc. But then $f_1\vec{t_1}$ occurs in $\vec{t_1}$, which contradicts the assumption that terms are finite. Hence $\triangleright$ is well–founded. □

To simplify the soundness proof even more we shall restrict the permutation steps to complete variable–sharing skeletons. Clearly, any skeleton can be extended to a complete skeleton without altering its properties wrt. closure. The permutation lemma below can be established for skeletons which are not variable–sharing if we allow nonsymmetrical schemes like the one presented at the end of section 2.6.

2.17. LEMMA. *If $\triangleright$ is a well–founded ordering over a complete, variable–sharing skeleton, the skeleton has a permutation variant which conforms to $\triangleright$.*

PROOF. Induction on the sub–skeletons, using lemma 2.14. □

2.18. THEOREM. *Let S be a provable sequent of closed formulae. Then S is valid.*

PROOF. Observe first that since each formula in S is closed, $S\sigma = S$ for each σ. As pointed out above we prove the case of a complete, variable–sharing skeleton δ' over S closed by a ground, homogeneous substitution σ. By lemma 2.16, $\triangleright$ is well–founded. By lemma 2.17, δ' has a permutation variant δ which conforms to $\triangleright$. It follows by routine induction on the skeleton that every sequent in $\delta\sigma$ is valid. The base step is trivial. For the inductive step, the quantifier inferences in $\delta\sigma$ are of the form

$$\frac{\Gamma, A\{x/t\} \vdash \Delta}{\Gamma, \forall x A \vdash \Delta} \qquad \frac{\Gamma, A\{x/f\vec{t}\} \vdash \Delta}{\Gamma, \exists x A \vdash \Delta} \qquad \frac{\Gamma \vdash A\{x/f\vec{t}\}, \Delta}{\Gamma \vdash \forall x A, \Delta} \qquad \frac{\Gamma \vdash A\{x/t\}, \Delta}{\Gamma \vdash \exists x A, \Delta}$$

where t is a ground term. For the $L\forall$ case, pick a model $(\mathbf{D}, w)$ which makes $\Gamma, \forall x A$ true. We can without loss of generality assume that $t \in \mathbf{D}$. Otherwise, t does not occur in $\Gamma, \forall x A \vdash \Delta$, in which case we may substitute a term in $\mathbf{D}$ for t in the proof of $\Gamma, \forall x A \vdash \Delta$ and get a proof of the appropriate form. So assume $t \in \mathbf{D}$. By definition, $\Gamma, A\{x/t\}$ is true in the model. By induction hypothesis, there is a formula in Δ which is true in the model.

For $L\exists$, pick a model $M = (\mathbf{D}, w)$ of $\Gamma, \exists x A$. By definition, there is a $t' \in \mathbf{D}$ such that $A\{x/t'\}$ is true in M. Let M' be the model $(\mathbf{D} \cup \{f\vec{t}\}, w \cup \{B\{t'/f\vec{t}\} \mid B \in w\})$. Since δ conforms to $\triangleright$, $f\vec{t}$ does not occur in the conclusion, hence M and M' agree on the formulae in Γ, Δ. By induction hypothesis, there is a formula in Δ true in M'. This formula is true also in M. The propositional rules are straightforward and are left for the reader. □

2.8. Model existence and completeness

A complete search procedure is a procedure which systematically expands all options in finite time This requires the formulation of expansion conditions for generative occurrences. A naive (and inefficient) search procedure for free variable LK is given below. Two derived rules are used instead of contraction, $L\forall$, and $R\exists$:

$$\frac{\Gamma, \forall x A, A\{x/y\} \vdash \Delta}{\Gamma, \forall x A \vdash \Delta} \; L C\forall \qquad\qquad \frac{\Gamma \vdash A\{x/y\}, \exists x A, \Delta}{\Gamma \vdash \exists x A, \Delta} \; R C\exists$$

The expansion conditions are defined relative to the term universe for the entire skeleton. In consequence a Skolem function introduced in one branch can make an occurrence in the leaf of another branch expandable. Let us say that the *variable set* of a formula $\forall x B$ in a branch β is the set of all free variables in β introduced by $L\forall$–inferences with principal formula of the form $\forall x B$. The variable set of $\exists x B$ is the set of free variables in β introduced by $R\exists$–inferences with principal formula of this form.

The search procedure generates a variable–sharing skeleton δ by a fair repetition of the following three steps:

- Check if there is a substitution which closes the skeleton δ. If there is such a substitution σ, terminate: $\delta\sigma$ is a proof. As shown in examples above this test can be formulated as a unification problem.
- If there is no substitution which closes δ and no branch is expandable, terminate: the endsequent is not classically valid.
- Otherwise, modify δ by expanding an expandable formula in a leaf.

Let β be a branch and A be a leaf occurrence. If A is an antecedent occurrence of the form $\forall x B$ or a succedent occurrence of the form $\exists x B$, A is *expandable* if there is no bijection from the variable set of A in β into the term universe. If A is any other nonatomic occurrence, A is expandable.

A procedure of this kind presents the information coded in the endsequent in a more explicit form. To show completeness, it is fruitful to view the process as a stepwise approximation to a model. If it terminates with a proof, the model construction has failed; a proof shows that what looked like a model in fact is no model at all.

Assume that the procedure generates a limit object δ_ω such that each quantifier substitution fails to close at least one branch. Observe initially that the set of free variables in the limit object is a disjoint union of variable sets. We are interested in quantifier substitutions which are disjoint unions of bijections from variable sets into the term universe. Substitutions in this form are *uniform*. If σ is uniform and does not close the branch β, the information in $\beta\sigma$ can be displayed in a countermodel.

2.19. EXAMPLE. Let ψ be $\exists x(Px \land Qx)$. The systematic search procedure may generate the following skeleton:

$$
\cfrac{
  \cfrac{
    \cfrac{
      \cfrac{
        \cfrac{
          \cfrac{
            \cfrac{Pa, Qb \vdash \psi, Py, Px \quad Pa, Qb \vdash \psi, Qy, Px}{Pa, Qb \vdash \psi, Py \land Qy, Px}
          }{Pa, Qb \vdash \psi, Px} \quad Pa, Qb \vdash \psi, Qx
        }{Pa, Qb \vdash \psi, Px \land Qx}
      }{Pa, Qb \vdash \psi}
    }{Pa, \exists x Qx \vdash \psi}
  }{\exists x Px, \exists x Qx \vdash \psi}
}{}
$$

The term universe is $\{a, b\}$. Let us call the rightmost branch β_3. Since the variable set of ψ in β_3 is $\{x\}$, there is no bijection into the universe. The leaf occurrence of ψ in this branch is hence expandable. Expansion generates the following two inferences (and hence splits β_3):

$$
\cfrac{
  \cfrac{Pa, Qb \vdash \psi, Py, Qx \quad Pa, Qb \vdash \psi, Qy, Qx}{Pa, Qb \vdash \psi, Py \land Qy, Qx}
}{Pa, Qb \vdash \psi, Qx}
$$

The resulting skeleton is a limit object which cannot be closed. There are two uniform substitutions: one maps x to b and y to a, the other interchanges the values. Each of them defines a countermodel. The model defined by the former is $(\{a, b\}, \{Pa, Qb\})$ and is given by the second branch from the left.

2.20. THEOREM. *Every unprovable sequent of closed formulae has a countermodel.*

PROOF. Assume that the procedure generates δ_ω. Let σ be any uniform quantifier substitution. By assumption, there must be a branch β which is not closed by σ (using König's lemma in the usual way). Let $\beta\sigma^+$ be the set of formulae with an antecedent occurrence in $\beta\sigma$ and $\beta\sigma^-$ be the set of formulae with a succedent occurrence in $\beta\sigma$. Let $\mathbf{D}$ be the term universe for δ_ω and x be the set of atomic formulae in $\beta\sigma^+$. It follows by routine induction that each formula in $\beta\sigma^+$ is true in $(\mathbf{D}, x)$ and each formula in $\beta\sigma^-$ is false in $(\mathbf{D}, x)$. The base step in the induction follows directly from definition and the assumption that the branch is not closed. The inductive steps follow by the following line of argument: Any nonatomic formula is the principal formula of an inference. Apply the induction hypothesis to its side formulae in β and conclude by the model definition. □

2.21. COROLLARY. *Every valid sequent is provable.*

PROOF. By a *reductio* argument from the Model existence theorem. □

2.9. From calculus to search procedure

I will now resume the line of thought I was pursuing in section 2.1, comparing free variable rules with rules with eigenparameter conditions. While the aim of section

2.1 is to clarify the conditions for connection-driven search, I shall in this section focus on termination properties and redundancy in the search space. These issues are of course related. If the search does not terminate as soon as possible, it makes a number of redundant steps, and *vice versa*.

The Eigenparameter conditions in LK and ground tableau systems facilitate the formulation of termination conditions. Part of this task is to constrain the instantiation (and hence duplication) of generative quantifier occurrences. The use of eigenparameters allows us to constrain these instantiations branchwise: only the term universe induced by formulae in the branch is relevant. It is an open question whether this is possible also for free variable systems, even though some speed–up results are known. The results can be explained by reference to the search procedure used in the previous section.

There are two different kinds of free variable systems: matrix systems and free variable tableaux. A key point in the exposition of classical logic has been to show that free variable LK can accommodate both of these by different strategies for selecting free variables. The procedure in section 2.8 generates variable–sharing (matrix related) skeletons, but can easily be modified to generate skeletons of the other type. It regulates expansion by the term universe of the whole skeleton. This is, however, not the only source of its inefficiency. As it stands it uses exponential space and makes inefficient use of unification. Since the procedure generates variable–sharing skeletons it introduces redundant copies of free variables, but the permutation properties caused by this tactic are not exploited by the use of connections. The procedure serves its function for the Model existence theorem, but is from the point of view of efficiency very naive. Below I shall briefly discuss some ways of improving the procedure.

One kind of redundancy stems from multiple copies of variables in variable–sharing skeletons. Bibel [1982a] proposed a matrix mechanism to overcome this, called *splitting by need*. Although well understood for clauses, splitting is not well analyzed for nonclausal formulae. But even if we turn the procedure into a procedure for free variable tableaux, it is still likely to give rise to redundancies compared to procedures for ground tableaux, cnf. the discussion of the termination problem for free variable tableaux in [Letz 1999]. *Universal variables* have been proposed to reduce this redundancy [Beckert and Hähnle 1992]. Another remedy is the δ^{++}–rule which implements a sharing of Skolem functions. The rule reduces the size of the term universe and can give rise to a nonelementary decrease in proof length; further optimalizations are possible [Baaz and Fernmüller 1995]. It is important to note that even if these proposals give significant speed–up, they do not eliminate the redundancy problems caused by free variables. Moreover, the precise relationship between Bibel's splitting method and the use of universal variables in tableaux has, up to my knowledge, not been clarified.

We may of course simulate a tableau procedure in the free variable system, but this will undermine the whole point of using free variables. Nevertheless, this is the simplest way to construct countermodels. For most nonclassical systems in this chapter I shall prove completeness in this way. I leave it open whether the constructions transfer directly to variable–sharing skeletons, and hence to matrices. The point is addressed further in section 4.4.

The procedure in the previous section makes very inefficient use of the unification algorithm, since one has to check the whole skeleton for closure after each expansion. What we would need is a mechanism which distributes most general unifiers as global constraints, so that the search can run in a least commitment way and the solutions to the partial unification problems be recorded.

I have deliberately neglected connections in this discussion. Since many authors cover the material in depth, there is no need to repeat this rich theory in a chapter about nonclassical logics. Many of the connection procedures have been transformed to a tableau setting, though mostly for clausal forms; an exception is [Hähnle and Klingenbeck 1996]. For references about search procedures and general overviews of the field, consult Bibel and Eder [1993] and [Letz and Stenz 2001] (Chapter 28 of this Handbook).

Finally, a word about implementation. Due to the complex structure of multiplicities, it is tricky to implement a connection–driven procedure for classical logic which does not rely on normal form. If we assume normal form, the task is much simpler. Theorem provers for classical logic have for good reasons been restricted to input in clausal form, cnf. [Letz and Stenz 2001] (Chapter 28 of this Handbook). Up to my knowledge virtually all published material on the implementation of connection–driven proof procedures makes this assumption. I shall follow up this point in the discussion of proof procedures for intuitionistic logic in section 4.4.

3. Labelled systems

3.1. Introduction

From the point of view of this chapter analytic proof systems for modal and intuitionistic logic have developed in three stages: destructive systems, ground prefixed systems and systems with free variables in prefixes.

The oldest analytic systems are *destructive* in the sense that one sometimes, in the course of a search, has to discharge parts of the built–up structure. A case in point is Gentzen's sequent calculus LJ for intuitionistic logic [Gentzen 1934–35]. In LJ only sequents with at most one formula in the succedent are permitted; otherwise the rules are as for LK. The logical rules of LJ are given in figure 10 on page 1550. Let us try to prove the sequent $\neg P \vdash \neg(P \vee Q) \vee (P \supset Q)$ in LJ. We may first expand the right disjunction. But in doing this we must choose between the disjuncts, i.e. we must opt for one of them and temporarily discard the other. Selecting the left disjunct gives rise to the leftmost derivation in figure 4. Since this option fails, we must backtrack and try the other. As the rightmost derivation in figure 4 shows, this leads to a proof.

LJ is the first intuitionistic sequent calculus. A multi–succedent version was later introduced by Maehara [1954]. The first modal systems of this kind seem to appear in the fifties in the works of Curry [1952], Kanger [1957] and Ohnishi and Matsumoto

$$\frac{\dfrac{\dfrac{\dfrac{\dfrac{P \vdash P \quad Q \vdash P}{P \vee Q \vdash P}}{\neg P, P \vee Q \vdash}}{\neg P \vdash \neg(P \vee Q)}}{\neg P \vdash \neg(P \vee Q) \vee (P \supset Q)}}$$

$$\frac{\dfrac{\dfrac{\dfrac{\dfrac{P \vdash P}{\neg P, P \vdash}}{\neg P, P \vdash Q}}{\neg P \vdash P \supset Q}}{\neg P \vdash \neg(P \vee Q) \vee (P \supset Q)}}$$

Figure 4: Two attempts to prove the endsequent in LJ.

[1957b, 1957a, 1959]. Tableau methods are used extensively in the pioneering works of Kripke [1959, 1963] and the related contributions of Hintikka [1962] and Schütte [1968]. Systems of this kind are comprehensively surveyed in the recent volume *Handbook of Tableau Methods*. The collection of papers in that volume contains an up–to–date treatment of a number of nonclassical systems, including chapters on modal and temporal logics [Goré 1999] and intuitionistic logic [Waaler and Wallen 1999].

As witnessed by the previous example the early sequent calculi are cumbersome to use, both as pen–and–pencil devices and as bases for implementation. Pushing metaphors we might say that the objects constructed under a proof–search have the structure of a forest. Prefixed (labelled) systems remedy the situation. Up to my knowledge the first prefixed system is the S5 system of "spotted formulae" due to Kanger [1957]. The same idea underlies a short note by Fitch [1966] and is worked out in more detail as systems of tableaux by Fitting [1983]. The idea of using prefixes has later been generalized by Gabbay into Labelled Deductive Systems [Gabbay 1996] and proposed as a general logical framework. Labels also serve a key function in Mints' work on cut–elimination in modal systems [Mints 1997].

The basic idea of labelled systems is to 'prefix' formulae by a new kind of terms and use these terms to separate the classical component from the nonclassical. Some authors, like Mints [1997], prefix sequents rather than formulae. In many cases the labels can be motivated by reference to Kripke models. The basis for the model–theoretical interpretation is that the structure of Kripke models can be defined by appropriate closure operations on trees; this property holds for all logics addressed in this chapter. Since prefixes in a tableau can naturally be interpreted as points in a tree one can define Kripke models by closure operations on "prefix trees". A prefix denotes, from this perspective, a point in a model under construction. Different logics can be characterized by different closure operations. In Fitting's modal systems this is reflected directly in the closure rules of the tableaux. Fitting's rule for closing a tableau is system–specific [Fitting 1983].

Recently, Massacci has proposed a refinement of Fitting's prefixed systems for modal propositional logic [Massacci 1994, Massacci 2000]. Just as in Fitting's systems the prefixes are taken as points in the tree which spans a Kripke model. The systems are called *single step tableaux* to reflect that prefixes of the principal and side formulae of an inference denote points which are at most one step away. Massacci thereby gains a high degree of modularity in the definition of the modal systems. This holds in particular for symmetrical and Euclidean logics, where the single step approach allows him to jump smoothly from one world to another. Moreover, all systems have the same closure rules; the systems are distinguished solely by their logical rules. And even though one can argue that the proofs in some of Massacci's systems are not as direct as they are in other logical systems, it is not likely that this side effect is computationally significant. Besides Massacci's own papers, his systems are thoroughly presented in the overview chapter by Goré [1999].

The ground prefix systems have conditions on prefix parameters which correspond to the Eigenparameter condition in Gentzen's LK. These conditions run contrary to the idea of connection–driven search. The dependencies captured by the parameter conditions are part of the logical consequence relation and can as such not be eliminated. But just as in classical first–order logic we can introduce free variables into the labels and use them to recast the dependency constraints into properties on the labels. Labels can then be tested for the crucial properties by means of unification algorithms.

This brilliant technical step was first proposed by Wallen [1987]. Rather than viewing the labels as points in a Kripke structure, Wallen argues for a proof–theoretical interpretation in terms of a relation on inferences [Wallen 1990]. As long as we have a Kripke structure at our disposal, the different perspectives just reflect different levels of abstraction. In this chapter we shall use Wallen's reduction ordering on inferences in the soundness proofs. The semantical perspective is, on the other hand, justified by the existence of soundness and completeness results. The proof–theoretical interpretation has the advantage that it carries over to systems without a Kripke semantics. The adaptation of the technique to a system of first–order dependent types illustrates the point [Pym and Wallen 1990].

It is fruitful to view the free variable systems in relation to the ground systems. Wallen's matrix systems generalize Fitting's systems of prefixed tableaux. Beckert and Goré [1997] obtain a slightly different family of modal systems by generalizing Massacci's single step tableaux; they also cover a larger class of systems than Wallen. Beckert and Goré have formulated their systems to facilitate their compact "lean–type" implementation.

Another class of labelled modal calculi employs a language called *KEM* [Artosi and Governatori 1994, Governatori 1995, Governatori and Rotolo 2000]. *KEM* is a language with free variables, but unlike the languages addressed in this chapter *KEM* also labels the subformulae of a given formula. The language has been applied in an original treatment of modal identity [Artosi, Benassi, Governatori and Rotolo 1998].

Labelled modal systems are not limited to tableau–style systems. A similar idea has been used by Ohlbach in the design of resolution systems for modal logics [Ohlbach 1988, Ohlbach 1990]. Despite technical differences in the systems, the unification problems induced by the resolution systems are identical to those induced by the corresponding matrix systems. By comparing the systems in this chapter with [Ohlbach et al. 2001] (Chapter 21 of this Handbook), the reader will find numerous points of intersection and mutual illumination.

I have decided to base the chapter on a sequent–style rendition of Wallen's systems. These systems are the most well–known, and they also transfer directly to first–order logic. One must observe that original sources should in any case be consulted. This is particularly important as long as the field is only on its way to be settled.

Wallen's matrix systems for modal and intuitionistic logic generalize Bibel's version of the classical connection calculus. To show the general nature of these systems I shall give two simple examples. Let us first address a modal variant of the propositional formula discussed at the beginning of section 2.1. Below is a matrix for the indexed modal formula $\Diamond(P^0 \vee R^1) \vee ((\Box(\neg P^2 \wedge Q^3) \vee \Diamond \neg Q^4) \wedge \neg P^5)$.

$$\left[\begin{array}{ccc} P^0[U] & R^1[U] & \left[\begin{array}{cc} \overline{P}^2[a] & \overline{Q}^4[V] \\ Q^3[a] & \\ & \overline{P}^5[] \end{array} \right] \end{array} \right]$$

Up to the parameter a and the free variables U and V the matrix above is identical to the propositional matrix in section 2.1. There are three connections: $\{P^0[U], \overline{P}^2[a]\}$, $\{P^0[U], \overline{P}^5[]\}$, and $\{Q^3[a], \overline{Q}^4[V]\}$. The free variables U and V are called *prefix variables* to distinguish them from the free variables generated by quantifiers. Different modal systems are distinguished by unification conditions. For instance, the assignment of the empty string ε to the variable U, which makes $\{P^0[U], \overline{P}^5[]\}$ complementary, is valid only for T–logics. Since the equation set $\{U = a, U = \varepsilon, V = a\}$ has no solution, the set of connections is not spanning. We may, however, duplicate the subformula $\Diamond(P^0 \vee R^1)$ and get the matrix

$$\left[\begin{array}{ccccc} P^6[W] & R^7[W] & P^0[U] & R^1[U] & \left[\begin{array}{cc} \overline{P}^2[a] & \overline{Q}^4[V] \\ Q^3[a] & \\ & \overline{P}^5[] \end{array} \right] \end{array} \right]$$

The matrix defines the set of connections $\{P^0[U], \overline{P}^2[a]\}$, $\{P^6[W], \overline{P}^5[]\}$, and $\{Q^3[a], \overline{Q}^4[V]\}$, which is spanning wrt. the substitution $\{U/a, V/a, W/\varepsilon\}$. The formula is hence provable in the modal system T.

The matrix method can reduce the complexity of search considerably for a particular class of invalid sequents. Let us say that the classical kernel of a modal formula is the formula obtained by stripping off every modal operator. If the kernel is classically invalid, the modal formula is invalid. One can now let the proof–search procedure implement a computationally cheap test for validity of the classical kernel prior to any operations on the labels, either at the level of paths or at the level of matrices. The matrix is generated with labels attached, but the labels are ignored in the classical test. If the test fails, the search simply terminates. Otherwise, we address the labels and check if the closure conditions hold also when labels are taken into account. If this is the case, we have a matrix proof. Otherwise, we must check if a proof can be found by increasing multiplicities. We know that every larger matrix is also a proof of the classical kernel, so we can include the labels in the closure test of an extended matrix directly. This is repeated as long as the closure test fails. Clearly, the process should have a termination condition. We shall discuss this approach to proof–search in labelled systems closer in the exposition of intuitionistic logic in section 4.4.

As the reader will notice, the example above illustrates this approach. Observe that the classical kernel of the modal formula is identical to the sample formula addressed in section 2.1. Hence, if we ignore labels in the first modal matrix above, the matrix is identical to the classical matrix at the beginning of the section 2.1. However, since the labels show that the conditions for a modal proof cannot be met, the multiplicity of $\Diamond(P^0 \vee R^1)$ is increased, resulting in the second matrix above. This matrix happens to satisfy the constraints for the modal logic T.

The example from intuitionistic propositional logic at the beginning of this section is slightly more involved. Figure 6 on page 1528 gives a sequent calculus formulation of the intuitionistic matrix system. The following is a well–defined skeleton:

$$\frac{\dfrac{\dfrac{\dfrac{P[a] \vdash P[U], P \supset Q \quad Q[a] \vdash P[U], P \supset Q}{P \vee Q[a] \vdash P[U], P \supset Q}}{\neg P, P \vee Q[a] \vdash P \supset Q} \, U}{\neg P \vdash \neg(P \vee Q), P \supset Q} \, a}{\neg P \vdash \neg(P \vee Q) \vee (P \supset Q)}$$

Recall the two LJ derivations in figure 4. Under the substitution $\{U/a\}$ the skeleton above corresponds, with one proviso, to the leftmost of the LJ derivations. Note that the substitution closes the left branch and fails to close the other. The proviso is due to the implication. The fact that we do not discard implications in the labelled system makes it possible to let the search resume and continue to expand the skeleton. Expanding the implication in the leftmost branch, we must introduce a new parameter b. This yields the following inference.

$$\frac{P[a], P[b] \vdash P[U], Q[b]}{P[a] \vdash P[U], P \supset Q} \, b$$

Assume that we add this inference to the skeleton above; let us call the resulting skeleton δ. The substitution $\{U/b\}$ closes the left branch of δ; the other branch is, however, still open. One way to construct a proof is to expand the implication in the other branch as well and use the same parameter b. The resulting skeleton will then be closed by $\{U/b\}$:

$$\frac{\dfrac{\dfrac{\dfrac{\dfrac{P[a], P[b] \vdash P[U], Q[b]}{P[a] \vdash P[U], P \supset Q} \, b \quad \dfrac{Q[a], P[b] \vdash P[U], Q[b]}{Q[a] \vdash P[U], P \supset Q} \, b}{P \vee Q[a] \vdash P[U], P \supset Q}}{\neg P, P \vee Q[a] \vdash P \supset Q} \, U}{\neg P \vdash \neg(P \vee Q), P \supset Q} \, a}{\neg P \vdash \neg(P \vee Q) \vee (P \supset Q)}$$

But this is redundant. We can avoid this step by *pruning* δ. The key observation is that the principal formula $P \vee Q[a]$ of the branching inference in δ has a label incompatible with b. Since no axiom label in the sub–skeleton above the left premiss of the inference contains a, the branching inference can simply be ignored. Hence the sub–skeleton above the rightmost premiss can also be ignored. Removing the branching inference from δ leaves us with a proof which corresponds to the rightmost LJ proof in figure 4 (up to the order of inferences).

On the implementational side Kreitz and Otten [1999] have introduced a uniform proof procedure for the first–order nonclassical systems. Extending the connection–driven classical search procedures, the uniform procedure specifies a search algorithm for nonclassical logics at a high level of detail. In doing this, the authors also improve on the formulation of the intuitionistic system [Otten and Kreitz 1995]. In the formulation of his intuitionistic system Wallen exploits the Gödel S4 mapping; the intuitionistic system can hence be taken as an application of the matrix system for S4. The syntax of the intuitionistic part of Kreitz and Otten's uniform procedure is formulated more carefully, as is Otten's implementation [1997]. The procedure has been extended to fragments of linear logic [Kreitz, Mantel, Otten and Schmitt 1997, Mantel and Kreitz 1998] and been applied in an attempt to model inductive reasoning [Kreitz and Pientka 2000]

The relationship between intuitionistic matrix proofs and proofs in Gentzen–style sequent calculi has been investigated in great detail with an eye to applications in program development systems [Kreitz and Schmitt 2000, Egly and Schmitt 1998, Egly and Schmitt 1999]. The papers include algorithmic transformations of intuitionistic matrix proofs into LJ proofs and include new results about the relationship between LJ and its multi–succedent variant [Egly and Schmitt 1999, Egly 2000].

Presenting the matrix systems in the form of a sequent calculus in effect separates pure logic from implementational considerations. The separation is not only fruitful for the presentation of ideas. It is also instructive for the design of matrix systems for new logics in general. The perspective suggests that one in such cases should take the sequent calculus as a point of departure, should there be one available, and try to design a sequent calculus with full permutability. This can be achieved by the introduction of term structures which capture dependencies between rules, so that global conditions on the proofs can be replaced by unification conditions on the terms. Given this system, one must try to design a matrix representation of the search space. In a sense this agenda summarizes the whole project of characterizing nonclassical provability in terms of matrices.

3.2. Syntax of labels

There exists a number of different variants of label syntax. Most authors let the labels prefix the formulae, others prefer to use them as suffix. I guess these variations are just a matter of personal taste. The terms 'prefix' and 'label' are used synonymously.

The object language extends the propositional fragment of the language in section 2.2 by a set of terms. A *prefix term* is either a *prefix variable* or a *prefix parameter*. Lower case letters from the beginning of the alphabet range over prefix parameters; upper case letters range over prefix variables. If p and q are strings of prefix terms, pq denotes the concatenation of p and q. We shall identify a string p with εp and $p\varepsilon$. $p \prec q$ denotes that p is a proper initial sequence of q. By convention, $\varepsilon \prec q$ for any q. If the language is not first–order, i.e. if there are no quantifier terms, we shall refer to prefix terms just as *terms*.

To conform with the work on unification, the class of admissible strings must be limited. Let us say that a *label* is a string of prefix terms, including the empty string ε, which contains at most one occurrence of a given term. The symbols p and q are used for labels. If t is a prefix term which occurs in a label q and $pt \preceq q$, then p is the *prefix of t in q*. A set of labels Θ satisfies the *Unique prefix property* if every prefix term has the same prefix in all labels in Θ in which it occurs. The property was identified in [Ohlbach 1988] and [Auffray and Enjalbert 1992]. Beckert and Goré [1997] base their free variable calculus on a weaker property.

A *label substitution* is a partial function from prefix variables into a set of labels. The set of labels in a skeleton will always satisfy the Unique prefix property, as well as being closed under $\prec$. It is crucial for the consistency of the systems that label substitutions preserve the Unique prefix property. There is a simple test which can be used to check this. Let Θ be a set of labels closed under $\prec$. We say that a substitution σ is *bounded by* Θ if the following condition holds for each U: if $\sigma(U) = q't$, there are labels pU and qt in Θ such that $(pU)\sigma = (qt)\sigma$.

3.1. LEMMA. *Let Θ be closed under $\prec$ and satisfy the Unique prefix property. Let σ be an idempotent label substitution bounded by Θ. Then $\Theta\sigma$ satisfies the Unique prefix property.*

PROOF. Let us say that the *prefix complexity* of a variable U in $\mathrm{dom}(\sigma)$ is the number of variables in $\mathrm{dom}(\sigma)$ which occurs in the prefix of U in Θ. Let σ_n be the restriction of σ to the variables with prefix complexity $\leq n$. The lemma holds if $\Theta\sigma_n$ satisfies the Unique prefix property for each n, which we prove by induction. Let U have prefix complexity n and t occur in $\sigma(U)$. By the boundedness condition, the prefix of t in $\Theta\sigma_n$ is identical to its prefix in $\Theta\sigma_{n-1}$. By idempotency, $\Theta\sigma_n = \Theta\sigma_{n-1}\sigma_n$ for each n (let $\Theta\sigma_{-1}$ be Θ). By induction hypothesis, $\Theta\sigma_{n-1}$ satisfies the Unique prefix property. We are done.   □

A *labelled formula* is a formula which is attached a label in brackets as suffix, like $P[a]$. A *labelled sequent* is an expression of the form $\Gamma \vdash \Delta$, where Γ and Δ are finite multisets of labelled formulae. A sequent is *empty labelled* if all formulae in the sequent are labelled with ε, like $P[\varepsilon] \vdash Q[\varepsilon]$. If Z is a syntactical object of one of the labelled calculi in this chapter (e.g., formula, sequent, skeleton), $\widehat{Z}$ denotes the unlabelled variant obtained by removing every label from Z. $\widehat{Z}$ is then an object of a calculus for classical logic. An empty labelled sequent S is identified with $\widehat{S}$, e.g., $P[\varepsilon] \vdash Q[\varepsilon]$ and $P \vdash Q$ are identified.

3.3. Unification

The search for a closing substitution for labelled skeletons can be posed as a unification problem. The unification problems for the nonclassical matrix systems have been defined in a particularly clear way as systems of simultaneous equations by Otten and Kreitz [1996]. This section presents their unification algorithm for S4. The algorithm also works for the intuitionistic matrix system of Wallen and is closely linked to the unification problems induced by the intuitionistic systems in section 4. Otten and Kreitz have adapted their algorithm to the other modal systems addressed in this chapter as well; further details can be found in the above cited paper. The algorithm improves on the algorithm defined by Ohlbach [1988] by computing a minimal set of most general unifiers.

The presentation follows the conventions used in this chapter. In particular, t is used both for prefix variables and prefix parameters. The unification algorithm takes a set of equations $\{p_1 = q_1, \ldots, p_n = q_n\}$ as input on condition that $\{p_1, q_1, \ldots, p_n, q_n\}$ satisfies the Unique prefix property. Let Γ be the initial set of equations. The substitution σ is a *unifier* for Γ if it is a solution to the equations, i.e. if $p_i\sigma = q_i\sigma$ for each i. A substitution τ is an *instance* of σ if there is an η such that $\tau = \sigma\eta$. A nonempty set Σ is a *complete set of unifiers* for Γ if each σ in Σ is a unifier and each unifier for Γ is an instance of a unifier in Σ. Σ is a *most general set of unifiers* if it is also *minimal*, i.e. if the following holds for every σ and τ in Σ: if τ is an instance of σ, then $\sigma = \tau$.

The unification algorithm makes essential use of the assumed Unique prefix property. To see the strength of this principle, take two arbitrary strings p and q. Assume that p is p_1p_2 and q is q_1q_2. Assume further that σ_1 unifies p_1 and q_1 and σ_2 unifies p_2 and q_2. Thanks to the Unique prefix property we know that $\sigma_1 \cup \sigma_2$ is a unifier for p and q. It is precisely for this reason that the unification algorithm below always terminates.

Observe that this is not the case for string unification in general. If p is Ua and q is bU, it is clear that $\sigma_1 = \{U/b\}$ unifies U and b and that $\sigma_2 = \{U/a\}$ unifies a and U. But since the two substitutions disagree on U, $\sigma_1 \cup \sigma_2$ does not unify p and q. This situation cannot arise for strings which satisfy the Unique prefix property.

The general idea of the algorithm is presented in the next example.

3.2. EXAMPLE. To unify the labels $aBcDEf$ and $aBGhiJ$ we have to look for a mapping which assigns a substring of the former to each variable in the latter, and vice versa. The unifiers can be visualized in the following way:

- arrange equal terms underneath each other,
- put a parameter within the range of a variable in the other string,
- stretch the range of a variable so that it either overlaps with a variable in the other string or ends between two constants of the other string or ends at the end of the other string.

Here is one example:

Rule	Equation	$\rightarrow$	Equation	Binding
$\top$	$\varepsilon = \vert\varepsilon$	$\rightarrow$	$\top$	
$\bot 1$	$ap = \vert\varepsilon$	$\rightarrow$	$\bot$	
$\bot 2$	$ap = \vert bq$	$\rightarrow$	$\bot$	
E1	$\varepsilon = \vert tp$	$\rightarrow$	$tp = \vert\varepsilon$	
E2	$ap = \vert Uq$	$\rightarrow$	$Uq = \vert ap$	
A1	$tp = \vert tq$	$\rightarrow$	$p = \vert q$	
A2	$Utp = \vert Vq$	$\rightarrow$	$Vq = U\vert tp$	
A3	$U = q\vert V$	$\rightarrow$	$U = qV\vert\varepsilon$	
A4	$Up = q_1\vert Vtq_2$	$\rightarrow$	$Up = q_1 V\vert tq_2$	
A5	$Up = q_1\vert aq_2$	$\rightarrow$	$Up = q_1 a\vert q_2$	
B1	$Up = q\vert\varepsilon$	$\rightarrow$	$p = \vert\varepsilon$	U/q
B2	$Up = \vert aq$	$\rightarrow$	$p = \vert aq$	U/ε
B3	$Up = q_1\vert abq_2$	$\rightarrow$	$p = \vert bq_2$	$U/q_1 a$
B4	$Ut_1 p = t_2 q_1\vert Vq_2$	$\rightarrow$	$Vq_2 = X\vert t_1 p$	$U/t_2 q_1 X$

Table 1: Transformation rules for the unification algorithm. $U \neq V$ in A2–A4. X is fresh in B4

Two new variables, X and Y, have also found their way into the figure. They are needed for the sake of obtaining most general solutions. The unifier $\sigma_1 = \{G\backslash cX, D\backslash XhiY, J\backslash YEf\}$ can be derived on the basis of the figure. To get *all* most general unifiers we simply line up all the options:

This gives rise to the following unifiers, which form a most general set:

$\sigma_0 = \{G\backslash cX, D\backslash Xh, E\backslash iY, J\backslash Yf\}$ (first row),

$\sigma_1 = \{G\backslash cX, D\backslash XhiY, J\backslash YEf\}$ (second row),

$\sigma_2 = \{G\backslash cDX, E\backslash XhiY, J\backslash Yf\}$ (third row).

The core of the unification algorithm is the set of transformation rules listed in table 1. Each rule transforms an equation into another equation and a (possibly empty) substitution. To facilitate the formulation of the rules we shall use the symbol '|' as a reading mark. The upper group of rules consists of one rule which generates the success mark $\top$ and two rules which generate the failure mark $\bot$.

The reading mark is used only at the right hand side and serves to single out potential values for variables at the front of the left hand side. This requires that the equations be in a particular form. There are seven rules used to achieve this: two exchange rules and five rules used to advance the reading mark. We shall call these rules E1, E2 and A1–A5. In the rules A2–A4 it is essential that $U \neq V$. Observe that at most one rule in the middle group can apply to a given equation.

There are four rules which produce bindings. In B4 the variable X is fresh. With the full set of rules more than one rule may apply to a given equation. More precisely, this holds for the following pairs of rules: A4 and B4; A5 and B2; A5 and B3; B2 and B3. The pairs show where there is OR–branching in the search space. Thanks to this the number of most general unifiers is in the worst case exponential in the length of the input equations.

The rules in the two uppermost groups generate no new bindings. We shall say that they transform the left hand equation into the right hand equation and the empty substitution. The other rules generate the singleton substitution given by the binding.

The algorithm operates on pairs of the form (Δ, σ), where Δ is a set of equations with the reading mark at the right hand side and σ is a label substitution. Pick an equation E in Δ and a rule which transforms E to E' and τ. Let Δ' be $\Delta\{E/E'\}\tau$ minus $\{\top\}$. Then $(\Delta', \sigma \cup \tau)$ is *obtained from* (Δ, σ) *by reduction on* E. The success mark $\top$ signifies that an equation has been solved and is therefore promptly removed from the equation set. (Δ, σ) *reduces to* (Δ', σ') if there is a sequence of reductions leading from (Δ, σ) to (Δ', σ'). Note that (Δ, σ) cannot reduce to $(\emptyset, \sigma')$ if $\bot \in \Delta$.

If Γ is the initial set of equations, we let Γ_0 be the set of all strings $p = |q$ such that $p = q$ is in Γ. The *success set for* Γ is the set of all σ such that $(\Gamma_0, \emptyset)$ reduces to $(\emptyset, \sigma)$.

3.3. EXAMPLE. Let Γ_0 be $\{Uab = |cV\}$. Figure 5 depicts all reductions from $(\Gamma_0, \emptyset)$ and shows that the success set is the singleton set $\{\{U/cX, V/Xab\}\}$. A graphical display of the solution is:

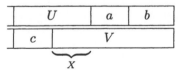

3.4. LEMMA. *Let Γ be a set of equations which satisfies the Unique prefix property and σ be in the success set for Γ. Then σ is idempotent and $\Gamma\sigma$ satisfies the Unique prefix property.*

PROOF. Idempotence is immediate from the Unique prefix property of Γ and the fact that all equations are instantiated once a new binding is computed in the reduction process. As to the second part it is immediate that all rules except B4

Line	Δ_i	σ_i	Rule to line
1	$\{Uab = \lvert cV\}$	$\emptyset$	
2	$\{ab = \lvert cV\}$	$\{U/\varepsilon\}$	B2 to 1
3	$\{\perp\}$	$\{U/\varepsilon\}$	$\perp$2 to 2
4	$\{Uab = c\lvert V\}$	$\emptyset$	A5 to 1
5	$\{V = X\lvert ab\}$	$\{U/cX\}$	B4 to 4
6	$\{\varepsilon = \lvert b\}$	$\{U/cX, V/Xa\}$	B3 to 5
7	$\{b = \lvert\varepsilon\}$	$\{U/cX, V/Xa\}$	E1 to 6
8	$\{\perp\}$	$\{U/cX, V/Xa\}$	$\perp$1 to 7
9	$\{V = Xa\lvert b\}$	$\{U/cX\}$	A5 to 5
10	$\{V = Xab\lvert\varepsilon\}$	$\{U/cX\}$	A5 to 9
11	$\{\varepsilon = \lvert\varepsilon\}$	$\{U/cX, V/Xab\}$	B1 to 10
12	$\emptyset$	$\{U/cX, V/Xab\}$	$\top$ to 11

Figure 5: All reductions from (Δ_1, σ_1). σ_{12} is the only solution.

preserve the Unique prefix property. B4 introduces a variable X which does not occur in the equations. However, this variable is fresh and cannot itself be bound to a value by any of the substitutions in the success set. To see this, note that the reading mark cannot move backwards and that X occurs to the left of the mark in the resulting equation in B4. Hence the prefix of X in $\Gamma\sigma$ is unique. □

3.5. LEMMA. *The reduction relation is well–founded.*

PROOF. Define a function h and a well–founded relation $<$ such that if (Δ', σ') is obtained from (Δ, σ) by reduction, then $h(\Delta') < h(\Delta)$. This can be done in many ways and is left for the reader. □

3.6. THEOREM. *Let Γ be a finite set of equations and Σ be the success set for Γ. Then Σ is a most general set of unifiers and is computable in exponential time.*

PROOF. Let $\tau \in \Sigma$. There must then be a reduction sequence from $(\Gamma_0, \emptyset)$ to $(\emptyset, \tau)$. We show that τ is a unifier for the equations in Γ by proving the following statement by induction on the length of the reduction sequence: *for each pair (Δ, σ) in the sequence, $\tau \setminus \sigma$ is a solution to Δ*. The base step is trivial since $\emptyset$ is a solution to $\emptyset$. For the inductive step, assume that (Δ', σ') is obtained from (Δ, σ) by reduction on E. We must now argue case by case.

Let us take one of the cases in detail. Assume that E is $Up = q\lvert\varepsilon$ and B1 has been used to generate $p = \lvert\varepsilon$ and the binding U/q. Then $\sigma' = \sigma \cup \{U/q\}$ and $\tau\setminus\sigma = (\tau\setminus\sigma')\cup\{U/q\}$. By induction hypothesis, $\tau\setminus\sigma'$ is a solution to $\Delta\{E/p = \lvert\varepsilon\}$. By inspection of the equation, it is evident that $\tau \setminus \sigma$ is a solution to Δ.

The other cases are similar. That the members of Σ are complete can be seen by inspecting the potential forms of unifiers (cnf. remarks in [Otten and Kreitz 1996]). Minimality of Σ follows since every two substitutions in Σ disagree on at least one binding in a way which blocks one substitution from being an instance of the other. This can, again, be seen from the transformation rules.

It follows from lemma 3.5 that Σ is computable. Clearly there can be exponentially many most general unifiers. $\qquad\square$

3.4. Unification by constraints

The unification algorithm above computes a set of most general unifiers for a set of equations Γ by calculating the unifiers incrementally for each equation in Γ. The technique is strong enough to derive *all* unifiers of Γ. In the context of proof–search it is, however, sufficient to find *one* solution. Since the number of most general unifiers may grow exponentially with the number and length of the strings in Γ, this observation is significant. Moreover, even if we compute only one unifier for Γ, it is not efficient to compute it by incrementally unifying the equations in Γ and backtrack in case of failure.

The unification algorithm presented in [Otten and Kreitz 2001] uses constraints to characterize variable substitutions. Several substitutions are characterized by a single constraint for each prefix. The constraints are introduced step by step for each equation, and if the resulting set of constraints is consistent, there is at least one unifier for all equations. The idea is illustrated in the example below.

3.7. EXAMPLE. Consider the set of equations $\Gamma = \{UV = a, WX = Ub, W = U\}$. There are two solutions to the first equation, namely $\{U/\varepsilon, V/a\}$ (applying B2, A5, B1, and T) and $\{U/a, V/\varepsilon\}$ (applying A5, B1, B1, and T). Depending on which solution is chosen there are five possible unifiers for the second equation: $\{W/\varepsilon, X/b\}$, $\{W/b, X/\varepsilon\}$ (in case U/ε) and $\{W/\varepsilon, X/ab\}$, $\{W/a, X/b\}$, $\{W/ab, X/\varepsilon\}$ (in case U/a). We can characterize the solutions to the first equation by the constraint $[UV] = \{a\}$ expressing the fact that the first character of the string assigned to UV must be the constant a. For the second equation we introduce the constraint $[WX] = \{a, b\}$, expressing that the first character of the string assigned to WX must be either a or b. The two constraints therefore encode each of the five unifiers listed above.

In general such a *domain constraint* has the form $U_1 U_2 \ldots U_n = \{a_1, a_2, \ldots, a_m\}$, denoting that the first character of the string assigned to $U_1 U_2 \ldots U_n$ must be an element from the *domain set* $\{a_1, a_2, \ldots, a_m\}$. From the first two constraints we deduce $[W] = \{a, b\}$ and $[U] = \{a\}$. To solve the third equation the first character of the strings assigned to W and U must be the same, i.e. we have to restrict both domain sets to $[W] = [U] = \{a, b\} \cap \{a\} = \{a\}$. In general for two constraints $[V_1 V_2 \ldots V_j \ldots V_n] = D_1$ and $[V_1 V_2 \ldots V_j] = D_2$ their domain sets D_1 and D_2 must be equal, since every substitution assigning the first character a to $V_1 V_2 \ldots V_j$ also assigns it to $V_1 V_2 \ldots V_j \ldots V_m$. If all constraints satisfy this property (and some others; see [Otten and Kreitz 2001]) they are said to be *consistent*. In order to get a

$$\frac{\Gamma, A[p], B[p] \vdash \Delta}{\Gamma, A \wedge B[p] \vdash \Delta} \; L\wedge \qquad\qquad \frac{\Gamma \vdash A[p], \Delta \quad \Gamma \vdash B[p], \Delta}{\Gamma \vdash A \wedge B[p], \Delta} \; R\wedge$$

$$\frac{\Gamma, A[p] \vdash \Delta \quad \Gamma, B[p] \vdash \Delta}{\Gamma, A \vee B[p] \vdash \Delta} \; L\vee \qquad\qquad \frac{\Gamma \vdash A[p], B[p], \Delta}{\Gamma \vdash A \vee B[p], \Delta} \; R\vee$$

$$\frac{\Gamma \vdash A[pU], \Delta \quad \Gamma, B[pU] \vdash \Delta}{\Gamma, A \supset B[p] \vdash \Delta} \; L\supset \qquad\qquad \frac{\Gamma, A[pb] \vdash B[pb], \Delta}{\Gamma \vdash A \supset B[p], \Delta} \; R\supset$$

$$\frac{\Gamma \vdash A[pU], \Delta}{\Gamma, \neg A[p] \vdash \Delta} \; L\neg \qquad\qquad\qquad \frac{\Gamma, A[pb] \vdash \Delta}{\Gamma \vdash \neg A[p], \Delta} \; R\neg$$

Figure 6: Propositional free variable rules.

consistent constraint set for our example we have to refine the constraint $[WX] = \{a, b\}$ to $[WX] = \{a\}$. Applying the only induced substitution $\{U/aU', W/aW'\}$ (where U' and V' are fresh variables) to Γ yields a set of equations with the same first character a on both side of each equation. It can therefore be deleted from all equations. From the resulting set of equations the final unifier $\{U/a, V/\varepsilon, W/a, X/b\}$ can be calculated easily.

The *consistency algorithm* illustrated in the previous example and described in detail in [Otten and Kreitz 2001] is considerably more efficient than the *backtracking algorithm* presented in the previous section if only one unifier needs to be calculated.

4. Propositional intuitionistic logic

The exposition of intuitionistic logic relies heavily on the concepts introduced for classical logic in section 2. Section 4.1 covers the free variable sequent calculus up to the Soundness theorem as well as matrix syntax. Completeness is established in section 4.2 through a system with ground labels.

4.1. Free variable systems

The free variable sequent calculus adopts the structural LK rules in figure 1 with the proviso that the rules now operate on labelled formulae. Contraction hence looks like this:

$$\frac{\Gamma, A[p], A[p] \vdash \Delta}{\Gamma, A[p] \vdash \Delta} \; LC \qquad\qquad \frac{\Gamma \vdash A[p], A[p], \Delta}{\Gamma \vdash A[p], \Delta} \; RC$$

The logical rules are given in figure 6. Recall that the symbol p ranges over labels, which means that it can be either ε or a prefix term or a sequence of prefix terms. The inferences of type $R\supset$ and $R\neg$ are *parameter–labelled*. Instances of $L\supset$ and $L\neg$ are *variable–labelled*. If r is one of the parameter–labelled inferences in figure 6, r is said to *belong* to the parameter b in the premiss. A variable–labelled inference in figure 6 *belongs* to its variable U. A *skeleton* is a tree regulated by the rules which satisfies the *Skeleton condition:* if r and r' belong to the same prefix parameter, the principal formulae of the respective inferences are contextual equivalents.

An *axiom* is a sequent of the form $\Gamma, P[p] \vdash P[q], \Delta$ with $p \preceq q$. A sequent S is a σ–*axiom* if $S\sigma$ is an axiom. A skeleton δ is a σ–*derivation* provided that σ is idempotent and the labels in $\delta\sigma$ satisfy the Unique prefix property. We shall say that $\delta\sigma$ is a *derivation*. A finite derivation $\delta\sigma$ with endsequent S is a *proof* of S if its leaves are all axioms. We shall say that σ *closes* δ and that δ is a σ–*proof*.

4.1. EXAMPLE. The Skeleton condition is a necessary soundness condition, as witnessed by the sequent $\neg(P \wedge Q) \vdash \neg P \vee \neg Q$. The sequent is not intuitionistically valid. Nevertheless one can construct the following tree:

$$
\dfrac{\dfrac{P[a] \vdash P[U], \neg Q}{\vdash P[U], \neg P, \neg Q}\; a \quad \dfrac{Q[a] \vdash Q[U], \neg P}{\vdash Q[U], \neg P, \neg Q}\; a}{\dfrac{\dfrac{\vdash P \wedge Q[U], \neg P, \neg Q}{\neg(P \wedge Q) \vdash \neg P, \neg Q}\; U}{\neg(P \wedge Q) \vdash \neg P \vee \neg Q}}
$$

By convention, brackets are omitted when the label is ε. Observe that the tree violates the Skeleton condition, which blocks it from being a proof wrt. $\{U/a\}$.

We shall assume that the set of labels in skeletons satisfies the Unique prefix property. This is not required for consistency, but simplifies the exposition. The property is tacitly assumed in the matrix systems in the literature.

Variable–pure and variable–sharing skeletons are as in definition 2.5. Moreover, we shall assume that the condition which pertains to variables in variable–sharing skeletons also holds for prefix parameters: two parameter–labelled inferences belong to the same prefix parameter if and only if they are contextually equivalent.

It is easy to see that the permutation results for free variable LK can be lifted to the intuitionistic free variable system. In particular lemma 2.14 holds. Observe that sharing of variables is required for symmetrical permutation schemes in situations where the lowermost inference is branching. Consider a case of a $R\neg$ over a $L\vee$:

$$
\dfrac{\dfrac{A, C[a] \vdash}{A \vdash \neg C}\; a \quad \dfrac{B, C[b] \vdash}{B \vdash \neg C}\; b}{A \vee B \vdash \neg C}
$$

The inferences permute symmetrically if and only if $a = b$. The system also admits nonsymmetrical schemes using contraction and weakening [Waaler 2001]. Like in LK, these schemes apply to pure variable skeletons.

Labelled sequents are evaluated in two stages. Kripke models are used to interpret unlabelled formulae in the usual way, whereas labels are mapped into points in the Kripke structure.

Formally, a *model* is a tuple which consists of a Kripke model and a label interpretation function. A *Kripke model* is a triple $(\mathbf{U}, \leq, \Vdash')$, where

- the *universe* $\mathbf{U}$ is a nonempty set partially ordered by $\leq$,
- $\Vdash'$ is a binary relation between $\mathbf{U}$ and the set of atomic formulae which satisfies the *Monotonicity condition:* if $x \Vdash' P$ and $x \leq y$, then $y \Vdash' P$.

The forcing relation $\Vdash$ is the weakest relation which contains $\Vdash'$ and is closed under the following rules:

$$
\begin{array}{lll}
x \Vdash P & \text{iff} & x \Vdash' P, \ P \text{ atomic}, \\
x \Vdash A \wedge B & \text{iff} & x \Vdash A \text{ and } x \Vdash B, \\
x \Vdash A \vee B & \text{iff} & x \Vdash A \text{ or } x \Vdash B, \\
x \Vdash \neg A & \text{iff} & y \not\Vdash A \text{ for each } y \geq x, \\
x \Vdash A \supset B & \text{iff} & y \not\Vdash A \text{ or } y \Vdash B \text{ for each } y \geq x.
\end{array}
$$

A *label interpretation function* is a function φ from a set of labels satisfying the Unique prefix property into the universe $\mathbf{U}$ such that for all labels s, t:

$$\varphi(s) \leq \varphi(t) \text{ if } s \preceq t.$$

$A[s]$ is *true* in the model if $\varphi(s) \Vdash A$, otherwise it is *false*. A model is a *countermodel* to a sequent S if every antecedent formula in S is true and every succedent formula in S is false. S is *valid* if it has no countermodels. This completes the specification of basic syntax and semantics.

The proof of the Soundness theorem for classical logic contains three parts: well-foundedness of the reduction ordering, permutation of the skeleton into a form which conforms to the reduction ordering, and an induction over the resulting proof. The argument below follows the same pattern. Moreover, the technical steps can be motivated in exactly the same way (cnf. the discussion preceding theorem 2.18).

4.2. DEFINITION. Let σ be a label substitution over a skeleton. The relations $\gg$ and $\sqsupset$ are binary relations over the inferences in a skeleton. They are the weakest relations closed under the following two conditions:

- if the principal formula of r_1 is an ancestor to a side formula of r_2, then $r_1 \gg r_2$,
- if r_1 belongs to U, $\sigma(U) \neq U$, $\sigma(U) \neq \varepsilon$, and r_2 belongs to the last prefix term in $\sigma(U)$, then $r_1 \sqsupset r_2$.

The *reduction ordering* $\triangleright$ induced by σ is defined as the transitive closure of $\gg \cup \sqsupset$. The skeleton *conforms to* $\triangleright$ if there are no two inferences r and r' such that $r \triangleright r'$ and r is below r'.

4.3. LEMMA. *Let σ be an idempotent label substitution which preserves the Unique prefix property of the underlying skeleton. Then the reduction ordering $\triangleright$ induced by σ is well–founded.*

PROOF. Four properties of $\sqsupset$ are used in the proof. Assume that $r_1 \sqsupset r_2$ and $r_3 \sqsupset r_4$. Let the side formula label of r_i be p_i. Then

(i) $p_1\sigma = p_2\sigma$,

(ii) $r_2 \not\geqq r_1$,

(iii) $r_2 \neq r_3$,

(iv) if $r_2 \gg r_3$, then $p_3\sigma$ is shorter than $p_2\sigma$.

In clause (ii), $\geqq$ denotes the reflexive closure of $\gg$. Let us first draw some simple consequences of the assumptions. Since $r_1 \sqsupset r_2$, r_1 belongs to a variable U and r_2 belongs to the last prefix term in $\sigma(U)$. Denote this term t, such that r_2 belongs to t. Hence U is the last term in p_1 and t is the last term in p_2. To prove (i), observe that both $p_1\sigma$ and $p_2\sigma$ end with t. The Unique prefix property gives that $p_1\sigma = p_2\sigma$. To prove (ii), assume for a contradiction that $r_2 \geqq r_1$. The assumption entails that U occurs in p_2; this is clear from the way that labels propagate in a skeleton. Assume first that U occurs in $\sigma(U)$. By idempotence, $\sigma(U) = U$. But then $t = U$, contrary to the definition of $\sqsupset$. Hence U does not occur in $\sigma(U)$. But if U occurs in p_2 and does not occur in $\sigma(U)$, U occurs in the prefix of t in p_2. Then $p_2\sigma$ contains two occurrences of t; the t in $\sigma(U)$, which results from substitution of U, comes in addition to the one which already is in p_2. This contradicts the assumption that σ preserves the Unique prefix property. For (iii), note that the only way that r_2 can equal r_3 is that r_3 belongs to a variable V and $\sigma(U) = V$. But lemma 2.1 holds and entails that $\sigma(V) = V$. This contradicts the irreflexivity of $\sqsupset$. As for (iv), let $r_2 \gg r_3$. By (iii) and the assumption that r_2 belongs to t, it follows that r_3 belongs to a variable in p_2 in the prefix of t. Hence $p_3 \prec p_2$. The only way that $p_3\sigma$ can have the same length as $p_2\sigma$ is that t is a variable V and $\sigma(V) = \varepsilon$. But since V occurs in $\sigma(U)$ and $V \in \text{dom}(\sigma)$, lemma 2.1 gives that $\sigma(V) = V$, contradicting the claim that $\sigma(V) = \varepsilon$. This proves (iv).

To prove the lemma, assume that $\rhd$ is cyclic. By (iii), the cycle must be of the form

$$r_1 \gg r_1', r_1' \sqsupset r_2, \ \ldots \ r_n \gg r_n', r_n' \sqsupset r_1.$$

By (ii), n must be at least 2. By (i) and (iv), the length of $p_1\sigma$ must be less than the length of $p_1\sigma$. Contradiction. $\qquad\square$

4.4. THEOREM. *A provable empty labelled sequent is valid.*

PROOF. Like for free variable LK, the proof is simplified by assuming a complete variable–sharing skeleton closed by σ. By lemma 4.3, the induced reduction ordering $\rhd$ is well–founded. Since lemma 2.14 holds, the skeleton has a permutation variant δ which conforms to $\rhd$. δ is closed by σ. By induction on the length of $\delta\sigma$ we show that every sequent in $\delta\sigma$ is valid.

Base step: the endsequent is an axiom $\Gamma, P[p] \vdash P[q], \Delta$ with $p \preceq q$. Take a model of $\Gamma, P[p]$ with label function φ. By the model condition for φ, $\varphi(p) \leq \varphi(q)$. By the Monotonicity condition, $\varphi(q) \Vdash P$, i.e. $P[q]$ is true in the model. For the inductive step we treat the cases of the last inference in $\delta\sigma$ being one of the implication rules:

$$\frac{\Gamma \vdash A[pq], \Delta \quad \Gamma, B[pq] \vdash \Delta}{\Gamma, A \supset B[p] \vdash \Delta} \qquad \frac{\Gamma, A[pb] \vdash B[pb], \Delta}{\Gamma \vdash A \supset B[p], \Delta}$$

In the $L \supset$ case q may be any string such that pq is a label. Pick a model of $\Gamma, A \supset B[p]$. Without loss of generality we may assume that the point pq is in the domain of the label interpretation function φ. We have to show that one member of Δ is true in the model. By the induction hypothesis applied to the proof of the left premiss, either $A[pq]$ or a formula in Δ is true. In the latter case we are done. In the former case the truth of $B[pq]$ follows from the model definition and the assumption that $\varphi(p) \leq \varphi(pq)$. Conclude by the induction hypothesis applied to the proof of the right premiss.

In the case of $R\supset$ let φ be the label interpretation function of an arbitrary model of Γ. If φ makes one formula in Δ true, we are done. Otherwise, let s be a point such that $\varphi(p) \leq s$. Assume that $s \Vdash A$. Observe that since δ conforms to σ, b does not occur in Γ. We may therefore assume that pb is not in the domain of φ. There must then be an extension φ' of φ which maps pb to s. Clearly, φ' agrees with φ on the evaluation of formulae in Γ. By induction hypothesis, $s \Vdash B$. Since s is arbitrarily chosen, $\varphi(p) \Vdash A \supset B$.   □

The rules of the sequent calculus define a tableau system and a matrix system exactly as in section 2. The reduction rules defining matrices are straightforward generalizations of the classical rules in section 2.5, illustrated below for implication (U and a fresh symbols).

$$(A \supset B)[p] \quad \rightsquigarrow \quad \left[\begin{array}{cc} \overline{A}[pa] & B[pa] \end{array} \right] \qquad \overline{(A \supset B)}[p] \quad \rightsquigarrow \quad \left[\begin{array}{c} A[pU] \\ \hline \overline{B}[pU] \end{array} \right]$$

Intuitionistic matrices differ from their classical counterparts in two ways. The connection $\{\overline{P}[p], P[q]\}$ is σ–complementary if σ is a label substitution such that $p\sigma \preceq q\sigma$. Signed formula of the form $\overline{(A \supset B)}[p]$ or $\neg A[p]$ are generative. Besides this, matrices are as in definition 2.7. The notion of a multiplicity is as in definition 2.9. A sequent S is *matrix provable* if there is a multiplicity μ such that the matrix of S with multiplicity μ contains a spanning set of σ–complementary connections; σ idempotent and preserving the Unique prefix property of the labels in the matrix.

4.5. EXAMPLE. Let χ be $\psi \supset P$ and ψ be $(P \supset Q) \supset P$. The sequent $\neg\chi \vdash$ expresses that *Peirce's law* cannot be consistently negated. An intuitionistically labelled variant of a *classical* proof of the sequent may look like this:

$$\cfrac{\cfrac{\cfrac{P[UaVb] \vdash Q[UaVb], P[Ua]}{\vdash P \supset Q[UaV], P[Ua]} \; b \qquad P[UaV] \vdash P[Ua]}{\psi[Ua] \vdash P[Ua]} \; V}{\cfrac{\vdash \chi[U]}{\neg\chi \vdash} \; U} \; a$$

Observe that if all labels are removed, the skeleton is an LK–proof. The matrix form gives a more compact representation:

$$\left[\begin{array}{ccc} \overline{P}[UaVb] & Q[UaVb] & \\ & & P[Ua] \\ \overline{P}[UaV] & & \end{array} \right]$$

The generative occurrences $\overline{\neg\chi}$ and $\overline{\psi}[Ua]$ in the reduction sequence which generates the matrix have multiplicity 1. Note that the matrix gives rise to a proof if and only if there is a solution to the set of equations $\{UaVb \preceq Ua, UaV \preceq Ua\}$. The equations are clearly unsolvable.

The matrices above are essentially equivalent to matrices in Wallen's system. The syntax is slightly different as he defines the labels (or 'prefixes') on positions in the formation tree of a formula rather than by explicit rules. From a logical perspective the formulation of the syntax makes no difference. Like in free variable LK intuitionistic matrices correspond to a class of variable–sharing skeletons. The intuitionistic matrix system is thus sound. Permutation properties can still be used to argue that the set of all variable–sharing skeletons differs only insignificantly from the set of all matrices (cnf. section 2.6).

4.2. A ground single step system

The labelled system presented in this section shares some of the features of Massacci's prefixed modal systems [Massacci 1994, Massacci 2000]. We shall therefore call it the *single step system*.

The rules of the single step system are designed for the formulation of a systematic search procedure. There is only one essential structural rule, which we shall call the *left monotonicity* rule:

$$\frac{\Gamma, A[pa] \vdash \Delta}{\Gamma, A[p] \vdash \Delta} \; LM$$

The rule reflects the Monotonicity condition for Kripke models. As usual p is a label and a is a parameter. As contraction is built directly into the logical rules, no other structural rules are needed. Weakening is, however, used for garbage collection.

The *logical rules* consist of the rules for disjunction and conjunction in figure 6 (page 1528) and the negation and implication rules in figure 7. In contrast to the free variable system there is a parameter condition in the single step system. The Parameter condition applies to $R\supset$ and $R\neg$. It regulates the order of inferences, since a right inference which belongs to a parameter a must occur below an instance of LM which applies a. Note that a now functions as an eigenparameter. A *derivation* is a tree regulated by the rules of the system. A *proof* is a finite derivation in which each leaf is an axiom of the form $\Gamma, P[p] \vdash P[q], \Delta$ with $p \preceq q$.

I shall now introduce a search procedure and use this to establish a model existence theorem. The procedure is a decision procedure for intuitionistic propositional logic. It uses the same termination criterion as [Sahlin, Franzén and Haridi 1992].

$$\frac{\Gamma, A \supset B[p] \vdash A[p], \Delta \quad \Gamma, B[p] \vdash \Delta}{\Gamma, A \supset B[p] \vdash \Delta} \; LC\supset' \qquad \frac{\Gamma, A[pa] \vdash B[pa], \Delta}{\Gamma \vdash A \supset B[p], \Delta} \; R\supset$$

$$\frac{\Gamma, \neg A[p] \vdash A[p], \Delta}{\Gamma, \neg A[p] \vdash \Delta} \; LC\neg' \qquad \frac{\Gamma, A[pa] \vdash \Delta}{\Gamma \vdash \neg A[p], \Delta} \; R\neg$$

Parameter condition: In $R\supset$ and $R\neg$ a cannot occur in the conclusion.

Figure 7: Implication and negation rules of the single step system. The rules for conjunction and disjunction ($L\wedge$, $R\wedge$, $L\vee$, $R\vee$) are as in figure 6.

The procedure is formulated with an explicit OR–branching which allows us to keep a tight control over contraction. It is perfectly possible to avoid the OR–branching, but this will result in derivations which require a massive amount of pruning.

The procedure generates an exponential number of derivations; each derivation is deviced so as to minimize redundancy. The main idea is this. The process starts by generating an initial derivation. A derivation π generated at any stage is extended by adding smaller derivations to open branches. These smaller derivations are generated in parallel by the *kernel* of the search procedure. One can in general define many different extensions of π in this way, which is why the number of derivations grows exponentially.

The definition of the procedure applies some new concepts. Let us say that a ground label is a *point*. A point *owns* an inference if it is the label of the side formulae. A *common point derivation (cpd)* is a derivation in which all inferences are owned by the same point. A cpd constructed over an empty labelled endsequent is called an *initial* cpd. All inferences in an initial cpd are owned by ε.

The initial cpd is the simplest derivation generated by the search procedure. An initial cpd is generated by logical rules other than parameter–labelled ones. The part of the kernel comprised of these steps is called *expansion*.

Expansion: Expand branchwise with logical rules other than $R\supset$ and $R\neg$ until each branch is either an axiom or all possible expansions have been made. For each branch avoid repetitions of $LC\supset'$ and $LC\neg'$ on the same formula.

It is easy to check that if these steps are applied to a sequent in which all formulae have identical label, which will always be the case when the expansion part is invoked, the result is a cpd. In particular this holds for the initial cpd, since the endsequent by assumption is empty labelled.

Observe also that after the expansion part is finished the leaf of each branch is either an axiom or of the form

$$\Gamma, B_1[p], \ldots, B_k[p] \vdash C_1[p], \ldots, C_m[p], \Delta$$

where each $B_i[p]/C_j[p]$ is a negation or an implication. This holds for the initial cpd and will hold for all cpds generated by the procedure. The formulae in Γ, Δ are atomic, but not necessarily labelled with p. We shall say that the sequent above has *branching degree* m.

Using the new notions we can formulate the general structure of the procedure with greater precision. The derivations are composed of cpds stacked on one another. Each cpd is generated by the kernel of the procedure, which consists of two parts: transition and expansion. As pointed out the initial cpd is an exception since it is determined exclusively by the expansion part applied to the endsequent. The function of the transition part is to create a jump to a new point. Its role is to initiate the new cpd and prepare for further expansion steps. The reason why the initial cpd is generated without the transition part is simply that we have to generate the inferences owned by ε before any further points can be analyzed.

Besides defining the steps initiating a new cpd, the transition part also implements the termination test. The following notion is crucial.

4.6. DEFINITION. The point q in a branch β is an *endpoint* wrt. β if, for each antecedent formula $A[q]$ in β, there is an antecedent β–occurrence of $A[p]$ for a $p \prec q$.

A branch is *finished* if its leaf is either an axiom or contains an endpoint or has branching degree 0. Hence the leaf of an unfinished branch has nonzero branching degree.

We can now describe how cpds are generated and how they give rise to new derivations. Assume that π is generated at some stage of the procedure. Assume further that π has an unfinished branch β and that the leaf of β is the sample sequent above with branching degree m. The branch gives rise to m new cpds, where cpd i is generated as follows. The *transition* part is first invoked.

Transition: Perform in sequence:

1. Remove each succedent occurrence by weakening except $C_i[p]$.
2. Expand $C_i[p]$ using a fresh parameter a. This generates an antecedent occurrence of a formula $A[pa]$.
3. If there is an antecedent occurrence of $A[q]$ in β for a $q \prec pa$, terminate: pa will be an endpoint in the resulting derivation.
4. If the leaf is an axiom, terminate.
5. For each $B_j[p]$, generate $B_j[pa]$ by the rule *LM*.

Clause 1 is strictly speaking not needed; its function is simply to remove garbage. Assuming that C_i is of the form $\neg A[p]$, the transition steps generate the cpd

$$\cfrac{\cfrac{\cfrac{\Gamma, B_1[pa], \ldots, B_k[pa], A[pa] \vdash}{\Gamma, B_1[p], \ldots, B_k[p], A[pa] \vdash} \; LM}{\Gamma, B_1[p], \ldots, B_k[p] \vdash \neg A[p]} \; r}{\Gamma, B_1[p], \ldots, B_k[p] \vdash C_1[p], \ldots, C_m[p], \Delta} \; RW$$

We can now apply the expansion steps to the leaf sequent of this cpd. In general this results in a larger cpd owned by pa.

This procedure can be applied to each unfinished branch in π to construct cpds in parallel. If there are n unfinished branches and the branching degree of branch i is m_i, one can generate $m_1 + \ldots + m_n$ cpds by the kernel of the algorithm. Using these cpds we can construct extensions of π as follows: for each unfinished branch i in π, put one of the m_i cpds on top of the branch. This can be done in $m_1 \times \ldots \times m_n$ different ways, which is the number of extensions of π.

The search procedure for the single step system follows the procedure above and generates derivations in a fair way. The procedure terminates in propositional logic. For each derivation we will eventually generate a finished leaf in all branches.

4.7. EXAMPLE. Our sample sequent is $\neg(P \wedge Q) \vdash \neg P \vee \neg Q$, cnf. example 4.1. The search procedure may generate the following initial cpd:

$$\cfrac{\cfrac{\neg(P \wedge Q) \vdash P, \neg P, \neg Q \quad \neg(P \wedge Q) \vdash Q, \neg P, \neg Q}{\neg(P \wedge Q) \vdash P \wedge Q, \neg P, \neg Q}}{\cfrac{\neg(P \wedge Q) \vdash \neg P, \neg Q}{\neg(P \wedge Q) \vdash \neg P \vee \neg Q}}$$

Both branches are open; let β_1 be the leftmost branch in the initial cpd and β_2 be the rightmost branch. Both leaves have branching degree 2. The leftmost leaf gives rise to two cpds. One of them is below.

$$\cfrac{\cfrac{\cfrac{\cfrac{\cfrac{\neg(P \wedge Q)[a], P[a] \vdash P[a] \quad \neg(P \wedge Q)[a], P[a] \vdash Q[a]}{\neg(P \wedge Q)[a], P[a] \vdash P \wedge Q[a]}}{\neg(P \wedge Q)[a], P[a] \vdash}}{\neg(P \wedge Q), P[a] \vdash}}{\neg(P \wedge Q) \vdash \neg P} \; a}{\neg(P \wedge Q) \vdash P, \neg P, \neg Q}$$

A candidat for the second is:

$$\cfrac{\cfrac{\cfrac{\cfrac{\cfrac{\neg(P \wedge Q)[b], Q[b] \vdash P[b] \quad \neg(P \wedge Q)[b], Q[b] \vdash Q[b]}{\neg(P \wedge Q)[b], Q[b] \vdash P \wedge Q[b]}}{\neg(P \wedge Q)[b], Q[b] \vdash}}{\neg(P \wedge Q), Q[b] \vdash}}{\neg(P \wedge Q) \vdash \neg Q} \; b}{\neg(P \wedge Q) \vdash Q, \neg P, \neg Q}$$

Observe that β_1 and β_2 in the initial cpd have almost identical leaves. Hence one can construct cpds for β_2 which are almost identical to the two cpds above. The initial cpd has hence 4 extensions. Let us for further reference say that π_1 is a derivation obtained from the initial cpd by adding the first of the cpds above to β_1 and π_2 is a derivation obtained by adding the second cpd to β_1 (we neglect what is added to β_2). Neither of them is proof, none of them are further expandable.

To prove the Model existence theorem we must investigate the set of derivations generated over an unprovable sequent. The goal is to show that they contain enough information for the construction of a countermodel. In classical logic this is straightforward, since a single open branch of a limit object contains sufficient information. In intuitionistic logic, on the other hand, we must select a collection of open branches. The branches are selected on the basis of the following property.

4.8. DEFINITION. Consider a sequence of derivations generated by the search procedure. A sequent is *open–ended* if the following holds for each derivation π in the sequence: if the sequent occurs in π, then it occurs in an open branch in π.

Open–ended sequents can be selected so that they form a tree structure. We shall see a proof of this in lemma 4.11. The construction relies on two crucial observations:

- if a sequent is open–ended and it occurs as the conclusion of a 1–premiss inference, then the premiss is open–ended,
- if a sequent is open–ended and it occurs as the conclusion of a branching inference, then at least one premiss is open–ended.

Observe in particular that if a leaf $\Gamma \vdash C_1[p], \ldots, C_m[p], \Delta$ with branching degree m is open–ended, and this leaf is expanded, each sequent $\Gamma \vdash C_i[p]$ is also open–ended.

The construction which leads to the Model existence theorem can be formalized by a system of *refutation rules*, comprised of

- all 1–premiss rules of the single step system except right weakening, i.e. $L\wedge$, $R\vee$, $R\supset$, $LC\neg'$, $R\neg$, LM. The Parameter condition pertains to $R\supset$ and $R\neg$;
- left and right projections of the branching rules:

$$\frac{\Gamma \vdash A[p], \Delta}{\Gamma \vdash A \wedge B[p], \Delta} \qquad \frac{\Gamma, A[p] \vdash \Delta}{\Gamma, A \vee B[p] \vdash \Delta} \qquad \frac{\Gamma, A \supset B[p] \vdash A[p], \Delta}{\Gamma, A \supset B[p] \vdash \Delta}$$

$$\frac{\Gamma \vdash B[p], \Delta}{\Gamma \vdash A \wedge B[p], \Delta} \qquad \frac{\Gamma, B[p] \vdash \Delta}{\Gamma, A \vee B[p] \vdash \Delta} \qquad \frac{\Gamma, B[p] \vdash \Delta}{\Gamma, A \supset B[p] \vdash \Delta}$$

Let us give the left projection rules subscript 1 and the right projection rules subscript 2, such that the uppermost implication rule is denoted $LC\supset'_1$;
- the following branching rule:

$$\frac{\Gamma, \Theta \vdash C_1[p] \quad \ldots \quad \Gamma, \Theta \vdash C_m[p]}{\Gamma, \Theta \vdash C_1[p], \ldots, C_m[p], \Delta} \; Split$$

where Θ is a collection of implications and negations labelled with p and each formula in Γ, Δ is atomic, but not neccesarily labelled with p. The inference above is owned by p.

It may at a first glance seem odd that the refutation rules for conjunction and disjunction are almost identical. But recall that the rules shall be used to present *open–ended* sequents. The refutation trees below serve a different purpose than proofs; quite to the contrary they justify unprovability. The method of refutation trees is inspired by the technique in [Pinto and Dyckhoff 1995]. It was used in [Waaler and Wallen 1999] in a model existence argument for the multi–succedent intuitionistic calculus. The presence of labels in the single step system facilitates the formulation of the argument.

4.9. DEFINITION. Consider a tree regulated by the refutation rules. A *segment* is a maximal block of successive inferences owned by the same point. A segment may contain at most one instance of *Split*, and this instance has to be the uppermost inference. Two successive instances of *Split* hence occur in different segments. A *refutation tree* for the intuitionistic single step system is a tree regulated by the refutation rules such that

- the tree contains no axioms,
- two inferences are owned by the same point iff they occur in the same segment,
- if a sequent contains an endpoint wrt. its branch, it is a leaf sequent.

A refutation tree is *complete* if it is not a proper subtree of a larger refutation tree.

4.10. LEMMA. *Let S be the uppermost sequent in the segment of inferences owned by q. Assume that there is an occurrence of $A[p]$ in the refutation tree and that $p \preceq q$. Then either $A[p]$ occurs in S or there is an occurrence of $A[p]$ in a sequent below S.*

PROOF. If $A[p]$ is either in S or in the endsequent, we are done. Otherwise, $A[p]$ is the side formula of an inference r. Let S be the premiss of r'. Since every inference belongs to a unique segment, r belongs to the same segment as r' if $p = q$. If $p \prec q$, it belongs to the segment of inferences owned by p. However, since labels increase as the tree grows, inferences which belong to a term in p must be below those who belong to a term which is in q but not in p. Hence r occurs below r'. ☐

Split characterizes all ways of expanding a sequent with positive branching degree and plays a crucial role in the characterization. Observe in particular that when refutation rules are used to represent a branch, sequences of right weakenings disappear. A premiss in *Split* contains the sequent obtained by selecting one succedent negation/implication and removing the rest of the succedent, i.e. the sequent which results from the first step of *transition*.

4.11. LEMMA. *If a sequent is not provable by the search procedure for the single step system, it has a finite, complete refutation tree.*

PROOF. All derivations generated over a given sequent agree trivially on the endsequent. By definition, the endsequent is open–ended iff none of the derivations are proofs. Hence the endsequent is open–ended. As observed above, an inference with an open–ended conclusion has at least one open–ended premiss. Starting with the endsequent we may hence construct a refutation tree from below by tracing branches in derivations, successively selecting an open–ended premiss and replacing blocks of right weakenings with a premiss in *Split*. The resulting limit object is

$$\frac{\neg(P \wedge Q)[a], P[a] \vdash Q[a]}{\neg(P \wedge Q)[a], P[a] \vdash P \wedge Q[a]}$$
$$\frac{}{\neg(P \wedge Q)[a], P[a] \vdash}$$
$$\frac{}{\neg(P \wedge Q), P[a] \vdash}$$
$$\frac{}{\neg(P \wedge Q) \vdash \neg P} \; a$$

$$\frac{\neg(P \wedge Q)[b], Q[b] \vdash P[b]}{\neg(P \wedge Q)[b], Q[b] \vdash P \wedge Q[b]}$$
$$\frac{}{\neg(P \wedge Q)[b], Q[b] \vdash}$$
$$\frac{}{\neg(P \wedge Q), Q[b] \vdash}$$
$$\frac{}{\neg(P \wedge Q) \vdash \neg Q} \; b$$

$$\frac{}{\neg(P \wedge Q) \vdash P, \neg P, \neg Q} \; Split$$
$$\frac{}{\neg(P \wedge Q) \vdash P \wedge Q, \neg P, \neg Q}$$
$$\frac{}{\neg(P \wedge Q) \vdash \neg P, \neg Q}$$
$$\frac{}{\neg(P \wedge Q) \vdash \neg P \vee \neg Q}$$

Figure 8: A complete refutation tree.

a complete refutation tree. Since every open–ended sequent eventually generates a finished branch, the tree is finite. □

A refutation tree ρ defines *collector sets* ρ^+ and ρ^-, where ρ^+ is the set of all formulae with an antecedent occurrence in a sequent in ρ and ρ^- is the set of all formulae with a succedent occurrence in ρ. The collector sets have a structure which is close to the structure of Kripke models for intuitionistic logic. The Kripke model $(\mathbf{U}, \preceq, \Vdash')$ *induced by* ρ is given by:

- $\mathbf{U}$ is the set of points in ρ which are not endpoints,
- $q \Vdash' P$ iff there is a $P[p] \in \rho^+$ for a $p \preceq q$.

The associated label interpretation function ι is given by: $\iota(q)$ is the point p in $\mathbf{U}$ which is largest wrt. $\prec$ and which satisfies $p \preceq q$. Hence, for each point q which occurs in ρ, $\iota(q) = q$ iff q is not an endpoint. Since the labels in ρ are closed under $\prec$, ι is well–defined. Observe that for each p and q in ρ, $\iota(p) \preceq \iota(q)$ iff $p \preceq q$.

4.12. EXAMPLE. Let us continue example 4.7 and construct a refutation tree from π_1 and π_2. Branch nr. 2 from the left in π_1 and the leftmost branch in π_2 are open. The complete refutation tree ρ in figure 8 is constructed out of these two branches. Its collector sets are:

$$\rho^+ = \{P[a], Q[b], \neg(P \wedge Q)\},$$
$$\rho^- = \{P, P[b], Q[a], P \wedge Q, P \wedge Q[a], P \wedge Q[b], \neg P, \neg Q, \neg P \vee \neg Q\}.$$

The Kripke model $(\mathbf{U}, \preceq, \Vdash')$ induced by ρ is given by: $\mathbf{U} = \{\varepsilon, a, b\}$, $a \Vdash' P$, $b \Vdash' Q$. Since there are no endpoints, the associated label interpretation function is the identity function. It is easy to see that this is a countermodel to the endsequent.

4.13. LEMMA. *If $x \Vdash A$ and $x \preceq y$, then $y \Vdash A$.*

PROOF. Induction on A. □

4.14. THEOREM. *If an empty labelled sequent is not provable in the single step system, it has a finite countermodel.*

PROOF. Assume that the sequent is not provable in the single step system. It is then not provable by the search procedure. By lemma 4.11, there is a finite refutation tree ρ over the sequent. We prove that the model $(\mathbf{U}, \preceq, \Vdash')$ induced by ρ, and the associated label interpretation function ι, satisfy:

- for each $A[p] \in \rho^+$, $\iota(p) \Vdash A$,
- for each $A[p] \in \rho^-$, $\iota(p) \nVdash A$.

This is proved by induction and establishes the lemma. The case that an atomic $P[p]$ is in ρ^+ is trivial: $\iota(p) \Vdash P$ by definition. The other cases of the induction require an argument. Let us complete the base step and take the implication cases.

For the base step, let $P[q] \in \rho^-$. Take the uppermost sequent S in the segment of inferences owned by q. There is a succedent occurrence of $P[q]$ in S. Assume for a contradiction that $\iota(q) \Vdash P$. There must then be a $P[p] \in \rho^+$ for a $p \preceq \iota(q)$. Since $\iota(q) \preceq q$, $p \preceq q$. By lemma 4.10 there is an antecedent occurrence of $P[p]$ either in S or below S. Since no atomic antecedent occurrence is removed by weakening, S contains an antecedent occurrence of $P[p]$. But then S is an axiom, contradicting the assumption that ρ is a refutation tree. Hence $\iota(q) \nVdash P$. This concludes the base step.

Let $A \supset B[p] \in \rho^+$. We show that for any $q \in \mathbf{U}$ such that $\iota(p) \preceq q$, either $q \Vdash B$ or $q \nVdash A$. There are two cases.

Case 1: there is an s such that $\iota(p) \preceq \iota(s) \preceq q$ and $B[s] \in \rho^+$. By induction hypothesis, $\iota(s) \Vdash B$. By lemma 4.13, $q \Vdash B$.

Case 2: otherwise. There is then an antecedent occurrence of $A \supset B[q]$ in ρ. To see this, note that either $\iota(p) = q$ or $\iota(p) \prec q$. If $\iota(p) = q$, either $p = q$, which is a trivial case, or p is an endpoint. In both cases $A \supset B[q] \in \rho^+$. If $\iota(p) \prec q$, then $p \prec q$; this follows by definition of ι. It is clear from lemma 4.10 that there is an antecedent occurrence of $A \supset B[p]$ below the formulae labelled with q. By the construction of ρ there are repetitions of LM so that there is an antecedent occurrence of $A \supset B[q]$ in ρ. $LC\supset'_1$ is applied to one of these occurrences, which yields $A[q] \in \rho^-$. By induction hypothesis, $q \nVdash A$.

Finally, let $A \supset B[p] \in \rho^-$. By construction, there is a parameter a such that $A[pa] \in \rho^+$ and $B[pa] \in \rho^-$. By induction hypothesis, $\iota(pa) \Vdash A$ and $\iota(pa) \nVdash B$. Since $\iota(p) \preceq \iota(pa)$, $\iota(p) \nVdash A \supset B$. $\qquad \square$

4.15. COROLLARY. *The search procedure for the single step system is a decision procedure.*

4.3. Completeness of the free variable system

The search procedure for the single step system can be simulated in the free variable system. The idea is to successively generate skeletons by following the steps in the construction of single step derivations. However, instead of generating m cpds for a branch with branching degree m, we generate *one* skeleton δ and substitutions $\sigma_1, \ldots, \sigma_m$ such that cpd π_i corresponds to $\delta \sigma_i$. This procedure is defined in detail in [Waaler 2001] along with a model existence argument. The procedure develops pure variable skeletons in a normal form which respects a particular ordering on inferences. The normal form, in turn, makes it easy to formulate termination conditions local to the branch.

The model existence result for the free variable system presented below is established nonconstructively. This saves us for a number of technical details. It works by relating a skeleton δ in the free variable system to a derivation π in the single step system. The basic idea is to view a substitution σ as a projection from δ onto π. The proof hence relies on the constructive proof in the previous section. In the proof of the lemma below we shall apply the derived rules $LC\supset$ and $LC\neg$ in the construction of a skeleton with free variables:

$$\frac{\Gamma, A \supset B[p] \vdash A[pU], \Delta \quad \Gamma, B[pU] \vdash \Delta}{\Gamma, A \supset B[p] \vdash \Delta} \; LC\supset \qquad \frac{\Gamma, \neg A[p] \vdash A[pU], \Delta}{\Gamma, \neg A[p] \vdash \Delta} \; LC\neg$$

4.16. LEMMA. *Let π be a derivation in the single step system with empty labelled endsequent. There is then a skeleton δ with the same structure as π, and a ground substitution σ, such that $\delta\sigma$ is a proof in the free variable system if π is a proof in the single step system.*

PROOF. We develop δ and σ inductively from π, starting with the endsequent, and prove that $\delta\sigma$ satisfies the following two properties:

(i) for each antecedent occurrence of $A[p]$ in π there is a corresponding antecedent occurrence of $A[q]$ in $\delta\sigma$ such that $q \preceq p$,

(ii) for each succedent occurrence of $A[p]$ in π there is a corresponding succedent occurrence of $A[p]$ in $\delta\sigma$.

The lemma follows from this. If π is just an endsequent, put $\delta = \pi$ and $\sigma = \emptyset$. $\delta\sigma$ satisfies (i) and (ii). Let r be an uppermost inference in π and π' be the derivation resulting from π by removing r (so that the conclusion of r is a leaf in π'). By induction hypothesis there is a δ' and a σ' such that $\delta'\sigma'$ satisfies (i) and (ii) wrt. π'. Assume that r is

$$\frac{\Gamma, \neg A[p] \vdash A[p], \Delta}{\Gamma, \neg A[p] \vdash \Delta} \; LC\neg'$$

The leaf in π' is hence $\Gamma, \neg A[p] \vdash \Delta$; assume that the leaf in δ' is $\Gamma', \neg A[p'] \vdash \Delta'$. By (i), $p'\sigma' \preceq p$. We now select a fresh variable U and add the following inference to δ':

$$\frac{\Gamma', \neg A[p'] \vdash A[p'U], \Delta'}{\Gamma', \neg A[p'] \vdash \Delta'} \; LC\neg$$

This results in δ. Since $p'\sigma' \preceq p$, there must be a ground label g such that $p'\sigma g = p$. Put $\sigma = \sigma' \cup \{U/g\}$. Note that r preserves properties (i) and (ii) wrt. $\delta\sigma$. If r is $LC\supset'$, we apply $LC\supset$ and reason in exactly the same way. If r is LM, put $\delta = \delta'$

and $\sigma = \sigma'$. If r is any other inference, just add the same inference to δ' and put $\sigma = \sigma'$. ☐

Observe that lemma 4.16, together with the soundness result for the free variable system, also entails soundness of the single step system.

4.17. COROLLARY. *If an empty labelled sequent is unprovable in the free variable system, it has a finite countermodel.*

PROOF. Assume that the sequent is not provable in the free variable system. By lemma 4.16, it is not provable in the single step system. By theorem 4.14, it has a finite countermodel. ☐

4.4. Connection–driven proof–search

We finally address connection–driven search in the free variable system with special emphasis on matrices. Not much has been done in this area. The only published work I am aware of is the connection–based procedure of Kreitz and Otten [1999], which works uniformly for all the logics presented in this chapter. Since this implementation does not rely on normal form, it is of interest also for classical logic. However, even if the procedure works fine for propositional classical logic, the non-classical versions are clearly open for improvements.

The source of the problem lies in the administration of multiplicities. The procedure of Kreitz and Otten in effect increases all multiplicities in an outer loop if the search for a proof with smaller multiplicities fails. What we would need is a procedure which increases multiplicities on demand. This is fairly easy to provide for first–order classical logic if we assume clausal form, but there has up to my knowledge not been published any algorithm which works for any nonclausal input. The complexity of the few prototype systems I am aware of indicates that a proper solution is not straightforward, even though the basic idea is easy to grasp. I shall leave the discussion of multiplicities here.

In the rest of this section I shall briefly sketch one way of utilizing connections. More generally, I shall discuss an adaptation of an arbitrary proof procedure for classical matrices which is independent of clausal form. We shall in particular see that the problem of restricting the term universe, discussed for free variable LK in section 2.9, also pertains to free variable search in the intuitionistic system.

Let us formulate a classical search procedure for the free variable system along the same lines as the procedure for classical logic in section 2.8. The algorithm implements a complete separation of an intuitionistical component from a classical component. To control contraction, we shall use the two derived rules $LC{\supset}$ and $LC{\neg}$ introduced in section 4.3 instead of contraction, $L{\supset}$, and $L{\neg}$. The search strategy applies a "classical tactic", typically some kind of connection–driven procedure, but follows the syntax of the labelled system. The definition below makes use of a yet undefined notion of expandability.

4.18. DEFINITION. The *classical search procedure* generates a skeleton over an end-sequent S as follows:

1. Apply the classical tactic to generate a variable–sharing skeleton δ over S. If $\widehat{\delta}$ is not an LK–proof, terminate: S is not intuitionistically valid.
2. Repeat the following steps:
   (a) Invoke the unification algorithm to check if there is a substitution which closes δ. If there is such a substitution σ, terminate: $\delta\sigma$ is a proof of S.
   (b) If there is no substitution which closes δ and no branch is *expandable*, terminate: S is not intuitionistically valid.
   (c) Otherwise, modify δ by applying the tactic to *expandable* formulae in the leaves until a new classical proof is found.

A main idea behind the algorithm is to put the generation to sleep while the skeleton is tested for closure. If unification fails, the search resumes and continues to develop the classical construction. This is achieved by successively increasing the multiplicity.

4.19. EXAMPLE. The procedure may, of course, be implemented on matrices rather than on skeletons. Let us adopt matrix syntax and continue example 4.5. The matrix given in that example may be the output of step 1 of the classical procedure. As pointed out the classical proof represented by this matrix fails intuitionistically. Hence step 2 is invoked. In step 2c the procedure continues to develop the matrix by increasing the multiplicities. Incrementing the multiplicity of $\overline{\neg\chi}$ gives the matrix

$$
\begin{bmatrix}
\overline{P}[U'a'V'b'] \quad Q[U'a'V'b'] & & \overline{P}[UaVb] \quad Q[UaVb] & \\
& P[U'a'] & & P[Ua] \\
\overline{P}[U'a'V'] & & \overline{P}[UaV] &
\end{bmatrix}
$$

The connections $\{\overline{P}[UaVb], P[U'a']\}$ and $\{\overline{P}[UaV], P[Ua]\}$ are spanning. They give rise to the equations $\{UaVb \preceq U'a', UaV \preceq Ua\}$, whose most general solution yields the closing substitution $\{V/\varepsilon, U'/Uab\}$.

Rather than completing the construction of the whole classical proof before testing the labels, it is in many cases more efficient, in particular wrt. space, to finish the treatment of one branch at a time. The classical procedure is formulated as it is to make one central point clear. Since classical unprovability entails intuitionistic unprovability, connection–driven search is particularly useful for sequents which are not even classically valid. Through an initial test for classical provability the intuitionistic search may in fact exploit the NP–hardness of the classical propositional decision problem: if the test fails, the procedure terminates; otherwise, specific label–sensitive mechanisms are invoked. There is hence a significant class of sequents, i.e. the classically invalid sequents, for which the complexity of the intuitionistic decision problem can be reduced from PSPACE–completeness [Statman 1979] to NP–completeness.

There are three key factors in the realization of the idea. First, the development of a single skeleton gives rise to redundancy. To avoid this effect, skeletons must be pruned. Second, the efficiency of the algorithm depends on the use of unification algorithms. Third, to prevent expansion beyond necessity, one must control contraction.

The first point is illustrated in the intuitionistic example in section 3.1. Pruning has not been addressed explicitly for proof–search procedures, even though Schmitt and Kreitz [2000] perform pruning operations in their translation of matrix proofs into Gentzen–style proofs.

The unification problem for the intuitionistic system is almost identical to the problem addressed in section 3.3, only differing in the test for '$\preceq$' rather that '$=$'. The problem is how one can integrate the procedure in a least commitment search. This has up to now not been addressed in the literature.

To control contraction we must define expansion conditions for generative occurrences. No such conditions have been given in the literature. The following example illustrates why the termination condition used in the search procedure for the single step system does not work for variable–sharing skeletons.

4.20. EXAMPLE. The following skeleton may be generated in step 1 in the classical search procedure.

$$\cfrac{\cfrac{\cfrac{\neg(P \vee Q), P[a] \vdash P[V], Q[V]}{\neg(P \vee Q) \vdash P[V], Q[V], \neg P}\, a}{\neg(P \vee Q) \vdash P \vee Q[V], \neg P}}{\neg(P \vee Q) \vdash \neg P}\, V \qquad \cfrac{\cfrac{\cfrac{\neg(P \vee Q), Q[b] \vdash P[V], Q[V]}{\neg(P \vee Q) \vdash P[V], Q[V], \neg Q}\, b}{\neg(P \vee Q) \vdash P \vee Q[V], \neg Q}}{\neg(P \vee Q) \vdash \neg Q}\, V$$
$$\neg(P \vee Q) \vdash \neg P \wedge \neg Q$$

There are two candidates for closure. $\{V/a\}$ closes the left branch, but fails to close the right branch. Observe in particular that the parameter a does not occur in the right branch. Similarly with the other candidate: $\{V/b\}$ closes the right branch, but not the left, and it assigns a value to V which is absent from the left branch. The skeleton cannot be closed. It seems reasonable to expand the left leaf further and generate:

$$\cfrac{\cfrac{\neg(P \vee Q), P[a] \vdash P[W], Q[W], P[V], Q[V]}{\neg(P \vee Q), P[a] \vdash P \vee Q[W], P[V], Q[V]}}{\neg(P \vee Q), P[a] \vdash P[V], Q[V]}\, W$$

The resulting skeleton is closed by $\{V/b, W/a\}$. Note that the information generated by one of the inferences which belongs to V is simply redundant. We obtained a proof by generating a new variable W, but the left leaf occurrences labelled with V play no role in the proof.

In all fairness the redundancy of the previous example can be eliminated if we follow Beckert and Goré and use universal variables [Beckert and Goré 1997]. However, the problem with their method is that universal variables do not distribute over branching inferences. It is then easy to construct more complex examples of the above kind which cannot in any obvious way be resolved by universal variables.

The tight control over contraction in the search procedure for the single step system is achieved through constraints on inference order. As pointed out at the beginning of this section the single step procedure can be simulated in the free variable system by constructing pure variable skeletons in a particular normal form. We may then define a tight termination condition. But once we relax these requirements and generate variable–sharing skeletons, the termination condition is no longer valid. Exactly as for free variable LK the source of this problem lies in the redundant inferences in variable–sharing skeletons. Observe that if we rename the variable in one branch of the skeleton in example 4.20, making it variable–pure, the inference introducing the W is not needed for closure.

Even though termination conditions for intuitionistic matrix search have not been given, [Korn and Kreitz 1997] contains material which is related to this problem. The idea behind their work is to formulate the model conditions for Kripke models in classical propositional logic and use this formulation as a premiss in an analysis of a translation of the initial formula into classical propositional logic. Moreover, Wallen [1990] gives termination conditions for the modal system S5, and this provides a solution to a fragment of intuitionistic logic.

There seems to be a trade–off between sharing and independence of variables. Sharing of variables gives full permutability and hence prepares the ground for connection–driven search methods. However, the closure of a branch must then be determined by global considerations; it is in general not sufficient to constrain the range of possible substitutions to the parameters in the branch. This is, on the other hand, possible for pure variable skeletons.

5. First–order intuitionistic logic

In classical first–order logic the quantificational structure can be separated from the underlying propositional structure in a clear–cut way. This is expressed by a number of fundamental properties like the prenex normal form, Gentzen's 'midsequent' theorem [Gentzen 1934–35], and Herbrand's theorem [Herbrand 1967, Bibel 1982c]. All of these properties fail for the nonclassical systems addressed in this chapter. In intuitionistic logic the separation is blocked by a nontrivial dependency between the quantifiers and implication/negation. In modal logics quantifiers do not distribute over modal operators.

The dependency between quantifiers and propositional structure in intuitionistic logic is addressed in detail by Shankar [1992] and Voronkov [1996]. Voronkov introduces a free variable extension of Gentzen's LJ in which constraints are developed and propagated; the constraints express the complex quantifier dependencies in intuitionistic logic in a clear way. However, LJ is a nonsymmetrical system with exceptions to permutation and is therefore not well suited for connection–driven search. Since both of these contributions are based on LJ, I shall not address them further.

$$\frac{\Gamma, A\{x/y[pU]\}[pU] \vdash \Delta}{\Gamma, \forall x A[p] \vdash \Delta} \; L\forall \qquad \frac{\Gamma \vdash A\{x/f[pa](\vec{y})\}[pa], \Delta}{\Gamma \vdash \forall x A[p], \Delta} \; R\forall$$

$$\frac{\Gamma, A\{x/f[p](\vec{y})\}[p] \vdash \Delta}{\Gamma, \exists x A[p] \vdash \Delta} \; L\exists \qquad \frac{\Gamma \vdash A\{x/y[p]\}[p], \Delta}{\Gamma \vdash \exists x A[p], \Delta} \; R\exists$$

$\vec{y}$ is a list of all labelled quantifier variables which occur free in the principal formula.

Figure 9: Free variable quantifier rules.

5.1. Term language

The term language simply combines the term language of classical first–order logic with the language of labels used in section 4. I shall refer to the terms of classical logic as *standard* terms; they are composed out of *parameter functions* f, g, h of every arity and *quantifier variables* x, y, z. *Labels* are finite strings of prefix terms without repetitions of any term. Prefix terms are divided into *prefix variables* U, V, W and *prefix parameters* a, b, c. The letters p and q are reserved for labels. Using these conventions we define the set of *labelled standard terms* by:

- the *labelled quantifier variable* $x[p]$ is a standard term labelled with p,
- if $\vec{t}$ is a list of n labelled standard terms and f has arity n, then $f[p](\vec{t})$ is a standard term labelled with p.

A *substitution* is a function which maps labelled quantifier variables into labelled standard terms and prefix variables into labels. A substitution σ has *projections* σ_Q and σ_I, defined as the restrictions of σ to, respectively, the set of labelled quantifier variables and the set of prefix variables. A substitution may satisfy the Cumulativity condition:

> *Cumulativity condition for* σ: for each $x[p]$ in $\text{dom}(\sigma)$, if $x[p]$ is mapped to a term labelled with q, then $q\sigma \preceq p\sigma$.

A set of labels Θ satisfies the *Unique prefix property* if every prefix term has the same prefix in all labels in Θ in which it occurs. A substitution σ is *bounded by* Θ if the following condition holds. Let $\sigma_I(U) = q't$. Then there are labels pU and qt in Θ such that $(pU)\sigma = (qt)\sigma$. Boundedness by Θ preserves the Unique prefix property; it is immediate that lemma 3.1 holds also in the first–order language.

5.2. A free variable system

The rules of the first–order free variable system consist of the structural rules in figure 1 (page 1498), the propositional rules in figure 6 (page 1528) and the quantifier rules in figure 9. A *skeleton* is a tree of inferences which satisfies the *Skeleton condition*: for any r and r' which belong to the same prefix term, the principal formulæ of the respective inferences are contextual equivalents and have identical labels in their side formulæ.

Let σ be a substitution which satisfies the Cumulativity condition and δ be a skeleton. The image of δ under σ, $\delta\sigma$, is a *derivation* if it satisfies the Unique prefix property. It is a *proof* if it is finite and every leaf is an axiom, i.e. a sequent of the form $\Gamma, A[p] \vdash A[q], \Delta; \ p \preceq q$. If $\delta\sigma$ is a proof, σ can be viewed as the solution to a set of equations over δ. The equations are induced by the standard terms, the Cumulativity condition and the condition on axioms.

5.1. EXAMPLE. Consider a skeleton over $\neg\neg\forall x P(x) \vdash \forall x \neg\neg P(x)$:

$$
\cfrac{
\cfrac{
\cfrac{
\cfrac{
\cfrac{
\cfrac{P(x[UaV])[UaV] \vdash P(f[c])[cbW]}{\forall x P(x)[Ua] \vdash P(f[c])[cbW]} \ V
}{\vdash \neg\forall x P(x)[U], P(f[c])[cbW]} \ a
}{\neg P(f[c])[cb] \vdash \neg\forall x P(x)[U]} \ W
}{\vdash \neg\forall x P(x)[U], \neg\neg P(f[c])[c]} \ b
}{\vdash \neg\forall x P(x)[U], \forall x \neg\neg P(x)} \ c
}{\neg\neg\forall x P(x) \vdash \forall x \neg\neg P(x)} \ U
$$

The skeleton induces a set of equations: $x = f$, $c \preceq UaV$, and $UaV \preceq cbW$. The first of these is simply an equation of standard terms defined by ignoring all labels. The second is induced by the Cumulativity condition. The third stems from the condition on axioms. A ground solution σ is given by: $\sigma(U) = cb$, $\sigma(V) = \varepsilon$, $\sigma(W) = a$.

5.2. DEFINITION. Let σ be a substitution. The projections σ_Q and σ_I induce relations $\sqsupset_Q$ and $\sqsupset_I$ defined as follows:
- let r_1 belong to U and $\sigma(U) \neq \varepsilon$. If r_2 belongs to the last prefix term in $\sigma(U)$, and this term is different from U, then $r_1 \sqsupset_I r_2$,
- if r_1 belongs to $x[p]$, r_2 belongs to $y[q] \neq x[p]$, and $\sigma(x[p]) = y[q]$, then $r_1 \sqsupset_Q r_2$,
- if r_1 belongs to $x[p]$, r_2 belongs to $f[q]$, and $\sigma(x[p]) = f[q](\cdot)$, then $r_1 \sqsupset_Q r_2$.

The *reduction ordering* $\rhd$ induced by σ is the transitive closure of $\rhd_I \cup \rhd_Q$, where $\rhd_I$ is the transitive closure of $\gg \cup \sqsupset_I$ and $\rhd_Q$ is the transitive closure of $\gg \cup \sqsupset_Q$. The skeleton *conforms to* $\rhd$ if there are no two inferences r and r' such that $r \rhd r'$ and r is below r'.

Observe that the skeleton in example 5.1 conforms to the induced reduction ordering. In fact, none of the other permutation variants conform to this relation.

5.3. LEMMA. *Let r_1 and r_2 have side formula labels p_1 and p_2, and let $\rhd$ be the reduction ordering induced by σ. Assume that σ preserves the Unique prefix property. If $r_1 \rhd r_2$, then $p_2\sigma \preceq p_1\sigma$.*

PROOF. The statement follows by repeated application of the following three cases. *Case 1:* $r_1 \gg r_2$. Then $p_2 \preceq p_1$, i.e. $p_2\sigma \preceq p_1\sigma$. *Case 2:* $r_1 \sqsupset_I r_2$. If r_1 belongs to

U and $\sigma(U) = q't$, then r_2 belongs to t. Thus $p_1 = pU$ and $p_2 = qt$. The term t has a unique prefix in $\delta\sigma$ and this prefix is $q\sigma$. Hence $pU\sigma = qt\sigma$, i.e. $p_2\sigma = p_1\sigma$. *Case 3:* $r_1 \sqsupseteq_Q r_2$. Let r_1 belong to $x[p_1]$, $\sigma(x[p_1]) = f[p_2](\vec{t})$, and r_2 belong to $f[p_2]$. By the Cumulativity condition, $p_2\sigma \preceq p_1\sigma$.   □

Like we did for classical first–order logic we shall restrict the soundness argument to skeletons closed by ground, homogeneous substitutions. This saves us from a number of technical details without destroying the main structure. A substitution σ is homogeneous wrt. δ if the following property holds. If $\sigma(x[p]) = f[q](\vec{t})$ and $f[q'](\vec{y})$ occurs in δ, then $f[q](\vec{t}) = f[q'](\vec{y})\sigma$.

5.4. LEMMA. *Let σ be a ground, homogeneous substitution which preserves the Unique prefix property of the underlying skeleton. Then the reduction ordering $\rhd$ induced by σ is well–founded.*

PROOF. Let r_1, r_2, and r_3 be inferences with side formula labels p_1, p_2, p_3. We first prove that (†) if $r_1 \sqsupseteq_I r_2$ and $r_2 \rhd r_3$, then $p_3\sigma \prec p_1\sigma$. To see this, assume that $r_1 \sqsupseteq_I r_2$ and $r_2 \rhd r_3$. By lemma 5.3, $p_3\sigma \preceq p_2\sigma$ and $p_2\sigma \preceq p_1\sigma$. Observe that since σ is ground, r_2 belongs to a prefix parameter a. Thus p_2 is of the form qa and $p_3 \preceq q$. Hence $p_3\sigma \prec p_2\sigma \preceq p_1\sigma$.

Should $\rhd$ be cyclic, the side formula labels of each inference in the cycle must be equal under σ, otherwise lemma 5.3 would be contradicted. By (†) we can conclude that $\rhd$ is cyclic only if $\rhd_Q$ is cyclic. But by exactly the same argument as the proof of lemma 2.16 it follows that $\rhd_Q$ is well–founded. Hence $\rhd$ is also well–founded. □

A *model* is a pair of a Kripke model and a label interpretation function. An intuitionistic Kripke model for a first–order language without labels is a quadruple $(\mathbf{U}, \mathbf{D}, \leq, \Vdash')$, where $\mathbf{U}$ is a nonempty set of points partially ordered by $\leq$ and

- $\mathbf{D}$ is a function which maps each point in $\mathbf{U}$ into a nonempty set of terms such that if $x \leq y$, then $\mathbf{D}(x) \subseteq \mathbf{D}(y)$,
- $\Vdash'$ is a binary relation between $\mathbf{U}$ and the set of atomic formulae such that
  - if $x \Vdash' P(t_1, \ldots, t_n)$, then $t_1, \ldots, t_n \in \mathbf{D}(x)$,
  - if $x \Vdash' P(\vec{t})$ and $x \leq y$, then $y \Vdash' P(\vec{t})$.

The forcing relation $\Vdash$ is the weakest extension of $\Vdash'$ closed under:

$$\begin{array}{lll}
x \Vdash P(\vec{t}) & \text{iff} & x \Vdash' P(\vec{t}), \ P(\vec{t}) \text{ atomic,} \\
x \Vdash A \wedge B & \text{iff} & x \Vdash A \text{ and } x \Vdash B, \\
x \Vdash A \vee B & \text{iff} & x \Vdash A \text{ or } x \Vdash B, \\
x \Vdash \neg A & \text{iff} & y \nVdash A \text{ for each } y \geq x, \\
x \Vdash A \supset B & \text{iff} & y \nVdash A \text{ or } y \Vdash B \text{ for each } y \geq x, \\
x \Vdash \forall z A & \text{iff} & \text{for each } y \geq x \text{ and each } t \in \mathbf{D}(y), \ y \Vdash A\{z/t\}, \\
x \Vdash \exists z A & \text{iff} & \text{there is a } t \in \mathbf{D}(y) \text{ such that } x \Vdash A\{z/t\}.
\end{array}$$

A *label interpretation function* is a function φ from a set of labels which meets the Unique prefix property into the universe $\mathbf{U}$ such that $\varphi(p) \leq \varphi(q)$ if $p \preceq q$. φ

interprets a set of labelled formulae Γ provided that the set of labels attached to formulae in Γ satisfies the Unique prefix property. There is also a condition on the term universes which must be fulfilled: if t is a standard term labelled with p which occurs in a formula in Γ, then $\hat{t} \in \mathbf{D}(\varphi(p))$. A formula $A[s]$ is *true* in the model if $\varphi(s) \models \widehat{A[s]}$, otherwise it is *false*.

5.5. THEOREM. *Let S be an empty labelled sequent provable in the free variable system. Then S is valid.*

PROOF. The proof is a direct extension of the proof of theorem 4.4 for the propositional language. So assume a complete, variable–sharing skeleton closed by a ground, homogeneous substitution σ. By lemma 5.4, the induced reduction ordering $\rhd$ is well–founded. It is easy to check that lemma 2.14 holds; this gives a permutation variant δ which conforms to $\rhd$ and is closed by σ. The propositional cases in the induction over $\delta\sigma$ are as in the proof of theorem 4.4. Let us show that the rules for the universal quantifier preserve validity in $\delta\sigma$.

$$\frac{\Gamma, A\{x/t_1\}[pq] \vdash \Delta}{\Gamma, \forall x A[p] \vdash \Delta} \ L\forall \qquad\qquad \frac{\Gamma \vdash A\{x/t_2\}[pa], \Delta}{\Gamma \vdash \forall x A[p], \Delta} \ R\forall$$

Consider first the $L\forall$–instance. Take a model $(\mathbf{U}, \mathbf{D}, \leq, \Vdash')$ and a label interpretation function φ which makes $\Gamma, \forall x A[p]$ true. Let B be $A\{x/t_1\}[pq]$. By the Cumulativity condition we know that t_1 is a term labelled with a $q_1 \preceq pq$. We may without loss of generality assume that $\hat{t_1} \in \mathbf{D}(\varphi(q_1))$ (otherwise argue as in the proof of theorem 2.18). By the model condition, $\hat{t_1} \in \mathbf{D}(\varphi(pq))$. Hence $\varphi(pq) \Vdash \hat{B}$. By induction hypothesis, one formula in Δ is true.

For the $R\forall$–inference, take a model $(\mathbf{U}, \mathbf{D}, \leq, \Vdash')$ and a label interpretation function φ which makes every formula in Γ true and every formula in Δ false. Since δ conforms to σ, neither a nor t_2 occurs in Γ, Δ. We may therefore assume that pa is not in the domain of φ and that there is no $x \in \mathbf{U}$ such that $\hat{t_2} \in \mathbf{D}(x)$. Take any point s such that $\varphi(p) \leq s$ and any term $t \in \mathbf{D}(s)$. Extend the Kripke model such that for each $y \geq s$ and each atomic P,

- $\hat{t_2} \in \mathbf{D}(y)$,
- $y \Vdash' P\{t/\hat{t_2}\}$ iff $y \Vdash' P$.

Extend φ such that $\varphi(pa) = s$. The extension is possible and does clearly not change the evaluation of formulae in the conclusion of the rule. By induction hypothesis, it makes $A\{x/t_2\}[pa]$ true. Since this argument holds for any s and t, the model makes $\forall x A[p]$ true. The original model agrees on this, which shows the validity of the rule. $\qquad\square$

5.3. Completeness

A ground single step system is defined by adding quantifier rules to the system in section 4.2. The system is as follows:

Single step system: **LJ:**

$$\frac{\Gamma, A[p], B[p] \vdash \Delta}{\Gamma, A \wedge B[p] \vdash \Delta} \; L\wedge \qquad\qquad \frac{\Gamma, A, B \vdash \Delta}{\Gamma, A \wedge B \vdash \Delta} \; L\wedge$$

$$\frac{\Gamma \vdash A[p], \Delta \quad \Gamma \vdash B[p], \Delta}{\Gamma \vdash A \wedge B[p], \Delta} \; R\wedge \qquad\qquad \frac{\Gamma \vdash A \quad \Gamma \vdash B}{\Gamma \vdash A \wedge B} \; R\wedge$$

$$\frac{\Gamma, A[p] \vdash \Delta \quad \Gamma, B[p] \vdash \Delta}{\Gamma, A \vee B[p] \vdash \Delta} \; L\vee \qquad\qquad \frac{\Gamma, A \vdash \Delta \quad \Gamma, B \vdash \Delta}{\Gamma, A \vee B \vdash \Delta} \; L\vee$$

$$\frac{\Gamma \vdash A[p], B[p], \Delta}{\Gamma \vdash A \vee B[p], \Delta} \; R\vee \qquad \frac{\Gamma \vdash A}{\Gamma \vdash A \vee B} \; R\vee_1 \qquad \frac{\Gamma \vdash B}{\Gamma \vdash A \vee B} \; R\vee_2$$

$$\frac{\Gamma, \neg A[p] \vdash A[p], \Delta}{\Gamma, \neg A[p] \vdash \Delta} \; LC\neg' \qquad\qquad \frac{\Gamma \vdash A}{\Gamma, \neg A \vdash} \; L\neg$$

$$\frac{\Gamma, A[pa] \vdash \Delta}{\Gamma \vdash \neg A[p], \Delta} \; R\neg \qquad\qquad \frac{\Gamma, A \vdash}{\Gamma \vdash \neg A} \; R\neg$$

$$\frac{\Gamma, A \supset B[p] \vdash A[p], \Delta \quad \Gamma, B[p] \vdash \Delta}{\Gamma, A \supset B[p] \vdash \Delta} \; LC\supset' \qquad\qquad \frac{\Gamma \vdash A \quad \Gamma, B \vdash \Delta}{\Gamma, A \supset B \vdash \Delta} \; L\supset$$

$$\frac{\Gamma, A[pa] \vdash B[pa], \Delta}{\Gamma \vdash A \supset B[p], \Delta} \; R\supset \qquad\qquad \frac{\Gamma, A \vdash B}{\Gamma \vdash A \supset B} \; R\supset$$

$$\frac{\Gamma, A\{x/f[p]\}[p] \vdash \Delta}{\Gamma, \exists x A[p] \vdash \Delta} \; L\exists' \qquad\qquad \frac{\Gamma, A\{x/f\} \vdash \Delta}{\Gamma, \exists x A \vdash \Delta} \; L\exists$$

$$\frac{\Gamma \vdash A\{x/f[q]\}[p], \exists x A[p], \Delta}{\Gamma \vdash \exists x A[p], \Delta} \; RC\exists' \qquad\qquad \frac{\Gamma \vdash A\{x/f\}}{\Gamma \vdash \exists x A} \; R\exists$$

$$\frac{\Gamma, \forall x A[p], A\{x/f[q]\}[p] \vdash \Delta}{\Gamma, \forall x A[p] \vdash \Delta} \; LC\forall' \qquad\qquad \frac{\Gamma, A\{x/f\} \vdash \Delta}{\Gamma, \forall x A \vdash \Delta} \; L\forall$$

$$\frac{\Gamma \vdash A\{x/f[pa]\}[pa], \Delta}{\Gamma \vdash \forall x A[p], \Delta} \; R\forall' \qquad\qquad \frac{\Gamma \vdash A\{x/f\}}{\Gamma \vdash \forall x A} \; R\forall$$

Eigenparameter condition for LJ: In $L\exists$ and $R\forall$, f cannot occur in the conclusion.
Parameter condition: In $L\exists'$ and $R\forall'$, a and f cannot occur in the conclusion.
Cumulativity condition: In $LC\forall'$ and $RC\exists'$, $q \preceq p$.

Figure 10: Logical rules for the single step system and for LJ. In LJ Δ is either empty or singleton.

Axioms of the form $\Gamma, A[p] \vdash A[q], \Delta$ with $p \preceq q$.

Structural rules: contraction, weakening and left monotonicity *(LM)*.

Logical rules in figure 10. Note the Parameter and Cumulativity conditions.

The *LM* rule must be used together with contraction. The search procedure for this system is faced with a difficulty not present in the propositional system. Semantically, this can be explained by reference to the natural first–order models. Points in these models may have infinite domains. A blind expansion of the points may hence be unfair. A simple sequent which illustrates this is

$$\forall x \exists y P(x, y) \vdash \neg (A \supset A).$$

If we exhaustively add inferences owned by ε, we will not find the proof. A direct adaptation of the proof procedure for the propositional system is hence unfair.

We may go around these problems by using an exhaustive search in which all formulae are expanded in every branch. A procedure of this kind is used in [Fitting and Mendelsohn 1998] to establish a model existence theorem for a number of first–order modal logics. This search procedure generates an unlimited number of redundant steps.

Rather than applying this method, we shall prove completeness of the single step system by relating it to the cut–free fragment of LJ. It is well–known that LJ without cut is complete (see e.g. [van Dalen 1986]). In this way LJ is used to illuminate the single step system. We shall use the following formulation of LJ:

Axioms of the form $\Gamma, A \vdash A$.

Structural rules: contraction on the left and weakening.

Logical rules in figure 10.

5.6. THEOREM. *The single step system for first–order intuitionistic logic is complete.*

PROOF. Let π be a derivation in LJ. The idea is to label every formula in π, starting with the endsequent, and prove that every labelled sequent in the resulting derivation π' satisfies the following invariants:

(i) the labels in the sequent are linearly ordered by $\preceq$,

(ii) if the sequent has one succedent occurrence, the label of this occurrence is maximal in the sequent wrt. $\preceq$.

The conditions entail that the set of all labels in a branch are linearly ordered by $\preceq$. We will have to apply structural rules in the process and add inferences to the LJ–derivation, otherwise its labelled variant will not be a well–formed derivation in the single step system. Condition (ii) entails that if π is an LJ–proof and π' is closed under the invariants, then π' is a proof in the single step system. This follows since every axiom in the LJ–proof is then mapped to an axiom in the single step system.

We proceed by induction on the size of π. If π is just the endsequent, π' is the empty labelled variant of the endsequent. Since ε is the only label in this sequent, π' satisfies (i) and (ii).

Consider the uppermost inference r in a branch in π. If the principal formula of r is a conjunction, disjunction, or existential quantifier, the argument is simple. Example:

$$\frac{\Gamma \vdash A}{\Gamma \vdash A \vee B} \, r \qquad\qquad \frac{\dfrac{\Gamma' \vdash A[p]}{\Gamma' \vdash A[p], B[p]}}{\Gamma' \vdash A \vee B[p]}$$

π' is constructed by constructing a single step derivation with leaf $\Gamma' \vdash A \vee B[p]$ and replacing r with the two inferences to the right. The existence of the single step derivation follows from the induction hypothesis. It is immediate from the induction hypothesis that the leaf $\Gamma' \vdash A[p]$ satisfies the invariants.

If r is $R\neg$, $R\supset$, or $R\forall$, the situation is equally simple, the only difference is that we must choose a fresh prefix parameter for the single step inference and, in the case of $R\forall$, remember that the eigenparameter shall also be labelled. Note that condition (ii) is preserved.

If r is $L\neg$, $L\supset$, or $L\forall$, we must use structural rules. Assume, as an example, that r is the $L\forall$–inference below. By induction hypothesis there is a single step derivation with leaf $\Gamma', \forall x A[p] \vdash \Delta'$. The term f must occur below r in the LJ–derivation. In the single step derivation it occurs with a label, say q. Since the labels in a branch are linearly ordered by $\preceq$, either $q \preceq p$ or $p \preceq q$. In the former case let p' be p, in the latter case let p' be q. Use contraction on $\forall x A[p]$ and derive $\forall x A[p']$ by LM. Double bar denotes structural rules. Figure:

$$\frac{\Gamma, A\{x/f\} \vdash \Delta}{\Gamma, \forall x A \vdash \Delta} \, r \qquad\qquad \frac{\dfrac{\dfrac{\Gamma', A\{x/f[q]\}[p'] \vdash \Delta'}{\Gamma', \forall x A[p'], A\{x/f[q]\}[p'] \vdash \Delta'}}{\Gamma', \forall x A[p'] \vdash \Delta'}}{\Gamma', \forall x A[p] \vdash \Delta'}$$

Observe that the instantiation of the quantifier must satisfy the Cumulativity condition. This concludes the argument. □

5.7. THEOREM. *The free variable system for first–order intuitionistic logic is complete.*

PROOF. Let π be a derivation in the single step system with empty labelled endsequent. We prove that there is a free variable skeleton δ with the same structure as π, and a ground substitution σ, such that $\delta\sigma$ is a proof if π is a proof.

The proof simply extends the proof of lemma 4.16. We shall use the details in that proof verbatim and just comment on new cases arising from the labelled standard terms and the quantifiers. In constructing δ and σ from π we have to show that $\delta\sigma$ satisfies the following property in addition to properties (i) and (ii):

(iii) each labelled standard term $f[p]$ in π corresponds to a unique ground term in $\delta\sigma$ of the form $f[p](\vec{t})$.

Let r be an uppermost inference in π. It is immediate that axioms and propositional inferences preserve property (iii). Assume that r is:

$$\frac{\Gamma, \forall x A[p], A\{x/f[q]\}[p] \vdash \Delta}{\Gamma, \forall x A[p] \vdash \Delta} \ LC\forall'$$

π' is the derivation resulting from π by removing r. The induction hypothesis gives us a skeleton δ' and a substitution σ'; assume that the leaf in δ' is $\Gamma', \forall x A[p'] \vdash \Delta'$. Select fresh variables z and U and add the following inference to δ':

$$\frac{\Gamma', \forall x A[p'], A\{x/z[p'U]\}[p'U] \vdash \Delta'}{\Gamma', \forall x A[p'] \vdash \Delta'} \ LC\forall$$

By induction hypothesis, $p'\sigma' \preceq p$. There must hence be a ground label g such that $p'\sigma'g = p$. The term $f[q]$ in π is either the dummy element 0 or a term which occurs as an eigenparameter in an inference below r. In the former case let us say that t is 0, in the latter case t is the term in $\delta'\sigma'$ which corresponds to $f[q]$; this term exists by clause (iii) and the induction hypothesis, and is labelled with q. Let σ be $\sigma' \cup \{z[p'U]/t\} \cup \{U/g\}$. Observe that since r satisfies the Cumulativity condition, $q \preceq p$; hence $q \preceq p'U\sigma$. The substitution σ thus satisfies the Cumulativity condition. Clearly, $\delta\sigma$ satisfies properties (i), (ii) and (iii). Assume next that r is the leftmost inference below:

$$\frac{\Gamma \vdash A\{x/f[pa]\}[pa], \Delta}{\Gamma \vdash \forall x A[p], \Delta} \ R\forall \qquad \frac{\Gamma \vdash A\{x/f[p'a](\vec{y})\}[p'a], \Delta}{\Gamma \vdash \forall x A[p'], \Delta} \ R\forall$$

We construct $\delta\sigma$ by adding the rightmost inference to δ' and putting $\sigma = \sigma'$. By induction hypothesis and (ii), $p = p'\sigma'$. Hence $pa = p'a\sigma$, which shows that property (ii) is preserved. The term $f[pa]$ in π corresponds to $f[p'a](\vec{y})\sigma$; observe that since each variable in $\vec{y}$ is in $\mathrm{dom}(\sigma)$, this term is ground and unique. Hence property (iii) is also preserved. The rules for the existential quantifier are treated in a similar way. $\qquad \square$

6. Normal modal logics up to S4

Section 6.1 contains a general introduction to normal modal systems. The exposition of systems up to S4 begins in section 6.2, while some stronger systems are addressed in section 7.

6.1. Modal systems: language and models

The language of propositional modal logic adds unary operators $\Diamond$ and $\Box$ to the usual connectives and quantifiers. The set of *formulae* is defined inductively from these logical constants, a set of standard terms and a set of atomic formulae in the usual way.

Modal logic is a conservative extension of classical logic. In the literature the various systems of modal logic are classified according to the strength of the modal principles they support. Let us first address propositional principles. We shall focus on a fairly small class of normal modal logics. The weakest normal modal logic is denoted K (after 'Kripke'). If we take $\Diamond$ as shorthand for $\neg\Box\neg$, its theorems can be defined inductively as the least set closed under the following axiom and rule schemes:

A, where A is classically valid,

$\Box(A \supset B) \supset (\Box A \supset \Box B)$,

$$\frac{A \quad A \supset B}{B} \text{ MP},$$

$$\frac{A}{\Box A} \text{ RN}.$$

The first scheme in this Hilbert–style axiomatic system covers all substitution instances of valid formulae in classical propositional logic. The formula $\Box P \supset \Box P$ is, e.g., obtained from $A \supset A$ by substitution and is hence an axiom. The distribution axiom $\Box(A \supset B) \supset (\Box A \supset \Box B)$ is simply denoted 'K'. MP is the rule of proof which the medieval logicians called *modus ponendo ponens*. RN, the rule of necessitation, states that provability entails necessity.

In combination with RN the K principle can be viewed as a defining principle for normal systems. Other principles of interest for this chapter are:

D: $\Box A \supset \Diamond A$,

T: $\Box A \supset A$,

4: $\Box A \supset \Box\Box A$,

5: $\Diamond A \supset \Box\Diamond A$.

It turns out that an axiomatic presentation of the modal systems can be defined simply by adding the respective principles to the set of axioms for the system K; for this reason there is a direct correspondence between the names of the *schemes* and the names of the corresponding *systems*. The relationships between the systems addressed in this chapter form a lattice structure:

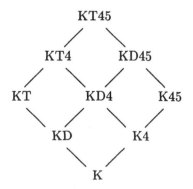

The lattice represents deductive strength. If a sequent is provable in, say K4, it is also provable in KD4, but not necessarily vice versa. KT4 is identical to the

Lewis–system S4, while KT45 is identical to S5. The schemes 4 and 5 receive their names from the connection to these historically important systems. We shall mostly use the Lewis notation for these systems. D is called the *deontic* principle due to its role in von Wright's pioneering work in deontic logic. T is the *truth* principle. The modal principles are in themselves not central for the logical systems in this section since we shall use conditions on terms to distinguish logical systems.

There are two first–order principles of particular interest: the *Barcan formula* and the *Converse Barcan formula*. They define different forms of distribution of the universal quantifier and the necessity operator:

BF: $\forall x \Box A \supset \Box \forall x A$,

CBF: $\Box \forall x A \supset \forall x \Box A$.

Different first–order extensions of the modal propositional systems can be characterized using these principles.

Contemporary applications of modal logic are often semantically motivated. We shall in this chapter always use Kripke models in combination with a label interpretation function, suitably restricted to ensure that there are enough terms in the domains. I shall close the section with the introduction of the Kripke model component of the semantical structure.

A *Kripke model* for the modal language is a quadruple $(\mathbf{U}, \mathbf{D}, R, V)$, where

- the *universe* $\mathbf{U}$ is a nonempty set of points (or "possible worlds"),
- the *domain function* $\mathbf{D}$ maps each point in $\mathbf{U}$ into a nonempty set of ground terms,
- the *accessibility relation* R is a binary relation on $\mathbf{U}$,
- V is a function which assigns a subset of $\mathbf{U}$ to each atomic formula, intuitively the set of points at which the atomic formula is true.

The satisfaction relation $\models$ is the weakest relation closed under the following clauses.

$$
\begin{array}{lll}
x \models P & \text{iff} & x \in V(P), \ P \text{ atomic}, \\
x \models A \wedge B & \text{iff} & x \models A \text{ and } x \models B, \\
x \models A \vee B & \text{iff} & x \models A \text{ or } x \models B, \\
x \models \neg A & \text{iff} & x \not\models A, \\
x \models A \supset B & \text{iff} & x \not\models A \text{ or } x \models B, \\
x \models \forall y A & \text{iff} & x \models A\{y/c\} \text{ for each } c \in \mathbf{D}(x), \\
x \models \exists y A & \text{iff} & x \models A\{y/c\} \text{ for at least one } c \in \mathbf{D}(x), \\
x \models \Box A & \text{iff} & y \models A \text{ for each } y \text{ such that } xRy, \\
x \models \Diamond A & \text{iff} & y \models A \text{ for at least one } y \text{ such that } xRy.
\end{array}
$$

If, for all x, y, xRy implies $\mathbf{D}(x) \subseteq \mathbf{D}(y)$, the model has *cumulative domains*. If $\mathbf{D}(x) = \mathbf{D}(y)$ for all x, y, the model has *constant domains*. Otherwise the domains are *varying*. A model for the propositional systems is simply a triple $(\mathbf{U}, R, V)$.

Models for the normal propositional systems in the lattice are defined by constraining R through combinations of the following conditions:

K: no constraints,

D: seriality, i.e. $\forall x \exists y (xRy)$,

T: reflexivity,

4: transitivity,

5: Euclideaness, i.e. $\forall x \forall y \forall z (xRy \wedge xRz \rightarrow yRz)$.

If L is a system in the lattice, a model is an *L–model* if the accessibility relation possesses the set of properties corresponding to the letters in the name of the system. A model of KT45 (S5) is hence a model in which R is reflexive, transitive and Euclidean, i.e. an equivalence relation. For further information about the systems, consult one of the standard texts on the subject, e.g. [Chellas 1980, Hughes and Cresswell 1968, Hughes and Cresswell 1984, Fitting 1993], or the survey chapter [Bull and Segerberg 1984] in the *Handbook of Philosophical Logic*. The latter text contains a comprehensive list of historical references.

The theory of quantified modal logic contains a wide variety of systems; for an overview of the field consult [Garson 1984]. A recent monograph based on prefixed tableaux is [Fitting and Mendelsohn 1998]. I have in this section opted for simplicity in the formulation of the systems and have neglected the complications caused by terms in modal semantics. The quantified modal systems in this chapter contain no treatment of terms beside those induced by Skolem functions. Systems with general terms can be obtained by attaching the intensional context to the function symbols [Ohlbach 1988]. Cialdea Mayer and Cerrito [2000] introduce prefixed tableau systems for a number of quantified modal systems with special emphasis on the treatment of terms.

6.2. Free variable propositional systems

The modal systems use the labelled language introduced in section 3.2. Recall that labels are finite strings over prefix variables and prefix parameters. Variables are denoted U, V, W; parameters are denoted a, b. A prefix term is either a prefix parameter or a prefix variable. A label p is either ε, a prefix term or a sequence of prefix terms. As usual we do not write labels when they are ε.

Let Θ be a set of labels which satisfies the Unique prefix property and $(\mathbf{U}, R, V)$ be an L–model. A function φ from Θ into the universe $\mathbf{U}$ is a *label interpretation function* provided that $\varphi(p) R \varphi(pt)$ for all labels p and pt in Θ; t a prefix term. Label interpretation functions for the logics K, K4 and K45 are only defined for sets of ground labels. For other systems, Θ may contain labels with free variables.

A set of labelled formulae is evaluated relative to an L–model and a label interpretation function φ provided all labels which occur in the set are in the domain of φ (and hence satisfies the Unique prefix property). $A[s]$ is *true* if $\varphi(s) \models \widehat{A[s]}$, otherwise it is *false*. The pair of the L–model and φ is an *L–countermodel* to a sequent S if every antecedent formula in S is true and every succedent formula in S is false. S is *L–valid* if it has no L–countermodels.

The structural rules of the system are as in figure 1 on page 1498. The logical rules for the propositional connectives are given in figure 11. Figure 12 contains the rules for the modal operators. The variable–labelled inferences of type $L\square$ and $R\Diamond$ *belong* to their free variables; instances of $R\square$ and $L\Diamond$ are parameter–labelled and

$$\frac{\Gamma, A[p], B[p] \vdash \Delta}{\Gamma, A \wedge B[p] \vdash \Delta} \ L\wedge \qquad\qquad \frac{\Gamma \vdash A[p], \Delta \quad \Gamma \vdash B[p], \Delta}{\Gamma \vdash A \wedge B[p], \Delta} \ R\wedge$$

$$\frac{\Gamma, A[p] \vdash \Delta \quad \Gamma, B[p] \vdash \Delta}{\Gamma, A \vee B[p] \vdash \Delta} \ L\vee \qquad\qquad \frac{\Gamma \vdash A[p], B[p], \Delta}{\Gamma \vdash A \vee B[p], \Delta} \ R\vee$$

$$\frac{\Gamma \vdash A[p], \Delta \quad \Gamma, B[p] \vdash \Delta}{\Gamma, A \supset B[p] \vdash \Delta} \ L\supset \qquad\qquad \frac{\Gamma, A[p] \vdash B[p], \Delta}{\Gamma \vdash A \supset B[p], \Delta} \ R\supset$$

$$\frac{\Gamma \vdash A[p], \Delta}{\Gamma, \neg A[p] \vdash \Delta} \ L\neg \qquad\qquad \frac{\Gamma, A[p] \vdash \Delta}{\Gamma \vdash \neg A[p], \Delta} \ R\neg$$

Figure 11: Propositional rules for the modal sequent calculus.

belong to their prefix parameter. A *modal skeleton* is a tree constructed according to the rules which satisfies the Skeleton condition: if r and r' belong to the same prefix parameter, the principal formulæ of the respective inferences are contextual equivalents. Variable–sharing and pure variable skeletons are as in definition 2.5.

The concept of a *derivation* relies on label substitutions, i.e. partial functions from prefix variables into labels. Not all label substitutions are admissible in every modal system. A *typing constraint* pertains to the logics between K and S4 in the lattice, given if table 2 for a substitution σ.

L	L–admissible type of $\sigma(U)$
K	parameter
KD	parameter or variable
KT	parameter, variable, or ε
K4	ground label except ε
KD4	label except ε
KT4	label including ε

Table 2: Typing constraints for admissible substitutions.

Let δ be a modal skeleton and σ be a label substitution. If L is KD, KT, KD4, or KT4, σ is *L–admissible* if it is idempotent and each value in the range of σ is of an appropriate type. $\delta\sigma$ is an *L–derivation* if its labels satisfy the Unique prefix property and σ is L–admissible. An *axiom* is a sequent of the form $\Gamma, P[p] \vdash P[p], \Delta$. An *L–proof* is a finite L–derivation in which every leaf is an axiom.

$$\frac{\Gamma, A[pU] \vdash \Delta}{\Gamma, \Box A[p] \vdash \Delta} \; L\Box \quad \frac{\Gamma \vdash A[pa], \Delta}{\Gamma \vdash \Box A[p], \Delta} \; R\Box \quad \frac{\Gamma, A[pa] \vdash \Delta}{\Gamma, \Diamond A[p] \vdash \Delta} \; L\Diamond \quad \frac{\Gamma \vdash A[pU], \Delta}{\Gamma \vdash \Diamond A[p], \Delta} \; R\Diamond$$

Figure 12: Modality rules for the free variable system.

If L is K or K4, two additional constraints must be placed on a proof $\delta\sigma$. First, in an axiom $\Gamma, P[p] \vdash P[p], \Delta$ the axiom label p must be ground. Second, σ must satisfy the Neighbourhood condition in order to be L–admissible.

Neighbourhood condition: if the term t occurs in $\sigma(U)$, then there is a branch in the skeleton which contains an occurrence of U and an occurrence of t.

The Neighbourhood condition is a sensible constraint for all systems addressed in this chapter. It is, however, a necessary consistency condition for the systems K and K4, as well as for the K45 system addressed in the next section.

6.1. EXAMPLE. The skeleton δ below shows that the modal systems satisfy the distribution axiom.

$$\frac{\dfrac{\dfrac{\dfrac{P[V] \vdash P[U], Q[a] \quad Q[U], P[V] \vdash Q[a]}{P \supset Q[U], P[V] \vdash Q[a]} \; a}{P \supset Q[U], P[V] \vdash \Box Q} \; V}{P \supset Q[U], \Box P \vdash \Box Q}}{\Box(P \supset Q), \Box P \vdash \Box Q} \; U$$

δ is a proof wrt. $\{U/a, V/a\}$. $\delta\{U/a, V/a\}$ is hence a proof in all the modal systems under discussion. Observe in particular that all the requirements for the system K are met: the substitution assigns a parameter to the variables, the parameter occurs in a branch which also contains the variables, and the axiom labels in the proof are ground.

6.2. EXAMPLE. The skeleton δ below is a proof (i.e. wrt. the empty substitution $\emptyset$) in systems at least as strong as KD.

$$\frac{\dfrac{\dfrac{P[U] \vdash P[U]}{\vdash P \supset P[U]}}{\vdash \Diamond(P \supset P)} \; U \quad \dfrac{\dfrac{P[a] \vdash P[a]}{\vdash P \supset P[a]}}{\vdash \Box(P \supset P)} \; a}{\vdash \Diamond(P \supset P) \wedge \Box(P \supset P)}$$

However, $\emptyset$ fails to make the axiom label in the leftmost leaf ground. $\delta\emptyset$ is hence not a K–proof. The substitution $\{U/a\}$ remedies this situation, but clashes with the Neighbourhood condition. $\delta\{U/a\}$ is hence not a K–proof either. In fact, the endsequent is not K–valid.

Matrices are, as before, defined by means of logical reduction rules; the rules for modalities are:

$$\overline{\Box A}[p] \quad \rightsquigarrow \quad \overline{A}[pU] \qquad \Box A[p] \quad \rightsquigarrow \quad A[pa]$$

$$\overline{\Diamond A}[p] \quad \rightsquigarrow \quad \overline{A}[pa] \qquad \Diamond A[p] \quad \rightsquigarrow \quad A[pU]$$

Consult definition 2.7 for the definition of matrices. Except that generative formulae are of the form $\overline{\Box A}[p]$ and $\Diamond A[p]$ the multiplicity of a reduction sequence is as in definition 2.9. The key definitions for the modal matrix system are: A substitution σ is L–admissible if it is idempotent and its values are of appropriate types. If L is at least as strong as KD, this is sufficient for L–admissibility, otherwise σ must also satisfy the Neighbourhood condition (replacing "branch" with "path"). The connection $\{\overline{P}[p], P[q]\}$ is σ–complementary if $p\sigma = q\sigma$. S is *matrix provable* if there is a multiplicity μ such that the matrix of S with multiplicity μ contains a spanning set of σ–complementary connections; σ L–admissible and preserving the Unique prefix property of the labels in the matrix.

6.3. EXAMPLE. A matrix over the truth axiom $\Box P \vdash P$ is:

$$\left[\begin{array}{cc} \overline{P}[U] & P \end{array} \right]$$

Every path through the matrix contains a $\{U/\varepsilon\}$–complementary connection. Observe that the substitution is not admissible in K, KD or K4. A matrix over the 4–instance $\Box P \vdash \Box\Box P$ is:

$$\left[\begin{array}{cc} \overline{P}[U] & P[ab] \end{array} \right]$$

Every path through the matrix contains a $\{U/ab\}$–complementary connection. $\Box P \vdash \Box\Box P$ is matrix provable in systems at least as strong as K4.

6.4. LEMMA. *Let Θ be a set of labels which satisfies the Unique prefix property and is closed under $\prec$, and let t be any prefix term with prefix p in Θ. Let σ preserve the Unique prefix property and $\varphi : \Theta\sigma \to \mathbf{U}$ be a label interpretation function into the L–model $(\mathbf{U}, R, V)$. Then $\varphi(p\sigma)R\varphi(pt\sigma)$.*

PROOF. Observe first that if $t\sigma$ is a prefix term, $\varphi(p\sigma)R\varphi(pt\sigma)$ by the assumption that φ is a label interpretation function. This proves the lemma for the case that t is a parameter and the case that t is a variable U and L is either K or KD. Assume that t is a variable U, L is K4 or KD4, and $\sigma(U) = t_1 \ldots t_n$. Let q_0 be $p\sigma$ and q_i be $pt_1 \ldots t_i\sigma$, so that $pU\sigma = q_n$. Θ is closed under $\prec$, hence $q_i \in \Theta\sigma$ for each $i \leq n$. By construction, $\varphi(q_i)R\varphi(q_{i+1})$; $i < n$. R is by assumption transitive, hence $\varphi(p\sigma)R\varphi(pU\sigma)$. If L is one of the T–systems, $\sigma(U)$ may also be ε. In this case R is reflexive, which yields $\varphi(p\sigma)R\varphi(p\sigma)$. $\qquad\square$

6.5. THEOREM. *Let L be between K and KT4 and S be an empty labelled L-provable sequent. Then S is L-valid.*

PROOF. Let π be a complete, variable–sharing skeleton over S closed by σ. Like we have observed in the soundness proofs for classical and intuitionistic logics, the assumption about sharing of variables is connected to the permutation schemes and is not essential for the argument. Exactly as in the proof of theorem 4.4 we can show that the reduction ordering $\rhd$ induced by σ is well–founded and that there is a permutation variant δ of π which conforms to $\rhd$ and is closed by σ. The argument for the latter statement applies lemma 2.14, which holds for all the modal systems. By induction on the length of $\delta\sigma$ we show that every sequent in $\delta\sigma$ is L–valid.

An axiom $\Gamma, P[p] \vdash P[p], \Delta$ is trivially valid. For the inductive step, we treat the cases of the last inference in $\delta\sigma$ being of one of the forms:

$$\frac{\Gamma, A[pq] \vdash \Delta}{\Gamma, \Box A[p] \vdash \Delta} \qquad\qquad \frac{\Gamma \vdash A[pa], \Delta}{\Gamma \vdash \Box A[p], \Delta}$$

In the $L\Box$ case q may be any string such that pq is a label. Pick an arbitrary model of $\Gamma, \Box A[p]$. We may without loss of generality assume that pq is in the domain of the label interpretation function φ. Note that the occurrence of $A[pq]$ in $\delta\sigma$ corresponds to an occurrence in δ of the form $A[p'U]$ such that $U\sigma = q$. Hence lemma 6.4 applies and allows us to infer that $\varphi(p)R\varphi(pq)$. By the truth conditions, Γ and $A[pq]$ hold in the model. By induction hypothesis, one formula in Δ is true.

In the case of $R\Box$ let φ be the label interpretation function of an arbitrary model of Γ and s be a point such that $\varphi(p)Rs$. Since δ conforms to σ, a does not occur in the conclusion. We may therefore assume that pa is not in the domain of φ. If φ makes a formula in Δ true, we are done. Otherwise, there must be a function φ' which agrees with φ on the evaluation of the formulae in the conclusion and which maps pa to s. By induction hypothesis, $s \Vdash A$. Since s is an arbitrary point, $\varphi(p) \models \Box A$. $\qquad\Box$

6.3. Single step propositional systems

Single step rules corresponding to the free variable systems in the previous section have been introduced by Massacci [1994]. Massacci has given rules for a number of other systems as well; all of these logics have also been given a free variable formulation in [Beckert and Goré 1997].

Following the pattern used for intuitionistic logic in section 4.2 I shall formulate a search procedure and use refutation trees to establish completeness. For the logics K4, KD4 and S4 the procedure implements a termination condition based on loop–checking. The loop–checking mechanism is defined by Fitting [1983] and has been investigated further by Demri [1995].

Loop–checking is computationally expensive. An alternative to loop–checking is to constrain contraction by numerical bounds. A result of this kind is established by Cerrito and Cialdea Mayer [1997] based on a technique introduced by Ladner

$$\frac{\Gamma, A[pa] \vdash \Delta}{\Gamma, \Box A[p] \vdash \Delta} \, LK \qquad \frac{\Gamma, \Box A[p], A[p] \vdash \Delta}{\Gamma, \Box A[p] \vdash \Delta} \, LT \qquad \frac{\Gamma, \Box A[pa] \vdash \Delta}{\Gamma, \Box A[p] \vdash \Delta} \, L4$$

$$\frac{\Gamma \vdash A[pa], \Delta}{\Gamma \vdash \Diamond A[p], \Delta} \, RK \qquad \frac{\Gamma \vdash A[p], \Diamond A[p], \Delta}{\Gamma \vdash \Diamond A[p], \Delta} \, RT \qquad \frac{\Gamma \vdash \Diamond A[pa], \Delta}{\Gamma \vdash \Diamond A[p], \Delta} \, R4$$

$$\frac{\Gamma \vdash A[pa], \Delta}{\Gamma \vdash \Box A[p], \Delta} \, R\Box \qquad\qquad \frac{\Gamma, A[pa] \vdash \Delta}{\Gamma, \Diamond A[p] \vdash \Delta} \, L\Diamond$$

Parameter condition for $R\Box$ and $L\Diamond$: a cannot occur in the conclusion.
Side condition for LK and RK: a occurs in the branch.

Figure 13: Single step modality rules.

[1977]. The authors define a mapping of the input sequent S into a set $f(S)$ such that the length the formulae in $f(S)$ is polynomially bounded by the length of S. They then prove that S is S4–contradictory if and only if $f(S)$ is T–contradictory and use this to define a contraction–free proof procedure for S4.

The results of Cerrito and Cialdea Mayer are defined for unlabelled sequent and tableau systems. By exploiting the structure of labels in single step tableaux Massacci has sharpened these results. More precisely, Massacci has established bounds on the *length* of prefixes and showed that a sequent is provable if and only it has a single step proof with the length of all labels constrained by the bound. For K4, KD4 and S4 the bound is quadratic in the length of the input sequent. For the other logics addressed in this section the bound is linear. Since he has also proved confluence results (up to an ordering on inferences), the bounds give rise to decision procedures. For further information about these results, and for a general discussion of approaches to termination, consult [Massacci 2000].

The structural rules and the propositional rules in figure 11 (page 1557) are shared by all the single step systems. Modality rules are given in figure 13. Observe that the Parameter condition for $L\Diamond$ and $R\Box$ gives rise to rule dependencies. The systems are specified by collecting modality rules according to table 3.

We shall now prove completeness of the single step systems by a similar procedure as we used for intuitionistic logic. Recall that the main idea is to generate derivations comprised of common point derivations (cpds) stacked above each other. A cpd is generated by the kernel of the procedure. An initial cpd over the empty labelled endsequent is generated by a succession of expansion steps. All other cpds are generated by a series of transition steps followed by a series of expansion steps. Derivations grow by inserting cpds above open leaves. It is clear that since the expansion steps terminate with sequents of a particular form, the sequents to which the transition steps are applied will always be of this form. We shall use this fact below, both in the formulation of termination conditions and in the definition of

L	$L\Diamond$ $R\Box$	LK RK	side cond.	LT RT	$L4$ $R4$
K	×	×	×		
KD	×	×			
KT	×	×		×	
K4	×	×	×		×
KD4	×	×			×
KT4	×	×		×	×

Table 3: Typing constraints for admissible substitutions.

the transition part of the cpd–generating kernel. For the 4–logics termination relies on the following concept.

6.6. DEFINITION. Let $p \prec q$. The point q is a *copy of p in* β if, for each A, there is an antecedent (succedent) occurrence of $A[q]$ in β iff there is an antecedent (succedent) occurrence of $A[p]$. If there is such a point p, we say that q is an *endpoint* wrt. β.

The expansion part of the kernel governs application of inferences which do not change labels. LT and RT are the only modality rules in this category. Observe the implicit contraction in LT and RT.

Expansion: Expand every formula whose principal symbol is a propositional connective. In T–logics one may also apply LT and RT, but avoid repeated expansion of the same formula in a branch.

The form of the open leaves are determined by such expansion steps. They are of the form

$$\Gamma, \Gamma', C_1[p], \ldots, C_k[p] \vdash C_{k+1}[p], \ldots, C_m[p], \Delta, \Delta'$$

where the formulae in Γ, Δ are all atomic; each formula in $\Gamma', C_{k+1}[p], \ldots, C_m[p]$ is of the form $\Box A[p]$, and each formula in $C_1[p], \ldots, C_k[p], \Delta'$ is of the form $\Diamond A[p]$. This sequent has *branching degree* m. The conditions for further expansion depend on the logic. We shall say that the sequent above is *finished* if one of the following conditions holds.

- If the sequent is an axiom, it is finished.
- If $m = 0$ and the logic is not KD or KD4, it is finished.
- If the logic is K4, KD4 or KT4, the sequent is finished if it contains an endpoint wrt. its branch.

Let π be a derivation with an unfinished branch β. Assume that the leaf of β has branching degree m. The branch gives rise to m new cpds, where cpd i is generated as follows. The *transition* part is first invoked to create a jump to a new point. Assuming that the form of the sequent is as above, the transition part is comprised of the following steps.

Transition: Perform the following logic–sensitive steps:
1. Remove each $C_j[p]$ by weakening except $C_i[p]$. Remove all formulae in Γ, Δ.
2. Expand $C_i[p]$ using a fresh parameter a; $i > 0$.
   KD, KD4: if $m = 0$, proceed as if a fresh parameter a had been introduced.
3. K4, KD4, KT4: generate $B[pa]$ using $L4$ or $R4$ for each $B[p]$ in Γ', Δ'.
   K4 and KD4: apply first contraction to $B[p]$.
4. K, KD, KD4, K4: generate $B[pa]$ using LK and RK for each $B[p]$ in Γ', Δ'.

This gives rise to a succession of inferences. The first step generates the following form (if $j > k$):

$$\frac{\Gamma_i' \vdash C_j[p], \Delta_i'}{\Gamma_i, \Gamma_i', C_1[p], \ldots, C_k[p] \vdash C_{k+1}[p], \ldots, C_{m_i}[p], \Delta_i, \Delta_i'} \, RW$$

Step 2 in the transition part invokes either $R\Box$ or $L\Diamond$. After the transition part is completed the expansion part of the procedure is invoked.

Assume that the original derivation π has n unfinished branches and the branching degree of branch i is m_i. If each m_i is greater than 0, π gives rise to $m_0 + \ldots + m_n$ cpds. Using these cpds we can construct $m_1 \times \ldots \times m_n$ extensions of π by putting one of the m_i cpds on top of branch i for each i. If the logic is at least as strong as KD, let m_i' be m_i if $m_i > 1$, otherwise m_i' is 1. Then π gives rise to $m_0' + \ldots + m_n'$ cpds, from which we can construct $m_1' \times \ldots \times m_n'$ extensions.

The definition of refutation trees follows definition 4.9 in section 4.2, but employs a slightly modified set of refutation rules. The refutation rules for the respective modal systems consist of

- all 1–premiss rules of the single step system except right weakening, i.e. $L\wedge$, $R\vee$, $R\supset$, $L\neg$, $R\neg$, and the modality rules,
- left and right projections of the branching rules; left projections shown below:

$$\frac{\Gamma \vdash A[p], \Delta}{\Gamma \vdash A \wedge B[p], \Delta} \qquad \frac{\Gamma, A[p] \vdash \Delta}{\Gamma, A \vee B[p] \vdash \Delta} \qquad \frac{\Gamma \vdash A[p], \Delta}{\Gamma, A \supset B[p] \vdash \Delta}$$

- the *Split* rule:

$$\frac{\Gamma', C_1[p] \vdash \Delta' \quad \ldots \quad \Gamma' \vdash C_m[p], \Delta'}{\Gamma, \Gamma', C_1[p], \ldots, C_k[p] \vdash C_{k+1}[p], \ldots, C_m[p], \Delta, \Delta'} \, Split$$

Γ, Δ contains atomic formulae; each formula in $\Gamma', C_{k+1}[p], \ldots, C_m[p]$ is of the form $\Box A[p]$, and each formula in $C_1[p], \ldots, C_k[p], \Delta'$ is of the form $\Diamond A[p]$.

The proof of the Model existence theorem for intuitionistic logic makes use of two properties of refutation trees:

- a sequent which is not provable by the search procedure has a finite, complete refutation tree (lemma 4.11),
- if S is the uppermost sequent in the segment of inferences owned by q, $p \preceq q$, there is an occurrence of $A[p]$ in S or in a sequent below S (lemma 4.10).

The two properties hold also in the modal systems and are used below. The proofs of the properties transfer directly from the intuitionistic refutation system to the modal systems at hand.

6.7. THEOREM. *Let L be one of the propositional modal logics up to S4. If an empty labelled sequent is not provable in the single step system for L, it has a finite countermodel.*

PROOF. Assume that the endsequent is not provable in the single step system for L. There is then a complete refutation tree ρ over the sequent. Let the collector sets ρ^+ and ρ^- be given by: ρ^+ is the set of all formulae with an antecedent occurrence in a sequent in ρ, ρ^- is the set of all formulae with a succedent occurrence in ρ. The Kripke model $(\mathbf{U}, R, V)$ induced by ρ is defined in terms of a relation R_0 and the diagonal relation Δ on $\mathbf{U}$. R_0^+ and R_0^* denote, respectively, the transitive and the reflexive, transitive closures of R_0. R_0 is the weakest relation such that

- pR_0pa for each point $pa \in \mathbf{U}$,
- if $q \in \mathbf{U}$ is a copy of p and $s \in \mathbf{U}$, then pR_0s iff qR_0s.

Given R_0 the model $(\mathbf{U}, R, V)$ is defined by:

- $\mathbf{U}$ is the set of points attached to formulae in ρ,
- $R = \begin{cases} R_0 & \text{for K and KD,} \\ R_0 \cup \Delta & \text{for T,} \\ R_0^+ & \text{for K4 and KD4,} \\ R_0^* & \text{for S4,} \end{cases}$
- $p \in V(P)$ iff $P[p]$ occurs in ρ^+.

Clearly the model is of the appropriate type for the respective systems. The identity function serves as label interpretation function. We prove that:

- for each $A[p] \in \rho^+$, $p \models A$,
- for each $A[p] \in \rho^-$, $p \not\models A$.

This is established by a double induction over A and p. More precisely, the induction is over pairs of the form (A, p) with the following lexicographical order: (A, p) is less than (B, q) iff A is a subformula of B or $A = B$ and $p \prec q$. The double induction is needed in case 2 and the case that $\Box B[p] \in \rho^-$.

The base step in the induction is exactly as in the proof of the Model existence theorem for intuitionistic logic (theorem 4.14). It is straightforward to establish the inductive step when the principal symbol of $A[p]$ is a truth–functional operator. The modal cases remain. Assume first that $\Box B[p] \in \rho^+$. We must show that for every s such that pRs, $s \models B$. There are 4 cases.

Case 1: s is pa for a parameter a. There must then be an antecedent occurrence of $\Box B[p]$ below the segment of inferences owned by pa. By construction, the rule LK has been applied and has generated an antecedent occurrence of $B[pa]$. By induction hypothesis, $pa \models B$.

Case 2: p is an endpoint. Assume that p is a copy of q. Then $q \prec p$. By definition, $\Box B[q] \in \rho^+$. By induction hypothesis, $q \models \Box B$. But qRs by construction of R. Hence $s \models B$.

Case 3: $s = p$. The logic is then a T–logic. The systems hence contains LT, and we must have that $B[p] \in \rho^+$. Conclude by induction hypothesis.

Case 4: s is pqa for a nonvoid label q and a parameter a. The logic is then a 4–logic. There must be an antecedent occurrence of $\Box B[p]$ below the segment of inferences owned by pq. The branch contains repeated applications of $L4$, which makes $\Box B[pq] \in \rho^+$. The LK rule has been applied to this so that $B[pqa] \in \rho^+$. By induction hypothesis, $pqa \models B$.

Assume that $\Box B[p] \in \rho^-$. By construction, either p is an endpoint or there has been an application of $R\Box$. Let us take the two cases separately. If p is an endpoint, p is a copy of a point $q \prec p$ such that $\Box B[q] \in \rho^-$. By induction hypothesis $q \not\models \Box B$. There is then a point s such that qRs and $s \not\models B$. Since p is a copy of q, pRs. Hence $p \not\models \Box B$. If there has been an application of $R\Box$, this application has created a succedent occurrence of $B[pa]$. The induction hypothesis gives $pa \not\models B$. By construction $pRpa$, hence $p \not\models \Box B$. Hence $p \not\models \Box B$ holds in both cases, which is what we have to prove. The $\Diamond$–cases are symmetrical.   □

6.8. COROLLARY. *Let L be one of the propositional modal logics up to $S4$. If an empty labelled sequent is unprovable in the free variable system for L, it has a finite countermodel.*

PROOF. The proof of the corresponding statement for intuitionistic logic relies on a mapping from proofs in the single step system to proofs in the free variable system (lemma 4.16). It is straightforward to define a mapping of this kind for the modal systems as well. The completeness result then follows from theorem 6.7.   □

6.4. First–order systems with cumulative or varying domains

Employing the term language introduced in section 5.1 it is straightforward to define cumulative and varying domain extensions of the propositional systems in section 6.2. The systems are obtained by including the quantifier rules in figure 14. To summarize, the systems consist of

- contraction and weakening (cnf. figure 1 on page 1498),
- the propositional rules in figure 11 on page 1557,
- the modality rules in figure 12 on page 1558,
- the quantifier rules in figure 14.

The systems are further defined by conditions on the set of admissible substitutions. The typing constraints in table 2 in section 6.2 transfer directly to the first–order systems. The systems are distinguished by the following conditions.

Cumulativity condition for σ: for each $x[p]$ in dom(σ), if $x[p]$ is mapped to a term labelled with q, then $q\sigma \preceq p\sigma$.

Varying domain condition for σ: for each $x[p]$ in dom(σ), if $x[p]$ is mapped to a term labelled with q, then $q\sigma = p\sigma$.

Let σ be a substitution which satisfies the Cumulativity condition and δ be a skeleton. $\delta\sigma$ is a *derivation* if it satisfies the Unique prefix property. It is a *proof* if

$$\frac{\Gamma, A\{x/y[p]\}[p] \vdash \Delta}{\Gamma, \forall x A[p] \vdash \Delta} \ L\forall \qquad\qquad \frac{\Gamma \vdash A\{x/f[p](\vec{y})\}[p], \Delta}{\Gamma \vdash \forall x A[p], \Delta} \ R\forall$$

$$\frac{\Gamma, A\{x/f[p](\vec{y})\}[p] \vdash \Delta}{\Gamma, \exists x A[p] \vdash \Delta} \ L\exists \qquad\qquad \frac{\Gamma \vdash A\{x/y[p]\}[p], \Delta}{\Gamma \vdash \exists x A[p], \Delta} \ R\exists$$

$\vec{y}$ is a list of all labelled quantifier variables which occur free in the principal formula.

Figure 14: Quantifier rules for first–order modal systems domains

it is finite and every leaf is an axiom, i.e. a sequent of the form $\Gamma, A[p] \vdash A[p], \Delta$. A substitution σ which closes δ can be viewed as the solution to a set of equations over δ induced by the standard terms, the Cumulativity/Varying domain conditions and the condition on axioms. The typing constraints on the substitutions restrict the space of possible solutions.

6.9. EXAMPLE. Below to the left is a matrix for the instance $\Box \forall x P(x) \supset \forall x \Box P(x)$ of the converse Barcan formula. A matrix for the instance $\forall x \Box P(x) \supset \Box \forall x P(x)$ of the Barcan formula is given to the right.

$$\left[\ \overline{P}(x[U])[U] \ \ P(f)[a] \ \right] \qquad \left[\ \overline{P}(f[a])[a] \ \ P(x)[U] \ \right]$$

The leftmost matrix is closed by the substitution $\{x[U]/f, U/a\}$. The substitution satisfies the Cumulativity condition but is not admissible for the varying domain logics. The matrix for the Barcan formula is closed by $\{x/f[a], U/a\}$, which fails to be admissible in both cumulative and varying domain systems. Note that the binding $x/f[a]$ is not admissible in these kind of systems because x is labelled with ε and $a \not\preceq \varepsilon$.

6.10. EXAMPLE. The sequent $\Box \exists x P(x) \vdash \exists x \Box P(x)$ is not valid in any of the modal systems. A matrix is:

$$\left[\ \overline{P}(f[U])[U] \ \ P(x)[a] \ \right]$$

The substitution $\{x/f[a], U/a\}$ fails to be admissible in both cumulative and varying domain systems. Observe that the sequent is unprovable for exactly the same reason as the Barcan formula.

In section 6.1 a Kripke model for the modal language was defined as a quadruple $(\mathbf{U}, \mathbf{D}, R, V)$. A *label interpretation function* is a function φ from a set of labels Θ into the universe $\mathbf{U}$ such that

- Θ satisfies the Unique prefix property,
- $\varphi(p)R\varphi(pt)$ for all labels p and pt in Θ.

$$\frac{\Gamma, \forall x A[p], A\{x/f[q]\}[p] \vdash \Delta}{\Gamma, \forall x A[p] \vdash \Delta} \ LC\forall' \qquad\qquad \frac{\Gamma \vdash A\{x/f[p]\}[p], \Delta}{\Gamma \vdash \forall x A[p], \Delta} \ R\forall'$$

$$\frac{\Gamma, A\{x/f[p]\}[p] \vdash \Delta}{\Gamma, \exists x A[p] \vdash \Delta} \ L\exists' \qquad\qquad \frac{\Gamma \vdash A\{x/f[q]\}[p], \exists x A[p], \Delta}{\Gamma \vdash \exists x A[p], \Delta} \ RC\exists'$$

Parameter condition: In $L\exists'$ and $R\forall'$ a and f cannot occur in the conclusion.
Cumulativity condition: In $LC\forall'$ and $RC\exists'$, $q \preceq p$.
Varying domain condition: In $LC\forall'$ and $RC\exists'$, $q = p$.

Figure 15: Quantifier rules of the single step system.

For quantified versions of K, K4 and K45 all labels in Θ must be ground. φ interprets a set of labelled formulae Γ provided that for each standard term t which occurs in a formula in Γ, if t is labelled with p, then $\widehat{t} \in \mathbf{D}(\varphi(p))$.

6.11. THEOREM. *Let S be an empty labelled sequent provable in the free variable system. Then S is valid.*

PROOF. The proof is a direct extension of the proof of theorem 6.5 for the propositional language. The quantifier rules are treated similarly to the soundness proof for first–order intuitionistic logic in theorem 5.5. Since the soundness proof adds little to the treatment of quantifiers in intuitionistic logic and the treatment of modalities in the propositional systems, details are left for the reader. □

A single step system is obtained by adding the quantifier rules in figure 15 to the propositional single step rules in figure 13 (page 1561) and the usual structural rules in figure 1. Contraction must in general be used on the principal formulae in L4 and R4. Table 3 transfers without modification. The system we obtain is a variant of the prefixed system for modal logics defined in [Kreitz and Schmitt 2000].

The Model existence theorem can be proved for the single step system using the same argument as for quantified prefixed tableaux in [Fitting and Mendelsohn 1998]. Moreover, the mapping of single step derivations into skeletons in the free variable system defined for intuitionistic logic extends straightforwardly to the modal systems, leading to the following conclusion.

6.12. THEOREM. *The free variable systems for first–order modal logic are complete.*

7. The S5 family

In this section we address first–order systems with constant domains for S5 and the "weak S5" systems K45 and KD45. The propositional versions of these systems enjoy a strong modal reduction property: every formula is equivalent to a formula without nested modalities. Semantically, Kripke models for this family of systems have a particularly simple structure.

The S5–like systems are hence simpler than the systems addressed in the previous section. This can be reflected directly in the logical rules. In fact there is no need to use labels longer than 1, not even for the first–order systems, which is one of the features of Kanger's pioneering system for S5 [Kanger 1957]. The systems below are formulated in the style of Kanger. Alternatively one could follow Massacci [1994] and define the systems as proper extensions of the weaker systems. By treating the S5 family differently from the weaker systems we loose modularity, but gain simplicity of rules.

It is natural to use constant domains in first–order models of these systems. This holds in particular for S5, since an S5 model with cumulative domains also has constant domains. The technique used below can be applied to constant domain versions of the systems in the previous section (not addressed in this chapter).

7.1. Term language

In the term language for cumulative and varying domain systems, introduced in section 5.1, there are two types of terms: labelled standard terms and prefix terms. The former class of terms depends on the latter, since the labels of the standard terms are comprised of prefix terms. But there is no dependency the other way around. This situation is different for the constant domain logics. Prefix parameters in this language are function symbols which take labelled standard terms as arguments. Moreover, quantifier variables are not labelled. Using the conventions from section 5.1 we define the set of *labelled standard terms* by:

- the quantifier variable x is a labelled standard term,
- if $\vec{t}$ is a list of n labelled standard terms and f has arity n, then $f[p](\vec{t})$ is a standard term labelled with p.

The set of *prefix terms* is inductively defined by

- a prefix variable U is a prefix term,
- if $\vec{t}$ is a list of n labelled standard terms and a is a prefix parameter with arity n, then $a(\vec{t})$ is a prefix term. (This differs from the language in section 5.1.)

Labels are inductively defined by

- ε is a label,
- if p is a label which does not contain a and $a(\vec{t})$ is a prefix term, then $pa(\vec{t})$ is a label,
- if p is a label which does not contain U, then pU is a label.

The systems in this section will only use labels with length less than 2. Labels of arbitrary length are, however, needed in constant domain versions of the systems in the previous section. Substitutions and the Unique prefix property are defined as in section 5.1.

$$\frac{\Gamma, A[U] \vdash \Delta}{\Gamma, \Box A[p] \vdash \Delta} \; L\Box \qquad \frac{\Gamma, A[a(\bar{y})] \vdash \Delta}{\Gamma, \Diamond A[p] \vdash \Delta} \; L\Diamond \qquad \frac{\Gamma, A\{x/y\}[p] \vdash \Delta}{\Gamma, \forall x A[p] \vdash \Delta} \; L\forall$$

$$\frac{\Gamma \vdash A[a(\bar{y})], \Delta}{\Gamma \vdash \Box A[p], \Delta} \; R\Box \qquad \frac{\Gamma \vdash A[U], \Delta}{\Gamma \vdash \Diamond A[p], \Delta} \; R\Diamond \qquad \frac{\Gamma \vdash A\{x/y\}[p], \Delta}{\Gamma \vdash \exists x A[p], \Delta} \; R\exists$$

Figure 16: Sequent calculus rules for the S5 constant domain family. $R\forall$ and $L\exists$ are as in figure 14.

7.2. Free variable systems

The systems have the same structural and propositional rules as the systems in section 6 (figure 1 page 1498 and figure 11 page 1557). Rules for modalities and quantifiers are listed in figure 16. The notion of a skeleton is as in section 6.2.

The table below defines the admissible values assumed by a label substitution σ. Given this, the notions of a derivation, a L–admissible substitution and a proof are exactly as in section 6.2. The Neighbourhood condition pertains to K45 derivations.

L	L–admissible type of $\sigma(U)$
K45	parameter
KD45	parameter or variable
S5	parameter, variable, or ε

7.1. EXAMPLE. The sequent $\Box(\Diamond P \supset P), \Diamond P \vdash \Box P$ is of interest in some systems of defeasible reasoning. It is provable in K45:

$$\cfrac{\cfrac{\cfrac{P[b] \vdash P[V], P[a]}{P[b] \vdash \Diamond P[U], P[a]} \; V \qquad P[U], P[b] \vdash P[a]}{\cfrac{\Diamond P \supset P[U], P[b] \vdash P[a]}{\cfrac{\Box(\Diamond P \supset P), P[b] \vdash P[a]}{\cfrac{\Box(\Diamond P \supset P), \Diamond P \vdash P[a]}{\Box(\Diamond P \supset P), \Diamond P \vdash \Box P} \; a} \; b} \; U}}$$

The skeleton is closed by the substitution $\{U/a, V/b\}$. None of the systems in section 6 are strong enough to prove the endsequent.

7.2. EXAMPLE. Let us repeat example 6.9 for the constant domain systems. The matrices are now:

$$\left[\; \overline{P}(x)[U] \;\; P(f)[a] \; \right] \qquad \left[\; \overline{P}(f[a])[a] \;\; P(x)[U] \; \right]$$

The leftmost matrix is closed by the substitution $\{x/f, U/a\}$, the rightmost is closed by $\{x/f[a], U/a\}$. There is no restriction on the substitution due to quantifier variables. Both the Barcan formula and its converse are hence provable in the constant domain systems.

7.3. EXAMPLE. The sequent $\Box \exists x P(x) \vdash \exists x \Box P(x)$ fails for the constant domain systems. In cumulative domain systems the proof is blocked by the substitution restrictions (cnf. example 6.10). However, as pointed out a proof of the Barcan formula in cumulative domain systems fails for the same reason. As shown above, the Barcan formula is provable in constant domain systems. Interestingly, an attempt to prove the sequent above for constant domains must therefore fail for another reason than it fails for cumulative domain systems. In the constant domain systems a proof is blocked by an occurs check failure. Inspect the matrix below:

$$\left[\ \overline{P}(f[U])[U] \quad P(x)[a(x)] \ \right]$$

The equations $x = f[U], U = a(x)$ have no finite solution.

7.4. DEFINITION. Let σ be a substitution. The projections σ_Q and σ_M induce relations $\sqsupset_Q$ and $\sqsupset_M$:

- let r_1 belong to U and $\sigma(U) \neq \varepsilon$. If r_2 belongs to the last prefix term in $\sigma(U)$, and this term is different from U, then $r_1 \sqsupset_M r_2$,
- if r_1 belongs to x, r_2 belongs to $y \neq x$, and $\sigma(x) = y$, then $r_1 \sqsupset_Q r_2$,
- if r_1 belongs to x, r_2 belongs to $f[q]$, and $\sigma(x) = f[q](\cdot)$, then $r_1 \sqsupset_Q r_2$.

The *reduction ordering* $\triangleright$ induced by σ is the transitive closure of $\triangleright_M \cup \triangleright_Q$, where $\triangleright_M$ is the transitive closure of $\gg \cup \sqsupset_M$ and $\triangleright_Q$ is the transitive closure of $\gg \cup \sqsupset_Q$. The skeleton *conforms to* $\triangleright$ if there are no two inferences r and r' such that $r \triangleright r'$ and r is below r'.

Lemma 7.5 below makes extensive use of the fact that prefix parameters assume labelled standard terms as arguments. It is the most interesting technical result in this section. The notion of a homogeneous substitution transfers to the extended language in a straightforward way. The property holds for σ if the following two conditions hold for all variables: If $\sigma(x) = f[q](\vec{t})$, and $f[p](\vec{y})$ occurs in the skeleton, then $f[q](\vec{t}) = f[p](\vec{y})\sigma$. If $a(\vec{t})$ occurs in $\sigma(U)$ and $a(\vec{y})$ occurs in the skeleton, then $a(\vec{t}) = a(\vec{y})\sigma$.

7.5. LEMMA. *The reduction ordering $\triangleright$ induced by a ground, homogeneous substitution which preserves the Unique prefix property is well-founded.*

PROOF. The proof is an adaptation of the proof for free variable LK (lemma 2.16). It is rewarding to use the same notation for both types of terms. Let X be either a prefix variable or a quantifier variable and F be either a parameter function or a prefix parameter. The expression $F[p](\vec{y})$ has different meaning depending on what F is. If F is a prefix parameter, $F[p](\vec{y})$ denotes that the prefix term $F(\vec{y})$ occurs

$$\frac{\Gamma, A[a] \vdash \Delta}{\Gamma, \Diamond A[p] \vdash \Delta} \; L\Diamond \qquad \frac{\Gamma, \Box A[p], \Box A[a] \vdash \Delta}{\Gamma, \Box A[p] \vdash \Delta} \; LC45 \qquad \frac{\Gamma, \Box A[p], A[p] \vdash \Delta}{\Gamma, \Box A[p] \vdash \Delta} \; LT$$

$$\frac{\Gamma \vdash A[a], \Delta}{\Gamma \vdash \Box A[p], \Delta} \; R\Box \qquad \frac{\Gamma \vdash \Diamond A[a], \Diamond A[p], \Delta}{\Gamma \vdash \Diamond A[p], \Delta} \; RC45 \qquad \frac{\Gamma \vdash A[p], \Diamond A[p], \Delta}{\Gamma \vdash \Diamond A[p], \Delta} \; RT$$

Parameter condition: In $L\Diamond$ and $R\Box$, a cannot occur in the conclusion.
Side condition for $L45$ and $R45$: The parameter a occurs in the branch.

Figure 17: Single step modality rules.

with prefix p (this prefix is unique by the Unique prefix property). If F is a standard function symbol, $F[p](\vec{y})$ denotes (as usual) a standard term labelled with p. $r(X)$ denotes that the inference r either belongs to X or occurs above an inference r' which belongs to X such that $r \triangleright r'$. Observe that if $r(X)$ belongs to F and $F[p](\vec{y})$ occurs in the skeleton, then X occurs in either p or $\vec{y}$.

If $\triangleright$ is not well-founded, there must be a cycle $r_1(X_1) \triangleright \ldots \triangleright r_n(X_n) \triangleright r_1(X_1); r_i$ belongs F_i and $\sigma(X_1) = F_2[q_2](\vec{t_2}), \ldots, \sigma(X_{n-1}) = F_n[q_n](\vec{t_n}), \sigma(X_n) = F_1[q_1](\vec{t_1})$. Since σ is homogeneous, $F_2[q_2](\vec{t_2})$ occurs in either q_1 or $\vec{t_1}$, $F_3[q_3](\vec{t_3})$ occurs in either q_2 or $\vec{t_2}$, etc. But then $F_1[q_1](\vec{t_1})$ occurs in either q_1 or $\vec{t_1}$. The former case contradicts the assumption that σ preserves the Unique prefix property, the latter case contradicts the assumption that terms are finite. $\Box$

7.6. THEOREM. *Let L be $K45$, $KD45$ or $S5$. If S is an empty labelled L-provable sequent, S is L-valid.*

PROOF. The proof follows the pattern of the other soundness proofs in the chapter, and applies lemma 7.5 at the obvious place in the argument. The propositional cases and the quantifier cases in the induction are straightforward. The modalized formulae are treated exactly as in the proof of theorem 6.5, except that the argument applies the following modification of lemma 6.4. *Let Θ be a set such that if $p \in \Theta$, then p is either ε or a prefix term. Let t_1 and t_2 be terms in Θ and $\varphi : \Theta\sigma \to U$ be a label interpretation function into the L-model (U, R, V). Then $\varphi(t_1)R\varphi(t_2)$.* Proof: By the model condition for φ, $\varphi(\varepsilon)R\varphi(t_1)$ and $\varphi(\varepsilon)R\varphi(t_2)$. Conclude by Euclideaness. $\Box$

7.3. Ground single step systems

Except for the modalities the single step systems have the same rules as the single step systems in the previous section. The propositional rules are listed in figure 11, page 1557; quantifier rules are in figure 15, page 1567; modality rules are in figure 17. Observe that both the quantifier rules and the modality rules are constrained by parameter conditions. Single step systems are defined by collections of modality rules:

L	$L\Diamond$ $R\Box$	$LC45$ $RC45$	side cond.	LT RT
K45	×	×	×	
KD45	×	×		
S5	×	×		×

7.7. THEOREM. *If an empty labelled sequent is not provable in the single step system for one of the three logics, it has a countermodel.*

PROOF. The proof exploits the strong similarity between the single step system and Gentzen's classical system LK. The similarity lies in the parameter conditions. More precisely, the Parameter condition which pertains to $L\Diamond$ and $R\Box$ in effect turns the parameter a in figure 17 into an eigenparameter.

The specification of a fair search procedure is straightforward and is left for the reader. A countermodel can be constructed out of an open branch β in the limit object; let β^+ be the set of formulae with an antecedent occurrence in β and β^- be the set of formulae with a succedent occurrence in β. The model $(\mathbf{U}, \mathbf{D}, R, V)$ is given by: $\mathbf{U}$ is the set of labels which occur in β; for each x, $\mathbf{D}(x)$ contains $\bar{t}$ for each labelled standard term t in β; $V(P)$ is the set of all points p in $\mathbf{U}$ such that $P[p]$ occurs in β^+. In S5 R is $\mathbf{U} \times \mathbf{U}$. In the two other systems R is $\mathbf{U} \times \mathbf{U}$ minus $\mathbf{U} \times \{\varepsilon\}$. We use the identity function as label interpretation function. It is then easy to show that for each $A[p] \in \beta^+$, $p \models \hat{A}$ and for each $A[p] \in \beta^-$, $p \not\models \hat{A}$. □

7.8. COROLLARY. *If an empty labelled sequent is unprovable in the free variable system, it has a countermodel.*

PROOF. Following the line of reasoning used in the proofs of lemma 4.16 and theorem 5.7 the mapping from a derivation in the single step system into a derivation in the free variable system is straightforward. Conclude by theorem 7.7. □

Acknowledgments

Some of the central views in this chapter have developed in discussions with Lincoln Wallen over a long period of time. The response from my readers has improved the quality of presentation significantly. Jens Otten has given significant help both for the conception and the presentation of unification. I have also received detailed and valuable criticism from Herman Ruge Jervell, Stephane Demri and Antonio Rotolo. Sincere thanks to all of them.

Bibliography

ANDREWS P. [1981], 'Theorem proving via general matings', *Journal of the ACM* **28**(2), 193–214.

ARTOSI A., BENASSI P., GOVERNATORI G. AND ROTOLO A. [1998], Shakesperian modal logic, *in* M. Kracht, M. de Rijke, H. Wansing and M. Zakharyaschev, eds, 'Advances in Modal Logic', CSLI Publications, Stanford, pp. 1–21.

ARTOSI A. AND GOVERNATORI G. [1994], Labelled model modal logic, *in* 'Proceedings of the CADE–12 Workshop on Automated Model Building', pp. 11–17.

AUFFRAY Y. AND ENJALBERT P. [1992], 'Modal theorem proving: An equational viewpoint', *Journal of Logic and Computation* **2**(3), 247–297.

AVRON A. [1991], 'Using hypersequents in proof systems for non-classical logics', *Annals of Mathematics and Artificial Intelligence* **4**, 225–248.

BAADER F. AND SNYDER W. [2001], Unification theory, *in* A. Robinson and A. Voronkov, eds, 'Handbook of Automated Reasoning', Vol. I, Elsevier Science, chapter 8, pp. 445–532.

BAAZ M. AND FERNMÜLLER C. G. [1995], Nonelementary speedups between different versions of tableaux, *in* P. Baumgartner, R. Hähnle and J. Posegga, eds, 'Proc. 4th. Workshop on Deduction with Tableaux and Related Methods', Vol. 918 of *LNCS*, Springer–Verlag, pp. 217–230.

BECKERT B. AND GORÉ R. [1997], Free variable tableaux for propositional modal logics, *in* D. Galmiche, ed., 'International Conference on Theorem Proving with Analythic Tableaux and Related Methods', Vol. 1227 of *LNAI*, Springer–Verlag, Berlin, pp. 91–106.

BECKERT B. AND HÄHNLE R. [1992], An improved method for adding equality to free variable semantic tableaux, *in* D. Kapur, ed., 'Proceedings, 11th. International Conference on Automated Deduction', LNCS 607, pp. 507–521.

BECKERT B. AND SCHMITT R. H. P. [1993], The even more liberalized δ-rule in free variable semantic tableaux, *in* 'Proceedings of the third Kurt Gödel Colloquium', Vol. 713 of *LNCS*, Springer–Verlag, pp. 108–119.

BELNAP N. D. [1982], 'Display logic', *Journal of Philosophical Logic* **11**, 375–417.

BIBEL W. [1981], 'On matrices with connections', *Journal of the ACM* **28**(4), 633–645.

BIBEL W. [1982a], *Automated Theorem Proving*, Vieweg, Braunschweig.

BIBEL W. [1982b], 'A comparative study of several proof procedures', *Artificial Intelligence* **18**(3), 269–293.

BIBEL W. [1982c], Computationally improved versions of Herbrand's Theorem, *in* J. Stern, ed., 'Proceedings of the Herbrand Symposium, Logic Colloquium '81', North-Holland Publishing Co., Amsterdam, pp. 11–28.

BIBEL W. [1987], *Automated Theorem Proving*, second revised edn., Vieweg, Braunschweig.

BIBEL W. AND EDER E. [1993], Methods and calculi for deduction, *in* D. Gabbay, C. Hogger and J. Robinson, eds, 'Handbook of logic in artificial intelligence and logic programming', Vol. 1, Clarendon Press, Oxford, pp. 68–182.

BOYER R. AND MOORE J. [1972], The sharing of structure in theorem-proving programs, *in* B. Meltzer and D. Michie, eds, 'Machine Intelligence', Vol. 7, Edinburgh University Press, pp. 101–116.

BULL R. AND SEGERBERG K [1984], Basic modal logic, *in* D. Gabbay and F. Guenthner, eds, 'Handbook of Philosophical Logic', Vol. 2, D. Reidel, pp. 1–88.

CERRITO S. AND CIALDEA MAYER M. [1997], 'A polynomial translation of S4 into T and contraction free tableaux for S4', *Logic Journal of the IGPL* .

CHELLAS B. [1980], *Modal Logic: An Introduction*, Cambridge University Press.

CIALDEA MAYER M. AND CERRITO S. [2000], Variants of first–order modal logics, *in* R. Dyckhoff, ed., 'Automated Reasoning with Analytic Tableaux and Related Methods', Vol. 1847 of *LNAI*, Springer–Verlag, pp. 175–189.

CURRY H. [1952], 'The elimination theorem when modality is present', *Journal of Symbolic Logic* **17**, 249–265.

DEMRI S. [1995], 'Uniform and non uniform strategies for tableaux calculi for modal logics', *Journal of Applied Non-Classical Logics* **5**(1), 77–96.

EGLY U. [2000], Properties of embeddings from Int to S4, *in* R. Dyckhoff, ed., 'Automated Reasoning with Analytic Tableaux and Related Methods', Vol. 1847 of *LNAI*, Springer–Verlag, pp. 205–220.

EGLY U. AND SCHMITT S. [1998], Intuitionistic proof transformation and their application to constructive program synthesis, *in* J. Calmet and J. Plaza, eds, 'Proc. AISC', Vol. 1476 of *LNAI*, Springer–Verlag, pp. 132–144.

EGLY U. AND SCHMITT S. [1999], 'On intuitionistic proof transformation, their complexity and application to constructive program synthesis', *Funaamenta Informaticae* **39**, 59–83.

FITCH F. [1966], 'Tree proofs in modal logic', *Journal of Symbolic Logic* **31**, 152.

FITTING M. [1983], *Proof methods for modal and intuitionistic logics*, Reidel, Dordrecht.

FITTING M. [1993], Basic modal logic, *in* D. Gabbay, C. Hogger and J. Robinson, eds, 'Handbook of logic in artificial intelligence and logic programming', Vol. 1, Clarendon Press, Oxford, pp. 368–448.

FITTING M. [1996], *First-Order Logic and Automated Theorem Proving*, Springer-Verlag.

FITTING M. AND MENDELSOHN R. [1998], *First–Order Modal Logic*, Kluwer Academic Publishers.

GABBAY D. [1996], *Labelled deductive systems*, Oxford University Press.

GARSON J. [1984], Quantification in modal logic, *in* D. Gabbay and F. Guenthner, eds, 'Handbook of Philosophical Logic', Vol. 2, D. Reidel, pp. 249–308.

GENTZEN G. [1934–35], 'Untersuchungen über das logische Schließen', *Mathematische Zeitschrift*, 39:176–210, 405–431, 1934-1935. English translation in M.E. Szabo *The Collected Papers of Gerhard Gentzen*, North-Holland, Amsterdam, 1969.

GORÉ R. [1999], Tableau methods for modal and temporal logics, *in* M. D'Agostino, D. Gabbay, R. Hähnle and J. Posegga, eds, 'Handbook of Tableaux Methods', Kluwer Academic Press, Dordrecht, pp. 297–396.

GOVERNATORI G. [1995], Labelled tableaux for multi–modal logics, *in* P. Baumgartner, r. Hähnle and J. Posegga, eds, 'Theorem Proving with Analytic Tableaux and Related Methods', Vol. 918 of *LNAI*, Springer Verlag, Berlin, pp. 79–94.

GOVERNATORI G. AND ROTOLO A. [2000], Labelled modal sequents, *in* R. Dyckhoff, ed., 'Automated Reasoning with Analytic Tableaux and Related Methods. Position Papers and Tutorials', CS/00/001, University of St. Andrews, School of Computer Science, Springer–Verlag, pp. 3–22.

HÄHNLE R. AND KLINGENBECK S. [1996], 'A-ordered tableaux', *Journal of Logic and Computation* **6**(6), 819–834.

HERBRAND J. [1967], Investigations in proof theory, *in* J. van Heijenoort, ed., 'From Frege to Gödel: A Source Book of Mathematical Logic', Harvard University Press, Cambridge, MA, pp. 525–581.

HINTIKKA J. [1962], *Knowledge and Belief*, Cornell University Press.

HUGHES G. AND CRESSWELL M. [1968], *An Introduction to Modal Logic*, Methuen, London.

HUGHES G. AND CRESSWELL M. [1984], *A Companion to Modal Logic*, Methuen, London.

KANGER S. [1957], *Provability in logic*, Stockholm Studies in Philosophy, Almquist and Wiksell, Stockholm.

KLEENE S. [1952], 'Permutability of inferences in Gentzen's calculi LK and LJ', *Memoirs of the American Mathematical Society* **10**, 1–26.

KORN D. AND KREITZ C. [1997], Deciding intuitionistic propositional logic via translation into classical logic, *in* '14th International Conference on Automated Deduction', Vol. 1249 of *LNAI*, Springer Verlag, Berlin, pp. 131–145.

KREITZ C., MANTEL H., OTTEN J. AND SCHMITT S. [1997], Connection-based proof construction in linear logic, *in* '14th International Conference on Automated Deduction', Vol. 1249 of *LNAI*, Springer Verlag, Berlin, pp. 207–221.

KREITZ C. AND OTTEN J. [1999], 'Connection-based theorem proving in classical and non-classical logics', *Journal for Universal Computer Science* **5**(3), 88–112.

KREITZ C. AND PIENTKA B. [2000], Matrix-based inductive theorem proving, *in* R. Dyckhoff, ed., 'International Conference TABLEAUX-2000', Vol. 1847 of *Lecture Notes in Artificial Intelligence*, Springer Verlag, pp. 294–308.

KREITZ C. AND SCHMITT S. [2000], 'A uniform procedure for converting matrix proofs into sequent-style systems', *Journal of Information and Computation* **162**(1–2), 226–254.

KRIPKE S. [1959], 'A completeness theorem in modal logic', *Journal of Symbolic Logic* **24**(1), 1–14.

KRIPKE S. [1963], 'Semantic analysis of modal logic I: Normal modal propositional calculi', *Zeitschrift für mathematische Logik und Grundlagen der Mathematik* **9**, 67–96.

LADNER R. E. [1977], 'The computational complexity of provability in systems of modal propositional logic', *SIAM Journal of Computation* **6**, 467–480.

LETZ R. [1999], Tableau methods for modal and temporal logics, *in* M. D'Agostino, D. Gabbay, R. Hähnle and J. Posegga, eds, 'Handbook of Tableaux Methods', Kluwer Academic Press, Dordrecht, pp. 125–196.

LETZ R. AND STENZ G. [2001], Model elimination and connection tableau procedures, *in* A. Robinson and A. Voronkov, eds, 'Handbook of Automated Reasoning', Vol. II, Elsevier Science, chapter 28, pp. 2015–2114.

MAEHARA S. [1954], 'Eine Darstellung der intuitionistische Logik in der klassischen', *Nagoya Mathematical Journal* **7**, 45–64.

MANTEL H. AND KREITZ C. [1998], A matrix characterization for MELL, *in* U. F. J. Dix, F. L. Del Cerro, ed., '6th European Workshop on Logics in AI (JELIA-98)', Vol. 1489 of *Lecture Notes in Artificial Intelligence*, Springer Verlag, pp. 169–183.

MASSACCI F. [1994], Strongly analytic tableaux for normal modal logics, *in* A. Bundy, ed., 'Proc. CADE–12', Vol. 814 of *LNAI*, Springer–Verlag, pp. 723–739.

MASSACCI F. [2000], 'Single step tableaux for modal logics', *Journal of Automated Reasoning* **24**(3), 319–364.

MINTS G. [1997], 'Indexed systems of sequents and cut-elimination', *Journal of Philosophical Logic* **26**(6), 671–696.

OHLBACH H.-J. [1988], A resolution calculus for modal logics, *in* E. Lusk and R. Overbeek, eds, 'Proc. 9th International Conference on Automated Deduction', Vol. 310 of *LNCS*, Springer–Verlag, pp. 500–516.

OHLBACH H.-J. [1990], 'Semantics-based translation methods for modal logics', *Journal of Logic and Computation* **1**(5), 691–746.

OHLBACH H., NONNENGART A., DE RIJKE M. AND GABBAY D. [2001], Encoding two-valued nonclassical logics in classical logic, *in* A. Robinson and A. Voronkov, eds, 'Handbook of Automated Reasoning', Vol. II, Elsevier Science, chapter 21, pp. 1403–1486.

OHNISHI M. AND MATSUMOTO K. [1957a], 'Corrections to our paper 'Gentzen method in modal calculi I'', *Osaka Mathematical Journal* **10**, 147.

OHNISHI M. AND MATSUMOTO K. [1957b], 'Gentzen method in modal calculi I', *Osaka Mathematical Journal* **9**, 113–130.

OHNISHI M. AND MATSUMOTO K. [1959], 'Gentzen method in modal calculi II', *Osaka Mathematical Journal* **11**, 115–120.

OTTEN J. [1997], ileanTAP: An Intuitionistic Theorem Prover, *in* D. Galmiche, ed., 'International Conference on Automated Reasoning with Analytic Tableaux and Related Methods', Vol. 1227 of *LNAI*, Springer Verlag, Berlin, pp. 307–312.

OTTEN J. AND KREITZ C. [1995], A connection based proof method for intuitionistic logic, *in* P. Baumgartner, R. Hähnle and J. Posegga, eds, 'Theorem Proving with Analytic Tableaux and Related Methods', Vol. 918 of *LNAI*, Springer Verlag, Berlin, pp. 122–137.

OTTEN J. AND KREITZ C. [1996], T-String-Unification: Unifying Prefixes in Non-Classical Proof Methods, *in* U. Moscato, ed., '5th Workshop on Theorem Proving with Analytic Tableaux and Related Methods', Vol. 1071 of *LNAI*, Springer–Verlag, Berlin, pp. 244–260.

OTTEN J. AND KREITZ C. [2001], Towards efficient prefix unification in non-classical theorem proving, Technical Report AIDA–00–03, Intellectics Group, Darmstadt University of Technology.

PINTO L. AND DYCKHOFF R. [1995], Loop-free construction of counter-models for intuitionistic propositional logic, *in* Behara, Fritsch and Lintz, eds, 'Symposia Gaussiana, Conf. A', Walter de Gruyter & Co, pp. 225–232.

PRAWITZ D. [1960], 'An improved proof procedure', *Theoria* **26**, 102–139.

PYM D. AND WALLEN L. [1990], Investigations into proof-search in a system of first-order dependent function types, *in* M. Stickel, ed., 'Tenth Conference on Automated Deduction, Lecture Notes in Computer Science 449', Springer-Verlag, pp. 236–250.

ROBINSON J. [1965], 'A machine oriented logic based on the resolution principle', *J.of the ACM* **12**(1), 23–41.

SAHLIN D., FRANZÉN T. AND HARIDI S. [1992], 'An Intuitionistic Predicate Logic Theorem Prover', *Journal of Logic and Computation* **2**(5), 619–656.

SCHÜTTE K. [1968], *Vollständige Systeme modaler und institutionistischer Logik*, Vol. 42 of *Ergebnisse der Mathematik und ihrer Grenzgebiete*, Springer Verlag, Berlin.

SCHWICHTENBERG H. AND TROELSTRA A. [1996], *Basic proof theory*, Vol. 43 of *Cambridge tracts in theoretical computer science*, Cambridge University Press, Cambridge.

SHANKAR N. [1992], Proof search in the intuitionistic sequent calculus, *in* D. Kapur, ed., 'Proceedings of 11th International Conference on Automated Deduction', Vol. 607 of *Lecture Notes in AI*, Springer Verlag, Berlin, pp. 522–536.

SMULLYAN R. [1968], *First-Order Logic*, Springer-Verlag, New York.

STATMAN R. [1979], 'Intuitionistic logic is polynomial-space complete', *Theor. Comp. Science* **9**, 73–81.

VAN DALEN D. [1986], Intuitionistic logic, *in* D. Gabbay and F. Guenthner, eds, 'Handbook of Philosophical Logic', Vol. III, D. Reidel Publishing Company, pp. 225–339.

VORONKOV A. [1996], Proof search in intuitionistic logic based on constraint satisfaction, *in* 'Proc. 5th TABLEAUX'96', Vol. 1071 of *LNAI*, Springer–Verlag, Berlin, pp. 312–329.

WAALER A. [2001], A sequent calculus for intuitionistic logic with classical permutation properties, Technical Report 285, Department of Computer Science, University of Oslo.

WAALER A. AND WALLEN L. [1999], Tableaux for intuitionistic logics, *in* M. D'Agostino, D. Gabbay, R. Hähnle and J. Posegga, eds, 'Handbook of Tableaux Methods', Kluwer Academic Press, Dordrecht, pp. 255–296.

WALLEN L. [1987], Matrix proof methods for modal logics, *in* J. McDermott, ed., '10th International Joint Conference on Artificial Intelligence', Morgan Kaufmann Inc., pp. 917–923.

WALLEN L. [1990], *Automated deduction in nonclassical logics*, MIT Press.

Index

Part VII

Decidable classes and model building

CHAPTER 23

Reasoning in Expressive Description Logics

Diego Calvanese   Giuseppe De Giacomo

Daniele Nardi   Maurizio Lenzerini

SECOND READERS: Enrico Franconi, Ian Horrocks, Maarten de Rijke, and
Ulrike Sattler.

Contents

HANDBOOK OF AUTOMATED REASONING
Edited by Alan Robinson and Andrei Voronkov
© 2001 Elsevier Science Publishers B.V. All rights reserved

1. Introduction

Knowledge Representation is the field of Artificial Intelligence which focuses on the design of formalisms that are both epistemologically and computationally adequate for expressing the knowledge an agent has about a particular domain. One of the main research lines of the field has been concerned with the idea that the knowledge structure should be expressed in terms of the classes of objects that are of interest in the domain, as well as the relevant relationships holding among such classes. One of the most important relationships is the one holding between two classes when one class is a subset of the other. Based on such a relationship, the organization of the set of classes used to characterize a domain of interest is based on hierarchical structures which not only provides for an effective and compact representation of information, but also allows one to perform the basic reasoning tasks in a computationally effective way.

The above principle formed the basis for the development of the first frame systems and semantic networks. However, such systems were in general not formally defined and the associated reasoning tools were strongly dependent on the implementation strategies. A fundamental step towards a logic-based characterization of such systems has been accomplished through the work on the KL-ONE system [Brachman and Schmolze 1985], which collected many of the ideas stemming from earlier semantic networks and frame-based systems, and provided a logical basis for interpreting objects, classes (or concepts), and relationships (or links, or roles) between them [see for example Woods and Schmolze 1992]. One of the basic goals of such a logical reconstruction was the precise characterization of the set of constructs used to build class and link expressions.

Providing a formal meaning to the constructs of the representation language has been fundamental, but knowledge representation systems should also come with reasoning procedures that are sound and complete with respect to a specified formal semantics. This is required to give the user a clear understanding of the results of reasoning in terms of well-established notions such as logical consequence. In addition, one should also give a precise characterization of the computational behavior of the inference system; thus, this aspect also is to be addressed with formal tools. With the article "The tractability of subsumption in Frame-Based Description Languages" by Brachman and Levesque [1984], a research line addressing the tradeoff between the expressiveness of KL-ONE like languages and the computational complexity of reasoning was originated. In fact, it was shown that an apparently minor extension of the language could make the basic deduction problem in the language computationally hard (even undecidable).

There has been a number of changes in terminology used in the area; these reflect the predominant aspects on which the research has concentrated. The descendants of KL-ONE have first been grouped under the label *terminological systems*, to emphasize the fact that classes and relationships were used to establish the basic terminology adopted in the modeled domain. Later, the emphasis was on the sets of concept forming constructs admitted in the language, giving rise to the name *concept languages*. Recently, after attention has been further moved towards the properties of the underlying logical systems, the term *Description Logics* has become popular, and will be the one used in this chapter.

A *knowledge base* expressed in a Description Logic (DL) is constituted by two components, traditionally called *TBox* and *ABox* (originally from "Terminological Box" and "Assertional Box" respectively). The TBox stores a set of universally quantified assertions, stating general properties of concepts and roles. For example, an assertion of this kind is the one stating that a certain concept, say `Parent`, is defined as a given expression using other concepts and roles, say "`Person` with at least one `child`". The ABox comprises assertions on individual objects, called instance assertions. A typical assertion in the ABox is the one stating that an individual is an instance of a certain concept. For example, one can assert that `Bill` is an instance of "`Person` with at least one `child`".

Several reasoning tasks can be carried out on a knowledge base of the above kind. The simplest form of reasoning involves computing the subsumption relation between two concept expressions, i.e., verifying whether one expression always denotes a subset of the objects denoted by another expression. In the above example, one can easily derive that `Parent` is a specialization of `Person`, i.e., `Person` subsumes `Parent`. A more complex reasoning task consists in checking whether a certain assertion is logically implied by a knowledge base. For example, we can infer from the above assertions that `Bill` is an instance of `Parent`.

The above observations emphasize that a DL system is characterized by four aspects:

1. The set of constructs constituting the language for building the concepts and the roles used in the TBox and in the ABox.

2. The kind of assertions that may appear in the TBox.

3. The kind of assertions that may appear in the ABox.

4. The inference mechanisms provided for reasoning on the knowledge bases expressible in the system.

The expressive power and the deduction capabilities of a DL system depend on the various choices and assumptions that the system adopts with regard to the above aspects. As to the fourth aspect, we concentrate in this chapter on inference mechanisms that are sound and complete with respect to the standard Tarskian semantics (see Sect. 2), although other choices are possible [Patel-Schneider 1989, Baader and Hollunder 1995, Donini, Lenzerini, Nardi, Nutt and Schaerf 1992].

The first aspect has been the subject of a lot of research work in the last decade. Indeed, most of the results on the computational complexity of DLs have been devised in a simplified context where both the TBox and the ABox are empty [Nebel 1988, Schmidt-Schauß and Smolka 1991, Donini, Lenzerini, Nardi and Nutt 1991, Donini, Lenzerini, Nardi and Schaerf 1996, Donini, Lenzerini, Nardi and Nutt 1997]. This is not surprising, since these works aimed at studying the language constructs in isolation, with the goal of singling out their impact on the complexity of subsumption between concept expressions.

The third aspect has been addressed by a few papers dealing with logical implication of ABox assertions under the simplifying assumption of an empty

TBox, again with the goal of studying how the various language constructs influence the reasoning on individuals [Hollunder 1996, Donini, Lenzerini, Nardi and Schaerf 1994, Schaerf 1994]. The complete setting, i.e., reasoning with both the TBox and the ABox, has been the subject of some investigations only recently. For example, Buchheit, Donini and Schaerf [1993] and De Giacomo and Lenzerini [1996] study two DL systems with powerful languages for expressing both the TBox and the ABox.

The second aspect, which is the focus of the present chapter, has first been analyzed under several simplifying assumptions, such as:

- The assertions in the TBox are restricted to so-called definitions, where a definition is an assertion stating that the extension of a concept denoted by a name is equal to the extension of another concept (typically a complex concept).

- For every concept C, at most one definition for C appears in the TBox.

- Definitions are acyclic, i.e., if we build a graph whose nodes are atomic concepts and whose arcs connect pairs of concepts such that one appears in the definition of the other, then the graph is acyclic.

It is easy to see that, in principle, when the TBox does not contain cycles, the reasoning tasks can be turned into reasoning on the concept expressions obtained by unfolding the definitions, i.e., by substituting the concepts defined in the knowledge base with their definitions. Interestingly, Nebel [1990] has shown that reasoning on assertions is computationally hard, even under the assumption of acyclicity (coNP-complete in this case).

More recently, there has been a strong interest in the problem of reasoning with TBox assertions without the acyclicity assumption [Nebel 1991, Baader 1991, Schild 1994, De Giacomo and Lenzerini 1994a, Calvanese, De Giacomo and Lenzerini 1995, Horrocks 1998, Horrocks and Sattler 1999]. One important outcome of this line of research is that, limiting the expressive power of the language with the goal of gaining tractability is useless in this setting, because the power of TBox assertions alone generally leads to high complexity in the inference mechanisms even in simple languages (see Sect. 3.3. For this reason, these investigations often refer to very powerful languages for expressing concepts and roles, and the property of interest is no longer tractability of reasoning, but rather decidability [Buchheit et al. 1993, Calvanese 1996c, De Giacomo 1995]. In addition, in the presence of assertions with no restrictions on cycles, there are languages which happen to lack the finite model property and, consequently, one has to distinguish between reasoning on finite and infinite models.

The goal of the chapter is to provide a thorough introduction to the recent results on reasoning on TBoxes in expressive DLs, i.e., DLs where:

1. The language used for building concepts and roles comprise all classical concept forming constructs, inverse roles, and general forms of number restrictions.

2. No restriction is posed on the assertions in the TBox.

We observe that expressive DLs are important in the light of the renewed interest in DLs that we find in disparate application areas. Indeed, DL systems are now advocated as suitable knowledge representation systems in many contexts, such as Information Systems [Catarci and Lenzerini 1993, Calvanese, De Giacomo and Lenzerini 1998*b*], Databases [Borgida 1995, Calvanese, Lenzerini and Nardi 1994, Bergamaschi and Sartori 1992, Sheth, Gala and Navathe 1993, Ullman 1997, Calvanese, Lenzerini and Nardi 1999], Software Engineering [Devambu, Brachman, Selfridge and Ballard 1991, Calvanese, De Giacomo and Lenzerini 1999], Intelligent Access to the Network [Levy, Rajaraman and Ordille 1996, Blanco, Illarramendi and Goñi 1994], action representation [Artale and Franconi 1994], and Planning [Weida and Litman 1992]. Many of the above papers point out that the full capabilities of a DL system (expressive language, general TBox assertions) are often required in the corresponding application fields [see also Doyle and Patil 1991].

The chapter is organized as follows. Sect. 2 presents syntax and semantics of a DL admitting a very powerful set of constructs. Such a logic, called $\mathcal{ALCQI}$, will be used as a basis in the paper. Also, Sect. 2 introduces the basic reasoning tasks in DLs, and provides a general discussion on the various techniques proposed to carry out such tasks. Sect. 3 addresses the correspondence between Description Logics and Propositional Dynamic Logics, which is the basis for several technical results that are presented in Sect. 4, where the problem of reasoning in unrestricted models is addressed. Sect. 5 presents results and techniques for reasoning on finite models. Finally, Sect. 6 provides a more complete picture of the decidability/undecidability borderline in expressive DLs.

2. Description Logics

The basic elements of DLs are *concepts* and *roles*, which denote classes and binary relations, respectively. Arbitrary concept and role expressions (in the following simply called *concepts* and *roles*) are formed by starting from a set of *atomic concepts* and *atomic roles*, i.e., concepts and roles denoted simply by a name, and applying concept and role *constructs*. Each variant of DLs is characterized by the set of constructors that can be used. We name a DL using calligraphic letters, according to the convention of using a certain symbol (either a letter or a subscript) for a specific set of constructs. All DLs we deal with include a set of basic constructs (see later), which give the prefix $\mathcal{AL}$ to the name.

In the following, we present the syntax of all constructs that are considered in this paper, which correspond to a language called $\mathcal{ALCQI}$. For a comprehensive discussion on the constructs used in DLs, see [Woods and Schmolze 1992, De Giacomo 1995, Calvanese 1996*c*, Donini et al. 1996].

2.1. Syntax and Semantics of the Logic $\mathcal{ALCQI}$

We introduce now the DL $\mathcal{ALCQI}$, in which concepts and roles are formed according to the following syntax:

$$C, C' \longrightarrow A \mid \neg C \mid C \sqcap C' \mid C \sqcup C' \mid \forall R.C \mid \exists R.C \mid \exists^{\geq n} R.C \mid \exists^{\leq n} R.C$$
$$R \longrightarrow P \mid P^-$$

where, A and P denote atomic concepts and atomic roles respectively, C and R denote arbitrary concepts and roles (either direct or inverse roles), and n denotes a positive integer. We also use the following abbreviations to increase readability:

- $\perp$ for $A \sqcap \neg A$ (where A is any atomic concept),
- $\top$ for $A \sqcup \neg A$,
- $C \Rightarrow D$ for $\neg C \sqcup D$,
- $\exists^{=n} R.C$ for $\exists^{\geq n} R.C \sqcap \exists^{\leq n} R.C$.

Let us comment on the constructs of $\mathcal{ALCQI}$.

Among the constructs used in forming concept expressions we find the basic set operators, namely set complement, intersection, and union that are denoted as *negation* ($\neg$), *conjunction* ($\sqcap$), and *disjunction* ($\sqcup$), respectively. DLs admit a restricted form of quantification which is realized through so-called *quantified role restrictions*, that are composed by a quantifier (existential or universal), a role, and a concept expression. Quantified role restrictions allow one to represent the relationships existing between the objects in two concepts, and the forms considered in $\mathcal{ALCQI}$ are general enough to capture the most common ways of establishing such relationships. For example, one can characterize the set of objects all of whose children are male as ∀child.Male, as well as the set of objects that have at least one male child as ∃child.Male. The former construct is called *universal role restriction* while the latter is called *(qualified) existential role restriction*. The simplest existence condition on a role is $\exists R.\top$, which is often abbreviated by $\exists R$ and is called *unqualified existential*. We obtain the basic language $\mathcal{AL}$ from $\mathcal{ALCQI}$ by allowing only atomic roles, and by restricting the concept constructs to conjunction, negation of atomic concepts only, universal role restriction, and unqualified existential. Adding to $\mathcal{AL}$ general negation, denoted by the letter $\mathcal{C}$, gives the language $\mathcal{ALC}$ [Schmidt-Schauß and Smolka 1991], in which also disjunction and qualified existential role restriction can be expressed. The letter $\mathcal{U}$ indicates the presence of disjunction in a language where negation is restricted to atomic concepts (such as for example $\mathcal{AL}$).

Number restrictions are used to constrain the number of *fillers*, i.e., the objects that are in a certain relationship with a given object. For example, $\exists^{=2}$child.Male characterizes the set of parents with exactly two male children. The form used here, called *qualified number restriction* [Hollunder and Baader 1991], is a very general one. It allows one to pose restrictions on the number of objects connected through a certain role, counting only those objects that satisfy a certain condition. The most common form of number restriction does not place any restriction on the concept the role fillers belong to. This form is called *unqualified*, and is written $\exists^{\geq n} R$, which stands for $\exists^{\geq n} R.\top$ (similarly for $\exists^{\leq n} R$ and $\exists^{=n} R$). Observe that the special cases of number restrictions where the number involved is equal to "1", express functionality ($\exists^{\leq 1} R$) and existence constraints ($\exists^{\geq 1} R$, i.e., $\exists R$), respectively. The presence of qualified number restrictions is specified by the letter $\mathcal{Q}$ in the name of the language; unqualified number restrictions are indicated by the letter $\mathcal{N}$, and when the number can be only "1", the letter used is $\mathcal{F}$.

In addition to concept forming constructs, $\mathcal{ALCQI}$ provides the *inverse role* construct, which allows us to denote the inverse of a given relation. One can for example state with $\exists^{\leq 2}child^-$ that someone has at most two parents, by making use of the inverse of the role child. It is worth noticing, that in a language without the inverse of roles, in order to express such a constraint one must use two distinct roles (e.g., child and parent) that cannot be put in the proper relation to each other. The presence in the language of inverse roles is specified by the letter $\mathcal{I}$.

From the semantic point of view, concepts are interpreted as subsets of a domain, and roles as binary relations over that domain. An *interpretation* $\mathcal{I} = (\Delta^{\mathcal{I}}, \cdot^{\mathcal{I}})$ over a set $\mathcal{A}$ of atomic concepts and a set $\mathcal{P}$ of atomic roles consists of a nonempty set $\Delta^{\mathcal{I}}$ (the *domain* of $\mathcal{I}$) and a function $\cdot^{\mathcal{I}}$ (the *interpretation function* of $\mathcal{I}$) that maps every atomic concept $A \in \mathcal{A}$ to a subset $A^{\mathcal{I}}$ of $\Delta^{\mathcal{I}}$ (the set of *instances* of A) and every atomic role $P \in \mathcal{P}$ to a subset $P^{\mathcal{I}}$ of $\Delta^{\mathcal{I}} \times \Delta^{\mathcal{I}}$ (the set of *instances* of P). The interpretation function can then be extended to arbitrary concepts and roles as follows[1]:

$$
\begin{aligned}
(\neg C)^{\mathcal{I}} &= \Delta^{\mathcal{I}} \setminus C^{\mathcal{I}} \\
(C \sqcap C')^{\mathcal{I}} &= C^{\mathcal{I}} \cap C'^{\mathcal{I}} \\
(C_1 \sqcup C_2)^{\mathcal{I}} &= C_1^{\mathcal{I}} \cup C_2^{\mathcal{I}} \\
(\forall R.C)^{\mathcal{I}} &= \{o \in \Delta^{\mathcal{I}} \mid \forall o'. (o, o') \in R^{\mathcal{I}} \rightarrow o' \in C^{\mathcal{I}}\} \\
(\exists R.C)^{\mathcal{I}} &= \{o \in \Delta^{\mathcal{I}} \mid \exists o'. (o, o') \in R^{\mathcal{I}} \wedge o' \in C^{\mathcal{I}}\} \\
(\exists^{\geq n} R.C)^{\mathcal{I}} &= \{o \in \Delta^{\mathcal{I}} \mid \sharp\{o' \mid (o, o') \in Q^{\mathcal{I}} \wedge o' \in C^{\mathcal{I}}\} \geq n\} \\
(\exists^{\leq n} R.C)^{\mathcal{I}} &= \{o \in \Delta^{\mathcal{I}} \mid \sharp\{o' \mid (o, o') \in Q^{\mathcal{I}} \wedge o' \in C^{\mathcal{I}}\} \leq n\} \\
(R^-)^{\mathcal{I}} &= \{(o, o') \in \Delta^{\mathcal{I}} \times \Delta^{\mathcal{I}} \mid (o', o) \in R^{\mathcal{I}}\}
\end{aligned}
$$

The basic reasoning tasks on concept expressions are concept satisfiability and concept subsumption.

- *Concept satisfiability* is the problem of deciding whether a concept has a nonempty interpretation.
- *Concept subsumption* (between C_1 and C_2) is the problem of deciding whether $C_1^{\mathcal{I}} \subseteq C_2^{\mathcal{I}}$ holds in every interpretation.

In $\mathcal{ALCQI}$, and in any language closed under negation, concept satisfiability and concept subsumption are obviously related to each other. Namely, a concept C is satisfiable if and only if it is not subsumed by $\perp$, while C_1 is subsumed by C_2 if and only if $C_1 \sqcap \neg C_2$ is unsatisfiable.

2.2. Knowledge Bases in $\mathcal{ALCQI}$

Usually, in DLs, a *knowledge base* is formed by two components, a *TBox*, expressing intensional knowledge about classes and relations, and an *ABox*, expressing exten-

---

[1] We use $\sharp S$ to denote the cardinality of a set S.

sional knowledge about objects. Here we concentrate on intensional knowledge only, and therefore we identify a knowledge base with a TBox.

Formally, an $\mathcal{ALCQI}$ knowledge base is constituted by a finite set of *inclusion assertions* of the form

$$C_1 \sqsubseteq C_2$$

with C_1 and C_2 arbitrary concept expressions.

The semantics of a knowledge base is specified through the notion of satisfaction of assertions. An interpretation $\mathcal{I}$ *satisfies* the assertion $C_1 \sqsubseteq C_2$ if $C_1^{\mathcal{I}} \subseteq C_2^{\mathcal{I}}$. An interpretation is a *model* of a knowledge base if it satisfies all assertions in it. A knowledge base is *satisfiable* if it admits a model.

Assertions of the form above are usually called *free* (or *general*) [Buchheit et al. 1993]. Special cases of assertions are also of interest. A *primitive inclusion assertion* is an inclusion assertion of the form $A \sqsubseteq C$, which specifies (by means of C) only *necessary* conditions for an object to be an instance of the atomic concept A. Thus, with only primitive inclusion assertions, an object cannot be inferred to be an instance of A, unless this is explicitly stated. Symmetrically, an assertion $C \sqsubseteq A$ specifies a *sufficient* condition for an object to be an instance of A. In contrast, an *equality assertion* $A \equiv C$, which corresponds to the pair of assertions $A \sqsubseteq C$ and $C \sqsubseteq A$, specifies both *necessary and sufficient* conditions for the instances of A. Observe that the inclusion assertion $A \sqsubseteq C$ is equivalent to the equality assertion $A \equiv A \sqcap C$, and that the inclusion assertion $C \sqsubseteq A$ is equivalent to $A \equiv A \sqcup C$. Equality assertions, are typical of the frame systems from which DLs originate, where assertions of this kind (without cycles, see later) are used to define a taxonomy of concepts.

For knowledge bases consisting only of primitive inclusion and/or equality assertions (and no free assertions), specific restrictions on the form of the assertions have been considered. For such knowledge bases it is usually assumed that each atomic concept may appear at most once on the left hand side of an assertion. Under this condition, allowing or not for the presence of so-called *(terminological) cycles*[2] becomes relevant. When cycles are not allowed, adding knowledge bases to a DL does not substantially change its properties. In particular, reasoning wrt a knowledge base can be straightforwardly reduced to concept subsumption. This is done by *unfolding*, i.e., by recursively replacing atomic concepts on the left hand side of a knowledge base assertion with the corresponding right hand side [Nebel 1991]. Instead, the presence of a cyclic knowledge base does have a strong impact on the DL. In this case, different types of semantics of a knowledge base may be defined, which differ in the interpretation of cycles (but coincide for acyclic knowledge bases). The semantics specified above is called *descriptive semantics* and is the only one that generalizes to free assertions. Alternatively, *fixpoint semantics* have been considered, in which the assertions are viewed as equations and only those interpretations that are (least or greatest) fixpoints of the equations are accepted as

---

[2]We remind the reader that a knowledge base contains a cycle if some concept in the right part of an assertion refers (either directly or indirectly through other assertions) to the atomic concept on the left part of the assertion.

models. For a detailed discussion on the different semantics, see [Nebel 1991, Buchheit et al. 1993, Buchheit, Donini, Nutt and Schaerf 1994, Schild 1994, De Giacomo and Lenzerini 1997]. Note that the presence of cycles increases also the computational complexity of reasoning [Baader 1996, Calvanese 1996b] and for this reason, until recently, it was ruled out in most knowledge representation systems based on DLs.

2.1. EXAMPLE. The following $\mathcal{ALCQI}$ knowledge base $\mathcal{K}_{file}$ models a file-system constituted by file-system elements (FSelem), each of which is either a Directory or a File. Each FSelem has a unique name and a unique parent (child$^-$). A Directory may have children while a File may not, and Root is a special directory which has no parent.

$$\texttt{FSelem} \sqsubseteq \exists^{\leq 1}\texttt{child}^-.\top$$

$$\texttt{FSelem} \sqsubseteq \exists\texttt{name.String} \sqcap \exists^{\leq 1}\texttt{name.}\top \qquad (2.1)$$

$$\texttt{FSelem} \equiv \texttt{Directory} \sqcup \texttt{File} \qquad (2.2)$$

$$\texttt{Directory} \sqsubseteq \neg\texttt{File} \qquad (2.3)$$

$$\texttt{Directory} \sqsubseteq \forall\texttt{child.FSelem} \qquad (2.4)$$

$$\texttt{File} \sqsubseteq \forall\texttt{child.}\bot$$

$$\texttt{Root} \equiv \texttt{Directory} \sqcap \forall\texttt{child}^-.\bot \qquad (2.5)$$

The assertions above are typical examples of data modeling constructs. In particular, assertions (2.2) and (2.3) state that FSelem is a *complete generalization* of Directory and File. Assertion (2.1) and assertion (2.4 represent a *has-a* constraint and a *has-many* constraint respectively, while assertion (2.5) provides a definition of the class Root in terms of a class expression, and implicitly contains an *is-a* constraint between the two classes Root and Directory.

In the following, we consider knowledge bases constituted by free assertions, hence without any restriction on their form. Knowledge bases of this form are in fact equivalent to knowledge bases constituted by primitive inclusion and equality assertions without restrictions. This follows easily by observing that a free assertion $C_1 \sqsubseteq C_2$ is equivalent to the pair of assertions $A \equiv C_1$, $A \sqsubseteq C_2$, where A is a newly introduced atomic concept. In Sect. 5 we deal also with so-called *primitive knowledge bases*, which are constituted only by primitive inclusion assertions. Such assertions correspond to the kind of constraints that can typically be expressed in conceptual data models [Calvanese et al. 1994], and reasoning on them is easier than with free assertions, if the underlying concept language is simple [Calvanese 1996b].

The constructs allowed in $\mathcal{ALCQI}$, in particular number restrictions and inverse roles, can interact in such a way that a knowledge base may admit no finite model, although it is satisfiable with an *infinite domain*. Similarly, a concept may be nonempty only in infinite interpretations [Cosmadakis, Kanellakis and Vardi 1990, Calvanese et al. 1994].

2.2. EXAMPLE. Let $\mathcal{K}_{guard}$ be the following knowledge base

$$\texttt{Guard} \quad \sqsubseteq \quad \exists\texttt{shields} \sqcap \forall\texttt{shields.Guard} \sqcap \exists^{\leq 1}\texttt{shields}^-$$

$$\texttt{FirstGuard} \quad \sqsubseteq \quad \texttt{Guard} \sqcap \forall\texttt{shields}^-.\bot$$

Intuitively, the assertions in $\mathcal{K}_{guard}$ state that: a guard is someone who shields guards and is shielded by at most one individual; a first guard is a guard who is not shielded by anyone. It is easy to see that the existence of a first guard implies the existence of an infinite sequence of guards, each one shielding the following one. This is due to the fact that all guards (including the first one) must have a shields successor, the first guard has no shields predecessor while any other guard can have at most one shields predecessor. Hence no guard can be reused to form a cycle of guards that shield each other, and the only possibility is to have an infinite chain (or tree). Summing up we can say that FirstGuard is consistent if we allow interpretations with a domain of arbitrary cardinality, but becomes inconsistent if we consider only interpretations with a finite domain.

This example shows that $\mathcal{ALCQI}$ lacks the *finite model property* [Ebbinghaus and Flum 1999], and hence reasoning with respect to unrestricted and finite domains are different. This fact becomes important when different assumptions on the domain being modeled are made. Finite interpretations (and thus models) are typically of interest in Databases, while a finite domain assumption is usually not considered in Knowledge Representation, and needs to be taken explicitly into account when devising reasoning procedures [Calvanese et al. 1994, Calvanese 1996a]. Therefore, we distinguish between unrestricted and finite model reasoning.

The basic reasoning tasks with respect to a given knowledge base are the following:

- *Knowledge base satisfiability* is the problem of deciding whether a knowledge base $\mathcal{K}$ is *satisfiable*, i.e., whether $\mathcal{K}$ admits a model $\mathcal{I}$.
- *Concept consistency* is the problem of deciding whether a concept C is *consistent* in a knowledge base $\mathcal{K}$, i.e., whether $\mathcal{K}$ admits a model $\mathcal{I}$ such that $C^{\mathcal{I}} \neq \emptyset$.
- *Logical implication* is the problem of deciding whether a knowledge base $\mathcal{K}$ *implies* an inclusion assertion $C_1 \sqsubseteq C_2$ (written as $\mathcal{K} \models C_1 \sqsubseteq C_2$), i.e., whether $C_1^{\mathcal{I}} \subseteq C_2^{\mathcal{I}}$ for each model $\mathcal{I}$ of $\mathcal{K}$.

Concept consistency and logical implication generalize concept satisfiability and concept subsumption, respectively, when we take into account a knowledge base.

For logics that do not have the finite model property, we distinguish between unrestricted and finite model reasoning. In particular, we talk about *unrestricted model reasoning*, when we consider arbitrary, and *finite model reasoning*, when we consider finite models only. When necessary, we distinguish between the two variants using the subscript "u" or "f".

2.3. EXAMPLE (2.1 CONTINUED). The assertions in $\mathcal{K}_{file}$ imply that in a model every object connected by a chain of role child of length n (for some n) to an instance of Root is an instance of FSelem. Formally, $\mathcal{K}_{file} \models \exists(\text{child}^-)^n.\text{Root} \sqsubseteq$ FSelem.

The basic reasoning tasks above can be reduced to each other (provided the language over which the knowledge base is built is sufficiently expressive). We have that logical implication $\mathcal{K} \models C_1 \sqsubseteq C_2$ can be reformulated as inconsistency of $C_1 \sqcap \neg C_2$ in $\mathcal{K}$, while consistency of C in $\mathcal{K}$ can be reformulated as $\mathcal{K} \not\models C \sqsubseteq \bot$. In addition, consistency of C in $\mathcal{K}$ can be reformulated as satisfiability of the knowledge base $\mathcal{K} \cup \{\top \sqsubseteq \exists P_{new}.C\}$, where P_{new} is a newly introduced atomic role. Finally, satisfiability of a knowledge base K can be reformulated as consistency of $\top$ in $\mathcal{K}$. Since the basic reasoning services can be reduced to each other, we can talk generically about *knowledge base reasoning*.

2.3. Reasoning Techniques

The study of suitable techniques for solving the reasoning problems in Description Logics has been developed starting with severe restrictions on the expressiveness of the language and on the form of the knowledge base. Consequently, the reasoning techniques have evolved over time, from specialized, ad-hoc methods to fully general ones.

The first approaches were developed under the assumption that one can embody the knowledge represented in the terminology directly into concept expressions, rather than assertions. Therefore, subsumption on concept expressions was regarded as the basic reasoning task.

The basic idea of the first algorithms for subsumption between concept expressions was to transform two input concepts into labeled graphs and test whether one could be embedded into the other; the embedded graph would correspond to the more general concept (the subsumer) [Borgida and Patel-Schneider 1994]. This method is called *structural comparison*, and the relation between concepts it computes is called *structural subsumption*. However, a careful analysis of the algorithms for structural subsumption shows that they are sound, but not always complete with respect to the semantics, provided the language is sufficiently expressive.

The studies on the trade-off between the expressiveness of a representation language and the difficulty of reasoning on the representations built using that language [Levesque and Brachman 1987] lead to the idea of carefully analyzing the various constructs of DLs, with the goal of characterizing the computational complexity of the reasoning tasks. This kind of research pointed out the need of a general approach to reasoning in DLs. Schmidt-Schauß and Smolka [1991] propose the notion of *constraint system* as a general technique to meet this need. Subsequent investigations showed that constraint systems can be seen as specialized forms of tableaux. Many results on algorithms for reasoning on concept expressions, and their complexity were then derived using tableau-based techniques [Donini et al. 1991, Buchheit et al. 1993, Donini et al. 1996, Donini et al. 1997, Horrocks 1998, Horrocks and Sattler 1999]. Such techniques, besides being intuitively appealing, provided a useful framework for modularizing the problem of designing reasoning algorithms for languages formed by different sets on constructs. In fact, a tableau-based algorithm essentially amounts to providing an expansion rule for each of the constructs in the language, and then show the correctness of each rule and the termination of the expansion process. The algorithms for concept satisfiability and subsumption obtained in this way have also lead to actual implementations by application of clever control strategies and optimization techniques [Horrocks and Patel-Schneider 1999].

One of the problems of tableau-based techniques for reasoning on concept expressions is that they do not easily extend to reasoning with assertions. Buchheit et al. [1993] present a first attempt to extend the tableau-based approach to (cyclic) knowledge bases. While providing an interesting result, this work points out the difficulties that can arise in proving termination of tableau-based algorithms. Such difficulties, combined with the reports from the first implementations of these methods (see for example the comparison of implemented systems by Baader, Hollunder, Nebel, Profitlich and Franconi [1992]), have shifted the attention to other techniques for reasoning in expressive DLs. In particular, the correspondence between DLs and Propositional Dynamic Logics (described in Sect. 3) have motivated the research on reasoning techniques for expressive DLs that are based on the translation into reasoning problems in Propositional Dynamic Logics, and therefore rely on the associated automata-based methods [Vardi and Wolper 1984, Vardi 1985, Vardi and Wolper 1986]. Such an approach is exactly the one reported in this chapter, in particular in Sect. 4.

It is worth noticing that the tableau-based approach has recently led to interesting developments towards DLs of the expressive power considered in this paper [Baader and Sattler 2000]. In particular it has led to the implementation of systems for reasoning on (free) assertions [Horrocks and Sattler 1999, Horrocks, Sattler and Tobies 1999, Horrocks and Patel-Schneider 1999].

All the above observations apply basically to unrestricted reasoning. However, as we mentioned before, unrestricted reasoning and finite model reasoning differ in expressive DLs. In Sect. 5 we describe the basic ideas of the techniques for finite model reasoning in expressive DLs.

3. Description Logics and Propositional Dynamic Logics

Propositional Dynamic Logics (PDLs) have been introduced by Fischer and Ladner [1979] as a formal system for reasoning about computer programs and they have since been studied extensively and extended in several ways [Kozen and Tiuryn 1990]. In this section we provide a brief overview of PDLs, and of the correspondence between PDLs and DLs.

3.1. Syntax and Semantics of PDLs

Syntactically, a PDL is constituted by expressions of two sorts: *programs* and *formulas*. Programs and formulas are built by starting from a set *Prog* of *atomic programs* and a set *Prop* of *propositional letters* and applying suitable operators. We denote propositional letters with A, arbitrary formulas with ϕ, atomic programs with P, and arbitrary programs with r, all possibly with subscripts. We focus on Converse-PDL [Fischer and Ladner 1979] whose abstract syntax is as follows:

$$\phi, \phi' \longrightarrow \top \mid \bot \mid A \mid \phi \wedge \phi' \mid \phi \vee \phi' \mid \phi \to \phi' \mid \neg\phi \mid \langle r \rangle \phi \mid [r]\phi$$

$$r, r' \longrightarrow P \mid r \cup r' \mid r; r' \mid r^* \mid r^- \mid \phi?$$

The basic propositional dynamic logic PDL [Fischer and Ladner 1979] is obtained from Converse-PDL by dropping converse programs r^-.

The semantics of Propositional Dynamic Logics [see for example Kozen and Tiuryn 1990] is based on the notion of a (Kripke) structure, which is defined as a triple $M = (\mathcal{S}, \{\mathcal{R}_P\}, \Pi)$, where $\mathcal{S}$ denotes a non-empty set of states, $\{\mathcal{R}_P\}$ is a family of binary relations over $\mathcal{S}$ such that each atomic program P is given a meaning through $\mathcal{R}_P$, and Π is a mapping from $\mathcal{S}$ to propositional letters such that $\Pi(s)$ determines the letters that are true in the state s. The basic semantical relation is "a formula ϕ holds at a state s of a structure M", which is written $M, s \models \phi$ and is defined by induction on the structure of ϕ:

$$
\begin{array}{ll}
M, s \models A & \text{iff } A \in \Pi(s) \\
M, s \models \top & \text{always} \\
M, s \models \bot & \text{never} \\
M, s \models \phi \wedge \phi' & \text{iff } M, s \models \phi \text{ and } M, s \models \phi' \\
M, s \models \phi \vee \phi' & \text{iff } M, s \models \phi \text{ or } M, s \models \phi' \\
M, s \models \phi \to \phi' & \text{iff } M, s \models \phi \text{ implies } M, s \models \phi' \\
M, s \models \neg\phi & \text{iff } M, s \not\models \phi \\
M, s \models \langle r \rangle \phi & \text{iff } \exists s' : (s, s') \in \mathcal{R}_r \text{ and } M, s' \models \phi \\
M, s \models [r]\phi & \text{iff } \forall s' : (s, s') \in \mathcal{R}_r \text{ implies } M, s' \models \phi
\end{array}
$$

where the family $\{\mathcal{R}_P\}$ is systematically extended so as to include, for every program r, the corresponding relation $\mathcal{R}_r$ defined by induction on the structure of r:

$$
\begin{array}{rcl}
\mathcal{R}_{r^-} & = & \{(s_1, s_2) \in \mathcal{S} \times \mathcal{S} \mid (s_2, s_1) \in \mathcal{R}_r\} \\
\mathcal{R}_{r \cup r'} & = & \mathcal{R}_r \cup \mathcal{R}_{r'} \\
\mathcal{R}_{r; r'} & = & \mathcal{R}_r \circ \mathcal{R}_{r'} \\
\mathcal{R}_{r^*} & = & (\mathcal{R}_r)^* \\
\mathcal{R}_{\phi?} & = & \{(s, s) \in \mathcal{S} \times \mathcal{S} \mid M, s \models \phi\}.
\end{array}
$$

If for each atomic program P the transition relation $\mathcal{R}_P$ is required to be a function that assigns to each state a unique successor state, then we are dealing with the *deterministic* variants of PDL [Ben-Ari, Halpern and Pnueli 1982, Vardi and Wolper 1986, Goldblatt 1992].

A structure $M = (\mathcal{S}, \{\mathcal{R}_P\}, \Pi)$ is called a *model* of a formula ϕ if there exists a state $s \in \mathcal{S}$ such that $M, s \models \phi$. A formula ϕ is *satisfiable* if there exists a model of ϕ, otherwise the formula is unsatisfiable.

The following two theorems show that satisfiability is EXPTIME-complete for both PDL and Converse-PDL.

3.1. THEOREM ([Fischer and Ladner 1979]). *Satisfiability in PDL is EXPTIME-hard.*

3.2. THEOREM ([Pratt 1979, Vardi and Wolper 1986]). *Satisfiability in Converse-PDL and in Deterministic-Converse-PDL can be decided in deterministic exponential time.*

3.2. The Correspondence between DLs and PDLs

The correspondence between DLs and PDLs, first pointed out by Schild [1991], is based on the similarity between the interpretation structures of the two logics: at the extensional level, individuals (members of $\Delta^{\mathcal{I}}$) in DLs correspond to states in PDLs, whereas links between two individuals correspond to state transitions. At the intensional level, concepts correspond to propositions, and roles correspond to programs.

More precisely, Schild [1991] showed that Converse-PDL corresponds to the DL $\mathcal{ALCI}_{reg}$ obtained from $\mathcal{ALCQI}$ by dropping qualified number restrictions and adding the constructs to form regular expressions on roles:

$$R, R' \longrightarrow P \mid R^- \mid R \sqcup R' \mid R \circ R' \mid R^* \mid id(C)$$

corresponding directly to the PDLs constructs on programs.

Formally, the correspondence is realized through a (one-to-one and onto) mapping δ from $\mathcal{ALCI}_{reg}$ concepts to Converse-PDL formulas, and from $\mathcal{ALCI}_{reg}$ roles to Converse-PDL programs. The mapping δ is defined inductively as follows (we assume $\sqcup$ and $\Rightarrow$ to be expressed by means of $\sqcap$ and $\neg$):

$$
\begin{aligned}
\delta(A) &= A & \delta(P) &= P \\
\delta(\neg C) &= \neg\delta(C) & \delta(R^-) &= \delta(R)^- \\
\delta(C \sqcap C') &= \delta(C) \wedge \delta(C') & \delta(R \sqcup R') &= \delta(R) \cup \delta(R') \\
\delta(\forall R.C) &= [\delta(R)]\delta(C) & \delta(R \circ R') &= \delta(R); \delta(R') \\
\delta(\exists R.C) &= \langle\delta(R)\rangle\delta(C) & \delta(R^*) &= \delta(R)^* \\
& & \delta(id(C)) &= \delta(C)?
\end{aligned}
$$

Given the above correspondence, all the DLs constructs that we shall consider can naturally be mapped into their PDLs analogues. However, DLs are normally used to define a knowledge base, while in PDLs such a notion has not been considered explicitly [see Fischer and Ladner 1979]. Consequently, the above correspondence is not sufficient to relate the reasoning problems. Therefore, Schild [1991] extends the mapping in such a way that a knowledge base formed by a set of assertions can be viewed as a PDL formula, and reasoning with respect to the knowledge base can be rephrased in terms of reasoning on such a PDL formula. We address this problem in the next section by showing how the assertions in a knowledge base can be turned into a DL concept.

Notice that, although the correspondence between PDLs and DLs has been exploited to provide reasoning methods for DLs, it has also lead to a number of interesting extensions to PDLs in terms of those constructs that are typical of DLs and have never been considered in PDLs. In particular, there is a tight relation between qualified number restrictions and *graded modalities* in modal logic [Van der Hoek 1992, Van der Hoek and de Rijke 1995, Fattorosi-Barnaba and De Caro 1985, Fine 1972].

3.3. Internalization of the Knowledge Base

One of the main results of the correspondence between DLs and PDLs is the understanding that a knowledge base can be "internalized" into a single concept, i.e., it is possible to build a concept that expresses all the assertions of the knowledge base [Schild 1991, Baader 1991].

Below we show that for the DLs $\mathcal{ALC}\cdot_{reg}$, with "·" standing for either nothing, $\mathcal{I}$, or additional constructs (e.g., number restrictions), reasoning on knowledge bases is in fact reducible to reasoning over concept expressions. We will see that such a reduction is possible because we consider DLs that are closed under negation and that are equipped with both union and reflexive-transitive closure of roles. Specifically, these constructs allow for denoting a "universal role", and this enables quantifying universally and existentially over all the objects in the interpretation domain, as shown below.

In the following we assume that $Q_1, \ldots, Q_m$ are all atomic roles and inverses of atomic roles present in the language, i.e., for logics without the inverse, $Q_1, \ldots, Q_m$ are all atomic roles, while for those equipped with inverse, $Q_1, \ldots, Q_m$ are all atomic roles and their inverse. Typically we assume that the atomic roles of the language are those occurring in the knowledge base and in the concepts under analysis.

Next we reformulate a standard result in modal logic, the so called generated submodel lemma [Goldblatt 1992], in terms of DLs, introducing the notion of *generated subinterpretation*.

Let $\mathcal{I} = (\Delta^{\mathcal{I}}, \cdot^{\mathcal{I}})$ be an interpretation and $r \in \Delta^{\mathcal{I}}$ an object in $\Delta^{\mathcal{I}}$. We call *r-generated subinterpretation of* $\mathcal{I}$ the interpretation $\mathcal{I}_r = (\Delta^{\mathcal{I}_r}, \cdot^{\mathcal{I}_r})$ defined as follows:

$$\Delta^{\mathcal{I}_r} = \{o \in \Delta^{\mathcal{I}} \mid (r, o) \in (\bigcup_{i=1,\ldots,m} Q_i^{\mathcal{I}})^*\}$$

$$A^{\mathcal{I}_r} = A^{\mathcal{I}} \cap \Delta^{\mathcal{I}_r} \quad \text{for each atomic concept } A$$

$$P^{\mathcal{I}_r} = P^{\mathcal{I}} \cap \Delta^{\mathcal{I}_r} \times \Delta^{\mathcal{I}_r} \quad \text{for each atomic role } P$$

3.3. PROPOSITION. *For every $\mathcal{ALC}\cdot_{reg}$ concept C, for every interpretation $\mathcal{I}$, and for every object $r \in \Delta^{\mathcal{I}}$, $r \in C^{\mathcal{I}}$ iff $r \in C^{\mathcal{I}_r}$.*

Prop. 3.3 is a direct consequence of the fact that DL concepts describe properties of an object r only in terms of those objects linked to it through role chains. The proof is a straightforward variant of that of the generated submodel lemma by Goldblatt [1992]. (Cf. also with the notion of *bisimulation* described in [Clarke and Schlingloff 2001], Chapter 24 of this Handbook.)

The main consequence of Prop. 3.3 is that, without loss of generality, we may restrict our attention to a special class of interpretations that we call "rooted connected interpretations". An interpretation $\mathcal{I} = (\Delta^{\mathcal{I}}, \cdot^{\mathcal{I}})$ is a *rooted connected interpretation* if and only if, for some $r \in \Delta^{\mathcal{I}}$ called "root"

$$\Delta^{\mathcal{I}} = \{o \mid (r,o) \in (\bigcup_{i=1,\dots,m} Q_i^{\mathcal{I}})^*\}.$$

Observe that if the DL we are considering is equipped with the inverse constructor then all $o \in \Delta^{\mathcal{I}}$ can be considered roots, while if it does not have inverse then there could be in fact only one root. Note also that generated subinterpretations are, by definition, rooted connected models. The following proposition ensures that we can restrict our attention to rooted connected interpretations.

3.4. PROPOSITION. *Let $\mathcal{K}$ be an $\mathcal{ALC} \cdot_{reg}$ knowledge base and C, C' two $\mathcal{ALC} \cdot_{reg}$ concepts. Then the following holds:*

- Knowledge base satisfiability. *$\mathcal{K}$ is satisfiable iff for some rooted connected interpretation $\mathcal{I}$, $\mathcal{I}$ is a model of $\mathcal{K}$.*
- Concept consistency. *C is consistent in $\mathcal{K}$ iff for some rooted connected interpretation $\mathcal{I}$ and some $s \in \Delta^{\mathcal{I}}$, $\mathcal{I}$ is a model of $\mathcal{K}$ and $s \in C^{\mathcal{I}}$.*
- Logical implication. *$\mathcal{K} \models C \sqsubseteq C'$ iff every rooted connected interpretation $\mathcal{I}$ that is a model of $\mathcal{K}$ is also a model of $C \sqsubseteq C'$.*

Observe that in $\mathcal{ALC} \cdot_{reg}$, the role $U = (\bigsqcup_{i=1,\dots,m} Q_i)^*$ is part of the language, and that such a role is interpreted as

$$(\bigcup_{i=1,\dots,m} Q_i^{\mathcal{I}})^*.$$

This means that, at least with respect to rooted connected interpretations, we have in fact a *universal role*, i.e., a role that reaches from the root every object in the domain[3]. Hence $\forall U.C$ expresses that every object in the domain is an instance of C, and $\exists U.C$ expresses that there exists an object of the domain that is an instance of C. With the notion of universal role in place we can *internalize* the knowledge base, i.e., we can encode tasks involving the knowledge base into tasks not involving it.

---

[3]The universal role corresponds to a *master modality* in modal logic, which becomes the so-called universal modality when connected models are considered [Blackburn, de Rijke and Venema 2000].

3.5. Proposition. *Let* $\mathcal{K} = \{C_1 \sqsubseteq D_1, \ldots, C_n \sqsubseteq D_n\}$ *be an* $\mathcal{ALC} \cdot_{reg}$ *knowledge base,* C, C' *two* $\mathcal{ALC} \cdot_{reg}$ *concepts, and let* $C_\mathcal{K} = (C_1 \Rightarrow D_1) \sqcap \cdots \sqcap (C_n \Rightarrow D_n)$. *Then the following holds:*

- Knowledge base satisfiability. *$\mathcal{K}$ is satisfiable iff $\forall U . C_\mathcal{K}$ is satisfiable.*
- Concept consistency. *C is consistent in $\mathcal{K}$ iff $C \sqcap \forall U . C_\mathcal{K}$ is satisfiable.*
- Logical implication. *$\mathcal{K} \models C \sqsubseteq D$ iff $(\forall U . C_\mathcal{K}) \Rightarrow (\forall U . (C \Rightarrow D))$ is satisfiable, or equivalently $(\forall U . C_\mathcal{K}) \sqcap (\exists U . (C \sqcap \neg D))$ is unsatisfiable, which can be further simplified to checking unsatisfiability of $(\forall U . C_\mathcal{K}) \sqcap (C \sqcap \neg D)$.*

An immediate consequence of Prop. 3.5 and of Th. 3.2 is the following.

3.6. Theorem. *Concept satisfiability and knowledge base satisfiability (and hence concept subsumption, concept consistency, and logical implication) in* $\mathcal{ALCI}_{reg}$ *are EXPTIME-complete.*

Observe that for DLs that do not include constructs for building regular expressions over roles, there is a sharp difference between reasoning techniques used in the presence of knowledge bases, and techniques used to reason on concept expressions. For example the logic $\mathcal{ALN}$ admits simple structural algorithms for deciding reasoning tasks not involving assertions that are sound and complete and require polynomial time [Borgida and Patel-Schneider 1994]. However, if free assertions are considered then decision procedures developed involve suitable termination strategies [Donini et al. 1996]. This difference is reflected by the computational properties of the associated decision problems. In particular, for the logic $\mathcal{ALC}$, reasoning tasks not involving knowledge bases are PSPACE-complete, while for knowledge base reasoning the following hardness result holds.

3.7. Theorem. *Concept consistency (and hence knowledge base satisfiability and logical implication) in* $\mathcal{ALC}$ *is EXPTIME-hard.*

This result follows directly from the proof of Thm. 3.1, by observing that the PDL formula used in the reduction has the form $\phi \wedge [P^*]\phi'$, where the only program appearing in ϕ and ϕ' is the atomic program P. By considering Prop. 3.5, satisfiability of such a formula corresponds to concept consistency in $\mathcal{ALC}$.

4. Unrestricted Model Reasoning

In this section we discuss the problem of reasoning with respect to unrestricted models in knowledge bases expressed in $\mathcal{ALCQI}$. We show that reasoning in $\mathcal{ALCQI}$ knowledge bases can be "compiled" into satisfiability in standard PDL. In order to do so we consider $\mathcal{ALC}\cdot$, with "·" standing for either nothing, $\mathcal{F}$, $\mathcal{I}$, or $\mathcal{FI}$, augmented by the reflexive-transitive closure operator on atomic and inverse roles (if present in the logic), with the proviso that such a role construct cannot appear in functional restrictions. In other words, functional restrictions (if present in the logic) are only applied to atomic roles or their inverse. We denote such logics by $\mathcal{ALC}\cdot_*$.

Without loss of generality we concentrate on knowledge base satisfiability. We provide a cascade of encodings[4] starting from knowledge base satisfiability in $\mathcal{ALCQI}$ and arriving to knowledge base satisfiability in $\mathcal{ALC}_*$. Since $\mathcal{ALC}_*$ is a sublanguage of $\mathcal{ALC}_{reg}$, which in turn corresponds to standard PDL, by internalizing the knowledge base we get to satisfiability in standard PDL.

The cascade of encodings of knowledge base satisfiability problems is as follows:

$$\mathcal{ALCQI} \longrightarrow \mathcal{ALCFI}_* \longrightarrow \mathcal{ALCI}_* \longrightarrow \mathcal{ALC}_*$$

More precisely, we first eliminate qualified number restrictions in favor of (unqualified) functional restrictions, which are the simplest form of number restriction considered in DLs –in doing this we need to introduce the reflexive-transitive closure of atomic and inverse roles; second, we eliminate completely functional restrictions; third, we eliminate inverse roles thus arriving to $\mathcal{ALC}_*$. Notably in encoding $\mathcal{ALCFI}_*$ knowledge bases into $\mathcal{ALCI}_*$ knowledge bases, we go from a logic that does not have the finite model property to a logic that has it.

The logics $\mathcal{ALC}_*$ and $\mathcal{ALCI}_*$ correspond to a restricted form of standard PDL and Converse-PDL respectively, which are both well known. We encode $\mathcal{ALCI}_*$ knowledge bases into $\mathcal{ALC}_*$ knowledge bases mainly for two reasons. First, the conceptual simplicity of encoding allows us to explain a general encoding technique in simple terms – the same encoding technique is also used to encode $\mathcal{ALCFI}_*$ knowledge bases into $\mathcal{ALCI}_*$ knowledge bases, although its application is much more subtle in that case. Second, since, as mentioned, $\mathcal{ALC}_*$ is a sublanguage of $\mathcal{ALC}_{reg}$, we can apply internalization and transform knowledge base reasoning in $\mathcal{ALC}_*$ into satisfiability in standard PDL, for which decision procedures can be effectively implemented (e.g., [Pratt 1980, De Giacomo and Massacci 2000] based on tableaux).

Each of the above encodings is polynomial[5]. Hence the overall compilation is polynomial as well. This allows us to conclude that knowledge base satisfiability (and hence concept consistency and logical implication) in $\mathcal{ALCQI}$ is EXPTIME-decidable, and hence EXPTIME-complete since knowledge base satisfiability in $\mathcal{ALC}$ is already EXPTIME-hard. Moreover such a cascade of encodings provides an algorithm to reason in $\mathcal{ALCQI}$ knowledge bases: first compile the $\mathcal{ALCQI}$ knowledge base into a $\mathcal{ALC}_*$ knowledge base (a polynomial step); then by internalization transform it into a standard PDL satisfiability problem (again a polynomial step); then run a PDL decision procedure (a possibly exponential step).

The rest of the section is organized as follows. First we present the notion of Fischer-Ladner closure of a knowledge base that is used in formulating the encodings. Then we present the encoding of knowledge bases, in order, from $\mathcal{ALCI}_*$ to $\mathcal{ALC}_*$, from $\mathcal{ALCFI}_*$ to $\mathcal{ALCI}_*$, and finally from $\mathcal{ALCQI}$ to $\mathcal{ALCFI}_*$.

---

[4]On encoding non-classical logics in classical logic see also [Ohlbach et al. 2001] (Chapter 21 of this Handbook) and on encoding modal logics in other modal logics see [Kracht and Wolter 2000].

[5]With the assumption, which is standard in DLs, that number restrictions are encoded in unary. Numbers encoded in binary are considered e.g., in [Tobies 1999b, Tobies 1999a].

4.1. Fisher-Ladner Closure of a Knowledge Base

We assume, without loss of generality, $\sqcup, \forall$ to be expressed by means of $\neg, \sqcap, \exists$. The *Fisher-Ladner closure* of an $\mathcal{ALCI}_*$ knowledge base $\mathcal{K}$, denoted $CL(\mathcal{K})$, is the least set of concepts F such that:

$$
\begin{array}{llll}
\text{if} & C \sqsubseteq C' \in \mathcal{K} & \text{then} & C, C' \in F \\
\text{if} & C \sqcap C' \in F & \text{then} & C, C' \in F \\
\text{if} & \neg C \in F & \text{then} & C \in F \\
\text{if} & C \in F & \text{then} & \neg C \in F \quad \text{(if } C \text{ is not of the form } \neg C') \\
\text{if} & \exists R.C \in F & \text{then} & C \in F \\
\text{if} & \exists R^*.C \in F & \text{then} & C, \exists R.\exists R^*.C \in F
\end{array}
$$

The notion of Fisher-Ladner closure of a knowledge base is closely related to the notion of Fisher-Ladner closure of a PDL formula [Fischer and Ladner 1979], which in turn is closely related to that of set of subformulas in simpler modal logics. Intuitively, given a knowledge base $\mathcal{K}$, $CL(\mathcal{K})$ includes all the concepts that play some role in establishing the truth-value of the concepts occurring in $\mathcal{K}$. In other words, $CL(\mathcal{K})$ includes all the concepts occurring in $\mathcal{K}$ and those generated by unfolding each concept of the form $\exists R^*.C$ into $C \sqcup \exists R.\exists R^*.C$. Both the number and the size of the concepts in $CL(\mathcal{K})$ are linearly bounded by the size of $\mathcal{K}$.

4.2. Inverse Roles

We show now that it is possible to eliminate the "inverse" operator from $\mathcal{ALCI}_*$ knowledge bases, while preserving the soundness and completeness of inference. Specifically, we present a polynomial encoding of $\mathcal{ALCI}_*$ knowledge bases into $\mathcal{ALC}_*$ knowledge bases that eliminates inverse roles but adds enough information so as not to destroy the original meaning of concepts with respect to the reasoning tasks. Such an encoding, first presented by De Giacomo [1996] in the context of PDLs, is the simplest illustration of a general technique for deriving reasoning procedures for expressive logics based on a (possibly polynomial) encoding of logics into simpler ones. Such a technique has led to several decidability and complexity results, as well as reasoning procedures in DLs. In particular, in the Sect. 4.3 it is used to eliminate functional restrictions.

Intuitively, the technique is based on two main points. Let the "Source Logic" be SL and the "Target Logic" be TL (in this section these logics are $\mathcal{ALCI}_*$ and $\mathcal{ALC}_*$ respectively):

1. Identify a finite set of assertion schemas in the language of TL capturing those characteristics that distinguish SL from TL (in the present case such assertion schemas are of the form $C \sqsubseteq \forall P.(\exists P^c.C)$, $C \sqsubseteq \forall P^c.(\exists P.C)$, and force the binary relation interpreting P^c to be the inverse of the one interpreting P).

2. Devise a function that, given an SL knowledge base $\mathcal{K}$, returns a finite "closed"[6] set of SL concepts, whose interpretation uniquely determines that of the concepts in $\mathcal{K}$, and that is used to instantiate the assertion schemas in (1) (in the present case such a set is simply the Fisher-Ladner closure of $\mathcal{K}$).

Indeed, by instantiating the assertion schemas in (1) to the concepts in (2), we can derive a TL knowledge base (in the present case, the so called $\mathcal{ALC}_*$-counterpart of an $\mathcal{ALCI}_*$ knowledge base, see below) which corresponds to the original SL knowledge base, in the sense that it preserves knowledge base satisfiability, concept consistency, and logical implication. If both the cardinality of the sets in (1) and (2) and the size of their elements are polynomially bounded by the original knowledge base, then so is the knowledge base we get.

We define the encoding ζ from $\mathcal{ALCI}_*$ knowledge bases $\mathcal{K}$ to $\mathcal{ALC}_*$ knowledge bases $\zeta(\mathcal{K})$, such that $\mathcal{K}$ is satisfiable if and only if $\zeta(\mathcal{K})$ is satisfiable. The knowledge base $\zeta(\mathcal{K})$, whose size is polynomial in the size of $\mathcal{K}$, is called the $\mathcal{ALC}_*$-counterpart of K.

4.1. DEFINITION. Let $\mathcal{K}$ be an $\mathcal{ALCI}_*$ knowledge base. The $\mathcal{ALC}_*$-counterpart $\zeta(\mathcal{K})$ of $\mathcal{K}$ is the union of two knowledge bases, $\zeta(\mathcal{K}) = \zeta_1(\mathcal{K}) \cup \zeta_2(\mathcal{K})$, where:

- $\zeta_1(\mathcal{K})$ is obtained from the original knowledge base $\mathcal{K}$ by replacing each occurrence of P^- with a new atomic role P^c, for every atomic role P occurring in $\mathcal{K}$.

- $\zeta_2(\mathcal{K})$ constitutes of a pair of assertions

$$C \;\sqsubseteq\; \forall P.\exists P^c.C$$

$$C \;\sqsubseteq\; \forall P^c.\exists P.C$$

for every $C \in CL(\zeta_1(\mathcal{K}))$ and every atomic program P occurring in $\mathcal{K}$.

In $\zeta_1(\mathcal{K})$ the inverse of atomic roles in $\mathcal{K}$ is replaced with new atomic roles. Each new role P^c is intended to represent P^- in $\zeta_1(\mathcal{K})$. $\zeta_2(\mathcal{K})$ constrains the models $\mathcal{I}$ of $\zeta(\mathcal{K})$ so that, for all $C \in CL(\zeta_1(\mathcal{K}))$, for all objects $o \in \Delta^{\mathcal{I}}$, if o is an instance of C then all the P-successors of o have a P^c-successor which is an instance of C as well, and similarly all the P^c-successors of o have a P-successor which is an instance of C. We show that, as far as knowledge base satisfiability is concerned (and hence concept consistency and logical implication), this allows us to correctly represent the inverse of P by means of P^c.

First of all, observe that if, instead of $\zeta_2(\mathcal{K})$, we impose the two *assertion schemas*:

$$X \;\sqsubseteq\; \forall P.\exists P^c.X$$

$$X \;\sqsubseteq\; \forall P^c.\exists P.X$$

where X is to be replaced by *every* concept of the language defined by the atomic concepts and roles in $\zeta_1(\mathcal{K})$, then the models of $\zeta_1(\mathcal{K})$ would be isomorphic to

---

[6]That is, the interpretation of each concept in the set depends only on the interpretation of the concepts already in the set.

the models of $\mathcal{K}$. In fact, the above two assertion schemas correspond to the ones used in the axiomatization of Converse-PDL to force each program P^- to be the converse of the program P. Hence the resulting logic would not be $\mathcal{ALC}_*$ but $\mathcal{ALCI}_*$ (where P^c instead of P^- denotes inverse programs). $\zeta_2(\mathcal{K})$ can be thought of as a *finite instantiation* of the above two schemas, with one instance for each concept in $CL(\zeta_1(\mathcal{K}))$. Although imposing the validity of such a finite instantiation does not suffice to guarantee the isomorphism of the models of $\zeta_1(\mathcal{K})$ and $\mathcal{K}$, it suffices to guarantee that $\mathcal{K}$ has a model if and only if $\zeta(\mathcal{K})$ has one.

To prove this result we define an operation that, given a model $\mathcal{I}$ of $\zeta(\mathcal{K})$, transforms it into a new special model $\mathcal{I}'$ of $\zeta(\mathcal{K})$, called c-closure of $\mathcal{I}$, which is isomorphic to a model of $\mathcal{K}$.

Let $\tilde{P}$ be an abstraction for both P and P^c, such that $\tilde{P}^c$ denotes P^c if $\tilde{P} = P$, and $\tilde{P}^c$ denotes P if $\tilde{P} = P^c$. Let $\mathcal{I} = (\Delta^{\mathcal{I}}, \cdot^{\mathcal{I}})$ be a model of $\zeta(\mathcal{K})$. We call the *c-closure* of $\mathcal{I}$, the interpretation $\mathcal{I}' = (\Delta^{\mathcal{I}'}, \cdot^{\mathcal{I}'})$, defined as follows:

- $\Delta^{\mathcal{I}'} = \Delta^{\mathcal{I}}$;
- $A^{\mathcal{I}'} = A^{\mathcal{I}}$, for each atomic concept A;
- $\tilde{P}^{\mathcal{I}'} = \tilde{P}^{\mathcal{I}} \cup \{(o', o) \mid (o, o') \in (\tilde{P}^c)^{\mathcal{I}}\}$, for each atomic role $\tilde{P}$.

Note that in the c-closure $\mathcal{I}'$ of a model $\mathcal{I}$, $P^{\mathcal{I}'}$ is obtained from $P^{\mathcal{I}}$ by including, for each pair (o, o') in $(P^c)^{\mathcal{I}}$, the pair (o', o) in $P^{\mathcal{I}'}$, and similarly $(P^c)^{\mathcal{I}'}$ is obtained from $(P^c)^{\mathcal{I}}$ by including, for each pair (o, o') in $P^{\mathcal{I}}$, the pair (o', o) in $(P^c)^{\mathcal{I}'}$. As a consequence, in the c-closure of an interpretation each atomic role P^c is interpreted as the inverse of P.

The next lemma relates models of $\zeta(\mathcal{K})$ to models of $\mathcal{K}$.

4.2. Lemma. *Let $\mathcal{K}$ be an $\mathcal{ALCI}_*$ knowledge base, $\zeta(\mathcal{K})$ its $\mathcal{ALC}_*$-counterpart, and $\mathcal{I}$ a model of $\zeta(\mathcal{K})$. Then the c-closure $\mathcal{I}'$ of $\mathcal{I}$ is a model of $\mathcal{K}$.*

From this lemma, and by observing that every model of $\mathcal{K}$ can be trivially transformed into a model of $\zeta(\mathcal{K})$ by interpreting P^c as P^-, we get the following result.

4.3. Theorem. *An $\mathcal{ALCI}_*$ knowledge base $\mathcal{K}$ is satisfiable if and only if its $\mathcal{ALC}_*$-counterpart $\zeta(\mathcal{K})$. is satisfiable.*

As a corollary of this theorem we get that knowledge base satisfiability (and hence concept consistency and logical implication) in $\mathcal{ALCI}_*$ and in $\mathcal{ALC}_*$ have the same computational complexity: they are both EXPTIME-complete. Observe however that such a result also follows directly from observing that reasoning with $\mathcal{ALCI}_*$ knowledge bases corresponds to reasoning with a restricted form of Converse-PDL and similarly, reasoning with $\mathcal{ALC}_*$ knowledge bases corresponds to reasoning with a restricted form of standard PDL.

4.3. Functional Restrictions

We now study reasoning in $\mathcal{ALCFI}_*$ knowledge bases. $\mathcal{ALCFI}_*$ is the DL obtained from $\mathcal{ALCI}_*$ by adding functional restrictions, i.e., number restrictions of the form

$\exists^{\leq 1} R$, where R is either an atomic role or the inverse of an atomic role. We show that knowledge base satisfiability (and hence concept consistency and logical implication) in $\mathcal{ALCFI}_*$ is EXPTIME-decidable, by following the technique already introduced above, and exhibiting an encoding of $\mathcal{ALCFI}_*$ knowledge bases into $\mathcal{ALCI}_*$ knowledge bases [De Giacomo and Lenzerini 1994a, De Giacomo 1995]. Although such an encoding has a simple form, proving its correctness requires quite sophisticated manipulations on interpretations. In particular, we observe that $\mathcal{ALCFI}_*$ knowledge bases *do not have* the finite model property, while $\mathcal{ALCI}_*$ knowledge bases *do have* it. Hence filtration arguments, usual in modal logics, cannot be applied directly.

We formally define the encoding γ from $\mathcal{ALCFI}_*$ knowledge bases $\mathcal{K}$ to $\mathcal{ALCI}_*$ knowledge bases $\gamma(\mathcal{K})$, such that $\mathcal{K}$ satisfiable if and only if $\gamma(\mathcal{K})$ is satisfiable. The size of $\gamma(\mathcal{K})$ is polynomial with respect to the size of $\mathcal{K}$. Since knowledge base satisfiability in $\mathcal{ALCI}_*$ can be decided in EXPTIME, this ensures that knowledge base satisfiability (and hence concept consistency and logical implication) in $\mathcal{ALCFI}_*$ can be decided in EXPTIME too.

We assume, without loss of generality, that $\mathcal{K}$ is in negation normal form (i.e., negations in concepts occurring in $\mathcal{K}$ are pushed inside as much as possible). It is easy to check that the transformation of any concept into negation normal form can be performed in linear time in the size of the concept.

4.4. DEFINITION. Let $\mathcal{K}$ be an $\mathcal{ALCFI}_*$ knowledge base in negation normal form. The $\mathcal{ALCI}_*$-*counterpart* $\gamma(\mathcal{K})$ of $\mathcal{K}$ is the union of two knowledge base, $\gamma(\mathcal{K}) = \gamma_1(\mathcal{K}) \cup \gamma_2(\mathcal{K})$, where:

- $\gamma_1(\mathcal{K})$ is obtained from the original knowledge base $\mathcal{K}$ by replacing each $\exists^{\leq 1} R$ with a new atomic concept $A_{\exists^{\leq 1}R}$, and each $\neg \exists^{\leq 1} R$ with $(\exists R.H_{\exists^{\leq 1}R}) \sqcap (\exists R.\neg H_{\exists^{\leq 1}R})$, where $H_{\exists^{\leq 1}R}$ is again a new atomic concept[7].

- $\gamma_2(\mathcal{K})$ constitutes of one assertion

$$(A_{\exists^{\leq 1}R} \sqcap \exists R.C) \sqsubseteq \forall R.C$$

  for every $A_{\exists^{\leq 1}R}$ occurring in $\gamma_1(\mathcal{K})$ and every $C \in CL(\gamma_1(\mathcal{K}))$, with the proviso that every concept of the form $\neg A_{\exists^{\leq 1}R}$ is replaced by $(\exists R.H_{\exists^{\leq 1}R}) \sqcap (\exists R.\neg H_{\exists^{\leq 1}R})$.

$\gamma_1(\mathcal{K})$ introduces the new concepts $A_{\exists^{\leq 1}R}$ and $H_{\exists^{\leq 1}R}$ in place of $\exists^{\leq 1} R$, so that positive occurrences of $\exists^{\leq 1} R$ are represented by the concept $A_{\exists^{\leq 1}R}$, and negative occurrences are represented by $(\exists R.H_{\exists^{\leq 1}R}) \sqcap (\exists R.\neg H_{\exists^{\leq 1}R})$. Note that every instance of $(\exists R.H_{\exists^{\leq 1}R}) \sqcap (\exists R.\neg H_{\exists^{\leq 1}R})$ has at least two R-successors.

The purpose of $\gamma_2(\mathcal{K})$ is less obvious. Intuitively, it constrains the models $\mathcal{I}$ of $\gamma(\mathcal{K})$ so that: for every object $o \in \Delta^{\mathcal{I}}$, if o is an instance of $A_{\exists^{\leq 1}R}$ and o_1 and o_2 are two R-successors of o, then o_1 and o_2 are instances of exactly the same concepts of $CL(\gamma_1(\mathcal{K}))$. This condition is sufficient to build a new model in which o_1 and o_2 are merged into a single object.

---

[7]We recall that only atomic roles or inverse of atomic roles can appear inside functional restrictions.

Observe that if, instead of adding $\gamma_2(\mathcal{K})$, we impose the assertion schema

$$A_{\exists \leq^1 R} \sqcap \exists R.X \sqsubseteq \forall R.X$$

where X is to be replaced by every concept of the language defined by the atomic concepts and roles in $\gamma_1(\mathcal{K})$, then the models of $\gamma_1(C)$ would be isomorphic to models of the original $\mathcal{ALCFI}_*$ knowledge base. However, the problem of verifying whether an $\mathcal{ALCI}_*$ concept is logically implied by an assertion schema is in general undecidable [Kozen and Tiuryn 1990]. So, adding the above schema to $\mathcal{ALCI}_*$ is of no use in establishing the decidability of reasoning in $\mathcal{ALCFI}_*$ knowledge bases.

Instead, the knowledge base $\gamma_2(\mathcal{K})$ can be thought of as a finite instantiation of the schema above, with one instance for each concept in $CL(\gamma_1(\mathcal{K}))$. Intuitively, imposing the validity of such finite instantiation is sufficient to guarantee that if $\gamma(\mathcal{K})$ has a model then $\mathcal{K}$ has a model as well, and vice-versa.

The main part in showing this result is showing that, given a model of $\gamma(\mathcal{K})$ we can build a model of $\mathcal{K}$. We proceed in two main steps:

1. Given a model $\mathcal{I}$ of $\gamma(\mathcal{K})$, we construct a special tree-like model $\mathcal{I}^t$.

2. Then, by suitably modifying $\mathcal{I}^t$, we construct a new model $\mathcal{I}^f$, in which all functional restriction requirements are satisfied, i.e., every object in which $A_{\exists \leq^1 R}$ holds has at most one R-successor.

The model of $\gamma(\mathcal{K})$ thus obtained is isomorphic to a model of the original $\mathcal{ALCFI}_*$ knowledge base $\mathcal{K}$. The constructions of $\mathcal{I}^t$ and $\mathcal{I}^f$ are quite sophisticated and we state only the final result.

4.5. THEOREM. *An $\mathcal{ALCFI}_*$ knowledge base $\mathcal{K}$ is satisfiable if and only if its $\mathcal{ALCI}_*$-counterpart $\gamma(\mathcal{K})$. is satisfiable.*

Observe that we cannot use a standard filtration argument [Goldblatt 1992] to prove the theorem above. In general, the ability to get a filtration of a model by a finite set of concepts (as $CL(\gamma_1(\mathcal{K}))$) leads to a finite model property. But $\mathcal{ALCFI}_*$ knowledge bases do not have the finite model property, so filtration techniques are not suitable to prove decidability. The construction sketched above instead builds, from a given model of $\gamma(\mathcal{K})$, a model of $\mathcal{K}$ that can be an infinite tree. Overall it is notable that reasoning in $\mathcal{ALCFI}_*$ knowledge bases, which do not have the finite model property, can be encoded, in a simple way, to reasoning in $\mathcal{ALCI}_*$ knowledge bases, which do have it.

The above result allows for establishing the decidability of reasoning in $\mathcal{ALCFI}_*$ knowledge bases. Moreover, since the encoding is polynomial, we get a characterization of the computational complexity.

4.6. THEOREM. *Knowledge base satisfiability (and hence concept consistency and logical implication) in $\mathcal{ALCFI}_*$ is EXPTIME-complete.*

4.4. Qualified Number Restrictions

We now study reasoning in $\mathcal{ALCQI}$ knowledge bases by exhibiting an encoding from $\mathcal{ALCQI}$ knowledge bases to $\mathcal{ALCFI}_*$ knowledge bases [De Giacomo and Lenzerini 1995b, De Giacomo 1995]. The encoding is based on the notion of reification (see later). As the encoding is polynomial, we get as a result the EXPTIME-decidability of reasoning in $\mathcal{ALCQI}$ knowledge bases. However, before discussing reasoning in $\mathcal{ALCQI}$ knowledge bases, we discuss some of the issues involved in the simpler logic $\mathcal{ALCQ}$ obtained by dropping inverse roles. This allows us to gain some intuition about results for $\mathcal{ALCQI}$.

4.4.1. Reasoning in $\mathcal{ALCQ}$ Knowledge Bases

Let us first ignore qualified number restrictions. Concepts of $\mathcal{ALCQ}$ without qualified number restrictions –i.e., concepts of $\mathcal{ALC}$– correspond directly to standard PDL formulas (of a restricted form). It is well-known that PDL formulas can be reduced to Deterministic-PDL formulas [Parikh 1981]. The basic idea, reformulated in DLs terms, is to replace each atomic role P by $F_P \circ G_P^*$, where F_P and G_P are new atomic roles that are globally functional (the assertion $\top \sqsubseteq \exists^{\leq 1} F_P \sqcap \exists^{\leq 1} G_P$ holds). Thus we encode $\mathcal{ALC}$ knowledge bases into $\mathcal{ALCF}_*$ knowledge bases of a special form. Let us call the resulting knowledge base $\mathcal{K}'$. We have that $\mathcal{K}$ is satisfiable if and only if it $\mathcal{K}'$ is satisfiable.

We briefly sketch the reasoning behind the proof of this statement. The if direction is straightforward, since any model $\mathcal{I}'$ of $\mathcal{K}'$ can be transformed into a model of $\mathcal{K}$ by interpreting P as $(F_P \circ G_P^*)^{\mathcal{I}'}$. The only if direction is as follows. Both $\mathcal{ALC}$ knowledge bases and $\mathcal{ALCF}_*$ knowledge bases have the *tree model property*: if a knowledge base has a model then it has a tree model, i.e., a model having the form of a *tree*. Hence, without loss of generality, we can restrict our attention to tree models only. Now, there is a one-to-one transformation from tree models $\mathcal{I}_T$ of $\mathcal{K}$ to (tree) models $\mathcal{I}_B$ of $\mathcal{K}'$. Indeed, we take $\Delta^{\mathcal{I}_B} = \Delta^{\mathcal{I}_T}$, $A^{\mathcal{I}_B} = A^{\mathcal{I}_T}$, and given an object $o \in \Delta^{\mathcal{I}_T}$ having as P-successors $o_1, \ldots, o_l$ we take $(o, o_1) \in F_P^{\mathcal{I}_B}$, and $(o_i, o_{i+1}) \in G_P^{\mathcal{I}_B}$, for $i = 1, \ldots, l - 1$. In this way we have $(o, o_i) \in P^{\mathcal{I}_T}$ if and only if $(o, o_i) \in (F_P \circ G_P^*)^{\mathcal{I}_B}$. Note that this construction is similar to the one often used in programming to transform an n-ary tree into a binary tree by coding children of a node as the combination of one child and its siblings.

We remark that $\mathcal{I}_T$ is required to be a tree because, once we get $\mathcal{I}_B$, we need to recover the "original" P-predecessor o of an object o_i, and thus $(F_P \circ G_P^*)^-$ needs to be *functional*. Otherwise, given an object o_i, we would not know which of the various $(F_P \circ G_P^*)^-$-successors is its original P-predecessor o, and therefore we would not be able to reconstruct $\mathcal{I}_T$ from $\mathcal{I}_B$.

Now let us consider again $\mathcal{ALCQ}$ knowledge bases. Representing an atomic role P as $F_P \circ (F_P')^*$, where F_P and F_P' are functional roles, makes it easy to express qualified number restrictions as constraints on the chain of $F_P \circ G_P^*$-successors of an object. For example, denoting the transitive closure of a role F as F^+, i.e.,

$F^+ \doteq F \circ F^*$, the concept $\exists^{\leq 3} P.C$ can be expressed by

$$\forall (F_P \circ G_P^* \circ id(C) \circ G_P^+ \circ id(C) \circ G_P^+ \circ id(C) \circ G_P^+).\neg C$$

which is equivalent to

$$\forall F_P.\forall G_P^*.(C \Rightarrow \forall G_P^+.(C \Rightarrow \forall G_P.\forall G_P^*.(C \Rightarrow \forall G_P.\forall G_P^*.\neg C))).$$

This concept can be read as "everywhere along the chain $F_P \circ G_P^*$ there are at most three objects that are instances of C", which corresponds exactly to the intended meaning.

The concept $\exists^{\geq 3} P.C$ can be expressed by

$$\exists (F_P \circ G_P^* \circ id(C) \circ G_P^+ \circ id(C) \circ G_P^+).C$$

which is equivalent to

$$\exists F_P.\exists G_P^*.(C \sqcap \exists G_P.\exists G_P^*.(C \sqcap \exists G_P.\exists G_P^*.C))$$

and can be read as "somewhere along the chain $F_P \circ G_P^*$ there are at least three objects that are instances of C", which again corresponds exactly to the intended meaning.

4.4.2. Reification of Roles

The construction above does not apply directly to $\mathcal{ALCQI}$ knowledge bases, since the presence of inverse roles does not allow us to restrict the attention to tree-like interpretations of the above form[8]. In order to carry out a similar construction we first need to *reify* atomic roles.

Atomic roles are interpreted as binary relations. Reifying a binary relation means creating for each pair of objects (o_1, o_2) in the relation an object which is connected by means of two special roles V_1 and V_2 to o_1 and o_2, respectively. The set of such objects represents the set of pairs forming the relation. However, the following problem arises: in general, there may be two or more objects being all connected by means of V_1 and V_2 to o_1 and o_2 respectively, and thus all representing the same pair (o_1, o_2). Obviously, in order to have a correct representation of a relation such a situation must be avoided.

Given an atomic role P, we call its *reified form* the complex role

$$V_1^- \circ id(A_P) \circ V_2$$

where A_P is a new atomic concept denoting objects representing the tuples of the relation associated with P, and V_1 and V_2 denote two functional roles that connect each object in A_P to the first and the second component respectively of the tuple represented by the object. Note that there is a clear symmetry between the role

---

[8]Indeed the presence of inverse roles allows for restricting the attention to "two-way" tree interpretations, as opposed to the "one-way" tree interpretations needed here.

$V_1^- \circ id(A_P) \circ V_2$ and its inverse $V_2^- \circ id(A_P) \circ V_1$. Observe that such complex roles are not part of $\mathcal{ALCQI}$, however given a concept of the form $\exists (V_1^- \circ id(A_P) \circ V_2).C$ we can immediately transform it into an $\mathcal{ALCQI}$ concept, namely $\exists V_1^-.(A_P \sqcap \exists V_2.C)$. Similarly for universal and number restrictions.

4.7. DEFINITION. Let $\mathcal{K}$ be an $\mathcal{ALCQI}$ knowledge base. The *reified-counterpart* $\xi_1(\mathcal{K})$ of $\mathcal{K}$ is the union of two knowledge bases, $\xi_1(\mathcal{K}) = \xi_0(\mathcal{K}) \cup \Theta_1$, where:

- $\xi_0(\mathcal{K})$ is obtained from the original knowledge base $\mathcal{K}$ by recursively replacing, for every atomic role P, every existential restriction, universal restriction and qualified number restriction as follows:

$$
\begin{array}{lll}
\exists P.C & \text{by} & \exists V_1^-.(A_P \sqcap \exists V_2.C), \\
\forall P.C & \text{by} & \forall V_1^-.(A_P \Rightarrow \forall V_2.C), \\
\exists^{\leq n} P.C & \text{by} & \exists^{\leq n} V_1^-.(A_P \sqcap \exists V_2.C), \\
\exists^{\geq n} P.C & \text{by} & \exists^{\geq n} V_1^-.(A_P \sqcap \exists V_2.C), \\
\exists P^-.C & \text{by} & \exists V_2^-.(A_P \sqcap \exists V_1.C), \\
\forall P^-.C & \text{by} & \forall V_2^-.(A_P \Rightarrow \forall V_1.C), \\
\exists^{\leq n} P^-.C & \text{by} & \exists^{\leq n} V_2^-.(A_P \sqcap \exists V_1.C), \\
\exists^{\geq n} P^-.C & \text{by} & \exists^{\geq n} V_2^-.(A_P \sqcap \exists V_1.C),
\end{array}
$$

  where V_1 and V_2 are new atomic roles (the only ones present after the transformation) and A_P is a new atomic concept.
- $\Theta_1 = \{\top \sqsubseteq \exists^{\leq 1} V_1 \sqcap \exists^{\leq 1} V_2\}$.

The next lemma guarantees us that, without loss of generality, we can restrict our attention to models of $\xi_1(\mathcal{K})$ that correctly represent relations associated with atomic roles, i.e., models in which each tuple of such relations is represented by a single object.

4.8. LEMMA. *If $\xi_1(\mathcal{K})$ has a model $\mathcal{I}$, then it has a model $\mathcal{I}'$ such that for each $(o, o') \in (V_1^- \circ id(A_{P_i}) \circ V_2)^{\mathcal{I}'}$ there is exactly one $o_{oo'}$ such that $(o_{oo'}, o) \in V_1^{\mathcal{I}'}$ and $(o_{oo'}, o') \in V_2^{\mathcal{I}'}$. That is, for all $o_1, o_2, o, o' \in \Delta^{\mathcal{I}'}$ such that $o_1 \neq o_2$ and $o \neq o'$, the following condition holds:*

$$
o_1, o_2 \in A_{P_i}^{\mathcal{I}'} \quad \rightarrow \quad \neg((o_1, o) \in V_1^{\mathcal{I}'} \wedge (o_2, o) \in V_1^{\mathcal{I}'} \wedge (o_1, o') \in V_2^{\mathcal{I}'} \wedge (o_2, o') \in V_2^{\mathcal{I}'}).
$$

The proof of Lem. 4.8 exploits the *disjoint union model property*: let $\mathcal{K}$ be an $\mathcal{ALCQI}$ knowledge base and $\mathcal{I} = (\Delta^{\mathcal{I}}, \cdot^{\mathcal{I}})$ and $\mathcal{J} = (\Delta^{\mathcal{J}}, \cdot^{\mathcal{J}})$ be two models of $\mathcal{K}$, then also the interpretation $\mathcal{I} \uplus \mathcal{J} = (\Delta^{\mathcal{I}} \uplus \Delta^{\mathcal{J}}, \cdot^{\mathcal{I}} \uplus \cdot^{\mathcal{J}})$ which is the disjoint union of $\mathcal{I}$ and $\mathcal{J}$, is a model of $\mathcal{K}$. We remark that most DLs have such a property, which is, in fact, typical of modal logics. Without going into details, we just mention that the model $\mathcal{I}'$ is constructed from $\mathcal{I}$ as the disjoint union of several copies of $\mathcal{I}$, in which the extension of role V_2 is modified by exchanging, in those instances that cause a wrong representation of a role, the second component with a corresponding object in one of the copies of $\mathcal{I}$. To prove that $\mathcal{I}'$ is indeed a model one can exploit, e.g., bisimulation, see also [Clarke and Schlingloff 2001] (Chapter 24 of this Handbook).

By using Lem. 4.8 we can prove the result below.

4.9. LEMMA. *Let $\mathcal{K}$ be an $\mathcal{ALCQI}$ knowledge base and $\xi_1(\mathcal{K})$ its reified-counterpart. Then $\mathcal{K}$ is satisfiable if and only if $\xi_1(\mathcal{K})$ is satisfiable.*

4.4.3. Reducing $\mathcal{ALCQI}$ Knowledge Bases to $\mathcal{ALCFI_*}$ Knowledge Bases

By Lemma 4.9, we can concentrate on the reified-counterparts of $\mathcal{ALCQI}$ knowledge bases. Note that these are $\mathcal{ALCQI}$ knowledge bases themselves, but their special form allows us to convert them into $\mathcal{ALCFI_*}$ knowledge bases. We adopt a technique resembling the one exploited for encoding $\mathcal{ALCQ}$ knowledge bases into $\mathcal{ALCF_*}$ knowledge bases. Intuitively, we represent the role V_i^- $(i = 1, 2)$, which is not functional (while V_i is so), by the role $F_{V_i} \circ G_{V_i}^*$, where F_{V_i} and G_{V_i} are new functional roles. The main point of such a transformation is that now qualified number restrictions can be encoded as constraints on the chain $F_{V_i} \circ G_{V_i}^*$. Formally, we define the $\mathcal{ALCFI_*}$-counterpart of an $\mathcal{ALCQI}$ knowledge base as follows.

4.10. DEFINITION. Let $\mathcal{K}$ be an $\mathcal{ALCQI}$ knowledge base and $\xi_1(\mathcal{K}) = \xi_0(\mathcal{K}) \cup \Theta_1$ its reified-counterpart. The $\mathcal{ALCFI_*}$-*counterpart* $\xi_2(\mathcal{K})$ of $\mathcal{K}$ is the union of two knowledge bases, $\xi_2(\mathcal{K}) = \xi_0'(\mathcal{K}) \cup \Theta_2$, where:

- $\xi_0'(\mathcal{K})$ is obtained from $\xi_0(\mathcal{K})$ by recursively replacing, for V_i $(i = 1, 2)$, every existential restriction, universal restriction and qualified number restriction as follows:

$$
\begin{array}{lll}
\exists V_i.C & \text{by} & \exists (G_{V_i}^-)^*.\exists F_{V_i}^-.C \\
\forall V_i.C & \text{by} & \forall (G_{V_i}^-)^*.\forall F_{V_i}^-.C \\
\exists V_i^-.C & \text{by} & \exists F_{V_i}.\exists G_{V_i}^*.C \\
\forall V_i^-.C & \text{by} & \forall F_{V_i}.\forall G_{V_i}^*.C \\
\exists^{\leq n} V_i^-.C & \text{by} & \forall F_{V_i}.\forall G_{V_i}^*.(C \Rightarrow \forall G_{V_i}^+)^n.\neg C \\
\exists^{\geq n} V_i^-.C & \text{by} & \exists F_{V_i}.\exists G_{V_i}^*.(C \sqcap \exists G_{V_i}^+)^{n-1}.C
\end{array}
$$

where F_{V_i} and G_{V_i} are new atomic roles and $(C \Rightarrow \forall G_{V_i}^+)^n.\neg C$ stands for

$$(C \Rightarrow \forall G_{V_i}.\forall G_{V_i}^*.(\cdots (C \Rightarrow \forall G_{V_i}.\forall G_{V_i}^*.\neg C) \cdots))$$

in which the pattern $C \Rightarrow \forall G_{V_i}.\forall G_{V_i}^*.\cdot$ is repeated n times. Similarly, for $(C \sqcap \exists G_{V_i}^+)^{n-1}.C$.

- $\Theta_2 = \{\theta_1, \theta_2\}$, with θ_i of the form:

$$\top \sqsubseteq \exists^{\leq 1} F_{V_i} \sqcap \exists^{\leq 1} G_{V_i} \sqcap \exists^{\leq 1} F_{V_i}^- \sqcap \exists^{\leq 1} G_{V_i}^- \sqcap \neg(\exists F_{V_i}^-.\top \sqcap \exists G_{V_i}^-.\top).$$

Observe that Θ_2 constrains the models $\mathcal{I}$ of $\xi_2(\mathcal{K})$ so that the relations $F_{V_i}^{\mathcal{I}}$, $G_{V_i}^{\mathcal{I}}$, $(F_{V_i}^-)^{\mathcal{I}}$, $(G_{V_i}^-)^{\mathcal{I}}$ are partial functions, and each object cannot be linked to other objects by both $(F_{V_i}^-)^{\mathcal{I}}$ and $(G_{V_i}^-)^{\mathcal{I}}$. As a consequence we get that $((F_{V_i} \circ G_{V_i}^*)^-)^{\mathcal{I}}$ is a partial function. This condition is required to prove the lemma below.

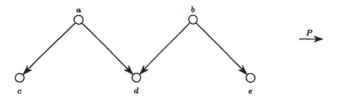

Figure 1: A model of the knowledge base $\mathcal{K} = \{C_0 \equiv \exists P.(\exists^{=2} P^-.(\exists^{=2} P.\top))\}$

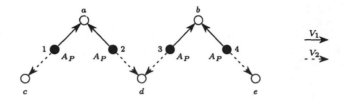

Figure 2: A model of the reified-counterpart $\xi_1(\mathcal{K})$ of $\mathcal{K}$

4.11. LEMMA. *Let $\mathcal{K}$ be a $\mathcal{ALCQI}$ knowledge base, $\xi_1(\mathcal{K})$ its reified-counterpart, and $\xi_2(\mathcal{K})$ its $\mathcal{ALCFI}_*$-counterpart. Then $\xi_1(\mathcal{K})$ is satisfiable if and only if $\xi_2(\mathcal{K})$ is satisfiable.*

As an immediate consequence of Lem. 4.11 and Lem. 4.9 we get the main result of this subsection.

4.12. THEOREM. *Let $\mathcal{K}$ be a $\mathcal{ALCQI}$ knowledge base and $\xi_2(\mathcal{K})$ its $\mathcal{ALCFI}_*$-counterpart. Then $\mathcal{K}$ is satisfiable if and only if its $\xi_2(\mathcal{K})$ is satisfiable.*

Since the size of $\xi_2(\mathcal{K})$ is polynomial in the size of $\mathcal{K}$, we get the following complexity characterization for reasoning in $\mathcal{ALCQI}$ knowledge bases [9].

4.13. THEOREM. *Knowledge base satisfiability (and hence concept consistency and logical implication) in $\mathcal{ALCQI}$ is EXPTIME-complete.*

Let us illustrate with an example the basic relationships between models of an $\mathcal{ALCQI}$ knowledge base and those of its reified-counterpart and $\mathcal{ALCFI}_*$-counterpart.

4.14. EXAMPLE. Let $\mathcal{K}$ be the following $\mathcal{ALCQI}$ knowledge base:

$$\{\ C_0 = \exists P.(\exists^{=2} P^-.(\exists^{=2} P.\top))\ \}$$

Figure 1 depicts a model $\mathcal{I}$ of $\mathcal{K}$ with $a \in C_0^{\mathcal{I}}$. In Figure 2 the model $\mathcal{I}$ of $\mathcal{K}$ is transformed into a model $\mathcal{I}'$ of its reified-counterpart $\xi_1(\mathcal{K})$. Finally, in Figure 3

---

[9]We remind that we assume unary coding of numbers in number restrictions.

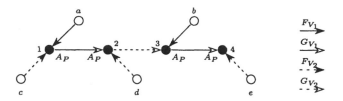

Figure 3: A model of the $\mathcal{ALCFI}_*$-counterpart $\xi_2(\mathcal{K})$ of $\mathcal{K}$

the model $\mathcal{I}'$ of $\xi_1(\mathcal{K})$ is transformed into a model $\mathcal{I}''$ of the $\mathcal{ALCFI}_*$-counterpart $\xi_2(\mathcal{K})$ of $\mathcal{K}$. Notice that from $\mathcal{I}''$ we can easily reconstruct $\mathcal{I}'$, and from $\mathcal{I}'$ the model $\mathcal{I}$ of the original knowledge base.

5. Finite Model Reasoning

As shown in Sect. 2, a DL which contains constructs for inverse roles and functionality in combination with cyclic assertions lacks the finite model property. Therefore, it becomes necessary to devise specific techniques to reason with respect to finite models only. In this section we discuss the problem of reasoning with respect to finite models in knowledge bases, and propose methods to solve this problem for various sublanguages of $\mathcal{ALCQI}$. These methods are based on an idea introduced by Lenzerini and Nobili [1990] and further developed and extended by Calvanese and Lenzerini [1994a, 1994b] and Calvanese [1996a].

When we restrict the attention to finite models, some properties that are essential for the reasoning techniques developed in Sect. 4 fail. In particular, all reductions exploiting the tree-model property cannot be applied since this property does not hold when only finite models are considered. An intuitive justification can be given by observing that, whenever a (finite) model contains a cycle, the unraveling of such a model into a tree generates an infinite structure. The following example shows that there are indeed cases where any finite model of a knowledge base must necessarily contain a cycle.

5.1. EXAMPLE. Let $\mathcal{K}_c$ be the $\mathcal{ALUNI}$ knowledge base consisting of one assertion:

$$\text{Node} \sqsubseteq \forall \text{edge}^-.\text{Node} \sqcap \exists^{\leq 1}\text{edge}^- \sqcap \forall \text{edge}.\text{Node} \sqcap \exists \text{edge}$$

As in Example 2.2, the above assertion forces in any model of $\mathcal{K}_c$ in which Node has a nonempty extension the existence of a sequence of objects each connected to the following one by means of the role edge. However, differently from Example 2.2, the assertion does not rule out that the $\text{edge}^{\mathcal{I}}$ relation forms a cycle. It is easy to verify that each finite model of $\mathcal{K}_c$ will be constituted by a finite number of such cycles.

If number restrictions (and in particular functionality) are not used, the finite model property does not fail. Therefore, a procedure for finite model reasoning must specifically address the presence of number restrictions. The method we present here is based on an encoding of the number restrictions that appear in a knowledge base into a system of linear inequalities. The method represents a generalization of the one developed by Lenzerini and Nobili [1990] for a simple data model based on disjoint classes and relationships. We first briefly describe the method on knowledge bases of a restricted form, which captures the data model of Lenzerini and Nobili [1990]. We then show how to extend it to capture finite model reasoning in knowledge bases built using more expressive languages, namely $\mathcal{ALUNI}$ and $\mathcal{ALCNI}$.

5.1. Finite Model Reasoning Using Linear Inequalities

To illustrate the reasoning technique we consider $\mathcal{ALNI}$ knowledge bases containing only assertions of a simplified form. Such knowledge bases essentially correspond to schemas expressed in the data model used by Lenzerini and Nobili [1990] (with roles representing binary relationships), which is a simplified form of the Entity-Relationship model [Chen 1976] without ISA relationships between classes. A knowledge base $\mathcal{K}$ of this form contains for each atomic role P an assertion

$$\top \sqsubseteq \forall P.A_2 \sqcap \forall P^-.A_1, \tag{5.1}$$

where A_1 and A_2 are two atomic concepts, and for each pair of distinct atomic concepts A and A', an assertion

$$A \sqsubseteq \neg A'. \tag{5.2}$$

These assertions enforce that in all models of $\mathcal{K}$ the following properties hold:

(Cond$_1$) The atomic concepts have pairwise disjoint extensions.

(Cond$_2$) Each role is "typed", i.e., its domain is included in the extension of an atomic concept A_1, and its codomain is included in the extension of an atomic concept A_2.

The only additional assertions that are present in $\mathcal{K}$ are used to impose cardinality constraints on roles and inverse roles, and are of the form

$$\top \sqsubseteq \exists^{\geq m_1} P \sqcap \exists^{\leq n_1} P$$
$$\top \sqsubseteq \exists^{\geq m_2} P^- \sqcap \exists^{\leq n_2} P^-, \tag{5.3}$$

where m_1, n_1, m_2, and n_2 are positive integers with $m_1 \leq n_1$ and $m_2 \leq n_2$.

Due to the restrictions on the use of constructs and assertions (which reflect the limited expressiveness of the data model), a knowledge base of the above form is always both satisfiable and finitely satisfiable, and all atomic concepts in it are consistent. However, due to the use of number restrictions some of the atomic concepts may not be finitely consistent.

In order to check for finite concept consistency , we construct from $\mathcal{K}$ a system $\Psi_\mathcal{K}$ of linear inequalities with one unknown $\mathrm{Var}(X)$ for each atomic concept or role

X in $\mathcal{K}$. The system contains inequalities

$$
\begin{aligned}
m_1 \cdot \mathrm{Var}(A_1) \;\leq\; \mathrm{Var}(P) \;\leq\; n_1 \cdot \mathrm{Var}(A_1) \\
m_2 \cdot \mathrm{Var}(A_2) \;\leq\; \mathrm{Var}(P) \;\leq\; n_2 \cdot \mathrm{Var}(A_2)
\end{aligned}
\tag{5.4}
$$

corresponding to the assertions (5.3), and for each atomic concept or role X, an inequality

$$
\mathrm{Var}(X) > 0. \tag{5.5}
$$

It can be shown that all atomic concepts in $\mathcal{K}$ are simultaneously consistent if and only if the associated system of inequalities $\Psi_{\mathcal{K}}$ admits a solution.

The proof of this result exploits the possibility of associating to a positive integer solution of $\Psi_{\mathcal{K}}$ a model of $\mathcal{K}$ in such a way that the cardinality of the extension of each atomic concept and role equals the value assigned by the solution to the corresponding unknown. One direction is easy, since from any model of $\mathcal{K}$ one can obtain an integer solution of $\Psi_{\mathcal{K}}$ by assigning to each unknown the cardinality of the extension of the corresponding atomic concept or role. The converse direction needs more attention. First of all, since the system is homogeneous, if it admits a solution then it admits also a solution S such that (i) for each atomic concept and role E the value $S(E)$ assigned by S to $\mathrm{Var}(E)$ is a positive integer, and (ii) for each P, A_1, A_2 appearing in an assertion of the form (5.1), it holds that $S(P) \geq S(A_1) \cdot S(A_2)$ [Lenzerini and Nobili 1990]. From such a solution S one can construct a model $\mathcal{I}$ of the knowledge base in which $X^{\mathcal{I}}$ has cardinality $S(X)$, for each atomic concept and role X. Assertions of the form (5.2) are satisfied by assigning to all atomic concepts disjoint extensions. In order to satisfy assertions (5.1), the extension $P^{\mathcal{I}}$ of each atomic role P is obtained as a set of pairs of instances of A_1 and A_2. Moreover, since S satisfies all inequalities (5.4), $P^{\mathcal{I}}$ can be constructed in such a way that also all assertions (5.3) involving number restrictions are satisfied. The reason is that conditions (Cond$_1$) and (Cond$_2$) allow one to regard all instances of an atomic concept as equivalent with respect to the participation in roles. Therefore the number restrictions (5.3), which are local conditions on the number of connections of single objects, are correctly encoded by means of the inequalities (5.4), which express global conditions on the total number of instances.

Since verifying the existence of a solution of $\Psi_{\mathcal{K}}$ can be done in time polynomial in the size of $\Psi_{\mathcal{K}}$[10], and hence time polynomial in the size of $\mathcal{K}$, we have an efficient method for verifying concept consistency in the knowledge bases considered so far.

The technique presented above is only suitable if one needs to verify the simultaneous consistency of *all* atomic concepts, which is reflected in the use of inequalities (5.5). In general, however, one may want to check the consistency of single concepts without posing any restrictions on other concepts of the knowledge base. Therefore, the solutions of the system of inequalities need to reflect also the case where in a model some atomic concept A, and hence all roles that are typed with A, have an empty extension. This means that when a solution of the system assigns the value 0 to the unknown corresponding to A, it must assign the value 0 also to all

---

[10]We assume to use a suitable encoding of $\Psi_{\mathcal{K}}$ in which numbers are represented in binary.

unknowns corresponding to the roles typed with A. Such a condition is not satisfied by every solution of the system, and we call a solution in which the condition holds *acceptable*.

To verify the existence of acceptable solutions of the system of inequalities derived from an $\mathcal{ALNI}$ knowledge base of the simple form above one can exploit a result about the complexity of integer programming, which essentially states that the existence of integer solutions of a system of inequalities implies the existence of solutions of bounded size [Papadimitriou 1981]. Such a result, combined with the technique presented by Calvanese and Lenzerini [1994*b*] allows one to show that the existence of acceptable solutions can be verified in polynomial time in the size of the system of inequalities [Calvanese 1996*c*].

5.2. Finite Model Reasoning on Primitive $\mathcal{ALUNI}$ Knowledge Bases

The method we have presented in Sect. 5.1 is not immediately applicable to more expressive languages and more general forms of knowledge bases. The reason is that conditions (Cond$_1$) and (Cond$_2$), which are necessary to construct a model of a knowledge base from a solution of the corresponding system of linear inequalities, are in general not satisfied. In fact, to correctly encode number restrictions by means of linear inequalities, it is sufficient that the following generalization of condition (Cond$_2$) is satisfied:

(Cond$_2'$) For each atomic role P and each concept expression C appearing in $\mathcal{K}$, the domain of P is either included in the extension of C or disjoint from it. Similarly for the codomain of P.

This condition guarantees that, in a model, all instances of a concept "behave" in the same way, and thus the local conditions encoded by number restrictions can be correctly captured by the global constraints represented by the system of inequalities.

It is possible to enforce conditions (Cond$_1$) and (Cond$_2'$) by performing a transformation on the knowledge base, and deriving from the transformed version the system of inequalities. A technique that makes use of this idea for finite model reasoning in expressive modeling formalisms was first introduced by Calvanese and Lenzerini [1994*b*] for an extended semantic database model, and successively extended to deal with primitive $\mathcal{ALUNI}$ knowledge bases [Calvanese et al. 1994] and for reasoning in an expressive object-oriented database model [Calvanese and Lenzerini 1994*a*]. We illustrate the technique for reasoning on primitive $\mathcal{ALUNI}$ knowledge bases by means of an example, using a slight variation of the knowledge base in Example 5.1.

5.2. EXAMPLE. Let $\mathcal{K}_b$ be the $\mathcal{ALUNI}$ knowledge base consisting of the assertions:

$$\texttt{Root} \quad \sqsubseteq \quad \exists^{\leq 0}\texttt{edge}^- \sqcap \forall\texttt{edge}.\texttt{OtherNode} \sqcap \exists^{\geq 1}\texttt{edge} \sqcap \exists^{\leq 2}\texttt{edge}$$

$$\texttt{OtherNode} \quad \sqsubseteq \quad \forall\texttt{edge}^-.(\texttt{Root} \sqcup \texttt{OtherNode}) \sqcap \exists^{=1}\texttt{edge}^- \sqcap$$
$$\forall\texttt{edge}.\texttt{OtherNode} \sqcap \exists^{\geq 1}\texttt{edge} \sqcap \exists^{\leq 2}\texttt{edge} \sqcap \neg\texttt{Root}.$$

$\mathcal{K}_b$ describes the properties of binary trees, where each node has at most one predecessor and at most two successors. In fact, we distinguish between nodes that have no predecessor (Root) and those that have one (OtherNode). Additionally, we require that each node has at least one successor. This combination of requirements makes the concept Root finitely inconsistent. The concept OtherNode, on the other hand, can be populated in a finite model of the knowledge base, although the model we obtain is somewhat counterintuitive, since it necessarily contains a cycle in the edge relation.

First of all, it is easy to see that, by introducing at most a linear number of new atomic concepts, we can transform the knowledge base into an equivalent one in which the nesting of constructs is eliminated. Specifically, in such a knowledge base, which we call *normalized*, the concept on the right hand side of an inclusion assertion is of the form L, $L_1 \sqcup L_2$, $\forall R.L$, $\exists^{\geq n} R$, or $\exists^{\leq n} R$, where L is an atomic or negated atomic concept.

5.3. EXAMPLE (5.2 CONTINUED). In the normalized $\mathcal{ALUNI}$ knowledge base $\mathcal{K}_n$ corresponding to $\mathcal{K}_b$ we introduce an additional concept Node to replace the disjunction Root $\sqcup$ OtherNode nested within the universal quantification, thus obtaining:

Node	$\sqsubseteq$	Root $\sqcup$ OtherNode	OtherNode	$\sqsubseteq$	$\forall$edge$^-$.Node
			OtherNode	$\sqsubseteq$	$\exists^{\geq 1}$edge$^-$
Root	$\sqsubseteq$	$\exists^{\leq 0}$edge$^-$	OtherNode	$\sqsubseteq$	$\exists^{\leq 1}$edge$^-$
Root	$\sqsubseteq$	$\forall$edge.OtherNode	OtherNode	$\sqsubseteq$	$\forall$edge.OtherNode
Root	$\sqsubseteq$	$\exists^{\geq 1}$edge	OtherNode	$\sqsubseteq$	$\exists^{\geq 1}$edge
Root	$\sqsubseteq$	$\exists^{\leq 2}$edge	OtherNode	$\sqsubseteq$	$\exists^{\leq 2}$edge
			OtherNode	$\sqsubseteq$	$\neg$Root.

Then, to ensure that conditions (Cond$_1$) and (Cond$'_2$) are satisfied, we use instead of atomic concepts, sets of atomic concepts, called *compound concepts*, and instead of atomic roles, so called *compound roles*. Each compound role is a triple $(P, \widehat{D}_1, \widehat{D}_2)$ constituted by an atomic role P and two compound concepts $\widehat{D}_1$ and $\widehat{D}_2$ typing respectively the first and second component of the instances of P. Intuitively, the instances of a compound concept $\widehat{D}$ are all those objects of the domain that are instances of all concepts in $\widehat{D}$ and are not instances of any concept not in $\widehat{D}$. A compound role $(P, \widehat{D}_1, \widehat{D}_2)$ is interpreted as the restriction of role P to the pairs whose first component is an instance of $\widehat{D}_1$ and whose second component is an instance of $\widehat{D}_2$.

This ensures that two different compound concepts have necessarily disjoint extensions, and hence that the property corresponding to (Cond$_1$) holds. The same observation holds for two different compound roles $(P, \widehat{D}_1, \widehat{D}_2)$ and $(P, \widehat{D}'_1, \widehat{D}'_2)$ that correspond to the same role P. Moreover, for compound roles the property corresponding to property (Cond$_2$) holds by definition, and, considering that the knowledge base is primitive and has been normalized, also (Cond$'_2$) holds.

The assertions in the knowledge base that do not involve number restrictions, force certain compound concepts and compound roles to be *inconsistent*, i.e., to have an empty extension in all models of the knowledge base. For example, the assertion $A_1 \sqsubseteq \neg A_2$ makes all compound concepts that contain both A_1 and A_2 inconsistent. Similarly, the assertion $A_1 \sqsubseteq \forall P.A_2$ makes all compound roles $(P, \widehat{D}_1, \widehat{D}_2)$ such that $\widehat{D}_1$ contains A_1 and $\widehat{D}_2$ does not contain A_2 inconsistent. One can check in polynomial time in the size of the knowledge base whether a compound concept or role is inconsistent. Observe however, that since the total number of compound concepts and roles is exponential in the number of atomic concepts in the knowledge base, doing the check for all compound concepts and roles takes in general exponential time. One can then encode the assertions involving number restrictions in the normalized knowledge base into assertions involving number restrictions on compound concepts.

5.4. EXAMPLE (5.3 CONTINUED). For the normalized knowledge base $\mathcal{K}_n$, the set of consistent compound concepts is $\widehat{\mathcal{D}}_n = \{E, R, O, RN, ON\}$, where $E = \emptyset$, $R = \{Root\}$, $O = \{OtherNode\}$ $RN = \{Node, Root\}$, and $ON = \{Node, OtherNode\}$, and the set of consistent compound roles is $\widehat{\mathcal{U}}_n = \{(edge, RN, O), (edge, RN, ON), (edge, ON, O),$ $(edge, ON, ON), (edge, E, R), (edge, E, RN), (edge, E, E)\}$. The assertions that derive from the assertions in $\mathcal{K}_n$ and which impose number restrictions on compound concepts are the following:

R	$\sqsubseteq$	$\exists^{\leq 0} edge^-$	RN	$\sqsubseteq$	$\exists^{\leq 0} edge^-$
R	$\sqsubseteq$	$\exists^{\geq 1} edge$	RN	$\sqsubseteq$	$\exists^{\geq 1} edge$
R	$\sqsubseteq$	$\exists^{\leq 2} edge$	RN	$\sqsubseteq$	$\exists^{\leq 2} edge$
O	$\sqsubseteq$	$\exists^{\geq 1} edge^-$	ON	$\sqsubseteq$	$\exists^{\geq 1} edge^-$
O	$\sqsubseteq$	$\exists^{\leq 1} edge^-$	ON	$\sqsubseteq$	$\exists^{\leq 1} edge^-$
O	$\sqsubseteq$	$\exists^{\geq 1} edge$	ON	$\sqsubseteq$	$\exists^{\geq 1} edge$
O	$\sqsubseteq$	$\exists^{\leq 2} edge$	ON	$\sqsubseteq$	$\exists^{\leq 2} edge$.

We construct now a system $\Psi_\mathcal{K}$ of linear inequalities which contains one unknown for each consistent compound concept and role (the inconsistent compound concepts and roles are not considered anymore). The inequalities are obtained by encoding the assertions in the knowledge base involving number restrictions on compound concepts, in a way similar to inequalities (5.4). Differently from the previous case, now each inequality involves one unknown corresponding to a compound concept and a sum of unknowns corresponding to compound roles. For example, the assertion $\widehat{D} \sqsubseteq \exists^{\geq n} P$, where $\widehat{D}$ is a compound concept and P is an atomic role, results in the inequality

$$n \cdot \mathrm{Var}(\widehat{D}) \leq \sum_{(P, \widehat{D}, \widehat{D}_2)} \mathrm{Var}((P, \widehat{D}, \widehat{D}_2)),$$

where the sum ranges over all consistent compound roles involving P and typed with $\widehat{D}$ on the first component.

5.5. Example (5.4 continued). The system $\Psi_{\mathcal{K}_n}$ derived from $\mathcal{K}_n$ consists of the inequalities

$0 \cdot r$	$\geq$	$e_{E,R}$	$0 \cdot rn$	$\geq$	$e_{E,RN}$
$1 \cdot r$	$\leq$	0	$1 \cdot rn$	$\leq$	$e_{RN,0} + e_{RN,ON}$
$2 \cdot r$	$\geq$	0	$2 \cdot rn$	$\geq$	$e_{RN,0} + e_{RN,ON}$
$1 \cdot o$	$\leq$	$e_{RN,0} + e_{ON,0}$	$1 \cdot on$	$\leq$	$e_{RN,ON} + e_{ON,ON}$
$1 \cdot o$	$\geq$	$e_{RN,0} + e_{ON,0}$	$1 \cdot on$	$\geq$	$e_{RN,ON} + e_{ON,ON}$
$1 \cdot o$	$\leq$	0	$1 \cdot on$	$\leq$	$e_{ON,0} + e_{ON,ON}$
$2 \cdot o$	$\geq$	0	$2 \cdot on$	$\geq$	$e_{ON,0} + e_{ON,ON},$

where we have denoted the unknown corresponding to a compound concept with the name of the compound concept in lower-case letters, and the unknown corresponding to a compound role (edge, X, Y) with $e_{X,Y}$.

It is possible to show that *acceptable* nonnegative integer solutions of $\Psi_{\mathcal{K}}$ (suitably defined), can be put into correspondence with finite models of the knowledge base $\mathcal{K}$, in which each compound concept and compound role has a number of instances that is equal to the value assigned by the solution to the corresponding unknown.

Hence, in order to check whether a concept A in a primitive $\mathcal{ALUNI}$ knowledge base is finitely consistent, we can proceed as follows: We derive from the knowledge base the system of inequalities. We then add an additional (non-homogeneous) inequality that forces the solutions of the system to assign a positive value to at least one of the unknowns corresponding to the compound concepts containing A. By exploiting the correspondence between acceptable solutions of the system of inequalities and models of the knowledge base we get the following characterization of finite concept consistency in primitive $\mathcal{ALUNI}$ knowledge bases.

5.6. Theorem. *Let $\mathcal{K}$ be a knowledge base, A an atomic concept in $\mathcal{K}$, and $\Psi_{\mathcal{K}}$ the system of inequalities derived from $\mathcal{K}$. Then A is finitely consistent in $\mathcal{K}$ if and only if*

$$\Psi_{\mathcal{K}}^{A} = \Psi_{\mathcal{K}} \bigcup \left\{ \sum_{\hat{D}|A\in\hat{D}} Var(\hat{D}) \geq 1 \right\}$$

admits an acceptable nonnegative integer solution.

5.7. Example (5.5 continued). To check whether the concept Root is finitely consistent in $\mathcal{K}_0$, we add to the system $\Psi_{\mathcal{K}_n}$ the inequality $r + rn \geq 1$, which forces R or RN to be populated, obtaining (after some simplifications)

$$r = o = 0$$
$$e_{RN,0} = e_{ON,0} = e_{E,R} = e_{E,RN} = 0$$
$$rn \leq e_{RN,ON} \leq 2 \cdot rn$$
$$on \leq e_{ON,ON} \leq 2 \cdot on$$

$$\text{on} = e_{RN,ON} + e_{ON,ON}$$
$$r + rn \geq 1.$$

It is easy to see that the inequalities in $\Psi_{\mathcal{K}_n}$ force both r and rn to get assigned value 0, and therefore the whole system admits no solution. This shows that the concept Root cannot be populated in any finite model of $\mathcal{K}_0$.

Similarly, to check whether the concept OtherNode is finitely consistent in $\mathcal{K}_0$, we can add the following inequality to $\Psi_{\mathcal{K}_n}$:

$$o + \text{on} \geq 1.$$

All solutions of the resulting system are acceptable. By simplifying the system we can verify that every solution assigns 0 to all unknowns except to on and to $e_{ON,ON}$, to which it assigns the same value. Let Sol be such a solution which assigns to on and to $e_{ON,ON}$ the positive integer k. We can obtain from Sol a finite model $\mathcal{I}$ of $\mathcal{K}_0$. Since ON must have k instances and it is the only compound concept with a nonempty extension, we define $\Delta^{\mathcal{I}} = \text{ON}^{\mathcal{I}} = \text{OtherNode}^{\mathcal{I}} = \{o_1, \ldots, o_k\}$. By setting $(\text{edge}, \text{ON}, \text{ON})^{\mathcal{I}} = \text{edge}^{\mathcal{I}} = \{(o_i, o_i) \mid i \in \{1, \ldots, k\}\}$, we obtain indeed a model of $\mathcal{K}_0$, although not one in which the edge relation has a tree-like structure.

The above result can be used for arbitrary concepts as well. An arbitrary concept C is consistent in $\mathcal{K}$ if and only if A_C is consistent in $\mathcal{K} \cup \{A_C \sqsubseteq C\}$, where A_C is an atomic concept not appearing in $\mathcal{K}$. As for the computational complexity of the method, since the existence of an acceptable solution of a system of inequalities can be verified in polynomial time in the size of the system, by Th. 5.6 we obtain the following upper bound for finite concept consistency.

5.8. THEOREM. *Whether a concept C is finitely consistent in a primitive $\mathcal{ALUNI}$ knowledge base $\mathcal{K}$ can be decided in worst case deterministic exponential time in the size of $\mathcal{K}$ plus the size of C.*

Since already for primitive $\mathcal{ALU}$ knowledge bases verifying concept consistency is EXPTIME-hard [Calvanese 1996b], the above method provides a computationally optimal reasoning procedure.

5.9. THEOREM. *Finite concept consistency in primitive $\mathcal{ALUNI}$ knowledge bases is EXPTIME-complete.*

The method we have described to decide concept consistency with respect to primitive $\mathcal{ALUNI}$ knowledge bases can be extended to handle also a wider class of knowledge bases, in which a negated atomic concept and, more in general, an arbitrary boolean combination of atomic concepts may appear on the left hand side of assertions. In particular, this makes it possible to deal also with knowledge bases containing definitions of concepts that are boolean combinations of atomic concepts, and perform finite model reasoning on such knowledge bases in deterministic exponential time.

Since $\mathcal{ALUNI}$ is not closed under negation we cannot immediately reduce logical implication to concept consistency. However, by making use of the observation above, the technique for deciding concept consistency can be extended to decide also finite logical implication $\mathcal{K} \models_f C_1 \sqsubseteq C_2$ in relevant cases in deterministic exponential time. More precisely, C_1 can be an arbitrary $\mathcal{ALUNI}$ concept and C_2 is required either to not contain the construct for universal quantification or to be of the form $\forall R.C'$ with C' a boolean combination of atomic concepts (see [Calvanese 1996c] for details). For the more general case, where also C_2 is an arbitrary concept expression, we need to resort to more involved techniques of higher computational complexity, which we briefly sketch in the next section.

5.3. Finite Model Reasoning in $\mathcal{ALCNI}$ and $\mathcal{ALCQI}$ Knowledge Bases

The method described in Section 5.2 can also be extended to solve the problem of finite model reasoning on free $\mathcal{ALCNI}$ knowledge bases [Calvanese 1996a]. Again, one can construct a system of linear inequalities and relate the existence of models for the knowledge base to the existence of particular solutions of the system. However the presence of arbitrary free inclusion assertions, and the higher expressiveness of the underlying language (in particular the presence of qualified existential quantification) make the construction of the system more involved than in the previous case. Indeed, while for primitive $\mathcal{ALUNI}$ knowledge bases it is sufficient to construct a system of inequalities whose size is simply exponential in the size of the knowledge base, the extension of the technique to $\mathcal{ALCNI}$ introduced by Calvanese [1996a] is based on and additional "expansion" step, which introduces an additional exponential blowup.

The additional expansion step becomes necessary due to the presence of assertions of the form $L_1 \sqsubseteq \exists R.L_2$. The most direct way to handle such assertions would be to leave their treatment to the system of inequalities (similarly to what is done for number restrictions). A natural extension of the system of inequalities would be to add for each assertion of the form $L_1 \sqsubseteq \exists P.L_2$ an inequality

$$\sum_{\substack{(P,\widehat{D}_1,\widehat{D}_2)\ | \\ L_1 \in \widehat{D}_1 \wedge L_2 \in \widehat{D}_2}} \mathrm{Var}((P,\widehat{D}_1,\widehat{D}_2)) \geq \sum_{\widehat{D}\ |\ L_1 \in \widehat{D}} \mathrm{Var}(\widehat{D}),$$

and a similar inequality for each assertion of the form $L_1 \sqsubseteq \exists P^-.L_2$. Unfortunately, imposing such conditions does not guarantee that from each acceptable nonnegative integer solution of the system a model of the knowledge base can be constructed, in which the number of instances of each compound concept and compound role is given by the value assigned by the solution to the corresponding unknown. The intuitive reason why this simple approach does not lead to the desired result for $\mathcal{ALCNI}$ knowledge bases, is that it relies on the fact that all objects that are instances of the same compound concept are characterized by the same properties. As already observed, the system of inequalities encodes local constraints on the number of connections that a single object may have, by means of global constraints on the total number of connections of a certain type. The differences on the types of connections between instances of different concepts are removed by considering compound concepts and roles. Once this is done, all instances of the same compound concept can be regarded as equivalent. The approach works for $\mathcal{ALUNI}$ knowledge bases, where no concept expression can distinguish between different instances of the same compound concept. This is no longer true if the concept expressions may contain qualified existential quantification, in which case splitting the domain into compound concepts is not sufficient to ensure that the instances have the same properties.

The problem can be dealt with by making a more fine-grained splitting of concepts and roles, which takes into account also the existence of connections of certain types. The resulting system of linear inequalities, whose acceptable solutions can be put into correspondence with finite models of the knowledge base, is doubly exponential in the size of the knowledge base (see [Calvanese 1996a] for details).

5.10. THEOREM. *Whether a concept C is finitely consistent in an $\mathcal{ALCNI}$ knowledge base $\mathcal{K}$ can be decided in worst case deterministic double exponential time in the size of $\mathcal{K}$ plus the size of C.*

Since $\mathcal{ALCNI}$ is closed under negation, the previous result provides also an upper bound for finite logical implication.

5.11. THEOREM. *Finite logical implication $\mathcal{K} \models_f C_1 \sqsubseteq C_2$ in $\mathcal{ALCNI}$ knowledge bases can be decided in worst case deterministic double exponential time in the sum of the sizes of $\mathcal{K}$, C_1, and C_2.*

The method can also be extended to knowledge bases containing qualified number restrictions, by making a separation of concepts based not only on the existence but also on the number of links of a certain type. It turns out that it is in fact sufficient to consider only intervals of numbers of links, where the ranges of these intervals are given by the numbers that effectively appear in the knowledge base. In this way it is still possible to keep the size of the resulting system of linear inequalities doubly exponential in the size of the knowledge base, and the same upper bounds as for $\mathcal{ALCNI}$ hold also for finite model reasoning over $\mathcal{ALCQI}$ knowledge bases.

An EXPTIME lower bound for finite model reasoning in $\mathcal{ALCNI}$ can be obtained by observing that e.g., $\mathcal{ALC}$ is a sublanguage of $\mathcal{ALCNI}$ which has the finite model property and for which (unrestricted and hence finite model) reasoning over a knowledge base is EXPTIME-hard. This leaves an exponential complexity gap between the known upper and lower bounds for finite model reasoning over $\mathcal{ALCNI}$ knowledge bases.

6. Beyond Basic Description Logics

Several additional constructs for building concept expressions besides those already present in $\mathcal{ALCQI}$ have been proposed in the literature. In this section we discuss the most important of these extensions, how they influence the reasoning process, and what modifications to the reasoning procedures are needed to take the additional constructs into account. Roughly speaking, the extensions for which a logic remains decidable are those for which the tree-model property is preserved [Vardi 1997], possibly after having performed a satisfiability preserving transformation of the knowledge base[11]. We remind the reader that this chapter concentrates on TBox reasoning only. Other extensions to $\mathcal{ALCQI}$ have been investigated that allow one to model and reason on individuals and ABoxes. We refer to [De Giacomo and Lenzerini 1996] for basic results on this subject.

6.1. Complex Roles

The EXPTIME-completeness result presented in Sect. 4 for unrestricted model reasoning on $\mathcal{ALCQI}$ knowledge bases has been extended to $\mathcal{ALCQI}_{reg}$, which is the DL obtained from $\mathcal{ALCQI}$ by adding the role constructs of PDLs, i.e., chaining, union, reflexive-transitive closure, and the identity role (tests in PDLs). In particular, qualified number restrictions, which are allowed only on atomic roles and inverse of atomic roles (called *basic roles* in the following), can be encoded as shown in Sect. 4.4, while reasoning in the resulting logic $\mathcal{ALCFI}_{reg}$ can be dealt with techniques based on automata on infinite trees [Calvanese 1996c, Calvanese, De Giacomo and Lenzerini 1999], which extend the techniques used for Converse-PDL by Vardi and Wolper [1986] and Vardi [1985].

$\mathcal{ALCQI}_{reg}$ and $\mathcal{ALCFI}_{reg}$ correspond to variants of PDLs whose computational properties had not been studied before. The PDL corresponding to $\mathcal{ALCQI}_{reg}$ is an extension of Converse-PDL with "graded modalities" [Fattorosi-Barnaba and De Caro 1985, Van der Hoek and de Rijke 1995] on atomic programs and their converse. While the PDL corresponding to $\mathcal{ALCFI}_{reg}$ is an extension of Deterministic-Converse-PDL [Vardi and Wolper 1986], in which determinism of both atomic programs and their inverse is determined by the properties of the starting state.

6.2. Boolean Constructs on Roles

The role constructs of $\mathcal{ALC} \cdot_{reg}$ allow one to build roles which are regular expressions over a set of basic roles. Since regular languages are closed under intersection and complementation, the intersection of roles and the complement of a role are already expressible in $\mathcal{ALC} \cdot_{reg}$, provided that we consider them as operators on the regular languages denoted by the role expressions. However, the more common approach both in PDLs and DLs is to consider boolean operators as applied to the binary relations denoted by the roles. The logics thus obtained are more expressive than traditional PDL [Harel 1984], but they lack for example the tree model property, and reasoning in the presence of these constructs is usually harder. We notice that

---

[11]The logics discussed by Danecki [1984] and Lutz and Sattler [2000] are an exception, being decidable without having the tree model property.

the semantics immediately implies that intersection of roles can be expressed by means of union and complementation.

Unrestricted satisfiability in PDL augmented with intersection of programs is decidable in deterministic double exponential time [Danecki 1984], and so is satisfiability in $\mathcal{ALC}_{reg}$ augmented with intersection of roles, even though these logics have neither the tree nor the finite model property. On the other hand, satisfiability in PDL augmented with complementation of programs is undecidable [Harel 1984] (Th. 2.34), and so is reasoning in $\mathcal{ALC}_{reg}$ augmented with complementation of roles. Also, Deterministic-PDL augmented with intersection of roles is highly undecidable [Harel 1985, Harel 1986], and since global functionality of roles (which corresponds to determinism of programs) can be expressed by means of local functionality, the undecidability carries over to $\mathcal{ALCF}_{reg}$ augmented with intersection of roles.

The proof of undecidability by Harel [1985] exploits a reduction from the unbounded *tiling* (or *domino*) *problem* [Berger 1966, Robinson 1971], which is the problem of checking whether a quadrant of the integer plane can be tiled using a finite set of tile types (i.e., square tiles with a color on each side), in such a way that adjacent tiles have the same color on the sides that touch[12]. We sketch the idea of the proof using the terminology of DLs, instead of that of PDLs. The reduction uses two roles right and up which are globally functional (i.e., $\forall(\text{right} \sqcup \text{up})^*.(\exists^{\le 1}\text{right} \sqcap \exists^{\le 1}\text{up})$) and denote pairs of tiles that are adjacent in the x and y directions, respectively. By means of intersection of roles (i.e., $\forall(\text{right} \sqcup \text{up})^*.\exists((\text{right} \circ \text{up}) \sqcap (\text{up} \circ \text{right}))$), right and up are constrained to effectively define a two-dimensional grid. Notice that to achieve this, it is necessary to impose for each point of the grid, that by following right $\circ$ up one reaches the same point as by following up $\circ$ right. The use of intersection of role chains turns out to be essential to force this condition. Transitive closure (i.e., $\forall(\text{right}\sqcup\text{up})^*.C$) is then exploited also to impose the required local matching constraints on all tiles of the grid.

The reduction above requires intersection to be applied to complex roles containing concatenations. The question therefore arises if decidability can be preserved if one restricts boolean operations to basic roles. This is indeed the case if complementation of basic roles is used only to express difference of roles. In fact, decidability in deterministic exponential time of unrestricted model reasoning holds for full $\mathcal{ALCQI}_{reg}$ extended with intersection and difference of basic roles, with the additional limitation that intersection or difference between an atomic role and an inverse atomic role may not be used [De Giacomo and Lenzerini 1995b, De Giacomo 1995]. The proof is based on the reification of roles (see Sect. 4.4.2) and exploits the possibility to impose boolean conditions on the objects that represent the reified instances of a role. Intersection of basic roles can also be expressed in the $\mathcal{SHIQ}$ DL [Horrocks and Sattler 1999], which extends $\mathcal{ALCQI}$ with transitive roles and role hierarchies.

---

[12]In fact the reduction is from the Π_1^1-complete –and thus highly undecidable– recurring tiling problem [Harel 1986], where one additionally requires that a certain tile occurs infinitely often on the x-axis.

Using a direct encoding into nonemptiness of automata on infinite trees, Lutz and Sattler [2000] show that $\mathcal{ALC}$ extended with full boolean operators on atomic roles (which are the only roles in the logic) is EXPTIME-complete. Observe that, by means of role negation, axioms can be internalized: the concept $\forall P.(C \Rightarrow C') \sqcap \forall \neg P.(C \Rightarrow C')$ corresponds to the assertion $C \sqsubseteq C'$.

Reification of roles can also be exploited to show decidability of finite model reasoning in knowledge bases in $\mathcal{ALCQI}$ augmented with intersection and difference of basic roles, with the same limitations as above. To this end qualified number restrictions are needed in order to express even unqualified number restrictions on the reified roles. For example, the concept $\exists^{\leq 2}$edge becomes, after reifying the role edge, $\exists^{\leq 2} V_1^-.A_{edge}$.

6.3. Role Value Maps

Another construct that stems from frame-systems and that provides additional useful means to specify structural properties of concepts is the so called *role value map* [Brachman and Schmolze 1985]. An object o is an instance of a role value map $(R_1 = R_2)$ if the set of objects that are connected to o via role R_1 equals the set of objects connected to o via role R_2. A generalization of role value map is *role value inclusion*, denoted $(R_1 \subseteq R_2)$, whose semantics is defined analogously to that of role value map, using set inclusion instead of set equality. Using these constructs one can denote, for example, by means of (owns $\subseteq$ lives_in $\circ$ made_in$^-$) the set of all persons that own only products manufactured in the country they live in.

When role value map is added, the logic looses the tree model property, and this construct leads immediately to undecidability of reasoning. For $\mathcal{ALC}_{reg}$ this can be shown by a reduction from the tiling problem in a similar way as to what is done by Harel [1985] for Deterministic-PDL with intersection of roles. In this case, role value map (i.e., $\forall$(right $\sqcup$ up)*.(right $\circ$ up = up $\circ$ right)) is used instead of role intersection to define the constraints on the grid. Undecidability holds however already for concept subsumption (with respect to the empty knowledge base) in $\mathcal{AL}$ augmented with role value map, where the involved roles are concatenations of atomic roles [Schmidt-Schauß 1989]. This is shown by a reduction from the word problem for semigroups, which is undecidable [Boone 1959].

Again, in order to show undecidability it is necessary to apply role value map to concatenations of roles. Indeed, if the application of role value map is restricted to boolean combinations of basic roles, it can be added to $\mathcal{ALCQI}_{reg}$ without influencing decidability and worst case complexity of reasoning. This follows directly from the decidability results for the extension with boolean constructs on basic roles, by observing that $(R_1 \subseteq R_2)$ is equivalent to $\forall (R_1 \sqcap \neg R_2).\bot$, and thus can be expressed using difference of roles. We observe also that *universal* and *existential role agreements* introduced by Hanschke [1992], which allow one to define concepts by posing various types of constraints that relate the sets of fillers of two roles, can be expressed by means of intersection and difference of roles. Thus reasoning in the presence of role agreements is decidable, provided these constructs are applied only to basic roles.

Another way to take role value map into account without loosing decidability is to restrict the use of such construct to functional roles, as usually done in the area of Feature Logics [Carpenter 1992]. Finally, we note that the role value map construct is also related to the notion of *path constraints* in database modeling [Buneman, Fan and Weinstein 1998].

6.4. Number Restrictions on Complex Roles

In $\mathcal{ALCQI}_{reg}$, the use of (qualified) number restrictions is limited to basic roles, which guarantees that the logic has the tree model property. This property is lost, together with decidability, if number restrictions may be imposed on arbitrary roles. The reduction to show undecidability is analogous to the one used for intersection of roles, except that now functionality of a complex role (i.e., $\exists^{\leq 1}(\text{right} \circ \text{up}) \sqcup (\text{up} \circ \text{right})$) is used instead of role intersection to define the grid.

Again, if one limits number restrictions to basic roles, as in $\mathcal{ALCQI}_{reg}$, then reasoning remains decidable. By exploiting reification of roles, De Giacomo and Lenzerini [1995b] show that decidability is not lost if one can impose number restrictions on roles that are composed by applying union, intersection, and difference to basic roles, with the same proviso as above, that direct and inverse roles may not appear together in such a boolean combination (see also [De Giacomo 1995] for details).

Another example of a decidable logic that does not have the tree model property is obtained by allowing the use of concatenation (but not transitive closure) inside number restrictions. Let us denote with $\mathcal{N}(X)$, where X is a subset of $\{\circ, \sqcup, \sqcap, ^-\}$, unqualified number restrictions applied to roles that are obtained by applying to atomic roles the role constructs in X. As shown by Baader and Sattler [1996, 1999], concept satisfiability in $\mathcal{ALCN}(\circ, \sqcap, \sqcup)$ is decidable in deterministic exponential time if intersection and union are restricted to *role chains* (i.e., concatenations of atomic roles) of the same length. Notice that, by the considerations above, decidability holds only for reasoning on concept expressions and is lost if one considers reasoning with respect to a knowledge base (or alternatively adds reflexive-transitive closure of roles). However, reasoning even with respect to the empty knowledge base is undecidable if one adds to $\mathcal{ALCN}$ number restrictions on more complex roles. In particular, this holds for $\mathcal{ALCN}(\circ, \sqcap)$ (if no constraints on the lengths of the chains are imposed) and for $\mathcal{ALCN}(\circ, \sqcup, ^-)$ [Baader and Sattler 1996, Baader and Sattler 1999]. The reductions again exploit the tiling problem, and make use of number restrictions on complex roles to simulate a universal role that is used for imposing conditions that hold for all points of the grid. Using a more complex reduction, Baader and Sattler [1999] show also that concept consistency in $\mathcal{ALCN}(\circ)$ (or concept satisfiability in $\mathcal{ALC}_{reg}\mathcal{N}(\circ)$) is undecidable.

Summing up, we can state that the borderline between decidability and undecidability of reasoning in the presence of number restrictions on complex roles has been traced quite precisely, although there are still some open problems. In particular, it is not known whether concept satisfiability in $\mathcal{ALCN}(\circ,^-)$, $\mathcal{ALC}_{reg}\mathcal{N}(\sqcap)$, or $\mathcal{ALC}_{reg}\mathcal{N}(\sqcup)$ is decidable [Baader and Sattler 1999]. Notice that decidability of knowledge base reasoning in $\mathcal{ALCN}(\sqcap,\sqcup,^-)$ follows from the decidability of $C2$, i.e., first order logic with two variables and counting quantifiers [Grädel, Otto and Rosen 1997, Grädel and Otto 1999].

6.5. Relations of Arbitrary Arity

DLs allow one to define concepts which denote classes of objects with common properties. These properties are defined by establishing relationships to other objects by means of roles. In traditional DLs, roles denote binary relations only, while some real world situations would be modeled more naturally by making use of relations of arity greater that two. Extensions of DLs with relations of arbitrary arity, which are interpreted as tuples of objects of the domain of interpretation, have been proposed in [Schmolze 1989, Catarci and Lenzerini 1993, De Giacomo and Lenzerini 1994b, De Giacomo 1995]. In order to use these relations for the specification of concepts, the notion of role is generalized to include also projections of relations on two of their components.

By exploiting reification (cfr. Sect. 4.4.2), reasoning in the presence of relations can be reduced to reasoning on ordinary DLs. A relation is reified by introducing a new concept and as many roles as the arity of the relation. A tuple of the relation is represented in the reified counterpart of the knowledge base by an instance of the corresponding concept, which is linked through each of the associated roles to an object representing the component of the tuple. Performing the reification requires however some attention, since, according to the standard semantics, in a relation there may not be two equal tuples (i.e., constituted by the same components in the same positions) in its extension. In the reified counterpart, on the other hand, one cannot explicitly rule out (e.g., by using specific assertions) that there are two objects o_1 and o_2 "representing" the same tuple, i.e., that are connected to exactly the same objects denoting the components of the tuple. A model of the reified counterpart of a knowledge base in which this situation occurs may not correspond directly to a model of the original knowledge base containing relations, since the two equivalent objects in general cannot be collapsed into a single object (representing the tuple) without violating assertions (e.g., cardinality constraints). However, a result analogous to Lem. 4.8 holds for relations of arbitrary arity. Therefore one does not need to take this constraint explicitly into account when reasoning on the reified counterpart of a knowledge base with relations.

By exploiting this idea, Calvanese, De Giacomo and Lenzerini [1997] introduce the DL $\mathcal{DLR}$, which extends $\mathcal{ALCQI}$ by boolean combinations of n-ary relations, and show that reasoning over $\mathcal{DLR}$ knowledge bases is again EXPTIME-decidable. Calvanese, De Giacomo and Lenzerini [1998a] propose a mechanism for specifying (unions of) conjunctive queries in $\mathcal{DLR}$, and present techniques for checking query containment. The problem of answering conjunctive queries using views over a $\mathcal{DLR}$ knowledge base is addressed by Calvanese, De Giacomo and Lenzerini [2000].

A method to reason with respect to finite models in the presence of relations of arbitrary arity is presented by Calvanese and Lenzerini [1994b, 1994a] in the context of a semantic and an object-oriented database model, respectively. The reasoning procedure, which represents a direct generalization of the one proposed in Sect. 5.2 to relations of arbitrary arity, does not exploit reification to handle relations but encodes directly the constraints on them into a system of linear inequalities.

6.6. Structured Objects, Well Foundedness, and Fixpoints

An alternative way to overcome the limitations that result from the restriction to unary and binary relationships, is to consider the interpretation domain as being constituted by objects with a complex structure, and extend the DLs with constructs that allow one to specify such structure [De Giacomo and Lenzerini 1995b]. This approach is in the spirit of object-oriented data models [Lecluse and Richard 1989, Bancilhon and Khoshafian 1989, Hull 1988, Bergamaschi and Nebel 1994]. In contrast with the idea of introducing n-ary relations, all aspects of the domain to be modeled can be represented in a uniform way, namely as concepts whose instances have certain structures. In particular, objects can either be unstructured or have the structure of a *set* or of a *tuple*. For objects having the structure of a set a particular role allows one to refer to the members of the set, and similarly each component of a tuple can be referred to by means of the (implicitly functional) role that labels it.

Reasoning in the presence of constructs for specifying structured objects is based on a reduction to reasoning in traditional DLs by exploiting reification of tuples and sets, and thus can be done in deterministic exponential time [De Giacomo and Lenzerini 1995a].

A limitation of the above approach is that there is no way to limit the depth of the structure of an object, and thus one cannot rule out non well-founded structures, such as a set that has itself as one of its elements, or a tuple that refers to itself via one of its components. To overcome this problem, Calvanese et al. [1995] and Calvanese [1996a] propose a *well-founded* construct $wf(R)$, which allows one to state that certain substructures of a model have to be finite. Formally $wf(R)$ is interpreted as the set of those objects which are not the starting point of an infinite sequence of objects, each connected to the next by means of role R. Thus it corresponds directly to the negation of a *repeat formula* in ΔPDL [Harel and Sherman 1982, Streett 1982]. By means of the well-founded construct one can express not only that the instances of a certain concept have a structure of finite depth, but also define inductive structures such as lists, finite trees, or directed acyclic graphs [Calvanese et al. 1995]. The technique to reason in $\mathcal{ALCQI}_{reg}$ extended with the well-founded construct is based on a reduction by means of reification to reasoning in ΔPDL extended with local functionality on direct and inverse programs, which is dealt with using automata-theoretic techniques [Calvanese 1996c].

Formulas including the well-founded construct can be considered as particular forms of fixpoint formulas. Fixpoints incorporated directly in the semantics of DLs have been first studied by Nebel [1991] and Baader [1996] for simple DLs. Fixpoints on concepts in their full generality have been investigated by Schild [1994] and De Giacomo and Lenzerini [1997]. The logics studied in these articles include constructs to define concepts which are least or greatest fixpoints of concept-equations. Decidability in deterministic exponential time for variants of these logics which include number restrictions has been established by exploiting a correspondence with the propositional μ-calculus [Kozen 1983, Streett and Emerson 1989]. Finally, Calvanese, De Giacomo and Lenzerini [1999] present the logic $\mathcal{ALCQI}_\mu$ which extends $\mathcal{ALCQI}_{reg}$ with the most general form of fixpoint on concepts. It also introduces $\mathcal{DLR}_\mu$, which in addition includes n-ary relations. Reasoning in $\mathcal{ALCQI}_\mu$ and in $\mathcal{DLR}_\mu$ is proved to be EXPTIME-decidable by a reduction to nonemptiness of two-way alternating automata on infinite trees [Vardi 1998].

7. Conclusions

DLs have been thoroughly investigated in the last fifteen years, especially with the goal of devising logic-based Knowledge Representation formalisms with a good compromise between expressive power and complexity of reasoning. Although the first studies on DLs concentrated on logics with limited sets of constructs, and tractable reasoning procedures, recent investigations on the features required in applications show the need for expressive DLs with decidable reasoning tasks. In this chapter, we have illustrated the main ideas that lead to the development of reasoning techniques for expressive DLs. Most of the described techniques rely on the correspondence between expressive DLs and Propositional Dynamic Logics. Such a correspondence does not allow one to directly derive sound and complete reasoning procedures for DLs. Indeed, we have illustrated several sophisticated techniques for reducing reasoning in expressive DLs to reasoning in Propositional Dynamic Logics. Also, we have presented specialized techniques for finite model reasoning in expressive DLs.

Besides being of interest from a scientific point of view, the decidability results described in this chapter have stimulated the investigation of implemented systems that are able to reason on expressive DLs. Interesting results on this aspect are reported by Horrocks and Sattler [1999], Horrocks et al. [1999], and Horrocks and Patel-Schneider [1999].

Bibliography

Artale A. and Franconi E. [1994], A computational account for a description logic of time and action, *in* J. Doyle, E. Sandewall and P. Torasso, eds, 'Proc. of the 4th Int. Conf. on the Principles of Knowledge Representation and Reasoning (KR'94)', Morgan Kaufmann, Los Altos, Bonn (Germany), pp. 3–14.

Baader F. [1991], Augmenting concept languages by transitive closure of roles: An alternative to terminological cycles, *in* 'Proc. of the 12th Int. Joint Conf. on Artificial Intelligence (IJCAI'91)', Sydney (Australia).

Baader F. [1996], 'Using automata theory for characterizing the semantics of terminological cycles', *Ann. of Mathematics and Artificial Intelligence* **18**, 175–219.

BAADER F. AND HOLLUNDER B. [1995], 'Embedding defaults into terminological knowledge representation formalisms', *J. of Automated Reasoning* **14**, 149–180.

BAADER F., HOLLUNDER B., NEBEL B., PROFITLICH H.-J. AND FRANCONI E. [1992], An empirical analysis of optimization techniques for terminological representation systems, in 'Proc. of the 3rd Int. Conf. on the Principles of Knowledge Representation and Reasoning (KR'92)', Morgan Kaufmann, Los Altos, pp. 270–281.

BAADER F. AND SATTLER U. [1996], Number restrictions on complex roles in description logics: A preliminary report, in 'Proc. of the 5th Int. Conf. on the Principles of Knowledge Representation and Reasoning (KR'96)', pp. 328–338.

BAADER F. AND SATTLER U. [1999], 'Expressive number restrictions in description logics', *J. of Logic and Computation* **9**(3), 319–350.

BAADER F. AND SATTLER U. [2000], Tableau algorithms for description logics, in R. Dyckhoff, ed., 'Proc. of the 4th Int. Conf. on Analytic Tableaux and Related Methods (TABLEAUX 2000)', Vol. 1847 of *Lecture Notes in Artificial Intelligence*, Springer-Verlag, pp. 1–18.

BANCILHON F. AND KHOSHAFIAN S. [1989], 'A calculus for complex objects', *J. of Computer and System Sciences* **38**(2), 326–340.

BEN-ARI M., HALPERN J. Y. AND PNUELI A. [1982], 'Deterministic propositional dynamic logic: Finite models, complexity, and completeness', *J. of Computer and System Sciences* **25**, 402–417.

BERGAMASCHI S. AND NEBEL B. [1994], 'Acquisition and validation of complex object database schemata supporting multiple inheritance', *Applied Intelligence* **4**(2), 185–203.

BERGAMASCHI S. AND SARTORI C. [1992], 'On taxonomic reasoning in conceptual design', *ACM Trans. on Database Systems* **17**(3), 385–422.

BERGER R. [1966], 'The undecidability of the dominoe problem', *Mem. Amer. Math. Soc.* **66**, 1–72.

BLACKBURN P., DE RIJKE M. AND VENEMA Y. [2000], Modal logic. To appear.

BLANCO J. L., ILLARRAMENDI A. AND GOÑI A. [1994], 'Building a federated relational database system: An approach using a knowledge-based system', *J. of Intelligent and Cooperative Information Systems* **3**(4), 415–455.

BOONE W. W. [1959], 'The word problem', *Ann. of Mathematics* **2**(70), 207–265.

BORGIDA A. [1995], 'Description logics in data management', *IEEE Trans. on Knowledge and Data Engineering* **7**(5), 671–682.

BORGIDA A. AND PATEL-SCHNEIDER P. F. [1994], 'A semantics and complete algorithm for subsumption in the CLASSIC description logic', *J. of Artificial Intelligence Research* **1**, 277–308.

BRACHMAN R. J. AND LEVESQUE H. J. [1984], The tractability of subsumption in frame-based description languages, in 'Proc. of the 4th Nat. Conf. on Artificial Intelligence (AAAI'84)', pp. 34–37.

BRACHMAN R. J. AND SCHMOLZE J. G. [1985], 'An overview of the KL-ONE knowledge representation system', *Cognitive Science* **9**(2), 171–216.

BUCHHEIT M., DONINI F. M., NUTT W. AND SCHAERF A. [1994], Terminological systems revisited: Terminology = schema + views, in 'Proc. of the 12th Nat. Conf. on Artificial Intelligence (AAAI'94)', Seattle (USA), pp. 199–204.

BUCHHEIT M., DONINI F. M. AND SCHAERF A. [1993], 'Decidable reasoning in terminological knowledge representation systems', *J. of Artificial Intelligence Research* **1**, 109–138.

BUNEMAN P., FAN W. AND WEINSTEIN S. [1998], Path constraints on semistructured and structured data, in 'Proc. of the 17th ACM SIGACT SIGMOD SIGART Symp. on Principles of Database Systems (PODS'98)', pp. 129–138.

CALVANESE D. [1996a], Finite model reasoning in description logics, in L. C. Aiello, J. Doyle and S. C. Shapiro, eds, 'Proc. of the 5th Int. Conf. on the Principles of Knowledge Representation and Reasoning (KR'96)', Morgan Kaufmann, Los Altos, pp. 292–303.

CALVANESE D. [1996*b*], Reasoning with inclusion axioms in description logics: Algorithms and complexity, *in* W. Wahlster, ed., 'Proc. of the 12th Eur. Conf. on Artificial Intelligence (ECAI'96)', John Wiley & Sons, pp. 303–307.

CALVANESE D. [1996*c*], Unrestricted and Finite Model Reasoning in Class-Based Representation Formalisms, PhD thesis, Dipartimento di Informatica e Sistemistica, Università di Roma "La Sapienza". Available at http://www.dis.uniroma1.it/pub/calvanes/thesis.ps.gz.

CALVANESE D., DE GIACOMO G. AND LENZERINI M. [1995], Structured objects: Modeling and reasoning, *in* 'Proc. of the 4th Int. Conf. on Deductive and Object-Oriented Databases (DOOD'95)', Vol. 1013 of *Lecture Notes in Computer Science*, Springer-Verlag, pp. 229–246.

CALVANESE D., DE GIACOMO G. AND LENZERINI M. [1997], Conjunctive query containment in Description Logics with *n*-ary relations, *in* 'Proc. of the 1997 Description Logic Workshop (DL'97)', pp. 5–9.

CALVANESE D., DE GIACOMO G. AND LENZERINI M. [1998*a*], On the decidability of query containment under constraints, *in* 'Proc. of the 17th ACM SIGACT SIGMOD SIGART Symp. on Principles of Database Systems (PODS'98)', pp. 149–158.

CALVANESE D., DE GIACOMO G. AND LENZERINI M. [1998*b*], What can knowledge representation do for semi-structured data?, *in* 'Proc. of the 15th Nat. Conf. on Artificial Intelligence (AAAI'98)', pp. 205–210.

CALVANESE D., DE GIACOMO G. AND LENZERINI M. [1999], Reasoning in expressive description logics with fixpoints based on automata on infinite trees, *in* 'Proc. of the 16th Int. Joint Conf. on Artificial Intelligence (IJCAI'99)', pp. 84–89.

CALVANESE D., DE GIACOMO G. AND LENZERINI M. [2000], Answering queries using views over description logics knowledge bases, *in* 'Proc. of the 17th Nat. Conf. on Artificial Intelligence (AAAI 2000)', pp. 386–391.

CALVANESE D. AND LENZERINI M. [1994*a*], Making object-oriented schemas more expressive, *in* 'Proc. of the 13th ACM SIGACT SIGMOD SIGART Symp. on Principles of Database Systems (PODS'94)', ACM Press and Addison Wesley, Minneapolis (Minnesota, USA), pp. 243–254.

CALVANESE D. AND LENZERINI M. [1994*b*], On the interaction between ISA and cardinality constraints, *in* 'Proc. of the 10th IEEE Int. Conf. on Data Engineering (ICDE'94)', IEEE Computer Society Press, Houston (Texas, USA), pp. 204–213.

CALVANESE D., LENZERINI M. AND NARDI D. [1994], A unified framework for class based representation formalisms, *in* J. Doyle, E. Sandewall and P. Torasso, eds, 'Proc. of the 4th Int. Conf. on the Principles of Knowledge Representation and Reasoning (KR'94)', Morgan Kaufmann, Los Altos, Bonn (Germany), pp. 109–120.

CALVANESE D., LENZERINI M. AND NARDI D. [1999], 'Unifying class-based representation formalisms', *J. of Artificial Intelligence Research* 11, 199–240.

CARPENTER B. [1992], *The Logic of Typed Feature Structures*, Cambridge University Press.

CATARCI T. AND LENZERINI M. [1993], 'Representing and using interschema knowledge in cooperative information systems', *J. of Intelligent and Cooperative Information Systems* 2(4), 375–398.

CHEN P. P. [1976], 'The Entity-Relationship model: Toward a unified view of data', *ACM Trans. on Database Systems* 1(1), 9–36.

CLARKE E. AND SCHLINGLOFF H. [2001], Model checking, *in* A. Robinson and A. Voronkov, eds, 'Handbook of Automated Reasoning', Vol. II, Elsevier Science, chapter 24, pp. 1635–1790.

COSMADAKIS S. S., KANELLAKIS P. C. AND VARDI M. [1990], 'Polynomial-time implication problems for unary inclusion dependencies', *J. of the ACM* 37(1), 15–46.

DANECKI R. [1984], Nondeterministic Propositional Dynamic Logic with intersection is decidable, *in* 'Proc. of the 5th Symp. on Computation Theory', Vol. 208 of *Lecture Notes in Computer Science*, Springer-Verlag, pp. 34–53.

DE GIACOMO G. [1995], Decidability of Class-Based Knowledge Representation Formalisms, PhD thesis, Dipartimento di Informatica e Sistemistica, Università di Roma "La Sapienza".

DE GIACOMO G. [1996], 'Eliminating "converse" from Converse PDL', *J. of Logic, Language and Information* **5**, 193–208.

DE GIACOMO G. AND LENZERINI M. [1994a], Boosting the correspondence between description logics and propositional dynamic logics, in 'Proc. of the 12th Nat. Conf. on Artificial Intelligence (AAAI'94)', AAAI Press/The MIT Press, pp. 205–212.

DE GIACOMO G. AND LENZERINI M. [1994b], Description logics with inverse roles, functional restrictions, and n-ary relations, in 'Proc. of the 4th Eur. Workshop on Logics in Artificial Intelligence (JELIA'94)', Vol. 838 of *Lecture Notes in Artificial Intelligence*, Springer-Verlag, pp. 332–346.

DE GIACOMO G. AND LENZERINI M. [1995a], Enhanced propositional dynamic logic for reasoning about concurrent actions (extended abstract), in 'Working Notes of the AAAI 1995 Spring Symposium on Extending Theories of Action: Formal and Practical Applications', pp. 62–67.

DE GIACOMO G. AND LENZERINI M. [1995b], What's in an aggregate: Foundations for description logics with tuples and sets, in 'Proc. of the 14th Int. Joint Conf. on Artificial Intelligence (IJCAI'95)', pp. 801–807.

DE GIACOMO G. AND LENZERINI M. [1996], TBox and ABox reasoning in expressive description logics, in L. C. Aiello, J. Doyle and S. C. Shapiro, eds, 'Proc. of the 5th Int. Conf. on the Principles of Knowledge Representation and Reasoning (KR'96)', Morgan Kaufmann, Los Altos, pp. 316–327.

DE GIACOMO G. AND LENZERINI M. [1997], 'A uniform framework for concept definitions in description logics', *J. of Artificial Intelligence Research* **6**, 87–110.

DE GIACOMO G. AND MASSACCI F. [2000], 'Combining deduction and model checking into tableaux and algorithms for converse-pdl', *Information and Computation* **160**(1–2).

DEVAMBU P., BRACHMAN R. J., SELFRIDGE P. J. AND BALLARD B. W. [1991], 'LASSIE: A knowledge-based software information system', *Communications of the ACM* **34**(5), 36–49.

DONINI F. M., LENZERINI M., NARDI D. AND NUTT W. [1991], Tractable concept languages, in 'Proc. of the 12th Int. Joint Conf. on Artificial Intelligence (IJCAI'91)', Sydney (Australia), pp. 458–463.

DONINI F. M., LENZERINI M., NARDI D. AND NUTT W. [1997], 'The complexity of concept languages', *Information and Computation* **134**, 1–58.

DONINI F. M., LENZERINI M., NARDI D., NUTT W. AND SCHAERF A. [1992], Adding epistemic operators to concept languages, in 'Proc. of the 3rd Int. Conf. on the Principles of Knowledge Representation and Reasoning (KR'92)', Morgan Kaufmann, Los Altos, pp. 342–353.

DONINI F. M., LENZERINI M., NARDI D. AND SCHAERF A. [1994], 'Deduction in concept languages: From subsumption to instance checking', *J. of Logic and Computation* **4**(4), 423–452.

DONINI F. M., LENZERINI M., NARDI D. AND SCHAERF A. [1996], Reasoning in description logics, in G. Brewka, ed., 'Principles of Knowledge Representation', Studies in Logic, Language and Information, CSLI Publications, pp. 193–238.

DOYLE J. AND PATIL R. S. [1991], 'Two theses of knowledge representation: Language restrictions, taxonomic classification, and the utility of representation services', *Artificial Intelligence* **48**, 261–297.

EBBINGHAUS H.-D. AND FLUM J. [1999], *Finite Model Theory*, second edition edn, Springer-Verlag.

FATTOROSI-BARNABA M. AND DE CARO F. [1985], 'Graded modalities I', *Studia Logica* **44**, 197–221.

FINE K. [1972], 'In so many possible worlds', *Notre Dame J. of Formal Logic* **13**(4), 516–520.

FISCHER M. J. AND LADNER R. E. [1979], 'Propositional dynamic logic of regular programs', *J. of Computer and System Sciences* **18**, 194–211.

GOLDBLATT R. [1992], *Logics of Time and Computation*, Vol. 7 of *Lecture Notes*, second edn, Center for the Study of Language and Information.

GRÄDEL E. AND OTTO M. [1999], 'On logics with two variables', *Theoretical Computer Science* **224**, 73–113.

GRÄDEL E., OTTO M. AND ROSEN E. [1997], Two-variable logic with counting is decidable, in 'Proc. of the 12th IEEE Symp. on Logic in Computer Science (LICS'97)', pp. 306–317.

HANSCHKE P. [1992], Specifying role interaction in concept languages, in 'Proc. of the 3rd Int. Conf. on the Principles of Knowledge Representation and Reasoning (KR'92)', Morgan Kaufmann, Los Altos, pp. 318–329.

HAREL D. [1984], Dynamic logic, in 'Handbook of Philosophical Logic', Vol. 2, D. Reidel, Dordrecht (Holland), pp. 497–640.

HAREL D. [1985], 'Recurring dominoes: Making the highly undecidable highly understandable', Ann. of Discrete Mathematics 24, 51–72.

HAREL D. [1986], 'Effective transformations of infinite trees, with applications to high undecidability, dominoes, and fairness', J. of the ACM 33(1), 224–248.

HAREL D. AND SHERMAN R. [1982], 'Looping vs. repeating in dynamic logic', Information and Computation 55, 175–192.

HOLLUNDER B. [1996], 'Consistency checking reduced to satisfiability of concepts in terminological systems', Ann. of Mathematics and Artificial Intelligence 18(2–4), 133–157.

HOLLUNDER B. AND BAADER F. [1991], Qualifying number restrictions in concept languages, Technical Report RR-91-03, Deutsches Forschungszentrum für Künstliche Intelligenz (DFKI), Kaiserslautern (Germany). An abridged version appeared in Proc. of the 2nd Int. Conf. on the Principles of Knowledge Representation and Reasoning (KR'91).

HORROCKS I. [1998], Using an expressive description logic: FaCT or fiction?, in 'Proc. of the 6th Int. Conf. on Principles of Knowledge Representation and Reasoning (KR'98)', pp. 636–647.

HORROCKS I. AND PATEL-SCHNEIDER P. F. [1999], 'Optimizing description logic subsumption', J. of Logic and Computation 9(3), 267–293.

HORROCKS I. AND SATTLER U. [1999], 'A description logic with transitive and inverse roles and role hierarchies', J. of Logic and Computation 9(3), 385–410.

HORROCKS I., SATTLER U. AND TOBIES S. [1999], Practical reasoning for expressive description logics, in H. Ganzinger, D. McAllester and A. Voronkov, eds, 'Proc. of the 6th Int. Conf. on Logic for Programming and Automated Reasoning (LPAR'99)', number 1705 in 'Lecture Notes in Artificial Intelligence', Springer-Verlag, pp. 161–180.

HULL R. [1988], A survey of theoretical research on typed complex database objects, in J. Paredaens, ed., 'Databases', Academic Press, pp. 193–256.

KOZEN D. [1983], 'Results on the propositional μ-calculus', Theoretical Computer Science 27, 333–354.

KOZEN D. AND TIURYN J. [1990], Logics of programs, in J. van Leeuwen, ed., 'Handbook of Theoretical Computer Science — Formal Models and Semantics', Elsevier Science Publishers (North-Holland), Amsterdam, pp. 789–840.

KRACHT M. AND WOLTER F. [2000], 'Normal modal logics can simulate all others', J. of Symbolic Logic . To appear.

LECLUSE C. AND RICHARD P. [1989], Modeling complex structures in object-oriented databases, in 'Proc. of the 8th ACM SIGACT SIGMOD SIGART Symp. on Principles of Database Systems (PODS'89)', pp. 362–369.

LENZERINI M. AND NOBILI P. [1990], 'On the satisfiability of dependency constraints in entity-relationship schemata', Information Systems 15(4), 453–461.

LEVESQUE H. J. AND BRACHMAN R. J. [1987], 'Expressiveness and tractability in knowledge representation and reasoning', Computational Intelligence 3, 78–93.

LEVY A. Y., RAJARAMAN A. AND ORDILLE J. J. [1996], Query answering algorithms for information agents, in 'Proc. of the 13th Nat. Conf. on Artificial Intelligence (AAAI'96)', pp. 40–47.

LUTZ C. AND SATTLER U. [2000], Mary likes all cats, in F. Baader and U. Sattler, eds, 'Proc. of the 2000 Description Logic Workshop (DL 2000)', CEUR Electronic Workshop Proceedings http://sunsite.informatik.rwth-aachen.de/Publications/CEUR-WS/Vol-33/, pp. 213–226.

NEBEL B. [1988], 'Computational complexity of terminological reasoning in BACK', Artificial Intelligence 34(3), 371–383.

NEBEL B. [1990], 'Terminological reasoning is inherently intractable', *Artificial Intelligence* **43**, 235–249.

NEBEL B. [1991], Terminological cycles: Semantics and computational properties, *in* J. F. Sowa, ed., 'Principles of Semantic Networks', Morgan Kaufmann, Los Altos, pp. 331–361.

OHLBACH H., NONNENGART A., DE RIJKE M. AND GABBAY D. [2001], Encoding two-valued nonclassical logics in classical logic, *in* A. Robinson and A. Voronkov, eds, 'Handbook of Automated Reasoning', Vol. II, Elsevier Science, chapter 21, pp. 1403–1486.

PAPADIMITRIOU C. H. [1981], 'On the complexity of integer programming', *J. of the ACM* **28**(4), 765–768.

PARIKH R. [1981], Propositional dynamic logic of programs: A survey, *in* 'Proc. of the 1st Workshop on Logics of Programs', Vol. 125 of *Lecture Notes in Computer Science*, Springer-Verlag, pp. 102–144.

PATEL-SCHNEIDER P. F. [1989], 'A four-valued semantics for terminological logic', *Artificial Intelligence* **38**(1), 319–351.

PRATT V. R. [1979], Models of program logic, *in* 'Proc. of the 20th Annual Symp. on the Foundations of Computer Science (FOCS'79)', pp. 115–122.

PRATT V. R. [1980], 'A near-optimal method for reasoning about action', *J. of Computer and System Sciences* **20**, 231–255.

ROBINSON R. [1971], 'Undecidability and nonperiodicity of tilings on the plane', *Inventiones Math.* **12**, 177–209.

SCHAERF A. [1994], 'Reasoning with individuals in concept languages', *Data and Knowledge Engineering* **13**(2), 141–176.

SCHILD K. [1991], A correspondence theory for terminological logics: Preliminary report, *in* 'Proc. of the 12th Int. Joint Conf. on Artificial Intelligence (IJCAI'91)', Sydney (Australia), pp. 466–471.

SCHILD K. [1994], Terminological cycles and the propositional μ-calculus, *in* J. Doyle, E. Sandewall and P. Torasso, eds, 'Proc. of the 4th Int. Conf. on the Principles of Knowledge Representation and Reasoning (KR'94)', Morgan Kaufmann, Los Altos, Bonn (Germany), pp. 509–520.

SCHMIDT-SCHAUSS M. [1989], Subsumption in KL-ONE is undecidable, *in* R. J. Brachman, H. J. Levesque and R. Reiter, eds, 'Proc. of the 1st Int. Conf. on the Principles of Knowledge Representation and Reasoning (KR'89)', Morgan Kaufmann, Los Altos, pp. 421–431.

SCHMIDT-SCHAUSS M. AND SMOLKA G. [1991], 'Attributive concept descriptions with complements', *Artificial Intelligence* **48**(1), 1–26.

SCHMOLZE J. G. [1989], Terminological knowledge representation systems supporting n-ary terms, *in* 'Proc. of the 1st Int. Conf. on the Principles of Knowledge Representation and Reasoning (KR'89)', pp. 432–443.

SHETH A. P., GALA S. K. AND NAVATHE S. B. [1993], 'On automatic reasoning for schema integration', *J. of Intelligent and Cooperative Information Systems* **2**(1), 23–50.

STREETT R. S. [1982], 'Propositional dynamic logic of looping and converse is elementarily decidable', *Information and Computation* **54**, 121–141.

STREETT R. S. AND EMERSON E. A. [1989], 'An automata theoretic decision procedure for the propositional μ-calculus', *Information and Computation* **81**, 249–264.

TOBIES S. [1999a], On the complexity of counting in description logics, *in* 'Proc. of the 1999 Description Logic Workshop (DL'99)', CEUR Electronic Workshop Proceedings http://sunsite.informatik.rwth-aachen.de/Publications/CEUR-WS/Vol-22/, pp. 105–109.

TOBIES S. [1999b], A PSPACE algorithm for graded modal logic, *in* H. Ganzinger, ed., 'Proc. of the 16th Int. Conf. on Automated Deduction (CADE'99)', Vol. 1632 of *Lecture Notes in Artificial Intelligence*, Springer-Verlag, pp. 52–66.

ULLMAN J. D. [1997], Information integration using logical views, *in* 'Proc. of the 6th Int. Conf. on Database Theory (ICDT'97)', Vol. 1186 of *Lecture Notes in Computer Science*, Springer-Verlag, pp. 19–40.

Van der Hoek W. [1992], 'On the semantics of graded modalities', *J. of Applied Non-Classical Logics* **2**(1), 81–123.

Van der Hoek W. and de Rijke M. [1995], 'Counting objects', *J. of Logic and Computation* **5**(3), 325–345.

Vardi M. Y. [1985], The taming of converse: Reasoning about two-way computations, *in* R. Parikh, ed., 'Proc. of the 4th Workshop on Logics of Programs', Vol. 193 of *Lecture Notes in Computer Science*, Springer-Verlag, pp. 413–424.

Vardi M. Y. [1997], Why is modal logic so robustly decidable, *in* 'DIMACS Series in Discrete Mathematics and Theoretical Computer Science', Vol. 31, American Mathematical Society, pp. 149–184.

Vardi M. Y. [1998], Reasoning about the past with two-way automata, *in* 'Proc. of the 25th Int. Coll. on Automata, Languages and Programming (ICALP'98)', Vol. 1443 of *Lecture Notes in Computer Science*, Springer-Verlag, pp. 628–641.

Vardi M. Y. and Wolper P. [1984], Automata-theoretic techniques for modal logics of programs, *in* 'Proc. of the 16th ACM SIGACT Symp. on Theory of Computing (STOC'84)', pp. 446–455.

Vardi M. Y. and Wolper P. [1986], 'Automata-theoretic techniques for modal logics of programs', *J. of Computer and System Sciences* **32**, 183–221.

Weida R. and Litman D. [1992], Terminological reasoning with constraint networks and an application to plan recognition, *in* 'Proc. of the 3rd Int. Conf. on the Principles of Knowledge Representation and Reasoning (KR'92)', Morgan Kaufmann, Los Altos, pp. 282–293.

Woods W. A. and Schmolze J. G. [1992], The KL-ONE family, *in* F. W. Lehmann, ed., 'Semantic Networks in Artificial Intelligence', Pergamon Press, pp. 133–178. Published as a special issue of *Computers & Mathematics with Applications*, Volume 23, Number 2–9.

Index

CHAPTER 24

Model Checking

Edmund M. Clarke

Bernd-Holger Schlingloff

SECOND READERS: Nikolaj Bjorner and Perdita Stevens.

Contents

HANDBOOK OF AUTOMATED REASONING
Edited by Alan Robinson and Andrei Voronkov

1. Introduction

Model checking is an automatic technique for verifying correctness properties of safety-critical reactive systems. This method has been successfully applied to find subtle errors in complex industrial designs such as sequential circuits, communication protocols and digital controllers [Browne, Clarke and Dill 1985, Clarke, Emerson and Sistla 1986, Clarke, Long and McMillan 1991, Burch, Clarke, Dill, Long and McMillan 1994]. It is expected that besides classical quality assurance measures such as static analysis and testing, model checking will become a standard procedure in the design of reactive systems.

A *reactive system* [Harel and Pnueli 1985, Manna and Pnueli 1992, Manna and Pnueli 1995] consists of several components which are designed to interact with one another and with the system's environment. In contrast to *functional* (or *transformational*) systems, in which the semantics is given as a function from input to output values, a reactive system is specified by its temporal properties. A (temporal) *property* is a set of desired behaviors in time; the system satisfies the property if each execution of the system belongs to this set. From a logical viewpoint, the system is described by a semantical (Kripke-)*model*, and a property is described by a logical *formula*. Arguing about system correctness, therefore, amounts to determining the *truth of formulas in models*.

In order to be able to perform such a verification, one needs a *modelling language* in which the system can be described, a *specification language* for the formulation of properties, and a deductive *calculus* or *algorithm* for the verification process. Usually, the system to be verified is modeled as a (finite) state transition graph, and the properties are formulated in an appropriate propositional temporal logic. An efficient search procedure is then used to determine whether or not the state transition graph satisfies the temporal formulas. When model checking was first developed in 1981 [Clarke and Emerson 1981, Emerson and Clarke 1982, Quielle and Sifakis 1981], it was only possible to handle concurrent systems with a few thousand states. In the last few years, however, the size of the concurrent systems that can be handled has increased dramatically. By using sophisticated data structures and heuristic search procedures, it is now possible to check systems many orders of magnitude larger [Burch, Clarke, McMillan, Dill and Hwang 1992].

Much of the success of model checking is due to the fact that it is a fully automatic verification method. Interactive methods are more general but harder to use; automatic methods have a limited range but are more likely to be accepted. In interactive verification, the user provides the overall proof strategy; the machine augments this by

- checking the correctness of each step,
- maintaining a list of assumptions and subgoals,
- applying the rules and substitutions which the user indicates, and by
- searching for applicable transformation rules and assumptions.

Sophisticated tools are also able to prove certain lemmas automatically, usually by applying a heuristic search. Although there has been considerable research on the use of theorem provers, term rewriting systems and proof checkers for verification, these techniques are time consuming and often require a great deal of manual intervention. Moreover, since most interactive provers are designed for undecidable languages (e.g., first or higher order logic), the proof process can never be completely automatic. User interaction is required, e.g., to find loop invariants or inductive hypotheses, and only an experienced user can perform a nontrivial proof.

On the other hand, with model checking all the user has to provide is a model of the system and a formulation of the property to be proven. The verification tool will either terminate with an answer indicating that the model satisfies the formula or show why the formula fails to hold in the model. These counterexamples are particularly helpful in locating errors in the model or system.

With the completely automatic approach it may be necessary for the model checking algorithm to traverse all reachable states of the system. This is only possible if the state space is finite. Whereas other automated deduction methods may be able to handle some infinite-state problems, model checking usually is constrained to a finite abstraction. In fact, model checking algorithms can be regarded as decision procedures for temporal properties of finite-state reactive systems. However, many interesting systems like sequential circuits or network protocols are finite state. Moreover, in the design of safety critical systems it is often possible to separate the (finite state) control structure from the (infinite state) data structure of a given module. Finally, in many cases it is possible to *abstract* an infinite domain into an appropriate finite one, such that "interesting" properties are preserved. In an 'a posteriori' verification, some efforts may be necessary to construct such an abstraction from a given program. In a structured software development process, however, the abstract system often arises naturally during an early design phase.

A main impediment of the fully automatic approach is the state explosion: if any state of the system is uniquely described by n state bits, then there are 2^n possible states the system can be in. At the present time, the number of states that can be represented *explicitly* (e.g., by lists or hash tables) is approximately 10^6. In [Burch, Clarke, McMillan, Dill and Hwang 1992, McMillan 1993], *binary decision diagrams* (BDDs) were used to represent state spaces *symbolically*. With this technique, models with several hundred state bits and more than 10^{100} reachable states can be checked. Because of this and other technical advances in the available tools it is now possible to verify reactive systems of realistic industrial complexity, and a number of major companies including Intel, Motorola, ATT, Fujitsu and Siemens have started using symbolic model checkers to verify actual designs.

We now describe a concrete example of a nontrivial application, where model checking has been used to improve a proposed international standard. Consider the cache coherence protocol described in the draft IEEE Futurebus+ standard [IEEE 1994]. This protocol is required to insure *coherence*: consistency of data in hierarchical systems composed of many processors and caches interconnected by multiple bus segments. Such protocols are notoriously complex and, therefore, quite difficult to debug. The Futurebus+ protocol maintains coherence by having the individual caches observe all bus transactions. In order to increase performance, the protocol allows transactions to be *split*. That is, the completion of a transaction may be delayed and the bus freed. Then, it is possible to service local requests while the remote request is being processed. At some later time, an explicit response is issued to complete the transaction. Consider a sample configuration with two processors P_1 and P_2 accessing data from a common memory via a single bus (see Fig. 1 on page 1640). Initially, neither processor has a copy of the data in its cache; they are said to be in the invalid state. Processor P_1 issues a read_shared request to obtain a readable copy of the data from memory. P_2 may observe this transaction and also obtain a readable copy, such that at the end of the transaction, both caches contain a shared_unmodified copy of the data. Next, if P_1 decides to modify the data, the copy held by P_2 must be eliminated in order to maintain coherence. Therefore, P_1 issues an invalidate transaction on the bus. When P_2 notices this transaction, it purges the data from its cache. After executing the invalidate-transaction, P_1 now has an exclusive copy of the data.

The standard specifies the possible states of the cache data within each processor and how this state is updated during each possible transaction. It consists of roughly 300 so-called *attributes*, which are essentially boolean variables together with some rules for setting and clearing them. In the automated verification of the Futurebus+ protocol described in [Clarke, Grumberg, Hiraishi, Jha, Long, McMillan and Ness 1993], these attributes were transformed into the input language of the SMV model checker [McMillan 1993]. For example, the following SMV code fragment indicates how the cache state is updated when the cache issues a read_shared transaction:

```
next(state) :=
  case CMD=read_shared:
    case state=invalid:
      case !SR & !TF: exclusive_unmodified;
            !SR       : shared_unmodified;
            1         : invalid;
      esac;
      ...
    esac;
    ...
  esac;
```

If the transaction is not split (!SR), then the data will be supplied to the cache. Either no other caches will read the data (!TF), in which case the cache obtains an exclusive_unmodified copy, or some other cache also obtains the data, and everyone obtains shared_unmodified copies. If the transaction is split, the cache data remains in the invalid state.

The model for the cache coherence protocol consists of approximately 2300 lines of SMV code (not counting comments). The model is highly nondeterministic, both to reduce the complexity of verification by hiding details, and to cover allowed design choices. This model is compiled into an internal BDD representation by the SMV program. Correctness properties are formulated in the temporal logic **CTL**. For example, cache consistency is described by requiring that if two caches have copies of a cache line, then they agree on the data in that line:

    AG (P1.readable & P2.readable -> P1.data = P2.data)

This formula is evaluated automatically on the BDD representation of the model. SMV finds that it is not valid and exhibits a scenario which could lead to the error: initially, both caches are invalid. Processor P_1 obtains an exclusive_unmodified copy of the data (say, data1) as described above and the data of P_2 is invalid (see Fig. 1). Then, P_2 issues a read_modified, which P_1 splits for invalidation. That is, the memory supplies a copy of the data to P_2, and P_1 postpones the invalidation of cache data until local actions are completed. Still having an exclusive_unmodified copy of data1, P_1 now modifies the data (say, into data2) and transitions to exclusive_modified. At this point, P_1 and P_2 are inconsistent. This bug can be fixed by requiring P_1 to go to the shared_unmodified state when it splits the read_modified transaction for invalidation.

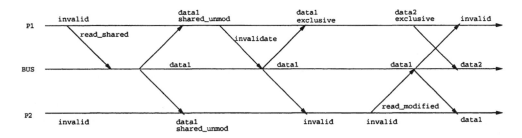

Figure 1: Error scenario in the Futurebus+ protocol

Given a formal model of a system to be verified, and a formulation of the properties the system should satisfy, there are three possible results which an automated model checker can produce:

1. either it finds a *proof* for the formula in the model and outputs "verified", or
2. it constructs a *refutation*, i.e., an execution of the (model of the) system which dissatisfies the (formulation of the) property, or
3. the complexity of the verification procedure exceeds the given memory limit or time bound.

If there is not sufficient space or time, in some cases it is possible to use bigger and faster machines for verification. Alternatively, one can use a coarser abstraction of the system and its properties. The third possibility is to employ heuristics which improve the performance of the verifier. Some of these heuristics are discussed in Sections 10 and 11.

In some sense it is more interesting to get a refutation than to get a proof. With a refutation, one can decide whether it is due to the modelling and formulation, or whether this undesired sequence of events could indeed happen in reality. In the former case, the unrealistic behavior can be eliminated by additional assumptions on the model or formula. In the latter case, one has found a bug, and the system and model can be changed appropriately. One of the major advantages of the fully automatic approach is that there is almost no additional overhead for the new verification of the changed system.

If the model checker is able to prove all specified formulas for the given model, then the verification is successfully completed. However, there can never be any guarantee that a system which has been verified by a computer tool will function correctly in reality. Even if we could assume that the verifier's hard- and software is correct (which we can not), there is a fundamental source of inaccuracy involved. Verification proves theorems about models of systems and formulations of properties, not about physical systems and desired behavior; we can never know to what extent our models and formulations reflect physical reality and intuitions. It is not possible to guarantee that a physical system will behave correctly in unexpected (i.e., unmodeled) situations. It would be unreasonable, however, to reject formal methods because they cannot offer such guarantees. Civil engineering can never *prove* that a certain building will not collapse. Nevertheless it uses mathematical models to calculate loads and wall thicknesses and so on. Similarly, we can never *prove* that our model adequately represents the reality. Therefore we can never *prove* that a system will function as planned. Nevertheless, compared to current practice, the use of formal methods can significantly decrease the amount of errors in complex software systems. A temporal logic specification adds redundancy to the design by restating an intended property in a (different) concise formalism. Computer aided verification can help to *locate errors* and to *increase reliability* of these systems. In the future, formal verification by model checking will augment classical software design tools such as structured analysis, code review and testing.

In this survey, we give a tutorial on the theoretical foundations and techniques used in model checking. Starting with elementary material on propositional temporal logics and automata we derive basic model checking algorithms from completeness results and tableau decision procedures. Then we discuss applications and techniques for efficient implementation of these algorithms. We extend the results to more expressive logics and models. Finally, we discuss some open problems and future research directions in the area. At the end of this chapter, the reader can find a list of all symbols and notations and an index of topics.

2. Logical Languages, Expressiveness

One of the major concerns of philosophical logic is to find an appropriate language for the formalization of natural language reasoning. The first and probably most successful of these languages is first order logic. Almost all mathematical statements and proofs can be formulated in this language. However, certain concepts important for computer science like well-foundedness and transitive closure require more expressive languages.

Temporal logic was invented to formalize natural language sentences about events in time, which use temporal adverbs like "eventually" and "constantly". Temporal logics have proved to be useful for specifying concurrent systems, because they can describe the ordering of events without introducing time explicitly. There have been many variants of temporal logic proposed in the literature. Temporal logics can be classified as

- state- or transition- (interval-) based, depending on whether the formulated properties involve one or more reference points,
- linear or branching time, depending on the intuition of time as a sequence or as a tree of events,
- star-free or regular, depending on the formal languages which can be defined by formulas of the logic, and
- propositional or first-order, depending on the cardinality of the nontemporal domains.

In principle, these classifications are orthogonal; in practice, however, only certain combinations are widely used. In this survey, we concentrate on propositional modal logic, linear temporal logic, computation tree logic, and fixpoint calculus. Restrictions and extensions of these logics are introduced whenever appropriate.

2.1. Propositional and First Order Logic

We assume a set $\mathcal{P} = \{p, q, p_1, ...\}$ of (atomic) propositions which can be either true or false. [1] For example, the proposition stack_is_empty denotes the fact that "the stack is empty". The *propositional logic* **PL** is built from $\mathcal{P}$ with the following syntax:

$$\mathbf{PL} \quad ::= \quad \mathcal{P} \mid \perp \mid (\mathbf{PL} \rightarrow \mathbf{PL})$$

That is,

- Every $p \in \mathcal{P}$ is a well-formed formula of propositional logic,
- $\perp$ is a well-formed formula ("the falsum"),
- if φ and ψ are well-formed formulae, then so is $(\varphi \rightarrow \psi)$, and
- nothing else is a formula.

$\mathcal{P}$ is a parameter of the logic; the special case $\mathcal{P} = \{\}$ is allowed. Other connectives can be defined as usual: $\neg\varphi \triangleq (\varphi \rightarrow \perp)$, $\quad \top \triangleq \neg\perp$, $\quad (\varphi \vee \psi) \triangleq (\neg\varphi \rightarrow \psi)$, $(\varphi \wedge \psi) \triangleq \neg(\neg\varphi \vee \neg\psi)$, and $(\varphi \leftrightarrow \psi) \triangleq ((\varphi \rightarrow \psi) \wedge (\psi \rightarrow \varphi))$. The precedence of these operators is fixed by $(\neg, \wedge, \vee, \rightarrow, \leftrightarrow)$, and parentheses are omitted in formulas whenever appropriate. Atomic propositions and negated propositions are called *literals*.

An *interpretation* $\mathcal{I}$ for the propositions is a function assigning a truth value from $\{\mathbf{true}, \mathbf{false}\}$ to every proposition. (For example, the proposition stack_is_empty is interpreted differently on a farm, in a library, or in front of a computer terminal.) A *propositional model* $\mathcal{M} \triangleq (U, \mathcal{I})$ consists of the fixed binary domain $U \triangleq \{\mathbf{true}, \mathbf{false}\}$ and an interpretation for $\mathcal{P}$. (Later on, we will consider logics

---

[1] A list of syntactic categories and other symbols is given in the appendix.

over arbitrary nonbinary domains.) The most basic semantical notion is the *validation relation* $\models$ between a model $\mathcal{M}$ and a formula φ. It is defined by the following clauses.

- $\mathcal{M} \models \mathrm{p}$ iff $\mathcal{I}(\mathrm{p}) = \mathbf{true}$,
- $\mathcal{M} \not\models \bot$, and
- $\mathcal{M} \models (\varphi \rightarrow \psi)$ iff $\mathcal{M} \models \varphi$ implies $\mathcal{M} \models \psi$.

That is, $\mathcal{M} \models (\varphi \rightarrow \psi)$ iff $\mathcal{M} \not\models \varphi$ or $\mathcal{M} \models \psi$. If $\mathcal{M} \models \varphi$, then we say that $\mathcal{M}$ *validates* φ, or, equivalently, φ is *valid in* $\mathcal{M}$.

Propositional logic is not well-suited to formalize statements about events in time. Even though the interpretation of a statement can be fixed, its truth value may vary in time. This cannot be expressed directly in **PL**.

To express such temporal dependencies, first order logic can be used. The set $\mathcal{P}$ is redefined to be a set of *monadic predicates*. That is, each $\mathrm{p} \in \mathcal{P}$ is augmented with an additional parameter denoting time, for example, $\mathtt{stack\_is\_empty}(t)$.

For sake of simplicity, we do not include function symbols (or constants) in the first-order language. Assume in addition to the set $\mathcal{P}$ of unary predicates a fixed set $\mathcal{R} \triangleq \{R, a, b, ...\}$ of *accessibility relations*, and let $\mathcal{R}^+ \triangleq \mathcal{R} \cup \{\prec, <, =\}$. Furthermore, let $\mathcal{T}$ be a set of *first-order variables* $\mathcal{T} \triangleq \{t, t_0, ...\}$ for points in time (which is assumed to be infinite unless stated otherwise).

$$\mathbf{FOL} \quad ::= \quad \mathcal{P}(\mathcal{T}) \mid \bot \mid (\mathbf{FOL} \rightarrow \mathbf{FOL}) \mid \mathcal{R}^+(\mathcal{T}, \mathcal{T}) \mid \exists \mathcal{T} \; \mathbf{FOL}$$

When writing formulas, we often use infix notation for relational terms: $t_1 R t_2 \triangleq R(t_1, t_2)$. The notation $\forall t \; \varphi$ is an abbreviation for $\neg \exists t \; \neg \varphi$, the string $x > y$ stands for $y < x$, and $x \leq y$ for $(x < y \vee x = y)$, etc.

To assign a truth value to a formula containing (free) variables, we assume that we are given a nonempty *universe* U of *points* in time, and that the *interpretation* $\mathcal{I}$ assigns to every proposition $\mathrm{p} \in \mathcal{P}$ a subset of points $\mathcal{I}(\mathrm{p}) \subseteq U$, and to every relation symbol $R \in \mathcal{R}$ a binary relation $\mathcal{I}(R) \subseteq U \times U$. For the special relation signs $=$, $\prec$, and $<$ we require that $\mathcal{I}(=) \triangleq \{(w, w) \mid w \in U\}$ is the *equality relation*, $\mathcal{I}(\prec) \triangleq \bigcup\{\mathcal{I}(R) \mid R \in \mathcal{R}\}$ is the *transition relation*, and $\mathcal{I}(<)$ is the transitive closure of $\mathcal{I}(\prec)$, the *reachability relation*. A *variable valuation* $\mathbf{v}$ assigns to any variable $t \in \mathcal{T}$ a point $w \in U$. A first-order model $\mathcal{M} \triangleq (U, \mathcal{I}, \mathbf{v})$ consists of a universe U, an interpretation $\mathcal{I}$, and a variable valuation $\mathbf{v}$. As in the propositional case, we define when a formula holds in a model:

- $\mathcal{M} \models \mathrm{p}(t)$ iff $\mathbf{v}(t) \in \mathcal{I}(\mathrm{p})$;
- $\mathcal{M} \not\models \bot$, and
- $\mathcal{M} \models (\varphi \rightarrow \psi)$ iff $\mathcal{M} \models \varphi$ implies $\mathcal{M} \models \psi$;
- $\mathcal{M} \models R(t_0, t_1)$ iff $(\mathbf{v}(t_0), \mathbf{v}(t_1)) \in \mathcal{I}(R)$;
- $\mathcal{M} \models \exists t \; \varphi$ iff $(U, \mathcal{I}, \mathbf{v}') \models \varphi$ for some $\mathbf{v}'$ which differs from $\mathbf{v}$ at most in t.

This language is rather expressive: consider the following example formulas.

(1) $(\texttt{stack\_is\_empty}(t_0) \to \exists t_1 (put(t_0, t_1) \land \neg \texttt{stack\_is\_empty}(t_1)))$

If $\texttt{stack\_is\_empty}$, then it is possible to perform a *put* such that not $\texttt{stack\_is\_empty}$ holds.

(2) $\forall t_1 ((t_0 \leq t_1 \land \texttt{req}(t_1)) \to \exists t_2 (t_1 < t_2 \land \texttt{ack}(t_2)))$

Every request is eventually acknowledged.

(3) $\forall t_1 ((t_0 \leq t_1 \land \texttt{req}(t_1)) \to \exists t_2 ((t_1 < t_2 \land \texttt{ack}(t_2)) \land$
$$\forall t_3 ((t_1 < t_3 \land t_3 < t_2) \to \texttt{req}(t_3))))$$

No request is withdrawn before it is acknowledged.

2.2. Multimodal and Temporal Logic

First order logic has been criticized by theoretical linguists for not being intuitive. Except from text in mathematical books, one can hardly find English sentences which explicitly use variables to refer to objects. Natural language statements use modal adverbs like "possibly" and "necessarily" to refer to an alternative state of affairs. Temporal phrases in natural language use the adverbs "eventually" and "constantly" (or "sometime" and "always") to refer to future points in time. Modal logic was invented to formalize these modal and temporal adverbs [Lewis 1912, Prior 1957, Prior 1967]. The idea is to suppress first-order variables $t \in \mathcal{T}$; propositions $\texttt{p} \in \mathcal{P}$ are nullary again. In modal logics, the meaning of a proposition like $\texttt{stack\_is\_empty}$ is intended to be "the stack is empty *now*". Thus, in a temporal interpretation, every formula describes a certain state of affairs *at a given point*.

To be able to describe properties depending on the relations between points, in multimodal logic for every $R \in \mathcal{R}$ a new operator $\langle R \rangle\, \varphi$ is introduced. The meaning of $\langle R \rangle\, \varphi$ is "possibly φ", i.e., "there exists some t accessible via R such that φ holds at t". Dually, $[R]\, \varphi \triangleq \neg \langle R \rangle\, \neg \varphi$ means "necessarily φ"; "for all t accessible via R, it is the case that φ holds at t".

$$\mathbf{ML} \quad ::= \quad \mathcal{P} \ \mid \ \bot \ \mid \ (\mathbf{ML} \to \mathbf{ML}) \ \mid \ \langle \mathcal{R} \rangle\, \mathbf{ML}.$$

Intuitively, the above example (1) could be written

$$(\texttt{stack\_is\_empty} \to \langle put \rangle\, \neg\texttt{stack\_is\_empty}).$$

Assume again that U is a nonempty set of *points in time* (or "possible worlds"). An *interpretation* $\mathcal{I}$ for multimodal logic assigns to every $\texttt{p} \in \mathcal{P}$ and $R \in \mathcal{R}$ a subset $\mathcal{I}(\texttt{p}) \subseteq U$ and a relation $\mathcal{I}(R) \subseteq U \times U$, respectively. The tuple $\mathcal{F} \triangleq (U, \mathcal{I})$ is called a *frame* for $\mathcal{P}$ and $\mathcal{R}$. A (Kripke-) *model* (introduced in [Kripke 1963, Kripke 1975]) $\mathcal{M} \triangleq (U, \mathcal{I}, w_0)$ for multimodal logic consists of a frame $(U, \mathcal{I})$ and a *current point* $w_0 \in U$. If $\mathcal{M} = (U, \mathcal{I}, w_0)$, we say that $\mathcal{M}$ is *based on* the frame $\mathcal{F} = (U, \mathcal{I})$. Thus, a Kripke model for multimodal logic is similar to a first order model, where the variable valuation $\mathbf{v}$ is replaced by a single designated point w_0.

Note that our notion of frame and model is somewhat different from the traditional use of these terms, where a *frame* denotes the tuple $(U, \{\mathcal{I}(R) \mid R \in \mathcal{R}\})$, and a *model* is the triple $(U, \{\mathcal{I}(R) \mid R \in \mathcal{R}\}, \{\mathcal{I}(p) \mid p \in \mathcal{P}\})$. Historically, atomic propositions have been regarded as being "variable" in a formula, thus $\{\mathcal{I}(p) \mid p \in \mathcal{P}\}$ is a separate *valuation* for these variables. In this paper, a proposition denotes a fixed predicate, hence its meaning is given by the interpretation. In a later section we introduce a separate syntactic category of *proposition variables*, which can be *evaluated* differently in each context.

Validity of a modal formula in a Kripke model $\mathcal{M} \triangleq (U, \mathcal{I}, w_0)$ is defined as follows.

- $\mathcal{M} \models p$ iff $w_0 \in \mathcal{I}(p)$;
- $\mathcal{M} \not\models \bot$, and
- $\mathcal{M} \models (\varphi \to \psi)$ iff $\mathcal{M} \models \varphi$ implies $\mathcal{M} \models \psi$.
- $\mathcal{M} \models \langle R \rangle \varphi$ iff there exists $w_1 \in U$ with $(w_0, w_1) \in \mathcal{I}(R)$ and $(U, \mathcal{I}, w_1) \models \varphi$.

We write $w \models \varphi$ instead of $(U, \mathcal{I}, w) \models \varphi$ whenever the frame $(U, \mathcal{I})$ is given. A formula φ is *universally* valid (or *frame-valid*) in $(U, \mathcal{I})$, if for all $w \in U$ it holds that $w \models \varphi$.

As defined above, $\prec$ is interpreted as the *transition relation*, i.e., the union of all accessibility relations, $<$ is interpreted as the transitive closure of $\prec$, and $\leq$ as the reflexive transitive closure (the *reachability relation*). For these special relations $\sim \in \{\prec, <, =, \leq\}$, we henceforth simply write $v \sim w$ instead of $(v, w) \in \mathcal{I}(\sim)$. We introduce the special operators $\mathbf{X}$, $\mathbf{F}^+$ and $\mathbf{F}^*$:

- $w_0 \models \mathbf{X}\,\varphi$ iff there exists $w_1 \in U$ such that $w_0 \prec w_1$ and $w_1 \models \varphi$,
- $w_0 \models \mathbf{F}^+\varphi$ iff there exists $w_1 \in U$ such that $w_0 < w_1$ and $w_1 \models \varphi$, and
- $w_0 \models \mathbf{F}^*\varphi$ iff there exists $w_1 \in U$ such that $w_0 \leq w_1$ and $w_1 \models \varphi$.

For the dual operators, we use the symbols $\mathbf{\bar{X}}\,\varphi \triangleq \neg\,\mathbf{X}\,\neg\varphi$, and $\mathbf{G}^+\varphi \triangleq \neg\,\mathbf{F}^+\,\neg\varphi$, and $\mathbf{G}^*\varphi \triangleq \neg\,\mathbf{F}^*\,\neg\varphi$. Traditionally, $\mathbf{X}$, $\mathbf{F}$, and $\mathbf{G}$ have been used to indicate neXt time, Future and Global operators[2]. Alternatively, $\mathbf{F}^+$ and $\mathbf{G}^+$ are called *sometime-* and *always*-operators. $\mathbf{\bar{X}}$ is referred to as *weak next-* operator.

Here are some historical remarks on the use of these operators. In the 1950's and 1960's, proof theory and model theory of modal logic was developed ([Rescher and Urquhart 1971, Hughes and Cresswell 1977] are historical, and [Blackburn, de Rijke and Venema 2000] is a modern textbook on this topic). Its applicability to computer science was discovered in the 1970's: [Burstall 1974] suggested a modal logic built upon $\mathbf{F}^+$ and $\mathbf{G}^+$ to describe program properties. [Kröger 1978] suggested to use both $\mathbf{X}$ and $\mathbf{F}^+$ for program verification. [Pnueli 1977] used a similar system for parallel programs. [Gabbay, Pnueli, Shelah and Stavi 1980] extended temporal logic for program specification by the binary connective *until* (explained below). The framework was further elaborated in [Pnueli 1981, Manna and Pnueli 1981, Manna and Pnueli 1982b, Manna and Pnueli 1982a, Pnueli 1984, Harel and Pnueli 1985,

---

[2]A note on notation: with the above convention, the $\mathbf{X}$, $\mathbf{\bar{X}}$, $\mathbf{F}^+$, $\mathbf{F}^*$, $\mathbf{G}^+$ and $\mathbf{G}^*$ operators could be written as $\langle\prec\rangle$, $[\prec]$, $\langle<\rangle$, $\langle\leq\rangle$, $[<]$ and $[\leq]$, respectively. In the literature, some authors use the symbols $\odot$, $\circ$, $\diamond$, and $\square$. An index of the notations used in this chapter is given in the appendix.

Manna and Pnueli 1987, Manna and Pnueli 1989]. The combination of $\langle R \rangle$- and $\mathbf{F}^+$-operators originates from *dynamic logic* [Salwicki 1970, Pratt 1976] (for an overview on dynamic logics, see [Harel 1984, Kozen and Tiuryn 1990]).

Intuitively, $\mathbf{X}\,\varphi$ indicates that φ holds at some point accessible via a single transition, $\mathbf{F}^+\,\varphi$ specifies that φ must hold in some point which can be reached by a nonempty sequence of transitions, and $\mathbf{F}^*\,\varphi$ means that φ holds at some reachable point (possibly now). Dually, $\mathbf{\overline{X}}\,\varphi$ holds if all successors satisfy φ, and $\mathbf{G}^*\,\varphi$ and $\mathbf{G}^+\,\varphi$ determine that all reachable points (except maybe the current point) must validate φ. With these operators, example (2) could be written

$$\mathbf{G}^*(\text{req} \to \mathbf{F}^+ \text{ack}).$$

From the definition, $w_0 \models \mathbf{\overline{X}}\,\varphi$ iff $w_1 \models \varphi$ for all $w_1 \in U$ such that $w_0 \prec w_1$. Similarly, $w_0 \models \mathbf{G}^+\,\varphi$ iff $w_1 \models \varphi$ for all $w_1 \in U$ such that $w_0 < w_1$. A point $w \in U$ is called *terminal*, if $\{w' \mid w \prec w'\} = \{\}$. A terminal point represents a final state of a terminating computation. Terminal points satisfy all $\mathbf{\overline{X}}$ - and $\mathbf{G}^+$-formulas vacuously: if w_0 has no accessible successors, then $w_0 \models \mathbf{\overline{X}}\,\varphi$ and $w_0 \models \mathbf{G}^+\,\varphi$ for any formula φ.

The difference between $\mathbf{F}^+$ and $\mathbf{F}^*$ is that in the latter "the future includes the present". Using the $\mathbf{X}$ operator, $\mathbf{F}^+$ and $\mathbf{F}^*$ can be mutually defined: clearly, the formula $(\mathbf{F}^*\,\varphi \leftrightarrow \varphi \vee \mathbf{F}^+\,\varphi)$ is valid. Therefore, the $\mathbf{F}^*$-operator can be expressed by $\mathbf{F}^+$. Using the equivalence $(\mathbf{F}^+\,\varphi \leftrightarrow \mathbf{X}\,\mathbf{F}^*\,\varphi)$, each occurrence of the operator $\mathbf{F}^+$ in a formula can be replaced by $\mathbf{F}^*$ and $\mathbf{X}$, with only a linear increase in formula length. It is not possible to define the $\mathbf{F}^+$-operator by $\mathbf{F}^*$ alone (without $\mathbf{X}$):

2.1. **Lemma.** *Without $\mathbf{X}$, the operator $\mathbf{F}^+$ is strictly more expressive than $\mathbf{F}^*$.*

Proof: Consider two models $\mathcal{M}_1$ and $\mathcal{M}_2$, where $U_1 \triangleq U_2 \triangleq \{w\}$, $\mathcal{I}_1(\prec) \triangleq \{\}$, $\mathcal{I}_2(\prec) \triangleq \{(w,w)\}$ and $\mathcal{I}_1(\text{p}) = \mathcal{I}_2(\text{p})$ for all $\text{p} \in \mathcal{P}$. Then $\mathcal{M}_1 \not\models \mathbf{F}^+\top$ and $\mathcal{M}_2 \models \mathbf{F}^+\top$. However, $w \models \mathbf{F}^*\,\varphi$ iff $w \models \varphi$ in both $\mathcal{M}_1$ and $\mathcal{M}_2$. Therefore, for all formulas φ which involve only propositions, boolean operators and $\mathbf{F}^*$ it holds that $\mathcal{M}_1 \models \varphi$ iff $\mathcal{M}_2 \models \varphi$. (The formal proof of this statement is omitted; it is a straightforward induction on the construction of such formulas.) Hence, there is no formula φ consisting only of propositions, boolean operators and $\mathbf{F}^*$ such that for all models $\mathcal{M}$ it holds that $\mathcal{M} \models \varphi$ iff $\mathcal{M} \models \mathbf{F}^+\top$. In other words, $\mathbf{F}^+\top$ is not expressible in this language. $\qquad\square$

A similar proof shows that modal operators cannot express statements about intervals. For example, there is no formula equivalent to example (3) of the above. To remedy this lack of expressiveness, [Kamp 1968] introduced a binary operator $(\varphi\,\mathbf{U}^+\,\psi)$ meaning "φ holds until ψ holds". We use the term *temporal logic* to refer to any modal logic which contains some sort of until-operator. In computer science, this operator was first used by [Gabbay et al. 1980] to classify important properties of concurrent programs. The semantics of $\mathbf{U}^+$ is defined as follows:

- $w_0 \models (\varphi\,\mathbf{U}^+\,\psi)$ iff there exists $w_1 \in U$ with $w_0 < w_1$ and $w_1 \models \psi$, and for all $w_2 \in U$ with $w_0 < w_2$ and $w_2 < w_1$, we have $w_2 \models \varphi$.

This situation is illustrated by the following picture.

As an example, the above formula (3) can be expressed with an until-operator as

$$\mathbf{G}^{\bullet}(\text{req} \to (\text{req}\,\mathbf{U}^{+}\,\text{ack})).$$

Various other operators can be defined via $\mathbf{U}^{+}$. Sometime-operator and nexttime operators (for discrete $\prec$) are obtained as follows:

- $\mathbf{X}\,\varphi \leftrightarrow (\bot\,\mathbf{U}^{+}\,\varphi)$
- $\mathbf{F}^{+}\,\varphi \leftrightarrow (\top\,\mathbf{U}^{+}\,\varphi)$

The proof of these equivalences is immediate from the definition: $w_0 \models (\bot\,\mathbf{U}^{+}\,\psi)$ iff there exists $w_1 \in U$ with $w_0 < w_1$ and $w_1 \models \psi$, and for all $w_2 \in U$ with $w_0 < w_2 < w_1$ it holds that $w_2 \models \bot$, which is impossible. In other words, $w_0 < w_1$, but there is no w_2 that satisfies $w_0 < w_2$ and $w_2 < w_1$. Therefore w_1 must be an immediate successor of w_0, i.e., $w_0 \prec w_1$. Consequently, $w_0 \models \mathbf{X}\,\varphi$. The second equivalence is obtained in a similar way.

The *reflexive until*-operator is defined as $(\varphi\,\mathbf{U}^{\bullet}\,\psi) \triangleq (\psi \vee \varphi \wedge (\varphi\,\mathbf{U}^{+}\,\psi))$.

As above, $\mathbf{F}^{\bullet}\,\varphi \leftrightarrow (\top\,\mathbf{U}^{\bullet}\,\varphi)$ and $(\varphi\,\mathbf{U}^{+}\,\psi) \leftrightarrow \mathbf{X}(\varphi\,\mathbf{U}^{\bullet}\,\psi)$. Without $\mathbf{X}$ it is not possible to define $\mathbf{U}^{+}$ or $\mathbf{F}^{+}$ from $\mathbf{U}^{\bullet}$. Hence, $\mathbf{X}$ cannot be defined by $\mathbf{U}^{\bullet}$.

The *unless* or *weak until*-operator is defined as

$$(\varphi\,\mathbf{W}^{+}\,\psi) \triangleq \neg(\neg\psi\,\mathbf{U}^{+}\,\neg(\varphi \vee \psi)).$$

Whereas $(\varphi\,\mathbf{U}^{+}\,\psi)$ requires that ψ eventually holds, $(\varphi\,\mathbf{W}^{+}\,\psi)$ is also true if ψ is never and φ always true. Intuitively, $(\varphi\,\mathbf{W}^{+}\,\psi)$ says that φ holds at least up to the next point where ψ holds. This can be seen as follows: assume that $w_0 \models \neg(\neg\psi\,\mathbf{U}^{+}\,\neg(\varphi \vee \psi))$. By definition, it is not the case that for some $w_1 > w_0$ both $w_1 \models \neg(\varphi \vee \psi)$ and $w_2 \models \neg\psi$ for all $w_0 < w_2 < w_1$. Thus, for all $w_1 > w_0$ it holds that $w_1 \models (\varphi \vee \psi)$, or $w_2 \models \psi$ for some $w_0 < w_2 < w_1$. In other words, if $w_1 > w_0$ then either $w_1 \models \varphi$ or there is some $w_0 < w_2 \leq w_1$ such that $w_2 \models \psi$. Therefore, if $w_2 \not\models \psi$ for all $w_0 < w_2 \leq w_1$, i.e. if w_1 is before the next point where ψ holds, then $w_1 \models \varphi$.

Note that by definition $(\varphi\,\mathbf{W}^{+}\,\bot) = \neg(\top\,\mathbf{U}^{+}\,\neg\varphi) = \mathbf{G}^{+}\,\varphi$. Some texts define the unless operator by $((\varphi\,\mathbf{U}^{+}\,\psi) \vee \mathbf{G}^{+}\,\varphi)$. In *natural models*, which consist of a sequence of points, these two definitions are equivalent:

2.2. LEMMA. *For natural models,* $(\varphi\,\mathbf{W}^{+}\,\psi) \leftrightarrow ((\varphi\,\mathbf{U}^{+}\,\psi) \vee \mathbf{G}^{+}\,\varphi)$.

PROOF: We must show that for all models $\mathcal{M}$ which are sequences, the following holds: (i) $\mathcal{M} \models ((\varphi\,\mathbf{W}^{+}\,\psi) \to ((\varphi\,\mathbf{U}^{+}\,\psi) \vee \mathbf{G}^{+}\,\varphi))$, (ii) $\mathcal{M} \models (\mathbf{G}^{+}\,\varphi \to (\varphi\,\mathbf{W}^{+}\,\psi))$

and (iii) $\mathcal{M} \models ((\varphi \, \mathbf{U}^+ \, \psi) \to (\varphi \, \mathbf{W}^+ \, \psi))$. For (i), assume that $w_0 \models (\varphi \, \mathbf{W}^+ \, \psi)$ and $w_0 \not\models \mathbf{G}^+ \varphi$. Then $w_1 \not\models \varphi$ for some $w_1 > w_0$. According to above, there is some $w_0 < w_2 \leq w_1$ such that $w_2 \models \psi$. Since the model is assumed to be a sequence, it is well-founded. Therefore there must be a smallest w_2 with this property; i.e. $w_0 < w_2 \leq w_1$, $w_2 \models \psi$, and $w_3 \not\models \psi$ for all $w_0 < w_3 < w_2$. Again, according to the above, if $w_0 < w_3 < w_2$ then $w_3 \models \varphi$. Therefore $w_0 \models (\varphi \, \mathbf{U}^+ \, \psi)$. Formula (ii) follows immediately from the definition: if $w_0 \models \mathbf{G}^+ \varphi$, then $w_1 \models \varphi$ for all $w_1 > w_0$. Therefore, it is not the case that some $w_1 > w_0$ exists which satisfies $w_1 \models \neg(\varphi \lor \psi)$. This implies $w_0 \not\models (\neg\psi \, \mathbf{U}^+ \, \neg(\varphi \lor \psi))$, i.e., $w_0 \models (\varphi \, \mathbf{W}^+ \, \psi)$. For implication (iii), we need the property that the model is linear: if $w_0 \models (\varphi \, \mathbf{U}^+ \, \psi)$, then there exists $w_1 > w_0$ such that $w_1 \models \psi$ and $w_2 \models \varphi$ for all $w_0 < w_2 < w_1$. Assume any point $w > w_0$. Then $w < w_1$ or $w \geq w_1$. In the first case, $w \models \varphi$. In the second case, there exists $w' = w_1$ such that $w' \models \psi$. Thus, for all $w > w_0$ it holds that $w \models \varphi$, or there exists $w_0 < w' \leq w$ such that $w' \models \psi$. This shows that $w_0 \models (\varphi \, \mathbf{W}^+ \, \psi)$. $\qquad\square$

This equivalence does not hold for dense time: for example, if $(U, \prec)$ is isomorphic to the rationals and $\mathcal{I}(\psi) \triangleq \{1/n \mid n \in \mathbf{N}\}$, then $\forall t_1 > 0 \exists t_2 > 0 \, (t_2 < t_1 \land \psi(t_2))$, hence $0 \models (\bot \, \mathbf{W}^+ \, \varphi)$. Moreover, $0 \not\models \mathbf{X} \top$ and $0 \models \mathbf{F}^+ \top$, hence $0 \not\models ((\bot \, \mathbf{U}^+ \, \psi) \lor \mathbf{G}^+ \bot)$. For more information on other models of time, see [van Benthem 1991, Gabbay, Hodkinson and Reynolds 1994]. An immediate consequence of Lemma 2.2 is that in natural models the operator $\mathbf{U}^+$ is definable by $\mathbf{W}^+$ and $\mathbf{F}^+$:

$$(\varphi \, \mathbf{U}^+ \, \psi) \leftrightarrow ((\varphi \, \mathbf{W}^+ \, \psi) \land \mathbf{F}^+ \, \psi).$$

With first order logic, it is possible to use reverse relations: $x > y$ iff $y < x$. In [Lichtenstein, Pnueli and Zuck 1985], the authors argue that the ability to refer to the past can facilitate program specifications. The temporal *past* or *since-* operator $\mathbf{U}^-$ is defined with the following semantics:

- $w_0 \models (\varphi \, \mathbf{U}^- \, \psi)$ iff there exists $w_1 \in U$ with $w_1 < w_0$ and $w_1 \models \psi$, and for all $w_2 \in U$ with $w_1 < w_2$ and $w_2 < w_0$, we have $w_2 \models \varphi$.

The syntax of linear temporal logic (**LTL**) is defined as follows:

$$\textbf{LTL} \quad ::= \quad \mathcal{P} \mid \bot \mid (\textbf{LTL} \to \textbf{LTL}) \mid (\textbf{LTL} \, \mathbf{U}^+ \, \textbf{LTL}) \mid (\textbf{LTL} \, \mathbf{U}^- \, \textbf{LTL}).$$

We write $\mathbf{F}^- \varphi$ and $\mathbf{G}^- \varphi$ for $(\top \, \mathbf{U}^- \, \varphi)$ and $\neg \mathbf{F}^- \neg\varphi$, respectively. Intuitively, these operators refer to "sometime in the past" and "always in the past". Moreover, $\mathbf{F}^\pm \varphi$ and $\mathbf{G}^\pm \varphi$ are abbreviations for $(\mathbf{F}^- \varphi \lor \varphi \lor \mathbf{F}^+ \varphi)$ and $\neg \mathbf{F}^\pm \neg\varphi$, respectively.

2.3. Expressive Completeness of Temporal Logic

How can first order and temporal logic be compared? Temporal logic can be regarded as a certain fragment of first order logic; this is explained more formally below. In contrast to modal or temporal logics, **FOL** formulas can mention several reference points (free variables). To be able to compare the expressiveness of both type of logics, we restrict **FOL** to formulas with at most one free variable.

The above semantics induces a translation "**FOL**" from modal or temporal to first order logic, where $\mathbf{FOL}(\varphi)$ has exactly one free variable t_0.

- $\mathbf{FOL}(\mathrm{p}) \triangleq \mathrm{p}(t_0)$
- $\mathbf{FOL}(\bot) \triangleq (t_0 \neq t_0)$
- $\mathbf{FOL}((\varphi \to \psi)) \triangleq (\mathbf{FOL}(\varphi) \to \mathbf{FOL}(\psi))$

- $\mathbf{FOL}(\langle R \rangle\, \varphi) \triangleq \exists t'(t_0 R t' \wedge \mathbf{FOL}(\varphi)\{t_0 := t'\})$
- $\mathbf{FOL}(\mathbf{X}\, \varphi) \triangleq \exists t'(t_0 \prec t' \wedge \mathbf{FOL}(\varphi)\{t_0 := t'\})$
- $\mathbf{FOL}(\mathbf{F}^+\, \varphi) \triangleq \exists t'(t_0 < t' \wedge \mathbf{FOL}(\varphi)\{t_0 := t'\})$
- $\mathbf{FOL}(\mathbf{F}^*\, \varphi) \triangleq \exists t'(t_0 \leq t' \wedge \mathbf{FOL}(\varphi)\{t_0 := t'\})$

- $\mathbf{FOL}((\varphi\, \mathbf{U}^+\, \psi)) \triangleq$
  $\exists t'(t_0 < t' \wedge \mathbf{FOL}(\psi)\{t_0 := t'\} \wedge \forall t''(t_0 < t'' < t' \to \mathbf{FOL}(\varphi)\{t_0 := t''\})).$
- $\mathbf{FOL}((\varphi\, \mathbf{U}^-\, \psi)) \triangleq$
  $\exists t'(t' < t_0 \wedge \mathbf{FOL}(\psi)\{t_0 := t'\} \wedge \forall t''(t' < t'' < t_0 \to \mathbf{FOL}(\varphi)\{t_0 := t''\})).$

This translation is sometimes called the *standard translation*[Blackburn et al. 2000]. In the translation of $\langle R \rangle\, \varphi$, ..., $(\varphi\, \mathbf{U}^+\, \psi)$, the symbols t' and t'' denote arbitrary variables which do not occur in $\mathbf{FOL}(\varphi)$ or $\mathbf{FOL}(\psi)$. The formula $\mathbf{FOL}(\psi)\{t_0 := t'\}$ denotes the formula $\mathbf{FOL}(\psi)$, where every (free) occurrence of the variable t_0 is replaced by the variable which is denoted by t'. The following example demonstrates the standard translation.

$\mathbf{FOL}(((\neg \mathrm{ack}\, \mathbf{U}^-\, \mathrm{req})\, \mathbf{U}^+\, \mathrm{ack}))$
$= \quad \exists t_1(t_0 < t_1 \wedge \mathrm{ack}(t_1) \wedge \forall t_2(t_0 < t_2 < t_1 \to \mathbf{FOL}((\neg \mathrm{ack}\, \mathbf{U}^-\, \mathrm{req}))\{t_0 := t_2\}))$
$= \quad \exists t_1(t_0 < t_1 \wedge \mathrm{ack}(t_1) \wedge \forall t_2(t_0 < t_2 < t_1 \to$
$\qquad\qquad\qquad \exists t_3(t_3 < t_2 \wedge \mathrm{req}(t_3) \wedge \forall t_4(t_3 < t_4 < t_2 \to \neg \mathrm{ack}(t_4))))).$

The standard translation of a modal or temporal formula is a first-order formula with exactly one free variable t_0. Correctness of the standard translation can formally be stated as follows:

2.3. FACT. For every $\varphi \in \mathbf{ML}$ or $\mathbf{LTL}$ there exists a first order formula $\mathbf{FOL}(\varphi)$ such that for every frame $(U, \mathcal{I})$, point $w_0 \in U$ and valuation $\mathbf{v}$ for which $\mathbf{v}(t_0) = w_0$ it holds that $(U, \mathcal{I}, w_0) \models \varphi$ iff $(U, \mathcal{I}, \mathbf{v}) \models \mathbf{FOL}(\varphi)$.

Hence, **FOL** is at least as expressive as **LTL**. A logic is called *expressively complete* (or *definitionally complete*), if there exists also a translation in the other direction: given any first-order formula with exactly one free variable, does an equivalent temporal formula exist?

For the translation of any given temporal formula into first order logic only three variables (say, t_0, t_1 and t_2) are really needed. Other variables can be reused; for example, the above $\mathbf{FOL}(((\neg \mathrm{ack}\, \mathbf{U}^-\, \mathrm{req})\, \mathbf{U}^+\, \mathrm{ack}))$ is equivalent to

$\exists t_1(t_0 < t_1 \wedge \mathrm{ack}(t_1) \wedge \forall t_2(t_0 < t_2 < t_1 \to$

$$\exists t_0 (t_0 < t_2 \land \mathbf{req}(t_0) \land \forall t_1 (t_0 < t_1 < t_2 \rightarrow \neg \mathbf{ack}(t_1)))))).$$

Similarly, modal logic can be translated into the so-called *guarded fragment* of first-order logic, which allows only two variables. In the first-order clause for $(\varphi \, \mathbf{U}^+ \, \psi)$ three variables are needed. This is the reason why the until-operator is not definable in modal logic. Likewise, **LTL** cannot express any property which "inherently" uses four variables. For example, the statement "there are three different connected points reachable from the current point" is not expressible in temporal logic.

$$\exists t_1, t_2, t_3 (t_0 < t_1 \land t_0 < t_2 \land t_0 < t_3 \land t_1 < t_2 \land t_1 < t_3 \land t_2 < t_3)$$

If $<$ is irreflexive, then a minimal model satisfying this formula is e.g. the following:

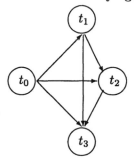

In case that $<$ is a linear order (antisymmetric and total) this is equivalent to

$$\exists t_1 (t_0 < t_1 \land \exists t_2 (t_1 < t_2 \land \exists t_3 (t_2 < t_3)))$$

in which we can rename t_3 by t_0 to get the equivalent

$$\exists t_1 (t_0 < t_1 \land \exists t_2 (t_1 < t_2 \land \exists t_0 (t_2 < t_0)))$$

which in turn can be expressed temporally as $\mathbf{F}^+ \, \mathbf{F}^+ \, \mathbf{F}^+ \, \top$.

Therefore, attention is restricted to certain classes of structures, like complete linear orders, or finitely-branching trees, etc. A *natural* model consists of a finite or infinite *sequence* of points. Formally, a natural model $\mathcal{M} \triangleq (U, \mathcal{I}, w_0)$ is a Kripke-model with only one accessibility relation, such that $(U, \prec)$ is isomorphic to the natural numbers or an initial segment of the natural numbers[3], where $\prec$ is the usual successor relation.

2.4. THEOREM (Kamp, Gabbay). *Temporal logic is expressively complete for natural models.*

The original proof of this theorem in [Kamp 1968, pp. 39–94] is extremely complicated. The proof given below follows [Gabbay 1989] and uses a certain property called *separation*. Call a temporal formula

---

[3] Some textbooks restrict attention to infinite models. Terminating computations are then modelled with an idle loop. In this survey, we use both finite and infinite computation sequences.

- *pure future*, if it is of form $(\varphi \, \mathbf{U}^+ \, \psi)$, where in both φ and ψ no $\mathbf{U}^-$-operator occurs, and
- *pure past*, if it is of form $(\varphi \, \mathbf{U}^- \, \psi)$, where in both φ and ψ no $\mathbf{U}^+$-operator occurs, and
- *pure present*, if it contains no $\mathbf{U}^+$ or $\mathbf{U}^-$-operators.

A *future formula* is a boolean combination of pure future and pure present formulas, i.e., one which does not contain any $\mathbf{U}^-$-operators. Similarly, a *past formula* does not contain any $\mathbf{U}^+$. A formula is *separated* if it is a boolean combination of future and past formulas. A logic has the *separation property* (for a given class of models), if for every formula there exists a separated formula which is equivalent for all models under consideration.

2.5. LEMMA. *The separation property implies expressive completeness.*

PROOF: This lemma is proven by induction on the structure of **FOL**-formulas. For the proof, we assume that **LTL** has the separation property for natural models. That is, for each linear temporal formula there exists an equivalent formula which is separated. We show that any first order formula $\varphi(t_0)$ which has exactly one free variable t_0 can be translated into a temporal formula $\mathbf{LTL}(\varphi)$. It suffices to consider first order logic where $\mathcal{R}^+ \triangleq \{<, =\}$: in natural models, there is a single accessibility relation, and every atomic subformula $t \prec t'$ can be equivalently replaced by $(t < t' \wedge \neg \exists t''(t < t'' \wedge t'' < t'))$. Furthermore, the scope of quantification can be minimized such that no sub-formula $\varphi \triangleq \exists t \, \psi$ contains a proposition $\mathrm{p}(t')$ where t' is free in φ. For example, $\exists t_1(t_1 > t_0 \wedge \mathrm{p}(t_0) \wedge \mathrm{p}(t_1))$ can be rewritten as $\mathrm{p}(t_0) \wedge \exists t_1(t_1 > t_0 \wedge \mathrm{p}(t_1))$.

The translation of $\mathrm{p}(t_0)$ is p. It is not necessary to give a translation for formulas $\mathrm{p}(t_1)$ or $t_0 \sim t_1$, since they involve other free variables than t_0. The translation of a boolean connective of sub-formulas is the boolean connective of the translation of the sub-formulas. The only remaining case are formulas $\varphi \triangleq \exists t_1 \, \psi(t_0, t_1)$. Since the scope of the quantifier $\exists t_1$ is minimal, φ does not contain any proposition $\mathrm{p}(t_0)$. That is, $\psi(t_0, t_1)$ is a boolean combination of formulas $\mathrm{p}(t_1)$, $t_0 \sim t_1$, and $\varphi' \triangleq \exists t_2 \, \psi'(t_0, t_1, t_2)$. Replace every sub-formula $t_0 < t$ by a new unary proposition $\mathtt{future}(t)$, replace every sub-formula $t_0 = t$ by a new unary $\mathtt{present}(t)$, and replace every $t < t_0$ by $\mathtt{past}(t)$. That is, φ now does not contain any t_0, and thus each φ' is a formula with exactly one free variable t_1. Since the nesting depth of existential quantifiers in each φ' is smaller than that of φ, we can apply the induction hypothesis to get temporal formulae $\mathbf{LTL}(\varphi')$. Reinserting these into ψ and replacing $\mathrm{p}(t_1)$ in ψ by p, and $\mathrm{q}(t_1)$ by q for $\mathrm{q} \in \{\mathtt{future}, \mathtt{present}, \mathtt{past}\}$ gives the temporal formula $\mathbf{LTL}(\psi)$. To translate $\varphi \triangleq \exists t_1 \, \psi$ we separate the temporal formula $(\mathbf{F}^- \, \mathbf{LTL}(\psi) \vee \mathbf{LTL}(\psi) \vee \mathbf{F}^+ \, \mathbf{LTL}(\psi))$. The resulting formula is a boolean combination of pure future, pure past and pure present formulas. Replace in this formula every $\mathtt{future}$ inside a pure future formula by $\top$, every other $\mathtt{future}$ by $\bot$. Similarly, replace every $\mathtt{past}$ inside a pure past formula by $\top$, and every other $\mathtt{past}$ by $\bot$. Finally, replace every $\mathtt{present}$ inside a pure present formula by $\top$, every other $\mathtt{present}$ by $\bot$. The resulting formula is the required translation $\mathbf{LTL}(\varphi)$.

Given any natural model $\mathcal{M} \triangleq (U, \mathcal{I}, w_0)$ for φ, define $\mathcal{I}(\mathtt{future}) \triangleq \{w \mid w >$

$w_0\}$, $\mathcal{I}(\text{present}) \triangleq \{w_0\}$ and $\mathcal{I}(\text{past}) \triangleq \{w \mid w < w_0\}$. Then every step in the above translation preserves validity in $\mathcal{M}$. Therefore, $\mathcal{M} \models \varphi$ iff $\mathcal{M} \models \mathbf{LTL}(\varphi)$. $\square$

To illustrate this construction, let us find the temporal equivalent of $\varphi \triangleq \exists t_1 (t_0 < t_1 \wedge p(t_1) \wedge \forall t_2 (t_0 < t_2 < t_1 \rightarrow q(t_2)))$. (We already know that the outcome should be $(q\, \mathbf{U}^+ p)$.) The first replacement results in $\exists t_1 \psi$, where $\psi \triangleq (\text{future}(t_1) \wedge p(t_1) \wedge \neg \exists t_2 (\text{future}(t_2) \wedge t_2 < t_1 \wedge \neg q(t_2)))$. The formula $\varphi'(t_1) = \exists t_2 (t_2 < t_1 \wedge \text{future}(t_2) \wedge \neg q(t_2)))$ inductively translates to $\mathbf{LTL}(\varphi') = \mathbf{F}^-(\text{future} \wedge \neg q) = \neg \mathbf{G}^-(\text{future} \rightarrow q)$. Thus $\mathbf{LTL}(\psi) = (\text{future} \wedge p \wedge \mathbf{G}^-(\text{future} \rightarrow q))$. To obtain $\mathbf{LTL}(\exists t_1 \psi)$ we have to separate $\mathbf{F}^\pm \mathbf{LTL}(\psi) = \mathbf{F}^+ \mathbf{LTL}(\psi) \vee \mathbf{LTL}(\psi) \vee \mathbf{F}^- \mathbf{LTL}(\psi)$. Separating $\mathbf{F}^+ \mathbf{LTL}(\psi) = \mathbf{F}^+(\text{future} \wedge p \wedge \mathbf{G}^-(\text{future} \rightarrow q))$ gives $\mathbf{G}^-(\text{future} \rightarrow q) \wedge (\text{future} \rightarrow q) \wedge ((\text{future} \rightarrow q)\, \mathbf{U}^+(\text{future} \wedge p))$ (see below). The disjuncts $\mathbf{F}^- \mathbf{LTL}(\psi) = \mathbf{F}^-(\text{future} \wedge p \wedge \mathbf{G}^-(\text{future} \rightarrow q))$ and $\mathbf{LTL}(\psi) = (\text{future} \wedge p \wedge \mathbf{G}^-(\text{future} \rightarrow q))$ are already separated. To obtain $\mathbf{LTL}(\varphi)$, we now replace every future inside a pure past or pure present formula by $\bot$ and every future inside a pure future formula by $\top$. Then $\mathbf{G}^-(\text{future} \rightarrow q) \wedge (\text{future} \rightarrow q)$ reduces to $\top$, and $((\text{future} \rightarrow q)\, \mathbf{U}^+(\text{future} \wedge p))$ reduces to $(q\, \mathbf{U}^+ p)$. The disjuncts $\mathbf{F}^- \mathbf{LTL}(\psi)$ and $\mathbf{LTL}(\psi)$ reduce to $\bot$. Therefore, $\mathbf{F}^\pm \mathbf{LTL}(\psi)$ reduces to $(q\, \mathbf{U}^+ p)$, which is the expected result for $\mathbf{LTL}(\psi)$.

In the above, we used the following equivalence to separate a nested occurrence of future- and past- operators:

$$\models \mathbf{F}^+(\varphi \wedge \mathbf{G}^- \psi) \leftrightarrow \mathbf{G}^- \psi \wedge \psi \wedge (\psi\, \mathbf{U}^+ \varphi)$$

PROOF: The left side of this formula states that sometimes in the future, φ and always in the past ψ holds. In other words, there is some $w_1 > w_0$ such that φ holds at w_1, and for all $w_2 < w_1$, the formula ψ holds at w_2. In a natural model, each such w_2 must be in the past ($w_2 < w_0$), present ($w_2 = w_0$) or future ($w_0 < w_2 < w_1$) of the current point w_0. Therefore, for each $w_2 < w_0$, the formula ψ holds, and ψ holds at w_0, and there is some $w_1 > w_0$ such that φ holds at w_1, and for all $w_0 < w_2 < w_1$, the formula ψ holds at w_2. This is stated by the right side of the formula. $\square$

A more convenient way to show the correctness of such formulas than by semantical reasoning is by an automated proof procedure. In Section 7, we will show that $\mathbf{LTL}$ is decidable. There are several automated provers freely available. In fact, the above formula is checked by the STeP system within milliseconds.

To show expressive completeness, it remains to prove the following:

2.6. LEMMA. $\mathbf{LTL}$ *has the separation property for natural models.*

PROOF: Consider the case of a non-separated formula $\varphi \triangleq (\varphi_1\, \mathbf{U}^+ \varphi_2)$, which contains a direct subformula $\psi \triangleq (\psi_1\, \mathbf{U}^- \psi_2)$ (i.e., ψ is a boolean component of φ_1 and/or φ_2, and does not occur elsewhere in φ_1 or φ_2). We write $\varphi_i^\top$ and $\varphi_i^\bot$ for $\varphi_i\{\psi := \top\}$ and $\varphi_i\{\psi := \bot\}$, respectively. By propositional reasoning,

$\varphi_1 \leftrightarrow ((\psi \vee \varphi_1^\perp) \wedge (\neg\psi \vee \varphi_1^\top))$ and $\varphi_2 \leftrightarrow ((\psi \wedge \varphi_1^\top) \wedge (\neg\psi \vee \varphi_2^\perp))$. Therefore, φ is equivalent to $(((\psi \vee \varphi_1^\perp) \wedge (\neg\psi \vee \varphi_1^\top)) \, \mathbf{U}^+ ((\psi \wedge \varphi_2^\top) \vee (\neg\psi \wedge \varphi_2^\perp)))$. By temporal reasoning, this in turn is equivalent to $(((\psi\vee\varphi_1^\perp) \, \mathbf{U}^+ (\psi\wedge\varphi_2^\top)) \vee ((\psi\vee\varphi_1^\perp) \, \mathbf{U}^+ (\neg\psi\wedge \varphi_2^\perp))) \wedge (((\neg\psi \vee \varphi_1^\top) \, \mathbf{U}^+ (\psi \wedge \varphi_2^\top)) \vee ((\neg\psi \vee \varphi_1^\top) \, \mathbf{U}^+ (\neg\psi \wedge \varphi_2^\perp)))$.

For each of the four boolean components of this formula, an equivalent separated formula is given in Fig. 2. Though these formulas are hard to read and difficult to prove manually, their validity can be easily checked bl an automated theorem prover. Intuitively, they are generalizations of the example given above. With the separating clauses, φ can be rewritten such that ψ is not in the scope of any $\mathbf{U}^+$.

Since the formulas of Fig. 2 still hold if $\mathbf{U}^+$ and $\mathbf{U}^-$ are interchanged, each $(\varphi_1 \, \mathbf{U}^- \, \varphi_2)$ containing a direct subformula $\psi \triangleq (\psi_1 \, \mathbf{U}^+ \, \psi_2)$ can be rewritten such that ψ does not occur in the scope of a $\mathbf{U}^-$. The general case of several different pasttime-subformulas nested within future-subformulas and vice versa can be handled by repeated application of these transformations. Formally, the claim follows by induction on the nesting depth and number of $\mathbf{U}^-$ sub-formulas within $\mathbf{U}^+$ and vice versa. □

Since in the separation step of this construction subformulas may be duplicated, the resulting **LTL** formula can be nonelementary larger than the original **FOL** formula.

(i) $(((\langle(\psi_1 \, \mathbf{U}^- \, \psi_2) \vee \varphi_1\rangle \, \mathbf{U}^+ \langle(\psi_1 \, \mathbf{U}^- \, \psi_2) \wedge \varphi_2\rangle) \leftrightarrow$
$\qquad (\psi_1 \, \mathbf{U}^+ \, \varphi_2) \wedge \langle\psi_2 \vee \psi_1 \wedge (\psi_1 \, \mathbf{U}^- \, \psi_2)\rangle \vee$
$\qquad\qquad ((\langle\psi_1 \vee \psi_2 \vee \neg(\neg\psi_2 \, \mathbf{U}^+ \, \neg\varphi_1)\rangle \, \mathbf{U}^+ \langle\psi_2 \wedge (\psi_1 \, \mathbf{U}^+ \, \varphi_2)\rangle) \wedge$
$\qquad\qquad\qquad\qquad (\neg(\neg\psi_2 \, \mathbf{U}^+ \, \neg\varphi_1) \vee \langle\psi_2 \vee \psi_1 \wedge (\psi_1 \, \mathbf{U}^- \, \psi_2)\rangle)$

(ii) $(((\langle(\psi_1 \, \mathbf{U}^- \, \psi_2) \vee \varphi_1\rangle \, \mathbf{U}^+ \langle\neg(\psi_1 \, \mathbf{U}^- \, \psi_2) \wedge \varphi_2\rangle) \leftrightarrow$
$\qquad ((\langle\varphi_1 \wedge \neg\psi_2\rangle \, \mathbf{U}^+ \, \varphi_2) \wedge \langle(\neg\psi_2 \wedge (\neg\psi_1 \vee \neg(\psi_1 \, \mathbf{U}^- \, \psi_2))\rangle) \vee$
$\qquad ((\langle\psi_1 \vee \psi_2 \vee (\varphi_1 \, \mathbf{U}^+ \langle\varphi_2 \vee \varphi_1 \wedge \psi_2\rangle)\rangle \, \mathbf{U}^+ \langle\neg\psi_1 \wedge \neg\psi_2 \wedge ((\varphi_1 \wedge \neg\psi_2) \, \mathbf{U}^+ \, \varphi_2)\rangle) \wedge$
$\qquad\qquad\qquad\qquad (\varphi_1 \, \mathbf{U}^+ \langle\varphi_1 \wedge \psi_2\rangle) \vee \langle\psi_2 \vee \psi_1 \wedge (\psi_1 \, \mathbf{U}^- \, \psi_2)\rangle)$

(iii) $((\langle\neg(\psi_1 \, \mathbf{U}^- \, \psi_2) \vee \varphi_1\rangle \, \mathbf{U}^+ \langle(\psi_1 \, \mathbf{U}^- \, \psi_2) \wedge \varphi_2\rangle) \leftrightarrow$
$\qquad (\langle\varphi_1 \wedge \psi_1\rangle \, \mathbf{U}^+ \, \varphi_2) \wedge \langle\psi_2 \vee \psi_1 \wedge (\psi_1 \, \mathbf{U}^- \, \psi_2)\rangle \vee$
$\qquad ((\langle\neg\psi_2 \vee (\varphi_1 \, \mathbf{U}^+ \langle\varphi_2 \vee \varphi_1 \wedge \neg\psi_1 \wedge \neg\psi_2\rangle)\rangle \, \mathbf{U}^+ \langle\psi_2 \wedge ((\varphi_1 \wedge \psi_1) \, \mathbf{U}^+ \, \varphi_2)\rangle) \wedge$
$\qquad\qquad\qquad\qquad ([\varphi_1 \, \mathbf{U}^+ \langle\varphi_1 \wedge \neg\psi_1 \wedge \neg\psi_2\rangle] \vee [\neg\psi_2 \wedge \langle\neg\psi_1 \vee \neg(\psi_1 \, \mathbf{U}^- \, \psi_2)\rangle])$

(iv) $((\langle\neg(\psi_1 \, \mathbf{U}^- \, \psi_2) \vee \varphi_1\rangle \, \mathbf{U}^+ \langle\neg(\psi_1 \, \mathbf{U}^- \, \psi_2) \wedge \varphi_2\rangle) \leftrightarrow$
$\qquad (\neg(\psi_1 \, \mathbf{U}^+ \, \neg\varphi_1) \vee \langle\neg\psi_2 \wedge (\neg\psi_1 \vee \neg(\psi_1 \, \mathbf{U}^- \, \psi_2))\rangle) \wedge$
$\qquad (\neg((\psi_1 \vee \psi_2 \vee \neg(\neg\psi_2 \, \mathbf{U}^+ \, \varphi_2)) \, \mathbf{U}^+ \langle\psi_2 \wedge (\psi_1 \, \mathbf{U}^+ \, \neg\varphi_1)\rangle) \vee$
$\qquad\qquad ((\neg\psi_2 \, \mathbf{U}^+ \, \varphi_2) \wedge \langle\neg\psi_2 \wedge (\neg\psi_1 \vee \neg(\psi_1 \, \mathbf{U}^- \, \psi_2))\rangle)))) \wedge$
$(\mathbf{F}^+[\neg\psi_1 \wedge \neg\psi_2 \wedge (\neg\psi_2 \, \mathbf{U}^+ \, \varphi_2)] \vee [(\neg\psi_2 \, \mathbf{U}^+ \, \varphi_2) \wedge (\neg\psi_2 \wedge (\neg\psi_1 \vee \neg(\psi_1 \, \mathbf{U}^+ \, \psi_2)))])$

Figure 2: Separation clauses for **LTL**

3. Second Order Languages

3.1. Linear and Branching Time Logics

As we have seen, linear temporal logic is expressively complete for natural models. The same result (with minor modifications) can be proved for finitely branching trees [Schlingloff 1992a, Schlingloff 1992b], and for certain partially ordered structures [Thiagarajan and Walukiewicz 1997]. In computer science, the possible executions of a program can be modelled as a *set of execution sequences*. Alternatively, it can be modelled as a unique *execution tree*, where branches denote nondeterministic decisions. This view is adopted in *branching time temporal logic* [Lamport 1980, Ben-Ari, Manna and Pnueli 1983, Emerson and Halpern 1986].

Statements about correctness of program can involve assertions about *all maximal paths* in a tree. A *path* in a model is a (finite or infinite) nonempty sequence of points $\sigma = (w_0, w_1, ...)$, where for each i with $0 \leq i < |\sigma|$ there exists an $R_i \in \mathcal{R}$ such that $(w_i, w_{i+1}) \in \mathcal{I}(R_i)$. A path is *maximal*, if each of its points which has a successor in the model also has a successor in the path. In other words, a maximal path is either infinite, or its final point w_n is terminal (there is no w such that $w_n \prec w$). Computation tree logic (**CTL**) [Clarke and Emerson 1981, Emerson and Clarke 1982] has the following syntax:

$$\textbf{CTL} \quad ::= \quad \mathcal{P} \mid \perp \mid (\textbf{CTL} \rightarrow \textbf{CTL}) \mid \textbf{E}(\textbf{CTL}\,\textbf{U}^+\,\textbf{CTL}) \mid \textbf{A}(\textbf{CTL}\,\textbf{U}^+\,\textbf{CTL}).$$

CTL is interpreted on *tree models*. A tree is defined as usual: it has a single root w_0, and every node w_n can be reached from w_0 by exactly one finite path. The transitive closure "<" of the successor relation "$\prec$" then denotes the usual tree-order: $(w_1, w_2) \in \mathcal{I}(<)$ iff w_1 is on the (unique) path from the root w_0 up to w_2.

- $w_0 \models \textbf{E}(\varphi\,\textbf{U}^+\,\psi)$ iff there exists $w_1 > w_0$ such that $w_1 \models \psi$, and for all $w_2 \in U$, if $w_0 < w_2 < w_1$ then $w_2 \models \varphi$.
- $w_0 \models \textbf{A}(\varphi\,\textbf{U}^+\,\psi)$ iff *for all maximal paths* p from w_0 there exists $w_1 > w_0$ *on path* p such that $w_1 \models \psi$, and for all $w_0 < w_2 < w_1$, $w_2 \models \varphi$.

Thus, the $\textbf{E}\,\textbf{U}^+$-operator is defined similar to the **LTL** until-operator. However, the intended models for **CTL** are trees, whereas **LTL** usually is interpreted on natural models. In **CTL** weak and derived operators can also be defined as abbreviations. However, in branching time, there are two variants of each derived operator.

$$\textbf{E}\,\textbf{X}\,\psi \triangleq \textbf{E}(\perp\,\textbf{U}^+\,\psi), \qquad\qquad \textbf{A}\,\textbf{X}\,\psi \triangleq \textbf{A}(\perp\,\textbf{U}^+\,\psi),$$
$$\textbf{E}\,\overline{\textbf{X}}\,\psi \triangleq \neg\textbf{A}\,\textbf{X}\,\neg\psi, \qquad\qquad \textbf{A}\,\overline{\textbf{X}}\,\psi \triangleq \neg\textbf{E}\,\textbf{X}\,\neg\psi,$$

$$\textbf{E}\,\textbf{F}^+\,\psi \triangleq \textbf{E}(\top\,\textbf{U}^+\,\psi), \qquad\qquad \textbf{A}\,\textbf{F}^+\,\psi \triangleq \textbf{A}(\top\,\textbf{U}^+\,\psi),$$
$$\textbf{E}\,\textbf{G}^+\,\psi \triangleq \neg\textbf{A}\,\textbf{F}^+\,\neg\psi, \qquad\qquad \textbf{A}\,\textbf{G}^+\,\psi \triangleq \neg\textbf{E}\,\textbf{F}^+\,\neg\psi,$$

$$\textbf{E}(\varphi\,\textbf{U}^*\,\psi) \triangleq (\psi \vee \varphi \wedge \textbf{E}(\varphi\,\textbf{U}^+\,\psi)), \qquad \textbf{A}(\varphi\,\textbf{U}^*\,\psi) \triangleq (\psi \vee \varphi \wedge \textbf{A}(\varphi\,\textbf{U}^+\,\psi)),$$
$$\textbf{E}\,\textbf{F}^*\,\psi \triangleq (\psi \vee \textbf{E}\,\textbf{F}^+\,\psi), \qquad\qquad \textbf{A}\,\textbf{F}^*\,\psi \triangleq (\psi \vee \textbf{A}\,\textbf{F}^+\,\psi),$$
$$\textbf{E}\,\textbf{G}^*\,\psi \triangleq (\psi \wedge \textbf{E}\,\textbf{G}^+\,\psi), \qquad\qquad \textbf{A}\,\textbf{G}^*\,\psi \triangleq (\psi \wedge \textbf{A}\,\textbf{G}^+\,\psi),$$

$$\mathbf{E}(\varphi \mathbf{W}^+ \psi) \triangleq \neg\mathbf{A}(\neg\psi \mathbf{U}^+ \neg(\varphi \vee \psi)), \qquad \mathbf{A}(\varphi \mathbf{W}^+ \psi) \triangleq \neg\mathbf{E}(\neg\psi \mathbf{U}^+ \neg(\varphi \vee \psi)).$$

Informally, $\mathbf{E}\mathbf{X}\psi$ means that some successor node satisfies ψ, and $\mathbf{A}\overline{\mathbf{X}}\psi$ holds if all successors are ψ. In a terminal point, $\mathbf{A}\overline{\mathbf{X}}\perp$ is valid, but $\mathbf{A}\mathbf{X}\perp$ not: if w_0 has no successors, then the only maximal path p from w_0 is the one-element sequence $\sigma = (w_0)$. On this unique path σ there is no $w_1 > w_0$, therefore each formula $\mathbf{A}(\varphi \mathbf{U}^+ \psi)$ and $\mathbf{E}(\varphi \mathbf{U}^+ \psi)$ must be invalid. As a special case, in such a point $\mathbf{E}\mathbf{X}\top$ is not valid, but $\mathbf{E}\overline{\mathbf{X}}\top$ and $\mathbf{E}\overline{\mathbf{X}}\perp$ are valid. In a nonterminal point, $(\mathbf{E}\mathbf{X}\varphi \leftrightarrow \mathbf{E}\overline{\mathbf{X}}\varphi)$ and $(\mathbf{A}\mathbf{X}\varphi \leftrightarrow \mathbf{A}\overline{\mathbf{X}}\varphi)$. Thus, if we restrict attention to models without terminal points, these operators coincide. The operators $\mathbf{A}\mathbf{X}$ and $\mathbf{E}\overline{\mathbf{X}}$ can be expressed by $\mathbf{E}\mathbf{X}$ and $\mathbf{A}\overline{\mathbf{X}}$ (with at most linear increase of formula length) via $(\mathbf{A}\mathbf{X}\varphi \leftrightarrow \mathbf{A}\overline{\mathbf{X}}\varphi \wedge \mathbf{E}\mathbf{X}\top)$ and $(\mathbf{E}\overline{\mathbf{X}}\varphi \leftrightarrow \mathbf{E}\mathbf{X}\varphi \vee \mathbf{A}\overline{\mathbf{X}}\perp)$, that is, $(\mathbf{E}\overline{\mathbf{X}}\varphi \leftrightarrow (\mathbf{E}\mathbf{X}\top \rightarrow \mathbf{E}\mathbf{X}\varphi))$. Thus, all **CTL** nexttime-operators can be expressed in terms of $\mathbf{E}\mathbf{X}$.

The formula $\mathbf{E}\mathbf{F}^*\psi$ means that some node in the computation tree satisfies ψ, and $\mathbf{A}\mathbf{F}^*\psi$ specifies that ψ must hold somewhere along every maximal computation path. Dually, $\mathbf{A}\mathbf{G}^*\psi$ means that every node in the (sub-) tree satisfies ψ, whereas $\mathbf{E}\mathbf{G}^*\psi$ indicates that ψ is globally valid along some path.

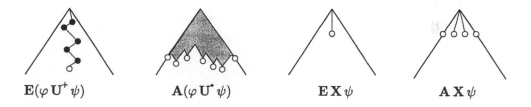

$$\mathbf{E}(\varphi \mathbf{U}^+ \psi) \qquad\qquad \mathbf{A}(\varphi \mathbf{U}^* \psi) \qquad\qquad \mathbf{E}\mathbf{X}\psi \qquad\qquad \mathbf{A}\mathbf{X}\psi$$

In the above picture, nodes satisfying φ are shown solid (or as a shaded area), whereas ψ nodes are indicated by a circle.

The operator $\mathbf{A}\mathbf{U}^+$ can be expressed by $\mathbf{E}\mathbf{U}^+$ and $\mathbf{A}\mathbf{F}^+$. This characterization is similar to the definition of the unless-operator in linear temporal logic, cf. page 1648:

$$\mathbf{A}(\varphi \mathbf{U}^+ \psi) \leftrightarrow (\mathbf{A}(\varphi \mathbf{W}^+ \psi) \wedge \mathbf{A}\mathbf{F}^+ \psi) = (\neg\mathbf{E}(\neg\psi \mathbf{U}^+ \neg(\varphi \vee \psi)) \wedge \mathbf{A}\mathbf{F}^+ \psi).$$

Therefore, it is sufficient to consider only the two basic operators $\mathbf{E}\mathbf{U}^+$ and $\mathbf{A}\mathbf{F}^+$ in formal proofs and algorithms. Similarly, the formula $\mathbf{E}(\varphi \mathbf{W}^+ \psi)$ can be replaced by $(\mathbf{E}(\varphi \mathbf{U}^+ \psi) \vee \mathbf{E}\mathbf{G}^+ \varphi)$. However, there is no negation-free "dual" characterization of $\mathbf{A}\mathbf{W}^+$ and $\mathbf{E}\mathbf{U}^+$.

We now give some examples of **CTL** formulas. The following properties are typical correctness requirements that might arise in the verification of a finite state concurrent program.

— $\mathbf{E}\mathbf{F}^+(\text{started} \wedge \neg\text{ready})$: it is possible to get to a state where started holds but ready does not hold.
— $\mathbf{A}\mathbf{G}^*(\text{req} \rightarrow \mathbf{A}\mathbf{F}^+ \text{ack})$: if a request occurs, then it will be eventually acknowledged

— $\mathbf{A\,G^*\,A\,F^*}$ stack_is_empty: the proposition stack_is_empty holds infinitely often on every computation path

— $\mathbf{A\,G^*\,E\,F^*}$ restart: from any state it is possible to get to a restart state.

For many **CTL** formulas it is possible to formulate similar correctness properties in **LTL**. *Possibility properties* like the last one mentioned above can not be formulated in **LTL**. On the other hand, certain *fairness properties* cannot be formulated in **CTL**.

How can we compare the expressivity of **CTL** with (the future fragment of) **LTL**? Direct comparison is difficult, since models are different: on natural models, which are special tree models with branching degree one, $\mathbf{A\,U^+}$ and $\mathbf{E\,U^+}$-operators coincide. On tree models with higher branching degree, **LTL** obviously cannot express $\mathbf{A}(\varphi\,\mathbf{U^+}\,\psi)$.

Therefore, one considers **LTL** and **CTL** on (nonlinear, non-tree) Kripke-models $(U, \mathcal{I}, w_0)$. In contrast to natural or tree models, Kripke-models can contain reflexive points, loops or even dense relations. We call an **LTL** future formula *sequence-valid* in a Kripke-model $\mathcal{M}$, if it is valid in all natural models $((w_0, w_1, ...), \mathcal{I}, w_0)$ which are *generated* from $\mathcal{M}$, that is, for all maximal paths $w_0, w_1, ...)$ in U starting from w_0. (A formal definition of this notion will be given in Section 4.) Similarly, a **CTL**-formula is called *tree-valid* in a Kripke-model, if it is valid in the root of the unique maximal tree generated from it.

With this definition, the expressivity of **LTL** and **CTL** can be compared. It turns out that on Kripke models, neither of both is strictly more expressive than the other one. For example, the **LTL** formula $\varphi \triangleq \mathbf{F^+\,G^+}\,p$ is not expressible in **CTL** (it is *not* the same property as $\mathbf{A\,F^+\,A\,G^+}\,p$). That is, there is no **CTL**-formula ψ such that ψ is tree-valid in exactly the same Kripke-models in which φ is sequence-valid. Similarly, $\mathbf{A\,G^+\,E\,F^+}\,p$ is not expressible in **LTL** (it is *not* the same as $\mathbf{G^+\,F^+}\,p$). For more information on the expressiveness of linear versus branching time see [Emerson and Lei 1985, Emerson and Halpern 1986, Clarke and Draghicescu 1988, Emerson 1990].

On Kripke-models, the logic $\mathbf{CTL^*}$ (see [Emerson and Lei 1985, Emerson and Halpern 1986]) subsumes **CTL** and **LTL** by separating path quantification (**E**) from temporal quantification ($\mathbf{U^+}$). Thus it is possible to write e.g. $\mathbf{E\,G^*\,F^*}\,p$. The logic $\mathbf{CTL^*}$ is strictly more expressive than both **CTL** and **LTL**. On binary trees, the expressiveness of $\mathbf{CTL^*}$ can be compared to first order logic with additional (second order) quantification on paths. For more information on the expressiveness and complexity of various sublogics of $\mathbf{CTL^*}$, see [Emerson 1990].

3.2. Propositionally Quantified Logics

Quantification over maximal paths is not a first-order notion. It is clear that for natural models, which consist of exactly one maximal path, this quantifier is not very useful. However, even for natural models, there might be other types of second-order quantification which could be interesting. Wolper remarked that "temporal logic can be more expressive"[Wolper 1982, Wolper 1983]. In temporal or first-order logic, it is not possible to specify that a certain proposition p holds on every *second* point of an execution sequence, without constraining the values of p in intermediate points. Formally, for a natural model where $U = (w_0, w_1, ...)$, define the new operator $\mathbf{G}^{2n}$ by

$$w_i \models \mathbf{G}^{2n} \varphi \quad \text{iff} \quad w_{i+2n} \models \varphi \text{ for all } n \geq 0$$

We will show that this operator can not be expressed in **LTL** or **FOL**. First, note that the following operators are not equivalent to $\mathbf{G}^{2n} \varphi$.

$$\mathbf{G}^{2n}_{\mathbf{LTL}} \varphi \triangleq \varphi \wedge \mathbf{G}^{\bullet}(\varphi \rightarrow \mathbf{X}\,\mathbf{X}\,\varphi)$$
$$(\mathbf{G}^{2n}_{\mathbf{FOL}} \varphi)(t_0) \triangleq \varphi(t_0) \wedge \forall t \geq t_0 (\varphi(t) \rightarrow \forall t_1, t_2 (t \prec t_1 \prec t_2 \rightarrow \varphi(t_2)))$$

These formulas define a stronger property than required: they imply that if φ holds in two adjacent states, it must hold always. Therefore, $\models (\mathbf{G}^{2n}_{\mathbf{LTL}} \varphi \rightarrow \mathbf{G}^{2n} \varphi)$. The reverse implication does not hold: there are models satisfying $\mathbf{G}^{2n} \varphi$ but not $\mathbf{G}^{2n}_{\mathbf{LTL}} \varphi$ or $\mathbf{G}^{2n}_{\mathbf{FOL}} \varphi(t_0)$, respectively.

3.1. THEOREM (Wolper). *Let* p *be any atomic proposition. There is no* **LTL**-*formula* φ *such that* $\models \varphi \leftrightarrow \mathbf{G}^{2n} \mathbf{p}$.

PROOF: Consider the following sequence $(\mathcal{M}_0, \mathcal{M}_1, \mathcal{M}_2, ...)$ of models. For each $i \geq 0$, define $\mathcal{M}_i \triangleq (U_i, \mathcal{I}_i, w_0^i)$, where $(U_i, \prec)$ is isomorphic to the integers: $U_i \triangleq (..., w_{-2}^i, w_{-1}^i, w_0^i, w_1^i, w_2^i, ...)$. Furthermore, define $\mathcal{I}_i(\mathbf{q}) \triangleq U_i \backslash w_i^i$ for all $\mathbf{q} \in \mathcal{P}$. That is, $w_n^i \models \mathbf{q}$ iff $i \neq n$ for all atomic propositions q. Since $(U_i, \mathcal{I}_i, w_0^i)$ is isomorphic to $(U_{i+1}, \mathcal{I}_{i+1}, w_1^{i+1})$, we have $w_0^i \models \varphi$ iff $w_1^{i+1} \models \varphi$ for all formulas φ. As a consequence, $w_0^i \models \varphi$ iff $w_0^{i+1} \models \mathbf{X}\varphi$.

In the next step, we prove that any **LTL** formula will almost always be **true** or almost always be **false** in the sequence $(\mathcal{M}_i)$: for any $\varphi \in \mathbf{LTL}$ there exists an i such that for all $j \geq i$ it holds that $\mathcal{M}_i \models \varphi$ iff $\mathcal{M}_j \models \varphi$. This is proved by induction on the structure of **LTL** formulas. The only interesting case is given by the until-connectives. We prove the case of $(\varphi \mathbf{U}^{\bullet} \psi)$. For this case, the induction hypothesis guarantees that there is an i such that for all $j \geq i$, both $w_0^j \models \varphi$ iff $w_0^{j+1} \models \varphi$ (*) and $w_0^j \models \psi$ iff $w_0^{j+1} \models \psi$ (**). We have to show that $w_0^j \models (\varphi \mathbf{U}^{\bullet} \psi)$ iff $w_0^{j+1} \models (\varphi \mathbf{U}^{\bullet} \psi)$. From the above consequence, $w_0^j \models (\varphi \mathbf{U}^{\bullet} \psi)$ iff $w_0^{j+1} \models \mathbf{X}(\varphi \mathbf{U}^{\bullet} \psi)$ (***). The following recursive characterization is valid: $\models (\varphi \mathbf{U}^{\bullet} \psi) \leftrightarrow (\psi \vee \varphi \wedge \mathbf{X}(\varphi \mathbf{U}^{\bullet} \psi))$. In particular, this implies $\models (\psi \rightarrow (\varphi \mathbf{U}^{\bullet} \psi))$ (†), $\models (\neg\psi \rightarrow ((\varphi \mathbf{U}^{\bullet} \psi) \leftrightarrow (\varphi \wedge \mathbf{X}(\varphi \mathbf{U}^{\bullet} \psi))))$ (††), and $\models (\neg\psi \rightarrow ((\varphi \mathbf{U}^{\bullet} \psi) \rightarrow \varphi))$ (†††).

If $w_0^j \models \psi$, then $w_0^j \models (\varphi \mathbf{U}^{\bullet} \psi)$ by (†). In this case, by (**), $w_0^{j+1} \models \psi$, hence also $w_0^{j+1} \models (\varphi \mathbf{U}^{\bullet} \psi)$ by (†). Therefore, if $w_0^j \models \psi$, then $w_0^j \models (\varphi \mathbf{U}^{\bullet} \psi)$ iff $w_0^{j+1} \models (\varphi \mathbf{U}^{\bullet} \psi)$. Now we consider the case that $w_0^j \not\models \psi$. By (†††), $w_0^j \models (\varphi \mathbf{U}^{\bullet} \psi)$ iff $w_0^j \models \varphi$ *and* $w_0^j \models (\varphi \mathbf{U}^{\bullet} \psi)$. By (*) and (***), this in turn holds iff $w_0^{j+1} \models \varphi$ and $w_0^{j+1} \models \mathbf{X}(\varphi \mathbf{U}^{\bullet} \psi)$. By (††), this is the case iff $w_0^{j+1} \models (\varphi \mathbf{U}^{\bullet} \psi)$.

To complete the proof, we now show that this eventual stability property does not hold for formulas which include the $\mathbf{G}^{2n}$ operator. It is not hard to see that $\mathcal{M}_i \models \mathbf{G}^{2n} \mathbf{p}$ iff i is odd: recall that $w_i^i \not\models \mathbf{p}$. Thus, if i is even, then for $n \triangleq i/2$

we have $w_{0+2n}^i \not\models p$, which means $w_0^i \not\models G^{2n} p$. If i is odd, however, then for all $n \geq 0$, $w_{0+2n}^i \models p$, and thus $w_0^i \models G^{2n} p$. Hence, we have shown that for every **LTL** formula φ there is a model $\mathcal{M}_i$ such that $\mathcal{M}_i \not\models (\varphi \leftrightarrow G^{2n} p)$. $\qquad\square$

The above proof shows that the G^{2n} operator cannot be defined in the basic temporal or first order language. However, it can be defined if additional propositions are allowed. To assert that $G^{2n} \varphi$ holds, it suffices to provide a "new" proposition q (not occurring in φ) such that $G_{LTL}^{2n} q$ holds, and that φ is valid wherever q is valid. This puts an additional constraint on the "auxiliary variable" q, which can be considered as an "implementation detail" in the context of φ. If we disregard the value of q, then the models satisfying $(G_{LTL}^{2n} q \wedge G^*(q \to \varphi))$ are exactly those satisfying $G^{2n} \varphi$. That is, for any model $\mathcal{M}$ such that $\mathcal{M} \models (G_{LTL}^{2n} q \wedge G^*(q \to \varphi))$ it holds that $\mathcal{M} \models G^{2n} \varphi$, and for every model $\mathcal{M}$ such that $\mathcal{M} \models G^{2n} \varphi$ it holds that $\mathcal{M}' \models (G_{LTL}^{2n} q \wedge G^*(q \to \varphi))$, where $\mathcal{M}'$ differs from $\mathcal{M}$ only in the fact that $\mathcal{I}(q) = \{w_0, w_2, w_4, ...\}$. Logically, this projection operation amounts to existential quantification on temporal propositions or sets of points:

$$G^{2n} \varphi \leftrightarrow \exists q (G_{LTL}^{2n} q \wedge G^*(q \to \varphi))$$
$$(G^{2n} \varphi)(t_0) \leftrightarrow \exists q ((G_{FOL}^{2n} q)(t_0) \wedge \forall t \geq t_0 (q(t) \to \varphi(t))))$$

The language used in the first of these formulas is called quantified temporal logic **qTL** [Sistla 1983], the language of the second item is *monadic second order logic* **MSOL**.

$$\textbf{qTL} ::= \mathcal{P} \mid \mathcal{Q} \mid \perp \mid (\textbf{qTL} \to \textbf{qTL}) \mid$$
$$(\textbf{qTL U}^+ \textbf{qTL}) \mid (\textbf{qTL U}^- \textbf{qTL}) \mid \exists \mathcal{Q} \textbf{ qTL}.$$

$$\textbf{MSOL} ::= \mathcal{P}(\mathcal{T}) \mid \mathcal{Q}(\mathcal{T}) \mid \perp \mid (\textbf{MSOL} \to \textbf{MSOL}) \mid$$
$$\mathcal{R}^+(\mathcal{T}, \mathcal{T}) \mid \exists \mathcal{T} \textbf{ MSOL} \mid \exists \mathcal{Q} \textbf{ MSOL}$$

To define this syntax, we used another syntactic category $\mathcal{Q} = \{q, q_0, ...\}$ of *proposition variables*. Any valuation in a model v assigns a set $\mathbf{v}(q) \subseteq U$ to each of these (second order) variables. The formula $\exists q \ \varphi$ is valid in a model $\mathcal{M} = (U, \mathcal{I}, \mathbf{v})$ if it is valid in some model $\mathcal{M}' = (U, \mathcal{I}, \mathbf{v}')$ which differs from $\mathcal{M}$ at most in the valuation of the proposition variable $q \in \mathcal{Q}$.

It is easy to lift the expressive completeness theorem 2.4 to second order.

3.2. LEMMA. *On natural models,* **qTL** *has the same expressiveness as* **MSOL**.

PROOF: In the proof of Theorem 2.4, it was shown how to construct the translation **LTL**(φ) of a first order formula φ. For any **MSOL** formula there is an equivalent prenex formula of the form $\sigma q_1 \sigma q_2 ... \sigma q_n \psi$, where ψ is a first order formula and each σ is a second order quantifier. Thus, defining **MSOL**$(\sigma q_1 \sigma q_2 ... \sigma q_n \psi)$ by $\sigma q_1 \sigma q_2 ... \sigma q_n$ **LTL**(ψ) gives a translation from **MSOL** into **qTL**. $\qquad\square$

3.3. LEMMA. *On natural models, the* $\mathbf{U}^+$*-operator in* **qTL** *is definable by the operators* $\mathbf{G}^{\pm}$ *and* $\mathbf{X}$:

$$(\varphi\,\mathbf{U}^+\,\psi) \leftrightarrow \forall q(\mathbf{G}^{\pm}(\mathbf{X}(\psi \vee \varphi \wedge q) \to q) \to q).$$

PROOF: Since this lemma is used several times in subsequent sections, we give a detailed proof. For one direction, assume that $(\varphi\,\mathbf{U}^+\,\psi)$ is valid in $\mathcal{M} \triangleq (U, \mathcal{I}, w_0)$. To prove that $\mathcal{M} \models \forall q(\mathbf{G}^{\pm}(\mathbf{X}(\psi \vee \varphi \wedge q) \to q) \to q)$, let $\mathcal{I}'(q)$ be an arbitrary set of points, and show that $(U, \mathcal{I}', w_0) \models (\mathbf{G}^{\pm}(\mathbf{X}(\psi \vee \varphi \wedge q) \to q) \to q)$. In other words, from the assumption $w_0 \models \mathbf{G}^{\pm}(\mathbf{X}(\psi \vee \varphi \wedge q) \to q)$ we have to show that $w_0 \models q$. In any natural model satisfying $w_0 \models (\varphi\,\mathbf{U}^+\,\psi)$, there are $w_1, ..., w_n \in U$ such that $w_i \prec w_{i+1}$ for all $0 \leq i < n$, and $\varphi(w_i)$ for all $0 < i < n$, and $w_n \models \psi$. If $w_0 \models \mathbf{G}^{\pm}(\mathbf{X}(\psi \vee \varphi \wedge q) \to q)$, then $w_i \models (\mathbf{X}(\psi \vee \varphi \wedge q) \to q)$ for all $i \geq 0$. Hence, $w_i \models (\mathbf{X}\,\psi \to q)$ and $w_i \models (\mathbf{X}(\varphi \wedge q) \to q)$ for all $i \geq 0$. From $w_n \models \psi$ it follows that $w_{n-1} \models \mathbf{X}\,\psi$. Since $w_{n-1} \models (\mathbf{X}\,\psi \to q)$, we have $w_{n-1} \models q$. Therefore $w_{n-1} \models (\varphi \wedge q)$, and $w_{n-2} \models \mathbf{X}(\varphi \wedge q)$. Since $w_{n-2} \models (\mathbf{X}(\varphi \wedge q) \to q)$, it follows that $w_{n-2} \models q$. Continuing inductively, we find that $w_i \models q$ for all $0 \leq i < n$. Therefore, $w_0 \models q$.

For the other direction, assume that $w_0 \models \forall q(\mathbf{G}^{\pm}(\mathbf{X}(\psi \vee \varphi \wedge q) \to q) \to q)$ and show that $w_0 \models (\varphi\,\mathbf{U}^+\,\psi)$. First, we show that there must be some $w > w_0$ satisfying $w \models \psi$. Assume for contradiction that this is not the case. Choose $\mathcal{I}(q) \triangleq \{w \mid \text{not } w \geq w_0\}$. In natural models, this is the set $\{w \mid w < w_0\}$. It follows that (i) $w \models q$ for all w such that not $w \geq w_0$, (ii) $w_0 \not\models q$, and (iii) $w \not\models q$ for all $w > w_0$. We show that (*): $w \models (\mathbf{X}(\psi \vee \varphi \wedge q) \to q)$ for all $w \in U$. According to the contradiction assumption, $w \not\models \psi$ for all $w > w_0$. With (iii), it follows that $w \not\models (\psi \vee \varphi \wedge q)$ for all $w > w_0$. Hence, $w \not\models \mathbf{X}(\psi \vee \varphi \wedge q)$ for all $w \geq w_0$. As a consequence, (*) holds for all $w \geq w_0$. If not $w \geq w_0$, then (*) is an immediate consequence of (i). From (*), we infer that $w_0 \models \mathbf{G}^{\pm}(\mathbf{X}(\psi \vee \varphi \wedge q) \to q)$. Therefore, $w_0 \models q$, which is a contradiction to (ii).

Let $w_1, ..., w_n$ be a set of points such that $w_i \prec w_{i+1}$ for all $0 \leq i < n$, and w_n is the smallest point satisfying ψ (i.e., $w_n \models \psi$ and $w_i \models \neg\psi$ for all $w_0 < w_i < w_n$). If $n = 1$, we are done: in this case $w_0 \models \mathbf{X}\,\psi$, which implies that $w_0 \models (\varphi\,\mathbf{U}^+\,\psi)$. If $n > 1$, to prove $w_0 \models (\varphi\,\mathbf{U}^+\,\psi)$ we additionally have to show that $w_i \models \varphi$ for any $0 < i < n$. Substitution of q with $\neg q$ in the assumption yields the following equivalent version: $w_0 \models \forall q(q \to \mathbf{F}^{\pm}(q \wedge \mathbf{X}(\psi \vee \varphi \wedge \neg q)))$. Choose $\mathcal{I}(q) \triangleq \{w \mid w_0 \leq w < w_i\}$. It follows that $w_0 \models \mathbf{F}^{\pm}(q \wedge \mathbf{X}(\psi \vee \varphi \wedge \neg q))$. That is, there is some $w \in U$ such that $w \models (q \wedge \mathbf{X}(\psi \vee \varphi \wedge \neg q))$. Since n is minimal, there is no $w \in \mathcal{I}(q)$ which satisfies $w \models \mathbf{X}\,\psi$. Therefore, it follows that there is a $w \geq w_0$ such that $w \models (q \wedge \mathbf{X}(\varphi \wedge \neg q))$. Since w_{i-1} is the only point with $w_{i-1} \models (q \wedge \mathbf{X}\,\neg q)$ we can conclude that $w_{i-1} \models \mathbf{X}\,\varphi$, i.e., $w_i \models \varphi$. $\qquad\square$

As a sideline we remark that this proof does not make essential use of the "past-component" of the $\mathbf{G}^{\pm}$-operator; in fact, the same proof holds verbatim if we replace $\mathbf{G}^{\pm}$ by $\mathbf{G}^*$ and $\mathbf{F}^{\pm}$ by $\mathbf{F}^*$. Thus, a corollary to Lemma 3.3 is $(\varphi\,\mathbf{U}^+\,\psi) \leftrightarrow \forall q(\mathbf{G}^*(\mathbf{X}(\psi \vee \varphi \wedge q) \to q) \to q)$. (Since $\mathbf{F}^+$ is somewhat more specific than $\mathbf{F}^{\pm}$ this could be considered as a somehow weaker result.)

The characterization of the $\mathbf{U}^+$-operator with second order quantification is a special case of the general scheme $\forall q(\mathbf{G}^\pm(\xi \to q) \to q)$, where $\xi \triangleq \mathbf{X}(\psi \vee \varphi \wedge q)$. Dually, the operator $(\varphi \, \mathbf{W}^+ \, \psi) \triangleq \neg(\neg\psi \, \mathbf{U}^+ \, \neg(\varphi \vee \psi))$ is characterized by

$$(\varphi \, \mathbf{W}^+ \, \psi) \leftrightarrow \neg\forall q(\mathbf{G}^\pm(\mathbf{X}(\neg(\varphi \vee \psi) \vee (\neg\psi \wedge q)) \to q) \to q)$$
$$\leftrightarrow \exists q(\neg q \wedge \mathbf{G}^\pm(\mathbf{X}((\neg\psi \wedge \neg\varphi) \vee (\neg\psi \wedge q)) \to q))$$
$$\leftrightarrow \exists q(\neg q \wedge \mathbf{G}^\pm(\neg q \to \neg \mathbf{X}(\neg\psi \wedge (\neg\varphi \vee q))))$$
$$\leftrightarrow \exists q(\neg q \wedge \mathbf{G}^\pm(\neg q \to \mathbf{\overline{X}}(\psi \vee (\varphi \wedge \neg q))))$$
$$\leftrightarrow \exists q(q \wedge \mathbf{G}^\pm(q \to \mathbf{\overline{X}}(\psi \vee \varphi \wedge q)))$$

This is an instance of the dual scheme $\exists q(q \wedge \mathbf{G}^\pm(q \to \xi))$ with $\xi \triangleq \mathbf{\overline{X}}(\psi \vee \varphi \wedge q)$.

For complexity reasons, it is not always advisable to allow quantifiers on arbitrary subsets of the universe U. Therefore, we introduce *fixpoint quantification*: quantification on sets which follows these schemes. This results in the *propositional μ-calculus μTL* [Emerson and Clarke 1980, Pratt 1981, Kozen 1983, Kozen and Parikh 1983]:

$$\mu\mathbf{TL} \quad ::= \quad \mathcal{P} \mid \mathcal{Q} \mid \bot \mid (\mu\mathbf{TL} \to \mu\mathbf{TL}) \mid \langle\mathcal{R}\rangle \, \mu\mathbf{TL} \mid \nu\mathcal{Q} \, \mu\mathbf{TL}.$$

The semantics of μTL can be defined by a translation into **MSOL**.

- **MSOL**(φ) is defined as in **FOL**(φ), for the cases $\mathrm{p} \in \mathcal{P}$, $\bot$, $(\psi_1 \to \psi_2)$, and $\langle\mathcal{R}\rangle \, \psi$
- **MSOL**$(q) \triangleq q(t_0)$, if $q \in \mathcal{Q}$
- **MSOL**$(\nu q \, \varphi) \triangleq \exists q(q(t_0) \wedge \forall t(q(t) \to \mathbf{MSOL}(\varphi)\{t_0 := t\}))$.

Recall that $\varphi\{t_0 := t\}$ denotes the formula which is formed from φ by replacing every free occurrence of t_0 by t. Similarly, $\varphi\{q := \psi\}$ denotes the formula which results from φ by replacing every free occurrence of q with ψ. The formula $\mu q \, \varphi$ is short for $\neg\nu q \, \neg(\varphi\{q := \neg q\})$. Thus, the translation of $\mu q \, \varphi$ evaluates to

- **MSOL**$(\mu q \, \varphi) = \neg\exists q(\neg q(t_0) \wedge \forall t(\neg q(t) \to \neg\mathbf{MSOL}(\varphi)\{t_0 := t\}))$
  $$= \forall q(q(t_0) \vee \neg\forall t(\neg q(t) \to \neg\mathbf{MSOL}(\varphi)\{t_0 := t\}))$$
  $$= \forall q(\forall t(\mathbf{MSOL}(\varphi)\{t_0 := t\} \to q(t)) \to q(t_0)).$$

In this chapter, we use ν as basic operator and μ as a defined operator, since the semantics of ν is a restricted *existential* quantification on sets of points, and μ is a restricted *universal* second order quantifier. However, $(\varphi \, \mathbf{U}^+ \, \psi)$, which is defined by an existential first order clause, is often associated with a μ-formula: when interpreting μTL on natural models, we use the operator $\mathbf{X}$ for the unique diamond operator $\langle R \rangle$. With this notation, Lemma 3.3 can be reformulated as follows.

3.4. COROLLARY. *For any natural model $\mathcal{M}$,*

$$\mathcal{M} \models (\varphi \, \mathbf{U}^+ \, \psi) \quad \textit{iff} \quad \mathcal{M} \models \mu q \, \mathbf{X}(\psi \vee \varphi \wedge q)$$

PROOF: With Lemma 3.3, the equivalence follows almost immediately from the definitions.

$$\mathbf{MSOL}(\mu q\, \mathbf{X}(\psi \vee \varphi \wedge q)) = \forall q(\forall t(\mathbf{MSOL}(\mathbf{X}(\psi \vee \varphi \wedge q))\{t_0 := t\} \rightarrow q(t)) \rightarrow q(t_0))$$
$$= \mathbf{MSOL}(\forall q(\mathbf{G}^{\pm}(\mathbf{X}(\psi \vee \varphi \wedge q) \rightarrow q) \rightarrow q))$$
$$\leftrightarrow \mathbf{FOL}((\varphi\, \mathbf{U}^+\, \psi)) \quad \text{(according to Lemma 3.3)} \qquad \square$$

Corollary 3.4 does not hold for more general Kripke models. In natural models, other operators can be characterized by similar $\mu\mathbf{TL}$ formulas:

$$\mathcal{M} \models \mathbf{F}^+\, \psi \qquad \text{iff} \qquad \mathcal{M} \models \mu q\, \mathbf{X}(\psi \vee q)$$

$$\mathcal{M} \models (\varphi\, \mathbf{W}^+\, \psi) \qquad \text{iff} \qquad \mathcal{M} \models \nu q\, \mathbf{\overline{X}}(\psi \vee \varphi \wedge q)$$

$$\mathcal{M} \models \mathbf{G}^*\, \psi \qquad \text{iff} \qquad \mathcal{M} \models \nu q\, (\psi \wedge \mathbf{\overline{X}}\, q)$$

$$\mathcal{M} \models (\varphi\, \mathbf{U}^*\, \psi) \qquad \text{iff} \qquad \mathcal{M} \models \mu q\, (\psi \vee \varphi \wedge \mathbf{X}\, q)$$

Similarly, on tree models all **CTL** operators can be defined by $\mu\mathbf{TL}$ formulas. The same holds for most other programming logics which can be found in the literature. A formal justification of this statement will be given below in Theorem 5.10.

For certain formulas, an alternative semantical description of the ν and μ quantifiers in terms of greatest and least fixed points can be given. A function $f : 2^U \rightarrow 2^U$ is called *monotonic*, if $P \subseteq Q$ implies that $f(P) \subseteq f(Q)$. A set $Q \subseteq U$ is called a *fixed point* of f, if $Q = f(Q)$.

Let $gfp(f) = \bigcup\{Q \mid Q \subseteq f(Q)\}$ and $lfp(f) = \bigcap\{Q \mid f(Q) \subseteq Q\}$. The Knaster-Tarski fixpoint theorem [Tarski 1955] states that if f is monotonic, then $gfp(f)$ and $lfp(f)$ are the *greatest* and *least fixed point* of f.

3.5. THEOREM (Knaster-Tarski). *Let* $f : 2^U \rightarrow 2^U$ *be monotonic. Then*
(a) $gfp(f) = f(gfp(f))$ *and* $lfp(f) = f(lfp(f))$, *and*
(b) If $Q = f(Q)$, *then* $Q \subseteq gfp(f)$ *and* $lfp(f) \subseteq Q$.

PROOF: Since gfp and lfp are dual, it suffices to prove the theorem for gfp.

If $Q = f(Q)$, then $Q \subseteq f(Q)$. If $Q \subseteq f(Q)$, then $Q \in \{Q \mid Q \subseteq f(Q)\}$, that is, $Q \subseteq \bigcup\{Q \mid Q \subseteq f(Q)\} = gfp(f)$. This proves (b). Furthermore, since f is monotonic, it implies that $f(Q) \subseteq f(gfp(f))$. Hence for each Q, if $Q \subseteq f(Q)$ then $Q \subseteq f(gfp(f))$ by transitivity of set inclusion. Since each individual Q is a subset of $f(gfp(f))$, this means that $\bigcup\{Q \mid Q \subseteq f(Q)\} \subseteq f(gfp(f))$, i.e., $gfp(f) \subseteq f(gfp(f))$. This is one part of (a). Now, we use this result to infer the converse inclusion of (a): since f is monotonic, $f(gfp(f)) \subseteq f(f(gfp(f)))$. Thus, $f(gfp(f)) \in \{Q \mid Q \subseteq f(Q)\}$, which means $f(gfp(f)) \subseteq \bigcup\{Q \mid Q \subseteq f(Q)\}$. Therefore, $f(gfp(f)) \subseteq gfp(f)$. $\qquad \square$

In fact, this proof shows that the second part of the theorem can be strengthened.

3.6. COROLLARY. *If* $f : 2^U \rightarrow 2^U$ *is monotonic, then*
- $Q \subseteq f(Q)$ *implies* $Q \subseteq gfp(f)$, *and*
- $f(Q) \subseteq Q$ *implies* $lfp(f) \subseteq Q$.

For a more detailed discussion of other fixpoint theorems, see [Davey and Priestley 1990, Gunter and Scott 1990].

In a frame $\mathcal{F} = (U, \mathcal{I})$, any formula φ defines a set $\varphi^{\mathcal{F}} \subseteq U$ of points in the universe, namely $\varphi^{\mathcal{F}} \triangleq \{w \mid (U, \mathcal{I}, w) \models \varphi\}$. Likewise, a formula φ with a free proposition variable q defines a function $\varphi_q^{\mathcal{F}} : U \to U$ from sets of points to sets of points (a *predicate transformer*): if $Q \subseteq U$, then $\varphi_q^{\mathcal{F}}(Q) \triangleq \{w \mid (U, \mathcal{I}', w) \models \varphi\}$, where $\mathcal{I}'$ differs from $\mathcal{I}$ only in $\mathcal{I}'(q) \triangleq Q$.

3.7. LEMMA. $(\nu q\ \varphi)^{\mathcal{F}} = \mathit{gfp}(\varphi_q^{\mathcal{F}})$ and $(\mu q\ \varphi)^{\mathcal{F}} = \mathit{lfp}(\varphi_q^{\mathcal{F}})$.

PROOF: According to the definitions, $w \in \mathit{gfp}(\varphi_q^{\mathcal{F}})$ iff $w \in \bigcup\{Q \mid Q \subseteq \varphi_q^{\mathcal{F}}(Q)\}$, that is, if there is some $Q \subseteq U$ such that $w \in Q$ and $Q \subseteq \varphi_q^{\mathcal{F}}(Q)$. In **MSOL** this condition can be denoted as $w \models \exists q(q(t_0) \wedge \forall t(q(t) \to \mathbf{MSOL}(\varphi)\{t_0 := t\}))$. This clause is exactly the semantical translation $\mathbf{MSOL}(\nu q\ \varphi$; thus $w \in \mathit{gfp}(\varphi_q^{\mathcal{F}})$ iff $w \models \nu q\ \varphi$. For $\mathit{lfp}(\varphi_q^{\mathcal{F}})$, the dual proof holds.   □

We say that a formula φ is *monotonic in q*, if the corresponding predicate transformer $\varphi_q^{\mathcal{F}}$ is monotonic. In other words, φ is monotonic in q iff $(\psi_1 \to \psi_2) \models (\varphi\{q := \psi_1\} \to \varphi\{q := \psi_2\})$ holds. φ is *monotonic*, if for each sub-formula $\nu q\ \psi$, the formula ψ is monotonic in q. Call an occurrence of a proposition variable q in a formula φ *positive* or *negative*, if it is under an even or odd number of negations. Formally, this notion is defined recursively: q is positive in the formula q. An occurrence of q in the formula $(\varphi \to \psi)$ is positive, if it is a negative occurrence in φ or a positive occurrence in ψ, and negative, if it is a positive occurrence in φ or a negative occurrence in ψ. An occurrence of q in $\langle R \rangle\ \varphi$ and $\nu q'\ \varphi$ is positive or negative, if it is positive or negative in φ, respectively. A formula φ is called *positive in q*, if every free occurrence of q in φ is positive. It is *positive*, if each sub-formula $\nu q\ \psi$ is positive in q.

3.8. LEMMA. *If φ is positive in q, then $\varphi_q^{\mathcal{F}}$ is a monotonic predicate transformer.*

PROOF: This statement can be proved by induction on the structure of φ. The induction basis, namely formulas which are atomic propositions, proposition variables or boolean constants, is immediate. For the inductive step, assume that $P \subseteq Q$. If $(\varphi \to \psi)$ is positive in q, then ψ must be positive and φ must be negative in q. Therefore, $\neg\varphi$ is positive in q. The induction hypothesis is that $\psi_q^{\mathcal{F}}(P) \subseteq \psi_q^{\mathcal{F}}(Q)$ and $\neg\varphi_q^{\mathcal{F}}(P) \subseteq \neg\varphi_q^{\mathcal{F}}(Q)$. From this we can infer that $\varphi_q^{\mathcal{F}}(Q) \subseteq \varphi_q^{\mathcal{F}}(P)$. Therefore, if $\varphi_q^{\mathcal{F}}(P) \subseteq \psi_q^{\mathcal{F}}(P)$ then $\varphi_q^{\mathcal{F}}(Q) \subseteq \psi_q^{\mathcal{F}}(Q)$. This follows from $\varphi_q^{\mathcal{F}}(Q) \subseteq \varphi_q^{\mathcal{F}}(P) \subseteq \psi_q^{\mathcal{F}}(P) \subseteq \psi_q^{\mathcal{F}}(Q)$. In other words, $(\varphi \to \psi)_q^{\mathcal{F}}(P) \subseteq (\varphi \to \psi)_q^{\mathcal{F}}(Q)$. For the case $\langle R \rangle\ \varphi$, the induction hypothesis is that $\varphi_q^{\mathcal{F}}(P) \subseteq \varphi_q^{\mathcal{F}}(Q)$. Then, $\{w \mid \exists w'(w, w') \in \mathcal{I}(R) \wedge w' \in \varphi_q^{\mathcal{F}}(P)\} \subseteq \{w \mid \exists w'(w, w') \in \mathcal{I}(R) \wedge w' \in \varphi_q^{\mathcal{F}}(Q)\}$. In other words, $(\langle R \rangle\ \varphi)_q^{\mathcal{F}}(P) \subseteq (\langle R \rangle\ \varphi)_q^{\mathcal{F}}(Q)$. Similarly, for formulas $\nu q'\varphi$, where q and q' are different variables, the induction hypothesis is that $\varphi_{q,q'}^{\mathcal{F}}(P, X) \subseteq \varphi_{q,q'}^{\mathcal{F}}(Q, X)$ for all X. Therefore, $X \subseteq (\varphi)_{q,q'}^{\mathcal{F}}(P, X)$ implies $X \subseteq (\varphi)_{q,q'}^{\mathcal{F}}(Q, X)$ for all X. Consequently, $\{w \mid \text{for some } X,\ w \in X \text{ and } X \subseteq \varphi_{q,q'}^{\mathcal{F}}(P, X)\} \subseteq \{w \mid \text{for some } X,\ w \in X \text{ and } X \subseteq \varphi_{q,q'}^{\mathcal{F}}(Q, X)\}$. According to the definition, this is the semantics of

$(\nu q' \varphi)_q^{\mathcal{F}}(P) \subseteq (\nu q' \varphi)_q^{\mathcal{F}}(Q)$. The last case is $\nu q \varphi$. Since this formula has no free occurrence of variable q, its denotation $(\nu q \varphi)_q^{\mathcal{F}}$ is a constant function. Trivially, constant functions are monotonic. □

The converse of this statement does not hold in general. In particular, [Ajtai and Gurevich 1987] shows that there is a formula which is monotonic on all finite structures but has no positive equivalent.

3.9. COROLLARY. *If φ is positive, then*

- $\models (\nu q\ \varphi \leftrightarrow \varphi\{q := \nu q\ \varphi\})$ *and* $\models (\mu q\ \varphi \leftrightarrow \varphi\{q := \mu q\ \varphi\})$.
- *If* $(U,\mathcal{I}) \models (\chi \leftrightarrow \varphi\{q := \chi\})$ *then both* $(U,\mathcal{I}) \models (\chi \rightarrow \nu q\ \varphi)$ *and* $(U,\mathcal{I}) \models (\mu q\ \varphi \rightarrow \chi)$.
- $(U,\mathcal{I}) \models (\chi \rightarrow \varphi\{q := \chi\})$ *implies* $(U,\mathcal{I}) \models (\chi \rightarrow \nu q\ \varphi)$, *and* $(U,\mathcal{I}) \models (\varphi\{q := \chi\} \rightarrow \chi)$ *implies* $(U,\mathcal{I}) \models (\mu q\ \varphi \rightarrow \chi)$

PROOF: If φ is positive in q, then $\varphi_q^{\mathcal{F}}$ is monotonic according to Lemma 3.8. Theorem 3.5 asserts that $gfp(\varphi_q^{\mathcal{F}}) = \varphi_q^{\mathcal{F}}(gfp(\varphi_q^{\mathcal{F}}))$. In the notation of Lemma 3.7, this means $(\nu q\ \varphi)^{\mathcal{F}} = \varphi_q^{\mathcal{F}}((\nu q\ \varphi)^{\mathcal{F}})$. Moreover, $\varphi_q^{\mathcal{F}}((\nu q\ \varphi)^{\mathcal{F}}) = (\varphi_q\{q := \nu q\ \varphi\})^{\mathcal{F}}$. Therefore, $\mathcal{M} \models (\nu q\ \varphi \leftrightarrow \varphi_q\{q := \nu q\ \varphi\})$. The other statements are shown similarly. □

According to Corollary 3.4, $(\varphi\,\mathbf{U}^+\,\psi)$ and $(\varphi\,\mathbf{W}^+\,\psi)$ in natural models are least and greatest fixed points of $\mathbf{X}(\psi \vee \varphi \wedge q)$ and $\overline{\mathbf{X}}(\psi \vee \varphi \wedge q)$, respectively. Therefore, the following *recursion* and *induction* axioms hold:

- $\models (\varphi\,\mathbf{U}^+\,\psi) \leftrightarrow \mathbf{X}(\psi \vee \varphi \wedge (\varphi\,\mathbf{U}^+\,\psi))$ and $\models (\varphi\,\mathbf{W}^+\,\psi) \leftrightarrow \overline{\mathbf{X}}(\psi \vee \varphi \wedge (\varphi\,\mathbf{W}^+\,\psi))$.
- $(U,\mathcal{I}) \models (\mathbf{X}(\psi \vee \varphi \wedge \chi) \rightarrow \chi)$ implies $(U,\mathcal{I}) \models ((\varphi\,\mathbf{U}^+\,\psi) \rightarrow \chi)$, and $(U,\mathcal{I}) \models (\chi \rightarrow \overline{\mathbf{X}}(\psi \vee \varphi \wedge \chi))$ implies $(U,\mathcal{I}) \models (\chi \rightarrow (\varphi\,\mathbf{W}^+\,\psi))$.

In particular, for $\mathbf{F}^+$, $\mathbf{G}^+$, $\mathbf{F}^*$ and $\mathbf{G}^*$, we have

- $\models (\mathbf{F}^+\,\psi) \leftrightarrow \mathbf{X}(\psi \vee \mathbf{F}^+\,\psi)$ and $\models (\mathbf{G}^+\,\varphi) \leftrightarrow \overline{\mathbf{X}}(\varphi \wedge \mathbf{G}^+\,\varphi)$.
- $\models (\mathbf{F}^*\,\psi) \leftrightarrow (\psi \vee \mathbf{X}\,\mathbf{F}^*\,\psi)$ and $\models (\mathbf{G}^*\,\varphi) \leftrightarrow (\varphi \wedge \overline{\mathbf{X}}\,\mathbf{G}^*\,\varphi)$.
- $(U,\mathcal{I}) \models (\mathbf{X}(\psi \vee \chi) \rightarrow \chi)$ implies $(U,\mathcal{I}) \models ((\mathbf{F}^+\,\psi) \rightarrow \chi)$, and $(U,\mathcal{I}) \models (\chi \rightarrow \overline{\mathbf{X}}(\varphi \wedge \chi))$ implies $(U,\mathcal{I}) \models (\chi \rightarrow \mathbf{G}^+\,\varphi)$.
- $(U,\mathcal{I}) \models ((\psi \vee \mathbf{X}\,\chi) \rightarrow \chi)$ implies $(U,\mathcal{I}) \models ((\mathbf{F}^*\,\psi) \rightarrow \chi)$, and $(U,\mathcal{I}) \models (\chi \rightarrow (\varphi \wedge \overline{\mathbf{X}}\,\chi))$ implies $(U,\mathcal{I}) \models (\chi \rightarrow \mathbf{G}^*\,\varphi)$.

As we have shown, positive $\mu\mathbf{TL}$ formulas denote greatest or least fixed points of predicate transformers. For nonmonotonic formulas, the existence of fixed points is not granted. For example, there is no $Q \subseteq U$ satisfying $Q = U \setminus Q$; thus, there is no fixed point of $(\neg q)_q^{\mathcal{F}}$. However, the **MSOL** semantics of $\nu q\ \neg q$ is $\exists q(q(t_0) \wedge \forall t(q(t) \rightarrow \neg q(t)))$, which is equivalent to the well-defined value $\bot$. On general Kripke-models, positive $\mu\mathbf{TL}$ is strictly weaker in expressiveness than unrestricted $\mu\mathbf{TL}$. Even unrestricted $\mu\mathbf{TL}$ can, in turn, express fewer properties of Kripke models than monadic second order logic:

3.10. LEMMA. *Consider the class of all Kripke models.*
  (a) *There is no positive μTL formula which is equivalent to $\nu q(\langle R \rangle \neg q)$.*
  (b) *There is no μTL formula which is equivalent to $\forall t p(t)$*

PROOF: For (a), consider $\varphi \triangleq \nu q(\langle R \rangle \neg q)$. Then $\mathbf{MSOL}(\varphi) = \exists q(q(t_0) \wedge \forall t(q(t) \to \exists t'(tRt' \wedge \neg q(t'))))$. This formula is equivalent to the first order condition $\exists t(t_0 R t \wedge t_0 \neq t)$: in one direction, if there is some q such that $w \in \mathcal{I}(q)$ and $w \models \forall t(q(t) \to \exists t'(tRt' \wedge \neg q(t')))$, then there must be a point reachable from w which is not in $\mathcal{I}(q)$, i.e., different from w. For the reverse implication, assume that $w \models \exists t(t_0 R t \wedge t_0 \neq t)$ and let $\mathcal{I}(q) \triangleq \{w\}$. Then $w \models q(t_0)$ and $w \models \forall t(q(t) \to \exists t'(tRt' \wedge \neg q(t')))$. Therefore, $w \models \varphi$.

There is no positive formula which can express this property: consider the frame $\mathcal{F} \triangleq (U, \mathcal{I})$, where $U \triangleq \{w_0, w_1\}$, $\mathcal{I}(R) \triangleq \{(w_0, w_0), (w_0, w_1), (w_1, w_1)\}$ and $\mathcal{I}(p) = \{\}$ for all $p \in \mathcal{P}$. Then $w_0 \models \varphi$ and $w_1 \not\models \varphi$. For each positive formula ψ, however, it holds that $w_0 \models \psi$ iff $w_1 \models \psi$. To prove this, we show by induction on the structure of ψ that $\psi^{\mathcal{F}} = \{\}$ or $\psi^{\mathcal{F}} = U$. For propositional formulas, this is immediate; the case $\langle R \rangle \psi$ follows from the definition of $\mathcal{F}$. The only remaining case are formulas $\nu q \psi$. According to the induction hypothesis, either $(\psi\{q := \top\})^{\mathcal{F}} = \{\}$ or $(\psi\{q := \top\})^{\mathcal{F}} = U$. In the first case, from the fact that $(\nu q \psi)^{\mathcal{F}} \subseteq \top^{\mathcal{F}}$ and monotonicity of ψ we infer that $(\psi\{q := \nu q \psi\})^{\mathcal{F}} \subseteq (\psi\{q := \top\})^{\mathcal{F}} = \{\}$. The first part of Theorem 3.5 implies that $(\nu q \psi)^{\mathcal{F}} \subseteq (\psi\{q := \nu q \psi\})^{\mathcal{F}}$; therefore, $(\nu q \psi)^{\mathcal{F}} = \{\}$. In the second case, $U = \top^{\mathcal{F}} = (\psi\{q := \top\})^{\mathcal{F}}$. With the second part of Theorem 3.5, it follows that $\top^{\mathcal{F}} \subseteq (\nu q \psi)^{\mathcal{F}}$, i.e., $(\nu q \psi)^{\mathcal{F}} = U$.

Statement (b) holds since the truth of μTL formulas is preserved under disjoint unions of models, whereas $\varphi \triangleq \forall t p(t)$ can be invalidated by adding an isolated point w with $w \not\models p$. Formally, consider the models $\mathcal{M}_0 \triangleq (U_0, \mathcal{I}, w_0)$ and $\mathcal{M}_1 \triangleq (U_1, \mathcal{I}, w_0)$, where $U_0 \triangleq \{w_0\}$, $U_1 \triangleq \{w_0, w\}$, $\mathcal{I}(R) \triangleq \{\}$ and $\mathcal{I}(p) \triangleq \mathcal{I}(q) \triangleq \{w_0\}$. Then $\mathcal{M}_0 \models \varphi$ and $\mathcal{M}_1 \not\models \varphi$, whereas for each μTL formula ψ it holds that $\mathcal{M}_0 \models \varphi$ iff $\mathcal{M}_1 \models \varphi$. As above, the only interesting case is $\nu q \psi$. If $\mathcal{M}_0 \models \nu q \psi$ then $w_0 \models \psi$, which implies $\mathcal{M}_1 \models \nu q \psi$. In the other direction, $\mathcal{M}_1 \models \nu q \psi$ implies that either $\mathcal{M}_1 \models \psi$ or $\mathcal{M}_1' \triangleq (U_1, \mathcal{I}_1, w_0) \models \psi$, where $\mathcal{I}_1(q) = U_1$. In the first case, $\mathcal{M}_0 \models \nu q \psi$ follows directly. In the second case, $\mathcal{M}_1 \models \psi\{q := \top\}$, which implies $\mathcal{M}_0 \models \psi\{q := \top\}$ by the induction hypothesis. From this, it follows that $\mathcal{M}_0 \models \nu q \psi$. □

If the model is *connected* (that is, $\forall w, w'(w < w' \vee w = w' \vee w > w')$), then every point is reachable from the current point. In this case, the operator $\mathbf{G}^{\pm}$ (the *universal modality*) can replace the first-order universal quantifier: $\mathcal{M} \models \forall t p(t)$ iff $\mathcal{M} \models \mathbf{G}^{\pm} p$. In this case,

$$\mathcal{M} \models \nu q\, \varphi \quad \text{iff} \quad \mathcal{M} \models \exists q(q \wedge \mathbf{G}^{\pm}(q \to \varphi)),$$

$$\mathcal{M} \models \mu q\, \varphi \quad \text{iff} \quad \mathcal{M} \models \forall q(\mathbf{G}^{\pm}(\varphi \to q) \to q).$$

Hence, on connected models (and, in particular, on natural models) μTL is at most as expressive as qTL (and MSOL). Since μTL does not contain any past-operators, there is no μTL formula which is equivalent to $\mathbf{F}^- \top$. Subsequently, however, we will show that for *initial validity* in natural models a translation from **qTL** (or **MSOL**) into positive μ**TL** exists. Since the proof uses ω-*regular languages* and ω-*automata*, it is postponed to subsection 3.4.

3.3. ω-automata and ω-languages

Given a (finite or infinite) natural model $\mathcal{M} \triangleq (U, \mathcal{I}, w_0)$, the interpretation $\mathcal{I}$ defines a mapping $\mathcal{I} : \mathcal{P} \to 2^U$ from propositions into subsets of the universe. Define a *labelling function* $\mathcal{L} : U \to 2^{\mathcal{P}}$ by

$$\mathrm{p} \in \mathcal{L}(w) \qquad \text{iff} \qquad w \in \mathcal{I}(\mathrm{p})$$

That is, $\mathcal{L}(w) \triangleq \{\mathrm{p} \mid w \in \mathcal{I}(\mathrm{p})\}$ is the *label* of point $w \in U$. If $U = (w_0, w_1, w_2, ...)$, then the sequence $\sigma = (\mathcal{L}(w_0), \mathcal{L}(w_1), \mathcal{L}(w_2), ...)$ is called the ω-*word* of $\mathcal{M}$ over the *alphabet* $\Sigma \triangleq 2^{\mathcal{P}}$. A set of ω-words is called an ω-*language*.

Let $\mathcal{F} \triangleq (U, \mathcal{I})$ be the frame of a natural model. Formula φ is *initially valid* in $\mathcal{F}$, if $(U, \mathcal{I}, w_0) \models \varphi$, where w_0 is the unique initial point of U (which has no predecessors). For any such frame $\mathcal{F}$ it holds that φ is universally valid iff $\mathbf{G}^* \varphi$ is initially valid, and φ is initially valid iff $(\mathbf{G}^- \perp \to \varphi)$ is universally valid.

We say that a linear-time logic formula *defines* the set of all natural frames in which it is initially valid. Thus every such formula defines the ω-language given by these frames. We now show that in order to define languages by formulas it suffices to restrict attention to the future fragment of temporal logic. The separation Lemma 2.6 states that any **LTL**-formula can be separated into a boolean combination of pure future, pure present and pure past formulas. It can be extended to **qTL**:

3.11. LEMMA. **qTL** *has the separation property on natural models.*

PROOF: Note that the formula $\exists q(\varphi \vee \psi) \leftrightarrow (\exists q\, \varphi \vee \exists q\, \psi)$ is valid. Moreover, if $\varphi_1, ..., \varphi_n$ are pure past, $\psi_1, ..., \psi_m$ are pure present and $\chi_1, ..., \chi_l$ are pure future, then $\exists q(\bigwedge \varphi_i \wedge \bigwedge \psi_j \wedge \bigwedge \chi_k)$ is equivalent to $(\exists q \bigwedge \varphi_i \wedge \exists q \bigwedge \psi_j \wedge \exists q \bigwedge \chi_k)$. Informally, this can be seen as follows: $\exists q(\varphi \wedge \psi) \to (\exists q\varphi \wedge \exists q\psi)$ is a tautology. In the other direction, assume that the past-formulas $\varphi_1, ..., \varphi_n$ are valid in the model $(U, \mathcal{I}, w_0)$ where $\mathcal{I}(q) \triangleq Q_1$, the present-formulas ψ_j are valid with $\mathcal{I}(q) \triangleq Q_2$, and the future-formulas χ_k are valid if $\mathcal{I}(q) \triangleq Q_3$, then the conjunction of past, present and future part is valid if $\mathcal{I}(q) \triangleq (\{w \mid w < w_0\} \cap Q_1) \cup (w_0 \cap Q_2) \cup (\{w \mid w > w_0\} \cap Q_3)$.

Now assume that $\varphi \triangleq \exists q\psi$, and show that there is an equivalent separated formula. The induction hypothesis is that for ψ there exists an equivalent formula ψ' which is a boolean combination of pure future, past and present formulas. Let $\psi'' \triangleq \bigvee \bigwedge (\varphi_i \wedge \psi_j \wedge \chi_k)$ be ψ' in disjunctive normal form, where all φ_i are pure past, ψ_j pure present and χ_k pure future. Applying the above formulas we see that $\exists q\psi'' \leftrightarrow \bigvee \bigwedge (\exists q\varphi_i \wedge \exists q\psi_j \wedge \exists q\chi_k)$. This formula is separated and equivalent to φ. $\square$

3.12. LEMMA. *For any* **LTL** *or* **qTL** *formula φ there exists an* **LTL** *or* **qTL** *future formula (without U^--operators) defining the same language.*

PROOF: Given a separated formula φ, let φ^+ be the formula φ where every subformula $(\varphi \, U^- \, \psi)$ is replaced by $\bot$. Then φ is initially valid in any natural model $\mathcal{M}$ iff ψ^+ is initially valid in $\mathcal{M}$. Thus φ and φ^+ define the same language.   □

Languages can also be defined by *(ω-)regular expressions* and by *finite (ω-) automata*.

The language of *(ω-)regular expression* is defined similar to the language of usual regular expressions, with an additional operation denoting infinite repetition of a subexpression.

- Every letter from the alphabet is an ω-regular expression.
- If α and β are ω-regular expressions, then so are ε, $(\alpha + \beta)$, $(\alpha; \beta)$ and α^+.
- If α is an ω-regular expression, then so is α^ω.

Every ω-regular expression defines an ω-language: the letter $a \subseteq \mathcal{P}$ defines $\{(a)\}$, i.e., a one-word language (one-element set) consisting of a one-letter word (one-element sequence). ε denotes the empty language, and $(\alpha + \beta)$, $(\alpha; \beta)$ and α^+ denote union, sequential composition and finite iteration of languages. α^ω denotes the language of all words consisting of an infinite concatenation of words from α. A language is called ω-regular if it can be defined by an ω-regular expression.

We use boolean terms over $\mathcal{P}$ to denote (unions of) letters. For example, if $\mathcal{P} = \{p1, p2\}$ then $(\neg p1 \wedge p2)$ denotes the letter $\{p2\}$, and $(\neg p1 \vee p2)$ denotes $\{\} + \{p2\} + \{p1, p2\}$.

As an example for an ω-regular expression, consider $(\neg p1)^\omega + (\top^+; p2)^\omega$. This expression defines the set of all infinite words $(\sigma_0, \sigma_1, \sigma_2, ...)$ such that either for all i it holds that $p1 \notin \sigma_i$, or for infinitely many i it holds that $p2 \in \sigma_i$. That is, it defines the set of natural models $\mathcal{M}$ such that $\mathcal{M} \models \mathbf{G}^*(\neg p1 \wedge \mathbf{X} \top) \vee \mathbf{G}^* \mathbf{F}^+ p2$. Since this formula implies $\mathbf{G}^* \mathbf{X} \top$, each of its natural models must be infinite.

An *ω-automaton* or *fair transition system* over the alphabet $\Sigma = 2^\mathcal{P}$ is defined like a usual (nondeterministic) automaton with an additional recurrence set ("fairness constraint"); it is a tuple $(S, \Delta, S_0, S_{acc}, S_{rec})$, where

- S is a set of states,
- $\Delta \subseteq S \times \Sigma \times S$ is the transition relation,
- $S_0 \subseteq S$ is the set of initial states,
- $S_{acc} \subseteq S$ is the set of accepting states (for finite words), and
- $S_{rec} \subseteq S$ is the set of recurring states (for infinite words).

A *Büchi-automaton* is a finite ω-automaton, that is, a fair transition system where the set S of states is finite. A *transition system* (or *labelled transition system*) is a fair transition system where $S_{acc} = S_{rec} = S$. A *weakly fair transition system* is an ω-automaton where $S_{rec} = S$ and $S_{acc} = \{s \mid \forall a, s'(s, a, s') \notin \Delta\}$. That is, in a weakly fair transition system all states are recurring, and states are accepting iff they are terminal. Usually, when talking about labelled and weakly fair transition systems, we omit the redundant components S_{acc} and S_{rec}.

A (finite or infinite) nonempty word $\sigma \triangleq (\sigma_0, \sigma_1, ...)$ is *accepted* by an automaton $(S, \Delta, S_0, S_{acc}, S_{rec})$, if there is a function ρ assigning to any $i < |\sigma|$ a state $\rho(\sigma_i) \in S$ of the automaton such that

- $\rho(0) \in S_0$,
- For all $0 \le i < n$, $(\rho(i), \sigma_i, \rho(i+1)) \in \Delta$, and
- $(\rho(n), \sigma_n, s) \in \Delta$ for some $s \in S_{acc}$, if σ is finite with last letter w_n, and
- $inf(\rho) \cap S_{rec} \neq \{\}$, if σ is infinite, where $inf(\rho)$ is the set of states that appear infinitely often in the range of ρ. That is, at least one recurring state must be selected infinitely often.

For alternative acceptance conditions, see [Thomas 1990][4]. We say that an automaton accepts a natural model $\mathcal{M}$, if it accepts the ω-word of $\mathcal{M}$. The language of a transition system consists of all paths through the transition graph; this language is prefix-closed (for any word in the language, all of its prefixes are also contained). The language defined by a weakly fair transition system consists of all maximal paths through the graph.

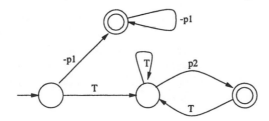

Figure 3: A Büchi automaton accepting $(\neg p1)^\omega + (\top^+; p2)^\omega$

As an example of a Büchi-automaton, consider Figure 3. This automaton accepts (i.e., defines) exactly the same language as the example ω-regular expression above. In general, for any ω-regular expression we can construct such a Büchi-automaton and vice versa; Büchi-automata can define all and only ω-regular languages.

3.13. LEMMA. *ω-regular expressions and Büchi-automata are of equal expressive power.*

PROOF: The proof of this statement is similar as for automata on finite words: for one direction, we have to show that the Büchi acceptance condition can be captured

---

[4]In the literature, a fairness constraint in a transition systems is sometimes defined to be a set of pairs (s, e), where $s \in S$ is a state and $e \in \Delta$ is an edge. It imposes the condition that if s appears infinitely often, then e must be taken infinitely often in each accepted word. It can be shown that for our purposes these definitions are equivalent. See [Anuchitanukul 1995] for the relationships and translations between these two notions for various acceptance conditions.

by an appropriate regular expression. Let $L(s_i, s_j)$ be a regular expression for the language of finite nonempty words sending an automaton from state s_i into state s_j. Then the ω-regular expression associated with any Büchi-automaton is

$$\Sigma\{L(s_0, s) \mid s_0 \in S_0, \ s \in S_{acc}\} + \Sigma\{L(s_0, s); L(s, s)^\omega \mid s_0 \in S_0, \ s \in S_{rec}\}$$

For the other direction it must be shown that Büchi-automata are closed under single letters, the empty language, union, concatenation, and finite and infinite repetition. All of these constructions are straightforward extensions of the appropriate constructions for automata on finite words [Hopcroft and Ullman 1979]. □

The automaton resulting from this proof is highly nondeterministic. An automaton is called *deterministic*, if its transition relation is a function $\Delta : S \times \Sigma \to S$. For each nondeterministic finite automaton on finite words an equivalent deterministic one is given by the well known powerset construction of Rabin and Scott [Hopcroft and Ullman 1979]. The same holds for finite transition systems. In contrast, for nondeterministic Büchi-automata it is not always possible to construct an equivalent deterministic one. For example, consider the language $\mathcal{L}$ of all words containing only finitely many p. This language is defined by the formula $\mathbf{F}^* \mathbf{G}^+ \neg p$ or the ω-regular expression $(\top^+ + (\top^+; \neg p^\omega))$. However, there is no deterministic Büchi-automaton defining $\mathcal{L}$: Assume for contradiction that $\mathcal{L}$ is the language of $\mathcal{A}$. Then $\mathcal{A}$ must accept $(\sigma; (\neg p)^\omega)$ for any finite word σ. In particular, from any reachable state some recurring state is reached by a finite number of $\neg p$-transitions. Let m be the maximum of these numbers. Therefore, in the run of $\mathcal{A}$ on the word $(p; (\neg p)^m)^\omega$ infinitely often recurring states are visited. Thus, this word also is accepted by $\mathcal{A}$. This is a contradiction, since it is not in $\mathcal{L}$.

3.4. Automata and Logics

Büchi [Büchi 1962] showed that his automata are closed under complement; this is a highly nontrivial proof. The best known construction for complementing Büchi-automata was given in [Safra 1988]; it involves an exponential blowup of the number of states of the automaton. More precisely, if A has n states, then it can be shown that the smallest automaton accepting the complement language of A in general has $O(2^{n \log n})$ states. For more information on the complementation problem for Büchi automata, see [Sistla, Vardi and Wolper 1987, Thomas 1990].

Closure under complement can be used to show that Büchi-automata are at least as expressive as **qTL**.

3.14. LEMMA. *For every* **qTL** *formula there is a Büchi-automaton defining the same language.*

PROOF: According to Lemma 3.12 it suffices to give a translation for formulas without $\mathbf{U}^-$. An automaton for the proposition $p \in \mathcal{P}$ is given by the trivial two-state machine $(\{s_0, s_{acc}\}, \Delta, \{s_0\}, \{s_{acc}\}, \{\})$, where $(s_0, a, s_{acc}) \in \Delta$ iff $p \in a$. An automaton

for $\perp$ is one which never accepts. From an automaton for φ, an automaton for $\mathbf{X}\,\varphi$ and $\mathbf{F}^+\,\varphi$ can be built by an appropriate prefixing with a single step or loop on the initial states. According to the remark following Lemma 3.3, $\mathbf{U}^+$ can be expressed with $\mathbf{X}, \mathbf{F}^+$ and second order quantification. Implications $(\varphi \rightarrow \psi)$ can be written as $(\neg\varphi \vee \psi)$ and thus be reduced to unions and complements. Finally, existential second order quantification amounts to the projection of the automaton onto a smaller alphabet: given an automaton $A = (S, \Delta, S_0, S_{acc}, S_{rec})$ over the alphabet $2^{(\mathcal{P} \cup \mathcal{Q})}$ which accepts the models of φ, the automaton $A'(S, \Delta', S_0, S_{acc}, S_{rec})$ accepts all models of $\exists q\,\varphi$, where $(s_i, a, s_j) \in \Delta'$ iff $(s_i, a \setminus \{q\}, s_j) \in \Delta$ or $(s_i, a \cup \{q\}, s_j) \in \Delta'$.
$\qquad \square$

In particular, since $\mathbf{LTL}$ is a sublanguage of $\mathbf{qTL}$, for every $\mathbf{LTL}$ formula there exists a corresponding Büchi-automaton. In Section 7, we will describe a tableaux decision procedure, which can be seen as an efficient algorithm to construct a Büchi-automaton from a formula. Other aspects of the connections between temporal logics, monadic logics and automata can be found in [Thomas 1999].

We now show that ω-regular expressions are at most as expressive as $\mu\mathbf{TL}$:

3.15. LEMMA. *For every ω-regular expression there exists a $\mu\mathbf{TL}$-formula describing the same language.*

PROOF: The proof associates with every ω-regular expression φ a $\mu\mathbf{TL}$-formula $\mu\mathbf{TL}_q(\varphi)$ with at most one free proposition variable q indicating the end of the sequence.

- $\mu\mathbf{TL}_q(P) \triangleq (\bigwedge_{\mathbf{p} \in P} \mathbf{p} \wedge \bigwedge_{\mathbf{p} \notin P} \neg\mathbf{p} \wedge q)$, if $P \in 2^{\mathcal{P}}$
- $\mu\mathbf{TL}_q(\epsilon) \triangleq \perp$
- $\mu\mathbf{TL}_q(\varphi + \psi) \triangleq (\mu\mathbf{TL}_q(\varphi) \vee \mu\mathbf{TL}_q(\psi))$
- $\mu\mathbf{TL}_q(\varphi; \psi) \triangleq \mu\mathbf{TL}_q(\varphi)\{q := \mathbf{X}\,\mu\mathbf{TL}_q(\psi)\}$
- $\mu\mathbf{TL}_q(\varphi^+) \triangleq \mu q_1\,(\mu\mathbf{TL}_q(\varphi)\{q := q \vee \mathbf{X}\,q_1\})$
- $\mu\mathbf{TL}_q(\varphi^\omega) \triangleq \nu q_1\,(\mu\mathbf{TL}_q(\varphi)\{q := \mathbf{X}\,q_1\})$

If φ defines a language of infinite strings, then $\mu\mathbf{TL}_q(\varphi)$ does not contain any free occurrence of q. However, if φ defines a language of finite strings, then $\mu\mathbf{TL}_q(\varphi)$ contains the free proposition variable q denoting the final point. A finite string is characterized by the fact that in its last point the formula $\mathbf{\bar{X}} \perp$ holds. Therefore, the $\mu\mathbf{TL}$-formula corresponding to an ω-regular expression φ is defined as $\mu\mathbf{TL}(\varphi) \triangleq \mu\mathbf{TL}_q(\varphi)\{q := \mathbf{\bar{X}} \perp\}$. It can be shown that $\mu\mathbf{TL}(\varphi)$ defines the same language as the ω-regular expression φ.
$\qquad \square$

As an example, consider the expression $(\neg\mathrm{p1})^\omega + (\top^+; \mathrm{p2})^\omega$.

$\mu\mathbf{TL}((\neg\mathrm{p1})^\omega + (\top^+; \mathrm{p2})^\omega)$
$= \nu q_1\,(\mu\mathbf{TL}(\neg\mathrm{p1})\{q := \mathbf{X}\,q_1\}) \vee \nu q_2(\mu\mathbf{TL}(\top^+; \mathrm{p2})\{q := \mathbf{X}\,q_2\})$
$= \nu q_1\,((\neg\mathrm{p1} \wedge q)\{q := \mathbf{X}\,q_1\}) \vee \nu q_2((\mu\mathbf{TL}(\top^+)\{q := \mathbf{X}\,\mu\mathbf{TL}(\mathrm{p2})\})\{q := \mathbf{X}\,q_2\})$
$= \nu q_1\,(\neg\mathrm{p1} \wedge \mathbf{X}\,q_1) \vee$
$\qquad \nu q_2(\mu q_3(\top \wedge q)\{q := q \vee \mathbf{X}\,q_3\}\{q := \mathbf{X}(\mathrm{p2} \wedge q)\}\{q := \mathbf{X}\,q_2\})$

$$= \nu q_1 \, (\neg p1 \wedge \mathbf{X}\, q_1) \vee \nu q_2(\mu q_3(\mathbf{X}(p2 \wedge q) \vee \mathbf{X}\, q_3)\{q := \mathbf{X}\, q_2\})$$
$$= \nu q_1 \, (\neg p1 \wedge \mathbf{X}\, q_1) \vee \nu q_2(\mu q_3 \, \mathbf{X}(p2 \wedge \mathbf{X}\, q_2 \vee q_3))$$
$$\leftrightarrow \nu q_1 \, (\neg p1 \wedge \mathbf{X} \top \wedge \mathbf{\overline{X}}\, q_1) \vee \nu q_2(\mu q_3 \, \mathbf{X}(p2 \vee q_3) \wedge \mathbf{\overline{X}}\, q_2)$$
$$= \mathbf{G}^{\boldsymbol{\cdot}}(\neg p1 \wedge \mathbf{X} \top) \vee \mathbf{G}^{\boldsymbol{\cdot}}\, \mathbf{F}^+ p2$$

This lemma closes the circle in the expressiveness results of second order languages.

3.16. THEOREM (Büchi, Wolper, Sistla). *To define ω-languages, the following formalisms are of equal expressive power:*

   i. μ**TL**
   ii. **qTL**
   iii. **MSOL**
   iv. *Büchi-automata*
   v.   *ω-regular expressions*

PROOF: For every μ**TL**-formula there exists an equivalent **qTL**-formula by definition; on natural models **qTL** is equal in expressiveness to **MSOL** by Lemma 3.2; according to Lemma 3.14, for every **qTL** (or **MSOL**) formula there is a Büchi-automaton defining the set of its models; by Lemma 3.13, Büchi-automata are equivalent to ω-regular expressions; and these in turn can be described by μ**TL**-formulas as shown in Lemma 3.15.   □

Similar results can be proved about logics with past operators on integer models (bi-infinite words) and two-way automata, and about branching time logics (μ**TL/qTL** on tree models) and tree automata ($\Delta \subseteq S \times 2^P \times (\mathcal{R} \times S)^n$) (see [Niwinsky 1988, Thomas 1990, Schlingloff 1992b]).

4. Model Transformations and Properties

As we have seen, linear temporal formulas and ω-automata both can be used to describe sets of infinite sequences. The practical difference is, that logic tends to be more "descriptive", specifying *what* a system should do, whereas automata tend to be more "machine-oriented", indicating *how* it should be done. Logical formulas are "global", they are interpreted on the whole structure, whereas automata are "local", describing single states and transitions.

Therefore, traditionally automata or related models are used to give an abstract account of the *system* to be verified, whereas formulas are used to specify *properties* of these systems. But, since it is possible to translate between automata and formulas and back, this choice is a matter of complexity, of available algorithms and of taste. We could equally well define both system and properties in temporal logic; in this case we would have to prove an implication formula (Section 7 will explain how to do this). Another alternative is that both the implementation and the specification are given as automata, where the latter is more "abstract" than the former. Then we have to prove that one can *simulate* the other.

In the next sections, we describe various transformations between models such as simulations and refinements, and investigate the preservation of logical properties under these transformations.

4.1. Models, Automata and Transition Systems

The previous section related ω-automata and linear temporal formulas via the ω-language accepted by the automaton and the set of natural models in which the formula is initially valid. There is, however, a more direct connection on the structural level. Let $M = (U, \mathcal{I}, w_0)$ be a Kripke-model with predicates from $\mathcal{P}$ and accessibility relations from $\mathcal{R}$. Consider the alphabet $\Sigma = 2^{\mathcal{P}} \times \mathcal{R}$, and let $\sigma = (\sigma_0 \sigma_1 \sigma_2 ...)$ be an ω-word, where $\sigma_i = (a_i, R_i)$. We say that σ is *generated by* M if there exists a mapping ρ from indices of letters of σ into points of U, such that

- $\rho(0) = w_0$,
- if $\rho(i) = w$, then $a_i = \mathcal{L}(w)$,
- if $\rho(i) = w$ and $\rho(i+1) = w'$, then $(w, w') \in \mathcal{I}(R_i)$, and
- if σ is finite with last letter σ_n, and $\rho(n) = w$, then w is terminal (i.e., there is no w' such that $w \prec w'$).

(Recall that $\mathcal{L}(w) \triangleq \{ \mathrm{p} \mid \mathrm{p} \in \mathcal{I}(w) \}$ is the label of point w.) The fourth condition guarantees that generated words represent maximal paths in the model[5]. Define the *language generated by* M to be the set of all ω-words generated by M. With these definitions, Kripke-models can be regarded as weakly fair transition systems for the alphabet $\Sigma = 2^{\mathcal{P}} \times \mathcal{R}$. (Recall that in a weakly fair transition system all states are recurring, and all terminal states are accepting.)

4.1. LEMMA. *For any Kripke-model* $M = (U, \mathcal{I}, w_0)$ *there exists a weakly fair transition system* $M_A = (S, \Delta, S_0)$, *such that the language generated by* M *is equal to the language accepted by* M_A.

PROOF: To prove this lemma, there are several alternative constructions. One possibility is to define $S \triangleq U \cup \{stop\}$, where $stop$ is a special accepting state for finite paths. Furthermore, $S_0 \triangleq \{w_0\}$, and $(w, (P, R), s) \in \Delta$ iff $w \in U$, $\mathcal{L}(w) = P$, and either $(w, s) \in \mathcal{I}(R)$ or w is terminal and $s = stop$. Then, M_A accepts exactly the set of all natural models which are generated by M. □

Thus, models can be seen as automata. Likewise, formulas can be seen as automata: in the previous section we observed that for every **LTL** formula there exists an equivalent Büchi-automaton. Since this proof is constructive, it yields a method to obtain such an automaton. However, a much more concise way of constructing it is the tableau construction sketched in Section 7 below.

---

[5]Some texts omit this condition, with the consequence that all prefixes of a generated word are also generated. Other authors impose the even stronger condition that all generated words must be infinite; this implies that all points in a model should be nonterminal.

Let φ be an **LTL**-formula, and $\mathcal{M}$ be a Kripke-model with a single accessibility relation. Then φ is sequence-valid in $\mathcal{M}$ iff the language generated by $\mathcal{M}$ (i.e., the language accepted by the weakly fair transition system $\mathcal{M}_A$ for $\mathcal{M}$) is a subset of the language accepted by the Büchi-automaton $\mathcal{M}_\varphi$ for φ. That is,

$$\mathcal{M} \models \varphi \quad \text{iff} \quad L(\mathcal{M}_A) \subseteq L(\mathcal{M}_\varphi).$$

The latter condition is equivalent to $L(\mathcal{M}_A) \cap \overline{L(\mathcal{M}_\varphi)} = \{\}$, or $L(\mathcal{M}_A \times \mathcal{M}_{\neg\varphi}) = \{\}$. Here, $\mathcal{M}_1 \times \mathcal{M}_2$ denotes the product of ω-automata, where the product automaton $\mathcal{M}_1 \times \mathcal{M}_2$ accepts an infinite word σ iff each component automaton accepts σ. Formally, if $\mathcal{M}_i \triangleq (S_i, \Delta_i, S_{i,0}, S_{i,acc}, S_{i,rec})$ for $i = 1, 2$, then $\mathcal{M}_1 \times \mathcal{M}_2 \triangleq (S, \Delta, S_0, S_{acc}, S_{rec})$, where

- $S \triangleq S_1 \times S_2 \times \{1, 2\}$,
- $((s_1, s_2, i), a, (s_1', s_2', j)) \in \Delta$ iff $(s_1, a, s_1') \in \Delta_1$, $(s_2, a, s_2') \in \Delta_2$, and $i = j$, or $i = 1$ and $s_1 \in S_{1,rec}$ and $j = 2$, or $i = 2$ and $s_2 \in S_{2,rec}$ and $j = 1$.
- $S_0 \triangleq S_{1,0} \times S_{2,0} \times \{1\}$,
- $S_{acc} \triangleq S_{1,acc} \times S_{2,acc} \times \{0, 1\}$,
- $S_{rec} \triangleq S_{1,rec} \times S_{2,rec} \times \{2\}$,

Intuitively, the definition of S_{rec} enforces that in an infinite run of $\mathcal{M}_1 \times \mathcal{M}_2$ both a state from $S_{1,rec}$ and a state from $S_{2,rec}$ must be visited infinitely often. With this construction, model checking of **LTL** sequence-validity in finite models reduces to the nonemptyness problem of Büchi-automata: a feasible way to check whether $\mathcal{M} \models \varphi$ is to construct the Büchi-automata $\mathcal{M}_A$ for the model and $\mathcal{M}_{\neg\varphi}$ for $\neg\varphi$, and to check whether the language of the product automaton $\mathcal{M}_A \times \mathcal{M}_{\neg\varphi}$ is empty. This approach is implemented in the SPIN and COSPAN model checking tools [Holzmann 1991, Kurshan 1994].

If both system $\mathcal{M}$ and property φ are given as automata, then "specification" φ can be regarded as a "more abstract version" of the "implementation" $\mathcal{M}$. We write $\mathcal{M}_I \models \mathcal{M}_S$ if $L(\mathcal{M}_I) \subseteq L(\mathcal{M}_S)$, i.e., if (the language of) $\mathcal{M}_I$ is a subset of (the language of) $\mathcal{M}_S$. A *property* φ is defined to be just any ω-language $\varphi \subseteq \Sigma^\omega$, where $\Sigma = 2^P \times \mathcal{R}$.

4.2. THEOREM. *Let $\mathcal{M}_1$ and $\mathcal{M}_2$ be Büchi-automata. Then*
- $\mathcal{M}_1 \models \mathcal{M}_2$ *iff for all properties φ, if $\mathcal{M}_2 \models \varphi$ then $\mathcal{M}_1 \models \varphi$.*
- $\mathcal{M}_1 \models \mathcal{M}_2$ *iff for all ω-regular φ, if $\mathcal{M}_2 \models \varphi$ then $\mathcal{M}_1 \models \varphi$.*

PROOF: One direction is immediate by transitivity of the subset relation: if $L(\mathcal{M}_1) \subseteq L(\mathcal{M}_2)$ and $L(\mathcal{M}_2) \subseteq L(\varphi)$, then $L(\mathcal{M}_1) \subseteq L(\varphi)$. The other direction follows from instantiating φ with $L(\mathcal{M}_2)$ and, in the strong form, from the fact that the Büchi-automaton $\mathcal{M}_2$ defines a regular language. $\qquad\square$

This theorem can help to reduce the complexity of checking whether a model satisfies a formula. In order to prove $\mathcal{M}_1 \models \varphi$, it can be helpful to look for a "small" model $\mathcal{M}_2$ such that $\mathcal{M}_1 \models \mathcal{M}_2$ and $\mathcal{M}_2 \models \varphi$.

4.2. Safety and Liveness Properties

A similar characterization result as the above 4.2 holds for finite transition systems and a special class of ω-languages called *safety-properties*. For natural models $\mathcal{M}$ and $\mathcal{M}'$, let $\mathcal{M}^{[..i]}$ be the model consisting of the first i points of $\mathcal{M}$, and $\mathcal{M} \circ \mathcal{M}'$ be the concatenation of the two models $\mathcal{M}$ and $\mathcal{M}'$. (If $\mathcal{M}$ is infinite, then define $\mathcal{M} \circ \mathcal{M}' \triangleq \mathcal{M}$.)

- φ is a *safety property*, iff for every natural model $\mathcal{M}$,

$$\mathcal{M} \models \varphi \text{ if } \forall i \exists \mathcal{M}' : \mathcal{M}^{[..i]} \circ \mathcal{M}' \models \varphi$$

This definition is from [Alpern and Schneider 1985]. An ω-language φ is a safety property if for every model *not* satisfying φ there is a finite prefix $\mathcal{M}^{[..i]}$ which can not be completed by any continuation $\mathcal{M}'$ such that $\mathcal{M}^{[..i]} \circ \mathcal{M}' \models \varphi$. In other words, for every model dissatisfying φ something "bad" must have happened after some finite number of steps which cannot be remedied by any future good behavior. Hence, in Lamport's popular characterization, safety properties express that "something bad never happens" [Lamport 1983].

- φ is a *liveness property*, iff for every natural model $\mathcal{M}$,

$$\forall i \exists \mathcal{M}' : \mathcal{M}^{[..i]} \circ \mathcal{M}' \models \varphi$$

A liveness property φ, on the other hand, can never be refuted by observing only a finite prefix of some run. It holds, if and only if every finite sequence can be completed to a model satisfying φ, hence φ states that "something good eventually happens". Notice, however, that in contrast to the "bad thing" referred to above, the occurrence of the "good thing" does not have to be observable in any fixed time interval. Thus, liveness failures cannot be detected by testing.

Without proof we state some facts about safety and liveness from [Alpern and Schneider 1985]:

4.3. THEOREM. *(Properties of safety and liveness)*
- *Safety properties are closed under finite unions and arbitrary intersections.*
- *Liveness properties are closed under arbitrary unions, but not under intersections.*
- $\top$ *is the only property which is both a safety and a liveness property.*
- *For any property φ there exists a safety property φ_S and a liveness property φ_L such that $\varphi = (\varphi_S \cap \varphi_L)$.*

The last of these facts is known as the *decomposition theorem* and can be proved by topological arguments. The safety-part of a property φ is the topological closure of φ, that is, the least safety property containing φ. As an example, on natural models the **LTL**-formula $(\mathrm{p} \, \mathbf{U}^+ \, \mathrm{q})$ is equivalent to $((\mathrm{p} \, \mathbf{W}^+ \, \mathrm{q}) \wedge \mathbf{F}^+ \, \mathrm{q})$, where the language defined by $(\mathrm{p} \, \mathbf{W}^+ \, \mathrm{q})$ is a safety property and the language defined by $\mathbf{F}^+ \, \mathrm{q}$ is a liveness property. Similarly, total correctness statements about programs can be decomposed into invariance (safety) and termination (liveness).

We now give a syntactical characterization of **LTL** safety properties.

4.4. THEOREM. *Every temporal formula built from literals with* $\perp$, $\top$, $\wedge$, $\vee$ *and* $\mathbf{W}^+$ *defines a safety property.*

PROOF: The proof is by induction on the structure of the formula. The only interesting case is $(\varphi \mathbf{W}^+ \psi)$. Assume that any model $\mathcal{M}$ falsifying both φ and ψ has a finite prefix $\mathcal{M}^{[..i]}$ such that any extension of $\mathcal{M}^{[..i]}$ falsifies these formulas. If $\mathcal{M} \not\models (\varphi \mathbf{W}^+ \psi)$, then there is a $w_j > w_0$ such that $w_j \models (\neg\varphi \wedge \neg\psi)$, and $w_k \models \neg\psi$ for $w_0 < w_k < w_j$. Therefore, in any model $\mathcal{M}^{[..j+i]} \circ \mathcal{M}'$, the formula $(\varphi \mathbf{W}^+ \psi)$ must be invalid. $\qquad\square$

An alternative characterization of safety in linear temporal logic is with past-operators. Any **LTL** formula $\mathbf{G}^* \psi$, where ψ is a past formula, defines a safety property. Moreover, any **LTL**-definable safety property can be defined by a formula of this form [Lichtenstein et al. 1985].

A binary relation $\Delta \subseteq U \times U$ is called *image finite*, if for any $x \in U$ the set $\{y \in U \mid (x, y) \in \Delta\}$ is finite. In particular, any finite relation is image finite. We call a transition system (S, Δ, S_0) *finitary*, if S_0 is finite and Δ is image finite. Of course, any finite transition system is finitary. Intuitively, finitary transition systems allow only "finite nondeterminism". The following statement extends Theorem 4.4 to finitary transition systems:

4.5. THEOREM. *Any finitary transition system defines a safety property.*

PROOF: Consider the language L of a finitary transition system. We have to show that for every sequence σ, if $\forall i \exists \sigma' : \sigma^{[..i]} \circ \sigma' \in L$ then $\sigma \in L$. In other words, assume that any finite prefix of σ can be extended to a string in L and show $\sigma \in L$. If σ is finite, then it is a finite prefix of itself; thus there exists some σ' such that $\sigma \circ \sigma' \in L$. Since every state of a transition system is accepting, it follows that $\sigma \in L$. If σ is infinite, consider the following computation tree: each node is marked by $(s, \sigma^{[..i]})$, where s is a state of the transition system and $\sigma^{[..i]}$ is a finite prefix of σ. The root is marked $(s, ())$, where s is any state. For any initial state $s_0 \in S_0$ of the transition system there is a child of the root in the computation tree which is marked (s_0, σ_0), where $\sigma_0 = \sigma^{[..0]}$ is the first letter of σ. Given a node marked $(s, \sigma^{[..i-1]})$ (where $i > 0$), for any s' such that $(s, \sigma_{i-1}, s') \in \Delta$ there is a child node in the tree marked $(s', (\sigma_0, ..., \sigma_i))$. Thus there exists a node marked $(s, \sigma^{[..i]})$ iff there is a path from some initial state to state s which is labelled by $(\sigma_0, ..., \sigma_{i-1})$. Since S_0 is finite and Δ is image finite, the computation tree is finitely branching. Since every prefix of σ can be extended to a string which is accepted by the transition system, the tree contains infinitely many nodes. Thus, by König's lemma from elementary set theory, it must contain an infinite branch. Therefore, there is a path in the transition system labelled by σ. Since all states in a transition system are recurring, it accepts σ. □

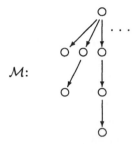

$\mathcal{M}:$

Figure 4: A non-finitary Kripke-model

Without the finitary restriction, Lemma 4.5 does not hold: consider the infinite transition system $\mathcal{M}$ of Figure 4. It shows a tree, such that for every natural number i a path of length i starts from the root. This transition system defines the set of all finite strings ($\mathbf{F}^{\cdot}\,\mathbf{X}\,\bot$), which is not a safety property. Similarly, the same language can be defined by an image finite transition system with infinitely many starting states. In particular, Lemma 4.5 implies that any finite transition system defines an ω-regular safety property. A weaker inverse statement also holds:

4.6. LEMMA. *For every ω-regular safety property there is a finite transition system defining this property.*

PROOF: Assume that a Büchi-automaton defining a certain safety property φ is given. We transform this automaton into a suitable normal form. First, any nonaccepting state s can either declared to be accepting or deleted, depending on whether an accepting state is reachable from s or not: since safety properties are prefix-closed languages, if there is an accepted path which passes through nonaccepting states, then there must be an equivalent path passing only through accepting states. Similarly, *nonaccepting SCCs* can be deleted: these are nontrivial strongly connected components in the automaton which do not contain a recurring state. Since φ is a safety property, for any accepted path ρ passing through states in a nonaccepting SCC there must be an equivalent path which avoids this SCC. Otherwise, assume that $\rho = \rho_1 \circ \rho_2$, where ρ_1 leads into the nonaccepting SCC. Consider the (nonaccepted) path $\rho_1 \circ \sigma^\omega$ which passes infinitely often through the nodes of this nonaccepting SCC. Any finite prefix $\rho_1 \circ \sigma^n$ of this path can be extended to the accepted path $\rho_1 \circ \sigma^n \circ \rho_2$; hence the whole path would have to be accepted. After the deletion of nonaccepting SCCs, each nontrivial SCC contains a recurring state. Therefore, the automaton accepts all finite and infinite paths through its state graph. Consider the transition system with the same state set and transition relation, where all states are accepting and recurring. The language of this transition system is the same as that of the (reduced) automaton.   □

For **LTL** safety properties φ, a deterministic transition system $\mathcal{M}_\varphi$ corresponding to φ can be obtained directly by a tableau procedure; see section 7.

Given a finite Kripke model $\mathcal{M}$ and an ω-regular safety property φ, checking whether $\mathcal{M}$ sequence-validates φ is especially easy. Let $\mathcal{M}_A$ be the weakly fair transition system corresponding to $\mathcal{M}$ according to Lemma 4.1, and let $\mathcal{M}_\varphi$ be a deterministic finite transition system defining the same language as φ. As above, $\mathcal{M} \models \varphi$ iff $L(\mathcal{M}_A) \subseteq L(\mathcal{M}_\varphi)$. Language containment can be decided by executing $\mathcal{M}_A$ (program) and $\mathcal{M}_\varphi$ (specification) in parallel and checking that for every step in $\mathcal{M}_A$ the corresponding step in $\mathcal{M}_\varphi$ exists. This approach is also used in *specification-based testing*, where a number of *test runs* $\sigma \in L(\mathcal{M}_A)$ is checked whether they conform to the specification, that is, $\sigma \in L(\mathcal{M}_\varphi)$. The test runs are either determined by the system under test, or selected by the specification according to some coverage strategy.

Safety properties can be used to characterize language containment for finitary transition systems just as ω-regular properties for Büchi-automata (cf. Fact 4.2). For finitary transition systems, it is sufficient to check whether $\mathcal{M}_2 \models \varphi$ implies $\mathcal{M}_1 \models \varphi$ for all *safety* properties φ in order to establish $\mathcal{M}_1 \models \mathcal{M}_2$:

4.7. THEOREM. *Let $\mathcal{M}_1$ and $\mathcal{M}_2$ be finitary transition systems. Then $\mathcal{M}_1 \models \mathcal{M}_2$ iff for all safety properties φ, if $\mathcal{M}_2 \models \varphi$ then $\mathcal{M}_1 \models \varphi$.*

PROOF: Assume that $\mathcal{M}_1 \models \mathcal{M}_2$, and that $\mathcal{M}_1 \not\models \varphi$. Then there exists a word σ accepted by $\mathcal{M}_1$ such that $\sigma \notin \varphi$. Since $L(\mathcal{M}_1) \subseteq L(\mathcal{M}_2)$, this counter model is also in the language of $\mathcal{M}_2$, hence $\mathcal{M}_2 \not\models \varphi$. For the other direction, since the set of all natural models generated from a finitary transition system is a safety property and by the fact that $\mathcal{M}_2 \models \mathcal{M}_2$ the assumption immediately reduces to $\mathcal{M}_1 \models \mathcal{M}_2$. □

4.3. Simulation Relations

The above characterization results concentrate on containment between the ω-languages generated by models and (linear time) formulas. However, there are two reasons to consider also weaker preorders between models than containment: firstly, for large nondeterministic transition systems language containment may not be easy to check. Secondly, sometimes it is desirable to formulate properties which depend on the *structure* of the system under consideration rather than on its *behavior*. Such properties may not be preserved even for systems generating the same language. For example, consider the two models $\mathcal{M}_1$ and $\mathcal{M}_2$ of Figure 5 over $\mathcal{P} = \{\}$ and $\mathcal{R} = \{a, b, c\}$.

Figure 5: Two sequence-equivalent but branching-inequivalent Kripke-models

Clearly, $L(\mathcal{M}_1) = L(\mathcal{M}_2)$, and therefore $\mathcal{M}_1 \models \mathcal{M}_2$. That is, if we observe sequences of transitions, then every possible behavior of $\mathcal{M}_1$ is also a possible behavior of $\mathcal{M}_2$. However, if we observe not only transitions which *are* taken, but also transitions which *could be* taken, then the behavior of $\mathcal{M}_1$ and $\mathcal{M}_2$ differs: if "possible continuations" are indicated by small light bulbs, then in the first system after performing a both the b and c lights will be lit, whereas in the second system only one of both is on. Formally, for every **LTL**-formula ψ it holds that ψ is sequence-valid in $\mathcal{M}_1$ iff ψ is sequence-valid in $\mathcal{M}_2$. For $\varphi \triangleq [a]([b] \perp \lor [c] \perp)$, it holds that $\mathcal{M}_2 \models \varphi$, but $\mathcal{M}_1 \not\models \varphi$.

Given two models $\mathcal{M}_1 = (U_1, \mathcal{I}_1, w_1)$ and $\mathcal{M}_2 = (U_2, \mathcal{I}_2, w_2)$, we say that $\mathcal{M}_1$ is a *submodel* of $\mathcal{M}_2$ (denoted by $\mathcal{M}_1 \sqsubseteq \mathcal{M}_2$), if $U_1 \subseteq U_2$, $\mathcal{I}_1 = \mathcal{I}_2 \downarrow U_1$ (the restriction of $\mathcal{I}_2$ to U_2), and $w_1 = w_2$. Intuitively, a submodel consists of some parts of the original model. In the proof of Lemma 4.6 we constructed a special submodel which preserves all execution sequences. Generally, all temporal properties are preserved when a model is replaced by the *generated submodel*, i.e., the submodel consisting of all points reachable from the current point. However, usually properties are not preserved when a model is replaced by an arbitrary submodel. Instead of simply omitting parts of a model, it is better to collapse several points into a single point.

For any two models $\mathcal{M}_1 = (U_1, \mathcal{I}_1, w_1)$ and $\mathcal{M}_2 = (U_2, \mathcal{I}_2, w_2)$, a relation $H \subseteq U_1 \times U_2$ is called a *simulation relation* between $\mathcal{M}_1$ and $\mathcal{M}_2$ if

- $(w_1, w_2) \in H$,
- For all $p \in \mathcal{P}$, $u \in U_1$, and $v \in U_2$, if $(u, v) \in H$ then $u \in \mathcal{I}_1(p)$ iff $v \in \mathcal{I}_2(p)$.
- For all u and v such that $(u, v) \in H$ and all R and u' such that $(u, u') \in \mathcal{I}_1(R)$ there is a v' with the property that $(v, v') \in \mathcal{I}_2(R)$ and $(u', v') \in H$.

Figure 6 illustrates the third condition.

We say that $\mathcal{M}_1$ *is simulated by* $\mathcal{M}_2$, or $\mathcal{M}_2$ *simulates* $\mathcal{M}_1$ (denoted by $\mathcal{M}_1 \overset{\rightarrow}{\sim} \mathcal{M}_2$), if there exists a simulation relation H between $\mathcal{M}_1$ and $\mathcal{M}_2$. Simulation relates a model $\mathcal{M}_1$ to an *abstraction* $\mathcal{M}_2$ of the model $\mathcal{M}_1$. It guarantees that every behavior of the model is also a possible behavior of the abstraction. However, since a point in the abstract model usually represents a set of points in the original model, the abstraction might have behaviors that have no counterpart in the original model. Thus, the term "simulation" is used as in "the PC simulates a gameboy" or "this program simulates the development of bacteria cultures".

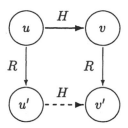

Figure 6: Simulation condition for u and v

4.8. FACT. $\stackrel{\rightarrow}{\sim}$ is a preorder on the class of all models.

PROOF: The proof of reflexivity is immediate. For transitivity, note that the relational product of two simulation relations is again a simulation relation.   □

If $\mathcal{M}_1 \sqsubseteq \mathcal{M}_2$, then $\mathcal{M}_1 \stackrel{\rightarrow}{\sim} \mathcal{M}_2$. Moreover, if $\mathcal{M}_1 \stackrel{\rightarrow}{\sim} \mathcal{M}_2$, then $\mathcal{M}_1 \models \mathcal{M}_2$: if $\mathcal{M}_2$ can simulate $\mathcal{M}_1$, then for every maximal run σ generated by $\mathcal{M}_1$ there exists a corresponding $\sigma' \in \mathcal{M}_2$.

A model is called *deterministic*, if for every $w \in U$ and $R \in \mathcal{R}$ there is at most one $w' \in U$ such that $(w, w') \in \mathcal{I}(R)$. (This definition is somewhat weaker than the definition of deterministic automata on page 1668.) For deterministic $\mathcal{M}_2$ also the converse holds: $\mathcal{M}_1 \models \mathcal{M}_2$ iff $\mathcal{M}_1 \stackrel{\rightarrow}{\sim} \mathcal{M}_2$. This is true because for any word there is at most one path through a deterministic transition system. Deterministic models and properties are an important special case. Whereas for many problems in nondeterministic transition systems an exponential search via backtracking is used, in the deterministic case the same problems can be solved with polynomial complexity.

4.9. LEMMA. *Let H be a simulation relation between $\mathcal{M}_1 = (U_1, \mathcal{I}_1, w_1)$ and $\mathcal{M}_2 = (U_2, \mathcal{I}_2, w_2)$, and $(w_1', w_2') \in H$. Then $(U_1, \mathcal{I}_1, w_1') \stackrel{\rightarrow}{\sim} (U_2, \mathcal{I}_2, w_2')$.*

PROOF: The proof is immediate from the definition of simulation relations.   □

A *modal box formula* is a formula not involving any diamond operator. More precisely, literals (propositions and negated propositions) and $\bot, \top$ are modal box formulas, and if φ and ψ are modal box formulas, then $(\varphi \wedge \psi)$, $(\varphi \vee \psi)$ and $[R]\varphi$ are modal box formulas. Similar to Lemmas 4.2 and 4.6, the following lemma relates simulations between models and preservation of modal box formulas:

4.10. LEMMA. *Let $\mathcal{M}_1 = (U_1, \mathcal{I}_1, w_1)$ and $\mathcal{M}_2 = (U_2, \mathcal{I}_2, w_2)$ be Kripke-models. $\mathcal{M}_1 \stackrel{\rightarrow}{\sim} \mathcal{M}_2$ implies that for all modal box formulas φ, if $\mathcal{M}_2 \models \varphi$ then $\mathcal{M}_1 \models \varphi$.*

PROOF: The proof is by induction on φ. The base cases $\bot, \top$ are trivial. For $p \in \mathcal{P}$, the assumption $(w_1, w_2) \in H$ implies $w_1 \in \mathcal{I}_1(p)$ iff $w_2 \in \mathcal{I}_2(p)$. For boolean operators $\wedge, \vee$, the statement is an immediate consequence of the induction hypothesis. Finally, if $w_1 \not\models [R]\varphi$, then there is a $w_1' \in U_1$ such that $(w_1, w_1') \in \mathcal{I}_1(R)$ and $w_1' \not\models \varphi$. Since $\mathcal{M}_1 \rightrightarrows \mathcal{M}_2$, there is a $w_2' \in U_2$ such that $(w_2, w_2') \in \mathcal{I}_2(R)$ and $(w_1', w_2') \in H$. Lemma 4.9 asserts that $(U_1, \mathcal{I}_1, w_1') \rightrightarrows (U_2, \mathcal{I}_2, w_2')$. According to the induction hypothesis, $w_2' \not\models \varphi$. Therefore, $w_2 \not\models [R]\varphi$, which was to be proved. □

This lemma makes it possible to check safety in the abstracted (small) model $\mathcal{M}_2$ rather than in the original (large) model $\mathcal{M}_1$: if $\mathcal{M}_1$ violates a modal box formula, then this violation will also occur in $\mathcal{M}_2$.

The above statement can be extended to more expressive logics. The logic **ACTL** [Long 1993, Clarke, Grumberg and Long 1994a, Clarke, Long and McMillan 1989, Josko 1993, Dams, Grumberg and Gerth 1994] is "**CTL** without **E** quantifier". That is, literals and $\top, \bot$ are **ACTL** formulas, and if φ and ψ are **ACTL** formulas, then $(\varphi \wedge \psi)$, $(\varphi \vee \psi)$, $\mathbf{A}(\varphi \mathbf{U}^+ \psi)$ and $\mathbf{A}(\varphi \mathbf{W}^+ \psi)$ are **ACTL** formulas, where $\mathbf{A}(\varphi \mathbf{W}^+ \psi) \triangleq \neg\mathbf{E}(\neg\psi \mathbf{U}^+ \neg(\varphi \vee \psi))$.

4.11. THEOREM. *Let $\mathcal{M}_1$ and $\mathcal{M}_2$ be Kripke-models and φ be an* **ACTL** *formula. If $\mathcal{M}_1 \rightrightarrows \mathcal{M}_2$ and $\mathcal{M}_2 \models \varphi$, then $\mathcal{M}_1 \models \varphi$.*

PROOF: Intuitively, this theorem is true because formulas in **ACTL** describe properties that are valid in all paths of a model. They cannot express the existence of a specific path in the model. If $\mathcal{M}_1 \rightrightarrows \mathcal{M}_2$, then every behavior of $\mathcal{M}_1$ is a behavior of $\mathcal{M}_2$. Thus every formula of **ACTL** that is valid in $\mathcal{M}_2$ must also be valid in $\mathcal{M}_1$.

Formally, the theorem is proved by induction on the structure of φ. Again, the only interesting cases are $\mathbf{A}\mathbf{U}^+$ and $\mathbf{A}\mathbf{W}^+$. We show the case of $\varphi \triangleq \mathbf{A}(\chi \mathbf{U}^+ \psi)$. Note that $\neg\mathbf{A}(\chi \mathbf{U}^+ \psi) \leftrightarrow (\mathbf{E}(\neg\psi \mathbf{U}^+ \neg(\chi \vee \psi)) \vee \mathbf{E}\mathbf{G}^+ \neg\psi)$ (cf. page 1655). Assume that $\mathcal{M}_1 \rightrightarrows \mathcal{M}_2$ and $\mathcal{M}_1 \not\models \varphi$, and show that $\mathcal{M}_2 \not\models \varphi$. If $w_1 \not\models \mathbf{A}(\chi \mathbf{U}^+ \psi)$, then in $\mathcal{M}_1$ there is either a finite sequence of nodes $w_1^1, w_1^2, \ldots, w_1^n$, such that $w_1^i \not\models \psi$ for $0 < i < n$, and $w_1^n \not\models (\chi \vee \psi)$, or a maximal path $w_1^1, w_1^2, w_1^3, \ldots$, such that $w_1^i \not\models \psi$ for all $i > 0$. Similar to the above, the induction hypothesis proves that a corresponding finite or infinite sequence $w_2^1, w_2^2, \ldots, w_2^n$ or $w_2^1, w_2^2, w_2^3, \ldots$, exists, such that $w_2^i \not\models \psi$ for $0 < i < n$, and $w_2^n \not\models (\chi \vee \psi)$, or $w_2^i \not\models \psi$ for all $i > 0$. Thus $w_2 \not\models \mathbf{A}(\chi \mathbf{U}^+ \psi)$. □

In general the converse of the above lemma and theorem are not valid. Essentially, this is due to the same reason why Lemma 4.5 fails to hold for non-finitary transition system: consider the counterexample of Figure 7.

Both models have infinitely many branches from the root, one branch of length one, one branch of length two, one branch of length three, and so on. $\mathcal{M}_1$ has an additional branch of infinite length. These two models cannot be distinguished by any modal formula:

4.12. LEMMA. *For any $\varphi \in$ **ML** it holds that $\mathcal{M}_1 \models \varphi$ iff $\mathcal{M}_2 \models \varphi$*

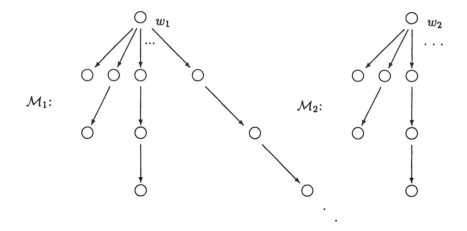

Figure 7: Two modally indistinguishable models

PROOF: The statement is proved by induction on φ. The crucial case is $\varphi = \langle R \rangle \psi$, $\mathcal{M}_1 \models \varphi$, and the successor w_1' of w_1 for which $w_1' \models \psi$ is on the additional infinite branch of $\mathcal{M}_1$. Choose any branch of $\mathcal{M}_2$ of length at least n, where n is the number of modal operators in φ. Denote the i-th point on the infinite branch of $\mathcal{M}_1$ and on the chosen branch of $\mathcal{M}_2$ by w_1^i and w_2^i, respectively (where $w_1^0 = w_1$ and $w_2^0 = w_2$). Then for all $i \leq n$ and all sub-formulas ξ_i of φ with at most $(n-i)$ modal operators it holds that $w_1^i \models \xi_i$ iff $w_2^i \models \xi_i$. This is proved by subinduction on $n - i$: if $n - i = 0$, then it holds by definition of the models. If $n - i > 0$ and $w_1^{i+1} \models \xi_{i+1}$ iff $w_2^{i+1} \models \xi_{i+1}$, then $w_1^i \models \langle R \rangle \xi_{i+1}$ iff $w_2^i \models \langle R \rangle \xi_{i+1}$. Especially, since φ has n modal operators, $w_1^0 \models \varphi$ iff $w_2^0 \models \varphi$. $\qquad \square$

In particular, Lemma 4.12 implies that for every modal box formula φ, if $\mathcal{M}_2 \models \varphi$ then $\mathcal{M}_1 \models \varphi$. Yet, $\mathcal{M}_2$ does not simulate $\mathcal{M}_1$: assume a simulation relation H mapping the first node w of the infinite path of $\mathcal{M}_1$ to any node w' of any finite path in $\mathcal{M}_2$. Then H must map the successor of w to the successor of w', the successor of the successor of w to the successor of the successor of w', and so on. There are finitely many successors from w', but infinitely many successors from w. Thus, after a finite number of steps, there will be nodes $u \in \mathcal{M}_1$ and $v \in \mathcal{M}_2$ such that $(u, v) \in H$, and u has a successor in $\mathcal{M}_1$, but v has no successor in $\mathcal{M}_2$.

This is a somewhat contrived counterexample. In "many" cases, the converse will hold. Recall that a model is called *image finite*, if every point has only finitely many successors.

4.13. THEOREM. *Let $\mathcal{M}_1$ and $\mathcal{M}_2$ be image finite Kripke-models. Then $\mathcal{M}_1 \stackrel{\rightarrow}{\rightrightarrows} \mathcal{M}_2$ iff for all modal box formulas φ, if $\mathcal{M}_2 \models \varphi$ then $\mathcal{M}_1 \models \varphi$.*

PROOF: Assume that all modal box formulas holding in $\mathcal{M}_2 \triangleq (U_2, \mathcal{I}_2, w_2)$ are also valid for $\mathcal{M}_1 \triangleq (U_1, \mathcal{I}_1, w_1)$, and construct a simulation between $\mathcal{M}_1$ and $\mathcal{M}_2$. Define H by $(u, v) \in H$ iff for all modal box formulas φ, if $v \models \varphi$ then $u \models \varphi$. Then $(w_1, w_2) \in H$ by definition, and $(u, v) \in H$ implies $\mathcal{L}_1(u) = \mathcal{L}_2(v)$, since literals are modal box formulas. Assume $(u, v) \in H$ and $(u, u') \in \mathcal{I}_1(R)$. We have to show that there is a v' such that $(v, v') \in \mathcal{I}_2(R)$ and for all modal box formulas φ, if $u' \not\models \varphi$ then $v' \not\models \varphi$. Assume for contradiction that for each v' with $(v, v') \in \mathcal{I}_2(R)$ there is a $\varphi_{v'}$ such that $u' \not\models \varphi_{v'}$ and $v' \models \varphi_{v'}$. Since $\mathcal{M}_2$ is image finite, $\bigvee \varphi_{v'}$ exists and is a modal box formula. Moreover, for all such v', we have $v' \models \bigvee \varphi_{v'}$, which means $v \models [R] \bigvee \varphi_{v'}$. This implies $u \models [R] \bigvee \varphi_{v'}$ and therefore $u' \models \bigvee \varphi_{v'}$. This is a contradiction to the assumption that $u' \not\models \varphi_{v'}$ for all $\varphi_{v'}$. □

We already mentioned that the above theorems can be used to reduce the complexity of model checking. To prove that $\mathcal{M}_1 \models \varphi$, it can help to find an appropriate abstraction $\mathcal{M}_2$, and to prove $\mathcal{M}_1 \stackrel{\rightarrow}{\rightrightarrows} \mathcal{M}_2$ and $\mathcal{M}_2 \models \varphi$. For more information, see [Bensalem, Bouajani, Loiseaux and Sifakis 1992].

Extremely efficient algorithms are known to check language inclusion for deterministic finite automata [Hopcroft and Ullman 1979]. These algorithms can be used to check the simulation preorder for deterministic models. For nondeterministic finite models $\mathcal{M}_1 = (U_1, \mathcal{I}_1, w_1)$ and $\mathcal{M}_2 = (U_2, \mathcal{I}_2, w_2)$, to check whether $\mathcal{M}_1 \stackrel{\rightarrow}{\rightrightarrows} \mathcal{M}_2$ we define a sequence of relations $H^0, H^1, \ldots$ on $U_1 \times U_2$ as follows:

- $(u, v) \in H^0$ iff for all $p \in \mathcal{P}$ it holds that $u \in \mathcal{I}_1(p)$ iff $v \in \mathcal{I}_2(p)$
- $(u, v) \in H^{n+1}$ iff $(u, v) \in H^n$ and for all R and $u' \in U_1$ such that $(u, u') \in \mathcal{I}_1(R)$ there is a v' with the property that $(v, v') \in \mathcal{I}_2(R)$ and $(u', v') \in H^n$.

The intersection H^* of all H^n is the largest simulation relation between $\mathcal{M}_1$ and $\mathcal{M}_2$. That is, $\mathcal{M}_1 \stackrel{\rightarrow}{\rightrightarrows} \mathcal{M}_2$ iff $(w_1, w_2) \in H^*$. Algorithmically, if $H^n = H^{n-1}$, then $H^* \triangleq H^n$ and the construction terminates. In other words, we construct the greatest fixed point of the one-step simulation relation. Since the structures are finite, there are only finitely many different H^n. Thus, termination is guaranteed. In Figure 8, $R(u)$ denotes the set $\{u' \mid (u, u') \in \mathcal{I}(R)\}$, and $|_1$ is the first component of a tuple. In the next section, a more elaborate implementation of a similar algorithm for symmetric simulation relations is given, which is based on partition refinement.

5. Equivalence reductions

In this section, we consider symmetric preorders, i.e., equivalences, and equivalence transformations between models. There are various possibilities for defining equivalences on models. For any preorder $\preceq$ from the preceding section, an equivalence can be defined by $\mathcal{M}_1 \simeq \mathcal{M}_2$ iff $\mathcal{M}_1 \preceq \mathcal{M}_2$ and $\mathcal{M}_2 \preceq \mathcal{M}_1$. In this way, the equivalence induced by the submodel ordering $\sqsubseteq$ is isomorphism. For $\mathcal{M}_1 \models \mathcal{M}_2$, the

---

procedure Sim_check (Model $(U_1, \mathcal{I}_1, w_1)$, Model $(U_2, \mathcal{I}_2, w_2)$) =
     $H^{new} := \{(u,v) \mid u \in U_1,\ v \in U_2,\ \mathcal{L}_1(u) = \mathcal{L}_2(v)\}$
    repeat
         $H^{old} := H^{new};\quad H^{new} := \{\}$
        for all $(u,v) \in H^{old}$ **do**
             $add := \top;$ **for all** $R \in \mathcal{R}$ **do**
                 if not $R(u) \subseteq ((R(u) \times R(v)) \cap H^{old})|_1$ **then** $add := \bot$
             if add **then** $H^{new} := H^{new} \cup \{(u,v)\}$
    until $H^{new} = H^{old};$
    if $(w_1, w_2) \in H^{new}$
    then print("$(U_1, \mathcal{I}_1, w_1)$ is simulated by $(U_2, \mathcal{I}_2, w_2)$")
    else print("There is no simulation between $(U_1, \mathcal{I}_1, w_1)$ and $(U_2, \mathcal{I}_2, w_2)$");

Figure 8: Algorithm for simulation checking

symmetric version is equality of the generated languages. Other model equivalences are introduced by equivalence with respect to logical formulas, and by symmetric simulations.

5.1. Bisimulations (p-morphisms)

A classical notion from modal logic is *p-morphism* [Segerberg 1968], [Segerberg 1971, p37] or *bisimulation* [Milner 1980, Park 1981]. A bisimulation is a relation $\leftrightarrow$ between the universes of two Kripke-models $(U_1, \mathcal{I}_1, w_1)$ and $(U_2, \mathcal{I}_2, w_2)$ such that

- $w_1 \leftrightarrow w_2$,
- If $u \leftrightarrow v$, then $u \in \mathcal{I}_1(\text{p})$ iff $v \in \mathcal{I}_2(\text{p})$
- If $u \leftrightarrow v$ and $(u, u') \in \mathcal{I}_1(R)$, then there exists v' such that $(v, v') \in \mathcal{I}_2(R)$ and $u' \leftrightarrow v'$.
- If $u \leftrightarrow v$ and $(v, v') \in \mathcal{I}_2(R)$, then there exists u' such that $(u, u') \in \mathcal{I}_1(R)$ and $u' \leftrightarrow v'$.

Two Kripke-models $\mathcal{M}_1$ and $\mathcal{M}_2$ are *bisimilar* (denoted by $\mathcal{M}_1 \leftrightarrow \mathcal{M}_2$), if there exists a bisimulation between them. Figure 9 shows some examples of bisimilar models.

This example demonstrates the following statements:

5.1. Fact.

- Each model is bisimilar to one where duplicate states (which have the same input and output) are removed,
- Each model is bisimilar to its unfolding, and

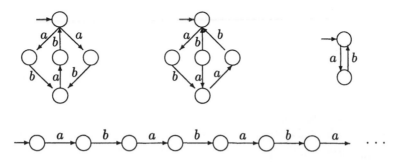

Figure 9: Bisimilar models

- Each model is bisimilar to its reachable part.

If $\mathcal{M}_1 \leftrightarrow \mathcal{M}_2$, then $\mathcal{M}_1 \rightrightarrows \mathcal{M}_2$ and $\mathcal{M}_2 \rightrightarrows \mathcal{M}_1$; the other direction of this statement is not necessarily true. For example, each of the models in Figure 10 simulates the other one, but they are not bisimilar.

Figure 10: Not-bisimilar models

Another important equivalence relation between models is that of being indistinguishable by formulas of a certain logic. We say that the models $\mathcal{M}_1$ and $\mathcal{M}_2$ are *equivalent with respect to the logic* $\mathbf{L}$ ($\mathcal{M}_1 \equiv_{\mathbf{L}} \mathcal{M}_2$) if for all well formed formulas of $\mathbf{L}$ it holds that $\mathcal{M}_1 \models \varphi$ iff $\mathcal{M}_2 \models \varphi$. The relation $\equiv_{FOL}$ is called *elementary equivalence*. Bisimulation relations are precisely those equivalences which preserve all modal formulas:

5.2. LEMMA. *Bisimilar models are modally equivalent: if* $\mathcal{M}_1 \leftrightarrow \mathcal{M}_2$, *then* $\mathcal{M}_1 \equiv_{\mathbf{ML}} \mathcal{M}_2$

The proof is by induction on the structure of φ, analogous to the proof of Lemma 4.10.

Hence, it is "safe" to substitute a model by a bisimilar one in a structured software development process: all multimodal formulas which are valid for the original model will remain valid for the substituted model. The converse of this lemma again requires image finiteness:

5.3. THEOREM (Segerberg71). *Image finite models are modally equivalent iff they are bisimilar: if M_1 and M_2 are image finite, then $M_1 \leftrightarrow M_2$ iff $M_1 \equiv_{ML} M_2$*

Again, the proof is similar to the proof of Theorem 4.13 in the previous section. The only difference is that bisimulation is a symmetric relation.

In general, this theorem does not hold for more expressive logics. For *finite* Kripke-models, however, it can be lifted even to logics like positive μ**TL**. Given any formula φ which is positive in q, and a natural number n, we define $\nu^0 q \, \varphi \triangleq \top$, and $\nu^{n+1} q \, \varphi \triangleq \varphi\{q := \nu^n q \, \varphi\}$. That is, $\nu^n q \, \varphi \triangleq \varphi\{q := \varphi\}\{q := \varphi\} \cdots \{q := \top\}$.

5.4. LEMMA. *Let $M \triangleq (U, I, w)$ be a finite model, where $|U| = n$, and let φ be a monotonic μ**TL** formula. Then $M \models \nu q \, \varphi$ iff $M \models \nu^n q \, \varphi$*

PROOF: One direction of this lemma follows from the fact that $\nu q \, \varphi$ denotes a fixed point, i.e., $(\nu q \, \varphi \rightarrow \varphi\{q := \nu q \, \varphi\})$. Since φ is monotonic, this implies $(\varphi\{q := \nu q \, \varphi\} \rightarrow \varphi\{q := \varphi\{q := \nu q \, \varphi\}\})$. By chain reasoning, $(\nu q \, \varphi \rightarrow \varphi\{q := \varphi\{q := \nu q \, \varphi\}\})$. By induction, $(\nu q \, \varphi \rightarrow \varphi\{q := \varphi\}\{q := \varphi\}...\{q := \nu q \, \varphi\})$. Again, since φ is monotonic in q, it holds that $(\varphi\{q := \nu q \, \varphi\} \rightarrow \varphi\{q := \top\})$, thus $(\nu q \, \varphi \rightarrow \nu^n q \, \varphi)$ is valid.

For the other direction, let $F \triangleq (U, I)$ be the frame on which M is based. Consider the sequence $((\nu^n q \, \varphi)^F)_{n \geq 0}$ of sets of points. Clearly, $(\nu^0 q \, \varphi)^F = \top^F = U \supseteq (\nu^1 q \, \varphi)^F$. Since φ_q^F is monotonic (cf. Fact 3.8), $(\nu^1 q \, \varphi)^F = \varphi_q^F((\nu^0 q \, \varphi)^F) \supseteq \varphi_q^F((\nu^1 q \, \varphi)^F) = (\nu^2 q \, \varphi)^F$. Continuing this argument, we conclude that $((\nu^n q \, \varphi)^F)_{n \geq 0}$ is a descending chain of sets. There are two possibilities: either there exists an $i < |U|$ such that $(\nu^i q \, \varphi)^F = (\nu^{i+1} q \, \varphi)^F$, hence $(\nu^i q \, \varphi)^F = (\nu^n q \, \varphi)^F$, or $(\nu^n q \, \varphi)^F = \{ \, \}$. In either case, the sequence stabilizes after at most $|U|$ steps: $(\nu^n q \, \varphi)^F = (\nu^{n+1} q \, \varphi)^F$. As a consequence, $(\nu^n q \, \varphi \rightarrow \nu^{n+1} q \, \varphi)$ is universally valid in F.

Now assume that $M \not\models \nu q \, \varphi$, and show that $M \not\models \nu^n q \, \varphi$. According to the definition on page 1660, $(U, I, w) \not\models \nu q \, \varphi$ means that for all $Q \subseteq U$ such that $w \in Q$ there exists a $v \in Q$ such that $(U, I', v) \not\models \varphi$, where $I'(q) = Q$. (*) Let $Q = (\nu^n q \, \varphi)^F$. If $w \notin Q$, then $(U, I, w) \not\models \nu^n q \, \varphi$ and we are done. If $w \in Q$, then by (*) for some v it holds that $(U, I, v) \models \nu^n q \, \varphi$, and $(U, I', v) \not\models \varphi$, where $I'(q) = (\nu^n q \, \varphi)^F$. In other words, $(U, I', v) \not\models \varphi\{q := \nu^n q \, \varphi\}$, which means that $(U, I, v) \not\models \nu^{n+1} \varphi$. Since $(U, I, v) \models (\nu^n q \, \varphi \rightarrow \nu^{n+1} q \, \varphi)$, this is a contradiction. □

This lemma is important for model checking of μ**TL** on finite Kripke models. Moreover, it allows to prove the following result.

5.5. THEOREM. *Finite models are monotonic μ**TL**-equivalent iff they are bisimilar: if M_1 and M_2 are finite, then $M_1 \leftrightarrow M_2$ iff $M_1 \equiv_{\mu TL} M_2$*

PROOF: Trivially, finite models are also image finite. Any two models which are equivalent with respect to monotonic μ**TL** are modally equivalent, since modal logic is a sublanguage of μ**TL**. Hence as an immediate consequence of Theorem 5.3, any two finite models which are μ**TL** equivalent are bisimilar.

For the other direction, assume that $\mathcal{M}_1 \models \varphi$ and $\mathcal{M}_2 \not\models \varphi$, where φ is a monotonic μ**TL**-formula. Let $n \triangleq \max(|U_1|, |U_2|)$, and φ^n be φ where every sub-formula $\nu q\ \psi$ is replaced by $\nu^n q\ \psi$. As a consequence of Lemma 5.4, $\mathcal{M}_i \models \varphi$ iff $\mathcal{M}_i \models \varphi^n$ for $i = 1, 2$. Therefore, $\mathcal{M}_1 \models \varphi^n$ and $\mathcal{M}_2 \not\models \varphi^n$. Since φ^n is a multimodal formula, $\mathcal{M}_1$ and $\mathcal{M}_2$ are modally inequivalent. Theorem 5.3 implies that $\mathcal{M}_1$ and $\mathcal{M}_2$ are not bisimilar. □

5.6. COROLLARY. *Any two finite Kripke-models which can be distinguished by a monotonic μ**TL**-formula can also be distinguished by a multimodal formula: if $\mathcal{M}_1$ and $\mathcal{M}_2$ are finite, then $\mathcal{M}_1 \equiv_{\mu\mathbf{TL}} \mathcal{M}_2$ iff $\mathcal{M}_1 \equiv_{\mathbf{ML}} \mathcal{M}_2$*

[Browne, Clarke and Grumberg 1988] proved that if two finite models can be distinguished by a formula of the logic **CTL***, then they can be distinguished by a **CTL** formula. Every **CTL*** formula has a positive μ**TL** equivalent [Dam 1994] (on tree models, **CTL*** can be translated into monadic second order logic, which is of the same expressiveness as μ**TL**). Therefore this result can be obtained as a consequence of the above.

5.2. Distinguishing Power and Ehrenfeucht-Fraïssé Games

The previous theorems showed that logics with different expressiveness can have the same distinguishing capabilities. We wish to formalize these notions. A logic **L2** is said to be *at least as expressive as* **L1** (or **L1** is *at most as expressive as* **L2**) iff for any formula $\varphi_1 \in \mathbf{L1}$ there exists a formula $\varphi_2 \in \mathbf{L2}$ such that for all models $\mathcal{M}$ we have $\mathcal{M} \models \varphi_1$ iff $\mathcal{M} \models \varphi_2$. **L1** and **L2** *have the same expressive power* if **L1** is at least as expressive as **L2** and **L2** is at least as expressive as **L1**. In other words, two logics have the same expressive power iff for any formula of one logic there is an equivalent formula from the other logic. For example, Theorem 2.4 states that on natural models, **FOL** and **LTL** have the same expressive power.

Logic **L2** is *at least as distinguishing as* **L1** (or **L1** is *at most as distinguishing as* **L2**) if any two models which are inequivalent with respect to **L1** are also inequivalent with respect to **L2**. That is, **L2** at least as distinguishing as **L1** iff $\mathcal{M}_1 \equiv_{\mathbf{L2}} \mathcal{M}_2$ implies $\mathcal{M}_1 \equiv_{\mathbf{L1}} \mathcal{M}_2$. **L1** and **L2** *have the same distinguishing power* if **L1** is at most as distinguishing as **L2** and **L2** is at most as distinguishing as **L1**. In other words, **L1** and **L2** have the same distinguishing power iff for all models $\mathcal{M}_1$ and $\mathcal{M}_2$ it holds that $\mathcal{M}_1 \equiv_{\mathbf{L1}} \mathcal{M}_2$ iff $\mathcal{M}_1 \equiv_{\mathbf{L2}} \mathcal{M}_2$.

Expressiveness is a finer equivalence relation on the class of all logics than distinguishability:

5.7. FACT. If **L1** is at most as expressive as **L2**, then it is at most as distinguishing. If **L1** and **L2** have the same expressive power, then they have the same distinguishing power (but not vice versa).

PROOF: Assume that for any formula $\varphi_1 \in \mathbf{L1}$ there exists an equivalent formula $\varphi_2 \in \mathbf{L2}$. Assume further two models $\mathcal{M}_1$ and $\mathcal{M}_2$ which are inequivalent with respect to **L1**, that is, for some $\varphi_1 \in$ **L1** we have $\mathcal{M}_1 \models \varphi_1$ and $\mathcal{M}_2 \not\models \varphi_1$ or vice versa. According to the first assumption there exists $\varphi_2 \in$ **L2** equivalent to φ_1. Therefore $\mathcal{M}_1 \models \varphi_2$ and $\mathcal{M}_2 \not\models \varphi_2$ or vice versa, which means that $\mathcal{M}_1$ and $\mathcal{M}_2$ are inequivalent with respect to **L2**. The second statement follows by symmetry. As example of logics with equal distinguishing power but different expressive power, consider multimodal logic and positive μ**TL**. $\square$

For any formula φ, we say that φ is *preserved under bisimulations*, if for all models $\mathcal{M}_1 \leftrightarrow \mathcal{M}_2$ it holds that $\mathcal{M}_1 \models \varphi$ iff $\mathcal{M}_2 \models \varphi$. A logic **L** is *bisimulation invariant*, if all well-formed formulas of **L** are preserved under bisimulations. Lemma 5.2 shows that multimodal logic is bisimulation invariant. In other words, if a property can be defined by a multimodal formula, then it is preserved under bisimulations. The same holds for more expressive logics like monotonic μ**TL**:

5.8. LEMMA. μ**TL** *is bisimulation invariant: if* $\mathcal{M}_1 \leftrightarrow \mathcal{M}_2$, *then for any positive* μ**TL** *formula* φ *it holds that* $\mathcal{M}_1 \models \varphi$ *iff* $\mathcal{M}_2 \models \varphi$.

In his thesis, van Benthem investigated the reverse direction, and gave a connection between bisimulations, first order and modal expressiveness (see [van Benthem 1983]). He showed that for first order formulas, bisimulation invariance implies multimodal definability:

5.9. THEOREM (Expressive completeness of **ML**). *For any first order formula* φ *(with one free variable) which is preserved under bisimulations there exists an equivalent multimodal formula.*

Thus, exactly those first order formulas which are preserved under bisimulations can be translated into modal logic. [Janin and Walukiewicz 1996] extended this theorem for second order formulas and μ**TL**, which is a converse to Lemma 5.8:

5.10. THEOREM (Expressive completeness of μ**TL**). *Let* φ *be any* **MSOL** *property. Then* φ *is preserved under bisimulations iff* φ *is definable by a positive* μ**TL** *formula.*

In particular, this result implies that every logic which is bisimulation invariant and has a semantical translation into **MSOL** can be also translated into mTL. As a corollary, many propositional logics of programs (CTL*, PDL, ...) which have been suggested can be translated into the μ-calculus.

Segerberg's theorem 5.3 relates modal equivalence to bisimilarity. Bisimilarity can also be defined in terms of a so-called *Ehrenfeucht-Fraïssé game* [Fraïssé 1954, Ehrenfeucht 1961]: there are two players, Ann and Bob. They play on a board on which two Kripke-models are drawn. Ann's goal is to show that these models are not bisimilar, whereas Bob's goal is to show that they are bisimilar. (So, this is not really a fair game, since the outcome is predetermined by the shape of the board.)

Each player has an unlimited amount of pebbles which are numbered consecutively: $a_0, a_1, a_2, ...$ and $b_0, b_1, b_2, ...$ To start the game, each player places his first pebble a_0, b_0 on the current point of one of the models. If the current points have a different label, Bob has lost immediately.

Thus, round 0 consists of placing a_0 and b_0 on the board. Similarly, round j consists of the placement of a_j and b_j: Ann chooses any point w_0 on one of the models on which some pebble (say, a_i or b_i for $i < j$) had been placed previously, and puts her next pebble a_j on some point w_1 which is an R-successor of w_0. Bob then locates the ith pebble (that is, b_i or a_i, respectively) on the other model, say in point w_0'. He looks for a point w_1' such that $w_0' R w_1'$, and w_1 and $w_{1'}$ have the same label. If he can't find such a point he has lost and the game ends; otherwise he chooses any such point and puts his next pebble b_j on it.

If the game continues forever, then Bob has won. Ann *can force a win within n rounds*, if she can place her pebble in such a way that Bob immediately loses the game, or if she can choose a point such that for each possible answer of Bob she can force a win within $n - 1$ rounds. Ann has a *winning strategy* if there is some n such that she can force a win within n rounds. Bob has winning strategy iff Ann does not have one; i.e., if in each round and for each possible move of Ann there is a response by Bob to continue the game.

Ehrenfeucht-Fraïssé games are a convenient way to imagine bisimulations.

5.11. THEOREM. *Ann has a winning strategy in this game iff the two models are not bisimilar; i.e., Bob has a winning strategy iff they are bisimilar.*

PROOF: From Bob's winning strategy, it is easy to construct a bisimulation between the two models: $w_i \leftrightarroweq w_i'$ iff Bob would have chosen w_i or w_i' as a reply to Ann's choosing w_i' or w_i, respectively. For the other direction, every bisimulation determines a winning strategy for Bob: he just replies by choosing any point which is related to the point chosen by Ann via the bisimulation relation. □

It is easy to modify the rules of the game such that it captures the equivalence of two models with respect to other logical languages. For example, in a game for **MSOL** we allow both Ann and Bob in any move to place an arbitrary *set* of pebbles on one of the models on the board. Then the two models can be distinguished by a monadic second order formula iff Ann has a winning strategy.

5.3. Auto-bisimulations and the Paige/Tarjan Algorithm

In this subsection we show how to minimize a given Kripke-model with respect to bisimulation equivalence. Note that our definitions did not exclude bisimulations from a model to itself (*auto-bisimulations*); i.e., some points in a model can be related by a bisimulation to other points in the *same* model.

5.12. LEMMA. *The union of any number of auto-bisimulations on a model is again an auto-bisimulation.*

PROOF: This follows directly from the definition of bisimulation relations. □

Thus, for any model, there exists a largest auto-bisimulation, namely, the union of all auto-bisimulations of this model. Additionally, the reflexive transitive symmetric closure of any auto-bisimulation is again an auto-bisimulation. Hence, for any auto-bisimulation $\leftrightarrow$ there is a largest equivalence relation $\equiv$ containing it ($\leftrightarrow\,\subseteq\,\equiv$) which is again an auto-bisimulation. And, the largest auto-bisimulation must be an equivalence relation on the set of points of a model.

Given any model $\mathcal{M} \triangleq (U, \mathcal{I}, w_0)$, and any equivalence relation $\equiv$ on U. Define the *quotient of $\mathcal{M}$ with respect to* $\equiv$ to be the model $\mathcal{M}^{\equiv} \triangleq (U^{\equiv}, \mathcal{I}^{\equiv}, w_0^{\equiv})$, where $U^{\equiv}$ is the set of equivalence classes of U with respect to $\equiv$, $w_0^{\equiv}$ is the equivalence class of w_0, $w^{\equiv} \in \mathcal{I}^{\equiv}(\mathbf{p})$ if there is some $w \in w^{\equiv}$ such that $w \in \mathcal{I}(\mathbf{p})$, and $(w_1^{\equiv}, w_2^{\equiv}) \in \mathcal{I}^{\equiv}(R)$ if there are $w_1 \in w_1^{\equiv}$ and $w_2 \in w_2^{\equiv}$ such that $(w_1, w_2) \in \mathcal{I}(R)$.

5.13. LEMMA. *If the equivalence relation $\equiv$ is an auto-bisimulation, then $\mathcal{M} \leftrightarrow \mathcal{M}^{\equiv}$.*

PROOF: Define $u \leftrightarrow v^{\equiv}$ iff $u \equiv v$. That is, each point in the original model is mapped to its equivalence class in the quotient model. We have to show that for this relation the four conditions defining a bisimulation (cf. page 1682) hold. For the initial point, $w_0 \leftrightarrow w_0^{\equiv}$ holds because $w_0 \equiv w_0$. Since $\equiv$ is a bisimulation, $u \equiv v$ implies that $\mathcal{L}(u) = \mathcal{L}(v)$. Thus if $u \leftrightarrow v^{\equiv}$ then $u \in \mathcal{I}(\mathbf{p})$ iff $v^{\equiv} \in \mathcal{I}^{\equiv}(\mathbf{p})$. Furthermore, if $(u_1, u_2) \in \mathcal{I}(R)$ and $u_1 \leftrightarrow v_1^{\equiv}$, then by definition $(u_1^{\equiv}, u_2^{\equiv}) \in \mathcal{I}^{\equiv}(R)$ and $u_1 \equiv v_1$. Therefore, $u_1^{\equiv} = v_1^{\equiv}$, i.e., $(v_1^{\equiv}, u_2^{\equiv}) \in \mathcal{I}^{\equiv}(R)$. For the last condition, assume that $(v_1^{\equiv}, v_2^{\equiv}) \in \mathcal{I}^{\equiv}(R)$ and $v_1^{\equiv} \leftrightarrow u_1$. Then there exist w_1 and w_2 such that $w_1 \equiv v_1$, $w_2 \equiv v_2$ and $(w_1, w_2) \in \mathcal{I}(R)$. From $v_1^{\equiv} \leftrightarrow u_1$ we infer $u_1 \equiv v_1$ and thus $u_1 \equiv w_1$. Since $\equiv$ is a bisimulation, there exists a $u_2 \equiv w_2$ such that $(u_1, u_2) \in \mathcal{I}(R)$. From $u_2 \equiv w_2$ and $w_2 \equiv v_2$ we conclude that $u_2 \equiv v_2$, i.e., $u_2 \leftrightarrow v_2^{\equiv}$.   □

The quotient of a model with respect to its largest auto-bisimulation can be regarded as a minimal representation of this model. In finite models, this minimal representation can be constructed very efficiently.

For any set of points $P \subseteq U$, let $\langle R \rangle P \triangleq \{w \mid \exists w' \in P, (w, w') \in \mathcal{I}(R)\}$. Given any partition of U into equivalence classes, call a component $w^{\equiv}$ *uniform*, if for all $\mathbf{p} \in \mathcal{P}$ it holds that $w^{\equiv} \subseteq \mathcal{I}(\mathbf{p})$ or $w^{\equiv} \cap \mathcal{I}(\mathbf{p}) = \{\}$. That is, $w^{\equiv}$ is uniform if $\mathcal{L}(w_1) = \mathcal{L}(w_2)$ for all $w_1, w_2 \in w^{\equiv}$. A component $w^{\equiv}$ is called *stable with respect to P*, if for all R either $w^{\equiv} \subseteq \langle R \rangle P$ or $w^{\equiv} \cap \langle R \rangle P = \{\}$. The partition is called *stable*, if all components are uniform and stable with respect to all components.

5.14. THEOREM. *The coarsest stable partition is the largest auto-bisimulation.*

PROOF: First, we show that any stable partition is an auto-bisimulation. Trivially, $w_0 \equiv w_0$. Since $u^{\equiv}$ is uniform, $u \equiv v$ implies $\mathcal{L}(u) = \mathcal{L}(v)$. If $(u, u') \in \mathcal{I}(R)$, then $u^{\equiv} \subseteq \langle R \rangle u'^{\equiv}$, because $u^{\equiv}$ is stable with respect to $u'^{\equiv}$. In other words, $u^{\equiv} \subseteq \{w \mid \exists w' \equiv u', (w, w') \in \mathcal{I}(R)\}$. Therefore, if $u \equiv v$, then there is a $v' \equiv u'$ such that $(v, v') \in \mathcal{I}(R)$. The symmetric condition is proved symmetrically. Vice versa, every auto-bisimulation defines a stable partition: to show that $u^{\equiv}$ is stable with respect to $v^{\equiv}$, assume that $u_1 \equiv u_2 \in u^{\equiv}$. Since $\equiv$ is a bisimulation, for every $(u_1, u_1') \in \mathcal{I}(R)$

and $u_1' \in v^=$ there must be a $u_2' \equiv u_1' \in v^=$ such that $(u_2, u_2') \in \mathcal{I}(R)$. Therefore, $u^= \subseteq \langle R \rangle v^=$ or $u^= \cap \langle R \rangle v^= = \{\}$. If $\equiv$ is the coarsest stable partition, then for any auto-bisimulation $\leftrightarrow$ it holds that $\leftrightarrow \subseteq \equiv$. Assuming for contradiction that u, v and $\leftrightarrow$ exist such that $u \leftrightarrow v$ and not $u \equiv v$, according to Lemma 5.12 the union of $\leftrightarrow$ and $\equiv$ would be a stable partition coarser than $\equiv$. □

The following algorithm can be used to construct the coarsest stable partition:

— Start with the trivial partition consisting of only one component
— Repeat
  – Choose a component $w_0^=$ and a proposition $p \in \mathcal{P}$;
  – Split $w_0^=$ into $w_0^= \cap \mathcal{I}(p)$ and $w_0^= \setminus \mathcal{I}(p)$

  or

  – Choose components $w_0^=$ and $w_1^=$, and a relation $R \in \mathcal{R}$;
  – Split $w_0^=$ into $w_0^= \cap \langle R \rangle w_1^=$ and $w_0^= \setminus \langle R \rangle w_1^=$

  until no new components can be obtained that way

The Paige-Tarjan algorithm [Paige and Tarjan 1987] given in Figure 11 is a sophisticated implementation of this idea; it maintains two partitions: a coarser one, C, and a finer one, F. All components in F are stable with respect to any component in C. The nondeterministic choice in the above *repeat*-loop is replaced by a systematic split of the finer partition with respect to all components of the coarser partition. Initially, C is the trivial partition and F is the split of C w.r.t. all $p \in \mathcal{P}$ and $R \in \mathcal{R}$. Then, a $w^= \in C$ is split into $w_1^= \in F$ and $w_2^= \triangleq w^= \setminus w_1^=$. Any $w_0^= \in F$ is split into four parts: First, it is split with respect to $\langle R \rangle w_1^=$, and then again with respect to $\langle R \rangle w_2^=$.

In this split of $w_0^=$, either the last or the first three parts must be empty: since $w_0^=$ is stable with respect to C, either $w_0^= \subseteq \langle R \rangle w^=$ or $w_0^= \cap \langle R \rangle w^= = \{\}$ for all R. If $w_0^= \subseteq \langle R \rangle w^=$, then $(w_0^= \setminus \langle R \rangle w_1^=) \setminus \langle R \rangle w_2^= = \{\}$. If $w_0^= \cap \langle R \rangle w^= = \{\}$, then both $w_0^= \cap \langle R \rangle w_1^= = \{\}$ and $w_0^= \cap \langle R \rangle w_2^= = \{\}$: since $w^= = w_1^= \cup w_2^=$, it holds that $\langle R \rangle w^= = \langle R \rangle w_1^= \cup \langle R \rangle w_2^=$.

The overall complexity of the algorithm is $O(m \cdot \log n)$, where n is the number of points in the original model, and m is the number of points (partitions) in the result.

6. Completeness

Logicians are interested in logical truths, i.e., in the set of formulas which are valid in *all* models of the logic. How does it help to know about the set of *all* valid formulas when we want to find out whether a particular formula φ holds for a given model or theory? The answer is to encode the model or theory as a set of *assumptions* Φ and check whether the formula in question *follows* from Φ.

In fact, a *logic* can be defined to be any set of well-formed formulas which is closed under provable consequence; and a *theory* is a set of well-formed formulas which is closed under semantical consequence.

Thus there are three notions of consequence involved here:

---

function Bisimulation_minimize (Model $(U, \mathcal{I}, v)$) : Model $=$
  $C := \{\{U\}\}$, $F := \{\{U\}\}$
  for all $p \in \mathcal{P}$ and $w^= \in F$ **do**
    $F := (F \setminus \{w^=\}) \cup \{w^= \cap \mathcal{I}(p),\ w^= \setminus \mathcal{I}(p)\}$;
  for all $R \in \mathcal{R}$ and $w^= \in F$ **do**
    $F := (F \setminus \{w^=\}) \cup \{w^= \cap \langle R \rangle \{U\},\ w^= \setminus \langle R \rangle \{U\}\}$;
  while $C \neq F$ **do**
    choose $w^= \in C \setminus F$ and $w_1^= \in F$ such that $w_1^= \subseteq w^=$
    $w_2^= := w^= \setminus w_1^=$; $C := (C \setminus \{w^=\}) \cup \{w_1^=,\ w_2^=\}$;
    for all $R \in \mathcal{R}$ and $w_0^= \in F$ **do**
      $F := F \setminus \{w_0^=\} \cup$
        $\{(w_0^= \cap \langle R \rangle\, w_1^=) \cap \langle R \rangle\, w_2^=,\ (w_0^= \cap \langle R \rangle\, w_1^=) \setminus \langle R \rangle\, w_2^=,$
        $\quad (w_0^= \setminus \langle R \rangle\, w_1^=) \cap \langle R \rangle\, w_2^=,\ (w_0^= \setminus \langle R \rangle\, w_1^=) \setminus \langle R \rangle\, w_2^=\ \}$
  end;
  return $(F, \mathcal{I}^=, v^=)$

Figure 11: Paige-Tarjan algorithm for bisimulation minimization

- $\Phi \mathrel{\Vdash} \varphi$ if φ follows from Φ,
  i.e. if any model in which all formulas from Φ are valid also validates φ,
- $\Phi \vdash \varphi$ if φ can be proved from Φ,
  i.e. if there is a proof of φ which uses only assumptions from Φ, and
- $(\Phi \to \varphi)$ if φ is implied by Φ.
  This is a statement of the object language which is only defined if Φ is a single formula. To be liberal, we can identify a finite set of formulas $\Phi \triangleq \{\varphi_1, ..., \varphi_n\}$ with the conjunction $\hat{\Phi} \triangleq (\varphi_1 \wedge ... \wedge \varphi_n)$.

Note that $\Phi \mathrel{\Vdash} \varphi$ is different from $\mathcal{M} \models \varphi$. The notations $\mathrel{\Vdash} \varphi$ and $\vdash \varphi$ are short for $\{\} \mathrel{\Vdash} \varphi$ and $\{\} \vdash \varphi$, respectively.

Of course, the semantical notion of *validity* sometimes is restricted to certain classes of models, e.g., to those satisfying certain axioms, or to natural or tree models.

Also, the algorithmic notion of *provability* sometimes is parameterized by a certain proof-system. In this section, we will use *Hilbert-style* proof-systems, consisting of a set of *axioms* and *derivation rules*. Although such proof systems are not very practical, often they can illustrate the principles underlying completeness proofs. Usually, axioms and derivation rules contain *proposition variables* $q \in \mathcal{Q}$ and a substitution rule allowing consistent replacement of proposition variables with formulas. Conceptually, proposition variables are not the same as propositions, though many authors do not distinguish between these syntactic categories. A free proposition variable in an axiom can be thought of more or less as if it were universally quantified.

To complicate things even more, there are two notions of validity of a formula: *local validity* $(U, \mathcal{I}, w_0) \models \varphi$ (in a model, where the evaluation point is given), and *universal validity* $(U, \mathcal{I}) \models \varphi$ in a frame $(U, \mathcal{I})$. Traditionally, focus has been on complete axiom systems for universal validity rather than for the local version; proofs are much simpler. Thus, in this section we are interested in formulas which are valid *in all models at all points*.

One of the major concerns after defining a logical language and its models is to find an *adequate* proof-system for the logic, i.e. one which is both *sound* and *complete*. That is, for any Φ and φ,

- if $\Phi \vdash \varphi$, then $\Phi \Vdash \varphi$ (Soundness), and
- if $\Phi \Vdash \varphi$, then $\Phi \vdash \varphi$ (Completeness).

It is obvious that any proof system should be sound: we don't want to be able to "prove" false statements. Usually is very easy to prove soundness. We just have to show that the axioms are valid, and that all formulas which can be deduced from valid formulas by the derivation rules are valid. Completeness is often much harder to show, if not impossible. However, it is important to strive for completeness. Firstly, we would like to make sure that any specification which is satisfied by a program can be proved from the program axioms, provided the specification is expressible in the logic. Secondly, and more important, in many cases decision algorithms for automated verification can be obtained from the completeness proofs or vice versa.

6.1. Deductions in Multimodal Logic

To illustrate the basic idea, we start with a simple deductive system for multimodal logic. A number of similar proofs can be found in [Burgess 1984]. We use the following axioms and rules:

(taut)	propositional tautologies
(MP)	$p, (p \to q) \vdash q$
(N)	$q \vdash [R]\,q$
(K)	$\vdash ([R](p \to q) \to ([R]\,p \to [R]\,q))$

Since this axiom system is based on the $[R]$-operator rather than the $\langle R \rangle$-operator, we identify $\langle R \rangle\,\varphi$ with $\neg\,[R]\,\neg\varphi$.

To prove $\Phi \vdash \varphi$ we have to give a *derivation* of φ from the assumptions Φ, i.e., a sequence of formulas such that the last element of this sequence is φ, and every element of this sequence is either from Φ, or a substitution instance of an axiom, or the substitution instance of the consequence of a rule, where all premises of the rule for this substitution appear already in the derivation.

As an example, let us assume (p → q) and derive some consequences:

1.	$(p \to q)$	(assumption)
2.	$[R](p \to q)$	(1, N)
3.	$([R](p \to q) \to ([R]\,p \to [R]\,q))$	(K)
4.	$([R]\,p \to [R]\,q)$	(2, 3, MP)

5.	$(\neg q \to \neg p)$	(1, taut)
6.	$([R]\neg q \to [R]\neg p)$	(5, as in 1-4)
7.	$(\neg [R]\neg p \to \neg [R]\neg q)$	(6, taut)
8.	$(\langle R \rangle p \to \langle R \rangle q)$	$(7, \langle R \rangle \varphi \triangleq \neg [R]\neg \varphi)$

Lines (4) and (8) form the basis for an inductive proof of the following replacement and monotonicity rules:

(repl) $(p \leftrightarrow q) \vdash (\varphi(p) \leftrightarrow \varphi(q))$,   and

(mon) $(p \to q) \vdash (\varphi(p) \to \varphi(q))$,   where $\varphi(q)$ is positive in q.

(mon) is a syntactical analog of Lemma 3.8. The requirement that $\varphi(q)$ is positive in q means that every occurrence of q is under an even number of negation signs (cf. the definition on Page 1662). For example, $[R]q$, $\langle R \rangle q$, and $(q \wedge [R](q \vee \langle R \rangle q))$ are positive in q.

6.1. THEOREM (Soundness of **ML** axiom system). *If $\Phi \vdash \varphi$ then $\Phi \Vdash \varphi$.*

PROOF: Soundness of **(taut)** and **(MP)** is immediate. **(N)** is the so called *necessitation rule*. Its validity depends on the universal interpretation of validity: f some formula is valid in every point of a model, it is valid in every point which is the R-successor of some other point in that model. **(K)** is the classical *Kripke*-axiom which holds for all normal modal logics. If in all accessible points p holds, and in all accessible points $(p \to q)$ holds, then in all accessible points q must hold.   □

The classical way to prove this theorem is the so–called Henkin-Hasenjäger construction. A set Ψ of formulas is *consistent with* Φ, if there is no finite subset $\{\psi_1, ..., \psi_n\} \subseteq \Psi$ such that $\Phi \vdash (\psi_1 \wedge ... \wedge \psi_n \to \bot)$. Given a set Φ of assumptions and a formula φ which is consistent with Φ, we will construct a model in which Φ is universally valid and φ is locally valid. Call a set w of formulas *maximal*, if for any formula ψ, either ψ or $\neg \psi$ is in w.

6.2. LEMMA (Lindenbaum's extension lemma). *For any formula φ which is consistent with Φ there exists a maximal consistent set w_0 such that $\varphi \in w_0$ and $\Phi \subseteq w_0$*

PROOF: Start with $\Phi \cup \{\varphi\}$; for every formula ψ according to a fixed enumeration add either ψ or $\neg \psi$ to w, whichever is consistent with the set constructed so far.□

The *canonical model* for Φ is $(U, \mathcal{I}, w)$, where
- U is the set of maximal consistent sets which include Φ,
- $\mathcal{I}(R) \triangleq \{(w_0, w_1) \mid q \in w_1 \text{ implies } \langle R \rangle q \in w_0\}$, and
- $\mathcal{I}(p) \triangleq \{w_0 \mid p \in w_0\}$, and
- w is any element from U such that $\varphi \in w$.

The following result is sometimes called the "truth" lemma. Intuitively, it states that any point in the canonical model contains exactly those formulas which are satisfied by this point.

6.3. Lemma (Truth lemma). *Let φ be any formula and w be a maximal consistent set in the canonical model. Then $\varphi \in w$ iff $(U, \mathcal{I}, w) \models \varphi$.*

Proof: The proof is by induction on the structure of φ. In the inductive step, there is one interesting case. We must show that $\langle R \rangle \, \varphi \in w_0$ iff $(U, \mathcal{I}, w_0) \models \langle R \rangle \, \varphi$. We first prove that $(U, \mathcal{I}, w_0) \models \langle R \rangle \, \varphi$ implies $\langle R \rangle \, \varphi \in w_0$. Since $w_0 \models \langle R \rangle \, \varphi$, there exists a w_1 such that $w_0 R w_1$ and $w_1 \models \varphi$. By definition of R, we have $\langle R \rangle \, q \in w_0$ for all $q \in w_1$. Since $w_1 \models \varphi$, the induction hypothesis implies $\varphi \in w_1$. Consequently, $\langle R \rangle \, \varphi \in w_0$.

For the other direction, assume that $\langle R \rangle \, \varphi \in w_0$. We have to show that there exists a maximal consistent set w_1 such that $(w_0, w_1) \in \mathcal{I}(R)$ and $\varphi \in w_1$. First observe that the formula $\vdash ((\langle R \rangle \, \varphi \wedge [R] \, \psi) \to \langle R \rangle (\varphi \wedge \psi))$ is derivable:

$$
\begin{array}{lll}
1. & [R](\psi \to \neg \varphi) \to ([R] \, \psi \to [R] \, \neg \varphi) & \textbf{(K)} \\
2. & (\neg [R] \, \neg \varphi \wedge [R] \, \psi) \to \neg [R](\psi \to \neg \varphi)) & (1, \text{taut}) \\
3. & (\langle R \rangle \, \varphi \wedge [R] \, \psi) \to \langle R \rangle (\varphi \wedge \psi) & (2, \textbf{repl}, \text{taut})
\end{array}
$$

Recall that $[R] \, \varphi$ is a syntactical abbreviation of $\neg \, \langle R \rangle \, \neg \varphi$. In line 3., we replaced $\neg \neg \varphi$ by φ and $\neg(\psi \to \neg \varphi)$ by $(\varphi \wedge \psi)$. This derivation can be generalized to obtain

$$
\vdash ((\langle R \rangle \, \varphi \wedge [R] \, \psi_1 \wedge \cdots \wedge [R] \, \psi_n) \to \langle R \rangle (\varphi \wedge \psi_1 \wedge \cdots \psi_n))
$$

Because of this result, the set $\{\varphi\} \cup \{\psi \mid [R] \, \psi \in w_0\}$ must be consistent with Φ. Otherwise, by the definition of consistency on page 1692, there would exist a finite set $\{\psi_1, ..., \psi_n\}$ of formulas such that $[R] \, \psi_i \in w_0$ for all $1 \leq i \leq n$, and $(\varphi \wedge \psi_1 \wedge \cdots \psi_n \to \bot)$ must be derivable from Φ. Since $\vdash (\langle R \rangle \, \bot \to \bot)$, we would have $\Phi \vdash (\langle R \rangle (\varphi \wedge \psi_1 \wedge \cdots \psi_n) \to \bot)$. Therefore, $\Phi \vdash ((\langle R \rangle \, \varphi \wedge [R] \, \psi_1 \wedge \cdots [R] \, \psi_n) \to \bot)$. Since $\{\langle R \rangle \, \varphi, [R] \, \psi_1, ..., [R] \, \psi_n\} \subseteq w_0$, the set w_0 would be inconsistent with Φ, which is a contradiction.

Since $\{\varphi\} \cup \{\psi \mid [R] \, \psi \in w_0\}$ is consistent with Φ, there exists some maximal consistent extension w_1 of this set. Moreover, if $\psi \in w_1$, then $[R] \, \neg \psi$ can not be in w_0 (otherwise, both ψ and $\neg \psi$ would be in w_1). Since w_0 is maximal, $\psi \in w_1$ implies $\neg [R] \, \neg \psi = \langle R \rangle \, \psi \in w_0$. From the definition of $\mathcal{I}(R)$, it follows that $(w_0, w_1) \in \mathcal{I}(R)$. Since $\varphi \in w_1$, the induction hypothesis gives $(U, \mathcal{I}, w_1) \models \varphi$. Together with $(w_0, w_1) \in \mathcal{I}(R)$ we have $(U, \mathcal{I}, w_0) \models \langle R \rangle \, \varphi$, which was to be shown. □

6.4. Lemma (Satisfiability of consistent formulas). *Every multimodal formula φ consistent with Φ is satisfiable in some model validating Φ.*

Proof: Since for the canonical model $(U, \mathcal{I}, w)$ it holds that $\Phi \subseteq w$ and $\varphi \in w$, Lemma 6.3 asserts that $(U, \mathcal{I}, w) \models \Phi$ and $(U, \mathcal{I}, w) \models \varphi$. Thus every consistent formula is satisfied in its canonical model. □

6.5. Theorem (Completeness). *The deductive system for **ML** is complete:*

$$
\textit{If } \Phi \Vdash \varphi \textit{ then } \Phi \vdash \varphi.
$$

PROOF: Without loss of generality, we can assume Φ to be consistent with itself: if Φ is inconsistent, then $\Phi \vdash \varphi$ holds trivially. If $\Phi \Vdash \varphi$, then no model in which Φ is universally valid contains a point which satisfies $\{\neg\varphi\}$; therefore with 6.4 it follows that $\{\neg\varphi\}$ is inconsistent with Φ, hence $\Phi \vdash (\neg\varphi \to \bot)$, which is $\Phi \vdash \varphi$.   □

We now show how this proof can be extended for natural models. Recall that a model is called *deterministic*, if all accessibility relations $R \in \mathcal{R}$ are *univalent*: for any given point w there is at most one R-successor of w. The following axiom describes this property.

(U) $\vdash (\langle R \rangle\, q \to [R]\, q)$

Soundness of this axiom in deterministic models is immediate: if there is any R-successor satisfying q, then all R-successors must satisfy q. In the completeness proof, axiom **U** forces the canonical model to be deterministic: for every $w_0 \in U$ of the canonical model and every $R \in \mathcal{R}$ there can be at most one w_1 with $(w_0, w_1) \in \mathcal{I}(R)$. To see why this is true, assume for contradiction that $(w_0, w_1) \in \mathcal{I}(R)$ and $(w_0, w_1') \in \mathcal{I}(R)$. If $w_1 \neq w_1'$, then there must be a formula ψ such that $\psi \in w_1$ and $\neg\psi \in w_1'$. Therefore $\langle R \rangle\, \psi \in w_0$ and $\langle R \rangle\, \neg\psi \in w_0$. This is a contradiction to the consistency of w_0: from axiom **U** it follows that if $\langle R \rangle\, \psi \in w_0$, then $\neg\, \langle R \rangle\, \neg\psi \in w_0$, since maximal consistent sets are closed under modus ponens. Thus, $\langle R \rangle\, \neg\psi \notin w_0$. Therefore, we have shown

6.6. THEOREM. **(U)** *is sound and complete for deterministic models.*

There are a number of other axioms which impose specific conditions on the canonical model. To investigate such connections is the topic of *correspondence theory*, see [van Benthem 1984]. Correspondences between modal axioms and relation algebraic expressions can be found in [Schlingloff and Heinle 1997]. (Such an expression is built from basic relation symbols with union, complement, concatenation, and transitive closure.)

As an example for the use of axiom **(U)** in verification, we prove

$$\{(\text{on} \to \langle R \rangle\, \neg\text{on} \ \wedge [S]\, \bot), \quad (\neg\text{on} \to \langle S \rangle\, \text{on} \ \wedge \langle R \rangle\, \neg\text{on})\} \quad \vdash \quad [R]\, \langle S \rangle\, [S]\, \bot.$$

The assumptions can be seen as describing the actions of a semaphore with two states, on and $\neg$on, which can be set with an S-operation when it is not on, and can be reset with an R-operation at any time. The semaphore cannot be set when it is in state on. We want to show that after a reset it is possible to set the semaphore once and only once; that is, for all points reachable with an R operation there exists an S successor from which no further S operation is possible.

1.	$\text{on} \to \langle R \rangle\, \neg\text{on} \wedge [S]\, \bot$	(assuumption)
2.	$\neg\text{on} \to \langle S \rangle\, \text{on} \wedge \langle R \rangle\, \neg\text{on}$	(assumption)
3.	$\text{on} \to \langle R \rangle\, \neg\text{on}$	(1, taut)
4.	$\neg\text{on} \to \langle R \rangle\, \neg\text{on}$	(2, taut)
5.	$\langle R \rangle\, \neg\text{on}$	(3, 4, taut)

6.	$\langle R \rangle \neg \text{on} \rightarrow [R] \neg \text{on}$	(U)
7.	$[R] \neg \text{on}$	(5, 6, MP)
8.	$\neg \text{on} \rightarrow \langle S \rangle \text{on}$	(2, taut)
9.	$[R] \neg \text{on} \rightarrow [R] \langle S \rangle \text{on}$	(8, mon)
10.	$[R] \langle S \rangle \text{on}$	(7, 9, MP)
11.	$\text{on} \rightarrow [S] \bot$	(1, taut)
12.	$[R] \langle S \rangle \text{on} \rightarrow [R] \langle S \rangle [S] \bot$	(11, mon)
13.	$[R] \langle S \rangle [S] \bot$	(10, 12, MP)

As we see, even in such simple examples it can be quite difficult to find a Hilbert-style proof "by hand"; therefore it is important to develop automatic proof methods. Algorithms for this purpose are the topic of Section 7.

Consider the case that the logic contains only one accessibility relation ($\mathcal{R} = \{R\}$). Then each path through a deterministic canonical model forms a natural model: let the formula φ be consistent with all substitution instances of the axiom **(U)**. Consider a sequence $\sigma \triangleq (w_0, w_1, w_2, ...)$ of points in the (deterministic) canonical model for φ such that $\varphi \in w_0$ and $w_i R w_{i+1}$ for all i. Obviously, σ is a natural model which initially satisfies φ. Therefore, with axiom **(U)** each consistent formula is satisfiable in a natural model; in other words, **(U)** is complete for monomodal logic in natural models. The same holds if we require univalence of the transition relation $\prec \triangleq \bigcup \mathcal{R}$:

(N) $q \vdash \maltese\, q$

(K) $\vdash (\maltese(p \rightarrow q) \rightarrow (\maltese\, p \rightarrow \maltese\, q))$

(U) $\vdash (\mathbf{X}\, q \rightarrow \maltese\, q)$

Together with **(taut)** and **(MP)**, these axioms are sound and complete for the **X**-operator in natural models.

6.2. Transitive Closure Operators

A major difference between temporal and modal logic is that temporal logic has operators for the transitive closure of the transition relation. In order to motivate the discussion in the completeness proofs for **CTL** and **LTL**, in this subsection we extend the above completeness proof to handle such operators. For simplicity, we first give the proof for the logic with operators **X** (or, equivalently **E X**) for the transition relation and **F*** (or **E F***) for its reflexive transitive closure (plus derived operators $\maltese\, \varphi \triangleq \neg\, \mathbf{X}\, \neg\varphi$, $\mathbf{G}^*\, \varphi \triangleq \neg\, \mathbf{F}^*\, \neg\varphi$, etc.). The necessary generalizations for **CTL** and **LTL** are indicated at the end of this subsection.

Close inspection of the semantics of **F*** reveals a fundamental problem, compared to the completeness proof given above. Consider the set $\Phi \triangleq \{\text{p}, \maltese\text{p}, \maltese\maltese\text{p}, \maltese\maltese\maltese\text{p}, ... \}$. Then clearly $\Phi \Vdash \mathbf{G}^*\, \varphi$. However, $\Phi \nvdash \mathbf{G}^*\, \varphi$, since every proof of $\mathbf{G}^*\, \varphi$ from Φ can use only a limited number of premises (proofs are *finite* sequences). But there does not exist a finite subset $\Phi_0 \subset \Phi$ such that the statement $\Phi_0 \vdash \mathbf{G}^*\, \varphi$ holds.

Thus, the above completeness proof fails. For an arbitrary set Φ, it may not be possible to construct a maximal consistent extension, since we can not apply an axiom to show the consistency of an infinite set of premisses.

When dealing with second order concepts like transitive closure we have to limit ourselves to a weaker form of completeness. An axiom system is called *weakly complete*, if $\Phi \Vdash \varphi$ implies $\Phi \vdash \varphi$ for all *finite* Φ.

In first order logic, the *deduction theorem* makes it possible to discard any finite set of assumptions: $\psi \Vdash \varphi$ iff $\Vdash (\forall \psi \to \varphi)$, where $\forall \psi$ is the universal closure of ψ. In temporal logic, a similar deduction theorem holds:

6.7. THEOREM (Deduction theorem). $\psi \Vdash \varphi$ *iff* $\Vdash (\mathbf{G}^* \psi \to \varphi)$.

Therefore, to prove weak completeness it is sufficient to prove that $\Vdash \varphi$ implies $\vdash \varphi$. We use the following axiom system (in addition to modus ponens (**MP**) and propositional tautologies (**taut**)):

(N)	$q \vdash \mathbf{X} q$
(K)	$\vdash (\mathbf{X}(p \to q) \to (\mathbf{X} p \to \mathbf{X} q))$
(Rec)	$\vdash (\mathbf{G}^* q \to (q \wedge \mathbf{X} \mathbf{G}^* q))$
(Ind)	$(p \to (q \wedge \mathbf{X} p)) \vdash (p \to \mathbf{G}^* q)$

Dually, the last axiom and rule can be written as

(Rec)	$\vdash ((q \vee \mathbf{X} \mathbf{F}^* q) \to \mathbf{F}^* q)$
(Ind)	$((q \vee \mathbf{X} p) \to p) \vdash (\mathbf{F}^* q \to p)$

(**N**) and (**K**) are "nexttime-versions" of the respective modal rule and axiom given above. In this subsection, we prove completeness for general Kripke structures (with a possibly nondeterministic accessibility relation), thus there is no need for the temporal version of (**U**). Axiom (**Rec**) and rule (**Ind**) are sometimes attributed to Segerberg. They reflect the definition of the transitive closure as the minimal transitive relation which includes all accessibility relations. (**Rec**) is the *recursion* axiom which can be used to unfold a $\mathbf{G}^*$-operator (cf. Subsection 3.2, Page 1663):

$$\mathbf{G}^* \varphi \to (\varphi \wedge \mathbf{X}(\varphi \wedge \mathbf{X}(\varphi \wedge ...))).$$

(**Ind**) is the *induction* rule which can be used to deduce a property $\mathbf{G}^* \varphi$ from an *invariant* ψ, i.e., from a formula ψ for which $(\psi \to \mathbf{X} \psi)$ and $(\psi \to \varphi)$ are derivable.

6.8. LEMMA. (**Rec**) *and* (**Ind**) *are sound:* $\vdash \varphi$ *implies* $\models \varphi$.

For the soundness of (**Rec**), observe that $w \models \mathbf{G}^* q$ means that for all $u \geq w$ it holds that $u \models q$. Thus $w \models q$, and for all $v \succ w$ and $u \geq v$ we have $u \models q$, which means $w \models \mathbf{X} \mathbf{G}^* \varphi$.

For the soundness of (**Ind**), assume that $(p \to (q \wedge \mathbf{X} p))$ is universally valid in a frame $\mathcal{F} \triangleq (U, \mathcal{I})$, that is, for any $w \in U$, if $w \models p$, then $w \models q$ and $v \models p$ for all $v \succ w$. Assume further that $w_0 \models p$, and show that $w \models q$ for all $w \geq w_0$. We show that $w \models p$ for all $w \geq w_0$. From this the claim follows since $w \models p$ implies $w \models q$. The proof is by induction on the length of the shortest path between w_0 and w. If this length is zero, then $w_0 = w$, and there is nothing to show. For the inductive step, assume that the shortest path from w_0 to w has $n + 1$ elements. Then there exists a predecessor $w' \prec w$ such that $w_0 \leq w'$, and the shortest path between w_0 and w' has n elements. From the induction hypothesis, $w' \models p$. Since $w' \prec w$, it follows that $w \models p$. $\qquad\square$

Next, we show that these axioms are complete for transitive closure. Up to the truth lemma, the proof is almost the same as for modal logic. But, we only use *finite* maximal consistent sets: we start with a single (finite) consistent formula φ for which we have to construct a model. The set $ESF(\varphi)$ of *extended sub-formulas* of φ (sometimes also called *Fischer-Ladner closure*, [Fischer and Ladner 1979]) is the following set of formulas:

- φ_1 and φ_2 are extended sub-formulas of $(\varphi_1 \rightarrow \varphi_2)$, (thus φ is an extended sub-formula of $\neg\varphi$)
- φ is an extended sub-formula of $\mathbf{X}\,\varphi$,
- φ and $\mathbf{X}\,\mathbf{F}^*\,\varphi$ are extended sub-formulas of $\mathbf{F}^*\,\varphi$,
- φ is an extended sub-formula of φ, and
- every extended sub-formula of an extended sub-formula of φ is an extended sub-formula of φ.

For any given φ, the set $ESF(\varphi)$ is finite. A consistent set of formulas is called *finitely maximal*, if it is maximal with respect to $ESF(\varphi)$; that is, for every extended sub-formula ψ of φ, either ψ or $\neg\psi$ is in the finitely maximal consistent set.

As in the infinite case, for any consistent formula φ there exists at least one consistent set w_0 which is finitely maximal with respect to $ESF(\varphi)$ such that $\varphi \in w_0$. Consider the following *finite canonical model* $(U, \mathcal{I}, w)$:

- U is the set of finitely maximal consistent sets,
- $\mathcal{I}(\prec) \triangleq \{(w_0, w_1) \mid \neg\mathbf{X}\,q \in w_0 \text{ implies } \neg q \in w_1\}$, and
- $\mathcal{I}(\mathrm{p}) \triangleq \{w_0 \mid \mathrm{p} \in w_0\}$, and
- w is any element from U such that $\varphi \in w$.

Compare this with the canonical model for modal logic on Page 1692. Similar as in Lemma 6.3, for any extended sub-formula φ and finitely maximal consistent set w, the following statement holds:

6.9. LEMMA (Truth lemma for transitive closure operators). $w \models \varphi$ *iff* $\varphi \in w$.

From this truth lemma, completeness follows exactly as in the multimodal case. PROOF: The proof is by induction on φ. The case $\varphi = \mathbf{X}\,\psi$ is proven almost exactly as in the completeness proof for modal logic. If $(U, \mathcal{I}, w_0) \models \mathbf{X}\,\psi$, then there exists a w_1 such that $w_0 \prec w_1$ and $w_1 \models \psi$. Assuming for contradiction that $\mathbf{X}\,\psi \notin w_0$, we have $\neg\mathbf{X}\,\psi \in w_0$, since the set of extended sub-formulas is closed under (single) negation. From the definition of $\mathcal{I}(\prec)$ we can infer that $\neg\psi \in w_1$, i.e., $\psi \notin w_1$. According to the induction hypothesis, $w_1 \not\models \psi$, which is a contradiction. In the other direction, assume that $\mathbf{X}\,\psi \in w_0$, and let w_1 be any finitely maximal consistent extension of $\{\psi\} \cup \{\neg\xi \mid \neg\mathbf{X}\,\xi \in w_0\}$. Since $\psi \in w_1$, the induction hypothesis gives $(U, \mathcal{I}, w_1) \models \psi$. According to the definition of $\mathcal{I}(\prec)$ it holds that $w_0 \prec w_1$. Therefore $(U, \mathcal{I}, w_0) \models \mathbf{X}\,\psi$.

Thus, it remains to show that $\mathbf{F}^*\,\psi \in w_0$ iff $(U, \mathcal{I}, w_0) \models \mathbf{F}^*\,\psi$. For one direction, assume that $\mathbf{F}^*\,\psi \notin w_0$. We have to prove that $w_0 \not\models \mathbf{F}^*\,\psi$. In other words, if $w_0 \leq w_n$ then it has to be shown that $w_n \not\models \psi$. Note that $w_0 \leq w_n$ iff there is a finite path $(w_0, w_1, ..., w_n)$ such that $w_i \prec w_{i+1}$ for all $i < n$. We show by induction on n that $\neg\mathbf{F}^*\,\psi \in w_n$, hence $\mathbf{F}^*\,\psi \notin w_n$. For $n = 0$, there is nothing to show. For $n > 0$, the induction hypothesis guarantees that $\mathbf{F}^*\,\psi \notin w_{n-1}$, i.e., $\neg\mathbf{F}^*\,\psi \in w_{n-1}$. Both $\mathbf{X}\,\mathbf{F}^*\,\psi$ and $\neg\mathbf{X}\,\mathbf{F}^*\,\psi$ are extended sub-formulas of $\mathbf{F}^*\,\varphi$, therefore one of them must be in w_{n-1}. From axiom **(Rec)**, the formula $(\neg\mathbf{F}^*\,\psi \to \neg\mathbf{X}\,\mathbf{F}^*\,\psi)$ can be derived. Consequently, $\neg\mathbf{X}\,\mathbf{F}^*\,\psi \in w_{n-1}$. Thus by the definition of $\mathcal{I}(\prec)$, we have $\neg\mathbf{F}^*\,\psi \in w_n$. Now we show that $w_n \not\models \psi$. Since axiom **(Rec)** derives $(\neg\mathbf{F}^*\,\psi \to \neg\psi)$ and $\neg\mathbf{F}^*\,\psi \in w_n$, the assumption $\psi \in w_n$ would contradict the consistency of w_n. Therefore, $\psi \notin w_n$. According to the induction hypothesis, $w_n \not\models \psi$.

Now we prove that $\mathbf{F}^*\,\psi \in w_0$ implies $w_0 \models \mathbf{F}^*\,\psi$. For any finitely maximal consistent set w and any (finite) set W of such sets, let $\hat{w} \triangleq \bigwedge\{\psi \mid \psi \in w\}$, and $\check{W} \triangleq \bigvee\{\hat{w} \mid w \in W\}$. Furthermore, let $X_w \triangleq \{w' \mid w \prec w'\}$. An important step is to prove

$$(*) \qquad \vdash (\hat{w} \to \mathbf{X}\,\check{X}_w)$$

Since $\vdash ((\mathbf{X}\,\psi_1 \wedge \mathbf{X}\,\psi_2) \to \mathbf{X}(\psi_1 \wedge \psi_2))$, we can infer $\vdash (\bigwedge\{\mathbf{X}\,\psi_i\} \to \mathbf{X}\,\bigwedge\{\psi_i\})$. Therefore, $\vdash (\hat{w} \to \mathbf{X}\,\bigwedge\{\neg q \mid \neg\mathbf{X}\,q \in w\})$. Since U is the set of *all* finitely maximal consistent sets, $\vdash \check{U}$ can be proven by propositional reasoning: for each φ and p, it is valid that $\varphi \vdash ((\varphi \wedge \mathrm{p}) \vee (\varphi \wedge \neg\mathrm{p}))$. Since $\check{U}$ is the disjunction of all possible conjunction of positive and negative literals from $\mathcal{P}$, it is derivable from this formula. Therefore, $\vdash (\hat{w} \to \mathbf{X}\,\check{U})$. Together, this gives $\vdash (\hat{w} \to \mathbf{X}(\check{U} \wedge \bigwedge\{\neg q \mid \neg\mathbf{X}\,q \in w\}))$. Consequently, $\vdash (\hat{w} \to \mathbf{X}\,\bigvee\{\hat{u} \wedge \bigwedge\{\neg q \mid \neg\mathbf{X}\,q \in w\} \mid u \in U\})$. If $w' \triangleq u \cup \{\neg q \mid \neg\mathbf{X}\,q \in w\}$ is inconsistent, then $\vdash (\hat{w}' \to \bot)$. If w' is consistent, then $w \prec w'$ according to the definition of $\mathcal{I}(\prec)$, i.e., $w' \in X_w$. Therefore, $\vdash (\hat{w} \to \mathbf{X}\,\bigvee\{\hat{w}' \mid w' \in X_w\})$, which proves $(*)$.

Since there are only finitely many extended sub-formulas, the universe U is finite. Let $W \triangleq \{w_0, w_1, ..., w_n\}$ be the set $\{w' \in U \mid w_0 \leq w'\}$. From $(*)$, it follows that $\vdash (\bigvee\{\hat{w} \mid w \in W\} \to \bigvee\{\mathbf{X}\,\check{X}_w \mid w \in W\})$. Furthermore, $\vdash (\bigvee\{\mathbf{X}\,\check{X}_w\} \to \mathbf{X}\,\bigvee\{\check{X}_w\})$. Since $\{X_w \mid w \in W\} \subseteq W$, it holds that $\vdash (\bigvee\{\hat{X}_w \mid w \in W\} \to \check{W})$. Therefore,

$$(**) \qquad \vdash (\check{W} \to \mathbf{X}\,\check{W})$$

Assume that $w_0 \not\models \mathbf{F}^*\,\psi$ and show that $\mathbf{F}^*\,\psi \notin w_0$. From the assumption, $w \not\models \psi$ for all $w \in W$. As above, the induction hypothesis implies that $\psi \notin w$ for all $w \in W$, i.e., $\neg\psi \in w$. Consequently, $(\hat{w} \to \neg\psi)$ for all $w \in W$, which implies $\vdash (\check{W} \to \neg\psi)$. Together with $(**)$ we have $\vdash (\check{W} \to (\neg\psi \wedge \mathbf{X}\,\check{W}))$. Thus, by **(Ind)**, $\vdash (\check{W} \to \mathbf{G}^*\,\neg\psi)$. Since $w_0 \in W$, it holds that $\vdash (\hat{w}_0 \to \check{W})$. Therefore, $\vdash (\hat{w}_0 \to \neg\mathbf{F}^*\,\psi)$. Since w_0 is consistent, $\mathbf{F}^*\,\psi \notin w_0$. □

6.10. LEMMA. *((N), (K), (Rec), (Ind)) is complete: if* $\models \varphi$ *then* $\vdash \varphi$.

PROOF: The theorem follows from Lemma 6.9 similar as Theorem 6.5 follows from Lemma 6.3 for multimodal logic. □

This completeness proof can easily be extended to **CTL** [Emerson and Halpern 1985]. The following axiom system (in addition to propositional logic) is sound and complete:

(N) $\qquad q \vdash \mathbf{A\, \ddot{X}}\, q$

(K) $\qquad \vdash (\mathbf{A\, \ddot{X}}(p \to q) \to (\mathbf{A\, \ddot{X}}\, p \to \mathbf{A\, \ddot{X}}\, q))$

(RecEU$^+$) $\quad \vdash (\mathbf{E\, X}(q_2 \vee q_1 \wedge \mathbf{E}(q_1 \mathbf{U^+} q_2)) \to \mathbf{E}(q_1 \mathbf{U^+} q_2))$

(RecAU$^+$) $\quad \vdash (\mathbf{A\, X}(q_2 \vee q_1 \wedge \mathbf{A}(q_1 \mathbf{U^+} q_2)) \to \mathbf{A}(q_1 \mathbf{U^+} q_2))$

(IndEU$^+$) $\quad (\mathbf{E\, X}(q_2 \vee q_1 \wedge p) \to p) \vdash (\mathbf{E}(q_1 \mathbf{U^+} q_2) \to p)$

(IndAU$^+$) $\quad (\mathbf{A\, X}(q_2 \vee q_1 \wedge p) \to p) \vdash (\mathbf{A}(q_1 \mathbf{U^+} q_2) \to p)$

For **LTL**, proving completeness for natural models is more intricate, since we have to construct a natural model from the canonical model. The axiom system for the future fragment uses suitable versions of (N), (K), (Rec), (Ind) and (U). For **LTL** with past operators, additional axioms are necessary which describe the relation between $\mathbf{U^+}$ and $\mathbf{U^-}$. Several elaborate proofs can be found in the literature [Prior 1957, Gabbay et al. 1980, Burgess 1984, Lichtenstein et al. 1985, Kröger 1987].

A sound and complete proof system for **qTL** was described in [Kesten and Pnueli 1995]. We just briefly indicate how the above axioms can be extended for μ**TL**:

(Recν) $\vdash (\nu q\, \varphi \to \varphi\{q := \nu q\, \varphi\})$

(Indν) $(p \to \varphi\{q := p\}) \vdash (p \to \nu q\, \varphi)$

An equivalent formulation which is based on the least fixpoint operator is

(Recμ) $\vdash (\varphi\{q := \mu q\, \varphi\} \to \mu q\, \varphi)$

(Indμ) $(\varphi\{q := p\} \to p) \vdash (\mu q\, \varphi \to p)$

All recursion and induction axioms above can be obtained as special cases of these very general axioms. For their soundness, we refer to the Knaster-Tarski fixpoint properties in Corollary 3.9. The completeness proof can be adapted to show completeness for a certain subclass of positive μ**TL** formulas, the *aconjunctive* ones [Kozen 1983]. This restriction enforces that if $\nu r\ \psi_1$ and $\nu s\ \psi_2$ are subformulas of $\nu q\ \psi$ each containing an occurrence of the same variable q, then no two occurrences of variables r and s are conjunctively related.

The problem of completeness of these axioms for *all* μ**TL** formulas was solved in [Walukiewicz 1995]. It can be shown that for any formula there exists an equivalent aconjunctive formula. Thereby it suffices to derive this aconjunctive formula from the axioms in order to prove any given formula.

In these proofs, there is a pattern which will frequently reappear in subsequent sections. An *invariance* is a negative occurrence of a least fixpoint operator, or a positive occurrence of a greatest fixpoint operator (e.g., $\mathbf{G^*}$, $\mathbf{W^+}$, ν). Dually, an *eventuality* ($\mathbf{F}^*$, $\mathbf{U}^+$, μ etc.) is a positive occurrence of a least fixpoint operator, or a negative occurrences of greatest fixpoint operator. In the completeness proof, invariances are unfolded via the recursion axiom, whereas eventualities are fulfilled using the recursion axiom.

7. Decision Procedures

In this section we derive *decision procedures* for some of the logics introduced above. As shown by Büchi and Rabin [Büchi 1962, Rabin 1969], monadic second order logic on natural and tree models is decidable. Therefore, all logics which have a validity-preserving standard translation into **MSOL** or **SnS** (second order logic of n successors) are decidable. However, this proof does not yield efficient decision algorithms. In this section, we will develop such algorithms from the completeness proofs of the previous section. Given a set of assumptions Φ and a formula φ, we want to decide whether $\Phi \vdash \varphi$ or not. By completeness, $\Phi \vdash \varphi$ iff $\Phi \Vdash \varphi$. Even though multimodal logic is complete, for arbitrary sets Φ of assumptions and a given formula φ it is not decidable whether $\Phi \Vdash \varphi$. Therefore, we restrict attention to finite sets of assumptions. Hence we need an algorithm which, given a formula φ and a finite set of assumptions Φ, decides whether there is a model which globally validates Φ such that φ is satisfied in the initial point.

If such a model exists, then often the size of the canonical model for Φ and φ can be bounded by a function of the length of the formulas $\hat{\Phi}$ and φ ("finite model property"). Therefore, many propositional modal and temporal logics are decidable: it is sufficient to check all models up to a certain size whether they are appropriate. However, this is not practical. In this section, we show how to construct a model effectively.

There are two main appraches. "Global" algorithms start with the largest possible model and shrink it to an appropriate size. "Local" algorithms start with a minimal model which is extended until it is a model for the formula. For technical reasons, global algorithms seem to be more adequate for the branching time approach, and local algorithms seem to be better suited for linear temporal logics.

7.1. Deciding Branching Time Logics

To decide whether a given multimodal formula φ is satisfiable with assumptions Φ, we try in a systematic way to construct the canonical model for $\Phi \Vdash \varphi$. In the universe of this model, points are maximal consistent sets of formulas. Since we assume that the set Φ of assumptions is finite, it is sufficient to consider maximality with respect to all sub-formulas of $\hat{\Phi}$ and φ. In the following, we assume that φ and Φ are given and write SF for the (finite) set of all of these sub-formulas. We use subsets of SF to represent maximal sets of sub-formulas. That is, a set $w \subseteq SF$ represents the maximal set $\{\psi \mid \psi \in w\} \cup \{\neg\psi \mid \psi \notin w\}$. A set $w \subseteq SF$ of subformulas is called *propositionally consistent*, if

- $\bot \notin w$, and
- if $(\psi_1 \rightarrow \psi_2) \in SF$, then $(\psi_1 \rightarrow \psi_2) \in w$ iff $\psi_1 \in w$ implies $\psi_2 \in w$.

That is, $(\psi_1 \rightarrow \psi_2) \in w$ iff $\psi_1 \notin w$ or $\psi_2 \in w$. Expanding the definitions it can be shown that

- if $\neg\psi \in SF$, then $\neg\psi \in w$ iff $\psi \notin w$,
- if $(\psi_1 \wedge \psi_2) \in SF$, then $(\psi_1 \wedge \psi_2) \in w$ iff $\psi_1 \in w$ and $\psi_2 \in w$, and
- if $(\psi_1 \vee \psi_2) \in SF$, then $(\psi_1 \vee \psi_2) \in w$ iff $\psi_1 \in w$ or $\psi_2 \in w$.

Any propositionally consistent set is "consistent for propositional logic": if we consistently replace any modal formula in w by a new proposition, then the resulting set of formulas is satisfiable in propositional logic. A satisfying interpretation is given by $\mathcal{I}(p) \triangleq \mathbf{true}$ iff $p \in w$.

To construct the canonical model of a consistent formula, let the universe U initially be the set of propositionally consistent sets of sub-formulas which contain all assumptions. That is, $U \triangleq \{w \subseteq SF \mid \Phi \subseteq w\}$. The obvious choice for $\mathcal{I}(p)$ then is $\{w \mid p \in w\}$. The initial interpretation of any $\langle R \rangle$ operator is the universal relation $U \times U$. The decision procedure iteratively deletes 'bad arcs' and 'bad points' until stabilization is reached. *Bad arcs* are pairs $(w_0, w_1) \in \mathcal{I}(R)$ such that w_0 contains $[R]\psi$ but it is not the case that $\psi \in w_1$. More precisely, an arc (w_0, w_1) is bad if for some sub-formula $\langle R \rangle \psi$ it holds that $\langle R \rangle \psi \notin w_0$ and $\psi \in w_1$. *Bad points* w_0 contain a formula $\langle R \rangle \psi$, but there does not (or no longer) exist a tuple $(w_0, w_1) \in \mathcal{I}(R)$ with $\psi \in w_1$. If upon termination there is a point w which was not deleted such that $\varphi \in w$, it returns "satisfiable", else it returns "unsatisfiable".

7.1. LEMMA. *The modal logic decision procedure is sound: φ is satisfiable in some model which universally validates Φ iff the procedure returns "satisfiable".*

PROOF: For one direction, let $\mathcal{M} = (U, \mathcal{I}, w_0)$ be the result of the above deletion procedure. That is, assume that $\mathcal{M}$ does not contain a bad arc or bad point, and that $w_0 \in U$ is some point with $\varphi \in w_0$. We show that $(U, \mathcal{I}) \models \Phi$ and $(U, \mathcal{I}, w_0) \models \varphi$. Similar to the truth Lemma 6.3, for every $w \in U$ and every $\psi \in SF$ it holds that $(\psi \in w)$ iff $(U, \mathcal{I}, w) \models \psi$. This is shown by induction on the structure of ψ: for atomic propositions and boolean combinations of formulas the statement is just a consequence of the respective definitions. For modal subformulas, it follows from the deletion rules in the decision procedure: if $[R]\psi \in w$, then for all $w' \in U$ such that $(w, w') \in \mathcal{I}(R)$ it must be the case that $\psi \in w'$. This holds since $\mathcal{M}$ does not contain any bad arcs. By the induction hypothesis, $w' \models \psi$, and therefore $w \models [R]\psi$. If $\langle R \rangle \psi \in w$, then there is some $w' \in U$ such that $(w, w') \in \mathcal{I}(R)$ and $\psi \in w'$. This holds since $\mathcal{M}$ does not contain any bad points. As above, it follows that $w \models \langle R \rangle \psi$. Thus, the assumption $\varphi \in w_0$ implies that $w_0 \models \varphi$. Moreover, since every $w \in U$ contains Φ we have shown that φ is satisfiable in a model which globally validates Φ.

For the other direction, assume that for some (finite or infinite) model $\mathcal{M} = (U, \mathcal{I}, w_0)$ it holds that $w_0 \models \varphi$, and $w \models \hat{\Psi}$ for all $w \in U$. We have to show that the above procedure terminates successfully. For any $w \in U$, let $w^\equiv \triangleq \{\psi \in SF \mid$

$w \models \psi\}$. Since SF is finite, there are only finitely many such $w^\equiv$. Let the *filtration* of $\mathcal{M}$ be $\mathcal{M}^\equiv \triangleq (U^\equiv, \mathcal{I}^\equiv, w_0^\equiv)$, where

- $U^\equiv \triangleq \{w \mid w = u^\equiv$ for some $u \in U\}$,
- $(w_1, w_2) \in \mathcal{I}^\equiv(R)$ iff there are $u_1, u_2 \in U$ such that $w_1 = u_1^\equiv$ and $w_2 = u_2^\equiv$ and $(u_1, u_2) \in \mathcal{I}(R)$,
- $w \in \mathcal{I}^\equiv(\mathrm{p})$ iff $\mathrm{p} \in w$, and
- $w_0^\equiv = \{\psi \in SF \mid w_0 \models \psi\}$.

Clearly, $\mathcal{M}^\equiv$ is a submodel of the initial model of our decision algorithm. Moreover, no point or arc of $\mathcal{M}^\equiv$ is ever removed by the decision procedure. Therefore, the algorithm terminates with a nonempty result. Since $w_0 \models \varphi$, it holds that $\varphi \in w_0^\equiv$. $\square$

Since the decision algorithm iterates over all of the points and sub-formulas, there are two ways to implement it. First, we can implement it by a search of all points using nested iteration for all sub-formulas of this point. The second technique is to use a bottom up search of all sub-formulas, where we check all points and arcs to see whether they are 'bad' with respect to this formula. In both cases, it is important to repeat the search after some deletions have taken place, until stabilization is reached. A pseudo-code description is given in Fig. 12. Recall that $R(w)$ denotes the set of successors of point w with respect to relation R. Furthermore, for any set of points U and formula ψ, let U_ψ denote $\{w \in U \mid \psi \in w\}$.

Depending on the data structures used for the representation of sets, it may not be necessary to implement set operations by a traversal of all elements of the set. For example, all set operations which are used in the comment lines of the pseudo-code can be implemented directly with a BDD representation for U and R as described in Section 10.

In a concrete implementation of this algorithm, there is a tradeoff between computation time and space: for any sub-formula $\psi \triangleq (\psi_1 \rightarrow \psi_2)$ and any point w, it can be determined whether $\psi \in w$ by deciding whether $\psi_1 \notin w$ or $\psi_2 \in w$. Hence, it is not necessary to represent a propositionally consistent set by the set of sub-formulas it consists of; boolean combinations of sub-formulas can be omitted. A point then is represented by

- the set of sub-formulas which are atomic propositions, and
- the set of sub-formulas which are of the kind $\langle R \rangle \psi$.

If we use this representation, then we may have to calculate the value of boolean combinations of formulas from their constituent parts. This value is needed in order to determine whether the representation of a point is propositionally consistent with the assumptions.

We now show how to extend this algorithm to transitive closure operators. The recursion axiom for the $\mathbf{F}^*$-operator can be written as follows: (cf. page 1696):

(Rec) $\vdash (\neg \mathbf{F}^* q \rightarrow \neg q \wedge \mathbf{X} \neg \mathbf{F}^* q)$

This axiom indicates that if $\mathbf{F}^* \psi \notin w_0$, then $\psi \notin w_0$ and for all w_1 such that $w_0 \prec w_1$ it should hold that $\mathbf{F}^* \psi \notin w_1$. Thus, in the model all points for which $\mathbf{F}^* \psi \notin w_0$ and $\psi \in w_0$ have to be deleted. Similarly, 'bad arcs' (w_0, w_1) are those for which $\mathbf{F}^* \psi \notin w_0$ and $\mathbf{F}^* \psi \in w_1$.

procedure ML_sat (Formula φ, Formulaset Φ) =

/* *Input Φ and φ, determine if φ satisfiable with global assumptions Φ* */

$\quad U := \{w \subseteq SF \mid \Phi \subseteq w, \perp \notin w\}$;

/* *delete propositionally inconsistent points* */

for all $\psi = (\psi_1 \rightarrow \psi_2) \in SF$ **do**

$\quad$ /* $U := U \cap ((U_\psi \setminus U_{\psi_1}) \cup (U_\psi \cap U_{\psi_2}) \cup (U_{\psi_1} \setminus U_\psi \setminus U_{\psi_2}))$ */

$\quad$ **for all** $w \in U$ **do**

$\qquad$ **if** $(\psi \in w \wedge \psi_1 \in w \wedge \psi_2 \notin w) \vee (\psi \notin w \wedge (\psi_1 \notin w \vee \psi_2 \in w))$

$\qquad$ **then** $U := U \setminus \{w\}$;

$R := U \times U$;

repeat until stabilization

$\quad$ **for all** $\psi = \langle R \rangle \psi_1 \in SF$ **do**

$\qquad$ /* *delete bad arcs* */

$\qquad$ /* $R := R \cap ((U_\psi \times U) \cup (U \times (U \setminus U_{\psi_1})))$ */

$\qquad$ **for all** $(w_0, w_1) \in R$ **do**

$\qquad\quad$ **if** $w_0 \notin U \vee w_1 \notin U \vee (\psi \notin w_0 \wedge \psi_1 \in w_1)$

$\qquad\quad$ **then** $R := R \setminus \{(w_0, w_1)\}$;

$\qquad$ /* *delete bad points* */

$\qquad$ /* $U := (U \setminus U_\psi) \cup (U \cap \{w \mid (R(w) \cap U_{\psi_1}) \neq \{\}\})$ */

$\qquad$ **for all** $w \in U$ **do**

$\qquad\quad$ **if** $(\psi \in w \wedge \forall w' \in R(w) \, (\psi_1 \notin w'))$ **then** $U := U \setminus \{w\}$;

if $U_\varphi = \{\}$

then print(φ, "is not satisfiable with assumptions", Φ)

else print(φ, "and the assumptions", Φ, "are satifiable in", U_φ)

Figure 12: Modal logic decision algorithm

In modal logic, a 'bad point' was defined to be one which contains $\langle R \rangle \psi$, but no R-successor contains ψ. For transitive closure operators, however, it is not sufficient to delete all points w_0 for which $\mathbf{F}^* \psi \in w_0$, $\psi \notin w_0$ and no successor contains $\mathbf{F}^* \psi$. There might be a closed loop of points all of which contain $\mathbf{F}^* \psi$, but no point containing ψ is reachable from the loop. A point is bad, if it *contains* $\mathbf{F}^* \psi$, but does not *fulfill* this eventuality, i.e., no reachable point w_n contains ψ. To check this condition, we need another iteration: for each sub-formula of the form $\mathbf{F}^* \psi$ we iteratively mark all points which can reach a point containing ψ. We initially mark all points which contain ψ. We then continue to mark all points which have a marked successor. After stabilization all formulas $\mathbf{F}^* \psi$ in unmarked points are unsatisfied and the respective points can be deleted. The algorithm, which is an extension of the algorithm in Figure 12, is given in Figure 13. For a correctness proof and an extension to **CTL**, see [Emerson and Sistla 1984, Emerson 1990]

---

for all $\psi = \mathbf{F}^{\bullet}\,\psi_1 \in SF$ **do**

/* delete bad 'arcs' */
$U := U \setminus \{w \mid \psi \notin w_0 \wedge \psi_1 \in w_0\};$
$R := R \setminus \{(w_0, w_1) \mid \psi \notin w_0 \wedge \psi \in w_1\};$

/* mark all points which can reach ψ_1 */
$New := \{w_0 \mid \exists w_1 \in U : (w_0, w_1) \in R \wedge \psi_1 \in w_1\};$
$Marked := New;$

repeat
    $New := \{w_0 \mid \exists w_1 \in New : (w_0, w_1) \in R\} \setminus Marked;$
    $Marked := Marked \cup New;$
until $New = \{\};$

/* delete bad points */
$U := U \setminus \{w \mid \psi_1 \in w \wedge w \notin Marked\};$

Figure 13: marking algorithm for transitive closure

7.2. Satisfiability Algorithms for Natural Models

The branching time decision procedures described in the previous subsection construct a "most general" model for any satisfiable formula. For any sub-formula, *all* propositionally consistent sets are traversed. The number of propositionally consistent sets of sub-formulas is exponential in the length of the formula; therefore, with an explicit representation of sets these algorithms are limited to "small" formulas.

Natural models for linear time logics are sequences of points. Each point determines a propositionally consistent set of sub-formulas, namely the set of those sub-formulas which are valid in this point. Often, the number of different propositionally consistent sets determined by a specific linear-time model is small, compared to the number of all propositionally consistent sets. Thus, in the decision procedure it can be more appropriate to build a model incrementally:

- Start with some initial point, and
- iteratively choose the next point for the constructed sequence.

In this way, only those propositionally consistent sets have to be stored which actually appear in the model. Of course, in the worst case all propositionally consistent sets will be traversed; however, we can expect a better average-case behavior.

This procedure involves a nondeterministic choice. Therefore, it is implemented using backtracking search. Similar to the presentation in the previous subsection, we first give an algorithm for modal logic before considering operators which involve recursion. Since we are aiming at natural models, we use deterministic monomodal logic, that is, modal logic with a single accessibility relation R for which axiom $\mathbf{U}$ is required (cf. page 1691).

We want to decide whether a formula φ is satisfiable in a natural model globally validating the assumptions Φ. We start with the set W of all propositionally consistent extensions of $\Phi \cup \{\varphi\}$. That is, $w \in W$ iff

- $\varphi \in w$,
- $\Phi \subseteq w$,
- $\perp \notin w$, and
- for all sub-formulas $\psi = (\psi_1 \rightarrow \psi_2)$ it holds that $\psi \in w$ iff $\psi_1 \in w$ implies $\psi_2 \in w$.

We choose some $w_0 \in W$ and try to construct a model with w_0 as initial point. At level i in the construction, we are given a propositionally consistent set w_i. If it does not contain any formula $\langle R \rangle \, \psi$, we are finished. In this case, we have found a finite model of length i with final point w_i. Otherwise, we construct the set

$$w_i^R \triangleq \{\psi \mid \langle R \rangle \, \psi \in w_i\} \cup \{\neg \psi \mid \neg \langle R \rangle \, \psi \in w_i\} \cup \Phi$$

We refer to $\{\psi \mid \langle R \rangle \, \psi \in w_i\}$ as the *positive future obligations* and to $\{\neg \psi \mid \neg \langle R \rangle \, \psi \in w_i\}$ as the *negative future obligations* of w_i. Thus, w_i^R is the set of all future obligations of w_i (with respect to R), plus the global assumptions. We then build the set S of all propositionally consistent extensions of w_i^R. Since there are only finitely many subformulas of $(\hat{\Phi} \wedge \varphi)$, the set S is finite. If w_i^R is not propositionally consistent, then $S = \{\}$. In this case, we backtrack to level $i - 1$ (or report failure, if $i = 0$). Otherwise, we choose some $w_{i+1} \in S$ as successor of w_i and continue *ad infinitum*. If we hit upon a point which is already contained in the constructed sub-model $w_0...w_i$, then the infinite cyclic model $w_0...w_i(w_{i+1}...w_i)^\omega$ initially satisfies φ and globally satisfies Φ. Since there are only finitely many maximal propositionally consistent sets, the construction must terminate. A pseudocode description of this algorithm is given in Figure 14.

---

procedure ML_sat_lin (Formula φ, Formulaset Φ) =
    $W := \{w \subseteq SF \mid \varphi \in w, \Phi \subseteq w, w$ propositionally consistent $\}$;
    $Stack := \{\}$;
    for all $w \in W$ **do** depth_first_search(w);
    print(φ, "is unsatisfiable with assumptions", Φ);

procedure depth_first_search (w) =
    if $w \in Stack$ **then** print(φ, Φ, "satisfiable by", $Stack$); **exit**;
    push(w, $Stack$);
    $pos := \{\psi \in SF \mid \langle R \rangle \, \psi \in w\}$; $neg := \{\psi \in SF \mid \langle R \rangle \, \psi \notin w\}$;
    if $pos = \{\}$ **then** print(φ, Φ, "satisfiable by", $Stack$); **exit**;
    $S := \{w \subseteq SF \mid pos \subseteq w, w \cap neg = \{\}, \Phi \subseteq w, w$ prop. consistent $\}$;
    for all $w' \in S$ **do** depth_first_search(w');
    pop($Stack$);

Figure 14: Modal logic decision algorithm for linear models

In this algorithm, there is some redundant calculation.

- Firstly, whenever we backtrack from a point, there cannot be a successful continuation from this point. Therefore, we can add all points which are popped from the stack to a list M. If procedure depth_first_search is called with an argument which is contained in M, it can backtrack immediately.
- Secondly, we already noted that it is not necessary to represent a propositionally consistent set by an enumeration of all sub-formulas it consists of. It is sufficient to mark for every proposition variable and for every sub-formula starting with an $\langle R \rangle$-operator whether they are contained in the maximal consistent set.
- Thirdly, in the calculation of the set S of possible successors of a point, it is sufficient to consider propositionally consistent sets which are subsets of ($pos \cup neg \cup \Phi$). That is, for sub-formulas ψ of φ which are neither future obligations of w nor sub-formulas of global assumptions from Φ, it is not necessary to fix their value in the successor w'. Both possible extensions, where $\psi \in w'$ or $\psi \notin w'$, are propositionally consistent and will lead to the same result. This improvement can be implemented for example by using a three-valued characteristic function for sub-formulas and propositionally consistent sets (contained, not contained, don't care) in the representation of points.

In Figure 15 we give a set of tableau rules for monomodal logic on deterministic models. The tableau rules can be seen as an implicit formulation of the algorithm in Figure 14, where the above improvements are included by definition. Similar tableau rules for modal logics can be found in [Fitting 1983] and for temporal logics in [Wolper 1985].

$$(\rightarrow) \frac{\Gamma, (\psi_1 \rightarrow \psi_2)}{\Gamma, \neg\psi_1 \quad \Gamma, \psi_2} \qquad (\neg \rightarrow) \frac{\Gamma, \neg(\psi_1 \rightarrow \psi_2)}{\Gamma, \psi_1, \neg\psi_2}$$

$$(\bot_1) \frac{\Gamma, \psi, \neg\psi}{*} \qquad (\bot_2) \frac{\Gamma, \bot}{*} \qquad (\top) \frac{\Gamma, \neg\bot}{\Gamma}$$

$$(\langle R \rangle) \frac{\Gamma, \langle R \rangle \varphi_1, ..., \langle R \rangle \varphi_n, \neg \langle R \rangle \psi_1, ..., \neg \langle R \rangle \psi_m}{\Phi, \varphi_1, ..., \varphi_n, \neg\psi_1, ..., \neg\psi_m} \qquad ([R]) \frac{\Gamma}{}$$

Figure 15: Tableau rules for monomodal logic on deterministic models

In these rules, Γ denotes any set of formulas, and Φ is the set of global assumptions. The double line in rules ($\langle R \rangle$) and ($[R]$) indicates a transition from one point in the constructed model to the next, and the star indicates that a branch is closed. Each tableau rule allows to derive zero, one or two sets of formulas from any set of formulas. Additional regulations are:

- Rule ($\rightarrow$) can only be applied if $\psi_2 \neq \bot$.
- Rules ($\langle R \rangle$) and ($[R]$) can only be applied if no other rule is applicable.
- Rule ($\langle R \rangle$) can only be applied if no other $\langle R \rangle \varphi$ or $\neg \langle R \rangle \psi$ is in Γ.

- Rule ($[R]$) can only be applied if no $\langle R \rangle \varphi$ is in Γ.

A *tableau* is a finite tree of sets of formulas such that

- The root of the tableau is $\Phi \cup \{\varphi\}$, and
- The children of each node are constructed according to some tableau rule.

A leaf is called *closed*, if it consists of the symbol $*$. It is called *open*, if it consists of a subset of formulas of some other node on the path from the root to this leaf. (In particular, if rule ($\langle R \rangle$) regenerates the root, the new leaf is open. Also, any empty node constructed by rule ($[R]$) is open). A tableau is *completed*, if any leaf is closed or open. A completed tableau is *successful*, if it contains an open leaf.

There is a strong connection between the tableau method and the local satisfiability algorithm sketched above. The propositional tableau rules systematically generate all necessary propositionally maximal consistent extensions of a given set of formulas, and the modal rules fix the structure of the accessibility relation(s) in the generated model graph.

For any given root, there are several different tableaus, since we did not specify any order in which the rules have to be applied. Nevertheless all these tableaus are equivalent: if there is *some* successful tableau for φ and Φ, then *every* completed tableau for it is successful.

7.2. THEOREM. *φ is satisfiable with assumptions Φ iff $\Phi \cup \{\varphi\}$ has a successful tableau.*

PROOF: For one direction, assume that there is some natural model $\mathcal{M} \triangleq ((w_0, w_1, w_2, ...), \mathcal{I}, w_0)$, where $w_0 \models \varphi$ and $w_i \models \Phi$ for every $i > 0$, and show that there is a completed tableau for φ and Φ with an open leaf. Equivalently, assume that any completed tableau for φ and Φ is given, and show that it contains an open leaf. We construct a sequence of tableau nodes n_i, and associate with any n_i a point $w(n_i)$ in the model. As an invariant of this construction, we show that for all formulas $\psi \in n_i$ it holds that $w(n_i) \models \psi$.

Initially n_0 is the root of the tableau, with $w(n_0) \triangleq w_0$. Since $w_0 \models \varphi$ and $w_0 \models \Phi$, the invariant is satisfied. Given any tableau node n_i with $w(n_i) = w_j$, no closing rules can be applicable, because this would contradict the invariant. Assume the child n_{i+1} of n_i is constructed by rule ($\neg \rightarrow$) or ($\top$). Then $w(n_{i+1}) \triangleq w_j$, and the invariant is preserved. If two children of n_i are constructed by rule ($\rightarrow$), then any one of them is chosen which preserves the invariant, and again $w(n_{i+1}) \triangleq w_j$. If n_i has a child obtained by rule ($\langle R \rangle$), then $w(n_{i+1}) \triangleq w_{j+1}$. The specific formulation of the rule guarantees that the invariant is preserved. Since the tableau is finite, and we can never apply one of the closing rules, we must hit an open leaf sooner or later.

For the other direction, we have to show that from any completed tableau with open leafs we can construct a model. The construction is similar to above. We consider the *unfolding* of the tableau. This is the tree arising from the repeated substitution of any open leaf with the subtableau rooted at the node subsuming this open leaf. In particular, an empty node generated by rule ($[R]$) can be replaced with any node on the path from the root to this node. If the tableau contains open leaves, then the unfolding contains infinite paths. In the unfolding, call any node whose child is constructed by rule ($\langle R \rangle$) or ($[R]$) a *pre-state*. It can be shown that the sequence of pre-states of any infinite path from the root constitutes an infinite model.   □

As an example for the tableau construction, consider the semaphore from page 1694. A linear time modelling of the transitions is given by

$$\Phi \triangleq \{(\text{on} \rightarrow r \ \wedge \langle R \rangle \neg \text{on}), \quad (\neg \text{on} \rightarrow r \ \wedge \langle R \rangle \neg \text{on} \vee s \ \wedge \langle R \rangle \text{on}), \quad \neg(r \wedge s)\}.$$

Here, r and s denote the semaphore-operations "reset" and "set", respectively. We prove that after a reset the semaphore can be set only once:

$$\varphi \triangleq (r \rightarrow [R](s \rightarrow [R](s \rightarrow \bot))).$$

To show that $\Phi \Vdash \varphi$, we construct the tableau with root $\Gamma \triangleq \Phi \cup \{\neg\varphi\}$ and show that it is closed. The tableau is given in Figure 16.

In this tableau, we omitted boolean decompositions. All leaves are closed because they contain both r and s. This is a contradiction to the assumption $\neg(r \wedge s)$ expressing that only one action is performed at a time.

Tableaus for LTL

We now extend these methods to linear time temporal logic. For simplicity, we restrict attention to the operators X and F^*. The algorithms are similar to the modal logic case described above. To decide whether a formula φ is satisfiable in a natural model, we apply the same depth-first search algorithm as sketched in Figure 14, where X replaces $\langle R \rangle$, and extended sub-formulas (ESF) are used instead of subformulas (SF). (Recall that both ψ and $X F^* \psi$ are extended sub-formulas of $F^* \psi$.)

There are two further modifications. Firstly, assume we are given a sub-formula $F^* \psi$ and a node w such that one of the following holds.
- $F^* \psi \in w$ and $\psi \notin w$ and $X F^* \psi \notin w$, or
- $F^* \psi \notin w$, and $\psi \in w$ or $X F^* \psi \in w$.

In this case, we can discard node w. Even though it may be *propositionally* consistent, it does not respect the recursion axiom

$$\vdash \ F^* \psi \leftrightarrow \psi \vee X F^* \psi.$$

Thus, this node cannot appear as a point in the model.

Secondly, when the depth-first-search finds a node w which is already on the stack, it would be preliminary to report a success. Consider the set of nodes $w \triangleq w_0, w_1, ..., w_n$, which are on the path from w to w. It could be the case that there is some sub-formula $F^* \psi$, such that each node contains both $F^* \psi$ and $X F^* \psi$, but none of them contains ψ. That is, the eventuality φ is *required* but not *fulfilled* in

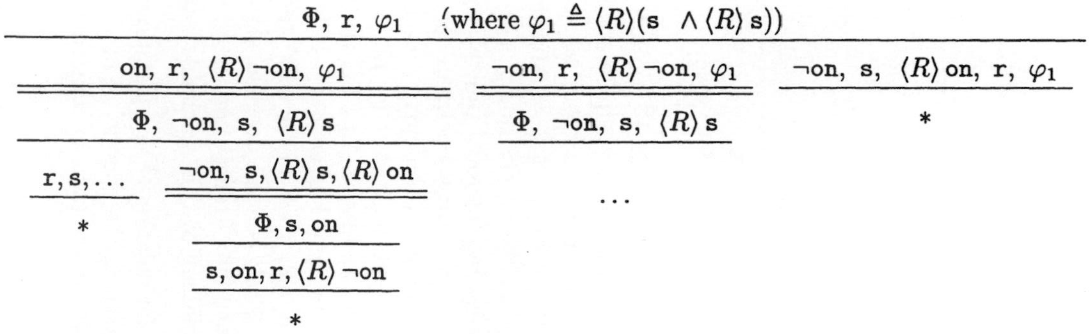

$$\Phi, r, \varphi_1 \quad (\text{where } \varphi_1 \triangleq \langle R \rangle (s \wedge \langle R \rangle s))$$

on, r, $\langle R \rangle \neg$on, φ_1 $\neg$on, r, $\langle R \rangle \neg$on, φ_1 $\neg$on, s, $\langle R \rangle$ on, r, φ_1 *

$\Phi, \neg$on, s, $\langle R \rangle$ s $\Phi, \neg$on, s, $\langle R \rangle$ s $\cdots$

r, s, $\ldots$ $\neg$on, s, $\langle R \rangle$ s, $\langle R \rangle$ on

* Φ, s, on

s, on, r, $\langle R \rangle \neg$on

*

Figure 16: Tableau for Φ and $(r \rightarrow [R](s \rightarrow [R](s \rightarrow \bot)))$.

$w_0, ..., w_n$. The fulfillment of $\mathbf{F}^* \varphi$ is "postponed forever" from each w_i to the next in a cyclic manner.

However, we cannot discard $w_0, w_1, ..., w_n$, because they might contribute to a satisfying model. Consider the following situation:

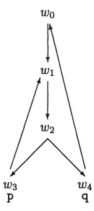

We assume that all nodes in this picture contain $\mathbf{F}^* p$ and $\mathbf{F}^* q$. The only node containing p is w_3, and the only node containing q is w_4. When the backtracking search encounters w_1 as child of w_3, it finds that in the loop w_1, w_2, w_3 the proposition q is required but not fulfilled. Thus it backtracks to w_2 and finds w_4 as second child. This time, in the loop w_0, w_1, w_2, w_4 the proposition p is required but not fulfilled. However, both p and q are satisfied in the model $(w_0, w_1, w_2, w_3, w_1, w_2, w_4)^\omega$.

Thus, when the depth-first-search finds a backward arc, it has to search the strongly connected component of nodes of the current node. A *strongly connected component* (SCC) is a set W of points such that for all $w_1, w_2 \in W$, if $w_1 \neq w_2$, then there is a path from w_1 to w_2 and back. An SCC W is called *terminal*, if for all $w \in W$, $w' \notin W$, it is not the case that $w \prec w'$. It is called *self-fulfilling*, if all required formulas are fulfilled, i.e., if for any $w \in W$ and $(\varphi_1 \mathbf{U}^+ \varphi_2) \in w$ there exists a $w' \in W$ such that $\varphi_2 \in w'$. For the decision algorithm, the depth-first-search graph has to be partitioned into strongly connected components. The given formula is satisfiable iff a self-fulfilling SCC is reachable from some initial node.

We postpone the algorithmic formulation of this partitioning to the next section, where the same algorithm is given in the context of model checking. Instead, we sketch the necessary modifications in the tableau construction. As additional rules to those of Figure 15, we add:

$$(\mathbf{F}^*) \; \frac{\Gamma, \mathbf{F}^* \psi}{\Gamma, \psi \qquad \Gamma, \mathbf{X}\,\mathbf{F}^* \psi} \qquad\qquad (\neg \mathbf{F}^*) \; \frac{\Gamma, \neg \mathbf{F}^* \psi}{\Gamma, \neg \psi, \neg \mathbf{X}\,\mathbf{F}^* \psi}$$

To deal with unfulfilled eventuality formulas, a backward loop can only be regarded as *open*, if for any $\mathbf{F}^* \psi$ which occurs in any w_i in the loop, there is a w_j in the loop such that $\psi \in w_j$ (*loop condition*). If the loop condition is not met, the unfolding of the tableau has to continue until all nodes of the SCC are contained in the loop. In this case, the respective branches are closed.

As an example for the loop condition, we show transitivity of $\leq$:

$$\vdash (\mathbf{F}^* \mathbf{F}^* p \rightarrow \mathbf{F}^* p)$$

The root of the tableau is marked with the negation of this formula, i.e. with $\mathbf{F}^* \mathbf{F}^* p$ and $\neg \mathbf{F}^* p$.

$$
\frac{\mathbf{F}^* \mathbf{F}^* p, \quad \neg \mathbf{F}^* p}{
\begin{array}{c|c}
\dfrac{\mathbf{F}^* p, \quad \neg \mathbf{F}^* p}{*} & \dfrac{\mathbf{X}\,\mathbf{F}^* \mathbf{F}^* p, \quad \neg \mathbf{F}^* p}{\dfrac{\mathbf{X}\,\mathbf{F}^* \mathbf{F}^* p, \quad \neg p, \quad \neg \mathbf{X}\,\mathbf{F}^* p}{\mathbf{F}^* \mathbf{F}^* p, \quad \neg \mathbf{F}^* p}}
\end{array}
}
$$

$$**$$

The leaf marked (*) closes because it is contradictory. The leaf (**) closes because it is subsumed by the root above, and the SCC to which it belongs contains the unfulfilled eventuality $\mathbf{F}^* \mathbf{F}^* p$.

There is a close connection between tableaus for temporal logics and ω-automata. The pre-states in the tableau (i.e., nodes immediately above a double line) can be seen as states of a generalized Büchi-automaton. The set of open leafs are the accepting states, and the recurring states are determined as follows: for any sub-formula $\varphi \triangleq \mathbf{F}^* \psi$ it must hold that φ is infinitely often not contained in an accepting run, or ψ is contained infinitely often. This can be formulated as generalized Büchi-acceptance condition on the states [Clarke, Grumberg and Hamaguchi 1997]. The formula then is satisfiable iff the language of the corresponding automaton is nonempty, and it is valid iff this language is Σ^ω (the set of all finite and infinite strings over Σ). Therefore, the decision problem for **LTL** can be regarded as an instance of the language problem of generalized Büchi automata [Wolper 1985, Emerson 1985, Vardi and Wolper 1986, Kurshan 1994]. In [Vardi 1995] other embeddings of tableau-based satisfiability procedures for temporal logics into decision algorithms for ω-automata, based on *alternating automata*, are described.

8. Basic Model Checking Algorithms

In this section, we will show how the most commonly used model checking procedures can be obtained from the above decision procedures.

Given a model $\mathcal{M}$ and a formula φ, the model checking problem is to decide whether $\mathcal{M} \models \varphi$. In principle, this can be done by encoding $\mathcal{M}$ as a set of assumptions ("premises" or "program axioms") Φ, and deciding whether $\Phi \vdash \varphi$. However, some experiments will quickly convince the reader that a naïve approach of doing so is doomed to failure. Usually, the program axioms all have a very special form, such as

$$(\texttt{state\_i} \rightarrow (\mathbf{X}\,\texttt{succ\_i1} \vee \cdots \vee \mathbf{X}\,\texttt{succ\_in}))$$

in a linear time modelling, or

$$(\texttt{state\_i} \rightarrow (\langle a_1\rangle\,\texttt{succ\_i1} \wedge \cdots \wedge \langle a_n\rangle\,\texttt{succ\_in}))$$

in a branching time approach. The decision procedure in general can not take advantage of this special form of the assumptions and will in every step break down all assumptions to its basic propositional components. This results in a very inefficient behavior; usually only very small systems can be verified and debugged that way.

Therefore, model checking algorithms avoid the encoding of the models as a set of program axioms; they use the models directly instead. Model checking determines whether a given specification formula is satisfied in a given Kripke-model, i.e., whether a tree or natural model satisfying the formula can be generated from it.

There are two variants of this task, depending on whether the initial or universal definition of satisfaction of a formula in a model is used. In the usual definition, a Kripke-model $\mathcal{M} \triangleq (U, \mathcal{I}, w_0)$ is given, which consists of universe U, accessibility relation(s) defined by $\mathcal{I}$, and current point $w_0 \in U$, and we have to check whether the formula φ is satisfied: $(U, \mathcal{I}, w_0) \models \varphi$. In the universal definition, we are given a frame $\mathcal{F} \triangleq (U, \mathcal{I})$ consisting of universe and interpretation, and want to know whether the formula is satisfied in *all* models based on this frame: $(U, \mathcal{I}) \models \varphi$ iff for all $w_0 \in U$ it holds that $(U, \mathcal{I}, w_0) \models \varphi$. Equivalently, we want to know whether $\varphi^{\mathcal{F}} = U$, where $\varphi^{\mathcal{F}} \triangleq \{w \in U \mid w \models \varphi\}$ is the set of points satisfying φ.

Of course, any algorithm which calculates $\varphi^{\mathcal{F}}$ can also be used to decide whether $(U, \mathcal{I}, w_0) \models \varphi$ holds: $w_0 \models \varphi$ iff $w_0 \in \varphi^{\mathcal{F}}$. Vice versa, if we have an efficient algorithm to decide whether $w_0 \models \varphi$, we can calculate $\varphi^{\mathcal{F}}$ by an iteration on all states.

The model checking problem has two parameters: model $\mathcal{M}$ and formula φ. Algorithms which iterate on the structure of φ and in each step traverse the whole of $\mathcal{M}$ are sometimes called *global*. Algorithms which iteratively extend the checked part of $\mathcal{M}$ and in each step determine the truth of each sub-formula of φ are sometimes called *local*. Although the theoretical worst-time complexity is not influenced by this choice, the average case behavior may differ significantly.

In principle, the three axes (branching/linear, universal/initial, global/local) are independent. In practice, however, for branching time logics mostly global algorithms for universal validity are used, whereas for linear time logics local algorithms for initial validity have been suggested.

8.1. Global Branching Time Model Checking

Given a Kripke frame $\mathcal{F} = (U, \mathcal{I})$ and a multimodal formula φ, the set $\varphi^{\mathcal{F}} \triangleq \{w \in U \mid w \models \varphi\}$ of points validating φ can be calculated by a recursive descent on the structure of φ:

- If p is an atomic proposition, then $p^{\mathcal{F}} \triangleq \mathcal{I}(p)$.
- $\perp^{\mathcal{F}} \triangleq \{\}$.
- $(\varphi \to \psi)^{\mathcal{F}} \triangleq (U \setminus \varphi^{\mathcal{F}}) \cup \psi^{\mathcal{F}}$.
- $(\langle R \rangle \, \psi)^{\mathcal{F}} \triangleq \{w \in U \mid \exists w' \in \psi^{\mathcal{F}}, (w, w') \in \mathcal{I}(R)\}$.

This algorithm seems to be just a trivial reformulation of the semantical definition for the logical operators. However, there are some important observations.

- Firstly, $(\langle R \rangle \, \psi)^{\mathcal{F}}$ can be calculated from $\psi^{\mathcal{F}}$ in two ways: we can check for each $w \in U$, whether the intersection of $\psi^{\mathcal{F}}$ and $R(w)$ is nonempty. Alternatively, we can calculate $\bigcup \{R^{-1}(w') \mid w' \in \psi^{\mathcal{F}}\}$, where $R^{-1}(w') \triangleq \{w \mid (w, w') \in \mathcal{I}(R)\}$ is the *inverse image* of point w under the relation R. This inverse image calculation can be accomplished by a traversal of all arcs $(w, w') \in \mathcal{I}(R)$: if $w' \in \psi^{\mathcal{F}}$, then $w \in (\langle R \rangle \, \psi)^{\mathcal{F}}$.
- Secondly, to avoid recalculation of common subformulas, we use a table, where for each sub-formula ψ the set $\psi^{\mathcal{F}}$ is stored. The size of $\psi^{\mathcal{F}}$ can be of the same order of magnitude as $|U|$. Thus, we need an efficient data structure for large sets of points.
- Thirdly, the overall *complexity* of this algorithm is linear in the number of different sub-formulas and in the size of the model. However, even for infinite models which are given by some symbolic description, e.g., Petri nets or Turing machines, some model checking problems can be decidable [Andersen 1994, Gurov, Berezin and Kapron 1996, Burkart and Esparza 1997]. In such cases, $\psi^{\mathcal{F}}$ can be of infinite size, and must be represented by a symbolic description as well.

Similar to the above modal logic procedure, the **CTL** model checking algorithm proceeds by marking each point with the set of sub-formulas which are valid for this point. Suppose we have already marked the set of points satisfying ψ_1 and the points satisfying ψ_2. To label the set of points satisfying $\varphi \triangleq \mathbf{E}(\psi_2 \, \mathbf{U}^+ \, \psi_1)$ or $\varphi \triangleq \mathbf{A}(\psi_2 \, \mathbf{U}^+ \, \psi_1)$, we use the fixpoint unfoldings

$$\mathbf{E}(\psi_2 \, \mathbf{U}^+ \, \psi_1) \leftrightarrow \mathbf{E} \, \mathbf{X}(\psi_1 \vee \psi_2 \wedge \mathbf{E}(\psi_2 \, \mathbf{U}^+ \, \psi_1))$$

$$\mathbf{A}(\psi_2 \, \mathbf{U}^+ \, \psi_1) \leftrightarrow \mathbf{A} \, \mathbf{X}(\psi_1 \vee \psi_2 \wedge \mathbf{A}(\psi_2 \, \mathbf{U}^+ \, \psi_1))$$

For $\varphi \triangleq \mathbf{E}(\psi_2 \, \mathbf{U}^+ \, \psi_1)$, we label all points with φ which have a successor that is labelled with ψ_1, or with ψ_2 and also φ. This process is repeated until stabilization is reached. For $\varphi \triangleq \mathbf{A}(\psi_2 \, \mathbf{U}^+ \, \psi_1)$, note that $\mathbf{A} \, \mathbf{X} \chi \leftrightarrow (\mathbf{E} \, \mathbf{X} \top \wedge \mathbf{A} \, \mathbf{X} \chi)$. Thus, we label all points with φ which have at least one successor, and for which all successors are labelled with ψ_1, or with ψ_2 and also φ. Again, this process must be repeated until no new points can be marked. The procedure is comparable to the marking algorithm in Figure 13. A recursive formulation of this algorithm is given in Fig. 17.

Since the Kripke-model has a finite number of points, each **repeat** in the algorithm stabilizes after at most $|U|$ passes. In the worst case, each pass searches the whole model ($|U|^2$ transitions), hence the complexity is linear in the number of different sub-formulas, and cubic in $|U|$.

```
procedure CTL_check (Model (U, I, w₀), Formula φ) =
    if w₀ ∈ eval(φ)
    then print("φ is satisfied at w₀ in (U, I)")
    else print("φ not satisfied at w₀ in (U, I)");

function eval (Formula φ): Pointset =
    case φ of
        p : return I(p);
        ⊥ : return {};
        (ψ₁ → ψ₂) : return U\ eval(ψ₁) ∪ eval(ψ₂);
        E(ψ₂ U⁺ ψ₁) :  E1 := eval(ψ₁);  E2 := eval(ψ₂);  E := {};
            repeat until stabilization
                E := E ∪ {w | (succ(w) ∩ (E1 ∪ (E2 ∩ E))) ≠ {}};
            return E;
        A(ψ₂ U⁺ ψ₁) :  E1 := eval(ψ₁);  E2 := eval(ψ₂);  E := {};
            repeat until stabilization
                E := E ∪ {w | {} ≠ succ(w) ⊆ E1 ∪ (E2 ∩ E)};
            return E;
function succ (Point w): Pointset = return {w' | (w, w') ∈ I(≺)};
```

Figure 17: naïve **CTL** model checking algorithm

This bound can be improved if the search is organized better. In [Clarke, Emerson and Sistla 1986], an algorithm is given which is linear in the size of the model as well. For the $\mathbf{E\,F^+}$-operator, the problem of marking all points for which $\mathbf{E\,F^+}\,\varphi$ holds, given the set of point satisfying φ, is equivalent to the *inverse reachability problem*: given a set of points, mark all points from which any finite path leads into the given set. Assuming that for any two points we can decide in constant time whether they are connected by an arc, this can be done with time complexity quadratic in the number of points.

```
function reach (Pointset Target): Pointset =
    Source := {};  Search := Target;
    while Search ≠ {} do
        Search := pred (Search) \ Source;
        Source := Source ∪ Search
    enddo;
    return Source;
function pred (Point w): Pointset = return {w' | (w', w) ∈ I(≺)};
```

Figure 18: Inverse reachability calculation

The algorithm given in Fig. 18 calculates the set *Source* of all points from which any point in given set *Target* is reachable. In this algorithm, every point enters the set *Search* in the **while** loop at most once. Moreover, all set operations can be performed in time linear in the size of these sets, i.e., in the number of points; thus the overall complexity is quadratic in $|U|$ or linear in the size of the Kripke-model.

For the $\mathbf{E}\mathbf{U}^+$-operator, this idea can be refined to give an evaluation procedure of linear complexity. The $\mathbf{A}\mathbf{U}^+$-operator can be expressed by

$$\mathbf{A}(\psi_2 \, \mathbf{U}^+ \, \psi_1) \leftrightarrow \neg(\mathbf{E}(\neg\psi_1 \, \mathbf{U}^+(\neg(\psi_1 \wedge \psi_2)) \vee \mathbf{E}\,\mathbf{G}^+ \, \neg\psi_1)$$

Thus, we only need a procedure marking all points for which $\mathbf{E}\,\mathbf{G}^+ \, \varphi$ holds. This can be done as follows:

- restrict the model to those states satisfying φ
- find the maximal strongly connected components in the restriction
- mark all points in the original model from which a nontrivial SCC or a point without successors can be reached by a path in the restricted model.

These operations can be accomplished with time complexity which is quadratic in U. Thus, the overall complexity of CTL model checking is linear in the size of the formula and in the size of the model.

Fairness Constraints

Some automated model checkers for **CTL** (for example, SMV [McMillan 1993] and SVE [Dingel and Filkorn 1995]) allow to specify a set of *constraints* Φ together with the Kripke-model. These constraints are assumed to hold in the whole model; i.e., they restrict the model to those parts where they are valid. This use of constraints is somewhat different from the assumptions in the previous sections, which were used to constrain the *set* of possible models. For example, an ω-automaton can be regarded as a Kripke-model, together with global eventuality and fairness constraints (accepting and recurring states). Constraints can be formulated in the same language in which the formula to be checked is specified; however, "mixed" approaches have been suggested [Josko 1993], where e.g. the constraints are described in **LTL** and the property is described in **CTL**.

As an example for the use of such constraints, often the path-quantifiers $\mathbf{A}$ and $\mathbf{E}$ are restricted to *fair* paths. *Simple* fairness constraints are of form $\mathbf{F}^+ \, \psi$, where ψ is a boolean combination of propositions. For example, the condition $\mathbf{F}^+ \top$ specifies that each run must be infinite. As another example for a simple fairness constraint, we might want to restrict our attention to execution sequences in which every component is always eventually scheduled. Streett fairness constraints are of form $(\mathbf{G}^+ \mathbf{F}^+ \psi_1 \rightarrow \mathbf{G}^+ \mathbf{F}^+ \psi_2)$ and are useful to restrict attention to *strongly fair* schedulers: if a component infinitely often requests a resource, it will be granted infinitely often. Historically, different fairness constraints were discussed in [Lehmann, Pnueli and Stavi 1981, Quielle and Sifakis 1982]. A comprehensive treatment of fairness concepts and proofs is given in [Francez 1986].

The above algorithm can be modified to deal with such fairness constraints by building the tableau of the **LTL**-assumption and checking the **CTL**-formula on the product of Kripke-model and tableau. The complexity increases by a factor which depends on the type of **LTL**-formulas in the assumption. For more information, see [Emerson and Lei 1986, Kupferman and Vardi 1996, Emerson, Jutla and Sistla 1993, Clarke, Grumberg and Long 1993].

8.2. Local Linear Time Model Checking

For a given Kripke-model $\mathcal{M} = (U, \mathcal{I}, w_0)$ and **CTL**-formula φ, the relation $\mathcal{M} \models \varphi$ holds iff the maximal tree generated from $\mathcal{M}$ at w_0 satisfies φ. For linear time logics, $\mathcal{M} \models \varphi$ is interpreted by *sequence-validity*. That is, we want to check whether *every maximal sequence* generated from $\mathcal{M}$ at w_0 satisfies φ. Equivalently, we have to decide whether $\neg\varphi$ is satisfiable in *some* natural model generated from $\mathcal{M}$. In some sense, this is a more complex question than the one for branching time, because a whole *set* of natural models has to be checked. Hence, we cannot simply mark a point in the Kripke-model with the set of linear-time formulas which are valid for this point: for example, $\mathbf{F}^+ \psi$ can be valid for one of the generated sequences, and not valid for another one.

We first consider sequence-validity of modal logic with a single accessibility relation R. Given a Kripke-model $\mathcal{M} = (U, \mathcal{I}, w_0)$ and a modal formula φ, we want to determine whether there is a maximal sequence generated from $\mathcal{M}$ at w_0 which satisfies φ in w_0. This is done by a depth-first-search in the product of the set of propositionally maximal consistent sets of sub-formulas and the set of points in the model.

Formally, an *atom* α is any pair (w, m), where $w \in U$ is a point, and $m \subseteq SF(\varphi)$ is a propositionally consistent set of sub-formulas. An atom is *admissible*, if w and m agree on the interpretation of propositions. That is, if $\mathbf{p} \in SF(\varphi)$, then $\mathbf{p} \in m$ iff $w \in \mathcal{I}(\mathbf{p})$.

An *initial atom* is any admissible atom $\alpha = (w_0, m_0)$, where w_0 is the current point of $\mathcal{M}$, and $\varphi \in m_0$. We define a relation X_R between admissible atoms: $X_R((w, m), (w', m'))$ holds iff the following conditions are met:

1. $(w, w') \in \mathcal{I}(R)$,
2. if $\langle R \rangle \psi \in SF(\varphi)$ and $\psi \in m'$, then $\langle R \rangle \psi \in m$,
3. if $\langle R \rangle \psi \in m$, then $\psi \in m'$, and
4. some $\langle R \rangle \psi \in m$.

The first condition reflects the fact that the steps in the generated sequence are predetermined by the Kripke-model. The second condition is imposed by the semantics of the $\langle R \rangle$-operator. The third condition is a reformulations of the axiom **(U)** and the corresponding tableau rule ($\langle R \rangle$) on page 1706. The fourth condition corresponds to the tableau rule ([R]); it allows the generated sequence to be finite when no $\langle R \rangle \psi$ is contained in a node.

Now we can construct a forest of atoms as follows:

- initial nodes are all initial atoms

- any node α has as children all α' such that $X_R(\alpha, \alpha')$

Since for any finite Kripke-model there are only finitely many atoms, each branch in this forest can be made finite by appropriate backward arcs. As in the tableau definition, a leaf is called *open*, if it has no $\langle R \rangle$ formulas in its first component (m); otherwise, it is *closed*.

An *accepting path* through the resulting structure starts with any initial node and is either infinite or ends with an open leaf. Any accepting path is a sequence generated from the Kripke-model which satisfies the given formula $\neg \varphi$, thereby forming a counterexample to the specification φ.

To implement the search for an accepting path, we perform a depth-first search with backtracking from the set of initial atoms to all of its successors. In order to be able to terminate loops in this search, we have to store all atoms which were encountered previously. Though there are several possibilities to represent such a set of atoms, the method of choice seems to be to employ a hash table. It is not necessary to use all components of m as hash indices, since the value of propositions is determined by w, and boolean combinations of formulas can be recovered from their constituent parts. Therefore, it is sufficient to store only the value of $\langle R \rangle$-subformulas.

In general, since we are only looking for *some* counter-model, we can terminate the search if a counter-model is found. Although in the worst case (if no counter-model exists) the whole forest must be searched, it is possible to find errors very quickly by an appropriate ordering of the depth-first search successors.

In the depth-first search, we have to remove closed atoms from the list of possible loop points. A better way is to *mark* these nodes as closed while backtracking; then the search will not recurse again if such an atom reappears. Also all other improvements mentioned on page 1706 can be used for this algorithm.

Extensions for LTL

We have seen that the local model checking algorithm for modal logic is almost the same algorithm as the local tableau decision procedure. Similarly, the local model checking for **LTL** is very close to its respective satisfiability algorithm. For simplicity, in this subsection we restrict attention to the future fragment of **LTL**.

In the definition of $X_R((w, m), (w', m'))$, we replace $\langle R \rangle$ by $\mathbf{X}$ and require in addition

5. if $\mathbf{F}^* \psi \in SF(\varphi)$ then $\mathbf{F}^* \psi \in m$ iff $\psi \in m$ or $\mathbf{X} \mathbf{F}^* \psi \in m$

This requirement corresponds to the recursion axiom $\vdash \mathbf{F}^* \psi \leftrightarrow \psi \vee \mathbf{X} \mathbf{F}^* \psi$. As in the case of modal logic, we try to thread an accepting path through the graph of atoms which arises from this definition. However, we can only accept those paths in which all eventualities $\mathbf{F}^* \psi$ are fulfilled. Since we can not guarantee that several eventualities are simultaneously fulfilled in some single loop, we have to calculate the strongly connected components of the reflexive transitive closure of X_R. An SCC W of atoms is called *self-fulfilling*, if for any $\mathbf{F}^* \psi$ in some $\alpha \in W$ there exists some $\alpha' \in W$ with $\psi \in \alpha'$. Any atom which does not contain positive future obligations $\mathbf{X} \psi$ is a trivial SCC, because it is a terminal node in the atom graph. Such a node forms a self-fulfilling SCC, because the above condition (5.) guarantees that for any $\mathbf{F}^{*}\,\psi \in \alpha$, also $\psi \in \alpha$. The given formula φ is satisfiable in $\mathcal{M}$ iff there exists a self-fulfilling SCC which is reachable from some initial atom. In this case, a natural model for φ generated by $\mathcal{M}$ is given by any sequence of atoms from an initial atom which ends in a terminal atom or infinitely often passes through all atoms of a self-fulfilling SCC.

For $\mathbf{U}^{+}$-operators, each positive occurrence $(\psi_1\,\mathbf{U}^{+}\,\psi_2)$ in some $\alpha \in W$ is an eventuality which has to be fulfilled at some point; thus the SCC W is defined to be self-fulfilling, if it is nontrivial and for any $(\psi_1\,\mathbf{U}^{+}\,\psi_2)$ in some $\alpha \in W$ there exists some $\alpha' \in W$ with $\psi_2 \in \alpha'$, or it is trivial and does not contain any $(\psi_1\,\mathbf{U}^{+}\,\psi_2)$.

To construct maximal SCCs, two different algorithms have been suggested(see, e.g. [Aho, Hopcroft and Ullman 1974]). For model checking, Tarjan's algorithm [Tarjan 1972] is particularly well-suited, since it enumerates the strong components of a graph during the backtrack from the depth-first search. If a maximal SCC W is found, all required and fulfilled eventualities in all nodes of W can be collected. W is self-fulfilling if all required eventualities are fulfilled. Thus model checking can be performed "on-the-fly" during the enumeration of the reachable atoms of the model. An appropriate depth–first–search **LTL** model checking algorithm is given in 19.

In this algorithm, the function `children` constructs for a given atom α the set of all possible successor atoms according to the transition relation of the Kripke-model and to the fixed point definition of the until-operator. One way to implement this function is to represent atoms by bitstrings which contain one bit for each proposition $p \in \mathcal{P}$ and one bit for each sub-formula $(\psi_2\,\mathbf{U}^{+}\,\psi_1) \in SF(\varphi)$. New atoms are included into a hash table, which contains one bitstring for each atom. For each entry into the hash table, the function `children` returns a list of pointers to the hash table. For more information on bitstate hashing techniques and state space caching, see [Courcoubetis, Vardi, Wolper and Yannakakis 1992, Holzmann 1995, Godefroid, Holzmann and Pirottin 1995].

The procedure `depth_first_search` realizes Tarjan's algorithm and the test whether an SCC is self-fulfilling. It recursively builds all atoms reachable from a given atom α. When the procedure backtracks, α is the root of a maximal SCC iff there are no atoms β in the subtree below α such that α is also in the subtree of β. In this case, the maximal SCC containing α consists of all nodes in the subtree below α, and this maximal SCC can be checked for acceptance. *table* is implemented as a hash table from atoms to natural numbers. *table*$[\alpha]$ contains

- UNDEFINED, as long as atom α has not occurred,
- the depth-first-number of α, when α is first encountered,
- the depth–first–number of the first encountered atom belonging to the same strongly connected component as α, after return from the recursive call, and
- MAXNAT (any value for which $\min(n, \text{MAXNAT})$ is always n), after the maximal strong component containing α has been analyzed.

To check whether an SCC is self-fulfilling, during its enumeration two sets are built: *required* contains the union of all eventualities which are required, and *fulfilled*

---

procedure LTL_check (Model $\mathcal{M}$, Formula φ) =
    Nat *depth_first_count* := 0;   /* *number of recursive call* */
    Atomset *stack* := {};   /* *Stack of searched atoms* */
    Natarray *table*;   /* *Hashtable from atoms to natural numbers* */
    Atomset *init* := {$\alpha \mid \alpha$ is an initial atom of $\mathcal{M}$ and φ};
    for all $\alpha \in$ *init* **do** depth_first_search(α);
    print("φ is not satisfiable in $\mathcal{M}$");

procedure depth_first_search (Atom α) =
    if (table [α] = UNDEFINED) **then**   /* α *is a new atom* */
        Nat *dfnumber* := *depth_first_count*;   /* *save current count* */
        depth_first_count := *depth_first_count*+1;
        table[α] := *dfnumber*;   /* *initialize with current depth* */
        push(*stack*, α);
        Atomset *succ* := children(α);
        for all ($\beta \in$ *succ*) **do**
            depth_first_search(β);
            table[α] := min(*table*[α], *table*[β]);   /* β *above* α? */
        if (*table*[α] = *dfnumber*) **then**   /* α *is the root of an SCC* */
        Formulaset *required* := {}, *fulfilled* := {};
        repeat
            β := pop(*stack*);
            table[β] := MAXNAT;
            required := *required* $\cup$ {$\psi_1 \mid (\psi_2 \, \mathbf{U}^+ \psi_1) \in \beta$};
            fulfilled := *fulfilled* $\cup$ {$\psi \mid \psi \in \beta$}
        until ($\alpha = \beta$);   /* *all elements of SCC are popped* */
        if *required* $\subseteq$ *fulfilled*   /* *SCC is self-fulfilling* */
        then print("φ satisfiable in $\mathcal{M}$"); **exit**;

function children (Atom (w, m)) : Atomset =
    if {$(\psi_2 \, \mathbf{U}^+ \psi_1) \in m$} = {} **then return** {}   /**no future obligations**/
    else return {$(w', m') \mid w \prec w'$,
            $(\psi_2 \, \mathbf{U}^+ \psi_1) \in m$ iff $\psi_1 \in m'$ or $\psi_2 \in m'$ and $(\psi_2 \, \mathbf{U}^+ \psi_2) \in m'$}

Figure 19: Depth–first–search **LTL** model checking algorithm

contains the union of all eventualities which are fulfilled in the atoms of this SCC. The SCC is self-fulfilling if *required*$\subseteq$*fulfilled*.

The main program calls depth_first_search for all initial atoms, where for an initial atom (w_0, m_0)

1. w_0 is the current point of $\mathcal{M}$, and
2. $m_0 \subseteq SF(\varphi)$ is any propositionally consistent set such that $\varphi \in m_0$.

If during the construction of the atom graph a maximal self-fulfilling SCC is found, the algorithm reports success; if the whole graph is searched without success we know that the formula is not satisfiable, and the program terminates with this result.

This algorithm is exponential in the number of $\mathbf{U}^+$-formulas, because every set of such sub-formulas determines a propositionally consistent set. It is linear in the size of the Kripke-model. In general, it can be shown that the problem of **LTL**-model checking (including past-operators) is PSPACE-complete in the size of the formula and NLOGSPACE in the size of the model (see [Sistla and Clarke 1986, Lichtenstein and Pnueli 1985]). The exponential complexity in the length of the formula usually is not very problematic, because specification formulas tend to be rather short. The linear complexity in the size of the model is a more serious limiting factor, since in the worst case (i.e., if the formula is unsatisfiable) all atoms have to be traversed. Current technology limits the applicability of such algorithms to models with approximately $10^5 - 10^6$ reachable atoms. In Section 11 we will discuss approaches which try to overcome this limit.

8.3. Model Checking for Propositional μ-Calculus

Both the local and the global model checking algorithms can be easily adapted to μ**TL**. Global model checking for **CTL** unfolds the fixpoint definition of the $\mathbf{A}\,\mathbf{U}^+$ and $\mathbf{E}\,\mathbf{U}^+$ operators. If we restrict our attention to *continuous* μ**TL**-formulas (see below), then this idea can be used to obtain a global model checking algorithm for these formulas. Moreover, as we will discuss in Section 10, this algorithm can be efficiently implemented using BDDs (see [Burch, Clarke, McMillan, Dill and Hwang 1992]).

According to the Knaster-Tarski theorem proved in Section 3.2,

$$(U, \mathcal{I}, w) \models \nu q\, \varphi \text{ iff } w \in \bigcup \{Q \mid Q \subseteq \varphi^{\mathcal{F}}\{q := Q\}\}$$

$$(U, \mathcal{I}, w) \models \mu q\, \varphi \text{ iff } w \in \bigcap \{Q \mid \varphi^{\mathcal{F}}\{q := Q\} \subseteq Q\}$$

A function $f : 2^U \to 2^U$ is called *union-continuous*, if $f(\bigcup_{i \in I} \{x_i\}) = \bigcup_{i \in I} f(x_i)$ for any index set I. If the functional defined by φ is union-continuous, then the fixpoints can be obtained as

$$\nu q\, \varphi = lim_{i \to \omega} \varphi^i(\top)$$

$$\mu q\, \varphi = lim_{i \to \omega} \varphi^i(\bot)$$

If U is finite, then every monotonic function is union-continuous. Moreover, according to Lemma 5.4, on finite models it is sufficient to consider the limit up to the cardinality of the universe:

$$\nu q\, \varphi = lim_{i \leq |U|} \varphi^i(\top)$$

$$\mu q\, \varphi = lim_{i \leq |U|} \varphi^i(\bot)$$

```
function eval (Formula φ): Pointset =
    case φ of
        p : return I(p); /* interpretation of proposition p */
        q : return v(q); /* valuation of proposition variable q */
        ⊥ : return {};
        (ψ₁ → ψ₂) : return U\ eval(ψ₁) ∪ eval(ψ₂);
        ⟨R⟩ ψ : return R⁻¹( eval(ψ));
        νq(ψ) : H := U;
            repeat until stabilization
                H := eval(ψ{q := H});
            return H;
        μq(ψ) : H := {};
            repeat until stabilization
                H := eval(ψ{q := H});
            return H;
```

Figure 20: naïve global branching time μ**TL** model checking algorithm

Consequently, for finite domains model checking of positive μ**TL** can be performed by extending the naïve global algorithm. The result is depicted in Figure 20.

Since every **repeat** in this algorithm can iterate up to $|U|$ times, the complexity is of order $|\varphi| \cdot |U|^{qd(\varphi)}$, where $qd(\varphi)$ is the depth of nesting of fixpoint operators in φ. This high complexity is due to the fact that the computation of any inner fixed point formula has to be restarted from scratch for every new iteration of an enclosing fixed point operator. For example, consider the **CTL**-formula $\mathbf{E}\,\mathbf{F}^*(p_1 \wedge \mathbf{E}\,\mathbf{F}^*\,p_2)$.

$$\mu\mathbf{TL}(\mathbf{E}\,\mathbf{F}^*(p_1 \wedge \mathbf{E}\,\mathbf{F}^*\,p_2)) = \mu q_1(\mathbf{X}\,q_1 \vee (p_1 \wedge \mu q_2(\mathbf{X}\,q_2 \vee p_2))).$$

This formula is *alternation-free*: in the inner fixed point formula $\mu q_2(\mathbf{X}\,q_2 \vee p_2)$ there is no occurrence of q_1. Therefore, in the evaluation of μq_1, this formula has a constant value. For such formulas, model checking can be done with linear time complexity [Emerson et al. 1993, Cleaveland and Steffen 1993]. In contrast, consider the μ**TL** formula

$$\mu q_1(p_1 \wedge \mu q_2(\mathbf{X}\,q_1 \vee \mathbf{X}\,q_2 \vee p_2)).$$

Here the inner formula $\mu q_2(\mathbf{X}\,q_1 \vee \mathbf{X}\,q_2 \vee p_2)$ is re-evaluated for every new iteration of q_1. That is, if $\psi(q_1, q_2) \triangleq (\mathbf{X}\,q_1 \vee \mathbf{X}\,q_2 \vee p_2)^{\mathcal{F}}$ and $\varphi(q_1) \triangleq (p_1 \wedge \mu q_2\psi(q_1, q_2))^{\mathcal{F}}$, we calculate $\mu q_1\varphi(q_1)$ by iterating

$$\varphi^0 \triangleq \bot,$$
$$\psi^{0,0} \triangleq \bot$$
$$\psi^{0,1} \triangleq \psi(\varphi^0, \psi^{0,0}) = (\mathbf{X}\bot \vee \mathbf{X}\bot \vee p_2),$$
$$\psi^{0,2} \triangleq \psi(\varphi^0, \psi^{0,1}) = (\mathbf{X}\bot \vee \mathbf{X}\,(\,\mathbf{X}\bot \vee p_2)\vee p_2),$$

$$\psi^{0,3} \triangleq \psi(\varphi^0, \psi^{0,2}) = (\mathbf{X} \perp \vee \mathbf{X} (\mathbf{X} \perp \vee \mathbf{X}(\mathbf{X} \perp \vee p_2) \vee p_2) \vee p_2),$$

...

$$\psi^{0,n+1} \triangleq \psi(\varphi^0, \psi^{0,n}) = \mu q_2 (\mathbf{X} \perp \vee \mathbf{X} \, q_2 \vee p_2), \text{ if } \psi^{0,n+1} = \psi^{0,n},$$
$$\varphi^1 \triangleq \varphi(\varphi^0) = (p_1 \wedge \mu q_2 (\mathbf{X} \perp \vee \mathbf{X} \, q_2 \vee p_2)) = (p_1 \wedge \psi^{0,n}),$$
$$\psi^{1,0} \triangleq \perp$$
$$\psi^{1,1} \triangleq \psi(\varphi^1, \psi^{1,0}) = (\mathbf{X} \, (p_1 \wedge \mu q_2 (\mathbf{X} \perp \vee \mathbf{X} \, q_2 \vee p_2)) \vee \mathbf{X} \perp \vee p_2),$$
$$\psi^{1,2} \triangleq \psi(\varphi^1, \psi^{1,1}) = (\mathbf{X} \, \varphi^1 \vee \mathbf{X} \, \psi^{1,1} \vee p_2),$$

...

and so on. A more sophisticated algorithm was given in [Emerson and Lei 1986]. Each sequence $\nu q_1 ... \nu q_n$ or $\mu q_1 ... \mu q_n$ of nested fixpoints of the same type can be calculated by a single loop. Since ψ is monotonic, and $\varphi^0 \subseteq \varphi^1$, we have $\psi^{0,n} \subseteq \psi^{1,n}$. To compute a least fixed point, it is sufficient to start with any value below the result. Therefore, $\psi^{1,0}$ can be initialized with $\psi^{0,n}$ instead of $\perp$. Generally, when restarting the computation of an inner fixed point of the same type, we can use the last approximation result as a starting value. Thus, the value of this inner fixed point can increase at most $|U|$ times. The overall complexity of this improved algorithm is $(|\varphi| \cdot |U|)^{ad(\varphi)}$, where $ad(\varphi)$ is the alternation depth of different fixpoint operators in φ.

In [Long, Browne, Clarke, Jha and Marrero 1994] the authors observe that by storing even more intermediate values, the time complexity for evaluating fixpoint formulas can be reduced to $O(|U|^{\lfloor ad/2 \rfloor + 1})$. It can be shown that the complexity of model checking μ**TL** is in NP $\cap$ co-NP; however, no lower bound is known to date. For more information, see [Berezin, Clarke, Jha and Marrero 1996].

For the local version, there have been a number of algorithms proposed in the literature [Winskel 1991, Cleaveland 1990, Bradfield and Stirling 1991, Stirling 1991]. We give a sketch of the tableau method from [Stirling and Walker 1991], which illustrates the basic ideas. The algorithm explores only a (small) part of the model by depth-first search. Each node in the tableau is marked by a sequence $\Delta, w \models \psi$, where $w \in U$ is a point in the model, ψ is a sub-formula of the given formula and Δ is a *definition list*. This is a sequence of declarations $(q_1 = \psi_1, ..., q_n = \psi_n)$, where the proposition variables q_i are pairwise disjoint and ψ_i uses at most variables from $q_1, ..., q_{i-1}$. For simplicity, we use $\vee$, $\wedge$, $\langle R \rangle$, $[R]$, μ and ν as basic operators and assume that negations only occur in literals. Furthermore, we assume that in the formula to be checked each μ and ν quantification binds a different proposition variable.

Since in [Stirling and Walker 1991] the μ-calculus is interpreted on branching structures, the tableau rules given in Figure 21 are nondeterministic. Any node marked $\Delta, w \models (\psi_1 \wedge \psi_2)$ has two children, where one is marked $\Delta, w \models \psi_1$ and the other $\Delta, w \models \psi_2$. For a node marked $\Delta, w \models (\psi_1 \vee \psi_2)$ there is only one child node which is either marked $\Delta, w \models \psi_1$ or $\Delta, w \models \psi_2$. Thus, for a given point w and formula φ, there are several nonequivalent completed tableaus; $w \models \varphi$ iff *some of* these tableaus is successful. A tableau is successful, if *each* leaf is successful. To turn the tableau method into a concrete model checking algorithm, we have to perform a depth-first search through all possible tableaus.

$$(\vee_i) \; \frac{\Delta, w \models (\psi_1 \vee \psi_2)}{\Delta, w \models \psi_i} \; (i \in \{1, 2\}) \qquad (\wedge) \; \frac{\Delta, w \models (\psi_1 \wedge \psi_2)}{\Delta, w \models \psi_1 \qquad \Delta, w \models \psi_2}$$

$$(\langle R \rangle) \; \frac{\Delta, w \models \langle R \rangle \, \psi}{\Delta, w' \models \psi} \qquad ([R]) \; \frac{\Delta, w \models [R] \, \psi}{\Delta, w_1 \models \psi \quad \cdots \quad \Delta, w_n \models \psi}$$

$$(\mu) \; \frac{\Delta, w \models \mu q \psi}{\Delta', w \models \psi} \qquad (\nu) \; \frac{\Delta, w \models \nu q \psi}{\Delta', w \models \psi}$$

$$(\text{PVar}) \; \frac{\Delta, w \models q}{\Delta, w \models \psi}$$

Figure 21: Tableau rules for branching time μ**TL**

The additional regulations for the tableau rules in Figure 21 are:
- Rule ($\langle R \rangle$) can only be applied if $w' \in R(w)$.
- In rule ($[R]$), it must hold that $R(w) = \{w_1, ..., w_n\}$.
- In rule (μ) and (ν), $\Delta' \triangleq \Delta \cup \{q = \psi\}$.
- Rule (PVar) can only be applied if $(q = \psi) \in \Delta$, and there is no ancestor node which is labelled $\Delta', w \models \psi$ (with the same w and ψ).

Intuitively, to check whether $\mu q \psi$ holds in point w, we record that q must be interpreted as a fixpoint of $\psi(q)$, and check whether ψ holds in w. Whenever we hit upon the proposition variable q in the further decomposition of $\psi(q)$, we can unfold this occurrence to ψ. However, to guarantee that the unfolding terminates, each proposition variable may be unfolded at most once in every branch of the tableau and every point of the model. Thus, for finite models each tableau is finite.

A tableau is maximal, if there is no leaf for which any rule is applicable. In a maximal tableau, a leaf $\Delta, w \models \psi$ is called *successful*, if
- $\psi = \mathrm{p} \in \mathcal{P}$ and $w \in \mathcal{I}(\mathrm{p})$, or $\psi = \neg \mathrm{p}$ and $w \notin \mathcal{I}(\mathrm{p})$,
- $\psi = q \in \mathcal{Q}$, $q \notin \Delta$, $w \in \mathbf{v}(q)$, or $\psi = \neg q$, $q \notin \Delta$, $w \notin \mathbf{v}(q)$, or
- $\psi = [R] \psi'$ and $R(w) = \{\}$ (Rule ($[R]$) produces no children),
- $\psi = q \in \mathcal{Q}$ and q was included in Δ by rule (ν).

In other words, a maximal tableau is not successful if it contains some unsuccessful leaf $\Delta, w \models \psi$ which satisfies
- $\psi = \mathrm{p} \in \mathcal{P}$ and $w \notin \mathcal{I}(\mathrm{p})$, or $\psi = \neg \mathrm{p}$ and $w \in \mathcal{I}(\mathrm{p})$,
- $\psi = q \in \mathcal{Q}$, $q \notin \Delta$, $w \notin \mathbf{v}(q)$, or $\psi = \neg q$, $q \notin \Delta$, $w \in \mathbf{v}(q)$, or
- $\psi = \langle R \rangle \psi'$ and $R(w) = \{\}$ (Rule ($\langle R \rangle$) not applicable),
- $\psi = q \in \mathcal{Q}$ and q was included in Δ by rule (μ).

With these definitions, soundness and completeness of the tableau decision method is stated in the following theorem, a proof of which can be found in [Stirling and Walker 1991].

8.1. THEOREM. $w \in \varphi^{\mathcal{F}}$ *iff there exists a successful tableau with root* $\{\}, w \models \varphi$.

More efficient local model checking algorithms for fragments of μ**TL** can be found in [Cleaveland and Steffen 1993, Bhat and Cleaveland 1996].

A somewhat different approach for model checking of μ-calculus was suggested in [Mader 1992]. It is based on *Gauss-elimination*: proving a formula in this approach is similar to solving a system of linear inequalities.

9. Modelling of Reactive Systems

Up to now, we assumed that a system is given as a single Kripke-model. However, real-life systems usually are composed of a number of smaller subcomponents. Even if the target system is a single sequential machine, it is often advantageous to model it as a set of processes running in parallel:

- usually the *functionality* suggests a certain decomposition into modules; sequentialization is not the primary issue in the design;
- certain subcomponents (e.g. hardware components) actually are independent of the rest of the system and, therefore, conceptually parallel,
- the *environment* can be seen as a process running in parallel to the system;
- software-reusability and object-oriented design require modularity.

9.1. Parallel Programming Paradigms

Hence, we have to consider systems of *parallel processes*, that is, processes which are executed during the same time period, and the synchronization between these processes. We distinguish between two main paradigms of parallel systems: *distributed* systems, where the subcomponents are seen as spatially apart from each other, and *concurrent* systems, where the subcomponents use common resources such as processor time or memory cells.

Message Passing vs. Shared Variables
Consequently, there are two main paradigms for synchronization between parallel processes: via *message passing* (for distributed systems), and via *shared variables* (for concurrent systems).

Of course, there is no clear distinction between distributed and concurrent programs. It is not possible to formalize the concept of being spatially apart, since this is dependent on one's own point of view: from the United States, all computers in a local area network in Europe can be regarded as a single system. From the processor's viewpoint, a hard disk controller can be regarded as a remote subsystem.

On the other side, every component of a distributed system shares *some* resource with *some* other component; if it were totally unrelated it would not make sense to regard it as being part of one system.

Consequently, from a certain point of view, passing a message between process A and B can be seen as process A writing into a shared variable which is read by B. On the other side, writing a shared variable can be seen as sending to all other processes which might use this variable the message that its value has changed. In fact, this transition from the message passing paradigm to an implementation via shared variables occurs in every network controller; and the transition from the shared variables paradigm to an implementation via message passing occurs in every distributed cache.

However, different paradigms produce different techniques; many parallel programming languages and many verification systems support only one of these two paradigms.

Synchronous vs. Asynchronous Systems

Another issue is the modelling of a process execution in time. In *discrete* processes a computation consists of a sequence of steps, whereas in *continuous* systems the value of state parameters changes gradually as time passes. *Hybrid systems* combine discrete and continuous components. Usually, the model of time which is used in verification is determined by the type of system under consideration.

For parallel systems of discrete processes, there are various ways to model their execution. *Synchronous* processing is characterized by the fact that in each step, every parallel component advances. For example, a circuit in which each gate switches at the pulse of a global clock can be seen as a synchronous system. In contrast, in an *asynchronous* execution in each step an arbitrary (nonempty) subset of all components proceeds. For example, a set of agents working independently and synchronizing via mailboxes is a typical asynchronous system. With synchronous processing, the transition relation of the system is the conjunction of the transition relations of the components, with asynchronous processing it is the disjunction.

If each process can perform an "idle" step at any time ("*stutter*"), then synchronous and asynchronous processing coincides. Both synchronous and asynchronous executions can be implemented by *interleaving*, where in each step at most one process is active. A typical example is a set of threads in a time-sharing operating system on a mono-processor machine. With interleaving execution, usually some fairness constraints are imposed on the scheduling to ensure that all processes can progress.

Related to the execution mode is the mode of interaction between parallel components. With *synchronous communication*, each component wishing to interact is blocked until all partners it requires are willing to participate in the communication. The information is then broadcast to all communication partners. With *asynchronous communication* each process decides whether it wants to wait at a certain point or not; usually some kind of buffering mechanism is used for messages which are not needed immediately.

Synchronous communication can be seen as a special case of asynchronous communication where the length of each buffer queue is limited to one, and each process decides to wait after writing into or before reading from that queue until the queue is empty or full again, respectively.

Vice versa, a buffer can be seen as a separate process in a synchronous system which is always willing to communicate with other processes. If the size of the buffer is unbounded, the system is not finite state. Even if their size is bounded, the buffers can be the biggest part of the modelling of an asynchronously communicating system.

9.2. Some Concrete Formalisms for Finite State Systems

Recall that a (labelled) *transition system* is a tuple (Σ, S, Δ, S_0), where
- Σ is a nonempty finite *alphabet*,
- S is a nonempty finite set of *states*,
- $\Delta \subseteq S \times \Sigma \times S$ is the *transition relation*, and
- $S_0 \subseteq S$ is the set of *initial states*.

A *parallel transition system* is a tuple $T = (T_1, ..., T_n)$ of transition systems, such that $S_i \cap S_j = \{\}$, for $i < j$. The *global* transition system T *associated with a* parallel transition system $(T_1, ..., T_n)$ is defined by $T = (\Sigma, S, \Delta, S_0)$, where
- $\Sigma = \bigcup \Sigma_i$
- $S = S_1 \times \cdots \times S_n$
- $S_0 = S_{10} \times \cdots \times S_{n0}$, and
- $((s_1, ..., s_n), a, (s'_1, ..., s'_n)) \in \Delta$ iff for all T_i
  — if $a \in \Sigma_i$, then $(s_i, a, s'_i) \in \Delta_i$, and
  — if $a \notin \Sigma_i$, then $s_i = s'_i$

Thus, in a parallel transition system synchronization between components is by the common alphabet. The size of the state space of the global transition system is the product of the sizes of all parallel components.

An *elementary Petri net* is a tuple $N = (P, T, F, s_0)$, where
- P is a finite set of *places*,
- T is a finite set of *transitions* ($P \cap T = \{\}$),
- $F \subseteq (P \times T) \cup (T \times P)$ is the *flow relation*, and
- $m_0 \subseteq P$ is the *initial marking* of the net.

A *marking* m of the net is any subset of P. By $\bullet t \triangleq \{p \mid (p, t) \in F\}$ and $t\bullet \triangleq \{p \mid (t, p) \in F\}$ we denote the *preset* and the *postset* of transition t, respectively. A transition t is *enabled* at marking m if $\bullet t \subseteq m$ (all its input places are occupied at m) and $t\bullet \cap m \subseteq \bullet t$ (all its output places are empty at m, or they are also input places). Marking m' is the *result of firing* transition t from marking m, if t is enabled at m and $m' = (m \setminus \bullet t) \cup t\bullet$. In contrast to condition-event Petri nets [Reisig 1998], where each place can be occupied by an arbitrary number of tokens, elementary Petri nets inherently are finite-state.

For every elementary Petri net there is an associated transition system: the alphabet is the set of transitions, the state set is the set of markings, the initial state is the initial marking, and $(m, t, m') \in \Delta$ iff m' is the result of firing t from m. The number of states of this transition system is exponential in the number of places of the net. Alternatively, for any elementary Petri net we can obtain a parallel transition system of the same order of magnitude: for each place p in the net there is a transition system with two states p^1 and p^0, denoting the fact that p is occupied or empty, respectively. For each $t \in T$, we let $(p^1, t, p^0) \in \Delta$ iff $p \in \bullet t \setminus t \bullet$ and $(p^0, t, p^1) \in \Delta$ iff $p \in t \bullet \setminus \bullet t$. Furthermore, $(p^1, t, p^1) \in \Delta$ iff $p \in \bullet t \cap t \bullet$. The language of the global transition system associated with this parallel transition system is the set of firing sequences of the net. Vice versa, every parallel transition system can be formulated as an elementary Petri net of the same order of magnitude. The construction is straightforward.

A *shared variables program* is a tuple (V, D, T, s_0), where

- $V = (v_1, ..., v_n)$ is a set of *program variables*,

- $D = D_1 \times \cdots \times D_n)$ is the *state space*, where each $D_i = \{d_{i1}, ..., d_{im_i}\}$ is a finite *domain* for variable v_i,

- $T \subseteq D \times D$ is a *transition relation*, and

- $s_0 = (d_{11}, ..., d_{n1})$ is the *initial state*.

A *state* of a shared variables program is a tuple $(d_1, ..., d_n)$, where each $d_i \in D_i$. Thus the number of states in a shared variables program is the product of the size of all domains. The transition relation T can be defined by a propositional formula φ_T with the set of atomic proposition $\mathcal{P} = \{(x = y) \mid x, y \in (V \cup V' \cup \bigcup D_i)\}$, where $V' = \{v'_1, ..., v'_n\}$. If $s = (d_1, ..., d_n)$ and $s' = (d'_1, ..., d'_n)$, then $(s, s') \in T$ iff $\mathcal{I} \models \varphi_T$, where $\mathcal{I}(v_i) = d_i$ and $\mathcal{I}(v'_i) = d'_i$.

Using relational semantics, a shared variables program can be obtained for almost all other models for concurrency. Therefore, shared variable programs are widely used to model reactive systems.

9.3. Example Applications

A Combinatorial Game

As a first example, we describe the use of model checking in a combinatorial search. Although this example is not very typical for real applications, it can demonstrate the capabilities and limits of present technology. A well-known puzzle from 1870 by the American Sam Loyd consists of a $h \times v$ grid in which there are $(h \cdot v) - 1$ numbered tiles and one blank space. A move consists in moving any tile into the position of the blank. The goal is to achieve a certain predetermined order on the tiles.

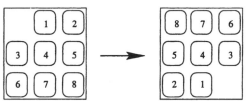

This puzzle can be described by a shared variables program as follows. For each tile there is a program variable which notes its horizontal and vertical position. Furthermore, there is a program variable **move** indicating whether the next move will be a shift up, down, left or right of the blank space. If the move would bring it out of the borders, nothing is changed; otherwise, its position is swapped with the respective adjacent tile.

```
MODULE main
DEFINE v := 3; h := 3;
VAR move: u,d,l,r;
    hpos: array 0..(h*v-1) of 1..h;
    vpos: array 0..(h*v-1) of 1..v;
ASSIGN
next(hpos[0]) := case
  (move=l) & !(hpos[0]=1) : hpos[0] - 1;
  (move=r) & !(hpos[0]=h) : hpos[0] + 1;
  1: hpos[0]; esac;
next(vpos[0]) := case
  (move=u) & !(vpos[0]=1) : vpos[0] - 1;
  (move=d) & !(vpos[0]=v) : vpos[0] + 1;
  1: vpos[0]; esac;
for all i:
next(hpos[i]) := case
  (move=l) & !(hpos[0]=1) & vpos[i]=vpos[0] & hpos[i]=hpos[0]+1 |
  (move=r) & !(hpos[0]=h) & vpos[i]=vpos[0] & hpos[i]=hpos[0]-1 : hpos[0];
  1: hpos[i]; esac;
next(vpos[i]) := case
  (move=u) & !(vpos[0]=1) & hpos[i]=hpos[0] & vpos[i]=vpos[0]-1 |
  (move=d) & !(vpos[0]=v) & hpos[i]=hpos[0] & vpos[i]=vpos[0]+1 : vpos[0];
  1: vpos[i]; esac;
init(vpos[i]) := i div h + 1; init(hpos[i]) := i mod h + 1;
DEFINE goal := /\_i(vpos[i] = v - (i div h) & hpos[i] = h - (i mod h))
SPEC !EF goal
```

Figure 22: SMV Code for Loyds Puzzle

The SMV code corresponding to this description[6] is shown in Figure 22. For $h = 3$ and $v = 3$, the internal representation of the transition relation takes about 3KB. There are $4 \cdot (h \cdot v)! = 1.4 \cdot 10^6$ states, of which 50% are reachable from any

---

[6]In the actual SMV code, variable array bounds or indices, e.g., vpos[i], are not allowed and have to be replaced by the respective constant values vpos[1],vpos[2],...

initial state. The specification claims that a certain final state is *not* reachable; the model checker contradicts this claim by showing a sequence of moves (rrddlluur-rddlluurrddlluurrdd) which gives a solution to the puzzle. The solution is found within a couple of minutes on a 32 MB Pentium 133.

For $h = 4$, $v = 3$, there are approximately 10^9 reachable states. Although the symbolic model checker detects rather quickly that some solution must exist, for the construction of a concrete solution sequence the state space has to be partitioned into strongly connected components. This requires several days of CPU time and approximately 1GB RAM on a Sparc Ultra. For model checking applications, virtual memory is not very useful; if the representation of the reachable state space exceeds the available main memory, then constant swapping occurs. To find a solution for $h = 4$, $v = 4$ by exhaustive state space exploration seems to be beyond the limits of present technology. In [Edelkamp and Reffel 1998], a combination of model checking and heuristic search is used to automatically construct solutions to this and other combinatorial games.

A Sequential Circuit

Our second example is from hardware verification. We consider a shift register for interfacing a parallel data bus. The register is from the 74x95 TTL family and is described in [Nowicki and Adam 1990]. It is used to exchange data between the bus and a serial device. It thus acts as parallel-serial converter and vice versa. A functional diagram of the register is given in Figure 23.

The register has a *mode control* input mc to choose between parallel or serial access mode. For each mode, there is a corresponding input clock (pc and sc). Parallel loading is performed if mc is high and a pc clock pulse arrives. In this case, data is read from the bus into the associated flip-flops. The data appears at the Q outputs at the pulse of the pc clock.

For serial loading, mode control should be low. Data is input serially with every tick of the sc clock. At each pulse the state of all flip-flops is transferred one stage to the right. After n cycles, the data is positioned at the parallel output and can be sent to the bus by an oc command. A right shift occurs if the serial input inp is held low. By a sequence of n right shifts, data which has been obtained in parallel from the bus can be written serially to the out port.

The register is implemented with SR-bistables which have the following characteristic function. If both inputs are low, the bistable keeps its state. The output Q

S	R	Q'
0	0	Q
1	0	1
0	1	0
1	1	-

is set if input S is high, and reset if input R is high. If both S and R are high, then Q

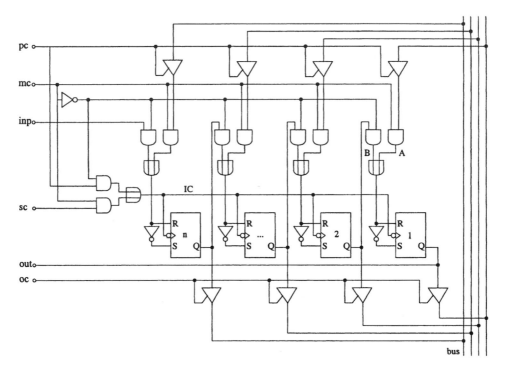

Figure 23: A shift register for data bus interfacing

is undefined. This can be modelled by a nondeterministic internal choice between high and low output. The latch is triggered by a negative edge of the clock pulse. That is, a change of output occurs only at the time instant when the clock line goes from high to low. If the value of the clock line is part of the state space, then the clock value would be low in every new state. For an accurate state-based model (e.g., of an asynchronous circuit), we would have to include timing information of all gates. However, if the clock is only used as trigger, an event based modelling is more adequate: the high-to-low change of the clock line is considered as an event occurrence. In each state, this event may or may not occur. To prevent executions in which the input or output clocks are indefinitely blocked, we require infinitely many input and output clock ticks in every infinite run.

The model is just a representation of the circuit's truth table, where the outputs are a boolean function of inputs and latch states. It can be derived automatically from any standard hardware description language; in fact, several model checkers support such front-end translations. Correctness of parallel and sequential input is expressed by the following formulas, where n is the width of the data bus:

$$\mathbf{A}\,\mathbf{G}^*(\mathrm{mc} \wedge \mathrm{pc} \to \bigvee_{i=1}^{n} (\mathrm{bus}\,[\mathtt{i}] \leftrightarrow \mathbf{A}((\mathrm{oc} \to \mathbf{A}\,\mathbf{X}\,\mathrm{bus}\,[\mathtt{i}])\,\mathbf{U}^+ \,\mathrm{ic})))$$

```
MODULE main
VAR Q, bus: array 1..n of boolean;   -- n SR-latches, n databits
    inp, mc, pc, sc, oc: boolean;    -- input lines
DEFINE out := Q[1]; ic := ((mc & pc) | (!mc & sc));
       A[i] := mc & pc & bus[i]; B[i] := !mc & Q[i+1];
       R[i] := !(A[i] | B[i]); S[i] := !R[i];
ASSIGN next(Q[i]) := case ic: case
                              !S[i] & !R[i]: Q[i];          --hold
                               S[i] & !R[i]: 1;             --set
                              !S[i] &  R[i]: 0;             --reset
                               S[i] &  R[i]: {0,1}; esac; --undef
                     !ic: Q[i]; esac; -- unchanged if no input
       next(bus[i]) := case oc: Q[i];  !oc: {0, 1}; esac;
FAIRNESS ic FAIRNESS oc
```

Figure 24: Model of shift register

$$\mathbf{A\,G^{*}}(\neg mc \wedge sc \rightarrow \bigvee_{i=2}^{n} (Q[i] \leftrightarrow \mathbf{A}(Q[i-1]\,\mathbf{U^{+}}\,ic)))$$

Intuitively, these formulas assure that data which is input into the register remains there until a new input occurs. If the mode control is set to parallel and there is a tick of the parallel clock, then the data which is currently on bus i will be delivered at each tick of the output clock, until a new input occurs. If the mode control is set to serial, and there is a tick of the serial clock, then the latches will remain stable until the next input.

The SMV model checker can verify these formulas for a bus width of 32 bit in less than a second. Similar formulas can be used to verify that after a sequence of n sequential load operations, the correct data word will be put onto the bus on a subsequent output pulse.

If the connection structure of wires within the circuit is "well-behaved", then automatic verification is successful even on much bigger circuits. A circuit is "well-behaved" if there exists an ordering of all wires such that the value of a wire only depends on the value of wires which are close in the ordering. For a formal definition of this condition see [McMillan 1993]. A large number of circuits with hundreds of storage places have been verified automatically in this way.

A Communication Protocol

The third example is a set of communicating processes within the operating system of a Siemens cellular phone. In this system, there are a number of basic processes communicating with one another by priority messages. Each of the processes implements a finite state machine, which is described by a set of SDL diagrams. Basically, a process waits in a certain state until it receives a message from some other process. It then performs some specified operations, sends a number of messages to other messages, and transitions to another state. Figure 25 shows part of the transition graph of a process and the corresponding SDL diagram. The displayed part is used to implement the following quote from the GSM international standard.

> "Initially the mobile station looks for a cell which satisfies the suitability constraints by checking cells in descending order of received signal strength. If a suitable cell is found, the mobile station camps on it and performs any registration necessary."

A property to be verified is that the system never deadlocks:

$$\mathbf{A\,G^*\,E\,F^*}\,\mathtt{init}$$

That is, no sequence of user actions can bring the phone into a state from where it cannot be reset. Since the number of merchandised units is expected to be very high, correctness is an important design issue. In this particular example, a number of potential problems in the design could be identified by model checking before the actual implementation took place [Schlingloff 1997].

In the model to be checked, there are five basic processes, plus the operating system kernel. There are approximately 50 different types of messages which can be sent by the processes, and each process has between 10 and 20 states. The operating system is responsible for the scheduling of processes according to a priority scheme, and for the storage and delivery of messages. Therefore, it has to maintain a buffer, in which for each process all messages are kept. The size of these buffers turns out to be the most important parameter in the verification. Basically, each buffer slot could be filled with every message; thus a combinatorial explosion similar to the one in our first example can occur. However, a buffer overflow almost certainly indicates an error in the implementation; for example, if some high-priority process keeps resending the same message, it will eventually fill up any bounded buffer. In the modelled system, a total number of 15-20 buffer slots was sufficient; a fairness assumption is used to select only those computations in which no buffer overflow occurs. Moreover, the buffer contents usually follows a regular pattern, therefore the above mentioned state explosion is avoided. In practical applications, an exponential growth in the number of reachable states almost certainly indicates an error. For buffers in which all messages have the same priority, the transition relation of a bounded buffer can be defined by the transition table in Figure 26.

In the right half of this table, an empty entry means that the respective program variable is set by the environment. An input value of nil in i indicates that there is no message to be sent; in this case the next value of i is determined by the sender. If this process has put a non-nil value x into i, then this value is appended to the buffer, and i is reset to nil. The last line indicates a buffer overflow: if a message is to be sent with the message buffer already filled, i remains stable. Thus, the formula $\mathbf{A\,G^*}(i \neq nil \rightarrow \mathbf{X}(i = nil))$ can be used to determine whether a buffer overflow can occur. If the output variable o is nil and there is a message to deliver, it is copied into o. When the operating system delivers a message y from o, it resets o to nil.

The content of the buffer b is given as a sequence $\langle x_1, ..., x_\nu \rangle$ of messages, where $\langle \rangle$ denotes the empty buffer. There are various possibilities to model such sequences. In Figure 27 we show a modelling which uses n program variables $b_1, ..., b_n$, such

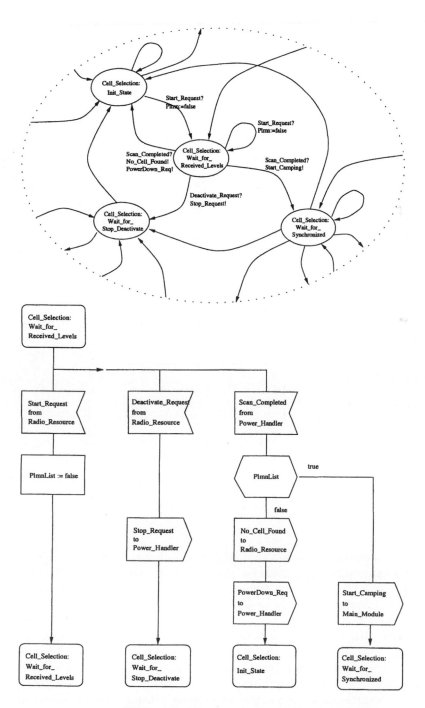

Figure 25: Transition graph and SDL diagram

i	b	o		i'	b'	o'
nil	$\langle\rangle$	nil			$\langle\rangle$	nil
x	$\langle\rangle$	nil		nil	$\langle\rangle$	x
nil	$\langle x_1, ..., x_\nu \rangle$	nil			$\langle x_1, ..., x_{\nu-1} \rangle$	x_ν
x	$\langle x_1, ..., x_\nu \rangle$	nil		nil	$\langle x, x_1, ..., x_{\nu-1} \rangle$	x_ν
nil	$\langle\rangle$	y			$\langle\rangle$	
x	$\langle\rangle$	y		nil	$\langle x \rangle$	
nil	$\langle x_1, ..., x_\nu \rangle$	y			$\langle x_1, ..., x_\nu \rangle$	
x	$\langle x_1, ..., x_\nu \rangle$	y	$(\nu < n)$	nil	$\langle x, x_1, ..., x_\nu \rangle$	
x	$\langle x_1, ..., x_n \rangle$	y		x	$\langle x_1, ..., x_n \rangle$	

Figure 26: Transition relation of a bounded buffer

that b_1 contains the front element of the message queue, and incoming messages are appended into the smallest b_ν which is empty (contains nil as value).

```
next(b[j]) := case
   (i=nil) & !(o=nil) : b[j];
   (i=nil) &  (o=nil) : b[j+1];
  !(i=nil) & !(o=nil) : if !(b[j-1]=nil) & b[j]=nil then i
                        else b[j] fi;
  !(i=nil) &  (o=nil) : if b[j]=nil then nil
                        else if b[j+1]=nil then i
                        else b[j+1] fi fi;          esac;
```

Figure 27: Model of bounded buffer

In this modelling, we rely on the fact that whenever $b_j = nil$, then for all $k \geq j$, also $b_k = nil$. This assumption only holds for the reachable states of a buffer which is initially empty; there are many transitions from illegal, i.e., non reachable states to other illegal states in this model. In an explicit representation of the transition relation, one should try to avoid these redundant entries. Below, we discuss symbolic representations with BDDs. With such a representation, even though the size of the transition relation is much bigger than the transition relation restricted to the reachable states, its representation is much smaller. Since the value of each buffer slot depends only on its immediate neighbors, in fact the size of the representation is linear in the (fixed) number and width of the buffer slots. For modelling unbounded queues, efficient data structures are discussed in [Boigelot and Godefroid 1996, Godefroid and Long 1996].

10. Symbolic Model Checking

Model checking methods derive a great deal of their success from the efficiency of the data structures that are used. A propositional formula can be regarded as a boolean function, mapping an interpretation of the propositions into {**true, false**}. Since very powerful techniques exist for manipulation of such functions, it makes sense to represent temporal and predicate logic formulas as well as frames in terms of boolean functions. The general idea is to *encode* each domain element by a boolean sequence. Predicates and relations are then represented by their characteristic functions. Temporal operators are interpreted algorithmically according to their fixpoint definitions.

For any shared variables program, we can obtain an equivalent shared variables program which uses only binary domains of the form $D = \{0, 1\}^n$. To do so, we use an arbitrary binary encoding of domain D_i and introduce for any program variable v_i over domain D_i new binary program variables $v_{i1}, ..., v_{ik}$, where $k = \lceil \log_2(|D_i|) \rceil$. This encoding is comparable to the implementation of arbitrary data types on digital computers, where each bit can take only two values.

If all program variables $V = \{v_1, ..., v_n\}$ of a shared variables program are over a binary domain, then any propositional formula φ over $\mathcal{P} = \{v_1, ..., v_n\}$ describes a set of states of the program, namely the set of all propositional models (interpretations) which validate the formula. Here we assume the substitution 0 for **false** and 1 for **true**. Vice versa, for any set of states there is a propositional formula describing this set. However, this formula is not uniquely determined; the problem of finding a shortest formula describing a given set of states is co-NP-hard.

The transition relation of a shared variables program with binary program variables $V = \{v_1, ..., v_n\}$ can be represented as an ordinary propositional formula over $\mathcal{P} = \{v_1, ..., v_n, v'_1, ..., v'_n\}$. If the transition relation is given as a propositional formula with equalities, we replace 0 by $\bot$, and 1 by $\top$, and $(v = v')$ by $(v \leftrightarrow v')$[7]. For example, the formula

$$v_1 = 0 \rightarrow ((v'_1 = 1) \wedge (v'_2 = v_2) \wedge (v'_3 \neq v_3))$$

in this notation becomes

$$\neg v_1 \rightarrow (v'_1 \wedge (v'_2 \leftrightarrow v_2) \wedge \neg(v'_3 \leftrightarrow v_3))$$

For a shared variables program with n program variables over binary domains the size of the state space is 2^n. Therefore e.g. the state space of a buffer of length 10 with values between 1 and 1000 is $2^{100} \simeq 10^{30}$. The *reachable* state space is a subset of this state space, which can be of the same order of magnitude. The transition relation for this buffer consists of pairs of states and therefore has a size of approximately 10^{60}.

To perform global model checking on systems of this or bigger size, we need an efficient representation of large sets.

---

[7] Recall that $\bot$ and $\top$ are propositional formulas, **false** and **true** are truth values and 0 and 1 are domain elements.

10.1. Binary Decision Diagrams

Clearly, a set could be represented by a table of boolean values. Containment of an element in such a set could then be calculated by selecting the appropriate element from the table. Another possible representation of a set is the explicit enumeration of its elements, e.g., as a list or array. However, these representations can be rather wasteful, since they pay no respect to the internal structure of the set. For example, given the domain $D = \{0, 1, ..., 15\}$, the explicit enumeration of the set "all numbers which are even or bigger than 11" is

$$S = \{0, 2, 4, 6, 8, 10, 12, 13, 14, 15\}$$

The bitstring representation is

$$S = (1010101010101111).$$

These representations take $O(|D| \cdot \lceil \log_2(|D|) \rceil)$ memory bits. Bitstrings provide extremely efficient (constant-time) access. In model checking applications, however, the space used by the data is usually more important than the execution time. So, it is desirable to have a concise data structure for representing large sets which still permits efficient access to the elements.

Given a binary encoding $\vec{v} = v_1 v_2 v_3 v_4$ of the domain D, the above explicit enumeration is

$$S = \{0000, 0010, 0100, 0110, 1000, 1010, 1100, 1101, 1110, 1111\}$$

This description corresponds to a propositional formula in disjunctive normal form. A much more succinct representation of the same set can be given by the formula

$$S = \{\vec{v} \mid v_4 = 0 \lor v_1 = 1 \land v_2 = 1\}$$

Usually it is hard to find a minimal propositional formula describing a given set of elements. Therefore attention is restricted to formulas in some normal form. A *binary decision diagram* (BDD, [Bryant 1986, Bryant 1992]) is such a canonical form for a propositional formula. BDDs often are substantially more compact than traditional normal forms such as conjunctive or disjunctive normal form, and they can be manipulated and evaluated very efficiently. Hence, they have become widely used for a variety of applications in computer-aided design applications. Many present tools in symbolic simulation and verification of combinational logic and sequential circuits use a BDD library for manipulating large sets. The size of the BDD depends more on the *structure* of the represented set than on its cardinality. For example, the BDD representation of the empty set and the full set are both of constant size one. Because of this dependence on the structure of the represented object, the description of a system with BDDs is sometimes called a *symbolic representation*, and techniques using BDDs to represent objects are called *symbolic techniques*. Subsequently, we describe symbolic model checking. For an alternative introduction to BDDs and BDD based algorithms in automated theorem proving, see [Moore 1994].

The use of BDDs in checking language containment for ω-automata is described in [Touati, Brayton and Kurshan 1991].

In model checking, binary decision diagrams are a preferred datatype for the representation of propositional formulas. They can be understood as an efficient implementation of binary decision trees. Usually, the BDD is much more succinct than the original decision tree. Efficiency is gained by sharing of subtrees and by elimination of unnecessary nodes.

Consider a three-place boolean connective Ite ("if-then-else"), such that

$$\mathsf{Ite}(\varphi, \psi_1, \psi_2) \triangleq ((\varphi \to \psi_1) \wedge (\neg\varphi \to \psi_2)).$$

Equivalently, $\mathsf{Ite}(\varphi, \psi_1, \psi_2) \leftrightarrow ((\varphi \wedge \psi_1) \vee (\neg\varphi \wedge \psi_2))$. Then $(\varphi \to \psi) \leftrightarrow \mathsf{Ite}(\varphi, \psi, \top)$, hence all boolean operators can be expressed with Ite, $\bot$ and $\top$. A formula ψ is said to be in *tree form*, if $\psi = \bot$, or $\psi = \top$, or $\psi = \mathsf{Ite}(v, \psi_1, \psi_2)$, where $v \in \mathcal{P}$ and ψ_1 and ψ_2 are in tree form. In other words, a formula ψ is in tree form, if it uses only Ite, $\bot$, $\top$, and propositions, and, additionally, for every subformula $\mathsf{Ite}(\varphi, \psi_1, \psi_2)$ of ψ, the formula φ is an (atomic) proposition, and ψ_1 and ψ_2 are not propositions. A tree form formula can be drawn as *binary decision tree*, where for each subformula $\mathsf{Ite}(v, \psi_1, \psi_2)$ there is a node labelled v which has ψ_2 and ψ_1 as left and right child nodes, respectively.

Assume a linear ordering $<$ on the set $\mathcal{P}$ of propositions. A tree form formula is said to be in *ordered tree form*, if for every subformula $\mathsf{Ite}(v_1, \varphi_1, \varphi_2)$ of φ, and every subformula $\mathsf{Ite}(v_2, \psi_1, \psi_2)$ of φ_1 or φ_2, it holds that $v_1 < v_2$. An ordered tree form formula is called *reduced*, if it does not contain any redundant subformula $\mathsf{Ite}(v, \psi, \psi)$ (with equal second and third argument). The sequence of leaves of the formula tree in a reduced ordered tree form formula is called the *logical spectrum* of the formula. For any given ordering, the reduced ordered tree form is a normal form. That is, for every propositional formula there is exactly one equivalent formula in reduced ordered tree form. This formula can be obtained by repeated application of the so-called *Shannon expansion*:

$$\varphi \leftrightarrow \mathsf{Ite}(v, \varphi\{v := \top\}, \varphi\{v := \bot\}),$$

and boolean reductions like $\mathsf{Ite}(v, \psi, \psi) \leftrightarrow \psi$ and $(\bot \to \top) \leftrightarrow \top$.

For example, truth table and tree form formula for the above set are given in Figure 28. The reader should also compare the tree form formula to the tree given on the following page.

The reduced ordered tree form formula for the ordering (v_1, v_2, v_3, v_4) of propositions is obtained by repeatedly replacing every redundant subformula $\mathsf{Ite}(v, \psi, \psi)$ in the above tree form formula by ψ:

$$S = \mathsf{Ite}(v_1, \mathsf{Ite}(v_2, \top, \mathsf{Ite}(v_4, \bot, \top)), \mathsf{Ite}(v_4, \bot, \top))$$

In a reduced ordered tree form formula, there might be several identical subformulas. In order to further reduce the length of the formula, we introduce names for subformulas. An *abbreviated* formula is a formula over the extended alphabet $\mathcal{P}_0 \triangleq \mathcal{P} \cup \{\delta_1, ..., \delta_n\}$, together with a (nonrecursive) list of *abbreviations*

v_1	v_2	v_3	v_4	S
1	1	1	1	1
1	1	1	0	1
1	1	0	1	1
1	1	0	0	1
1	0	1	1	0
1	0	1	0	1
1	0	0	1	0
1	0	0	0	1
0	1	1	1	0
0	1	1	0	1
0	1	0	1	0
0	1	0	0	1
0	0	1	1	0
0	0	1	0	1
0	0	0	1	0
0	0	0	0	1

$$S = \mathsf{Ite}(v_1,$$
$$\mathsf{Ite}(v_2,$$
$$\mathsf{Ite}(v_3,$$
$$\mathsf{Ite}(v_4, \top, \top),$$
$$\mathsf{Ite}(v_4, \top, \top)),$$
$$\mathsf{Ite}(v_3,$$
$$\mathsf{Ite}(v_4, \bot, \top),$$
$$\mathsf{Ite}(v_4, \bot, \top))),$$
$$\mathsf{Ite}(v_2,$$
$$\mathsf{Ite}(v_3,$$
$$\mathsf{Ite}(v_4, \bot, \top),$$
$$\mathsf{Ite}(v_4, \bot, \top)),$$
$$\mathsf{Ite}(v_3,$$
$$\mathsf{Ite}(v_4, \bot, \top),$$
$$\mathsf{Ite}(v_4, \bot, \top))))$$

Figure 28: Truth table and tree form formula

$(\delta_1 \triangleq \psi_1, \quad ..., \quad \delta_n \triangleq \psi_n)$. In each abbreviation, ψ_i is an abbreviated formula $\mathsf{Ite}(v, \varphi, \varphi')$ over the alphabet $\mathcal{P}_i \triangleq \mathcal{P} \cup \{\delta_{i+1}, ..., \delta_n\}$. The introduction of names for subformulas is comparable to the introduction of pointers in formula trees: an abbreviated formula can be drawn as a dag (directed acyclic graph), where each node represents a subformula or abbreviation. A formula is *maximally abbreviated*, if

1. no compound subformula $\mathsf{Ite}(v, \varphi_1, \varphi_2)$ appears twice, and
2. no two abbreviations have the same right hand side.

For the above example, a maximally abbreviated formula is

$$S = \mathsf{Ite}(v_1, \mathsf{Ite}(v_2, \top, \delta), \delta), \text{ where } \delta \triangleq \mathsf{Ite}(v_4, \bot, \top)$$

In an implementation an abbreviation can be a pointer or array index to the corresponding subformula. A maximally abbreviated formula is in *BDD form*, if for all subformulas $\mathsf{Ite}(v, \varphi, \psi)$, both φ and ψ are from $\{\bot, \top, \delta_1, ..., \delta_n\}$. In the example, this normal form can be obtained by introducing further definitions:

$$S = \mathsf{Ite}(v_1, \delta_1, \delta_2), \text{ where } \delta_1 \triangleq \mathsf{Ite}(v_2, \top, \delta_2) \text{ and } \delta_2 \triangleq \mathsf{Ite}(v_4, \bot, \top)$$

Actually, a BDD form formula is given by a list of abbreviations $(\delta_i \triangleq \mathsf{Ite}(v, \varphi_i, \psi_i))$ and an entry point to this list. It can be drawn as a *binary decision diagram*: for any $\delta \triangleq \mathsf{Ite}(v, \delta_1, \delta_2)$, draw a node labelled v with reference δ, which has the nodes referenced by δ_2 and δ_1 as left and right children, respectively. To illustrate these ideas with pictures, we give the binary decision tree for the above example S:

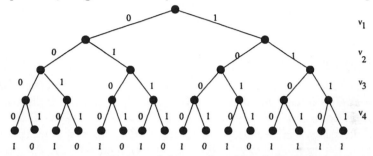

This tree is just a transcription of the truth table of S's characteristic function. It has many isomorphic subtrees. For any two isomorphic subtrees it is sufficient to maintain only one copy. We can replace the other one by a link to the corresponding subtree.

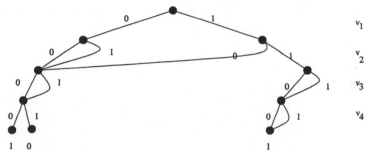

In the resulting structure, there are nodes for which both alternatives lead to the same subtree. These nodes represent redundant decisions and can be eliminated.

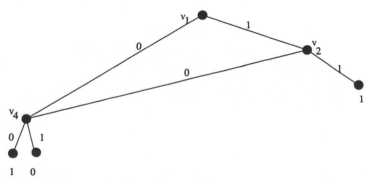

The resulting graph is the (ordered) binary decision diagram for this set with ordering (v_1, v_2, v_3, v_4). Given a variable ordering, there is a canonical BDD for every formula. It can be constructed using the Shannon expansion in a simple recursive descent:

$$\varphi(v_i...v_n) \leftrightarrow \mathsf{Ite}(v_i, \varphi\{v_i := \top\}(v_{i+1}...v_n), \varphi\{v_i := \bot\}(v_{i+1}...v_n))$$

This gives the unique binary decision tree for the chosen ordering. To obtain the BDD for $\varphi(v_i...v_n)$ we recursively calculate the BDD δ_1 for $\varphi\{v_i := \top\}(v_{i+1}...v_n)$ and δ_2 for $\varphi\{v_i := \bot\}(v_{i+1}...v_n)$. Upon backtrack, a new node $\delta \triangleq \mathsf{Ite}(v_i, \delta_1, \delta_2)$ is added to the BDD. However, we do *not* create a new node if both branches in the recursion are equal (return a common result), or if an equivalent node already exists in the BDD. To check this latter condition, we implement the set of BDD nodes $\delta \triangleq \mathsf{Ite}(v, \delta_1, \delta_2)$ as a hash table from (v, δ_1, δ_2) to δ.

Each entry in the hash-table is a quadruple $(\delta, v, \delta_1, \delta_2)$: pointers to BDD nodes are represented as integer numbers. A BDD is identified by its topmost node, and 0 is a pointer to $\bot$ and 1 is a pointer to $\top$. That is, the type "Bdd" is defined as "Int". Likewise, variable names are represented as integer numbers; for clarity we introduce the type "Bddvar" which is also defined as "Int". Thus, for each BDD node $(\delta, i, \delta_1, \delta_2)$ in the hash table, δ (of type "Bdd") is the number of the BDD node, i (of type "Bddvar") is the number of a BDD variable, and δ_1 and δ_2 (of type "Bdd") are links to other BDD nodes. For each (i, δ_1, δ_2) the hash table returns the pointer δ, if this node exists in the BDD.

The resulting algorithm is given in Figure 29. It takes as input a **PL** formula with $\mathcal{P} = \{v_1, ..., v_n\}$ and calculates the table of BDD nodes and a pointer to the topmost node for the variable ordering $(v_1, ..., v_n)$.

---

function PL2BDD (Formula φ) : (Nodeset, Bdd) =
   /* Calculates the BDD of φ
        as a set of nodes and a pointer to the topmost node */
   Nodeset *table* := {}; /* Table of BDD nodes $(\delta, i, \delta_1, \delta_2)$ */
   Bdd *max* := 1; /* Index of maximal table entry */
   Bdd *result* := BDD(φ,1); /* Index of topmost BDD node */
   return (*table*, *result*);

function BDD (Formula φ, Bddvar i) : Bdd =
   /* φ is the current subformula, i is the current BDD variable */
   /* Return value is a pointer to the maximal BDD node */
   if $i > n$ **then return** eval(φ) /* φ is a boolean constant */
   else δ_1 := BDD($\varphi\{v_i := \bot\}$, $i+1$); δ_2 := BDD($\varphi\{v_i := \top\}$, $i+1$);
      if $\delta_1 = \delta_2$ **then return** δ_1
      elsif $\exists \delta : (\delta, i, \delta_1, \delta_2) \in$ *table* **then return** δ
      else *max* := *max* + 1; *table* := *table* $\cup$ $\{(max, i, \delta_1, \delta_2)\}$; **return** *max*;

Figure 29: Transformation of propositional formulas into BDDs

In the BDD representation of sets, several operations can be performed very efficiently. Checking whether a given element w is contained in a set $W \subseteq U$ is done in time $O(\log |U|)$ by traversing the BDD of W according to the bitstring encoding $\vec{w}$

of w. Addition and deletion of elements as well as union and intersection of sets can be done by recursive descent. We now describe this procedure for the implication. Note that the Ite-operator commutes with other boolean connectives:

$$(\mathsf{Ite}(p, \varphi_1, \varphi_2) \to \psi) \quad \leftrightarrow \quad \mathsf{Ite}(p, (\varphi_1 \to \psi), (\varphi_2 \to \psi))$$
$$(\psi \to \mathsf{Ite}(q, \varphi_1, \varphi_2)) \quad \leftrightarrow \quad \mathsf{Ite}(q, (\psi \to \varphi_1), (\psi \to \varphi_2))$$

Similar equivalences hold for $\wedge$, $\vee$, etc. We prove only the first one of these equivalences. Recall that $\mathsf{Ite}(p, \varphi_1, \varphi_2)$ is defined by $\mathsf{Ite}(p, \varphi_1, \varphi_2) \leftrightarrow ((p \to \psi_1) \wedge (\neg p \to \psi_2))$.

$$
\begin{aligned}
(\mathsf{Ite}(p, \varphi_1, \varphi_2) \to \psi) \quad &\leftrightarrow \quad (((p \wedge \varphi_1) \vee (\neg p \wedge \varphi_2)) \to \psi) \\
&\leftrightarrow \quad (((\neg p \vee \neg \varphi_1) \wedge (p \vee \neg \varphi_2)) \vee \psi) \\
&\leftrightarrow \quad ((\neg p \vee \neg \varphi_1 \vee \psi) \wedge (p \vee \neg \varphi_2 \vee \psi)) \\
&\leftrightarrow \quad ((p \wedge (\varphi_1 \to \psi)) \vee (\neg p \wedge (\varphi_2 \to \psi))) \\
&\leftrightarrow \quad \mathsf{Ite}(p, (\varphi_1 \to \psi), (\varphi_2 \to \psi)) \qquad \square
\end{aligned}
$$

Given BDDs for φ and ψ, the BDD for $(\varphi \to \psi)$ can be constructed as follows. Since $BDD(\varphi)$ and $BDD(\psi)$ can be either 0, 1, or $\mathsf{Ite}(v, \delta_1, \delta_2)$, there are nine cases which have to be considered. If $BDD(\varphi)$ is 0 or $BDD(\psi)$ is 1, the resulting BDD is

```
function BDD_imp (Bdd φ, ψ) : Bdd =
    /* Calculates the BDD of (φ → ψ) from the BDDs of φ and ψ */
    if φ = 0 or ψ = 1 then return 1
    elsif φ = 1 then return ψ
    elsif ψ = 0 and (φ, i, φ₁, φ₂) ∈ table_φ
        then return new_node(i, BDD_imp(φ₁, 0), BDD_imp(φ₂, 0))
    else (φ, i, φ₁, φ₂) ∈ table_φ and (ψ, j, ψ₁, ψ₂) ∈ table_ψ
        if i = j then return new_node(i, BDD_imp(φ₁, ψ₁), BDD_imp(φ₂, ψ₂))
        elsif i < j then return new_node(i, BDD_imp(φ₁, ψ), BDD_imp(φ₂, ψ))
        elsif i > j then return new_node(j, BDD_imp(φ, ψ₁), BDD_imp(φ, ψ₂));

function new_node (Bddvar i, Bdd δ₁, δ₂) : Bdd =
    /* Returns a pointer to a new or existing BDD node */
    /* i is the number of a BDD variable, δ₁, δ₂ pointers to BDD nodes */
    if δ₁ = δ₂ then return δ₁
    elsif ∃δ : (δ, i, δ₁, δ₂) ∈ table then return δ
    else max := max + 1; table := table ∪ {(max, i, δ₁, δ₂)}; return max;
```

Figure 30: Combination of BDDs

1. If $BDD(\varphi)$ is 1, the resulting BDD is $BDD(\psi)$. If $BDD(\varphi)$ is an internal node $\mathsf{Ite}(v, \delta_1, \delta_2)$, and $BDD(\psi)$ is the leaf 0, we use the equivalence:

$$(\mathsf{Ite}(v, \delta_1, \delta_2) \to \bot) \quad \leftrightarrow \quad \mathsf{Ite}(v, (\delta_1 \to \bot), (\delta_2 \to \bot))$$

Since $\neg\varphi \triangleq (\varphi \to \bot)$, this means that the BDD for $\neg\varphi$ is constructed from the BDD for φ by exchanging all leafs 0 and 1. The only remaining case is that both $BDD(\varphi) = \mathsf{Ite}(v, \varphi_1, \varphi_2)$ and $BDD(\psi) = \mathsf{Ite}(v', \psi_1, \psi_2)$ are internal nodes. There are three subcases:

1. $v = v'$: $(\mathsf{Ite}(v, \varphi_1, \varphi_2) \to \mathsf{Ite}(v, \psi_1, \psi_2)) \leftrightarrow \mathsf{Ite}(v, (\varphi_1 \to \psi_1), (\varphi_2 \to \psi_2))$

2. $v < v'$ in the order of variables:
   $(\mathsf{Ite}(v, \varphi_1, \varphi_2) \to \mathsf{Ite}(v', \psi_1, \psi_2))$
   $$\leftrightarrow \mathsf{Ite}(v, \varphi_1 \to \mathsf{Ite}(v', \psi_1, \psi_2), \varphi_2 \to \mathsf{Ite}(v', \psi_1, \psi_2))$$

3. $v > v'$ in the order of variables:
   $(\mathsf{Ite}(v, \varphi_1, \varphi_2) \to \mathsf{Ite}(v', \psi_1, \psi_2))$
   $$\leftrightarrow \mathsf{Ite}(v', \mathsf{Ite}(v, \varphi_1, \varphi_2) \to \psi_1, \mathsf{Ite}(v, \varphi_1, \varphi_2) \to \psi_2)$$

In all of these subcases, the BDD for $(\varphi \to \psi)$ is constructed by a recursive call according to the indicated equivalence. Again, upon backtrack a new node is created only if both links are different and no equivalent node exists so far. The algorithm is given in Fig. 30. Some BDD implementations use negated edges to avoid the recursive descent for $\neg\varphi$. Other implementations hash subformulas, such that certain recursive descents can be avoided all together. For more information, see [Brace, Rudell and Bryant 1990].

The complexity of the function BDD_imp is linear in the size of the argument BDDs. In principle, all 16 two-argument boolean operations on BDDs can be implemented with linear complexity via this procedure. For example, the BDD for the intersection of two sets φ and ψ can be calculated from the BDDs of φ and ψ using the definition $(\varphi \land \psi) \leftrightarrow \neg(\varphi \to \neg\psi)$. In practice, however, most BDD libraries achieve a better performance by providing for each connective a special recursive procedure which takes symmetries and idempotences in the arguments into respect. [Bryant 1986] gives a uniform scheme to handle all 16 boolean connectives. In Fig. 31 this generic BDD_apply function is given; the idea of using a co-factoring function is from the BDD library by D. Long.

For a given boolean function, the size of the BDD depends critically on the ordering of the variables. For the example formula above (cf. page 10)

$$v_1 = 0 \to ((v'_1 = 1) \land (v'_2 = v_2) \land (v'_3 \neq v_3))$$

and the variable ordering $(v_1, v_2, v_3, v'_1, v'_2, v'_3)$, the above algorithm yields the following BDD. (We omit all branches leading to negative leaves.)

```
function BDD_apply (Fun ∘, Bdd φ, ψ) : Bdd =
    /* Calculates the BDD of (φ ∘ ψ) from BDDs of φ and ψ */
    if φ ∈ {0,1} and ψ ∈ {0,1} then return φ ∘ ψ
    else m := min_var(φ, ψ);
        (f₀, f₁) := co_factor(φ, m);   (g₀, g₁) := co_factor(ψ, m);
        δ₁ := BDD_apply(∘, f₀, g₀);   δ₂ := BDD_apply(∘, f₁, g₁);
        return new_node(m, δ₁, δ₂);

function min_var (Bdd φ, ψ) : Bddvar =
    /* Returns the minimal BDD variable in φ and ψ */
    if φ ∈ {0,1} and (ψ, j, ψ₁, ψ₂) ∈ table then return j
    elsif (φ, i, φ₁, φ₂) ∈ table and ψ ∈ {0,1} then return i
    elsif (φ, i, φ₁, φ₂) ∈ table and (ψ, j, ψ₁, ψ₂) ∈ table then return min(i, j);

function co_factor (Bdd δ, Bddvar m) : (Bdd, Bdd) =
    /* Returns two BDD pointers to combine */
    if δ ∈ {0,1} then return (δ, δ)
    else /* (δ, i, δ₁, δ₂) ∈ table */
        if i > m then return (δ, δ) else return (δ₁, δ₂);
```

Figure 31: Applying arbitrary functions to BDDs

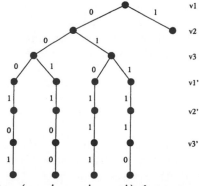

For the variable ordering $(v_1, v_1', v_2, v_2', v_3, v_3')$, however, we obtain the following much smaller BDD:

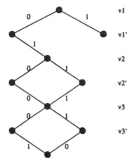

This is a common phenomenon when working with BDDs. In general, a good heuristics is to keep "dependent" variables as close together in the ordering as possible [Fuji, Ootomo and Hori 1993, Enders, Filkorn and Taubner 1993]. For a more formal treatment in the context of sequential circuits, see [Bermann 1991, McMillan 1993]. Unfortunately, the problem of finding an *optimal* variable ordering is NP-hard[Bryant 1991]. Basically, for every possible ordering one has to construct the BDD and compare their sizes, which is not feasible. Automatic reordering strategies usually proceed by steepest ascend heuristics [Felt, York, Brayton and Vincentelli 1993, Rudell 1993, Bern, Meinel and Slobodová 1995].

10.2. Symbolic Model Checking for CTL

In [Burch, Clarke, McMillan, Dill and Hwang 1992], the term *symbolic* model checking was introduced for algorithms which use a BDD representation of the Kripke model (cf. Page 1735).

Assume that the transition relation is given as a BDD over the variables $(v_1, ..., v_n, v_1', ..., v_n')$, and for each $p \in \mathcal{P}$ a BDD over $(v_1, ..., v_n)$ is given which represents the set $\mathcal{I}(p)$. We will show how the naïve **CTL** model checking algorithm in Fig. 17 on P. 1714 can be implemented directly with this representation.

Assume that φ is a propositional formula given as a BDD. Substitution $\varphi\{v := b\}$ of a proposition v in φ by a constant value $b \in \{\bot, \top\}$ can be done by assigning a pointer to the appropriate leaf (0 or 1) to each v node. Thus, the function that restricts some argument of a boolean function can be computed in time which is linear in the representation of the function. By using the substitution algorithm, boolean quantification $\exists v\ \varphi$ can be reduced to restriction by

$$(\exists v\ \varphi) \leftrightarrow (\varphi\{v := \bot\} \vee \varphi\{v := \top\})$$

Of course, it would be inefficient to implement simultaneous quantification $\exists \vec{w}\ \varphi$ on a set $\vec{w} \triangleq (v_1...v_n)$ of variables by a sequence of such substitutions and disjunctions. Fig. 32 shows how to calculate $\exists \vec{w}\ \varphi$ in a more direct way.

We now describe how to obtain a BDD representation of $\varphi^{\mathcal{F}}$ for any **CTL** formula φ from the given BDD representation of $\mathcal{F}$. The BDDs for $\bot$ and $p \in \mathcal{P}$ are trivial. The calculation of boolean composites of BDDs was described in the previous subsection. The evaluation of $\mathbf{E}\,\mathbf{U}^+$ and $\mathbf{A}\,\mathbf{U}^+$ involves computing a fixed

```
function BDD_exists (Set_of_Bddvar w, Bdd φ) : Bdd =
    /* w = {w₁...wₙ} is a set of BDD variables, φ the BDD of a formula */
    /* Result is a BDD for ∃w₁...∃wₙ φ */
    if φ ∈ {0,1} then return φ
    else /* (φ, i, φ₁, φ₂) ∈ table */
        δ₁ := BDD_exists(w, φ₁);  δ₂ := BDD_exists(w, φ₂);
        if i ∈ w then return BDD_apply(or, δ₁, δ₂)
        else return new_node(i, δ₁, δ₂);
```

Figure 32: Boolean quantification on BDDs

point. This is done according to the iteration given in Figure 17. In the evaluation of $\mathbf{E}(\psi_2 \mathbf{U}^+ \psi_1)$, we have to build the set $\{w \mid \exists w'(w \prec w' \wedge w' \in (\psi_1^{\mathcal{F}} \cup \psi_2^{\mathcal{F}} \cap E))\}$, where E is an intermediate result of the iteration. This formula is an instance of the scheme $\{w \mid \exists w'(\varphi(w') \wedge \psi(w, w'))\}$. Assume we are given a BDD for φ defined over the variables $\vec{w} \triangleq (v_1, ..., v_n)$, and a BDD for ψ in the variables $(v_1, ..., v_n, v_1', ..., v_n')$. The BDD for $\exists w'(\varphi(w') \wedge \psi(w, w'))$, which uses variables $(v_1, ..., v_n)$, can be obtained as follows. We first rename all variables v_i in the BDD for φ by v_i'. Then we intersect this BDD with the BDD for ψ to obtain a BDD over $(v_1, ..., v_n, v_1', ..., v_n')$. Finally, all primed variables are "thrown away" by existential quantification on $w' \triangleq (v_1', ..., v_n')$. The case of $\mathbf{A}(\psi_2 \mathbf{U}^+ \psi_1)$, where we have to calculate $\{w \mid \forall w'(w \prec w' \rightarrow w' \in (\psi_1^{\mathcal{F}} \cup \psi_2^{\mathcal{F}} \cap E))\}$, is similar.

In fact, all of the above BDD operations for one iteration step can be performed during a simple BDD traversal, if v_i and v_i' are always kept together in the variable order. This so-called *relational product algorithm* is similar to the BDD_apply and BDD_exists algorithms in Figs. 31 and 32. Assume that we are given BDD representations of φ and ψ, where the variable ordering in the BDD for φ is $w_1...w_n$ and in ψ it is $v_1...v_{2n}$, where $w_i = v_{2i-1}$ and $w_i' = v_{2i}$. Function relprod_BDD in Fig. 33 calculates the representation of $\exists \vec{w'}(\varphi\{\vec{w} := \vec{w'}\} \wedge \psi)$. The result contains BDD variables $v_1 v_3...v_{2n-1}$; renaming to $w_1...w_n$ can be done whenever a new node is created ($v_i = w_{i+1/2}$).

In theory, the complexity of the **CTL** model checking algorithm based on BDDs is not better than with an explicit representation. In practice, however, the BDD representation of large sets of points in realistic systems tends to be quite manageable. Moreover, the number of iteration steps required to reach a fixed point is often small ($\leq 10^3$). For hardware systems, that is, in the verification of sequential circuits, most states are reachable in very few steps, but the BDDs tend to grow exponentially in the first few steps. For software systems, especially if there is not much parallelism contained, the BDD often grows only linear with the number of steps, until the whole state space is traversed. The following picture shows the relation between the BDD size and number of steps in typical examples.

---

function BDD_relprod (Bdd φ, ψ) : Bdd =
  /* Calculates a BDD for $\exists w'(\varphi(w') \wedge \psi(w, w'))$ */
  /* φ has variables $1..n$ and ψ has variables $1...2n$ */
  /* Result contains BDD variables $1, 3, 5..., 2n - 1$ */
  if $\varphi = 0$ **or** $\psi = 0$ **then return** 0
  elsif $\psi = 1$ **then return** 1
  else $m := \text{min\_var\_2}(\varphi, \psi)$; /* *Substitution* $\{w := w'\}$ *in* φ */
      $(f_0, f_1) := \text{co\_factor}(\varphi, m \text{ div } 2)$; $(g_0, g_1) := \text{co\_factor}(\psi, m)$;
      $\delta_1 := \text{BDD\_relprod}(f_0, g_0)$; $\delta_2 := \text{BDD\_relprod}(f_1, g_1)$;
      if even(m) **then return** BDD_apply(or, δ_1, δ_2)
      else return new_node(m, δ_1, δ_2);

function min_var_2 (Bdd φ, ψ) : Bddvar /* *Ass.:* $(\psi, j, \psi_1, \psi_2) \in table_\psi$ */ =
  /* Returns an appropriate variable number for BDD_relprod */
  if $\varphi \in \{0, 1\}$ **then return** j
  else /* $(\varphi, i, \varphi_1, \varphi_2) \in table_\varphi$ */ **return** $\min(2 \cdot i, j)$;

Figure 33: Relational product on BDDs $(\exists w'(\varphi(w') \wedge \psi(w, w')))$

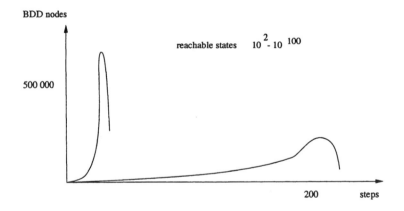

10.3. Relational μ-Calculus

The global algorithm for model checking the propositional μ-calculus can be implemented with BDDs similar as the **CTL** algorithm above. The relational product algorithm can be used to calculate each single step in the fixpoint iteration of modal formulas. We now show how this technique can be extended to a richer logical language which is closer to other programming paradigms. We use a relational μ-calculus similar to the one presented in [Park 1974]. In computer science, [Chandra and Harel 1980] were the first to use similar fixed point operators for the specification of queries in relational databases. In contrast to these papers, we do not use function symbols; they could be added easily to this framework as special relations. Informally, the relational μ-calculus can be seen as first order predicate logic with an additional recursion operator. More information on the logical properties of this calculus can be found in [Vardi 1982, Immerman 1986, Gurevich and Shelah 1986, Dawar, Lindell and Weinstein 1996].

A (typed) *structure* S consists of a collection of disjoint sets called *domains*, and a collection of relations over these domains. (In some textbooks, structures are called *algebras*.) Elements of the domains are called *objects*. Models for propositional temporal logics can be regarded to be special structures with a single domain U, unary predicates $P \subseteq U$ and binary relations $R \subseteq U \times U$ on this domain.

A *signature* $\Sigma = (\mathcal{D}, \mathcal{R})$ consists of a finite set $\mathcal{D}$ of *domain names*, and a finite set $\mathcal{R}$ of *relation symbols*. Associated with each relation symbol is its *type* τ, which is a sequence of domain names. Unary relation symbols are called *predicate symbols*.

An *interpretation* $\mathcal{I}$ for a signature Σ on a structure S is a mapping $\mathcal{I} : \Sigma \to S$ assigning a nonempty domain $\mathcal{I}(D)$ for each domain name D and a relation of appropriate arity for each relation symbol. That is, if $\tau(R) = (D_1, ..., D_n)$, then $\mathcal{I}(R) \subseteq (\mathcal{I}(D_1) \times \cdots \times \mathcal{I}(D_n))$. If the interpretation of a predicate symbol P is a singleton set, we say that P is a *constant*.

Given a signature Σ, let $\mathcal{V}$ be a set of variables, each of which is either an *individual variable* or a *relation variable*. Again, we assume that each variable has an appropriate type. In the relational μ-calculus, there are two more syntactic categories: *well-formed formulas* and *relation terms of type* τ. Assuming that the symbols $($, $)$, $\bot$, $\to$, $=$, $\exists$, μ and λ are not in the signature, a *well formed formula* φ is built according to the following syntax:

- $\bot$, $(\varphi \to \psi)$, where φ and ψ are well formed formulas,
- $(x_1 = x_2)$, where x_1 and x_2 are individual variables of the same type,
- $\exists x\, \varphi$, where φ is a well formed formula, and x is an individual variable, or
- $\rho\, x_1...x_n$, where ρ is a relation term of type $(D_1, ..., D_n)$ (see below), and x_i is an individual variable of type D_i for all $i \leq n$.

In first order logic, a relation term is just a relation symbol from the signature. In second order logic, a relation term can either be a relation symbol or a relation variable $q \in Q$. In the relational μ-calculus, more complex relations can be specified via λ-*abstraction* and μ-*recursion*. In this calculus, a *relation term* ρ of type $(D_1, ..., D_n)$ is

- a relation symbol R or relation variable X of type $(D_1, ..., D_n)$,
- $\lambda x_1...x_n\, \varphi$, where φ is a well formed formula and each x_i is an individual variable of type D_i, or
- $\mu X\, \rho$, where X is a relation variable of type $(D_1, ..., D_n)$, and ρ a relation term of the same type which is positive in X.

As in the propositional case, in this definition ρ is defined to be *positive* in X, if every occurrence of X is under an even number of negation signs. Positiveness ensures that the functional defined by ρ is monotonic in the lattice of values for X and thus the least fixpoint of the functional exists.

A *variable valuation* $\mathbf{v}$ is a mapping assigning an object $\mathbf{v}(x) \in D$ to every individual variable x of type D, and a relation $\mathbf{v}(X) \subseteq D_1 \times \cdots \times D_n$ to every relation variable X of type $(D_1, ..., D_n)$. A *relational model* $\mathcal{M} \triangleq (S, \mathcal{I}, \mathbf{v})$ for the signature Σ consists of a structure S, an interpretation $\mathcal{I}$, and a variable valuation $\mathbf{v}$. Similar to first order and temporal logics, we say that the model $\mathcal{M} \triangleq (S, \mathcal{I}, \mathbf{v})$ is *based* on the *frame* $\mathcal{F} \triangleq (S, \mathcal{I})$. Any relational model $\mathcal{M} \triangleq (S, \mathcal{I}, \mathbf{v})$ determines an object $x^{\mathcal{M}}$ for every individual variable x, a relation $\rho^{\mathcal{M}}$ of appropriate type for each relation term ρ, and a unique truth value $\varphi^{\mathcal{M}} \in \{\mathbf{true}, \mathbf{false}\}$ for any formula φ. This *denotation* of variables and formulas is defined in the usual way:

- $x^{\mathcal{M}} \triangleq \mathbf{v}(x)$, if $x \in \mathcal{V}$ is an individual variable,
- $\perp^{\mathcal{M}} \triangleq \mathbf{false}$,
- $(\varphi \rightarrow \psi)^{\mathcal{M}} = \mathbf{true}$ iff $\varphi^{\mathcal{M}} = \mathbf{true}$ implies $\psi^{\mathcal{M}} = \mathbf{true}$,
- $(x_1 = x_2)^{\mathcal{M}} = \mathbf{true}$ iff $x_1^{\mathcal{M}} = x_2^{\mathcal{M}}$; i.e., iff x_1 and x_2 denote the same object in S,
- $(\exists x\, \varphi)^{\mathcal{M}} = \mathbf{true}$ iff $\varphi^{(S, \mathcal{I}, \mathbf{v}')} = \mathbf{true}$ for some valuation $\mathbf{v}'$ which differs from $\mathbf{v}$ at most in x,
- $(\rho\, x_1...x_n)^{\mathcal{M}} = \mathbf{true}$ iff $(x_1^{\mathcal{M}}, ..., x_n^{\mathcal{M}}) \in \rho^{\mathcal{M}}$,
- $R^{\mathcal{M}} \triangleq \mathcal{I}(R)$, if R is a relation symbol,
- $X^{\mathcal{M}} \triangleq \mathbf{v}(X)$, if X is a relation variable,
- $(\lambda x_1...x_n\, \varphi)^{\mathcal{M}} \triangleq \{(d_1, ..., d_n) \mid \varphi^{\mathcal{F}}(d_1, ..., d_n) = \mathbf{true}\}$, where $\varphi^{\mathcal{F}}(d_1, ..., d_n) \triangleq \varphi^{(S, \mathcal{I}, \mathbf{v}')}$ and $\mathbf{v}'$ differs from $\mathbf{v}$ only in the assignment of d_i to x_i for $1 \leq i \leq n$; i.e., $(\lambda x_1...x_n(\varphi))^{\mathcal{M}}$ is the relation consisting of all tuples of objects for which φ is $\mathbf{true}$, and
- $(\mu X\, \rho)^{\mathcal{M}} \triangleq \bigcap \{Q \mid \rho^{\mathcal{F}}(Q) \subseteq Q\}$, where $\rho^{\mathcal{F}}(Q) \triangleq \rho^{(S, \mathcal{I}, \mathbf{v}')}$, and $\mathbf{v}'$ differs from $\mathbf{v}$ only in $\mathbf{v}'(X) = Q$; i.e., $\mu X(\rho)^{\mathcal{M}}$ is the least fixpoint of the functional $\rho^{\mathcal{F}}$.

The relational operators λ and μ are similar to the operators used in λ-calculus and in denotational semantics. In fact, we could define well formed formulas to be object terms of the special type $\{\mathbf{false}, \mathbf{true}\}$. Relation terms could then be defined as function terms with boolean result, and the λ abstraction builds such a function term from a boolean object term.

The relational μ-calculus extends first order logic in a similar way as the propositional μ calculus extends modal logic. In fact, the standard translation from modal into first order logic can be trivially extended into a standard translation from propositional into relational μ calculus. In addition, the relational μ calculus offers some restricted form of non-monadic second order quantification. It contains classical first-order logic as a sublanguage. Note, however, that in the relational μ-calculus there is no λ-abstraction on relation variables. This would result in a second-order calculus. In contrast to second order logic, there is no μ-calculus formula expressing that domain D is finite [Park 1974]. On the other hand, the minimization operator can be expressed in second order logic similar as in the propositional case (cf. Page 1660):

$$\mu X(\rho)\vec{x} \leftrightarrow \forall X (\forall \vec{x}(\rho \vec{x} \rightarrow X\vec{x}) \rightarrow X\vec{x})$$

Since the induction axiom for arithmetic can be formulated as a least fixpoint formula, the natural numbers have a categorical theory in the relational μ-calculus (for details, see also [Park 1974]). Therefore, the set of valid formulas is not recursively enumerable, and its expressiveness lies properly in between first and second order logic.

The μ-recursion operator can be used to give recursive definitions of boolean functions, similar to the use of recursion in functional and logic programming. As an example, the addition-relation on natural numbers can be defined from the constant Z (zero) and the successor relation S by $\mu X (\lambda xyz(Zx \wedge y = z \vee \exists uv(Sux \wedge Svz \wedge Xuyv)))$. All recursive functions of arithmetic can be defined in this way; therefore, on infinite domains, the relational μ-calculus has the expressive power of Turing machines. On finite domains, the model checking problem is polynomial in the size of the structure. Therefore, only those functions are definable which can be computed with time complexity polynomial in the size of the structure ([Chandra and Harel 1980]). For a restricted converse of this statement, see [Vardi 1982, Immerman 1986].

Given a finite relational frame $\mathcal{F} \triangleq (S, \mathcal{I})$ and a relational term ρ or formula φ, model checking can be used to determine the denotation $\rho^{\mathcal{F}}$ or $\varphi^{\mathcal{F}}$, respectively. In [Burch, Clarke, McMillan, Dill and Hwang 1992], a symbolic model checking algorithm for the relational μ-calculus is given (see Figure 34). Assume for simplicity that each domain is binary; for non–binary domains the algorithm can be extended by an appropriate encoding. In the frame, the interpretation $\mathcal{I}$ of a relation of type $(D_1, ..., D_n)$ is represented by a BDD with variables $v_1, v_2, ..., v_n$.

A term or formula with free individual variables $x_1, ..., x_m$ is represented as a BDD with additional BDD variables $x_1, ..., x_m$. A relation variable is represented by its name; each BDD node can contain (the name of) a relation variable as one of its successors. In other words, each BDD node is a tuple $(\delta, i, \delta_1, \delta_2)$, where δ is the name of this node, i is a variable from the set $\{v_1, ..., v_n, x_1, ..., x_m\}$, and each δ_j is one of the BDD constants 0 or 1, a name of another BDD node, or the name of a relation variable. Substitution of a relation variable with a relation in a BDD can be done by a simple BDD traversal.

The model checking algorithm is divided into two functions, BDD_form and BDD_term, which recurse over the structure of the formula and term. BDD_form inputs a formula φ and (the BDD representation of) the interpretation $\mathcal{I}$ in frame $\mathcal{F}$, and returns a BDD which is satisfied by a given valuation $\mathbf{v}$ iff $(S, \mathcal{I}, \mathbf{v}) \models \varphi$. The first five cases in the function derive directly from the respective semantic definitions and should require no explanation. The last case, application of a relation term ρ, uses the function BDD_term$(\rho, \mathcal{I})$ to find a representation of the relational term ρ (under the interpretation $\mathcal{I}$), then substitutes the argument variables $x_1, ..., x_n$ for the place-holder variables $v_1, ..., v_n$, producing a BDD which is satisfied iff ρ holds for $x_1, ..., x_n$.

The function BDD_term takes as arguments a relational term ρ and the BDD representation of the interpretation $\mathcal{I}$. It returns a BDD which represents the relation term in the manner described above. The first and second case in the definition of BDD_term, a relation symbol or relation variable, simply return the BDD representation of the relation in the interpretation or the name of the relation variable, respectively. The third case, λ-abstraction, produces a BDD with variables $v_1, ...,$

v_n substituted for the variables v_1, ..., v_n. This is the representation for an n-ary relation which holds iff its arguments satisfy the formula φ when assigned to x_1, ..., x_n. The most interesting case is the last: the fixed point operator μ. To find the fixed point of a relational term with respect to a free relation variable X we use the standard technique for finding the least fixed point of a monotonic functional in a finite domain. First we evaluate BDD_term($\rho, \mathcal{I}$) to get a BDD r for ρ. Then we compute the fixed point by a series of approximations X^0, X^1, ..., beginning with the empty relation (which is represented by the BDD constant 0). To compute the BDD X^{i+1} from X^i we substitute all occurrences of the variable X in the BDD r with X^i. Since the domain is finite and ρ is positive in X, the series must converge to the least fixed point (cf. Lemma 5.4 and Section 8.3). Convergence is detected when $X^{i+1} = X^i$. In this case, X^i is the BDD for $\mu X \rho$. Note that testing for convergence is easy, since with a hash-table implementation of BDD nodes equality can be determined in constant time (cf. the algorithm in Fig. 29).

The μcke model checker [Biere 1997] is one of the first tools for model checking the relational μ-calculus. For each non-binary domain, an appropriate binary en-

---

function BDD_form (Formula φ, Interpretation $\mathcal{I}$) : Bdd =
  /* Calculates the BDD of formula φ in the interpretation $\mathcal{I}$ */
  case φ **of**
    $x \in \mathcal{V}$: **return** lte($x, 1, 0$);
    $(x_1 = x_2)$: **return** lte(x_1, lte($x_2, 1, 0$), lte($x_2, 0, 1$));
    $\bot$: **return** 0;
    $(\varphi_1 \to \varphi_2)$: **return** BDD_imp(BDD_form($\varphi_1, \mathcal{I}$), BDD_form($\varphi_2, \mathcal{I}$));
    $\exists x \, \varphi$: **return** BDD_exists(x, BDD_form($\varphi, \mathcal{I}$));
    $\rho x_1 ... x_n$: **return** BDD_term($\rho, \mathcal{I}$)$\{v_1 := x_1\}...\{v_n := x_n\}$;

function BDD_term (RelationalTerm ρ, Interpretation $\mathcal{I}$) : Bdd =
  /* Calculates the BDD of term ρ in the interpretation $\mathcal{I}$ */
  case ρ **of**
    $R \in \mathcal{R}$: **return** $\mathcal{I}(R)$ /* pointer to BDD for R */;
    $X \in \mathcal{V}$: **return** X /* name of X */;
    $\lambda x_1 ... x_n \, \varphi$: **return** BDD_form($\varphi, \mathcal{I}$)$\{x_1 := v_1\}...\{x_n := v_n\}$;
    $\mu X \rho$: $r :=$ BDD_term($\rho, \mathcal{I}$);   **return** BDD_lfp($r, 0$);

function BDD_lfp (BDD r, BDD X^i) : BDD =
  /* Fixpoint iteration of BDD r for ρ with substitution $\{X := X^i\}$ */
  $X^{i+1} := r\{X := X^i\}$;
  if $X^{i+1} = X^i$ **then return** X^i
  else return BDD_lfp(r, X^{i+1});

Figure 34: Symbolic evaluation of formulas and terms

coding is generated automatically. The model is given in a C-like input language. It is compiled automatically into an internal BDD representation. Since μcke uses several sophisticated heuristics for the allocation of BDD variables, its performance is comparable to more specialized systems like SMV.

11. Partial Order Techniques

With symbolic methods we try to tackle the complexity problem which arises from the parallel composition of modules by using the BDD data structure which can handle very large sets. Partial order methods, on the other hand, try to avoid the generation of large sets: they only generate a minimal part of the state space which is necessary to evaluate the given formula.

Several variants have been suggested: *stubborn sets* ([Valmari 1990]), *sleep sets* ([Godefroid 1990, Godefroid and Wolper 1991, Godefroid and Pirottin 1993]), *interleaving* and *ample sets* [Katz and Peled 1988, Peled 1993], and others. Subsequently, we describe an algorithm for partial order model checking of linear time temporal logic properties which is based on [Yoneda, Nakade and Tohma 1989, Valmari 1990]. For an overview of other methods, see [Clarke, Grumberg, Minea and Peled 1999]. Partial order methods for branching time logics and symbolic methods have been investigated in [Gerth, Kuiper, Peled and Penczek 1995, Alur, Brayton, Henzinger, Quadeer and Rajamani 1997]. A somewhat different approach to partial order model checking by unfolding of Petri nets was suggested in [McMillan 1992, Esparza 1994].

The interleaving definition of parallel program semantics determines the state space of the global system to be the product of all state spaces of its parallel components. This can lead to wasteful algorithms. In general, each (nondeterministic) execution of a program generates a partial order, where points are ordered by causality. In interleaving semantics this partial order is represented by the set of all of its interleaving sequences.

For example, the following elementary Petri net represents a system with two processes synchronizing via t_0 and t_3:

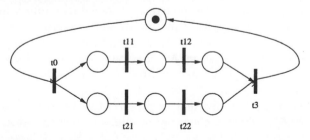

This system generates the following partial order:

Some of the interleaving sequences are

$t_0 \; t_{11} \; t_{12} \; t_{21} \; t_{22} \; t_3 \; ...$
$t_0 \; t_{11} \; t_{21} \; t_{12} \; t_{22} \; t_3 \; ...$
$t_0 \; t_{11} \; t_{21} \; t_{22} \; t_{12} \; t_3 \; ...$
$t_0 \; t_{21} \; t_{11} \; t_{22} \; t_{12} \; t_3 \; ...$
$t_0 \; t_{21} \; t_{11} \; t_{12} \; t_{22} \; t_3 \; ...$

However, it may not be necessary to consider *all* of these interleavings to determine, e.g., the truth value of the formula $\mathbf{G}^+ \mathbf{F}^* t_3$. The main idea of partial order methods is to try to inspect only some "representative" interleaving sequences for the formula in question. Thus, we do *not* alter the semantics to deal with "real" concurrency (where independent transitions can occur at the same time), and we do *not* extend the logic to be able to express partial order properties. On the contrary, we will limit the expressiveness of temporal logic and use the partial order to improve the efficiency of model checking.

11.1. Stuttering Invariance

Given an elementary Petri net N and a formula φ, we want to find whether there exists a run ρ of N satisfying φ. In general, there are infinitely many runs through the system; therefore we partition them into a finite number of equivalence classes, such that the existence of a satisfying run ρ implies that every element of the equivalence class $[\rho]$ satisfies φ. Thus we only have to check a finite number of equivalence classes, and a coarser partition yields a better algorithm.

To do so, we need a *stuttering invariant* temporal logic. Consider a formula with the atomic propositions $\{p_1, ..., p_k\} \subseteq \mathcal{P}$. Two natural models $\mathcal{M}$ and $\mathcal{M}'$ are *strongly equivalent* with respect to $\{p_1, ..., p_k\}$, if they are of the same cardinality, and for all $i \geq 0$ and all $p \in \{p_1, ..., p_k\}$ we have $w_i \in \mathcal{I}(p)$ iff $w'_i \in \mathcal{I}'(p)$. A point w_{i+1} in $\mathcal{M}$ is *stuttering* w.r.t. $\{p_1, ..., p_k\}$, if for all $p \in \{p_1, ..., p_k\}$ we have $w_i \in \mathcal{I}(p)$ iff $w_{i+1} \in \mathcal{I}(p)$. For any model $\mathcal{M} \triangleq (U, \mathcal{I}, w_0)$, define the *stutter-free kernel* $\mathcal{M}^o$ w.r.t. $\{p_1, ..., p_k\}$ to be the model obtained by eliminating all stuttering states from $\mathcal{M}$. More formally, $\mathcal{M}^o$ contains all non-stuttering points from $\mathcal{M}$, and $w \prec w'$ in $\mathcal{M}^o$ iff $w \prec w'$ in $\mathcal{M}$, or there are stuttering points $w_1, ..., w_n$ such that $w \prec w_1 \prec \cdots \prec w_n \prec w'$ in $\mathcal{M}$. Two models $\mathcal{M}_1$ and $\mathcal{M}_2$ are *stuttering equivalent* w.r.t. $\{p_1, ..., p_k\}$, if their stutter-free kernels are strongly equivalent w.r.t. $\{p_1, ..., p_k\}$.

A formula φ is *stuttering invariant* or *preserved under stuttering*, if for any two models $\mathcal{M}_1$ and $\mathcal{M}_2$ which are stuttering equivalent with respect to the set of atomic propositions of φ it holds that $\mathcal{M}_1 \models \varphi$ iff $\mathcal{M}_2 \models \varphi$. A language is stuttering invariant, if all of its formulas are stuttering invariant.

In general, formulas involving the operator $\mathbf{X}$ are not stuttering invariant. For example, the formula $\mathbf{X}\,\mathrm{p}$ holds in the model $(\{w_0, w_1, w_2\}, \mathcal{I}, w_0)$, where $\mathcal{I}(\mathrm{p}) = \{w_0, w_1\}$ and $w_0 \prec w_1 \prec w_2$, but not in the stuttering equivalent model $(\{w_0, w_2\}, \mathcal{I}, w_0)$. The next-operator has always been a topic of discussions in temporal specification [Lamport 1983]. Most notions of refinement of systems do not preserve properties with next-operators. Recall that $\mathbf{X}$ is definable with $\mathbf{U}^+$, but not with $\mathbf{U}^*$ (see Lemma 2.1 and Page 1647). Let $\mathbf{LTL} - \mathbf{X}$ be the logic built from propositions $\mathrm{p} \in \mathcal{P}$, boolean connectives $\bot$, $\rightarrow$ and the reflexive until operator $\mathbf{U}^*$.

11.1. LEMMA. *Any* $\mathbf{LTL} - \mathbf{X}$ *formula is stuttering invariant.*

PROOF: Assume that φ is an $\mathbf{LTL} - \mathbf{X}$ formula, $\mathcal{M} \triangleq (U, \mathcal{I}, w_0)$ a model and $\mathcal{M}^o \triangleq (U^o, \mathcal{I}^o, w_0)$ the stuttering-free kernel of φ w.r.t. the propositions in φ. Furthermore, for any $w \in U$, let $w^o \in U^o$ be the maximal non-stuttering point such that $w^o \leq w$. We show that for any $w \in U$

$$(*) \qquad (U, \mathcal{I}, w) \models \varphi \quad \text{iff} \quad (U^o, \mathcal{I}^o, w^o) \models \varphi.$$

In particular, since $w_0^o = w_0$, this implies that $\mathcal{M} \models \varphi$ iff $\mathcal{M}^o \models \varphi$. From this, the claim follows immediately: if $\mathcal{M}_1^o$ and $\mathcal{M}_2^o$ are strongly equivalent w.r.t. the atomic propositions of φ, then clearly $\mathcal{M}_1^o \models \varphi$ iff $\mathcal{M}_2^o \models \varphi$. If $\mathcal{M}_1$ and $\mathcal{M}_2$ are stuttering equivalent, then the stutter-free kernels $\mathcal{M}_1^o$ and $\mathcal{M}_2^o$ are strongly equivalent. Therefore, in this case $\mathcal{M}_1 \models \varphi$ iff $\mathcal{M}_1^o \models \varphi$ iff $\mathcal{M}_2^o \models \varphi$ iff $\mathcal{M}_2 \models \varphi$.

The proof of $(*)$ is by induction φ. For atomic propositions, $w_{i+1} \models \mathrm{p}$ iff $w_i \models \mathrm{p}$ for each point w_{i+1} which is stuttering w.r.t. $\{\mathrm{p}, \mathrm{p}_1, ..., \mathrm{p}_k\}$. Therefore $w \models \mathrm{p}$ iff $w^o \models \mathrm{p}$. For boolean connectives the statement is obvious. For the $\mathbf{U}^*$-operator, we treat only the case $\varphi = \mathbf{F}^* \psi = (\top\, \mathbf{U}^* \psi)$; the general case $\varphi = (\psi_2\, \mathbf{U}^* \psi_1)$ is similar. $(U, \mathcal{I}, w_0) \models \mathbf{F}^* \psi$ means that there is a $w_1 \geq w_0$ such that $(U, \mathcal{I}, w_1) \models \psi$. By the inductive hypothesis, this is equivalent to the claim that for some $w_1 \geq w_0$, $(U^o, \mathcal{I}^o, w_1^o) \models \psi$. This claim in turn holds iff for some $v_1 \in U^o$, $v_1 \geq w_0^o$ and $(U^o, \mathcal{I}^o, v_1) \models \psi_1$. This means that $(U^o, \mathcal{I}^o, w_0^o) \models \mathbf{F}^* \psi$. Note that this proof is not valid for the $\mathbf{F}^+$-operator, since it is possible that $w_1 > w_0$ but $w_1^o = w_0$. $\qquad \square$

In [Peled and Wilke 1997], a converse to this lemma is proved:

11.2. THEOREM. *Any* $\mathbf{LTL}$ *formula which is stuttering invariant is expressible in* $\mathbf{LTL} - \mathbf{X}$.

Stuttering invariance allows to group all stuttering equivalent runs into the same equivalence class, thereby reducing the average complexity of the model checking. Of course, the reduction will be better if φ uses fewer propositions. Usually, a given formula mentions only a small subset of the system, allowing the equivalence classes to be rather large. In particular, consider a system with two independent transitions t_1 and t_2 (a formal criterion of independence is given below). All runs which differ only in the interleaving of t_1 and t_2 are stuttering equivalent with respect to all atomic propositions not related to t_1 or t_2. Therefore, each $\mathbf{LTL} - \mathbf{X}$ formula not referring to t_1 and t_2 has the same truth value for all of these runs.

11.2. Partial Order Analysis of Elementary Nets

First, we need an appropriate stuttering-invariant restricted logical language to express "interesting" properties of elementary Petri nets. Recall that a state of the net is just a marking of its places. Thus, it is reasonable to use places as atomic propositions, where a proposition p is valid in a state iff the place p is marked in that marking.

Assume that we are given an elementary Petri net and an **LTL − X** formula describing a property of this net. Now, we define when two transitions are independent of one another. Firstly, independent transitions must neither disable nor enable each other; that is, if t_1 is enabled in s and s' is a successor of s with respect to the firing of t_1, then t_2 is enabled at s iff t_2 is enabled at s', and vice versa for t_2 firing. Secondly, if the independent transitions t_1 and t_2 are both enabled in s, then they must be able to commute; that is, each execution obtained by first firing t_1 and then t_2 must be stuttering equivalent (w.r.t. the property under consideration) to one obtained by first firing t_2 and then t_1.

However, it is not practical to check these two properties for all pairs of transitions in all global states of the system. Therefore, we use a syntactic condition which ensures that some transition is independent from another one.

Call a set T of transitions *persistent* in s, if whatever one does from s while remaining outside of T does not affect T. Formally, T is persistent in s iff for all $t \in T$ and all firing sequences $t_0, t_1, ..., t_n, t$ such that $t_i \notin T$ for all $0 \le i \le n$ there exists a stuttering equivalent firing sequence starting with t.

If T is persistent, we do not have to consider the firing of transitions outside of T when constructing the children of the given state in the depth-first-search; there will be a stuttering equivalent sequence constructed by the firing of some $t \in T$.

However, this definition still is not effective. There is no efficient way to compute a minimal persistent set of transitions for a given state. Therefore, we compute an approximation. There is a tradeoff between the amount of time spent in the calculation of minimal persistent sets, and the reduction of the state space obtained. As a general strategy, some simple heuristics can gain a lot, and sophisticated methods don't add too much.

We start with a single enabled transition $T = \{t\}$ and repeat until stabilization to add all transitions which can "interfere" with some transition in T. Here "interfere" means that they can enable or disable, or cannot commute with some transition in T.

Given any marking m, firable transition t_f and disabled transition t, we have to find a set of firable transitions such that the firing of any transition in this set could lead to the firing of t before t_f. A set $NEC(t, m)$ of transitions is *necessary* for t in m, if $NEC(t, m) = \{t' \mid p \in t' \bullet \}$ for some $p \in (\bullet t \setminus m)$. We use a functional notation here, since $NEC(t, m)$ is determined by the chosen heuristic strategy. Similarly, the set $NEC^*(t, m)$ is defined to be any set of transitions containing t which is transitively closed under necessity; that is, for any $t' \in NEC^*(t, m)$ such that t is disabled in m there exists a set $NEC(t', m)$ of transitions necessary for t' such that $NEC(t', m) \subseteq NEC^*(t, m)$. If t is disabled in m, then t cannot fire unless some transitions from $NEC^*(t, m)$ fire before.

If t is in conflict with t_f, then the firing of any transition in $NEC^*(t, m)$ could eventually enable t; therefore all transitions in $NEC^*(t, m)$ have to be fired as alternatives to the firing of t_f. But, there is still another class of dependent transitions. We want to obtain stuttering equivalence with respect to the atomic propositions in φ. Therefore, we have to take into account that φ might fix an order onto the firing of independent transitions. Usually, φ contains only a few propositions. Call a transition *visible* for φ, if $\bullet t \cup t \bullet$ contains any place p appearing in φ. If t is visible, the firing order with other visible transitions is important. A visible transition can be regarded to be in conflict with all other visible transitions. Define the *conflict* of t by

$$C(t) = \{t' \mid \bullet t' \cap \bullet t \neq \{\}\} \cup \{t\}.$$

The *extended conflict* of t is just the conflict of t, if t is invisible; otherwise, it is the conflict of t plus all other visible transitions. Now a *dependent set* $DEP(t_f, m)$ of t_f is any set of transitions such for any t in the extended conflict of t_f there exists a set $NEC(t, m) \subseteq DEP(t_f, m)$.

Finally, the set of transitions which are fired should be transitively closed under dependency; thus, let $READY(m)$ be any (smallest) nonempty set of firable transitions, such that

$$DEP(t_f, m) \subseteq READY(m) \quad \text{if} \quad t_f \in READY(m).$$

Correctness of this reduction method is guaranteed by the following theorem:

11.3. THEOREM. *For any firing sequence ρ of the net there exists a firing sequence ρ' generated only by firing ready transitions such that ρ and ρ' are equivalent with respect to all* **LTL** $-$ **X** *safety properties.*

Consider the depth-first model checking algorithm for **LTL** in Figure 19. During the construction of the set of children of a state in the depth first search we can neglect all firable transitions which are not ready. This can result in a considerable average case reduction; in fact, for examples with many concurrent and "almost" independent processes it can logarithmically reduce the state space which has to be traversed. Though the worst case complexity of constructing a ready set is cubic in the size of the net, in average examples it is only linear in the number of transitions.

The above construction can be extended to deal also with liveness and other linear temporal logic properties. To do so, we need to assure that whenever a state is reached for the second time, a different ready set is constructed, to make sure that no eventuality is delayed infinitely often. For a detailed exposition and an extension to real-time logics, see [Yoneda and Schlingloff 1997].

12. Bounded Model Checking

The model checking algorithms of the previous sections were based on the idea of calculating the greatest or least fixed point of a certain continuous function. Model checking can also be done by translating temporal logic into classical logic and using well-established automated deduction methods. In particular, in Subsection 2.3 on Page 1649 we defined a translation **FOL** from linear temporal logic to first order logic. If the model to be checked is finite, then each first order existential quantifier can be replaced by a finite disjunction, and every universal quantifier can be replaced by a finite conjunction of variables. Moreover, as described in section 10, each finite model can be coded as a boolean combination of atomic formulas $p(t)$ and $t \prec t'$. Likewise, for sequence-validity, the condition that a finite set $\{t_1, \ldots t_n\}$ of points forms a maximal path in a model can be coded as such a formula.

Consider the conjunction of the propositional translation of the formula and the boolean encoding of the model. This is a formula which can be tested for satisfiability by standard SAT algorithms. In [Biere, Cimatti, Fujita and Zhu 1999, Biere, Cimatti and Zhu 1999], the term *bounded model checking* is introduced for checking sequence-validity of future **LTL** formulas with this approach. The execution sequences of a Kripke model are enumerated by increasing length and combined with the translation of the formula. These are converted into conjunctive normal form and tested for satisfiability by propositional theorem provers. With appropriate heuristics, in some cases this method turned out to give even better results than BDD based methods.

12.1. An Example

Before giving the technical details, we show an example. Consider the Kripke model in Fig. 35. There are four points in the model. Each point w is represented by two

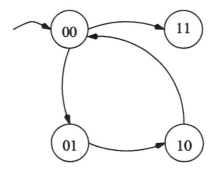

Figure 35: A two-bit model

state variables, $w \triangleq (v_1, v_0)$, denoting the value of the high bit and the low bit, respectively. The initial state is (00). Thus the initial state predicate $I(w)$ is defined as $(\neg v_1 \wedge \neg v_0)$. The only terminal state is (11), thus the terminal state predicate $T(w)$ is $(v_1 \wedge v_0)$. The transition relation is represented by the formula $R(w, w') \triangleq$
$(\neg v_1 \wedge \neg v_0 \wedge \neg v_1' \wedge v_0') \vee (\neg v_1 \wedge v_0 \wedge v_1' \wedge \neg v_0') \vee (v_1 \wedge \neg v_0 \wedge \neg v_1' \wedge \neg v_0') \vee (\neg v_1 \wedge \neg v_0 \wedge v_1' \wedge v_0')$

Suppose we are interested in the fact that any execution eventually reaches state (11). In **LTL**, this amounts to checking whether $\mathbf{F}^*(v_1 \wedge v_0)$ is sequence-valid. Equivalently, we can check whether there is a maximal path in the model in which state (11) is never reached. That is, we check whether $\mathbf{G}^* \neg(v_1 \wedge v_0)$ is satisfiable in the model. According to the definition, this is the case iff there is a path in the model starting in an initial point and ending in a terminal point or in a cycle, such that every point on the path satisfies $\neg v_1$ or $\neg v_0$. In bounded model checking, we restrict our attention to paths of length k, that is, paths with $k+1$ states. We start with $k = 0$, and increment k until a witness is found. Consider the case where k equals 2. We name the $k+1$ states as w^0, w^1, w^2. Since every state is encoded by two boolean variables, there are six propositional variables altogether: v_1^0, v_0^0, v_1^1, v_0^1, v_1^2, v_0^2. We now formulate a set of constraints on these variables in propositional logic which guarantee that the path $\sigma = (w^0, w^1, w^2)$ is indeed a witness for $\mathbf{G}^*(\neg v_1 \vee \neg v_0)$.

- First, σ must start in an initial point. This is expressed by $I(w^0)$ as described above: $\varphi_1 \triangleq (\neg v_1^0 \wedge \neg v_0^0)$

- Second, each w^{i+1} must be a successor of w^i according to the transition relation, i.e., $R(w^0, w^1) \wedge R(w^1, w^2)$ must hold. This expands to
$\varphi_2 \triangleq (\neg v_1^0 \wedge \neg v_0^0 \wedge \neg v_1^1 \wedge v_0^1) \vee (\neg v_1^0 \wedge v_0^0 \wedge v_1^1 \wedge \neg v_0^1) \vee$
$\qquad (v_1^0 \wedge \neg v_0^0 \wedge \neg v_1^1 \wedge \neg v_0^1) \vee (\neg v_1^0 \wedge \neg v_0^0 \wedge v_1^1 \wedge v_0^1) \wedge$
$\qquad (\neg v_1^1 \wedge \neg v_0^1 \wedge \neg v_1^2 \wedge v_0^2) \vee (\neg v_1^1 \wedge v_0^1 \wedge v_1^2 \wedge \neg v_0^2) \vee$
$\qquad (v_1^1 \wedge \neg v_0^1 \wedge \neg v_1^2 \wedge \neg v_0^2) \vee (\neg v_1^1 \wedge \neg v_0^1 \wedge v_1^2 \wedge v_0^2)$

- Third, the path must be either terminal or end in a loop. That is, either $T(w^2)$ holds, or there must be a transition from w^2 to one of w^0, w^1 or w^2. The formula $\varphi_3 \triangleq T(w^2) \vee R(w^2, w^0) \vee R(w^2, w^1) \vee R(w^2, w^2)$ is expanded similar to φ_2.

- Fourth, $\mathbf{G}^* \neg(v_1 \wedge v_0)$ must hold in the first point of the sequence, i.e., $\neg(v_1 \wedge v_0)$ must hold for w^0, w^1 and w^2. Therefore, $\varphi_4 \triangleq \bigwedge_{i=0}^{2} \neg(v_1^i \wedge v_0^i)$.

It is easy to see that there is a propositional model for $\varphi \triangleq \varphi_1 \wedge \varphi_2 \wedge \varphi_3 \wedge \varphi_4$ iff there is a maximal path consisting of three model states validating the given formula. Satisfiability of φ can be checked by SAT procedures like SATO [Zhang 1997] or Stålmarck's algorithm [Stålmarck 1989, Stålmarck and Säflund 1990, Borälv 1997]. Thus, by increasing the number of states allowed in the search, we get an alternative model checking procedure.

In this example, the formula is indeed satisfiable. The satisfying assignment corresponds to a counterexample that is a path from the initial point (00) over (01) to (10) followed by the loop from (10) to (00). If the transition from (10) to (00) is changed to point (11), then the original formula becomes unsatisfiable.

12.2. Translation into Propositional Logic

Assume that we are given a Kripke model $\mathcal{M}$, an **LTL** formula ψ and a bound k. Subsequently, each w^i is a vector of $\lceil \log |\mathcal{M}| \rceil$ boolean variables. We will construct a propositional formula in $w^0 \ldots w^k$ which is (propositionally) satisfiable iff there is a maximal path of length k in $\mathcal{M}$ validating ψ.

The initial and terminal state predicates $I(w)$ and $T(w)$ and the transition relation $R(w, w')$ are given by $\mathcal{M}$. The following propositional formula describes that the points to which the variables $w^1 \ldots w^k$ refer form a maximal path in $\mathcal{M}$:

$$[\mathcal{M}]_k \triangleq I(w^0) \wedge \bigvee_{i=1}^{k} R(w^{i-1}, w^i) \wedge \left(T(w^k) \vee \bigvee_{l=0}^{k} R(w^k, w^l) \right)$$

Now we define the translation $[\![\psi]\!]_k^i$ of a temporal formula ψ evaluated at point w^i in the sequence $(w^0 \ldots w^k)$. In general, the constraint imposed by the temporal specification depends on whether the path under consideration is terminating or not. Consider the formula $(\varphi \, \mathbf{U}^+ \, \psi)$ in a terminating path $(w^0 \ldots w^k)$. This formula holds in point w^i iff there is a $i < j \leq k$ such that such that ψ holds at w^j, and φ holds at all w^m such that $i < m < j$. This can be translated by a disjunction over all possible positions w^j at which ψ eventually might hold, and a conjunction for each of these positions ensuring that φ holds for all points between w^i and w^j. That is, in this case $[\![(\varphi \, \mathbf{U}^+ \, \psi)]\!]_k^i \triangleq \bigvee_{j=i+1}^{k} ([\![\psi]\!]_k^j \wedge \bigwedge_{m=i+1}^{j-1} [\![\varphi]\!]_k^m)$

Now consider the case that the path $(w^0 \ldots w^l \ldots w^k)$ ends with a loop from w^k to w^l. The formula $(\varphi \, \mathbf{U}^+ \, \psi)$ is satisfied in w^i iff one of the following holds:

- as for terminating sequences, there exists some $i < j \leq k$ such that ψ holds at w^j, and φ holds at all w^m such that $i < m < j$, or
- there exists some $l \leq j \leq i$ such that ψ holds at w^j, and φ holds at all w^m such that $i < m \leq k$, and φ holds at all w^m such that $l \leq m < j$.

Figure 36 visualizes these two possibilities.

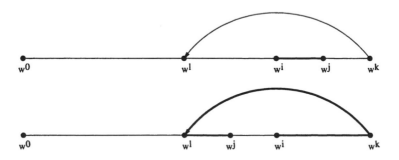

Figure 36: Two possibilities for "until" in a loop

The definition of $[\![\psi]\!]_k^i$ is by recursion on the structure of ψ, where the current point i changes but the length of the path k stays the same. For this translation, let $i \leq k$ be natural numbers, and let $(\bigvee_{j=l}^{i} \psi) \triangleq \bot$ for $l > i$.

- $[\![p]\!]_k^i \triangleq p(w^i)$
- $[\![\bot]\!]_k^i \triangleq \bot$
- $[\![(\varphi \rightarrow \psi)]\!]_k^i \triangleq ([\![\varphi]\!]_k^i \rightarrow [\![\psi]\!]_k^i)$

- $[(\varphi\, \mathbf{U}^+\, \psi)]_k^i \triangleq \bigvee_{j=i+1}^k ([\psi]_k^j \wedge \bigwedge_{m=i+1}^{j-1} [\varphi]_k^m) \vee$

$$\bigvee_{l=0}^k \left(\bigwedge_{m=i+1}^k [\varphi]_k^m \wedge R(w^k, w^l) \wedge \bigvee_{j=l}^i ([\psi]_k^j \wedge \bigwedge_{m=l}^{j-1} [\varphi]_k^m) \right)$$

For the last of these clauses, cf. Figure 36. Correctness of our translation can be stated as follows.

12.1. THEOREM. *There exists a maximal path of length k generated by $\mathcal{M}$ which initially validates ψ iff $([\mathcal{M}]_k \wedge [\psi]_k^0)$ is propositionally satisfiable. In other words, ψ is sequence-valid in $\mathcal{M}$ iff $([\mathcal{M}]_k \to [\psi]_k^0)$ is propositionally valid for all $k \geq 0$.*

An upper bound for the length k of the path to be considered is $|\mathcal{M}| \times 2^{|\psi|}$ (for the complexity of **LTL** model checking, see Sect. 8.2). In principle, bounded model checking could be extended to other specification logics such as $\mu\mathbf{TL}$. In practice, however, the number of boolean propositions which are introduced tends to be too big for currently available SAT provers.

13. Abstractions

Even though BDD representations, partial order methods and SAT procedures allow to apply model checking to rather large systems, one of the main topics still is the size of the models. To verify an implementation of several thousands of lines of code by model checking, it is necessary to find a suitable abstraction.

13.1. Abstraction functions

Numerous authors have considered the problem of reducing the complexity of verification by using abstractions, equivalences, preorders, etc. For example, in [Graf and Steffen 1990] a method is described for generating a reduced version of the global state space, given a description of how the system is structured and specifications of how the components interact. In [Wolper 1986] it is demonstrated how to do model checking for programs which are data independent. The method described in [Kurshan 1989], which is based on ω-language containment, was implemented in the COSPAN system [Har'El and Kurshan 1990, Kurshan 1994]. In this system, the user may give abstract models of the system and specification in order to reduce the complexity of the test for containment. To ensure soundness, the user specifies homomorphisms between actual and abstract processes. These homomorphisms are checked automatically. We describe a general framework elaborated in [Long 1993].

Traditionally, finite-state verification methods focus on the control flow of the system. Symbolic methods have made it possible to handle even some systems that involve nontrivial data manipulation, but the complexity of verification is often high. However, specifications of systems that include data paths usually involve fairly simple relationships among the data values in the system. For example, the correctness of a communications protocol might be independent of the particular data transmitted, provided that no two subsequent messages are identical. As another example, in verifying the addition operation of a microprocessor, we might require that the value in one register is eventually equal to the sum of the values in two other registers. The complexity of the verification can be reduced in such cases by suitable abstractions. An *abstraction* is specified by giving a mapping between the actual data values in the system and a small set of *abstract data values*. By extending the mapping to states and transitions, we can produce an abstract version of the system under consideration. The abstract system is often much smaller than the actual system, and, as a result, it is usually much simpler to verify properties at the abstract level.

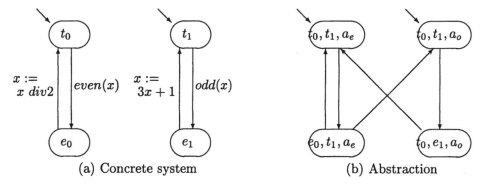

(a) Concrete system   (b) Abstraction

Figure 37: The dining mathematicians

For example, consider the program from Figure 37. This example called the "dining mathematicians" is from [Dams et al. 1994] and is reconsidered in [Merz 1997]. It consists of two processes communicating via a shared variable x which ranges over the domain D_x of all integers. Initially x is any positive integer. Both processes have a "thinking" and an "eating" state and start in the former. That is, the state space is $\{t_0, e_0\} \times \{t_1, e_1\} \times D_x$, and the initial states are $\{(t_0, t_1, d) \mid d > 0\}$. Note that both of these sets are infinite. The system ensures mutual exclusion to the eating phase and starvation-freeness for both processes.

Assume that we are interested in proving mutual exclusion: $\mathbf{A}\,\mathbf{G}^*\,\neg(e_0 \wedge e_1)$. We create a domain A_x of abstract values for x, with $A_x \triangleq \{a_z, a_e, a_o\}$, and define the *abstraction mapping* h_x from D_x to A_x as follows.

$$\alpha_x(d) \triangleq \begin{cases} a_z, & \text{if } d = 0, \\ a_e, & \text{if } d \text{ is even, and} \\ a_o, & \text{if } d \text{ is odd.} \end{cases}$$

Now we can use just three atomic propositions to express the abstract value of x: "$x \triangleq a_0$", "$x \triangleq a_e$", and "$x \triangleq a_o$". We can no longer express properties about the exact value of x using these atomic propositions. In many cases though, by judicious choice of the abstraction mapping, knowing just the abstract value is sufficient.

Two points $w_0 = (w_{00}, w_{01}, d_0)$ and $w_1 = (w_{10}, w_{11}, d_1)$ in the original Kripke model are *equivalent w.r.t.* the abstraction mapping α, if $w_{00} = w_{10}$, $w_{01} = w_{11}$ and $\alpha_x(d_1) = \alpha_x(d_2)$. That is, two points are equivalent if they have the same label, and the abstracted variable values in both points are equal. The α-*abstraction* is the quotient of the original model under this equivalence. Since the abstract domain A_x is finite, the α-abstraction is a finite Kripke model. Figure 37(b) shows the reachable part of the α-abstraction of 37(a). It is easy to see (and can be confirmed by model checking) that the abstracted system validates $\mathbf{A}\,\mathbf{G}^* \neg(e_0 \wedge e_1)$. As we will see below, this implies that the original systems also guarantees this property.

Formally, abstractions are formed by giving surjections $\alpha_1, \ldots, \alpha_n$ which map each D_i onto a set D_i^α of abstract values. The surjection $\alpha = (\alpha_1, \ldots, \alpha_n)$ then maps each program state to a corresponding abstract state. As explained above, this mapping may be applied in a natural way to the initial states and the transitions of the program. The resulting transition system is the α-abstraction of the original program. Applying abstractions to several or all of the program variables, the specification has a much smaller number of atomic propositions and points. For the abstracted system, various state space reductions discussed in previous sections can be applied.

One way of obtaining a representation of the α-abstraction of a concurrent program is to build a representation of the original state space and to construct the α-abstraction from it. However, if the original state space is infinite as in the above example, or it is too large to fit into memory, this may not be feasible. In the finite state case, it might be possible to represent the system using BDD-based methods, but the computational complexity of building the α-quotient from this representation can still be very high.

To circumvent these problems, another way of producing abstract models in a BDD-based verification tool is to start with a high level description of the system and the abstraction function. The system could be given, e.g., as a program in a hardware description language. From this, a BDD for the abstracted system is generated directly. In order to perform the compilation process effectively, an *approximation* to the α-abstraction is generated[Clarke, Grumberg and Long 1994a]. This approximation might be somewhat larger than the α-abstraction, but it can be built very efficiently. The techniques used in this construction are similar to those involved in *abstract interpretation* [Cousot and Cousot 1977, Cousot and Cousot 1979, Dams 1995]. This way, it is even possible to use abstractions to verify systems in which the data path is not completely specified. By modeling the data path as a collection of units that perform unspecified functions, the verification of the data path and the verification of the control can be largely decoupled.

To be able to interpret specification formulas with respect to both the original transition system and its abstraction, atomic formulas must be those specifying that a program variable has a particular abstract value. In Theorem 4.11 we showed that if $\mathcal{M}_1$ is simulated by $\mathcal{M}_2$, then any formula in the logic **ACTL** valid in $\mathcal{M}_2$ is also valid in $\mathcal{M}_1$. An abstraction is a special simulation; thus if an **ACTL** formula is true in the abstract system, we can conclude that it is also true in the original system. In addition, if the equivalence relations induced by the α_i are *congruences* with respect to the operations used in the program, then the formula is true in the abstract system iff it is true of the original system. [Loiseaux, Graf, Sifakis, Bouajjani and Bensalem 1995] discusses abstraction techniques which preserve properties specified in μTL.

It should be emphasized that the choice of suitable abstractions α_i is an interactive step in the verification. Usually, there are several possibilities to abstract a given system, all preserving different properties. In our above example, the chosen abstraction does not allow to prove starvation-freeness of the second process. However, this situation is not typical for industrial applications. In [Clarke, Grumberg and Long 1994a], the following abstractions are used to verify a pipelined arithmetic/logical unit with over 4000 state bits and 10^{1300} reachable states.

- congruence modulo an integer, for dealing with arithmetic operations;
- single bit abstractions, for dealing with bitwise logical operations;
- product abstractions, for computing abstractions such as the above; and
- symbolic abstractions. This is a powerful type of abstraction that allows to verify an entire class of formulas simultaneously.

Another approach at implementing abstraction functions is directly at the level of the BDD data structure. Given an abstraction function, we can reduce the size of a BDD by merging nodes that have the same abstract value. *Abstract BDDs* (ABDDs) are a generalization of Residue BDDs (RBDDs, see [Kimura 1995]). To obtain an ABDD it is not necessary to build the full BDD: ABDDs can be constructed directly from the abstraction function and the description of the system. For more information, see [Clarke, Jha, Lu and Minea 1997].

13.2. Symmetry Reductions

Most large hardware circuits are highly symmetric. For instance, one can find symmetry in memories, caches, register files, bus and network protocols — any type of hardware containing replicated structures. For symmetric systems, we can apply special abstractions to avoid searching the entire state space of the circuit and to reduce the size of the BDDs representing the transition relation[Starke 1991, Emerson and Sistla 1993, Clarke, Filkorn and Jha 1993, Ip and Dill 1993].

Suppose that we want to represent the boolean function (formula) $\varphi(v_1, ..., v_n)$ of n variables by a BDD. Symmetry in a boolean function is modeled in terms of a permutation group acting on the set of variables of the function. We say that φ is *invariant* under a permutation σ on v_1, ..., v_n, if the value of the function does not change when the permutation σ is applied to its arguments:

$$\varphi(v_1, ..., v_n) = \varphi(\sigma(v_1), ..., \sigma(v_n))$$

The function is said to be invariant under a group G of permutations, if it is invariant under each permutation σ in G. For example, let $\varphi(v_1, v_2, v_3, v_4)$ be the function which tests whether two 2-bit numbers (v_1, v_3) and (v_2, v_4) are equal. The function φ is clearly invariant under the transpositions (1 2) and (3 4). The first permutation corresponds to exchanging input bits v_1 and v_2. The second corresponds to exchanging v_3 and v_4. The function will, of course, also be invariant under the group generated by the two transpositions.

Let B^n be the set of boolean vectors of length n, and let G be a permutation group on $1, ..., n$. Assume that G acts on B^n in the natural way. For example, applying the transposition $(2\ 3)$ to $(0, 1, 0, 1)$ yields $(0, 0, 1, 1)$. We say that two vectors v^1 and v^2 are *equivalent with respect to* G if there is a permutation σ in G such that $v^1 = v^2$. Since G is a group, this relation is an equivalence relation on B^n and therefore partitions B^n into a number of equivalence classes. The number of equivalence classes may be much smaller than the number of boolean vectors in B^n.

A boolean function $\varphi(v_1, ..., v_n)$ is uniquely determined by the set of vectors in B^n that cause it to have the value $\top$. If φ is invariant under some group of permutations G, it may be possible to compact the BDD representation for φ: if any one of the boolean vectors in some equivalence class determined by G makes φ true, then all of the vectors in this equivalence class will. Consequently, in the BDD representation for φ it is necessary to keep at most one representative from each equivalence class. In many cases this significantly reduces the size of the BDD for φ.

Essentially the same idea can be used to reduce the size of the state space that must be searched by the symbolic model checking algorithm. Let U be the set of possible states of the system, which are determined by the values of $v_1, ..., v_n$. A permutation of these state variables induces a permutation on the state-space of the system. Let $\prec$ be the transition relation of the system and $\equiv$ be an equivalence relation. We say that $\prec$ *respects* $\equiv$ if whenever $w_1 \equiv w_1'$ and $w_2 \equiv w_2'$, then $w_1 \prec w_2$ iff $w_1' \prec w_2'$. When the transition relation R respects the equivalence relation $\equiv$ determined by a permutation group, it is possible to reduce the state space to the set of equivalence classes $U^{\equiv}$ determined by $\equiv$. The corresponding transition relation between these equivalence classes is $\prec^{\equiv}$. Since we only need one point for each equivalence class, the model $(U^{\equiv}, \prec^{\equiv})$ is often much smaller than the original model $(U, \prec)$.

Similar as with abstraction functions, the reduced BDD can be constructed directly from a description of the system and the permutation group. For more information, the reader is referred to [Kannan and Lipton 1986, Clarke, Filkorn and Jha 1993]. It is not clear, though, how the reductions obtained by symmetries interacts with other abstraction techniques and partial order methods.

13.3. Parameterized Systems

A special case of a symmetry is that the system consists of an arbitrary number of similar or identical processes. Systems of this type are commonplace – they occur in bus protocols and network protocols, I/O channels, and many other structures that are designed to be extensible by adding similar components. A number of methods have been proposed for extending model checking to such designs [Clarke, Grumberg and Browne 1986, Wolper and Lovinfosse 1989, German and Sistla 1992, Clarke, Grumberg and Jha 1995].

After using a model checker to determine the correctness of a system configured with a fixed number of processors or other components, it is natural to ask whether this number is enough in some sense to represent a system with any number of components. This question was approached in [Browne, Clarke and Grumberg 1989], who extended **CTL** to a logic called *indexed* **CTL**. This logic allows the restricted use of process quantifiers as in the formula $\bigwedge_i \varphi_i$, which means that the formula φ holds for all processes i. Restricting the use of these quantifiers and eliminating the next-time operator makes it impossible to write a formula which can distinguish the number of processes in a system. By establishing an appropriate relationship between a system with n processes and a system with $n + 1$ processes, one can guarantee that all systems satisfy the same set of formulas in the indexed logic. This method was used to establish the correctness of a mutual exclusion algorithm by exhibiting a bisimulation relation between an n-process system and a 2-process system, and applying model checking to the 2-process system.

One disadvantage of the indexing method is that the bisimulation relation must be proved "by hand" in an *ad hoc* manner. Finite state methods cannot be used to check it because it is a map between states of a finite state process and a process with an arbitrary number of states. A method without this disadvantage was proposed in [Kurshan and McMillan 1989], and independently in [Wolper and Lovinfosse 1989]. This method uses a process Q to act as an invariant, as the number of processes increases. If P represents one process in the system, then by showing that the possible executions of P composed with Q are contained in the possible executions of Q, we can conclude by induction that Q adequately represents a system of any finite number of processes. Since both P composed with Q and Q are finite state processes, the containment relation can be checked automatically. This method has been applied in [McMillan and Schwalbe 1992] to the Encore Gigamax cache consistency protocol. By slightly generalizing the model of one processor, an invariant process for this system could be obtained which stands for any number of processors on a bus.

These induction techniques have been generalized by a number of authors (e.g., [Marelly and Grumberg 1991]). However, the main problem in all of these verification methods is that of constructing the invariant process. Currently, the invariant process must be generated interactively. Counterexamples produced by model checking tools are helpful for guiding the construction, but it would be useful to have automated techniques for this purpose. To make these methods generally accepted, more results on the combination of model checking and inductive theorem proving and powerful heuristics are necessary.

14. Compositionality and Modular Verification

As explained in Section 9, most circuits and protocols are modeled as networks of communicating parallel processes. The complexity of these models grows exponentially in the number of processes; thus, monolithic verification of such designs can be hard. Therefore, it may be necessary to verify small components separately and, from that, derive the correctness of the whole design, without building a model for the entire system. This so-called *compositionality paradigm* has been investigated by a number of authors [deRoever, Langmaack and Pnueli 1998].

14.1. Model Checking and Theorem Proving

Assume a process consisting of a parallel composition of several subprocesses, where all subprocesses have associated formulas specifying their properties. Whenever a property of a parallel composition is to be proven, we can first prove for each component that the corresponding property holds, and then infer in an adequate proof system that the global property of the composition also holds. Model checking can be used to verify the individual components; then theorem proving techniques can be used to derive global properties of their parallel composition. The composition step substantially simplifies the verification problem, since it avoids building the global state space. Thus, the compositionality paradigm is a promising perspective for the combination of model checking with theorem proving.

Moreover, this approach supports the hierarchical design process. One can work out specifications for all parts of a complex system and prove that if every component satisfies its specification, then the whole system is correct. When the system is implemented it is sufficient to verify each component separately. It is also possible to change the actual implementation of some component without having to repeat the verification of the entire system as soon as the new implementation meets its local requirements.

For instance, consider the problem of verifying a communications protocol that is modelled by three processes: a transmitter, some type of network, and a receiver. Suppose that the specification for the system is that data is eventually transmitted correctly from the sender to the receiver. Such a specification might be decomposed into three local properties. First, the data should eventually be transferred correctly from the transmitter to the network. Second, the data should eventually be transferred correctly from one end of the network to the other. Finally, the data should eventually be transferred correctly from the network to the receiver. We might be able to verify the first of these local properties using only the transmitter and the network, the second using only the network, and the third using only the network and the receiver. By decomposing the verification in this way, we never have to compose all of the processes and therefore avoid the state explosion phenomenon.

Whereas model checking for the verification of the individual components is a well-understood technique, for the derivation of global system properties from local components properties an appropriate calculus is needed. There are two possibilities for implementing a proof system for such a calculus. The first is to incorporate the calculus into a general purpose theorem prover. For example, there are embeddings of Lamport's temporal logic of actions (TLA) into the theorem provers LARCH, PVS and Isabelle (see, e.g., [Abadi, Lamport and Merz 1996]). However, the computational complexity inherent in such an approach may prevent the resulting tool from being applicable for large industrial designs.

The second possibility is to build a special purpose theorem prover for the chosen calculus. Several suggestions for a concrete framework following this approach have been made. The proof system of [Stirling 1987] is, probably, the most compositional in the sense that it clearly reduces the verification problem to the verification of components. However, the logic which is used in this paper is too weak to be of much interest in practice. In [Andersen, Stirling and Winskel 1994] the parallel composition operator was eliminated basically by encoding one of the subprocesses into the formula. In the worst case this results in an exponential blow-up in the size of the formula, and the total complexity remains the same as for non-compositional model checking. The proof system of [Dam 1995] is complete for finite-state processes. However, it uses a silent τ action for all synchronizations, and in the τ-rule there have to be as many premises as there are actions in the model. Therefore, one can only have a fixed set of actions.

The STeP system [Bjørner, Browne, Chang, Colón, Kapur, Manna, Simpa and Uribe 1995, Bjørner, Browne, Chang, Colón, Kapur, Manna, Sipma and Uribe 1996] implements another approach to combining model checking and theorem proving under a single framework. However, the user must decide what has to be model checked and what to be derived in a theorem prover. It would be desirable to create the verification agenda automatically, such that the user will only have to supply some intermediate properties and possibly assist the theorem prover during a proof search.

14.2. Compositional Assume-Guarantee Reasoning

Ideally, compositional reasoning exploits the natural decomposition of a complex system into simpler components, handling one component at a time. In practice, however, when a component is verified it may be necessary to *assume* that the environment behaves in a certain manner. If the other components in the system *guarantee* this behavior, then we can conclude that the verified properties are valid in the entire system. These properties can be used to deduce additional global properties of the system.

The *assume-guarantee paradigm* (cf. e.g., [Pnueli 1984]) uses this method. Typically, a formula is a triple $\langle\psi\rangle\mathcal{M}\langle\varphi\rangle$ where ψ and φ are temporal formulas and $\mathcal{M}$ is a program. The formula is valid if whenever $\mathcal{M}$ is part of a system satisfying ψ, the system must also satisfy φ. A typical proof shows that $\langle\psi\rangle\mathcal{M}\langle\varphi\rangle$ and $\langle\top\rangle\mathcal{M}'\langle\psi\rangle$ hold and concludes that $\langle\top\rangle\mathcal{M} \parallel \mathcal{M}'\langle\varphi\rangle$ is valid. This proof strategy can also be expressed as an inference rule:

$$\frac{\langle\psi\rangle\mathcal{M}\langle\varphi\rangle \quad \langle\top\rangle\mathcal{M}'\langle\psi\rangle}{\langle\top\rangle\mathcal{M} \parallel \mathcal{M}'\langle\varphi\rangle}$$

The soundness of an assume-guarantee rule of this form is straightforward. A more powerful form that also involves pure temporal reasoning is:

$$\langle \psi_1 \rangle \mathcal{M}_1 \langle \varphi_1 \rangle$$
$$\langle \psi_2 \rangle \mathcal{M}_2 \langle \varphi_2 \rangle$$
$$\xi_1 \wedge \varphi_1 \rightarrow \psi_2$$
$$\xi_1 \wedge \varphi_2 \rightarrow \psi_1$$
$$\frac{\varphi_1 \wedge \varphi_2 \rightarrow \xi_2}{\langle \xi_1 \rangle \mathcal{M}_1 \parallel \mathcal{M}_2 \langle \xi_2 \rangle}$$

In the composed system $\mathcal{M}_1 \parallel \mathcal{M}_2$, the module $\mathcal{M}_2$ is part of the environment of $\mathcal{M}_1$ and vice versa. $\mathcal{M}_2$ guarantees via φ_2 that the assumption ψ_1 of $\mathcal{M}_1$ is met, provided that its own assumption ψ_2 holds. $\mathcal{M}_1$, in turn, guarantees the assumption of $\mathcal{M}_2$, provided that its assumption holds.

As shown in [Pnueli 1984], careless application of this rule may lead to a circular reasoning and, thus, may result in an erroneous conclusion. To avoid this, Pnueli suggested associating a parameter over some well–founded set with each temporal formula in the assume-guarantee rule. The rule then allows for a temporal formula to be deduced only from formulas with smaller parameters. For an abstract account of composition, see [Merz 1997]. Several tools have been developed that permit this type of reasoning to be automated [Josko 1993, Long 1993, Grumberg and Long 1994]. The tools provide a machinery for checking automatically the validity of formulas of the form $\langle \psi \rangle \mathcal{M} \langle \varphi \rangle$. These tools, however, suffer from two main deficiencies.

Firstly, they do not provide any mechanism to avoid or to locate circular reasoning. Thus, they count on the user "common sense" for correct application of the method. An open problem is to develop an algorithm for checking non-circularity in assume-guarantee reasoning. This could bridge the gap between the abstract assume-guarantee paradigm and its computerized version.

Secondly, in order to obtain a powerful method, the preorder and the semantics of the logics should both include a notion of *fairness*. This is essential for modelling systems (hardware or communication protocols) at the appropriate level of abstraction. Unfortunately, no efficient technique exists to check or compute *fair preorder* between models. In [Grumberg and Long 1994], it is suggested how to check the fair preorder in some simple cases. In the general case, the problem is PSPACE-hard [Kupferman and Vardi 1996]. A notion of fair preorder that, on the one hand, is suitable for computerized assume-guarantee reasoning, and on the other hand, can be checked efficiently, would make compositional reasoning less error prone and could widen the applicability of this type of reasoning.

15. Further Topics

There are several extensions to each of the topics presented here, and in many areas there is a lot of ongoing activity. Current research can be classified into two main tracks:

- improve efficiency and applicability of present model checking techniques, and

- extend the realm of application and merge model checking with other formal methods.

A number of papers on industrial case studies, advanced heuristics, and improved algorithms and data structures follows the first track. The second track encompasses papers on model checking for infinite state systems, integration with simulation and testing, as well as model checking for real-time, probabilistic and security related applications.

15.1. Combination of Heuristics

Partial order techniques attempt to alleviate the state explosion problem by constructing a reduced state space to be searched by the model checking algorithm. Originally introduced in the context of untimed models, they have been expanded to handle real time systems [Yoneda and Schlingloff 1997, Sloan and Buy 1997]. In turn, symbolic techniques have been applied to model checking for real-time systems. It seems to be a challenging task to combine the advantages of partial order reduction with a symbolic representation for real-time system verification. One of the intrinsic difficulties is that the partial order reduction, as described in section 11, needs to have access to the search history, which is trivially implemented for explicit state search but has no immediate correspondence in the symbolic case. Recent advances [Alur et al. 1997, Kurshan, Levin, Minea, Peled and Yenigun 1997] have shown that this technique can be combined with symbolic model checking, which in many cases allows much larger state spaces to be handled. One of these methods [Kurshan et al. 1997] allows partial order reduction to be performed statically, by analyzing the state graph of each asynchronous system component. Existing partial order methods for real-time models are dynamic in the sense that they use timing information obtained during the state space search. However, probably a significant part of the dependency information can be obtained statically as well, making the combination with symbolic techniques possible [Minea 1999].

Partial order methods mostly have been investigated within the context of (stutter-invariant) linear temporal logic model checking. The method reduces the complex part of the model checking problem, namely the size of the model. The tableau for an **LTL** specification is usually small. However, the state explosion problem is even more prevalent in the case of conformance checking and (bi-)simulation between automata. A problem here is how to apply partial order reduction simultaneously to both models.

A key factor that affects the efficiency of partial order reduction is the number of visible transitions, i.e., transitions that may change a predicate in the checked property. With more and more complex specifications, the number of visible transitions increases and less reduction can be achieved. Some approaches to alleviate this problem have been proposed in [Peled 1993]. One possibility is to take advantage of the structure of the specification and rewrite it as a combination of simpler properties. However, no optimal solution is known to date.

Other issues that are important in conjunction with the combination of heuristics are abstraction and compositionality. It is still unknown how the efficiency improvement gained by symbolic representation and partial order analysis interact with abstraction techniques and compositional reasoning. To be able to verify even bigger systems, it is important to develop methods and tools that allow to combine the benefits of several methods.

15.2. Real Time Systems

Within the last few years, several attempts have been made to apply formal analysis methods also to *real time systems*. The ideas and techniques presented so far are well-suited for the verification of systems in which only *causal* aspects of time are important. In some applications it is desirable to consider *quantitative* aspects of timing behavior. We say that a system has to satisfy *hard real time constraints*, if its correctness depends on the value or progress of "the real" clock. In hard real-time systems, not only the relative order of events is important, but also their absolute duration with respect to a (conceptual) global clock. For example, in a traffic light controller, it might not be sufficient to show that if a pedestrian pushes a button, then *eventually* the green lights will be on. To allow approaching cars to pass, the light should stay red after the button has been pushed *for at least 10 seconds*. To avoid that pedestrians start crossing at red, it should also change *not later than 30 seconds* after the request. In this example, we assume that both the pedestrian and the traffic light controller have the same measure of the duration of a second. Of course, it is possible to model the global clock as separate concurrent part of the system. Then this global clock synchronizes the local clocks of both pedestrian and traffic light controller. Thus, it is possible to consider real-time verification as special case of the untimed methods described above. However, in hard real-time systems, global time is ubiquitous, therefore this approach may not be the most efficient.

It is important to note that "hard real time" does not mean "as fast as possible". As the above example shows, predictability of timing behavior can also mean that some events do not occur before a certain amount of time has elapsed. As another example, consider a real-time protocol, where all necessary computation steps *must* be performed in *exactly* a fixed time slot. Currently, hard real time systems are designed with trial and error: if a component is too fast, an idle waiting loop is incorporated; if it is too slow, more expensive hardware is used. This procedure has several disadvantages. Firstly, it can add intricate hardware-software dependencies to a system. Therefore the migration to new hardware generations is complicated. Secondly, the execution time of single statements can vary depending on input data, nondeterministic scheduling, cache behavior, etc. Timing measurement can not guarantee that the actual timing will be within required boundaries. Finally, in applications like the design of asynchronous circuits, an arbitrary delay of signals can be expensive.

In real time verification, clock values usually are assumed to be nonnegative real, rational or natural numbers. As opposed to untimed systems, there is no generally accepted representation of sets or regions of timing values. Common tools use *difference bound matrices* [Dill 1989] and *clock regions* [Alur, Courcoubetis and Dill 1990, Alur 1991] to represent timing constraints. Real time systems often are modelled with timed automata [Alur 1998, Alur and Dill 1990] or timed transition systems [Henzinger, Manna and Pnueli 1992]. For an overview on real time logics and models, see [Alur and Henzinger 1992]. Reachability and model checking algorithms for these models are given in [Alur et al. 1990]. Generally, the complexity of verifying real-time systems is much higher than that for untimed systems. Moreover, timing constructs are often represented using an explicit state representation. Consequently, the number of states that can be handled is relatively small ($10^5 - 10^7$). Thus, at present, only highly abstracted examples (e.g., [Archer and Heitmeyer 1996]) can be verified automatically by model checking tools like KRONOS [Yovine 1997, Yovine 1998] or UPPAAL [Larsen, Petterson and Yi 1997, Aceto, Bergueno and Larsen 1998].

It is a challenging research task to find a paradigm separating the real-time component from the functional and reactive component in the specification of typical real-time requirements. This could make model checking an integral component in the development of reactive real-time systems.

15.3. Probabilistic Model Checking

Some safety-critical systems have a stochastic behavior. This may be either due to the fact that some part of the outside world, which is stochastic in nature, is modelled as part of the system, or because of hardware failures which may happen stochastically. Available model checkers usually model the probabilistic behavior of such systems non-deterministically, missing the ability to assess how probable some system behavior is.

A number of theoretical papers have been written on probabilistic verification. Efficient algorithms have been given by several authors; for example, there is an LTL model checking algorithm which is exponential in the size of the formula and polynomial in the size of the Markov chain [Courcoubetis and Yannakakis 1995]. However, currently there are no probabilistic model checking tools available which can verify systems of realistic size. The bottleneck is the construction of the state space and the necessity to solve huge systems of linear equations. A more efficient alternative could be to perform the probability calculations using Multi-Terminal Binary Decision Diagrams (MTBDDs).

MTBDDs [Bahar, Frohm, Gaona, Hachtel, Macii, Pardo and Somenzi 1993, Clarke, Fujita, McGeer, Yang and Zhao 1993] differ from BDDs in that the leaves may have values other than 0 and 1; in this case the leaves contain transition probabilities. MTBDDs can be used to represent D–valued matrices efficiently. Consider a $2^m \times 2^m$–matrix A. Its elements a_{ij}, can be viewed as the values of a function $f_A : \{0, \ldots 2^m - 1\} \times \{0, \ldots 2^m - 1\} \to D$, where $f_A(i, j) = a_{ij}$. Using the standard encoding $c : B^m \to \{0, \ldots 2^m - 1\}$ of boolean sequences of length less than m into the integers, this function may be interpreted as a D–valued boolean function $f : B^m \to D$ where $f(x, y) = f_A(c(x), c(y))$ for $x = (x_0 \ldots x_{m-1})$ and $y = (y_0 \ldots y_{m-1})$. This transformation now allows matrices to be represented as MTBDDs. In order to obtain an efficient MTBDD–representation, the variables of f are permuted. Instead of the MTBDD for $f(x_0 \ldots x_{m-1}, y_0 \ldots y_{m-1})$, the MTBDD obtained from $f(x_0, y_0, x_0, y_0, \ldots x_{m-1}, y_{m-1})$ can be used. This convention imposes a recursive structure on the matrix from which efficient recursive algorithms for all standard matrix operations can be derived.

MTBDDs can be integrated with a symbolic model checker and have the potential to outperform other matrix representations because they are very compact. For example, in [Hachtel, Macii, Pardo and Somenzi 1996] symbolic algorithms were developed to perform steady-state probabilistic analysis for systems with finite state models of more than 10^{27} states. While it is difficult to provide precise time complexity estimates for probabilistic model checking using MTBDDs, the success of BDDs in practice indicates that this is likely to be a worthwhile approach.

The standard model used in probabilistic model checking are finite state discrete-time Markov chains ([Hansson and Jonsson 1989, Courcoubetis and Yannakakis 1995, Aziz, Singhal, Balarin, Brayton and Sangiovanni-Vincentelli 1995, Aziz, Sanwal, Singhal and Brayton 1996]). This model is a powerful notation for the dependability analysis of fault-tolerant real-time control systems, performance analysis of commercial computer systems and networks, and operation of automated manufacturing systems.

To specify properties of finite state discrete-time Markov chains, *Probabilistic Real Time Computation Tree Logic* (PCTL) was introduced in [Hansson and Jonsson 1989]. PCTL augments **CTL** with time and probability; it is a very expressive logic and offers simple model checking algorithms that can be implemented using symbolic techniques in a straightforward manner [Baier, Clarke, Hartonas-Garmhausen, Kwiatkowska and Ryan 1997].

However, in order to make model checking a standard method for probabilistic verification, more experiences with industrial size examples, typical requirements and efficient tools are necessary.

15.4. Model Checking for Security Protocols

Security protocols are another promising area for the application of model checking techniques. The increasing amount of confidential information (such as monetary transactions) sent over insecure communication links (such as the internet) requires more and more sophisticated encryption protocols. Like hardware designs, these protocols can have subtle bugs which are difficult to find. It may be possible to use the same exhaustive search techniques as in model checking to verify security protocols. By examining all possible execution traces of the protocol in the presence of a malicious adversary with well defined capabilities, it may be possible to determine if an attack on the protocol could be successful.

Typically, security protocols can be thought of as a set of principals which send messages to each other. The hope is that by requiring agents to produce a sequence of formatted and encrypted messages, the security goals of the protocol can be achieved. For example, if a principal A receives a message encrypted with a key known only by principal B, then principal A should be able to conclude that principal B created the message. However, it would be incorrect to conclude that principal A is talking to principal B. An adversary could be replaying a message overheard during a previous conversation between A and B. If the aim is to keep the message secret, then as long as the adversary does not learn the key, this security property is satisfied. If, however, the aim is to authenticate B to A, then clearly this is not satisfied since the message was not necessarily sent by B.

Since the reasoning behind the correctness of these protocols can be subtle, researchers have tried turning to formal methods to prove protocols correct. In [Burrows, Abadi and Needham 1989], a logic of belief is developed in which one could formally reason about security protocols by stating axioms about the protocol and trying to derive theorems about its security. [Kindred and Wing 1996] added some automation to this process by generating theory checkers for these logics. In [Meadows 1994], a different approach is taken by modelling a security protocol in terms of a set of rewrite rules. These rules capture the way that the adversary can learn new information using encryption and decryption, and by receiving replies to messages sent to participants of the protocol. In [Woo and Lam 1993], the authors propose a model for authentication and provide a number of inference rules that could be used for proving properties in this model. The paper [Mitchell, Mitchell and Stern 1997] investigated the use of Murφ, a previously existing model checker, for verifying security protocols.

A special purpose model checker for authentification protocols could contain two orthogonal components. The first is a *state exploration component*. Each honest agent can be described by the sequence of actions that it takes during a run of the protocol, and can be viewed as a finite-state machine. A trace of the actions performed by the asynchronous composition of these state machines corresponds to a possible execution of the protocol by the agents. By performing an exhaustive search of the state space of the composition, it can be determined if various security properties are violated.

The second component would be the *message derivation engine* which is used to model what the adversary is allowed to do. It can be implemented as a simple natural deduction theorem prover for constructing valid messages. The adversary can intercept messages, misdirect messages, and generate new messages using encryption, decryption, concatenation (pairing), and projection. Each time a message is sent, the adversary intercepts the message and adds it to the set of assumptions it can use to derive new messages. Whenever an honest agent receives a message, the message must have been generated by the derivation engine.

A first prototypical implementation shows that this framework can be successfully used to analyze threats and exhibit possible attacks in authentication protocols. It is also general enough to handle other kinds of security protocols such as key exchange and electronic commerce. Moreover, combining model checking with other automated deduction techniques could make it possible to verify both the encryption algorithm and the actual implementation at the same time. However, for a widespread use it is additionally necessary to integrate the model checking approach with other, more well-established security design methods.

Acknowledgments

We would like to thank Wolfgang Heinle for help with initial versions of this chapter, the editor for his patience with us during its preparation, and the referees for many useful comments and suggestions.

Bibliography

ABADI M., LAMPORT L. AND MERZ S. [1996], A TLA solution to the RPC–memory specification problem, *in* M. Broy, S. Merz and K. Spies, eds, 'Formal System Specification: The RPC–Memory Specification Case Study', Vol. 1169 of *LNCS*, Springer, pp. 21–66.

ACETO L., BERGUENO A. AND LARSEN K. [1998], Model checking via reachability testing for timed automata, *in* B. Steffen, ed., 'Proc. 4th Int. Workshop on Tools and Algorithms for the Construction and Analysis of Systems (TACAS '98)', Vol. 1384 of *LNCS*, Springer, Lisbon, pp. 281–297.

AHO A. V., HOPCROFT J. E. AND ULLMAN J. D. [1974], *The Design and Analysis of Computer Algorithms*, Addison–Wesley.

AJTAI M. AND GUREVICH Y. [1987], 'Monotone versus positive', *Journal of the ACM* **34**, 1004–1015.

ALPERN B. AND SCHNEIDER F. [1985], 'Defining liveness', *Information Processing Letters* **21**, 181–185.

ALUR R. [1991], Techniques for Automatic Verification of Real–Time Systems, PhD thesis, Stanford University.

ALUR R. [1998], Timed automata, *in* 'Verification of Digital and Hybrid Systems', NATO ASI Summer School Series, Springer.

ALUR R., BRAYTON R. K., HENZINGER T., QUADEER S. AND RAJAMANI S. K. [1997], Partial-order reduction in symbolic state space exploration, *in* 'Proc. 9th Int. Conf. on Computer Aided Verification (CAV '97)', Vol. 1254 of *LNCS*, Springer, Haifa, Israel, pp. 340–351.

ALUR R., COURCOUBETIS C. AND DILL D. [1990], Model–checking for real–time systems, *in* 'Proc. 5th Ann. IEEE Symp. on Logic in Computer Science (LICS '90)', IEEE Comp. Soc. Press, pp. 414–425.

ALUR R. AND DILL D. [1990], Automata for modelling real–time systems, *in* 'Proc. 17th Int. Conf. on Automata, Languages and Programming (ICALP '90)', Vol. 443 of *LNCS*, Springer, pp. 322–335.

ALUR R. AND HENZINGER T. A. [1992], Logics and models of real–time: A survey, *in* 'Real–Time: Theory in Practice', LNCS, Springer.

ANDERSEN H. R. [1994], On model checking infinite–state systems, *in* A. Nerode and Matiyasevich, eds, 'Logic at St. Petersburg. Symp. on Logical Foundations of Computer Science (LFCS '94)', Vol. 813 of *LNCS*, Springer, St. Petersburg, Russia, July 11–14.

ANDERSEN H. R., STIRLING C. AND WINSKEL G. [1994], A compositional proof system for the modal μ–calculus, *in* 'Proc. 9th Ann. IEEE Symp. on Logic in Computer Science (LICS '94)', IEEE Computer Society Press, Paris, France, pp. 144–153. BRICS Report RS-94-34.

ANUCHITANUKUL A. [1995], Synthesis of Reactive Programs, PhD thesis, Stanford.

ARCHER M. AND HEITMEYER C. [1996], Mechanical verification of timed automata: A case study, *in* 'IEEE Real–Time Technology and Applications Symp. (RTAS'96)', IEEE Computer Society Press, Boston MA.

AZIZ A., SANWAL K., SINGHAL V. AND BRAYTON R. K. [1996], Verifying continuous Markov chains, *in* R. Alur and T. Henzinger, eds, 'Proc. 8th Workshop on Computer Aided Verification (CAV '96)', Vol. 1102 of *LNCS*, Springer, pp. 269–276.

AZIZ A., SINGHAL V., BALARIN F., BRAYTON R. K. AND SANGIOVANNI-VINCENTELLI A. L. [1995], It usually works – the temporal logic of stochastic systems, *in* P. Wolper, ed., 'Proc. 7th Workshop on Computer Aided Verification (CAV '95)', Vol. 939 of *LNCS*, Springer, pp. 155–166.

BAHAR R. I., FROHM E. A., GAONA C. M., HACHTEL G. D., MACII E., PARDO A. AND SOMENZI F. [1993], Algebraic decision diagrams and their applications, *in* 'Proc. Int. Conf. on Computer Aided Design (ICCAD '93)', Santa Clara, pp. 188–191.

Baier C., Clarke E. M., Hartonas-Garmhausen V., Kwiatkowska M. and Ryan M. [1997], Symbolic model checking for probabilistic processes, in 'Proc. Int. Conf. on Automata, Languages and Programming (ICALP '97))', Vol. 1256 of *LNCS*, pp. 430–437.

Ben-Ari M., Manna Z. and Pnueli A. [1983], 'The temporal logic of branching time', *Acta Informatica* **20**, 207–226.

Bensalem S., Bouajani A., Loiseaux C. and Sifakis J. [1992], Property preserving simulations, in G. V. Bochmann and D. K. Probst, eds, 'Proc. 4th Int. Conf. on Computer Aided Verification (CAV '92)'.

Berezin S., Clarke E. M., Jha S. and Marrero W. [1996], Model checking algorithms for the μ-calculus, Technical Report CMU–CS–96–180, CMU.

Bermann C. L. [1991], 'Circuit width, register allocation and ordered binary decision diagrams', *IEEE Trans. on Computer–Aided Design* **10**(8), 1059–1066.

Bern J., Meinel C. and Slobodová A. [1995], Global rebuilding of BDDs – avoiding the memory requirement maxima, in P. Wolper, ed., 'Proc. 7th Workshop on Computer Aided Verification (CAV '95)', Vol. 939 of *LNCS*, Springer, pp. 4–15.

Bhat G. and Cleaveland R. [1996], Efficient local model checking for fragments of the modal μ-calculus, in T. Margaria and B. Steffen, eds, 'Proc. Tools and Algorithms for the Construction and Analysis of Systems (TACAS '96)', Vol. 1055 of *LNCS*, Springer, pp. 107–126.

Biere A. [1997], Effiziente Modellprüfung des μ-Kalküls mit binären Entscheidungsdiagrammen, PhD thesis, University of Karlsruhe, Germany.

Biere A., Cimatti A., Fujita M. and Zhu Y. [1999], Symbolic model checking using SAT procedures instead of BDDs, in 'Proc. 36th ACM/IEEE Design Automation Conference (DAC '99)'.

Biere A., Cimatti A. and Zhu Y. [1999], Symbolic model checking without BDDs, in 'Proc. Tools and Algorithms for the Analysis and Construction of Systems (TACAS'99)', Vol. 1579 of *LNCS*, Springer.

Bjørner N., Browne A., Chang E., Colón M., Kapur A., Manna Z., Simpa H. B. and Uribe T. E. [1995], STeP: The Stanford theorem prover – user's manual, Technical Report STAN–CS–TR–95–1562, Department of Computer Science, Stanford University.

Bjørner N., Browne A., Chang E., Colón M., Kapur A., Manna Z., Sipma H. B. and Uribe T. E. [1996], STeP: Deductive–algorithmic verification of reactive and real–time systems, in 'Proc. 8th Workshop Computer Aided Verification (CAV '96)', Vol. 1102 of *LNCS*, Springer.

Blackburn P., de Rijke M. and Venema Y. [2000], *Modal Logic*, Elsevier. draft, 395 pp.

Boigelot B. and Godefroid P. [1996], Symbolic verification of communication protocols with infinite state spaces using qdds, in R. Alur and T. Henzinger, eds, 'Proc. 8th Workshop on Computer Aided Verification (CAV '96)', Vol. 1102 of *LNCS*, Springer, pp. 1–12.

Borälv A. [1997], The industrial success of verification tools based on stålmarck's method, in O. Grumberg, ed., 'Proc. 9th Workshop on Computer Aided Verification (CAV '97)', Vol. 1254 of *LNCS*, Springer.

Brace K. S., Rudell R. L. and Bryant R. E. [1990], Efficient implementation of a BDD package, in 'Proc. 27th ACM/IEEE Design Automation Conference (DAC '90)', pp. 40–45.

Bradfield J. and Stirling C. [1991], Local model checking for infinite state spaces, in 'Proc. 3rd Workshop on Computer Aided Verification (CAV '91)', LNCS, Springer.

Browne M. C. and Clarke E. M. [1986], SML: A high level language for the design and verification of finite state machines, in 'IFIP WG 10. 2 Int. Working Conf. from HDL Descriptions to Guaranteed Correct Circuit Designs', IFIP, Grenoble, France.

Browne M. C., Clarke E. M. and Dill D. [1985], Checking the correctness of sequential circuits, in 'Proc. 1985 Int IEEE Conf. on Computer Design', IEEE, Port Chester, New York.

Browne M. C., Clarke E. M. and Dill D. [1986], Automatic circuit verification using temporal logic: Two new examples, in 'Formal Aspects of VLSI Design', Elsevier Science Publishers (North Holland).

BROWNE M. C., CLARKE E. M. AND GRUMBERG O. [1988], 'Characterizing finite Kripke structures in propositional temporal logic', *Theoretical Computer Science* **59**(1–2), 115–131.

BROWNE M. C., CLARKE E. M. AND GRUMBERG O. [1989], 'Reasoning about networks with many identical finite–state processes', *Information and Computation* **81**(1), 13–31.

BROWNE M., CLARKE E. M., DILL D. AND MISHRA B. [1986], 'Automatic verification of sequential circuits using temporal logic', *IEEE Trans. on Computers* **C-35**(12), 1035–1044.

BRYANT R. E. [1986], 'Graph–based algorithms for Boolean function manipulation', *IEEE Trans. on Computers* **C-35**(8), 677–691.

BRYANT R. E. [1991], 'On the complexity of VLSI implementations and graph representations of Boolean functions with application to integer multiplication', *IEEE Trans. on Computers* **40**(2), 205–213.

BRYANT R. E. [1992], 'Symbolic Boolean manipulation with ordered binary decision diagrams', *ACM Computing Surveys* **24**(3), 293–317.

BÜCHI J. R. [1962], On a decision method in restricted second order arithmetic, *in* 'Proc. Int. Congr. Logic, Method and Philosophy of Science 1960', Stanford University Press, Palo Alto, CA, USA, pp. 1–12.

BURCH J. R., CLARKE E. M., DILL D., LONG D. E. AND MCMILLAN K. L. [1994], 'Symbolic model checking for sequential circuit verification', *IEEE Trans. on Computer Aided Design of Integrated Circuits* **13**(4), 401–424.

BURCH J. R., CLARKE E. M., GRUMBERG O., LONG D. E. AND MCMILLAN K. L. [1992], 'Automatic verification of sequential circuit designs', *Phil. Trans. R. Soc. Lond. A* **339**, 105–120.

BURCH J. R., CLARKE E. M. AND LONG D. E. [1991*a*], Representing circuits more efficiently in symbolic model checking, *in* 'Proc. 28th ACM/IEEE Design Automation Conference (DAC '91)'.

BURCH J. R., CLARKE E. M. AND LONG D. E. [1991*b*], Symbolic model checking with partitioned transition relations, *in* A. Halaas and P. B. Denyer, eds, 'Proc. Int. Conf. on Very Large Scale Integration (VLSI '91)', Edinburgh, Scotland.

BURCH J. R., CLARKE E. M., MCMILLAN K. L., DILL D. AND HWANG L. J. [1992], 'Symbolic model checking: 10^{20} states and beyond', *Information and Computation* **98**(2), 142–170. also in 5th IEEE LICS 90.

BURCH J. R., CLARKE E. M., MCMILLAN K. L. AND DILL D. L. [1990], Sequential circuit verification using symbolic model checking, *in* 'Proc. 27th ACM/IEEE Design Automation Conference (DAC '90)'.

BURGESS J. [1984], Basic tense logic, *in* F. G. D. Gabbay, ed., 'Handbook of Philosophical Logic', Reidel, chapter II. 2, pp. 89–134.

BURKART O. AND ESPARZA J. [1997], 'More infinite results', *Electronic Notes in Theoretical Computer Science* **6**. http://www. elsevier. nl/locate/entcs/volume6. html.

BURROWS M., ABADI M. AND NEEDHAM R. [1989], A logic of authentication, Technical Report 39, DEC Systems Research Center.

BURSTALL M. [1974], Program proving as hand simulation with a little induction, *in* 'Proc. IFIP Congress, Stockholm', North Holland, pp. 308–312.

CHANDRA A. AND HAREL D. [1980], 'Computable queries for relational databases', *J. of Computer and System Sciences* **21**, 156–178.

CLARKE E. M. AND DRAGHICESCU I. A. [1988], Expressibility results for linear time and branching time logics, *in* 'Linear Time, Branching Time and Partial Order in Logics and Models for Concurrency', Vol. 354 of *LNCS*, Springer, pp. 428–437.

CLARKE E. M., DRAGHICESCU I. A. AND KURSHAN R. P. [1990], A unified approach for showing language containment and equivalence between various types of ω–automata, *in* A. Arnold and N. D. Jones, eds, 'Proc. 15th Coll. on Trees in Algebra and Programming', Vol. 407 of *LNCS*, Springer.

CLARKE E. M. AND EMERSON E. A. [1981], Synthesis of synchronization skeletons for branching time temporal logic, in 'Proc. Workshop on Logic of Programs', Vol. 131 of *LNCS*, Springer, Yorktown Heights, NY.

CLARKE E. M., EMERSON E. A. AND SISTLA A. P. [1986], 'Automatic verification of finite–state concurrent systems using temporal logic specifications', *ACM Transactions on Programming Languages and Systems* **8**(2), 244–263.

CLARKE E. M., FILKORN T. AND JHA S. [1993], Exploiting symmetry in temporal logic model checking, in C. Courcoubetis, ed., 'Proc. 5th Workshop on Computer Aided Verification (CAV '93)', Vol. 697 of *LNCS*, Springer, Elounda, Crete.

CLARKE E. M., FUJITA M. AND HEINLE W. [1997], Hybrid spectral transform diagrams, in 'Proc. 1st Int. Conf. on Information, Communications and Signal Processing (ICICS '97)'.

CLARKE E. M., FUJITA M., MCGEER P., YANG J. AND ZHAO X. [1993], Multi–terminal binary decision diagrams: An efficient data structure for matrix representation, in 'Proc. Int. Workshop on Logic Synthesis (IWLS '93)', Tahoe City.

CLARKE E. M., FUJITA M. AND ZHAO X. [1995], Hybrid decision diagrams — overcoming the limitations of MTBDDs and BMDs, in 'Proc. IEEE Int. Conf. on Computer Aided Design (ICCAD '95)', IEEE Computer Society Press, pp. 54–60.

CLARKE E. M., FUJITA M. AND ZHAO X. [1996], Multi–terminal binary decision diagrams and hybrid decision diagrams, in T. Sasao and M. Fujita, eds, 'Representations of Discrete Functions', Kluwer academic publishers, chapter 4, pp. 93–108.

CLARKE E. M. AND GRUMBERG O. [1987a], Avoiding the state explosion problem in temporal model checking algorithms, in 'Proc. 6th Ann. ACM Symp. on Principles of Distributed Computing', pp. 294–303.

CLARKE E. M. AND GRUMBERG O. [1987b], Research on automatic verification of finite–state concurrent systems, Technical Report CMU-CS-87-105, Carnegie Mellon University.

CLARKE E. M., GRUMBERG O. AND BROWNE M. C. [1986], Reasoning about networks with many identical finite-state processes, in 'Proc. 5th Ann. ACM Symp. on Principles of Distributed Computing', ACM, pp. 240–248.

CLARKE E. M., GRUMBERG O. AND HAMAGUCHI K. [1997], 'Another look at LTL model checking', *Formal Methods in System Design* **10**, 47–71.

CLARKE E. M., GRUMBERG O., HIRAISHI H., JHA S., LONG D. E., MCMILLAN K. L. AND NESS L. A. [1993], Verification of the Futurebus+ cache coherence protocol, in L. Claesen, ed., 'Proc. 11th Int. Symp. on Computer Hardware Description Languages and their Applications', North–Holland.

CLARKE E. M., GRUMBERG O. AND JHA S. [1995], Parametrized networks, in S. Smolka and I. Lee, eds, 'Proc. 6th Int. Conf. on Concurrency Theory (CONCUR '95)', Vol. 962 of *LNCS*, Springer.

CLARKE E. M., GRUMBERG O. AND LONG D. E. [1993], Model checking, in M. Broy, ed., 'Deductive Program Design', Springer NATO ASI series F, pp. 305–350.

CLARKE E. M., GRUMBERG O. AND LONG D. E. [1994a], 'Model checking and abstraction', *ACM Transactions on Programming Languages and Systems* **16**(5), 1512–1542. also in 19th ACM POPL '92.

CLARKE E. M., GRUMBERG O. AND LONG D. E. [1994b], Verification tools for finite–state concurrent systems, in J. W. de Bakker, W. P. de Roever and G. Rozenberg, eds, 'A Decade of Concurrency – Reflections and Perspectives', Vol. 803 of *LNCS*, Springer, pp. 124–175. REX School/Symposium, Nordwijkerhout, The Netherlands, June 1993.

CLARKE E. M., GRUMBERG O., MCMILLAN K. AND ZHAO X. [1994], Efficient generation of counterexamples and witnesses in symbolic model checking, Technical Report CMU–CS–94–204, Carnegie Mellon University, Pittsburgh.

CLARKE E. M., GRUMBERG O., MINEA M. AND PELED D. [1999], 'State space reductions using partial order techniques', *Int. Journal on Software Tools for Technology Transfer* . to appear.

CLARKE E. M., GRUMBERG O. AND PELED D. [1999], *Model Checking*, MIT Press, Boston, MA.

CLARKE E. M., JHA S., LU Y. AND MINEA M. [1997], Equivalence checking using abstract BDDs. manuscript.

CLARKE E. M., KHAIRA K. AND ZHAO X. [1993], Word level model checking — a new approach for verifying arithmetic circuits, in 'Proc. 30th ACM/IEEE Design Automation Conference (DAC '93)', IEEE Computer society press.

CLARKE E. M., KIMURA S., LONG D. E., MICHAYLOV S., SCHWAB S. A. AND VIDAL J. P. [1992], Symbolic computation algorithms on shared memory multiprocessors, in N. Suzuki, ed., 'Shared Memory Multiprocessing', MIT Press, pp. 53–80.

CLARKE E. M., LONG D. E. AND MCMILLAN K. L. [1989], Compositional model checking, in 'Proc. 4th Ann. IEEE Symp. on Logic in Computer Science (LICS '89)', Asilomar, Calif.

CLARKE E. M., LONG D. E. AND MCMILLAN K. L. [1991], 'A language for compositional specification and verification of finite state hardware controllers', Proc. IEEE 79(9), 1283–1292.

CLARKE E. M., MCMILLAN K. L., ZHAO X., FUJITA M. AND YANG J. [1993], Spectral transforms for large Boolean functions with applications to technology mapping, in 'Proc. 30th ACM/IEEE Design Automation Conference (DAC '93)', IEEE Computer Society Press, pp. 54–60.

CLARKE E. M. AND MISHRA B. [1984], Automatic verification of asynchronous circuits, in 'Proc. Workshop on Logics of Programs', Vol. 164 of LNCS, Springer, pp. 101–115.

CLARKE E. M. AND ZHAO X. [1994], Combining symbolic computation and theorem proving: some problems of Ramanujan, in A. Bundy, ed., '12th Int. Conf. on Automated Deduction (CADE '94)', Vol. 814 of LNCS, Springer, Nancy, France, pp. 758–763.

CLEAVELAND R. [1990], 'Tableau–based model checking in the propositional μ–calculus', Acta Informatica 27(8), 725–747.

CLEAVELAND R. AND STEFFEN B. [1993], 'A linear–time model–checking algorithm for the alternation–free modal μ–calculus', Formal Methods in System Design 2(2), 121–147.

COURCOUBETIS C., VARDI M. Y., WOLPER P. AND YANNAKAKIS M. [1992], 'Memory efficient algorithms for the verification of temporal properties', Formal Methods in System Design 1, 275–288.

COURCOUBETIS C. AND YANNAKAKIS M. [1995], 'The complexity of probabilistic verification', Journal of the ACM 42(4), 857–907.

COUSOT P. AND COUSOT R. [1977], Abstract interpretation: a unified lattice model for static analysis of programs by construction or approximation of fixpoints, in 'Proc. 4th Ann. ACM Symp. on Principles of Programming Languages (POPL '77)'.

COUSOT P. AND COUSOT R. [1979], Systematic design of program analysis frameworks, in 'Proc. 6th Ann. ACM Symp. on Principles of Programming Languages (POPL '79)'.

DAM M. [1994], 'CTL* and ECTL* as fragments of the modal μ–calculus', Theoretical Computer Science 126, 77–96.

DAM M. [1995], Compositional proof systems for model checking infinite state processes, in 'Proc. 6th Int. Conf. on Concurrency Theory (CONCUR '95)', Vol. 962 of LNCS, Springer, pp. 12–26.

DAMS D. [1995], Abstract interpretation and partition refinement for model checking, PhD thesis, Technical University Eindhoven.

DAMS D., GRUMBERG O. AND GERTH R. [1994], Abstract interpretation of reactive systems: Abstractions preserving ∀CTL*, ∃CTL* and CTL*, in E.-R. Olderog, ed., 'Programming Concepts, Methods and Calculi (PROCOMET '94)', IFIP Transactions, North Holland / Elsevier, Amsterdam, pp. 561 – 581.

DAVEY A. A. AND PRIESTLEY H. A. [1990], Introduction to Lattices and Order, Cambridge Mathematical Textbooks, Cambridge University Press.

DAWAR A., LINDELL S. AND WEINSTEIN S. [1996], First order logic, fixed point logic and linear order, in H. Kleine-Büning, ed., 'Proc. Computer Science Logic (CSL '95)', Vol. 1092 of LNCS, Springer, pp. 161–177.

DEROEVER, W., LANGMAACK, H. AND PNUELI, A., EDS [1998], Compositionality: The Significant Difference, Vol. 1536 of LNCS, Springer.

DILL D. [1989], Timing assumptions and verification of finite–state concurrent systems, *in* J. Sifakis, ed., 'Proc. Int. Workshop on Automatic Verification Methods for Finite State Systems', Vol. 407 of *LNCS*, Springer, Grenoble, France, pp. 197–212.

DILL D. L. AND CLARKE E. M. [1986], 'Automatic verification of asynchronous circuits using temporal logic', *IEEE Proceedings* **133**(5).

DINGEL J. AND FILKORN T. [1995], Model checking for infinite state systems using data abstraction, assumption–commitment style reasoning and theorem proving, *in* P. Wolper, ed., 'Proc. 7th Workshop on Computer Aided Verification (CAV '95)', Vol. 939 of *LNCS*, Springer, pp. 45–69.

EDELKAMP S. AND REFFEL F. [1998], OBDDs in heuristic search, *in* O. Herzog and A. Günter, eds, 'Proc. KI-98: Advances in Artificial Intelligence', Vol. 1504 of *LNCS/LNAI*, Springer, pp. 81–92.

EHRENFEUCHT A. [1961], 'An application of games to the completeness problem for formalized theories', *Fund. Math.* **49**, 129–141.

EMERSON E. A. [1985], Automata, tableaux, and temporal logic, *in* R. Parikh, ed., 'Proc. Int. Conf. on Logics of Programs', Vol. 193 of *LNCS*, Springer, pp. 79–88.

EMERSON E. A. [1990], Temporal and modal logic, *in* J. van Leeuwen, ed., 'Handbook of Theoretical Computer Science', Vol. B, Elsevier, pp. 997–1072.

EMERSON E. A. AND CLARKE E. M. [1980], Characterizing correctness properties of parallel programs using fixpoints, *in* 'Proc. 17th Int. Coll. on Automata, Languages and Programming (ICALP '80)', Vol. 85 of *LNCS*, EATCS, Springer, pp. 169–181.

EMERSON E. A. AND CLARKE E. M. [1982], 'Using branching time logic to synthesize synchronization skeletons', *Science of Computer Programming* **2**, 241–266.

EMERSON E. A. AND HALPERN J. Y. [1985], 'Decision procedures and expressiveness in the temporal logic of branching time', *Journal of Computer and System Sciences* **30**(1), 1–24.

EMERSON E. A. AND HALPERN J. Y. [1986], '"sometimes" and "not never" revisited: on branching time vs. linear time', *Journal of the ACM* **33**, 151–178.

EMERSON E. A., JUTLA C. S. AND SISTLA A. P. [1993], On model–checking for fragments of μ–calculus, *in* C. Courcoubetis, ed., 'Proc. 5th Workshop on Computer Aided Verification (CAV '93)', Vol. 697 of *LNCS*, Springer.

EMERSON E. A. AND LEI C. L. [1985], Modalities for model checking: Branching time strikes back, *in* 'Proc. 12th Symp. on Principles of Programming Languages (POPL '85)', New Orleans, La.

EMERSON E. A. AND LEI C. L. [1986], Efficient model checking in fragments of the propositional μ–calculus, *in* 'Proc. 1st Symp. on Logic in Computer Science (LICS '86)', Boston, Mass.

EMERSON E. A. AND SISTLA A. P. [1984], 'Deciding full branching time logic', *Information and Control* **61**, 175–201.

EMERSON E. A. AND SISTLA A. P. [1993], Symmetry and model checking, *in* C. Courcoubetis, ed., 'Proc. 5th Workshop on Computer Aided Verification (CAV '93)', Vol. 697 of *LNCS*, Springer, Elounda, Crete.

ENDERS R., FILKORN T. AND TAUBNER D. [1993], 'Generating BDDs for symbolic model checking', *Distributed Computing* **6**, 155–164.

ESPARZA J. [1994], 'Model checking using net unfoldings', *Science of Computer Programming* **23**(2–3), 151–195.

FELT E., YORK G., BRAYTON R. AND VINCENTELLI A. S. [1993], Dynamic variable reordering for BDD minimization, *in* 'Proc. European Design Automation Conference (EuroDAC '93)', pp. 130–135.

FISCHER M. J. AND LADNER R. E. [1979], 'Propositional dynamic logic of regular programs', *Journal of Computer and System Sciences* **18**(2), 194–211.

FITTING M. [1983], *Proof methods for modal and intuitionistic logics*, Reidel, Dordrecht.

FRAÏSSÉ R. [1954], Sur quelques classifications des systèmes de relations, Séries A 1, Publications Scientifiques de l'Universit'e d'Algerie.

FRANCEZ N. [1986], *Fairness*, Text and Monographs in Computer Science, Springer.

FUJI H., OOTOMO G. AND HORI C. [1993], Interleaving based variable ordering methods for ordered binary decision diagrams, *in* 'Proc. Int. Conf. on Computer Aided Design (ICCAD '93)', IEEE.

GABBAY D. [1989], The declarative past and imperative future: Executable temporal logic for interactive systems, *in* B. Banieqbal, ed., 'Temporal Logic in Specification', Vol. 398 of *LNCS*, Springer, pp. 431–448.

GABBAY D., HODKINSON I. AND REYNOLDS M. [1994], *Temporal Logic: Mathematical Foundations and Computational Aspects*, Vol. 1, Clarendon Press, Oxford.

GABBAY D., PNUELI A., SHELAH S. AND STAVI J. [1980], On the temporal analysis of fairness, *in* 'Proc. 7th ACM Symp. on Principles of Programming Languages (POPL '80)', pp. 163–173.

GERMAN S. M. AND SISTLA A. P. [1992], 'Reasoning about systems with many processes', *Journal of the ACM* **39**, 675–735.

GERTH R., KUIPER R., PELED D. AND PENCZEK W. [1995], A partial order approach to branching time logic model checking, *in* 'Proc. 3rd Israel Symp. on the Theory of Computing and Systems (ISTCS '95)', IEEE Computer Society Press, pp. 130–140.

GODEFROID P. [1990], Using partial orders to improve automatic verification methods, *in* 'Proc. 2nd Workshop on Computer Aided Verification (CAV '90)', Vol. 531 of *LNCS*, Springer, Rutgers, New Brunswick, pp. 176–185.

GODEFROID P., HOLZMANN G. J. AND PIROTTIN D. [1995], 'State–space caching revisited', *Formal Methods in System Design* **7**(3), 1–15.

GODEFROID P. AND LONG D. E. [1996], Symbolic protocol verification with queue BDDs, *in* 'Proc. 11th Ann. IEEE Symp. on Logic in Computer Science (LICS '96)', New Brunswick.

GODEFROID P. AND PIROTTIN D. [1993], Refining dependencies improves partial-order verification methods, *in* 'Proc. 5th Workshop on Computer Aided Verification (CAV '93)', Vol. 697 of *LNCS*, Springer, Elounda, Crete, pp. 438–449.

GODEFROID P. AND WOLPER P. [1991], A partial approach to model checking, *in* 'Proc. 6th Ann. IEEE Symp. on Logic in Computer Science (LICS '91)', Amsterdam, pp. 406–415.

GRAF S. AND STEFFEN B. [1990], Compositional minimization of finite state processes, *in* R. Kurshan and E. M. Clarke, eds, 'Proc. 2nd Workshop on Computer Aided Verification (CAV '90)', Vol. 3 of *DIMACS Series in Discrete Mathematics and Theoretical Computer Science*, American Mathematical Society. Also in Springer LNCS 531.

GRUMBERG O. AND LONG D. E. [1994], 'Model checking and modular verification', *ACM Transactions on Programming Languages and Systems* **16**, 843–872.

GUNTER C. A. AND SCOTT D. S. [1990], Semantic domains, *in* J. van Leeuwen, ed., 'Handbook of Theoretical Computer Science', Vol. B, Elsevier, pp. 633–674.

GUREVICH Y. AND SHELAH S. [1986], 'Fixed–point extensions of first–order logic', *Annals of Pure and Applied Logic* **32**, 265–280.

GUROV D., BEREZIN S. AND KAPRON B. M. [1996], A modal μ–calculus and a proof system for value passing processes, *in* 'Proc. Int. Workshop on Verification of Infinite State Systems (INFINITY '96)', Electronic Notes in Theoretical Computer Science, Pisa, pp. 149–163. Report, University of Passau, MIP-9614 July 1996.

HACHTEL G. D., MACII E., PARDO A. AND SOMENZI F. [1996], 'Markovian analysis of large finite state machines', *IEEE Transactions on Computer–Aided Design of Integrated Circuits and Systems* **15**(12), 1479–1493.

HANSSON H. AND JONSSON B. [1989], A framework for reasoning about time and reliability, *in* 'Proc. 10th IEEE Real-Time Systems Symp.', pp. 102–111.

HAREL D. [1984], Dynamic logic, *in* F. G. D. Gabbay, ed., 'Handbook of Philosophical Logic', Reidel, chapter II. 10, pp. 488–604.

HAREL D. AND PNUELI A. [1985], On the development of reactive systems, *in* K. R. Apt, ed., 'Logics and Models of Concurrent Systems', Vol. F13 of *NATO ASI Series*, Springer, pp. 477–498.

HAR'EL Z. AND KURSHAN R. P. [1990], 'Software for analytical development of communications protocols', *AT&T Tech. J.* **69**(1), 45–59.

HENZINGER T., MANNA Z. AND PNUELI A. [1992], Timed transition systems, Technical Report TR 92-1263, Dept. of CS, Cornell Univ.

HOLZMANN G. [1991], *Design and Validation of Computer Protocols*, Software Series, Prentice Hall.

HOLZMANN G. [1995], An analysis of bitstate hashing, in 'Proc. 15th Int. Conf. on Protocol Specification, Testing and Verification', INWG/IFIP, Chapman and Hall, Warsaw, pp. 301–314.

HOPCROFT J. E. AND ULLMAN J. D. [1979], *Introduction to Automata Theory, Languages, and Computation*, Addison-Wesley.

HUGHES G. E. AND CRESSWELL M. J. [1977], *An Introduction to Modal Logic*, Methuen.

IEEE [1994], *IEEE Standard for the Futurebus+ Logical Protocol Specification*, IEEE Computer Society. IEEE Standard 896. 1, 1994 Edition.

IMMERMAN N. [1986], 'Relational queries computable in polynomial time', *Information and Control* **68**, 86–104.

IP C. W. AND DILL D. [1993], Better verification through symmetry, in L. Claesen, ed., 'Proc. 11th Int. Symp. on Computer Hardware Description Languages and their Applications', North–Holland.

JANIN D. AND WALUKIEWICZ I. [1996], On the expressive completeness of the propositional μ–calculus with respect to monadic second order logic, in 'Proc. 7th Int. Conf. on Concurrency Theory (CONCUR '96)', Vol. 1119 of *LNCS*, Springer, Pisa, Italy.

JOSKO B. [1993], 'Modular specification and verification of reactive systems', Habilitationsschrift, University of Oldenburg.

KAMP H. W. [1968], Tense Logic and the Theory of Linear Order, PhD thesis, Univ. of Calif. , Los Angeles.

KANNAN R. AND LIPTON R. J. [1986], 'Polynomial–time algorithm for the orbit problem', *Journal of the ACM* **33**(4), 808–821.

KATZ S. AND PELED D. [1988], An efficient verification method for parallel and distributed programs, in deBakker et al., ed., 'Linear Time, Branching Time and Partial Order in Logics and Models for Concurrency', Vol. 354 of *LNCS*, Springer.

KESTEN Y. AND PNUELI A. [1995], A complete axiomatization of qptl, in 'Proc. 10th Ann. IEEE Symp. on Logic in Computer Science (LICS '95)', pp. 2–12.

KIMURA S. [1995], Residue BDD and its application to the verification of arithmetic circuits, in 'Proc. 32nd Int. Design Automation Conference (DAC '95)'.

KINDRED D. AND WING J. M. [1996], Fast, automatic checking of security protocols, in 'USENIX 2nd Workshop on Electronic Commerce'.

KOZEN D. [1983], 'Results on the propositional μ–calculus', *Theoretical Computer Science* **27**, 333–354.

KOZEN D. AND PARIKH R. [1983], A decision procedure for the propositional μ–calculus, in 'Proc. Int. Symp. Logic of Programs'.

KOZEN D. AND TIURYN J. [1990], Logics of programs, in J. van Leeuwen, ed., 'Handbook of Theoretical Computer Science', Vol. B, Elsevier, pp. 791–839.

KRIPKE S. A. [1963], 'Semantical considerations on modal logic', *Acta Philosophica Fennica* **16**, 83–94.

KRIPKE S. A. [1975], 'Outline of a theory of truth', *Journal of Philosophy* **72**, 690–716.

KRÖGER F. [1978], A uniform logical basis for the description, specification and verification of programs, in 'Proc. IFIP Work. Conf. Formal Desription of Programming Concepts', North Holland, St. Andrews, Canada, pp. 441–457.

KRÖGER F. [1987], *Temporal logic of Programs*, number 8 in 'EATCS monographs on TCS', Springer.

KUPFERMAN O. AND VARDI M. Y. [1996], Verification of fair transition systems, *in* R. Alur and T. Henzinger, eds, 'Proc. 8th Workshop on Computer Aided Verification (CAV '96)', Vol. 1102 of *LNCS*, Springer, pp. 372–382.

KURSHAN R. P. [1989], Analysis of discrete event coordination, *in* J. W. de Bakker, W. P. de Roever and G. Rozenberg, eds, 'Proc. REX Workshop on Stepwise Refinement of Distributed Systems, Models, Formalisms, Correctness', Vol. 430 of *LNCS*, Springer.

KURSHAN R. P. [1994], *Computer–Aided Verification of Coordinating Processes: The Automata–Theoretic Approach*, Princeton University Press, Princeton, New Jersey.

KURSHAN R. P., LEVIN V., MINEA M., PELED D. AND YENIGUN H. [1997], Verifying hardware in its software context, *in* 'Proc. Int. Conf. on Computer Aided Design (ICCAD '97)', IEEE, San Jose, CA, USA.

KURSHAN R. P. AND MCMILLAN K. L. [1989], A structural induction theorem for processes, *in* 'Proc. 8th Ann. ACM Symp. on Principles of Distributed Computing', ACM Press.

LAMPORT L. [1980], "sometimes" is sometimes "not never", *in* 'Proc. 7th Ann. ACM Symp. on Principles of Programming Languages (POPL '80)', ACM, Las Vegas, pp. 174–185.

LAMPORT L. [1983], What good is temporal logic?, *in* 'Proc. IFIP', pp. 657–668.

LARSEN K., PETTERSON P. AND YI W. [1997], 'Uppaal in a nutshell', *Software Tools for Technology Transfer* 1(1/2).

LEHMANN D., PNUELI A. AND STAVI J. [1981], Impartiality, justice, and fairness: The ethics of concurrent termination, *in* 'Proc. Int. Conf. on Automata, Languages, and Programming (ICALP '81)', Vol. 115 of *LNCS*, Springer.

LEWIS C. I. [1912], 'Implication and the algebra of logic', *Mind* **21**, 522–531.

LICHTENSTEIN O. AND PNUELI A. [1985], Checking that finite state concurrent programs satisfy their linear specification, *in* 'Proc. 12th Ann. ACM Symp. on Principles of Programming Languages (POPL '85)', ACM press, New Orleans, La.

LICHTENSTEIN O., PNUELI A. AND ZUCK L. [1985], The glory of the past, *in* 'Proc. Int. Conf. Logics of Programs', Vol. 193 of *LNCS*, Springer, pp. 196–218.

LOISEAUX C., GRAF S., SIFAKIS J., BOUAJJANI A. AND BENSALEM S. [1995], 'Property preserving abstractions for the verification of concurrent systems', *Formal Methods in System Design* **6**(1), 11–44. also in CAV '92, LNCS 663.

LONG D. E. [1993], Model Checking, Abstraction and Compositional Verification, PhD thesis, CMU School of Computer Science, CMU–CS–93–178.

LONG D. E., BROWNE A., CLARKE E. M., JHA S. AND MARRERO W. R. [1994], An improved algorithm for the evaluation of fixpoint expressions, *in* 'Proc. 6th Workshop on Computer Aided Verification (CAV '94)', LNCS, Springer, pp. 338–350.

MADER A. [1992], Tableau recycling, *in* 'Proc. 4th Workshop on Computer Aided Verification (CAV '92)', LNCS, Springer.

MANNA Z. AND PNUELI A. [1981], 'Verification of concurrent programs: The temporal framework'.

MANNA Z. AND PNUELI A. [1982a], Verification of concurrent programs: Temporal proof principles, *in* D. Kozen, ed., 'Proc. Workshop on Logics of Programs', Vol. 131 of *LNCS*, Springer, pp. 200–252.

MANNA Z. AND PNUELI A. [1982b], Verification of concurrent programs: The temporal framework, *in* R. S. Boyer and J. S. Moore, eds, 'The Correctness Problem in Computer Science', Academic Press, London, pp. 215–273.

MANNA Z. AND PNUELI A. [1987], A hierarchy of temporal properties, *in* 'Proc. 6th Ann. ACM Symp. on Principles of Distributed Computing', Stanford University Press, Stanford, CA 94305.

MANNA Z. AND PNUELI A. [1989], The anchored version of the temporal framework, *in* 'Linear Time, Branching Time and Partial Order in Logics and Models for Concurrency', Vol. 354 of *LNCS*, Springer, pp. 201–284.

MANNA Z. AND PNUELI A. [1992], *The Temporal Logic of Reactive and Concurrent Systems – Specification*, Springer.

MANNA Z. AND PNUELI A. [1995], *Temporal Verifications of Reactive Systems – Safety*, Springer.

MARELLY R. AND GRUMBERG O. [1991], Gormel — grammar oriented model checker, Technical Report 697, The Technion.

MCMILLAN K. [1992], Using unfoldings to avoid the state space explosion problem in the verification of asynchronous circuits, *in* 'Proc. 4th Workshop on Computer Aided Verification', Vol. 663 of *LNCS*, Springer, Montreal, Canada, pp. 164–177.

MCMILLAN K. L. [1993], *Symbolic Model Checking*, Kluwer Academic Publishers.

MCMILLAN K. L. AND SCHWALBE J. [1992], Formal verification of the Encore Gigamax cache consistency protocol, *in* N. Suzuki, ed., 'Proc. Int. Symp. on Shared Memory Multiprocessing', MIT Press, pp. 111–134.

MEADOWS C. [1994], The NRL protocol analyzer: An overview, *in* 'Proc. 2nd Int. Conf. on the Practical Applications of Prolog'.

MERZ S. [1997], Abstraction as a proof rule, Technical report, Universität München.

MILNER R. [1980], *A Calculus of Communicating Systems*, Vol. 92 of *LNCS*, Springer.

MINEA M. [1999], Partial order reduction for model checking of timed automata, *in* 'Proc. Concur 99', LNCS, Springer.

MISHRA B. AND CLARKE E. M. [1985], 'Hierarchical verification of asynchonous circuits using temporal logic', *Theoretical computer science* 38, 269–291.

MITCHELL J. C., MITCHELL M. AND STERN U. [1997], Automated analysis of cryptographic protocols using Murφ, *in* 'Proc. 1997 IEEE Symp. on Security and Privacy', IEEE Computer Society Press.

MOORE J. S. [1994], 'Introduction to OBDD algorithm for the ATP community', *Journal of automated reasoning* 12, 33–45.

NIWINSKY D. [1988], Fixed points vs. infinite generation, *in* 'Proc. 3rd Ann. IEEE Symp. on Logic in Computer Science (LICS '88)', pp. 402–409.

NOWICKI J. R. AND ADAM L. J. [1990], *Digital Circuits*, Edward Arnold.

PAIGE R. AND TARJAN R. [1987], 'Three efficient algorithms based on partition refinement', *SIAM journal on computing* 16(6).

PARK D. M. [1974], Finiteness is mu–ineffable, Theory of Computation Report 3, University of Warwick.

PARK D. M. [1981], Concurrency and automata on infinite sequences, *in* P. Deussen, ed., 'Theoretical Computer Science: 5th GI–Conference, Karlsruhe', Vol. 104 of *LNCS*, Springer, pp. 167–183.

PELED D. [1993], All from one, one for all: on model checking using representatives, *in* C. Courcoubetis, ed., 'Proc. 5th Workshop Computer Aided Verification (CAV '93)', Vol. 697, Springer, Elounda, Crete.

PELED D. AND WILKE T. [1997], 'Stutter–invariant temporal properties are expressible without the nexttime operator', *Information Processing Letters* .

PNUELI A. [1977], The temporal logic of programs, *in* 'Proc. 18th Ann. IEEE Symp. on Found. of Comp. Science (FOCS '77)', pp. 46–57.

PNUELI A. [1981], 'The temporal semantics of concurrent programs', *Theoretical Computer Science* 13, 45–60.

PNUELI A. [1984], In transition from global to modular temporal reasoning about programs, *in* K. R. Apt, ed., 'Logics and Models of Concurrent Systems', Vol. 13 of *NATO ASI series*, Springer.

PRATT V. [1976], Semantic considerations on Floyd-Hoare logic, *in* 'Proc. 17th IEEE Symp. on Foundations of Comp. Sci. (FOCS'76)', pp. 109–121.

PRATT V. [1981], A decidable μ–calculus, *in* 'Proc. Ann. ACM Symp. on Foundations of Computer Science (FOCS '81)'.

PRIOR A. [1967], *Past, Present and Future*, Clarendon Press, Oxford.

PRIOR A. N. [1957], *Time and Modality*, Oxford University Press.

QUIELLE J. P. AND SIFAKIS J. [1981], Specification and verification of concurrent systems in CESAR, *in* 'Proc. 5th Int. Symp. on Programming'.

QUIELLE J. P. AND SIFAKIS J. [1982], Fairness and related properties in transition systems, Technical Report 292, IMAG.

RABIN M. O. [1969], 'Decidability of second order theories and automata on infinite trees', *Trans. AMS* **141**, 1–35.

REISIG W. [1998], *Elements of Distributed Algorithms*, Springer.

RESCHER N. AND URQUHART A. [1971], *Temporal Logic*, Springer.

RUDELL R. L. [1993], Dynamic variable reordering for ordered binary decision diagrams, *in* 'Proc. IEEE/ACM Int. Conf. on Computer Aided Design (ICCAD '93)', pp. 42–47.

SAFRA S. [1988], On the complexity of omega–automata, *in* 'Proc. 29th IEEE Symp. on Foundations of Computer Science (FOCS '88)', White Plains.

SALWICKI A. [1970], 'Formalized algorithmic languages', *Bull. Acad. Polon. Sci. , Ser. Sci. Math. Astron. Phys.* **18**, 227–232.

SCHLINGLOFF H. [1992a], 'Expressive completeness of temporal logic of trees', *Journal of Applied Non–Classical Logics* **2**. **2**, 157–180.

SCHLINGLOFF H. [1992b], On the expressive power of modal logic on trees, *in* A. Nerode and M. Taitslin, eds, 'Proc. 2nd Int. Symp. Logical Foundations of Computer Science ("Logic at Tver")', Vol. 620 of *LNCS*, Springer, pp. 441–451.

SCHLINGLOFF H. [1997], 'Verification of finite–state systems with temporal logic model checking', *South African Computer Journal* **19**, 27–52.

SCHLINGLOFF H. AND HEINLE W. [1997], Relational algebra and modal logics, *in* C. Brink, W. Kahl and G. Schmidt, eds, 'Relational Methods in Computer Science', Advances in Computing Science, Springer, chapter 5.

SEGERBERG K. [1968], 'Decidability of S4.1', *Theoria* **34**, 7–20.

SEGERBERG K. [1971], An essay in classical modal logic, Technical Report Filosofiska Studier 13, Department of Philosophy, University of Uppsala.

SISTLA A. P. [1983], Theoretical Issues in the Design and Verification of Distributed Systems, PhD thesis, CMU Dept. of Computer Science, CMU–CS–83–146.

SISTLA A. P. AND CLARKE E. M. [1986], 'Complexity of propositional temporal logics', *Journal of the ACM* **32**(3), 733–749.

SISTLA A. P., VARDI M. Y. AND WOLPER P. [1987], 'The complementation problem for Büchi automata with applications to temporal logic', *Theoretical Computer Science* **49**, 217–237.

SLOAN R. H. AND BUY U. [1997], 'Stubborn sets for real–time Petri nets', *Formal Methods in System Design* **11**(1), 23–40.

STÅLMARCK G. [1989], 'A system for determining propositional logic theorems by applying values and rules to triplets that are generated from a formula', Swedish Patent No. 467076 (1992), US Patent No. 5 276 897 (1994), European Patent No. 0404 454 (1995).

STÅLMARCK G. AND SÄFLUND M. [1990], Modelling and verifying systems and software in propositional logic, *in* B. K. Daniels, ed., 'Proc. Int. Conf. on Safety of Computer Control Systems (SAFECOMP '90)', Pergamon Press, pp. 31–36.

STARKE P. H. [1991], 'Reachability analysis of Petri nets using symmetries', *Syst. Anal. Model. Simul.* **8**(4/5), 293–303.

STIRLING C. [1987], 'Modal logics for communicating systems', *Theoretical Computer Science* **49**, 311–348.

STIRLING C. [1991], Modal and temporal logics, *in* S. Abramsky, D. Gabbay and T. Maibaum, eds, 'Handbook of Logic in Computer Science', Oxford University Press.

STIRLING C. AND WALKER D. J. [1991], 'Local model checking in the modal μ–calculus', *Theoretical Computer Science* **89**(1), 161–177. also in Proc. TAPSOFT '89, Springer LNCS 351, 369–386, 1989.

TARJAN R. E. [1972], 'Depth first search and linear graph algorithms', *SIAM Journal of Computing* **1**, 146–160.

TARSKI A. [1955], 'A lattice–theoretical fixpoint theorem and its applications', *Pacific J. Math.* **5**, 285–309.

THIAGARAJAN P. S. AND WALUKIEWICZ I. [1997], An expressively complete linear time temporal logic for Mazurkiewicz traces, *in* 'Proc. 12th Ann. IEEE Symp. on Logic in Computer Science (LICS '97)', pp. 183–194.

THOMAS W. [1990], Automata on infinite objects, *in* J. van Leeuwen, ed., 'Handbook of Theoretical Computer Science', Vol. B, Elsevier.

THOMAS W. [1999], Languages, automata, and logic, *in* G. Rozenberg and A. Salomaa, eds, 'Handbook of Formal Language Theory', Vol. III, Springer, pp. 389–455.

TOUATI H. J., BRAYTON R. K. AND KURSHAN R. P. [1991], Testing language containment for ω–automata using BDDs, *in* 'Proc. 1991 Int. Workshop on Formal Methods in VLSI Design'.

VALMARI A. [1990], A stubborn attack on state explosion, *in* 'Proc. 2nd Workshop on Computer Aided Verification (CAV '90)', Vol. 531 of *LNCS*, Springer, Rutgers, New Brunswick, pp. 156–165.

VAN BENTHEM J. [1983], *Modal Logic and Classical Logic*, Bibliopolis, Naples.

VAN BENTHEM J. [1984], Correspondence theory, *in* F. G. D. Gabbay, ed., 'Handbook of Philosophical Logic', Reidel, chapter II. 4, pp. 167–249.

VAN BENTHEM J. [1991], *The Logic of Time*, 2nd edn, Kluwer, Dordrecht.

VARDI M. [1995], Alternating automata and program verification, *in* J. van Leeuwen, ed., 'Computer Science Today: Recent Trends and Developments', Vol. 1000 of *LNCS*, Springer.

VARDI M. Y. [1982], The complexity of relational query languages, *in* 'Proc. 14th Int. ACM Symp. on the Theory of Computing', pp. 137–146.

VARDI M. Y. AND WOLPER P. [1986], An automata–theoretic approach to automatic program verification, *in* 'Proc. 1st Symp. on Logic in Computer Science (LICS '86)', Boston, Mass.

WALUKIEWICZ I. [1995], Completeness of Kozen's axiomatisation of the propositional μ–calculus, *in* 'Proc. 10th Ann. IEEE Symp. on Logic in Computer Science (LICS '95)', pp. 14–24.

WINSKEL G. [1991], 'A note on model checking the modal ν–calculus', *Theoretical Computer Science* **83**, 157–167. also in Proc. ICALP '89, Ausiello et. al. (ed.), LNCS 372, 761–772.

WOLPER P. [1982], Specification and synthesis of communicating processes using an extended temporal logic, *in* 'Proc. 9th Int. Symp. on Principles of Programming Languages (POPL '82)', Albuquerque, pp. 20–33.

WOLPER P. [1983], 'Temporal logic can be more expressive', *Information and Control* **56**(1–2), 72–99.

WOLPER P. [1985], 'The tableau method for temporal logic: An overview', *Logique et Analyse* **110–111**, 119–136.

WOLPER P. [1986], Expressing interesting properties of programs in propositional temporal logic, *in* 'Proc. 13th ACM Symp. on Principles of Programming Languages (POPL '86)'.

WOLPER P. AND LOVINFOSSE V. [1989], Verifying properties of large sets of processes with network invariants, *in* J. Sifakis, ed., 'Proc. Int. Workshop on Automatic Verification Methods for Finite State Systems', Vol. 407 of *LNCS*, Springer.

WOO T. Y. C. AND LAM S. S. [1993], A semantic model for authentication protocols, *in* 'Proc. IEEE Symp. on Research in Security and Privacy'.

YONEDA T., NAKADE K. AND TOHMA Y. [1989], A fast timing verification method based on the independence of units, *in* 'Proc. of 19th Int. Symp. on Fault-tolerant Computing', pp. 134–141.

YONEDA T. AND SCHLINGLOFF H. [1997], 'Efficient verification of parallel real–time systems', *Formal Methods in System Design* **11**(2), 187–215.

YOVINE S. [1997], 'Kronos: A verification tool for real–time systems', *Software Tools for Technology Transfer* **1**(1/2).

YOVINE S. [1998], Model–checking timed automata, *in* G. Rozenberg and F. Vandraager, eds, 'Embedded Systems', LNCS, Springer.

ZHANG H. [1997], SATO: An efficient propositional prover, *in* 'Proc. Int. Conf. on Automated Deduction (CADE '97)', Vol. 1249 of *LNCS/LNAI*, Springer, pp. 272–275.

List of symbols used in this chapter

Syntactic categories

Operators

Logics

Semantical notions

Index

CHAPTER 25

Resolution Decision Procedures

Christian G. Fermüller   Alexander Leitsch

Ullrich Hustadt   Tanel Tammet

Contents

HANDBOOK OF AUTOMATED REASONING
Edited by Alan Robinson and Andrei Voronkov

1. Introduction

The design of an algorithmic method which decides the truth of sentences is an old and important problem of mathematics and philosophy. It was Gottfried Wilhelm Leibniz who formulated already in the seventeenth century the fascinating vision of a *calculus ratiocinator* [Leibniz 1923], which reduces the solution of arbitrary problems to purely "mechanical" computation, once they have been formulated in an adequate formalism. About two centuries later Gottlob Frege [1884] developed the formalism of (what we now call) predicate logic, the first formal system with a strong potential of general knowledge representation. This allowed Leibniz's vision to materialize in the more moderate though also more concrete project to find a decision algorithm for the validity of formulas in predicate logic. Already Löwenheim [1915] presented results that (at least with hindsight) can be understood to define, on the one hand, a decision procedure for monadic first-order logic with equality, and on the other hand reduce the decision problem for full first-order logic to one with binary predicate symbols only. However, Hilbert should be credited for clear formulations (in his lectures around 1920 and most prominently in [Hilbert and Ackermann 1928]) of the *Entscheidungsproblem*, i.e. the problem to "decide the validity (respectively satisfiability) of a given logical expression by a finite number of operations". The importance of the decision problem is emphasized by the list of prominent scientists who contributed to it (by finding solvable subclasses): Löwenheim, Skolem, Ackermann, Bernays, Schönfinkel and Gödel *inter alii*. A. Church [1936] and—independently, in a more convincing form—A. Turing [1936/37] succeeded to prove the undecidability of the problem. Despite the unsolvability in its general form, the problem retained its vigor and importance. With the development of computers and automated theorem proving in the 1960s the implementation of a small but real *calculus ratiocinator* eventually became reality. In particular the invention of the unification principle and of resolution by J. A. Robinson [Robinson 1965b] paved the way for efficient ATP-programs. As theorem provers are essentially semi-decision procedures for first-order logic (i.e. proofs for all valid sentences can be effectively constructed) the challenge consists in guaranteeing *termination* of proof search procedures on decidable fragments of full first-order logic. The first prover of this type was designed by S. Y. Maslov [1968]; the underlying calculus combines sequent calculus and unification in a clever way. An interesting decision procedure for the so-called Gödel class was described in [Kallik 1969]. It is related to Robinson's resolution rule, but does not use unification. Somewhat later J. H. Joyner [1973] showed in his thesis that resolution can be turned into a decision procedure for many classes of clause sets that correspond to classical solvable classes.

On the basis of Joyner's approach we present resolution as decision procedure; that means we systematically investigate resolution refinements with respect to their potential as decision procedures. In Section 2 we introduce notations and basic definitions used throughout the paper. In Section 3 we investigate ordering refinements from the point of view of the decision problem. In some interesting cases we have to augment the ordering restrictions by saturation mechanisms in order to guarantee termination of the proof search or use nonliftable orderings that are not complete in general. Section 4 is dedicated to hyperresolution and not only presents classes of clause sets decidable by this refinement, but also shows how to extend the resolution prover to an automated model building procedure. In Section 5, we give an application of resolution decision procedures to a problem in description logic. In particular we show that the satisfiability problem for general knowledge bases over the description logic $\mathcal{ALB}$, an extension of $\mathcal{ALC}$, can be reduced to that of formulas in various solvable fragments of first-order logic, which in turn can be solved by an appropriate resolution refinement. We conclude with some hints to related work in Section 6.

2. Notation and definitions

We provide definitions for the basic notions of clause logic and also introduce some more special terminology. Although we assume the reader to be familiar with the concept of resolution we review the fundamental definitions for sake of clarity. Additional terminology will be introduced in later sections whenever this assists precise formulations.

Concerning the language of clause logic we assume that there is an infinite supply of *variable symbols* V, *constant symbols* CS, *function symbols* FS, and *predicate symbols* PS. As usual each function and predicate symbol is associated with some fixed *arity* which we denote by $arity(F)$ for $F \in PS$ or FS. We call a predicate or function symbol *unary* if it is of arity 1; *binary* if the arity is 2; and, in general, *n-place* for arity n. If S is some set of expressions, clauses or clause sets then $CS(S)$, $FS(S)$, and $PS(S)$, refers to the set of constant, function and predicate symbols, respectively, that occur in S.

We define the notions *term, atom, literal, expression* and *clause* formally:

2.1. DEFINITION. A *term* is defined inductively as follows:
1. Each variable and each constant is a term.
2. If $t_1, \ldots, t_n$ are terms and f is an *n*-place function symbol, then $f(t_1, \ldots, t_n)$ is also a term.

If a term t is of form $f(t_1, \ldots, t_n)$, $n \geq 1$, we call it *functional*; the set of arguments of t, $args(t)$, is $\{t_1, \ldots, t_n\}$;

2.2. DEFINITION. If $t_1, \ldots, t_n$ are terms and P is an *n*-place predicate symbol then $A = P(t_1, \ldots, t_n)$ is an *atom*; $args(A)$ is the set $\{t_1, \ldots, t_n\}$.

2.3. DEFINITION. A *literal* is either an atom or an atom preceded by a negation sign.

2.4. DEFINITION. An *expression* is either a term or a literal.

2.5. DEFINITION. A *clause* is a finite set of literals. The *empty clause* is denoted by $\square$.

Throughout this chapter we shall speak of classes of clause sets, by this we always mean sets of finite sets of clauses.

2.6. DEFINITION. If a literal L is unnegated, i.e. if it is identical with an atom A, then the *dual* of L—L^d—equals $\neg A$. Otherwise, if L is of the form $\neg A$ then $L^d = A$. For a set of literals $C = \{L_1, \ldots, L_n\}$ we define $C^d = \{L_1^d, \ldots, L_n^d\}$.

Additionally we introduce the following notation:

2.7. DEFINITION. C_+ is the set of *positive literals* (unnegated atoms) of a clause C, analogously C_- denotes the set of *negative literals* (negated atoms) in C. A clause C is called *positive* if $C_+ = C$ and *negative* if $C_- = C$.
If S is a set of clauses then $P(S)$ denotes the subset of all positive clauses in S.

2.8. DEFINITION. C is a *Horn clause* if it contains at most one positive literal, i.e. $|C_+| \leq 1$.

2.9. DEFINITION. The *term depth* of a term t, $\tau(t)$, is defined as follows:
1. If t is a variable or a constant, then $\tau(t) = 0$.
2. If $t = f(t_1, \ldots, t_n)$, where f is an n-place function symbol, then $\tau(t) = 1 + \max\{\tau(t_i) \mid 1 \leq i \leq n\}$.
The term depth of a literal L is defined as $\tau(L) = \max\{\tau(t) \mid t \in args(L)\}$. The term depth of a clause C is defined as $\tau(C) = \max\{\tau(L) \mid L \in C\}$. For a set S of clauses we define $\tau(S) = \max\{\tau(C) \mid C \in S\}$.

The *set of all variables* occurring in E is denoted by $V(E)$; if C is a clause, then $V(C)$ is the union over all $V(P_i)$ for all atoms P_i in C.

2.10. DEFINITION. Expressions or clauses E_1 and E_2 are called *variable disjoint* if $V(E_1) \cap V(E_2) = \emptyset$.
An expression or a clause is called *ground* if no variables occur in it. We call it *constant free* if no constants occur in it, and *function free* if it does not contain function symbols.

2.11. DEFINITION. $\tau_{\min}(t, s)$ is defined as the *minimal depth of occurrence* of a term t within a term s; i.e.
1. If $t = s$ then $\tau_{\min}(t, s) = 0$.
2. Otherwise, if $s = f(s_1, \ldots, s_n)$, where f is an n-place function symbol, then $\tau(t, s) = 1 + \min\{\tau(t, s_i) \mid t \text{ occurs in } s_i\}$.
(If t does not occur in s then $\tau_{\min}(t, s)$ remains undefined.)
For a literal $L = (\neg)P(t_1, \ldots, t_n)$, $\tau_{\min}(t, L) = \min\{\tau_{\min}(t, t_i) \mid t \text{ occurs in } t_i\}$. If C is a clause, then $\tau_{\min}(t, C)$ denotes the minimum of $\tau_{\min}(t, P_i)$ for all atoms P_i of C.

The *maximal depth of occurrence* $\tau_{\max}$ is defined analogously.

2.12. EXAMPLE. Let $P_1 = P(x, f(f(y)))$, $P_2 = Q(f(x))$ and $C = \{P_1, \neg P_2\}$. Then $\tau(P_1) = 2$, $\tau(P_2) = 1$, $\tau(C) = 2$, $\tau_{\min}(x, C) = 0$, $\tau_{\max}(x, C) = 1$, $\tau_{\min}(y, C) = \tau_{\max}(y, C) = 2$.

2.13. DEFINITION. The *maximal variable depth* of an expression E is defined as $\tau_v(E) = \max\{\tau_{\max}(x, E) \mid x \in V(E)\}$.
For clauses C we define $\tau_v(C) = \max\{\tau_v(L) \mid L \in C\}$;
analogously for clause sets S $\tau_v(S) = \max\{\tau_v(C) \mid C \in S\}$.

The *number of occurrences* of a variable x in a set of expressions is written as $OCC(x, E)$.

2.14. DEFINITION. Let V be the set of variables and T be the set of terms. A *substitution* is a mapping $\sigma : V \to T$ such that $\sigma(x) = x$ almost everywhere. We call the set $\{x \mid \sigma(x) \neq x\}$ *domain* of σ and denote it by $dom(\sigma)$, $\{\sigma(x) \mid x \in dom(\sigma)\}$ is called *range* of σ ($rg(\sigma)$). σ is called a *ground substitution* if $V(rg(\sigma)) = \emptyset$.
 A *(variable) renaming* is an injective substitution σ such that $rg\,\sigma \subseteq V$.

We occasionally specify a substitution as a (finite) set of expressions of the form $x_i \leftarrow t_i$ with the intended meaning $\sigma(x_i) = t_i$. Compositions of substitutions are written in postfix notation, i.e. $\sigma\vartheta$ stands for $\vartheta \circ \sigma$; if E is a set of expressions then $E\sigma$ represents the set $\sigma(E) = \{\sigma(e) \mid e \in E\}$.

2.15. DEFINITION. We say that a substitution σ is *based on a clause set* S if no other constant and functions symbols besides that in $CS(S)$ and $FS(S)$, respectively, occur in the terms of $rg(\sigma)$.

2.16. DEFINITION. An expression or set of expressions E_1 is an *instance* of another expression (or set of expressions) E_2 if there exists a substitution σ such that $E_1 = E_2\sigma$. If $V(E_2\sigma) = \emptyset$ then $E_2\sigma$ is called a *ground instance*.

We may compare expressions, substitutions and clauses using the following ordering relation.

2.17. DEFINITION. Let E_1 and E_2 be expressions, then $E_1 \leq_s E_2$—read: E_1 *is more general than* E_2—if there exists a substitution σ such that $E_1\sigma = E_2$. For substitutions ρ and θ we define analogously: $\rho \leq_s \theta$ if there exists a substitution σ such that $\rho\sigma = \theta$. Similarly, if C and D are clauses, then $C \leq_{ss} D$ if there exists a substitution σ such that $C\sigma \subseteq D$. In this case we also say, in accordance with the usual resolution terminology, that C *subsumes* D.

2.18. DEFINITION. A set of expressions M is *unifiable* by a substitution σ (called *unifier* of M) if $E_i\sigma = E_j\sigma$ for all $E_i, E_j \in M$. σ is called *most general unifier* (*mgu*) of M if for every other unifier ρ of M: $\sigma \leq_s \rho$.
 We shall also say that E_1 *is unifiable with* E_2 if $\{E_1, E_2\}$ is unifiable.

Remember that any two different mgus of a set of expressions only differ in the names of the variables.

2.19. DEFINITION. A *factor* of a clause C is a clause $C\theta$, where θ is an mgu of some $C' \subseteq C$.

2.20. DEFINITION. A clause C is called *condensed* if there exists no factor of C which is a proper subclause of C. If C' is a condensed factor of C such that $C' \subseteq C$ then C' is called a *condensation* of C; condensations are unique up to renaming [Joyner 1976].

By the *condensation rule* we mean the principle that—during proof-search—every clause is immediately replaced by its condensation.

2.21. EXAMPLE. $\{P(x,y), P(y,x)\}$ is condensed. $\{P(x,y), P(x,a)\}$ is not condensed; its condensation is $\{P(x,a)\}$.

For the *resolvent* we retain the original definition of Robinson [1965b], which combines factorization and (binary) resolution.

2.22. DEFINITION. If C and D are variable disjoint clauses and M and N are subsets of C and D respectively, such that $N^d \cup M$ is unifiable by the mgu θ, then $E = (C - M)\theta \cup (D - N)\theta$ is a *(Robinson-)resolvent* of C and D.

If M and N are singleton sets then E is called *binary resolvent* of C and D.

The atom A of $(N^d \cup M)\theta$ is called the *resolved atom*. We also say that E is *generated via* A. The elements of N and M are called the *literals resolved upon*.

2.23. DEFINITION. For a clause set S we define $Res(S)$ as the set of Robinson-resolvents of S. Additionally we define:

$$R(S) = S \cup Res(S)$$

$$R^0(S) = S, \quad R^{i+1}(S) = R(R^i(S)), \qquad \text{and}$$

$$R^*(S) = \bigcup_{i \geq 0} R^i(S).$$

We say that a clause C is *derivable from* a clause set S if $C \in R^*(S)$.

In the following sections we use various *refinements* of Robinson's resolution procedure. By a refinement (call it x) of resolution we mean a computable operator ρ_x such that

$$\rho_x(S) \subseteq R^*(S)$$

for all clause sets S. We define

$$R_x(S) = S \cup \rho_x(S).$$

R_x^i and the deductive closure R_x^* are defined in the obvious way. Particularly we write $R_<$ for operators based on an A-ordering $<$ and R_H for hyperresolution.

In contrast to resolution refinements we shall also define *variants of resolution*: For resolution variants we allow ordinary resolvents to be replaced by certain instances of it. This technique is also called *saturation*.

In Section 3, we sometimes refer to the well known splitting rule. To make the argumentation more precise we present a formal definition.

2.24. DEFINITION. Let L and L' be literals in a clause C; we define $L \sim_v L'$ if $V(L) \cap V(L') \neq \emptyset$ and $\sim_{v*}$ as the transitive closure of $\sim_v$. An equivalence class under $\sim_{v*}$ is called *component* of C. A clause is called *decomposed* if it consists of only one component and *disconnected* if every component consists of one literal only.

2.25. EXAMPLE. Let $C_1 = \{P(x), R(x,y), Q(y)\}$, $C_2 = \{P(x), Q(y)\}$ and $C_3 = \{P(x), R(x,y), Q(z)\}$. Then C_1 is decomposed (note that $P(x) \sim_v R(x,y)$, $R(x,y) \sim_v Q(y)$ and thus $P(x) \sim_{v*} Q(y)$). C_2 is disconnected and C_3 is neither decomposed nor disconnected.

2.26. DEFINITION. For any clause set S let $SPLIT(S)$ denote the set of clause sets obtained by *splitting* all members of S as far as possible. More accurately we define recursively:

1. $\Sigma_0 = \{S\}$.
2. If for all $S' \in \Sigma_i$ and all $C \in S'$ C is decomposed then

$$\Sigma_{i+1} = \Sigma_i.$$

3. If there is some $S' \in \Sigma_i$ such that for some $C \in S'$ C is can be decomposed into C' and C'' then

$$\Sigma_{i+1} = (\Sigma_i - \{S'\}) \cup ((S' - \{C\}) \cup \{C'\}) \cup ((S' - \{C\}) \cup \{C''\}).$$

(A proper C is chosen nondeterministically)

Now we may define $SPLIT(S) = \Sigma_k$ where $k = \min\{l \mid \Sigma_l = \Sigma_{l+1}\}$.

The *splitting rule* says that we have to apply resolution to all members of $SPLIT(S)$ separately to test for the unsatisfiability of S. (Recall that S is unsatisfiable iff S' is unsatisfiable for all $S' \in SPLIT(S)$.)

For the semantic of clause logic we refer, as usual, to the terminological machinery inspired by Jaques Herbrand. We review the basic definitions:

2.27. DEFINITION. The *Herbrand universe* $\mathbf{H}_S$ of a clause set S is the set of all ground terms built up from $CS(S)$ and $FS(S)$. (If $CS(S)$ is empty we introduce a special constant symbol to prevent $\mathbf{H}_S$ from being empty).

2.28. DEFINITION. An *Herbrand instance* of an atom or a clause C in S is a ground instance $C\theta$ of C such that θ is based on S.

2.29. DEFINITION. The *Herbrand base* $\hat{\mathbf{H}}_S$ is the set of all Herbrand instances of atoms appearing in clauses of S.

2.30. DEFINITION. An *Herbrand interpretation* $\mathbf{HI}_S$ for a clause set S is a subset of $\hat{\mathbf{H}}_S$ with the intended meaning that the truth value **true** is assigned to all elements of $\mathbf{HI}_S$ and the truth value **false** is assigned to all atoms in $\hat{\mathbf{H}}_S - \mathbf{HI}_S$.

We shall make use of the following naming conventions: For variable symbols we use letters from the end of the alphabet (u, v, w, x, y, z); for constant symbols, letters a, b, c are used; function symbols are denoted by f, g or h; as metavariables for terms we use t or s; capital letters will denote atoms, literals, clauses or certain sets of expressions. Whenever needed these letters are augmented by indices.

2.31. DEFINITION. The set of *first-order formulas* over a signature (CS, FS, PS) and a set of variables V is inductively defined as follows: (i) every atom is a first-order formula, (ii) if φ and ψ are formulas and x is a variable, then $\neg\varphi$, $\varphi \vee \psi$, $\varphi \wedge \psi$, $\varphi \rightarrow \psi$, $\varphi \leftrightarrow \psi$, $(\forall x)\,\varphi$, and $(\exists x)\,\varphi$ are first-order formulas.

The notions of scope of a universal quantifier $\forall$ and an existential $\exists$, and free and bound variables are defined in the usual way. We use $(Qx)\varphi$ to denote either $(\forall x)\,\varphi$ or $(\exists x)\,\varphi$. The *matrix* of a formula φ is the formula ψ obtained from φ by deleting all occurrences of quantifiers. By $\varphi[x/t]$ we denote the formula obtained from φ by replacing every free occurrence of the variable x by the term t.

2.32. DEFINITION. A formula is *rectified* if every quantifier binds a different variable and free variables are different from bound ones. It is easy to see that every first-order formula is logically equivalent to a rectified one.

A formula φ is in *prenex form* if $\varphi = (Q_1 x_1) \ldots (Q_n x_n)\psi$ where $Q_1, \ldots, Q_n$ are quantifiers and the formula ψ is quantifier free. The sequence of quantifiers $(Q_1 x_1) \ldots (Q_n x_n)$ is the *prefix* of φ. A formula in prenex form is also called *prenex formula*. For every formula φ there exists an equivalent formula $prenex(\varphi)$ in prenex form.

A formula φ is in *negation normal form* if for every subformula $\neg\psi$ of φ, ψ is an atomic formula and φ contains no occurrences of the binary operators $\rightarrow$ and $\leftrightarrow$. For every formula φ there exists an equivalent formula $nnf(\varphi)$ in negation normal form.

Let φ be a rectified formula in negation normal form. The *structural Skolem form* $sSkf(\varphi)$ of φ is obtained by exhaustively applying the following rule to φ:

$$(\exists x)\,\psi \Rightarrow \psi[x/f(y_1, \ldots, y_n)]$$

where $y_1, \ldots, y_n$ are the universally quantified variables in the scope of which $(\exists x)\,\psi$ occurs and f is a new function symbol.

2.33. EXAMPLE. The structural Skolem form of $(\forall x)\,(\exists x_2)\,(\forall z_1)\,(((\neg p(x) \vee q(x_2)) \wedge (\neg q(x_2) \vee p(x))) \wedge \neg r(x, z_1))$ is $(\forall x)\,(\forall z_1)\,(((\neg p(x) \vee q(f(x))) \wedge (\neg q(f(x)) \vee p(x))) \wedge \neg r(x, z_1))$.

The structural Skolem form is only one of the possible Skolem normal forms of first-order formula. For an in-depth discussion of various different skolemization techniques see [Baaz et al. 2001] (Chapter 5 of this Handbook).

2.34. DEFINITION. Let φ be a rectified first-order formula. The *standard clausal form* of φ is given by $cls(cnf(sSkf(prenex(nnf(\varphi)))))$ where cnf denotes a syntax preserving transformation of first-order formulas to conjunctive normal form based on the rule of distributivity, and cls is defined by

$$cls(\psi) = \{\{L_1,\ldots,L_n\} \mid L_1 \vee \ldots \vee L_n \text{ is a conjunct in } \psi\}.$$

2.35. EXAMPLE. The standard clausal form of $(\forall x)\,(\forall z_1)\,(((\neg p(x) \vee q(f(x))) \wedge (\neg q(f(x)) \vee p(x))) \wedge \neg r(x,z_1))$ is $\{\{\neg p(x), q(f(x))\}, \{\neg q(f(x)), p(x)\}, \{\neg r(x,z_1)\}\}$.

Note that the size of $cnf(\psi)$ and therefore the size of the standard clausal form of ψ can be exponential in the size of ψ, due to the duplication of subformulas in applications of the rule of distributivity. One solution is the use of *structural transformations* [Baaz, Fermüller and Leitsch 1994, Plaisted and Greenbaum 1986] in the process of transforming formulas into conjunctive normal form. The use of structural transformations in the computation of the clausal form of a first-order formula is discussed in detail in [Baaz et al. 2001, Nonnengart and Weidenbach 2001] (Chapters 5 and 6 of this Handbook).

In the following we describe a particular instance of structural transformations, namely, the computation of the *definitional form* of a first-order formula.

2.36. DEFINITION. Let $\mathrm{Pos}(\varphi)$ be the set of positions of a first-order formula φ. If λ is a position in φ, then $\varphi|_\lambda$ denotes the subformula of φ at position λ and $\varphi[\lambda \leftarrow \psi]$ is the result of replacing the subformula of φ at position λ by ψ.

We associate with each element λ of $\Lambda \subseteq \mathrm{Pos}(\varphi)$ a new predicate symbol Q_λ and a new literal $Q_\lambda(x_1,\ldots,x_n)$, where x_1, ..., x_n are the free variables of $\varphi|_\lambda$. Let

$$\mathrm{Def}_\lambda^+(\varphi) = (\forall x_1)\ldots(\forall x_n)\,(Q_\lambda(x_1,\ldots,x_n) \to \varphi|_\lambda) \quad \text{and}$$
$$\mathrm{Def}_\lambda^-(\varphi) = (\forall x_1)\ldots(\forall x_n)\,(\varphi|_\lambda \to Q_\lambda(x_1,\ldots,x_n)).$$

The *definition* of Q_λ is the formula

$$\mathrm{Def}_\lambda(\varphi) = \begin{cases} \mathrm{Def}_\lambda^+(\varphi) & \text{if } \varphi|_\lambda \text{ has positive polarity,} \\ \mathrm{Def}_\lambda^-(\varphi) & \text{if } \varphi|_\lambda \text{ has negative polarity,} \\ \mathrm{Def}_\lambda^+(\varphi) \wedge \mathrm{Def}_\lambda^-(\varphi) & \text{otherwise.} \end{cases}$$

Now, define $\mathrm{Def}_\Lambda(\varphi)$ inductively by:

$$\mathrm{Def}_\emptyset(\varphi) = \varphi \quad \text{and}$$
$$\mathrm{Def}_{\Lambda \cup \{\lambda\}}(\varphi) = \mathrm{Def}_\Lambda(\varphi) \wedge \mathrm{Def}_\Lambda(\varphi[\lambda \leftarrow Q_\lambda(x_1,\ldots,x_n)])),$$

where λ is maximal in $\Lambda \cup \{\lambda\}$ with respect to the prefix ordering on positions. The corresponding clauses will be called *definitional clauses*. A *definitional form* of φ is $\mathrm{Def}_\Lambda(\varphi)$, where Λ is a subset of positions of subformulas (usually, nonatomic or nonliteral subformulas).

If a formula φ contains no occurrences of equivalence, then for any position λ, $\varphi|_\lambda$ will have either positive or negative polarity. In this case the third case in the definition of $\mathrm{Def}_\lambda(\varphi)$ is obsolete.

2.37. EXAMPLE. Consider the first-order formula

$$\varphi = (\exists x)\,(\forall y)\,(\neg R(x,y) \vee (\neg q(y) \vee (\exists z)\,(R(y,z) \wedge q(z))))$$

Let λ_1, λ_2, and λ_3 denote the positions of the subformulas $(\exists z)\,(R(y,z) \wedge q(z))$, $(\neg q(y) \vee (\exists z)\,(R(y,z) \wedge q(z)))$, and $(\forall y)\,(\neg R(x,y) \vee (\neg q(y) \vee (\exists z)\,(R(y,z) \wedge q(z))))$ in φ, respectively. Then

$$\begin{aligned}
\mathrm{Def}_{\{\lambda_1,\lambda_2,\lambda_3\}}(\varphi) &= \mathrm{Def}_{\lambda_1}(\varphi) \wedge \mathrm{Def}_{\{\lambda_2,\lambda_3\}}(\varphi[\lambda_1 \leftarrow Q_{\lambda_1}(y)]) \\
&= (\forall x)\,(Q_{\lambda_1}(x) \to (\exists z)\,(R(y,z) \wedge q(z))) \wedge \\
&\quad \mathrm{Def}_{\{\lambda_2,\lambda_3\}}((\exists x)\,(\forall y)\,(\neg R(x,y) \vee (\neg q(y) \vee Q_{\lambda_1}(y)))) \\
&= (\forall y)\,(Q_{\lambda_1}(y) \to (\exists z)\,(R(y,z) \wedge q(z))) \wedge \\
&\quad \mathrm{Def}_{\lambda_2}((\exists x)\,(\forall y)\,(\neg R(x,y) \vee (\neg q(y) \vee Q_{\lambda_1}(y)))) \wedge \\
&\quad \mathrm{Def}_{\{\lambda_3\}}((\exists x)\,(\forall y)\,(\neg R(x,y) \vee Q_{\lambda_2}(y))) \\
&= (\forall y)\,(Q_{\lambda_1}(y) \to (\exists z)\,(R(y,z) \wedge q(z))) \wedge \\
&\quad (\forall y)\,(Q_{\lambda_2}(y) \to (\neg q(y) \vee Q_{\lambda_1}(y))) \wedge \\
&\quad \mathrm{Def}_{\{\lambda_3\}}((\exists x)\,(\forall y)\,(\neg R(x,y) \vee Q_{\lambda_2}(y))) \\
&= (\forall y)\,(Q_{\lambda_1}(y) \to (\exists z)\,(R(y,z) \wedge q(z))) \wedge \\
&\quad (\forall y)\,(Q_{\lambda_2}(y) \to (\neg q(y) \vee Q_{\lambda_1}(y))) \wedge \\
&\quad \mathrm{Def}_{\lambda_3}((\exists x)\,(\forall y)\,\neg R(x,y) \vee Q_{\lambda_2}(y)) \wedge \\
&\quad \mathrm{Def}_{\emptyset}((\exists x)\,Q_{\lambda_3}(x)) \\
&= (\forall x)\,(Q_{\lambda_1}(y) \to (\exists z)\,(R(y,z) \wedge q(z))) \wedge \\
&\quad (\forall x)\,(Q_{\lambda_2}(y) \to (\neg q(y) \vee Q_{\lambda_1}(y))) \wedge \\
&\quad (\forall x)\,(Q_{\lambda_3}(x) \to (\forall y)\,(\neg R(x,y) \vee Q_{\lambda_2}(y))) \wedge \\
&\quad (\exists x)\,Q_{\lambda_3}(x).
\end{aligned}$$

2.38. PROPOSITION. *Let φ be a first-order formula and let Λ be a subset of $\mathrm{Pos}(\varphi)$.*
1. *φ is satisfiable iff $\mathrm{Def}_\Lambda(\varphi)$ is satisfiable.*
2. *$\mathrm{Def}_\Lambda(\varphi)$ can be computed in polynomial time.*
3. *If Λ contains all positions of non-literal subformulas of φ, then the size of the standard clausal form of $\mathrm{Def}_\Lambda(\varphi)$ is linear in the size of φ.*

The p-definitional form of a closed first-order formula defined in [Baaz et al. 2001, page 310] (Chapter 5 of this Handbook) Chapter 5 is a special case of Definition 2.36. The length-optimizing form of [Boy de la Tour 1992] is based on a similar principle, as well as the formula renaming technique described in [Nonnengart and Weidenbach 2001] (Chapter 6 of this Handbook).

3. Decision procedures based on ordering refinements

3.1. Motivation

Very different types of resolution refinements can be turned into effective means for deciding satisfiability of certain classes of clause sets. In Section 4 hyperresolution will be investigated from this point of view. However, the ground breaking work of William H. Joyner [Joyner 1973, Joyner 1976] and Russian scholars—in particular S. J. Maslov (see [Maslov 1968] and [Zamov 1989])—that introduced the paradigm of "resolution as a decision procedure" (or, equivalently, "inverse method as a decision procedure") was based on ordering refinements, sometimes augmented by saturation mechanisms. In this section we review some generalizations of these results.

Traditionally, investigations into the decision problem concentrated on prefix classes of first-order formulas without function symbols. It turns out that certain (completeness preserving) ordering strategies allow to control effectively the nesting of terms in resolvents of clauses corresponding (via skolemization) to formulas with certain types of quantifiers prefixes. In particular the initially extended Ackermann class (prefix $\exists^*\forall\exists^*$), the initially extended Gödel class (prefix $\exists^*\forall\forall\exists^*$), the Skolem class (see Subsection 3.5) and the related class $\mathcal{K}$ of Maslov can be shown decidable by such methods. Once the role of ordering restrictions is understood it is easy to generalize these classes to classes of clause sets that allow for more complex term structures than those obtained by skolemization of function free formulas.

As a motivating example consider the *monadic class*, i.e. the class of all first-order formulas (without function symbols) that contain only monadic predicate symbols. Obviously, the atoms of clauses corresponding to such formulas are all of form $P(x)$ or $P(f(x_1, \ldots, x_n))$, where f denotes a skolem function. To define a proof search procedure which generates only finitely many different resolvents from such sets of clauses we have to prevent the derivation of "deep" resolvents. Observe that unrestricted resolution allows to derive all clauses of form

$$\{P(f^n(x))\} \quad \text{where } n \geq 1$$

from the clause set

$$S = \{\{\neg P(x), P(f(x))\}, \{P(x)\}\}$$

corresponding to the monadic formula $\forall x \exists y([P(x) \supset P(y)] \wedge P(x))$. However, suppose we order atoms (and correspondingly literals) by defining

$$P(f(x_1, \ldots, x_n))\sigma \succ Q(x_i)\sigma \quad (1 \leq i \leq n), \text{ and}$$

$$P(f(x_1, \ldots, x_n))\sigma \succ Q(g(x_1, \ldots, x_m))\sigma \quad \text{if } n > m$$

for all monadic predicate symbols P, Q, function symbols f, g, and substitutions σ. If we allow to resolve only upon maximal literals in clauses then no clause at all is derivable from S. It is easy to see that no clauses with nested function symbols are derivable from any clause set corresponding to a monadic formula if we employ the mentioned resolution refinement, which is well known to preserve completeness (see below). Still, clauses of arbitrary length could be derivable. But this can be prevented either by decomposing clauses into their variable disjoint subclauses or by applying the condensation rule mentioned in Section 2, above. Summarizing we get that $R_x^*(S)$ is finite for all clause sets S corresponding to a formula in the monadic class, where R_x is a properly defined resolution operator. By the completeness of R_x, we have just described a decision procedure for the monadic class since we only have to check whether $\square \in R_x^*(S)$.

Traditionally, decidability results like that for monadic class have been solved by quite different methods (see [Dreben and Goldfarb 1979]). E.g., it can be shown that any model of a monadic formula F can be mapped into a model of F of cardinality $\leq 2^p$, where p is the number of different predicate symbols in F. Clearly, the resolution based decision procedure is more feasible than an exhaustive search for a model among all possible interpretations of cardinality $\leq 2^p$ (unless p is extremely small). Moreover, it has the advantage that any resolution based prover (e.g., OTTER [McCune 1995], SPASS [Weidenbach, Gaede and Rock 1996], or Gandalf [Tammet 1997]) can be used for that purpose, provided it allows to define simple ordering restrictions as mentioned above.

3.2. A-orderings

The ordering that we have used for the monadic class in the example above is just a special case of the well known concept of A-orderings introduced in Kowalski and Hayes [1969]. We present a definition, that is slightly more general than that of Kowalski and Hayes.

3.1. DEFINITION. An A-ordering $<$ is a binary relation on atoms such that
1. $<$ is irreflexive,
2. $<$ is transitive,
3. for all atoms A,B and all substitutions θ: $A < B$ implies $A\theta < B\theta$.

A subtle point concerns the definition of the resolvents that obey the A-ordering restriction. Whereas Kowalski and Hayes demand that the atoms to be resolved upon are maximal with respect to the ordering, we use the following definition which is due to Joyner [1976].

3.2. DEFINITION. For any clause set S and any A-ordering $<$: $E \in R_<(S)$ if E is a (Robinson-)resolvent of clauses in S such that for no atom B in E: $A < B$, where A is the resolved atom.

This means that we use an *a posteriori criterion* as opposed to an *a priori criterion* for the applicability of the resolution rule.

It is interesting to observe that in order to guarantee the termination of proof search we have to insist on the stronger a posteriori criterion in some cases.

The completeness of A-ordering resolution is readily shown by a semantic tree argument. The importance of this proof technique lies in the fact that additional techniques like condensation, subsumption and certain saturation techniques can be shown to preserve completeness by the same argument. For a proof of this fact and the theorems and lemmas below, we refer to [Fermüller, Leitsch, Tammet and Zamov 1993].

3.3. Covering terms and atoms

Instead of investigating "classical" decision classes (i.e., the prefix classes described in [Dreben and Goldfarb 1979]) in a case by case manner we first introduce some additional terminology that reveals common features of the term structure in corresponding clauses and, more importantly, leads to natural generalizations of those classes in the context of clause logic.

Throughout the next sections we speak of terms, atoms and literals characterized by special properties which we call *covering* and *weakly covering*, respectively.

3.3. DEFINITION. A functional term t is called *covering* if for all functional subterms s occurring in t we have $V(s) = V(t)$. An atom or literal A is called *covering* if each argument of A is either a constant or a variable or a covering term t such that $V(t) = V(A)$.

3.4. DEFINITION. A functional term t is called *weakly covering* if for all non ground, functional subterms s of t: $V(s) = V(t)$. Similarly to Definition 3.3, an atom or literal A is called *weakly covering* if each argument of A is either a ground term or a variable or a weakly covering term t such that $V(t) = V(A)$.

3.5. EXAMPLE. $g(h(x), a, f(x,x))$ is a covering term; $f(x, g(h(a), f(y,x), y))$ is weakly covering but not covering; $g(f(x,y), x, h(x))$ is neither covering nor weakly covering. $P(h(x), x)$ is a covering and $Q(f(x, f(x,y)), f(y,x), h(a))$ a weakly covering atom; $P(f(a, h(b)), h(c))$, like any ground atom, is covering, too. $P(h(x), y)$ and $P(h(x), f(x,y))$ are not weakly covering.

Clearly, all covering atoms or terms are also weakly covering, but the converse does not hold. Covering atoms originate for instance by skolemization of (function free) prenex formulas where the existential quantifiers are in the scope of all or none of the universal quantifiers. Also observe that any atom or term that contains at most one variable is weakly covering.

The essential facts needed to establish a bound on the term depth as well as the length of resolvents for certain classes of clause sets, are summarized in the following lemmas.

3.6. LEMMA. *Let θ be an mgu of two covering atoms A and B. Then the following properties hold for $A\theta$ ($= B\theta$):*
1. *$A\theta$ is covering,*
2. *$\tau(A\theta) = \max(\tau(A), \tau(B))$*
3. *$|V(A\theta)| \leq \max(|V(A)|, |V(B)|)$.*

Similar properties can be shown to hold for weakly covering atoms as well. The following property of covering atoms is essential, too:

3.7. LEMMA. *Let A and B be two (weakly) covering atoms such that $V(A) = V(B)$. For any substitution θ: If $A\theta$ is (weakly) covering then $B\theta$ is (weakly) covering, too.*

3.4. Classes $\mathcal{E}_1$ and $\mathcal{E}^+$

The concept of (weakly) covering literals permits concise definitions of some decision classes. Consider, e.g., the following class of clause sets:

3.8. DEFINITION *($\mathcal{E}_1$)*. A clause set S belongs to $\mathcal{E}_1$ if the following holds for all clauses C in S:
1. All literals in C are covering, and
2. for all literals $L, M \in C$ either $V(L) = V(M)$ or $V(L) \cap V(M) = \emptyset$.

3.9. EXAMPLE. Let $C_1 = \{P(f(x,y),a), Q(y,x,x)\}$, $C_2 = \{P(f(x,f(x,a))), Q(z,y,a)\}$, $C_3 = \{P(x,f(a))\}$ and $C_4 = \{Q(x,y,a), P(x,x)\}$. Then $\{C_1, C_2\} \in \mathcal{E}_1$, but any clause set containing C_3 or C_4 is not in $\mathcal{E}_1$.

$\mathcal{E}_1$ may be regarded as an extension of the initially extended Ackermann class (characterized by the prefix type $\exists^*\forall\exists^*$).

The class $\mathcal{E}_1$ has the pleasant property that for every clause set S in $\mathcal{E}_1$ and every resolvent or factor C of clauses in S, the number of variables in any split component of C will not exceed the maximal number of variables in its parent clauses. However, there is no bound on the term depth of clauses in $R(S)$. To guarantee a term depth limit for resolvents of clauses in $\mathcal{E}_1$, a simple A-ordering strategy can be used.

3.10. DEFINITION. Let A and B be two atoms, then $A <_d B$ if
1. $\tau(A) < \tau(B)$, and
2. for all $x \in V(A)$: $\tau_{\max}(x, A) < \tau_{\max}(x, B)$
   (implying $V(A) \subseteq V(B)$).

It is easy to show that $<_d$ is an A-ordering. It can also be proved that, for every $S \in \mathcal{E}_1$, every resolvent in $R_{<_d}(S)$ fulfills the defining conditions of class $\mathcal{E}_1$ and is smaller or equal with respect to term depth than its parent clauses. This is mainly a consequence of Lemma 3.6 and Lemma 3.7. To get a decision procedure we have to bound the length of resolvents, too. For this we may either use the splitting rule (see Definition 2.26) or the condensation rule (see Definition 2.20).

3.11. Theorem. *The class $\mathcal{E}_1$ is decidable; $R_{<_d}$ combined with the splitting or condensation rule provides a decision procedure.*

$\mathcal{E}_1$ remains decidable if we slightly generalize it as follows:

3.12. Definition ($\mathcal{E}^+$). A clause set S belongs to $\mathcal{E}^+$ if, for all clauses C in S, the following properties hold:

1. All literals in C are weakly covering, and
2. for all literals $L, M \in C$ either $V(L) = V(M)$ or $V(L) \cap V(M) = \emptyset$.

3.13. Example. Let $C_1 = \{P(f(x,y),a), Q(y,x,x)\}$, $C_2 = \{P(f(x,f(x,a)), Q(z,y,a)\}$, $C_3 = \{P(x,f(a))\}$ and $C_4 = \{Q(x,y,a), P(x,x)\}$. Then $\{C_1, C_2, C_3\} \in \mathcal{E}^+$, but any clause set containing C_4 is not in $\mathcal{E}^+$.

$\mathcal{E}^+$ clearly is a strict superset of $\mathcal{E}_1$, because arbitrary ground terms are now additionally allowed to occur everywhere in the clauses. $\mathcal{E}^+$ also contains the class of clause sets only consisting of clauses C such that $|V(C)| \leq 1$. This subclass has first been proved decidable by Y. Gurevich [1973] and is often called class $\mathcal{E}$, which motivated the name $\mathcal{E}^+$ for the class defined above.

$R_{<_d}$ combined with the splitting rule or condensation also provides a decision procedure for $\mathcal{E}^+$ [de Nivelle 1998a]. However, unlike $\mathcal{E}_1$, the term depth as well as the maximal variable depth of a resolvent can be greater than the term depth and maximal variable depth of its parent clauses.

3.14. Example. Consider the clauses $C_1 = \{\neg P(x, s(s(0))), P(s(x), s(s(0)))\}$ and $C_2 = \{\neg P(y, s(s(0))), P(s(y), s(s(0)))\}$. Clearly, $\{C_1, C_2\} \in \mathcal{E}^+$. The resolvent of C_1 and C_2 using the most general unifier $\sigma = \{y \leftarrow s(x)\}$ is $C_3 = \{\neg P(x, s(s(0))), P(s(s(x)), s(s(0)))\}$. Note that in $C_1\sigma = C_1$ and in $C_2\sigma = \{\neg P(s(x), s(s(0))), P(s(s(x)), s(s(0)))\}$ both literals are maximal with respect to $<_d$. The maximal variable depth of C_3 is greater than the maximal variable depth of C_1 and C_2.

The resolvent $\{Q(s(0), y, f(s(0), y))\}$ of $\{P(x, y, f(x,y)), Q(x, y, f(x,y))\}$ and $\{\neg P(s(0), y, z)\}$ has a greater term depth than its parent clauses.

It can be proved that for every $S \in \mathcal{E}^+$, every resolvent C in $R_{<_d}(S)$ fulfills the defining conditions of class $\mathcal{E}^+$, and the maximal variable depth and the term depth of C does not exceed $\tau_v(S) + \tau(S)$ [de Nivelle 1998a].

3.15. Theorem. *The class $\mathcal{E}^+$ is decidable; $R_{<_d}$ combined with the splitting or condensation rule provides a decision procedure.*

It is mandatory that $<_d$ is used as an a posteriori criterion as the following example illustrates.

3.16. EXAMPLE. Consider the clauses $C_1 = \{\neg P(x, s(s(0))), \ P(s(x), s(s(0)))\}$ and $C_4 = \{P(0, s(s(0)))\}$. We have already observed in the previous example, that both literals in C_1 are maximal with respect to $<_d$. Thus, if $<_d$ is used as an a priori criterion, then we obtain an unbounded sequence of clauses $\{P(s(0), s(s(0)))\}$, $\{P(s(s(0)), s(s(0)))\}, \ldots, \{P(s^i(0)), s^2(0)\}, \ldots$ by resolving on the first literal of C_1.

There are various alternative decision procedures for the class $\mathcal{E}^+$. In Section 3.7 we present a resolution refinement based on a nonliftable ordering which is able to decide $\mathcal{E}^+$. A decision procedure based on a combination of ordering refinements with a saturation mechanism has been used in [Fermüller et al. 1993, chapter 5]. We illustrate this approach in the next section for the more interesting case of the Skolem class.

3.5. An extension of the Skolem class

The (initially extended) Skolem class is the class of prenex formulas with a prefix of the form $(\exists z_1) \cdots (\exists z_l)(\forall y_1) \cdots (\forall y_m)(\exists x_1) \cdots (\exists x_n)$ such that each atom of the matrix has among its arguments either

1. at least one of the x_i, or
2. at most one of the y_i, or
3. all of $y_1, \ldots y_m$.

In this section we consider a class of clause sets which strongly generalizes the initially extended Skolem class.

3.17. DEFINITION $(\mathcal{S}^+)$. A clause set S belongs to $\mathcal{S}^+$ if for all clauses C in S and all literals L in C:

1. If t is a functional term occurring in C then $V(t) = V(C)$.
2. $|V(L)| \leq 1$ or $V(L) = V(C)$.

Class $\mathcal{S}^+$ contains the clause forms of all formulas in the initially extended Skolem class, which in turn contains the initially extended Gödel class (i.e. the prefix class with quantifier prefix type $\exists^* \forall \forall \exists^*$).

$\mathcal{S}^+$ is related to $\mathcal{E}_1$. In fact we have:

$$E \in R_{<_d}(\{C, D\}) \qquad \text{implies} \qquad \tau(E) \leq \tau(\{C, D\})$$

if $\{C, D\} \in \mathcal{S}^+$. The only problem is that in general $R_{<_d}(S) \notin \mathcal{S}^+$ for clause sets $S \in \mathcal{S}^+$. Atoms may be generated which, besides covering terms, have arbitrary variables as arguments.

To be able to argue more accurately we define:

3.18. DEFINITION. An atom or literal A is called *essentially monadic on a term t* if t is an argument of A and each other argument is either equal to t or a constant. A is called *almost monadic on t* if t is functional and, besides t and constants, also at least one variable that is not in $V(t)$ occurs among the arguments of A.

3.19. EXAMPLE. The literal $P(g(x), b, g(x))$ is essentially monadic on $g(x)$. The literal $P(f(f(z)), x, a, f(f(z)))$ is almost monadic on $f(f(z))$. In contrast, $P(x, y, a, x)$ and $Q(f(x), f(y))$ are neither essentially monadic nor almost monadic (on any term).

As mentioned above $R_{<_d}$ provides a term depth limit for the resolvents of $\mathcal{S}^+$. But by resolving such clauses, almost monadic atoms may be generated besides covering ones.

3.20. EXAMPLE. Let $C = \{P(x), Q(x, y)\}$ and $D = \{\neg P(f(z)), Q(g(z), z)\}$. The only $R_{<_d}$-resolvent of C and D is $E = \{Q(f(z), y), Q(g(z), z)\}$. The first literal of E is almost monadic on $f(z)$; the second literal is covering and essentially monadic.

Observe that, for the class $\mathcal{S}^+$, noncovering (but almost covering) atoms are generated by $R_{<_d}$ only if one of the parent clauses is function free, and the atom(s) resolved upon in this clause contain(s) one variable only, whereas other atoms must also have additional variables as arguments. In all other cases all atoms of a resolvent are covering. It is an easy task to refine the ordering $<_d$ in a way such that it becomes sufficiently restrictive to terminate on all inputs from $\mathcal{S}^+$ (and many other classes). We just have to add

    4. $V(A) \subset V(B)$ implies $A <_d B$ for function free atoms A and B

to the defining conditions for $<_d$ (Definition 3.10). Unfortunately, the resulting resolution variant is not an A-ordering. Still, using techniques developed by Hans de Nivelle one can show that completeness is preserved if the inputs are from $\mathcal{S}^+$ [de Nivelle n.d.]. However, one looses compatibility with subsumption and other deletion strategies. Here, we describe another useful method to guarantee termination *and* completeness, namely *saturation*.

For any almost monadic atom we define a corresponding set of essentially monadic atoms.

3.21. DEFINITION. Let A be almost monadic on some functional term t and CS be some set of constants. The *monadization* $MON(A, \mathrm{CS})$ consists of atoms that are like A except for replacing each variable that occurs as argument of A (but not of t) by t or some constant in CS. More exactly: Let $\Sigma_{t,\mathrm{CS}}$ be the set of all substitutions of the form $\{x_i \leftarrow t_i \mid x_i \in V(A) - V(t)\}$ where $t_i = t$ or $t_i \in \mathrm{CS}$ then $MON(A, \mathrm{CS}) = \{A\sigma \mid \sigma \in \Sigma_{t,\mathrm{CS}}\}$.

We extend the definition of MON to clauses and clause sets: If all almost monadic atoms A of a clause C are almost monadic on the same functional term t then $MON(C, \mathrm{CS}) = \{C\sigma' \mid \sigma' \in \Sigma'_{t,\mathrm{CS}}\}$ where Σ'_t is the set of substitutions $\{x_i \leftarrow t_i \mid x_i \in V(C) - V(t)\}$, such that $t_i = t$ or $t_i \in \mathrm{CS}$.

If C is function free and there is one and only one variable x, such that all literals $L \in C$ with $|V(L)| \geq 2$ contain x then $MON(C, \mathrm{CS}) = \{C\sigma \mid \sigma \in \Sigma_{x,\mathrm{CS}}\}$ where $\Sigma_{x,\mathrm{CS}}$ is the set of substitutions $\{x_i \leftarrow t_i \mid x_i \in V(C) - V(t)\}$, such that $t_i = x$ or $t_i \in \mathrm{CS}$.

In all other cases $MON(C, \mathrm{CS}) = \{C\}$.

For any clause set S: $MON(S) = \bigcup_{C \in S} MON(C, CS(S))$ (where $CS(S)$ is the set of all constants occurring in clauses of S).

3.22. REMARK. As we only use the monadization operator in the context of finite clause sets S we will implicitly assume that the set of constants occurring in S is always used for the monadization of atoms or clauses. For sake of readability we therefore suppress the second argument and write $MON(A)$ and $MON(C)$ instead of $MON(A, CS)$ and $MON(C, CS)$, respectively. Observe that, in our context, $MON(A)$ and $MON(C)$ are always finite.

3.23. EXAMPLE. For all examples we assume that there is just one constant a. Let $A = P(f(x,y), z)$ then $MON(A) = \{P(f(x,y), f(x,y)), P(f(x,y), a)\}$. Let $C = \{Q(u, x, f(x,a)), P(u, f(x,a))\}$ then $MON(C) = \{\{Q(f(x,a), x, f(x,a)), P(f(x,a), f(x,a))\}, \{Q(a, x, f(x,a)), P(a, f(x,a))\}$. For $D = \{P(x,x), Q(u,a,x), P(x,v)\}$ we have $MON(D) = \{\{P(x,x), Q(x,a,x)\}, \{P(x,x), Q(x,a,x), P(x,a)\}, \{P(x,x), Q(a,a,x)\}, \{P(x,x), Q(a,a,x), P(x,a)\}\}$.

We may now define a new resolution variant R_m which is based on $R_{<_d}$.

3.24. DEFINITION. For any clause set S:

$$R_m(S) = MON(R_{<_d}(S)).$$

The members of $R_m(S)$ are called R_m-resolvents.

It can be shown that for any $\{C, D\} \in S^+$ and $E \in R_m(\{C, D\})$ we have $\tau(E) \leq \tau(\{C, D\})$. Moreover, the subclauses of E resulting from splitting fulfill the defining conditions of S^+.

We thus arrive at the following result:

3.25. THEOREM. S^+ *is decidable; R_m combined with the splitting rule or condensation provides a decision procedure.*

3.6. Nonliftable orderings

We have seen above that refinements based on A-orderings can be used to define decision procedures for various classes of clause sets. However, other types of ordering restrictions are important, as well. In order to achieve new decidability results or more efficient decision procedures, it will be important to pay attention to these refinements. Therefore we conclude with a discussion of the particularly interesting case of the so-called *nonliftable orderings*.

Recall the Definition 3.1 of A-orderings. The binary relation $<_R$ is an A-ordering iff it is irreflexive, transitive and satisfies the *liftability* condition: for all atoms A, B and all substitutions θ: $A <_R B$ implies $A\theta <_R B\theta$.

Although sufficient, liftability is not always a necessary condition for an irreflexive and transitive relation $<_R$ to be complete. First of all the definition of liftability can be weakened to deal not with arbitrary instances but only with ground instances appearing in an unsatisfiable set of ground instances. This observation is used in [de Nivelle 1998a] to define a resolution refinement which is complete and terminating on $\mathcal{E}^+$, but also liftable in the weaker sense. On $\mathcal{E}^+$ this ordering coincides with the A-ordering $<_d$ and thus yields an (a posteriori) A-ordering decision procedure for this class.

Moreover there exist a number of criteria which guarantee completeness for strong nonliftable orderings. A minimal requirement for a nonliftable ordering $\succ$ to be compatible with the resolution inference rule is that $\succ$ is invariant under renaming:

3.26. DEFINITION. An ordering $\succ$ is invariant under renaming if for any two literals A and B such that $V(A) = V(B)$ and any renamings ϑ_1 and ϑ_2 with $rg(\vartheta_1) = rg(\vartheta_2)$, $A \succ B$ implies $A\vartheta_1 \succ B\vartheta_2$.

The renaming condition ensures that we can rename the variables of clauses C and D to ensure variable-disjointness before deriving a resolvent of C and D without affecting the $\succ$-maximality of literals:

3.27. LEMMA. Let $\succ$ be an ordering which is invariant under renaming. Let C be a clause and σ be a variable renaming. If a literal L is $\succ$-maximal in C, then $L\sigma$ is $\succ$-maximal in $C\sigma$.

Now, the following question is an important open problem:

Does every ordering that is invariant under renaming define a complete resolution refinement?

Partial solutions to this problem have been presented by H. de Nivelle and T. Tammet. H. de Nivelle [1997] shows the completeness for orderings invariant under renaming on Krom clauses. A proof by Tammet [1996] shows that the following orderings $<_g$ and $<_{ng}$ are complete, if the a priori criterion is used to select the resolvent:

3.28. DEFINITION. For any two literals A and B, $A <_g B$ if A is not ground and B is ground. Analogously, $A <_{ng} B$ if A is ground and B is not ground.

Completeness is preserved if $<_g$ is strengthened by arbitrary completeness-preserving orderings for the ground and nonground cases:

3.29. DEFINITION. Let $<_s$ be a completeness-preserving ordering of nonground literals and $<_r$ be an ordering of ground literals. Then, for any two literals A and B, $A <_{gsr} B$ if either A is not ground and B is ground, both A and B are ground and $A <_r B$ or both A and B are nonground and $A <_s B$.

The resolution refinement based on $<_g$ is also complete if used as a posteriori criterion. However, this is not true for the ordering $<_{ng}$ as the following example shows.

3.30. EXAMPLE. Let $C_1 = \{\neg P(a)\}$, $C_2 = \{\neg Q(a)\}$, and $C_3 = \{P(x), Q(y)\}$. The set $S = \{C_1, C_2, C_3\}$ is obviously unsatisfiable. There are only two resolution inference steps possible on S. We can either resolve C_1 and C_3 with most general unifier $\sigma_1 = \{x \leftarrow a\}$ or C_2 and C_3 with most general unifier $\sigma_2 = \{y \leftarrow a\}$. However, the literal $P(a)$ is not maximal in $C_3\sigma_1 = \{P(a), Q(y)\}$ with respect to $<_{ng}$ nor is $Q(a)$ maximal in $C_3\sigma_2 = \{P(x), Q(a)\}$. If we use $<_{ng}$ as a posteriori criterion, then none of these resolution inference steps by the resolution refinement based on $<_{ng}$ is possible. Hence, we obtain no refutation of S.

De Nivelle [1995] shows that any irreflexive and transitive relation $\succ$ which is invariant under renaming is complete for sets of *decomposed clauses*, i.e. clauses where all literals contain the same variables (the orderings are applied a priori).

Although nonliftable orderings are useful to obtain resolution decision procedures for a variety of classes, as exemplified in the following section, they are typically not compatible with the strategies of full subsumption and tautology removal. Moreover we cannot use the a posteriori but only the a priori criterion for selecting resolvents.

3.7. Classes decidable by nonliftable orderings

The book [Fermüller et al. 1993] presents a few orderings which are nonliftable, but are complete for some classes, for example the class $\mathcal{E}^+$ and the class $\mathcal{K}$ of Maslov.

It follows from the result of de Nivelle [1995] that completeness for $\mathcal{E}^+$ is preserved if the condition (1): $\tau(A) < \tau(B)$ is dropped from the previous Definition 3.10 of an A-ordering $<_d$, keeping only the condition (2): for all $x \in V(A)$: $\tau_{\max}(x, A) < \tau_{\max}(x, B)$. Although the ordering fulfilling just (2) does not obey the renaming condition in general, it does so on $\mathcal{E}^+$. There it coincides with the ordering $<_\tau$ defined as: $A <_\tau B$ iff $\tau_v(A) < \tau_v(B)$. The ordering $<_\tau$ is invariant under renaming and thus is complete on $\mathcal{E}^+$ but it is not an A-ordering. As discussed in Section 3.4, class $\mathcal{E}^+$ can be decided also by a liftable a posteriori ordering.

The class $\mathcal{K}$ was introduced by Maslov [1971]. The following definitions are based on [Fermüller et al. 1993, chapter 6].

3.31. DEFINITION ($\mathcal{K}$). Let φ be a closed formula in negation normal form without nonconstant function symbols such that no variable is bound by two different quantifier occurrences. Let ψ be a subformula of φ. The φ-prefix of the formula ψ is a sequence of quantifiers of the schema φ which bind the free variables of ψ.

Then φ belongs to the class $\mathcal{K}$ if there exist variables $x_1, \ldots, x_k$, $k \geq 0$, which are not in the scope of any existential quantifier, and for every atomic subformula ψ of φ the φ-prefix of φ

1. either has length less or equal to 1, or
2. ends with an existential quantifier, or
3. is of the form $(\forall x_1)(\forall x_2) \ldots (\forall x_k)$

It is straightforward to see that $\varphi \in \mathcal{K}$ iff $cnf(prenex(\varphi)) \in \mathcal{K}$, where cnf denotes a syntax preserving transformation of first-order formulas to conjunctive normal form based on the rule of distributivity. Thus, without loss of generality we can restrict ourselves to formulas in prenex form whose matrix is in conjunctive normal form, that is, formulas in $\mathcal{K}$ have the form

$$(\forall x_1)\ldots(\forall x_k)(Q_1 z_1)\ldots(Q_l z_l) \bigwedge_{i=1,\ldots,n} \bigvee_{j=1,\ldots,m_i} L_{i,j} \qquad (3.1)$$

where $m \geq 0$, $k \geq 0$, $l \geq 0$, $n > 0$, $m_i > 0$, and $L_{i,j}$ are literals. The class of clause sets obtained from formulas (3.1) in $\mathcal{K}$ is denoted by $\mathcal{KC}$.

We define an ordering on terms and literals as follows.

3.32. DEFINITION. Let s and t be terms, then $s \lesssim_Z t$ if at least one of the following conditions is satisfied:

1. $t = f(t_1,\ldots,t_n)$, $s = g(t_1,\ldots,t_m)$, $n \geq m \geq 0$.
2. s is a variable and either $s \in args(t)$ or $s = t$.

Let A and B be two atoms, then $A \lesssim_Z B$ if for every nonconstant argument term s of B there exists a nonconstant argument term t of A such that $t \lesssim_Z s$.

We define $\sim_Z$ as $\lesssim_Z \cap \lesssim_Z^{-1}$ and $<_Z$ as $\lesssim_Z / \sim_Z$ on terms and atoms.

The ordering $<_Z$ is not liftable, but it is invariant under renamings. It follows from the results in [Fermüller et al. 1993] that any derivation from a clause set S in $\mathcal{KC}$ by a combination of $R_{<_Z}$ and splitting terminates. By the result of de Nivelle [1995], the refinement $R_{<_Z}$ is complete.

3.33. THEOREM. $\mathcal{KC}$ is decidable; $R_{<_Z}$ combined with the splitting rule provides a decision procedure.

Recently, Hustadt and Schmidt [1999b] have shown that $\mathcal{KC}$ as well as the class $\mathcal{DKC}$ containing the clause sets obtained from conjunctions of formulas in $\mathcal{K}$ are decidable using a resolution refinement based on a liftable ordering.

A fragment of first-order logic which currently attracts much attention is the *guarded fragment* proposed by Andréka, van Benthem and Németi [1995, 1998]. It is an attempt to characterise a class of first-order formulas sharing properties like decidability, the finite model property and the tree model property with modal logics.

3.34. DEFINITION ($\mathcal{GF}$). The guarded fragment $\mathcal{GF}$ is a subclass of first-order logic without nonconstant function symbols which is inductively defined as follows:

1. $\top$ and $\bot$ are in $\mathcal{GF}$,
2. if A is an atom, then A is in $\mathcal{GF}$,
3. $\mathcal{GF}$ is closed under boolean combinations,
4. if φ is in $\mathcal{GF}$, A is an atom, and $\bar{x}$ is a sequence of variables, such that every free variable of φ is an argument of A, then $(\forall \bar{x})(A \to \varphi)$ and $(\exists \bar{x})(A \land \varphi)$ are in $\mathcal{GF}$. The atom A is called a *guard*.

Andréka, van Benthem and Németi [1995] show that every satisfiable formula in the guarded fragment has a model of finite size. Thus, the guarded fragment is decidable. The first resolution decision procedure for the guarded fragment has been described by de Nivelle [1998b].

Let φ be a guarded formula in negation normal form. Let Λ_φ be the set of positions of subformulas in φ of the form $\forall \bar{x}(\neg A \vee \psi)$. By $\Xi_{\mathcal{GF}}$ we denote the transformation taking φ to its definitional form $\mathrm{Def}_{\Lambda_\varphi}(\varphi)$.

3.35. EXAMPLE. The definitional form of the guarded formula

$$(\exists x)\,(Q(x) \wedge (\forall y)\,(\neg R(x,y) \vee (\forall z)\,(\neg P(x,z) \vee (\exists v)\,(R(v,z) \wedge (B(z,z) \vee C(v))))))$$

is

$$(\exists x)\,(Q(x) \wedge Q_1(x))$$
$$\wedge\;(\forall x)(Q_1(x) \rightarrow (\forall y)\,(\neg R(x,y) \vee Q_2(x)))$$
$$\wedge\;(\forall x)(Q_2(x) \rightarrow (\forall z)\,(\neg P(x,z) \vee (\exists v)\,(R(v,z) \wedge (B(z,z) \vee C(v))))).$$

The standard clausal form consists of the clauses

$$\{Q(x)\}, \{Q_1(x)\},$$
$$\{\neg Q_1(x), \neg R(x,y), Q_2(x)\},$$
$$\{\neg Q_2(x), \neg P(x,z), R(f(x,z),z)\},$$
$$\{\neg Q_2(x), \neg P(x,z), B(z,z), C(f(x,z))\}.$$

Observe that $\Xi_{\mathcal{GF}}$ applied to a guarded formula φ yields again a guarded formula. Furthermore, all remaining universal quantifiers are outermost and any existential quantifier occurs in the scope of all universally quantified variables. The standard clausal form of $\Xi_{\mathcal{GF}}(\varphi)$ can then be characterized as follows.

3.36. DEFINITION *(Weakly guarded clause)*. A clause C is *weakly guarded* if
1. all literals $L \in C$ are weakly covering,
2. if C is nonground, then there is a negative literal $L \in C$ with $\tau_v(L) = 0$ and $V(L) = V(C)$, and
3. if $\tau_v(L) > 0$, then $V(L) = V(C)$.

A literal L is *simple* if L is covering and the term depth of L is less than or equal to 1. If we replace the first condition above by the requirement that all literals L in C are simple, then C is a *guarded clause*. A clause set is *(weakly) guarded* if its clauses are (weakly) guarded. By $\mathcal{GC}$ and $\mathcal{WGC}$ we denote the class of all guarded and weakly guarded clause sets, respectively.

It is straightforward to see that the class $\mathcal{GC}$ is a subclass of $\mathcal{WGC}$.

3.37. THEOREM. *Let φ be a conjunction of guarded formulas. The standard clausal form of $\Xi_{\mathcal{GF}}(\varphi)$ is a guarded clause set.*

The resolution decision procedure of de Nivelle [1998b] is based on the following ordering $<_{\mathcal{GF}}$: $L_1 <_{\mathcal{GF}} L_2$ if $\tau_v(L_1) < \tau_v(L_2)$ or $V(L_1) \subset V(L_2)$. The ordering $<_{\mathcal{GF}}$ is not liftable, but is invariant under renaming. Every guarded clause C contains a literal L which is $<_{\mathcal{GF}}$-maximal in C and L contains all variables of C.

3.38. THEOREM. $\mathcal{WGC}$ is decidable; $R_{<_{\mathcal{GF}}}$ provides a decision procedure.

Recently, Ganzinger and de Nivelle [1999] presented a resolution decision procedure for the class $\mathcal{GC}$ with equality based on the superposition calculus of Bachmair and Ganzinger [1994]. In contrast to the approach of de Nivelle [1998b], it makes use of a liftable ordering and an additional selection function on negative literals. Ganzinger and de Nivelle [1999] also show that the satisfiability problem for the class $\mathcal{WGC}$ with equality is undecidable.

4. Hyperresolution as decision procedure

4.1. Classes decidable by hyperresolution

Refinements based on A-orderings or on other types of orderings do not suffice to obtain decision procedures for all relevant decision classes. Particularly in the case of the Bernays-Schönfinkel class and of many functional clause classes hyperresolution is superior to ordering refinements. On the other hand hyperresolution is not suited as decision method for the one-variable or for the Ackermann class. Thus we will discuss some syntactic features, which characterize the applicability of decision methods of different types. First we give formal definitions of hyperresolution and the corresponding refinement operator:

4.1. DEFINITION. Let C, D be condensed clauses, where D is positive. The condensation of a binary resolvent of C and a factor of D is called a *PRF-resolvent* (PRF abbreviates "positive, restricted factoring").

Remark. Throughout this section we assume that clauses always appear in condensed form, mostly without mentioning this fact explicitly.

4.2. DEFINITION. Let C be a nonpositive clause and let the clauses D_i, for $1 \leq i \leq n$, be positive. Then the sequence $\Gamma = (C; D_1, \ldots, D_n)$ is called a *clash sequence*.
    Let $C_0 = C$ and C_{i+1} be a PRF-resolvent of C_i and D_{i+1} for $i < n$. If C_n is positive then it is called a *clash (or hyper)resolvent* defined by Γ.

Hyperresolution is the oldest refinement of resolution [Robinson 1965a] and exemplifies the principle of macro inference. It only produces positive clauses or the empty clause $\square$. In variance to the standard definition of hyperresolution we have included a restriction on factoring. The concept of "semi-factoring" is investigated in [Noll 1980], where—inter alia—it is shown that positive hyperresolution based on PRF-resolution is complete.

Below, we do not need to refer to hyperresolution deductions themselves but rather are interested in the set of derived clauses. For this purpose the following operator based description of hyperresolution seems most adequate.

4.3. DEFINITION. Let S be a set of clauses. By $\rho_H(S)$ we denote the set of all clash resolvents definable by clash sequences of clauses in S. The hyperresolution operator R_H and its closure R_H^* is defined by:

$$R_H(S) = S \cup \rho_H(S),$$

$$R_H^0(S) = S \text{ and } R_H^{i+1}(S) = R_H(R_H^i(S)) \text{ for } i \leq 0.$$

$$R_H^*(S) = \bigcup_{i \geq 0} R_H^i(S).$$

The satisfiability problem of the following class of first-order formulas is decidable, as the Herbrand universes of the corresponding skolemized forms are finite. Although decidability is easy to prove by model theoretic means, the behavior of resolution on this class is problematic.

4.4. DEFINITION. Let $\mathcal{BS}$ be the class of all closed formulas of the form

$$(\exists x_1) \ldots (\exists x_m)(\forall y_1) \ldots (\forall y_m)M,$$

where M is quantifier-free and all terms occurring in M are variables. Then $\mathcal{BS}$ is called the Bernays-Schönfinkel class. If, in addition, M is a conjunction of Horn clauses then we obtain the subclass $\mathcal{BSH}$.

Because the skolemization M' of a formula M in $\mathcal{BS}$ does not contain function symbols, all Herbrand interpretations of M' have a fixed finite domain. Thus a trivial decision procedure for satisfiability consists in evaluating M' over all its Herbrand interpretations. Here, however, we are interested in the termination behavior of resolution refinements on $\mathcal{BS}$ and $\mathcal{BSH}$. For this purpose we have to define clauses classes corresponding to $\mathcal{BS}$ and $\mathcal{BSH}$.

4.5. DEFINITION. $\mathcal{BS}^*$ is the class of all finite sets of clauses S such that for all $C \in S : \tau(C) = 0$. $\mathcal{BSH}^*$ is the subclass of $\mathcal{BS}^*$ containing sets of Horn clauses only.

The condition $\tau(C) = 0$ in Definition 4.5 guarantees that there are no function symbols in S. All constant symbols appearing in a set $S \in \mathcal{BS}^*$ can be thought to have been introduced by skolemization. Thus $\mathcal{BS}^*$ is exactly the clause class corresponding to $\mathcal{BS}$; similarly $\mathcal{BSH}^*$ is the clause class corresponding to $\mathcal{BSH}$. $\mathcal{BS}^*$ and $\mathcal{BSH}^*$ can be decided by (total) saturation:

Take a $S \in \mathcal{BSH}^*$, replace S by the set of all ground instances S' and then decide S' by a propositional method (e.g. propositional resolution or the Davis-Putnam method).

This method can be very inefficient due to the fact that S' may be much larger than S itself. It is also an interesting fact that $\mathcal{BS}$ is of highest computational complexity among the classical prefix classes [Denenberg and Lewis 1984].

We now investigate how A-ordering refinements behave on $\mathcal{BS}$ and $\mathcal{BSH}$.

4.6. EXAMPLE. Let $S : \{C_1, C_2, C_3, C_4\}$ be the following set of clauses in $\mathcal{BSH}^*$:
$C_1 = \{P(a,b)\}$, $C_2 = \{P(x,y), \neg P(y,x)\}$, $C_3 = \{P(x,z), \neg P(x,y), \neg P(y,z)\}$,
$C_4 = \{\neg P(b,c)\}$.

C_2 represents symmetry and C_3 transitivity. S is satisfiable because $\{P(b,c)\}$ cannot be obtained from $\{P(a,b)\}$ using the rules of symmetry and transitivity. We show now that all A-ordering refinements are nonterminating on S, i.e. there exists no A-ordering refinement which decides $\mathcal{BSH}$ (note that S even is a set of Horn clauses).

Indeed $R^*_{<_A}(\{C_2, C_3\}) = R^*_{\emptyset}(\{C_2, C_3\})$ for every A-ordering $<$. The reason for this effect is the unifiability of resolved atoms with all atoms in the resolvent (for all R-derivable clauses); therefore the case $L < M$ can never occur and no resolvents can be excluded. Particularly $R^*_{<_A}(\{C_2, C_3\})$ contains the infinite sequence of clauses

$$C_n = \{P(x_1, x_n), \neg P(x_1, x_2) \ldots, \neg P(x_k, x_{k+1}) \ldots, \neg P(x_{n-1}, x_n)\}$$

for $n \geq 2$. These clauses cannot be removed by subsumption nor do they "collapse" by condensing (they are in fact condensed). Thus, even with subsumption, no A-ordering terminates on S. On the other hand we obtain

$$R^*_H(S) = S \cup \{\{P(b,a)\}, \{P(a,a)\}, \{P(b,b)\}\}$$

and thus R^*_H terminates on S. Moreover the set of unit clauses

$$\mathcal{M} = \{\{P(a,b)\}, \{P(b,a)\}, \{P(a,a)\}, \{P(b,b)\}\}$$

defines an atomic representation of a Herbrand model of S.

We show now that termination of R^*_H can be guaranteed on $\mathcal{BSH}^*$.

4.7. PROPOSITION. *Hyperresolution decides $\mathcal{BSH}^*$, i.e. $R^*_H(S)$ is finite for all S in $\mathcal{BSH}^*$.*

PROOF. Let S be in $\mathcal{BSH}^*$. Then S is in Horn form and the positive clauses in $R^*_H(S)$ are all unit. There are no function symbols in S and no function symbols can be introduced by resolution. Therefore we obtain for the set $\mathcal{D}$ of atoms of positive clauses in $R^*_H(S)$:

$$\mathcal{D} \subseteq \{A \mid A \text{ is an atom over } \Sigma(S), \tau(A) = 0\}.$$

Moreover all unit clauses with atoms from $\mathcal{D}$ are (trivially) condensed and normalized with respect to renaming of variables; so we obtain that the set $\mathcal{D}$ is finite. $\square$

4.8. EXAMPLE.

$$S = \{\{P(x_1, x_1, a)\}, \ \{P(x, z, u), \neg P(x, y, u), \neg P(y, z, u)\},$$

$$\{P(x, y, u), P(y, z, u), \neg P(x, z, u)\}, \ \{\neg P(x, x, b)\}\}.$$

S is non-Horn and even "essentially" non-Horn; that means there exists no sign renaming transforming S into a set of Horn clauses. In renaming P by $\neg P$ we only exchange the roles of a and b, otherwise S remains as it is. R_H^* neither terminates on S nor on the renamed form S'. R_H^* produces clauses of arbitrary length on S—even if we add subsumption (i.e. we replace R_H^* by $R_{H_s}^*$). Thus $R_{H_s}^*$ + sign renaming does not terminate on S. That means hyperresolution cannot decide the Bernays-Schönfinkel class. Moreover none of the "standard" refinements terminates on S. There is, however, general semantic clash resolution over arbitrary models $\mathcal{M}$ as defined by J. Slagle [Slagle 1967]; in such a refinement only clauses which are false in $\mathcal{M}$ are derivable. So, in case S is satisfiable, we only have to choose a model of S; on such a model all clauses are true and thus semantic clash resolution does not produce any resolvents. This trick, however, can hardly be recommended as a method in resolution decision theory. Note that models should be the outcome of our procedures, not the starting point!

Of course there is the brute force method to decide $\mathcal{BS}^*$ by ground saturation. We will see later that, by an appropriate use of hyperresolution, saturation can be reduced considerably.

We show now how hyperresolution can be applied as decision procedure on functional clauses classes. These classes can be considered as generalizations of DATALOG [Ceri, Gottlob and Tanca 1990]. Formally DATALOG is a subclass of $\mathcal{BSH}$ such that all positive clauses are ground and $V(C_+) \subseteq V(C_-)$ for all other clauses.

4.9. DEFINITION. A set of clauses S belongs to $\mathcal{PVD}$ (positive variable dominated) if for all $C \in S$:

PVD-1) $V(C_+) \subseteq V(C_-)$ (C is ground for $C_- = \square$),
PVD-2) $\tau_{\max}(x, C_+) \leq \tau_{\max}(x, C_-)$ for all $x \in V(C_+)$.

$\mathcal{PVD}$ corresponds to a subclass of a class named $\mathcal{PVD}$ in [Fermüller et al. 1993], where the properties above were "relativized" under settings. That means there might be some sign renaming γ such that $\gamma(S) \in \mathcal{PVD}$ even if S itself is not in $\mathcal{PVD}$. Take for example the set of clauses

$$S = \{\{P(x_1), Q(g(x_1, x_1))\}, \ \{R(f(x_1), x_2)\}, \ \{P(a)\}, \ \{R(x, y), \neg Q(y)\},$$

$$\{\neg P(x), \neg P(f(x))\}, \ \{\neg R(a, a), \neg R(f(b), a)\}\}$$

Obviously S is not in $\mathcal{PVD}$ (there are positive clauses containing variables and $\{R(x, y), \neg Q(y)\}$ violates PVD-1)).

But let γ be the sign renaming mapping Q to $\neg Q$, R to $\neg R$ and P remaining unchanged. Then

$$\gamma(S) = \{\{P(x_1), \neg Q(g(x_1, x_1))\}, \ \{\neg R(f(x_1), x_2)\}, \ \{P(a)\}, \ \{Q(y), \neg R(x, y)\},$$
$$\{\neg P(x), \neg P(f(x))\}, \ \{R(a, a), R(f(b), a)\}\}$$

and $\gamma(S) \in \mathcal{PVD}$.

The example above suggests the following generalization of $\mathcal{PVD}$:

4.10. DEFINITION. A set of clauses S belongs to $\mathcal{PVD}_r$ if there exists a sign renaming γ such that $\gamma(S)$ belongs to $\mathcal{PVD}$.

The idea behind $\mathcal{PVD}$ is that the positive parts are always "smaller" than the negative ones. As hyperresolution produces positive clauses only, we may hope that the produced clauses are small too (i.e. small enough to achieve termination). Indeed the following theorem holds (see also [Leitsch 1993] and [Fermüller et al. 1993]):

4.11. THEOREM. *Hyperresolution decides* $\mathcal{PVD}$, *i.e. for every* $S \in \mathcal{PVD}$ *the set* $R_H^*(S)$ *is finite.*

PROOF. Let S be a set of clauses in $\mathcal{PVD}$. Obviously $R_H^*(S)$ is finite if the following conditions (a), (b) hold:
(a) $R_H^*(S) - S$ contains only (positive) ground clauses and
(b) $\tau(D) \leq r$ for all $D \in R_H^*(S) - S$ and $r = \max\{\tau(C_+) \mid C \in S\}$
Thus it remains to prove (a) and (b).

By Definition 4.9 $V(C_+) \subseteq V(C_-)$ for all $C \in S$; in particular $P(S)$ consists of ground clauses only. Now consider a clash sequence $\Gamma : (C; D_1, \ldots, D_n)$ for $C \in S$ and positive ground clauses $D_1, \ldots, D_n$; let E be a clash resolvent of Γ. Then $E = C_+\lambda$ where λ is the "total" substitution corresponding to the clash resolution (in fact λ is obtained by concatenation of the mgus corresponding to the single PRF-resolvents of Γ). Let L be an arbitrary (negative) literal in C_-; then, by definition of λ, $\lambda(L) = \neg A$ for some ground atom A in a clause D_i. Consequently, as all D_i are ground clauses, λ is a ground substitution. By $V(C_+) \subseteq V(C_-)$ it follows that the resolvent $E : C_+\lambda$ is a ground clause too. This proves (a).

For (b) consider, like above, a clash $\Gamma : (C; D_1, \ldots, D_n)$ and its corresponding total substitution λ. Let us assume that the D_i are all ground clauses with $\tau(D_i) \leq r$. By definition of λ we get $C_-\lambda \subseteq D_1 \cup \cdots \cup D_n$ and thus $\tau(C_-\lambda) \leq r$. We have to show $\tau(C_+\lambda) \leq r$.

If $\tau(C_+\lambda) = \tau(C_+)$ then, by definition of r, we get $\tau(C_+\lambda) \leq r$ and we are done.
If $\tau(C_+\lambda) > \tau(C_+)$ then there exists a variable $x \in V(C_+)$ with

$$\tau(C_+\lambda) = \tau_{\max}(x, C_+) + \tau(x\lambda).$$

By property PVD-2) $\tau_{\max}(x, C_+) \leq \tau_{\max}(x, C_-)$ and so

$$\tau(C_+\lambda) \leq \tau_{\max}(x, C_-) + \tau(x\lambda) \leq \tau(C_-\lambda).$$

But $\tau(C_-\lambda) \leq r$ and so $\tau(C_+\lambda) \leq r$.

$\square$

The decision procedure for $\mathcal{PVD}$ can easily be modified to the following decision procedure for $\mathcal{PVD}_r$:

1. Search for a renaming γ such that $\gamma(S)$ is in $\mathcal{PVD}$ (if there is no such γ then $S \notin \mathcal{PVD}_r$).

2. Apply R_H^* to $\gamma(S)$.

Note that there are only finitely many sign renamings on a set of clauses and that the properties PVD-1) and PVD-2) are decidable. Thus we can always decide whether a set of clauses is in $\mathcal{PVD}_r$. Once we have found the right renaming γ, we replace S by $\gamma(S)$ and apply hyperresolution.

The class $\mathcal{PVD}$ is relatively "tight" with respect to undecidability: If we add the clause

$$T^- = \{P(x_1, x_2), P(x_2, x_3), \neg P(x_1, x_3)\}$$

(i.e. the transitivity of $\neg P$) we can encode the word problem of any equational theory (see [Fermüller et al. 1993] chapter 3.3). From the fact that there are equational theories with undecidable word problems (e.g. the theory of combinators [Stenlund 1971]) it follows that

$$\Gamma = \{S \cup \{T^-\} \mid S \in \mathcal{PVD}\}$$

is an undecidable class of clause sets.

The main point in the proof of Theorem 4.11 consists in showing that all positive clauses in $R_H^*(S)$ are ground and $\tau(R_H^*(S)) \leq d$ for some constant d. While the property PVD-1) is essential (note that T^- does not fulfil PVD-1)), PVD-2) can be replaced by a more general condition (term depth is only a specific complexity measure for literals and clauses). Particularly we obtain a more general decision class in replacing term depth by arbitrary *atom complexity measures* α fulfilling the following axioms:

1. $\alpha(A) \leq \alpha(A\theta)$ for substitutions θ and atom formulas A.
2. For all $k \in \mathbb{N}$ the set $\{A\theta \mid \theta \in \Theta_0, \alpha(A\theta) \leq k\}$ is finite, where Θ_0 is the set of all ground substitutions over a finite signature.
3. α is extended to literals by $\alpha(A) = \alpha(\neg A)$ and to clauses by $\alpha(\{L_1, \ldots, L_n\}) = \max\{\alpha(L_i) \mid 1 \leq i \leq n\}$.

For such an α we have to postulate that there exists a constant d such that for all ground substitutions θ either $\alpha(C_+\theta) \leq d$ or $\alpha(C_+\theta) \leq \alpha(C_-\theta)$ [Leitsch 1993].

If we relax the condition on $\mathcal{PVD}$, that positive clauses must be ground, we must add a somewhat stronger restriction on the behavior of the parts C_+ and C_- relative to each other. This idea leads to the class $\mathcal{OCC1}$ where the positive parts of clauses are "linear" (i.e. every variable occurs only once).

4.12. DEFINITION. $\mathcal{OCC1}$ is the set of all sets of clauses S such that for all $C \in S$:

1. $\mathrm{OCC}(x, C_+) = 1$ for all $x \in V(C_+)$ and

2. $\tau_{max}(x, C_+) \leq \tau_{min}(x, C_-)$ for all $x \in V(C_+) \cap V(C_-)$.

Like in the case of $\mathcal{PVD}$ we can define a class $\mathcal{OCCI}_r$ via renamings and reduce the decidability of $\mathcal{OCCI}_r$ to that of $\mathcal{OCCI}$.

4.13. THEOREM. *Hyperresolution decides* $\mathcal{OCCI}$, *i.e. for every* $S \in \mathcal{OCCI}$ *the set* $R_H^*(S)$ *is finite.*

PROOF. In [Fermüller et al. 1993].   □

While for deciding $\mathcal{PVD}$ condensing of clauses is not necessary, it is required for $\mathcal{OCCI}$ (otherwise the size of clauses diverges). Of course we can always apply an even stricter (but complete) refinement like hyperresolution with forward subsumption or replacement in order to decide $\mathcal{PVD}$ and $\mathcal{OCCI}$.

$\mathcal{BS}^*$ is not a subclass of $\mathcal{PVD}_r$. But we will define a method to transform $\mathcal{BS}^*$ into $\mathcal{BS}^* \cap \mathcal{PVD}$ under preservation of sat-equivalence. This method is more subtle and more efficient than complete ground saturation. The basic idea is the following:

Let S be in $\mathcal{BS}^*$. Search for a renaming γ such that $\gamma(S) \in \mathcal{PVD}$. If there is such a γ then apply R_H^* to $\gamma(S)$, else select some arbitrary γ and transform $\gamma(S)$ into a set of clauses $\mathcal{D} \in \mathcal{PVD}$ by partial saturation of the variables which violate PVD-1); afterwards apply R_H^* to $\mathcal{D}$. Let us call this procedure BSALG. Then BSALG is indeed a decision algorithm for $\mathcal{BS}^*$. For the actual performance of BSALG the right selection of a renaming is crucial; clearly one should try to select a γ for which the set $\mathcal{D}$ becomes minimal. In the next example we compare brute force saturation with BSALG. For this purpose we replace R_H^* by the more restrictive operator R_{Hs}^* (hyperresolution + forward subsumption). This leads to a further increase of efficiency, but without loss of correctness and termination (note that R_{Hs}^* is complete and $R_{Hs}^*(S) \subseteq R_H^*(S)$ for all sets of clauses S).

4.14. EXAMPLE. We take the set of clauses from Example 4.8, i.e.

$$S = \{\{P(x_1, x_1, a)\}, \{P(x, z, u), \neg P(x, y, u), \neg P(y, z, u)\},$$

$$\{P(x, y, u), P(y, z, u), \neg P(x, z, u)\}, \{\neg P(x, x, b)\}\}.$$

We already know that R_H^* does not terminate on S. Clearly $S \notin \mathcal{PVD}$ but $S \in \mathcal{BS}^*$. We compute the set $\mathcal{D}$ (without renaming the predicate symbol P) and obtain

$$\mathcal{D} = \{\{P(a, a, a)\}, \{P(b, b, a)\}, \{P(x, z, u), \neg P(x, y, u), \neg P(y, z, u)\},$$

$$\{P(x, a, u), P(a, z, u), \neg P(x, z, u)\},$$

$$\{P(x, b, u), P(b, z, u), \neg P(x, z, u)\}, \{\neg P(x, x, b)\}\}$$

$\mathcal{D} \in \mathcal{PVD}$ and $|\mathcal{D}| = |S| + 2 = 6$.

$$R_{Hs}^*(\mathcal{D}) = \mathcal{D} \cup \{\{P(a, b, a), P(b, a, a)\}\}.$$

Thus $R_{H_s}^*$ terminates on $\mathcal{D}$ producing only one additional clause ($|R_{H_s}^*(\mathcal{D})| = 7$). Note that in the second generation of hyperresolvents we obtain the clauses

$$\{P(b,a,a), P(a,a,a), P(a,b,a)\} \ \{P(b,b,a), P(b,a,a), P(a,b,a)\}$$

which are both subsumed by the clauses of the first generation and therefore are deleted.

Using the brute force saturation method we obtain a set of ground clauses $\mathcal{D}'$ which contains 36 clauses. Moreover $\mathcal{D}'$ has still to be tested for satisfiability. Thus we see that BSALG may be much faster than the pure saturation method.

4.2. Model building by hyperresolution

If S is a set of Horn clauses then $P(R_H^*(S))$, the set of all positive clauses derivable from S by hyperresolution, defines a Herbrand model; this is a well-known result in the semantics of logic programming. Indeed, for Horn sets, $P(R_H^*(S))$ consists of unit clauses only which form the atomic representation of a Herbrand model. That means, in the Herbrand base of S, all instances of $P(R_H^*(S))$ are set to true and the other ground atoms to false. $P(R_H^*(S))$ is an atomic representation of an H-model even in the more general case that the nonpositive clauses in S may be arbitrary, but $P(R_H^*(S))$ consists of unit clauses only. By resolution decision theory we possess means to guarantee termination of R_H^* on certain clause classes. If S is a set of Horn clauses and R_H^* terminates on S then (clearly) we obtain a finite atom representation of a Herbrand model of S. Particularly we obtain such finite representations on the classes $\mathcal{PVD} \cap$ Hornlogic and $\mathcal{OCC1} \cap$ Hornlogic by the Theorems 4.11 and 4.13. Our main purpose here is to show, how we can extract atomic representations of Herbrand models from finite sets of clauses which are invariant under the operator of hyperresolution with replacement R_{Hr}; the positive clauses in this set need not be unit clauses. Particularly we will define a procedure which extracts a Herbrand model from every satisfiable set of clauses in $\mathcal{PVD} \cup \mathcal{OCC1}$; this procedure is free of backtracking and does not rely on search. Note that our basic resolution operator, however, will not be R_H (the standard operator of hyperresolution) but the reduction operator R_{Hr}. The choice of R_{Hr} is based on some particular mathematical properties of subsumption-reduced sets which turn out to be fruitful to model building.

For the remaining part of this section we identify unit clauses with atoms and write clauses as disjunctions; this is more natural for automated model building and makes the argumentation more transparent.

Hyperresolution + replacement is a reduction method rather than a deduction method; instead of deleting only clauses which are subsumed by clauses derived before, we subject the whole set of derived clauses to subsumption tests periodically. The formal definition is:

$$R_{Hr}(S) = \mathrm{sub}(R_H(S)), \quad R_H(S) = S \cup \rho_H(S)$$

where sub is a reduction operator which produces subsumption-minimal sets (i.e. there are no different clauses C and D such that $C \leq_{ss} D$) and $\rho_H(S)$ is the set of all hyperresolvents definable from clauses in S. Contrary to R_H the operator R_{Hr} is not monotonic and thus the union of the sets $R^i_{Hr}(S)$ does not describe the set of clauses "eventually" obtained. Note that, by the completeness of R^*_{Hr}, for unsatisfiable sets of clauses S there exists an iteration number i such that $\square \in R^i_{Hr}(S)$ and therefore $R^i_{Hr}(S) = \{\square\}$ ($\square$ subsumes all other clauses). If the sequence of the $R^i_{Hr}(S)$ "converges" on a class of clause sets Γ then R^*_{Hr} is a decision procedure for Γ; in this case we have to compute $R^i_{Hr}(S)$ till we obtain a k such that $R^k_{Hr}(S) = R^{k+1}_{Hr}(S)$. The final set of clauses obtained that way is "stable" (sometimes also called saturated) i.e. it remains unchanged under further reductions (it is in fact in normal form with respect to R^*_{Hr}). We denote it by $R^*_{Hr}(S)$.

4.15. DEFINITION. Let S be a set of condensed clauses. Then S is called (R_{Hr}-) *stable* if $R_{Hr}(S) = S$.

If a R_{Hr}-sequence $(R^i_{Hr}(S))_{i \in \mathbb{N}}$ converges to $R^k_{Hr}(S)$ then, by Definition 4.15, $R^k_{Hr}(S)$ is stable and a fixed point of the operator R_{Hr}. Let us assume that an R_{Hr}-sequence converges and yields a (stable) set S' such that all positive clauses in S' are unit. Then, by the following lemma, these clauses form an atom representation of a Herbrand model of S'; this lemma is a generalization of a well-known theorem in Horn logic. For the remaining part of this section we write "AR" for atomic representation and "stable" for R_{Hr}-stable.

4.16. LEMMA. *Let S be a finite set of nonpositive condensed clauses and $\mathcal{A}$ be a finite set of atoms such that $S \cup \mathcal{A}$ is satisfiable and stable. Then $\mathcal{A}$ is an AR of a Herbrand model of $S \cup \mathcal{A}$ (over the signature of $S \cup \mathcal{A}$).*

Lemma 4.16 suggests the following strategy of finding a model: Suppose that a R_{Hr}-sequence converges to S such that $\square \notin S$ (what is equivalent to $S \neq \{\square\}$). Then search for a finite set of atoms $\mathcal{A}$ such that $(S - P(S)) \cup \mathcal{A}$ is finite, satisfiable and implies S. The resulting set $\mathcal{A}$ is an AR of a Herbrand model of $(S - P(S)) \cup \mathcal{A}$ which is also a model of S itself. Before we develop a method to obtain such a set of atoms $\mathcal{A}$ we have to investigate where R_{Hr}-reduction actually terminates. $\mathcal{PVD}$ and $\mathcal{OCC1}$ (see Definitions 4.10 and 4.12) are not only decision classes under R_H but also under R_{Hr}; a characteristic feature of both classes is the decomposed form of the positive clauses (and of all derivable positive clauses). The model building procedure to be described below works on all decision classes of hyperresolution with disconnected positive clauses.

4.17. DEFINITION. We call S *positively disconnected* (and write $S \in \mathcal{PDC}$) if $R^*_H(S)$ is finite and all clauses in $P(R^*_H(S))$ are disconnected (see Definition 2.24).

There are technical reasons for using R^*_H instead of R^*_{Hr} in Definition 4.17 [Fermüller and Leitsch 1996].

The application of the operator R_{Hr}^* to $\mathcal{PDC}$ gives us finite R_{Hr}^*-stable sets and provides the raw material for our model building method. For every set $S \in \mathcal{PDC}$ we obtain a set $R_{Hr}^k(S)$ such that $R_{Hr}^k(S)$ is stable. If S is satisfiable then, by the logical equivalence of S and $R_{Hr}^k(S)$, every model of $R_{Hr}^k(S)$ is also a model of S. If the positive clauses in $R_{Hr}^k(S)$ are all unit then, by Lemma 4.16, we already have an AR of a Herbrand model of S.

The following lemma gives us the key technique for the transformation of a stable set into another stable set, where all positive clauses are unit. Essentially we show that, for stable sets of clauses, positive clauses can be replaced by proper subclauses under preservation of satisfiability.

4.18. LEMMA. *Let* $S \in \mathcal{PDC}$ *such that* S *is satisfiable and stable and let* D *be a positive nonunit clause in* S. *Let* P *be an (arbitrary) atom in* D. *Then*

(1) $(S - \{D\}) \cup \{P\}$ *is satisfiable and*

(2) $(S - \{D\}) \cup \{P\} \to S$ *is valid.*

Remark:

(1) and (2) together imply the existence of a model of $(S - \{D\}) \cup \{P\}$ *which is also a model of* S.

PROOF. (sketch) A detailed proof can be found in [Fermüller and Leitsch 1996].

(2) trivially holds since P implies D.

It remains to prove (1). We use proof by contradiction assuming that the set $S' : (S - \{D\}) \cup \{P\}$ is unsatisfiable. Then $\square \in R_H^*(S')$; note that we use the monotonic operator R_H instead of R_{Hr}.

Let $D' = D - \{P\}$; then the clauses in $R_H^*(S')$ differ from those in $R_H^*(S)$ "at most by D'". More exactly: if $C \in R_H^*(S')$ then either $C \in R_H^*(S)$ or there exists a variable renaming η with $V(C) \cap V(D'\eta) = \emptyset$ such that the condensed form of $C \cup D'\eta$ is in $R_H^*(S)$. We express this relation by

$$(*) \quad R_H^*(S') \leq_{D'} R_H^*(S).$$

(*) is a nontrivial property and only holds because $S \in \mathcal{PDC}$ and by the condensed form of the clauses.

By $\square \in R_H^*(S')$ we thus obtain $H \in R_H^*(S)$ where H is the condensed form of D' (note that $\square \notin S$ as S is satisfiable!). Since $R_{Hr}^*(S)$ subsumes $R_H^*(S)$ and since S is R_{Hr}-stable there must be a clause $G \in S$ s.t. $G \leq_{ss} H$. By definition of D and D' we obtain $D' \leq_{ss} D$ and thus $H \leq_{ss} D$; moreover $H \neq D$—otherwise D is not condensed. Moreover D does not subsume H and thus does not subsume G (note that $\leq_{ss}$ is transitive). Therefore we obtain two clauses D and G in S with $G \leq_{ss} D$ and $D \not\leq_{ss} G$. This, however, contradicts the assumption that S is stable under subsumption. We conclude that S' is satisfiable. $\square$

The validity of Lemma 4.18 is essentially based on the stability of the set of clauses S. It is very easy to see that the result becomes wrong for nonstable sets S: Just take $S = \{\{P(a), P(b)\}, \{\neg P(a)\}\}$.

Trivially S is satisfiable. But if we replace $\{P(a), P(b)\}$ by $\{P(a)\}$ we obtain the set of clauses $S_1 : \{\{P(a)\}, \{\neg P(a)\}\}$ which is unsatisfiable. But note that S is not stable; rather we have $R_{Hr}(S) = \{\{P(b)\}, \{\neg P(a)\}\}$ and the replacement sequence converges to the set $\{\{P(b)\}, \{\neg P(a)\}\}$.

The example also shows that the theorem becomes wrong if we replace the non-monotonic operator R_{Hr} by (the monotonic) R_H; thus we see that subsumption is necessary to guarantee the correctness of the reduction.

The transformation of S into $(S - \{D\}) \cup \{P\}$ can be described by an operator α which (deterministically) selects a clause D and a literal P in D; if $P(S)$ consists of unit clauses only we define $\alpha(S) = S$. Then we may iterate the application of α and R_{Hr}-closure on the new sets of clauses. Note that $(S - \{D\}) \cup \{P\}$ need not be stable, even if S is stable. Therefore we have to compute a reduction sequence on $\alpha(S)$ in order to obtain the next stable set.

Let us assume that the reduction sequence $(R_{Hr}^i(S))_{i \in \mathbb{N}}$ converges to its limit $R_{Hr}^*(S)$. The iterated reduction process can conveniently be defined by an operator on stable sets of clauses.

4.19. DEFINITION *(the operator T)*. T is defined on stable sets of clauses in $\mathcal{PDC}$ by $T(S) = R_{Hr}^*(\alpha(S))$.

The iteration of T is defined by:

$$T^0(S) = S \text{ and } T^{i+1}(S) = T(T^i(S))$$
if $T^i(S)$ is a stable set in $\mathcal{PDC}$ and $i \in \mathbb{N}$.

It is easy to verify that for all stable sets in $\mathcal{PDC}$ all $T^i(S)$ are again stable sets in $\mathcal{PDC}$. Therefore $T^i(S)$ is well-defined for all stable sets $S \in \mathcal{PDC}$ and $i \in \mathbb{N}$.

Let S be a stable set in $\mathcal{PDC}$. Then, by Lemma 4.18 we know that $\alpha(S) \to S$ is valid and that $\alpha(S)$ is satisfiable, provided S is satisfiable. Thus also $T(S)$ is satisfiable (by the correctness of R_{Hr}^*) and $T(S) \to S$ is valid. Therefore we already know that $T^i(S) \to S$ is valid and that $T^i(S)$ is satisfiable for all $i \in \mathbb{N}$. But, unfortunately, we have not yet reached our goal. We still have to show that the sequence $(T^i(S))_{i \in \mathbb{N}}$ converges, i.e. that there exists a number k such that $T^k(S) = T^{k+1}(S)$; we obtain such a k when all positive clauses in $T^k(S)$ are unit clauses and $\alpha(T^k(S)) = T^k(S)$. In this case $P(T^k(S))$ is an AR of a Herbrand model of S.

In order to prove the convergence of the sequence $(T^i(S))_{i \in \mathbb{N}}$ to a stable set of clauses $\mathcal{D}$ such that $P(\mathcal{D})$ consists of unit clauses only, we have to introduce a Noetherian ordering $\prec$ on sets of clauses and to show that the $T^i(S)$ are decreasing with respect to $\prec$.

4.20. DEFINITION. Let S and $\mathcal{D}$ be two finite sets of condensed clauses. We define $S \prec \mathcal{D}$ if

(1) $S \leq_{ss} \mathcal{D}$,
(2) for all $C \in S$ there exists a $D \in \mathcal{D}$ s.t. $C \leq_{ss} D$ and $|C| \leq |D|$ and
(3) $\mathcal{D} \not\leq_{ss} S$.

It is not hard to show that $\prec$ is irreflexive, transitive and Noetherian; for a proof we refer to [Fermüller and Leitsch 1996]. From $\prec$ we would expect $T(S) \prec S$ for stable sets in $\mathcal{PDC}$; unfortunately this does not hold (a counterexample is defined in [Fermüller and Leitsch 1996]). Instead we have the following weaker property of $\prec$:

4.21. LEMMA. *Let S be a R_{Hr}-stable set in $\mathcal{PDC}$ containing a positive nonunit clause. Then $R_H^*(T(S)) \prec R_H^*(S)$.*

PROOF. (sketch) A detailed proof can be found in [Fermüller and Leitsch 1996].

First of all we reduce the problem to $R_H^*(\alpha(S)) \prec R_H^*(S)$; note that $T(S) = R_{Hr}^*(\alpha(S))$.

Condition (1) of Definition 4.20 is easy to prove: By definition of α we have $\alpha(S) \leq_{ss} S$. Because $\leq_{ss}$ is preserved under R_H we obtain $R_H^*(\alpha(S)) \leq_{ss} R_H^*(S)$.

In order to show condition (3) of Definition 4.20 we have to prove that there exists a $C \in R_H^*(\alpha(S))$ s.t. $R_H^*(S) \not\leq_{ss} \{C\}$. Let E be the nonunit positive clause selected by α. Then there exists an atom P in E with $\alpha(S) = (S - \{E\}) \cup \{P\}$. Then $P \in R_H^*(\alpha(S))$ and $R_H^*(S) \not\leq_{ss} \{P\}$.

Condition (2) of Definition 4.20 follows from the following more general property (which can be proved by induction on n):

(*) For all $n \geq 0$ and for all $C \in R_H^n(\alpha(S))$ there exists a $D \in R_H^*(S)$ s.t. $|C| \leq |D|$ and a renaming substitution η with $C\eta \subseteq D$.

For the proof of (*) it is crucial to have the monotone operator R_H instead of R_{Hr}.

This eventually yields $R_H^*(\alpha(S)) \prec R_H^*(S)$. It remains to show $R_H^*(T(S)) \prec R_H^*(S)$. By definition of T we have

$$R_H^*(T(S)) = R_H^*(R_{Hr}^*(\alpha(S))) \subseteq R_H^*(R_H^*(\alpha(S))) = R_H^*(\alpha(S)).$$

Moreover, by definition of R_H^* and R_{Hr}^* and the subsumption relation for sets of clauses we also obtain

$$T(S) = R_{Hr}^*(\alpha(S)) =_{ss} R_H^*(\alpha(S))$$

and $R_H^*(T(S)) =_{ss} R_H^*(\alpha(S))$. By this last property and by $R_H^*(T(S)) \subseteq R_H^*(\alpha(S))$, $R_H^*(\alpha(S)) \prec R_H^*(S)$ we eventually obtain

$$R_H^*(T(S)) \prec R_H^*(S).$$

$\square$

4.22. EXAMPLE.
Consider the following set of condensed clauses

$$S = \{\{E(a), S(a)\}, \{Q(a), R(a)\}, \{P(x), Q(x), \neg R(x), \neg S(x)\},$$
$$\{\neg P(a), \neg Q(a)\}\}.$$

S is in $\mathcal{PVD}$ (and thus in $\mathcal{PDC}$) but S is not stable. We compute the reduction sequence $(R_{Hr}^i(S))_{i \in \mathbb{N}}$ which converges and gives

$$R_{Hr}^*(S) = R_{Hr}^1(S) = S \cup \{\{E(a), P(a), Q(a)\}\}.$$

By writing S_1 for $R_{Hr}^1(S)$ and applying α we obtain

$$\alpha(S_1) = (S_1 - \{\{E(a), S(a)\}\}) \cup \{\{S(a)\}\}.$$

By Lemma 4.18 we know that $\alpha(S_1)$ is satisfiable and that every of its models is a model of S too.

Again $\alpha(S_1)$ is not stable and we compute its corresponding R_{Hr}-reduction sequence.

Then let $S_2 = T(S_1) = R_{Hr}^*(\alpha(S_1))$. So we get

$$S_2 = \{\{S(a)\}, \{Q(a), R(a)\}, \{P(a), Q(a)\}, \{P(x), Q(x), \neg R(x), \neg S(x)\},$$
$$\{\neg P(a), \neg Q(a)\}\}.$$

Note that in the computation of S_2 we obtain the new clash resolvent $\{P(a), Q(a)\}$ which subsumes $\{E(a), P(a), Q(a)\}$. On S_2 we define

$$\alpha(S_2) = (S_2 - \{\{P(a), Q(a)\}\}) \cup \{\{Q(a)\}\}.$$

Then $S_3 = R_{Hr}^*(\alpha(S_2)) = T(S_2) =$

$$\{\{S(a)\}, \{Q(a)\}, \{P(x), Q(x), \neg R(x), \neg S(x)\}, \{\neg P(a), \neg Q(a)\}\}.$$

Clearly $\alpha(S_3) = S_3$ and our procedure stops with $T(S_3) = S_3$ and $S_3 = T^2(S_1)$ (in fact S_3 is a fixed point of T). By the validity of $T^2(S_1) \to S$ and by the satisfiability of $T^2(S_1)$—via the model $\mathcal{M} = \{S(a), Q(a)\}$—we obtain $\mathcal{M}$ as model of S itself.

We are now in the position to formulate our main result, the convergence of the sequence $(T^i(S))_{i \in \mathbb{N}}$ on stable set of clauses S for $S \in \mathcal{PDC}$. From this result we will extract an algorithm which, on satisfiable sets of clauses $S \in \mathcal{PVD}$, always terminates with an atomic representation of a Herbrand model of S (if S is unsatisfiable then $R_{Hr}^*(S) = \{\Box\}$ and the model building procedure does not start at all).

4.23. THEOREM. *Let S be a stable and satisfiable set of clauses in $\mathcal{PDC}$. Then the sequence $(T^i(S))_{i \in \mathbb{N}}$ converges to a set of clauses $\mathcal{D}$ such that $P(\mathcal{D})$ is an atomic representation of a Herbrand model of S.*

PROOF. We have to prove the existence of an iteration number i with $T^i(S) = T^{i+1}(S)$. From Lemma 4.21 we know that, for every satisfiable, R_{Hr}-stable set $\mathcal{D}$ containing positive nonunit clauses, $R_H^*(T(\mathcal{D})) \prec R_H^*(\mathcal{D})$. Then Lemma 4.18 implies that $\alpha(\mathcal{D})$ is satisfiable and implies $\mathcal{D}$; clearly the same holds for $T(\mathcal{D})$. By iterating this argument we obtain a descending chain of satisfiable sets of clauses

$$\cdots \prec R_H^*(T^{k+1}(S)) \prec R_H^*(T^k(S)) \prec \cdots R_H^*(S).$$

Because $\prec$ is Noetherian this chain is finite and there exists a minimal element $R_H^*(T^i(S))$. We have to show that $T^i(S) = T^{i+1}(S)$:

Let us assume that $T^i(S) \neq T^{i+1}(S)$; then, by definition of T, $\alpha(T^i(S)) \neq T^i(S)$. This, however, implies the existence of a nonunit positive clause in $T^i(S)$; by Lemma 4.21 we obtain $R_H^*(T^{i+1}(S)) \prec R_H^*(T^i(S))$ contradicting the assumption of minimality. This implies $T^i(S) = T^{i+1}(S)$.

We have also seen that $\alpha(T^i(S)) = T^i(S)$, i.e. all positive clauses in $T^i(S)$ are unit; by Lemma 4.16 $P(T^i(S))$ is an AR of a Herbrand model of $T^i(S)$. By the validity of $T^i(S) \supset S$, $P(T^i(S))$ is also an AR of a Herbrand model of S. $\qquad\square$

If the sequence $(T^i(S))_{i \in \mathbb{N}}$ converges then we denote the limit by $T^*(S)$. By Theorem 4.23 we always may apply the following algorithm to sets of clauses in $\mathcal{PDC}$:

MB:

a) Compute $R_{Hr}^*(S)$.

b) If $\square \in R_{Hr}^*(S)$ then stop else compute $T^*(R_{Hr}^*(S))$.

MB is correct and complete; that means MB yields $\square$ for unsatisfiable sets of clauses S in $\mathcal{PVD}$ and Herbrand models for satisfiable ones. R_{Hr}^* is complete and always terminates on $\mathcal{PDC}$. Thus if S is satisfiable we obtain a stable set of clauses S' which is in $\mathcal{PDC}$ too. But then, by Theorem 4.23, $T^*(S')$ is defined and $P(T^*(S'))$ is an AR of a Herbrand model of S'. $S' \to S$ is valid and thus $P(T^*(S'))$ is also an AR of a Herbrand model of the set of input clauses S. Note that MB is free of backtracking and search; indeed the computation of T^* is purely "iterative". By $\mathcal{PVD} \cup \mathcal{OCCI} \subseteq \mathcal{PDC}$ the procedure MB works on the decision classes for hyperresolution defined in the beginning of this section. The output of MB is a representation of a (mostly) infinite model $\mathcal{M}$; however one can show that the models $\mathcal{M}$ constructed by MB on $\mathcal{PVD} \cup \mathcal{OCCI}$ can always be transformed into finite models [Fermüller and Leitsch 1996].

The whole model building method can be extended to the classes $\mathcal{PVD}_r$ and $\mathcal{OCCI}_r$ (see Definition 4.10): Given a set of clauses S, search for a sign renaming γ such that $\gamma(S) \in \mathcal{PVD}$ and then apply MB to $\gamma(S)$. MB then yields an AR of a Herbrand model of $\gamma(S)$; by changing the signs backwards one obtains an atom representation of a Herbrand model of S.

4.24. EXAMPLE. We define the following satisfiable set of clauses:

$$S = \{\{P(b)\}, \{P(f(x)), \neg P(x)\}, \{\neg P(a), \neg P(f(a))\}\}.$$

S is not in $\mathcal{PVD}$ and $(R_{Hr}^i(S))_{i \in \mathbb{N}}$ is divergent. Note that for all $i \geq 1$:

$$\{P(f^i(b))\} \in R_{Hr}^i(S) - R_{Hr}^{i-1}(S)$$

. But $S \in \mathcal{PVD}_r$ as can be seen by computing $\gamma(S)$ for the renaming γ exchanging P and $\neg P$. Indeed

$$\{\{\neg P(b)\}, \{P(x), \neg P(f(x))\}, \{P(a), P(f(a))\}\}$$

is in $\mathcal{PVD}$.
By setting $S_1 = \gamma(S)$ we obtain

$$R^0_{Hr}(S_1) = S_1 \text{ and } R^1_{Hr}(S_1) = \{\{\neg P(b)\}, \{P(x), \neg P(f(x))\}, \{P(a)\}\}.$$

Clearly $\rho_H(R^1_{Hr}(S_1)) = \emptyset$ and $R^2_{Hr}(S_1) = R^1_{Hr}(S_1)$.
We see that $(R^i_{Hr}(S))_{i \in \mathbb{N}}$ converges and

$$R^*_{Hr}(S_1) = \{\{\neg P(b)\}, \{P(x), \neg P(f(x))\}, \{P(a)\}\}.$$

By Lemma 4.16 (and clearly visible in this case) $\mathcal{A} : \{P(a)\}$ is an atomic representation of a Herbrand model of S_1 ($\mathcal{A}$ is also a ground representation of this model).

Therefore $\mathcal{M} : \{P(b)\} \cup \{P(f(t)) | t \in H(S)\}$ is a ground representation of a Herbrand model of S. By the principle of forward chaining (S is in Horn form) the set $P(R^*_H(S))$ must be an atomic representation of a Herbrand model of S. Indeed $P(R^*_H(S)) = \{P(f^n(b)) \mid n \in \mathbb{N}\} \subseteq \mathcal{M}$, but as the set is infinite the computation of R^*_H on S does not yield a syntactic model representation. However we can compute a finite AR of the model $\mathcal{M}$ directly out of $\mathcal{A}$ itself; such a representation is $\mathcal{B} : \{P(b), P(f(x))\}$ (over $H(S)$). Note that $\mathcal{M}$ does not represent a minimal Herbrand model, in contrast to $P(R^*_H(S))$.

It is not hard to show that the complement set of a finite ground representation always possesses a finite AR too; this property even holds for linear representations, i.e. for finite AR's $\mathcal{A}$ such that for all $A \in \mathcal{A}$, A contains every variable at most once [Fermüller and Leitsch 1993]. Moreover these representations can be obtained algorithmically.

Models do not only represent counterexamples but are also useful in refining resolution itself. In these model-based refinements only clauses are derived which are false in a predefined model $\mathcal{M}$. In order to automatize such a method we need an algorithm to evaluate clauses over $\mathcal{M}$; for finite models there are straightforward algorithms for this purpose. But the situation becomes more complex for representations of (infinite) Herbrand models. However there are algorithms (again based on hyperresolution) evaluating clauses over AR's constructed by the procedure MB [Fermüller and Leitsch 1996]. So we see that hyperresolution, being an efficient standard refinement in automated deduction, can be used 1. as *decision procedure*, 2. as *model building method* and 3. as *evaluation algorithm* over Herbrand models.

Considering the practical and conceptual importance of constructing counterexamples, the body of knowledge about model generation is relatively small. But in more recent times many different methods and techniques have been invented, analyzed and applied. Automated model building (sometimes also called model generation) is becoming a discipline on its own and one of the most fascinating applications of automated deduction. In this section we presented automated model building as an application of resolution decision theory, but there are several other approaches too. We just mention those of T. Tammet [1991], R. Manthey and F. Bry [1988], S. Klingenbeck [1996], P. Baumgartner and U. Furbach [1996],

P. Baumgartner, U. Furbach, and I. Niemelä [1996], R. Caferra and N. Zabel [1992], N. Peltier [1997a], J. Slaney [1992], M. Fujita, J. Slaney, and F. Bennet [1993], and C. Fermüller and A. Leitsch [1996, 1998].

Tammet's approach, like the one presented above, is based on resolution decision procedures. But while Tammet's method directly yields finite models, the method presented in this section produces *symbolic representations* of Herbrand models; finite models then are extracted from Herbrand models in a postprocessing step. Tammet used narrowing and worked with equations (in the object language); his method yields models of formulas from the union of the Ackermann and the monadic class (via the clausal form).

Caferra and Zabel defined an extension (called RAMC) of the resolution calculus by an equational constraint logic, which is specifically designed for the purpose of model building. Their method is symbolic and yields (like that in [Fermüller and Leitsch 1996]) complete representations of Herbrand models. In his Ph.D. thesis Nicolas Peltier gave a thorough discussion and comparison of the different model building methods [Peltier 1997a] and developed several new techniques; in particular it is shown that RAMC can simulate hyperresolution extending the range of model building beyond $\mathcal{PDC}$.

Manthey and Bry describe a hyperresolution prover called SATCHMO which is based on a model generation paradigm [Manthey and Bry 1988]. Their method of model building, although similar concerning the use of hyperresolution, differs from that presented in this section in several aspects. They essentially use splitting of positive clauses and backtracking, features that are both avoided in the method presented here. Moreover we make use of subsumption and replacement in an essential way and guarantee termination on specific syntax classes.

The approaches of S. Klingenbeck and of Baumgartner and Furbach are based on tableaux calculi instead on resolution. There countermodels are typically represented by open branches. The hypertableau method of Baumgartner and Furbach can be considered as an improvement of SATCHMO. A very strong tableau method, called RAMCET, has been developed by Nicolas Peltier ([Peltier 1997b]); in RAMCET equational constraints are used to prune infinite branches leading to a much better termination behavior than obtained by ordinary tableaux.

In [Fermüller and Leitsch 1998] model building is extended to clause logic with equality. In particular it is shown that $\mathcal{PVD}$ remains decidable if extended by ground equality (it becomes undecidable for full equality). The iteration method, similar to the one defined above, is based on positive resolution and ordered paramodulation. Although the admissible equations are ground the expressivity (for models) is increased considerably.

Slaney [1992] devised the program FINDER that identifies finite models (of reasonable small cardinality) of clause sets whenever they exist. The algorithm is based on a clever variant of exhaustive search through all finite interpretations and does not refer to resolution or another first-order inference system. Fujita, Slaney and Bennett [1993] defined SCOTT, a combination of FINDER with the resolution theorem prover OTTER [McCune 1995]. His method was applied successfully to solve open problems in algebra. In comparison to the other methods mentioned above,

Slaney's method behaves like a "numeric" versus a symbolic one.

Despite the differences all methods aim at more intelligent inference systems which, besides producing proofs efficiently, are also apt to construct counterexamples.

5. Resolution decision procedures for description logics

Two research areas where decidability issues play a particularly prominent role are: extended modal logics and description logics. Although it is not difficult to see that most of the logics under consideration can be translated to first-order logic, it is not obvious what the characteristics of the corresponding classes of first-order formulas are which make these logics decidable. Furthermore, the fact that the class of first-order formulas resulting from the translation of modal formulas or expressions in a description logic is decidable, does not necessarily indicate whether and how a resolution-based decision procedure for this class can be obtained. Following Hustadt and Schmidt [1999a, 1999c] and Hustadt [1999] we present various classes of clause sets into which nonclassical logics can be embedded by the use of suitable translation morphisms.

We focus on a language called $\mathcal{ALB}$ which is defined as follows. A *(terminological) signature* is given by a tuple $\Sigma = (\mathsf{O}, \mathsf{C}, \mathsf{R})$ of three disjoint alphabets, the set C of *concept symbols*, the set R of role symbols, and the set O of *object symbols*. Concept symbols and role symbols are also called *atomic concepts* and *atomic roles*.

The set of concept terms (or just concepts) and role terms (or just roles) is inductively defined as follows. Every concept symbol is a concept term and every role symbol is a role term. Now assume that C and D are concepts, and R and S are roles. Then

- $\top$ (top concept), $\bot$ (bottom concept), $C \sqcap D$ (concept intersection), $C \sqcup D$ (concept union), $\neg C$ (concept complement), $\forall R.C$ (universal restriction), and $\exists R.C$ (existential restriction) are concept terms,
- ∇ (top role), $\triangle$ (bottom role), $R \sqcap S$ (role intersection), $R \sqcup S$ (role union), $\neg R$ (role complement), R^{-1} (role converse), $R|C$ (domain restriction), and $R|C$ (range restriction) are role terms.

Concept term and role terms are (terminological) expressions. We obtain the well-known description logic $\mathcal{ALC}$ [Schmidt-Schauß and Smolka 1991] by restricting $\mathcal{ALB}$ role terms to role symbols.

5.1. EXAMPLE. Let Cheese and Beef be concept symbols and eats a role symbol. Then $\forall \neg \text{eats}.\neg\text{Cheese}$ and $\forall \nabla.\text{Cheese}$ are $\mathcal{ALB}$ concepts, but not $\mathcal{ALC}$ concepts. Person $\sqcap \exists$ eats.Beef and Cheese $\sqcup$ Beef are both $\mathcal{ALB}$ concepts and $\mathcal{ALC}$ concepts.

A *knowledge base* has two parts: A *TBox* comprising of terminological sentences and an *ABox* comprising of assertional sentences. *Terminological sentences* are of the form $C \sqsubseteq D$, $C \doteq D$, $R \sqsubseteq S$, and $R \doteq S$, and *assertional sentences* are of the form $a \in C$ and $(a, b) \in R$, where C and D are concepts, R and S are roles, and a and b are object symbols.

5.2. EXAMPLE. The following is a small $\mathcal{ALB}$ knowledge base.

TBox :	Person $\dot{\sqsubseteq}$ Male $\sqcup$ Female
	Parent $\doteq$ Person $\sqcap$ $\exists$ hasChild.Person
	Person $\sqcap$ Professor $\dot{\sqsubseteq}$ $\exists$ hasDegree.PhD
	CheeseLover $\doteq$ Person $\sqcap$ $\forall$ $\neg$eats.$\neg$Cheese
ABox :	bob $\in$ Person $\qquad$ jim $\in$ Person
	bob $\in$ Professor $\qquad$ cheddar $\in$ Cheese
	(bob, jim) $\in$ hasChild $\quad$ (bob, cheddar) $\in$ $\neg$eats

The knowledge base consists of four terminological sentences and six assertional sentences. Intuitively, the first sentence of the TBox defines that the concept Person is a subset of the union of the concepts Male and Female, that is, every element of the set Person is either an element of the set Male or an element of the set Female. The first sentence of the ABox defines that the object bob is an element of the concept Person. The formal semantics of knowledge bases will be presented in Definition 5.6.

5.3. DEFINITION. A symbol S_0 *uses* a symbol S_1 *directly* in a TBox T if and only if T contains a sentence of the form $S_0 \doteq E$ or $S_0 \dot{\sqsubseteq} E$ such that S_1 occurs in E. A symbol S_0 *uses* S_n if and only if there is a chain of symbols $S_0, \ldots, S_n$ such that S_i uses S_{i+1} directly, for every i, $1 \le i \le n-1$. A knowledge base Γ is said to contain a *terminological cycle* if and only if some symbol uses itself in the TBox of Γ.

5.4. EXAMPLE. In the knowledge base of Example 5.2 the concept symbol Parent uses the concept symbol Person directly and Person uses Male and Female directly. So, Parent uses Male and Female. It is straightforward to check that the knowledge base contains no terminological cycles.

The standard definition of knowledge bases imposes the following restrictions on the set of admissible terminological sentences: (i) The left-hand sides of terminological sentences have to be concept symbols or role symbols, (ii) any concept or role symbol occurs at most once on the left-hand side of any terminological sentence, and (iii) there are no terminological cycles. Knowledge bases obeying these restrictions are known as *descriptive knowledge bases*. In this context terminological sentences are called *definitions*. When no restrictions are imposed, we speak of *general knowledge bases*.

5.5. EXAMPLE. The first terminological sentence of the knowledge base above obeys restrictions (ii) and (iii), but it violates restriction (i) of the definition of descriptive knowledge bases. Thus, it is a general knowledge base.

5.6. DEFINITION. An *interpretation* $\mathcal{I} = (\Delta^{\mathcal{I}}, \cdot^{\mathcal{I}})$ over a signature $\Sigma = (\mathsf{O}, \mathsf{C}, \mathsf{R})$ consists of a nonempty *domain* $\Delta^{\mathcal{I}}$ and an *interpretation function* $\cdot^{\mathcal{I}}$ mapping every object symbol in O to an element of $\Delta^{\mathcal{I}}$, such that $a^{\mathcal{I}} \neq b^{\mathcal{I}}$ if $a \neq b$, every concept symbol A in C to a subset $C^{\mathcal{I}}$ of Δ and every role symbol P in R to a subset of $\Delta \times \Delta$.

The interpretation function is extended to arbitrary concepts and roles as follows:

$$\top^{\mathcal{I}} = \Delta^{\mathcal{I}}$$
$$\bot^{\mathcal{I}} = \emptyset$$
$$(\neg C)^{\mathcal{I}} = \Delta^{\mathcal{I}} - C^{\mathcal{I}}$$
$$(C \sqcap D)^{\mathcal{I}} = C^{\mathcal{I}} \cap D^{\mathcal{I}}$$
$$(C \sqcup D)^{\mathcal{I}} = C^{\mathcal{I}} \cup D^{\mathcal{I}}$$
$$(\forall R.C)^{\mathcal{I}} = \{d \mid (\forall e)\, (d, e) \in R^{\mathcal{I}} \rightarrow e \in C^{\mathcal{I}}\}$$
$$(\exists R.C)^{\mathcal{I}} = \{d \mid (\exists e)\, (d, e) \in R^{\mathcal{I}} \wedge e \in C^{\mathcal{I}}\}$$

$$\nabla^{\mathcal{I}} = \Delta^{\mathcal{I}} \times \Delta^{\mathcal{I}}$$
$$\triangle^{\mathcal{I}} = \emptyset$$
$$(\neg R)^{\mathcal{I}} = \Delta^{\mathcal{I}} \times \Delta^{\mathcal{I}} - R^{\mathcal{I}}$$
$$(P \sqcap Q)^{\mathcal{I}} = P^{\mathcal{I}} \cap Q^{\mathcal{I}}$$
$$(P \sqcup Q)^{\mathcal{I}} = P^{\mathcal{I}} \cup Q^{\mathcal{I}}$$
$$R \lfloor C^{\mathcal{I}} = R^{\mathcal{I}} \cap (\Delta^I \times C)$$
$$R \rceil C^{\mathcal{I}} = R^{\mathcal{I}} \cap (C \times \Delta^I)$$
$$R^{-1\mathcal{I}} = \{(d, e) \mid (e, d) \in R^{\mathcal{I}}\}$$

An interpretation $\mathcal{I}$ satisfies the assertional and terminological sentences of $\mathcal{ALB}$

$$a \in C \quad \text{if} \quad a^{\mathcal{I}} \in C^{\mathcal{I}}$$
$$C \sqsubseteq D \quad \text{if} \quad C^{\mathcal{I}} \subseteq D^{\mathcal{I}}$$
$$C \doteq D \quad \text{if} \quad C^{\mathcal{I}} = D^{\mathcal{I}}$$

$$(a, b) \in R \quad \text{if} \quad (a^{\mathcal{I}}, b^{\mathcal{I}}) \in R^{\mathcal{I}}$$
$$R \sqsubseteq S \quad \text{if} \quad R^{\mathcal{I}} \subseteq S^{\mathcal{I}}$$
$$R \doteq S \quad \text{if} \quad R^{\mathcal{I}} = S^{\mathcal{I}}.$$

An interpretation $\mathcal{I}$ is a *model* of a knowledge base Γ if and only if $\mathcal{I}$ satisfies all sentences in Γ.

A terminological expression E_1 is in *negation normal form* if for every subexpression $\neg E_2$ of E_1, E_2 is a concept or role symbol. For every terminological expression E_1 there exists a terminological expression E_2 in negation normal form such that for every interpretation $\mathcal{I}$, $E_1^{\mathcal{I}} = E_2^{\mathcal{I}}$.

It is well known that description logics can be embedded into sublanguages of first-order logic (with equality), Figure 1 specifies one possible embedding of $\mathcal{ALB}$ expressions into first-order logic, the so so-called *standard* or *relational translation*. In Section 5.2 we discuss an alternative embedding, the optimized functional translation.

5.7. EXAMPLE. The translation of the knowledge base in Example 5.2 is the following first-order formula:

$$(\forall x)\, (p_{\text{Person}}(x) \rightarrow (p_{\text{Male}}(x) \vee p_{\text{Female}}(x)))$$
$$\wedge (\forall x)\, (p_{\text{Parent}}(x) \leftrightarrow (p_{\text{Person}}(x) \wedge (\exists y)\, (p_{\text{hasChild}}(x, y) \wedge p_{\text{Person}}(y))))$$
$$\wedge (\forall x)\, ((p_{\text{Person}}(x) \wedge p_{\text{Professor}}(x)) \rightarrow (\exists y)\, (p_{\text{hasDegree}}(x, y) \wedge p_{\text{PhD}}(y)))$$
$$\wedge (\forall x)\, (p_{\text{CheeseLover}}(x) \leftrightarrow (p_{\text{Person}}(x) \wedge (\forall y)\, (\neg p_{\text{eats}}(x, y) \rightarrow \neg p_{\text{Cheese}}(y))))$$
$$\wedge p_{\text{Person}}(\text{bob}) \wedge p_{\text{Person}}(\text{jim}) \wedge p_{\text{Professor}}(\text{bob}) \wedge p_{\text{Cheese}}(\text{cheddar})$$
$$\wedge p_{\text{hasChild}}(\text{bob}, \text{jim}) \wedge \neg p_{\text{eats}}(\text{bob}, \text{cheddar}).$$

Embedding of sentences:

$$\Pi(C \sqsubseteq D) = (\forall x)\,(\pi(C, x) \to \pi(D, x)) \qquad \Pi(R \sqsubseteq S) = (\forall x)(\forall y)\,(\pi(R, x, y) \to \pi(S, x, y))$$
$$\Pi(C \doteq D) = (\forall x)\,(\pi(C, x) \leftrightarrow \pi(D, x)) \qquad \Pi(R \doteq S) = (\forall x)(\forall y)\,(\pi(R, x, y) \leftrightarrow \pi(S, x, y))$$
$$\Pi(a \in C) = \pi(C, \underline{a}) \qquad\qquad \Pi((a, b) \in R) = \pi(R, \underline{a}, \underline{b})$$

where $\underline{a}$ and $\underline{b}$ are constants uniquely associated with a and b.
Embedding of terms:

$$\pi(A, X) = p_A(X) \qquad\qquad\qquad \pi(P, X, Y) = p_P(X, Y)$$
$$\pi(\neg C, X) = \neg\pi(C, X) \qquad\qquad \pi(\neg R, X, Y) = \neg\pi(R, X, Y)$$
$$\pi(\top, X) = \top \qquad\qquad\qquad\quad \pi(\nabla, X, Y) = \top$$
$$\pi(\bot, X) = \bot \qquad\qquad\qquad\quad \pi(\triangle, X, Y) = \bot$$
$$\pi(C \sqcap D, X) = \pi(C, X) \wedge \pi(D, X) \qquad \pi(R \sqcap S, X, Y) = \pi(R, X, Y) \wedge \pi(S, X, Y)$$
$$\pi(C \sqcup D, X) = \pi(C, X) \vee \pi(D, X) \qquad \pi(R \sqcup S, X, Y) = \pi(R, X, Y) \vee \pi(S, X, Y)$$
$$\pi(\forall R.C, X) = (\forall y)\,(\pi(R, X, y) \to \pi(C, y)) \qquad \pi(R {\restriction} C, X, Y) = \pi(R, X, Y) \wedge \pi(C, Y)$$
$$\pi(\exists R.C, X) = (\exists y)\,(\pi(R, X, y) \wedge \pi(C, y)) \qquad \pi(R {\restriction} C, X, Y) = \pi(R, X, Y) \wedge \pi(C, X)$$
$$\pi(R^{-1}, X, Y) = \pi(R, Y, X)$$

where X and Y are meta-variables for variables and constants, and p_A (respectively p_P) denotes a unary (binary) predicate symbol uniquely associated with the concept symbol A (role symbol P).

Figure 1: The standard embedding of $\mathcal{ALB}$ into first-order logic

In the case of $\mathcal{ALB}$ all common inferential services for knowledge bases, like subsumption tests for concepts, TBox classification, realization, retrieval, can be reduced to tests of the satisfiability of a knowledge base.

5.1. Decidability by ordered resolution

The conversion to clausal form of first-order formulas resulting from the translation of $\mathcal{ALB}$ knowledge bases, makes use of the following structural transformation. For ease of presentation we assume any first-order formula ϕ is in negation normal form.

Recall the notion of a definitional form of a first-order formula from Section 2. Note that the embedding Π preserves the structure of $\mathcal{ALB}$ expression, that is, with every occurrence of an $\mathcal{ALB}$ expression in a knowledge base Γ we can uniquely associate an occurrence in the first-order formulae $\Pi(\Gamma)$. Let Λ^r be the set of positions of nonatomic concepts and nonatomic roles in the knowledge base Γ. By Ξ_r we denote the transformation taking $\Pi(\Gamma)$ to its *definitional form* $\mathrm{Def}_{\Lambda^r}(\Pi(\Gamma))$. We assume that the variable ordering in a literal $Q_\lambda(x, y)$ introduced by Ξ_r follows the convention we have used in the definition of π, that is, for a subformulae like $R(x, y) \star S(x, y)$ associated with $R \star S$ and subformulae like $R(y, x)$ associated with

R^{-1} we introduce $Q_\lambda(x, y)$ (not $Q_\lambda(y, x)$).

5.8. THEOREM. *Let* Γ *be any* $\mathcal{ALB}$ *knowledge base.* $\Xi_r \Pi(\Gamma)$ *can be computed in polynomial time, and* Γ *is satisfiable iff* $\Xi_r \Pi(\Gamma)$ *is satisfiable.*

PROOF. It is straightforward to see that the translation of Γ and the computation of the definitional form can be performed in polynomial time. That Π is satisfiability equivalence preserving can be checked with respect to the semantics given in Definition 5.6. By Proposition 1 Ξ_r is also satisfiability equivalence preserving. $\square$

Next we characterise a class of clauses which we call *DL-clauses*. Let C be a clause and L a literal in C. We refer to a literal L as *embracing* in C if for every L' in C, $V(L') \cap V(L) \neq \emptyset$ implies $V(L') \subseteq V(L)$ (that is, it contains all variables occurring in the split component in which it occurs). A term t in C is called *embracing* if for every L' in C, $V(L') \cap V(t) \neq \emptyset$ implies $V(L) \subseteq V(t)$. A literal L is *singular* if it contains no functional term and $V(L)$ is a singleton. A literal is *flat* if it is nonground and contains no functional term.

5.9. DEFINITION *(DL-clause)*. A literal L is a *DL-literal* if the following is true.
   1. L is simple (see Definition 3.36),
   2. L is either monadic or dyadic, and contains at most 2 variables,
   3. L is ground whenever it contains a constant symbol, and
   4. the maximal arity of any function symbol in L is 1.
A clause C is a *DL-clause*, if
   1. when C contains a functional term t, then t is embracing,
   2. C is ground whenever C contains a constant symbol,
   3. all literals in C are DL-literals, and
   4. the argument multisets of all flat, dyadic literals coincide.

Property (4) is important to enable us to use a liftable ordering for our resolution decision procedure. It excludes clauses like $\{p(x, x), q(x, y)\}$. In order to avoid possibly unbounded chains of variables across literals we would need to restrict resolution inferences to the literal $q(x, y)$. But, when such clauses are present it is in general not possible to devise a liftable ordering such that only the second literal is maximal. By contrast, clauses like $\{p(x, x), q(x, x)\}$ and $\{p(x, y), q(x, y)\}$ are DL-clauses, and may occur in a derivation from $\Xi_r \Pi(\Gamma)$.

5.10. LEMMA. *Let* Γ *be an* $\mathcal{ALB}$ *knowledge base. Every clause in the standard clausal form of* $\Xi_r \Pi(\Gamma)$ *belongs to the class of DL-clauses.*

We define an A-ordering $<_{cov}$ on atoms as follows.

5.11. DEFINITION. Let A and B be two atoms, then $A <_{cov} B$ if either the multiset of arguments of A is a strict sub-multiset of the multiset of arguments of B or for every argument s of A there exists an argument t of B such that s is a strict subterm of t.

Hustadt and Schmidt [1999a] show that ordered resolution and ordered factoring on DL-clauses with respect to $<_{\infty\nu}$ will result in DL-clauses.

5.12. LEMMA. *Let $C = \{L_1, L_2\} \cup D$ be an indecomposable, DL-clause with σ a most general unifier of L_1 and L_2. The split components of $(\{L_1\} \cup D)\sigma$ are DL-clauses.*

PROOF. Since C is indecomposable and contains at least two literals, it is not a ground clause. By property (2) it contains no constants. So, the most general unifier σ will not introduce any constant symbols. Also, there are no functional terms in the range of σ, since all functional terms in C are embracing. Therefore, σ is a variable renaming. It is straightforward to see that variable renamings preserve the properties (1)–(4). $\qquad\square$

5.13. LEMMA. *DL-clauses are preserved under $<_{\infty\nu}$-ordered resolution; more precisely: Let $C_1 = \{A_1\} \cup D_1$ and $C_2 = \{\neg A_2\} \cup D_2$ be two variable-disjoint, indecomposable, DL-clauses such that A_1 and A_2 are unifiable with most general unifier σ, and there is no literal $A_3\sigma$ in $(D_1 \cup D_2)\sigma$ such that $A_1\sigma <_{\infty\nu} A_3\sigma$. Then the split components of $(D_1 \cup D_2)\sigma$ are DL-clauses.*

PROOF. It is not difficult to show that the following holds:
1. A_1 is embracing in C_1.
2. If A_1 is a flat, singular literal, then C_1 contains only flat, singular literals.
3. If A_1 is flat, then C_1 contains no functional term.
4. If $A_1\sigma$ contains a functional term t, then for no variable x in C_2 is $x\sigma$ a functional term, and t is embracing in $(D_1 \cup D_2)\sigma$.
5. If A_1 contains a functional term t, then for no variable x in C_1, is $x\sigma$ a functional term and t is embracing in $(D_1 \cup D_2)\sigma$.

Analogously, for $\neg A_2$ and C_2. Let $(D_1 \cup D_2)\sigma$ be nonempty and E be a split component of it.
1. It follows that no functional term in E has a functional term argument and that functional terms in E are embracing.
2. Suppose $A_1\sigma$ contains a constant. Then either A_1 or A_2 is ground. Since A_1 and $\neg A_2$ are embracing, E is a unit ground clause.
3. It follows from (1) and (2) that all literals in E are DL-literals.
4. Only if $A_1\sigma = A_2\sigma$ is a flat, dyadic literal does E possibly contain a flat, dyadic literal $L\sigma$. The argument multiset of L coincides with that of either A_1 or A_2. Therefore, the argument multiset of $L\sigma$ coincides with $A_1\sigma$. So does the argument multiset of any flat, dyadic literal in E. $\qquad\square$

5.14. THEOREM. *Let Γ be an $\mathcal{ALB}$ knowledge base and let S be the standard clausal form of $\Xi_r\Pi(\Gamma)$. Then any derivation from S by a combination of $R_{<_{\infty\nu}}$ and the splitting or condensation rule terminates.*

PROOF. By Theorem 5.8 and Lemmas 5.10, 5.12 and 5.13; because any set of nonvariant, indecomposable DL-clauses built from finitely many predicate and function symbols is finitely bounded; and the fact that any application $R_{<\infty_v}$ is followed immediately by applications of the splitting rule.   □

5.15. COROLLARY. *The satisfiability problem for $\mathcal{ALB}$ knowledge bases is decidable; the transformation $\Xi_r \Pi$ and $R_{<\infty_v}$ combined with the splitting or condensation rule provide a decision procedure.*

Given an $\mathcal{ALB}$ knowledge base Γ, the characteristics of clauses in the standard clausal form of $\Xi_r \Pi(\Gamma)$ are rather simple. It is therefore not surprising that there exists a variety of alternative solvable classes into which we can embed satisfiability problem for $\mathcal{ALB}$ knowledge bases.

Tammet [1992, 1995] has introduced the following fragment of first-order logic:

5.16. DEFINITION. Any formula φ of the predicate logic without equality and without nonconstant function symbols belongs to the class One-free if any subformula of φ starting with a quantifier contains no more than one free variable.

It is straightforward to see that for any knowledge base Γ, $\Pi(\Gamma)$ is in the class One-free. Furthermore, Ξ_r transforms any formula φ in One-free into a conjunction of formulas of the class $\mathcal{K}$. The standard clausal form of $\Xi_r(\varphi)$ is an element of $\mathcal{KC}$. Therefore, the refinement $R_{<z}$ defined in Section 3.6 combined with the splitting rule provides a decision procedure for the class One-free as well as for the satisfiability problem of $\mathcal{ALB}$ knowledge bases.

5.17. THEOREM. *The class One-free is decidable; $R_{<z}$ combined with the splitting rule provides a decision procedure.*

5.18. COROLLARY. *The transformation $\Xi_r \Pi$ and $R_{<z}$ combined with the splitting rule provides a decision procedure for the satisfiability problem of $\mathcal{ALB}$ knowledge bases.*

5.2. Variations of $\mathcal{ALB}$

A closer inspection of the formulas we obtain from translating $\mathcal{ALB}$ knowledge bases into first-order logic reveals, that only the presence of the top role ∇ and role complement prevents $\Pi(\Gamma)$ from being guarded for arbitrary knowledge bases Γ.

5.19. EXAMPLE. Consider the $\mathcal{ALB}$ expressions $\forall \nabla.A$ and $\forall \neg P.A$. The translation of these expression is $(\forall y)\,(\top \rightarrow A(y))$ and $(\forall y)\,(\neg P(x,y) \rightarrow A(y))$, respectively. In both cases the first-order formulas lack an appropriate guard to satisfy the definition of guarded formulas.

Consequently, the reduct of $\mathcal{ALB}$ without the top role and role complement allows for the use of the resolution decision procedures for the guarded fragment.

5.20. COROLLARY. $R_{<_{\mathcal{G}\mathcal{F}}}$ provides a decision procedure for the satisfiability problem of knowledge bases over the reduct of $\mathcal{ALB}$ without the top role and role complement.

If we restrict ourselves even further, namely to descriptive knowledge bases over $\mathcal{ALC}$, then all the inferential services for knowledge bases can be reduced to tests of the satisfiability of concept terms [Donini et al. 1994]. See also [Calvanese et al. 2001] (Chapter 23 of this Handbook) for a discussion of inferential services in description logics and their interrelationships. Since $\mathcal{ALC}$ is a notational variant of basic multi-modal logic, the techniques described in [Ohlbach et al. 2001] (Chapter 21 of this Handbook) are applicable. In particular, the optimized functional translation [Schmidt 1997, Schmidt 1998] can be used instead of the standard translation described in Section 5 to map concept terms into first-order logic.

The optimized functional translation maps concept terms of $\mathcal{ALC}$ into a logic, called *basic path logic*, which is a monadic fragment of sorted first-order logic with sorts AF_R uniquely associated with the role symbols and an additional sort W, binary function symbols $[\_\_]_{AF_R}$ of sort $W \times AF_R \to W$, and one constant ϵ of sort W. For better readability we write $[\_\_]$ instead of $[\_\_]_{AF_R}$, since the sort of $[\_\_]_{AF_R}$ is uniquely determined by the sort of its second argument.

5.21. EXAMPLE. Let AF_{R_1} and AF_{R_2} be sorts associated with the role symbols R_1 and R_2, respectively. Let the constant symbol c be of sort AF_{R_1} and the variable x of sort AF_{R_2}. Then $[[\epsilon\, c]\, x]$ is a term of sort W.

The optimized functional translation consists of a sequence of transformations. The first transformation Π_f maps a concept term C to its so-called functional translation defined by $(\forall x)\, \pi_f(\varphi, x)$, where π_f is given by

$$\pi_f(A, s) = A(s)$$
$$\pi_f(\neg C, s) = \neg \pi_f(C, s)$$
$$\pi_f(C \sqcap D, s) = \pi_f(C, s) \wedge \pi_f(D, s)$$
$$\pi_f(C \sqcup D, s) = \pi_f(C, s) \vee \pi_f(D, s)$$
$$\pi_f(\forall R.C, s) = def_R(s) \to (\forall x{:}AF_R)\, \pi_f(C, [s\, x])$$
$$\pi_f(\exists R.C, s) = def_R(s) \wedge (\exists x{:}AF_R)\, \pi_f(C, [s\, x]).$$

The second transformation applies the so-called quantifier exchange operator Υ, which moves existential quantifiers inwards over universal quantifiers using the rule '$(\exists x)(\forall y)\, \psi$ becomes $(\forall y)(\exists x)\, \psi$'. The two transformation are combined into a the function $\overline{\Pi}_f$ mapping concept terms C to $\neg\Upsilon\Pi_f(\neg C)$.

The mapping $\overline{\Pi}_f$ is satisfiability equivalence preserving for $\mathcal{ALC}$, that is, a concept term C is satisfiable if and only if $\neg\Upsilon\Pi_f(\neg C)$ is satisfiable [Ohlbach and Schmidt 1997]. Note that in the closed first-order formula $\overline{\Pi}_f(C)$ no existential quantifier occurs in the scope of a universal quantifier. Thus, all skolem functions in the standard clausal form of $\overline{\Pi}_f(C)$ are constants. The following theorem is a consequence of the results of Ohlbach and Schmidt [1997] for basic path logic.

5.22. THEOREM. *Let C be an ALC concept term. Then any derivation by unrefined resolution combined with the splitting or condensation rule from $\overline{\Pi}_f(C)$ terminates.*

5.23. COROLLARY. *The mapping $\overline{\Pi}_f$ and unrefined resolution combined with the splitting or condensation rule provide a decision procedure for the satisfiability problem of ALC concept terms.*

By additional transformations we can embed the basic path logic into a subclass of the Bernays-Schönfinkel class. First, we replace all occurrences of literals $P(s)$ where s is a path of the form $[[[\epsilon \, \alpha_{R_1}^1] \, \alpha_{R_2}^2] \ldots \alpha_{R_n}^n]$ where $\alpha_{R_j}^j$ is a variable or constant of sort AF_{R_j}, for $1 \leq j \leq n$, by $P_{n+1}(\epsilon, \alpha_{R_1}^1, \ldots, \alpha_{R_n}^n)$ where P_{n+1} is an $(n+1)$-ary predicate symbol uniquely associated with P and n. Second, the sort information associated with the variables and constants occurring in the literals in the clause set can be encoded in the predicate symbols of the literals. So, we can replace all occurrences of literals $P_{n+1}(\epsilon, \alpha_{R_1}^1, \ldots, \alpha_{R_n}^n)$ by $P_{R_1 \ldots R_n}(\epsilon, \alpha^1, \ldots, \alpha^n)$ where $P_{R_1 \ldots R_n}$ is a predicate symbol uniquely associated with the predicate symbol P_{n+1} and the sorts $AF_{R_1}, \ldots, AF_{R_n}$. The variables and constants $\alpha^1, \ldots, \alpha^n$ no longer carry any sort information. Finally, we observe that all literals in the transformed clause set share the first argument ϵ, which we can eliminate safely.

This sequence of three transformations can be combined in one:

$$P([[[\epsilon \, \alpha_{R_1}^1] \, \alpha_{R_2}^2] \ldots \alpha_{R_n}^n]) \quad \text{becomes} \quad P_{R_1 \ldots R_n}(\alpha^1, \ldots, \alpha^n).$$

We denote this transformation by Ξ_{BS}.

5.24. THEOREM. *For every ALC concept term C, the first-order formula $\Xi_{BS}\overline{\Pi}_f(C)$ is satisfiable if and only if C is satisfiable and $\Xi_{BS}\overline{\Pi}_f(C)$ is an element of the Bernays-Schönfinkel class.*

Note that not every formula of the Bernays-Schönfinkel class is in the range of $\Xi_{BS}\overline{\Pi}_f$. For the particular subclass of BS we obtain from $\Xi_{BS}\overline{\Pi}_f$ that Theorem 5.22 is still valid. Since the number of ground instances of formulas in the Bernays-Schönfinkel class is finite it is also possible to use propositional theorem proving methods to obtain decision procedures for the satisfiability problem of ALC concept terms.

5.3. Decidability by hyperresolution

Following [Hustadt and Schmidt 1999a] we define a decision procedure based on hyperresolution combined with the splitting rule for the satisfiability problem of ALC concept terms. The derivations are in essence exactly as for tableaux calculi for description logics. However, compared to tableaux calculi the procedure has the advantage that (i) it provides more flexibility concerning the theorem proving strategy, and (ii) it allows for the application of general redundancy criteria.

Let C be an ALC concept term. Let the clause set S be the standard clausal form of $\Xi_r\Pi(C)$. There is exactly one positive ground unit clause in S and all other clauses contain negative literals. The clauses containing negative literals alone cannot form a clash sequence.

In all clauses except those of the form

$$\{\neg p_A(x), \neg p_R(x,y), p_B(y)\} \tag{5.1}$$

there is a unary negative literal containing all variables of the clause, and with the exception of

$$\{\neg p_A(x), p_R(x, f(x))\} \tag{5.2}$$

and

$$\{\neg p_A(x), p_B(f(x))\} \tag{5.3}$$

no variables occur as arguments of functional terms.

Given these observations it is straightforward to prove by induction that all hyperresolvents derivable from the standard clausal form of $\Xi_r \Pi(C)$ are ground clauses. With eager applications of the splitting rule to hyperresolvents we can ensure that all positive clauses in a derivation are ground unit clauses. However, in inference steps by hyperresolution involving clauses of the forms (5.2) and (5.3) as nonpositive premises the term depth of the hyperresolvent is greater than the term depth of the positive premise of the inference. So, to ensure termination of hyperresolution we have to show that there is an upper bound on the term depth of hyperresolvents.

Recall, that the standard translation Π into first-order logic preserves the structure of concepts and roles and that the application of the transformation Ξ_r to a formula φ establishes a correspondence between subformula of φ and the new predicate symbols introduced by Ξ_r. Consequently, the subexpression relation on the concept term C induces an acyclic relation on the predicate symbols in $\Xi_r \Pi(C)$. Formally, define a dependency relation $\succ_c^1$ on the predicate symbols in $\Xi_r \Pi(C)$ by $p_A \succ_c^1 p_B$, if there is a definition $(\forall \bar{x})\, (\phi \to \psi)$ in $\Xi_r \Pi(\overline{C})$ such that p_A occurs in ϕ and p_B occurs in ψ. Let $\succ_S$ be an ordering on the predicate symbols in $\Xi_r \Pi(\overline{\Gamma})$ which is compatible with the transitive closure of $\succ_c^1$. Since the subexpression relation on C is acyclic, it is always possible to find such an ordering. We will use the ordering $\succ_S$ to show the termination of hyperresolution on the standard clausal form of $\Xi_r \Pi(C)$.

Next, define a measure μ_S on ground unit clauses occurring in a derivation from the clausal form S of $\Xi_r \Pi(C)$ by

$$\mu_D(C) = \begin{cases} (p_A, p_A), & \text{if } C = \{p_A(t)\} \\ (p_A, p_R), & \text{if } C = \{p_R(s,t)\} \text{ has been derived from} \\ & \quad \{\neg p_A(x), p_R(x, f(x))\} \in S \end{cases}$$

That is, the measure associated with a ground unit clause is a pair of predicate symbols. Measures are compared by the lexicographic combination $\succ_S^2 = (\succ_S, \succ_S)$. Since $\succ_S$ is well-founded, also $\succ_S^2$ is well-founded.

Note that any clause of the form $\{p_R(s,t)\}$ occurring in a derivation from S is derived by resolving a unit clause $\{p_A(s)\}$ with a clause of the form (5.2). Thus,

μ_S is well-defined, i.e. it assigns a pair of predicate symbols to every ground unit clause occurring in a derivation from S.

It is straightforward to check that for any inference step by hyperresolution on S the conclusion of the inference step is smaller or equal to the measure of one of its positive premises. Termination then follows from the well-foundedness of $\succ_S^2$.

Note that we can use μ_S and $\succ_S^2$ to define an atom complexity measure as described on page 1819. Then the following theorem is a consequence of the results in [Leitsch 1993].

5.25. THEOREM. *Let C be an $\mathcal{ALC}$ concept term and let S be the standard clausal form of $\Xi_r \Pi(C)$. Then any derivation from S by hyperresolution combined with the splitting rule terminates.*

5.26. COROLLARY. *The transformation $\Xi_r \Pi$ and hyperresolution combined with the splitting rule provide a decision procedure for the satisfiability problem of $\mathcal{ALC}$ concept terms.*

Hustadt and Schmidt [1999c] extend the approach presented in this section to general knowledge bases over the description logic $\mathcal{ALC}$.

5.4. Simulation of tableaux decision procedures for $\mathcal{ALC}$

Hustadt and Schmidt [1999a] also consider the relation between the decision procedure based on hyperresolution and a standard tableaux decision procedure for the satisfiability problem of $\mathcal{ALC}$ concept terms.

Given an $\mathcal{ALC}$ concept term C we start with an initial constraint system $\{a \in C\}$ for an arbitrary object symbol a and apply the following transformation rules:

1. $\Delta \Rightarrow_\sqcap \Delta \cup \{a \in C, a \in D\}$, if $a \in (C \sqcap D)$ is in Δ, $a \in C$ and $a \in D$ are not both in Δ.
2. $\Delta \Rightarrow_\sqcup \Delta \cup \{a \in E\}$, if $a \in (C \sqcup D)$ is in Δ, neither $a \in C$ nor $a \in D$ is in Δ, and $E = C$ or $E = D$.
3. $\Delta \Rightarrow_\exists \Delta \cup \{(a,b) \in R, b \in C\}$, if $a \in \exists R.C$ is in Δ, there is no c such that both $(a,c) \in R$ and $c \in C$ are in Δ, and b is a new object symbol with respect to Δ.
4. $\Delta \Rightarrow_\forall \Delta \cup \{b \in C\}$, if $a \in \forall R.C$ and $(a,b) \in R$ are in Δ, and $b \in C$ is not in Δ.
5. $\Delta \Rightarrow_\perp \Delta \cup \{a \in \perp\}$, if $a \in A$ and $a \in \neg A$ are in Δ, where A is a concept symbol.

Let $\Rightarrow_{TAB}$ be the transitive closure of the union of the transformation rules given above. A constraint system Δ contains a *clash* if $\{a \in \perp\} \subset \Delta$. A constraint system Δ is satisfiable iff there exists a constraint system Δ' such that (i) $\Delta \Rightarrow_{TAB} \Delta'$, (ii) no further applications of $\Rightarrow_{TAB}$ to Δ' are possible, and (iii) Δ' is clash-free. A concept term C is satisfiable if and only if the constraint system $\{a \in C\}$ is satisfiable.

The correspondence between the tableaux decision procedure and the decision procedure based on hyperresolution presented in Section 5.3 is not difficult to see.

Remember that for every concept C and every role R, which may possibly occur in an ABox during a satisfiability test, there exist corresponding predicate symbols p_C and p_R in the standard clausal form of $\Xi_r \Pi(\overline{\Gamma})$. Likewise for every object symbol a we will have a corresponding term t_a.

Transformation by the inference rules is simulated as follows:

1. An application of the $\Rightarrow_\sqcap$ rule corresponds to hyperresolution inference steps between a ground clause $\{p_{C \sqcap D}(t_a)\}$ and clauses $\{\neg p_{C \sqcap D}(x), p_C(x)\}$ and $\{\neg p_{C \sqcap D}(x), p_D(x)\}$, generating the hyperresolvents $\{p_C(t_a)\}$ and $\{p_D(t_a)\}$.

2. An application of the $\Rightarrow_\sqcup$ rule corresponds to an inference step between a ground unit clause $\{p_{C \sqcup D}(t_a)\}$ and $\{\neg p_{C \sqcup D}(x), p_C(x), p_D(x)\}$. We then apply the splitting rule to the conclusion $\{p_C(t_a), p_D(t_a)\}$ which will generate two branches, one on which our set of clauses contains $\{p_C(t_a)\}$ and one on which it contains $\{p_D(t_a)\}$.

3. An application of the $\Rightarrow_\exists$ rule corresponds to two hyperresolution inference steps between the clauses $\{p_{\exists R.C}(t_a)\}$, $\{\neg p_{\exists R.C}(x), p_R(x, f(x))\}$, and $\{\neg p_{\exists R.C}(x), p_C(f(x))\}$. This will add $\{p_R(t_a, f(t_a))\}$ and $\{p_C(f(t_a))\}$ to the clause set. The term $f(t_a)$ corresponds to the new object symbol b introduced by the $\Rightarrow_\exists$ rule, that is, $t_b = f(t_a)$.

4. An application of the $\Rightarrow_\forall$ rule corresponds to a hyperresolution inference step with nonpositive premise $\{\neg p_{\forall R.C}(x), \neg p_R(x, y), p_C(y)\}$ and positive premises $\{p_{\forall R.C}(t_a)\}$ and $\{p_R(t_a, t_b)\}$.

5. An application of the $\Rightarrow_\perp$ rule corresponds to a hyperresolution inference step with nonpositive premise $\{\neg p_{\neg A}(x), \neg p_A(x)\}$ and positive premises $\{p_A(t_a)\}$ and $\{p_{\neg A}(t_a)\}$. The hyperresolvent is the empty clause showing that the current clause set is unsatisfiable.

5.27. THEOREM. *The hyperresolution decision procedure p-simulates tableaux decision procedures for $\mathcal{ALC}$.*

5.5. Model generation

As with tableaux-based procedures and the approach presented in Section 4.2 hyperresolution lends itself for the construction of a model when the empty clause was not derived. We briefly describe how this can be done.

First, define a translation mapping which maps the first-order syntax back to the original syntax. This exploits the one to one correspondence between ground terms and objects, and predicate symbols and concept and role subexpressions, respectively. For any ground term t_a, let $\hat{t}_a$ denote the object symbol a uniquely associated with t_a. Let $\widehat{C}$ and $\widehat{R}$ denote the concept and role obtained by replacing any occurrences of $\overline{I}$ by $\neg A$, and P^u and P^d by P, respectively. Now, define the mapping Π^{-1} by $\Pi^{-1}(\{p_C(t_a)\}) = \hat{t}_a \in \widehat{C}$, $\Pi^{-1}(\{p_R(t_a, t_b)\}) = (\hat{t}_a, \hat{t}_b) \in \widehat{R}$ and the straightforward extension to clauses and sets of clauses. Given a set S of unit ground clauses, $\Pi^{-1}(S)$ is a set of assertional sentences.

Second, we denote by $\widehat{\mathcal{I}}$ the function mapping a set of assertional sentences to an interpretation $(\Delta^{\mathcal{I}}, \cdot^{\mathcal{I}})$ in the sense of Definition 5.6 which is defined as follows. Given a set Γ of assertional sentences, the domain $\Delta^{\mathcal{I}}$ of $\widehat{\mathcal{I}}(\Gamma)$ is the set of all object symbols in Γ. For every concept symbol A, an element a of $\Delta^{\mathcal{I}}$ is in $A^{\mathcal{I}}$ iff the assertional sentence $a \in A$ is an element of Γ. Correspondingly, for every role symbol P, a pair (a, b) of elements of $\Delta^{\mathcal{I}}$ is in $P^{\mathcal{I}}$ iff the assertional sentence $(a, b) \in P$ is an element of Γ.

Recall from Section 4.2 the notion of an atomic representation of a Herbrand model of a set S of clauses.

5.28. THEOREM. *Let Γ be a descriptive knowledge base, S the standard clausal form of $\Xi_r \Pi(\overline{\Gamma})$, and let $\mathcal{A}$ be $P(R_H^*(S))$. Then $\mathcal{A}$ is a finite, ground AR of S, and $\widehat{\mathcal{I}}(\Pi^{-1}(\mathcal{A}))$ is a model of Γ.*

PROOF. As noted before, during the derivation only ground unit clauses are generated. To prove that $\mathcal{A}$ is a model of $R_H^*(S)$ we have to show that any ground instance of a clause C in $R_H^*(S)$ is true in $\mathcal{A}$. This obviously holds for any of the positive ground unit clauses in $R_H^*(S)$. Also, any negative ground unit clause $\{\neg A\}$ is true in $\mathcal{A}$. Let $C = \{\neg A_1\sigma, \ldots, \neg A_n\sigma\} \cup D\sigma$, where $D\sigma$ contains no negative literals, be the ground instance of clause in $R_H^*(S)$. If one of the $A_i\sigma$, $1 \leq i \leq n$ is not in $\mathcal{A}$, then C is true. Otherwise, $R_H^*(S)$ contains the unit clauses $\{A_i\sigma\}$, $1 \leq i \leq n$, and we have derived $D\sigma$ at one stage of the derivation. Consequently, one of the split components of $D\sigma$ is in $R_H^*(S)$. The split components of a ground clause are unit ground clauses, for which we have already shown that they are true in $\mathcal{A}$. It follows that C is true in $\mathcal{A}$. Hence $\mathcal{A}$ is a model of $R_H^*(S)$ and also S.

By Theorem 5.27 and the correspondence between predicate symbols and ground terms in the clause set and the symbols in the knowledge base, it follows that $\Pi^{-1}(\mathcal{A})$ is identical to a clash-free knowledge base Γ' derivable from Γ such that no further applications of $\Rightarrow_{TAB}$ are possible. It follows from the results of [Schmidt-Schauß and Smolka 1991] that $\widehat{\mathcal{I}}(\Pi^{-1}(\mathcal{A}))$ is a model of Γ.   □

The finite model property is an immediate consequence of Theorems 5.14 and 5.28.

5.29. COROLLARY. *Let Γ be a descriptive knowledge base. If Γ is satisfiable, then it has a model of finite size.*

6. Related work

There are several extensions and applications of resolution decision procedures not described in the sections above which deserve attention. We just mention two types:

- extensions to clause logic with equality and
- extensions to constraint logic.

Almost all decision classes discussed above become undecidable if the equality predicate is allowed to occur. In particular this holds for the classes $\mathcal{E}_1$, $\mathcal{E}^+$, $\mathcal{S}^+$ and $\mathcal{PVD}$ (but not for the Bernays-Schönfinkel class). Important decidable classes remaining decidable under addition of equality are the (initially extended) Ackermann class and the monadic class. A decision procedure for an extension of the Ackermann class with equality is defined in [Fermüller and Salzer 1993]; it is based on ordered resolution and ordered paramodulation. A modification of the superposition calculus was applied to decide the monadic class with equality [Bachmair, Ganzinger and Waldmann 1993]. Both methods use extension by new constant symbols. In [Fermüller and Salzer 1993] new constant symbols (in equations) are introduced in a preprocessing step in order to guarantee termination; in [Bachmair et al. 1993] the extension by constants is part of the inference rule. This indicates that "ordinary" equational inference systems are not strong enough to handle more complicated equational decision problems. Nevertheless both methods mentioned above are sufficiently efficient to be applied as ordinary theorem provers as well. Although the class $\mathcal{PVD}$ becomes undecidable under addition of equality, it remains decidable if equality appears in ground form only; a corresponding decision procedure can be obtained by positive resolution and ordered paramodulation [Fermüller and Leitsch 1998]. In equational clause logic ordering is even more important than in ordinary clause logic: Note that unrestricted paramodulation does not even terminate on ground problems like $\{f(a) = a, P(a)\}$.

Another important extension of clause logic is that by equational constraints. In [Pichler 1998] it is shown that many clause classes remain decidable under addition of (equational) constraints; the corresponding decision procedures can be obtained from those in pure clause logic in a natural way.

Bibliography

ANDRÉKA H., NÉMETI I. AND VAN BENTHEM J. [1998], 'Modal languages and bounded fragments of predicate logic', *Journal of Philosophical Logic* **27**(3), 217–274.

ANDRÉKA H., VAN BENTHEM J. AND NÉMETI I. [1995], 'Back and forth between modal logic and classical logic', *Bulletin of the IGPL* **3**(5), 685–720.

BAAZ M., EGLY U. AND LEITSCH A. [2001], Normal form transformations, *in* A. Robinson and A. Voronkov, eds, 'Handbook of Automated Reasoning', Vol. I, Elsevier Science, chapter 5, pp. 273–333.

BAAZ M., FERMÜLLER C. AND LEITSCH A. [1994], A non-elementary speed-up in proof length by structural clause form transformation, *in* 'Proceedings of the 9th Annual IEEE Symposium on Logic in Computer Science (LICS'94)', IEEE Computer Society Press, pp. 213–219.

BACHMAIR L. AND GANZINGER H. [1994], 'Rewrite-based equational theorem proving with selection and simplification', *Journal of Logic and Computation* **4**(3), 217–247.

BACHMAIR L., GANZINGER H. AND WALDMANN U. [1993], Superposition with simplification as a decision procedure for the monadic class with equality, *in* 'Computational Logic and Proof Theory, Third Kurt Gödel Colloquium, KGC'93, Brno, Czech Republic, August 1993, *Proceedings*', Vol. 713 of *Lecture Notes in Computer Science*, Springer Verlag, pp. 83–96.

BAUMGARTNER P. AND FURBACH U. [1996], 'Hyper Tableaux. Part I: Proof Procedure and Model Generation', Dagstuhl-Seminar Reports *Disjunctive logic programming and databases: Nonmonotonic aspects*.

Baumgartner P., Furbach U. and Niemelä I. [1996], Hyper Tableaux, in 'Logics in AI, Proc. JELIA'96', Vol. 1126 of *Lecture Notes in Artificial Intelligence*, Springer Verlag, pp. 1–17.

Boy de la Tour T. [1992], 'An optimality result for clause form translation', *J. of Symbolic Computation* 14, 283–301.

Caferra R. and Zabel N. [1992], 'A method for simultaneous search for refutations and models by equational constraint solving', *J. Symbolic Computation* 13, 613–641.

Calvanese D., Giacomo G. D., Lenzerini M. and Nardi D. [2001], Reasoning in expressive description logics, in A. Robinson and A. Voronkov, eds, 'Handbook of Automated Reasoning', Vol. II, Elsevier Science, chapter 23, pp. 1581–1634.

Ceri S., Gottlob G. and Tanca L. [1990], *Logic Programming and Databases*, Springer Verlag.

Church A. [1936], 'A note on the entscheidungsproblem', *J. Symbolic Logic* 1, 40–44.

de Nivelle H. [1995], Ordering Refinements of Resolution, PhD thesis, Delft University of Technology.

de Nivelle H. [1997], A classification of non-liftable orders for resolution, in W. McCune, ed., 'Automated Deduction – CADE-14', Vol. 1249 of *Lecture Notes in Artificial Intelligence*, Springer Verlag, pp. 336–350.

de Nivelle H. [1998a], Deciding the E^+-class by an a posteriori, liftable order, ILLC Report ML-1998-030, University of Amsterdam, The Netherlands.

de Nivelle H. [1998b], Resolution decided the guarded fragment, ILLC report CT-98-01, University of Amsterdam, The Netherlands.

de Nivelle H. [n.d.], A family of resolution decision procedures, in 'Workshop on Logic, Language and Computation, Palo Alto USA, 1998'. To appear.

Denenberg L. and Lewis H. R. [1984], Logical syntax and computational complexity, Vol. 1104 of *Lecture Notes in Mathematics*, Springer Verlag, pp. 101–115.

Donini F. M., Lenzerini M., Nardi D. and Schaerf A. [1994], 'Deduction in concept languages: from subsumption to instance checking', *Journal of Logic and Computation* 4(4), 423–452.

Dreben B. and Goldfarb W. D. [1979], *The Decision Problem*, Addison-Wesley.

Fermüller C. and Leitsch A. [1993], Model building by resolution, in E. B. et al., ed., 'Computer Science Logic, 6th Workshop, CSL'92 San Miniato, Italy, September/Oktober 1992, Selected Papers', Vol. 702 of *Lecture Notes in Computer Science*, Springer Verlag, pp. 134–148.

Fermüller C. and Leitsch A. [1996], 'Hyperresolution and automated model building', *J. Symbolic Computation* 6(2), 173–230.

Fermüller C. and Leitsch A. [1998], 'Decision procedures and model building in equational clause logic', *Logic Journal of the Interest Group in Pure and Applied Logics (IGPL)* 6(1), 17–41.

Fermüller C., Leitsch A., Tammet T. and Zamov N. [1993], *Resolution Methods for the Decision Problem*, Vol. 679 of *Lecture Notes in Artificial Intelligence*, Springer Verlag.

Fermüller C. and Salzer G. [1993], Ordered paramudulation and resolution as decision procedure, in A. Voronkov, ed., 'Logic Programming and Automated Reasoning, 4th International Conference, LPAR'93, St. Petersburg, Russia, July 1993, Proceedings', Vol. 698 of *Lecture Notes in Artificial Intelligence*, Springer Verlag, pp. 122–133.

Frege G. [1884], *Die Grundlagen der Arithmetik. Eine logisch-mathematische Untersuchung über den Begriff der Zahl*, Breslau.

Fujita M., Slaney J. and Bennett F. [1993], Automatic generation of some results in finite algebra, in 'Proc. 13th IJCAI', pp. 52–57.

Ganzinger H. and de Nivelle H. [1999], A superposition decision procedure for the guarded fragment with equality, in 'Proceedings of the 14th Annual IEEE Symposium on Logic in Computer Science (LICS'99)', IEEE Computer Society Press, pp. 295–304.

Gurevich Y. [1973], Formuly s odnim ∀ (formulas with one ∀), in 'Izbrannye Voprosy Algebry i Logiki (Selected Questions in Algebra and Logic—in Memory of A. Mal'cev)', Nauka, Novosibirsk, pp. 97–100.

HILBERT D. AND ACKERMANN W. [1928], *Grundzüge der theoretischen Logik*, Berlin.

HUSTADT U. [1999], Resolution-Based Decision Procedures for Subclasses of First-Order Logic, PhD thesis, Universität des Saarlandes, Saarbrücken, Germany.

HUSTADT U. AND SCHMIDT R. A. [1999a], Issues of decidability for description logics in the framework of resolution, *in* R. Caferra and G. Salzer, eds, 'Automated Deduction in Classical and Non-Classical Logics: Selected Papers', Vol. 1761 of *Lecture Notes in Artificial Intelligence*, Springer Verlag, pp. 192–206.

HUSTADT U. AND SCHMIDT R. A. [1999b], Maslov's class K revisited, *in* H. Ganzinger, ed., 'Proceedings of the 16th International Conference on Automated Deduction (CADE-16)', Vol. 1632 of *Lecture Notes in Artificial Intelligence*, Springer Verlag, pp. 172–186.

HUSTADT U. AND SCHMIDT R. A. [1999c], On the relation of resolution and tableaux proof systems for description logics, *in* T. Dean, ed., 'Proceedings of the 16th International Joint Conference on Artificial Intelligence (IJCAI'99)', Morgan Kaufmann, pp. 110–115.

JOYNER W. H. [1973], Automated Theorem Proving and the Decision Problem, PhD thesis, Harvard University.

JOYNER W. H. [1976], 'Resolution strategies as decision procedures', *J. Association of Computing Machinery* **23**(1), 398–417.

KALLIK B. [1969], A decision procedure based on the resolution method, *in* 'Information Processing 68 (IFIP 68)', Vol. 1, North-Holland Publishing Company, pp. 269–275.

KLINGENBECK S. [1996], Counter Examples in Semantic Tableaux, PhD thesis, University of Karlsruhe.

KOWALSKI R. AND HAYES P. J. [1969], Semantic trees in automated theorem proving, *in* B. Meltzer and D. Michie, eds, 'Machine Intelligence 4', Edinburgh University Press, pp. 87–101.

LEIBNIZ G. W. [1923], Calculus ratiocinator, *in* P. A. der Wissenschaften, ed., 'Sämtliche Schriften und Briefe', Reichel, Darmstadt.

LEITSCH A. [1993], 'Deciding clause classes by semantic clash resolution', *Fundamenta Informaticae* **18**, 163–182.

LÖWENHEIM L. [1915], 'Über Möglichkeiten im Relativkalkül', *Mathematische Annalen* **68**, 169–207.

MANTHEY R. AND BRY F. [1988], Satchmo: a theorem prover implemented in Prolog, *in* '9th Conference on Automated Deduction', Vol. 310 of *Lecture Notes in Computer Science*, Springer Verlag, pp. 415–434.

MASLOV S. Y. [1968], 'The inverse method for establishing deducibility for logical calculi', *Proc. Steklov Inst. Math.* **98**, 25–96.

MASLOV S. Y. [1971], The inverse method for establishing deducibility for logical calculi, *in* V. P. Orevkov, ed., 'The Calculi of Symbolic Logic I: Proceedings of the Steklov Institute of Mathematics edited by I.G. Petrovskiĭ and S. M. Nikol'skiĭ, number 98 (1968)', American Mathematical Society, pp. 25–96.

MCCUNE W. [1995], Otter 3.0 Users Guide, Technical report, Argonne National Laboratory, Argonne (Ill.).

NOLL I. [1980], A note on resolution: How to get rid of factoring without loosing completeness, *in* '5th Conference on Automated Deduction', Vol. 87 of *Lecture Notes in Computer Science*, Springer Verlag, pp. 250–263.

NONNENGART A. AND WEIDENBACH C. [2001], Computing small clause normal forms, *in* A. Robinson and A. Voronkov, eds, 'Handbook of Automated Reasoning', Vol. I, Elsevier Science, chapter 6, pp. 335–367.

OHLBACH H. J. AND SCHMIDT R. A. [1997], 'Functional translation and second-order frame properties of modal logics', *J. of Logic and Computation* **7**(5), 581–603.

OHLBACH H., NONNENGART A., DE RIJKE M. AND GABBAY D. [2001], Encoding two-valued nonclassical logics in classical logic, *in* A. Robinson and A. Voronkov, eds, 'Handbook of Automated Reasoning', Vol. II, Elsevier Science, chapter 21, pp. 1403–1486.

PELTIER N. [1997a], 'Increasing the capabilities of model building by constraint solving with terms with integer exponents', *Journal of Symbolic Computation* **24**, 59–101.

PELTIER N. [1997b], Simplifying formulae in tableaux. Pruning the search space and building models, in 'Proceeding of Tableaux'97', Vol. 1227 of *Lecture Notes in Artificial Intelligence*, Springer Verlag, pp. 313–327.

PICHLER R. [1998], Extending decidable clause classes via constraints, Technical report, Institut f. Computersprachen, TU Wien.

PLAISTED D. A. AND GREENBAUM S. [1986], 'A structure-preserving clause form translation', *J. of Symbolic Computation* **2**, 293–304.

ROBINSON J. A. [1965a], 'The generalized resolution principle', *Intern. Journal of Computer Mathematics* **1**, 227–334.

ROBINSON J. A. [1965b], 'A machine oriented logic based on the resolution principle', *J. Association of Computing Machinery* **12**(1), 23–41.

SCHMIDT R. A. [1997], Optimised Modal Translation and Resolution, PhD thesis, Universität des Saarlandes, Saarbrücken, Germany.

SCHMIDT R. A. [1998], Resolution is a decision procedure for many propositional modal logics, in M. Kracht, M. de Rijke, H. Wansing and M. Zakharyaschev, eds, 'Advances in Modal Logic, Volume 1', Vol. 87 of *Lecture Notes*, CSLI Publications, Stanford, pp. 189–208.

SCHMIDT-SCHAUSS M. AND SMOLKA G. [1991], 'Attributive concept description with complements', *Artificial Intelligence* **48**, 1–26.

SLAGLE J. R. [1967], 'Automatic theorem proving with renamable and semantic resolution', *J. Association of Computing Machinery* **14**(4), 687–697.

SLANEY J. [1992], Finder (finite domain enumerator): notes and guide, Technical report, Australian National University Automated Reasoning Project, Canberra.

STENLUND S. [1971], *Combinators λ–Terms and Proof Theory*, Reidel Publ. Comp.

TAMMET T. [1991], Using resolution for deciding solvable classes and building finite models, in 'Baltic Computer Science', Vol. 502 of *Lecture Notes in Computer Science*, Springer Verlag, pp. 33–64.

TAMMET T. [1992], Resolution Methods for Decision Problems and Finite Model Building, PhD thesis, Chalmers University of Technology and University of Göteborg.

TAMMET T. [1995], Using resolution for extending KL-ONE-type languages, in N. Pissinou, A. Silberschatz, E. K. Park and K. Makki, eds, 'Proceedings of the Fourth International Conference on Information and Knowledge Management (CIKM'95)', ACM Press.

TAMMET T. [1996], Separate orderings for ground and non-ground literals preserve completeness of resolution. Unpublished manuscript.

TAMMET T. [1997], 'Gandalf', *Journal of Automated Reasoning* **18**(2), 199–204.

TURING A. [1936/37], 'On computable numbers with an application to the Entscheidungsproblem', *Proc. of the London Math. Soc.* **Ser. 2**(42), 230–265.

WEIDENBACH C., GAEDE B. AND ROCK G. [1996], SPASS and FLOTTER, version 0.42 (system description, in M. McRobbie and J. Slaney, eds, 'Automated Deduction – CADE-15', Vol. 1104 of *Lecture Notes in Artificial Intelligence*, Springer Verlag, pp. 141–145.

ZAMOV N. K. [1989], 'Maslov's inverse method and decidable classes', *Annals of Pure and Applied Logic* **42**, 165–194.

Index

Part VIII

Implementation

CHAPTER 26

Term Indexing

R. Sekar

I.V. Ramakrishnan

Andrei Voronkov

Contents

1. Introduction

1.1. Motivation

First-order terms constitute the basic representational unit of information in several disciplines of computer science such as automated deduction, term rewriting, symbolic computing, and logic and functional programming. Computation is done by operations germane to manipulating terms such as unification, pattern matching, and subsumption. Often these operations are performed on collections of terms. For instance, in logic programming, deductive databases, and theorem-proving by model elimination we need to select all candidate clause-heads in the program that unify with a given goal. In automated deduction, term rewriting and functional programming, the selection criteria may be based on unifiability (e.g., in resolution), matching (e.g., in normalization) or subsumption. Such retrieval of *candidate terms* that bear a specific relationship to a given *query term* (or set of query terms) is a central operation in automated theorem provers, deductive databases, and logic and functional programming systems. In the absence of techniques for speeding up the retrieval of candidate terms, the time spent in identifying candidates may overshadow the time spent in performing other useful computation. The problem is especially important in contexts where the data sets get large and/or keep growing, as in automated theorem provers and deductive databases. Clearly, a naive approach based on linear search through the set of terms degrades very quickly when large data sets are involved. It is fast enough to start with, but as the term set grows, more and more time is spent in the search for suitable candidates. This leads to a rapid and monotonic drop in performance of the system, as pointed out by Wos [1992]:

> "*After a few CPU minutes of use, a reasoning program typically makes deductions at less than 1% of its ability at the beginning of a run.*"

This factor has led to a lot of research interest in *term indexing* techniques, which refers broadly to techniques for the design and implementation of structures that facilitate rapid retrieval of a set of candidate terms satisfying some property (such as generalizations, instances, unifiability, etc.) from a large collection of terms. Use of term indexing techniques have resulted in dramatic speed improvements, ranging from one to several orders of magnitude, in all major theorem provers, including (in the alphabetical order) BLIKSEM [de Nivelle 2000], E [Schulz 1999], FIESTA [Nieuwenhuis, Rivero and Vallejo 1997], GANDALF [Tammet 1997], OTTER [McCune 1994a, McCune and Wos 1997], SETHEO [Moser, Ibens, Letz, Steinbach, Goller, Schumann and Mayr 1997], SNARK [Stickel, Waldinger, Lowry, Pressburger and Underwood 1994, Stickel, Waldinger and Chaudhry 2000], SPASS [Weidenbach, Gaede and Rock 1996], VAMPIRE [Riazanov and Voronkov 1999], and WALDMEISTER [Hillenbrand, Buch, Vogt and Löchner 1997]. Term indexing techniques enable theorem provers to continue performing deductions at a steady pace, as opposed to the rapid degradation observed in the absence of term indexing. For instance, Wos [1992] observed that "... OTTER makes deductions at the rate of 550 per second in the first few seconds, and at the rate of 460 per second after 19 CPU hours ...".

HIPER runs 20 to 30 times faster on small and moderate sized problems, with the asymptotic speedup approaching infinity [Christian 1993]. The benefits are less dramatic in functional and logic programming, but nevertheless very significant — use of indexing leads to typical improvements in speeds of such programs by between 20% to 200%. Effective term indexing techniques have hence become an integral component of high-performance declarative programming and automated reasoning systems.

Since the early results demonstrating the effectiveness of indexing techniques, research into term indexing has acquired major momentum. In particular a variety of new techniques were invented and implemented for term indexing. One reason for developing so many techniques is that the conditions under which terms are retrieved differ for different operations. For instance in pattern matching we have to retrieve terms that are generalizations of an input term, whereas for generating critical pairs we retrieve terms that unify with the input term. In addition, indexing algorithms tend to exhibit tradeoffs in retrieval speed and space usage. Thus no one indexing technique can cater to all applications.

This paper presents a survey of the main indexing techniques that have been developed in the past. We formulate these techniques within a uniform framework that makes it easier to understand the advantages, disadvantages and trade-offs in developing and using term indexing.

1.2. Formulation of the term indexing problem

The problem of term indexing can be formulated abstractly as follows. Given a set $\mathcal{L}$ (called the *set of indexed terms*), a binary relation R over terms (called the *retrieval condition*) and a term t (called the *query term*), identify the subset $\mathcal{M}$ of $\mathcal{L}$ consisting of all of the terms l such that $R(l, t)$ holds. If $R(l, t)$ holds, we say that l is R-compatible with t, or simply *compatible* when R is clear from the context.

In some applications it is enough to search for a superset of $\mathcal{M}$, i.e., to also retrieve terms l for which $R(l, t)$ does not hold, but we would naturally like to minimize the number of such terms in order to increase the effectiveness of indexing. In other applications, it is acceptable to retrieve only some R-compatible indexed terms, i.e., a subset of $\mathcal{M}$. If the set of the retrieved terms is guaranteed to coincide with the set of R-compatible terms, then the indexing technique is said to perform *perfect filtering*. Otherwise, indexing performs *imperfect filtering*.

In the context of term indexing, it is usually the case that the relation R of interest is such that $R(s, t)$ holds if there exists substitutions σ and β such that $s\sigma = t\beta$, and furthermore, these substitutions satisfy certain additional constraints. For instance, if σ and β are constrained to be renaming substitutions, the relation $R(s, t)$ simply becomes a variant check. Likewise, if β is constrained to be the empty substitution, the relation $R(s, t)$ becomes an instance check. In addition to identifying R-compatible terms, we sometimes need to compute the substitutions σ and β as well.

The principal parameters associated with term indexing are:

- *Retrieval condition*, expressed by the relation R that determines the subset $\mathcal{M}$ of the indexed terms that need to be identified. The most common examples of retrieval condition are unification, matching, subsumption, etc.
- *Retrieval mode*, which determines whether the entire set $\mathcal{M}$ is returned, or whether the elements of this set are returned one at a time. In some cases we are only interested in nonemptiness of the candidate set.

1.3. Early research in indexing

Traditional notions of indexing. In very general terms, *indexing* refers to the ability to quickly filter out a set of candidate elements that satisfy specific criteria from a (typically) large data set. One of the oldest examples include card indexes in libraries, where the data set consists of all the books in the library, and the selection criteria may be based on author names, titles or keywords. Another example is that of indexes in books, where the data set includes all the pages in the book, and the selection criteria is based on the appearance of keywords in a page. A more formal treatment of indexing was developed in the context of databases, where the data set consisted of all the records in the database, and the selection criteria were based on the values of one or more of the fields in the record.

This paper deals with the same general problem as captured by the above examples, but in the context of automated reasoning, declarative programming and deductive databases. In these contexts, the principal data of interest are *first-order terms*, which are much more expressive and complex as compared to the simple data values that arise in text indexing or databases. Whereas selection criteria are traditionally based on single attributes (i.e., retrieval of all records that have the specified value of an attribute), for terms, it is based on complex operations such as unification and matching on these terms. In addition, these operations may have to be performed in the context of an equational theory, the most common such theory arising in the context of AC symbols. Finally, we may be interested in multiterm indexing problems discussed later.

Attribute-based indexing. In *attribute-based indexing*, we map some features of a term t into a simple-valued (say, integer-valued) attribute a_t. Indexing is then based on identifying a relation R_A on attributes of t and s such that $R(s,t) \Rightarrow R_A(a_s, a_t)$ (or $R_A(a_s, a_t) \Rightarrow R(s,t)$). For instance, if the retrieval relation is *inst*, then the attribute can be the number of function symbols in a term. (Observe that if t is an instance of s then the number of function symbols in t is greater than or equal to that of s.) We consider several examples of attribute-based indexing below:

- *Matching pretest* makes use of the fact that for a term t to be an instance of l, the number of symbols in t is greater than or equal to the number of symbols in l.
- *Outline indexing* makes use of the fact that t and l are unifiable only if they agree at all nonvariable positions. It employs a bit-vector to encode the nonvariable positions and the corresponding symbols [Henschen and Naqvi 1981].

- *Superimposed codewords*: the attribute is obtained by logical-or operations on the bit representations of function symbols at specified positions within a term [Wise and Powers 1984, Ramamohanarao and Shepherd 1986]

Attribute-based indexing is based on the assumption that a relation involving simple-valued attributes is much easier to compute than performing term matching or unification. Thus, it can be used as a coarse filter for the likely candidates. However, it has several disadvantages. Firstly, the accuracy of attribute-based indexing is typically low. Second, if the index set is large, the coarse filter, while an improvement over the naive approach of matching or unifying with every term in the indexed set, may still be inefficient as it may involve checking the relation R_A for each term in the set.[1] Due to these disadvantages, we will focus on symbol-based indexing (defined below) for the rest of this paper.

Function symbol based indexing. The retrieval condition is typically based on identification of a unifying substitution between the query and indexed terms, with various constraints placed on the substitutions. Thus, the question of whether the retrieval condition holds between the query term and an indexed term is determined by the function symbols in both these terms. For instance, in every position where both the query term and candidate term contain a function symbol, these symbols must be identical. Therefore we can make use of some or all of the function symbols in the indexed terms in determining the candidate terms. Most known term indexing techniques are based on this observation, and we refer to such techniques broadly as *function symbol based indexing*, or simply as *symbol-based indexing*. The rest of this paper presents a survey of some of the most important symbol-based indexing techniques.

1.4. Overview of organization

This paper is organized into five parts.

1. In Section 2, we provide the requisite background, including notations and definitions. We formulate the term indexing problem and its context. In Section 3 we outline the basic representation and implementation techniques related to terms and indexing.
2. In Section 4 we show how term indexing can be formulated in terms of string matching. The common framework enables us to understand many indexing methods as instances of the generic framework. The framework also makes it easier to compare and contrast known approaches. Most importantly, the framework distills out essential characteristics of different techniques as elaborated in Section 16.

---

[1] It would be desirable to choose attributes and the relation on the attribute such that the candidate terms can be identified quickly, without having to try all of terms in the indexed set. For instance, in the case of the *inst* relation, we can store the index set as an array (or tree) that is sorted on the value of the size attribute. We can then perform a search in $O(\log n)$ time to identify all terms that are larger than the query term.

3. The third part of this paper presents a survey of many indexing techniques: path indexing (Section 5), discrimination trees (Section 6), adaptive automata (Section 7), automata-driven indexing (Section 8), substitution trees (Section 10), unification factoring (Section 12), code trees (Section 9), and context trees (Section 11). To keep this part down to a reasonable size, not all known methods are surveyed. Instead, we have made an effort to capture diverse methods. Particular emphasis have been given to works that provide a formal treatment of space/time complexity and optimality.

4. The fourth part of this paper treats some advanced indexing techniques: multi-term indexing (Section 13), issues in perfect filtering (Section 14), and indexing modulo the AC-theory (Section 15).

5. The fifth (and the last) part of this paper summarizes the indexing techniques considered so far, discusses implementations of indexing in logic and functional programming, and also in theorem provers, and discusses new directions for term indexing. In Section 16, we summarize the indexing techniques considered so far by providing a list of "basic elements" of term indexing techniques. Many of these elements are in fact based on concepts well known in string-matching automata. The common framework developed in Section 4 enables us to lift these concepts from the domain of string matching to the domain of term-indexing. We describe each of these elements and the issues and trade-offs in employing them in indexing methods. We also provide a summary of how these elements have been combined in indexing methods proposed so far. In Section 17 we briefly describe indexing as implemented in some declarative programming systems and theorem provers. In Section 18 we sketch possible new directions for indexing.

2. Background

2.1. *Notations and definitions*

We begin this section with the notations and concepts used in the rest of this paper. We assume familiarity with the basic concept of a *term*. The symbols in a term are drawn from a nonempty *alphabet* Σ and a countable set of variables $\mathcal{V}$. A term is *ground* if it contains no occurrences of variables. With each symbol s in the alphabet is associated a nonnegative integer, called the *arity* of s, denoted $arity(s)$. We assume that the terms are well-formed, i.e., every symbol in the term has the correct number of arguments, as given by the arity of the symbol. We will use a, b, c, d and f to denote nonvariable symbols (which are sometimes referred to as *function symbols*) and x, y, z (with or without subscripts and primes) to denote variables. We also denote variables using a wildcard symbol $*$, with or without subscripts. The symbol $*$ written without subscripts will have two uses, depending on context. In some contexts it means an occurrence of a unique variable. For example, $f(x, x, *, *)$ denotes any term of the form $f(x, x, y, z)$, where y, z are distinct variables different from x. In other contexts it will be used as a wildcard symbol denoting any variable.

root(*t*) denotes the *top symbol* of *t*, i.e., the symbol appearing at the root of a term *t*. We will also (somewhat ambiguously) use the wildcard ? in terms. This wildcard will always denote a term whose top symbol is different from a certain set of function symbols, depending on the context. In some sections, the symbol $\neq$ is used as a wildcard symbol.

In order to refer to subterms of a term, we develop the following concept of a *position*[2]:

2.1. DEFINITION *(Position)*. A *position* is either the empty string Λ, or *p.i*, where *p* is a position and *i* an integer. The notions of a *position in a term* and the *subterm of t at a position p*, denoted *t/p*, are defined as follows.

- Λ is a position in *t* and $t/\Lambda = t$;
- If $t/p = f(t_1, \ldots, t_n)$, where $n > 0$, then $p.1, \ldots, p.n$ are positions in *t* and $t/p.i = t_i$, for all $i \in \{1, \ldots, n\}$.

Instead of $\Lambda.i$ we will write simply *i*. We use $\mathcal{P}$ to denote the set of all positions. The notation $\mathcal{P}(t)$ denotes all the positions in a term *t*, and $\mathcal{P}_v(t)$ and $\mathcal{P}_f(t)$ denote the subset of these positions at which *t* has variables and function symbols respectively. The set $\mathcal{P}_v(t)$ is called the *fringe* of *t*. We use $t[s]_p$ to denote the term obtained from *t* by replacing t/p by *s*.

We illustrate these concepts using the term $t = f(a(x), b(a(y), c))$. Here, $t/\Lambda = t$, $t/2 = b(a(y), c)$, $t/2.1 = a(y)$, and $t/2.2 = c$. The term $t[c]_2 = f(a(x), c)$ is obtained by replacing the second argument of *f* by (the term) *c*. The fringe of *t* is $\{1.1, 2.1.1\}$.

A *substitution* is a mapping from variables to terms. Given a substitution β, we denote by $t\beta$ the term obtained by replacing every variable *x* in *t* by $\beta(x)$. We say that *t* is an *instance* of *s* if $s\beta = t$ for some substitution β. If *t* is an instance of *u* then we write $u \leq t$ and call *u* a *prefix* of *t*. The inverse of $\leq$ relation is denoted by $\geq$.

We denote by $\{x_1 \mapsto t_1, \ldots, x_n \mapsto t_n\}$ the substitution β defined as follows:

$$\beta(x) = \begin{cases} t_i, & \text{if } x = x_i; \\ x, & \text{otherwise.} \end{cases}$$

For example, for the term $t = f(a(x), b(y, z))$ and the substitution $\beta = \{x \mapsto b(x', x''), y \mapsto c\}$ we have $t\beta = f(a(b(x', x'')), b(c, z))$.

Terms *t* and *s* are called *unifiable*, if there exists a substitution β such that $s\beta = t\beta$.

2.2. The problem context

In this section, we describe the term indexing problem in the context of theorem proving, logic programming and deductive databases, and functional programming.

---

[2]The terminology *occurrence* and *path* are sometimes used in the literature to denote the same concept.

2.2.1. Theorem proving

First-order theorem provers can generally be divided into two kinds. The first kind is the *saturation-based* provers that implement various kinds of resolution or the inverse method. The second kind can be characterized as the *tableau-based* provers that implement semantic tableaux or model elimination.

Saturation-based provers. Examples are FIESTA [Nieuwenhuis et al. 1997], GANDALF [Tammet 1997], OTTER [McCune 1994b], SPASS [Weidenbach et al. 1996], VAMPIRE [Riazanov and Voronkov 1999], and WALDMEISTER [Hillenbrand et al. 1997]. Such provers generate new clauses from a given set of clauses using suitable inference rules (binary resolution, hyperresolution, etc.) and add the new clauses to the set of already inferred ones (i.e., *saturate* a set of clauses under applications of the inference rules). More information on saturation-based provers can be found in [Lusk 1992, McCune 1994b, Riazanov and Voronkov 2000] and [Weidenbach 2001] (Chapter 27 of this Handbook).

In addition to inference rules, saturation-based provers also use *simplification rules* which either "simplify" clauses in the search space (i.e., replace them by "simpler" clauses) or remove them from the search space completely. There is a variety of retrieval conditions used to identify applicability of inference or simplification rules, including instance, generalization, unifiability, miltiliteral forward and backward subsumption, and variance check.

To give the reader an example of the number of clauses processed by one run, we give figures obtained by a 270 seconds run of VAMPIRE on the problem LCL-129-1.p of the PTTP library [Sutcliffe and Suttner 1998] using a 230MHz SPARC processor. During the run 8,272,207 clauses were generated, of which 5,203,928 were not included in the search space because their weights exceeded the specified weight limit. Of the remaining 3,068,279 clauses, at the end of the run 8,053 were retained, and 3,060,226 were rejected by *forward subsumption* (i.e., identified as instances of other clauses in the search space). Even if we assume that all the runtime was spent for checking subsumption, this means that VAMPIRE was performing, on the average, over 10,000 subsumption-checks per second, each of these checks identifies if a clause is an instance of several thousand other clauses in the search space. An example term of weight 16 (i.e., with 16 symbols) participating in the proof is $t(e(e(x_0, e(x_1, x_2)), e(e_i x_0, e(x_3, x_2)), e(x_1, x_3))))$. Most clauses had weights between 20 and 24, but there were some clauses with weights as high as 40. Doing such a large number of subsumption-checks per second without using term indexing is hardly possible.

Tableau-based provers. The most known tableau-based prover is SETHEO [Letz, Schumann, Bayerl and Bibel 1992, Moser et al. 1997]. Such provers start with a set of input clauses, and construct a tree-like proof object, whose nodes are literals or clauses. At each step of the algorithm, one selects a node in the tree and applies some inference rule that produces a set of children of the selected node. Usually, this inference rule is resolution against one of the input clauses, and the set of the input clauses does not change during the run.

This can be implemented in the same way as SLD-resolution rule is implemented in logic programming (as observed by Stickel [1988]), because every input clause $A_1 \vee \ldots A_n$ can be regarded as n Prolog clauses, each one of the form

$$A_i \; :\!- \; \neg A_1, \ldots, \neg A_{i-1}, \neg A_{i+1}, \ldots, \neg A_n.$$

Another commonly exploited inference rule is *resolution against a lemma*, i.e., a previously derived literal. The set of lemmas is dynamically changing and can be large. In addition to these rules, backward and forward subsumption on the set of lemmas can be performed.

The performance of the tableau-based provers can drastically improve if all the main operations (resolutions against an input clause and against a lemma; and subsumption on lemmas) are implemented using term indexing.

2.2.2. Logic programming and deductive databases

In *logic programming languages* such as Prolog and *deductive databases*, a program is defined by a sequence of *clauses*. The evaluation of such programs may proceed in either a top-down fashion, similar in operation to tableau-based provers, or in a bottom-up fashion, which is similar to saturation-based provers.

In top-down evaluation, the evaluator identifies the substitutions which unify a literal in the goal clause with the heads of the program clauses. After this, the literal is replaced by the terms in the body of a unifying clause. Thus, the indexing problem in this context is based on unifiability of a term with one of the clause heads. When a subgoal is ground, we can make use of term matching, which is more efficient than unification. (Groundness can often be deduced using a procedure called *mode analysis*.) When goals are known to be ground, the indexing problem is one of identifying clause heads that are generalizations of the subgoals.

Tabled logic programming combines the goal-directed nature of top-down evaluation with the stronger completeness properties of bottom-up evaluation. Operationally, a tabled evaluator operates like a top-down evaluator, but remembers the results of previous evaluation to eliminate repeated computations involving any one subgoal. Thus, in addition to the problem of identifying unifiable clause heads, we are also interested in identifying if a new subgoal has been encountered earlier. In the simplest case, this may be determined by checking if the new goal is a *variant* of a previously encountered subgoal. In a more general case, we are interested in identifying subgoals that are *subsumed* by previously evaluated subgoals.

2.2.3. Functional programming and term rewriting

In *functional programming* and *term rewriting*, we are interested in computing the *normal form* of a term t with respect to a set of rewrite rules. Specifically, we identify a rewrite rule $l \to r$ such that its left-hand side l is a generalization of a subterm t' of t. We then replace t' in t by the corresponding instance of r. This process is repeated until we obtain a term t'' that contains no instances of any left-hand side. Thus, one of the main indexing problem of interest here is that of retrieving terms that are generalizations of a given term. Moreover, it is important to develop indexing strategies that can select not only candidate left-hand sides of rewrite rules, but also subterms within the input term where reductions are to be applied.

2.2.4. Summary of retrieval problems

In summary, we are interested in the following retrieval problems:

- atoms *unifiable* with a given atom (logic programming, deductive databases, different resolution rules);
- subgoals that are *variants* of previously attempted subgoals (tabled logic programming and deductive databases) [Chen and Warren 1996, Ramakrishnan 1991], naming in splitting without backtracking [Riazanov and Voronkov 2001];
- atoms that are *instances* of previously computed atoms (tabled logic programming, deductive databases [Rao, Ramakrishnan and Ramakrishnan 1996], forward subsumption and demodulation in resolution-based theorem provers);
- atoms that are *generalizations* of previously computed or stored atoms (functional programming, optimization in logic programming when predicates are known to be called with bound arguments, backward subsumption and demodulation in resolution-based theorem provers).

For some of these retrieval problems, their multiliteral analogues exists (e.g., simultaneous unifiability, forward and backward subsumption, and the clause variance problem). This leads to *multiterm indexing* discussed in Section 13.

2.3. Term indexing operations

Retrieval of candidate terms. Given a query term t and the indexed set $\mathcal{L}$, the retrieval operation is concerned with the identification of the subset $\mathcal{M}$ of those terms in $\mathcal{L}$ that have the specified relation R to t. The retrieval relation R identifies those terms $l \in \mathcal{L}$ that need to be selected. Some of the retrieval conditions discussed above are:

$$
\begin{aligned}
unif(l, t) &\Leftrightarrow \exists \sigma \; l\sigma = t\sigma; \\
inst(l, t) &\Leftrightarrow \exists \sigma \; l = t\sigma; \\
gen(l, t) &\Leftrightarrow \exists \sigma \; l\sigma = t; \\
var(l, t) &\Leftrightarrow \exists \sigma \; (l\sigma = t \wedge \sigma \text{ is a renaming substitution}).
\end{aligned}
$$

More complex conditions specific to indexing on multiliteral clauses will be introduced later.

Index construction and maintenance. In order to support rapid retrieval of candidate terms, we need to process the indexed set into a data structure called the *index*. *Index construction* operation is concerned with the initial construction of this data structure for a given operation R and indexed set $\mathcal{L}$. After the initial construction, we may need to make changes to the indexed set via insertion or deletion of terms. *Index maintenance* operations start with an index for a set $\mathcal{L}$, and incrementally construct an index for another set $\mathcal{L}'$ that is obtained by insertion or deletion of terms in or from $\mathcal{L}$.

Different choices of indexing techniques typically reflect a different trade-off among the costs for performing each of the above three tasks (namely, retrieval, index construction, and index maintenance). For instance, in the context of functional and logic programming, the indexed set is essentially fixed and so there are no index maintenance operations. Moreover, the index is constructed at compile-time. Thus the indexing techniques are aimed at optimizing the retrieval time, possibly at the expense of increasing the cost of index construction and maintenance. In some of the other applications such as tabled logic programming, insertions in the index may be frequent, but deletions do not occur. In other applications, such as automated theorem proving, the indexed set is generated at runtime and/or changes frequently, so it is necessary to minimize the costs of all three tasks.

2.4. Variations in term indexing operations

Nonlinearity. In general, the query and indexed terms may be *nonlinear*, i.e., may have repeated occurrences of variables. The multiple occurrences may occur all within one of the two terms involved, or a single variable may occur in both the query term and an indexed term. In either case, it is necessary to check the consistency among the substitutions received by multiple occurrences of the same variable. For instance, consider the problem of determining if the term $f(t_1, t_2)$ is an instance of $f(x, x)$. In this case, the first occurrence of x gets t_1 as its matching substitution, whereas the second occurrence of x gets t_2 as the substitution. In order for $f(t_1, t_2)$ to be an instance of $f(x, x)$, these two substitutions for x must be consistent, i.e., t_1 must be the same as t_2. Consistency checking is typically an expensive operation, and unless treated very carefully, consideration of nonlinearity at the indexing stage can lead to performance degradation. As such, many techniques ignore nonlinearity at the indexing stage, and rely on a post-processing step to carry out the consistency checks. Other methods postpone all of the consistency checking operations after the less expensive operations that merely check local term structure. For these reasons, we will deal mainly with linear terms towards the beginning of this paper. We will moreover assume that no variables are shared between the query term and indexed terms.

Equational theories. The retrieval condition may be based on an *equational theory* E, e.g., whether the query term t is an instance of a term from $\mathcal{L}$ with respect to E, i.e., there exists a term $l \in \mathcal{L}$ and a substitution β such that $E \vdash l\beta = t$. For instance, in the context of automated reasoning, we are interested in matching and unification in the presence of associative-commutative operators. In lazy functional programming, we are interested in matching in the context of the equational theory given by the program.

Priorities. In many contexts, the terms in the indexed set are associated with *priorities*, which need to be respected by the retrieval operation. In some contexts, such as functional programming, we may be interested in retrieving only the highest priority patterns, i.e., such terms l that

$$R(l, t) \wedge \forall l' \in \mathcal{L} \ (priority(l') > priority(l) \Rightarrow \neg R(l', t)).$$

In other contexts such as logic programming and deductive databases, the retrieval operation may be required to return candidate terms from $\mathcal{L}$ in a decreasing order of priority. Priorities arise in the context of automated reasoning as well, where they may be used to encode heuristics aimed at generating "simpler," "more general" or "more useful" theorems first. For instance, in completion procedures we may prefer to generate critical pairs from "smaller" terms before using "larger" terms.

Computing substitutions. In many applications, we are not only interested in identifying the candidate terms from the indexed set, but also in identifying a substitution or substitutions under which the query term and the candidate term satisfy the retrieval condition. In theory, computation of such substitutions can be performed after indexing, but this approach increases the post-processing cost after identification of the candidate terms. As such, many indexing techniques are designed to compute the substitutions as part of the indexing operation and return them. The *one-at-a-time* retrieval mode is particularly suited for such techniques.

Many-to-many operations. *Many-to-many* indexing problems arise in the context of operations that are performed collectively on groups of terms. Some of the most common examples are multiliteral subsumption, hyperresolution, and unit-resulting resolution. Substantial speedups have been reported by using many-to-many indexing operations in these cases, as compared to just using one-to-many indexing. In particular, the many-to-many problems require that we deal with a set Q of query terms, rather than a single query term.

Since the term "many-to-many" is ambiguous and may refer to an operation on two indexes, while all the above mentioned operations require one indexed set of terms and several query terms, we will use the term *multiterm* indexing. We postpone the discussion of multiterm indexing until Section 13.

Subterm-based retrieval conditions. Sometimes, we may be interested in considering all subterms of the query term as query terms themselves. For instance, in term rewriting, we want to identify an indexed term l (which corresponds to the lhs of a rewrite rule) and a *subterm* t/p of the given term such that t/p is an instance of l.

Similarly, we may want to index on all of the subterms of a given set of indexed terms. For example, in *completion procedures* or *paramodulation-based theorem proving* (see [Nieuwenhuis and Rubio 2001], Chapter 7 of this Handbook) we have to

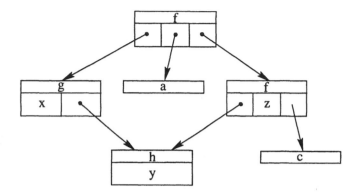

Figure 1: DAG representation of the term $f(g(x, h(y)), a, f(h(y), z, c))$

identify all subterms of given terms that are unifiable with, or instances of, a query term.

Although all of these cases can be handled either by multiterm indexing or by a straightforward inclusion of all subterms in the index, it would be advantageous to exploit the fact that a term and its subterms share common structures in order to develop space and time-efficient indexing algorithms.

Consideration of subterm-based retrieval conditions is beyond the scope of this paper.

3. Data structures for representing terms and indexes

3.1. Data structures for representing terms

There are several data structures for representing terms. We present a short summary of three such structures: conventional representations using trees or DAGs, flatterm representation and Prolog term representation.

3.1.1. Conventional representation of terms

Given the inductive definition of terms, the most obvious way to represent them is to use trees or *directed acyclic graphs (DAGs)*. The root node of the tree representation for a term t contains the root symbol of t and pointers to nodes that correspond to immediate subterms of t. These pointers may be stored either in an array or as a linked list. The conventional representation is a versatile one and readily supports common operations such as traversing a term in different ways, skipping subterms, etc.

An example of a DAG representation is shown in Figure 1. As compared to a tree representation, a DAG representation presents an opportunity to *share subterms*. Such sharing can contribute to as much as an exponential decrease in the size of the term. The benefits of sharing are significant in practice — for instance, in term rewriting and functional programming, rules such as $f(x) \rightarrow g(x,x)$ occur commonly, and a tree-representation would require duplication of the (arbitrarily large) term that appears as the substitution for x in the term being reduced. In contrast, using a dag representation, we can achieve the same effect by duplicating the pointer to the substitution, without having to duplicate the substitution.

Some systems employ dag representations with *aggressive sharing*, also called *perfect sharing* where we ensure that only a single copy of a term exists, regardless of the number of contexts in which it occurs. Aggressive sharing is used in some theorem provers, such as OTTER and VAMPIRE, especially for long-lived terms (terms that are *kept*). Aggressive sharing also simplifies nonlinear matching, since the task of consistency checking across multiple substitutions for the same variable simplifies to comparing the pointers to all the respective terms, rather than checking whether the substitutions are structurally identical. Particularly efficient representations have been developed for such aggressive sharing in the context of the congruence closure problem [Nelson and Oppen 1980]. The overhead of aggressive sharing is typically too high in programming applications such as functional and logic programming systems. However, in some contexts, a further optimized representation known as *hashed cons* has been found to be useful.

3.1.2. Flatterms

Flatterm is a representation for terms introduced in [Christian 1989, Christian 1993]. Flatterm is a linear structure that corresponds to a linked-list representation of the nodes visited in a preorder traversal of a term. In this paper, we will use *preorder traversal* as synonym for depth-first, left-to-right inspection of the subterms. To facilitate skipping of subterms, a node n corresponding to a subterm has pointers to the node that follows immediately after all of the children of n. The flatterm representation of the term $f(g(a, h(y)), h(y), x)$ is shown below, where the following notations are used:

Symbol: symbol at the current node
Next: next node in preorder traversal of term
Prev: previous node in preorder traversal
End: last node (in preorder traversal) in the subtree rooted at the current node.

Observe that most operations on terms require some form of traversal of a term. If we restrict ourselves to a preorder traversal, then flatterm provides a more efficient way to traverse the term as compared to conventional terms. Moreover, each node in a flatterm has a fixed structure with the same number of fields. This implies that the sizes of all nodes are identical, which, in turn, simplifies memory management. (In contrast, the size of a node in a conventional term depends on the number of children of the node.) The constant size of the nodes means also that they can be put in an array, which eliminates the need in the **Next** and **Prev** references and leads to a smaller memory consumption and faster traversal.

Flatterms are particularly efficient when used in conjunction with left-to-right discrimination trees (see Section 6). They are not well-suited in situations where

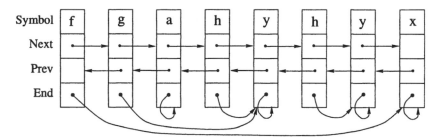

Figure 2: Flatterm representation of $f(g(a, h(y)), h(y), x)$

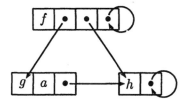

Figure 3: Prolog representation of $f(g(a, h(y)), h(y), x)$

the traversal order may be different from left-to-right. Another difficulty is that this representation does not support structure sharing. Flatterms are used in several theorem provers to represent query terms, for which structure is unimportant.

3.1.3. Prolog terms

Prolog uses an optimized version of the conventional term representation, where each node is tagged as a *const*, *fun* or *ref* node, which are used to store constants (i.e., function symbols with arity zero), function symbols (with arity > 0), and pointers to other terms respectively. The variable nodes are represented as references to the node itself, which enables particularly efficient implementation of variable binding via setting of the pointer to the term to be bounded. Note that neither the var nodes, nor the const nodes have any children. Hence Prolog implementations store such values within the corresponding parent nodes. Finally, the function nodes are represented using variable-sized nodes, with both the function symbol and references to the children represented using the same array. The Prolog representation of terms is illustrated in Figure 3.

3.2. Variable banks

There are situation where the same term may be used with different sets of variables during the same retrieval operation. For example, the (indexed) literal $f(y, g(y))$ can be used n times for performing a hyperresolution inference with the clause

$$\neg f(x_0, x_1) \lor \neg f(x_1, x_2) \lor \neg f(x_{n-1}, x_n) \lor h(x_0, x_n).$$

To perform this hyperresolution inference, one needs to use n copies of $f(y, g(y))$ with y instantiated by the terms $x_0, g(x_0), \ldots, g^{n-1}(x_0)$.

A typical implementation technique for such situations is the use of *variable banks*. Suppose that we have an indexed term l with the variables $y_1, \ldots, y_n$ which can be used several times with different instantiations for $y_1, \ldots, y_n$. Then we create several copies of the sequence $y_1, \ldots, y_n$:

$$y_{11}, \quad \cdots \quad , y_{1n},$$
$$\cdots$$
$$y_{m1}, \quad \cdots \quad , y_{mn}.$$

Each copy is called a variable bank. When, during retrieval, we perform kth operation with the index, we use the variable bank $y_{k1}, \ldots, y_{kn}$ instead of $y_1, \ldots, y_n$. To increase efficiency, variable banks are usually allocated only once as an array, and each variable bank is also implemented as an array containing a large enough number of variables.

Variable banks are used (under different names) in OTTER, FIESTA, and VAMPIRE. The term "variable banks" is taken over from [Rivero 2000].

3.3. Data structures for representing indexes

There are two broad categories of representations for indexes. The first category consists of representations similar to finite-state automata or tries, which are "interpreted" at retrieval time. The second category consists of representations that use some form of code that is executed in order to perform retrieval.

3.3.1. Automata-based representations

The *automata-like representations* deal with issues very similar to those that arise in *string-matching automata*, and these issues have been studied well in the literature. Perhaps the most important aspect is the representation for outward transitions from a state. A variety of techniques have been studied that attempt to minimize the storage needed for representing these transitions, yet try to achieve $O(1)$ expected time for identifying the applicable transition based on the symbol in the input string (or term). The different data structures studied are:

- *Array:* fast, but high memory consumption since the number of outward transitions may be very small compared to the alphabet size.

- *Linked list*: economical in terms of space, but slow for making transitions
- *Hash table:* storage requirements slightly more than linked list representation, but significantly faster. However, collisions can become a problem.
- *Jump table:* specialized data-structures that combine the benefits of array representation with low memory requirements [Dawson, Ramakrishnan and Ramakrishnan 1995].

In jump tables, the symbol's value is directly used as an index, as in the case of the array representation. However, to reduce the storage requirements, the tables for different automaton states are "overlapped." The problem of optimizing the space requirement is NP-complete, but effective heuristics have been developed that work well in practice [Dawson, Ramakrishnan and Ramakrishnan 1995].

3.3.2. Code trees

It is usual in automated deduction to compile the query term into a code that is executed on the index. If the compilation time is small compared to the retrieval time, this compilation pays off.

It is less usual to compile the index itself to a code that will be executed on the query term in order to perform retrieval. We may compile the code for a real machine, as for functional programming language compilers, or for a virtual machine, as in the case of Prolog's WAM (see, e.g., [Aït-Kaci 1991]). In the case of automated deduction, the dynamic nature of indexed sets and the modern computer architecture work against a fully compiled approach, so a virtual machine is the only alternative. Such an approach to indexing is demonstrated in [Voronkov 1994, Voronkov 1995, Riazanov and Voronkov 2000*b*], where the index is represented as a structure called *code tree*. Code trees will be discussed in Section 9.

4. A common framework for indexing

Symbol-based indexing techniques can be described abstractly as follows. Candidate terms selected are those that have identical function symbols as the (subset of) positions in the query and the indexed terms. In order to select the candidate terms, we need to examine these subset of positions in the query term in some order. In effect, the whole process can be viewed as constructing a string of symbols from the query term, and identify if this string "matches" the string constructed from the indexed terms. Thus, most symbol-based indexing techniques can be unified under the broad theme of *string matching based indexing*.

Given this analogy between string matching and term indexing, we can readily see the applicability of previously known techniques for string-matching, such as the use of trie and finite-state automata based data structures for fast matching. Specifically, we can build a trie or an automaton consisting of all the strings obtained from the indexed terms. At retrieval time, a string corresponding to the query term is constructed (implicitly or explicitly) and "run through" the automaton to identify the strings in the automaton that are compatible with this string. Finally, the compatible strings in the automaton are mapped into the corresponding candidate set of terms. The key advantage of using an automaton (or a trie) representation is that those operations that are common for matching against multiple strings can be "factored out." This advantage results in substantial speedups over a naive approach that would repeatedly test the query term against each one of the indexed terms.

In this section we first develop the concepts needed to relate string matching operations and the corresponding relations among terms. We then proceed to describe the basic techniques, many of which are drawn from string-matching, that can be used to improve the speed of retrieval and/or reduce the size of the index. Our description of indexing techniques in subsequent sections will draw upon the concepts developed in this section. This approach enables one to understand many known indexing methods as instances of a more generic set of techniques, thus shedding light on the fundamental advantages and disadvantages of each of these methods and making it easier to compare and contrast them.

4.1. Position strings

In order to make use of string-matching techniques, we first need to convert the terms into a string representation. One way to do this is to write out the symbols occurring in a term in some sequence, thus arriving at a string. However, such an approach may lose some of the information captured by the term structure. To preserve this information, we can capture each symbol in a term together with its position in the string. For instance, we can represent the term $f(a, g(b, c))$ as a string

$$\langle \Lambda, f \rangle \langle 1, a \rangle \langle 2, g \rangle \langle 2.1, b \rangle \langle 2.2, c \rangle. \tag{4.1}$$

Rather than generating a single string from a term, we may choose to generate multiple strings. For instance, we may generate the following set of strings from the same term:

$$\{\langle \Lambda, f \rangle \langle 1, a \rangle, \langle \Lambda, f \rangle \langle 2, g \rangle \langle 2.1, b \rangle, \langle \Lambda, f \rangle \langle 2, g \rangle \langle 2.2, c \rangle\}. \tag{4.2}$$

We refer to strings (4.1) and those in (4.2) as *position strings*, or *p-strings* for short. Intuitively, a p-string is simply a string representation of some term. More formally,

4.1. DEFINITION *(Position strings)*. A *position string* (abbreviated *p-string*) S over an alphabet Σ is a nonempty string of the form $\langle p_1, s_1 \rangle \langle p_2, s_2 \rangle \cdots \langle p_n, s_n \rangle$ where $p_i \in \mathcal{P}$ and $s_i \in \Sigma \cup \mathcal{V}$ such that:

- for all $1 \leq i, j \leq n$, if p_i is a proper prefix of p_j then $i < j$;
- there exists a term t, called the *characteristic term for S* such that
  - for every $1 \leq i \leq n$ we have $root(t/p_i) = s_i$; and
  - $p_1, \ldots, p_n$ are exactly the set of positions in t.

Intuitively, we can view the positions $p_1, \ldots, p_n$ in a p-string as capturing a way to traverse a term, with $s_1, \ldots, s_n$ being the symbols visited in this traversal order. If the order of traversal is fixed *a priori* (e.g., we use a depth-first or breadth-first traversal order), then the position information becomes redundant. If we do not want to constrain ourselves with any one fixed way of visiting symbols in a term, then the position information is important.

In a term structure, it is typically meaningless and/or impossible to visit a node before first visiting all of its parents. This is the reason for imposing the first condition in the above definition. Secondly, we want the p-string to represent a term, which we call the characteristic term. Note that the characteristic term is unique, up to replacement of variables by other variables.

Sometimes, we may abbreviate p-strings in such a way that we drop one or more variables from them. For instance, we abbreviate the p-string

$$\langle \Lambda, f \rangle \langle 1, * \rangle \langle 2, g \rangle \langle 2.1, * \rangle \langle 2.2, c \rangle$$

as $\langle \Lambda, f \rangle \langle 2, g \rangle \langle 2.2, c \rangle$. We will use the notation $ct(S)$ to denote the characteristic term of a string S. The characteristic term for the above p-strings is $f(*, g(*, c))$.

4.2. P-string compatibility and indexing

We now proceed to describe how p-strings generated from the indexed terms can be used as the basis for identifying those terms that are compatible with a given query term. For this purpose, we need to extend the notion of R-compatibility to operate between p-strings and terms:

4.2. Definition *(p-string compatibility).* Given a term t and a p-string S, define the S-*prefix* of t, denoted $t \backslash S$, to be a term t' obtained from t by replacing every position in t that is not contained in S by a new distinct variable. S is said to be R-*compatible* with the term t if $R(ct(S), t')$ holds.

We will overload the notation $R(S, t)$ to denote R-compatibility between the string S and term t. For instance, the p-string $\langle \Lambda, f \rangle \langle 2, g \rangle \langle 2.2, c \rangle$, whose characteristic term is $f(*, g(*, c))$, is compatible with the query term $f(a, g(b, x))$ with respect to the retrieval condition *unif*. On the other hand, the p-string $\langle \Lambda, f \rangle \langle 1, c \rangle \langle 2, g \rangle \langle 2.2, c \rangle$ is not *unif*-compatible with this term. Moreover, $\langle \Lambda, f \rangle \langle 2, g \rangle \langle 2.2, c \rangle$ is not compatible with this term with respect to the relation *gen*.

A simple technique for determining if $R(l, t)$ can possibly hold is to first generate one or more p-strings from l and then check if each of these p-strings are R-compatible with t. To ensure that an indexing technique based on this approach will be *sound* (i.e., identify all indexed terms that are potentially R-compatible with t), we require that these p-strings be *characteristic strings* of l as defined below:

4.3. Definition *(Characteristic set of strings).* A set $\{S_1, \ldots, S_k\}$ of p-strings is called *characteristic for a term l* if for any term t, we have $R(l, t) \Rightarrow \bigwedge_{1 \leq i \leq k} R(S_i, t)$.

This condition ensures that any term that is potentially compatible with t is identified by the filter. We will use the notation S_t to denote a characteristic set of strings for a term t. If this set is singleton, then we use S_t to refer to this string. For a set $\mathcal{L}$ of terms, we use the notation $S_\mathcal{L}$ to refer to the union of characteristic sets for all terms in t, i.e., $S_\mathcal{L}$ denotes a set $\bigcup_{l \in \mathcal{L}} S_l$.

Symbol-based indexing techniques are based on constructing a characteristic set $S_\mathcal{L}$ of strings for the indexed set $\mathcal{L}$ of terms, and constructing an automaton (or trie) of all these strings. Such an automaton can be used to quickly identify those p-strings that are compatible with a given query term. This information about compatibility with individual p-strings needs to be combined to identify which of the indexed terms are potentially compatible with the query term. In particular, we consider each indexed term l, and ask the question if the query term was compatible with strings of its characteristic set. In the worst case, the combination step will hence take time $O(\sum_{l \in \mathcal{L}} |S_l|)$. However, in practice, several additional constraints are placed upon the traversal orders for generating characteristic strings, which enable the indexing to be performed faster.

To illustrate the concepts developed so far, consider the indexed set $\mathcal{L} = \{f(*, a, b), f(b, a, a), f(b, a, *)\}$ under the retrieval condition *gen*. Suppose that we generate one characteristic string from each of the terms in the indexed set, so that we get

$$S_\mathcal{L} = \{\langle \Lambda, f \rangle \langle 2, a \rangle \langle 3, b \rangle, \langle \Lambda, f \rangle \langle 2, a \rangle \langle 3, a \rangle \langle 1, b \rangle, \langle \Lambda, f \rangle \langle 2, a \rangle \langle 3, * \rangle \langle 1, b \rangle\}.$$

An automaton for these three strings is shown in Figure 4(a). In this figure, the leaves are annotated with the number(s) of term(s) from which the p-string corresponding to the state was generated.

Given a query term $t = f(b, a, c)$ and the retrieval condition *gen*, we can use this automaton for indexing as follows. First, we inspect the position Λ of t, note that the symbol f at this position is identical to that on the transition from state 2 to state 3, and thus move to state 3 of the automaton. Next, we inspect position 2 of t, match with the symbol a on the transition leading to state 5. Next we inspect position 3, and note that it is compatible with $*$ on the transition leading to state 8. Finally, we inspect position 1 and then reach the final state 13 that is marked with $\{3\}$. Since the query term is compatible with only the p-string derived from the indexed term $f(b, a, *)$, we can immediately conclude that the query term is potentially compatible with this term alone.

Backtracking may be needed while performing retrieval operation in some cases. For instance, for the query term $f(b, a, b)$, we can use the automaton of Figure 4(a) to reach the final state marked with $\{1\}$. However, this term is compatible with the p-string generated from the term $f(b, a, *)$ as well, and this can be detected only by backtracking to state 6 and following down the transition to state 8.

Now consider the same set of indexed terms, but with different sets of p-strings and the retrieval condition *unif*. Let the p-strings be:

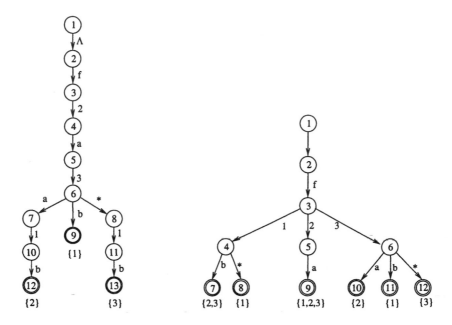

Figure 4: Example indexing automata

$$\mathcal{S}_{f(*,a,b)} = \{\langle\Lambda, f\rangle\langle 1, *\rangle, \langle\Lambda, f\rangle\langle 2, a\rangle, \langle\Lambda, f\rangle\langle 3, b\rangle\},$$
$$\mathcal{S}_{f(b,a,a)} = \{\langle\Lambda, f\rangle\langle 1, b\rangle, \langle\Lambda, f\rangle\langle 2, a\rangle, \langle\Lambda, f\rangle\langle 3, a\rangle\},$$
$$\mathcal{S}_{f(b,a,*)} = \{\langle\Lambda, f\rangle\langle 1, b\rangle, \langle\Lambda, f\rangle\langle 2, a\rangle, \langle\Lambda, f\rangle\langle 3, *\rangle\}.$$

Note that there is one p-string corresponding to each of the root-to-leaf paths in each indexed term. The automaton for these p-strings, shown in Figure 4(b), thus captures the *path indexing* technique proposed in [Stickel 1989, Ramesh, Ramakrishnan and Warren 1990] and discussed in the next section. We can use this automaton for retrieving terms that are unifiable with the query term $t = f(b, *, b)$. We need to retrieve the indexed terms such that all of the p-strings generated from them are compatible with t. We use the automaton to inspect t. We match the root symbol f, and then proceed to follow down on each of the transitions down from state 3. Specifically, we inspect position 1 in t at state 4, and see that it is compatible (under unification) with both transitions leading out of state 4. Thus, t is compatible with the first p-strings of all of the indexed terms. We now match against the second strings by following the second transition out of state 3. Again, we see that under unification, t is compatible with all of these p-strings as well. Finally, we follow the third transition out of state 3, and find that states 11 and 12 are compatible with t. At this point, we have information about the compatibility of t with all of the p-strings, from which we can conclude that t is potentially compatible with terms 1 and 3.

5. Path indexing

5.1. Overview of path indexing

We first describe *path indexing* using the general scheme presented in Section 4. In path indexing, we generate multiple p-strings from each indexed term, each one corresponding to a traversal of one root-to-leaf path in the term. We then build a trie of these p-strings, which is used to perform the retrieval operation.

By exploiting the nature of root-to-leaf traversals, we can use a more optimized representation for positions. In particular, since successive positions inspected correspond to parent and child, it is sufficient to denote which child is being included in a p-string, rather than specifying the position of the child. For instance, consider the path from the root of the term $f(b, g(f(x), a))$ to the variable x. Rather than using a p-string $\langle \Lambda, f \rangle \langle 2, g \rangle \langle 2.1, f \rangle \langle 2.1.1, * \rangle$, we can use the simpler representation $f.2.g.1.f.1.*$. For the rest of our discussion on path indexing, we will make use of the simplified representation for p-strings. We will also use the alternative term *path strings* to refer to such p-strings.

The second optimization is in the way we combine the results of matches on p-strings into a match for (some of) the indexed terms using set intersection operations. We illustrate this using the example set of indexed terms

$$(1)\ f(g(a, *), c),\quad (2)\ f(g(*, b), *),\quad (3)\ f(g(a, b), c),$$
$$(4)\ f(g(*, c), b),\quad (5)\ f(*, *).$$

The path strings generated from these terms, together with an identification of which indexed terms produced the path strings, are shown below:

$f.1.*$	$\{5\}$	$f.2.*$	$\{2, 5\}$
$f.1.g.1.*$	$\{2, 4\}$	$f.2.c$	$\{1, 3\}$
$f.1.g.1.a$	$\{1, 3\}$	$f.2.b$	$\{4\}$
$f.1.g.2.*$	$\{1\}$		
$f.1.g.2.b$	$\{2, 3\}$		
$f.1.g.2.c$	$\{4\}$		

A trie for these strings is shown in Figure 5. We have annotated each leaf node in this trie with the set of indexed terms that generated the path string corresponding to the leaf.

Some of the earliest ideas related to path indexing can be found in the coordinate indexing scheme [Hewitt 1971]. Path indexing was proposed independently by Ramesh et al. [1990] in the context of logic programming, and Stickel [1989] in the context of automated reasoning. Path indexing and its many variants have been extensively studied by McCune [1992] and Graf [1992, 1996].

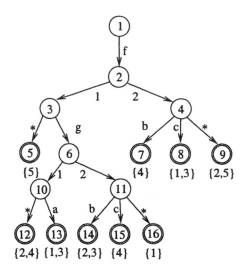

Figure 5: Path index for $\{f(g(a, *), c), f(g(*, b), *), f(g(a, b), c), f(g(*, c), b), f(*, *)\}$

5.2. Indexing algorithms

The construction and maintenance operations involve insertion and deletion of terms from the index. Below we describe algorithms for insertion, deletion, and retrieval.

5.2.1. Index construction

Index construction proceeds by successive insertion of path strings from each of the indexed terms. The insertion process is straightforward. We generate path strings corresponding to each of the root-to-leaf paths in the term to be inserted. For those path strings that already appear in the index, we simply need to insert the new indexed term in the candidate set associated with the final state corresponding to the string. Those path strings that do not already exist in the trie are inserted into the trie, and the final state corresponding to the string is annotated with the singleton set containing the newly inserted indexed term. Figure 6 shows the result of inserting the term $f(g(b, c), *)$ in the index of Figure 5. Note that two of the path strings generated from the term, namely, $f.1.g.2.c$ and $f.2.*$, already exist in the trie. The candidate sets of the corresponding final states (labelled 15 and 9 respectively) are updated to include the newly included term, which is identified by the number 6. The third path string, $f.1.g.1.b$ is a new path string, and it is inserted into the trie. The corresponding new final state, labelled 17, is associated with the candidate set $\{6\}$.

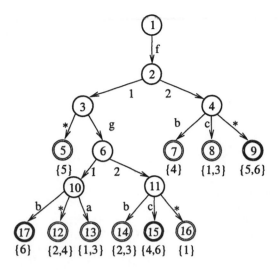

Figure 6: Path index after insertion of $f(g(b,c), *)$ to Figure 5

5.2.2. Index maintenance

Index maintenance involves insertion and deletion of terms from the indexed terms. Insertion of new terms has already been covered. Deletion of terms is also simple. We first generate the path strings from the term to be deleted. For each of these strings, we identify the corresponding final state in the trie and delete the indexed term from the associated candidate set. If this operation results in an empty candidate set, we can then delete the final state from the trie. If the parent of the final state has no children now, we can delete the parent as well and proceed higher up in the trie. This process is repeated until we reach a trie node that has nonzero number of descendants. The deletion operation is illustrated in Figure 7, which shows the index obtained by deleting the term $f(g(*,c), b)$ (which is identified by the number 4 in the indexed set) from the index of Figure 6. Note that this term generates three path strings $f.1.g.1.*$, $f.1.g.2.c$, and $f.2.b$, which are associated with final states labelled 12, 15, and 7 respectively. We delete 4 from the candidate sets associated with these states. Observe that this results in the candidate set of state 7 becoming empty. We therefore delete this state. Observe that the parent state 4 has other descendants, so we stop without deleting this state.

5.2.3. Retrieval of generalizations

Retrieval of generalizations corresponds to the one-to-many matching problem, where we are interested in rapid selection of terms such that the query term matches these terms. It is an important operation that plays a central role in term rewriting and functional programming. Even in the case of logic programming and deductive databases, one-to-many matching occurs frequently as an optimization of the unification operation when some arguments are known to be bound.

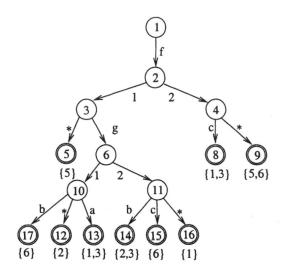

Figure 7: Path index after deleting $f(g(*,c),b)$ from Figure 6

The retrieval process is best described using the algorithm of Figure 8. The algorithm takes two parameters, one representing a state within the trie, and the second a subterm of the query term t. It is initially invoked as $retrieve(s_0, t)$, where s_0 is the root of the trie. We use the notation $\mathcal{M}_s$ to denote the candidate set associated with a final state s.

We can perform one optimization to avoid set unions at retrieval time. This can be accomplished as follows. Let s be a state in the trie that has a transition on $*$ to another state s'. Then we duplicate the indexed terms in $\mathcal{M}_{s_*}$ in the candidate sets associated with all the descendent states of s. This optimization reduces the cost of retrievals, but can increase the cost of insertions and deletions to the indexed set. When a new path string terminating with a $*$ is inserted in (or deleted from) the index, we have to not only update the candidate set associated with s_*, but also the candidate sets associated with all of the descendants of s. Even worse, when we delete a t from such an index, we have to check if some other terms having $*$ in nonvariable positions of t should be removed from the branches previously used by t.

5.2.4. Retrieval of instances

Retrieval of instances is an important problem that arises in the context of backward subsumption and demodulation in automated theorem-proving, and tabled resolution in logic programming and deductive databases. We describe a retrieval algorithm in Figure 9.

In identifying indexed terms that are instances of the query term, observe that variables in the indexed term play no role. (Once again, this is because we are ignoring nonlinearity during indexing.) However, variables in the query terms

function *retrieve*(Trie state s, term u) returns set of terms $\mathcal{M}$
1. $\mathcal{M} := \phi$
2. if u is nonvariable and $\exists$ a transition
          from state s to another state s' labelled with $root(u)$ then
3.   if s' is a final state then
4. $\mathcal{M} := \mathcal{M}_{s'}$
5.   else
6.   let $\mathcal{I}$ be the set of numbers i such that $\exists$
                  a transition from s' to s_i labelled by i
7. $\mathcal{M} := \bigcap_{i \in \mathcal{I}} retrieve(s_i, u/i)$
8.   endif
9.   endif
10. if $\exists$ a transition from s to a state s_* labelled with $*$ then
11. $\mathcal{M} := \mathcal{M} \cup \mathcal{M}_{s_*}$
12. return $\mathcal{M}$

Figure 8: Algorithm for retrieval of generalizations from a path index

function *retrieve*(Trie state s, term u) returns set of terms $\mathcal{M}$
1. if $u = *$ then
2.   let $\mathcal{F}$ be the set of all final states that are descendants of s
3. $\mathcal{M} = \bigcup_{s' \in \mathcal{F}} \mathcal{M}_{s'}$
4. else if $\exists$ a transition from s to a state s' labelled with $root(u)$ then
5.   if s' is a final state then
6. $\mathcal{M} := \mathcal{M}_{s'}$
7.   else
8.   let $\mathcal{I}$ be the set of numbers i such that $\exists$
              a transition from s' to s_i labelled by i
9. $\mathcal{M} := \bigcap_{i \in \mathcal{I}} retrieve(s_i, u/i)$
10.   endif
11. endif
12. return $\mathcal{M}$

Figure 9: Algorithm for retrieval of instances from a path index

are significant. In particular, if the query term has a path string of the form $s_1.p_2.s_2.p_3\ldots.p_{k-1}.s_{k-1}.p_k.*$, then this path string is compatible with all path strings in the index of the form $s_1.p_2.s_2.p_3\ldots.p_{k-1}.s_{k-1}\ldots$. Thus, we take the union of all the candidate sets corresponding to all such path strings at step 2 of the algorithm. If u is not a variable, then the retrieval proceeds as usual by taking the transition from s that is labelled with the root symbol of u.

Observe that the set $\mathcal{F}$ of the descendants of the state s identified at step 2 can be large, and as such, the union operation quite expensive. We can reduce this cost by precomputing the union and storing it at each state of the trie. Note that unlike the optimization for avoiding unions in the case of retrieval of generalizations, this optimization does not increase the cost of either insertion or deletion of indexed terms, but may considerably increase memory consumption. In particular, let C_s denote the set

$$\bigcup_{s' \in \mathcal{F}}$$

(see step 3 of the algorithm). Then, whenever a path string S is inserted into the trie, it is added to C_s for every state s that is on the root-to-leaf path in the trie corresponding to S. Deletion of indexed terms simply reverses this process.

5.2.5. Retrieval of unifiable terms

Retrieval of unifiable terms is an important operation in automated theorem proving in tasks such as resolution and critical-pair generation, and in logic programming and deductive databases. We present the algorithm for retrieving unifiable terms below.

Observe that unification treats the indexed term and the query term symmetrically. In particular, if either term contains a variable at some position p, then all path strings that are identical in the other term up to p, are compatible with this path string. Thus, the retrieval algorithm for unification is obtained by essentially combining the retrieval algorithm for generalizations and instances. The combination is in some sense like a union, as the candidate sets obtained are the larger of the sets obtained at step 2 of Figure 9 and step 13 of Figure 8.

The optimizations mentioned earlier for avoiding the unions at steps 3 and 15 can again be applied, with essentially the same tradeoffs as in the case of retrieval of generalizations and instances.

5.2.6. Retrieval of variants

This operation is also symmetric with respect to the indexed and query terms. However, unlike unification, we treat variables in this case just like nonvariable symbols. The algorithm for retrieval is given in Figure 11.

5.2.7. Implementation issues

The set union and intersection operations can be made efficient by using bitvector representations for sets. This ensures that we can perform the unions and intersections very fast (e.g., in a few machine instructions) even for index sets

function *retrieve*(Trie state s, term u) returns set of terms $\mathcal{M}$
1.   if $u = *$ then
2.   let $\mathcal{F}$ be the set of all final states that are descendants of s
3. $\mathcal{M} = \bigcup_{s' \in \mathcal{F}} \mathcal{M}_{s'}$
4.   else
5. $\mathcal{M} := \emptyset$
6.   if $\exists$ a transition from s to a state s' labelled with $root(u)$ then
7.   if s' is a final state then
8. $\mathcal{M} := \mathcal{M}_{s'}$
9.   else
10.   let $\mathcal{I}$ be the set of numbers i such that $\exists$
                  a transition from s' to s_i labelled by i
11. $\mathcal{M} := \bigcap_{i \in \mathcal{I}} retrieve(s_i, u/i)$
12.   endif
13.   endif
14.   if $\exists$ a transition from s to a state s_* labelled with $*$ then
15. $\mathcal{M} := \mathcal{M} \cup \mathcal{M}_{s_*}$
16.   return $\mathcal{M}$

Figure 10: Algorithm for retrieval of unifiable terms from a path index

with a few hundreds of terms. However, problems can arise when the sets contain larger numbers of terms, for example over 20,000 as reported in [Riazanov and Voronkov 2001a].

5.3. Variations of path indexing

Use of bitvectors for compact representation of the sets $\mathcal{M}$ and $\mathcal{C}$ was suggested in [Ramesh et al. 1990]. It is especially appropriate in applications where the number of terms involved is small to moderate (up to a few hundred terms). If such compact and efficient representation was usable, further optimizations are possible. In particular, [Ramesh et al. 1990] suggests that we use the candidate terms identified so far (i.e., in indexing using the first k path strings in the query term) to prune the candidate set for subsequent path strings (i.e, $k + 1$st path string). More precisely, we carry around the current candidate set $\mathcal{D}$ at all times. We set $\mathcal{M} := \mathcal{M}_{s'} \cap \mathcal{D}$ at step 8 in Figure 10. Moreover, before we descend into a state s' at step 6 of the algorithm, we check to ensure that there exists some term in $\mathcal{D}$ that is a descendant of s'. Using these optimizations, we can identify failures early, and moreover avoid inspecting some positions that are not necessary to determine the candidate set.

A variant of path indexing is obtained by limiting the maximum lengths of path strings. Those path strings longer than this length are truncated. This variation has

function *retrieve*(Trie state s, term u) returns set of terms $\mathcal{M}$
1. if $\exists$ a transition from state s to another state s' labelled with $root(u)$ then
2.   if s' is a final state
3.   then $\mathcal{M} := \mathcal{M}_{s'}$
4.   else
5.   let $\mathcal{I}$ be the set of numbers i such that $\exists$
             a transition from s' to s_i labelled by i
6. $\mathcal{M} := \bigcap_{i \in \mathcal{I}} retrieve(s_i, u/i)$
7.   endif
8. endif
9. return $\mathcal{M}$

Figure 11: Algorithm for retrieval of variants from a path index

been proposed and studied by McCune [1992] in the OTTER system. By controlling the maximum length, we can control the size of the trie. The savings are particularly significant in McCune's version, since it stores the sets C_s at each node in the trie. As these sets are represented as lists, the storage required per node in the trie is substantial. Graf [1992] uses an alternative approach where the sets C are not stored, and this representation is less sensitive to this optimization. Other techniques for reducing the size, such as pruned and collapsed tries, have not been studied. As compared to length limiting the paths, the pruning and collapsing techniques have the advantage that no accuracy is lost by these techniques.

Graf [1992] proposes a variation of path indexing in which the candidate set elements are retrieved one-at-a-time. To accomplish this, we can explicitly construct a data structure (called the *query tree*) that captures the union and intersection operations performed by the retrieval algorithms presented above. In particular, as we traverse the trie, we construct the query tree that represents the set operations to be performed, rather than performing them directly. This query tree can then be evaluated to yield the candidate set elements one at a time. In particular, we can try to compute the first element in the candidate set, then the second element, and so on. One of the advantages of this approach is that it can deal with insertions to the index concurrent with the retrieval. Assume that the indexed terms are given integer identifiers in such a manner that terms created later on have a larger id than terms created earlier. We now evaluate the query tree to get the candidate terms in the increasing order of the id. This approach ensures that if new terms were to be added to the query tree in the middle of the retrieval process, these terms would get larger identifiers than the terms already existing in the index, and hence will be retrieved after all of the terms already in the index. This ability to process concurrent retrieval and insertion is particularly convenient in applications where the retrieved term may be processed in such a way that new terms may have to be inserted into the index.

Riazanov and Voronkov [2001a] discuss a modification of path indexing that also works for multiliteral clauses. Their modification also uses skip lists to store sets of literals or clauses at each node. There are no union operations since every node stores the list of all literals or clauses stored in the leaves descendent from this node. Intersection operations are optimized by changing the order of intersections and using fast traversal of skip lists.

5.4. Summary of advantages and disadvantages

Path indexing has been studied extensively by McCune [1992], Graf [1992], [Riazanov and Voronkov 2001a] in the context of automated theorem proving, and by Ramesh et al. [1990], Chen, Ramakrishnan and Ramesh [1992] in the context of logic programming. The slight variations in these implementations were outlined earlier. Specifically, McCune's [1992] implementation uses hashing instead of tries, and moreover, stores the sets C_s. In contrast, Graf uses tries and also avoids storing the C_s sets. As such, the latter approach utilizes less memory than the former.

One of the main advantages of path indexing is that it is economical in terms of memory usage, more so than any other indexing technique discussed in this paper. The best performance in terms of memory usage is obtained when we use tries to represent the index, and store the candidate sets only at the leaves of the index, but not at the intermediate nodes. Another aspect of memory usage is that is can be further reduced by placing depth restrictions on indexing, or possibly by using techniques such as pruning and collapsing.

A second advantage is that path indexing involves no backtracking. Symbols in the query term are inspected at most once, thus leading to better retrieval time. The insertion and deletion operations on the index are also very efficient, typically beating the times for insertion and deletion operations for other indexing techniques.

One of the main disadvantages is the cost of combining intermediate results. This leads to decreased retrieval performance. As compared to the other indexing techniques, path indexing can be useful for retrieving instances or implementing backward subsumption. The performance becomes worse for retrieving unifiable terms or generalizations.

6. Discrimination trees

6.1. Overview

In *discrimination tree* indexing, we generate a single p-string from each of the indexed terms. This p-string is obtained via a preorder traversal of the terms. We then build a trie consisting of these p-strings.

By exploiting the nature of preorder traversals, we can develop a more optimized representation for the p-strings. In particular, note that given that the function symbols have predefined arities, there is a unique correspondence between the string

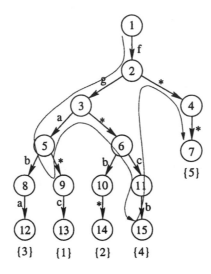

Figure 12: Example of discrimination tree indexing

obtained by preorder traversal and the term, even when the position information is completely ignored. Thus, we can use a simplified representation where the position information is no longer used. Moreover, we can annotate the final states in the trie with the candidate set $\mathcal{M}$ corresponding to the state. There is no need for (potentially expensive) combination operations that were required in the case of path indexing.

We illustrate discrimination tree indexing with the following example.

$$(1)\ f(g(a, *), c), \quad (2)\ f(g(*, b), *), \quad (3)\ f(g(a, b), a),$$
$$(4)\ f(g(*, c), b), \quad (5)\ f(*, *).$$

The following p-strings are obtained from these terms. We have omitted the position information from the p-strings.

$$
\begin{array}{ll}
f.g.a. * .c & \{1\} \\
f.g. * .b.* & \{2\} \\
f.g.a.b.a & \{3\} \\
f.g. * .c.b & \{4\} \\
f. * .* & \{5\}
\end{array}
$$

The index for retrieval of generalizations of the query term $f(g(a, c), b)$ is shown in Figure 12. To understand the process of indexing, note that the string corresponding to the query term is $f.g.a.c.b$. We compare the symbols in this string successively with the symbols on the edges in the path from the root to state 5. At this point, we cannot take the left path, as the symbol b on this edge conflicts with the symbol c

in the query term. However, the symbol * on the edge leading to state 9 is entirely plausible, since taking this edge corresponds finding a generalization (namely, a variable) of the subterm c of the query term. However, we cannot proceed further from state 9, so we have to backtrack to state 3. At this point, we can follow down the * branch all the way down the final state 15, identifying candidate term 4. If we are interested in all generalizations, we have to backtrack further to state 2, and then finally follow down to state 7, identifying candidate term 5.

Finally, we note that in order to perform retrieval of unifiable terms and instances, we must efficiently deal with situations where the query term has a variable at a point where the indexed terms contain a function symbol. In such a case, we need a mechanism to efficiently skip the corresponding subterms in the indexed terms. We can make use of *jump lists* for this purpose.

Earliest known implementations of discrimination trees are due to Greenbaum [1986]. Subsequently, Christian [1989] developed the flatterm representation for use in discrimination trees, and this resulted in excellent speedups [Christian 1989, Christian 1993]. Discrimination trees have been further studied extensively by McCune [1992] and Graf [1996]. They are used extensively in the provers OTTER, WALDMEISTER, and E.

6.2. Indexing algorithms

6.2.1. Index construction and maintenance

Construction of a discrimination tree is straightforward. We start with an empty tree, and successively insert each of the indexed terms into the tree. This is accomplished by constructing the preorder string from the term to be inserted, and then inserting this string into the tree. Since the index is a trie, algorithms for inserting strings into the trie are well known and not discussed further here. Figure 13 illustrates the insertion operation on discrimination trees.

Deletion operation can also be performed readily, since it amounts to deleting the corresponding preorder string from a trie. Deletion operation is illustrated in Figure 14. Introduction of jump lists complicates the insertion and deletion algorithms. Effectiveness of jump lists in practice was not studied.

6.2.2. Term traversal operations

In this and following sections we introduce algorithms for several retrieval operations. These algorithms will use functions for term traversal introduced below.

For technical purposes we extend $\mathcal{P}(t)$ by a special object ε called the *end position* in t. The set $\mathcal{P}(t) \cup \{\varepsilon\}$ will be denoted by $\mathcal{P}^+(t)$. When it is necessary to tell the end position from the other positions, we call the positions in $\mathcal{P}(t)$ *proper positions*.

We denote by $<$ the lexicographic ordering on positions extended in the following way: $p < \varepsilon$ for any proper position p. To perform traversal of a term t we will need two operations on proper term positions: $next_t$ and $after_t$, which can be informally explained as follows. Represent the term t as a tree and imagine a term traversal in the left-to-right, depth-first direction. Suppose $t/p = s$. Then $t/next_t(p)$ is the

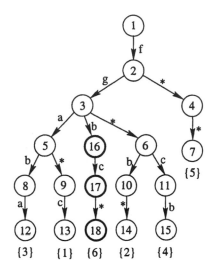

Figure 13: Insertion of term $f(g(b, c), *)$

subterm of t visited immediately after s, and $t/after_t(p)$ is the subterm visited immediately after traversal of all subterms of s. Formally, let $\Lambda = p_1 < \ldots < p_n < p_{n+1} = \varepsilon$ be all positions in t. Then $next_t(p_i) = p_{i+1}$ for all $i \leq n$. The definition of $after_t$ is as follows: $after_t(p_i) = p_j$, where j is the smallest number such that $j > i$ and for all $i < k < j$ the position p_i is a prefix of p_k.

Figure 15 illustrates the behavior of *next* and *after* on the positions in the term $f(f(a, a), a)$.

6.2.3. Retrieval of generalizations

An algorithm for retrieval of generalizations from a discrimination tree is shown in Figure 16.

Even though the automata for path indexing look quite different from those for discrimination tree indexing, the retrieval algorithms have much in common. In particular, only steps 6 and 10 in the above algorithm are different from path indexing retrieval algorithm. Out of these two steps, the difference at step 6 arises due to (a) the fact that no intersection operations need to be performed in discrimination tree, and (b) because the next position to visit is implicit, and needs to be computed based on the current position being inspected and the query term t itself. The difference at step 10 arises because V_* would be a final state in a path index, whereas in a discrimination tree, it will have further descendants in general, and hence the trie needs to be traversed further. The second difference arises again because of implicit traversal, which in this case, requires us to skip all positions in u that are the children of p. The problem is caused by *embedded variables*, i.e., the variables at the position p in the query term such that some indexed terms have a nonvariable at the position p.

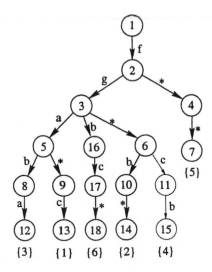

Figure 14: Deletion of term $f(g(*, c), b)$

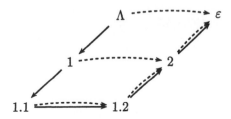

Figure 15: $next_t$ and $after_t$ on the positions in $t = f(f(a, a), a)$. Solid straight lines and dashed arcs depict $next_t$ and $after_t$ respectively.

Note that instead of returning the entire set, it may be preferable to return the candidate terms one at a time. This can be accomplished by using a backtracking algorithm. In particular, instead of computing a union at step 10, we would set a choice point. Later on, in order to retrieve the next candidate term, we would backtrack to this choice point, and then explore the '*' transition.

function *retrieve*(index state V, term t, position p) returns set of terms C
1. $C := \phi$
2. if $\exists$ a transition from state V to another state V' labeled with $root(t/p)$ then
3.   if V' is a final state
4.   then $C := C_{V'}$
5.   else
6. $C := retrieve(V', t, next_t(p))$
7.   endif
8. endif
9. if $\exists$ a transition from V to a state V_* labeled with $*$
10.   then $C := C \cup retrieve(V_*, t, after_t(p))$
11. return C

Figure 16: Algorithm for retrieval of generalizations from a discrimination tree

function *retrieve*(index state V, term t, position p) returns set of terms C
1. if $t/p = {}^{\prime}*{}^{\prime}$
2.   then $C = \bigcup_{V' \in JumpList(V)} retrieve(V', t, next_t(p))$
3. else
4. $C := \phi$
5.   if $\exists$ a transition from state V to a state V' labeled with $root(u/p)$ then
6.   if V' is a final state
7.   then $C := C_{V'}$
8.   else
9. $C := retrieve(V', t, next_t(p))$
10.   endif
11.   endif
12.   if $\exists$ a transition from V to a state V_* labeled with $*$
13.   then $C := C \cup retrieve(V_*, t, after_t(p))$
14. endif
15. return C

Figure 17: Algorithm for retrieval of unifiable terms from a discrimination tree

6.2.4. Retrieval of unifiable terms

An algorithm for retrieval of unifiable terms from a discrimination tree is shown in Figure 17. In this figure we denote by $JumpList(V)$ the jump list for a state V.

Note again that the algorithm for retrieval of unifiable terms is similar to the corresponding algorithm for path indexing. The differences arise mainly because of the reasons as before: the traversal order is implicit in discrimination trees, so the next position to visit has to be computed explicitly. Also, when a variable is inspected in the query term, we need to skip the corresponding portions of the indexed terms, which is accomplished using the jump lists.

Figure 18 illustrates this algorithm. We need to make use of the jump lists for

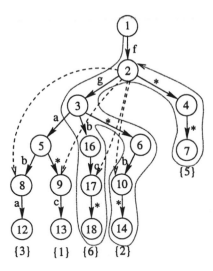

Figure 18: Retrieval of terms unifiable with $f(g(b, *), a)$

efficiently skipping portions of the discrimination tree that correspond to a variable in the query term. In the general case, there is a jump link from every node in the tree to all its descendent states that examine the position immediately after all of the positions within the current subterm. The storage for such links can be substantial, and would clutter the picture. So, we have shown jump lists only for those nodes where jump links go to a state different from the immediate child of a node.

6.3. Variations

Perfect discrimination trees were proposed by McCune [1992]. Such trees deal with nonlinearity, and are hence perfect filters. To deal with nonlinearity, these trees use named variables, as opposed to the anonymous variable '*' in standard discrimination trees. However, using different variables in different terms will adversely affect the ability to share prefixes of preorder strings in the tree, and hence lead to extensive backtracking. To avoid this, variables in indexed terms are *normalized* so that the same set of variables can be used across different indexed terms in a consistent manner. For instance, we could use x_i to denote the ith distinct variable in an indexed term. Then the term $f(y, g(y, z))$ will be represented as $f(x_1, g(x_1, x_2))$. Another possibility is to linearize the term, i.e., represent every occurrence of a variable as a distinct variable and also store in the index *equality constraints* indicating which variables in the indexed term are equal. For example, the term $f(y, g(y, z))$ will be represented as $f(x_1, g(x_2, x_3))$ plus the equality constraint $x_1 = x_2$. Equality constraints are used in [Rivero 2000, Riazanov and Voronkov 2000b].

Depth-limiting [McCune 1992] is an approach to limiting the size of the discrimination tree, possibly at the expense of retrieval time.

Deterministic discrimination trees [Graf 1991] are a variation that avoids backtracking altogether. Thus, in a single scan of the "relevant portions" of the query term, we can determine all of the candidate terms. Deterministic trees have been proposed mainly in the context of retrieving generalizations. They avoid states that have transitions on variables and nonvariables, since such states necessitate backtracking. This is accomplished by selectively instantiating some of the variable positions in each indexed term t to obtain a set of instances $\mathcal{T}$ of the indexed term such that the set of ground instances of t is identical to the set of ground instances of all of the terms in $\mathcal{T}$. For instance, the set of terms

$$\{f(g(a,*),c), f(g(*,b),*), f(g(*,c),b)\}$$

would be expanded into the set

$$\{f(g(a,b),c), f(g(a,b),\neq), f(g(a,c),c), f(g(a,c),b), f(g(a,\neq),c), f(g(\neq,c),b)\},$$

where the symbol $\neq$ is a wildcard symbol that matches every function symbol except those occurring at that position in the original terms. Note that such expansion results in an explosion in the number of indexed terms — in fact, the blow up can be exponential. Deterministic automata are used in applications where the indexed terms change very infrequently, e.g., functional programming and term rewriting with (almost) fixed set of rules. We will consider a generalized version of deterministic automata in the next section.

6.4. Summary of advantages and disadvantages

Discrimination trees improve over path indexing in avoiding the expensive set intersection operations that are required to obtain candidate terms from candidate p-strings. One disadvantage is that they tend to use more storage, since we cannot share states for examining symbols at a position p from multiple indexed terms unless they have identical symbols in every position p' that precedes p in preorder traversal. Similar sharing in path indexing only requires that the terms are identical in positions that are ancestors of p. Space usage is exacerbated significantly if jump lists are maintained. Maintenance of jump links also makes insertion and deletion operations significantly more expensive. A second disadvantage is that backtracking is typically required in retrieval operations, necessitating reexamination of symbols. However, this overhead is typically small as compared to the cost of set intersection operations in path indexing.

Perfect discrimination trees improve on standard trees in their ability to incorporate tests for consistency of substitutions in the index. Moreover, the binding operations (i.e., operations for computing substitutions) can be shared across multiple indexed terms. However, since consistency checking operations can be very expensive (e.g., when the substitutions being compared are large), introduction of these operations into the index can degrade performance. It would be better to postpone these expensive operations so that they occur after the simpler operations of checking for the occurrence of a symbol at a position. Such reordering is possible with some of the techniques described later on in this paper.

Deterministic discrimination trees improve upon standard trees in that no backtracking is required for retrieval. The downside is that they can be very large – whereas the size of standard discrimination trees (measured as the number of nodes) is linear in the sum of sizes of indexed terms, the worst case size of deterministic trees can be exponential in the number of indexed terms. This also means that insertion and deletion operations in the index are expensive. Thus, deterministic trees are suitable primarily for applications where retrieval performance is important, and efficiency of maintenance operations is not a concern.

7. Adaptive automata

7.1. Overview

For constructing adaptive automata, we generate one p-string from each indexed term. The traversal order for generating the p-string is not fixed *a priori*, as in the case of discrimination trees. Instead, the traversal order is *adapted* to suit the set of indexed terms. The adaptation is designed to minimize the size of the automaton and the retrieval time.

Although adaptive automata can use backtracking, they have been studied primarily in the context of deterministic automata for retrieving generalizations. In particular, this means that no state in the automaton has a transition on a function symbol and a variable. The traversal order for generating the p-strings is designed in such a way as to avoid constructing such states. When such branches become unavoidable, the indexed term containing the variable is instantiated at this position with all possible symbols that can appear in this context. Index construction then proceeds with these instances in place of the term containing the variable.

In generating p-strings for adaptive automata, we ensure that all p-strings with a common prefix examine the same position after this prefix. When we construct a trie of such p-strings, we have a unique transition out of any automaton state that examines a position. Thus, we can optimize the representation by storing the next position to inspect as part of an automaton state, rather than creating a transition based on this position. A second optimization, which applies to all deterministic automata, is that the final states directly yield all possible candidate terms — there is no need to search any further.

In this section we assume that the set of indexed terms is prioritized, i.e., we have a function $priority(l)$, which allows us to compare priorities of indexed terms, i.e., checking if $priority(l) \geq priority(l')$ holds for given indexed terms l, l'. Let us give an example. Consider the set consisting of the following three terms:

$$(1) \ f(x,a,b), \quad (2) \ f(b,a,a), \quad (3) \ f(x,a,y),$$

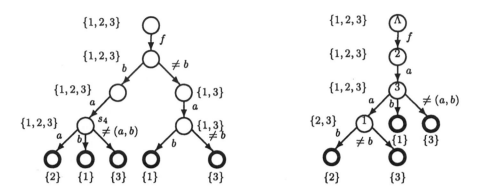

Figure 19: A left-to-right automaton and an adaptive automaton

where the terms with the smaller number have the largest priority. Figure 19 shows a left-to-right automaton and an adaptive automaton for this set of terms.

Adaptive traversals, as embodied in adaptive automata, possess the following advantages over fixed-order traversals such as the left-to-right traversal used in discrimination trees:

- adaptive automata are typically smaller, e.g., 8 states vs. 11 states in the example. The reduction factor can even become exponential.

- retrieval requires lesser time, e.g., left-to-right automaton needs to inspect four positions to announce a match of the query term $f(c, a, b)$ against indexed term 1, whereas the adaptive automaton inspects only a proper subset of these positions. Examining unnecessary symbols is especially undesirable in the context of lazy functional languages.

In the rest of this section, we use the term "matching automata" synonymously with index.

The origins of adaptive indexing can be traced back to the development of complete normalization strategies for a subset of orthogonal rewrite systems [Dershowitz and Jouannaud 1990] called *strongly sequential systems* [Huet and Levy 1978, Huet and Levy 1991]. This work was extended for lazy functional languages in [Laville 1988, Laville 1987, Puel 1990, Maranget 1992, Kennaway 1990]. The technique was studied in the context of arbitrary terms in [Sekar, Ramesh and Ramakrishnan 1992].

7.2. Indexing algorithms

In this section, we develop algorithms for constructing adaptive automata for a prioritized set of indexed terms, and using them for retrieval of generalizations of a query term. The idea behind the construction of adaptive automata is the following. We "guess" the query term t position by position, and build an automaton for retrieval of generalizations of t using the information about currently known positions. The "so far guessed" part of t is a linear term that will be denoted by u. We have $u \leq t$; this implies that every indexed term l compatible with t (i.e., $l \leq t$) must also unify with u. Sometimes, we can find the match for t without complete inspection of t, but only using partial information about t available in u. This happens when we find out that some indexed term l is compatible with u but no indexed term l' of a higher priority is unifiable with u). This suggests the following definition.

7.1. DEFINITION. A term $l \in \mathcal{L}$ $\mathcal{L}$-matches u if $l \leq u$, and no $l' \in \mathcal{L}$ with priority greater than that of l unifies with u. Given a term u, we define its match set, denoted by $\mathcal{L}_u$, as the set of terms in $\mathcal{L}$ unifiable with u.

Intuitively, $\mathcal{L}_u$ consists of all indexed terms that can potentially be generalizations of t. We will use the wildcard $\neq$ in the term u in the following way: $\neq$ unifies with any variable, but does not unify with a nonvariable symbol.

7.2.1. Index construction

The algorithm *Build* for constructing an adaptive automaton is shown in Figure 20. A state V of the automaton remembers the prefix u of a query term that would have been inspected while reaching that state from the start state. Suppose that p is the next position inspected from V. Then there are transitions from V on each distinct symbol c that appears at p for any $l \in \mathcal{L}_u$. There will also be a transition from V on $\neq$ which will be taken on inspecting a symbol different from those on the other edges leaving V.

The symbol $\neq$ appearing at a position p denotes the inspection of a symbol in the input that does not occur at p in any indexed term in $\mathcal{L}_u$. This implies that if a prefix u has $\neq$ at a position p then every indexed term that could potentially match an instance of u must have a variable at or above p.

Procedure *Build* is recursive, and the automaton is constructed by invoking $Build(s_0, x)$ where s_0 is the start state of the automaton. *Build* takes two parameters: V, a state of the automaton and u, the prefix examined in reaching V. The invocation $Build(V, u)$ constructs the subautomaton rooted at V.

At line 2, the termination condition is checked. By the definition of indexed term match, we need to rule out possible matches with higher priority indexed terms before declaring a match for a lower priority indexed term. Since the match set $\mathcal{L}_u$ contains all indexed terms that could possibly match the prefix u, we simply need to check that each indexed term in the match set is either already in l or has a lower priority than l.

If the termination conditions are not satisfied then the automaton construction is continued at lines 5 through 12. At line 5, the next position p to be inspected is selected and this information is recorded in the current state in line 6. Lines 7, 8 and 9 create transitions based on each symbol that could appear at p for any indexed term in $\mathcal{L}_u$. In line 9, *Build* is recursively invoked with the prefix extended

Procedure $Build(index\,state\,V, term\,u)$
1.   let $\mathcal{M}$ denote the set of all indexed terms that match u.
2.   if $\mathcal{M} = \{l\}$ and $\forall\, l' \in \mathcal{L}_u\ priority(l) \geq priority(l')$ then
3.   mark V with $\{l\}$ and terminate
4.   else
5. $p = select(u)$; /* $select$ is a function to choose the next position to inspect */
6. $pos[V] = p$; /* Next position to inspect is recorded in the pos field */
7.   for each nonvariable symbol c for which $\exists l \in \mathcal{L}_u$ with $root(l/p) = c$ do
8.   create a new node V_c and an edge from V to V_c labeled c;
9. $Build(V_c, u[c(y_1,\ldots,y_n)]_p)$ /* $y_1,\ldots,y_n$ are new variables, n is the arity of c */
10.   if $\exists l \in \mathcal{L}_u$ with a variable at p or above p then
11.   create a new node $V_{\neq}$ and an edge from V to $V_{\neq}$ labeled $\neq$;
12. $Build(V_{\neq}, u[\neq]_p)$

Figure 20: Construction of adaptive automata

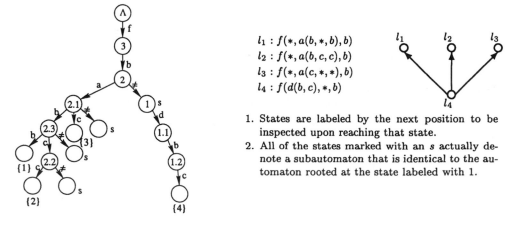

$l_1 : f(*, a(b, *, b), b)$
$l_2 : f(*, a(b, c, c), b)$
$l_3 : f(*, a(c, *, *), b)$
$l_4 : f(d(b, c), *, b)$

1. States are labeled by the next position to be inspected upon reaching that state.
2. All of the states marked with an s actually denote a subautomaton that is identical to the automaton rooted at the state labeled with 1.

Figure 21: Example of an adaptive indexing automaton

to include the symbols seen on the transitions created at line 8. If there is an indexed term in $\mathcal{L}_u$ with a variable at or above p then a transition on $\neq$ is created at line 11 and $Build$ is recursively invoked at line 12. The recursive calls initiated at lines 9 and 12 together will complete the construction of the subautomaton rooted at state V. An example adaptive automaton built using this algorithm is shown in Figure 21.

7.2.2. Retrieval of generalizations

An algorithm for retrieval of generalizations is shown in Figure 22.

As compared to discrimination trees, the retrieval algorithm is further simplified: there is no backtracking involved, and the final state reached directly yields all of the candidate terms. In addition to specifying all of the candidate terms, the final

function *retrieve*(*IndexState V, Term t*) returns set of terms
1. if ∃ a transition from V to another state V'
       labeled with $root(t/pos[V])$ or else with $\neq$ then
2.   if V' is a final state labeled with $\{l\}$ then
3.   return $\{l\}$
4.   else
5.   return *retrieve*(V', t)
6.   endif
7. else
8.   return $\emptyset$
9. endif

Figure 22: Retrieval of generalizations from adaptive automata

state can also store the substitution for each of the candidate terms, i.e., there would be no need to explicitly compute the substitution at retrieval time.

7.2.3. Time and space complexity

The primary objective of a selection function is to reduce the automaton size and/or the matching time. Therefore it is important to know how we measure these quantities. A natural measure of the size of an automaton is the number of states in it. However, this measure has the drawback that minimization of total number of states is NP-complete, even for the simple case of indexed terms with no variables [Comer and Sethi 1976]. This makes it impossible to develop efficient algorithms that build an automaton of smallest size, unless P = NP. Even so, we would still like to show that certain algorithms are always better than others for reducing the size. One way to do this is to choose an alternative measure of size that is closely related to the original size measure, yet does not have the drawback of NP-completeness of its minimization. A natural choice in this case is the breadth of the automaton, which is closely related to the total number of states.

As for matching time, it is easy to define the time to match a given term using a given automaton: it is simply the length of the path in the automaton from the root to the final state that accepts the given term. However, what we would like is a time measure that does not refer to input terms. We could associate an average matching time with an automaton, but this would require information that is not easily obtained: the relative frequencies with which each of the paths in the automaton are taken[3]. Therefore, instead of defining a time measure that totally orders the automata for a specific distribution of input terms, we use the following measure that partially orders them *independent* of the distribution. Let $MT(s, A)$ denote the length of the path in (automaton) A from the start state to the accepting state of the *ground* term s. If s is not accepted by A then $MT(s, A)$ is undefined.

---

[3]It is possible to assume that all terms over Σ are equally likely and derive a matching time on this basis, but such assumptions are seldom justified or useful in practice.

Class of Terms	Lower bound on space	Upper bound on space	Lower bound on time	Upper bound on time
Unambiguous, no priority	$\Omega(2^{\sqrt{\alpha}})$	$O(\prod_{i=1}^{n}|l_i|)$	$\Omega(\alpha)$	S
Unambiguous, with priority	$\Omega(\alpha^{n-1})$	$O(\prod_{i=1}^{n}|l_i|)$	$\Omega(S)$	S
Ambiguous	$\Omega(\alpha^{n-1})$	$O(\prod_{i=1}^{n}|l_i|)$	$\Omega(S)$	S

Notation

l_i : i^{th} indexed term

n : Number of Indexed Terms

S : Total number of nonvariable symbols in indexed terms

α : Average number of nonvariable symbols in indexed terms

Figure 23: Space and matching time complexity of adaptive automata.

We now examine upper and lower bounds on the space and matching time complexity of adaptive tree automata for several classes of terms. Since the traversal order itself is a parameter here, we first need to clarify what we mean by upper and lower bounds. By an upper bound, we refer to an upper bound obtained by using the best possible traversal for a set of indexed terms, i.e., a traversal that minimizes space (or time, as the case may be). The rationale for this definition is that for every set of indexed terms, there exist traversal orders that can result in the worst possible time or space complexity. Clearly, it is not interesting to talk about the upper bound on size of the automaton obtained using such a (deliberately chosen) nonoptimal traversal order. Our lower bounds refer to the lower bounds obtained for any possible traversal order.

The complexity results on size and matching time of adaptive automata are shown in Figure 23. In this figure, "unambiguos" means that the indexed terms do not unify with one another.

7.2.4. Greedy strategies for minimizing space

Representative Sets. Consider the indexed terms in Figure 21 and the prefix $u = f(*, a(b, *, b), *)$. Although $\mathcal{L}_u = \{l_1, l_4\}$, observe that a match for l_4 can be declared only if the 3rd argument of f is b. In such a case we declare a match for the higher priority indexed term l_1.

Inspecting any position only on behalf of a indexed term such as l_4 is wasteful, e.g., inspection of position 1 for u is useless since it is irrelevant for declaring a match for l_1. We can avoid inspecting such positions by considering the representative set instead of a match set for a prefix u. A representative set is defined formally as follows:

7.2. DEFINITION. A *representative set* $\overline{\mathcal{L}_u}$ of a prefix u with respect to a set of indexed terms $\mathcal{L}$ is a minimal subset $\mathcal{S}$ such that the following condition holds for every l in $\mathcal{L}$:

$$\forall t \geq u \ (l \leq t) \Rightarrow \exists l' \in \mathcal{S} \ [(l' \leq t) \wedge (priority(l') \geq priority(l))]. \tag{7.1}$$

All these strategies select the next position based on *local information* such as the prefix and the representative set associated with v or its children. Let p denote the next position to be selected.

1. Select a p such that the number of distinct nonvariables at p, taken over all indexed terms in $\overline{\mathcal{L}_u}$ is *minimized*. This strategy attempts to minimize the size by local minimization of breadth of the automata. It does not attempt to reduce matching time.

2. Select a p such that the number of distinct nonvariables at p, taken over all indexed terms in $\overline{\mathcal{L}_u}$ is *maximized*. The rationale here is that by maximizing the breadth, a greater degree of discrimination is achieved. If we can quickly distinguish among the indexed terms, then the (potentially) exponential blow-up can be contained. Furthermore, once we distinguish one indexed term from the others, we no longer inspect unnecessary symbols and so matching time can also be improved.

3. Select a p such that the number of indexed terms having nonvariables at p is maximized. The motivation for this strategy is that only indexed terms with variables at p are duplicated in the representative sets of the descendants of the current state v of the automaton. By minimizing this number of indexed terms that are duplicated, we can contain the blow-up. Furthermore, this choice minimizes the probability of inspecting an unnecessary position: it is a necessary position for the most number of indexed terms.

4. Let $\overline{\mathcal{L}_1}, \ldots, \overline{\mathcal{L}_r}$ be the representative sets of the children of v. Select a p such that $\Sigma_{i=1}^r |\overline{\mathcal{L}_i}|$ is minimized. Note that the main reason for exponential blow-up is that many indexed terms get duplicated among the representative sets of the children of v. This strategy locally minimizes such duplication (since $\Sigma_{i=1}^r |\overline{\mathcal{L}_i}|$ is given by the size of $\overline{\mathcal{L}_u}$ plus the number of indexed terms that are duplicated among the representative sets of the children states.) For improving time, this strategy again locally minimizes the number of indexed terms for which an unnecessary symbol is examined at each of the children of v.

All of the above greedy strategies suffer from the drawback that:

7.3. THEOREM. *For each of the above strategies there exist indexed term sets for which automata of smaller size can be obtained by making a choice different from that given by the strategy.*

The proof is established by providing indexed term sets for which automata of smaller size can be obtained by using a strategy different from each of those mentioned above. The contrived nature of the example, however, shows that although it is possible for these strategies to fail, such failures may be atypical. Even when they fail, as in the above example, they still appear to be significantly better than fixed order traversals.

7.2.5. Reducing matching time by selecting index positions

We now propose another important local strategy that does not suffer from the drawbacks of the greedy strategies discussed in the previous section. The key idea is to inspect the so-called index positions in u whenever they exist. This strategy yields automata of smaller (or same) size and superior (or same) matching time than that obtainable by any other choice.

We call an *index position* any position p in the fringe of u such that every instance of u for which there is a match in $\mathcal{L}$, u/p is a nonvariable. A set of terms is called *constructor-based* if the outermost symbol in every term is different from all of the nonoutermost symbols in all other terms. It is strongly sequential if every prefix of every indexed term has an index position.

7.4. Theorem. *Adaptive automata are space and time optimal for strongly sequential constructor systems.*

This result is very important in the context of complete normalization strategies for constructor-based orthogonal systems. Such systems form the basis of lazy functional programming languages such as Haskell and Hope. In lazy functional languages, evaluation (of input terms) is closely coupled with matching. Specifically, a subterm of the input term is evaluated only when its root symbol needs to be inspected by the matcher. If there are subterms whose evaluation does not terminate, then an evaluator that uses an algorithm that identifies matches without inspection of such subterms can terminate, whereas use of algorithms that do inspect such subterms will lead to nontermination.

Since the set of positions inspected to identify a match is dependent on the traversal order used, the termination properties also depend upon the traversal order. In order to make sure that the program terminates on input terms of interest to the programmer, the programmer may have to reason about the traversal order used. In particular, the programmer can code his/her program in such a way that (for terms of interest to him/her) the matcher will inspect only those subterms whose evaluation will terminate. This implies that the programmer must be made aware of the traversal order used *even before the program is written* — thereby ruling out synthesis of *arbitrary* traversal orders at compile time. Given this constraint on preserving termination properties, a natural question is whether the traversal order can be "internally changed" by the compiler in a manner that is transparent to the programmer. Thus, given a traversal order T that is assumed by a programmer, can we make use of another traversal order S internally such that S is typically better than T, and is formally guaranteed to be no worse than T. We define such a traversal order below, based on the notion of index positions.

Given a traversal order T, denote by $S(T)$ the traversal order such that, for a prefix u, $S(T)$ selects the next position p in fringe of u such that:

- p is an index position, if u has index positions;
- p that is chosen by T, otherwise.

7.5. Theorem. *(i) $S(T)$ is no worse than T in terms of space consumption as well as retrieval time. (ii) In lazy functional programs, every program that terminates when matching using T is used will also terminate with $S(T)$.*

7.2.6. Minimizing space usage using DAG-automata

One of the main reason for the exponential space requirement is the use of tree structure in representing the automaton. Lack of sharing in trees results in duplication of functionally identical subautomata leading to wastage of space. A natural solution to this problem is to implement sharing with the help of dag structure (instead of tree).

An obvious way to achieve sharing is to use standard FSA minimization techniques. A method based on this approach first constructs the automaton (using algorithm *Build*) and then converts it into a (optimal) dag. However, the size of the tree automaton can be exponentially larger than that of the dag automaton. Therefore use of FSA minimization technique is bound to be very inefficient. To overcome this problem we must construct the dag automaton without generating its tree structure first. This means we must identify equivalence of two states *without even generating* the subautomata rooted at these states.

Central to our construction (of dag automaton) is a technique that detects equivalent states based on the representative sets. Consider two prefixes u and u' that have the same representative set $\overline{\mathcal{L}_u}$. Suppose that u and u' differ only in those positions where every indexed term in $\overline{\mathcal{L}_u}$ has a variable. Since such positions are irrelevant for determining a match, these two prefixes are equivalent. On the other hand, it can also be shown that if they have different representative sets or differ in any other position then they are not equivalent. Based on this observation, we define the relevant prefix of u as follows. Let $p_1, p_2, \ldots, p_k$ denote (all of the) positions in u such that for each p_i there is at least one indexed term in $\overline{\mathcal{L}_u}$ that has a variable at p_i and all other indexed terms in $\overline{\mathcal{L}_u}$ have a variable either at p_i or above it. The relevant prefix of u is then

$$u[\neq]_{p_1}[\neq]_{p_2} \cdots [\neq]_{p_k}.$$

7.6. Theorem. *The automaton obtained by merging states with identical relevant prefixes is optimal.*

Merging equivalent states as described above can substantially reduce the space required by the automata, e.g., the tree automaton in Figure 21 has 25 states which can now be reduced to 16 by sharing.

We can show that the upper bound on size of dag automata is $O(2^n S)$ which is much smaller than the corresponding bound $O(\prod_{i=1}^{n} |l_i|)$ for tree automata. We can also establish a lower bound of $O(2^\alpha)$ for ambiguous indexed terms. For unambiguous indexed terms, it is unknown whether the lower bound on size is exponential.

7.2.7. Computational complexity for building adaptive automata

Some of the central problems in computing adaptive automata are the computation of index positions and computation of representative sets. Both problems can be solved in quadratic time in the worst case for untyped languages. However, in the presence of types:

- Computing index positions is coNP-complete for typed terms, but there exists a polynomial time algorithm for untyped terms.
- Computing a representative set is NP-complete for typed terms, but takes polynomial time for untyped terms.

7.3. Summary of advantages and disadvantages

The primary advantage of adaptive automata are that they can be more compact and faster than discrimination trees. Like deterministic discrimination trees, they require no backtracking, but in general, this is achieved with a smaller automaton. A disadvantage is that index maintenance operations may be more expensive. However, this is hard to assess, since the cost of these operations is closely related to the size of the index.

The benefits of adaptive automata outweigh the costs in applications where retrieval cost is to be minimized, while the cost of index construction or maintenance operations is not a concern. This is particularly true in declarative language implementations. Adaptive indexing technique provides the basis for complete evaluation algorithms for (lazy) functional languages.

While the size of adaptive automaton can be large in general, the algorithm for sharing equivalent states reduces this space requirement significantly. The same algorithm is applicable for deterministic discrimination trees as well. The space savings produced by this algorithm are more significant in the case of deterministic discrimination trees.

Backtracking adaptive automata provide an alternative approach that does not suffer from the space blowups associated with deterministic automata. The insertion and deletion operations are also rendered faster. Backtracking adaptive indexing still provides advantages over discrimination trees in terms of space usage as well as size.

8. Automata-driven indexing

8.1. Overview

Automata-driven indexing is an indexing technique that is based on string-matching. When a query term is checked for compatibility with a set of indexed terms, the substitution operations may have to be repeated for each candidate term, as the substitutions computed for different indexed terms may be different. For this reason, this technique focuses exclusively on sharing of the comparison operations that involve nonvariable symbols in the indexed and query terms. Specifically, the index in this approach is built from *preorder strings*, obtained from each indexed term as follows:

- traverse the term in preorder;
- break the p-string thus obtained at variable positions to get several strings, possibly as many as the number of variables in the term plus one.

For instance, consider the query term and indexed term shown in Figure 24, which will be used as the running example to illustrate the technique in the rest of this section. We have deliberately used an example with just a single indexed term in order to simplify the illustrations. The indexed term $f(g(a, a, h(y)), h(a))$ shown in the figure gives rise to two preorder strings: $\langle \Lambda, f \rangle \langle 1, g \rangle \langle 1.1, a \rangle \langle 1.2, a \rangle \langle 1.3, h \rangle$ and $\langle 2, h \rangle \langle 2.1, a \rangle$. The term $f(a, x, y)$ (not shown in the figure) generates just a single preorder string $\langle \Lambda, f \rangle \langle 1, a \rangle$.

In automata-driven indexing, a string-matching automaton is constructed from the preorder strings obtained from the indexed terms. The preorder strings from the query term are run through this automaton. The automaton states reached in this process capture all of the information relating to the nonvariable symbols in the query term. This information will be sufficient to determine the candidate terms from the indexed set, i.e., there will be no need to examine the query term symbols again. In principle, this technique can be used to retrieve unifiable terms, generalizations as well as instances. Another important feature of this technique is that it can be easily applied to retrieve indexed terms that are instances of (or are unifiable with) all subterms of the query term, rather than being limited to root matches only [Ramesh, Ramakrishnan and Sekar 1994]. We will, however, limit ourselves to the problem of unifiability of indexed terms with a query term.

Note that the preorder strings obtained in the manner described above do not fit the definition of p-strings, since some of the preorder strings can contain descendant positions without containing the ancestor positions. We can rework the definition of p-strings to accommodate this, but it is in fact simpler to define the notion of unifiability with respect to preorder strings.

8.1. DEFINITION *(preorder string unifiability)*. A preorder string $S \equiv \langle p_1, s_1 \rangle \langle p_2, s_2 \rangle \cdots \langle p_n, s_n \rangle$ is said to be *unifiable* with another preorder string $S' \equiv \langle p'_1, s'_1 \rangle \langle p'_2, s'_2 \rangle \cdots \langle p'_m, s'_m \rangle$ if and only if $\forall 1 \leq i \leq n \ \forall 1 \leq j \leq m \ p_i = p'_j \Rightarrow s_i = s'_j$.

The following preorder strings result from the terms shown in Figure 24:
S_s^1: $\langle \Lambda, f \rangle \langle 1, g \rangle \langle 1.1, a \rangle$
S_s^2: $\langle 1.2, h \rangle \langle 1.2.1, a \rangle \langle 2, h \rangle \langle 2.1, a \rangle$
S_t^1: $\langle \Lambda, f \rangle \langle 1, g \rangle \langle 1.1, a \rangle \langle 1.2, a \rangle \langle 1.3, h \rangle$
S_t^2: $\langle 2, h \rangle \langle 2.1, a \rangle$.

The above definition of preorder string unifiability requires that two preorder strings agree at every position that is common among them. Due to the nature of preorder strings, note that the subset of common positions must occur together. Therefore preorder string compatibility can be reduced to questions involving string matching. Specifically, four scenarios arise when checking the unifiability of two preorder

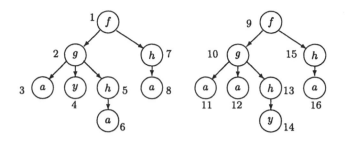

Figure 24: A query term s and an indexed term t.

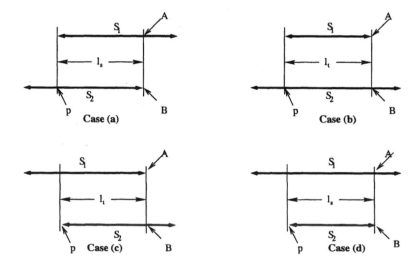

Figure 25: Scenarios for preorder string compatibility

strings, as shown in Figure 25. In this figure, the preorder string S_t is from an indexed term t, whereas S_s is a preorder string from the query term s. These two strings are shown so that they are aligned with each other at the common positions. p denotes the first common position among S_t and S_s, while l_t and l_s represent their respective lengths from this common position p. From the figure, it is easy to see that the string matching questions that need to be answered to determine preorder string unifiability are:

Q1: (Cases (a) and (b)) Does a prefix of S_t of length $\min(l_t, l_s)$ occur in S_s at p? In the example of Figure 24, case (b) arises between S_t^1 and S_s^1, with $p = \Lambda$, $l_s = 3$ and $l_t = 5$.

Q2: (Cases (c) and (d)) Does a prefix of S_s of length $\min(l_t, l_s)$ occur in S_t at p? In the example, case (c) arises between S_s^2 and S_t^2, with $l_s = l_t = 2$.

The index is built in such a fashion that all the information required to answer these questions can be obtained in a single scan through the query term. After this, each of these string matching questions will be answered in $O(1)$ time.

The origins of automata-driven indexing arose in the context of tree pattern matching [Ramesh and Ramakrishnan 1992]. It was then extended to deal with indexing of Prolog clauses in [Ramesh et al. 1990]. An implementation of this technique was developed [Chen, Ramakrishnan and Ramesh 1994] and integrated into the ALS Prolog system. Finally, it has been extended to the problem of retrieving clauses that are unifiable with a given query term or any of its subterms [Ramesh et al. 1994].

8.2. Indexing algorithms

8.2.1. Index construction
Index construction proceeds by first constructing all of the preorder strings corresponding to the indexed terms. Since the position information is redundant in preorder strings, this information is dropped. For the indexed term $f(g(a, a, h(y)), h(a))$ shown in Figure 24, this leads to the strings $fgaah$ and ha.

We then build an Aho-Corasick automaton to recognize these strings, as well as the substrings of these strings. This automaton serves as the index that supports retrieval of terms unifiable with a set of indexed terms. (For the rest of this section, we use the "automaton" and "index" interchangeably.) Figure 26 shows the automaton obtained for the preorder strings for the above indexed term. This automaton has two types of links: *goto* and *failure*. The *goto* links are forward links that are taken whenever we see a symbol in the input term that matches the symbol associated with the link. The *failure* link is taken when the input symbol does not match the symbol associated with any of the forward links.

From the Aho-Corasick automaton, we can obtain a *goto tree* by deleting all the failure links. Similarly, we obtain a *fail tree* by deleting all the forward links and *reversing* the fail links. The fail tree for the automaton in Figure 26 is given in Figure 27(a). We say that the state A in the automaton represents string S if the (unique) path in the goto tree between the root (i.e., start state) and A spells S. For example, state A_9 in the automaton represents gaa.

The following properties of the automaton are essential for answering Q1 and Q2.

1. Every substring of every preorder string from every indexed term is represented by a unique state in the automaton. This implies: (a) each prefix of an indexed string is represented, and (b) every prefix of a query string that occurs in any indexed string is represented.

2. While scanning the string $a_1 a_2 \ldots a_n$ if the automaton reaches a state A that represents a string S on reading a_j then S is the longest suffix of $a_1 a_2 \ldots a_j$ among the strings represented by the automaton states.

3. If S_1 and S_2 are the strings represented by states A and B respectively then S_1 is a suffix of S_2 iff A is an ancestor of B in the fail tree.

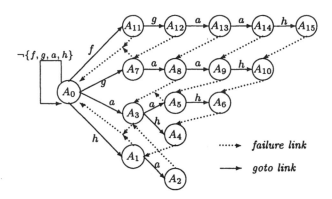

Figure 26: Automaton for suffixes of strings generated from indexed term.

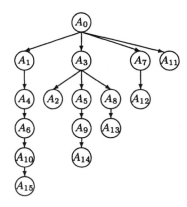

Figure 27: Fail tree corresponding to automaton of Figure 26

8.2.2. Retrieval of unifiable terms

The selection begins by scanning the preorder strings from the query term using the Aho-Corasick automaton and recording with each symbol the state reached upon reading it. Figure 28 shows the states of the index reached for our running example. The figure also shows the states reached on scanning preorder strings from the indexed term, this information being known at automaton construction time.

We now recall the string-matching questions that arise and describe how we can answer them (see Figure 25):

Q1: Does a prefix of S_t of length $l \equiv min(l_t, l_s)$ occur in S_s at p? We (i) obtain the state A representing the prefix of S_t of length l in the automaton, (ii) obtain the state B stored at $(p+l)$th position in S_q, and (iii) verify if A is an ancestor of B in the fail tree.

Q2: Does a prefix of S_s of length $l \equiv min(l_t, l_s)$ occur in S_t at p? We (i) obtain

Indexed-term info (computed at	states	A_{11}	A_{12}	A_{13}	A_{14}	A_{15}	?	A_1	A_2
index construction time)	preorder	f	g	a	a	h	Y	h	a
Query-term info (computed at	preorder	f	g	a	X	h	a	h	a
retrieval time)	states	A_{11}	A_{12}	A_{13}		A_1	A_2	A_1	A_2

Figure 28: Illustration of states reached when the strings from the indexed term and query term are scanned using the automaton of Figure 26

the state A reached on inspecting a prefix of S_t that extends to a length of l after the position p; (ii) obtain the state B representing the state reached on examining the prefix of S_s of length l; (iii) ensure that B actually represents the prefix of S_s of length l, i.e., ensure that $depth(B) = l$ in the goto tree[4]; (iv) verify whether B is an ancestor of A.

The detailed algorithm for retrieving unifiable terms is shown below in Figure 29. Procedure *Index* uses two arrays T and S that contain information about the symbols inspected in a preorder traversal of t and s respectively. These arrays are thus indexed by preorder numbers of nodes in the terms t and s. Each record in T has four fields: *label*, *varposn*, *subtree* and *state*. The *label* field is used to specify the functor/variable symbol at the ith position in a preorder traversal of the indexed term t. The *varposn* field at $T[i]$ is set to the preorder number of the nearest variable node that appears after i in preorder in t. The *subtree* field of $T[i]$ is set to the preorder number of the last node in the subtree rooted at node i. The *state* field specifies the state of the automaton reached on reading the symbol at i while scanning t. The structure of array S is identical to T. In addition the algorithm uses variables n_s, n_t, l_s, l_t and v_s. The variables n_s and n_t correspond to preorder numbers of nodes in s and t respectively up to which the retrieval procedure has proceeded without failure. The variables l_s and l_t store the lengths of remaining portions of query and indexed strings. v_s is set to true if the immediately preceding substitution was made to a variable in s. pf and nd are functions that return the preorder number and the number of descendants of a state in the fail tree respectively whereas function *depth* returns the depth of a state in the goto tree.

At run time the query term s is scanned prior to selection of any rule and all the fields in each record of S are filled. Note that T is filled at index construction time. Now procedure *Index* is then invoked to select t.

We illustrate the above method using Figure 28. After initialization at step 1, we proceed to step 10 where l is set to the minimum of the lengths of indexed term and query term strings. In this case, the query string is smaller ($l = 3$). We proceed through to step 15, where we verify that the state A_{13} representing the prefix fga

---

[4]This step is necessary since it is possible that failure transitions may have been taken while examining the prefix of S_s. In such a case, B would represent a proper substring of S_s and not a prefix. The depth check ensures that no failure transitions were taken. Note that this check is not required for preorder strings from the indexed term, as such strings are known to be represented in the index.

Procedure *Index*

1. $n_s := n_t := 1; fail := false; v_s := false;$
2.   while $(\neg fail) \wedge$ (s and t are not completely scanned) do
3.   if $S[n_s].label$ is a variable then
4. $v_s := true;$
5. $n_s := n_s + 1; n_t := T[n_t].subtree + 1;$
6.   elsif $T[n_t].label$ is a variable then
7. $v_s := false;$
8. $n_t := n_t + 1; n_s := S[n_s].subtree + 1;$
9.   else
10. $l := min(S[n_s].varposn - n_s + 1, T[n_t].varposn - n_t + 1);$
11. $n_s := n_s + l; n_t := n_t + l$
12. $pre_s := pf(S[n_s - 1].state); pre_t := pf(T[n_t - 1].state);$
13.   if $\neg v_s$ then /* instance of Q1 */
14. $nd_t := nd(T[n_t - 1].state);$
15. $fail := \neg(pre_t \le pre_s \le pre_t + nd_t);$
16.   else /* instance of Q2 */
17. $nd_s := nd(S[n_s - 1].state);$
18. $d_s := depth(S[n_s - 1].state);$
19. $fail := \neg(pre_s \le pre_t \le pre_s + nd_s) \vee \neg(l_s = d_s)$
20.   endif
21.   endif;
22. end

Figure 29: Procedure *Index* for retrieval of unifiable terms

is (trivially) an ancestor of the state A_{13} stored with the 3rd symbol in the query string. The algorithm loops back to step 3, where we skip the variable in the query term. Also, v_s is set at step 4. The algorithm proceeds to step 10. Here, l is set to 1, which corresponds to the remaining length of the indexed string. Since v_s is set, we proceed through steps 17 through 19, where we check whether the second query-term string prefix h occurs at the fifth position in the first string from the indexed term. Clearly, A_1 represents the prefix h (see Figure 43(c)). Furthermore, the state representing the first string from indexed term, namely A_{15}, is a descendant of A_1 in the fail tree. Hence the second string-matching step also succeeds. In the next string matching step, we look for the occurrence of the second string from indexed term starting at the 3rd position in the second string from the query term. Again we note that the state stored with the last symbol in the second string from the query term is the same as that representing the second string from the indexed term. Therefore this string-matching step also succeeds and the indexed term is selected to be included as a candidate term.

When multiple indexed terms are present, we sequence through the indexed terms one-by-one, asking this series of questions on behalf of each indexed term. Note that although the questions are asked on a per-indexed-term basis, the string matching operations themselves are performed just once, and the symbols from the query term are also inspected at most once. Although this operation of sequencing through the indexed terms may appear very inefficient, it is in general unavoidable in techniques that generate multiple strings from each indexed term, such as path indexing and automata-driven indexing. Moreover, the impact of such sequencing can be minimized in practice using "coarse filtering" techniques (such as those described below) that quickly filter out indexed terms that are candidates.

8.2.3. Implementation issues

A straightforward way to perform rule selection is to invoke function *retrieve* once for every rule. However such a method regards every indexed term as a likely candidate, and will hence waste time on many indexed terms that can be readily ruled out. To do this, the above algorithm can be modified as follows. Specifically, we can construct a coarsely filtered set of indexed terms such that the first string of every one of these indexed terms is either a prefix of the first string from the query term or vice versa. This is done by taking all of the first preorder strings from all of the indexed terms and constructing an automaton to recognize these strings[5]. Let A be any state of the automaton, and let S_A be the string represented by A. Then this state is annotated with the set $\mathcal{M}$ of indexed terms such that for every $l \in \mathcal{M}$, the first string of l is a prefix of S_A or vice-versa. For retrieval, we traverse the coarse filtering automaton with the query term, stopping either when we encounter a final state of the automaton or when we reach the end of the first string in the query term. The set of indexed terms associated with the automaton state at this point will be taken as the coarse-filtered set of indexed terms. We can now restrict our attention to this subset of indexed terms, sequencing through them to answer string-matching questions for the subsequent strings in these indexed terms.

Several other optimizations are possible with automata-driven indexing. With these optimizations, the automata-driven indexing has been integrated into the ALS Prolog system. Use of this technique resulted in speed improvements of 0% (i.e., no performance degradation for any program) to 30% for typical programs. This implementation performs indexing in *multiple stages*. Each stage starts off with a filtered set of candidate terms, and uses the indexing approach implemented within the stage to further reduce the candidate set. Successive stages perform increasingly complex operations for indexing. In the *ALS* implementation, the first stage performed first-argument indexing, the second stage used the coarse filtering technique above, while the final stage performed the full-blown version of automata-driven indexing. Although this particular implementation required three stages to gain consistent performance improvement, it is possible to integrate the first and second stages without suffering performance penalty. Thus, speed improvements could be gained with this approach by just using the coarse-filtering stage before

---

[5]The resulting automaton would look like a discrimination tree for the indexed term, except every path in this tree is truncated at the first transition that is labelled with a '*'.

the full-blown automata-driven indexing stage.

8.3. Summary of advantages and disadvantages

Automata-driven indexing factors the operations involved in matching the function symbols of the query term with those from the indexed terms. In particular, it ensures that *no symbol in the query term is ever examined more than once*. This contrasts with some of the indexing techniques described earlier (e.g., discrimination trees) where symbols may have to be reexamined (potentially many times) due to backtracking. Although adaptive indexing avoids reexamination of symbols, this is achieved at the cost of a potential exponential blow-up in the size of the index, which is avoided in automata-driven indexing. On the negative side, note that this technique generates multiple preorder strings from each indexed term, similar to path indexing. Combining the results involving individual preorder strings (so as to determine compatibility of the indexed and query terms) is time-consuming, as we have to sequence through many indexed terms. Automata-driven indexing shares this drawback with path indexing, which may also end up spending a substantial amount of time sequencing through the indexed terms in the combination step. In practice, however, we find that the overhead of such combination steps is lower in the case of path indexing than automata driven indexing. On the other hand, automata driven indexing generates fewer strings from each indexed term than path indexing, and thus the number of combination steps is reduced.

In the worst-case, automata-driven indexing requires $O(|s| + \sum_{i=1}^{i=n} t_i)$ time to index n indexed terms $t_1, ..., t_n$. We note that the worst-case performance of automata-driven indexing cannot be improved upon in general. This is because in the worst case, all of the indexed terms are unifiable with a query term, and so we need to compute the substitutions for all of the variables in all of the indexed terms. This leads us to a lower bound that is the same as the runtime complexity of automata-driven indexing. In practice, however, techniques such as unification factoring are better suited for dealing with root-unifications.

It must be emphasized that a key benefit of automata-driven indexing is that the ideas are applicable to handle indexing questions that involve all of the subterms of the query term. None of the other indexing techniques discussed in this paper are able to reuse the efforts involved in unifying the query term at the root for operations involving unification of the subterms. The interested reader is referred to [Ramesh et al. 1994] for details.

9. Code trees

Code trees were introduced in [Voronkov 1994, Voronkov 1995]. A code tree is an index consisting of pieces of code instead of strings. Every piece of code is an instruction of an abstract machine able to perform the retrieval operation.

The general scheme of this indexing technique is as follows. Suppose that we have a retrieval condition R. For every indexed term l, we compile l into a sequence of instructions $i_1, \ldots, i_n$ of the abstract machine. This sequence represents a function I_l such that for every possible query term t we have $I_l(t) \Leftrightarrow R(l, t)$. The sequence of instructions may, in general, not execute sequentially. For example, it may have branching or jump instructions.

Given a collection $\mathcal{L}$ of terms, the code tree for this collection is constructed as follows. For every $l \in L$ we compile the corresponding sequence of instructions representing I_l. Then we integrate this sequence of instructions into a (large) automaton called *code tree*. The code tree represents the function $I_{\mathcal{L}}$ such that $I_{\mathcal{L}}(t)$ returns the list of all $l \in \mathcal{L}$ such that $R(l, t)$.

Code trees are used in VAMPIRE to implement retrieval of generalizations (used in *forward demodulation*) and multiliteral subsumption (see Section 13.2).

9.1. Retrieval of generalizations

Algorithms for performing retrieval on different representations of a query term may differ in a number of details. For example, when we perform depth-first traversal of a query term $f(s, t)$ represented as a tree and go down from the symbol f to the subterm s we have to memorize the subterm t, since t should be traversed after the traversal of s has been completed. If we use the flatterm representation of query terms, memorizing t is unnecessary, since we will arrive at the term t anyhow when the traversal of s will have been completed.

Since a code tree represents a code for performing retrieval, the code contains instructions for performing traversal of the query term and thus the set of instructions used in code trees may depend on the chosen representation of query terms. In this section we choose the *flatterm* representation considered in *partially adaptive code trees*partially adaptive code treecode tree!partially adaptive [Riazanov and Voronkov 2000b]. A version of code trees working with nearly an arbitrary representation of query terms is presented in [Voronkov 1995].

We will use the term traversal functions $next_t$ and $after_t$ introduced in Section 6.2.2.

We denote by $|t|$ the *size* of a term t. Using flatterms, a term t is represented by an array of the size $|t| + 1$. Let $p_1 < \ldots < p_n$ be all positions in t. Then the i-th element of the array is a pair $\langle s, j \rangle$, where $s = root(t/p_i)$ and $p_j = after_t(p_i)$. For example, the term $f(x, g(a))$ is represented by the structure shown on Figure 30.

In can be seen that computation of our two major term traversal operations on positions, $next_t$ and $after_t$, can be done very efficiently on such a representation. $next_t$ is computed by a simple incrementation of the corresponding subscript, so $next_t(p_i) = p_{i+1}$, and the subscript of $after_t(p_i)$ is given in the ith element explicitly. Another serious advantage of this representation in comparison with tree-like terms is that equality of two subterms t/p_i and q/t_j can be checked efficiently, without using stack operations.

Let us fix a term l. Let $\Lambda = p_1 < p_2 < \ldots < p_n$ be all proper positions in l. Then for $i \in \{1, \ldots, n\}$, $pos_i(l)$ will denote p_i.

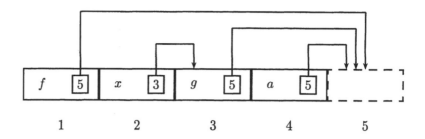

Figure 30: Flatterm structure for $f(x, g(a))$

Let us give several definitions that will be used in the description of subsumption algorithms below. Let $p_{k_1} < \ldots < p_{k_m}$ be all variable positions in l. The i-th *variable position* in l, denoted by $vp_i(l)$, is defined as $vp_i(l) = p_{k_i}$. For $i > m$ $vp_i(l)$ is undefined. The *normalized form* of a term l, denoted by $norm(l)$, is the term obtained from l be replacing the subterm of l at the ith variable position by the variable $*_i$, for all i. For example, the normalized form of $f(x_1, a, g(x_1, x_2))$ is $f(*_1, a, g(*_2, *_3))$.

The *variable equivalence relation* for a term l, denoted $\mathcal{E}_t$, is the equivalence relation on $\{1, \ldots, m\}$ such that: $\langle i, j \rangle \in \mathcal{E}_t$ if and only if $root(t/vp_i(l)) = root(t/vp_j(l))$. For example, the variable equivalence relation for $f(x_1, a, g(x_1, x_2))$ consists of two equivalence classes: $\{1, 2\}$ and $\{3\}$. Note that two terms s, t are variants of each other if and only if the pair $\langle norm(s), \mathcal{E}_s \rangle$ coincides with the pair $\langle norm(l), \mathcal{E}_t \rangle$. If $\mathcal{B}$ is a binary relation, $\mathcal{B}^\approx$ denotes the transitive, reflexive and symmetric closure of $\mathcal{B}$. If $\mathcal{E}$ is an equivalence relation and $\mathcal{B}$ is such a binary relation that $\mathcal{B}^\approx = \mathcal{E}$, then $\mathcal{B}$ is called a *frame* of $\mathcal{E}$. A frame is called *minimal* if no proper subset of it is a frame. Throughout the rest of this paper we consider only equivalence relations over finite sets of the form $\{1, \ldots, m\}$. A finite sequence $\langle u_1, v_1 \rangle, \ldots, \langle u_k, v_k \rangle$ of pairs of integers is called a *computation sequence* for $\mathcal{E}$ if the relation $\{\langle u_1, v_1 \rangle, \ldots, \langle u_k, v_k \rangle\}$ is a minimal frame of $\mathcal{E}$ and $u_i < v_i$ for all $i \in \{1, \ldots, k\}$. Such a computation sequence is called *canonical* if each u_i is the minimal element of its equivalence class in $\mathcal{E}$ and for $i < j$ we have $\langle u_1, v_1 \rangle <_{lex} \ldots <_{lex} \langle u_k, v_k \rangle$, where $<_{lex}$ is the standard lexicographic (i.e., componentwise) order on integers. Note that the canonical computation sequence is uniquely defined.

Consider an example: equivalence relation consisting of two equivalence classes: $\{1, 3, 5, 7\}$ and $\{2, 4\}$. The canonical computation sequence for this relation is $\{\langle 1, 3 \rangle, \langle 1, 5 \rangle, \langle 1, 7 \rangle, \langle 2, 4 \rangle\}$. Another computation sequence for this equivalence relation is $\{\langle 1, 3 \rangle, \langle 3, 5 \rangle, \langle 3, 7 \rangle, \langle 2, 4 \rangle\}$.

```
procedure Subsume(l, t)
begin
  /* First phase: term traversal */
  let subst be an array for storing positions in l;
  pos_l := Λ;
  pos_t := Λ;
  while pos_l ≠ ε
    if norm(l)/pos_l = *_i then
      subst[i] := pos_t;
      pos_t := after_t(pos_t);
      pos_l := after_l(pos_l);
    else /* l/pos_l is not a variable */
      if root(l/pos_l) ≠ root(t/pos_t) then
        return failure;
      else
        pos_t := next_t(pos_t);
        pos_l := next_l(pos_l);
      endif;
    endif;
  end while;
  /* Second phase: comparison of terms */
  let ⟨u_1, v_1⟩, ..., ⟨u_n, v_n⟩ be the canonical computation sequence for E_l.
  forall i ∈ {1, ..., n}
    if t/subst[u_i] ≠ t/subst[v_i] then return failure;
  end forall
  return success;
end
```

Figure 31: A term subsumption algorithm

9.2. Compilation for forward subsumption by one term

In order to define instructions of an abstract machine for performing subsumption, we will first define a subsumption algorithm. On unit clauses, subsumption is equivalent to matching. We are going to solve the following problem: given a term l and a query term t we have to check if l subsumes t. Figure 31 shows a deterministic algorithm that implements forward subsumption.

Following [Voronkov 1995] we specialize this general subsumption algorithm $Subsume$ for each indexed term l, obtaining its specialized version $Subsume_l$. The specialized version has the property $Subsume_l(t) = Subsume(l, t)$, for each query term t. The specialized algorithm is represented as a sequence of instructions of an abstract machine. In other words, we *compile* the term into code of the abstract machine. Then this code is submitted, together with the query term t, to the interpreting procedure. Before presenting technical details, let us consider a simple example.

procedure $Subsume_l(t)$
begin

$p := \Lambda;$	$initl : Initialize(m_1)$
if $root(t/p) \neq f$ return failure;	$m_1 :$ $Check(f, m_2, faill)$
$p := next_t(p);$	
if $root(t/p) \neq g$ return failure;	$m_2 :$ $Check(g, m_3, faill)$
$p := next_t(p);$	
$subst[1] := p;$	$m_3 :$ $Put(1, m_4, faill)$
$p := after_t(p);$	
$subst[2] := p;$	$m_4 :$ $Put(2, m_5, faill)$
$p := after_t(p);$	
if $root(t/p) \neq h$ return failure;	$m_5 :$ $Check(h, m_6, faill)$
$p := next_t(p);$	
$subst[3] := p;$	$m_6 :$ $Put(3, m_7, faill)$
$p := after_t(p);$	
$subst[4] := p;$	$m_7 :$ $Put(4, m_8, faill)$
$p := after_t(p);$	
if $t/subst[1] \neq t/subst[3]$ return failure;	$m_8 :$ $Compare(1, 3, m_9, faill)$
if $t/subst[1] \neq t/subst[4]$ return failure;	$m_9 :$ $Compare(1, 4, m_{10}, faill)$
return success;	$m_{10} :$ $Success$
end	$faill :$ $Failure$

Figure 32: The algorithm *Sub-sume* specialized for the term $l = f(g(x_1, x_2), h(x_1, x_1))$

Figure 33: The corresponding sequence of instructions

9.1. EXAMPLE. Let $l = f(g(x_1, x_2), h(x_1, x_1))$ be an indexed term. The specialised version of the matching algorithm for this term is shown in Figure 32.

This specialized version can be rewritten in a more formal way using special instructions *Initialize, Check, Put, Compare, Success* and *Failure* as shown in Figure 33. The semantics of these instructions should be clear from the example, but will also be formally explained later.

9.3. Abstract subsumption machine

Now we are ready to describe the abstract machine, its instructions, compilation process, and interpretation formally. Memory of the abstract machine is divided into the following "registers":

1. substitution register *subst* which is an array of positions in the query term;

2. register p for storing the current position in the query term;

3. a register *instr* for storing the label of the current instruction.

$Initialize(m_1)$	$p := \Lambda$; goto m_1

$Check(s, m_1, m_2)$	if $root(t/p) = s$
	   then
	     $p := next_t(p)$;
	     goto m_1
	   else goto m_2

$Put(n, m_1, m_2)$	$subst[n] := p$; $p := after_t(p)$; goto m_1

$Compare(m, n, m_1, m_2)$	if $t/subst[m] = t/subst[n]$
	   then goto m_1;
	   else goto m_2

$Success$	return success
$Failure$	return failure

Figure 34: Semantics of instructions in code sequences

To identify instructions in code we will use *labels*. We distinguish two special labels: *initl*, and *faill*. A *labeled instruction* will be written as a pair of the form $m : I$, where m is a label and I is the instruction itself. The instruction set of our abstract machine consists of *Initialize*, *Check*, *Put*, *Compare*, *Success* and *Failure*. *Success* and *Failure* have no arguments. Other instruction have the following form:

- *Initialize*(m_1), where m_1 is a label;
- *Check*(f, m_1, m_2), where f is a function symbol and m_1, m_2 are labels;
- *Put*(n, m_1, m_2), where n is a positive integer and m_1, m_2 are labels;
- *Compare*(n_1, n_2, m_1, m_2), where n_1, n_2 are positive integers and m_1, m_2 are labels.

For convenience, we define two functions on instructions, *cont* and *back*. On all the above instructions *cont* returns m_1 and *back* returns m_2. Intuitively, *cont* is the label of the instructions that should be executed after the current instruction (if this instruction succeeds), and *back* is the label of the instruction that is executed if the current instruction fails.

The semantics of the instructions is shown in Figure 34. At the moment the last argument of *Put* is dummy. It will be used when we discuss the case of many indexed terms.

For a given indexed term l, compilation of instructions for *Subsume$_l$* results in a set of labeled instructions, called the *code for l*. It consists of two parts: *traversal code* and *compare code* plus three standard instructions: *initl* : *Initialize*(m_1), *succl* : *Success* and *faill* : *Failure*.

Suppose $p_1 < p_2 < \ldots < p_k$ are all positions in l. The *traversal code* for l is the set of labeled instructions $\{m_1 : I_1, \ldots, m_k : I_k\}$, where m_i's are labels and I_i's are defined as follows:

$$I_i = \begin{cases} Check(root(l/p_i), m_{i+1}, faill), & \text{if } l/p_i \text{ is not a variable;} \\ Put(k, m_{i+1}, faill), & \text{if } norm(l)/p_i = *_k. \end{cases}$$

Let $\langle u_1, v_1 \rangle, \ldots, \langle u_n, v_n \rangle$ be the canonical computation sequence for $\mathcal{E}_l$. Then the *compare code* for l is the set of instructions $m_{k+i} : Compare(u_i, v_i, m_{k+i+1}, faill)$ for $i \in \{1, \ldots, n\}$, where $m_{k+n+1} = succl$. In Figure 33 from example 9.1 instructions m_1–m_7 and m_8, m_9 form the traversal and the compare code respectively.

The code for l is executed on the query term according to the semantics of instructions shown in Figure 34, beginning with the instruction *Initialize*. The following statement is unlikely to surprise anybody: execution of the code for l on any query term t terminates and returns *success* if and only if l subsumes t. Observe that code for l has a linear structure: instructions can be executed sequentially. In view of this observation we will call code for l also the *code sequence* for l.

9.4. Code tree for a set of indexed terms

Recall that our main problem is to find if any term l in a large set L of indexed terms subsumes a given query term t. Using compilation described in the previous subsection, one can solve the problem by the execution of the codes for all terms in L. This solution is inappropriate for large sets of terms. However, code sequences for terms can still be useful as we can share many instructions from code for different terms. We rely on the following observation: in most instances in automated theorem proving the set L contains many terms having similar structure. Code sequences for similar terms often have long coinciding prefixes. It is natural to combine the code sequences into one indexing structure, where the equal prefixes of code sequences are shared. Due to the tree-like form of such structures we call them *code trees*. Nodes of code trees are instructions of the abstract subsumption machine. Linking of different code sequences is done by setting appropriate values to the *cont* and *back* arguments of the instructions. A branch of such a tree is a code sequence for some indexed term interleaved by some instructions of code sequences for other indexed terms. Apart from reducing memory consumption, combining code sequences in one index results in tremendous improvements in time-efficiency, since during a subsumption check shared instructions are executed once for several terms in the indexed set. To illustrate this idea, let us compare the code sequences for the terms $l_1 = f(f(x_1, x_2), f(x_1, x_1))$ and $l_2 = f(f(x_1, x_2), f(x_2, x_2))$ given in Figure 35.

Sharing the first eight instructions of this results in the code given in Figure 36. This figure also illustrates control flow of this code.

We can execute this code as follows. First, the eight shared instructions are executed. If none of them results in failure, we continue by executing instructions m_8, m_9, m_{10}. If the *Success* instruction m_{10} is reached the whole process terminates

$initl : Initialize(m_1)$
$m_1 : Check(f, m_2, faill)$
$m_2 : Check(f, m_3, faill)$
$m_3 : Put(1, m_4, faill)$
$m_4 : Put(2, m_5, faill)$
$m_5 : Check(f, m_6, faill)$
$m_6 : Put(3, m_7, faill)$
$m_7 : Put(4, m_8, faill)$
$m_8 : Compare(1, 3, m_9, faill)$
$m_9 : Compare(1, 4, m_{10}, faill)$
$m_{10} : Success$

$initl : Initialize(m_1)$
$m_1 : Check(f, m_2, faill)$
$m_2 : Check(f, m_3, faill)$
$m_3 : Put(1, m_4, faill)$
$m_4 : Put(2, m_5, faill)$
$m_5 : Check(f, m_6, faill)$
$m_6 : Put(3, m_7, faill)$
$m_7 : Put(4, m_8, faill)$
$m_8 : Compare(2, 3, m_9, faill)$
$m_9 : Compare(2, 4, m_{10}, faill)$
$m_{10} : Success$

Figure 35: Code sequences for two terms

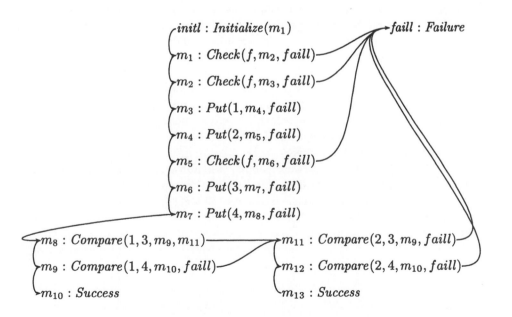

Figure 36: Code tree for two terms

with success. Otherwise, if any of the equality checks m_8, m_9, failed, we have to backtrack and resume the execution from the instruction m_{11}.

In general, to maintain a code tree $C_{\mathcal{L}}$ for a dynamically changing set $\mathcal{L}$, one has to implement two operations: integration of new code sequences into the tree, when a term is inserted in $\mathcal{L}$, and removal of sequences when a term is deleted from $\mathcal{L}$. The integration of a code sequence C_l into a code tree $C_{\mathcal{L}}$ can be done as follows. We move simultaneously along the sequence C_l and a branch of $C_{\mathcal{L}}$ beginning from the *Initialize* instructions. If the current instruction $I_{\mathcal{L}}$ in $C_{\mathcal{L}}$ coincides with the current instruction I_l in C_l up to the label arguments, we follow down the instructions in their *cont* arguments. If $I_{\mathcal{L}}$ differs from I_l we have to consider two cases:

1. If $back(I_{\mathcal{L}})$ is not the *Failure* instruction, then in the code tree we move to this instruction and continue integration.

2. If $back(I_{\mathcal{L}})$ is *Failure*, we set the *back* argument of $I_{\mathcal{L}}$ to the label of I_l. Thus, the rest of the code sequence C_l together with the passed instructions in C_l forms a new branch in the tree.

Removal of obsolete branches is also very simple: we remove from the code all unshared instructions corresponding to the removed term and link the remaining instructions in an appropriate manner. Due to postponing *Compare* instructions, code trees maintained in this manner have an important property: traversal codes for any terms having the same normalized form are shared completely.

Code trees are executed nearly the same way as code sequences, but with one difference due to possible backtrack points. As soon as an instruction with a backtrack argument is found, we store its backtrack argument and the current position in the query term in special stacks *backtrPos* and *backtrInstr*. Semantics of instructions in code trees is shown in Figure 37.

It is worth noting that all operations in the semantics of the instructions can be executed very efficiently on flatterms. Riazanov and Voronkov [2000*b*] consider *partially adaptive code trees*, in which the *Compare* instruction do not necessarily correspond to the canonical sequence for $\mathcal{E}_l$. Moreover, these instructions can be moved up and down the code tree.

The experiments described in Nieuwenhuis, Hillenbrand, Riazanov and Voronkov [2001] have shown that, for retrieval of generalization, code trees (as implemented in VAMPIRE) are faster than perfect discrimination trees (as implemented in WALD-MEISTER) by about a factor of 1.4 and faster than context trees implemented in FIESTA by about a factor of 1.9. Code trees use about 1.2 times more space compared to context trees and about 4.6 time less space than discrimination trees.[6]

---

[6]WALDMEISTER's discrimination trees are array-based, so every node occupies a considerable amount of memory, even if only one term is stored in this node.

$Initialize(m_1)$	$p := \Lambda;$ $backtrPos := empty\ stack;$ $backtrInstr := empty\ stack;$ goto m_1

$Check(s, m_1, m_2)$	if $root(t/p) = s$ then
	   $push(m_2, backtrInst);$
	   $push(p, backtrPos);$
	   $p := next_t(p);$
	   goto m_1
	 else goto m_2

$Put(n, m_1, m_2)$	$push(m_2, backtrInst);$ $push(p, backtrPos);$ $subst[n] := p;$ $p := after_t(p);$ goto m_1

$Compare(k, n, m_1, m_2)$	if $l/subst[k] = l/subst[n]$ then
	   $push(m_2, backtrInst);$
	   $push(p, backtrPos);$
	   goto m_1
	 else goto m_2

$Success$	return success
$Failure$	if $backtrPos$ is empty then return failure $p = pop(backtrPos);$ goto $pop(backtrInst)$

Figure 37: Semantics of instructions in code trees

10. Substitution trees

10.1. Overview

Substitution trees [Graf 1995] extend the model of indexing presented earlier so that comparisons in the index no longer involve simple tests of equality on nonvariable symbols, but can test for unifiability among terms. This is achieved by storing substitutions rather than terms or p-strings. The idea of using arbitrary unification operations in the index can be traced to abstraction trees [Ohlbach 1990]. As a result of this, substitution trees can be smaller in size. Moreover, substitution trees can factor out the computation of substitutions, as opposed to just matching operations

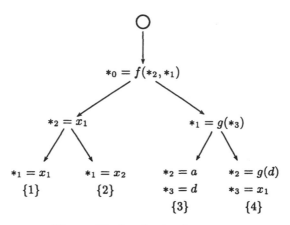

Figure 38: A substitution tree

involving nonvariable symbols.

We will use *normalized variables* in the indexed terms as defined on page 1889. For instance, we rename the indexed terms $f(x, a)$ into $f(x_1, a)$ and $f(x_1, x_2)$. In addition to the normalized variables $x_1, x_2, \ldots$ we will use a sequence of variables $*_0, *_1, \ldots$, disjoint from the variables of indexed or query terms, to represent substitutions. Substitution of a term t for a variable $*_i$ will be denoted by an equality $*_i = t$. In substitution trees, instead of storing a term t, we store a substitution $*_0 = t$ represented as a composition of substitutions for $*_i$. For example, the term $f(g(a, x_1))$ can be stored as a composition of such substitutions in several different ways, including $*_0 = f(g(a, x_1))$ and $*_0 = f(g(*_1, x_1))$, $*_1 = a$. Substitution trees share common parts of substitutions rather than common prefixes. Every branches in a substitution tree represents an indexed term, obtained by composing the substitutions on this branch and applying the resulting substitution to $*_0$.

10.1. EXAMPLE. We illustrate substitution tree indexing with an example set consisting of four indexed terms

$$(1)\ f(x_1, x_1), \quad (2)\ f(x_1, x_2),$$
$$(3)\ f(a, g(d)), \quad (4)\ f(g(d), g(x_1)).$$

in Figure 38. By composing the substitutions on e.g., the rightmost branch:

$$*_0 = f(*_2, *_1), \ *_1 = g(*_3), \ *_2 = g(d), \ *_3 = x_1,$$

we obtain the substitution of $f(g(d), g(x_1))$ for $*_0$ representing indexed term 4.

10.2. Index maintenance

Before discussing indexing algorithms, let us note one feature of substitution trees: the order of term traversal is not fixed in advance. For example, for the substitution tree of Figure 38, the substitution for the first argument of f is done before the substitution for its second argument in indexed terms $1, 2$, but it is done after in indexed terms $3, 4$. So when we traverse indexed terms $1, 2$, we traverse the arguments of f left-to-right, while for indexed terms $3, 4$ we traverse them right-to-left. This feature may lead to very compact substitution trees, but it also has some undesirable consequences for the indexing algorithms:

1. There may be several different ways to *insert* a term in a substitution tree. For example, if we insert $f(x_1, g(x_2))$ in the substitution tree of Figure 38, we may follow down any of the transitions coming out from $*_0 = f(*_1, *_2)$. If we follow the left one, we share the substitution $*_1 = x_1$, if we follow the right one, we share $*_2 = g(x_3)$. This property can be used to find an optimal way of inserting a term and lead to even more compact substitution trees, but optimal insertion requires more complex algorithms.

2. When we *delete* a term t from a substitution tree, if there are several transitions coming out from a node, we cannot decide which transition corresponds to t by simply looking at the children of this node. Therefore, algorithms for deletion of a term from a substitution tree involve some kind of backtracking.

3. *Retrieval* may result in a larger amount of backtracking steps compared to other indexing techniques. For example, if all of the indexed terms and the query term are ground, retrieval using all previously studied indexing techniques will be deterministic, but retrieval using substitution trees may require backtracking even in this case.

In this paper we present a version of substitution trees called *linear substitution trees* of Graf [1996]. In linear substitution trees, on any root-to-leaf path, each variable $*_i$ occurs at most once in right-hand sides of substitutions. For example, the substitution $*_0 = f(*_1, *_1)$ cannot occur in a linear substitution tree. Likewise, two substitutions $*_1 = f(*_3)$ and $*_2 = g(*_3)$ cannot occur on the same branch. However, the substitution $*_0 = f(x_1, x_1)$ is perfectly legal.

Insertion of indexed terms $l_1, ..., l_n$ is viewed as insertion of the substitutions $*_0 = l_1, ..., *_0 = l_n$. The insertion process works by following down a path in the tree that is *compatible* with the substitution ρ to be inserted. To formally define insertion and deletion of substitutions, let us introduce a few notions.

Let l_1, l_2 be terms and V be a set of variables $\{*_i, *_{i+1}, *_{i+2}, ...\}$ for some $i \geq 0$, such that V is disjoint from the variables of l_1, l_2. The *most specific linear common generalization* of l_1 and l_2 with respect to V, denoted $mslcg(l_1, l_2, V)$ is defined as follows.[7]

1. If either l_1 or l_2 is a variable $*_k$, then $mslcg(l_1, l_2)$ is $*_k$.

---

[7]Our notion of most specific linear common generalization is slightly nonstandard, since we treat variables in $\{*_0, *_1, ...\}$ differently from other variables. However, one can prove that the result is always the most general linear term that generalizes both l_1 and l_2.

2. Otherwise, if l_1 coincides with l_2, then $mslcg(l_1, l_2) = l_1$.

3. Otherwise, let p be the first (in the preorder traversal order) position in both l_1 and l_2 such that the top symbols of l_1/p and l_2/p are different. Consider two cases

(a) Either l_1/p or l_2/p is a variable $*_k$. Define $l'_1 = l_1[*_k]_p$ and $l'_2 = l_2[*_k]_p$. Then define $mslcg(l_1, l_2, V)$ to be the most specific linear common generalization of l'_1 and l'_2 with respect to V.

(b) Otherwise, define $l'_1 = l_1[*_i]_p$ and $l'_2 = l_2[*_i]_p$. Then define $mslcg(l_1, l_2, V)$ to be the most specific linear common generalization of l'_1 and l'_2 with respect to $V - \{*_i\}$.

For example, the most specific linear common generalization of $f(g(x_1), g(x_1))$ and $f(x_1, g(x_2))$ with respect to $\{*_2, \ldots\}$ is the term $f(*_2, g(*_3))$. Likewise, the most specific linear common generalization of $f(g(x_1), g(*_1))$ and $f(x_1, g(x_2))$ with respect to $\{*_2, \ldots\}$ is the term $f(*_2, g(*_1))$.

Let σ_1 and σ_2 be two substitutions and V be a set of variables such that both V and the domains of σ_1 and σ_2 are subsets of $\{*_0, *_1, \ldots\}$. The *most specific linear common generalization* of σ_1 and σ_2 with respect to V, denoted $mslcg(\sigma_1, \sigma_2, V)$, is defined as follows. Consider the set X of all variables x such that $x\sigma_1$ and $x\sigma_2$ have the same top symbol and $x\sigma_1 \neq x$. Let $X = \{*_1, \ldots, *_j\}$ such that $i < \ldots < j$. Take any function symbol h and let s be the most specific linear common generalization of the terms $h(*_i\sigma_1, \ldots, *_j\sigma_1)$ and $h(*_i\sigma_2, \ldots, *_j\sigma_2)$ with respect to V. Then s has the form $h(s_i, \ldots, s_j)$ for some terms $s_i, \ldots, s_j$. Define $mslcg(\sigma_1, \sigma_2, V)$ to be the substitution $\{*_i = s_i, \ldots, *_j = s_j\}$.

10.2. Example. The most specific linear common generalization of the substitutions

$$\sigma_1 = \{*_1 = g(a), *_2 = f(c, x_1), *_3 = g(c)\}$$
$$\sigma_2 = \{*_1 = g(b), *_2 = x_1, *_3 = g(x_2)\}$$

with respect to $\{*_4, \ldots\}$ is computed as follows. First, the set X consists of the variables $*_1$ and $*_3$ because σ_1 and σ_2 disagree on the top symbols of $*_2$. Then we have to compute the most specific linear common generalization of $h(g(a), g(c))$ and $h(g(b), g(x_2))$, that is $h(g(*_4), g(*_5))$. Therefore, the most specific linear common generalization of σ_1 and σ_2 is the substitution $\rho = \{*_1 = g(*_4), *_3 = g(*_5)\}$.

Two substitutions σ_1 and σ_2 are called *compatible* if their most specific linear common generalization is nonempty. Let σ and ρ be two substitutions. If there exists a substitution τ such that for every variable x in the domain of σ we have $x\rho\tau = x\sigma$, we denote τ by σ/ρ. It is not hard to argue that for any compatible substitutions σ_1, σ_2 and their most specific linear common generalization ρ, both σ_1/ρ and σ_2/ρ are defined. For instance, for the substitutions of Example 10.2, we have

$$\sigma_1/\rho = \{*_2 = f(c, x_1), *_4 = a, *_5 = c\};$$
$$\sigma_2/\rho = \{*_2 = x_1, *_4 = b, *_5 = x_2\}.$$

function *insert*(node n, substitution σ)
1.   if $\exists$ a child n' of n labelled by ρ such that ρ is compatible with σ then
2. $\tau := mslcg(\sigma, \rho)$;
3.   if $\tau = \rho$ then
4.   *insert*$(n', \sigma/\rho)$
5.   else
6.   change label of n' to ρ/τ;
7.   insert a new node n'' labelled by τ between n and n';
8.   add to n'' as a child a new leaf labelled by σ/τ
9.   endif
10. else
11.   add to n as a child a new leaf labelled by σ
12. endif

Figure 39: Algorithm for insertion into a substitution tree

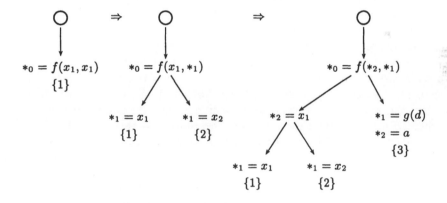

Figure 40: Insertion of terms into a substitution tree

An algorithm for insertion in substitution trees is given in Figure 39. To insert a term l in the substitution tree, one should call the insertion function *insert* using, as arguments, the top node of the tree and the substitution $*_0 = l$.

We will illustrate this algorithm on the terms used in Example 10.1, assuming that they are inserted in the order of their numbers. The substitution tree containing all four terms was already shown in Figure 38. The intermediate substitution trees consisting of the terms (1), (1)–(2), and (1)–(3) are shown in Figure 40. In general, a different order of inserting indexed terms in a substitution tree may result in different trees.

Deletion of a term l from a substitution tree is quite straightforward except that backtracking is required to find the leaf corresponding to the substitution $*_0 = l$

to be deleted. When the leaf is found, we delete all nodes that correspond only to this substitution and repair the tree, by collapsing sequences of nodes with a single child into one node. For example, deletion of term (4) from the substitution tree of Figure 38 results in the rightmost substitution tree among those in Figure 40.

10.3. Retrieval of unifiable terms

When an indexing technique is used as a perfect filter, some retrieval conditions may be more difficult to handle than others. For example, for discrimination trees retrieval of generalizations is straightforward, but retrieval of unifiable terms of instances is more difficult to implement because of embedded variables.

Substitution trees differ from other indexing techniques in this aspect: all retrieval operations have quite a straightforward implementation on substitution trees. As a result, some provers (SPASS and FIESTA) use substitution trees as a single indexing data structure. This feature is due to storing substitutions rather than symbols at nodes. The price to pay is that an operation performed at visiting a node is not a simple comparison of symbols, but may involve complex operations, like unification. We will demonstrate this by retrieval of unifiable terms from substitution trees.

Retrieval proceeds by following down all paths in the substitution tree that contain only substitutions compatible with the given query term. Specifically, we follow down each edge in the substitution tree, starting from the root, until we hit a leaf or we reach a substitution that is incompatible with the query term. In the former case, the indexed terms associated with the leaf are added to the candidate set, whereas in the latter case we prune the search operation at this node. It is convenient to perform this operation using a backtracking algorithm, as with discrimination trees. As an example, consider the substitution tree of Figure 38 and the query term $f(f(a, y_1), y_1)$.

Retrieval is demonstrated in Figure 41. We use dashed arrows to show the nodes visited successfully. The computed substitutions are illustrated at the left-hand side of the picture.

Graf [1996] describes some variations of substitution trees. Here we presented linear substitution trees, but they can also be nonlinear, containing substitutions like $*_0 = f(*_1, *_1)$. In *weighted substitution trees* we maintain additional information about size of substitutions. This information can be used to prune some of the unsuccessful paths in the tree very quickly, rather than proceeding until a point where an incompatible substitution is seen.

11. Context trees

Context trees is a data structure for indexing introduced only recently by Ganzinger, Nieuwenhuis and Nivela [2001]. Since we learned about this technique just a couple of weeks before this volume goes to print, we present it here only sketchily.

Context trees generalize of substitution trees so that one can use variables ranging

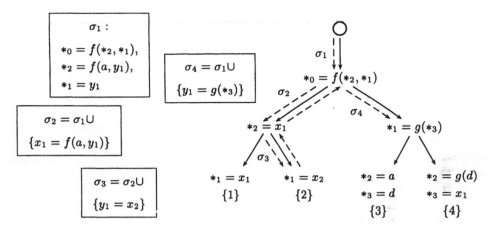

Figure 41: Retrieval of terms unifiable with $f(f(a, y_1), y_1)$ from a substitution tree

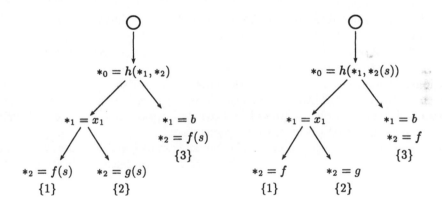

Figure 42: A substitution tree and a context tree

over function symbols. For example, the term $f(a, b)$ can be represented using a composition of substitutions $*_0 = *_1(a, b), *_1 = f$. Thus, terms with different function symbols can be shared, too.

Consider an example taken from [Ganzinger et al. 2001]. The set of indexed terms consists of the following three terms:

$$(1) \ h(x_1, f(s)), \quad (2) \ h(x_1, g(s)), \quad (3) \ h(b, f(s)).$$

where s is an arbitrary term. Figure 42 shows a left-to-right substitution tree (i.e., the traversal order is always left-to-right) and a context tree for this set of terms.

Context trees are more compact than substitution trees. Retrieval time depends on the query term. For example, for the query term $h(b, f(r))$ and unification as the retrieval condition the term r will be unified three times with s in the substitution tree, and only once in the context tree of Figure 42. On the contrary, for the query term $h(b, k(r))$ the terms r and s will be unified once in the context tree, but no unification or r against s will take place in the substitution tree.

Context trees can be made even more compact when function symbols of different arities can be shared as well. The technique for this is presented in [Ganzinger et al. 2001] based on the idea of *curried terms*. Essentially, if we want to share the top function symbols in the terms $f(a, b)$ and $h(a)$, we introduce a new function symbol $\cdot$ to denote function application, and consider the terms with their arguments reversed, i.e., $(f \cdot b) \cdot a)$ and $h \cdot a$. Details can be found in [Ganzinger et al. 2001].

12. Unification factoring

12.1. Overview

Unification factoring [Dawson, Ramakrishnan, Ramakrishnan, Sagonas, Skiena, Swift and Warren 1995] is an indexing technique that is similar to substitution trees, but developed independently in the context of logic programming. It shares most of the advantages of substitution trees, including the ability to factor out substitutions. In addition, Dawson, Ramakrishnan, Ramakrishnan, Sagonas, Skiena, Swift and Warren [1995] studied *optimal* algorithms for construction of factoring automata. In this section, we provide a brief description of unification factoring, followed by a discussion of the optimality results.

Unification factoring was developed in the context of logic programming, where programs consists of a collection of *predicate definitions*. Each predicate definition is made up of *clauses* of the form

$$Head :- Body.$$

The set of indexed terms consist of all clause heads that define a single predicate,[8] and the retrieval condition is unifiability.

12.2. Complexity of constructing optimal automata

As with substitution trees, there are many possible ways to build an index, each with a differing performance. The interesting problem then is the design of *optimal* unification factoring that minimizes the cost of retrieval. One possible measure of cost is the number of edges traversed to perform a retrieval operation. This measure is reasonable if the cost of all unification operations in the index are of the same order. In the presence of nonlinear indexed terms, this can no longer be assured: note that the time required to perform an operation such as $X = Y$ will depend on the actual terms appearing in the query term in place of X and Y. As such, we

---

[8]The idea is to build different indexes for different predicates.

limit our discussion to only linear indexed terms in this section, which will ensure that we never have to perform operations that require us to compare arbitrarily large terms.

Although counting the number of edges traversed appears to be a natural way to measure cost, it suffers from the drawback that the cost becomes a function of the query term. This makes it difficult to talk about cost of the automaton as a whole. In order to develop a measure that is independent of the query term, we can make use of the worst-case cost, which corresponds to a query term that has a single nonvariable symbol at its root, with all arguments being distinct variables. (This is the worst case since such a term will unify with every indexed term.) It has been shown [Dawson, Ramakrishnan, Ramakrishnan, Sagonas, Skiena, Swift and Warren 1995] that construction of optimal index is very hard in the case of *nonsequential automata* that deal with indexed terms with no priorities. They also present a polynomial time algorithm for optimal *sequential automata* that deal with indexed terms that are totally ordered in priority. Such sequential automata capture Prolog's strategy of sequentially trying the clauses defining a predicate. The complexity is also dependent on the availability of *mode* information, which specifies in advance (i.e., at index construction time) whether certain subterms in the query term will always be ground terms or always be (free) variables.

	Sequential	*Nonsequential*
Without modes	P (dynamic programming)	NP-complete
With modes	NP-hard in Π_2^p	NP-hard

12.3. *Construction of optimal automata*

We will annotate each state in the sequential unification factoring automaton (SFA) with (a) the prefix of the query term that would be inspected on the path from the root to that state, and (b) the set of indexed terms that are compatible with that prefix. We can treat the compatible set as a sequence, which would allow us to capture the (totally ordered) priority information. The following three properties are used in the construction of an optimal SFA.

1. In an SFA, the transitions from a state partition its compatible set into *subsequences*.

2. In an optimal SFA for a sequence of terms, states and transitions specifying unification operations common to the entire sequence form a "chain" (i.e., a sequence of nodes, each of which has only one outgoing transition).

3. Each subautomaton of an optimal SFA is itself optimal.

For the last point, we note that each sub-SFA will be associated with a different prefix at its root state which reflects the symbols that have been inspected already in reaching that state from the root of the entire SFA. We will hence talk about SFA as being parametrized with respect to the prefix and the compatible set (sequence) associated with its root state.

The construction of an optimal automaton is a recursive process in which, at each state starting with the root, the automaton is expanded based on the compatible set C of indexed terms and the prefix u associated with that state. We consider each position in the fringe of u, and select a position p such that costs of the optimal sub-SFA's created after inspecting p are minimized. From the properties of optimal SFA stated above, it follows that an SFA constructed in this manner will be optimal. The recursive construction process lends itself to a dynamic programming solution as described below. As mentioned earlier, we deal only with linear indexed terms.

We use a function *part* to partition the compatible sequence C into the minimum number of subsequences that share unification operations at this position.

12.1. DEFINITION *(Partition)*. Given a sequence $C = \langle l_1, \ldots, l_n \rangle$ of terms and a position π, the *partition of C by π*, denoted $part(C, \pi)$, is the set of all triples (a, j, j'), $1 \le j \le j' \le n$, such that all $\langle l_j, \ldots, l_{j'} \rangle$ is a maximal subsequence of $\langle l_1, \ldots, l_n \rangle$ having the same symbol a at the position π.

For example, the partition of the sequence $\langle p(a, a), p(a, b), p(b, c), p(a, d) \rangle$ at position 1 is the set $\{(a, 1, 2), (b, 3, 3), (a, 4, 4)\}$ corresponding to the following three maximal subsequences

$$\langle p(a, a), p(a, b) \rangle, \quad \langle p(b, c) \rangle, \quad \langle p(a, d) \rangle.$$

Each triple (a, j, j') computed by *part* corresponds to a transition from an SFA state with prefix u and compatible sequence C. Note that all terms in the subsequence $\langle l_j, \ldots, l_{j'} \rangle$ possess identical symbols at the position p and possibly some of the other positions. Specifically, they are identical in all nonvariables in $mslcg(l_j, \ldots, l_{j'})$. It is clear from the above properties of optimal SFA's that the unification operations corresponding to the common positions (which are not already present in u) will be shared by the indexed terms in the subsequence. Thus, we can build an optimal SFA by identifying the choice of p that minimizes the cost (as per the equation given below), computing the partitions of S with respect to this position, introducing transitions corresponding to each subsequence $\langle l_j, ..., l_{j'} \rangle$, and then using a recursive procedure to complete the sub-SFA reached by these transitions. Observe that the prefix corresponding to the new state reached by the transition (a, j, j') will be $mslcg(l_j/p, \ldots, l_{j'}/p)$. Therefore, we can compute the cost of a minimal SFA for a subsequence $\langle l_i, ..., l_{i'} \rangle$ using the formula

$$cost(i, i', u) = \min_{\pi \in \mathcal{P}_v(u)} \left(\sum_{\substack{(a, j, j') \in \\ part(\langle l_i, \ldots, l_{i'} \rangle, \pi)}} (cost(j, j', u') + |u'| - |u|) \right), \quad (12.1)$$

where u' stands for $mslcg(l_j, ..., l_{j'})$, and $|t|$ denotes the number of nonvariable symbols in t. It is easy to see that the third parameter u of $cost(i, i', u)$ in the above equation is always $mslcg(l_i, ..., l_{i'})$, and is hence uniquely determined by i and i'. Thus, we can eliminate u from the above equation, and compute the minimal SFA using a dynamic programming technique using a two-dimensional table indexed by i and i' for all values $1 \leq i \leq i' \leq n$.

12.2. EXAMPLE. Construction of an optimal SFA for the indexed terms of Figure 43a begins with the computation of its cost, using Equation 12.1. The root position (Pos) and cost ($Cost$) of the lowest cost sub-SFA computed for a subsequence with end points (i, i') at any point in the computation are stored in a table (see Figure 43b) at the entry (i, i'), where i is the row and i' the column. Boldface numbers in the table represent the position and cost for the optimal subautomaton computed for the corresponding subsequence, while italic numbers represent the position and the cost of the discarded (sub-optimal) sub-SFA.

13. Multiterm indexing

In this section we deal with multiterm indexing. There are two cases when the need in multiterm indexing arises:

- The retrieval condition is specified in terms of a finite set of query terms rather than a single query term.
- We deal with an indexed set of *clauses* rather than single terms.

Typical retrieval conditions for multiterm indexing are:

- simultaneous unification;
- forward subsumption;
- backward subsumption;
- clause variance [Riazanov and Voronkov 2001].

We introduce several definitions and then discuss these retrieval conditions in detail.

13.1. DEFINITION *(clause)*. A *clause* is usually defined to be a finite set (or multiset) of literals. For the purposes of this section, it is enough to consider a clause as a *set of terms*. A clause which is a singleton set is called a *unit clause*. When we deal with clauses that may have cardinality ≥ 2 we will speak about *multiliteral clauses*.

We will denote clauses either as a sequence of their terms, $t_1, \ldots, t_n$, or as a disjunction $t_1 \vee \ldots \vee t_n$.

13.1. Simultaneous unification

Simultaneous unification is the following retrieval condition. Given a set of indexed terms $\mathcal{L}$ and a *sequence* of query terms $t_1, \ldots, t_n$, find all sequences of indexed

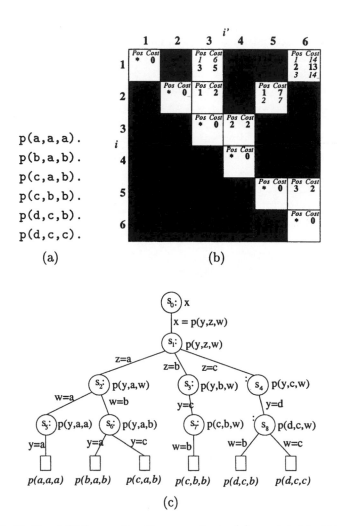

Figure 43: Optimal SFA construction: predicate (a), cost table (b), SFA (c)

terms $l_1, \ldots, l_n$ such that there exist substitutions $\sigma_1, \ldots, \sigma_n, \sigma$ such that

$$l_1 \sigma_1 = t_1 \sigma, \ldots, l_n \sigma_n = t_n \sigma.$$

Simultaneous unification is useful for implementing the hyperresolution and unit-resulting resolution inference rules. The hyperresolution inference rule can be formulated as follows:

$$\frac{l_1 \vee C_1 \quad \cdots \quad l_n \vee C_n \quad \neg t_1 \vee \ldots \vee \neg t_n \vee D}{(C_1 \vee \ldots \vee C_n \vee D)\sigma},$$

where σ is a most general unifier of the sequences $(l_1, \ldots, l_n)$ and $(t_1, \ldots, t_n)$. In this rule, the premises are assumed to be variable-disjoint. However in practice, $t_i \vee C_i$ and $t_j \vee C_j$ for $i \neq j$ can be two copies of the same clause, so l_i and l_j will be the same term in the index. So we use $\sigma_1, \ldots, \sigma_n$ instead of σ in the corresponding retrieval condition.

A hyperresolution inference can be considered as a sequence of binary resolution inferences, but implementation of hyperresolution through binary resolution can be expensive. Hyperresolution is especially valuable when the input set of clauses consists of Horn clauses only. Then the rule can be reformulated in a simpler way:

$$\frac{l_1 \quad \cdots \quad l_n \quad \neg t_1 \vee \ldots \vee \neg t_n \vee t}{t\sigma},$$

so only unit clauses have to be dealt with.

13.2. Subsumption

Multiliteral subsumption is the following retrieval condition on clauses. Given two clauses C and D, does there exist a substitution τ such that $C\tau \subseteq D$. If such a substitution exists, we say that C *subsumes* D. If both C and D are singletons, i.e., $C = \{s\}$ and $D = \{t\}$, it is easy to see that C subsumes D if and only if t is an instance of s. Therefore, when we retrieve candidates for subsumption among unit clauses, we can use the indexing techniques developed so far, retrieval of generalizations for forward subsumption and retrieval of instances for backward subsumption.

Among the retrieval conditions considered so far we distinguished two instance-related problems: retrieval of instances and retrieval of generalizations. Their analogues in multiterm indexing are respectively backward and forward subsumption.

13.2. DEFINITION. *Backward subsumption* is the following retrieval condition: given a set of indexed clauses $\mathcal{C}$ and a query clause D, find all clauses $C \in \mathcal{C}$ such that D subsumes C. *Forward subsumption* is the following retrieval condition: given a set of indexed clauses $\mathcal{C}$ and a query clause D, does there exist a clause $C \in \mathcal{C}$ such that C subsumes D.

Subsumption on unit clauses reduces to matching, so it can be checked in linear time. Multiliteral subsumption is NP-complete. If we consider the set of indexed clauses as constant and vary only the query clause, then forward subsumption can be solved in polynomial time while backward subsumption is still NP-complete. Some provers treat multiliteral clauses as multisets of literals. Then a clause C subsumes a clause D if there exists a substitution σ such that $C\sigma$ is a *submultiset* of D. On multisets, subsumption is still NP-complete, but both forward and backward subsumption are polynomial. Moreover, backward subsumption on multisets can be checked in the time constant in the size of the query clause, but the constant can be exponential in the size of the index.

In practice, both forward and backward subsumption are very expensive operations. For some benchmarks forward subsumption may take over 90% of the overall running time of a prover. Forward subsumption is indispensable: with forward subsumption turned off resolution-based provers are unable to solve problems that are rather trivially solved with forward subsumption turned on. Backward subsumption works very well on some problems but is not very useful on other problems. For example, on some problems VAMPIRE forward subsumes several million clauses while no clause at all is backward subsumed. For this reason, some provers employ incomplete backward subsumption algorithms or even turn backward subsumption off on some problems. Some provers, for example E, use incomplete forward subsumption algorithms.

13.3. Algorithms and data structures for multiterm indexing

There is a variety of algorithms and data structures for multiterm indexing. The techniques used in multiterm indexing are based on the techniques for term indexing. However, generalization to the multiterm case can be quite nontrivial, especially when one wants to achieve perfect filtering.

There are two main approaches to multiterm indexing.

1. Use the standard term indexing data structures and index on a small subset of the set of query terms, for example on two literals only. In this case the candidate set is obtained by the intersection of the candidate sets for the selected query terms. The size of the candidate set may be very large compared to the set of all compatible indexed clauses.

2. Design special data structures, obtained by modification of the corresponding data structures for term indexing. The retrieval algorithms may be quite complex compared to their term indexing counterparts. The aim is to achieve perfect filtering.

There are some issues to multiterm indexing which do not occur in term indexing. Typical examples are the following.

1. *The order of terms in the query set matters.* Consider the situation when the query set consists of two terms t_1, t_2 such that the set of candidate clauses for t_2 is empty while the set of candidate terms for t_1 is large. Obviously, it is better

to begin retrieval with t_2 than with t_1, then the retrieval of candidates for t_2 can be omitted. Moreover, adaptive retrieval algorithms may play a major role.

2. For imperfect filtering based on selection of a subset of query terms *selection of the terms matters*. Ideally, the terms which give smaller candidate sets should be preferred.

3. For some indexing techniques, the *indexed clauses may be reordered before insertion into index*, to achieve a better degree of sharing and/or faster retrieval.

We will illustrate some of these concepts, when we consider code trees for forward subsumption.

13.4. Algorithms for multiliteral forward subsumption

A subsumption algorithm for multiliteral forward subsumption can be obtained from a subsumption algorithm for forward subsumption on terms in the following way. Suppose that we have an indexed clause $C = l_1, \ldots, l_n$ and a query clause $D = t_1, \ldots, t_m$. The clause C subsumes D if for every term l_i in C there exist a term t_{k_i} in D such that l_i subsumes t_{k_i} with some substitution θ_i, and the substitutions $\theta_1, \ldots, \theta_n$ agree on all variables on which they are defined.

For example, let $C = \{g(x_1, f(x_2)), g(x_1, f(f(x_3)))\}$ and $D = \{g(y, f(f(y)))\}$. Then the first literal of C subsumes the first literal of D with the substitution $\theta_1 = \{x_1 \mapsto y, x_2 \mapsto f(y)\}$, and the second literal of C subsumes the first literal of D with the substitution $\theta_2 = \{x_1 \mapsto y, x_3 \mapsto y\}$. The substitutions θ_1 and θ_2 are both defined on x_1, and $\theta_1(x_1) = \theta_2(x_1)$, so C subsumes D.

The main difference between the subsumption algorithm for multiliteral clauses and that for terms is that for each term l_i of the indexed clause $C = l_1, \ldots, l_n$ we have to *find* a corresponding term t_{k_i} of the query clause D. The search for t_{k_i} can be implemented, for example, by a backtracking algorithm which tries the values $1, \ldots, m$ for k_i one by one.

To define a multiliteral subsumption algorithm, let us define some notions related to positions in a clause. From now on we view a clause as a *sequence* of its literals rather than a set.

Consider a clause $C = l_1, \ldots, l_n$. A *position in* C is any pair (m, p) such that $1 \leq m \leq n$ and each p is a proper position in l_m. The order $<$ on positions in C is defined as follows: $(m, p) < (m', p')$ if either $m < m'$ or $(m = m'$ and $p < p')$. As in the case of terms, we extend the set of positions in C by a special position ε called the *end position* in C; this positions is the greatest in the ordering $<$.

We will now define the functions $next_C$ and $after_C$ similar to the corresponding functions on terms. Let $\Lambda = p_1 < \ldots < p_m < p_{m+1} = \varepsilon$ be all positions in C. Then $next_C(p_i) = p_{i+1}$ for all $i \leq m$. The definition of $after_C$ is as follows:

$$after_C(m, p) = \begin{cases} (m, after_{l_m}(p)), & \text{if } after_{l_m}(p) \neq \varepsilon; \\ undefined, & \text{otherwise} \end{cases}$$

We introduce a new relation and two functions on positions in clauses which are related to the literal structure. Let $C = l_1, \ldots, l_n$ be a clause whose proper positions are $p_1, \ldots, p_m$. The partial functions $next\_literal_C$ and $previous\_literal_C$ are defined on the positions of C of the form (m, Λ) as follows:

$$next\_literal_C(m, \Lambda) \quad = \quad \begin{cases} (m+1, \Lambda), & \text{if } m < n; \\ \varepsilon, & \text{otherwise.} \end{cases}$$

$$previous\_literal_C(m, \Lambda) \quad = \quad \begin{cases} (m-1, \Lambda), & \text{if } m > 1; \\ \varepsilon, & \text{otherwise.} \end{cases}$$

One can introduce a data structure on which the functions $next_C$, $after_C$, $next\_literal_C$, $previous\_literal_C$ can be evaluated efficiently. For example, one can use a double-linked list of flatterms.

The notions of *normalized form* of a clause C, denoted by $norm(C)$ and *variable equivalence relation* for a clause C, denoted $\mathcal{E}_C$, are defined in the same way as for terms.

Now we can define a clause-to-clause subsumption algorithm. Such an algorithm is given in Figure 44. Some parts of this algorithm are similar to the corresponding parts of the term subsumption algorithm, other parts implement iteration of literals $l_1, \ldots, l_n$ in the indexed clause C, search for t_{k_i} in the clause D, and backtracking. We use several labels and **goto** statements because the resulting algorithm will be easier to transform into instructions of an abstract subsumption machine than a more structured algorithm.

The algorithm traverses literals in C one by one (see the **first** label). If a match for a particular literal l_i was not found, the algorithm tries to use a different match for the previous literal l_{i-1} (see the use of $previous\_literal_C$ in **backtrack**). If a match of a particular literal in D against l_i fails, the next literal in D is tried (see the use of $next\_literal_D$ in **backtrack**). To remember the latest tried literal in D, we use the stack $backtrPos$ of literal positions in D. When a new literal in D is tried, the position of this literal is pushed on $backtrPos$. This position is popped from $backtrPos$ upon backtracking.

13.5. Code trees for forward subsumption

As in the case of term subsumption, we will now specialize the general subsumption algorithm *Subsume* for each indexed term C, obtaining its specialized version $Subsume_C$, and then represented the specialized version as a sequence of instructions of an abstract machine. The specialized version has the property $Subsume_C(D) = Subsume(C, D)$, for each query term D. The instructions of the abstract machine are very similar to those use for term subsumption, except that added are new instructions for iterating literals in the indexed and query clauses and for backtracking. The code for each particular literal in the indexed clause is compiled almost in the same way as for the term subsumption, except that instead of the label *faill* we use the label of the appropriate backtracking instruction.

```
procedure Subsume(C, D)
begin
  let subst be an array for storing positions in C;
  let backtrPos be a stack for storing positions in D;
  pos_C := (0, Λ);
  first: /* try the first literal in D */
    pos_C := next_literal_C(pos_C);
    pos_D := (1, Λ);
    push(Λ, backtrPos);
    goto next;
  backtrack:
    pos_D := next_literal_D(pop(backtrPos));
    if pos_D = ε then
      if pos_C = Λ then return failure;
      pos_C := previous_literal_C(pos_C);
      goto backtrack;
    else
      push(pos_D, backtrPos);
    endif
  next: /* trying the next literal in D */
    do
      if norm(C)/pos_C = *_i then
        subst[i] := pos_D;
        pos_D := after_D(pos_D);
        pos_C := after_C(pos_C);
      else /* C/pos_C is not a variable */
        if root(C/pos_C) ≠ root(D/pos_D) then goto backtrack;
        pos_D := next_D(pos_D);
        pos_C := next_C(pos_C);
      endif;
    while pos_C is defined;
    /* literal matched successfully */
    if pos_C ≠ ε goto first;
    /* All literals traversed, comparison of terms */
    let ⟨u_1, v_1⟩, ..., ⟨u_n, v_n⟩ be the canonical computation sequence for ℰ_C.
    forall i ∈ {1, ..., n}
      if D/subst[u_i] ≠ D/subst[v_i] then goto backtrack;
    return success;
end
```

Figure 44: A clause-to-clause subsumption algorithm

13.3. EXAMPLE. Let $C = g(x_1, c), h(x_1, x_1)$ be an indexed clause. The specialised version of the subsumption algorithm for this clause and the corresponding sequence of instructions are shown in Figures 45 and 46.

In order to represent the specialized algorithm, two new kinds of instructions have been added: *First* and *Backtrack*. The semantics of these instructions in code trees is given in Figure 47. The instruction *First* sets the current position p to the first position in D and memorizes the address of the following *Backtrack* instruction in the backtrack stack *backtrInst*. The instruction *Backtrack* iterates over other literals in D. This instruction can be reexecuted several times, since it repeatedly pushes its own address on the backtrack stack, until no more literals in the query clause can be found.

Codes for several clauses can be compiled into a code tree, as in the case of forward subsumption for unit clauses. However, we obtain a more considerable gain in efficiency for multiliteral clauses when the backtrack points in different clauses are shared. This happens when the normal forms of one or more initial literals in the index clauses coincide. Consider, for example, two clauses $g(x_1, c), h(x_1, x_1)$ and $g(x_1, c), h(c, x_1)$. The code tree for these clauses and the dataflow of the retrieval algorithm are shown in Figure 48. The very expensive backtracking-related instructions are shared, both for the first and for the second literal in the clauses.

14. Issues in perfect filtering

Up to now, we did not pay major attention to perfect filtering. For some applications, perfect filtering is easy to achieve. A typical example is search for generalizations when all indexed terms are linear (functional programming).

In theorem proving perfect filtering is important because the sets of indexed terms often easily contain 10^5–10^6 terms, so imperfect filtering can results in too many candidates or too few candidates. In this section we consider issues that arise in perfect filtering.

14.1. Normalization of variables

The most typical source of imperfect filters is normalization of terms which "forgets" the variable names. For example, if the term $f(x, x)$ is stored in the index as $f(*_1, *_2)$, one cannot achieve perfect filtering for any of standard retrieval conditions. There are two ways of coping with this problem: normalization of variables and equality constraints.

Normalization of variables. Variables are enumerated in the order of their first occurrences in the indexed term. For example, both terms $f(x, y, x)$ and $f(y, x, y)$ will be turned into $f(*_1, *_2, *_1)$. The main disadvantage of this technique is a relatively small degree of sharing, when indexed terms contain many occur-

procedure $Subsume_C(D)$
begin $initl:$ $Initialize(m_1)$
  first1: $m_1:$ $First(m_3, m_2)$
    $p := \Lambda;$
    $push(\Lambda, backtrPos);$
    goto **next1**;
  backtrack1: $m_2:$ $Backtrack(m_3)$
    $p := next\_literal_D(pop(backtrPos));$
    if $p = \varepsilon$ then return failure;
    $push(p, backtrPos);$
  next1:
    if $root(D/p) \neq g$ then goto **backtrack1**; $m_3:$ $Check(g, m_4, faill)$
    $p := next_D(p);$
    $subst[1] := p;$ $m_4:$ $Put(1, m_5, faill)$
    $p := after_D(p);$
    if $root(D/p) \neq c$ then goto **backtrack1**; $m_5:$ $Check(c, m_6, faill)$
    $p := next_D(p);$
  first2: $m_6:$ $First(m_8, m_7)$
    $p := \Lambda;$
    $push(\Lambda, backtrPos);$
    goto **next2**;
  backtrack2: $m_7:$ $Backtrack(m_8)$
    $p := next\_literal_D(pop(backtrPos));$
    if $p = \varepsilon$ then goto **backtrack1**;
    $push(p, backtrPos);$
  next2:
    if $root(D/p) \neq h$ then goto **backtrack2**; $m_8:$ $Check(h, m_9, faill)$
    $p := next_D(p);$
    $subst[2] := p;$ $m_9:$ $Put(2, m_{10}, faill)$
    $p := after_D(p);$
    $subst[3] := p;$ $m_{10}:$ $Put(3, m_{11}, faill)$
    $p := after_D(p);$
  if $D/subst[1] \neq D/subst[2]$ $m_{11}:$ $Compare(1, 2, m_{12}, faill)$
    then goto **backtrack2**; $m_{12}:$ $Compare(1, 3, m_{13}, faill)$
  if $D/subst[1] \neq D/subst[3]$ $m_{13}:$ $Success$
    then goto **backtrack2**; $faill:$ $Failure$
  return success;
end

Figure 45: The algorithm *Subsume* specialized for the clause $g(x_1, c), h(x_1, x_1)$

Figure 46: The corresponding sequence of instructions

$First(m_1, m_2)$	$p := \Lambda;$ $push(m_2, backtrInst);$ $push(\Lambda, backtrPos);$ goto $m_1;$
$Backtrack(m_1)$	$p := next\_literal_D(pop(backtrPos));$ if $p = \varepsilon$ then goto $faill;$ $push(self, backtrInst);$ $push(p, backtrPos);$ goto $m_1;$

Figure 47: Semantics of additional instructions in code trees

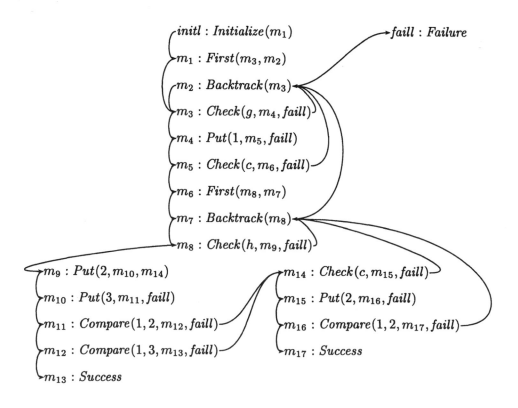

Figure 48: Code tree for two clauses $g(x_1, c), h(x_1, x_1)$ and $g(x_1, c), h(c, x_1)$

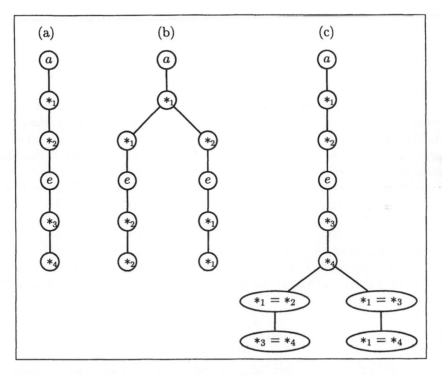

Figure 49: Three ways of representing variables: (a) using imperfect filtering; (b) enumerating variables; (c) using equality constraints

rences of variables. To illustrate this, consider Figure 49 showing three techniques of representing variables in an index storing the set of two terms $\{a(x_1, x_1, e(x_2, x_2)), \; a(x_1, x_2, e(x_1, x_1))\}$ in a discrimination tree.

In (a) imperfect filtering is used, in (b) variables are enumerated, and in (c) equality constraints (described below) are used. Of the three techniques, variable enumeration is likely to consume the largest amount of space when the term sets are large.

Equality constraints. An indexed term l is considered as a pair $\langle l', E \rangle$, where l' is obtained from l by "forgetting" variable names as in the case of imperfect filtering; and E is a set of *equality constraints* of the form $*_i = *_j$ which encode dependencies among the variables of l. A pair $*_i = *_j$ belongs to the equality constraint if $i < j$ and the variable $*_i$ represents the first occurrence of $*_j$ in l. For example $f(x_1, x_1, g(x_2, x_1))$ will be represented by the pair $\langle f(*_1, *_2, g(*_3, *_4)), \{*_1 = *_2, *_1 = *_4\}\rangle$. The index consists of nodes of two kinds: ordinary nodes plus equality constraints.

Using equality constraints results in indexes of smaller sizes. Usually, their use reduces both time for retrieval and memory used by the index. Retrieval is usually faster due to the following observation: each variable creates a potential backtrack point. When variable enumeration is used, each different variable creates an "early" backtrack point. When equality constraints are used, these backtrack points are delayed until the whole term has been processed.

When perfect filtering is required, another problem may arise, both for variable enumeration and equality constraint techniques. This problem arises when multi-literal clauses are used. In multiliteral clauses, one cannot normalize variables in a single literal, because variables are not local to a literal, but may be shared by different literals in a clause. The only sound way to normalize variables is by normalizing them within a clause. Thus, a clause $P(x, y), Q(y, z)$ will be normalized into $P(*_1, *_2), Q(*_2, *_3)$. If we want to store both terms $P(*_1, *_2)$ and $Q(*_2, *_3)$ in the index, then the index may contain nonnormalized literals, for example, $Q(*_2, *_3)$ instead of $Q(*_1, *_2)$. Storing terms that are not normalize can decrease sharing in the index. An interesting technique implemented in some indexes in Vampire is storing normalized terms plus substitutions. For example, when we have to store $Q(*_2, *_3)$, we will store $Q(*_1, *_2)$ instead, but store it together with the substitution $\{*_1 \mapsto *_2, *_2 \mapsto *_3\}$.

14.2. Multiple copies of variables

There is a problem that arises in some indexing operations: for some indexed terms, their multiple copies should be used. A typical example is when search for generalizations is used to reduce a term to its normal form. During reduction to normal form, a term can be rewritten several times, by the same indexed terms, but with different substitutions. For example, if we derived an ordered unit equality $f(x) = g(x)$, it can be used twice to rewrite the query term $h(f(f(y)))$. The first rewriting uses the substitution $\{x \mapsto f(y)\}$ to rewrite the query term into $h(g(f(y)))$; then the second rewriting uses the substitution $\{x \mapsto y\}$ to rewrite this term into $h(g(g(y)))$. When such a sequence of rewritings is performed, several different substitutions can be made for the variables of an indexed term. Therefore, representation of variables (or substitutions) in the index must allow for several different substitutions to be done.

Several provers, including Otter, Vampire, and Fiesta, use *variable banks* use discussed above in Section 3.2. A variable bank is a data structure (usually an array) which represents a (substitution for a) collection of variables. For example, if the index uses variables $*_1, \ldots, *_n$, we can use an array of size n whose elements are references to terms. Each time a sequence of indexing operation is to be performed, for each operation in the index a new variable bank is used.

15. Indexing modulo AC-theories

Many mathematical functions used and modelled in automated reasoning are associative and commutative, as captured by the following two axioms:

$$f(x, f(y, z)) = f(f(x, y), z); \qquad (A)$$
$$f(x, y) = f(y, x). \qquad (C)$$

We write $f \in AC$ if f is such an associative-commutative symbol and write $s =_{AC} t$ to indicate that s and t are equivalent under associativity and commutativity.

15.1. DEFINITION *(Flattened Term)*. *Flattened representation* of a term t is obtained by reducing it to its normal form using rewrite rules of the following form for each AC-symbol f:

$$f(X, f(Y), Z) \quad \rightarrow \quad f(X, Y, Z).$$

Here X, Y and Z denote arbitrary sequences of terms. We denote the flattened form of a term t by $\bar{t}$.

In this section we will often use the flatten form of a term instead of the term itself, and thus treat $f \in AC$ as a function symbol of a nonfixed arity.

   AC-indexing refers to the variation of indexing problem that arises when the relationship between the indexed and query term is augmented to take the AC-properties into account. In this section, we discuss an indexing technique for selecting AC-generalizations of a given query term. More formally, the problem is to select those indexed terms l such that there exists a substitution σ with $l\sigma =_{AC} t$. If such a substitution exists we say that t AC-matches l, l is an AC-generalization of t, and t is an AC-instance of l.

   Consider an example. Let $f \in AC$, $l = f(a, x, b)$, and $t = f(b, c, d, a)$. Then for $\sigma = \{x \mapsto f(c, d)\}$ we have $l\sigma =_{AC} t$. AC-matching has been studied extensively (see, for example [Gottlob and Leitsch 1987, Benanav, Kapur and Narendran 1987, Socher 1989, Kounalis and Lugiez 1991, Nicolaita 1992, Verma and Ramakrishnan 1992, Lugiez and Moysset 1993, Bachmair, Chen and Ramakrishnan 1993, Bachmair, Chen, Ramakrishnan, Anantharaman and Chabin 1995, Eker 1995]). AC-matching is NP-complete in general but can be performed in polynomial time for linear query terms [Benanav et al. 1987].

   If $f \in AC$, we use the notation $\sim$ to denote the smallest symmetric rewrite relation (also called the *permutation congruence*) for which $f(X, u, Y, v, Z) \sim f(X, v, Y, u, Z)$. Observe that l is an AC-generalization of t if and only if $l\sigma \sim \bar{t}$, for some substitution σ.

   The *top-layer* of a term l, denoted by $\hat{l}$, is obtained by replacing all occurrences of an AC-symbol f by a constant, also denoted by f. For example, if $f \in AC$ and $g \notin AC$, then the top-layer of $g(x, f(b, f(x, c)))$ is $g(x, f)$. Let l and t be two flattened terms with $l\sigma \sim t$. Then we have

(i) $\hat{l} \leq \hat{t}$. For example, the term $g(a, g(a, a))$ cannot be an AC-instance of $g(x, f(b, c))$ as the respective top-layers do not match.

(ii) if p is a position of an AC-symbol in the top-layer of l, then $(l/p)\sigma \sim t/p$, i.e., if the top-layers of the given terms match,then we need to consider the stripped-off subterms at the positions of f and recursively determine whether suitable AC-matches can be found.

Conversely, if (i) and (ii) are satisfied for some substitution σ, then $l\sigma \sim t$. In other words, AC-matching is completely characterized by conditions (i) and (ii).

Condition (i) represents a standard (i.e., non-AC) matching problem. Condition (ii) leads to a bipartite graph matching problem as shown below. Suppose that $l/p = f(l_1, \ldots, l_m)$ and $t/p = f(t_1, \ldots, t_n)$, where $f \in AC$. Let us also assume, without loss of generality, that for some k, $0 \leq k \leq m$, no term $l_1, \ldots, l_k$ is a variable, while all terms $l_{k+1}, \ldots, l_m$ are variables. Define a bipartite graph $G = (V_1 \cup V_2, E)$, with $V_1 = \{t_1, \ldots, t_n\}$, $V_2 = \{l_1, \ldots, l_k\}$, and E consisting of all pairs (t_i, l_j), such that $l_j\sigma \sim t_i$, for some substitution σ. It can easily be seen that if

• $n = m$ or $n > m > k$, and
• there is a maximum bipartite matching of size k in the bipartite graph G

then $f(l_1, \ldots, l_m)\sigma \sim f(t_1, \ldots, t_n)$, for some substitution σ and hence condition (ii) is satisfied.

Based on the above discussion, we can perform indexing in two phases. In the first phase, we use *associative-commutative (or AC-) discrimination trees* for indexing. An *AC-discrimination tree* for a set of terms $\mathcal{I}$ is a hierarchically structured collection of standard discrimination trees. The top of the hierarchy is a standard discrimination tree for the set of top-layers of terms in $\mathcal{I}$; and at each node with an incoming edge labeled by an AC-symbol another AC-discrimination tree is attached that represents the corresponding set of nonvariable subterms of terms in $\mathcal{I}$.

The AC-discrimination tree for the terms

$$k(f(a, b), c, f(y, c)) \text{ and } k(f(a, x), c, f(a, b))$$

is shown in Figure 50. The associated top-layers are $k(f, c, f)$ and $k(f, c, f)$. The first subtree represents the terms $f(a, b)$ and $f(a, x)$, the second subtree the terms $f(y, c)$ and $f(a, b)$.

To use this tree, we

• traverse the individual standard trees in the hierarchy as usual, and then
• use bipartite graph matching to combine the results from different levels of the hierarchy.

To illustrate this process, consider using the above tree to retrieve generalizations of $k(f(b, a), c, f(a, b))$. The top-level tree is successfully traversed to the first AC-node, call it v, at which point the two subterms b and a are provided as inputs to the first subtree. Traversal of the subtree yields two bipartite graphs, one for each element of the set $L_v = \{f(a, b), f(a, x)\}$. The size of each respective maximum matching indicates that the input term $f(b, a)$ is an AC-instance of both $f(a, b)$

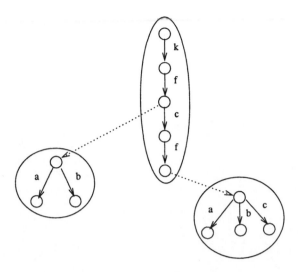

Figure 50: Example of an AC-discrimination tree.

and $f(a, x)$. Traversal of the top-level tree resumes at node v and continues on to the second AC-node, call it v', with L-$v' = \{f(y, c), f(a, b)\}$. The input terms for the second subtree are a and b. The subterm $f(a, b)$ of the input is found to be an AC-instance of $f(a, b)$, but not $f(y, c)$. Thus, only the indexed term $k(f(a, x), c, f(a, b))$ is identified as an AC-generalization. The running time for the first stage (i.e., AC-matching linear terms) using AC-Discrimination trees has polynomial complexity. In fact, the running time of the algorithm is dominated by the cost of doing bipartite graph matching, which takes $O(mn^{1.5})$, where n is the size of t and m is the sum of the sizes of all indexed terms in $\mathcal{I}$.

The bipartite graphs that arise are of the form $G = (V_1 \cup V_2, E)$, where $V_1 = \{t_1, \ldots, t_n\}$ is a set of subterms of the query term, $V_2 = \{l_1, \ldots, l_k\}$ is a set of indexed subterms, and E contains an edge (t_i, l_j) if and only if l_j AC-matches t_i. Note that V_2 depends only on the indexed terms; it remains fixed for a given AC-tree and a node therein. We can design special techniques to efficiently handle bipartite graph matching for cases where V_2 is small, say $k \leq 4$. The graph G is computed stepwise, via a sequence of bipartite graphs $G_1, G_2, \ldots, G_n$. Traversal of the subtree for query t_1 determines the edges incident on that node, thereby defining G_1. Traversal of the subtree for t_2 determines the edges incident on t_2, which are added to G_1 to yield G_2; and so on.

Suppose $V_2 = \{t_1, t_2\}$. Each traversal of the subtree for a term s_i yields a bitstring b_i of length two; the bitstring 10 is obtained if s_i is an AC-instance of t_1 but not of t_2; and the strings 00, 01 and 11 are interpreted correspondingly. The size of a maximum matching on the bipartite graph G_i can be readily determined from b_i and the size of a maximum matching on G_{i-1}. We compute this efficiently using

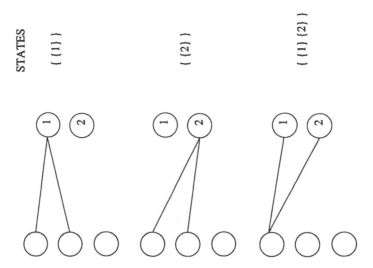

Figure 51: Example of bipartite graph matching automata.

Bipartite Graph Matching Automata. [9] Let $|V_2| = k$ and Π_d denote all subsets of d vertices ($d \leq k$). Encode by a state all possible bipartite graphs that have maximum bipartite matchings of size d and incident on one or more of the subsets in Π_d. Figure 51 shows an example bipartite graph matching automata for the case $d = 1, k = 2$ and $\Pi_1 = \{\{1\}, \{2\}\}$.

We use the adjacency matrix to represent the bipartite graph. The element in the ith row and jth column is 1 if and only if s_i AC-matches t_j. The symbol on which a transition is made is a bitstring of length k (each such bitstring represents a possible row in the adjacency matrix). A transition is made from a state representing a maximum matching of size d to a state representing a maximum matchings of size $d + 1$. Denote by S_k the bipartite graph matching automata for finding maximum matchings of size k. For $|V_2| = k$ use S_k.

The initial state of the automaton represents graphs with a maximum matching of size 0. Its three successor states represents three different types of graphs with maximum matchings of size 1. The three cases are: (i) t_1 can be matched, but not t_2; (ii) t_2 can be matched, but not t_1; (iii) both t_1 and t_2 can be matched, but not at the same time. The final state represents graphs with a maximum matching of size 2. Finally, we read the rows of the adjacency matrix representing the bipartite graph one by one and make transitions accordingly. There is a maximum bipartite matching of size k if and only if the final state in S_k is reached.

By using bipartite graph matching automata in conjunction with AC-discrimination trees for doing AC-matching we can show that for the first stage, all bipartite matching problems at all AC-nodes visited during traversal of an AC-discrimination

---

[9]Bachmair et al. [1993] call these *Secondary Automata*.

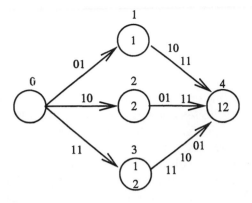

Figure 52: Example

tree for a set of flat terms with total size m, on an input term of size n can be done in $O(mn)$ time.

16. Elements of term indexing

In this section, we provide a list of "basic elements" of term indexing techniques such that new indexing techniques can be devised via a suitable combination of these elements. This enables us to understand many known indexing methods as instances of the generic framework. The common framework also makes it easier to compare and contrast the known approaches. Most importantly, the framework distills out essential characteristics of different techniques, so that (a) one can easily combine these characteristics to get new indexing techniques, (b) understand the trade-offs involved and be able to predict/explain performance of different techniques.

16.1. Deterministic and backtracking automata

An indexing automaton that requires reinspection of symbols in the query term is called a *backtracking automaton*. If all query terms can be processed without such reinspection, the automaton is said to be *deterministic*. The reinspection of symbols in the query term is necessitated when there exist two p-string prefixes (i.e., prefixes of p-strings) S_1 and S_2 such that:

- there exists a term t compatible with both S_1 and S_2;
- S_1 and S_2 are respectively of the form SS_1' and SS_2', where S is the maximal common prefix of S_1 and S_2;
- S_1' and S_2' examine at least one common position, say, p.

The first part of the condition implies that, when the index is traversed to find p-strings compatible with t, the states s_1 and s_2 representing S_1 and S_2 would have to be visited. Otherwise we would miss out some p-strings compatible with t. The second condition implies that neither of these states would be a descendant of another, but have a common ancestor s that represents their maximal common prefix S. The retrieval algorithm would thus follow the path from the root of the index to s and on to s_1, and then will need to backtrack back to s and then follow down the path to s_2. In this process, the symbol at p is first inspected on the path from s to s_1, and then inspected again on the path from s to s_2.

Techniques for avoiding reinspection fall into several different categories that can be related to the above criteria:

- use of augmented sets of indexed terms that enable one to ignore one of S_1 or S_2 completely, without losing correctness. In particular, this would require that every indexed term that is compatible with t can be found by following just the path to s_1; there would be no need to backtrack and retry the match by following the path to s_2.
- use of traversal orders that avoid generation of p-strings that satisfy the above criteria. For instance, path-indexing ensures that after visiting a common prefix S, two different path-strings would visit the same exact set of positions (if they correspond to the same root-to-leaf paths), or a completely disjoint set of positions (if they correspond to completely different paths).
- use of *failure links* that enable us to reuse the information seen about the symbol at p while matching S_2. The automata-driven indexing technique follows this approach, and thus avoids reexamination.

Of these, the first technique is the one that has been studied from the point of building deterministic indexes [Graf 1991, Sekar, Ramesh and Ramakrishnan 1995], so we consider only this technique in this section. Other techniques are discussed separately in the following sections.

To understand how a set of indexed terms can be augmented so as to avoid reinspection of symbols, consider the set of indexed terms

$$\{f(b, a, a), f(*, a, b), f(b, a, *)\}.$$

An index for retrieval of generalizations was illustrated in Figure 4(a). The p-strings $\langle \Lambda, f \rangle \langle 2, a \rangle \langle 3, b \rangle$ and $\langle \Lambda, f \rangle \langle 2, a \rangle \langle 3, * \rangle \langle 1, b \rangle$ satisfy the conditions laid out above that necessitate reinspection of symbols. These two strings correspond to S_1 and S_2 mentioned in the condition: both strings correspond to generalizations of the query term $f(b, a, b)$, with a common prefix $\langle \Lambda, f \rangle \langle 2, a \rangle$, and position 3 requiring reinspection. To avoid the reinspection, we can augment the above term set to include the terms $f(b, a, b)$ and $f(?, a, b)$. We then annotate each leaf of the index with the set of *all* indexed terms that generalizations of the p-string reaching that leaf. The new index that incorporates these modifications is shown in Figure 53(a). Retrieval of generalizations using this automaton requires no backtracking.

The augmented set of indexed terms is typically not constructed explicitly. Instead, it is constructed implicitly by the index construction algorithm. For instance, in the *Build* algorithm of Section 7, we define the notion of a match set so as to ensure that it is sufficient to follow down a single path in the index.

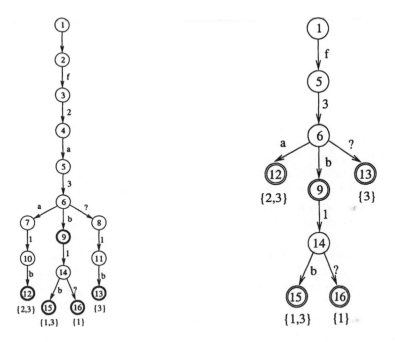

Figure 53: Deterministic and pruned/collapsed index

The trade-off in using deterministic automata is one of space (and construction time) versus retrieval time. Observe that these considerations are very similar to that of deterministic versus nondeterministic finite-state automata.

16.1.1. Issues and trade-offs

- Deterministic indexes require no backtracking for retrieval. The final states can also store substitutions, in addition to the candidate terms. These factors lead to fast retrieval times.
- Deterministic indexes are expensive in terms of space and construction/modification time—they can be exponential in size and number of indexed terms for retrieval of generalizations, possibly worse for other retrieval conditions. (*Compare with the trade-offs between NFAs and DFAs.*)

16.2. Traversal orders: multiple vs single p-string

One of the main decisions to be taken when developing an indexing technique is the order in which indexed terms are traversed to generate p-strings. Some indexing techniques use traversal orders that generate a single p-string from each indexed term, whereas others generate multiple p-strings. For instance, discrimination trees and adaptive automata generate single p-strings. In contrast, path indexing generates multiple p-strings from each indexed term. The primary advantage of generating a single p-string is that a compatible p-string directly yields a compatible indexed term. When multiple p-strings are generated from a single indexed term, we need to ensure compatibility of all these p-strings with the query term. Viewed in another way, nontrivial operations need to be performed on sets of compatible p-strings in order to obtain compatible indexed terms.

On the other hand, generating multiple strings typically leads to shorter strings, which in turn leads to increased sharing among strings, and thus reduced storage requirements. Moreover, techniques that generate multiple p-strings can avoid situations where reinspection of symbols may be needed. For instance, path indexing uses a traversal order where the conditions laid out in the previous section regarding symbol reinspection will never be satisfied.

An important consideration in the choice of traversal orders is whether they yield p-strings that contain variables (or '*' symbol in them). The presence of such embedded variables introduces the need for backtracking in an index. For instance, in the example discussed in the previous section, the need for reinspection of symbols arose because there were two p-strings such that the first position where they differ correspond to a variable in one of the p-strings, but a nonvariable in another. Similarly, scanning past a variable in the query term often requires us to have forward links for skipping appropriate subterms (e.g., jump-lists in discrimination trees).

16.2.1. Issues and trade-offs

- Path indexing produces many p-strings such that no variables are embedded within the strings. Moreover, these strings do not contain any pair of positions that do not have an ancestor-descendant relationship. The first property ensures that there is never a need to skip a subterm in a query term, while the second property ensures that we need not have jump lists that need to be taken when we inspect variables in the query term. The main results from the point of view of indexing are:
  - the automata are completely deterministic;
  - the automaton size (i.e., the number of nodes in it) is linear in the size of indexed terms;
  - but we require many operations for combining intermediate results (obtained as a result of matching individual p-strings) to compute the set of compatible terms.
- Automata-driven indexing produces fewer strings than paths, and shares the property with path indexing in that they do not contain embedded variable. The net result is that:
  - the automaton is completely deterministic;
  - it uses space quadratic in the size of the indexed terms;
  - this method also requires many operations for combining results of p-string matches to identify candidate terms, but the intermediate sets are always smaller than those for path indexing.

- Discrimination trees produce just a single p-string from each indexed term, which contains several embedded variables and subterms. The net effect is that:
  - indexing requires significant amount of backtracking (nondeterministic);
  - automata require significant storage for jump lists to skip subterms;
  - no effort needs to be spent for combining intermediate results.
- Adaptive automata produce p-strings with no embedded variables, but to do this, they generate many instances of the original set of indexed terms. The net effect for computing generalizations of a query term is that:
  - indexing requires no backtracking;
  - no need for combining intermediate results;
  - worst case space requirement is exponential in the size of indexed terms.

16.3. Adaptive and fixed-order traversals

For adaptive traversals, the next set of positions to inspect can depend on all of the symbols inspected so far. Fixed-order traversals, on the other hand, select the next position as a function of the fringe positions of the prefix inspected.

Adaptive traversal orders are utilized in adaptive automata, substitution trees, and unification factoring. Fixed-order traversals are used in path indexing, discrimination trees, and automata-driven indexing. The trade-offs in using adaptive versus fixed order of traversals is related to the complexity of algorithms for generating adaptive traversals (these algorithms can be simple or complex), as well as the interaction of adaptive traversal orders with other optimizations such as failure links.

16.3.1. Issues and trade-offs

- Adaptive traversals can minimize the number of variables embedded within p-strings, which reduces the amount of backtracking needed.
- Computing the traversal order may add overhead to index construction and maintenance operations, but retrieval time is improved.
- With fixed-order traversals, the only mechanism to minimize embedded variables is by producing multiple p-strings.

16.4. Pruned and collapsed indexes

We can borrow and/or adapt techniques for reducing space requirements for tries in order to reduce the space requirements for the index. In particular, we can borrow the idea of *pruned tries*, where we stop examining symbols as soon as we identify a unique string that is compatible with the query string. We can adapt the idea of *collapsed tries*, where sequences of states all of which have a unique successor are eliminated from the trie. For both these techniques, the idea is that inspection of positions eliminated by the technique does not reduce our ability to discriminate among them.

We can apply both these techniques to term indexes as well. In particular, we can use the pruning technique to replace a subtree of the index that contains at most one final state by the final state. Note that such pruning does not adversely affect the accuracy of filtering — in the worst case, the query term may not be compatible with the p-string corresponding to the final state, but we have at most one indexed term that has been incorrectly identified as being compatible with the query term. This slight decrease in accuracy may be well worth the savings in space.

We can easily extend the above technique so that we not only replace subtrees with single final states, but also subtrees with less than k final states, for some small k. Once again, the decrease in accuracy (proportional to k) may be small as compared to the savings in space usage.

In order to apply the collapsing technique, note that we may not be able to eliminate some intermediate states because they examine positions whose children will later be examined. Nevertheless, we may be able to "compress" all such transitions using a single operation that examines multiple positions in the query term. We will use the term *augmented edge* to denote such edges.

Figure 53(b) shows the result of applying the pruning and collapsing techniques on the automaton of Figure 53(a). Note that the terminal sequence of states examining position 1 have been eliminated in the leftmost and rightmost paths in the indexing automaton. We have also eliminated the inspection of position 2, which occurred immediately after inspecting position 1 in Figure 53. Observe that we could eliminate this test since no children of a are being examined further down in the automaton. Had this not been the case, we would have collapsed the inspection of the root symbol and position 2. One possible way to represent this in the automaton is by using $f(*, a, *)$ on the outward transition from state 1, rather than the label f. Whether the collapsed representation leads to actual space reduction at the implementation level is unclear. If the index is represented as code as in Section 9, the collapsed representation may end up being as expensive as (or perhaps more expensive than) the uncollapsed representation. If the index is represented using traditional representations for finite-state machines, then collapsing can lead to some improvements in space usage. However, if significant amount of auxiliary information is to be stored with each trie state, then the storage savings due to collapsing can be significant.

Finally, note that we can apply the collapsing technique more generally to replace subcomponents of the trie that are deep but have few branches. We can collapse each root-to-leaf path (i.e., paths from the root of the subcomponent to its leaf, which may or may not coincide with the leaves of the whole trie) in such components into an augmented edge. We may use techniques such as hashing to identify which of the augmented edges are to be taken.

The benefits and trade-offs associated with pruned/collapsed indexes are as follows:

- Pruning and collapsing can save space, without necessarily losing discrimination (unlike techniques such as depth-bounding).

- Increased time for making transitions, as pruned edges are associated with complex conditions for transition. (Note that there would be fewer transitions that are taken, so the total time spent in making transitions may not be affected.)
- But overall retrieval time may be reduced, as these techniques enable incremental construction of good adaptive traversals — note that decision regarding order of inspection of symbols corresponding to pruned/collapsed portions of the trie is not fixed prematurely, but determined as more terms are inserted in the index.
- Note that each transition in the index may result in a binding operation to variables in the query term. By reducing the number of transitions (using pruning/collapsing) we can reduce the time spent in performing such bindings.

16.5. Failure links

Most of the indexing techniques studied so far have the property that, once a failure is encountered, they backtrack to the lowest ancestor node where either a '*' transition could have been taken, or a variable was encountered in the query term. At this point, they follow down the next possible transition from this state. If there is failure along this path, then we look for the next outermost branch and so on. In general, this can lead to wasted effort in rescanning portions of the query term again and again, as we follow down each of these alternate paths in the index. Failure links exploit information known about the structure of the query term at the point of failure in order to prune away alternate paths that are bound to fail.

Recall that failure links are another well-known concept in string matching, pioneered in the Knuth-Morris-Pratt algorithm [Knuth, Morris and Pratt 1977]. Among known indexing techniques, it has been used only in automata-driven indexing [Ramesh et al. 1990] and threaded automata for subsumption [Rao et al. 1996], although it is readily applicable to any backtracking index. One of the benefits of studying the indexing technique within a common framework is that we can easily identify components such as this which can be developed in the context of one technique and then applied to other techniques.

16.5.1. Issues and trade-offs

- reduces backtracking and/or the computation involved in backtracking;
- may increase space usage;
- increases the cost of index construction/maintenance operations.

16.6. Sharing equivalent states

For deterministic indexes, two states are equivalent if the subindexes rooted at these states are identical. By identifying such subautomata and merging them, we can build dag automata that use significantly less space than the original indexes.

Even better, if we can identify the equivalence of states even before constructing the subautomata, then we can save significant amount of time in construction of the automata.

Identification of equivalent states is somewhat harder in backtracking indexes, since the equivalence of two states cannot be determined just by inspecting the subautomata rooted at these states. This is because the states inspected when backtracking out of the two subautomata may be different. As such, sharing of equivalent states has been studied primarily in the context of deterministic automata.

16.6.1. Issues and trade-offs

- Sharing can lead to significant reduction in space usage
- Direct construction of minimal automata (i.e., without first constructing unminimized automata) is crucial
- No significant negative effects

16.7. Factoring computation of substitutions

In the model described so far, the primitive steps in the retrieval operation consisted of checking whether the query term had a specific nonvariable symbol at a position. For collapsed tries, this operation generalizes to checking multiple positions. If this is to be extended for indexing nonlinear terms, one may add more powerful operations to the index, specifically, the operation of testing for unifiability of two variables. Such operations can be used to perform consistency checks among substitutions, especially in the context of problems such as simultaneous unification, multiliteral subsumption, etc. They also provide a convenient way to factorize the substitutions themselves. Such extensions have been studied in the context of several indexing techniques, although many of the techniques known to date restrict themselves to linear terms. Even when a technique deals with nonlinear indexed terms, the more complex operations for consistency checking (of substitutions) are typically performed after all other operations.

16.7.1. Issues and trade-offs

- Treats indexing and computation of substitutions as a single process, rather than as separate phases, which avoids re-examination of symbols
- Shares not only common matching operations but also common variable substitutions, which leads to more efficient handling of nondeterminism.
- Can make an imperfect filtering technique into a perfect one.

16.8. Prioritized indexing

One way to deal with priorities is to ignore them completely during the indexing phase – instead, we identify all compatible terms using indexing, and then eliminate all except the terms with maximal priorities. In many applications, this may be unacceptable, since we may generate a large intermediate set of candidate terms first before eliminating most of them in the second step. Therefore, an indexing approach that only computes the terms with maximal priority is desirable. Among the indexing techniques described through the rest of the paper, some (e.g., adaptive pattern matching and unification factoring) methods incorporate priorities into the index, whereas a few other techniques (e.g., path indexing) handle them at retrieval time.

16.8.1. Issues and trade-offs

- Construction vs. retrieval time — handling priorities makes the index construction more expensive, but retrieval is accelerated, e.g., in adaptive automata, the need to handle priorities increases construction time as well as size of the automata, but in an application where retrieval time is most important, this is a good trade-off.
- Priorities may make it possible to design (more) optimal algorithms, e.g., in unification factoring, optimal automata can be developed for linearly ordered indexed terms, but not for the unprioritized case; in adaptive automata, priority information can be used to build optimal automata for classes of terms for which no optimal automata exists in the unprioritized case.
- It is sometimes possible to perform the priority-related operations efficiently at runtime. For instance, in dynamic path indexing, path automata are constructed without taking priority into account, but at retrieval time, we compute the elements of this set in an order consistent with the priorities. When efficient methods exist for handling priority related operations at retrieval time, it may not be worth the additional cost of dealing with priorities in the index construction and maintenance operations.

16.9. Summary of indexing techniques

Based on the terminology developed so far, we can classify the known term indexing techniques as shown in Table 1.

17. Indexing in practice

17.1. Logic programming and deductive databases.

Absence of indexing in logic programming systems will result in unnecessary backtracking, leading to poor performance. Almost all systems use some form of indexing. Specifically:

- Most logic programming systems use the outermost symbol of the first argument for indexing.
- The ALS system uses full indexing as described in [Chen et al. 1992].

technique name	perfect filtering	priorities	number of strings	adaptive	deterministic	pruned/collapsed	fail link/dags	subst. factoring	retrieval condition
path indexing	NL	N	≥ 1	N	Y	N	N/A	N	all
automata-driven	NL	Y	≥ 1	N	Y	N	Y	N	unif
discrimination tree	Y,NL	N	1	N	N	N	N	N	all
adaptive automata	NL	Y	1	N	Y	N	Y	N	gen
substitution trees	Y	N	1	Y	N	Y	N	Y	all
unification factoring	Y	Y	1	Y	N	N	N	Y	unif
AC-discrimination tree	NL	N	≥ 1	N	N	N	N	N	gen
AC-path indexing	N	N	≥ 1	N	Y	N	N/A	N	all
code tree	Y	N	1	Y,N	N	N	Y	Y	subsumption

Table 1: Classification of term indexing techniques

Here NL means modulo nonlinearity, i.e., the retrieval is being done without any regard to variables that may occur multiple times in the indexed terms or the query term. In other words, the filtering performed would be perfect if all the indexed terms and the query term were linear.

- The XSB system [Sagonas, Swift, Warren, Freire and Rao 1997] uses unification factoring described in [Dawson, Ramakrishnan, Skiena and Swift 1996].
- The SICStus Prolog system [Int 2000] allows one to specify the positions in terms on which indexing is to be performed.

Experimental results show that unification factoring is a practical technique that can achieve substantial speedups for logic programs, while requiring no changes in the WAM. The speedups observed may be even more substantial when unification factoring is applied to programs which are themselves produced by transformations. For instance, the HiLog transformation [Cheng, Kifer and Warren 1993] increases the declarativeness of programs by allowing unification on predicate symbols. If implemented naively, however, HiLog can cause a decrease in efficiency for clause access. Experiments have shown that unification factoring can lead to speedups of 3 to 4 on HiLog code.

17.2. Functional programming

Adaptive indexing is essential for doing lazy evaluation based on Huet-Levy style [Huet and Levy 1991]. Two systems that use such techniques are: Equals [Kaser, Pawagi, Ramakrishnan, Ramakrishnan and Sekar 1992, Kaser, Ramakrishnan, Ramakrishnan and Sekar 1997] and Gaml [Maranget 1992]. Some functional languages such as Haskell use a variation of standard and deterministic discrimination trees [Wadler 1987].

17.3. Theorem provers

In this section we overview the data structures and indexing techniques used by the modern resolution-based theorem provers. The information about particular provers is kindly provided[10] by Hans de Nivelle, Thomas Hillenbrand, Bill McCune, Robert Nieuwenhuis, Alexandre Riazanov, Stephan Schulz, and Christoph Weidenbach.

17.3.1. BLIKSEM

BLIKSEM uses imperfect *substitution trees* for forward subsumption and forward demodulation. For forward subsumption, only one term of each clause is stored in the tree.

For backward subsumption and demodulation BLIKSEM uses an interesting trick. Essentially, no special algorithms for backward subsumption or demodulation are implemented. But occasionally all clauses are rechecked, as if they were just generated, with the forward subsumption and demodulation checks.

For unification no indexing is used.

---

[10]In alphabetical order. The list of provers is also given in the alphabetical order.

17.3.2. E

- *Perfect discrimination trees with weight constraints* for forward subsumption and forward demodulation. In addition, for forward demodulation age constraints are used.[11] For nonunit forward subsumption the use of discrimination trees gives an imperfect indexing technique, so for the nonunit case E uses sequential search with various prefilters (weight, class, individual literal matches).

- For backward demodulation E uses sequential search on *perfectly shared term structures* with reducibility markers and weight filtering.[12]

- For backward subsumption sequential search with prefilters as above is used. Unification is also implemented using sequential search, but the unification algorithm is equation-solving optimized for early mismatch detection.

17.3.3. Fiesta

Until recently, for all indexing algorithms Fiesta *substitution trees* were used. Currently, *context trees* are under implementation.

17.3.4. Otter

- *Discrimination trees* are used for forward subsumption and forward demodulation.

- *Path indexing* is used for backward subsumption, backward demodulation, and unification.

Multiliteral operations in Otter implement imperfect filtering, since the index contains literals, not clauses. However, the substitution computed during indexing on the literal level is used to complete the retrieval operation on the clause level.

17.3.5. Spass

Spass uses *substitution trees* for all indexing operations: forward subsumption and demodulation, backward subsumption and demodulation, and unification. For all operations perfect filtering is implemented and the retrieval operations deliver always the binding representing the substitution. The binding can then be used, without being applied to any term, to e.g., to verify ordering restrictions.

17.3.6. Vampire

- *Partially adaptive code trees* for forward subsumption and forward demodulation. In the case of forward demodulation, for nonoriented unit equalities the index also contains precompiled ordering constraints.

---

[11]Experiments described in [Riazanov and Voronkov 2000b] have shown no gain of efficiency of the use of weight constraints for code trees as implemented in Vampire.

[12]This is only used to find clauses which have to be eliminated from the set of processed clauses (because a term in a maximal or selected literal can be rewritten in a way that makes reprocessing necessary). Also note that during the search, normal form dates of irreducible subterms are updated, so that the age constraints of the PDTs make interreduction and actual rewriting very cheap. Interreduction as well as the actual rewriting are then performed using the perfect discrimination trees.

- *Path indexing* for backward subsumption and backward demodulation. The algorithm for retrieval uses optimization based on *database joins* and *skip lists*.
- *Perfectly shared terms* for storing terms occurring in kept clauses.
- *Flatterms* for representing terms occurring in temporary clauses.

17.3.7. Waldmeister

For unification, forward demodulation, and forward subsumption Waldmeister employs *perfect discrimination trees* with the pruning refinement that every branch leading to only one leaf node is shrunk.

At least in the unit equational case, keeping the clauses in SOS permanently normalized does not pay off.[13] So Waldmeister spends most of its runtime in the forward operations, especially in demodulation and subsumption; and backward subsumption and demodulation are implemented by sequential search.

18. Conclusion

Efficient indexing techniques have been developed for many retrieval operations arising in logic and functional programming, and theorem proving. In spite of this, important improvements of the existing indexing techniques are still possible and needed, and other techniques for previously not considered retrieval conditions need to be developed.

However, there are research directions in term indexing that need to be further investigated. In this section we sketch some possible research directions.

18.1. Comparison of indexing techniques

Until recently, it was difficult to compare the practical efficiency of term indexing methods in a unified framework. Previous comparisons suffered from two major problems. First, experimental results about performance of indexing technique were designed in such a way so that it was impossible to compare these results with a different implementation. As a result, superiority of a particular indexing technique was demonstrated by comparing a tightly coded implementation of this technique with nonoptimized experimental implementations of other techniques by the same person. Second, benchmarks for comparison were often nonrepresentative, for example, randomly generated.

A practical comparison method *COMPIT* (a method for *COMP*aring *I*ndexing *T*echniques) was described in a recent paper by Nieuwenhuis et al. [2001]. The idea of this method is the following. First, benchmarks for the method can be generated by running different provers. The method used for creating such benchmarks for a given prover is to add instructions making the prover write to a log file a trace each time an operation on the index takes place, and then run it on the given problem.

---

[13]Thomas Hillenbrand, private communication.

For example, each time a term t is inserted (deleted, unified with), a trace like $+t$ (resp. $-t$, ut) is written to the file. Moreover, we require to store the traces along with information about the result of the operation (e.g., success/failure), which allows one to detect cases of incorrect behaviour of the indexing methods being tested.

The main part of the evaluation process is to test a given implementation of indexing on such a benchmark file. This given implementation is assumed to provide operations for querying and updating the indexing data structure, as well as a translation function for creating terms in its required format from the benchmark format. In order to avoid overheads and inexact time measurements due to translations and reading terms from the disk, the evaluation process first reads a large block of traces, storing them in main memory. After that, all terms read are translated into the required format. Then time measuring is switched on, and a loop is started which calls the corresponding sequence of operations, and time is turned off before reading the next block of traces from disk, and so on.

The method was applied in Nieuwenhuis et al. [2001] to compare the implementations of content trees in Dedam [Ganzinger et al. 2001], partially adaptive code trees in Vampire [Riazanov and Voronkov 2000b], and perfect discrimination trees in Waldmeister, for the retrieval of generalizations.

Based on this experiments the library *LIBERTI* (*LI*rary of *B*enchmarks for *E*fficient *R*etrieval and *T*erm *I*ndexing) was created. When benchmarks for other retrieval conditions are added to the library, we will have more empirical evidence about the comparative efficiency of various term indexing methods.

18.2. Indexing in presence of constraints

Constraints have two major uses in automated deduction. *Orderings constraints* are used for restricting the applicability of inference rules and eliminating redundant clauses, see [Bachmair and Ganzinger 2001, Nieuwenhuis and Rubio 2001] (Chapters 2 and 7 of this Handbook). Constraints are also used to present knowledge about built-in domains, for example integers or finite domains, see [Bockmayr and Weispfenning 2001] (Chapter 12).

When ordering constraints are used, it is often the case that after term retrieval an ordering constraint should be checked; and when the constraint is not satisfied, the retrieval process continues. Checking ordering constraints may be expensive, so it is desirable to built-in constraint checking in the retrieval process. The first step towards building-in constraint checking was done in Vampire: when retrieval of instances is used to implement backward demodulation, ordering constraints are compiled. When retrieval is finished, the compiled constraint is checked against the substitution that is computed as the result of retrieval.

18.3. Other retrieval conditions

There are several important retrieval conditions not covered in this paper but important enough for efficient implementation of theorem provers. Some examples are

- Retrieval conditions for multiliteral clauses, for example, forward and backward subsumption, and simultaneous unification. Some results and techniques appear in [Voronkov 1995] for forward subsumption and in [de Nivelle 1998] for simultaneous unification.

- Developing indexing methods for subterms. Bottom-up techniques for this problem is reported in [Hoffmann and O'Donnel 1982]. While some preliminary work based on top-down traversal appears in [Ramesh and Ramakrishnan 1992, Ramesh et al. 1994] there is still a need for faster methods.

Bibliography

AÏT-KACI H. [1991], *Warren's Abstract Machine: a Tutorial Reconstruction*, The MIT Press.

BACHMAIR L., CHEN T. AND RAMAKRISHNAN I. [1993], Associative-commutative discrimination nets, *in* M.-C. Gaudel and J.-P. Jouannaud, eds, 'Proceedings of the 4th International Joint Conference on Theory and Practice of Software Development (TAPSOFT)', Vol. 668 of *Lecture Notes in Computer Science*, Springer Verlag, Orsay, France, pp. 61–74.

BACHMAIR L., CHEN T., RAMAKRISHNAN I., ANANTHARAMAN S. AND CHABIN J. [1995], Experiments with associative-commutative discrimination nets, *in* C. Mellish, ed., 'International Joint Conference on Artificial Intelligence', Vol. 1, Montréal, pp. 348–355.

BACHMAIR L. AND GANZINGER H. [2001], Resolution theorem proving, *in* A. Robinson and A. Voronkov, eds, 'Handbook of Automated Reasoning', Vol. I, Elsevier Science, chapter 2, pp. 19–99.

BÉNANAV D., KAPUR D. AND NARENDRAN P. [1987], 'Complexity of matching problems', *Journal of Symbolic Computation* 3, 203–216.

BOCKMAYR A. AND WEISPFENNING V. [2001], Solving numerical constraints, *in* A. Robinson and A. Voronkov, eds, 'Handbook of Automated Reasoning', Vol. I, Elsevier Science, chapter 12, pp. 749–842.

CHEN T., RAMAKRISHNAN I. AND RAMESH R. [1992], Multistage indexing algorithms for speeding Prolog execution, *in* K. Apt, ed., 'Proceedings of the Joint International Conference and Symposium on Logic Programming (JICSLP-92)', MIT Press, pp. 639–653. Revised version [Chen et al. 1994].

CHEN T., RAMAKRISHNAN I. V. AND RAMESH R. [1994], 'Multistage indexing algorithms for speeding Prolog execution', *Software — Practice and Experience* 24(12), 1097–1119.

CHEN W. AND WARREN D. S. [1996], 'Tabled evaluation with delaying for general logic programs', *Journal of the ACM* 43(1), 20–74.

CHENG W., KIFER M. AND WARREN D. [1993], 'HILOG: a foundation for higher-order logic programming', *Journal of Logic Programming* 15(3), 187–230.

CHRISTIAN J. [1989], Fast Knuth-Bendix completion: A summary, *in* N. Dershowitz, ed., 'Proceedings of the 3rd International Conference on Rewriting Techniques and Applications', Vol. 355 of *Lecture Notes in Computer Science*, Springer Verlag, pp. 551–555.

CHRISTIAN J. [1993], 'Flatterms, discrimination nets, and fast term rewriting', *Journal of Automated Reasoning* 10(1), 95–113.

COMER D. AND SETHI R. [1976], Complexity of trie index construction (extended abstract), *in* '17th Annual Symposium on Foundations of Computer Science', IEEE, Houston, Texas, pp. 197–207.

DAWSON S., RAMAKRISHNAN C. AND RAMAKRISHNAN I. [1995], Design and implementation of jump tables for fast indexing of logic programs, *in* M. V. Hermenegildo and S. D. Swierstra, eds, 'Programming Languages: Implementations, Logics and Programs, 7th International Symposium, PLILP'95', Vol. 982 of *Lecture Notes in Computer Science*, Springer Verlag, Utrecht, The Netherlands, pp. 133–150.

Dawson S., Ramakrishnan C., Ramakrishnan I., Sagonas K., Skiena S., Swift T. and Warren D. [1995], Unification factoring for efficient execution of logic programs, *in* 'ACM Symposium on Principles of Programming Languages', ACM Press, pp. 247–258.

Dawson S., Ramakrishnan C., Skiena S. and Swift T. [1996], 'Principles and practice of unification factoring', *ACM Transactions on Programming Languages and Systems* 18(5), 528–563.

De Nivelle H. [1998], 'An algorithm for the retrieval of unifiers from discrimination trees', *Journal of Automated Reasoning* 20(1/2), 5–25.

De Nivelle H. [2000], *Bliksem 1.10 User's Manual*, MPI für Informatik, Saarbrücken.

Dershowitz N. and Jouannaud J.-P. [1990], Rewrite systems, *in* J. Van Leeuwen, ed., 'Handbook of Theoretical Computer Science', Vol. B: Formal Methods and Semantics, North Holland, Amsterdam, chapter 6, pp. 243–309.

Eker S. M. [1995], 'Associative-commutative matching via bipartite graph matching', *Computer Journal* 38(5), 381–399.

Ganzinger H., Nieuwenhuis R. and Nivela P. [2001], Context trees. Submitted to IJCAR.

Gottlob G. and Leitsch A. [1987], 'On the efficiency of subsumption algorithms', *Journal of the ACM* 32(2), 280–295.

Graf A. [1991], Left-to-right tree pattern matching, *in* R. Book, ed., 'RTA'91', Vol. 488 of *Lecture Notes in Computer Science*, Springer Verlag, pp. 323–334.

Graf P. [1992], Path indexing for term retrieval, Technical Report MPI-I-92-237, Max-Planck-Institut für Informatik, Saarbrucken, Germany.

Graf P. [1995], Substitution tree indexing, *in* J. Hsiang, ed., 'Rewriting Techniques and Applications', Vol. 914 of *Lecture Notes in Computer Science*, pp. 117–131.

Graf P. [1996], *Term Indexing*, Vol. 1053 of *Lecture Notes in Computer Science*, Springer Verlag.

Greenbaum S. [1986], Input transformations and resolution implementation techniques for theorem-proving in first-order logic, PhD thesis, University of Illinois at Urbana-Champaign.

Henschen L. and Naqvi S. [1981], An improved filter for literal indexing in resolution systems, *in* '6th Int'l Joint Conference on Artifical Intelligence (IJCAI)', pp. 528–529.

Hewitt C. [1971], Description and theoretical analysis of Planner: A language for proving theorems and manipulating models in a robot, PhD thesis, Department of Mathematics, MIT.

Hillenbrand T., Buch A., Vogt R. and Löchner B. [1997], 'Waldmeister: High-performance equational deduction', *Journal of Automated Reasoning* 18(2), 265–270.

Hoffmann C. M. and O'Donnel M. J. [1982], 'Pattern matching in trees', *Journal of the ACM* 29(1), 68–95.

Huet G. and Levy J.-J. [1978], Computation in nonambiguous linear term rewriting systems, Technical Report 359, IRIA, Le Chesney, France. Revised version in [Huet and Levy 1991].

Huet G. and Levy J.-J. [1991], Computation in orthogonal rewriting systems, I and II, *in* J.-L. Lassez and G. Plotkin, eds, 'Computational Logic. Essays in Honor of Alan Robinson.', MIT Press, pp. 395–443. Earlier version appeared as [Huet and Levy 1978].

Int [2000], *Sictus Prolog User's Manual. Release 3.8.4*.

Kaser O., Pawagi S., Ramakrishnan C., Ramakrishnan I. and Sekar R. [1992], Fast parallel implementation of lazy languages — the EQUALS experience, *in* '1992 ACM Conference on Lisp and Functional Programming', ACM Press, pp. 335–344.

Kaser O., Ramakrishnan C., Ramakrishnan I. and Sekar R. [1997], 'EQUALS — a parallel implementation of a lazy language', *Journal of Functional Programming* 7(2), 183–217.

Kennaway J. [1990], The specificity rule for lazy pattern matching in ambiguous term rewriting systems, *in* N. Jones, ed., 'ESOP'90, 3rd European Symposium on Programming', Vol. 432 of *Lecture Notes in Computer Science*, Springer Verlag, Copenhagen, Denmark, pp. 256–270.

Knuth D., Morris J. and Pratt V. [1977], 'Fast pattern matching in strings', *SIAM Journal of Computing* **6**(2), 323–350.

Kounalis E. and Lugiez D. [1991], Compilation of pattern matching with associative-commutative functions, *in* S. Abramsky and T. Maibaum, eds, 'Proceedings of the International Joint Conference on Theory and Practice of Software Development, volume 1: Colloquium on Trees in Algebra and Programming', number 493 *in* 'Lecture Notes in Computer Science', Springer Verlag, Brighton, U.K., pp. 57–73.

Laville A. [1987], Lazy pattern matching in the ML language, *in* K. Nori, ed., 'Foundations of Software Technology and Theoretical Computer Science, 7th Conference', Vol. 287 of *Lecture Notes in Computer Science*, Springer Verlag, Pune, India, pp. 400–419.

Laville A. [1988], Implementation of lazy pattern matching algorithms, *in* 'Proceedings of the European Symposium on Programming', Vol. 300 of *Lecture Notes in Computer Science*, Springer Verlag, pp. 298–316.

Letz R., Schumann J., Bayerl S. and Bibel W. [1992], 'SETHEO: A high-performance theorem prover', *Journal of Automated Reasoning* **8**(2), 183–212.

Lugiez D. and Moysset J. [1993], Complement problems and tree automata in AC-like theories, *in* P. Enjalbert, A. Finkel and K. W. Wagner, eds, 'Proceedings of the Symposium on Theoretical Aspects of Computer Science (STACS'93)', Vol. 665 of *Lecture Notes in Computer Science*, Springer Verlag, pp. 515–524.

Lusk E. [1992], Controlling redundancy in large search spaces: Argonne-style theorem proving through the years, *in* A. Voronkov, ed., 'Logic Programming and Automated Reasoning. International Conference LPAR'92.', Vol. 624 of *Lecture Notes in AI*, St.Petersburg, Russia, pp. 96–106.

Maranget L. [1992], Compiling lazy pattern matching, *in* 'ACM Conference on Lisp and Functional Programming', pp. 21–31.

McCune W. [1992], 'Experiments with discrimination-tree indexing and path indexing for term retrieval', *Journal of Automated Reasoning* **9**(2), 147–167.

McCune W. [1994a], OTTER 3.0 reference manual and guide, Technical Report ANL-94/6, Argonne National Laboratory/IL, USA.

McCune W. [1994b], OTTER 3.0 reference manual and guide, Technical Report ANL-94/6, Argonne National Laboratory.

McCune W. and Wos L. [1997], 'Otter—the CADE-13 competition incarnations', *Journal of Automated Reasoning* **18**(2), 211–220.

Moser M., Ibens O., Letz R., Steinbach J., Goller C., Schumann J. and Mayr K. [1997], 'SETHEO and E-SETHEO—the CADE-13 systems', *Journal of Automated Reasoning* **18**, 237–246.

Nelson G. and Oppen D. [1980], 'Fast decision procedures based on congruence closure', *Journal of the ACM* **27**(2), 356–364.

Nicolaita D. [1992], An indexing scheme for AC-equational theories, Technical report, Research Institute for Infomatics, Bucharest, Romania.

Nieuwenhuis R., Hillenbrand T., Riazanov A. and Voronkov A. [2001], Let's COMPIT: a method for COMParing Indexing Techniques in theorem provers, Preprint CSPP-11, Department of Computer Science, University of Manchester.
URL: *http://www.cs.man.ac.uk/preprints/index.html*

Nieuwenhuis R., Rivero J. and Vallejo M. [1997], 'The Barcelona prover', *Journal of Automated Reasoning* **18**(2), 171–176.

Nieuwenhuis R. and Rubio A. [2001], Paramodulation-based theorem proving, *in* A. Robinson and A. Voronkov, eds, 'Handbook of Automated Reasoning', Vol. I, Elsevier Science, chapter 7, pp. 371–443.

Ohlbach H. [1990], Abstraction tree indexing for terms, *in* 'Proceedings of the 9th European Conference on Artificial Intelligence', Pitman Publishing, London, pp. 479–484.

PUEL L. [1990], Compiling pattern matching by term decomposition, in 'ACM Conference on Lisp and Functional Programming', pp. 273–281.

RAMAKRISHNAN R. [1991], 'Magic templates: A spellbinding approach to logic programs', *Journal of Logic Programming* **11**(3 & 4), 189–216.

RAMAMOHANARAO K. AND SHEPHERD J. [1986], A superimposed codewords indexing scheme for very large Prolog databases, in E. Shapiro, ed., 'Proceedings of the Third International Conference on Logic Programming', Vol. 225 of *Lecture Notes in Computer Science*, Springer Verlag, London, pp. 569–576.

RAMESH R., RAMAKRISHNAN I. AND SEKAR R. [1994], Automata-driven efficient subterm unification, in P. S. Thiagarajan, ed., 'Foundations of Software Technology and Theoretical Computer Science, 14th Conference', Vol. 880 of *Lecture Notes in Computer Science*, Springer Verlag, Madras, India, pp. 288–299.

RAMESH R. AND RAMAKRISHNAN I. V. [1992], 'Nonlinear pattern matching in trees', *JACM* **39**(2), 295–316.

RAMESH R., RAMAKRISHNAN I. AND WARREN D. [1990], Automata-driven indexing of Prolog clauses, in 'Seventh Annual ACM Symposium on Principles of Programming Languages', San Francisco, pp. 281–290. Revised version [Ramesh, Ramakrishnan and Warren 1995].

RAMESH R., RAMAKRISHNAN I. AND WARREN D. [1995], 'Automata-driven indexing of Prolog clauses', *Journal of Logic Programming* **23**(2), 151–202.

RAO P., RAMAKRISHNAN C. AND RAMAKRISHNAN I. [1996], A thread in time saves tabling time, in M. Maher, ed., 'Proceedings of the 1996 Joint International Conference and Symposium on Logic Programming', MIT Press, pp. 112–126.

RIAZANOV A. AND VORONKOV A. [1999], Vampire, in H. Ganzinger, ed., 'Automated Deduction— CADE-16. 16th International Conference on Automated Deduction', Vol. 1632 of *Lecture Notes in AI*, Trento, Italy, pp. 292–296.

RIAZANOV A. AND VORONKOV A. [2000a], Limited resource strategy in resolution theorem proving, Preprint CSPP-7, Department of Computer Science, University of Manchester.
    URL: *http://www.cs.man.ac.uk/preprints/index.html*

RIAZANOV A. AND VORONKOV A. [2000b], Partially adaptive code trees, in M. Ojeda-Aciego, I. de Guzmán, G. Brewka and L. Pereira, eds, 'Logics in Artificial Intelligence. European Workshop, JELIA 2000', Vol. 1919 of *Lecture Notes in AI*, Springer Verlag, Málaga, Spain, pp. 209–223.

RIAZANOV A. AND VORONKOV A. [2001a], An efficient algorithm for backward subsumption using path indexing and database joins, Preprint, Department of Computer Science, University of Manchester. To appear.
    URL: *http://www.cs.man.ac.uk/preprints/index.html*

RIAZANOV A. AND VORONKOV A. [2001b], Splitting without backtracking, Preprint CSPP-10, Department of Computer Science, University of Manchester.
    URL: *http://www.cs.man.ac.uk/preprints/index.html*

RIVERO J. [2000], Data Structures and Algorithms for Automated Deduction with Equality, Phd thesis, Universitat Politècnica de Catalunya, Barcelona.

SAGONAS K., SWIFT T., WARREN D., FREIRE J. AND RAO P. [1997], The XSB programmer's manual: version 1.7, Technical report, SUNY at Stony Brook.

SCHULZ S. [1999], System abstract: E 0.3, in H. Ganzinger, ed., 'Automated Deduction—CADE-16. 16th International Conference on Automated Deduction', Lecture Notes in AI, Trento, Italy, pp. 297–301.

SEKAR R. C., RAMESH R. AND RAMAKRISHNAN I. V. [1995], 'Adaptive pattern matching', *SIAM Journal on Computing* **24**(6), 1207–1234.

SEKAR R., RAMESH R. AND RAMAKRISHNAN I. [1992], Adaptive pattern matching, in W. Kuich, ed., 'Proceedings of the 19th International Colloquium on Automata, Languages and Programming', number 623 in 'Lecture Notes in Computer Science', Springer Verlag, Vienna, pp. 247–260. Revised version [Sekar et al. 1995].

SOCHER R. [1989], A subsumption algorithm based on characteristic matrices, *in* N. Dershowitz, ed., 'Rewriting Techniques and Applications, 3rd International Conference, RTA-89', Vol. 355 of *Lecture Notes in Computer Science*, Springer Verlag, Chapel Hill, North Carolina, USA, pp. 573–581.

STICKEL M. [1988], 'A PROLOG technology theorem prover: Implementation by an extended Prolog compiler', *Journal of Automated Reasoning* 4, 353–380.

STICKEL M. E. [1989], The path-indexing method for indexing terms, Technical Report 473, SRI International, Menlo Park, California, USA.

STICKEL M., WALDINGER R. AND CHAUDHRY V. [2000], *A Guide to SNARK*, SRI International. **URL:** *www.ai.sri.com/hpkb/snark/tutorial*

STICKEL M., WALDINGER R., LOWRY R., PRESSBURGER T. AND UNDERWOOD I. [1994], Deductive composition of astronomical software from subroutine libraries, *in* A. Bundy, ed., 'Automated Deduction — CADE-12. 12th International Conference on Automated Deduction', Vol. 814 of *Lecture Notes in AI*, Nancy, France, pp. 341–355.

SUTCLIFFE G. AND SUTTNER C. [1998], 'The TPTP problem library — CNF release v. 1.2.1', *Journal of Automated Reasoning* 21(2).

TAMMET T. [1997], 'Gandalf', *Journal of Automated Reasoning* 18(2), 199–204.

VERMA R. M. AND RAMAKRISHNAN I. [1992], 'Tight complexity bounds for term matching problems', *Information and Computation* 101(1), 33–69.

VORONKOV A. [1994], An implementation technique for a class of bottom-up procedures, *in* M. Hermenegildo and J. Penjam, eds, 'Programming Languages Implementation and Logic Programming. 6th International Symposium, PLILP'94', Vol. 844 of *Lecture Notes in Computer Science*, Madrid, pp. 147–164.

VORONKOV A. [1995], 'The anatomy of Vampire: Implementing bottom-up procedures with code trees', *Journal of Automated Reasoning* 15(2), 237–265.

WADLER P. [1987], Efficient compilation of pattern matching, *in* S. P. Jones, ed., 'The Implementation of Functional Programming Languages', Prentice Hall, chapter 5.

WEIDENBACH C. [2001], Combining superposition, sorts and splitting, *in* A. Robinson and A. Voronkov, eds, 'Handbook of Automated Reasoning', Vol. II, Elsevier Science, chapter 27, pp. 1965–2013.

WEIDENBACH C., GAEDE B. AND ROCK G. [1996], Spass & flotter version 0.42, *in* M. McRobbie and J. Slaney, eds, 'Automated Deduction — CADE-13', Vol. 1104 of *Lecture Notes in Computer Science*, New Brunswick, NJ, USA, pp. 141–145.

WISE M. AND POWERS D. [1984], Indexing Prolog clauses via superimposed codewords and field encoded words, *in* 'Proceedings of the International Symposium on Logic Programming', Computer Society Press, pp. 203–210.

WOS L. [1992], 'Note on McCune's article on discrimination trees', *Journal of Automated Reasoning* 9(2), 145–146.

Index

CHAPTER 27

Combining Superposition, Sorts and Splitting

Christoph Weidenbach

Contents

HANDBOOK OF AUTOMATED REASONING
Edited by Alan Robinson and Andrei Voronkov
© 2001 Elsevier Science Publishers B.V. All rights reserved

1. What This Chapter is (not) About

This article is about the implementation of first-order saturation based clausal theorem provers. At the heart of such an implementation is a first-order calculus. It consists of inference rules that generate new clauses and reduction rules that reduce the number of clauses or transform clauses into simpler ones. In this chapter we introduce a great variety of clause set[1] based inference and reduction rules that can be composed to various sound and complete first-order calculi. The clause store data structure together with such a calculus are the basis for most of today's theorem proving systems. In this chapter we go one step further by introducing a splitting rule that supports explicit case analysis. This generalizes the standard clause store based approach to a clause store collection[2] approach where different clause stores represent the different cases. Therefore, the splitting rule introduces a second dimension in automated theorem proving.

The third dimension we consider here are constraints, extra information attached to a clause restricting its semantics and/or usage with respect to the calculus. Well-known constraints are ordering constraints, forcing substituted terms to satisfy the attached ordering restrictions, basicness constraints, forbidding paramodulation inferences on certain terms in the clause, or type constraints guaranteeing that instantiations for variables conform to the attached type of the variable, see [Nieuwenhuis and Rubio 2001, Dowek 2001] (Chapters 7 and 16 of this Handbook).

From an abstract implementation point of view the handling of constraints is always the same. The information is attached to a clause, it is maintained during the inference/reduction application process and it is exploited by constraint specific algorithms/deduction mechanisms to restrict inferences/reductions or to even eventually delete a clause. As a typical example for the implementation of constraints this chapter introduces sort constraints, specific type constraints for variables where the type (sort) theory is itself expressed by clauses.

When it comes to an actual implementation, building a (competitive) first-order theorem prover is a non-trivial effort. It results in a serious software project. A theorem-proving software project is always a compromise between different software design goals like maintainability, efficiency, flexibility, readability, short development time, modularity, etc. Foe example, if we believe that the highest impact on the performance of a prover is a result of a sophisticated calculus, a "good theory", then an implementation should focus on maintainability, flexibility, modularity and readability in order to support (future) progress in theory, motivated by implementation/experimentation experience. If we want to build a prover for a particular time critical application, then efficiency and short development time may be our guides to a successful system. Therefore, we won't study the implementation of provers at the level of data structures, object hierarchies or module design. Instead, we will discuss the needs for an efficient implementation of the various inference/reduction rules and the impacts that the top-level search algorithms have

---

[1] From an implementation point of view we consider clause multisets, called *clause stores*.

[2] A *clause store collection* is a multiset of clause stores.

on an actual implementation. This together with a specific design goal decision can then lead to a design concept for a real prover.

Heuristics are also not in focus of this chapter, although they can play an important rôle in automated theorem proving. For example, the heuristic that chooses the next clause for inferences inside a typical "main loop" of a saturation based prover (see Table 1 on page 1) can have a great impact on the success/non-success of a search attempt for a proof. However, it is the nature of heuristics that they are sometimes useful and sometimes make things even worse. In the context of automated theorem proving, it is often not predictable what will be the case as long as we don't restrict our attention to specific problems (problem classes). Therefore, the main focus of this chapter is on inference/simplification/reduction techniques. For these techniques we know, e.g., that they can be composed to decision procedures for a variety of syntactically identifiable subclasses of first-order logic [Bachmair, Ganzinger and Waldmann 1993, Nieuwenhuis 1996, Jacquemard, Meyer and Weidenbach 1998, Weidenbach 1999]. Our level of abstraction is often lower compared to chapters of this volume that solely are concerned with theory, because we want to emphasize on the implementation relevant aspects of inference/simplification/reduction techniques. Hence, we always refrain from "more elegant" formulations in order to make the consequences for an (efficient) implementation more explicit.

The design concepts introduced and discussed in this chapter are not necessarily original contributions of the author. For example, the combination of saturation and splitting is original, but the use of indexing techniques (see also [Ramakrishnan et al. 2001], Chapter 26 of this Handbook) is a widely used method. Many of the design ideas introduced in this chapter are "common knowledge" among the developers of first-order saturation based theorem provers and are regularly discussed among these. Thus it is hard to say where the origin of some idea comes from and I refer to my colleagues listed in the acknowledgments.

In this chapter I frequently use the notion *in practice* to argue for design decisions. This refers to the problem domains we have been interested in so far: Problems resulting from the analysis/verification of software [Fischer, Schumann and Snelting 1998], from the area of automatic type inference [Frühwirth, Shapiro, Vardi and Yardeni 1991, Charatonik, McAllester, Niwinski, Podelski and Walukiewicz 1998], from the analysis of security protocols [Heintze and Clarke 1999, Weidenbach 1999], planning problems [Kautz and Selman 1996], modal logic problems [Hustadt and Schmidt 1997], and problems from the TPTP problem library [Sutcliffe and Suttner 1998]. If we say that some technique/design/calculus is preferred over some other technique/design/calculus *in practice*, this is always meant with respect to the above mentioned problem domains.

After a section on notation and notions (Section 2), an introduction to major design aspects of saturation-based provers (Section 3), we discuss a wide set of inference/reduction rules (Section 4). For each rule we provide a formal definition and explain specific aspects of its pragmatics and implementation. In Section 5 we evolve the global design of a prover from all these rules.

2. Foundations

If not stated otherwise, we use here exactly the notions/notation of [Nonnengart and Weidenbach 2001] (Chapter 6 of this Handbook).

A *multiset* over a set A is a function M from A to the natural numbers. Intuitively, $M(a)$ specifies the number of occurrences of a in M. We say that a is an element of M if $M(a) > 0$. The union, intersection, and difference of multisets are defined by the identities $(M_1 \cup M_2)(x) = M_1(x) + M_2(x)$, $(M_1 \cap M_2)(x) = \min(M_1(x), M_2(x))$, and $(M_1 \setminus M_2)(x) = max(0, M_1(x) - M_2(x))$. We use a set-like notation to describe multisets.

A first-order language is constructed over a signature $\Sigma = (\mathcal{F}, \mathcal{R})$, where $\mathcal{F}$ and $\mathcal{R}$ are non-empty, disjoint, in general infinite sets of function and predicate symbols, respectively. Every function or predicate symbol has some fixed arity. In addition to these sets that are specific for a first-order language, we assume a further, infinite set $\mathcal{X}$ of variable symbols disjoint from the symbols in Σ. Then the set of all *terms* $\mathcal{T}(\mathcal{F}, \mathcal{X})$ is recursively defined by: (i) every function symbol $c \in \mathcal{F}$ with arity zero (a *constant*) is a term, (ii) every variable $x \in \mathcal{X}$ is a term and (iii) whenever $t_1, \ldots, t_n$ are terms and $f \in \mathcal{F}$ is a function symbol with arity n, then $f(t_1, \ldots, t_n)$ is a term. A term not containing a variable is a *ground term*. If $t_1, \ldots, t_n$ are terms and $R \in \mathcal{R}$ is a predicate symbol with arity n, then $R(t_1, \ldots, t_n)$ is an *atom*. An atom or the negation of an atom is called a *literal*. Disjunctions of literals are *clauses* where all variables are implicitly universally quantified. Clauses are often denoted by their respective multisets of literals where we write multisets in usual set notation. A clause consisting of exactly one literal is called a *unit*.

The set of *free* variables of an atom (term) denoted by $vars(\phi)$[3] is defined as follows: $vars(P(t_1, \ldots, t_n)) = \cup_i vars(t_i)$ and $vars(f(t_1, \ldots, t_n)) = \cup_i vars(t_i)$, $vars(x) = \{x\}$. The function naturally extends to literals, clauses and (multi)sets of terms (literals, clauses).

A *substitution* σ is a mapping from the set of variables to the set of terms such that $x\sigma \neq x$ for only finitely many $x \in \mathcal{X}$. We define the *domain* of σ to be $dom(\sigma) = \{x \mid x\sigma \neq x\}$ and the co-domain of σ to be $cdom(\sigma) = \{x\sigma \mid x\sigma \neq x\}$. Hence, we can denote a substitution σ by the finite set $\{x_1 \mapsto t_1, \ldots, x_n \mapsto t_n\}$ where $x_i\sigma = t_i$ and $dom(\sigma) = \{x_1, \ldots, x_n\}$. A *ground substitution* σ has no variable occurrences in its co-domain, $vars(cdom(\sigma)) = \emptyset$. An injective substitution σ where $cdom(\sigma) \subset \mathcal{X}$ is called a *variable renaming*. The application of substitutions to terms is given by $f(t_1, \ldots, t_n)\sigma = f(t_1\sigma, \ldots, t_n\sigma)$ for all $f \in \mathcal{F}$ with arity n. We extend the application of substitutions to literals and clauses as usual: $P(t_1, \ldots, t_n)\sigma = P(t_1\sigma, \ldots, t_n\sigma)$ (accordingly for literals) and $\{L_1, \ldots, L_n\}\sigma = \{L_1\sigma, \ldots, L_n\sigma\}$.

Given two terms (atoms) s, t, a substitution σ is called a *unifier* for s and t if $s\sigma = t\sigma$. It is called a *most general unifier* (mgu) if for any other unifier τ of s, t there exists a substitution λ with $\sigma\lambda = \tau$. A substitution σ is called a *matcher* from

---

[3]Please recall that we reuse notation of [Nonnengart and Weidenbach 2001] (Chapter 6 of this Handbook), so ϕ denotes an atom (formula).

s to t if $s\sigma = t$. The notion of a mgu is extended to atoms, literals in the obvious way. We say that σ is a unifier for a sequence of terms (atoms, literals) $t_1, \ldots, t_n$ if $t_i\sigma = t_j\sigma$ for all $1 \leq i, j \leq n$ and σ is a mgu if in addition for any other unifier τ of $t_1, \ldots, t_n$, there exists a substitution λ with $\sigma\lambda = \tau$.

A *position* is a word over the natural numbers. The set $pos(f(t_1, \ldots, t_n))$ of positions of a given term $f(t_1, \ldots, t_n)$ is defined as follows: (i) the empty word ϵ is a position in any term t and $t|_\epsilon = t$, (ii) if $t|_\pi = f(t_1, \ldots, t_n)$, then $\pi.i$ is a position in t for all $i = 1, \ldots, n$, and $t|_{\pi.i} = t_i$. We write $t[s]_\pi$ for $t|_\pi = s$. With $t[\pi/s]$, where $\pi \in pos(t)$, we denote the term (atom) obtained by replacing $t|_\pi$ by s at position π in t. The *length* of a position π is defined by $length(\epsilon) = 0$ and $length(i.\tau) = 1 + length(\tau)$. The notion of a position can be extended to atoms, literals and even formulae in the obvious way.

As an alternative to the already mentioned multiset notation of clauses, we also write clauses in the form $\Theta \,\|\, \Gamma \to \Delta$ where Θ is a multiset of monadic atoms[4] and Γ, Δ are multisets containing arbitrary atoms. Logically, the atoms in Θ and Γ denote negative literals while the atoms in Δ denote the positive literals in the clause. The empty clause $\square$ denotes $\bot$ (falsity). The multiset Θ is called the *sort constraint* of $\Theta \,\|\, \Gamma \to \Delta$. A sort constraint Θ is *solved* in a clause $\Theta \,\|\, \Gamma \to \Delta$ if it does not contain non-variable terms and $vars(\Theta) \subseteq vars(\Gamma \cup \Delta)$. If the clause is determined by the context, we simply say that a sort constraint is solved. In case we are not interested in a separation of the negative literals in a clause, we write clauses in the form $\Gamma \to \Delta$. We often abbreviate disjoint set union with sequencing, e.g., we write $\Theta \,\|\, \Gamma \to \Delta, R(t_1, \ldots, t_n)$ for $\Theta \,\|\, \Gamma \to \Delta \cup \{R(t_1, \ldots, t_n)\}$ Equality atoms are written $l \approx r$ and are mostly distinguished from non-equality atoms. The latter are named A, B. In case we don't want to distinguish these two different kinds of atoms we use the letter E (possibly indexed) to denote an arbitrary atom. Inferences and reductions where equations are involved are applied with respect to the symmetry of $\approx$.

A clause $\Theta_1 \,\|\, \Gamma_1 \to \Delta_1$ *subsumes* a clause $\Theta_2 \,\|\, \Gamma_2 \to \Delta_2$ if $\Theta_1\sigma \subseteq \Theta_2$, $\Gamma_1\sigma \subseteq \Gamma_2$ and $\Delta_1\sigma \subseteq \Delta_2$ for some matcher σ. The relation "is subsumed by" between clauses is a quasi-ordering on clauses. Please recall that we consider clauses to be multisets. Hence, e.g., the clause $\{P(x), P(y)\}$ (also possibly written $\to P(x), P(y)$) does not subsume the clause $\{P(x)\}$ (possibly written $\to P(x)$).

The function *size* maps terms, atoms, literals to the number of symbols they are built from, e.g., $size(t) = |pos(t)|$. In case of a literal, we don't consider the negation symbol for its size. The *depth* of a term, literal is the maximal length of a position in the term, literal, e.g., $depth(t) = max(\{length(\pi) \mid \pi \in pos(t)\}$. The depth of a clause is the maximal depth of its literals. The size of clause is the sum of its literal sizes.

For the definition of our inference/reduction rules we shall often need the notion of an ordering to compare terms. This notion is then lifted to tuples, sets, clauses and (multi)sets of clauses. A *partial order* is a reflexive, transitive and antisymmetric relation. A *strict order* is a transitive and irreflexive relation. Every partial order

---

[4]These are atoms with a monadic predicate as their top symbol that form the sort constraint.

$\succeq$ induces a strict order $\succ$ by $t \succ s$ iff $t \succeq s$ and $t \neq s$. The lexicographic extension $\succ^{lex}$ on tuples of some strict order $\succ$ is defined by $(t_1, \ldots, t_n) \succ^{lex} (s_1, \ldots, s_n)$ if for some $1 \leq i \leq n$ we have $t_i \succ s_i$ and for all $1 \leq j < i$ it is the case that $t_i = s_i$. The multiset extension $\succ^{mul}$ is defined by $M \succ^{mul} N$ if $N \neq M$ and for all $n \in N \setminus M$ there exists an $m \in M \setminus N$ with $m \succ n$. A *reduction ordering* $\succ$ is a well-founded, transitive relation satisfying for all terms t, s, l, positions $p \in pos(l)$ and substitutions σ that whenever $s \succ t$ then $l[p/s\sigma] \succ l[p/t\sigma]$. For the purpose of this chapter, we are only interested in reduction orderings that are total on ground terms, possibly up to some congruence on the ground terms. Any (reduction) ordering $\succ$ on terms (atoms) can be extended to clauses in the following way. We consider clauses as multisets of *occurrences* of equations and atoms. The occurrence of an equation $s \approx t$ in the antecedent is identified with the multiset $\{\{s, t\}\}$, the occurrence of an atom A in the antecedent is identified with the multiset $\{\{A, \top\}\}$, the occurrence of an equation in the succedent is identified with the multiset $\{\{s\}, \{t\}\}$ and the occurrence of an atom in the succedent is identified with the multiset $\{\{A\}, \{\top\}\}$. We always assume that $\top$ is the minimal constant with respect to $\succ$. Now we overload $\succ$ on literal occurrences to be the twofold multiset extension of $\succ$ on terms (atoms) and $\succ$ on clauses to be the multiset extension of $\succ$ on literal occurrences. If $\succ$ is well-founded (total) on terms (atoms), so are the multiset extensions on literals and clauses.

Observe that an occurrence of an equation $s \approx t$ (an atom) in the antecedent is strictly bigger than an occurrence of $s \approx t$ in the succedent. The atoms in the sort constraint will not be subject to ordering restrictions but will be processed by specific inference/reduction rules.

An antecedent or succedent occurrence of an equation $s \approx t$ (an atom A) is *maximal* in a clause $\Theta \| \Lambda \to \Pi$ if there is no occurrence of an equation or atom in $\Lambda \to \Pi$ that is strictly greater than the occurrence $s \approx t$ (the atom A) with respect to $\succ$. An antecedent or succedent occurrence of an equation $s \approx t$ is *strictly maximal* in a clause $\Theta \| \Lambda \to \Pi$ if there is no occurrence of an equation in $\Lambda \to \Pi$ that is greater or equal than the occurrence $s \approx t$ with respect to $\succ$. A clause $\Theta \| \Lambda \to \Pi, s \approx t$ (clause $\Theta \| \Lambda \to \Pi, A$) is *reductive* for the equation $s \approx t$ (the atom A), if $s \approx t$ (the atom A) is a strictly maximal occurrence of an equation (atom) and $t \not\succ s$.

For the specific constraint approach introduced here, monadic Horn theories are of particular importance. Such theories provide a natural representation of sort/type information (see Section 4.2). A *Horn clause* is a clause with at most one positive literal. A *monadic Horn theory* is a set of Horn clauses where all occurring predicates are monadic. A *declaration* is a clause $S_1(x_1), \ldots, S_n(x_n) \to S(t)$ with $\{x_1, \ldots, x_n\} \subseteq vars(t)$. It is called a *term declaration* if t is not a variable and a *subsort declaration* otherwise. A subsort declaration is called *trivial* if $n = 0$. A term t is called *shallow* if t is a variable or is of the form $f(x_1, \ldots, x_n)$ where the x_i are not necessarily different variables. A term t is called *linear* if every variable occurs at most once in t. It is called *semi-linear* if it is a variable or of the form $f(t_1, \ldots, t_n)$ such that every t_i is semi-linear and whenever $vars(t_i) \cap vars(t_j) \neq \emptyset$ we have $t_i = t_j$ for all i, j. A term declaration is called *shallow* (*linear, semi-linear*) if t is shallow (linear, semi-linear). Note that shallow term declarations don't include arbitrary ground terms. However, any ground term declaration can be equivalently represented, with respect to the minimal model semantics, by finitely many shallow term declarations. For example, the ground term declaration $\to S(f(a))$ can be represented by the shallow declarations $T(x) \to S(f(x))$, $\to T(a)$. A *sort theory* is a finite set of declarations. It is called *shallow (linear, semi-linear)* if all term declarations are shallow (linear, semi-linear).

A *clause store* is a multiset of clauses. A *clause store collection* is a multiset of clause stores. The inference and reduction rules discussed in this chapter operate on clauses occurring in a clause store of a clause store collection. There are inference rules

$$\mathcal{I} \frac{\Theta_1 \,\|\, \Gamma_1 \to \Delta_1 \quad \cdots \quad \Theta_n \,\|\, \Gamma_n \to \Delta_n}{\Psi \,\|\, \Pi \to \Lambda}$$

reduction rules

$$\mathcal{R} \frac{\Theta_1 \,\|\, \Gamma_1 \to \Delta_1 \quad \cdots \quad \Theta_n \,\|\, \Gamma_n \to \Delta_n}{\Psi_1 \,\|\, \Pi_1 \to \Lambda_1}$$
$$\vdots$$
$$\Psi_k \,\|\, \Pi_k \to \Lambda_k$$

and splitting rules.

$$\mathcal{S} \frac{\Theta \,\|\, \Gamma \to \Delta}{\begin{array}{c|c} \Psi_{1,1} \,\|\, \Pi_{1,1} \to \Lambda_{1,1} & \Psi_{1,2} \,\|\, \Pi_{1,2} \to \Lambda_{1,2} \\ \vdots & \vdots \\ \Psi_{n,1} \,\|\, \Pi_{n,1} \to \Lambda_{n,1} & \Psi_{m,2} \,\|\, \Pi_{m,2} \to \Lambda_{m,2} \end{array}}$$

The clauses $\Theta_i \,\|\, \Gamma_i \to \Delta_i$ are called the *parent clauses* or *premises* of the splitting (reduction, inference) rule and the clauses $\Psi_{i(,j)} \,\|\, \Pi_{i(,j)} \to \Lambda_{i(,j)}$ the *conclusions*. A rule is applied to a clause store collection P by selecting a clause store N out of P such that the premises of an inference (reduction, splitting) rule are contained in N. In this case, N is called the *current* clause store. If an inference is performed, the conclusion of the inference is *added* to N. If a reduction is performed, the premises are *replaced* in N by the conclusions. As a special case, if no conclusion is present, the premises are deleted from N. If a splitting rule is applied, the current store N is *replaced* in P by two stores

$$N \setminus \{\Theta \,\|\, \Gamma \to \Delta\} \cup \{\Psi_{j,1} \,\|\, \Pi_{j,1} \to \Lambda_{j,1} \mid 1 \le j \le n\}$$
$$N \setminus \{\Theta \,\|\, \Gamma \to \Delta\} \cup \{\Psi_{j,2} \,\|\, \Pi_{j,2} \to \Lambda_{j,2} \mid 1 \le j \le m\}$$

One can think of more general splitting rules but the above schema is sufficient for a general understanding of the implementation consequences caused by such a rule. Semantically, clause stores represent conjunctions of their clauses whilst clause store collections represent disjunctions of their contained clause stores. So a clause store collection P represents a disjunction (clause stores) of conjunctions (of universally quantified clauses) of disjunctions (of literals).

A clause store N is *saturated* with respect to a set of inference and reduction rules (no splitting rules), if any conclusion of an inference rule application to N yields a clause that can eventually be deleted by a sequence of reduction rule applications. This definition of saturation provides an operational point of view. For the underlying semantic concept, see [Bachmair and Ganzinger 2001, Nieuwenhuis and Rubio 2001] (Chapters 2 and 7 of this Handbook).

3. A First Simple Prover

In this section, we discuss the implementation of a simple resolution based calculus. Although the calculi implemented in today's saturation based provers are much more sophisticated than the simple resolution calculus considered here, some important design decisions can already be explained on the basis of such a simple example. The resolution calculus consists of the inference rules resolution, factoring and the reduction rules subsumption deletion and tautology deletion

Resolution
$$\mathcal{I}\frac{\Gamma_1, A \to \Delta_1 \quad \Gamma_2 \to \Delta_2, B}{(\Gamma_1, \Gamma_2 \to \Delta_1, \Delta_2)\sigma}$$

Factoring Right
$$\mathcal{I}\frac{\Gamma \to \Delta, A, B}{(\Gamma \to \Delta, A)\sigma}$$

Subsumption Deletion
$$\mathcal{R}\frac{\Gamma_1 \to \Delta_1 \quad \Gamma_2 \to \Delta_2}{\Gamma_1 \to \Delta_1}$$

Factoring Left
$$\mathcal{I}\frac{\Gamma, A, B \to \Delta}{(\Gamma, A \to \Delta)\sigma}$$

Tautology Deletion
$$\mathcal{R}\frac{\Gamma, A \to \Delta, A}{}$$

where σ is a most general unifier (mgu) of the atoms A and B for the rules resolution, factoring and in order to apply subsumption, the clause $\Gamma_1 \to \Delta_1$ must subsume the clause $\Gamma_2 \to \Delta_2$.

For the resolution rule to be complete, it is required that the parent clauses $\Gamma_1, A \to \Delta_1$ and $\Gamma_2 \to \Delta_2, B$ have no variables in common. Actual implementations of the rule satisfy this requirement in different ways. They all have in common that variables are represented by (natural) numbers, so this is our assumption for the rest of this paragraph. The first solution explicitly renames the clauses such that they have no variables in common. The second solution accepts clauses that share variables, but when running the unification algorithm the variables are separated by adding an offset to the variables of one clause.[5] A typical offset is the value of the maximal, with respect to number greater, variable of the other clause. The third solution also accepts clauses that share variables and solves the problem by employing two substitutions, one for each clause. This requires some modifications

---

[5] Please recall that we assume variables to be represented by naturals.

to the standard unification algorithms,[6] because the terms of the different atoms need to be explicitly separated. In order to test applicability of the resolution rule, it is sufficient to explicitly or implicitly rename the variables of the considered atoms, not the overall clause.

For the factoring rule there is an extra variant for positive (Factoring Right) and negative literals (Factoring Left). We could have presented both variants in one rule, by denoting clauses as disjunctions of literals. However, our representation is closer to actual implementations of the rule. All clause data structures used in well-known provers explicitly separate positive from negative literals. The reason is efficiency and already becomes obvious for factoring: Whenever we search for a partner literal for a positive literal it does not make sense to consider negative literals at all. Similar situations arise for other inference/reduction rules. Therefore, the decision in this chapter is always to distinguish positive and negative literals when presenting inference/reduction rules.

Now let us compose the inference/reduction rules to an actual prover. The input of the prover is a clause store containing clauses without equality and the output on termination is a proof or a saturated clause store. The above resolution calculus is complete, so we also want our search procedure to be complete in the sense that if resources don't matter and our procedure is called with an unsatisfiable clause store then it will eventually find a proof (the empty clause). In order to achieve this goal, we have to guarantee that the considered clause set is saturated in the limit. This includes that all inferences between clauses have been performed. An easy way to remember which inferences have already been performed is to split the input clause store in a set Wo of clauses (Worked off clauses) where all inferences between clauses in this set already took place and a set Us of clauses (Usable clauses) which still have to be considered for inferences. Then a main loop iteration of the prover consists of selecting a clause from the Us set, moving it to the Wo set and then adding all inferences between the selected clause and the clauses in Wo to the Us set. If the selection is fair, i.e., no clause stays arbitrarily long in the Us set without being selected, this results in a complete procedure. It remains to build reductions into this loop. The idea for this loop is due to the Otter theorem prover and its predecessors [McCune and Wos 1997].

The reduction rules tautology deletion and subsumption deletion decrease the number of clauses in the clause store while the inference rules increase the number of clauses. Hence, exhaustive application of the reduction rules terminates and produces smaller clause stores. In practice, small clause sets are preferred over large ones, hence reductions are preferred over inferences. This consideration together with the idea of the main-loop introduced above leads to *ResolutionProver1* depicted in Table 1. Note that subsumption and tautology deletion are independent in the sense that once all tautologies have been removed, subsumption does not generate new tautologies. Analyzing such dependencies between reductions is one key for an efficient implementation.

---

[6] For a discussion on syntactic unification algorithms, consider [Baader and Snyder 2001] (Chapter 8 of this Handbook).

```
1  ResolutionProver1 (N)
2    Wo := ∅;
3    Us := taut(sub(N));
4    While (Us ≠ ∅ and □ ∉ Us)  {
5      (Given, Us):= choose(Us);
6      Wo        := Wo ∪ {Given};
7      New       := res(Given, Wo) ∪ fac(Given);
8      New       := taut(sub(New));
9      New       := sub(sub(New, Wo), Us);
10     Wo        := sub(Wo, New);
11     Us        := sub(Us, New) ∪ New;
12   }
13   If (Us = ∅) then print "Completion Found";
14   If (□ ∈ Us) then print "Proof Found";
```

Table 1: A First Resolution Based Prover

For the description of theorem proving procedures we use the following abbreviations: $fac(C)$ is the set of all factoring inference conclusions (left and right) from the clause C, $res(C, D)$ is the set of all resolution inference conclusions between two clauses C and D, $taut(N)$ is the set N after exhaustive application of tautology deletion and $sub(N, M)$ is the set of all clauses from N that are not subsumed by a clause in M. We overload sub for one argument, where $sub(N)$ denotes the set N after exhaustive application of subsumption deletion to the clauses in N. We overload res by defining $res(C, N)$ to be the set of all resolution inferences between the clause C and a clause in N. The function $choose$ selects and removes a clause from its argument clause store and returns the selected clause as well as the updated argument clause store.

As already motivated, the procedure $ResolutionProver1$ operates on two clause stores: Wo and Us. The store Wo holds all clauses that have already been selected for inferences, while the store Us contains all candidate clauses to generate inferences. The prover $ResolutionProver1$ is called with a finite clause store N and tests those for unsatisfiability. Lines 2 and 3 initialize the sets Wo and Us. Note that Us is not initialized with N, but its completely inter-reduced equivalent. This step is called *input reduction*. The search for the empty clause (a saturation) is implemented by the lines 4–12. The while-loop starting at line 4 terminates if the empty clause is found or the set Us is empty. We will argue below that this implies that the set Wo is saturated. If Us is not empty and the body of the while-loop is entered, the function *choose* selects at line 5 a clause out of the usable set. The function is fair, if no clause stays in *Us* for an infinite number of iterations through the while loop. A widely used, fair implementation (heuristic) of *choose* is to select a lightest clause that is a clause of smallest size. This selection function is fair, because there are only finitely many different clauses with respect to subsumption having less than k symbols, for any constant k.[7] Many refinements of the *choose* function are possible: using different weights for variable and signature symbols , preferring clauses with more/fewer variables, preferring clauses that contain certain atoms/term structures or considering in addition the depth of a clause in the search space. The depth of a clause in the search space is zero for all input clauses and every conclusion of an inference has the maximal depth of their parent clauses plus one. Many provers use a combination of weight and depth selection, e.g., choosing four times clauses by minimal weight and every fifth time by minimal depth. This combination again goes back to Otter where the ratio can be controlled by the *pick-given* ratio parameter.

Then the clause *Given* is selected, removed from *Us* and added to *Wo* (lines 5, 6). Next (line 7) all resolution inference conclusions between *Given* and *Wo* and all factoring inference conclusions from *Given* are stored in *New*. Note that since *Given* is already contained in *Wo* these inferences include self resolution inferences. The clauses generated so far are called *derived* clauses. The lines 8–11 are devoted to reduction. First, all tautologies and subsumed clauses are removed from *New*. Then all clauses that are subsumed by a clause in *Wo* or *Us* are deleted from *New*. This operation is called *forward subsumption*. Clauses remaining in *New* are then used for *backward subsumption*, the subsumption of clauses in the sets *Wo* and *Us* by clauses from *New*. Finally, the clauses from *New* are added to *Us*. These clauses are usually called *kept* clauses.

There are two invariants that hold each time line 4 is executed:

- Any resolution inference conclusion from two clauses in *Wo* (factoring inference conclusion from a clause in *Wo*) is either contained in *Wo*, *Us* or is subsumed by a clause in *Wo*, *Us* or is a tautology.

- The sets *Wo* and *Us* are completely inter-reduced:
  $Wo \cup Us = taut(Wo \cup Us)$ and
  $Wo \cup Us = sub(Wo \cup Us)$.

A consequence of these invariants to hold is that if the procedure stops then the set *Wo* is saturated. Furthermore, if the function *choose* is fair, then the *ResolutionProver1* is complete.

In case that for the set N a satisfiable subset N' is known, e.g., if the clauses represent a proof attempt of a conjecture with respect to some theory that is known to be satisfiable, we could also initialize the sets by $Wo := N'$ and $Us := (N \setminus N')$, obtaining the so called set of support (SOS) strategy [Wos, Robinson and Carson 1965]. The SOS strategy preserves completeness.

---

[7]Note that since the input set N is finite, the relevant signature is finite, too.

Many other saturation based provers (e.g., Otter, SPASS, Waldmeister, see Appendix A) have a search algorithm based on two sets of clauses.[8]

For example, we simulate a run of *ResolutionProver1* on the clauses

$$1: \qquad\qquad\qquad \rightarrow P(f(a))$$
$$2: \qquad\qquad P(f(x)) \rightarrow P(x)$$
$$3: \quad P(f(a)), P(f(x)) \rightarrow$$

shown in Table 2. For each while-loop iteration, we show the content of the *Wo* and *Us* set at line 4, the selected *Given* clause and the content of *New* before execution of line 8. Newly generated clauses are printed in full detail while we refer to a clause in the sets *Wo* and *Us* only by its unique clause number. The function *choose* selects lightest clauses.

Every box in Table 2 represents one while-loop iteration. For newly generated clauses we also show the applied inference rule and parent clauses/literals. Here *Res* indicates a resolution inference, *Fac* a factoring inference and the notion $n.m$ refers to literal m of clause n. So, for example, clause 7 is generated by a resolution inference between the first literal of clause 1 and the second literal of clause 3 where literals are counted from left to right. Iteration 4 shows already some common phenomena of saturation based calculi. First, these calculi are typically redundant in the sense that the very same clause can be generated in various, different ways. For example, clause 7 and clause 10 are logically identical, although the former is generated by a resolution inference while the latter is the result of a factoring application. As a consequence, subsumption is indispensable for saturation based calculi to cut down the number of kept clauses. The situation gets even more dramatic in the context of equality, where a single loop iteration can already cause an explosion in the number of newly generated clauses. This will be discussed in more detail in Section 4. Coming back to our run, note that in the reduction part of while-loop iteration 4, the clauses 2, 3, 5, 7–10 are all subsumed by clause 6. Second, even for this simple example, it happened that the selection of the *Given* clause is not always unique when choosing lightest clauses. During iteration 4, the clauses 3 and 5 have both size 6, but choosing clause 5 instead of clause 3 would have caused an additional while loop iteration before the empty clause is derived. Of course, the function *choose* could be refined and we will in fact discuss such refinements, but in practice it happens (and must happen) frequently that several clauses have the same precedence with respect to *choose*. Then selecting the right clause (by accident) can enable a prover to find a proof where it gets lost in the search space by selecting a different one. This phenomenon is common to all theorem provers and can be observed at the yearly CADE CASC system competitions (e.g., see [Sutcliffe and Suttner 1999]), where the performance of provers varies depending on the ordering of the input problem clauses.

If *ResolutionProver1* is ran on non-trivial examples, the *Us* set rapidly gets much larger than the *Wo* set. It easily happens that after some iterations the size increases by a factor of 1000. In particular, it is common in the context of problems containing equality. Therefore, at least with respect to the number of clauses that have to be

---

[8] However, they use different names for the sets. So don't be confused.

Iteration 1

$Wo = \emptyset$	$Us = \{1, 2, 3\}$
$Given = $ 1: $\to P(f(a))$	
$New = $ $\emptyset$	

Iteration 2   ↓

$Wo = \{1\}$	$Us = \{2, 3\}$
$Given = $ 2: $P(f(x)) \to P(x)$	
$New = $ $\{4:[\text{Res}:1.1,2.1]$ $\to P(a),$	
$5:[\text{Res}:2.1,2.2]$ $P(f(f(x))) \to P(x) \}$	

Iteration 3   ↓

$Wo = \{1, 2\}$	$Us = \{3, 4, 5\}$
$Given = $ 4: $\to P(a)$	
$New = $ $\emptyset$	

Iteration 4   ↓

$Wo = \{1, 2, 4\}$	$Us = \{3, 5\}$
$Given = $ 3: $P(f(a)), P(f(x)) \to$	
$New = $ $\{$ 6:$[\text{Res}:1.1,3.1]$ $P(f(x)) \to,$	
7:$[\text{Res}:1.1,3.2]$ $P(f(a)) \to,$	
8:$[\text{Res}:2.2,3.1]$ $P(f(f(a))), P(f(x)) \to,$	
9:$[\text{Res}:2.2,3.2]$ $P(f(a)), P(f(f(x))) \to,$	
10:$[\text{Fac}:3.1,3.2]$ $P(f(a)) \to \}$	

Iteration 5   ↓

$Wo = \{1, 4\}$	$Us = \{6\}$
$Given = $ 6: $P(f(x)) \to$	
$New = $ $\{11:[\text{Res}:1.1,6.1]$ $\square \}$	

Table 2: A Run of *ResolutionProver1*

```
 1  ResolutionProver2(N)
 2    Wo         := ∅;
 3    Us         := taut(sub(N));
 4    While (Us ≠ ∅ and □ ∉ Us)  {
 5      (Given, Us):= choose(Us);
 6      if (sub({Given}, Wo) ≠ ∅)  {
 7        Wo         := sub(Wo, {Given});
 8        Wo         := Wo ∪ {Given};
 9        New        := res(Given, Wo) ∪ fac(Given);
10        New        := taut(sub(New));
11        New        := sub(New, Wo);
12        Us         := Us ∪ New;
13      }
14    }
15    If (Us = ∅) then print "Completion Found";
16    If (□ ∈ Us) then print "Proof Found";
```

Table 3: A Second Resolution Based Prover

considered, the subsumption tests with respect to the Us set are the most expensive parts of the algorithm. Typical runs of *ResolutionProver1* show a behavior where more than 95% of the overall time is spent for subsumption checks. This motivates the design of *ResolutionProver2* shown in Table 3.

ResolutionProver2(N) does not perform any subsumption tests with respect to the Us set and back subsumption is only performed with respect to the actually selected given clause. The two invariants for *ResolutionProver2* are

- Any resolution inference conclusion from two clauses in Wo (factoring inference conclusion from a clause in Wo) is either contained in Wo, Us or is subsumed by a clause in Wo or is a tautology.
- The set Wo is completely inter-reduced:
  $Wo = taut(Wo)$ and
  $Wo = sub(Wo)$.

These two invariants are still strong enough to guarantee that if the while loop terminates, the Wo set is saturated. Note that although New is always reduced with respect to Wo at line 11, the set Us is in general not reduced with respect to Wo, i.e., $Us \neq sub(Us, Wo)$.

If we assume that *choose* selects light clauses there is a further motivation to leave out subsumption tests with respect to the Us set. If a clause C subsumes a clause D, then $size(C) \leq size(D)$. So small clauses have a higher probability to subsume other clauses than larger clauses. Therefore, because we always select the lightest given clause, the hope is that not too many clauses that could have been subsumed stay in the Us set. In practice, *ResolutionProver2* saves about 10% of the time spent for reductions (subsumption) compared to *ResolutionProver1*. For the simple resolution calculus we studied so far, *ResolutionProver2* is mostly in favor of *ResolutionProver1* when run in practice (see [Riazanov and Voronkov 2000] for a comparison). As soon as our reduction techniques include rules that produce lighter clauses (see Section 4) the choice is no longer obvious in general. There are examples where an overall interreduction easily yields the empty clause, but for a *ResolutionProver2* style algorithm sophisticated heuristics are needed to still find a proof.

Running *ResolutionProver2* on the example clause store, the result is similar to the run of *ResolutionProver1* (Table 2). The first three iterations are identical, but at iteration 4, the clauses 2, 3, 5, 7–10 are not subsumed but stay in their respective sets. Then, in iteration 5, where clause 6 is selected as given clause, the clauses 2, 3 are removed from the Wo set (line 7 of *ResolutionProver2*, Table 3) and the empty clause is derived.

There are many possible alternatives, variations, refinements for the two loops suggested here. Let us discuss some aspects. First, concerning factoring, any clause store can be finitely saturated with respect to factoring, since a factor has strictly fewer literals than its parent. So one could get the idea to keep the Wo set always saturated with respect to factoring. The disadvantage of this approach is that the number of factors that can be generated out of one clause grows worst case exponentially in the number of literals. The prover Bliksem allows a user to prefer factors (see Appendix A).

Second, concerning resolution and the selection of the given clause, we could also a priori built for each loop iteration all one step resolvents between the clauses in the Us set and between one parent from the Us set and one parent from the Wo set. Then instead of picking a *Given* clause, we pick one resolvent, use it for (back and/or forward) reduction and finally add it to the Wo set. This approach results in a more fine grained development of the search space. This design for a proof search is closely related to clause graph resolution [Eisinger 1991].

Third, on the implementation side, if we once decide to implement *Resolution-Prover2*, the only information we need for the clauses in Us are their properties with respect to the *choose* function and how these clauses can be generated. For all clauses except the input clauses it suffices to store references for the parents and the used inference. This way it is possible to store all Us clauses in a compact way. In practice constant space suffices for any clause. This dramatically decreases memory consumption and results in an extra speed up. The necessary regeneration of clauses once they are selected, plays no rôle concerning performance. The Waldmeister prover follows this approach. Fourth, another way to keep the Us set small is to throw away clauses with respect to certain weight or complexity restrictions on the newly generated clauses. Either these clauses are just thrown away resulting in an incomplete procedure, this is supported by Otter, SPASS and Vampire (see

Appendix A), or the restrictions can be set in a way such that only finitely many clauses can pass the restriction test and once the search results in such a saturated set, the restrictions are adjusted and the search is restarted. This design is supported by Bliksem, SPASS and Fiesta. Such an exploration of the search space can be particularly useful in the context of unit equational problems.

4. Inference and Reduction Rules

In this section we describe a variety of inference/reduction rules. For every rule, we start with a formal definition of the rule and then, if necessary, discuss aspects of its pragmatics, complexity, interaction with other rules or design concepts and its implementation and usage. Some rules are stated in a general, possibly non-effective form (e.g., see the conflict rule, Definition 4.19). In this case we also discuss effective instantiations. The rules don't form a particular calculus, instead several well-known calculi can be implemented by forming appropriate groups of rules. An example is the simple resolution calculus considered in Section 3.

Many reduction rules can be simulated by one or several inference rule applications followed by a (trivial) subsumption step. As long as the inference rule set is complete this observation is not too surprising, since we require all our rules to be sound. So one might think that the sophisticated reduction machinery introduced in this section is not really necessary but just a waste of resources when implemented. However, it is just the other way round. Reduction rules always lead to "simpler" clause stores by deleting some clause or by replacing a clause by a "simpler" one. This often ensures the termination of exhaustive application of (groups of) such rules and enables application of these rules to *all* clauses. Therefore, in the context of an implementation, reduction rules cannot be simulated by inference rule applications since those don't terminate when applied exhaustively. Inference rules are only applied to some selected *Given* clause. Reduction rules should be viewed as restricted inference rules that eventually lead to simpler clause stores and help to explore the "easy" parts of the search space (problem). They replace search space exploration by (efficient) calculation. In fact, some of the reduction rules introduced in this section are motivated by decidability results for various first-order logic fragments.

4.1. Reduction Orderings

For many of the inference/reduction rules defined in the sequel, maximality restrictions on literals, terms play an important rôle. The two most popular orderings are the Knuth-Bendix ordering (KBO) [Knuth and Bendix 1970, Peterson 1983] and the recursive path ordering with status (RPOS) [Dershowitz 1982]. For a broad introduction to orderings, consider the article by Dershowitz [1987] and the more recent book by Baader and Nipkow [1998]. The definitions below differ in some details from other definitions found in the literature, but reflect implementation experience.

Nearly all orderings used in todays provers are variations of the KBO and the RPOS. In particular, weaker versions the orderings are often used. For example, purely weight based orderings or variants of the RPOS without recursive considera-tion of subterms. These weaker versions have the advantage of cheaper computation and when used to restrict inference rules (see Section 4.3) of a broader exploration of the search space. This can be useful for the search of short proofs.

Let $>$ be a strict order on the set of signature symbols (functions, predicates), called a *precedence*. Let *weight* be a mapping from the set of signature symbols into the non-negative integers. We call a weight function *admissible* for some precedence if for every unary function symbol f with $weight(f) = 0$, the function f is maximal in the precedence, i.e., $f \geq g$ for all other function symbols g. The function *weight* is extended to a weight function for terms (atoms) as follows: (i) if t is a variable, then $weight(t) = k$, where k is the minimum weight of any constant and (ii) if $t = f(t_1, \ldots, t_n)$, then $weight(t) = weight(f) + \sum_i weight(t_i)$. Let *occ* be a function returning the number of occurrences $occ(s, t)$ of a term s in a term t, defined by $occ(s, t) = |\{p \in pos(t) \mid t|_p = s\}|$ and let *status* be a mapping from the signature symbols to the set $\{left, right, mul\}$.

4.1. DEFINITION *(KBO)*. If t, s are terms, then $t \succ_{kbo} s$ if $occ(x, t) \geq occ(x, s)$ for every variable $x \in (vars(t) \cup vars(s))$ and

(1) $weight(t) > weight(s)$ or

(2) $weight(t) = weight(s)$ and $t = f(t_1, \ldots, t_k)$ and $s = g(s_1, \ldots, s_l)$ and

   (2a) $f > g$ in the precedence or

   (2b) $f = g$ and

      (2b1) $status(f) = left$ and $(t_1, \ldots, t_k) \succ_{kbo}^{lex} (s_1, \ldots, s_l)$ or

      (2b2) $status(f) = right$ and $(t_k, t_{k-1}, \ldots, t_1) \succ_{kbo}^{lex} (s_l, s_{l-1}, \ldots, s_1)$

Note that in case (2b) the condition $f = g$ implies $k = l$. Multiset status for function symbols can also be defined but does not pay off in practice for the KBO. If the weight function is admissible for the precedence, then the KBO is a reduction ordering [Baader and Nipkow 1998]. If the precedence $>$ is total, then the KBO is total on ground terms (atoms). For some finite set of signature symbols[9] and two terms s, t with $s \succ_{kbo} t$, there are finitely many terms s' with $s \succ_{kbo} s' \succ_{kbo} t$.

The motivation to consider unary function symbols with weight zero comes in particular from group theory. The standard group axioms can be turned into a convergent system (see [Dershowitz and Plaisted 2001], Chapter 9 of this Handbook) using the KBO with precedence $i > f > e$ and weights $weight(i) = 0$, $weight(f) = weight(e) = 1$ where i is the inverse function, f denotes group multiplication and e represents the neutral element. During the saturation (completion) process it is crucial to orient the derived equation $i(f(x, y)) \approx f(i(y), i(x))$ from left to right, for otherwise the saturation process won't terminate. The only way to achieve $i(f(x, y)) \succ f(i(y), i(x))$ is to assign weight 0 to the function symbol i.

---

[9]For an infinite set the condition does obviously not hold.

Implementation of the KBO can be done straightforward from the definition. For the RPOS we also assume $>$ to be a strict order (precedence) on the set of signature symbols (functions, predicates).

4.2. DEFINITION *(RPOS)*. If t, s are terms, then $t \succ_{rpos} s$ if

(1) $t \in vars(s)$ and $t \neq s$ or

(2) $t = f(t_1, \ldots, t_k)$ and $s = g(s_1, \ldots, s_l)$ and

  (2a) $t_i \succeq_{rpos} s$ for some $1 \leq i \leq k$ or

  (2b) $f > g$ and $t \succ_{rpos} s_j$ for all $1 \leq j \leq l$ or

  (2c) $f = g$ and

    (2c1) $status(f) = left$ and $(t_1, \ldots, t_k) \succ_{rpos}^{lex} (s_1, \ldots, s_l)$ and
    $t \succ_{rpos} s_j$ for all $1 \leq j \leq l$ or

    (2c2) $status(f) = right$ and $(t_k, t_{k-1}, \ldots, t_1) \succ_{rpos}^{lex} (s_l, s_{l-1}, \ldots, s_1)$ and
    $t \succ_{rpos} s_j$ for all $1 \leq j \leq l$ or

    (2c3) $status(f) = mul$ and $\{t_1, \ldots, t_k\} \succ_{rpos}^{mul} \{s_1, \ldots, s_l\}$

The RPOS is a reduction ordering as well and if the precedence $>$ is total RPOS is also total on ground terms (atoms), up to the congruence relation $=_{mul}$ generated from the symbols with multiset status. If f is a function symbol with $status(f) = mul$ then $f(t_1, \ldots, t_n) =_{mul} f(s_1, \ldots, s_n)$ if $\{t_1, \ldots, t_n\} =_{mul}^{mul} \{s_1, \ldots, s_n\}$, for example $f(a, f(a, b)) =_{mul} f(f(b, a), a)$. Even for some finite set of signature symbols and two terms s, t with $s \succ_{rpos} t$, there are in general infinitely many terms s' with $s \succ_{rpos} s' \succ_{rpos} t$.

The RPOS can for example be used to orient distributivity the "right way". If $f > g$, then the equation $f(x, g(y, z)) \approx g(f(x, y), f(x, z))$ is oriented by RPOS from left to right. Note that KBO cannot orient the equation from left to right, because the right hand side has one more occurrence of the variable x.

Given a specific theorem proving problem, the relevant signature is finite and fixed. In this case it can be useful to further refine an ordering by defining $t \succ s$ if $t\sigma \succ s\sigma$ for all ground substitutions σ where $(vars(t) \cup vars(s)) \subseteq dom(\sigma)$. Following this idea, RPOS can be instantiated to an ordering that totally orders all atoms by predicate symbols and only in second place considers possible argument terms, independently from variable occurrences! This can be achieved by making all (some) predicate symbols larger in the precedence than all function symbols. For example, with respect to the above suggested lifting and a signature with predicate symbols P, Q and function symbols f, a where $P > Q > f > a$ it holds that $P(x) \succ_{rpos} Q(f(x, y))$ because P is greater in the precedence than Q, f, a and hence any ground term that can be substituted for x or y. Such an application of RPOS can, e.g., be useful to make literals built from newly introduced formula renaming predicates minimal. This prevents the generation of the standard CNF via ordered resolution, see [Nonnengart and Weidenbach 2001] (Chapter 6 of this Handbook).

Straightforward recursive implementation of RPOS following the definition results in an algorithm with worst case exponential complexity. Using a dynamic programming idea, a polynomial algorithm can be devised [Snyder 1993]. However, in practice, it turns out that the straightforward implementation is superior to the dynamic programming approach, if the following filter is added. Whenever we test $t \succ_{rpos} s$ for two terms s, t, we first check $vars(s) \subseteq vars(t)$.

4.2. Sorts

The motivation for sorts comes from programming languages, where one likes to catch as many errors at compile time as possible. For example, if the addition function is only defined for number sorts (types) but used in a program with a list type, the compiler can complain about such a statement by exploiting the sort information. Of course, the sort checking must be tractable, i.e., it should at least be decidable and/or show acceptable performance for real world programs. A prerequisite for the sort information to be checked at compile time, is that the sort information is separated from the program and it is typically included in an extra declaration part.

Here we generalize this situation. The sort information is not separated from the first-order problem as, e.g., done in algebraic specification languages, but part of the problem itself. Therefore, we cannot check sort information at compile time, after or while reading the problem. Instead the sort information is used at run time, during proof search, to detect ill-sorted and therefore redundant clauses and to simplify the sort information contained in the clauses by specific algorithms. These algorithms exploit the sort information in a much more efficient way than their standard first-order reduction rule counterparts.

4.3. DEFINITION *(Sort Constraint Resolution).* The inference

$$\mathcal{I} \frac{T_1(t), \ldots, T_n(t), \Psi \| \Gamma \to \Delta \qquad \Theta_i \| \Gamma_i \to \Delta_i, T_i(s_i) \quad (1 \leq i \leq n)}{(\Theta_1, \ldots, \Theta_n, \Psi \| \Gamma_1, \ldots, \Gamma_n, \Gamma \to \Delta_1, \ldots, \Delta_n, \Delta)\sigma}$$

where (i) σ is the simultaneous mgu of $t, s_1, \ldots, s_n$, (ii) t is a non-variable term and there is no further literal $S(t) \in \Psi$, (iii) all Θ_i are solved, (iv) all $T_i(s_i)\sigma$ are reductive for $(\Theta_i \| \Gamma_i \to \Delta_i, T_i(s_i))\sigma$ is a *sort constraint resolution* inference.

Sort constraint resolution is a hyper resolution (see Definition 4.14) like inference rule. It simulates the rule weakening of sorted unification [Weidenbach 1998] on the relativization of sorted variables represented by the sort constraint.

4.4. DEFINITION *(Empty Sort).* The inference

$$\mathcal{I} \frac{T_1(x), \ldots, T_n(x), \Psi \| \Gamma \to \Delta \qquad \Theta_i \| \Gamma_i \to \Delta_i, T_i(s_i) \quad (1 \leq i \leq n)}{(\Theta_1, \ldots, \Theta_n, \Psi \| \Gamma_1, \ldots, \Gamma_n, \Gamma \to \Delta_1, \ldots, \Delta_n, \Delta)\sigma}$$

where (i) σ is the simultaneous mgu of $s_1, \ldots, s_n$, (ii) $x \notin vars(\Gamma \cup \Delta \cup \Psi)$ and no non-variable term occurs in Ψ, (iii) all Θ_i are solved, (iv) all $T_i(s_i)\sigma$ are reductive for $(\Theta_i \| \Gamma_i \to \Delta_i, T_i(s_i))\sigma$ is an *empty sort* inference.

Empty sort is similar to sort resolution and, in fact, in some of our papers (e.g., Jacquemard et al. [1998]) we unified both rules into one inference rule. For the purpose of the decidability results presented in these papers this is appropriate. For implementation, it makes sense to distinguish these rules, because the eventual success of empty sort, i.e., we are able to show that some sort is non-empty, does not rely on the particular sort constraint, but only on the set of monadic (sort) symbols that share their variable argument. We check emptiness of an intersection of sort symbols. Since there are only finitely many different such sorts with respect to some finite clause store, it may make sense to store constraints that resulted in successful non-emptiness proofs and to reuse them. One application domain are the proofs required in the context of static soft typing (Definition 4.6).

4.5. DEFINITION *(Sort Simplification).* Let N be the current clause store and $N' \subseteq N$ be exactly the set of all declarations in N. The reduction

$$\mathcal{R}\frac{S(t), \Theta \,\|\, \Gamma \to \Delta}{\Theta \,\|\, \Gamma \to \Delta}$$

where $N' \models \forall x_1, \ldots, x_n \,[S_1(x_1), \ldots, S_n(x_n) \supset S(t)]$ and $\{S_1(x_1), \ldots, S_n(x_n)\} \subseteq \Theta$ is the maximal subset of Θ for which $\{x_1, \ldots, x_n\} \subseteq vars(t)$ is called *sort simplification.*

Given an arbitrary sort theory N', the relation

$$N' \models \forall x_1, \ldots, x_n \,[S_1(x_1), \ldots, S_n(x_n) \supset S(t)]$$

is always decidable in polynomial time. In terms of sorted unification the problem means deciding well-sortedness [Weidenbach 1998]. A bottom-up algorithm based on dynamic programming yields the polynomial complexity whereas a simple top down approach results in an exponential procedure. The latter procedure would correspond to solve the problem with ordered resolution and an SOS strategy.

Sort simplification is one important reason why it makes sense to treat particular occurrences of monadic predicates in a special way. Sort simplification cannot be simulated via other standard reduction techniques like matching replacement resolution (see Definition 4.20) and cannot be extended to non-monadic predicates. For example, for binary relations, the undecidable problem whether two ground terms are contained in a transitive binary relation generated by some positive unit clauses [Schmidt-Schauß 1988] can be reduced to deciding applicability of an extended sort simplification rule for binary relations. So without further restrictions, sort simplification cannot be effectively used for other n-ary relations.

4.6. DEFINITION *(Static Soft Typing).* Let N be the current clause store over some fixed signature Σ and M be a sort theory such that $N \models S(t)$ implies $M \models S(t)$ for any ground monadic atom $S(t)$ over Σ where S occurs in some sort constraint in N. The reduction

$$\mathcal{R}\frac{\Theta \,\|\, \Gamma \to \Delta}{}$$

where $M \not\models \exists x_1, \ldots, x_n \, \Theta$ with $vars(\Theta) = \{x_1, \ldots, x_n\}$ is called *static soft typing*.

The above definition of static soft typing is not effective. The problem $M \not\models \exists x_1, \ldots, x_n \, \Theta$ is not decidable for arbitrary sort theories M and sort constraints Θ. It includes the general problem of sorted unification [Weidenbach 1998] that is well-known to be undecidable, in general. Furthermore, it is not obvious how the sort theory M can be constructed out of N such that it meets the requirements of Definition 4.6. A solution to all these problems is the following. First, all clauses that contain positive monadic atoms are safely approximated and restricted to the sort information they contain:

$$\mathcal{R} \frac{\Theta \| \Gamma \to \Delta, S_1(t_1), \ldots, S_n(t_n)}{\Theta_1 \| \to S_1(t_1)}$$

$$\vdots$$

$$\Theta_n \| \to S_n(t_n)$$

where no monadic atom occurs in Δ, Θ is solved and $\Theta_i = \{S(x) \mid S(x) \in \Theta$ and $x \in vars(S_i(t_i))\}$ for $1 \leq i \leq n$. By construction all Θ_i are solved and the rule does not modify declarations. If the initial clause set N does not contain positive equations, then the sort theory N' obtained by a fix-point computation of the above reduction on N approximates N in the desired way (see Definition 4.6). Second, the sort theory N' is approximated to a sort theory N'' such that satisfiability of sort constraints in N'' gets decidable.

$$\mathcal{R} \frac{\Theta \| \to S(f(t_1, \ldots, t_n))}{\Theta_1, T(x) \| \to S(f(s_1, \ldots, s_n))}$$

$$\Theta_2 \| \to T(t_i)$$

where t_i is not a variable and for all $1 \leq j \leq n$ we define $s_j = x$ if $t_j = t_i$ and $s_j = t_j$ otherwise. Furthermore, $\Theta_1 = \{S(y) \mid S(y) \in \Theta$ and $y \in vars(S(f(s_1, \ldots, s_n)))\}$ and Θ_2 is the restriction of Θ to atoms with argument $x \in vars(t_i)$.

By construction, the derived clauses have a solved sort constraint and N'' approximates N' as desired. The sort theory N'' is shallow and satisfiability of sort constraints with respect to shallow sort theories is decidable by the inference rules sort resolution, empty sort and the reduction rules sort simplification, subsumption deletion (Definition 4.16) and condensation (Definition 4.17) [Jacquemard et al. 1998, Weidenbach 1999]. Hence, this instance of static soft typing is effective.

So if we start with a clause store N that does not contain positive equations, we construct once the approximated sort theory N''. If this theory is not trivial, i.e., there is at least one monadic predicate S with $N'' \not\models \forall x \, S(x)$, the sort theory N'' is stored and static soft typing is applied to any input or derived clause. Since N'' is only approximated once, typically at the beginning of the inference process, the rule is called static soft typing. If in the input clause store all sort constraints are solved and there are no positive equations, static soft typing preserves completeness [Weidenbach 1996, Ganzinger, Meyer and Weidenbach 1997].

If equations occur in a clause store a dynamic soft typing approach seems to be more suitable. Consider Ganzinger et al. [1997] and Meyer [1999] for details.

4.3. Inference Rules

The introduced inference rules can be composed to a variety of (well-known) calculi. The calculi range from the ordinary resolution calculus investigated in Section 3 to a superposition calculus with selection, splitting and sort constraints that are subject to the basicness restriction. To cover all these cases, the rules defined here are given in generic way such that each definition covers several variants of the rule. In particular, all rules are available with a selection restriction of negative literals that does not destroy completeness [Bachmair and Ganzinger 1994]. For any clause we can select some negative literals with the effect that all inference rule applications taking this clause as a parent clause must involve the selected literals. For example, if we select the literal $R(x, y)$ in the clause $\| R(x, y), f(g(x), y) \approx f(y, z) \to$ then no equality resolution inference (see below) is possible from this clause.

4.7. DEFINITION *(Equality/Reflexivity Resolution).* The inference

$$\mathcal{I} \frac{\Theta \| l \approx r, \Gamma \to \Delta}{(\Theta \| \Gamma \to \Delta)\sigma}$$

where (i) σ is the mgu of l and r, (ii) Θ is solved, (iii) $l \approx r$ is selected or $(l \approx r)\sigma$ is maximal in $(\Theta \| l \approx r, \Gamma \to \Delta)\sigma$ and no literal is selected in Γ is called an *equality resolution* inference. If condition (iii) is replaced by $l \approx r$ is selected or no literal is selected in Γ, the inference is called *reflexivity resolution*.

4.8. DEFINITION *((Ordered) Paramodulation/Superposition Left).* The inferences

$$\mathcal{I} \frac{\Theta_1 \| \Gamma_1 \to \Delta_1, l \approx r \quad \Theta_2 \| s[l']_p \approx t, \Gamma_2 \to \Delta_2}{(\Theta_1, \Theta_2 \| s[p/r] \approx t, \Gamma_1, \Gamma_2 \to \Delta_1, \Delta_2)\sigma}$$

and

$$\mathcal{I} \frac{\Theta_1 \| \Gamma_1 \to \Delta_1, l \approx r \quad \Theta_2 \| A[l']_p, \Gamma_2 \to \Delta_2}{(\Theta_1, \Theta_2 \| A[p/r], \Gamma_1, \Gamma_2 \to \Delta_1, \Delta_2)\sigma}$$

where (i) σ is the mgu of l' and l, (ii) l' is not a variable, (iii) Θ_1 and Θ_2 are solved (iv) no literal in Γ_1 is selected, (v) $s \approx t$ (the atom A) is selected or no literal in Γ_2 is selected, is called a *paramodulation left* inference. If, in addition, $r\sigma \not\succ l\sigma$ the inference is an *ordered paramodulation left* inference. If, in addition, $l\sigma \approx r\sigma$ is reductive for $(\Theta_1 \| \Gamma_1 \to \Delta_1, l \approx r)\sigma$, (v) is replaced by $s\sigma \approx t\sigma$ (the atom $A\sigma$) is selected or it is maximal in $(\Theta_2 \| s \approx t, \Gamma_2 \to \Delta_2)\sigma$ (in $(\Theta_2 \| A, \Gamma_2 \to \Delta_2)\sigma$) and no literal in Γ_2 is selected and $t\sigma \not\succ s\sigma$ then the inference is called a *superposition left* inference.

Note that no paramodulation/superposition inference is performed into the sort constraint. Hence, the sort constraint is subject to the basicness restriction. In case all sort constraints of an initial clause store were solved, the basicness restriction preservers completeness, see [Nieuwenhuis and Rubio 2001] (Chapter 7 of this Handbook).

4.9. DEFINITION *((Ordered) Paramodulation/Superposition Right).* The inferences

$$\mathcal{I}\frac{\Theta_1 \,\|\, \Gamma_1 \to \Delta_1, l \approx r \qquad \Theta_2 \,\|\, \Gamma_2 \to \Delta_2, s[l']_p \approx t}{(\Theta_1, \Theta_2 \,\|\, \Gamma_1, \Gamma_2 \to \Delta_1, \Delta_2, s[p/r] \approx t)\sigma}$$

and

$$\mathcal{I}\frac{\Theta_1 \,\|\, \Gamma_1 \to \Delta_1, l \approx r \qquad \Theta_2 \,\|\, \Gamma_2 \to \Delta_2, A[l']_p}{(\Theta_1, \Theta_2 \,\|\, \Gamma_1, \Gamma_2 \to \Delta_1, \Delta_2, A[p/r])\sigma}$$

where (i) σ is the mgu of l' and l, (ii) l' is not a variable, (iii) Θ_1 and Θ_2 are solved (iv) no literal in Γ_1, Γ_2 is selected is a *paramodulation right* inference. If, in addition, $r\sigma \not\succ l\sigma$ the inference is an *ordered paramodulation right* inference. If, in addition, $l\sigma \approx r\sigma$ is reductive for $(\Theta_1 \,\|\, \Gamma_1 \to \Delta_1, l \approx r)\sigma$, $s\sigma \approx t\sigma$ $(A\sigma)$ is reductive for $(\Theta_2 \,\|\, \Gamma_2 \to \Delta_2, s \approx t)\sigma$ $(\Theta_2 \,\|\, \Gamma_2 \to \Delta_2, A)\sigma$ the inference is called a *superposition right* inference.

In an actual implementation the parallel extensions of the above defined paramodulation/superposition left/right inferences [Benanav 1990] are preferred. Whenever such an inference rule is applicable, we don't only replace the initially found occurrence of $l\sigma$ in the second clause by $r\sigma$, but all occurrences. On the ground level the parallel replacement corresponds to an application of the inference rules exactly the way they are defined above plus exhaustive application of non-unit rewriting with the left premise (Definition 4.21) on the conclusion.

Note that the ordering conditions of the above inference rules as well as the ordering conditions of the inference rules defined below, are checked with respect to the found unifier. This is called the a posteriori ordering check. An implementation of the inference rules that have ordering restrictions, first orders the clauses as they are and only searches for inferences with respect to the found candidates (maximal literals, maximal sides of equations). This is called the a priori ordering check. Then, after having found a second candidate clause together with a unifier, the a posteriori check is evaluated. This second check is more expensive than the first, because it has to be dynamically computed with respect to any found unifier. However, since most of the time in a saturation prover is spent with reduction (see Section 3), the extra time for the a posteriori check does not matter, but needs some effort for an (efficient) implementation.

The following example shows that the a posteriori check can in fact prevent the generation of extra clauses. Consider the two clauses

$$\to f(x,y) \approx f(y,x)$$
$$\to P(f(a,b))$$

The equation $f(x, y) \approx f(y, x)$ cannot be oriented by any reduction ordering. So without an a posteriori ordering check, we can derive the clause $\to P(f(b, a))$ by a superposition right inference. Now consider the very same example where we use an RPOS with precedence $f > b > a$ and $status(f) = left$. This implies $f(b, a) \succ_{rpos} f(a, b)$ and therefore the a posteriori ordering check for the potential superposition right inference conclusion $\to P(f(b, a))$ fails. No inference is possible between the above two clauses.

Next we define three factoring rules, namely (ordered) factoring, equality factoring and merging paramodulation. The different rules are needed to obtain completeness results with respect to different inference rule sets. For the standard resolution/paramodulation calculus [Robinson 1965, Robinson and Wos 1969, Chang and Lee 1973, Peterson 1983] the factoring rule without ordering restrictions suffices for completeness. For the ordered resolution/superposition calculus, ordered factoring has to be combined with either equality factoring or merging paramodulation to obtain completeness [Bachmair and Ganzinger 1994].

4.10. DEFINITION *((Ordered) Factoring)*. The inferences

$$\mathcal{I} \frac{\Theta \,\|\, \Gamma \to \Delta, E_1, E_2}{(\Theta \,\|\, \Gamma \to \Delta, E_1)\sigma}$$

and

$$\mathcal{I} \frac{\Theta \,\|\, \Gamma, E_1, E_2 \to \Delta}{(\Theta \,\|\, \Gamma, E_1 \to \Delta)\sigma}$$

where (i) σ is the mgu of E_1 and E_2, (ii) Θ is solved (iii) $(E_1, E_2$ occur positively, E_1 is maximal and no literal in Γ is selected) or $(E_1, E_2$ occur negatively, E_1 is maximal and no literal in Γ is selected or E_1 is selected) are called *ordered factoring right* and *ordered factoring left*, respectively. If condition (iii) is replaced by $(E_1, E_2$ occur positively and no literal in Γ is selected) or $(E_1, E_2$ occur negatively, E_1 is selected or no literal in Γ is selected) the inferences are called *factoring right* and *factoring left*, respectively.

There is an overlap between Ordered Factoring defined above and Equality Factoring defined below, because the rule ordered factoring also considers equations. We did so because for the ordered paramodulation calculus with respect to our definitions Equality Factoring is not needed for completeness. The rule Ordered Factoring suffices for completeness.

4.11. DEFINITION *(Equality Factoring)*. The inference

$$\mathcal{I} \frac{\Theta \,\|\, \Gamma \to \Delta, l \approx r, l' \approx r'}{(\Theta \,\|\, \Gamma, r \approx r' \to \Delta, l' \approx r')\sigma}$$

where (i) σ is the mgu of l' and l, (ii) $r\sigma \not\preceq l\sigma$, (iii) Θ is solved, (iv) no literal in Γ is selected, (v) $l\sigma \approx r\sigma$ is a maximal occurrence in $(\Theta \,\|\, \Gamma \to \Delta, l \approx r, l' \approx r')\sigma$ is called an *equality factoring* inference.

4.12. DEFINITION *(Merging Paramodulation).* The inference

$$\mathcal{I}\frac{\Theta_1 \,\|\, \Gamma_1 \to \Delta_1, l \approx r \qquad \Theta_2 \,\|\, \Gamma_2 \to \Delta_2, s \approx t[l']_p, s' \approx t'}{(\Theta_1, \Theta_2 \,\|\, \Gamma_1, \Gamma_2 \to \Delta_1, \Delta_2, s \approx t[p/r], s \approx t')\sigma}$$

where (i) σ is the composition of the mgu τ of l and l' and the mgu λ of $s\tau$ and $s'\tau$, (ii) the clause $(\Theta_1 \,\|\, \Gamma_1 \to \Delta_1, l \approx r)\sigma$ is reductive for $l\sigma \approx r\sigma$, (iii) Θ_1 and Θ_2 are solved, (iv) no literal in Γ_1, Γ_2 is selected, (v) the clause $(\Theta_2 \,\|\, \Gamma_2 \to \Delta_2, s \approx t, s' \approx t')\sigma$ is reductive for $s\sigma \approx t\sigma$, (vi) $s\tau \succ t\tau$, (vii) l' is not a variable is called a *merging paramodulation* inference.

4.13. DEFINITION *((Ordered) Resolution).* The inference

$$\mathcal{I}\frac{\Theta_1 \,\|\, \Gamma_1 \to \Delta_1, E_1 \qquad \Theta_2 \,\|\, E_2, \Gamma_2 \to \Delta_2}{(\Theta_1, \Theta_2 \,\|\, \Gamma_1, \Gamma_2 \to \Delta_1, \Delta_2)\sigma}$$

where (i) σ is the mgu of E_1 and E_2, (ii) Θ_1 and Θ_2 are solved, (iii) no literal in Γ_1 is selected, (iv) $E_1\sigma$ is strictly maximal in $(\Theta_1 \,\|\, \Gamma_1 \to \Delta_1, E_1)\sigma$, (v) the atom $E_2\sigma$ is selected or it is maximal in $(\Theta_2 \,\|\, E_2, \Gamma_2 \to \Delta_2)\sigma$ and no literal in Γ_2 is selected is called *ordered resolution.* If conditions (iv), (v) are replaced by E_2 is selected or no literal is selected in Γ_2, the inference is called *resolution.*

If, in Definition 4.13, one of the parent clauses of the inference is a unit, the inference is called *(ordered) unit resolution.* The standard resolution rule is an instance of this rule if we omit the conditions (ii)–(iv) and restrict our attention to non-equational atoms.

4.14. DEFINITION *((Ordered) Hyper Resolution).* The inference

$$\mathcal{I}\frac{\Theta \,\|\, E_1, \ldots, E_n \to \Delta \qquad \Theta_i \,\|\, \to \Delta_i, E_i' \quad (1 \le i \le n)}{(\Theta, \Theta_1, \ldots, \Theta_n \,\|\, \to \Delta, \Delta_1, \ldots, \Delta_n)\sigma}$$

(i) σ is the simultaneous mgu of $E_1, \ldots, E_n, E_1', \ldots, E_n'$, (ii) Θ as well as all Θ_i are solved, (iii) all $E_i'\sigma$ are strictly maximal in $(\Theta_i \,\|\, \Gamma_i \to \Delta_i, E_i')\sigma$ is called an *ordered hyper resolution* inference. If condition (iii) is dropped, the inference is called a *hyper resolution* inference.

In the application of the inference rule hyper resolution as well as the inference rules sort resolution (Definition 4.3) and empty sort (Definition 4.4) more than two parent clauses are involved, in general. So the search for candidate clauses gets more complicated. In particular, an appropriate ordering of the literals $E_1, \ldots, E_n$ for searching partner clauses can be indispensable for efficiency reasons. For example, if we search partners for the literals $P(x), Q(a, f(x))$ it may be the case that we find thousand potential partners for $P(x)$ (all clauses with a positive (maximal) literal $P(t)$) but only a few for $Q(a, f(x))$ (only clauses with a positive (maximal) literal $Q(a, f(t))$ or with variable occurrences at the positions of a, $f(t)$). So starting with $Q(a, f(x))$ for partner search is the more efficient way, since it will potentially provide instantiation of x when we subsequently search for partners of $P(x)$. So a good heuristic is to proceed at any time of the partner search with the literals that has a maximal number of symbols with respect to the already established partial unifier. Nevertheless, please note that the number of hyper resolvents grows in the worst case exponentially in n.

4.4. Reduction Rules

Our philosophy is that reduction rules are at the heart of successful automated theorem proving. The aim of reduction rules is to transform clauses (or even formulas, see [Nonnengart and Weidenbach 2001], Chapter 6 of this Handbook) in simpler ones. So whereas inference rules are at the search side of automated theorem proving, reduction rules are at the computation side.

4.15. DEFINITION *(Duplicate/Trivial Literal Elimination)*. The reductions

$$\mathcal{R}\frac{\Theta \,\|\, \Gamma \to \Delta, E, E}{\Theta \,\|\, \Gamma \to \Delta, E}$$

and

$$\mathcal{R}\frac{\Theta \,\|\, \Gamma, E, E \to \Delta}{\Theta \,\|\, \Gamma, E \to \Delta}$$

and

$$\mathcal{R}\frac{\Theta, A, A \,\|\, \Gamma \to \Delta}{\Theta, A \,\|\, \Gamma \to \Delta}$$

are called *duplicate literal eliminations*. The reductions

$$\mathcal{R}\frac{\Theta \,\|\, \Gamma, t \approx t \to \Delta}{\Theta \,\|\, \Gamma \to \Delta}$$

and

$$\mathcal{R}\frac{\|\, t \approx s \to}{\Box}$$

where for the final variant we assume that t and s are unifiable, are called *trivial literal eliminations*.

Please recall that although trivial literal elimination can be simulated by equality resolution or factoring, for these inference rules to apply a clause must first be selected as *Given* clause. Reduction rules like duplicate or trivial literal elimination apply to all (newly) generated clauses.

4.16. DEFINITION *(Subsumption Deletion)*. The reduction

$$\mathcal{R}\frac{\Theta_1 \,\|\, \Gamma_1 \to \Delta_1 \qquad \Theta_2 \,\|\, \Gamma_2 \to \Delta_2}{\Theta_1 \,\|\, \Gamma_1 \to \Delta_1}$$

where $\Theta_2 \parallel \Gamma_2 \to \Delta_2$ is subsumed by $\Theta_1 \parallel \Gamma_1 \to \Delta_1$ is called *subsumption deletion*.

Testing subsumption between two clauses is an *NP*-complete problem [Garey and Johnson 1979]. Nevertheless, subsumption is indispensable for saturation based theorem proving as we already discussed in Section 3. Hence, there exist a variety of papers presenting algorithms that show a polynomial behavior on certain subclasses of clauses (e.g., [Gottlob and Leitsch 1985]) or that introduce specific data structures to speed up the subsumption test in practice (e.g., [Socher 1988, Tammet 1998]). Many of todays provers use a variant of the Stillman [1973] algorithm for the subsumption test. Basically, the algorithm tries to find for every literal in $\Theta_1 \parallel \Gamma_1 \to \Delta_1$ a different instance in $\Theta_2 \parallel \Gamma_2 \to \Delta_2$ such that all single instantiations are compatible, i.e., identical variables are mapped to identical terms. This simple version is not tractable in practice. Prefilters must be added to the algorithm that make it tractable in practice. We discuss two filters [Nonnengart et al. 1998]. The first filter is based on the size of the clauses. A necessary condition for a subsumption deletion application over multisets is that $size(\Theta_1 \parallel \Gamma_1 \to \Delta_1) \leq size(\Theta_2 \parallel \Gamma_2 \to \Delta_2)$. Since the size of clauses is usually needed for selection heuristics (see the discussion on the *choose* function in Section 3), the size of a clause is typically stored in a clause data structure an therefore this test is almost for free. For every two clauses passing this test, the second prefilter checks whether for every literal in $\Theta_1 \parallel \Gamma_1 \to \Delta_1$ there exists some instance literal in $\Theta_2 \parallel \Gamma_2 \to \Delta_2$ at all. So we consider the literals in $\Theta_1 \parallel \Gamma_1 \to \Delta_1$ separately and don't check compatibility between the different substitutions. This check is again a necessary condition for the subsumption test to succeed and can be done in polynomial time. Clauses passing these two tests are then subject to the Stillman algorithm. In practice, more than 95% of all subsumption tests can already be rejected by the two filters.

Note that there is a subtle difference between multiset subsumption (considered here) and set subsumption. The clause $\to Q(a,x), Q(y,b)$ subsumes the clause $\to Q(a,b)$ if we consider clauses to be sets, but does not if we consider clauses to be multisets. Therefore, in our version of the Stillman algorithm we require matched literals to be different.

When integrated into a prover, subsumption deletion is not an operation applied to two clauses but applied to two sets of clauses or a clause and a set of clauses (see Table 1 and Table 3). The former test can be reduced to the latter by considering the clauses in one set separately. So it remains to test whether some clause C subsumes some clause in a set N or is subsumed by some clause in N. We already argued that the set N (in particular the Us set) can become very large. Then it is in practice intractable to traverse all clauses in N and then to apply the subsumption test to each clause. An additional filter is needed: Indexing, see [Ramakrishnan et al. 2001] (Chapter 26 of this Handbook). Indexing is the data base technology of automated theorem proving. The crucial operations provided by an index of a clause store N are: compute all clauses that include an atom that is an instance/a generalization/unifiable with some query atom. Typically, the result of such a query consists of the clauses together with the found atom. So in order to test whether some clause C is subsumed by a clause in an indexed clause store N, one picks a literal from C that has a low probability of being subsumed, searches the index for generalizations of that literal and then tests C and the found clauses for subsumption. Since the query and the result literal are already found, using appropriate data structures it is sufficient to test the clauses without these literals. So one needs a more general subsumption test with the possibility to hide at least one literal in each clause. This extended test is also needed for the reduction rules matching replacement resolution (Definition 4.20) and non-unit rewriting (Definition 4.21).

4.17. DEFINITION *(Condensation)*. The reduction

$$\mathcal{R} \frac{\Theta_1 \,\|\, \Gamma_1 \to \Delta_1}{\Theta_2 \,\|\, \Gamma_2 \to \Delta_2}$$

where $\Theta_2 \,\|\, \Gamma_2 \to \Delta_2$ subsumes $\Theta_1 \,\|\, \Gamma_1 \to \Delta_1$ and $\Theta_2 \,\|\, \Gamma_2 \to \Delta_2$ is derived from $\Theta_1 \,\|\, \Gamma_1 \to \Delta_1$ by instantiation and (exhaustive) application of trivial literal elimination is called *condensation*.

In the literature condensation is often defined on the basis of factoring applications. From an implementation point of view the above definition is much sharper, because it only suggests matchers to generate duplicate literals that can be eventually removed, not unifiers as suggested by a definition based on factoring. All these candidate instantiation substitutions can be effectively computed by subsequently searching for matchers σ such that $E_1\sigma = E_2$ for $E_1, E_2 \in \Gamma_1$ (respectively for Θ_1, Δ_1) and then testing whether $(\Theta_1 \,\|\, \Gamma_1 \setminus \{E_2\} \to \Delta_1)\sigma$ subsumes $\Theta_1 \,\|\, \Gamma_1 \to \Delta_1$. This idea leads to a procedure that is more efficient than the factoring based algorithm suggested by Joyner Jr. [1976] and related to the techniques presented by Gottlob and Fermüller [1993].

4.18. DEFINITION *(Tautology Deletion)*. The reduction

$$\mathcal{R} \frac{\Theta \,\|\, \Gamma \to \Delta}{}$$

where $\models \Theta \,\|\, \Gamma \to \Delta$ is called *tautology deletion*.

The above rule is sometimes also called semantic tautology deletion, since it is based on a semantic tautology test. This test corresponds to testing unsatisfiability of a set of ground literals. If we keep in mind that any literal can be coded as an (dis)equation, in order to test unsatisfiability of a set of ground literals it is sufficient to test congruence closure with respect to the positive equations. This can be done in polynomial time [Downey, Sethi and Tarjan 1980]. There are certain weaker syntactic conditions that can be checked in linear time:

$$\mathcal{R} \frac{\Theta \,\|\, \Gamma, E \to \Delta, E}{}$$

or

$$\mathcal{R}\frac{\Theta, A \parallel \Gamma \to \Delta, A}{}$$

or

$$\mathcal{R}\frac{\Theta \parallel \Gamma \to \Delta, t \approx t}{}$$

These conditions are implemented by nearly all todays theorem provers. The semantic check requires appropriate data structures for an efficient implementation. It is contained in the provers E, Saturate and SPASS.

4.19. DEFINITION *(Conflict).* The reduction

$$\mathcal{R}\frac{\Theta_1 \parallel \Gamma_1 \to \Delta_1 \quad \ldots \quad \Theta_n \parallel \Gamma_n \to \Delta_n}{\Box}$$

where $\Theta_1 \parallel \Gamma_1 \to \Delta_1, \ldots, \Theta_n \parallel \Gamma_n \to \Delta_n \models \Box$ is called *conflict.*

Even if n is fixed, the rule conflict is not effective, in general. It basically solves the general unsatisfiability problem of first-order logic. The rule sort simplification is an effective instance of this rule. Two further effective instantiations of this rule that are not related to specific theories are implemented in todays provers: *unit conflict* and the *terminator* [Antoniou and Ohlbach 1983]. The former is the rule

$$\mathcal{R}\frac{\parallel \to E_1 \qquad \parallel E_2 \to}{\Box}$$

such that E_1 and E_2 are unifiable. It seems that this rule is superfluous since it only detects a contradiction between two unit clauses. However, since we consider unification between E_1 and E_2, this rule cannot be simulated by, for example, matching replacement resolution (see Definition 4.20), but only by a resolution step. In the context of problems where the majority of generated clauses are units (e.g., unit equational problems or condensed detachment problems [McCune and Wos 1992]) the probability that both clauses are selected for inferences can become arbitrarily low. Then it can pay off to add this reduction rule that implements a (global) one step search for the empty clause.

The terminator is a generalization of unit conflict and a restriction of the general conflict rule to at most k non-unit clauses out of the n clauses, k fixed. For some given, finite set of clauses it is decidable whether we can derive the empty clause by resolution, if any derivation is restricted to contain at most k non-unit clauses. This is easy to see, since there are only finitely many different derivations using k non-unit clauses and resolving with a unit clause strictly reduces the length of the resolvent compared to the maximal length of one of its parent clauses. That's the terminator. In practice the terminator can be useful with values $k \leq 3$. Larger values rarely make sense, since the number of clauses that have to be considered for this rule grows exponentially in k times the length of the non-unit clauses. Note that if the terminator is applied to a Horn clause store without equality, it can be turned into a complete refutation procedure by subsequently increasing n.

As an exception from all other reduction rules, in practice the terminator is integrated in the search procedure like an inference rule, not like a reduction rule. It is too expensive to apply the terminator to all newly generated clauses and often it does not pay off. So the terminator is solely applied to the selected *Given* clauses, if it is activated.

4.20. DEFINITION *(Matching Replacement Resolution).* The reductions

$$\mathcal{R} \frac{\Theta_1 \,\|\, \Gamma_1 \to \Delta_1, E_1 \quad \Theta_2 \,\|\, \Gamma_2, E_2 \to \Delta_2}{\Theta_1 \,\|\, \Gamma_1 \to \Delta_1, E_1}$$
$$\Theta_2 \,\|\, \Gamma_2 \to \Delta_2$$

and

$$\mathcal{R} \frac{\Theta_1 \,\|\, \Gamma_1, E_1 \to \Delta_1 \quad \Theta_2 \,\|\, \Gamma_2 \to \Delta_2, E_2}{\Theta_1 \,\|\, \Gamma_1, E_1 \to \Delta_1}$$
$$\Theta_2 \,\|\, \Gamma_2 \to \Delta_2$$

and

$$\mathcal{R} \frac{\Theta_1 \,\|\, \Gamma_1 \to \Delta_1, A_1 \quad \Theta_2, A_2 \,\|\, \Gamma_2 \to \Delta_2}{\Theta_1 \,\|\, \Gamma_1 \to \Delta_1, A_1}$$
$$\Theta_2 \,\|\, \Gamma_2 \to \Delta_2$$

where (i) $E_1\sigma = E_2$ ($A_1\sigma = A_2$ for the third variant), (ii) $\Theta_1\sigma \subseteq \Theta_2$, $\Gamma_1\sigma \subseteq \Gamma_2$, $\Delta_1\sigma \subseteq \Delta_2$ are called *matching replacement resolutions.*

Matching replacement resolution is a restricted variant of replacement resolution, itself a restricted form of resolution where the conclusion must subsume one of its parent clauses. For matching replacement resolution we restrict the unifier of the complementary literals computed for replacement resolution to be a matcher. This speeds up the applicability test significantly.

The third variant of the rule that applies to the sort constraint cannot be simulated by sort simplification (Definition 4.5), because it also considers clauses that are not declarations. On the other hand, matching replacement resolution can also not simulate sort simplification. Consider the clauses

$$T(x), S(f(x)), \Theta_1 \,\|\, \Gamma_1 \to \Delta_1$$
$$R(x) \,\| \quad \to S(f(x))$$
$$T(x) \,\| \quad \to R(x)$$

The negative occurrence of $S(f(x))$ in the first clause cannot be eliminated by matching replacement resolution but by sort simplification.

4.21. DEFINITION *(Non-Unit Rewriting)*. The reductions

$$\mathcal{R}\frac{\Theta_1 \,\|\, \Gamma_1 \to \Delta_1, s \approx t \quad \Theta_2 \,\|\, \Gamma_2, E[s']_p \to \Delta_2}{\Theta_1 \,\|\, \Gamma_1 \to \Delta_1, s \approx t \\ \Theta_2 \,\|\, \Gamma_2, E[p/t\sigma] \to \Delta_2}$$

and

$$\mathcal{R}\frac{\Theta_1 \,\|\, \Gamma_1 \to \Delta_1, s \approx t \quad \Theta_2 \,\|\, \Gamma_2 \to \Delta_2, E[s']_p}{\Theta_1 \,\|\, \Gamma_1 \to \Delta_1, s \approx t \\ \Theta_2 \,\|\, \Gamma_2 \to \Delta_2, E[p/t\sigma]}$$

where (i) $s\sigma = s'$, (ii) $s\sigma \succ t\sigma$, (iii) $\Theta_1\sigma \subseteq \Theta_2$, $\Gamma_1\sigma \subseteq \Gamma_2$, $\Delta_1\sigma \subseteq \Delta_2$ are called *non-unit rewriting*.

The ordering restrictions for non-unit rewriting are a posteriori ordering restrictions, i.e., we compare the terms s and t with respect to the found matcher σ. An efficient implementation of this check is non-trivial because it requires a tight connection between indexing, ordering computation and subsumption. Therefore, many provers use the a priori ordering check, i.e., they verify $s \succ t$. See also the discussion on page 1988.

4.22. DEFINITION *(Unit Rewriting)*. The reductions

$$\mathcal{R}\frac{\| \to s \approx t \quad \| E[s']_p \to}{\| \to s \approx t \\ \| E[p/t\sigma] \to}$$

and

$$\mathcal{R}\frac{\| \to s \approx t \quad \| \to E[s']_p}{\| \to s \approx t \\ \| \to E[p/t\sigma]}$$

where (i) $s\sigma = s'$, (ii) $s\sigma \succ t\sigma$, are called *unit rewriting*.

Unit rewriting is an instance of the second version of non-unit rewriting where all Θ_i, Γ_i, Δ_i are empty. We mention it here explicitly, because it is the style of rewriting used in purely equational completion, a theorem proving discipline of its own. Furthermore, the a posteriori ordering check is much easier to implement, because we need no subsumption check.

In practice the rewriting reductions are among the most expensive reductions. Note that any subterm of any clause has to be considered and that subsequent rewriting steps to the same clause are common. Therefore, many provers don't use the full power of non-unit rewriting, but restrict the left clause to be a positive unit equation. They reduce non-unit clauses by positive unit equations.

Even the a posteriori check, condition (ii), can be further refined. Consider an equation where the left and right hand side don't share any variables. Then the a posteriori check will typically fail but may succeed by appropriate further instantiations. For example the equation $f(x,y) \approx g(z)$ cannot be oriented and hence the equation $f(a,b) \approx a$ cannot be rewritten by unit rewriting using the first equation. Now assume a RPOS with precedence $f > g > a > b$. Then the equation $f(a,b) \approx g(z)$ (the result of matching $f(x,y)$ with $f(a,b)$) can be turned into an oriented equation by instantiating z with a or b. This enables rewriting of $f(a,b)$ to $g(a)$ or $g(b)$. In general it is sufficient to consider the minimal constant and the crucial extra variables for further instantiation. Note also that the equation $f(x,y) \approx g(z)$ subsumes an equation like $f(x,y) \approx g(y)$ that is oriented and can therefore be used for rewriting in a straightforward way.

Another way to solve the problem of unorientable equations because of extra variables is to split equations. Given some equation $s \approx t$ where $vars(s) \not\subseteq vars(t)$ and $vars(t) \not\subseteq vars(s)$, we introduce a new function symbol h where the arity of h is exactly $|vars(s) \cap vars(t)|$. If $\{x_1, \ldots, x_n\} = vars(s) \cap vars(t)$ then the equation $s \approx t$ is replaced by the equations $s \approx h(x_1, \ldots, x_n)$ and $t \approx h(x_1, \ldots, x_n)$. Given a KBO or RPOS and a precedence where the new symbol h is smaller than the top symbols of s and t, both introduced equations are oriented from left to right. In order to obtain a complete calculus that includes splitting of equations splitting must not be applied infinitely many times.

The final reduction rule exploits particular equations of the form $x \approx t$ (called assignment equations), where x does not occur in t nor in the rest of the clause. Negative equations of this form can simply be removed from a clause. In order to remove positive assignment equations the domain structure shared by any model of the current clause store has to be examined. In particular, we exploit the case that the domain is non-trivial. Therefore, before this rule can be applied, certain properties of any clause store model must be checked. This can, e.g., be done by a sufficient criterion that can be tested syntactically.

4.23. DEFINITION *(Assignment Equation Deletion)*. Let N be the current clause store. The reductions

$$\mathcal{R} \frac{\Theta \,\|\, x \approx t, \Gamma \to \Delta}{\Theta \,\|\, \Gamma \to \Delta}$$

and

$$\mathcal{R} \frac{\Theta \,\|\, \Gamma \to x \approx t, \Delta}{\Theta \,\|\, \Gamma \to \Delta}$$

where for both variations of the rule we assume (i) $x \notin vars(t)$, (ii) $x \notin vars(\Theta \,\|\, \Gamma \to \Delta)$ and for the second variant, where we remove a positive equation, we assume in addition that $|\mathcal{D}| > 1$ for any interpretation $\mathcal{M}$ with $\mathcal{M} \models N$, are called *assignment equation deletion*.

This reduction rule is the clause version of the simplification rules suggested in [Nonnengart and Weidenbach 2001] (Chapter 6 of this Handbook). For the elimination of the positive equation it is necessary to guarantee a non-trivial domain for any model of the current clause store. A syntactic condition is the existence of a clause $\|\, s \approx t \rightarrow$ where s and t are arbitrary. If such a clause is contained in the clause store, the domain of any model is non-trivial and we can apply the second variant of the rule.

4.5. Splitting

The effect of a splitting rule application is not only to extend the current clause store but also to modify and extend the current clause store collection.

4.24. DEFINITION *(Splitting)*. The inference

$$\mathcal{S}\frac{\Theta_1, \Theta_2 \,\|\, \Gamma_1, \Gamma_2 \rightarrow \Delta_1, \Delta_2}{\Theta_1 \,\|\, \Gamma_1 \rightarrow \Delta_1 \quad | \quad \Theta_2 \,\|\, \Gamma_2 \rightarrow \Delta_2}$$

where $vars(\Theta_1 \,\|\, \Gamma_1 \rightarrow \Delta_1) \cap vars(\Theta_2 \,\|\, \Gamma_2 \rightarrow \Delta_2) = \emptyset$ and neither of the two derived split clauses is empty is called *splitting*.

Without the condition that the two split clauses must not share variables, Splitting is very much like the β-rule of free variable tableau, see [Hähnle 2001] (Chapter 3 of this Handbook). Since the clauses don't share variables, the two cases are completely independent and the derived clauses can be used for simplification/reduction without any restriction. For example, both clauses subsume the parent clause.

In case the first split part is ground, i.e., $vars(\overline{S(t)} \,\|\, \overline{E} \rightarrow \overline{E'}) = \emptyset$, where $\overline{S(t)} = S_1(t_1), \ldots, S_n(t_n)$, $\overline{E} = E_1, \ldots, E_m$ and $\overline{E'} = E'_1, \ldots, E'_l$ and $1 \leq i \leq n$, $1 \leq j \leq m$, $1 \leq k \leq l$, it is very useful to add the negation of the first split clause to the second part

$$\mathcal{S}\frac{\overline{S(t)}, \Theta_2 \,\|\, \overline{E}, \Gamma_2 \rightarrow \overline{E'}, \Delta_2}{\overline{S(t)} \,\|\, \overline{E} \rightarrow \overline{E'} \quad \left|\quad \begin{array}{l} \Theta_2 \,\|\, \Gamma_2 \rightarrow \Delta_2 \\ \quad\|\quad \rightarrow S_i(t_i) \\ \quad\|\quad \rightarrow E_j \\ \quad\| E'_k \rightarrow \end{array}\right.}$$

All these additional unit clauses can help a lot in reducing the clause set of the second part (see matching replacement resolution, Definition 4.20 or non-unit rewriting, Definition 4.21). In a purely propositional setting, a calculus solely based on unit conflict (see Definition 4.19) and extended splitting can polynomially simulate truth tables, whereas a calculus based on unit conflict and the simple splitting rule cannot [D'Agostino 1992].

Of course, for any first part split clause we could add its negation to the second part. However, in general this leads to the introduction of new Skolem constants, and in practice this tends to extend the search space for the second part. Note that in this case the ground units resulting from the negated first part cannot be used for matching replacement resolutions, because the introduced Skolem constants are new. As an alternative one could also record the ground instances of the variables in the first split clause used in the refutation of the first part and then add their negation as a disjunct to the second part. But it is questionable whether such an effort pays off in practice.

Splitting itself often tends to generate a huge search tree, so additional refinements are necessary. A natural one is to require that Δ_1 and Δ_2 are non-empty in Definition 4.24. So we only split non-Horn clauses into clauses having strictly less positive literals. The rationale behind this comes from the propositional level. For a set of propositional Horn clauses, satisfiability can be decided in linear time [Dowling and Gallier 1984], whereas satisfiability for arbitrary clauses is an *NP*-complete problem. The reduction rule matching replacement resolution (Definition 4.20) is also a decision procedure for propositional Horn clauses (although it results in a quadratic time implementation). Hence, non-Horn splitting and matching replacement resolution are a reasonable decision procedure for propositional clauses. In case a clause can be split into a propositional part (no variables) and a non-propositional one, it is very useful to split the clause that way and to add the negation of the propositional part to the second as indicated before.

An alternative to an explicit case analysis is to split clauses by the introduction of new propositional symbols. For example, the clause
$$S(x) \,\|\, f(x) \approx y \to Q(x,x), Q(a,z)$$
can be replaced by the clauses

$$
\begin{aligned}
S(x) \,\|\, f(x) &\approx y, A \to Q(x,x) \\
\| \quad & B \to Q(a,z) \\
\| \quad & \to A, B
\end{aligned}
$$

where A, B are new propositional symbols. The replacement preservers satisfiability of the current clause store and if it is only applied finitely many often during a proof attempt it also preserves completeness. If A, B are minimal in the ordering, no inference on A, B will be performed as long as other literals are contained in the respective clauses. So the different parts of the original clause don't interfere as long as they are completely resolved. This simulates splitting without the need to extend the notion of a clause store to a collection of clause stores and hence a less complicated implementation. The second advantage of this approach is that it does not introduce the inherent redundancy of an explicit splitting approach, see [Hähnle 2001] (Chapter 3 of this Handbook). The main disadvantage of this splitting style is that none of the generated clauses can be directly used for reductions, because the propositional variables A, B must be new. This splitting style is available in the provers Saturate and Vampire(see [Riazanov and Voronkov 2001]), explicit splitting (Definition 4.24) is available in SPASS.

```
1 PROVER(N)
2   Wo := ∅;
3   Us := ired(N, N);
4   While (Us ≠ ∅ and □ ∉ Us)  {
5     (Given, Us)      := choose(Us);
6     Wo               := Wo ∪ {Given};
7     New              := inf(Given, Wo);
8     (New, Wo, Us)    := ired(New, Wo, Us);
9   }
10  If (Us = ∅) then print "Completion Found";
11  If (□ ∈ Us) then print "Proof Found";
```

Table 4: The Overall Loop without Splitting

5. Global Design Decisions

5.1. Main-Loop

The main-loop without splitting, Table 4, is a generalization of the main-loop introduced in Section 3, Table 1.

Compared to the simple, resolution-based prover, all inferences are computed in the extra function *inf* and (inter)reduction takes place in the function *ired*. In the automatic mode of a typical prover, the inference rules applied in *inf* are chosen after an analysis of the input problem. For example, if the input problem contains no equality, the superposition/paramodulation rules are not activated or if the input problem is Horn, factoring rules are not needed.

The combination of the reduction rules gets more subtle compared to the combination of subsumption/tautology deletion presented in Section 3. The function *ired* serves this purpose, Table 6. Please recall that the terminator is integrated like an inference rule and hence does not show up. First, line 4, any newly derived clause is forward reduced with respect to the sets *Wo* and *Us*. The function *fred* is presented in detail in Table 5. The ordering of the tested forward reductions is determined by potential dependencies between the rules and by their respective implementation costs.

We don't consider the lazy reduction approach introduced in Section 3, Table 3. It is a bit tricky but not too difficult to develop it out of the presented full reduction algorithms. Inside the algorithms a redundant clause is not always directly deleted, but represented by the constant ⊤.

In practice, tautology deletion (Table 5, line 2), elimination of trivial literals

```
1  fred(Given, Wo, Us)
2    Given := taut(Given);
3    If (Given = ⊤) then return(⊤);
4    Given := obv(Given);
5    Given := cond(Given);
6    Given := aed(Given, Wo, Us);
7    If (fsub(Given, Wo, Us)) then return(⊤);
8    (Hit, Given) := frew(Given, Wo, Us);
9    If (Hit) then {
10     Given := taut(Given)
11     If (Given = ⊤) then return(⊤);
12     Given := obv(Given);
13     Given := cond(Given);
14     If (fsub(Given, Wo, Us)) then return(⊤);
15   }
16   Given := ssi(Given, Wo, Us);
17   Given := fmrr(Given, Wo, Us);
18   Given := unc(Given, Wo, Us);
19   Given := sst(Given, Wo, Us);
20   return(Given);
```

Table 5: Forward Reduction

(line 4), condensation (line 5) and assignment equation deletion (line 6) are cheap operations, because only the derived clause has to be considered for testing their applicability. This is not completely true for the assignment equation deletion (see Definition 4.23), but the suggested syntactic domain size criterion can be tested once at the beginning of the search process, so no extra effort is necessary. Clauses that pass these tests, are checked for forward subsumption with respect to Wo and Us (line 7) and for forward rewriting (line 8) where Hit is set to true, if a rewriting step actually took place. If a rewriting step is performed, the rules tautology deletion, elimination of duplicate/trivial literals, condensation and forward subsumption are checked a second time (lines 10–14). Below is a simple example that demonstrates dependencies between the different reduction rules.

```
1  ired(New, Wo, Us)
2    While (New ≠ ∅)  {
3      (Given, New) := choose(New);
4      Given        := fred(Given, Wo, Us);
5      If (Given ≠ ⊤) then {
6        (New, Wo, Us)   := bsub(Given, New, Wo, Us);
7        (New, Wo, Us)   := bmrr(Given, New, Wo, Us);
8        (New, Wo, Us)   := brew(Given, New, Wo, Us);
9        Us              := Us ∪ {Given};
10       }
11     }
12   return(∅, Wo, Us);
```

Table 6: Interreduction

$$
\begin{aligned}
&1: & &\rightarrow f(x) \approx x \\
&2: & &\rightarrow a \approx b \\
&3: & P(f(x)) &\rightarrow P(x) \\
&4: & P(f(x)), P(b) &\rightarrow \\
&5: & P(a), P(c) &\rightarrow \\
&6: & P(g(f(x))), P(g(x)) &\rightarrow
\end{aligned}
$$

The clauses 3–6 are completely interreduced with respect to the reductions presented in Section 4. Rewriting with clause 1 into clause 3 generates a syntactic tautology, rewriting with clause 1 into clause 4 enables a further condensation step on clause 4 resulting in $4':P(b) \rightarrow$ and rewriting clause 5 with clause 2 produces $5':P(b), P(c) \rightarrow$ (assuming $a \succ b$) that is forward subsumed by clause $4'$. After rewriting with clause 1, duplicate literal elimination can be applied to clause 6.

Finally the reductions sort simplification (line 16), forward clause reduction (line 17), unit conflict (line 18) and static soft typing are tested. These reduction rules don't enable further applications of other rules, because they either strictly reduce the number of literals or reduce the clause to ⊤ (static soft typing). In order to test the applicability of these rules the overall clause stores Wo and Us must be considered.

All clauses that pass forward reduction (Table 6, line 4) are used for back reduction (lines 6–8) and are finally added to the Us set (line 9). Backward subsumption (line 6) deletes all clauses from Wo and Us that are subsumed by $Given$. Backward matching replacement resolution (line 7) tests all clauses in Wo and Us for matching replacement resolution with $Given$. Reduced clauses are always deleted from their respective source set and added to *New*. Back rewriting (line 8) behaves the same, but tests rewriting. The clauses in *New* are not directly tested for all these reduction rules. They are tested after having entered the *Us* set. This is motivated by efficiency issues which we will discuss below.

The function *choose* (Table 6, line 3) selects a clause with the smallest number of symbols. Small clauses have a higher probability to reduce other clauses. For example, a subsuming clause must have fewer symbols (consider the discussion after Definition 4.16) than the clause it subsumes. For many other reductions like rewriting, selecting small clauses is still a good heuristic because the size ordering of terms is often included in the reduction ordering.

Note that a clause can be selected several times as *Given* clause in the while-loop of the interreduction algorithm, if it is successfully reduced several times. Selecting small *Given* clauses tries to minimize the number of such situations.

The main-loop presented in Table 7 extends the already discussed main-loop of Table 4 with splitting. In case splitting is not applied, executing the main-loop in Table 7 or Table 4 results in exactly the same behavior.

If splitting is possible (Table 7, line 10) it is preferred over all other inferences. The rationale behind this decision is that a splitting application results in a strictly smaller clause store collection. The exploration of the binary tree generated by the splitting rule is performed by a standard depth-first, backtracking search (lines 7, 11, 12).

All functions implementing inference/reduction operations have to be refined and must also consider the *split level* of a clause. Initially, all clauses have split level zero and the current split level is zero. Then any clause generated by a splitting inference gets the current split level plus one as its split level and the current split level is incremented. Clauses generated by all other inference/reduction rules get the maximal split level of their parent clauses as their new split level. Backtracking resets the current split level to the split level of the activated branch. But what happens if a clause C is now subsumed by a clause D with a greater split level? We must not delete C, but only remove it from the current clause store, store it at D's split level on the split stack and reinsert it if backtracking considers that level. Clauses that are rewritten or reduced by clauses with a higher split level must be copied and also kept appropriately on the split stack.

Basically that is all to integrate splitting into a saturation based prover. Nevertheless, some refinements are possible. First, since all clauses have a split level, also the empty clause has a split level. This level indicates where backtracking should start to consider open branches and all branches at a higher split level can be discarded. For example, if we derive the empty clause at split level zero, then we can immediately stop and don't have to consider any further possibly open branches. Second, if we don't only store the split level with each clause but also a bit array with length of the split level, the following improvement is possible. The bit array is updated together with the split level and indicates every level that contributed to the clause. If we now derive an empty clause at some split level and detect that it does not depend on some earlier levels above the previous backtracking level that

```
1 PROVER(N)
2   Wo    := ∅;
3   Us    := ired(N, N);
4   Stack := emptystack();
5   While (Us ≠ ∅ and (□ ∉ Us or not stackempty(Stack)))   {
6     If (□ ∈ Us) then
7       (Stack, Wo, Us)  := backtrack(Stack, Wo, Us);
8     else {
9       (Given, Us)    := choose(Us);
10      If (splittable(Given)) then {
11        New  := firstsplitcase(Given);
12        Stack := push(Stack, secondsplitcase(Given));
13      }
14      else {
15        Wo  := Wo ∪ {Given};
16        New  := inf(Given, Wo);
17      }
18      (New, Wo, Us)   := ired(New, Wo, Us);
19    }
20  }
21  If (Us = ∅) then print "Completion Found";
22  If (□ ∈ Us) then print "Proof Found";
```

Table 7: The Overall Loop with Splitting

have open branches left, we can erase these levels, their split clauses and all clauses depending on these. We call this operation *branch condensation* and it is indispensable to make splitting feasible in practice. In the AI literature branch condensation it often referred to as dependency directed backtracking.

The *choose* functions suggested so far have shown to be very useful in a setting without splitting. With an explicit splitting rule, additional criteria for the selection of the next given clause make sense. For example, we could prefer clauses that can be splitted and sort them according to their afterwards obtained reduction potential.

In Section 3 we also introduced a main-loop with lazy reduction, Table 3. Although we did not present it here, lazy reduction is also possible with the extended inference rule set and it is not too difficult to think of lazy extensions of the main-loops according to Table 3. Therefore, we omitted an extra presentation here.

5.2. Proof Documentation/Checking

Proof documentation is possible by implicitly or explicitly storing all clauses during the overall search process that might contribute to a proof. As a consequence, a run with proof documentation has a higher memory consumption and so causing the prover to slow down. This effect is further supported by splitting applications, where all clauses from all significant branches must be kept as well. Therefore, in favor of execution speed, many provers don't output proofs (saturated clause stores). Nevertheless, due to their efficient implementation, today's leading systems can handle proofs of several hundred thousand steps in reasonable time.

Automated proof checking is a very important topic in any theorem proving project. The inference/reduction rules are non-trivial to (efficiently) implement, so there is a high potential for bugs. Proofs of automated theorem provers cannot be checked by hand in practice. So there is a need for automated proof checking. One possibility is a separately implemented proof checker. The checker takes a proof and starts with an analysis of the splitting rule applications. The checker generates the binary tree resulting from subsequent splitting inference applications and tests whether all branches contain an empty clause, whether the split level assignments are done correctly and whether the splitting inference rule is applied in a sound way. Then the checker generates for every inference/reduction rule application the corresponding first-order theorem proving problem and provides it for a separate prover. The single step proof problems can typically be easily solved if they are correct. This way, it is possible to validate proofs up to several hundred thousand steps in reasonable time and that completely automatically. As such a proof checker solely relies on logical implication, it supports most of today's saturation-based inference systems.

5.3. Data Structures and Algorithms

In Section 3 we discussed a simple prover based on resolution. In Section 5.1 we extended this prover to cope with the inference/reduction rules of Section 4. For our simple resolution-based prover we already argued that

- the Us set grows very fast,
- reductions are indispensable to reduce the number of clauses in the Us set
- most of the time is spent with reductions.

The situation is getting even more dramatic if we consider the inference rules for equality introduced in Section 4 and the suggested main-loops (Table 4, Table 7). For example, if the selected *Given* clause C in the main-loop contains a positive equation, then any non-variable subterm of any literal of a clause in *Wo* that unifies with the left or right hand side of the equation generates a new clause by paramodulation. If the considered left hand side is a variable then any subterm of any different clause unifies with the variable and produces a new clause via paramodulation. An example for such a clause is one that forces a finite, two element domain: $\to x \approx a, x \approx b$. Ordering restrictions improve the situation (not for the finite domain clause), but we nevertheless have to find reasonable ways to store large Us sets and to efficiently find reduction/inference partners.

There are several solutions to these problems. We now focus on one solution and discuss alternatives at the end of this section. The first design decision is to store all atoms in Wo, Us in a shared way, respectively. That means every occurrence of any subterm of an atom in Us (Wo) exists exactly once and is shared by all superterms containing this subterm. The idea is to save space and to keep indexing structures small. As all terms are shared, any subterm is only submitted once to the indexing structure that provides retrieval for inferences/reductions. This works fine for ground terms, but in general clauses contain variables that are considered different if they occur in different clauses. Therefore, almost nothing can be shared between two different non-ground clauses. The solution to this problem is our second design decision that is to *normalize* variables of clauses. For any clause, if the clause is considered from left to right as a sequence of its literals, the variables are named with respect to their occurrence according to a fixed variable sequence. After normalization there is a high probability that clauses with variables share non-ground subterms. This is confirmed by experiments.

A consequence of this decision is that algorithms for unification/matching/generalization have to keep track of this fact. For example, we need variants of the unification algorithm that use two substitutions in order to store bindings between variables for two terms stemming from two different clauses in an appropriate way.[10]

Putting newly generated clauses into a sharing/indexing data structure is extra effort. Since newly generated clauses have a high probability of being subsumed or reduced by already existing clauses, the New set (Table 4, 7, 6) is kept unshared. Furthermore, reductions are (by definition) destructive, so they can only be efficiently applied to unshared clauses. Shared clauses have to be extracted/copied from the sharing structure before modification, because destructive manipulation of shared terms may also effect other clauses where the considered reduction is not permitted. So any forward reduction to the $Given$ clause inside the interreduction algorithm (Table 6) is done destructively, but before a back reduction operation can actually be performed (lines 6–8) the clause has to be extracted/copied from the Wo, Us sharing structure first. As it is unshared afterwards, it can be moved to the New set. At line 9 of the $ired$ function (Table 6), the $Given$ clause is inserted into the sharing/indexing structures of the Us set.

An alternative solution is to completely abstract from variable positions, e.g., by introducing one dummy variable for all occurring variables. We build one or several atom/term trees that represent all atoms/terms without considering variables to be different. These trees are then linked to the real atoms/terms and efficient algorithms can be devised to search for candidate atoms/terms out of such skeleton trees. Atoms/terms found this way are still candidates, because of the variable

---

[10]See the discussion in Section 3.

abstraction. They have then to be verified by the appropriate matching/unification test. The so called discrimination trees (see [Ramakrishnan et al. 2001], Chapter 26 of this Handbook) support such an approach.

If we resign from complete interreduction and focus on lazy reduction (see Table 3), no reduction rule needs to be tested with respect to the Us set. So inserting the Us clauses into an indexing structure for access is not needed. The Us clauses are only needed to provide a pool from which the next $Given$ clause is selected. To this end, we only need the necessary information for the $choose$ function and the clause itself. If the $choose$ function relies on size, the necessary information is simply a number. Since all Us clauses are children of two Wo clauses, instead of storing the clause, we store the numbers of the parents and the way it was generated represented by, say, one extra number. So, every clause in the Us set can be represented by four numbers, in practice in constant space. This results in a huge reduction of memory consumption and hence in an increase of execution speed. The Waldmeister system (see Appendix A) can treat the Us set this way. Note that the extra time needed to generate the $Given$ clause can be neglected. In case a parent of a selected $Given$ clause is no longer in the Wo set, it must have become redundant, hence the $Given$ clause is redundant as well and needs not to be considered.

A further possibility to restrict the number of clauses in the Us set is to simply throw away clauses. This may cause incompleteness of the theorem prover. Such techniques are available in Fiesta, Otter, SPASS and Vampire, see Appendix A.

Acknowledgments

Knowledge about the design of automated theorem provers is mostly distributed by discussions among the authors of such systems. I want to thank Bill McCune the author of Otter that is the father system of all today's "modern" automated saturation based theorem provers. We learned a lot about the implementation of theorem provers by inspecting Otter. My colleagues Arnim Buch, Thomas Hillenbrand, Bernd Löchner, authors of Waldmeister, Jörg Denzinger, author of Discount, Hans de Nivelle, author of Bliksem, Stephan Schulz, author of E, Harald Ganzinger, author of Saturate, Andrei Voronkov, co-author of Vampire, Robert Nieuwenhuis, author of Fiesta(and Saturate) contributed a lot to this chapter.

As mentioned in the introduction the development of a competitive theorem prover is a challenging software project, exemplified in the following for the SPASS theorem prover: Although there existed some preliminary versions of SPASS before 1994, the first version called SPASS was started in that year and was finished in 1995 by Bernd Gaede in the context of his diploma thesis. This version already relied on a library of data structures we called EARL.[11] The library already contained indexing support and was developed by Peter Graf and Christoph Meyer and myself. Clause normal form translation was added to SPASS by Georg Rock as a diploma project. Further development of SPASS took place in paid student projects that

---

[11] Efficient Automated Reasoning Library

typically lasted for several months each. Christian Cohrs introduced splitting to SPASS, Enno Keen was responsible for inference rules and parsing support, Thorsten Engel wrote our proof checker, Dalibor Topic significantly improved our memory management module and contributed to the implementation of reduction rules and Christian Theobalt wrote a whole bunch of documentation support scripts and mastered the challenge to port SPASS to the Windows world. As a prerequisite he developed a neat graphical user interface. Bijan Afshordel contributed to reductions on the formula level and programmed the atom definition module, Uwe Brahm was indispensable for putting SPASS on the Web and Christof Brinker added the most recent development, the detection and deletion of non-syntactic tautologies. Thanks to all of them.

Finally, I'm indebted to Thomas Hillenbrand, Enno Keen and Andreas Nonnengart for many comments on this chapter that lead to significant improvements. The numerous detailed comments of Andrei Voronkov were indispensable to make the chapter what it is now.

Bibliography

ANTONIOU G. AND OHLBACH H. J. [1983], Terminator, in A. Bundy, ed., 'Proceedings of 8th International Joint Conference on Artificial Intelligence, IJCAI-83', pp. 916–919.

BAADER F. AND NIPKOW T. [1998], *Term Rewriting and All That*, Cambridge University Press.

BAADER F. AND SNYDER W. [2001], Unification theory, in A. Robinson and A. Voronkov, eds, 'Handbook of Automated Reasoning', Vol. I, Elsevier Science, chapter 8, pp. 445–532.

BACHMAIR L. AND GANZINGER H. [1994], 'Rewrite-based equational theorem proving with selection and simplification', *Journal of Logic and Computation* **4**(3), 217–247. Revised version of Max-Planck-Institut für Informatik technical report, MPI-I-91-208, 1991.

BACHMAIR L. AND GANZINGER H. [2001], Resolution theorem proving, in A. Robinson and A. Voronkov, eds, 'Handbook of Automated Reasoning', Vol. I, Elsevier Science, chapter 2, pp. 19–99.

BACHMAIR L., GANZINGER H. AND WALDMANN U. [1993], Superposition with simplification as a decision procedure for the monadic class with equality, in G. Gottlob, A. Leitsch and D. Mundici, eds, 'Computational Logic and Proof Theory, Third Kurt Gödel Colloquium', Vol. 713 of *LNCS*, Springer, pp. 83–96.

BENANAV D. [1990], Simultaneous paramodulation, in M. E. Stickel, ed., 'Proceedings of the 10th International Conference on Automated Deduction', Vol. 449 of *LNAI*, Springer, pp. 442–455.

CHANG C.-L. AND LEE R. C.-T. [1973], *Symbolic Logic and Mechanical Theorem Proving*, Computer Science and Applied Mathematics, Academic Press.

CHARATONIK W., MCALLESTER D., NIWINSKI D., PODELSKI A. AND WALUKIEWICZ I. [1998], The horn mu-calculus, in 'Proceedings 13th IEEE Symposium on Logic in Computer Science, LICS'98', IEEE Computer Society Press, pp. 58–69.

D'AGOSTINO M. [1992], 'Are tableaux an improvement on truth-tables?', *Journal of Logic, Language and Information* **1**, 235–252.

DERSHOWITZ N. [1982], 'Orderings for term-rewriting systems', *Theoretical Computer Science* **17**, 279–301.

DERSHOWITZ N. [1987], 'Termination of rewriting', *Journal of Symbolic Computation* **3**(1), 69–115.

DERSHOWITZ N. AND PLAISTED D. [2001], Rewriting, in A. Robinson and A. Voronkov, eds, 'Handbook of Automated Reasoning', Vol. I, Elsevier Science, chapter 9, pp. 533–608.

Dowek G. [2001], Higher-order unification and matching, *in* A. Robinson and A. Voronkov, eds, 'Handbook of Automated Reasoning', Vol. II, Elsevier Science, chapter 16, pp. 1009–1062.

Dowling W. F. and Gallier J. H. [1984], 'Linear-time algorithms for testing the satisfiability of propositional horn formulae', *Journal of Logic Programming* **1**(3), 267–284.

Downey P. J., Sethi R. and Tarjan R. E. [1980], 'Variations on the common subexpression problem', *Journal of the ACM* **27**(4), 758–771.

Eisinger N. [1991], *Completeness, Confluence, and Related Properties of Clause Graph Resolution*, Research Notes in Artificial Intelligence, Pitman Ltd., London.

Fischer B., Schumann J. and Snelting G. [1998], Deduction-based software component retrieval, *in* W. Bibel and P. H. Schmitt, eds, 'Automated Deduction - A Basis for Applications', Vol. 3 of *Applied Logic*, Kluwer, chapter 11, pp. 265–292.

Frühwirth T., Shapiro E., Vardi M. Y. and Yardeni E. [1991], Logic programs as types for logic programs, *in* A. R. Meyer, ed., 'Proceedings of the 6th Annual IEEE Symposium on Logic in Computer Science, LICS'91', IEEE Computer Society Press, pp. 300–309.

Ganzinger H., Meyer C. and Weidenbach C. [1997], Soft typing for ordered resolution, *in* 'Proceedings of the 14th International Conference on Automated Deduction, CADE-14', Vol. 1249 of *LNAI*, Springer, Townsville, Australia, pp. 321–335.

Garey M. R. and Johnson D. S. [1979], *Computers and intractability : A guide to the theory of NP-completeness*, Mathematical Sciences Series, Freeman, New York.

Gottlob G. and Fermüller C. G. [1993], 'Removing redundancy from a clause', *Artificial Intelligence* **61**, 263–289.

Gottlob G. and Leitsch A. [1985], 'On the efficiency of subsumption algorithms', *Journal of the ACM* **32**(2), 280–295.

Hähnle R. [2001], Tableaux and related methods, *in* A. Robinson and A. Voronkov, eds, 'Handbook of Automated Reasoning', Vol. I, Elsevier Science, chapter 3, pp. 100–178.

Heintze, N. and Clarke, E., eds [1999], *Workshop on Formal Methods and Security Protocols*, Self Publishing, Trento, Italy.

Hillenbrand T., Jaeger A. and Löchner B. [1999], Waldmeister – improvements in performance and ease of use, *in* H. Ganzinger, ed., '16th International Conference on Automated Deduction, CADE-16', LNAI, Springer, pp. 232–236.

Hustadt U. and Schmidt R. A. [1997], On evaluating decision procedures for modal logics, *in* 'Proceedings of 15th International Joint Conference on Artificial Intelligence, IJCAI-97', pp. 202–207.

Jacquemard F., Meyer C. and Weidenbach C. [1998], Unification in extensions of shallow equational theories, *in* T. Nipkow, ed., 'Rewriting Techniques and Applications, 9th International Conference, RTA-98', Vol. 1379 of *LNCS*, Springer, pp. 76–90.

Joyner Jr. W. H. [1976], 'Resolution strategies as decision procedures', *Journal of the ACM* **23**(3), 398–417.

Kautz H. and Selman B. [1996], Pushing the envelope: Planning, propositional logic and stochastic search, *in* 'Proceedings of the 13th National Conference on AI, AAAI'96', Vol. 2, AAAI Press / MIT Press, pp. 1194–1201.

Knuth D. E. and Bendix P. B. [1970], Simple word problems in universal algebras, *in* I. Leech, ed., 'Computational Problems in Abstract Algebra', Pergamon Press, pp. 263–297.

McCune W. and Wos L. [1992], Experiments in automated deduction with condensed detachment, *in* '11th International Conference on Automated Deduction, CADE-11', Vol. 607 of *LNCS*, Springer, pp. 209–223.

McCune W. and Wos L. [1997], 'Otter', *Journal of Automated Reasoning* **18**(2), 211–220.

Meyer C. [1999], Soft Typing for Clausal Inference Systems, Dissertation, Technische Fakultät der Universität des Saarlandes, Saarbrücken, Germany.

Nieuwenhuis R. [1996], Basic paramodulation and decidable theories (extended abstract), *in* 'Proceedings 11th IEEE Symposium on Logic in Computer Science, LICS'96', IEEE Computer Society Press, pp. 473–482.

NIEUWENHUIS R. AND RUBIO A. [2001], Paramodulation-based theorem proving, *in* A. Robinson and A. Voronkov, eds, 'Handbook of Automated Reasoning', Vol. I, Elsevier Science, chapter 7, pp. 371–443.

NIVELA P. AND NIEUWENHUIS R. [1993], Saturation of first-order (constrained) clauses with the *Saturate* system, *in* C. Kirchner, ed., 'Rewriting Techniques and Applications, 5th International Conference, RTA-93', Vol. 690 of *Lecture Notes in Computer Science, LNCS*, Springer, Montreal, Canada, pp. 436–440.

NONNENGART A., ROCK G. AND WEIDENBACH C. [1998], On generating small clause normal forms, *in* C. Kirchner and H. Kirchner, eds, '15th International Conference on Automated Deduction, CADE-15', Vol. 1421 of *LNAI*, Springer, pp. 397–411.

NONNENGART A. AND WEIDENBACH C. [2001], Computing small clause normal forms, *in* A. Robinson and A. Voronkov, eds, 'Handbook of Automated Reasoning', Vol. I, Elsevier Science, chapter 6, pp. 335–367.

PETERSON G. E. [1983], 'A technique for establishing completeness results in theorem proving with equality', *SIAM Journal of Computation* 12(1), 82–100.

RAMAKRISHNAN I., SEKAR R. AND VORONKOV A. [2001], Term indexing, *in* A. Robinson and A. Voronkov, eds, 'Handbook of Automated Reasoning', Vol. II, Elsevier Science, chapter 26, pp. 1853–1964.

RIAZANOV A. AND VORONKOV A. [1999], Vampire, *in* H. Ganzinger, ed., '16th International Conference on Automated Deduction, CADE-16', Vol. 1632 of *LNAI*, Springer, pp. 292–296.

RIAZANOV A. AND VORONKOV A. [2000], Limited resource strategy in resolution theorem proving, Preprint CSPP-7, Department of Computer Science, University of Manchester.
URL: *http://www.cs.man.ac.uk/preprints/index.html*

RIAZANOV A. AND VORONKOV A. [2001], Splitting without backtracking, Preprint CSPP-10, Department of Computer Science, University of Manchester.
URL: *http://www.cs.man.ac.uk/preprints/index.html*

ROBINSON G. AND WOS L. [1969], Paramodulation and theorem-proving in first-order theories with equality, *in* B. Meltzer and D. Michie, eds, 'Machine Intelligence 4', pp. 135–150.

ROBINSON J. A. [1965], 'A machine-oriented logic based on the resolution principle', *Journal of the ACM* 12(1), 23–41.

SCHMIDT-SCHAUSS M. [1988], 'Implication of clauses is undecidable', *Theoretical Computer Science* 59, 287–296.

SCHULZ S. [1999], System abstract: E 0.3, *in* H. Ganzinger, ed., '16th International Conference on Automated Deduction, CADE-16', Vol. 1632 of *LNAI*, Springer, pp. 297–301.

SNYDER W. [1993], 'On the complexity of recursive path orderings', *Information Processing Letters* 46, 257–262.

SOCHER R. [1988], A subsumption algorithm based on characteristic matrices, *in* E. Lusk and R. Overbeek, eds, '9th International Conference on Automated Deduction, CADE-9', Vol. 310 of *LNCS*, Springer, pp. 573–581.

STILLMAN R. B. [1973], 'The concept of weak substitution in theorem-proving', *Journal of the ACM* 20(4), 648–667.

SUTCLIFFE G. AND SUTTNER C. B. [1998], 'The tptp problem library – cnf release v1.2.1', *Journal of Automated Reasoning* 21(2), 177–203.

SUTCLIFFE G. AND SUTTNER C. B. [1999], 'The cade-15 atp system competition', *Journal of Automated Reasoning* 23(1), 1–23.

TAMMET T. [1998], Towards efficient subsumption, *in* C. Kirchner and H. Kirchner, eds, '15th International Conference on Automated Deduction, CADE-15', Vol. 1421 of *LNAI*, Springer, pp. 427–441.

WEIDENBACH C. [1996], Computational Aspects of a First-Order Logic with Sorts, Dissertation, Technische Fakultät der Universität des Saarlandes, Saarbrücken, Germany.

WEIDENBACH C. [1998], Sorted unification and tree automata, *in* W. Bibel and P. H. Schmitt, eds, 'Automated Deduction - A Basis for Applications', Vol. 1 of *Applied Logic*, Kluwer, chapter 9, pp. 291–320.

WEIDENBACH C. [1999], Towards an automatic analysis of security protocols in first-order logic, *in* H. Ganzinger, ed., '16th International Conference on Automated Deduction, CADE-16', Vol. 1632 of *LNAI*, Springer, pp. 378–382.

WEIDENBACH C., AFSHORDEL B., BRAHM U., COHRS C., ENGEL T., KEEN E., THEOBALT C. AND TOPIC D. [1999], System description: Spass version 1.0.0, *in* H. Ganzinger, ed., '16th International Conference on Automated Deduction, CADE-16', Vol. 1632 of *LNAI*, Springer, pp. 314–318.

WOS L., ROBINSON G. AND CARSON D. [1965], 'Efficiency and completeness of the set of support strategy in theorem proving', *Journal of the ACM* **12**(4), 536–541.

Appendix

A. Links to Saturation Based Provers

| Bliksem | by Hans de Nivelle |
| | http://www.mpi-sb.mpg.de/~nivelle/ |

Discount — by Jörg Denzinger
http://agent.informatik.uni-kl.de/denzinge/denzinger.html

E — by Stephan Schulz [Schulz 1999]
http://wwwjessen.informatik.tu-muenchen.de/personen/schulz.html

Fiesta — by Robert Nieuwenhuis, Pilar Nivela, and Guillem Godoy
http://www.lsi.upc.es/~roberto/

Gandalf — by Tanel Tammet
http://www.cs.chalmers.se/~tammet/gandalf/

Otter — by William McCune [McCune and Wos 1997]
http://www-unix.mcs.anl.gov/AR/otter/

Saturate — by Harald Ganzinger, Robert Nieuwenhuis, and Pilar Nivela [Nivela and Nieuwenhuis 1993]
http://www.mpi-sb.mpg.de/SATURATE/

SPASS — by Christoph Weidenbach, Bijan Afshordel, Enno Keen, Christian Theobalt, and Dalinor Topić [Weidenbach et al. 1999]
http://spass.mpi-sb.mpg.de/

Vampire — by Alexandre Riazanov and Andrei Voronkov [Riazanov and Voronkov 1999]
http://www.cs.man.ac.uk/fmethods/vampire/

Waldmeister — by Arnim Buch, Thomas Hillenbrand, Roland Vogt, Bernd Löchner, and Andreas Jaeger [Hillenbrand, Jaeger and Löchner 1999]
http://agent.informatik.uni-kl.de/waldmeister/

Index

CHAPTER 28

Model Elimination and Connection Tableau Procedures

Reinhold Letz

Gernot Stenz

SECOND READERS: Peter Baumgartner and Uwe Petermann.

Contents

HANDBOOK OF AUTOMATED REASONING
Edited by Alan Robinson and Andrei Voronkov

1. Introduction

The last years have seen many efforts in the development, implementation and application of automated deduction systems. Currently, the most successful theorem provers for classical first-order logic are either based on resolution or on model elimination [Sutcliffe and Suttner 1998]. While resolution is treated in other chapters of this Handbook, see [Bachmair and Ganzinger 2001, Weidenbach 2001] (Chapters 2 and 27), this chapter presents the state-of-the-art of theorem proving using model elimination. Historically, model elimination has been presented in different conceptual frameworks. While the very first paper [Loveland 1968] used a tree-oriented format, a restricted and more resolution-oriented chain notation [Loveland 1969, Loveland 1978] has become the standard for some twenty years.

This changed about ten years ago, when it was recognized that it is more natural to view model elimination as a particular refinement of the tableau calculus, in which connections are employed as a control mechanism for guiding the proof search. In order to emphasize this approach, we introduced the term "connection tableaux" [Schumann and Letz 1990, Letz, Schumann, Bayerl and Bibel 1992, Letz 1993, Letz, Mayr and Goller 1994]. This view had a very fruitful effect on the research in the field. In the meantime, many calculi and proof procedures developed in automated deduction, such as SLD-Resolution, the connection method or systems like Satchmo and MGTP, have been reformulated in tableau style. As a positive result of these activities, the similarities and differences between many calculi with formerly unclear relations could be identified. Furthermore, new calculi have been developed which are based on tableaux and integrate connections in different manners, see, e.g., [Hähnle 2001] (Chapter 3 of this Handbook). The main advantages of viewing model elimination as a tableau calculus are the following. On the one hand, more powerful search pruning mechanisms can be identified. On the other hand, the completeness proofs are simplified significantly.

Since model elimination is one of the main paradigms in automated deduction, a wealth of methods for improving the basic proof procedure have been developed. Many of these methods, however, have a very limited effect, since they improve the performance only for few, often pathological examples. Therefore, we have concentrated on methods that have generally proven successful. Furthermore, we have put emphasis on the presentation of the main paradigms for an efficient implementation of model elimination and its refinements.

When trying to classify the methods of redundancy elimination developed for model elimination, one naturally ends up with three categories. Since in model elimination or connection tableaux the manipulated inferential objects are not clauses but tableaux, which are entire deductions, a significant number of techniques have been developed which permit to identify certain deductions as redundant just because of their internal structures. These techniques, among which the property of regularity is most important, constitute the first class of improvements, which may be termed as *structural* or *local* methods of search pruning. Another source of redundancy in proof search results from the fact that typically certain deductions are redundant in the presence of other ones. These *global* approaches of inter-tableau pruning form the second class of methods for redundancy elimination. A prominent example of such a method is failure caching. The final improvement of pure model elimination has to do with the length of proofs. Even minimal proofs may become rather long when compared with other calculi. This is because pure model elimination is *cut-free* and the generated deduction objects are trees. Consequently, a proof may contain the same subproof more than once. A further difference between model elimination and calculi such as resolution is that free variables in a tableau are normally considered as *rigid*, in the sense that every variable can be used in one instantiation only. We describe the main methods to overcome these deficiencies, which are controlled cuts and universal variables.

When it comes to the implementation of a theorem prover based on model elimination, we have a very special situation. This is because model elimination is very close to SLD-resolution, which is the basic inference system of the programming language Prolog. Consequently, one can take advantage of this proximity by using as much as possible from the implementation techniques developed for Prolog. One successful such approach is to extend abstract machine technology from the Horn case to the full clausal case. Another possibility consists in taking Prolog itself as a programming language, by which reasonably efficient implementations of model elimination can often be obtained with no or only very little implementational effort. Both of these approaches will be described in detail. But the close relation of model elimination to Prolog may also have negative effects. Especially, it is very difficult to implement refinements of model elimination which do not fit with the basic working principles of Prolog. For example, there is no easy way of integrating equality handling or theory reasoning into an abstract machine. Or, when using Prolog as programming language, it is very difficult to implement a different backtracking mechanism. This has motivated us to develop and present a further implementation architecture which is more modular and flexible and which strongly differs from the ones based on Prolog or Prolog techniques. The key idea for achieving high efficiency in this approach is the extensive re-use of the results of expensive operations.

The development of a redundancy elimination technique is one thing, its efficient implementation is another one. Fortunately, many of the refinements developed for model elimination may be formulated in a uniform general setting, as conditions on the instantiations of variables, so-called disequation constraints. In the final section, we develop the general framework of disequation constraints including universal variables and normalization, and we describe in detail how efficient constraint handlers may be implemented.

2. Clausal Tableaux and Connectedness

2.1. Preliminaries

Before starting with the presentation of clausal tableaux, the meaning of some basic concepts and notations has to be defined. We are working on formulae in clause logic and use standard conventions for denoting logical symbols and formulae. Our alphabet consists of individual *variables, function* and *predicate symbols* with arities ≥ 0, the logical *connectives* $\neg$ (negation), $\vee$ (disjunction) and $\wedge$ (conjunction), the *universal* and the *existential quantifiers* $\forall$ respectively $\exists$, plus the comma and the parentheses as punctuation symbols. A *term* is either a variable or a string of the form $\alpha(t_1, \ldots, t_n)$ where α is a function symbol of arity n and the t_i are terms. An *atomic formula* is a string of the form $\alpha(t_1, \ldots, t_n)$ where α is a predicate symbol of arity n and the t_i are terms. Expressions of the form $\alpha()$ are conveniently abbreviated by writing just α. First-order formulae, occurrences of expressions in other expressions, the scope of quantifier occurrences, and what it means that a variable occurs free or bound in an expression are defined as usual.

We emphasize the special notions used in this work. The *complement* of a formula F is G if F is of the form $\neg G$, and $\neg F$ otherwise; the complement of a formula is abbreviated as $\sim F$. A *literal* is either an atomic formula or an atomic formula with a negation sign in front of it. A *clause* is a disjunction of literals, i.e., either a literal, called a *unit clause*, or a string of the form $L_1 \vee \cdots \vee L_n$ where the L_i are literals. A *Horn clause* is a clause containing at most one positive literal. A *clausal formula* is a conjunction of clauses, i.e., either a clause or a string of the form $c_1 \wedge \cdots \wedge c_n$ where the c_i are clauses.

A *substitution* σ is any mapping of variables to terms; for any (sequence of) expression(s) F, we abbreviate with $F\sigma$ the (sequence of) expression(s) obtained by simultaneously replacing every free occurrence of a variable in F with its value under σ; $F\sigma$ is called an *instance* of F. The tuples $\langle x, t \rangle$ in a substitution with $x \neq t$ are called *bindings* and abbreviated by writing x/t. Normally, a substitution will be denoted by giving the set of its bindings. If $\{x_1/t_1, x_2/t_2, x_3/t_3, \ldots\}$ is (the set of bindings of) a substitution σ, then $\{x_1, x_2, x_3, \ldots\}$ and $\{t_1, t_2, t_3, \ldots\}$ are called the *domain* and the *range* of σ, respectively. Given two (sequences of) expressions F and G, when a substitution σ satisfies $F\sigma = G\sigma$, then σ is called a *unifier* for F and G. Some specializations of the unifier concept are of high importance. A unifier σ for F and G is termed a *most general unifier* if, for every unifier τ for F and G, there is a substitution θ with $\sigma\theta = \tau$; σ is a *minimal unifier* if the set of its bindings has minimal cardinality. To illustrate the difference, given three distinct variables x, y, z, then $\{x/y\}$ is a minimal unifier for the terms x and y whereas the substitution $\{x/y, z/x\}$ is a most general unifier, but no minimal unifier. Finally, a unifier σ is *idempotent* if $\sigma = \sigma\sigma$. It holds that any minimal unifier is idempotent and most general. Since nearly all unification algorithms return minimal unifiers, we will prefer that term throughout this chapter.

Subsequently, we will preferably employ special meta-expressions for the denotation of formulae and their components. For individual variables we will normally use the letters u, v, w, x, y, z; *constants* are nullary function symbols and are denoted with the letters a, b, c, d; for function symbols of arity > 0 we use f, g, h; predicate symbols are denoted with P, Q, R, nullary predicate symbols are denoted with lower case letters; subscripts will be used when needed.

2.2. Inference Rules of Clausal Tableaux

Clausal tableaux are trees labelled with literals (and other control information) inductively defined as follows.

2.1. DEFINITION *(Clausal tableau).* Let S be a set or conjunction of clauses $c_1, \ldots, c_n$. A tree consisting of just one unlabelled node is a *clausal tableau for* S. The single branch of this tree is considered as *open*. If B is an open branch in a clausal tableau T for S with leaf node N (called *subgoal*), then the formula trees obtained from the following two inference rules are *clausal tableaux for* S:

    (Expansion rule) Select a clause c_i in S and simultaneously replace all its variables with distinct new variables not occurring in T. Let $L_1 \vee \cdots \vee L_n$ be the resulting clause. Then attach n new nodes as successors of the subgoal N and label them with the literals $L_1, \ldots, L_n$, respectively. The new branches are considered as *open*.

    (Closure or reduction rule) If the subgoal N with literal label K has an ancestor node N' with literal L on the branch B such that there exists a minimal unifier σ for K and the complement $\sim L$ of L, then obtain the tableau $T\sigma$, that is, apply the substitution σ to the literals in T. Now the branch B is considered as *closed*.[1]

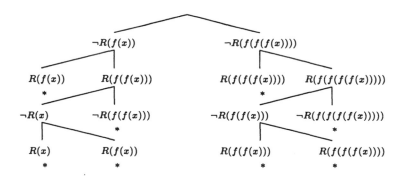

Figure 1: A closed clausal tableau for the formula S consisting of the two clauses $R(x) \vee R(f(x))$ and $\neg R(x) \vee \neg R(f(f(x)))$.

Figure 1 displays a closed clausal tableau, i.e., a tableau with the closure rule applied to all its branches, which we indicate with an asterisk at the end of each branch. In the figure, the unifiers resulting from the closure steps are already applied to the tableau. In general, variables in clausal tableaux are considered as *rigid*, i.e., just as place holders for arbitrary ground terms. In Section 5, it will be shown that this condition can be weakened for certain variables. The example shows the

---

[1]A branch is closed by applying an inference rule. There are no implicit branch closures.

necessity of renaming variables. Without renaming it would be impossible to unify the second literal in the first clause with the complement of the second literal in the second clause, which is done, for example, in the second closure step on the left. Furthermore, multiple copies of the same input clauses are needed.

Let us make some remarks regarding the peculiarities of this definition as compared with the more familiar definition of tableaux. For one thing, we carry the input set or formula S alongside the tableau and do not put its members at the beginning of the tableau, we leave the root unlabelled instead. This facilitates the comparison of tableaux for different input sets. For example, one tableau may be an instance of another tableau, even if their input sets differ. Also, a branch is considered as closed only if the closure rule was explicitly applied to it, all other branches are considered as open, even when they are complementary. This precaution simplifies the presentation, in particular, of the proof of the Lifting Lemma (Lemma 6.5), and more adequately reflects the actual situation when implementing tableaux.

The clausal tableau calculus is *sound* and *complete*, that is, for every set of clauses S, there exists a closed clausal tableau for S if and only if S is unsatisfiable. Furthermore, the clausal tableau calculus is *(proof) confluent*, i.e., every clausal tableau for an unsatisfiable input formula S can be completed to a closed clausal tableau for S.

Clausal tableaux provide a large potential for refinements, i.e., for imposing additional restrictions on the tableau construction. For instance, one can integrate *ordering restrictions* [Klingenbeck and Hähnle 1994] as they are successfully used in resolution-based systems (see also Chapter 3 in this Handbook). The most important structural refinement of clausal tableaux with respect to automated deduction, however, is to use links or *connections* to guide the proof search.

2.3. Connection Tableaux

Some additional notation will be useful.

2.2. Definition *(Tableau clause)*. For any non-leaf node N in a clausal tableau, the set of nodes $N_1, \ldots, N_m$ immediately below N is called the node *family below* N; if the nodes $N_1, \ldots, N_m$ are labelled with the literals $L_1, \ldots, L_m$ respectively, then the clause $L_1 \vee \cdots \vee L_m$ is named the *tableau clause below* N; The tableau clause below the root node is called the *start* or *top clause* of the tableau.

A closer look at the tableau displayed in Figure 1 reveals an interesting structural property. In every node family below the start clause, at least one node has a complementary ancestor. This property can be formulated in two variants, a weaker one and a stronger one.

2.3. DEFINITION *(Path connectedness, connectedness)*.

1. A clausal tableau is said to be *path connected* (or *weakly connected*) iff, in every node family below the start clause, there is one node with a complementary ancestor.

2. A clausal tableau is said to be *connected* (or *tightly connected*) iff, in every node family below the start clause, there is one node which is complementary to its predecessor.

A (path) connected tableau is also called *(path) connection* tableau.

With the connection conditions, every clause has a certain relation to the start clause. This allows a goal-oriented form which may be used to guide the proof search.

Let us make some brief historical remarks on the rôle of connections in tableaux. The notion of a connection is a central concept in automated deduction whereas tableau calculi, traditionally, have no reference to connections—as an example, note that the notion does not even occur in [Fitting 1996]. On the other hand, it was hardly noticed in the field of automated deduction and logic programming that calculi like *model elimination* [Loveland 1968, Loveland 1978], the *connection calculi* in [Bibel 1987], or *SLD-resolution* [Kowalski and Kuehner 1970] should proof-theoretically be considered as tableau calculi. This permits, for instance, to view the calculi as *cut-free* proof systems. The relation of these calculi to tableaux has not been recognized, although, for example, the original presentation of model elimination [Loveland 1968] is clearly in tableau style. The main reason for this situation may be that until recently both communities (tableaux and automated deduction) were almost completely separated. As a further illustration of this fact, note that unification was not really used in tableaux before the end of the eighties [Reeves 1987, Fitting 1990]. In Section 2.7, we will clarify the relation of connection tableaux with model elimination, SLD-resolution, and the connection method.

In order to satisfy the connectedness conditions, for every tableau expansion step except the first one, the closure rule has to be applied to one of the newly attached nodes. This motivates to amalgamate both inference rules into a new macro inference rule.

2.4. DEFINITION *((Path) extension rule)*. The *(path) extension rule* is defined as follows: perform a clausal expansion step immediately followed by a closure step unifying one of the newly attached literals, say L, with the complement of the literal at its predecessor node (at one of its ancestor nodes); the literal L and its node are called *entry* or *head literal* and *entry* or *head node*, respectively.

The building of such macro inference rules is a standard technique in automated deduction to increase efficiency. With these new rules, the clausal tableau calculi can be reorganized.

2.5. DEFINITION *((Path) connection tableau calculus)*. The *(path) connection tableau calculus* consists of the following three inferences rules:

- the (path) extension rule,
- the closure or reduction rule,
- and the *start rule*, which is simply the expansion rule, but restricted to only one application, namely the attachment of the start clause.

A fundamental proof-theoretical property of the two connection tableau calculi is that they are not proof confluent, as opposed to the general clausal tableau calculus. This can easily be recognized, for instance, by considering the unsatisfiable set of unit clauses $S = \{p, q, \neg q\}$. If we select p as start clause, then the tableau cannot be completed to a closed tableau without violating the (path) connectedness condition. In other terms, using the (path) connectedness condition, one can run into dead ends. The important consequence to be drawn from this fact is that, for those tableau calculi, systematic branch saturation procedures of the type presented in [Smullyan 1968] do not exist. Since an open connection tableau branch that cannot be expanded does not guarantee the existence of a model, connection tableaux are therefore not suited for *model generation*. Weaker connection conditions that are compatible with model generation are described in [Billon 1996, Baumgartner 1998, Baumgartner, Eisinger and Furbach 1999] and in [Hähnle 2001] (Chapter 3 of this Handbook).

2.4. Proof Search in Connection Tableaux

When using non-confluent deduction systems like the connection tableau calculi, in order to find a proof, in general, all possible deductions have to be enumerated in a fair manner until the first proof is found. The *search space* for a tableau enumeration procedure can be defined as a tree of tableaux.

2.6. DEFINITION *((Tableau) search tree).* Let S be a set of formulae and C a tableau calculus. The *corresponding (tableau) search tree* is a tree T labelled with tableaux defined by induction on its depth.
  1. The root of T is labelled with the trivial tableau, consisting just of a root node.
  2. Every non-leaf node N of depth n in T has as many successor nodes as there are successful applications of a single inference step in the tableau calculus C applied to the tableau at the node N and using formulae from S; the successor nodes of N of depth $n+1$ are labelled with the resulting tableaux, respectively.
The leaf nodes of a (tableau) search tree can be partitioned into two sets of nodes, the ones labelled with tableaux that are closed, called *success nodes*, and the others which are labelled with open tableaux to which no successful inference steps can be applied, called *failure nodes*. Closed tableaux occurring in a search tree are *proofs*.

It is important to note that the search spaces of tableau calculi cannot be represented by familiar *and-or-trees* in which the and-nodes represent the tableau clauses and the or-nodes the alternatives for expansion. Such a more compact representation is not possible in the first-order case, because the branches in a free-variable tableau cannot be treated independently.

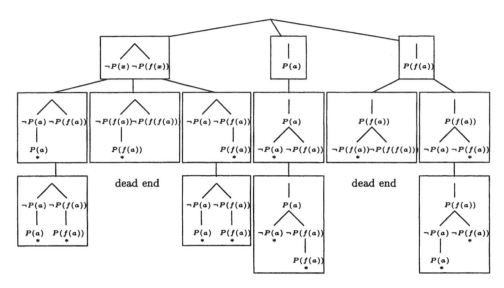

Figure 2: The connection tableau search tree for the set S consisting of the three clauses $\neg P(x) \vee \neg P(f(x))$, $P(a)$, and $P(f(a))$.

In Figure 2, the complete connection tableau search tree for a set of clauses is given. For this simple example, the search tree is finite. Note that the search space of the general clausal tableau calculus (without a connection condition) is infinite for S. This is but one example for the search pruning effect achieved by the connection conditions.

In order to find a connection tableau proof, the corresponding (normally infinite) search tree has to be explored. This can be done *explicitly* by constructing all tableaux in a *breadth-first* manner and working down the search tree level-wise from top to bottom, such a calculus was discussed in [Baumgartner and Brüning 1997]. The explicit construction of all tableaux, however, suffers from an enormous consumption of memory, since the number and the sizes of the generated proof objects significantly grow during the proof process. Furthermore, the computational effort for creating new tableaux increases with the depth of the search tree, since the sizes of the tableaux increase. In contrast, for resolution procedures the *number* of new proof objects (clauses) is generally considered the critical parameter. This sufficiently demonstrates why an explicit tableau enumeration approach should not be pursued in practice.

The customary and successful paradigm therefore is to explore a tableau search tree in an *implicit* manner, using *consecutively bounded depth-first iterative deepening search* procedures. In this approach, iteratively larger finite initial parts of a search tree $\mathcal{T}$ are explored, by imposing so-called *completeness bounds* on the structure of the permitted tableaux. Due to the construction process of tableaux from the root to the leaves, many tableaux have identical or structurally identical subparts. This suggests exploring finite initial segments in a *depth-first* manner, by employing *structure sharing* techniques and using *backtracking*. More precisely, at each time only one tableau is in memory, which is extended following the branches of the search tree; backtracking occurs when a leaf node of the current initial segment of the search tree has been reached. If no proof was found on one level, then the next level of the iteration is started. A more elaborate description of this proof search procedure will be given in Section 7. Even though according to this methodology initial parts of the search tree are explored several times, no significant efficiency is lost if the initial segments increase exponentially [Korf 1985]. The advantage is that, due to the application of Prolog techniques, very high inference rates can be achieved.

2.5. *Completeness Bounds*

In this section, different important completeness bounds will be introduced. Formally, a completeness bound can be viewed as a particular size function on tableaux.

2.7. DEFINITION *(Completeness bound)*. A *size bound* is a total mapping s assigning to any tableau T a non-negative integer n called the *s-size* of T. A size bound s is called a *completeness bound* for a (clausal) tableau calculus C if, for any finite set S of formulae (clauses) and any $n \geq 0$, the search tree corresponding to C and S contains only finitely many tableaux with s-size less or equal to n.

The finiteness condition qualifies completeness bounds as suitable for iterative deepening search. Given a completeness bound s and an iterative deepening level with size limit n, an implicit deduction enumeration procedure works as follows. Whenever an inference step is applied to a tableau, it is checked whether the s-size of the new tableau is $\leq n$, otherwise backtracking is performed.

2.5.1. *Inference bound*
The most natural completeness bound is the so-called *inference bound* which counts the number of inference steps that are needed to construct a closed tableau. Using the inference bound, the search tree is explored level-wise; that is, for size n, the search tree is explored until depth $\leq n$. The search effort can be reduced by using *look-ahead* information as follows. As soon as a clause is selected for attachment, its length is taken into account for the current inference number, since obviously, for every subgoal of the clause at least one inference step is necessary to solve it. This enables us to detect the exceeding of the current size limit as early as possible. For example, considering the search tree given in Figure 2, with inference limit 2, one can avoid an expansion step with the first clause $\neg P(x) \vee \neg P(f(x))$, since any closed tableau with this clause as start clause will at least need 3 inference steps. This method was first used in [Stickel 1988].

2.5.2. Depth bound

A further simple completeness bound is the *depth bound*, which limits the length of the branches of the tableaux considered in the current search level. In connection tableaux, one can relax this bound so that it is only checked when non-unit clauses are attached. This implements a kind of unit preference strategy. An experimental comparison of the inference bound and the relaxed depth bound is contained in [Letz et al. 1992].

Both of the above bounds have certain deficiencies in practice. Briefly, the inference bound is too optimistic, since it implicitly assumes that subgoals which are not yet processed may be solved with just one inference step. The weakness of the depth bound, on the other hand, is that it is too coarse in the sense that the number of tableaux in a search tree with depth $\leq n+1$ is usually much larger than the number of tableaux with depth $\leq n$. In fact, in the worst case, the increase function is doubly exponential whereas, in the case of the inference bound, the increase function is exponential at most. Furthermore, both bounds favour tableaux of completely different structures. Using the inference bound, trees containing few long branches are preferred, whereas the depth bound prefers symmetrically structured trees.

2.5.3. A divide-and-conquer optimization of the inference bound

In [Harrison 1996], the following method was applied for avoiding some of the deficiencies of the inference bound. In order to comprehend the essence of the method, assume N_1 and N_2 to be two subgoals (among others) in a tableau and let the number of remaining inferences be k. Now it is clear that one of the two subgoals must have a proof of $\leq k/2$ inferences in order to meet the size limit. This suggests the following two-step algorithm. First, select the subgoal N_1 and attempt to solve it with inference limit $k/2$; if this succeeds, solve the rest of the tableau with whatever is left over from k. If this has been done for all solutions of the subgoal N_1, repeat the entire process for N_2. The advantage of this method is that the exploration of N_1 and N_2 to the full limit k is often avoided. Its disadvantage is that pairs of solutions of the subgoals with size $\leq k/2$ will be found twice, which increases the search space. In order to keep this method from failing in the recursive case, methods of failure caching as presented in Section 4.3 are needed. In practice, this method performs better if smaller limits like $k/3$ or $k/4$ are used instead of $k/2$, although those do not guarantee that all proofs on the respective iterative deepening level can be found. A possible explanation for this improved behavior is that the latter methods tend to prefer short or unit clauses which is a generally successful strategy in automated deduction (see also Section 2.6.2 where a similar effect may be achieved with a method based on a different idea).

2.5.4. Clause dependent depth bounds

Other approaches aim at improving the depth bound. The depth bound is typically implemented as follows. For a given tableau depth limit, say k, every node in the tableau is labelled with the value $k - d$ where d is the distance from the root node. If this value of a node is 0, then no tableau extension is permitted at this node.

Accordingly, one may call this value of a node its *resource*. This approach permits a straightforward generalization of the depth bound. Instead of giving the open successors $N_1, \ldots, N_m$ of a tableau node N with resource i the resource $j = i - 1$, the resource j of each of $N_1, \ldots, N_m$ is the value of a function r of two arguments, the resource i of N and the number m of new subgoals in the attached clause. We call such bounds *clause dependent depth bounds*. With clause dependent depth bounds a smoother increase of the iterative deepening levels can be obtained. Two such clause dependent depth bounds have been used in practice, one defined by $r(i, m) = i - m$ (this bound is available in the system SETHEO since version V.3 [Goller, Letz, Mayr and Schumann 1994]) and the other by $r(i, m) = (i - 1)/m$ (this bound was called *sym* in [Harrison 1996]).

2.5.5. (Inference) weighted depth bounds

Although a higher flexibility can be obtained with clause dependent depth bounds, all these bounds are pure depth bounds in some sense, since the resource j of a node is determined at the time the node is attached to the tableau. In order to increase the flexibility and to permit an integration of features of the inference bound, the so-called *weighted depth bounds* have been developed. The main idea of the weighted depth bounds is to use a bound such as the clause dependent depth bound as a basis, but to take the inferences into account when eventually allocating the resource to a subgoal. In detail, this is controlled by three parameterized functions w_1, w_2, w_3 as follows. When entering a clause with m subgoals from a node with resource i, first, the maximally available resource j for the new subgoals is computed according to a clause dependent depth bound, i.e., $j = w_1(i, m)$. Then, the value j is divided into two parts, a *guaranteed* part $j_g = w_2(j, m) \le j$ and an *additive* part $j_a = j - j_g$. Whenever a subgoal is selected, the additive part is modified depending on the inferences Δi performed since the clause was attached to the tableau,[2] i.e., $j_a' = w_3(j_a, \Delta i)$. The resource finally allocated for a selected subgoal then is $j_g + j_a'$.

Depending on the parameter choices for the functions w_1, w_2, w_3, the respective weighted depth bound can simulate the inference bound ($w_1(i, m) = i - m$, $w_2(j, m) = 0$, $w_3(j_a, \Delta i) = j_a - \Delta i$) or the (clause dependent) depth bound(s) or any combination of them.

A parameter selection which represents a simple new completeness bound combining inference and depth bound is, for example, $w_1(i, m) = i - 1$, $w_2(j, m) = j - (m - 1)$, $w_3(j_a, \Delta i) = j_a/(1 + \Delta i)$. For certain formula classes, this bound turned out to be much more successful than each of the other bounds [Moser, Ibens, Letz, Steinbach, Goller, Schumann and Mayr 1997]. One reason for the success of this strategy is that it also performs a unit preference strategy.

---

[2] We assume that the look-ahead optimization is used, according to which reduction steps and extension steps into unit clauses do not increase the current inference value. This implies that $\Delta i = 0$ if no extension steps into non-unit clauses have been performed on subgoals of the current clause.

2.6. Subgoal Processing

There is a source of indeterminism in the clausal tableau calculi presented so far that can be removed without any harm. This indeterminism concerns the selection of the next subgoal at which an expansion, extension, or closure step is to be performed.

2.8. DEFINITION *(Subgoal selection function)*. A *(subgoal) selection function* ϕ is a mapping assigning an open branch with subgoal N to every open tableau T. Let ϕ be a subgoal selection function and $S = T_1, \ldots, T_n$ a sequence of tableaux. If each tableau T_{i+1} in S can be obtained from T_i by performing an inference step on the subgoal $\phi(T_i)$, then we say that S and T_n are *constructed according to* ϕ.

Most complete refinements and extensions of clausal tableau calculi developed to date are *independent of the subgoal selection*, i.e., the completeness holds for any subgoal selection function (for exceptions see Section 6.2 and Section 7 in [Letz et al. 1994]). If a calculus has this property, then it is possible to choose one subgoal selection function ϕ in advance and ignore all tableaux in the search tree that are not constructed according to ϕ. This way the search effort can be reduced significantly. As an illustration of this method of *search pruning*, consider the search tree displayed in Figure 2. For this simple tree, one can only distinguish two subgoal selection functions ϕ_1 and ϕ_2. ϕ_1 selects the left subgoal and ϕ_2 the right subgoal in the start clause. When deciding for ϕ_2, the three leftmost lower boxes will vanish from the search tree. In case ϕ_1 is used, only two boxes will be pruned away.

For the clausal tableau calculi presented up to this point, even the following stronger independence property holds.

2.9. PROPOSITION (Strong independence of subgoal selection). *Given any closed (path) (connection) tableau T for a set of clauses S constructed with n inference steps, then for any subgoal selection function ϕ, there exists a sequence $T_0, \ldots, T_n$ of (path) (connection) tableaux constructed according to ϕ such that T_n is closed and T is an instance of T_n, i.e. $T = T_n\sigma$ for some substitution σ.*

PROOF. See [Letz 1999]. □

In case a calculus is strongly independent of the subgoal selection, not only completeness is preserved, but minimal proof lengths as well. Furthermore, if a completeness bound of the sort described above is used, then the iterative deepening level on which the first proof is found is always the same, independent of the subgoal selection. Note that the strong independence of the subgoal selection (and hence minimal proof lengths) will be lost for certain extensions of the clausal tableau calculus such as *folding up* [Letz et al. 1994] and the *local* closure rule which is discussed below.

One particular useful form of choosing subgoals is *depth-first* selection, i.e., one always selects the subgoal of an open branch of maximal length in the tableau. *Depth-first left-most/right-most* selection always chooses the subgoal on the left-most/right-most open branch (which automatically has maximal depth). Depth-first left-most selection is the built-in subgoal selection strategy of Prolog. Depth-first selection has a number of advantages, the most important being that the search is kept relatively local. Furthermore, very efficient implementations are possible.

2.6.1. Subgoal reordering

The order of subgoal selection has influences on the size of the search space, as shown by the search tree above. This is because subgoals normally share variables and thus the solution substitutions of one subgoal have an influence on the solution substitutions of the other subgoals.

A general *least commitment* paradigm is to prefer subgoals that produce fewer solutions. In order to identify a non-closable connection tableau as early as possible, the solutions of a subgoal should be exhausted as early as possible. Therefore, subgoals for which probably only few solutions exist should be selected earlier than subgoals for which many solutions exist. This results in the *fewest-solutions* principle for subgoal selection.

Depth-first selection means that all subgoal alternatives stem from one clause of the input set. Therefore, the selection order of the literals in a clause can be determined *statically*, i.e., once and for all before starting the proof search, as in [Letz et al. 1992]. But subgoal selection can also be performed *dynamically*, whenever the literals of the clause are handled in a tableau. The static version is cheaper (in terms of performed comparisons), but often an optimal subgoal selection cannot be determined statically, as can be seen, for example, when considering the transitivity clause $P(x, z) \vee \neg P(x, y) \vee \neg P(y, z)$. Statically, none of the literals can be preferred. Dynamically, however, when performing an extension step entering the transitivity clause from a subgoal $\neg P(a, z)$, the first subgoal $\neg P(x, y)$ is instantiated to $\neg P(a, y)$. Since it contains only one variable now, it should be preferred according to the fewest-solutions principle. Entering the transitivity clause from a subgoal $\neg P(x, a)$ leads to preference of the second subgoal $\neg P(y, a)$.

2.6.2. Subgoal alternation

When a subgoal in a tableau has been selected for solution, a number of complementary unification partners are available, viz. the connected path literals and the connected literals in the input clauses. Together they form the so-called *choice point* of the subgoal. One common principle of standard backtracking search procedures in model elimination (and in Prolog) is that, whenever a subgoal has been selected, its choice point must be completely finished, i.e., when retracting an alternative in the choice point of a subgoal, one has to stick to the subgoal and try another alternative in its choice point. This standard methodology has an interesting search-theoretic weakness.

This can be shown by the following generic example, variants of which often occur in practice. Given the subgoals $\neg P(x, y)$ and $\neg Q(x, y)$ in a tableau, assume the following clauses to be in the input.

(1) $P(a, a)$,
(2) $P(x, y) \vee \neg P'(x, z) \vee \neg P'(y, z)$,

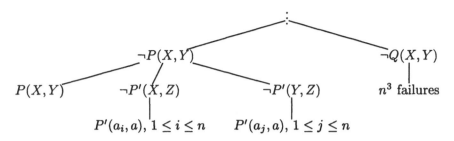

Figure 3: Effort in case of standard subgoal processing.

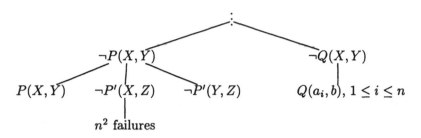

Figure 4: Effort when switching to another subgoal.

(3) $P'(a_i, a)$, $1 \leq i \leq n$,
(4) $Q(a_i, b)$, $1 \leq i \leq n$.

Suppose further we have decided to select the first subgoal and perform depth-first subgoal selection. The critical point, say at time t, is after unit clause (1) in the choice point was tried and no compatible solution instance for the other subgoal was found. Now we are forced to enter clause (2). Obviously, there are n^2 solution substitutions (unifications) for solving clause (2) (the product of the solutions of its subgoals). For each of those solutions, we have to perform n unifications with the Q-subgoal, which all fail. Including the unifications spent in clause (2), this amounts to a total effort of $1 + n + n^2 + n^3$ unifications (see Figure 3). Observe now what would happen when at time t we would not have entered clause (2), but would switch to the Q-subgoal instead. Then, for each of the n solution substitutions $Q(a_i, b)$, one would jump to the P-subgoal, enter clause (2) and perform just n failing unifications for its first subgoal. This sums up to a total of just $n + n(1 + n) = 2n + n^2$ unifications (see Figure 4).

It is apparent that this phenomenon is related to the fewest-solutions principle. Clause (2) generates more solutions for the subgoal $\neg P(X, Y)$ than the clauses in the choice point of the subgoal $\neg Q(X, Y)$. This shows that taking the remaining alternatives of *all* subgoals into account provides a choice which can better satisfy the fewest-solution principle. As a general principle, *subgoal alternation* always switches to the subgoal the current connected clause of which is likely to produce the fewest solutions.

One might argue that with a different subgoal selection, selecting the Q-subgoal first could also avoid the cubic effort. But it is apparent that the example could be extended so that the Q-subgoal would additionally have a longer clause as an alternative, so that the total number of its solutions would be even larger than that of the P-subgoal. In this case, with subgoal alternation one could jump back to the P-subgoal and try clause (2) next, in contrast to standard subgoal selection. Another possibility of jumping to the Q-subgoal *after* having entered clause (2) would be free subgoal selection. In fact, subgoal alternation under depth-first subgoal selection comes closer to standard free subgoal selection, but both methods are not identical.

The question is, when it is worthwhile to stop the processing of a choice point and switch to another subgoal? As a matter of fact, it cannot be determined in advance, how many solutions a clause in the choice point of a subgoal produces for that subgoal. A useful criterion, however, is the *shortest-clause* principle, since, in the worst case, the number of subgoal solutions coming from a clause is the product of the numbers of solutions of its subgoals.[3]

In summary, subgoal alternation works as follows. The standard subgoal selection and clause selection phases are combined and result in a single selection phase that is performed before each derivation step. The selection yields the subgoal for which the most suitable unification partner exists wrt. the number of solutions probably produced. This is done by comparing the unification partners of all subgoals with each other using, for instance, the shortest-clause principle. If more than one unification partner is given the mark of 'best choice', their corresponding subgoals have to be compared due to the principles for standard subgoal selection, namely the first-fail principle and the fewest-solutions principle.

In order to compare the way subgoal alternation (using the shortest-clause principle) works to the standard non-alternating variant, consider two subgoals A and B with clauses of lengths 1,3,5 and 2,4,6 in their choice points, respectively. Table 1 illustrates the order in which clauses are tried.

Subgoal alternation has a number of interesting effects when combined with other methods in model elimination. First note that the method leads to the preference of short clauses. A particularly beneficial effect of preferring short clauses, especially the preference of unit clauses, is the early instantiation of variables. Unit clauses are usually more instantiated than longer clauses, because they represent the "facts" of the input problem, whereas longer clauses in general represent the axioms of the underlying theory. Since normally variables are shared between several subgoals, the solution of a subgoal by a unit clause usually leads to instantiating variables in other subgoals. These instantiations reduce the number of solutions of the other subgoals and thus reduce the search space to be explored when selecting them. Advantage is also taken from subgoal alternation when combined with local failure caching considered in Section 4.3. Failure caching can only exploit information from *closed*

---

[3] Also, the number of variables in the *calling* subgoal and in the *head* literal of a clause matter for the number of solutions produced.

standard backtracking	subgoal alternation
A1 B2	A1 B2
A1 B4	A1 B4
A1 B6	A1 B6
A3 B2	℧ B2 A3
A3 B4	B2 A5
A3 B6	℧ A3 B4
A5 B2	A3 B6
A5 B4	℧ B4 A5
A5 B6	℧ A5 B6

Table 1: Order of tried clauses for subgoals A and B with clauses of lengths 1,3,5 and 2,4,6 in their choice points, respectively. ℧ indicates subgoal alternations.

sub-tableaux, thus a large number of small subproofs provides more information for caching than a small number of large sub-tableaux that cannot be closed. Since subgoal alternation prefers short clauses and hence small subproofs, the local failure caching mechanism is supported.

Subgoal alternation leads to the simultaneous processing of several choice points. This provides the possibility of computing *look-ahead information* concerning the minimal number of inferences still needed for closing a tableau. A simple estimate of this inference value is the number of subgoals plus the number of all subgoals in the shortest alternative of each subgoal. In general, when using standard subgoal selection, every choice point with literal L except the current one contains connected path literals and connected unit clauses, that is, possibly L can be solved in one inference step. Using subgoal alternation, the reduction steps and the extension steps with unit clauses have already been tried at several choice points, so that only the unification partners *in non-unit clauses* are left in the choice points of several subgoals. Thus more information about the required inference resources can be obtained than in the standard procedure. This *look-ahead information* can be used for search pruning, whenever the number of inferences has an influence on the search bound.[4]

However, under certain circumstances alternating between subgoals may be disadvantageous. If a subgoal cannot be solved at all, switching to another subgoal may be worse than sticking to the current choice point, since the latter may lead to an earlier retraction of the whole clause. This is important for ground subgoals in particular, because they have at most one solution substitution in the Horn case. Since ground subgoals do not contain free variables, they normally cannot profit from early instantiations achieved by subgoal alternation, i.e., switching to brother

---

[4]This technique is also used by the SETHEO system [Moser et al. 1997].

subgoals and instantiating their free variables cannot lead to instantiations within a ground subgoal. Therefore, when processing a ground subgoal, the fewest-solutions principle for subgoal selection becomes more important than the shortest-clause principle for subgoal alternation. For this reason, subgoal alternation should not be performed when the current subgoal is ground.

2.7. Connection Tableaux and Related Calculi

Due to the fact that tableau calculi work by building up tree structures whereas other calculi derive new formulae from old ones, the close relation of tableaux with other proof systems is not immediately evident. There exist similarities of tableau proofs to deductions in other calculi. In order to clarify the interdependencies, it is helpful to reformulate the process of tableau construction in terms of formula generation procedures. There are two natural formula interpretations of tableaux which we shall mention and which both have their merits.

2.10. DEFINITION. The *branch formula* of a formula tree T is the disjunction of the conjunctions of the formulae on the branches of T.

Another finer view is preserving the underlying tree structure of the formula tree.

2.11. DEFINITION *(Formula of a formula tree (inductive))*.
1. The *formula* of a one-node formula tree labelled with the formula F is simply F.
2. The *formula* of a complex formula tree with root N (with label F) and immediate formula subtrees $T_1, \ldots, T_n$, in this order, is $F \wedge (F_1 \vee \cdots \vee F_n)$ (or simply $F_1 \vee \cdots \vee F_n$ if N is unlabelled) where F_i is the formula of T_i, for every $1 \leq i \leq n$.

Evidently, the branch formula and the formula of a formula tree are equivalent. Futhermore, it is clear that the following proposition holds, from which, as a corollary, also follows the soundness of the method of clausal tableaux.

2.12. PROPOSITION. *If F is the (branch) formula of a clausal tableau for a set of clauses S, then F is a logical consequence of S.*

PROOF. Trivial. □

With the formula notation of tableaux, one can identify a close correspondence of tableau deductions to calculi of the *generative* type. This way, the relation between tableaux and Gentzen's *sequent system* was shown in [Smullyan 1968] using so-called *block tableaux*. We are interested in recognizing similarities to calculi from the field of automated deduction. For this purpose, it is helpful to only consider the *open parts* of tableaux, which we call *goal trees*.

2.13. DEFINITION *(Goal tree)*. The *goal tree of* a tableau T is the formula tree obtained from T by cutting off all closed branches.

The goal tree of a tableau contains only the open branches of a tableau. Obviously, for the continuation of the refutation process, all other parts of the tableau may be disregarded without any harm.

2.14. DEFINITION *(Goal formula)*.
 1. The *goal formula* of any closed tableau is the falsum $\bot$.
 2. The *goal formula* of any open tableau is the formula of the goal tree of the tableau.

Using the goal formula interpretation, the tableau construction can be viewed as a linear deduction process in which a new goal formula is always deduced from the previous one until eventually the falsum is derived. In Example 2.15, we give a goal formula deduction that corresponds to the construction of the tableau in Figure 1, under a branch selection function ϕ that always selects the right-most branch.

2.15. EXAMPLE *(Goal formula deduction)*. The set of clauses $S = \{R(x) \vee R(f(x)),$ $\neg R(x) \vee \neg R(f(f(x)))\}$ has the following goal formula refutation.

$\neg R(x) \vee \neg R(f(f(x)))$
$\neg R(x) \vee (\neg R(f(f(x))) \wedge R(f(f(f(x)))))$
$\neg R(x) \vee (\neg R(f(f(x))) \wedge R(f(f(f(x)))) \wedge \neg R(f(x)))$
$\neg R(x) \vee (\neg R(f(f(x))) \wedge R(f(f(f(x)))) \wedge \neg R(f(x)) \wedge R(f(f(x))))$
$\neg R(x)$
$\neg R(f(x)) \wedge R(f(f(x)))$
$\neg R(f(x)) \wedge R(f(f(x))) \wedge \neg R(x)$
$\neg R(f(x)) \wedge R(f(f(x))) \wedge \neg R(x) \wedge R(f(x))$
$\bot$

2.16. PROPOSITION. *The goal formula of any clausal tableau T is logically equivalent to the formula of T.*

PROOF. Trivial.   □

2.7.1. Model elimination chains

Using the goal tree or goal formula notation, one can easily identify a close similarity of connection tableaux with the model elimination calculus as presented in [Loveland 1978], which we will discuss in some more detail. As already mentioned, model elimination was originally introduced as a tree-based procedure with the full generality of subgoal selection in [Loveland 1968], although the deductive object of a tableau is not explicitly used in this paper. As Don Loveland has pointed out, the linearized version of model elimination presented in [Loveland 1969, Loveland 1978] was the result of an adaptation to the resolution form. Here, we treat a subsystem of model elimination without factoring and lemmata, called *weak model elimination* in

[Loveland 1978], which is still refutation-complete. The fact that weak model elimination is indeed a specialized subsystem of the connection tableau calculus becomes apparent when considering the goal formula deductions of connection tableaux. The weak model elimination calculus can be considered as the special case of the connection tableau calculus where the selection of open branches is performed in a *depth-first right-most* or *left-most* manner, i.e., always the right-most (left-most) open branch has to be selected. Let us choose the right-most variant for now. Due to this restriction of the subgoal selection, a one-dimensional "chain" representation of goal formulae is possible in which no logical operators are necessary. The transformation from goal formulae with a depth-first right-most selection function to model elimination chains works as follows. To any goal formula generated with a depth-first right-most selection function, apply the following operation: replace every conjunction $L_1 \wedge \cdots \wedge L_n \wedge F$ with $[L_1 \cdots L_n]F$ and delete all disjunction symbols.

In a model elimination chain, the occurrences of bracketed literals denote the non-leaf nodes and the occurrences of unbracketed literals denote the subgoals of the goal tree of the tableau. For every subgoal N corresponding to an occurrence of an unbracketed literal L, the bracketed literal occurrences to the left of L encode the ancestor nodes of N. The model elimination proof corresponding to the goal formula deduction given in Example 2.15 is depicted in Example 2.17.

2.17. EXAMPLE *(Model elimination chain deduction).* The set $\{R(x) \vee R(f(x)),$ $\neg R(x) \vee \neg R(f(f(x)))\}$ has the following model elimination chain refutation.

$\neg R(x) \ \neg R(f(f(x)))$
$\neg R(x) \ [\ \neg R(f(f(x))) \ ] \ R(f(f(f(x))))$
$\neg R(x) \ [\ \neg R(f(f(x))) \ R(f(f(f(x)))) \ ] \ \neg R(f(x))$
$\neg R(x) \ [\ \neg R(f(f(x))) \ R(f(f(f(x)))) \ \neg R(f(x)) \ ] \ R(f(f(x)))$
$\neg R(x)$
$[\ \neg R(f(x)) \ ] \ R(f(f(x)))$
$[\ \neg R(f(x)) \ R(f(f(x))) \ ] \ \neg R(x)$
$[\ \neg R(f(x)) \ R(f(f(x))) \ \neg R(x) \ ] \ R(f(x))$
$\perp$

It is evident that weak model elimination is a refinement of the connection tableau calculus, in which a fixed depth-first selection function is used. Viewing chain model elimination as a tableau refinement has various proof-theoretic advantages concerning generality and the possibility of defining extensions and refinements of the basic calculus. Also the soundness and completeness proofs of chain model elimination are immediate consequences of the soundness and completeness proofs of connection tableaux, which are very short and simple if compared with the rather involved proofs in [Loveland 1978]. Subsequently, we will adopt the original and more general view of model elimination as intended by Don Loveland [Loveland 1968] and use the terms connection tableaux and model elimination synonymously.

It is straightforward to recognize that SLD-resolution, although traditionally introduced as a resolution refinement, can also be viewed as a restricted form of model elimination where the reduction steps are omitted. If the underlying formula is a *Horn formula*, i.e., contains Horn clauses only, then it is obvious that this restriction on model elimination preserves completeness.[5]

2.7.2. The connection method

Another framework in automated deduction which is related with tableaux is the *connection method* [Andrews 1981, Bibel 1987]. We briefly mention the fundamental concepts of the connection method here, since they will be used for a search pruning technique presented in Section 4.1.

2.18. DEFINITION *(Path, connection, mating, spanning property)*. Given a set of clauses $S = \{c_1, \ldots, c_n\}$, a *path through* S is a set of n literal occurrences in S, exactly one from each clause in S. A *connection in* S is a two-element subset of a path through S such that the corresponding literals are complementary. Any set of connections in S is called a *mating in* S. A mating M is said to be *spanning for* S if every path through S is a superset of a connection in M.

A set of ground clauses S is unsatisfiable if and only if there is a spanning mating for S. The most natural method for finding and identifying a spanning mating as such is to use a tree-oriented path checking procedure which decomposes the formula, much the same as in the tableau framework, but guided by connections. The majority of those connection *calculi* in [Bibel 1987] can therefore be considered as connection *tableau* calculi, using the weaker path connectedness condition. Thus, every closed (path) connection tableau for a set S determines a spanning mating for S. In the first-order case, the notions of multiplicities and unification come into play, which we will not treat here. For a more detailed comparison, see [Letz et al. 1994, Letz 1998b].

3. Further Structural Refinements of Clausal Tableaux

The pure calculus of connection tableaux is only moderately successful in automated deduction. This is because the corresponding search trees are still full of redundancies. In general, there are different methodologies for reducing the search effort of tableau search procedures. In this section, we consider methods which attempt to restrict the tableau *calculus*, that is, disallow certain inference steps if they produce tableaux of a certain *structure*—note that the connection condition is such a structural restriction on general clausal tableaux. The effect on the tableau search tree is that the respective nodes together with the dominated subtrees can be ignored so that the branching rate of the tableau search tree decreases. These *structural* methods of redundancy elimination are *local* pruning techniques in the sense that they can be performed by looking at single tableaux only.

---

[5]When starting with an all-negative clause, reduction steps are not possible for syntactic reasons.

3.1. Regularity

A fundamental structural refinement of tableaux is the so-called regularity condition.

3.1. DEFINITION *(Regularity).* A clausal tableau is *regular* if on no branch a literal occurs more than once.

The term "regular" has been used to emphasize the analogy to the definition of *regular* resolution [Tseitin 1970]. Imposing the regularity restriction has some important consequences. First, for general clausal tableaux, every closed tableau of minimal size is guaranteed to be regular. Therefore, regularity preserves minimal proof lengths. Furthermore, using regularity the tableau search space of any ground formula becomes finite. While the latter condition also holds for connection tableaux, minimal closed connection tableaux may not be regular. In [Letz et al. 1994] it is shown that regular connection tableaux cannot even polynomially simulate connection tableaux. Nevertheless, a wealth of experimental results clearly shows that this theoretical disadvantage is more than compensated for by the strong search pruning effect of regularity [Letz et al. 1992], so that this refinement is indispensable for any model elimination proof procedure.

3.2. Tautology Elimination

Normally, it is a good strategy to eliminate certain clauses from the input set which can be shown to be redundant for finding a refutation. Tautological clauses are of such a sort.[6] In the ground case, tautologies may be identified once and for ever in a preprocessing phase and can be eliminated before starting the actual proof search. In the first-order case, however, it may happen that tautologies are generated dynamically. Let us demonstrate this phenomenon with the example of the clause $\neg P(x, y) \lor \neg P(y, z) \lor P(x, z)$ expressing the transitivity of a relation. Suppose that during the construction of a tableau this clause is used in an extension step (for simplicity renaming is neglected). Assume further that after some subsequent inference steps the variables y and z are instantiated to the same term t. Then a tautological instance $\neg P(x, t) \lor \neg P(t, t) \lor P(x, t)$ of the transitivity formula has been generated. Since no tautological clause is relevant in a set of formulae, connection tableaux with tautological tableau clauses need not be considered when searching for a refutation. Therefore the respective tableau and any extension of it can be disregarded.

Please note that the conditions of tautology-freeness and regularity are partially overlapping. More specifically, the non-tautology condition on the one hand covers all occurrences of identical predecessor nodes, but not the more remote ancestors. The regularity condition on the other hand captures all occurrences of tautological

---

[6]Of course, tautologies may facilitate the construction of smaller tableau proofs, since they can be used to simulate the cut rule. Yet, an *uncontrolled* use of cuts is not desirable at all.

clauses for backward reasoning with Horn clauses (i.e. with negative start clauses only), but not for non-Horn clauses.

3.3. Tableau Clause Subsumption

An essential pruning method in resolution theorem proving is *subsumption deletion*, which during the proof process deletes any clause that is subsumed by another clause, and this way eliminates a lot of redundancy. Although no new clauses are generated in the tableau approach, a restricted variant of clause subsumption reduction can be used in the tableau framework, too. First, we briefly recall the definition of subsumption between clauses.

3.2. DEFINITION *(Subsumption for clauses)*. Given two clauses c_1 and c_2, we say that c_1 *subsumes* c_2 if there is a variable substitution σ such that the set of literals contained in $c_1\sigma$ is a subset of the set of literals contained in c_2.

Similar to the dynamic generation of tautologies, it may happen, that a clause which has been attached in a tableau step during the tableau construction process is instantiated and then subsumed by another clause from the input set. As an example, suppose the transitivity clause from above and a unit clause $P(a, b)$ are contained in the input set. Now, if the transitivity clause is used in a tableau and if after some inference steps the variables x and z are instantiated to a and b, respectively, then the resulting tableau clause $\neg P(a, y) \vee \neg P(y, b) \vee P(a, b)$ is subsumed by $P(a, b)$. Obviously, for any closed tableau using the former tableau clause a closed tableau exists which uses the latter clause instead.

Again there is the possibility of a pruning overlap with the regularity and the non-tautology conditions. Note that, strictly speaking, avoiding tableau clause subsumption is not a pure *tableau structure* restriction, since a case of subsumption cannot be defined by merely looking at the tableau. Additionally, it is necessary to take the respective input set into account.

3.4. Strong Connectedness

When employing an efficient transformation from the general first-order format to clausal form, new predicates are sometimes introduced which are used to abbreviate certain formulae [Eder 1984, Plaisted and Greenbaum 1986, Boy de la Tour 1990]. Assume, for instance, we have to abbreviate a conjunction of literals $a \wedge b$ with a new predicate d by introducing a biconditional $d \leftrightarrow a \wedge b$. This rewrites to the three clauses $\sim a \vee \sim b \vee d$, $a \vee \sim d$, and $b \vee \sim d$. Interestingly, every resolvent between the three clauses is a tautology. Applied to the tableau construction, this means that whenever one of these clauses is immediately below another one, then a hidden form of a tautology has been generated as shown in Figure 5. (This example also illustrates that the effect of the cut rule can be simulated by suitable definitions.)

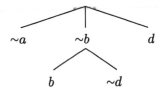

Figure 5: Hidden tautologies in tableaux.

Please note that certain cases of such hidden tautologies may be avoided. For this purpose the notion of connectedness was strengthened to *strong connectedness* in [Letz 1993].

3.3. DEFINITION *(Strong connectedness)*. Two clauses c_1 and c_2 are *strongly connected* if there is a substitution σ such that $c_1\sigma$ contains exactly one literal whose complement occurs in $c_2\sigma$, i.e. c_1 and c_2 can be used as the parent clauses of a non-tautological resolvent.

In Section 6.1, it will be proven that, for all pairs of adjacent tableau clauses, strong connectedness may be demanded without losing completeness. However, it is essential that the two clauses are adjacent, i.e. one must be located immediately below the other. For more distant pairs of tableau clauses one dominated by the other, the condition that they be strongly connected is not compatible with the condition of regularity. An example for this is given in Figure 6. This figure shows the only closed strongly connected regular tableau with top clause $\{\neg p, \neg q\}$. Note that the top clause and the clause $\{p, q\}$ have only tautological resolvents. This cannot be avoided even when additional inference rules like factorization or folding up (see Section 5) are available.

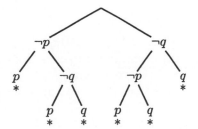

Figure 6: A strongly connected tableau for $\{\{p,q\}, \{p, \neg q\}, \{\neg p.q\}, \{\neg p.\neg q\}\}$.

3.5. Use of Relevance Information

By using *relevance information*, the set of possible start clauses can be minimized.

3.4. DEFINITION *(Essentiality, relevance, minimal unsatisfiability)*. A formula F is called *essential in* a set S of formulae if S is unsatisfiable and $S \setminus \{F\}$ is satisfiable. A formula F is named *relevant in* S if F is essential in some subset of S. An unsatisfiable set of formulae S is said to be *minimally unsatisfiable* if each formula in S is essential in S.

As will be shown in Section 6, the connection tableau calculus is complete in the strong sense that, for every relevant clause in a set S, there exists a closed connection tableau for S with this clause as the start clause. Since in any unsatisfiable set of clauses, some negative clause is relevant, it is sufficient to consider only negative clauses as start clauses. The application of this default pruning method achieves a significant reduction of the search space. In many cases, one has even more information concerning the relevance of certain clauses. Normally, a satisfiable subset of the input is well-known to the user, namely, the clauses specifying the theory axioms and the hypotheses. Such relevance information is also provided in the TPTP library [Sutcliffe, Suttner and Yemenis 1994]. A goal-directed system can enormously profit from the relevance information by considering only those clauses as start clauses that stem from the conjecture. As an example, consider an axiomatization of set theory containing the basic axiom that the empty set contains no set, which is normally expressed as a negative unit clause. Evidently, it is not very reasonable to start a refutation with this clause.

It is important to note, however, that when relevance information is being employed, then *all* conjecture clauses have to be tried as start clauses and not only the all-negative ones. Relevance information is normally more restrictive than the default method except when *all* negative clauses are stemming from the conjecture, in which case obviously the default mode is more restrictive.

4. Global Pruning Methods in Model Elimination

4.1. Matings Pruning

As already mentioned in Section 2.7.2, a mating, i.e. a set of connections, can be associated with any (path) connection tableau. However, this mapping is not injective in general. So one and the same mating may be associated with different tableaux. This means that the matings concept provides a more abstract view of the search space and enables us to group tableaux into equivalence classes. Under certain circumstances, it is not necessary to construct *all tableaux* in such a class but only *one representative*. In order to illustrate this, let us consider the set of propositional clauses

$$\{\neg P_1 \vee \neg P_2, \neg P_1 \vee P_2, P_1 \vee \neg P_2, P_1 \vee P_2\}.$$

As shown in Figure 7, the set has 4 closed regular connection tableaux with the all-negative start clause $\neg P_1 \vee \neg P_2$. If, however, the involved sets of connections are inspected, it turns out that the tableaux all have the same mating consisting of

6 connections. The redundancy contained in the tableau framework is that certain tableaux are *permutations* of each other corresponding to different possible ways of *traversing* a set of connections. Obviously, only one of the tableaux in such an equivalence class has to be considered.

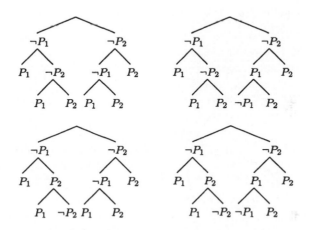

Figure 7: Four closed connection tableaux for the same spanning mating.

The question is, how exactly this redundancy can be avoided. A general line of development would be to store all matings that have been considered during the tableau search procedure and to ignore all tableaux which encode a mating which was already generated before. This approach would require an enormous amount of space. Based on preliminary work in [Letz 1993], a method was developed in [Letz 1998b] which can do with very little space and avoid the form of duplication shown in Figure 7. To comprehend the method, note that, in the example above, the source of the redundancy is that a certain connection can be used both in an extension step and in a reduction step. This causes the combinatorial explosion. The idea is now to block certain reduction steps by using an ordering $\prec$ on the occurrences of literals in the input set which has to be respected during the tableau construction, as follows. Assume, we want to perform a reduction step from a node N to an ancestor node N'. Let $N_1, \ldots, N_n$ be the node family below N'. The nodes $N_1, \ldots, N_n$ were attached by an extension step "into" a node complementary to N', say N_i. Now we do not permit the reduction step from N to N' if $N_i \prec N$ where the ordering $\prec$ is inherited from the literal occurrences in the input set to the tableau nodes. As can easily be verified, for any total ordering, in the example above, only one closed tableau can be constructed with this proviso. As shown in [Letz 1998b], using this method a super-exponential reduction of the search space can be achieved with almost no overhead.

On the other hand, there may be problems when combining this method with other search pruning techniques.

4.1.1. Matings pruning and strong connectedness

For instance, the method is not compatible with the condition of strong connectedness presented in Section 3.4. As a counterexample, consider the set of the four clauses given in Example 4.1.

4.1. EXAMPLE. $\{P \vee Q(a),\ P \vee \neg Q(a),\ \neg P \vee Q(a),\ \neg P \vee \neg Q(x)\}$.

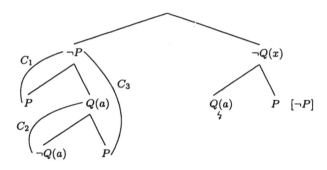

Figure 8: Deduction process for Example 4.1.

If we take the fourth clause, which is relevant in the set, as top clause, enter the first clause, then the second one by extension, and finally, perform a reduction step, then the closed subtableau on the left-hand side encodes the mating $\{C_1, C_2, C_3\}$. Now, any extension step at the subgoal labelled with $\neg Q(x)$ on the right-hand side immediately violates the strong connectedness condition. Therefore, backtracking is required up to the state in which only the top clause remains. Afterwards, the second clause must be entered, followed by an extension step into the first one. But now the mating pruning forbids a reduction step at the subgoal labelled with P, since it would produce a closed subtableau encoding the same mating $\{C_3, C_2, C_1\}$ as before. Since extension steps are impossible because of the regularity condition, the deduction process would fail and incorrectly report that the clause set is satisfiable.

4.2. Tableau Subsumption

A much more powerful application of the idea of subsumption between input clauses and tableau clauses consists in generalizing subsumption between clauses to subsumption between entire tableaux. For a powerful concept of subsumption between formula trees, the following notion of *formula tree contractions* proves helpful.

4.2. DEFINITION *((Formula) tree contraction)*. A (formula) tree T is called a *contraction* of a (formula) tree T' if T' can be obtained from T by attaching n (formula) trees to n non-leaf nodes of T, for some $n \geq 0$.

Figure 9: Illustration of the notion of tree contractions.

In Figure 9, the tree on the left is a contraction of itself, of the second and the fourth tree but not a contraction of the third one. Furthermore, the third tree is a contraction of the fourth one, which exhausts all contraction relations among these four trees. Now subsumption can be defined easily by building on the instance relation between formula trees.

4.3. DEFINITION *(Formula tree subsumption)*. A formula tree T *subsumes* a formula tree T' if some formula tree contraction of T' is an instance of T.

The subsumption relation can be extended considerably by considering the branches as sets, or even more by employing the positive refinement technique discussed in [Baumgartner and Brüning 1997].

Since the exploitation of subsumption between entire tableaux has not enough potential for reducing the search space, we favour the following form of subsumption deletion.

4.4. DEFINITION *(Subsumption deletion)*. For any pair of different nodes $\mathcal{N}$ and $\mathcal{N}'$ in a tableau search tree $\mathcal{T}$, if the goal tree of the tableau at $\mathcal{N}$ subsumes the goal tree of the tableau at $\mathcal{N}'$, then the whole subtree of the search tree with root $\mathcal{N}'$ is deleted from $\mathcal{T}$.

With subsumption deletion, a form of *global* redundancy elimination is achieved which is complementary to the purely tableau *structural* pruning methods discussed so far. In [Letz et al. 1994] it is shown that, for many formulae, cases of goal tree subsumption inevitably occur during proof search. Since this type of redundancy cannot be identified with tableau structure refinements like connectedness, regularity, or allies, methods for avoiding tableau subsumption are essential for achieving a well-performing model elimination proof procedure.

4.2.1. Tableau subsumption vs. regularity
Similar to the case of resolution where certain refinements of the *calculus*, i.e., restrictions of the resolution *inference rule*, become incomplete when combined with subsumption deletion, such cases also occur for refinements of tableau calculi. Formally, the compatibility with subsumption deletion can be expressed as follows.

4.5. DEFINITION *(Compatibility with subsumption)*. A tableau calculus is said to be *compatible with subsumption* if any of its tableau search trees $\mathcal{T}$ has the following property. For arbitrary pairs of nodes $\mathcal{N}$, $\mathcal{N}'$ in $\mathcal{T}$, if the goal tree S of the tableau T at $\mathcal{N}$ subsumes the subgoal tree S' of the tableau T' at $\mathcal{N}'$ and if $\mathcal{N}'$ dominates a success node, then $\mathcal{N}$ dominates a success node.

The (connection) tableau calculus is compatible with subsumption, but the integration of the regularity condition, for example, poses problems.

4.6. PROPOSITION. *The regular connection tableau calculus is incompatible with subsumption.*

Clauses: Tableau:

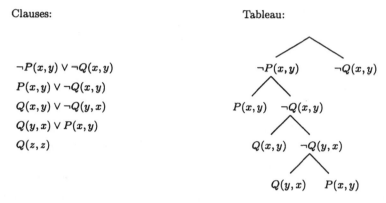

$$\neg P(x,y) \vee \neg Q(x,y)$$
$$P(x,y) \vee \neg Q(x,y)$$
$$Q(x,y) \vee \neg Q(y,x)$$
$$Q(y,x) \vee P(x,y)$$
$$Q(z,z)$$

Figure 10: The incompatibility of subsumption and regularity.

PROOF. We use the unsatisfiable set of clauses displayed on the left of Figure 10. Taking the first clause as top clause and employing the depth-first left-most selection function, the first subgoal N labelled with $\neg P(x,y)$ can be solved by deducing the tableau T depicted on the right of the figure. Since N has been solved optimally, i.e., without instantiating its variables, the subgoal tree of T subsumes the subgoal trees of all other tableaux working on the solution of N. Hence, all tableaux competing with T can be removed by subsumption deletion. But T cannot be extended to a solved tableau, due to the regularity condition, the crucial impediment being that an extension step into $Q(z, z)$ is not permitted, since it would render the already solved subtableau on the left irregular. To obtain a formula in which subsumption is fatal for *any* top clause, one can employ the *duplication trick* used in [Letz et al. 1994]. $\square$

The obvious problem with regularity is that it applies to entire tableaux whereas tableau subsumption considers only their subgoal trees. A straightforward solution therefore is to restrict regularity to subgoal trees, too. The respective weakening of regularity is called *subgoal tree regularity* . Similar incompleteness results can be achieved when combining tableau subsumption with tautology deletion. Here, a remedy is to ignore the non-tautology conditions of a tableau clause if some of its literals do not occur in the current subgoal tree. The same argument applies to the combination of tableau clause subsumption with formula tree subsumption.

4.3. Failure Caching

The observation that cases of subsumption inevitably will occur in practice suggests organizing the enumeration of tableaux in such a manner that cases of subsumption can really be detected. This could be achieved with a proof procedure which explicitly constructs competitive tableaux and thus investigates the search tree in a breadth-first manner. However, as already mentioned, the explicit enumeration of tableaux or goal trees is practically impossible. But when performing an implicit enumeration of tableaux by using iterative-deepening search procedures, only one tableau is in memory at any one time. This renders it very difficult to implement subsumption techniques in an adequate way. However, we discuss two methods by which a restricted concept of subsumption deletion can be implemented. The first paradigm employs *intelligent backtracking* [Neitz 1995]. This refinement of the standard Prolog backtracking technique searches the branch for the substitution that prevents a subgoal from being solved and backtracks to that point. Yet, this is difficult to do in the non-Horn case or in combination with other pruning mechanisms. The other paradigm is the use of so-called "failure caching" methods. The idea underlying this approach is to avoid the repetition of subgoal solutions which apply the same or a more special substitution to the respective branch. There are two approaches, one of which uses a permanent cache [Astrachan and Loveland 1991] and the other one uses a temporary cache [Letz et al. 1994]. We describe the latter method, which might be called "local failure caching" in more detail, because it turned out to be more successful in practice. Subsequently, we assume that only depth-first branch selection functions are used.

4.7. DEFINITION *(Solution -, failure substitution)*. Given a tableau search tree $\mathcal{T}$ for a tableau calculus and a depth-first branch selection function, let $\mathcal{N}$ be a node in $\mathcal{T}$, T the tableau at $\mathcal{N}$ and N the selected subgoal in T.

1. If $\mathcal{N}'$ with tableau T' is a node in the search tree $\mathcal{T}$ dominated by $\mathcal{N}$ such that all branches through N in T' are closed, let $\sigma' = \sigma_1 \cdots \sigma_n$ be the composition of substitutions applied to the tableau T on the way from $\mathcal{N}$ to $\mathcal{N}'$. Then the substitution $\sigma = \{x/x\sigma' \in \sigma' : x \text{ occurs in } T\}$, i.e., the set of bindings in σ' with domain variables occurring in the tableau T, is called a *solution (substitution) of N at $\mathcal{N}$ via $\mathcal{N}'$*.

2. If $\mathcal{T}'$ is an initial segment of the search tree $\mathcal{T}$ containing no proof at $\mathcal{N}'$ or below it, then the solution σ is named a *failure substitution for N at $\mathcal{N}$ via $\mathcal{N}'$ in $\mathcal{T}'$*.

Briefly, when a solution of a subgoal N with a substitution σ does not permit to solve the rest of the tableau under a given size bound, then this solution substitution is a failure substitution. We describe how failure substitutions can be applied in a search procedure which explores tableau search trees in a depth-first manner employing structure sharing and backtracking.

4.8. DEFINITION *(Generation, application, and deletion of a failure substitution)*. Let $\mathcal{T}$ be a finite initial segment of a tableau search tree.

1. Whenever a subgoal N selected in a tableau T at a search node $\mathcal{N}$ in $\mathcal{T}$ has been closed via (a sub-refutation to) a node $\mathcal{N}'$ in the search tree, then the computed solution σ is stored at the tableau node N. If the tableau at $\mathcal{N}'$ cannot be completed to a closed tableau in $\mathcal{T}'$ and the proof procedure backtracks over $\mathcal{N}'$, then σ is turned into a failure substitution.
2. In any alternative solution process of the tableau T below the search node $\mathcal{N}$, if a substitution $\tau = \tau_1 \cdots \tau_m$ is computed such that one of the failure substitutions stored at the node N is more general than τ, then the proof procedure immediately backtracks.
3. When the search node $\mathcal{N}$ (at which the tableau node N was selected for solution) is backtracked, then all failure substitutions at N are deleted.

	action	subgoals	substitution	fail.subs.
T_0	start step	$\neg P(x), \neg Q(y), \neg R(x)$	$\emptyset$	$\emptyset$
T_1	$P(a)$ entered	$\neg Q(y), \neg R(a)$	$\{x/a\}$	$\emptyset$
T_2	$Q(a)$ entered	$\neg R(a)$	$\{x/a, y/a\}$	$\emptyset$
	unification failure	$\neg R(a)$	$\{x/a, y/a\}$	$\emptyset$
	retract step 2	$\neg Q(y), \neg R(a)$	$\{x/a\}$	$\{y/a\}$
T_3	$Q(b)$ entered	$\neg R(a)$	$\{x/a, y/b\}$	$\{y/a\}$
	unification failure	$\neg R(a)$	$\{x/a, y/b\}$	$\{y/a\}$
	retract step 3	$\neg Q(y), \neg R(a)$	$\{x/a\}$	$\{y/a\}$
	retract step 1	$\neg P(x), \neg Q(y), \neg R(x)$	$\emptyset$	$\{x/a\}$
T_4	$P(x) \vee \neg Q(x)$ entered	$\neg Q(x), \neg Q(y), \neg R(x)$	$\{z/x\}$	$\{x/a\}$
T_5	$Q(a)$ entered	$\neg Q(y), \neg R(a)$	$\{z/a, x/a\}$	$\{x/a\}$
T_5	T_5 subsumed by T_1	$\neg Q(y), \neg R(a)$	$\{z/a, x/a\}$	$\{x/a\}$
	retract step 5	$\neg Q(x), \neg Q(y), \neg R(x)$	$\{z/x\}$	$\{x/a\}$
T_6	$Q(b)$ entered	$\neg Q(y), \neg R(b)$	$\{z/b, x/b\}$	$\{x/a\}$
T_7	$Q(a)$ entered	$\neg R(b)$	$\{z/b, x/b, y/a\}$	$\{x/a\}$
T_8	$R(b)$ entered		$\{z/b, x/b, y/a\}$	$\{x/a\}$

Figure 11: Proof search using failure substitutions.

4.9. EXAMPLE. In order to understand the mechanism, we show the method at work on a specific example.

Let S be the set of the five clauses

$$\neg P(x) \vee \neg Q(y) \vee \neg R(x), \quad P(a), \quad P(z) \vee \neg Q(z), \quad Q(a), \quad Q(b), \quad R(b).$$

A possible tableau construction for this clause set is documented in Figure 11. Assume, we start with the first clause in the set S and explore the corresponding tableau search tree using a depth-first left-to-right subgoal selection function, just like in Prolog. Accordingly, in inference step 1, the subgoal $\neg P(x)$ is solved using the clause $P(a)$. With this substitution, the remaining subgoals cannot be solved. Therefore, when backtracking step 1, the failure substitution $\{x/a\}$ is stored at the subgoal $\neg P(x)$. The search pruning effect of this failure substitution shows up in inference step 5 when the failure substitution is more general than the computed tableau substitution, i.e., the tableau T_5 is subsumed by the tableau T_1. Without this pruning method, steps 2 to 4 would have to be repeated.

Note also that one has to be careful to delete failure substitutions under certain circumstances, as expressed in step 3 of the procedure. This provision applies, for example, to the failure substitution $\{y/a\}$ generated at the subgoal $\neg Q(y)$ after the retraction of inference step 2. When the choice point of this subgoal is completely exhausted, then $\{y/a\}$ has to be deleted. Otherwise, it would prevent the solution process of the tableau when, in step 7, this subgoal is again solved using the clause $Q(a)$.

As already noted in Example 4.9, when the failure substitution $\{x/a\}$ at $\neg P(x)$ is more general than an alternative solution substitution of the subgoal, then the subgoal tree of the former tableau subsumes the one of the tableau generated later. The described method preserves completeness for certain completeness bounds, as stated more precisely in the following proposition.

4.10. PROPOSITION. *Let $\mathcal{T}$ be the initial segment of a connection tableau search tree defined by some subgoal selection function and the depth bound (Section 2.5.2) or some clause-dependent depth bound (Section 2.5.4) with size limitation k. Assume a failure substitution σ has been generated at a node N selected in a connection tableau T at a search node $\mathcal{N}$ in $\mathcal{T}$ via a search node $\mathcal{N}'$ according to the procedure in Definition 4.8. If T_c is a closed connection tableau in the search tree $\mathcal{T}$ below the search node $\mathcal{N}$ and τ the composition of substitutions applied when generating T_c from T, then the failure substitution σ is not more general than τ.*

PROOF. Assume indirectly, that σ is more general than τ, i.e., $\tau = \sigma\theta$. Let S_c and S be the subtableaux with root N in T_c respectively in the connection tableau at $\mathcal{N}'$. Then, replacing S_c in T_c with $S\theta$ results in a closed connection tableau T_c'. Furthermore, it is clear that T_c' satisfies the size limit k of the completeness bound used. Now the connection tableau calculus is strongly independent of the selection function. Consequently, a variant T_c'' of the tableau T_c' must be contained in the search tree $\mathcal{T}$ below the search node $\mathcal{N}'$. Since T_c'' must be closed, too, there must be a closed tableau below the search node $\mathcal{N}'$. But this contradicts the assumption of σ being a failure substitution.   □

The failure caching method described above has to be adapted when combined with other completeness bounds. While for the (clause-dependent) depth bounds exactly the method described above can be used, care must be taken when using the inference bound so as not to lose completeness. It may happen that a subgoal solution with solution substitution σ exhausts almost all available inferences so that there are not enough inferences left for the remaining subgoals, and there might exist another, smaller solution tree of the subgoal with the same substitution which would permit the solution of the remaining subgoals. Then the failure substitution σ would prevent this. Accordingly, in order to guarantee completeness, the number of inferences needed for a subgoal solution has to be attached to a failure substitution, and only if the solution tree computed later is greater or equal to the one associated with σ, σ may be used for pruning.

Furthermore, when using failure caching together with structural pruning methods such as regularity, tautology deletion, or tableau clause subsumption, phenomena like the one discussed in Proposition 4.6 may lead to incompleteness. A remedy is to restrict the structural conditions to the subgoal tree of the current tableau. But even if this requirement is complied with, completeness may be lost as demonstrated by the following example.

4.11. EXAMPLE. Let S be the set of the seven clauses

$$\neg P(x,b) \vee \neg Q(x), \ \ P(x,b) \vee \neg R(x) \vee \neg P(y,b), \ \ P(a,z), \ \ P(x,b), \ \ R(a), \ \ Q(a), \ \ R(x).$$

Using the first clause as start clause and performing a Prolog-like search strategy, the clause $P(x,b) \vee \neg R(x) \vee \neg P(y,b)$ is entered from the subgoal $\neg P(x,b)$. Solving the subgoal $\neg R(x)$ with the clause $R(a)$ leads to a tableau structure violation (irregularity or tautology) when $\neg P(y,b)\{x/a\}$ is solved with $P(a,z)$. This triggers the creation of a failure substitution $\{x/a\}$ at the subgoal $\neg R(x)$. The alternative solution of $\neg R(x)$ (with $R(x)$) and of $\neg P(y,b)$ (with $P(a,z)$) succeeds, so that the subgoal $\neg P(x,b)$ in the top clause is solved with the empty substitution $\emptyset$. The last subgoal $\neg Q(x)$ in the top clause, however, cannot be solved using the clause $Q(a)$ due to the failure substitution $\{x/a\}$ at $\neg R(x)$. This initiates backtracking, and the solution substitution $\emptyset$ at the subgoal $\neg P(x,b)$ is turned into a failure substitution. As a consequence, any alternative solution of this subgoal will be pruned, so that the procedure does not find a closed tableau, although the set of clauses is unsatisfiable. The problem is that the first tableau structure violation encountered has mutated to a failure substitution $\{x/a\}$. The reason for the failure is that the substitution $\{x/a\}$ leading to success (i.e. a regular tableau) is blocked by the previous computation of a *different* tableau that runs into a regularity violation. One possible solution is to simply ignore the fatal failure substitution x/a when the respective node $\neg P(x,b)$ is solved. In a more general sense, this results in the following modification of Definition 4.8.

4.12. DEFINITION (*Generation, application, and deletion of failure substitutions*). Items 1 and 3 are as in Definition 4.8, item 2 has to be replaced as follows.

2. In any alternative solution process *of the subgoal N* below the search node $\mathcal{N}$, if a substitution $\tau = \tau_1 \cdots \tau_m$ is computed such that one of the failure substitutions stored at the node N is more general than τ, then the proof procedure immediately backtracks.

In other terms, the failure substitutions at a subgoal have to be deactivated when the subgoal has been solved. This restricted usage of failure substitutions for search pruning preserves completeness. It would be interesting to investigate which weaker restrictions on failure caching and the structural tableau conditions would still guarantee completeness. With the failure caching procedure described in Definition 4.12 a significant search pruning effect can be achieved, as confirmed by a wealth of experimental results [Letz et al. 1994, Moser et al. 1997].

4.3.1. Comparison with other methods

The *caching* technique proposed in [Astrachan and Stickel 1992] suggests to record the solutions of subgoals independently of the path contexts in which the subgoals appear. Then, cached solutions can be used for solving subgoals by *lookup* instead of *search*. In the special case in which no solutions for a cached subgoal exist, the cache acts in the same manner as the local failure caching mechanism. One difference is that failure substitutions take the path context into account and hence are compatible with subgoal tree regularity whereas the caching technique mentioned above is not. On the other hand, permanently cached subgoals without context have more cases of application than the temporary and context-dependent failure substitutions. The main disadvantage of the context-ignoring caching technique, however, is that its applicability is restricted to the Horn case. Note that the first aspect of the caching technique mentioned, that is replacing search by lookup, cannot be captured with a temporary mechanism as described above, since lookup is mainly effective for *different* subgoals whereas failure substitutions are merely used on different solutions of *one and the same* subgoal.

In [Loveland 1978] a different concept of subsumption was suggested for model elimination chains. Roughly speaking, this concept is based on a proof transformation which permits to ignore certain subgoals if the set of literals at the current subgoals is subsumed by an input clause. Such a replacement is possible, for example, if the remaining subgoals can be solved without reduction steps into their predecessors. In terms of tableaux, Loveland's subsumption *reduces* the current subgoal tree while our approach tries to *prune* it.

5. Shortening of Proofs

The analytic tableau approach has proven successful, both proof-theoretically and in the practice of automated deduction. It is well-known, however, since the work of Gentzen [Gentzen 1935] that the purely analytic paradigm suffers from a fundamental weakness, namely, the poor *deductive power*. That is, for very simple examples, the smallest tableau proofs may be extremely large if compared with proofs in other calculi. In this section, we shall present methods which can remedy this weakness and lead to significantly shorter proofs. The methods we consider are of two different types. First, we describe mechanisms that amount to adding additional inference rules to the tableau calculus. The mechanisms are centered around a controlled integration of the (backward) cut rule. Those mechanisms have the widest application, since they already improve the behaviour of tableaux for propositional logic. Furthermore, we consider an improvement of tableaux which is first-order by its very nature, since it can be effective for tableaux with free variables only. It results from the fact that free variables in tableaux need not necessarily be treated as rigid. This results in a system in which the complexity of proofs can be significantly smaller than the so-called *Herbrand complexity*, which for a given set S of clauses is the complexity of the minimal unsatisfiable set of ground instances of clauses in S (see [Baaz and Leitsch 1992]).

5.1. Factorization

The *factorization* rule was introduced to the model elimination format in [Kowalski and Kuehner 1971] (see also [Loveland 1972]) and used in the connection calculus [Bibel 1987, Chapter III.6], but was applied to depth-first selection functions only due to format restrictions. On the general level of the (connection) tableau calculus, which permits arbitrary node selection functions, the rule can be motivated as follows. Consider a closed tableau containing two nodes N_1 and N_2 with the same literals as labels. Furthermore, suppose that all ancestor nodes of N_2 are also ancestors of N_1. Then, the closed tableau part T below N_2 could have been reused as a solution and attached to N_1, because all expansion and reduction steps performed in T under N_2 are possible in T under N_1, too. This observation leads to the introduction of *factorization* as an additional inference rule. Factorization permits to mark a subgoal N_1 as solved if its literal can be unified with the literal of another node N_2, provided that the set of ancestors of N_2 is a subset of the set of ancestors of N_1; additionally, the respective substitution has to be applied to the tableaux.

5.1. Example. For any set $\{A_1, \ldots, A_n\}$ of distinct propositional atoms, let S_n denote the set of all 2^n clauses of the shape $L_1 \vee \ldots \vee L_n$ where $L_i = A_i$ or $L_i = \neg A_i$, $1 \leq i \leq n$.

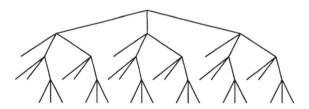

Figure 12: Tree structure of a minimal closed tableau for Example 5.1, $n = 3$.

As illustrated with Figure 12 the standard *cut-free* tableau calculi are intractable for this class of formulae [Letz 1993, Letz et al. 1994]. Used on the set of clauses

$$\{p \vee q, p \vee \neg q, \neg p \vee q, \neg p \vee \neg q\}$$

which denotes an instance of Example 5.1, for $n = 2$, factorization yields a shorter proof, as shown in Figure 13. Factorization steps are indicated by arcs. Obviously, in order to preserve soundness the rule must be constrained to prohibit solution cycles. Thus, in Figure 13 the factorization of subgoal N_4 on the right hand side with the node N_3 with the same literal on the left hand side is not permitted after the first factorization (node N_1 with node N_2) has been performed, because this would involve a reciprocal, and hence unsound, employment of one solution within the other. To avoid the cyclic application of factorization, tableaux have to be supplied with an additional factorization dependency relation.

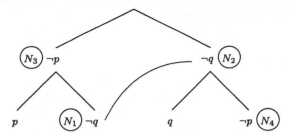

Figure 13: Factorization step in a connection tableau for Example 5.1, $n = 2$.

5.2. DEFINITION *(Factorization dependency relation).* A *factorization dependency relation on a tableau* T is a strict partial ordering $\prec$ on the tableau nodes ($N_1 \prec N_2$ means that the solution of N_2 depends on the solution of N_1).

5.3. DEFINITION *(Tableau factorization).* Given a tableau T and a factorization dependency relation $\prec$ on its nodes. First, select a subgoal N_1 with literal L and another node N_2 labelled with a literal K such that

1. there is a minimal unifier σ: $L\sigma = K\sigma$,
2. N_1 is dominated by a node N which has the node N_2 among its immediate successors, and
3. $N_3 \not\prec N_2$, where N_3 is the brother node of N_2 on the branch from the root down to and including N_1.[7]

Then mark N_1 as closed. Afterwards, modify $\prec$ by first adding the pair of nodes $\langle N_2, N_3 \rangle$ and then forming the transitive closure of the relation; finally, apply the substitution σ to the tableau. We say that the subgoal N_1 has been *factorized with* the node N_2. The tableau construction is started with an empty factorization dependency relation, and all other tableau inference rules leave the factorization dependency relation unchanged.

Applied to the example shown in Figure 13, when the subgoal N_1 is factorized with the node N_2, the pair $\langle N_2, N_3 \rangle$ is added to the previously empty relation $\prec$,

---

[7]Note that N_3 may be N_1 itself.

thus denoting that the solution of the node N_3 depends on the solution of the node N_2. After that, factorization of the subgoal N_4 with the node N_3 is not possible any more.

It is clear that the factorization dependency relation only relates brother nodes, i.e., nodes which have the same immediate predecessor. Furthermore, the applications of factorization at a subgoal N_1 with a node N_2 can be subdivided into two cases. Either, the node N_2 has been solved already, or the node N_2 or some of the nodes dominated by N_2 are not yet solved. In the second case we shall speak of an *optimistic* application of factorization, since the node N_1 is marked as solved *before* it is known whether a solution exists. Conversely, the first case will be called a *pessimistic* application of factorization.

Similar to the case of ordinary (connection) tableaux, if the factorization rule is added, the order in which the tableau rules are applied does not influence the structure of the tableau.

5.4. PROPOSITION (Strong node selection independency of factorization).
Any closed (connection) tableau with factorization for a set of clauses constructed with one selection function can be constructed with any other selection function.

PROOF. See [Letz et al. 1994].   □

Switching from one selection function to another may mean that certain optimistic factorization steps become pessimistic factorization steps and vice versa. If we are working with subgoal trees, i.e., completely remove solved parts of a tableau, as done in the chain format of model elimination, then for all *depth-first* selection functions solely optimistic applications of factorization can occur. Also, the factorization dependency relation may be safely ignored, because the depth-first procedure and the removal of solved nodes render cyclic factorization attempts impossible. It is for this reason, that the integration approaches of factorization into model elimination or into the connection calculus have not mentioned the need for a factorization dependency relation. Note also that if factorization is integrated into the chain format of model elimination, then the mentioned strong node selection independency does not hold, since pessimistic factorization steps cannot be performed.

The addition of the factorization rule permits the generation of significantly smaller (connection) tableaux proofs. Thus, for the critical formula class given in Example 5.1, for which no polynomial tableau proofs exist (see Figure 12), there exist linear closed connection tableaux with factorization, as shown in Figure 14. With the factorization rule connection tableaux linearly simulate truth tables. In fact, the factorization rule can be considered as being a certain restricted version of the *cut rule*, which permits to add two new nodes labelled with arbitrary formulae F and $\neg F$, respectively, to any tableau branch. We speak of an *atomic cut* when F is an atomic formula.

5.5. PROPOSITION. *Atomic cut tableaux can linearly simulate tableaux with fac-*

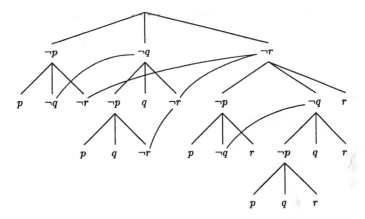

Figure 14: Linear closed connection tableau with factorization for Example 5.1, $n = 3$.

torization, and regular connection atomic cut tableaux can linearly simulate (con-nection) tableaux with factorization.

PROOF. We perform the simulation proof for atomic cut tableaux. Given a closed tableau with factorization, each factorization step of a node N_1 with a node N_2, both labelled with a literal L, can be simulated as follows. First, perform a cut step with $\sim L$ and L at the ancestor N of N_2, producing new nodes N_4 and N_5; thereupon, move the tableau part formerly dominated by N below N_4; then, remove the tableau part underneath N_2 and attach it to N_5; finally, perform reduction steps at N_1 and N_2. The simulation is graphically shown in Figure 15.   □

While it is an open problem whether clausal tableaux with factorization can polynomially simulate atomic cut tableaux, *connection* tableaux with factorization cannot even polynomially simulate pure clausal tableaux (without atomic cut), as will be discussed in the next subsection.

5.2. The Folding Up Rule

The so-called *folding up rule* is an inference rule which, for connection tableaux, is stronger than factorization concerning deductive power. Folding up generalizes the *c-reduction* rule introduced to the model elimination format in [Shostak 1976]. In contrast to factorization, for which the pessimistic and the optimistic application do not differ concerning their deductive power, the shortening of proofs achievable with folding up results from its pessimistic nature. The theoretical basis of the rule is the possibility of extracting *bottom-up lemmata* from solved parts of a tableau, which can be used on other parts of the tableau (as described in [Loveland 1968]

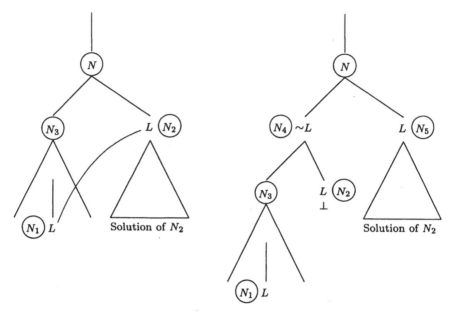

Figure 15: Simulation of factorization by cut rule applications.

and [Letz et al. 1992], or [Astrachan and Loveland 1991]). Folding up represents a particularly efficient realization of this idea.

We explain the rule with an example. Given the tableau displayed on the left of Figure 16, where the arrow points to the node at which the last inference step (a reduction step with the node 3 levels above) has been performed. With this step we have solved the dominating nodes labelled with the literals r and q. In the solutions of those nodes the predecessor labelled with p has been used for a reduction step. Obviously, this amounts to the derivation of two lemmata $\neg r \vee \neg p$ and $\neg q \vee \neg p$ from the underlying formula. The new lemma $\neg q \vee \neg p$ could be added to the underlying set and subsequently used for extension steps (this has already been described in [Letz et al. 1992]). The disadvantage of such an approach is that the new lemmata may be *non-unit* clauses, as in the example, so that extension steps into them would produce new subgoals, together with an unknown additional search space. The redundancy introduced this way can hardly be controlled.

With the folding up rule a different approach is pursued. Instead of adding lemmata of arbitrary lengths, so-called *context unit lemmata* are stored. In the discussed example, we may obtain two context unit lemmata:

$\neg r$, valid in the *(path)* context p, and
$\neg q$, valid in the context p.

Also, the memorization of the lemmata is not done by augmenting the input formula but *within* the tableau itself, namely, by "folding up" a solved node to the edge which dominates its solution context. More precisely, the folding up of a solved

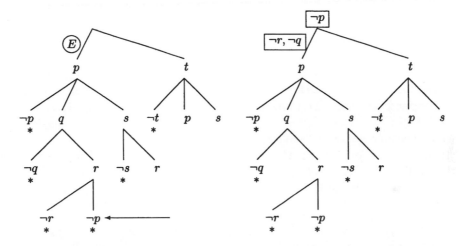

Figure 16: Connection tableau before and after folding up three times.

node N to an edge E means labelling E with the negation of the literal at N. Thus, in the example in Figure 16 the edge E above the p-node on the left-hand side of the tableau is successively labelled with the literals $\neg r$ and $\neg q$, as displayed on the right-hand side of Figure 16; lists of context-unit lemmata are shown as framed boxes. Subsequently, the literals in the boxes at the edges can be used for ordinary reduction steps. So, at the subgoal labelled with r a reduction step can be performed with the edge E, which was not possible before the folding up. After that, the subgoal s could also be folded up to the edge E, which we have not done in the figure, since after solving that subgoal the part below E is completely solved. But now the p-subgoal on the left is solved, and we can fold it up above the root of the tableau; since there is no edge above the root, we simply fold up *into* the root. This folding up step facilitates that the p-subgoal on the right can be solved by a reduction step.

The gist of the folding up rule is that only *unit* lemmata are added, so that the additionally imported indeterminism is not too large. Over and above that, the technique gives rise to a new form of pruning mechanism called *strong regularity*, which is discussed below. Furthermore, the folding up operation can be implemented very efficiently, since no renaming of variables is needed, as in a full lemma mechanism.

In order to be able to formally introduce the inference rule, we have to slightly generalize the notion of tableaux.

5.6. DEFINITION *((Marked) edge-labelled tableau)*. A *(marked) edge-labelled tableau (E-tableau)* is just a tableau as introduced in the Definitions 2.1 and 2.5 with the only modifications that also the edges and the root node are labelled by the labelling function λ, namely, with lists of literals. Additionally, in every extension and reduction step, the closed branch is *marked* with the respectively used ancestor literal. The *path set* of a non-root node N in an E-tableau is the union of the sets of literals at the nodes dominating N and in the lists at the root and at the edges dominating the immediate predecessor of N.

5.7. DEFINITION *(E-tableau folding up)*. Let T be an E-tableau, N a non-leaf node with literal L and the subtree below N be closed. The insertion position of the literal $\sim L$ is computed as follows. From the markings of all branches dominated by N select the set M of nodes which dominate N (M contains exactly the predecessor nodes on which the solution of N depends).

1. If M is empty or contains the root node only, then add the literal $\sim L$ to the list of literals at the root.
2. Otherwise, let N' be the deepest path node in M. Add the literal $\sim L$ to the list of literals at the edge immediately above N'.[8]

As an illustration, consider Figure 16, and recall the situation when the 'q'-node N on the left has been solved completely. The markings of the branches dominated by N are the 'r'-node below N and the 'p'-node above N. Consequently, $\neg q$ is added to the list at the edge E.

Additionally, the reduction rule has to be extended, as follows.

5.8. DEFINITION *(E-tableau reduction)*. Given a marked E-tableau T, select a subgoal N with literal L, then,

1. either select a dominating node N' with literal $\sim K$ and a minimal unifier σ for L and K, and mark the branch with N',
2. or select a dominating edge or the root E with $\sim K$ in $\lambda(E)$ and a minimal unifier σ for L and K; then mark the branch with the node immediately below the edge or with the root, respectively.

Finally, apply the substitution σ to the literals in the tableau.

The *tableau* and the *connection tableau calculus with folding up* result from the ordinary versions by working with edge-labelled tableaux, adding the folding up rule, substituting the old reduction rule by the new one, starting with a root labelled with the empty list, and additionally labelling all newly generated edges with the empty list. Subsequently, we will drop the prefix 'E-' and simply speak of 'tableaux'.

The soundness of the folding up operation is expressed in the following proposition.

5.9. PROPOSITION (Soundness of folding up). *Let N be any subgoal with literal L in a marked tableau T, P the path set of N, and S a set of clauses. Suppose T' is any tableau deduced from T incorporating folding up steps and employing only clauses from S in the intermediate extension steps. Then, for the new path set P' of N in T': $P \cup S$ logically implies P'.*

---

[8]The position of the inserted literal exactly corresponds to the *C-point* in the terminology used in [Shostak 1976].

PROOF. The proof is by induction on the number n of folding up steps between T and T'. The base case for $n = 0$ is trivial, since $P' = P$. For the induction step, let $P' = P^n$ be the path set of N after the n-th folding up step inserting a literal, say L', into the path above N. This step was the consequence of solving a literal $\sim L'$ with clauses from S and path assumptions from P^{n-1}, i.e., the path set of N before the n-th folding up step. This means that $P^{n-1} \cup S \cup \{\sim L'\}$ is unsatisfiable. Now, by the induction assumption, $P \cup S \models P^{n-1}$. Consequently, $P \cup S \models P^{n-1} \cup \{L'\} = P'$. $\square$

It is obvious that if a depth-first selection function is used and N is not yet solved in T', then all clauses in S are tableau clauses dominated by N or a brother node of N. This knowledge is used in the proof of Theorem 6.11 below.

In [Letz et al. 1994], it is proven that, for connection tableaux, the folding up rule is properly stronger concerning its deductive power than the factorization rule. In fact, the formula class used in this proof can also be used to show that connection tableaux with factorization cannot even polynomially simulate the pure clausal tableau calculus (without the atomic cut rule).

5.10. PROPOSITION. *Connection tableaux with factorization cannot polynomially simulate connection tableaux with folding up.*

PROOF. See [Letz et al. 1994]. $\square$

Conversely, for a certain class of selection functions, the polynomial simulation in the other direction is possible.

5.11. PROPOSITION. *For arbitrary depth-first selection functions, (connection) tableaux with folding up linearly simulate (connection) tableaux with factorization.*

PROOF. Given any closed (connection) tableau T with factorization, let $\prec$ be its factorization dependency relation. By the strong node selection independency of factorization (Proposition 5.4), T can be constructed with any selection function. We consider a construction $C = (T_0, \ldots, T_m, T)$ of T with a depth-first selection function ϕ which respects the partial order of the factorization dependency relation $\prec$, i.e., for any two nodes N_1, N_2 in the tableau, $N_1 \prec N_2$ means that N_1 is selected before N_2; such a selection function exists since $\prec$ solely relates brother nodes. The deduction process C can directly be simulated by the (connection) tableau calculus with folding up, as follows. Using the same selection function ϕ, any expansion (extension) and reduction step in C is simulated by an expansion (extension) and reduction step. But, whenever a subgoal has been completely solved in the simulation, it is folded up. Since in the original deduction process, due to the pessimistic application of factorization, the factorization of a node N_2 with a node N_1 (with literal L) involves that N_1 has been solved before, in the simulation the literal L must have been folded up before. Now, *any* solved node can be folded up at least one step, namely, to the edge E above its predecessor (or into the root). Since E

(or the root) dominates N_1, the original factorization step can be simulated by a reduction step. The simulation of factorization by folding up is graphically shown in Figure 17.   □

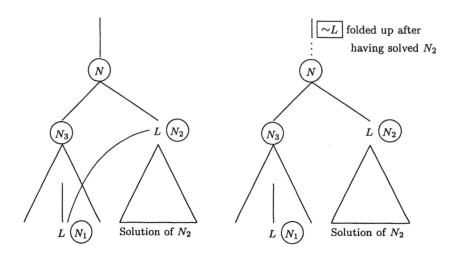

Figure 17: Simulation of factorization by folding up.

Finally, we show that the folding up rule, though properly more powerful than factorization, is still a hidden version of the cut rule.

5.12. PROPOSITION. *Atomic cut tableaux and atomic cut regular connection tableaux linearly simulate (connection) tableaux with folding up.*

PROOF. We perform the simulation proof for atomic cut tableaux. Given a tableau derivation with folding up, each folding up operation at a node N_0 adding the negation $\sim L$ of the literal L at a solved node to the label of an edge above a node N (or to the root), can be simulated as follows. Perform a cut step at the node N with the atom of L as the cut formula, producing two new nodes N_1 and N_2 labelled with L and $\sim L$, respectively; shift the solution of L from N_0 below the node N_1 and the part of the tableau previously dominated by N below its new successor node N_2; finally, perform a reduction step at the node N_0. It is obvious that the unmarked branches of both tableaux can be injectively mapped to each other such that all pairs of corresponding branches contain the same leaf literals and the same sets of path literals, respectively. The simulation is graphically shown in Figure 18. □

Connection tableaux with folding up can linearly simulate atomic cut tableaux. This is a straightforward corollary of a result proven in [Mayr 1993].

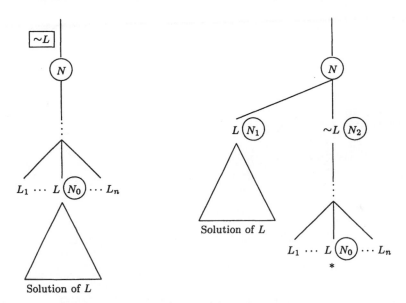

Figure 18: Simulation of folding up by the cut rule.

5.3. The Folding Down Rule

The simulation of factorization by folding up also shows how a restriction of the folding up rule can be defined which permits an *optimistic* labelling of edges. If a strict linear (dependency) ordering is defined on the successor nodes $N_1, \ldots, N_m$ of any node, then it is permitted to label the edge leading to any node N_i, $1 \le i \le m$, with the set of the negations of the literals at all nodes which are smaller than N_i in the ordering. We call this operation the *folding down* rule. The folding down operation can also be applied incrementally, as the ordering is completed to a linear one. The folding down rule is sound, since it can be simulated by the cut rule plus reduction steps, as illustrated in Figure 19. The rule is a very simple and efficient way of *implementing* factorization. Over and above that, if the literals on the edges are also considered as path literals in the regularity test, an additional search space reduction can be achieved this way which is discussed in the next section. It should be noted that it is very difficult to identify this refinement in the factorization framework. There, it is normally formulated in a restricted version, namely, as the condition that the set of literals at the *subgoals* of a tableau need to be consistent.

5.13. PROPOSITION. *(Regular) (connection) tableaux with folding down and (regular) (connection) tableaux with factorization linearly simulate each other.*

PROOF. See [Letz et al. 1994]. □

5.14. REMARK. Folding down is essentially *Prawitz reduction* [Prawitz 1960].

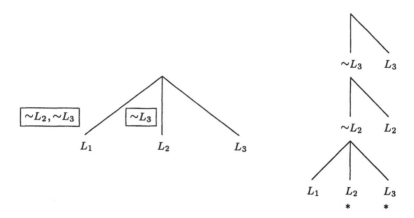

Figure 19: Simulation of folding down by cut.

Hence, by the above proposition, Prawitz reduction and factorization have the same deductive power when added to the connection tableau calculus, and Prawitz reduction is properly weaker than folding up and atomic cut.

5.4. Universal and Local Variables

The improvement of the tableau rules that we investigate in this part is of a quantificational nature. It deals with the problem that normally free variables in tableaux are considered as rigid, i.e., each as a place holder for an unknown ground term. Accordingly, every occurrence of a literal in a tableau can be used in one instance only. The simple reason is that tableau branches are disjunctively connected and the universal quantifier does not distribute over disjunctions. Under certain circumstances, however, such a distribution is possible and the respective variables may be read as universally quantified on the branch. The formulae containing such variables can then be used in different instances concerning the universal variables contained, which can permit a significant shortening of proofs. A very general definition of so-called *universal variables* is formulated in [Beckert and Hähnle 1992, Beckert 1998, Beckert and Hähnle 1998] as well as in [Hähnle 2001] (Chapter 3 of this Handbook). In its final reading, a variable x in a formula F on a branch of a general free-variable tableau T is *universal* if the formula $\forall x F$ may be added to the tableau branch and the formula of the resulting tableau is logically implied by the formula of T.

5.4.1. Local variables

Obviously, this definition is too general to be of any practical use, since this property of a variable is undecidable. One simple sufficient condition for being universal which applies to the case of clauses is that a variable occurs in only one literal of a clause. For connection tableaux, a proof shortening effect can only be achieved this way if this occurs in non-unit clauses, since unit clauses can be freely used in new instances without producing new open branches. Unfortunately, such non-unit clauses do rarely occur in practice. Consequently, in [Letz 1998a, Letz 1999], the notion of local variables has been developed, which has more applications in connection tableaux.

5.15. DEFINITION *(Local variable)*. Given an open tableau branch B of a clausal tableau, if a variable x occurs on B and on no other open branch of the tableau, then x is called *local (to B)*.

Obviously, every local variable is universal. How can this property of a variable be utilized in detail? If a variable x in a formula F is universal, then the formula $\forall x F$ could be added to the branch without affecting the soundness of the calculus. As a matter of fact, this *generalization rule* is merely of a theoretical interest. Since we are only interested in calculi performing atomic branch closure, it is clear that the new formulae have to be decomposed by the γ-rule of free-variable tableaux, thus producing a variant of the formula F in which the variable x is renamed. And, since in connection tableaux instantiations are only performed in inference steps closing a branch, one can perform the generalization implicitly, exactly at that moment. This naturally leads to a generalized version of the unification rule.

5.16. DEFINITION *(Local unification rule)*. Let K and L with universal variables $x_1, \ldots, x_n$ and $y_1, \ldots, y_n$ respectively be two literals to be unified in an inference step in a tableau T. Obtain K' by replacing all occurrences of $x_1, \ldots, x_n$ in K with distinct new variables not occurring in T; *afterwards* obtain L' by doing the same for L (i.e., perform no simultaneous replacement in K *and* L). If there is a (minimal) unifier for K' and L', apply σ to the tableau and close the respective branch.[9] If the set of universal variables is determined by the locality condition, we speak of the *local unification rule*.

The *local extension rule* and the *local reduction rule* are obtained from the standard rules by replacing standard unification with local unification.

The proof shortening effect of the local closure rule can be demonstrated by considering the set of the two clauses $R(x) \vee R(f(x))$ and $\neg R(x) \vee \neg R(f(f(x)))$, and the closed tableau shown in Figure 1. With the local unification rule one can obtain the significantly smaller closed tableau displayed in Figure 20. Assume the tableau construction is performed using a left-most branch selection function. The crucial difference occurs when the entire left subtree has been closed and the right-most subgoal $\neg R(f(f(f(x))))$ is extended using the first input clause with the first literal as entry literal. Since the variable x in the subgoal is local, it is renamed to, say y, which eventually leads to attachment of the tableau clause $R(f(f(f(y))))$

---

[9]Note that this rule is more powerful than the extension of unification defined in [Beckert and Hähnle 1998]. For example, a branch containing two formulae $P(x)$ and $\neg P(f(x))$ with universal variable x may be closed.

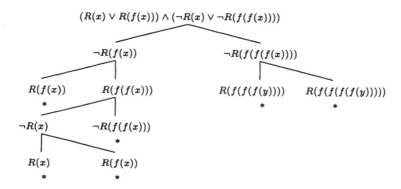

Figure 20: Closed clausal tableau with local unification rule.

and $R(f(f(f(f(y)))))$ and the closure of the left-most new branch. The remaining subgoal $R(f(f(f(f(y)))))$ can then be closed by a (local) reduction step.

Note that the tableau displayed in Figure 20 has no closed ground instance, in contrast to the tableau calculi developed so far that have the *ground projection property* [Baaz and Leitsch 1992], i.e., when substituting ground terms for the variables in a tableau proof for a set of clauses S, the resulting tableau remains closed and all tableau clauses are instances of clauses in S. The modified tableau system with the local unification rule permits to build refutations that are smaller than the so-called Herbrand complexity of the input, which normally is a lower bound to any standard tableau proof; the *Herbrand complexity* of an unsatisfiable set of clauses S is the complexity of the smallest unsatisfiable set of ground instances of clauses in S. It is evident, however, that tableau calculi containing the local unification rule are not independent of the branch selection function. If we would select the subgoals on the right before complete closure of the left subtree, x would not be local and hence the proof shortening effect would be blocked. Consequently, with the local unification rule, the order in which branches are selected can influence the size of minimal tableau proofs. Note that the same holds for the folding up rule discussed in Section 5.2.

6. Completeness of Connection Tableaux

In this section we will provide completeness proofs for the most important of the new calculi.

6.1. Structurally Refined Connection Tableaux

First, we consider the case of connection tableaux with the structural refinements of regularity, strong connectedness, and the use of relevance information, which were mentioned in Section 3. Since the path connectedness condition is less restrictive, it suffices to consider the full connectedness condition. Unfortunately, we cannot proceed as in the case of free-variable tableaux or general clausal tableaux. Since the connection tableau calculus lacks proof confluence, the standard completeness proof using Hintikka sets cannot be applied. Instead, an entirely different approach for proving completeness will be used. The proof consists of two parts. In the first part, we demonstrate the completeness for the case of ground formulae—this is the interesting part of the proof. In the second part, this result is lifted to the first-order case by a standard proof technique. Beforehand, we need some additional terminology.

6.1. DEFINITION *(Strengthening)*. The *strengthening* of a set of clauses S *by* a set of literals $P = \{L_1, \ldots, L_n\}$, written $P \rhd S$, is the set of clauses obtained by first removing all clauses from S containing literals from P and afterwards adding the n unit clauses $L_1, \ldots, L_n$.

6.2. EXAMPLE. For the set of propositional clauses $S = \{p \vee q, p \vee s, \neg p \vee q, \neg q\}$, the strengthening $\{p\} \rhd S$ is the set of clauses $\{p, \neg p \vee q, \neg q\}$.

Clearly, every strengthening of an unsatisfiable set of clauses is unsatisfiable. In the ground completeness proof, we will make use of the following further property.[10]

6.3. LEMMA (Strong Mate Lemma). *Let S be an unsatisfiable set of ground clauses. For any literal L contained in any relevant clause c in S there exists a clause c' in S such that*

(i) c' contains $\sim L$,

(ii) every literal in c' different from $\sim L$ does not occur complemented in c, and

(iii) c' is relevant in the strengthening $\{L\} \rhd S$.

PROOF. From the relevance of c follows that S has a minimally unsatisfiable subset S_0 containing c; every formula in S_0 is essential in S_0. Hence, there is an interpretation $\mathcal{I}$ for S_0 with $\mathcal{I}(S_0 \setminus \{c\}) = \text{true}$ and $\mathcal{I}(c) = \text{false}$, hence $\mathcal{I}(L) = \text{false}$. Define another interpretation $\mathcal{I}'$ by setting $\mathcal{I}'(L) = \text{true}$ and otherwise $\mathcal{I}' = \mathcal{I}$. Then $\mathcal{I}'(c) = \text{true}$. The unsatisfiability of S_0 guarantees the existence of a clause c' in S_0 with $\mathcal{I}'(c') = \text{false}$. We prove that c' meets the conditions (i) – (iii). First, the clause c' must contain the literal $\sim L$ and not the literal L, since otherwise $\mathcal{I}(c') = \text{false}$, which contradicts the selection of $\mathcal{I}$, hence (i). Additionally, for any literal L' in c' different from $\sim L$: $\mathcal{I}(L') = \mathcal{I}'(L') = \text{false}$. As a consequence, L' cannot occur complemented in c, since otherwise $\mathfrak{I}(c) = \text{true}$; this proves (ii). Finally, the essentiality of c' in S_0 entails that there exists an interpretation $\mathcal{I}''$ with $\mathcal{I}''(S_0 \setminus \{c'\}) = \text{true}$ and $\mathcal{I}''(c') = \text{false}$. Since $\sim L$ is in c', $\mathcal{I}''(L) = \text{true}$. Therefore, c' is essential in $S_0 \cup \{L\}$, and also in its unsatisfiable subset $\{L\} \rhd S_0$. From this conclusion and

---

[10]In terms of resolution, it expresses the fact that, for any literal L in a clause c that is relevant in a clause set S, there exists a non-tautological resolvent "over" L with another relevant clause in S.

from the fact that $\{L\} \triangleright S_0$ is a subset of $\{L\} \triangleright S$ follows that c' is relevant in $\{L\} \triangleright S$. □

6.4. PROPOSITION (Ground completeness of regular strong connection tableaux). *For any finite unsatisfiable set S of ground clauses and for any clause c which is relevant in S, there exists a closed regular strong connection tableau for S with top clause c.*

PROOF. Let S be a finite unsatisfiable set of ground clauses and c any relevant clause in S. A closed regular strong connection tableau T for S with top clause c can be constructed from the root to its leaves via a sequence of intermediate tableaux as follows. Start with a tableau consisting simply of c as the top clause. Then iterate the following non-deterministic procedure, as long as the intermediate tableau is not yet closed.

> Choose an arbitrary open leaf node N in the current tableau with literal L. Let c be the tableau clause of N and let $P = \{L_1, \ldots, L_m, L\}$, $m \geq 0$, be the set of literals on the path from the root up to the node N. Then, select any clause c' which is relevant in $P \triangleright S$, contains $\sim L$, is strongly connected to c, and does not contain literals from the path $\{L_1, \ldots, L_m, L\}$; perform an expansion step with c' at the node N.

First, note that, evidently, the procedure admits solely the construction of regular strong connection tableaux, since in any expansion step the attached clause contains the literal $\sim L$, no literals from the path to its parent node (regularity), nor does c' contain a literal different from $\sim L$ which occurs complemented in c. Due to regularity, there can be only branches of finite length. Consequently, the procedure must terminate, either because every leaf is closed, or because no clause c' exists for expansion which meets the conditions stated in the procedure. We prove that the second alternative does never occur, since for any *open* leaf node N with literal L there exists such a clause c'. This will be demonstrated by induction on the node depth. The induction base, $n = 1$, is evident, by the Strong Mate Lemma (6.3). For the step from n to $n + 1$, with $n \geq 1$, let N be an open leaf node of tableau depth $n + 1$ with literal L, tableau clause c, and with a path set $P \cup \{L\}$ such that c is relevant in $P \triangleright S$, the induction assumption. Let S_0 be any minimally unsatisfiable subset of $P \triangleright S$ containing c, which exists by the induction assumption. Then, by the Strong Mate Lemma, S_0 contains a clause c' which is strongly connected to c and contains $\sim L$. Since no literal in $P' = P \cup \{L\}$ is contained in a non-unit clause of $P' \triangleright S$ and because N was assumed to be open, no literal in P' is contained in c' (regularity). Finally, since S_0 is minimally unsatisfiable, c' is essential in S_0; therefore, c' is relevant in $P' \triangleright S$. □

The second half of the completeness proof uses a standard lifting argument.

6.5. LEMMA (Lifting Lemma). *Let S and S' be two sets of clauses such that every clause in S' is an instance of a clause in S. Let furthermore $T'_0, \ldots, T'_n$ be any sequence of successive (regular) (path) (connection) tableaux for S'. Then there* *exists a sequence $T_0, \ldots, T_n$ of successive (regular) (path) (connection) tableaux for the set S such that T'_n is an instance of T_n, i.e., $T'_n = T_n\sigma$, for some substitution σ, and, for every branch B' in T'_n, B' is closed if and only if its corresponding branch B in T_n is closed.*

PROOF. The proof is straightforward by induction on the length of the construction sequence. The induction base, $n = 1$, is trivial. For the induction step, let T'_{n+1} be obtained from T'_n by applying on a branch B' with subgoal N' either (1) a closure step or (2) an expansion or (3) a (path) extension step using a clause from S' with matrix c'. Now let B with subgoal N be the branch in T_n corresponding to B'. In case (1), N' must have a complementary ancestor node. Select one, say N'_a, and let N_a be its corresponding node in T_n. Since, by the induction assumption, T'_n is an instance of T_n, there exists a (minimal) unifier τ for the literal at N and the complement of the literal at N_a. Obtain T_{n+1} by applying τ to T_n and closing B. In case (2), select a clause c from S such that $c\tau = c'$, for some substitution τ (such a clause exists by assumption) and obtain T_{n+1} by performing an expansion step using c at B. Case (3) is just a combination of (2) and (1), because a (path) extension step is an expansion step followed by a certain closure step. In all cases, the same branches are closed in both tableaux and T'_{n+1} is an instance of T_{n+1}. Therefore regularity is preserved, since any tableau which has a regular instance must also be regular. $\square$

6.6. THEOREM. *For any unsatisfiable set S of clauses, there exists a closed regular connection tableau.*

PROOF. First, by Herbrand's completeness theorem, there exists a finite unsatisfiable set S' of ground instances of clauses in S. Let T' be a closed regular ground connection tableau for S' which exists by Proposition 6.4. The Lifting Lemma then guarantees the existence of a closed regular connection tableau T' for S. $\square$

6.2. Enforced Folding and Strong Regularity

The folding up operation has been introduced as an ordinary inference rule which, according to its indeterministic nature, may or may not be applied. Alternatively, we could have defined versions of the (connection) tableau calculi with folding up in which any solved node *must* be folded up immediately after it has been solved. It is clear that whether folding up is performed freely, as an ordinary inference rule, or in an enforced manner, the resulting calculi are not different concerning their deductive power, since the folding up operation is a monotonic operation which does *not decrease* the inference possibilities. But the calculi differ with respect to their search spaces, since by treating the folding up rule just as an ordinary inference rule, which may or may not be applied, an additional and absolutely useless form of indeterminism is imported. Consequently, the folding up rule should not be introduced as an additional inference rule, but as a tableau operation to be performed immediately after the solution of a subgoal. The resulting calculi will be called the *(connection) tableau calculi with enforced folding up*.

The superiority of the enforced folding up versions over the unforced ones also holds if the regularity restriction is added, according to which no two *nodes* on a branch can have the same literal as label. But the manner in which the folding up and the folding down rules have been introduced raises the question whether the regularity condition might be sharpened and extended to the literals in the labels of the edges as well. It is clear that such an extension of regularity is not compatible with folding up, since any folding up operation causes the respective closed branch to immediately violate the extended regularity condition. A straightforward remedy is to apply the extended condition to the *subgoal trees* of tableaux only.

6.7. DEFINITION *(Strong regularity)*. A tableau T is called *strongly regular* if it is regular and no literal at a subgoal N of T is contained in the path set of N.

When the strong regularity condition is imposed on the connection tableau calculus with enforced folding up, then a completely new calculus is generated which is no extension of the regular connection tableau calculus, that is, not every proof in the regular connection tableau calculus can be directly simulated by the new calculus. This is because after the application of a folding up operation certain inference steps previously possible for other subgoals may then become impossible. A folding up step may even lead to an immediate failure of the extended regularity test, as demonstrated below. Since the new calculus is no extension of the regular connection tableau calculus and therefore the completeness result for regular connection tableaux cannot be applied, its completeness is not to be taken for granted. In fact, the new calculus is *incomplete* for some selection functions.

6.8. PROPOSITION. *There is an unsatisfiable set S of ground clauses and a selection function ϕ such that there is no refutation for S in the strongly regular connection tableau calculus with enforced folding up.*

6.9. EXAMPLE. The set S consisting of the clauses

$$\neg p \vee \neg s \vee \neg r, \qquad p \vee s \vee r, \qquad \neg q \vee r, \qquad q \vee \neg r,$$
$$\neg p \vee t \vee u, \qquad p \vee \neg t \vee \neg u, \qquad \neg q \vee s, \qquad q \vee \neg s,$$
$$\neg q \vee t, \qquad q \vee \neg t,$$
$$\neg q \vee u, \qquad q \vee \neg u.$$

PROOF. Let S be the set of clauses given in Example 6.9, which is minimally unsatisfiable. The non-existence of a refutation with the top clause $p \vee s \vee r$ for a certain unfortunate selection function ϕ is illustrated in Figure 21. There, the tableau extension steps are shown using black lines while the grey lines indicate the different alternatives for such extensions. If ϕ selects the s-node, then two alternatives exist for extension. For the one on the left-hand side, if ϕ shifts to the p-subgoal above and completely solves it in a depth-first manner, then the enforced folding up of the p-subgoal immediately violates the strong regularity, indicated with a '⸁' below the responsible $\neg p$-subgoal on the left. Therefore, only the second alternative on the right-hand side may lead to a successful refutation. Following the figure, it can easily be verified that for any refutation attempt there is a selection possibility which either leads to extension steps which immediately violate the old regularity condition or produce subgoals labelled with $\neg p$ or $\neg r$. In those cases, the selection function always shifts to the respective p- or r-subgoal in the top clause, solves it completely and folds it up afterwards, this way violating the strong regularity. Consequently, for such a selection function, there is no refutation with the given top clause. The same situation holds for any other top clause selected from the set. This can be verified in a straightforward though tedious manner. □

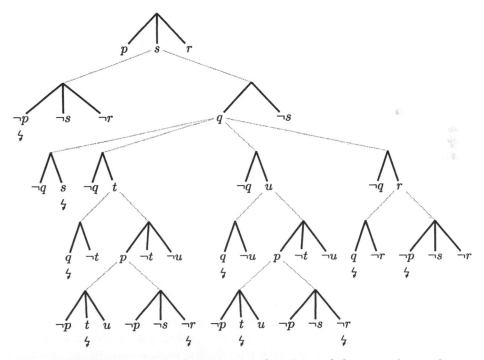

Figure 21: Incompleteness for free selection functions of the strongly regular connection tableau calculus with enforced folding up.

This result demonstrates that there is a trade-off between optimal selection functions and structural restrictions on tableaux. It would be interesting to investigate under which weakenings of the strong regularity the completeness for arbitrary selection functions might be obtained.

If we restrict ourselves to depth-first selection functions, however, the calculus is complete, as shown next.

We are now going to present completeness proofs for two calculi, for strongly regular connection tableaux with enforced folding up using depth-first selection functions and for strongly regular connection tableaux with enforced folding down using arbitrary selection functions. The completeness proofs are based on the following non-deterministic procedure for generating connection tableaux which is similar to the one used in the proof of proposition 6.4 However, in the following procedure a mapping α is carried along as an additional control structure which, upon selection of a subgoal N, associates with N a specific subset $\alpha(N)$ of the input clauses.

6.10. PROCEDURE. Let S_0 be a finite unsatisfiable set of ground clauses, c_0 any clause which is relevant in S_0, and ϕ any subgoal selection function. First, perform a start step with the clause c_0 at the root N_0 of a one-node tableau, select a subset S of S_0 with c_0 being essential in S, and set $\alpha(N_0) = S$. Then, as long as applicable, iterate the following procedure.

> Let N be the subgoal selected by ϕ, P the path set of N, L the literal and c the tableau clause at N, and $S = \alpha(N')$ where N' is the immediate predecessor node of N.
> If $\sim L \in P$, perform a reduction step at N.
> Otherwise, perform an extension step at N with a clause c' in S such that c' is relevant in $(P \cup \{L\}) \triangleright S$, select a subset S' of S with c' being essential in the set $(P \cup \{L\}) \triangleright S'$, and set $\alpha(N) = S'$.
> Additionally, depending on the chosen extension of the calculus, enforced folding up or folding down operations need to be applied.

It suffices to perform the completeness proofs for the ground case, since the lifting to the first-order case is straightforward, using the Lifting Lemma (6.5).

6.11. THEOREM (Completeness for enforced folding up). *For any finite unsatisfiable set S_0 of ground clauses, any depth-first subgoal selection function, and any clause c_0 which is relevant in S_0, there exists a refutation of S_0 with top clause c_0 in the strongly regular connection tableau calculus with enforced folding up.*

PROOF. Let S_0 be a finite unsatisfiable set of ground clauses, c_0 any relevant clause in S_0, and ϕ any depth-first subgoal selection function. We demonstrate that *any* deterministic execution of Procedure 6.10 including enforced folding up operations leads to a refutation in which only strongly regular connection tableaux are constructed. We start with a tableau consisting simply of c_0 as the top clause, and let α map the root to any subset S of S_0 in which c_0 is essential. Then we prove by induction on the number of inference steps needed for deriving a tableau that
  (i) any generated tableau T is strongly regular, and
  (ii) an inference step can be performed at the subgoal $\phi(T)$ according to Procedure 6.10.
The induction base, $n=0$, is evident. For the induction step, let T be a tableau generated with $n > 0$ inference steps, $N = \phi(T)$ with literal L and path set P, c the tableau clause at N, N' the immediate predecessor of N, and $\alpha(N') = S$. Two cases have to be distinguished.

Case 1. Either, the last node selected before N was N'. In this case, by the induction assumption and the fact that Procedure 6.10 only permits extension (or start) steps with clauses not containing literals from the path set P, it is guaranteed that T is strongly regular, hence (i). By the induction assumption, c is essential in $P \triangleright S$. Consequently, due to the Strong Mate Lemma, an inference step according to the procedure can be performed at N, therefore (ii).

Case 2. Or, the last inference step before the selection of N completely solved a brother node of N. In this case, after having entered the clause c, additional literals may have been inserted by intermediate folding up operations. We show that the resulting tableau is still strongly regular. For this purpose let N_i be an arbitrary subgoal in T, L_i the literal and c_i the clause at N_i, P_i its (extended) path set in T, and N_i' the immediate predecessor of N_i. With S_i we denote the clause set $\alpha(N_i')$. Furthermore, let $T^\star$ be the former tableau resulting from the extension step at N' into the clause c, and $P_i^\star$ the path set of N_i in $T^\star$. By the induction assumption, L_i is not contained in $P_i^\star$. According to Procedure 6.10, in the solutions of brother nodes of N_i only clauses from the set $S_i \setminus \{c_i\}$ are permitted for extension steps. Due to the depth-first selection function, the solution process of brother nodes of N is a subprocess of the solution process of brother nodes of N_i. Therefore, by the soundness of the folding up rule (Proposition 5.9), the set of literals K_i inserted into $P_i^\star$ during the derivation of T from $T^\star$ is logically implied by the satisfiable set $A_i = (P_i^\star \cup S_i) \setminus \{c_i\}$. Since, by the induction assumption, $A_i \cup \{c_i\}$ is unsatisfiable, $A_i \cup \{L_i\}$ is also unsatisfiable. Consequently, $L_i \notin K_i$, and hence $L_i \notin P_i$. Since this holds for all subgoals of T, T must be strongly regular, which proves (i). Furthermore, all c_i remain essential in the sets $P_i \cup S_i$. Therefore, by the Strong Mate Lemma, at the subgoal N in T an inference step according to Procedure 6.10 can be performed, hence (ii).

Now we have proven that the procedure produces only strongly regular connection tableaux and whenever the procedure terminates, it must terminate with a closed tableau. Finally, the termination of the procedure follows from the fact that, for any finite set of ground clauses, only strongly regular tableaux of finite depth exist. $\square$

6.12. THEOREM (Completeness for enforced folding down). *For any finite unsatisfiable set S_0 of ground clauses, any subgoal selection function, and any clause c_0 which is relevant in S_0, there exists a refutation of S_0 with top clause c_0 in the strongly regular connection tableau calculus with enforced folding down.*

PROOF. The structure of the proof is the same as the one for folding up, viz., by induction on the number of inference steps it has to be shown that properties (i) and (ii) from the proof of Theorem 6.11 apply. Therefore, only the induction step is carried out. Suppose a subgoal N is selected with literal L, tableau clause c, path set P, and $\alpha(N') = S$ for the immediate predecessor N' of N. The enforced folding down operation inserts the negations of the literals at the unsolved brother nodes of N into the edge leading to N *before* the subgoal N is solved. First, we prove that such steps always preserve the strong regularity condition. Clearly, folding down operations can only violate this condition for tautological tableau clauses. Since no tautological clause can be relevant in a set and Procedure 6.10 only permits the use of relevant clauses, no tautological clause can occur in a generated tableau, hence (i). It remains to be shown that any selected subgoal can be extended in accordance with Procedure 6.10. By the induction assumption, c is essential in $P \triangleright S$. Hence, there is an interpretation $\mathcal{I}$ with $\mathcal{I}(c) =$ false and $\mathcal{I}((P \triangleright S) \setminus \{c\}) =$ true. We prove that any folding down operation preserves the essentiality of the clause c. Let $P' = \{\sim K_1, \ldots, \sim K_n\}$ be the set of literals inserted above N in a folding down operation on the literals $K_1, \ldots, K_n$ at the other subgoals in c. Clearly, $\mathcal{I}(\sim K_i) =$ true, for all literals in P'. Therefore, c is essential in $P' \cup (P \triangleright S)$ and hence also in its unsatisfiable subset $(P' \cup P) \triangleright S$. Therefore (ii) also applies. $\qquad \square$

7. Architectures of Model Elimination Implementations

All competitive implementations of model elimination are iterative-deepening search procedures using backtracking. When envisaging the implementation of such a procedure, one has the choice between fundamentally different architectures, for reasons we will now explain. As indicated at the end of Section 2.7.1, it is straightforward to recognize that SLD-resolution (the inference system underlying Prolog) can be considered as a refinement of model elimination obtained by simply omitting the reduction inference rule. Since highly efficient implementation techniques for Prolog have been developed, one can profit from these efforts and design a *Prolog Technology Theorem Prover (PTTP)*. The crucial characteristic of Prolog technology is that input clauses are *compiled* into procedures of a virtual or actual machine which permits a very efficient execution of the extension operation. There are even two different approaches taking advantage of Prolog technology. On the one hand, one can build on some of the efficient implementation techniques of Prolog and add the ingredients needed for a sound and complete model elimination proof procedure. On the other hand, one can use Prolog itself as implementation language with the hope that its proximity to model elimination permits a short and efficient implementation of a model elimination proof search procedure. The PTTP approaches, both of which will be described in this section, have dominated the implementations of model elimination in the last years. The use of Prolog technology, however, has a severe disadvantage, namely, that the framework is not flexible enough for an easy integration of new techniques and new inference rules. This inflexibility has almost blocked the implementations of certain important extensions of model elimination, in particular, the integration of inference mechanisms for an efficient equality handling. Therefore, we also present a more natural and modular implementation architecture for model elimination, which is better suited for various extensions of the calculus. Although this approach cannot compete with the PTTP approaches concerning the efficiency by which new instances of input clauses are generated, this drawback can be compensated for by an intelligent mechanism of reusing clause copies, so that about the same high rates of inferences per seconds can be achieved for the typical problems occurring in automated deduction.

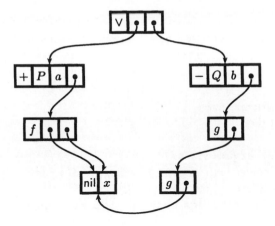

Figure 22: Internal representation of the clause $P(a, f(x, x)) \vee \neg Q(b, g(g(x)))$.

7.1. Basic Data Structures and Operations

When analyzing the actual implementations of model elimination, one can identify some data structures and operations that are more or less common to all successful approaches and hence form some kind of a standard framework. The first subject is the way formulae are represented internally in order to permit efficient operations on them. It has turned out that all terms, literals, and clauses may be represented in a natural tree manner except variables, which should be shared. In Figure 22, such a standard representation of a clause is illustrated. The treatment of variables needs some further explanation. Internally, variables are typically represented as structures consisting of their actual bindings and their print names with nil indicating that the variable is currently free. Variables are not identified and distinguished by their print names but by the addresses of their structures.

7.1.1. Unification

The next basic ingredient is the unification algorithm employed, which is specified generically in Table 2. In the displayed procedures, it is left open how variable bindings are performed and retracted. Unification is specified with two mutually recursive procedures, the first one for the unification of two lists of terms, the other one for the unification of two terms. The standard in model elimination implementations is that a binding is performed destructively by deleting nil from the variable cell and inserting a pointer to the term to be substituted for the variable. The resulting bound variable cell then does no more denote a variable but the respective term. The recursive function binding(term) returns term if term is not a bound variable cell, or otherwise binding(first(term)). On backtracking, variable bindings have to be retracted. This is done by simply reinserting nil in the first

```
procedure unify_lists( args₁,args₂ )
    if ( args₁ = ∅ ) then
      true;
    /* check first arguments */
    elseif ( unify( binding( first( args₁ ) ),binding( first( args₂ ) ) ) ) then
      unify_lists( rest( args₁ ),rest( args₂ ) );
    /* undo variable bindings made in this procedure */
    else
      unbind;
      false;
    endif;

procedure unify( arg₁,arg₂ )
    if ( is_var( arg₂ ) ) then
      if ( occurs( arg₂,arg₁ ) ) then
        false;
      else
        bind( arg₂,arg₁ );
        true;
      endif;
    elseif ( is_var( arg₁ ) ) then
      if ( occurs( arg₁,arg₂ ) ) then
        false;
      else
        bind( arg₁,arg₂ );
        true;
      endif;
    elseif ( functor( arg₁ ) == functor( arg₂ ) ) then
      unify_lists( args( arg₁ ),args( arg₂ ) );
    else
      false;
    endif;
```

Table 2: The unification procedures.

element of the respective bound variable cells, so that the original state is restored. unbind causes the bindings of the whole unification attempt to be retracted.

7.1.2. Polynomial unification

It is straightforward to recognize that this unification procedure is linear in space but exponential in time in the worst case. Although this is not a critical weakness for the typical formulae in automated deduction, one may easily improve the given procedure to a polynomial time complexity by using methods described in [Corbin and Bidoit 1983]. The key idea of such methods is that one attaches an additional tag to any complex term. This tag is employed to avoid that the same pairs of complex terms are successfully unified more than once during a unification operation. Furthermore, this tag can be used to reduce the number of occurs checks to a polynomial (see also [Letz 1993, Letz 1999]).

7.1.3. Destructive unification using the trail

In order to know which bound variables have to be unbound, the *trail* is used as a typical data structure. The trail is a global list-like structure in the program which contains the pointers to the bound variables in the order in which they have been bound. Since all standard backtracking procedures retract bindings exactly in the reversed order of their generation, a simple one-dimensional list-like structure is sufficient for the trail. The *trailmarker* is a global variable which gives the current position of the trail. The number of bindings performed may differ from one inference step to another. In order to know how many bindings have to be retracted when an inference step is retracted, there are two techniques. One possibility is to locally store either the number of performed bindings or the trail position at which the bindings of the previous inference step start. Alternatively, one can use a special stop label on the trail which is written in a trail cell whenever an inference step ends; in this case, no local information is needed. Depending on which solution is selected, the unification procedure has to be modified accordingly.

Figure 23 documents the entire binding process and the trail modifications performed during proof search for the set of the four clauses $\neg P(x, y) \vee \neg P(y, x)$, $P(a, z)$, $P(b, v)$, and $Q(a, b)$. The description begins after the start step in which the first input clause has been attached (a). First an extension step using the second input clause is performed, which produces two bindings (b). Then an extension step with the Q-subgoal is attempted: y (and implicitly z) are bound to a, but the unification fails when a (the binding of x) is compared with b (c). Next the two inferences are retracted (d). After extension steps using the third clause (e) and the fourth clause (f), the proof attempt succeeds. This technique permits that backtracking can be done very efficiently.

7.1.4. The connection graph

The connection condition from Definition 2.3 is a prerequisite for any model elimination extension step. Therefore it is advantageous to be able to quickly find the complementary literals for a selected subgoal. The set of connections between the

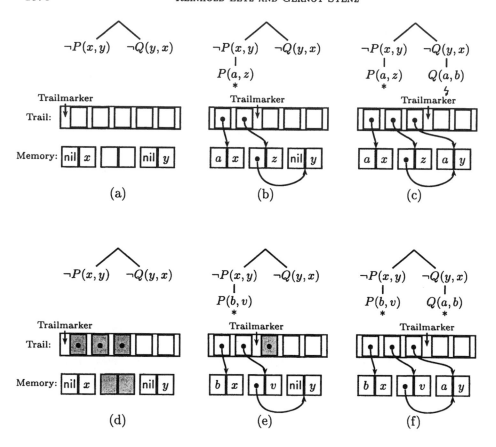

Figure 23: An example of the trail modifications during proof search.

literals of a clause set can be represented in an undirected graph, the so-called *connection graph*. When a subgoal is selected for an expansion step during the proof search, it is sufficient to consider the connections involving that subgoal.

7.1. EXAMPLE. To demonstrate the concept of the connection graph, we consider the clauses $\neg P(g(x)) \vee \neg Q(g(x)) \vee \neg Q(f(x))$, $Q(x) \vee \neg P(f(x))$, $Q(g(y)) \vee P(f(y))$ and $P(f(a))$. The connection graph of this set of clauses is shown in Figure 24. The connections are indicated by the solid lines between the literals. The faint dashed lines show the pairs of literals where, even though they have the same predicate symbol and complementary signs, the argument terms cannot be unified. These literals are not connected. Thus, when the literal $\neg P(g(x))$ has been chosen for an extension step, the clause $Q(g(y)) \vee P(f(y))$ need not be tried.

Since the variables in clauses are all implicitly universally quantified, the connections between literals are independent of any instantiations applied during the proof search. Therefore, the computation of the literal connections can be done statically and used as a filter. If, generally speaking, there is a connection (P, Q) in a set of clauses, then the literal P is also said to have a *link* to literal Q and vice versa. Thus, each literal has a list of links. The link lists for the literals in Example 7.1 are:

$$
\begin{aligned}
P(g(a)): &\quad \{\neg P(g(x))\} \\
\neg P(g(x)): &\quad \{P(g(a))\} \\
\neg Q(g(x)): &\quad \{Q(g(y)), Q(x)\} \\
\neg Q(f(x)): &\quad \{Q(x)\} \\
Q(x): &\quad \{\neg Q(g(x)), \neg Q(f(x))\} \\
\neg P(f(x)): &\quad \{P(f(y))\} \\
P(f(y)): &\quad \{\neg P(f(x))\} \\
Q(g(y)): &\quad \{\neg Q(g(x))\}
\end{aligned}
$$

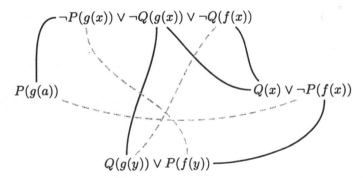

Figure 24: The connection graph for the clause set $\neg P(g(x)) \vee \neg Q(g(x)) \vee \neg Q(f(x))$, $Q(x) \vee \neg P(f(x))$, $Q(g(y)) \vee P(f(y))$ and $P(g(a))$.

7.1.5. The problem of generating clause variants

One of the main difficulties when implementing model elimination procedures is how to provide renamed variants of input clauses efficiently, because in every extension step a new variant of an input clause is needed. It is obvious that the generation of a new variant of an input clause by copying the clause and replacing its variables consistently with new ones is a time consuming operation, all the more since variables are shared and it is not a tree that has to be copied but a graph. The search for an efficient solution of this problem naturally leads to the use of Prolog technology.

7.2. Prolog Technology Theorem Proving

One reason for the high efficiency of current Prolog systems is the fact that many of the operations to be performed in SLD-resolution steps can be determined in advance depending on the respective clause and its entry literal. This information can be used for compiling every Prolog input clause $A :- A_1,\ldots,A_n$ (which corresponds to the clause $A \vee \sim A_1 \vee \cdots \vee \sim A_n$ with entry literal A) into procedures of some actual or virtual machine. Since SLD-resolution steps are nothing else but extension steps, this technique can also be applied to model elimination. The first one to use such a compilation method for model elimination was Mark Stickel [Stickel 1984] who called his system a PTTP, a Prolog Technology Theorem Prover.

In summary, the main deficiencies of Prolog as far as first-order automated reasoning is concerned are the following:

1. the incompleteness of SLD-resolution for non-Horn formulae,
2. the unsound unification algorithm, and
3. the unbounded depth-first search strategy.

To extend the reasoning capabilities of Prolog to full model elimination, it is necessary to extend SLD-resolution to the full extension rule and to add the start rule and the reduction rule.

7.2.1. Contrapositives

In order to implement the full extension rule and to further permit the compilation of input clauses into efficient machine procedures, one has to account for the fact that a clause may be entered at every literal. Accordingly, one has to consider all so-called *contrapositives* of a clause $L_1 \vee \cdots \vee L_n$, i.e., the n Prolog-style strings of the form $L_i :- \sim L_1,\ldots,\sim L_{i-1},\sim L_{i+1},\ldots,\sim L_n$. The start rule can also be captured efficiently, by adding a contrapositive of the form $\perp :- \sim L_1,\ldots,\sim L_n$ for every input clause $L_1 \vee \cdots \vee L_n$. Now, with the Prolog query ?- $\perp$ as the single start clause, all start steps can be simulated with extension steps. As a matter of fact, one can use relevance information here and construct such start contrapositives only for subsets of the input clause set containing a relevant start clause; by default, start contrapositives are generated for the set of all-negative input clauses.

7.2.2. Unification in Prolog

Prolog by default uses a unification algorithm that is designed for maximum efficiency but that can lead to incorrect results.[11] A Prolog program like

```
X < ( X + 1 ).
:- ( Y + 1 ) < Y.
```

can prove that there is a number whose successor is less than itself; the reason for the unsoundness is that no occurs check is performed in Prolog unification. Since the compilation of extension steps into machine procedures also concerns parts of the unification, this compilation process has to be adapted such that sound unification

---

[11]Some Prolog systems provide sound unification via compile time and/or runtime options or via libraries.

Contrapositive: $P(a, f(x,x))$:- $Q(b, g(g(x)))$

```
procedure P( arg₁,arg₂ )
    variable x,tq,arg₂₁,arg₂₂,trail_position;
    x := new_free_variable;
    arg₁ = binding( arg₁ );
    /* mark trail position */
    trail_position := trailmarker;
    /* unify clause head: check first arguments */
    if ( is_var( arg₁ ) or ( is_const( arg₁ ) and arg₁ == a ) ) then
      if ( is_var( arg₁ ) ) then bind( arg₁,a ); endif;
      /* first arguments unifiable, check second arguments */
      arg₂ = binding( arg₂ );
      if ( is_var( arg₂ ) ) then
        bind( arg₂,make_complex_term( f,x,x ) );
        tq := make_complex_term( g, make_complex_term( g,x ) );
        add_subgoal( Q(b,tq) );
        next_subgoal;
      elseif ( is_complex_term( arg₂ ) and functor( arg₂ ) == f ) then
        arg₂₁ := binding( get_arg( arg₂,1 ) );
        arg₂₂ := binding( get_arg( arg₂,2 ) );
        if ( unify( arg₂₁,arg₂₂ ) ) then
          tq := make_complex_term( g, make_complex_term( g,arg₂₁ ) );
          add_subgoal( Q(b,tq) );
          next_subgoal;
        endif;
      endif;
    endif;
    /* undo variable bindings made in this procedure */
    unbind( trail_position );
```

Table 3: Compilation of a contrapositive into a procedure.

is performed. In special cases, however, efficiency can be preserved, for example, if the respective entry literal L is *linear*, i.e., if every variable occurs only once in L. It is straightforward to recognize that in this case, no occurs check is needed in extension steps and the highly efficient Prolog unification can be used. For the general case, an ideal method takes advantage of this optimization by distinguishing the first occurrence of a variable in a literal from all subsequent ones. For every first occurrence, the occurs check may be omitted. In Table 3, a procedure is shown which performs an extension step including the generation of a new clause variant in a very efficient manner.

7.2.3. Path information and other extensions

Unfortunately, for the implementation of the reduction inference rule, one definitely has to provide additional data structures. While in SLD-resolution the ancestor literals of a subgoal are not needed, for model elimination the tableau paths have to be stored and every subgoal must have access to its path. This additional effort cannot be avoided. On the other hand, access to the ancestors of a subgoal is necessary for the implementation of basic refinements like regularity, which is also very effective in the pure Horn case.

Finally, the unbounded depth-first search strategy of Prolog has to be extended to incorporate completeness bounds like the inference bound, the depth bound or other bounds discussed in Section 2.5. It turned out in general that this can be achieved with the following additional data structures. In order to capture bounds which allocate remaining resources directly to subgoals such as the depth bound, every subgoal has to be additionally labelled with its current depth. When inference bounds are involved, a global counter is needed.

7.3. Extended Warren Abstract Machine Technology

As described in [Stickel 1984], PTTP implementations perform their tasks in two distinct phases. First the input formula is translated to Prolog code which in the second phase is compiled into (real or virtual) machine code. The main problem of such a two-step compilation, first to some real programming language and then to native code, is that the second compilation process takes too much time for typical applications, which require short response times. In order to avoid the second compilation phase, an interpreter for the code generated in the first compilation phase has to be used. Since the full expressive power of an actual programming language is not needed, this has caused the development of a very restricted abstract language tailored specifically to the processing of Prolog or model elimination, respectively. We begin with a description of the basics of such a machine for Prolog (see [Warren 1983] and [Schumann 1991] for a more detailed description).

7.3.1. The Warren Abstract Machine

D.H.D. Warren developed a virtual machine for the execution of Prolog programs [Warren 1983] which is called the Warren Abstract Machine (WAM). It combines high efficiency, good portability, and the possibility for compiling Prolog programs. The WAM is widely used and has become a kernel for commercial Prolog systems, implemented as software emulation or even micro-coded on dedicated hardware [Taki, Yokota, Yamamoto, Nishikawa, Uchida, Nakashima and Mitsuishi 1984, Benker, Beacco, Bescos, Dorochevsky, Jeffré, Pöhlmann, Noyé, Poterie, Sexton, Syre, Thibault and Watzlawik 1989]. The WAM is structured as a register-based multi-memory machine as shown in Figure 25. Its *memory* holds the program (as a sequence of WAM instructions) and data. The *register file* keeps a certain set of often used data and control information. The WAM instruction, located in the memory at the place where the *program counter* register points to,

Is fetched and executed by the *control unit*.

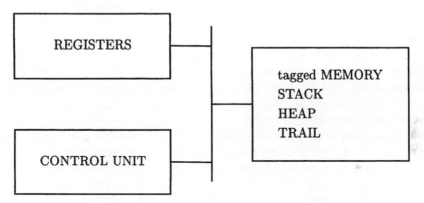

Figure 25: The Warren Abstract Machine

Next we will describe how a Prolog program is *compiled* into machine instructions of the WAM. We begin with the special case of a *deterministic* program which corresponds to a situation in which there is only one possibility for extending the subgoals of the clause. In this case no backtracking inside the clause is needed. The respective tableau is generated using a depth-first left-to-right selection function. Then the program can be executed in the same manner as in a *procedural* programming language, that is, the head of a clause is considered as the *head* of a procedure and the subgoals as the *procedure calls* of other procedures (the parameter passing, however, is quite different). Accordingly, this can be implemented on a machine level exactly in the way it is done in functional or procedural languages, using a *stack* with *environment control blocks* which hold the control information (return address, dynamic link) and the local variables. A detailed explanation of these concepts can be found e.g. in [Aho and Ullman 1977]. The local variables are addressed using a register E pointing to the beginning of the current environment. A Horn clause H :- G1,...,Gn. is executed using the following instructions[12].

```
H:                          % entry point for clause H.
        allocate            % generate new environment (on stack) with space for locals
        ...                 % pass parameters (discussed below)
        ...                 % set parameters for G1 (discussed below)
        call        G1      % call first subgoal, remember return address A
A: ...
        ...                 % set parameters for Gn (discussed below)
        call        Gn      % call last subgoal, remember return address
        deallocate          % deallocate control block and return
```

Each environment contains a pointer to the previous environment (*dynamic link*). The entire list, in effect, represents the *path* from the root to the current node in the

---

[12]Actually, the WAM provides a number of different instructions for the sake of optimization, e.g., for tail recursion elimination. Here, only the basic instructions are described.

tableau, the return addresses in the environments point to the code of the subgoals. The program terminates when the last call in the query returns.

The parameters of the head and the subgoals of the clauses are *terms* in a logical sense consisting of *constants*, *logical variables*, *lists*[13], and *structures* (complex terms). A Prolog term is represented by a *word* of the memory, containing a *value* and a *tag*. The tag distinguishes the type of the term, namely *reference*, *structure*, *list*, and *constant*. The tag type "reference" is used to represent the (logical) variables. Structures are represented in a non structure-sharing manner, i.e. they are copied explicitly with their functors.

For the purposes of parameter passing, the WAM uses two sets of registers, the registers $A_1, \ldots, A_n$ for keeping parameters and temporary registers $T_1, \ldots, T_n$. When a subgoal is to be called, its parameters are provided in the registers A_i by using put instructions. There exists one put instruction for each data type. In the head of a clause, the parameters in the A registers are fetched and compared with the respective parameter of the head, using a get or unify instruction. Here again, a separate instruction for each data type is provided. The matching algorithm has to check if constants and functors are equal. If a variable has to be bound to a constant, the value of the constant and the tag "constant" is written into the memory location where the variable resides; if the variable is bound to a structure, a pointer to that structure is written into the variable cell, together with the tag "reference". Structures themselves are created in a separate part of memory, the *heap*, to ensure their permanent storage.

An example illustrates the usage of the instructions to pass the parameters. Let us assume that a subgoal $P(a, z)$ calls a head of a clause $P(a, f(x, y))$:- .... The variables reside in the environment control block and are accessed via an offset from the register E pointing to the current environment. In [Warren 1983] they are noted as $Y_1, \ldots, Y_n$.

```
        put_constant     a,A1    % put first parameter (constant a) into register A1
        put_variable     Y4,A2   % put variable z (in variable cell #4) into A2
        call             P       % call the "P-clause"

P:
        allocate         2       % allocate space for 2 variables
        get_const        a,A1    % try to unify 1st parameter with constant a
        get_structure    f/2,A2  % get second argument: must be a structure or
                                 % a variable to be bound to a new structure
        unify_variable   Y1      % unify with first arg (in local cell #1)
        unify_variable   Y2      % unify with second arg (in local cell #2)
        ...                      % body of clause comes here
```

This example also shows that the get and unify instructions must operate in two modes ("read","write") according to the type of parameter they receive. If the variable z in the subgoal has been bound to some function symbol prior to this call, for example, to $f(a, b)$, then the list is taken apart by the get_list instruction and x and y in the head of P are bound to a respectively to b (read mode). If, however, z

---

[13]A list is considered as a data type of its own for reasons of efficiency. A list could also be represented as a binary structure: $list(Head, Tail)$ comparable to a Lisp *cons*-structure.

in the subgoal has not yet been bound to a function symbol, a *new* binary function symbol with two variables as arguments is created as a structure on the heap by the instructions get_structure and unify_variable (write mode). Note that the creation on the heap is necessary, since the newly created structure has to stay in existence even after the execution of the clause P.

Finally, let us consider the full case of nondeterministic programs, in which a subgoal of a clause unifies with more than one (complemented) head of a clause, in which case backtracking is needed. Backtracking is implemented by means of so-called *choice points*, control blocks which hold all the information for undoing an inference step. These choice points are pushed onto the stack. The basic information of a choice point is a link to its predecessor, a code address to the entry point of the next clause to be attempted, and the information that is needed to undo all extension steps executed since that choice point was created. This involves a copy of all registers of the WAM as well as the variables which have been bound since the generation of the choice point. For the latter purpose a *trail* is used, in the same manner as described in Section 7.1. Whenever a backtracking action has to be performed, all registers from the current choice point are loaded into the WAM, all stack modifications are undone, and the respective variables are unbound. Then the next clause is attempted. The WAM contains a last alternative optimization, according to which the choice point can be discarded if the last extension clause is tried. The list of different possibilities is coded by the instructions try_me_else, and trust_me_else_fail, the latter representing the last alternative. Assuming that there are three clauses c1, c2, c3 for extension, the compiled code is shown below.

```
    ...
    call    P               % call the P-clauses
P:                          % generate a choice-point.
c123:
    try_me_else C2a         % try c1; if this fails, try c2
c1:
    ...                     % code of clause c1
c2a:
    try_me_else C3a         % try c2; if this fails, try c3
c2:
    ...                     % code of clause c2
c3a:
    trust_me_else_fail      % there is only one alternative left
c3:
    ...                     % code of clause c3
```

The WAM has some additional instructions for optimization which we do not consider here. First, a *dynamic* preselection on the data type of the first parameter is done (switch_on_term). Its arguments give entry points of lists of clauses which have to be tried according to the type of the first parameter of the current subgoal (variable, constant, list, structure). Also hash tables are used for selection of a clause head, which is useful when there is a large number of head literals with constants as first arguments.

7.3.2. The SETHEO abstract machine

Inspired by the architecture of the WAM, the SETHEO model elimination prover [Letz et al. 1992] has been implemented. The central part of SETHEO is the SETHEO Abstract Machine (SAM), which is an extension of the WAM. The concepts introduced there had to be extended and enhanced for attaining a complete and sound proof procedure for the model elimination calculus, and for facilitating the use of advanced control structures and heuristics. A detailed description of all the instructions and registers of the original version is available as a manual [Letz, Schumann and Bayerl 1989]. The layout of the abstract machine is basically the same as in Figure 25, except that additional space is reserved for the *proof tree* and the *constraints*, which are discussed in Section 8. The *proof tree* stores the current state of the generated tableau, which can be displayed graphically to illustrate the structure of the proof. Additionally, there are global counters, e.g. for the number of inferences performed.

In the following we will point out and explain some of the most important differences between the SAM and the WAM.

The Reduction Step. In order to successfully handle non-Horn clauses in model elimination, extension steps and *reduction steps* are necessary. A subgoal in the tableau can be closed by a reduction step if there exists a complementary unifiable literal in the path from the root to the current node. The resulting substitution σ is then applied to the entire tableau. How can this reduction step be implemented within the concepts of an Abstract Machine? As described above, the tableau is implicitly represented in the stack of the machine, using a linked list of *environment control blocks*. This linked list just represents the path from the root of the tableau to the current node[14]. Thus, the instruction executing the reduction step searches through this list, starting from the current node, to find a complementary literal which is unifiable with the current subgoal. The respective unification is carried out in the standard way. This procedure, however, requires that additional information must be stored in each environment, namely, the *predicate symbol* of the head literal of a contrapositive, its *sign*, and a pointer to the *parameters* of that literal. The detailed structure of an environment of the SAM is displayed in Figure 26, the *base pointer* points to the current environment in the *stack*.

The reduction inference rule itself is nondeterministic in the sense that a subgoal may have more than one connected predecessor literal in the path. Hence, we have to store an additional *pointer* in every choice point, pointing to the environment which corresponds to the node which will be tried next for a reduction step.

Efficiency Considerations. To increase the efficiency of the SETHEO machine, a tagged memory is used. The basic types of variables, terms, constants and reference cells, which are used in the Warren Abstract Machine, are divided into further subtypes in order to gain a better performance (compare also [Vlahavas and Halatsis 1987]). Thus, for instance, the type 'variable' has the subtypes: 'free

---

[14]For this reason no *tail recursion* optimization is allowed as it is done in the WAM. This optimization tries to throw away environments as soon as possible, e.g., before executing the last subgoal of a clause.

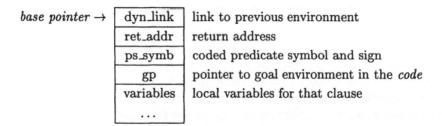

Figure 26: The SAM environment

variable' (T_FVAR), 'temporary variable' (T_TVAR), and 'bound variable', i.e. a reference cell (T_BVAR). Additionally, complex terms are tagged differently depending on whether they contain variables or not. The additional information contained in these tags can be used for optimizing the unification operation.

Parameter Transfer. In the original WAM, parameter transfer from a subgoal to a head of a clause is done via the A_i registers. As the number of registers had to be minimized and the ability to deal with a variable number of parameters was required, this solution was not suitable for the SAM. Instead, the parameters are transferred via an argument vector. This approach originates from [Vlahavas and Halatsis 1987], but had to be adapted. The number of parameters of a subgoal and their types are fixed. The only exception are variables, which may be unbound or bound to an arbitrary object. Consequently, an argument vector is generated in the code area during compilation which contains the values and data types of the parameters. For variables an offset into the current environment is given. After dereferencing this address, the object to which the variable is bound can be accessed. The only information directly passed during the execution of a `call` instruction is the address of the beginning of this argument vector. It is put into the register gp (goal pointer). After the selection of a head of a clause, the unification between the parameters of the goal and those of the head starts. For each parameter in the head, a separate unify instruction is used which tries the unification with the parameter gp points to, and, in the case of success, increments gp. The following example shows the construction of the argument vector. Consider a subgoal $P(a, x, f(x))$. It will generate something like the following argument vector consisting of three words.

```
gp:     T_CONST    16     % 1st argument: constant a as index into symbol table
        T_VAR1     1      % 2nd: variable x with offset 1 (w.r.t.\ environment)
        T_CREF     term1  % 3rd: pointer to term f(x)
        ...
term1:  T_NGTERM   17     % functor f with index 17
        T_VAR2     1      % variable x (second occurrence)
        T_EOSTR    0      % end of the structure
```

7.4. Using Prolog as an Implementation Language

The preceding section has shown that implementing model elimination by extending Prolog technology requires considerable effort. Since SLD-resolution is very similar to model elimination, many newer implementations of model elimination are done directly in Prolog. We will now consider the potential of using Prolog as an implementation language. It is easy to see that a basic implementation of model elimination can be obtained in Prolog with a few straightforward additions. For this purpose, we need to explicitly create all contrapositives and a mechanism for performing reduction steps has to be provided. Both can be done in a simple and methodical way, as will be demonstrated with the following formula proposed by J. Pelletier in [Pelletier and Rudnicki 1986]. We have written the problem in Prolog-like notation, i.e., with variables in capital letters and function and predicate symbols in lower case letters. A semi-colon is used when more than one positive literal is in a clause.

```
< - p(a,b).
< - q(c,d).
p(X,Z) < - p(X,Y), p(Y,Z).
q(X,Z) < - q(X,Y), q(Y,Z).
p(X,Y) < - p(Y,X).
p(X,Y) ; q(X,Y) < -.
```

The transformation starts by forming the Horn contrapositives for the input clauses, as shown in Section 7.2.1. To simulate the negation sign, predicate symbols are preceded with labels, p_ for positive literals and n_ for negative literals. Additionally, start clauses are added as Prolog queries.

Furthermore, to overcome the incompleteness of Prolog for non-Horn formulae, we need to simulate the reduction operation. This is done as follows. First, the paths are added as additional arguments to the logical arguments of the respective literals. For optimization purposes, we use two path lists, one for the positive and one for the negative literals in the respective path. In each extension step, the respective path list is extended by the respective literal. Finally, for actually enabling the performance of reduction steps, an additional clause is added for each predicate symbol and sign that tries all unifiable literals in the path list. The output then looks as follows.

```
% Start clauses
false :- p_p(a,b, [ ],[ ]).

false :- p_q(c,d, [ ],[ ]).

% Contrapositives
n_p(a,b, P, N).

n_q(c,d, P, N).

p_p(X,Z, P,N) :- N1 = [ p(X,Z) | N ], p_p(X,Y, P,N1), p_p(Y,Z, P,N1).
n_p(X,Y, P,N) :- P1 = [ p(X,Y) | P ], n_p(X,Z, P1,N), p_p(Y,Z, P1,N).
```

```
n_p(Y,Z, P,N) :- P1 = [ p(Y,Z) | P ], n_p(X,Z, P1,N), p_p(X,Y, P1,N).


p_q(X,Z, P,N) :- N1 = [ q(X,Z) | N ], p_q(X,Y, P,N1), p_q(Y,Z, P,N1).
n_q(X,Y, P,N) :- P1 = [ q(X,Y) | P ], n_q(X,Z, P1,N), p_q(Y,Z, P1,N).
n_q(Y,Z, P,N) :- P1 = [ q(Y,Z) | P ], n_q(X,Z, P1,N), p_q(X,Y, P1,N).


p_p(X,Y, P,N) :- N1 = [ p(X,Y) | N ], p_p(Y,X, P,N1).
n_p(Y,X, P,N) :- P1 = [ p(Y,X) | P ], n_p(X,Y, P1,N).


p_p(X,Y, P,N) :- N1 = [ p(X,Y) | N ], n_q(X,Y, P,N1).
p_q(X,Y, P,N) :- N1 = [ q(X,Y) | N ], n_p(X,Y, P,N1).


% Clauses for performing reduction steps
n_p(X,Y, P,N) :- member(p(X,Y), N).
p_p(X,Y, P,N) :- member(p(X,Y), P).
n_q(X,Y, P,N) :- member(q(X,Y), N).
p_q(X,Y, P,N) :- member(q(X,Y), P).


member(X,[ X | R ]).
member(X,[ Y | R ]) :- member(X,R).
```

What is missing in order to perform a complete proof search, is the implementation of a completeness bound and the iterative deepening. We consider the case of the tableau depth bound (Section 2.5.2), which can be implemented by adding the remaining depth resource D as an additional argument to the literals in the contrapositives and start clauses. After having entered a contrapositive, it is checked whether the current depth resource is > 0, in which case it is decremented by 1 and the new resource is passed to the subgoals of the clause. For start clauses, the depth may be passed unchanged to the subgoals.

```
% for contrapositives
P(...,D) :- D > 0, D1 is D-1, P1(...,D1), ..., Pn(...,D1).


% for start clauses
false(D):- P1(...,D), ..., Pn(...,D).
```

When posing the query, say, `false(5)`, the Prolog backtracking mechanism will automatically ensure that all connection tableaux up to tableau depth 5 are examined. Finally, the iterative deepening is handled by simply adding the following clause to the end of the program.

```
false(D) :- D1 is D+1, false(D1).
```

After having loaded such a program into Prolog (in some Prolog systems the clauses have to be ordered such that all predicates occur consecutively), one can start the proof search by typing in the query: `?- false(1)`.

For the discussed example, the Prolog unification (which in general is unsound) poses no problem, since no function symbol of arity > 0 occurs. In the general case, however, one has to use sound unification. Some Prolog systems offer sound unification, often in various ways. Either the system has a sound unification predicate in its library or sound unification can be switched on by setting a global flag. While the latter is more comfortable, it may lead to unnecessary run-time inefficiencies, since the occurs check is always performed even if it would not be needed according to the optimizations discussed in the previous sections. Such an optimization may also be achieved in a Prolog implementation by linearization of the clause heads (for which Prolog unification may be used then) and a subsequent sound unification of the remaining critical terms (see, for example, [Plaisted 1984]).

In summary, this illustrates how surprisingly simple it is to implement a pure model elimination proof search procedure in Prolog. Furthermore, such an implementation also yields a very high performance in terms of inference steps performed per second. The approach of using Prolog, however, becomes more and more problematic when trying to implement model elimination proof procedures with more advanced search pruning mechanisms such as the ones discussed in Section 3 and Section 4.

7.5. A Data Oriented Architecture

The prover architectures described so far all rely on the approach of compiling the input clauses and some parts of the inference system into procedures, the ones creating Prolog source code and the ones generating native or abstract machine instructions. The inference rules and important subtasks such as the unification algorithm, the backtracking mechanism, or the subgoal processing are deeply intertwined and standardized in order to achieve high efficiency. Such an approach is suitable when a certain kind of optimized proof procedure has evolved for which no obvious improvements are known. In automated theorem proving, however, this is not the case. New techniques are constantly developed which may lead to significant improvements. Against this background, the most important shortcoming of Prolog technology based provers is their inflexibility. Changing the unification such as to add sorts, for example, or adding new inference rules, e.g., for equality handling, or generalizing the backtracking procedure becomes extremely cumbersome if not impossible in such an architecture.

Accordingly, as the last of the architectures, we discuss a more natural or straightforward implementation of the model elimination procedure, in the sense that the components of the program are modularized and can be identified more naturally with their mathematical definitions. Since the most important difference to Prolog technology style provers is that clauses are represented as data structures and do not become part of the prover program, such an approach will be called a data oriented proof procedure, as opposed to the clause compilation procedures. Unlike the WAM-based architectures, which heavily rely on the implicit encoding of the proof in the program execution scheme, the proof object here is the clausal tableau, which is completely stored in memory. Although this leads to a larger memory consumption, it causes no problems in practice, as today's computers have enough main storage space to contain the proof trees for practically all *feasible* proof problems. Only very large proofs, that means proofs with more than, say, 100,000 inferences become unfeasible with the data oriented concept.

An implementation of this data oriented approach, the SETHEO-based prover system Scheme-SETHEO, has been partially completed.

7.5.1. The basic data structures

The data objects used in this approach can be categorized into *formula data objects* and *proof data objects*. The basic formula data objects are the (input) formula, the clauses, the clause copies and the subgoals. From these objects, the formula is implicitly represented by the set of its clauses (as there is only one input formula). Reasonable data structures for the other objects are given here.

Clauses. The most important elements of the clause structure are the original or *generic* literals and the list of clause copies used in the proof. Since clauses may be entered at any subgoal, it is not necessary to compute contrapositives.

	Generic Literals			
V	Clause Number	...	$P(x), \neg Q(y), \ldots$	...	List of clause copies

Clause copies. In every extension step, a renamed copy of the original clause has to be made and added to the tableau.

Subgoals			Predecessor	
V_c	$sg_1, \ldots, sg_n$	...	Clause	...	Path

Subgoals. Subgoal objects contain the information about the literal they represent, i.e. the sign, predicate symbol, the argument terms, etc.

sg	Sign	Predicate Symbol	Argument Terms	Extension	Clause Copy	Links	Selection Tag	...

As a matter of fact, additional control information can be included in these data objects, which is omitted here for the sake of clarity. Further important data structures utilized in the proof process are the variable trail (which was described in Section 7.1.3) and the list of subgoals. The variable trail is one of the few concepts adopted from the Prolog technology architecture, since a device for manual bookkeeping of the variable instantiations is required.

Global subgoal list. This is the central global data object. It consists of the sequence of subgoals of all clause copies hitherto introduced to the current tableau. Figure 27 illustrates how the subgoals of the clause copies constitute the global subgoal list. The dotted lines refer to the underlying tree structure, the dashed arrows indicate the linking between the elements of the global subgoal list. In any inference step, the literal at which an extension or reduction step is performed, is marked as selected, as illustrated in Figure 27 by a grey shading of the subgoals.

The global access to the list of subgoals relieves us from the need to conform to some sort of depth-first search. Instead, a subgoal selection function can be em-

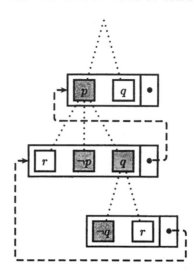

Figure 27: The global subgoal list and the implied tableau structure.

ployed that chooses an arbitrary subgoal for the next inference step. This way, new heuristics become feasible that operate globally on the proof object. For example, free subgoal reordering can be performed easily.

In Figure 28, a detailed snapshot of the subgoal and clause copy data structures of a certain proof state is shown. The tableau structure is only given implicitly. In fact, all information needed to move through the tableau, as, for instance, during a folding up operation, is provided by extensive cross-referencing among the different data objects. The figure shows the connections between data objects of the various kinds (data objects for original clauses are not contained in the tableau). Again, selected subgoals are highlighted by grey shading. The subgoal p has been chosen for an extension step with the clause $C = \{r, \neg p, q\}$. A copy C' of C is linked to p via the extension pointer. The subgoals of C' are accessible via the subgoal vector pointed to by C'. This subgoal vector is appended to the global subgoal list. To allow upward movement through the tableau, the copy is linked to the extended subgoal, while the new subgoals are linked to the clause copy. The subgoals p and $\neg p$ are immediately marked as selected, the subgoal q becomes selected in the next extension step. It should be noted that, since we rely on clauses instead of contrapositives, the connected literal need not be the first literal in the clause, as is the case here.

7.5.2. The proof procedure

Table 4 shows a simplified data oriented proof procedure (not featuring the reduction rule or start clause selection). Based on the connection graph of the input formula, the list of associated links is attached to each subgoal. The procedure

```
procedure solve( sg, links, resource )
    if ( links ≠ ∅ ) then
        extension( sg, first( links ), resource );
        /* try next alternative */
        solve( sg, rest( links ), resource );
    endif;

procedure extension( sg, link, resource )
    dec_resource := decrement_resource( resource );
    if ( dec_resource > 0 ) then
        clause := new_clause_copy( link );
        head := head( clause, link );
        trail_pos := trailmarker;
        if ( unify_literals( ~sg, head ) ) then
            old_subgoals := subgoals;
            make_new_subgoals( clause, sg, head );
            new_sg := select_subgoal;
            if ( new_sg )
                new_links := links( new_sg );
                new_resource := resource( new_sg );
                solve( new_sg, new_links, new_resource );
            else
                proof_found;
                abort;
            endif;
            /* backtracking */
            unbind( trailpos );
            subgoals := old_subgoals;
        endif;
    endif;
```

Table 4: A rudimentary model elimination proof procedure.

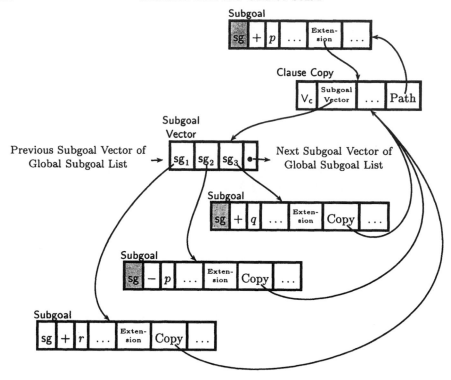

Figure 28: Cross-referencing between clause copy and subgoal data structures.

solve explores the search space by successively applying the extension rule using the elements in the link list of its subgoal argument *sg*. The reduction rule can be incorporated easily as an additional inferential alternative. The procedure extension checks the resource bound, adds the linked clause to the proof tree, and modifies the global subgoal list. When a literal can be selected, solve is called again with the new subgoals, otherwise a proof has been found and the procedure aborts.

7.5.3. Reuse of clause instances

How can high performance be achieved with such an architecture? It turns out that the most time consuming procedure in this approach is the generation of a new instance of an input clause, which has to be performed in every extension step. One of the main reasons for the high performance of the PTTP based model elimination procedures is that this operation is implemented very efficiently. But the question is, whether it is really necessary to generate a new clause instance in every extension step. Typically, proof search procedures based on model elimination process relatively small tableaux, but a large number of them. That is, in model elimination theorem proving, the degree of backtracking is extremely high if compared with typical Prolog applications. Many Prolog executions require deep deduction trees including optimizations like tail recursion. For those applications, a new generation of clause instances is indispensable. This striking difference between the deduction trees considered in Prolog and in theorem proving shows that central ingredients of Prolog technology will rarely be needed in theorem proving.

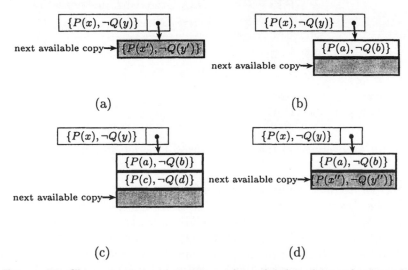

Figure 29: Clause instance creation and availability during backtracking

The key idea for achieving high performance when clause copying is time consuming is the *reuse* of clause instances. The clause copies created once are not discarded when backtracking but are kept in a list of available copies for later reuse, as illustrated with the example in Figure 29. At startup (subfigure (a)), one uninstantiated copy is provided for each clause. This copy is used in an extension step and instantiated, as shown in subfigure (b). Now no other copy is available. When the clause is selected for an extension step again, a new copy has to be created. This situation is shown in subfigure (c). When backtracking occurs during the search process and the extension step that initiated the creation of the copy in subfigure (c) is undone, the copy remains in the list of clause copies and only the pointer to the next available copy is moved backward. This situation is displayed in subfigure (d). This way, over the duration of the proof, a monotonically growing list of clause copies is built and in most cases clause copies can be reused instead of having to be created. As a matter of fact, this requires that all variable bindings are retracted. However, when using destructive unification and the trail concept this can be done very efficiently. Experimental results have shown that with such an architecture inference rates may be obtained that are comparable to the ones achieved with PTTP implementations.

7.6. Existing Model Elimination Implementations

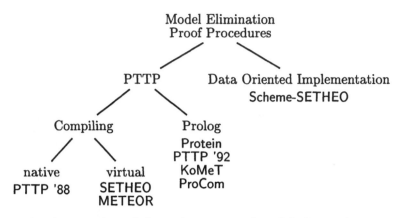

Figure 30: An overview of the architectures of model elimination systems.

In Figure 30, existing implementations of model elimination are classified according to the descriptions given in this section. The references for the listed systems are: PTTP '88 [Stickel 1988], SETHEO [Letz et al. 1992], METEOR [Astrachan and Loveland 1991], Protein [Baumgartner and Furbach 1994], PTTP '92 [Stickel 1992], KoMeT [Bibel, Bruening, Egly and Rath 1994], ProCom [Neugebauer and Petermann 1995, Neugebauer 1995], Scheme-SETHEO (see Section 7.5).

8. Implementation of Refinements by Constraints

When considering the presented tableau refinements such as regularity, tautology, or subsumption-freeness, the question may be raised whether it is possible with reasonable effort to check these conditions after each inference step. Note that a unification operation in one part of a tableau can produce instantiations which may lead to an irregularity, tautology, or subsumed clause in another distant part of the tableau. The structure violation can even concern a closed part of the tableau. Fortunately, there exists a *uniform* and *highly efficient* technique for implementing many of the search pruning mechanisms presented in the previous sections: *Syntactic disequation constraints.*

8.1. Reformulation of Refinements as Constraints

8.1.1. Tautology elimination

Let us demonstrate the technique first using an example of dynamic tautology elimination. Recall that certain input clauses may have tautological instances, which can be avoided as tableau clauses. When considering the transitivity clause

$\neg P(x, y) \vee \neg P(y, z) \vee P(x, z)$, there are two classes of instantiations which may render the formula tautological. Either x and y are instantiated to the same term, or y and z. Obviously, the generation of a tautological instance can be avoided if the unification operation is constrained by forbidding that the respective variables are instantiated to the same terms. In general, this leads to the formulation of *disequation constraints* of the form $s_1, \ldots, s_n \neq t_1, \ldots, t_n$ where the s_i and t_i are terms. Alternatively, one could formulate this instantiation prohibition as a disjunction $s_1 \neq t_1 \vee \cdots \vee s_n \neq t_n$. A disequation constraint is violated if *every* pair $\langle s_i, t_i \rangle$ in the constraint is instantiated to the same term. For the transitivity clause, the two disequation constraints $x \neq y$ and $y \neq z$ can be generated and added to the transitivity formula. The non-tautology constraints for the formulae of a given input set can be generated in a preprocessing phase *before* starting the actual proof process. Afterwards, the tableau construction is performed with *constrained clauses*. Whenever a constrained clause is to be used for tableau expansion, the formula and its constraints are consistently renamed, the tableau expansion is performed with the clause part, and the constraints are added. If the constraints are violated, then a tautological tableau clause has been generated, in which case one can immediately perform backtracking.

8.1.2. Regularity

Regularity can also be captured using disequation constraints. In contrast to non-tautology constraints, however, regularity constraints have to be generated dynamically during the proof search. Whenever a new renamed variant c of a (constrained) clause is attached to a branch in an extension step, then, for every literal L with argument sequence $s_1, \ldots, s_n$ in the clause c and for every branch literal with the same sign and predicate symbol with arguments $t_1, \ldots, t_n$, a disequation constraint $s_1, \ldots, s_n \neq t_1, \ldots, t_n$ must be generated.

8.1.3. Tableau clause subsumption

Tableau clause subsumption is essentially treated in the same manner as tautology elimination. Recall the example from Section 3.3 where in addition to the transitivity clause a unit clause $P(a, b)$ is assumed to be in the input set. Then, the disequation constraint $x, z \neq a, b$ may be generated and added to the transitivity clause. Like non-tautology constraints, non-subsumption constraints can be computed and added to the formulae in the input set before the actual proof process is started.[15] Please note that this mechanism does not capture certain cases of tableau clause subsumption, as demonstrated with the following example. Assume that the transitivity clause and a unit clause $P(f(v), g(v))$ are contained in the input set. In analogy to the other example, a disequation constraint $x, z \neq f(v), g(v)$ could be added to the transitivity formula. But now the constraint contains the variable v, which does not occur in the transitivity clause. Since clauses (and their con-

---

[15]Note, however, that due to the NP-completeness of subsumption, it might be advisable not to generate *all* possible non-subsumption constraints, since this could involve an exponentially increasing preprocessing time.

straints) are always renamed before being integrated into a tableau, the renaming of the variable v will occur in the constraint only and nowhere else in the tableau. Consequently, this variable can never be instantiated by tableau inference steps, so that the constraint can never be violated and is therefore absolutely useless for search pruning. Clearly, the case of full subsumption cannot be captured in this manner. The constraint mechanism should prevent x and z from being instantiated to any terms which have the *structures* $f(t)$ and $g(t)$, respectively, regardless what t is. This can be conveniently achieved by using *universal variables* in addition to the *rigid variables*. The respective disequation constraint then reads $\forall v\ x, z \neq f(v), g(v)$, which is violated exactly when x and z are instantiated to any terms of the structures $f(s)$ and $g(t)$ with $s = t$.

More general disunification problems are discussed in [Comon and Lescanne 1989].

8.2. Disequation Constraints

After this explanation of the potential of constraints, we will now more rigorously present the framework of disequation constraints, with respect to their use in pruning the proof search in model elimination.

8.1. DEFINITION *(Disequation constraint).* A *disequation constraint* C is either true or of the form $\forall u_1 \cdots \forall u_m\ l \neq r\ (m \geq 0)$ with l and r being sequences of terms $s_1, \ldots, s_n$ and $t_1, \ldots, t_n$ $(n \geq 0)$, respectively. For any disequation constraint C of the latter form, $l \neq r$ is called the *kernel* of C, n its *length*, $u_1, \ldots, u_m$ its *universal variables*, and the disequation constraints $s_i \neq t_i$ are termed the *subconstraints* of C. Occasionally, we will use the *disjunctive form* of a disequation constraint kernel, which is $s_1 \neq t_1 \vee \cdots \vee s_n \neq t_n$.

An example of a disequation constraint of length $n = 1$ and with one universal variable is
$$\forall z\ f(g(x, a, f(y)), v) \neq f(g(z, z, f(z)), v).$$

Since all considered constraints will be disequation constraints, we will simply speak of constraints in the sequel. Next, we will discuss the meaning of constraint violation.

8.2. DEFINITION *(Constraint violation, equivalence).* No substitution *violates* the constraint true. A substitution σ *violates* a constraint of the form $\forall u_1 \cdots \forall u_m\ l \neq r$ if there is a substitution τ with domain $u_1, \ldots, u_m$ such that $l\tau\sigma = r\tau\sigma$. When a violating substitution exists for a certain constraint, we say that the constraint *can be violated*; a constraint *is violated*, if all substitutions violate it. Two constraints are *equivalent* if they have the same set of violating substitutions.

For example, the substitution $\sigma = \{x/f(a)\}$ violates the constraint $\forall y\ x \neq f(y)$, since $x\tau\sigma = f(y)\tau\sigma$ for $\tau = \{y/a\}$.

8.2.1. Constraint normalization

How may the violation of a constraint be detected in an efficient manner? The basic characteristic of constraints permitting an efficient constraint handling is that these constraints can often be simplified. For example, the complex constraint given after Definition 8.1 is equivalent to the simpler constraint $x, y \neq a, a$, which obviously can be handled more efficiently. Constraints can always be expressed in a specific form.

8.3. DEFINITION *(Constraint in solved form)*. A constraint is in *solved form* if it is either true or if its kernel has the form $x_1, \ldots, x_n \neq t_1, \ldots, t_n$ where all variables on the left-hand side are pairwise distinct and non-universal (i.e., do not occur in the quantifier prefix of the constraint), and no variable x_i occurs in terms of the right-hand side.

For example, the constraint $x, y \neq a, a$ is in solved form whereas the equivalent constraint $x, y \neq y, a$ is not. Every constraint can be rewritten into solved form by using the following nondeterministic algorithm.

8.4. DEFINITION *(Constraint normalization)*. Let C be any disequation constraint as input. If the constraint is true or if the two sides l and r of its kernel are not unifiable, then the constraint true is a *normal form* of C. Otherwise, let σ be any minimal unifier for l and r that contains no binding of the form x/u where u is a universal variable of C and x is not. Let $\{x_1/t_1, \ldots, x_n/t_n\}$ be the set of all bindings in σ with the x_i being non-universal in C, and let $u_1, \ldots, u_m$ be the universal variables in C that occur in some of the terms t_i. Then the constraint $\forall u_1 \cdots \forall u_m \ x_1, \ldots, x_n \neq t_1, \ldots, t_n$ is a *normal form* of C.

Note that, for preserving constraint equivalence and for achieving a solved form, the use of a minimal unifier is needed in the procedure, employing merely most general unifiers will not always work. Consider, for example, the constraint $f(y) \neq x$ and the most general unifier $\{x/f(x), y/x\}$. This would yield the constraint $x, y \neq f(x), x$ as a normal form, which is not equivalent to $f(y) \neq x$ and which cannot even be violated.

Let us demonstrate the effect of the normalization procedure by applying it to the complex constraint $\forall z \ f(g(x, a, f(y)), v) \neq f(g(z, z, f(z)), v)$ mentioned above. First, we obtain the minimal unifier $\{x/a, z/a, y/a\}$. Next, the binding z/a is deleted, since z is universal, which eventually yields the normal form constraint $x, y \neq a, a$. As shown with this example, some constraint variables may vanish in the normalization process. On the other hand, the length of a constraint may also increase during normalization.

8.5. PROPOSITION. *Any normal form of a constraint C is in solved form and equivalent to C.*

PROOF. If C is true or if the two sides of its kernel are not unifiable, then the normal form of C is true, which is in solved form and equivalent to C. It remains to consider the case of a constraint $C = \forall u_1 \cdots u_m \; l \neq r$ with unifiable l and r. When normalizing C according to the procedure in Definition 8.4, first, a minimal unifier σ for l and r is computed which does not bind non-universal variables to universal ones. The kernel $l' \neq r'$ of the corresponding normal form C' of C contains exactly the subconstraints $x_i \neq t_i$ for every binding $x_i/t_i \in \sigma$ with non-universal x_i. Since minimal unifiers are idempotent, no variable in the domain of σ occurs in terms of its range. Therefore, C' is in solved form. For considering the equivalence of C and C', first note the following. Since σ is a minimal unifier for l and r, it is idempotent and more general than any unifier for l and r. Therefore, a substitution ρ unifies l and r if and only if $v\rho = s\rho$ for every binding $v/s \in \sigma$. Let now θ be any substitution.

Case 1. If θ violates C, then there exists a substitution τ with domain $\{u_1, \ldots, u_m\}$ and $l\tau\theta = r\tau\theta$. Therefore, for any binding $v/s \in \sigma$, $v\tau\theta = s\tau\theta$, i.e., $\tau\theta$ is a unifier for l' and r'. Let τ' be the set of bindings in τ with domain variables occurring in C'. Then $\tau'\theta$ unifies l' and r'. Consequently, θ violates C'.

Case 2. If θ violates C', then there exists a substitution τ with its domain being the universal variables in C' and $l'\tau\theta = r'\tau\theta$. Let σ' be the set of bindings in σ which bind universal variables. Then, for any binding $v/s \in \sigma$, $v\sigma'\tau\theta = s\sigma'\tau\theta$, and hence $\sigma'\tau\theta$ unifies l and r. Since $\sigma'\tau$ is a substitution with domain $\{u_1, \ldots, u_m\}$, θ violates C. □

8.3. Implementing Disequation Constraints

We will discuss now how the constraint handling can be efficiently integrated into a model elimination proof search procedure. First, we consider the problem of generating constraints in normal form.

8.3.1. Efficient constraint generation

Unification is a basic ingredient of the normalization procedure mentioned above. In the successful implementations of model elimination, a destructive variant of the unification procedure specified in Table 2 is used. If slightly extended, this procedure can also be used for an efficient constraint generation. First, universal variables must be distinguished from non-universal ones. The best way to do this is to extend the internal data structure for variables with an additional cell where it is noted whether the variable is universal or not. The advantage of this approach is that the type of a variable may change during the proof process which nicely goes together with the feature of local variables mentioned in Section 5.4.1. Then, the mentioned unification operation must be modified in order to prevent the binding of a non-universal variable to a universal one. After these modifications, the generation and normalization of a constraint can be implemented efficiently by simply using the new unification procedure, as follows.

8.6. DEFINITION *(Constraint generation).* Given any two sequences l and r of terms that must not become equal by instantiation.

1. Destructively unify l and r and push the substituted variables onto the trail.
2. Collect the respective bindings of the non-universal variables only.
3. Finally undo the unification.

After these operations the term sequences l and r are in their original form, and the collected bindings represent the desired disequation constraint in normal form.

8.3.2. Efficient constraint propagation

During proof search with disequation constraints, every tableau is accompanied by a set of constraints. When an inference step is performed, it produces a substitution which is applied to the tableau. In order to achieve an optimal pruning of the search space, it should be checked after each inference step whether the computed substitution violates one of the constraints of the tableau. If so, the respective inference step can be retracted and we call this a *constraint failure*. If not, the substitution σ has to be propagated to the constraints, i.e., every constraint C has to be replaced by $C\sigma$ before the next inference step is being executed. As a matter of fact, if some of the new constraints can no longer be violated, they should be ignored for the further proof attempt. This is important for reducing the search effort, since normally, a wealth of constraints will be generated during proof search.

If the constraints are always kept in normal form, then the mentioned operations can be performed quite efficiently. Assume, for example, that a substitution $\sigma = \{x/a\}$ is applied to the current tableau. Then it is obvious that all constraints in which x does not occur on the left-hand side may be ignored. In case no constraint of the current tableau is violated by the substitution σ, a new constraint $C\sigma$ has to be created and afterwards normalized for every constraint C containing x on the left-hand side, which is still a considerable effort. In order to do this efficiently, new constraints should not be generated explicitly, but the old constraints should be reused and modified appropriately. For this purpose, it is more comfortable to keep the constraints in disjunctive form. Then, for any such constraint C, only the respective subconstraint $(x \neq t)\sigma$ needs to be normalized to, say C', and the former subconstraint $x \neq t$ in C can be replaced with the subconstraints of C'. This operation may also change the *actual length* of the former constraint. In summary, this results in the following procedure for constraint propagation.

8.7. DEFINITION *(Constraint propagation).* All constraints are assumed to be normalized and in disjunctive form. Suppose a substitution $\sigma = \{x_1/s_1, \ldots, x_n/s_n\}$ is performed during the tableau construction. Then, for every subconstraint $C_i = x_i/t_i$ (i.e., with x_i in the domain of σ) of every constraint C, successively compute the normal form C_i' of $s_i \neq t_i\sigma$ with length, say k, and perform the following operations:

1. If $C_i' = \text{true}$, ignore C for the rest of the proof attempt (it cannot be violated),
2. If $k = 0$, decrement the actual length of C by 1; if the actual length 0 is reached, perform backtracking (the constraint is violated),
3. Otherwise replace C_i with C_i' and modify the actual length of C by adding $k - 1$.

In order to guarantee efficiency, all modifications performed on the constraints
have to be stored intermediately and undone on backtracking.

8.3.3. Internal representation of constraints

Obviously, a prerequisite for the efficiency of the constraint handling is a suitable
internal representation of the constraints. When analyzing the described constraint
handling algorithms, such a representation has to meet the following requirements.

1. After the instantiation of any variable x, a quick access to all subconstraints of
   the form $x \neq t$ is needed.

2. If a subconstraint C_i of a constraint C is violated, it must be easy to check
   whether C is violated without considering the other subconstraints of C.

3. Whenever a subconstraint C_i of a constraint C normalizes to true, then it must
   be easy to deactivate C and all other subconstraints of C.

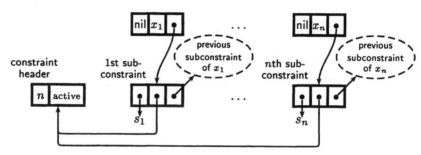

Figure 31: Internal representation of a constraint $x_1, \ldots, x_n \neq s_1, \ldots, s_n$.

This can be achieved by using a data structure as displayed in Figure 31. In
order to have immediate access from a variable x to all subconstraints of the form
$x \neq t$, it is reasonable to maintain a list of the subconstraints corresponding to each
variable. The best solution is to extend the data structure of a variable by a pointer
to the last element in its subconstraint list. From this subconstraint the previous
subconstraint of the variable x can be accessed, and so forth. (The aforementioned
tag which expresses whether a variable is universal or not is omitted in the figure.)

A constraint itself is separated into a *constraint header* and its subconstraints.
The header contains the actual length of the constraint and a tag whether the
constraint is already true or whether it can still be violated (active). From each
subconstraint there is a pointer to the respective constraint header. Now if a subconstraint is violated, then the length counter in the header is decremented by 1.
If, on the other hand, a subconstraint normalizes to true, then the tag in the header
is set to true. Because of the shared data structure, both modifications are immediately visible and can be used from all other subconstraints of the constraint. Please
note that an explicit access from a constraint header to its subconstraints is not
needed.

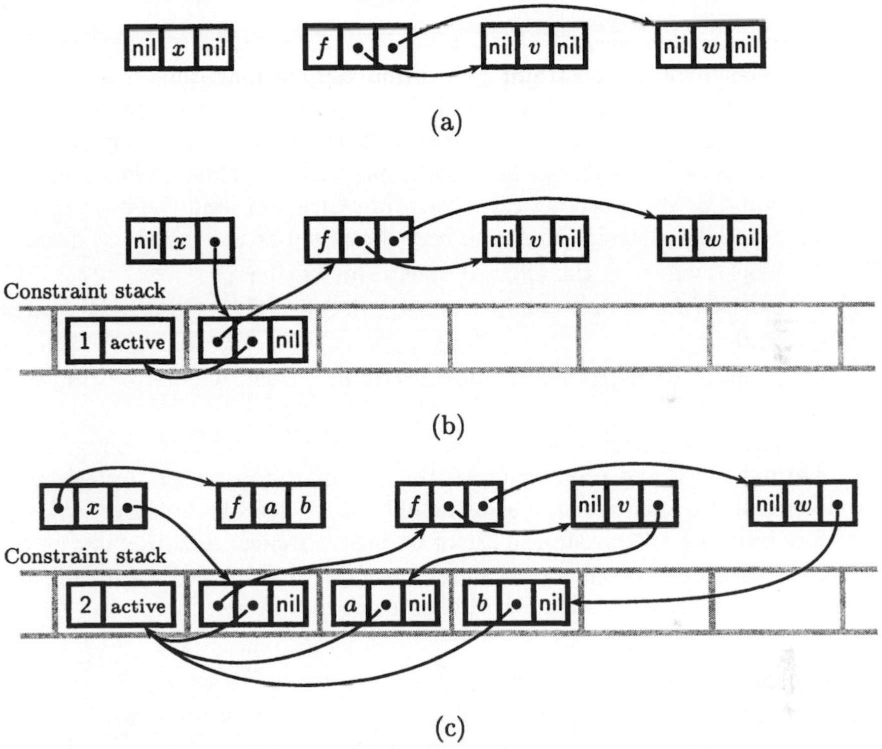

Figure 32: The constraint stack.

It is comfortable to reserve a special part of the memory for the representation of constraints, which we call the *constraint stack*. In order to understand the modifications of the constraint stack during the proof process for the case of a more complex normalization operation, consult Figure 32. Assume we are given a tableau with subgoals $P(x)$ and $\neg Q(x)$ and a predecessor literal $P(f(v,w))$. Assume that no constraints for the variables x, v and w exist (a). Now, a regularity constraint $x \neq f(v,w)$ may be generated, which requires that a constraint header and a subconstraint are pushed onto the constraint stack (b). Assume that afterwards an extension step is performed at the subgoal $\neg Q(x)$ with an entry literal $Q(f(a,b))$. The unifier $\sigma = \{x/f(a,b)\}$ has to be propagated to the constraints. This is done by pushing the two new subconstraints $v \neq a$ and $w \neq b$ onto the constraint stack, which were obtained after normalization. Furthermore, the subconstraint lists of v and w have to be extended. Finally, the counter in the constraint header has to be incremented by 1. Note that nothing has to be done about the old subconstraint $x \neq f(v,w)$. Since the variable x has been bound, the old subconstraint will simply be ignored by all subsequent constraint checks.

8.3.4. Constraint backtracking

The entire mechanism of constraint generation and propagation has to be embedded into the backtracking driven proof search procedure of model elimination. Accordingly, also all modifications performed on the constraint stack and in the subconstraint lists of the variables have to be properly undone when an inference step is retracted. For this purpose, after each inference step and the corresponding modifications in the constraint area, one has to remember the following data.

1. The old length values in the affected constraint headers,
2. the old values (active or true) in the second cells of the affected constraint headers, and
3. the old pointers to the previous subconstraints in the affected variables and subconstraints.

   This is exactly the information that has to be stored for backtracking. A comfortable method for doing this would be the use of a *constraint trail* similar to the variable trail, except that here also the old values need to be stored while the variable trail only has to contain the list of bound variables. Additionally, in order to permit the reuse of the constraint stack, one has to remember the top of the constraint stack before each sequence of constraint modifications.

8.3.5. Disequation constraints in Prolog

Some Prolog implementations offer the possibility of formulating disequation constraints. As an example, we consider the Prolog system Eclipse [Wallace and Veron 1993]. Here, using the infix predicate ˜= one can formulate syntactic disequation constraints. This permits that constraints resulting from structural tableau conditions can be easily implemented. We describe the method for regularity constraints on the first contrapositive of the transitivity clause

```
p_p(X,Z, P,N) :- N1 = [ p(X,Z) | N ], p_p(X,Y, P,N1), p_p(Y,Z, P,N1).
```

taken from the Prolog example in Section 7.4. We show how regularity can be integrated by modifying the clause as follows.

```
p_p(X,Z, P,N) :- N1 = [ p(X,Z) | N ],
                 not_member(p(X,Z), P),
                 not_member(p(X,Y), N1),
                 not_member(p(Y,Z), N1),
                 p_p(X,Y, P,N1), p_p(Y,Z, P,N1).
```

where not_member is defined as:

```
not_member(_,[ ]).
not_member(E,[F|R]) :- E ˜= F, not_member(E,R).
```

With similar methods an easy integration of tautology and subsumption constraints can be achieved. However, when it comes to the integration of more sophisticated constraints such as the ones considered next, it turns out that an efficient Prolog implementation is very difficult to obtain.

8.4. Constraints for Global Pruning Methods

8.4.1. Improving the matings pruning with constraints

In Section 4.1, a method was described which can guarantee that certain permutations of matings are not generated more than once. The idea was to impose an ordering on the literals in the input formula, which is inherited to the tableau nodes. Now, a reduction step from a subgoal N to an ancestor node N' may be avoided if the entry node N'' immediately below N' is smaller than N in the ordering. In fact, this method can also be implemented and even improved by using disequation constraints, as follows. The prohibition to perform a reduction step on N using N' may be reexpressed as a disequation constraint $l \neq r$ where l and r are the argument sequences of the literals at N and N', respectively. Such a constraint does prune not only the respective reduction step, but all tableaux in which the literals at N and N'' become equal by instantiation. In [Letz 1998b] it is proven that this extension of the matings pruning preserves completeness, the main reason being that the matings pruning is compatible with regularity.

8.4.2. Failure caching using constraints

The failure caching mechanism described in Section 4.3 can also be implemented using disequation constraints. Briefly, the method requires that when a subgoal N is solved with a solution substitution σ on the variables of the respective path and the remaining subgoals cannot be solved with this substitution, then σ is turned into a failure substitution as defined in Section 4.3 and, for any alternative solution substitution τ for N, σ must not be more general than τ.

8.8. Definition (*Constraint of a failure substitution*). Let $\sigma = \{x_1/t_1, \ldots, x_n/t_n\}$ be a failure substitution generated at a subgoal N and V the set of variables on the path with leaf N in the last tableau in which the subgoal N was selected for an inference step. The *constraint of the failure substitution* σ is the normal form of the constraint $\forall u_1 \cdots \forall u_m \ x_1, \ldots, x_n \neq t_1, \ldots, t_n$ where $u_1, \ldots, u_m$ are the variables occurring in terms of σ that are not in V.

It is straightforward to recognize that a failure substitution σ of a tableau node N is more general than a solution substitution τ of N if and only if the constraint of the failure substitution σ is violated by τ. Consequently, the constraint handling mechanism can be used to implement failure caching. In order to adequately implement failure caching by using constraints, the use of universal variables is also necessary, such as for the case of tableau clause subsumption (Section 8.1.3). This can be seen by considering, for example, a subgoal N with failure substitution $\sigma = \{x/f(z, z)\}$

where z is a variable not occurring in the set V. The constraint of σ is $\forall z\; x \neq f(z, z)$. When N can be solved with a solution substitution $\tau = \{x/f(a, a)\}$, then σ is more general than τ and, in fact, the constraint $\forall z\; x \neq f(z, z)$ is violated by τ. Obviously, it is impossible to capture such a case without universal variables.

8.4.3. Centralized management of constraints

It is apparent that structural constraints resulting from different sources, tautology, regularity, subsumption, or matings, need not be distinguished in the tableau construction. Furthermore, in general, the constraints need not even be tied to the respective tableau clauses, but the constraint information can be kept separate in a special constraint storage space. This also fits in with the method of forgetting closed parts of a tableau and working with subgoal trees instead, because all relevant structure information of the solved part of the tableau is contained in the constraints. However, when structural constraints are used in combination with constraints resulting from failure substitutions, constraints have to be deactivated in certain states of the proof process, as shown in Section 4.3. In this case, it is necessary to take the tableau positions into account at which the respective constraints were generated.

9. Experimental Results

In the previous sections we introduced numerous refinements of model elimination. But, as we are also discussing implementation techniques in this text, knowing about the soundness and completeness of these refinements is not sufficient, it is also of vital importance to know how all these refinements behave when implemented and applied in practice. This section presents a number of experimental results to give an idea of the actual performance of model elimination refinements.

9.1. Test Problem Set and Experimental Environment

All our experiments were conducted in a uniform manner on a subset of the TPTP problem library [Sutcliffe et al. 1994] (version 2.2.1). Starting with the entire set of 4004 TPTP problems, we eliminated all non-clausal problems, all satisfiable problems and all unit equality and pure equality problems. Of the remaining problem set, we selected those problems which at least one of the model elimination search strategies in use with our current e-SETHEO system could solve within 300 seconds. This selection process left us with a test set of 1057 problems. One experiment has been restricted to the test problems containing equality predicates, 431 of which were in our test set.

All experiments were conducted on a Sun Ultra-60 workstation. Each strategy was run on each problem with a time resource of 300 seconds.

Finally, it should be noted that the success of all possible enhancements of model elimination procedures depends on a diligent implementation of the same. The additional effort induced by a bad implementation can more than nullify the gains of a potentially successful technique.

We have tested the most important refinements of model elimination, the results of these tests can be found in the following sections.

9.2. Regularity

The concept of regularity, as introduced in Section 3.1, is one of the most successful single improvement techniques, as can readily be seen in Figure 33. We compared two strategies using simple iterative deepening without further refinements, one with regularity constraints and one without.

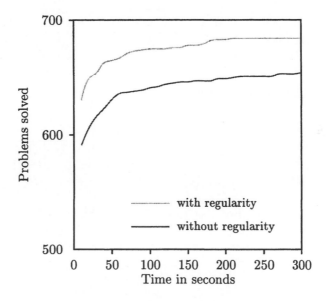

Figure 33: Performance of the depth bound without and with regularity.

9.3. Completeness Bounds

As detailed in Section 2.5, different completeness bounds may be used by the model elimination procedure. We have compared the depth bound, the weighted depth bound and the inference bound. The results of our experiments, however, were ambiguous. In Figure 34, we can see the results on the entire test set.

It is apparent from that figure that the depth bound is the most successful strategy if no knowledge about the problem is available. Yet, distinguishing problems according to some very basic criteria can yield a different picture.

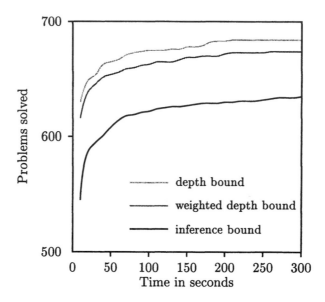

Figure 34: Entire problem set: performance of various completeness bounds with regularity.

Figure 35 depicts the test results for Horn problems only. Here, the weighted depth bound is more successful than the depth bound. A similar result is obtained when restricting the experiments to problems containing the equality predicate, as shown in Figure 36, where we omitted the generally least successful inference bound.

9.4. Relevance Information

As explained in Section 3.5, the use of relevance information can significantly reduce the search space by limiting the number of possible start clauses. The TPTP library [Sutcliffe et al. 1994] provides such relevance information by introducing input clause types. When relevance information is used, only conjecture type clauses are selected as start clauses, whereas in the standard case all negative clauses are potential start clauses.

The result of a comparison between proving with and without relevance information can be seen in Figure 37. As expected, better results are obtained with the use of relevance information.

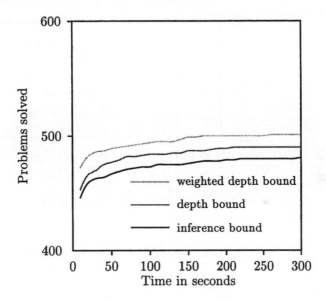

Figure 35: Horn problems: performance of various completeness bounds with regularity.

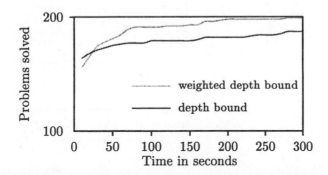

Figure 36: Equality problems: performance of various depth bounds with regularity.

9.5. Failure Caching

The technique of failure caching as described in Section 4.3 has been implemented in SETHEO with the use of constraints, as described in Section 8.4.2. As becomes apparent from Figure 38, the use of this technique has a considerable influence on the test results.

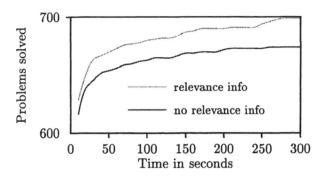

Figure 37: The effect of the use of relevance information (with weighted depth bound and regularity).

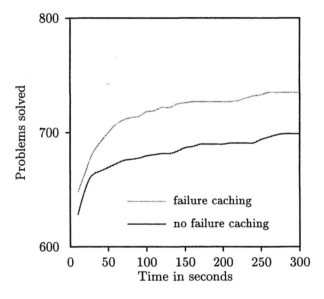

Figure 38: The effect of failure caching (with weighted depth bound and regularity).

9.6. Folding Up

Introduced in Section 5.2, the folding up technique has also been implemented as a model elimination refinement in SETHEO and has turned out to be very successful. Figure 39 shows three curves: The lowest curve indicates the proofs found with the use of regularity only, while the middle curve gives the number of proofs using regularity and folding up. Finally, the curve with the highest number of proofs shows the result of combining folding up with the full use of constraints (enabling both regularity and failure caching).

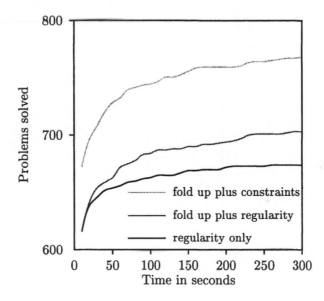

Figure 39: Enhancements through the use of the folding up technique and failure caching (with weighted depth bound).

9.7. Dynamic Subgoal Reordering

The concept of subgoal reordering was introduced in Section 2.6.1. As can be seen in Figure 40, even a local (this means only within the selected clause) subgoal selection according to the fewest solution principle can have a positive effect.

9.8. Summary

The experimental results presented in this section show that the refinements described in this chapter are applicable in automated theorem proving and that they may also be combined in several ways to accumulate the gains of the individual refinements. Among all these refinements, regularity and failure caching stand out in particular as being the most important and successful ones.

10. Outlook

The model elimination or connection tableau approach is an efficient and successful paradigm in automated deduction. There are, however, a number of deficiencies, which have to be addressed in the future. One of the fundamental weaknesses of connection tableaux is the handling of equality. The naïve approach to simply add the congruence axioms of equality, suffers from the weakness that equality specific

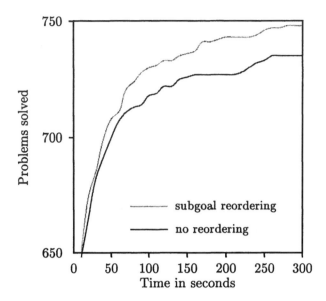

Figure 40: Performance of the weighted depth bound with constraints, with and without dynamic subgoal reordering.

redundancy elimination techniques are ignored. The most successful paradigm for treating equality in saturation-based theorem proving, *ordered paramodulation*, is not compatible with connection tableaux. There have been attempts to integrate *lazy paramodulation*, a variant of paramodulation without orderings which is compatible with model elimination. This method is typically implemented by means of a transformation (like Brand's modification method [Brand 1975]), which eliminates the equality axioms and compiles certain equality inferences into the formula. A certain search space pruning might be obtained by using limited ordering conditions [Bachmair, Ganzinger and Voronkov 1998], preferably implemented as ordering constraints. This would fit well with the constraint technology applicable in connection tableaux.

Another, more general weakness of the search procedure is that it typically performs poorly on formulae with relatively long proofs. On the one hand, this has directly to do with the methodology of iterative-deepening search. On the other hand, when proofs are becoming longer, the goal-orientedness loses its reductive power. To prove difficult formulae in one big leap by reasoning backwards from the conjecture is very difficult. An interesting perspective here is the use of *lemmata*, intermediate results typically deduced in a forward manner from the axioms. Some progress has been made in this direction by the development of powerful filtering techniques.

A further interesting line of research could be the use of pruning methods based on semantic information. One could, for example, use small models of the axioms in order to detect the unsolvability of certain subgoals. Finally, the consideration of a confluent and possibly even nondestructive integration of connection conditions into the tableau framework definitely deserves attention.

Acknowledgments

We would like to thank Peter Baumgartner and Uwe Petermann for their valuable comments on an earlier version of this chapter. Furthermore we want to thank Herbert Stenz for his exceptionally thorough proofreading and Rajeev Goré for his linguistic advice. This work was partially funded by the *Deutsche Forschungsgemeinschaft (DFG)* as part of the *Schwerpunktprogramm Deduktion* and the *Sonderforschungsbereich (SFB) 342*.

Bibliography

AHO A. V., SETHI R. AND ULLMAN J. D. [1986], *Compilers – Principles, Techniques, and Tools*, Addison-Wesley, Reading, MA.

AHO A. V. AND ULLMAN J. D. [1977], *Principles of Compiler Design*, Addison-Wesley, Reading, MA. See also the widely expanded subsequent book [Aho, Sethi and Ullman 1986].

ANDREWS P. B. [1981], 'Theorem proving through general matings', *Journal of the ACM* **28**, 193–214.

ASTRACHAN O. L. AND LOVELAND D. W. [1991], METEORs: High performance theorem provers using model elimination, Technical Report DUKE–TR–1991–08, Department of Computer Science, Duke University.

ASTRACHAN O. AND STICKEL M. [1992], Caching and Lemmaizing in Model Elimination Theorem Provers, *in* D. Kapur, ed., 'Proceedings, 11th International Conference on Automated Deduction (CADE-11), Saratoga Springs, NY, USA', Vol. 607 of *LNAI*, Springer, Berlin, pp. 224 – 238.

BAAZ M. AND LEITSCH A. [1992], 'Complexity of resolution proofs and function introduction', *Annals of Pure and Applied Logic* **57**(3), 181–215.

BACHMAIR L. AND GANZINGER H. [2001], Resolution theorem proving, *in* A. Robinson and A. Voronkov, eds, 'Handbook of Automated Reasoning', Vol. I, Elsevier Science, chapter 2, pp. 19–99.

BACHMAIR L., GANZINGER H. AND VORONKOV A. [1998], Elimination of Equality via Transformation with Ordering Constraints, *in* C. Kirchner and H. Kirchner, eds, 'Proceedings, 15th International Conference on Automated Deduction (CADE-15), Lindau, Germany', Vol. 1421 of *LNAI*, Springer, Berlin, pp. 175–190.

BAUMGARTNER P. [1998], Hyper Tableau — The Next Generation, *in* H. de Swart, ed., 'Proceedings of the International Conference on Automated Reasoning with Analytic Tableaux and Related Methods (TABLEAUX-98), Oisterwijk, The Netherlands', Vol. 1397 of *LNAI*, pp. 60–76.

BAUMGARTNER P. AND BRÜNING S. [1997], 'A Disjunctive Positive Refinement of Model Elimination and its Application to Subsumption Deletion', *Journal of Automated Reasoning* **19**(2), 205–262.

BAUMGARTNER P., EISINGER N. AND FURBACH U. [1999], A Confluent Connection Calculus, *in* H. Ganzinger, ed., 'Proceedings of the 16th International Conference on Automated Deduction (CADE-16)', Vol. 1632 of *LNAI*, Springer, Berlin, pp. 329–343.

BAUMGARTNER P. AND FURBACH U. [1994], PROTEIN: A PROver with a Theory Extension INterface, *in* A. Bundy, ed., 'Proceedings of the 12th International Conference on Automated Deduction (CADE-12)', Vol. 814 of *LNAI*, Springer, Berlin, pp. 769–773.

BECKERT B. [1998], Integrating and Unifying Methods of Tableau-based Theorem Proving, PhD thesis, University of Karlsruhe, Department of Computer Science.

BECKERT B. AND HÄHNLE R. [1992], An Improved Method for Adding Equality to Free Variable Semantic Tableaux, *in* D. Kapur, ed., 'Proceedings, 11th International Conference on Automated Deduction (CADE-11), Saratoga Springs, NY, USA', LNCS 607, Springer, Berlin, pp. 507–521.

BECKERT B. AND HÄHNLE R. [1998], Analytic Tableaux, *in* W. Bibel and P. H. Schmitt, eds, 'Automated Deduction — A Basis for Applications', Vol. I: Foundations, Kluwer, Dordrecht, pp. 11–41.

BENKER H., BEACCO J. M., BESCOS S., DOROCHEVSKY M., JEFFRÉ T., PÖHLMANN A., NOYÉ J., POTERIE B., SEXTON A., SYRE J. C., THIBAULT O. AND WATZLAWIK G. [1989], KCM: A Knowledge Crunching Machine, *in* M. Yoeli and G. Silberman, eds, 'Proceedings of the 16th Annual International Symposium on Computer Architecture, Jerusalem, Israel', IEEE Computer Society Press, New York, pp. 186–194.

BIBEL W. [1987], *Automated Theorem Proving*, second revised edn, Vieweg, Braunschweig.

BIBEL W., BRUENING S., EGLY U. AND RATH T. [1994], KoMeT, *in* 'Proceedings, 12th International Conference on Automated Deduction (CADE-12), Nancy, France', Vol. 814 of *LNAI*, Springer, Berlin, pp. 783–787.

BILLON J.-P. [1996], The disconnection method: a confluent integration of unification in the analytic framework, *in* P. Migliolo, U. Moscato, D. Mundici and M. Ornaghi, eds, 'Proceedings of the 5th International Workshop on Theorem Proving with Analytic Tableaux and Related Methods (TABLEAUX)', Vol. 1071 of *LNAI*, Springer, Berlin, pp. 110–126.

BOY DE LA TOUR T. [1990], Minimizing the Number of Clauses by Renaming, *in* M. E. Stickel, ed., '10th International Conference on Automated Deduction (CADE-10), Kaiserslautern, Germany', LNCS, Springer, Berlin, pp. 558–572.

BRAND D. [1975], 'Proving Theorems with the Modification Method', *SIAM Journal on Computing* 4(4), 412–430.

COMON H. AND LESCANNE P. [1989], 'Equational Problems and Disunification', *Journal of Symbolic Computation* 7(3–4), 371–425.

CORBIN J. AND BIDOIT M. [1983], A Rehabilitation of Robinson's Unification Algorithm, *in* 'Information Processing', North Holland, Amsterdam, pp. 909–914.

EDER E. [1984], An Implementation of a Theorem Prover Based on the Connection Method, *in* W. Bibel and B. Petkoff, eds, 'Proceedings of the International Conference on Artificial Intelligence: Methodology, Systems and Applications (AIMSA), Varna, Bulgaria', North Holland, Amsterdam, pp. 121–128.

FITTING M. C. [1990], *First-Order Logic and Automated Theorem Proving*, Springer, Berlin.

FITTING M. C. [1996], *First-Order Logic and Automated Theorem Proving*, second revised edn, Springer, Berlin.

GENTZEN G. [1935], 'Untersuchungen über das logische Schließen', *Mathematische Zeitschrift* **39**, 176–210, 405–431. English translation in M. E. Szabo, editor, *The Collected Papers of Gerhard Gentzen*, pages 68–131. North Holland, Amsterdam, 1969.

GOLLER C., LETZ R., MAYR K. AND SCHUMANN J. M. P. [1994], SETHEO V3.2: Recent developments, *in* A. Bundy, ed., 'Proceedings of the 12th International Conference on Automated Deduction (CADE-12)', Vol. 814 of *LNAI*, Springer, Berlin, pp. 778–782.

HÄHNLE R. [2001], Tableaux and related methods, *in* A. Robinson and A. Voronkov, eds, 'Handbook of Automated Reasoning', Vol. I, Elsevier Science, chapter 3, pp. 100–178.

HARRISON J. [1996], Optimizing proof search in model elimination, *in* M. A. McRobbie and J. K. Slaney, eds, 'Proceedings of the 13th International Conference on Automated Deduction (CADE-13)', Vol. 1104 of *LNAI*, Springer, Berlin, pp. 313–327.

KLINGENBECK S. AND HÄHNLE R. [1994], Semantic Tableaux with Ordering Restrictions, *in* A. Bundy, ed., 'Proceedings, 12th International Conference on Automated Deduction (CADE-12), Nancy, France', LNCS 814, Springer, Berlin, pp. 708–722.

KORF R. E. [1985], Iterative-Deepening-A: An Optimal Admissible Tree Search, *in* A. Joshi, ed., 'Proceedings of the 9th International Joint Conference on Artificial Intelligence', Morgan Kaufmann, Los Angeles, CA, pp. 1034–1036.

KOWALSKI R. A. AND KUEHNER D. [1970], Linear resolution with selection function, Technical report, Metamathematics Unit, Edinburgh University, Edinburgh, Scotland.

KOWALSKI R. AND KUEHNER D. [1971], 'Linear Resolution with Selection Function', *Artificial Intelligence* **2**, 227–260.

LETZ R. [1993], First-order calculi and proof procedures for automated deduction, PhD thesis, Technische Hochschule Darmstadt, Darmstadt, Germany.

LETZ R. [1998*a*], Clausal Tableaux, *in* W. Bibel and P. H. Schmitt, eds, 'Automated Deduction — A Basis for Applications', Vol. I: Foundations, Kluwer, Dordrecht, pp. 43–72.

LETZ R. [1998*b*], Using Matings for Pruning Connection Tableaux, *in* C. Kirchner and H. Kirchner, eds, 'Proceedings, 15th International Conference on Automated Deduction (CADE-15), Lindau, Germany', Vol. 1421 of *LNAI*, Springer, Berlin, pp. 381–396.

LETZ R. [1999], First-Order Tableaux Methods, *in* M. D'Agostino, D. Gabbay, R. Hähnle and J. Posegga, eds, 'Handbook of Tableau Methods', Kluwer, Dordrecht, pp. 125–196.

LETZ R., MAYR K. AND GOLLER C. [1994], 'Controlled Integration of the Cut Rule into Connection Tableau Calculi', *Journal of Automated Reasoning* **13**(3), 297–338.

LETZ R., SCHUMANN J. AND BAYERL S. [1989], SETHEO: A SEquentiell THEOrem Prover for first order logic, Technical Report FKI-97-89, Technische Universität München, Munich, Germany.

LETZ R., SCHUMANN J., BAYERL S. AND BIBEL W. [1992], 'SETHEO: A High-Performance Theorem Prover', *Journal of Automated Reasoning* **8**(2), 183–212.

LOVELAND D. W. [1968], 'Mechanical Theorem Proving by Model Elimination', *Journal of the ACM* **15**(2), 236–251. Reprinted in: [Siekmann and Wrightson 1983].

LOVELAND D. W. [1969], 'A Simplified Format for the Model Elimination Theorem-Proving Procedure', *Journal of the ACM* **16**(3), 349–363.

LOVELAND D. W. [1972], 'A Unifying View of Some Linear Herbrand Procedures', *Journal of the ACM* **19**(2), 366–384.

LOVELAND D. W. [1978], *Automated theorem proving: A logical basis*, North Holland, Amsterdam.

MAYR K. [1993], Refinements and Extensions of Model Elimination, *in* A. Voronkov, ed., 'Proceedings of the 4th International Conference on Logic Programming and Automated Reasoning (LPAR'93), St. Petersburg, Russia', Vol. 698 of *LNAI*, Springer, Berlin, pp. 217–228.

MOSER M., IBENS O., LETZ R., STEINBACH J., GOLLER C., SCHUMANN J. AND MAYR K. [1997], 'SETHEO and E-SETHEO—The CADE-13 Systems', *Journal of Automated Reasoning* **18**(2), 237–246.

NEITZ W. [1995], Untersuchungen zum selektiven Backtracking in zielorientierten Kalkülen des automatischen Theorembeweisens, PhD thesis, University of Leipzig.

NEUGEBAUER G. [1995], ProCom/CaPrI *and the Shell* ProTop. *User's Guide*, FB IMN, HTWK Leipzig. ftp://www.koralle.imn.htwk-leipzig.de/pub/ProCom/procom.html.

NEUGEBAUER G. AND PETERMANN U. [1995], Specifications of Inference Rules and their Automatic Translation, *in* P. Baumgartner, R. Hähnle and J. Posegga, eds, 'Proceedings of the 4th International Workshop on Theorem Proving with Analytic Tableaux and Related Methods (TABLEAUX)', Vol. 918 of *LNAI*, Springer, Berlin, pp. 185–200.

PELLETIER F. J. AND RUDNICKI P. [1986], 'Non-obviousness', *AAR Newsletter* (6), 4–5.

PLAISTED D. A. [1984], The Occur-check Problem in Prolog, *in* '1984 International Symposium on Logic Programming', IEEE Computer Society Press, New York.

PLAISTED D. A. AND GREENBAUM S. [1986], 'A Structure Preserving Clause Form Translation', *Journal of Symbolic Computation* **2**(3), 293–304.

Prawitz D. [1960], 'An improved proof procedure', *Theoria* **26**, 102–139. Reprinted in [Siekmann and Wrightson 1983].

Reeves S. V. [1987], 'Adding Equality to Semantic Tableaux', *Journal of Automated Reasoning* **3**, 225–246.

Schumann J. [1991], Efficient Theorem Provers based on an Abstract Machine, PhD thesis, Technische Universität München.

Schumann J. and Letz R. [1990], PARTHEO: A High-Performance Parallel Theorem Prover, *in* M. E. Stickel, ed., 'Proceedings, 10th International Conference on Automated Deduction (CADE-10), Saratoga Springs, NY, USA', LNAI 449, Springer, Berlin, pp. 40–56.

Shostak R. E. [1976], 'Refutation Graphs', *Artificial Intelligence* **7**, 51–64.

Siekmann, J. and Wrightson, G., eds [1983], *Automation of Reasoning*, Springer, Berlin. Two volumes.

Smullyan R. [1968], *First-Order Logic*, Springer, Berlin.

Stickel M. E. [1984], A Prolog Technology Theorem Prover, *in* '1984 International Symposium on Logic Programming', IEEE Computer Society Press, New York.

Stickel M. E. [1988], A Prolog Technology Theorem Prover, *in* E. Lusk and R. Overbeek, eds, '9th International Conference on Automated Deduction (CADE-9), Argonne, Ill', LNCS, Springer, Berlin, pp. 752–753.

Stickel M. E. [1992], 'A Prolog technology theorem prover: a new exposition and implementation in Prolog', *Theoretical Computer Science* **104**, 109–128.

Sutcliffe G. and Suttner C. B. [1998], The CADE-14 ATP System Competition, Technical Report JCU-CS-98/01, Department of Computer Science, James Cook University.
URL: *http://www.cs.jcu.edu.au/ftp/pub/techreports/98-01.ps.gz*

Sutcliffe G., Suttner C. and Yemenis T. [1994], The TPTP problem library, *in* A. Bundy, ed., 'Proceedings, 12th International Conference on Automated Deduction (CADE-12), Nancy, France', LNCS 814, Springer, Berlin, pp. 708–722. Current version available on the *World Wide Web* at the URL http://www.cs.jcu.edu.au/ftp/users/GSutcliffe/TPTP.HTML.

Taki K., Yokota M., Yamamoto A., Nishikawa H., Uchida S., Nakashima H. and Mitsuishi A. [1984], Hardware Design and Implementation of the Personal Sequential Inference Machine (PSI), *in* 'Proceedings of the International Conference on Fifth Generation Computer Systems', ICOT, Tokyo, Japan, pp. 398–409.

Tseitin G. [1970], 'On the Complexity of Proofs in Propositional Logics', *Seminars in Mathematics* **8**.

Vlahavas I. and Halatsis C. [1987], A New Abstract Prolog Instruction Set, *in* 'Expert systems and their applications (Proceedings)', Avignon, pp. 1025–1050.

Wallace M. and Veron A. [1993], Two problems – two solutions: One system – ECLiPSe, *in* 'Proceedings IEE Colloquium on Advanced Software Technologies for Scheduling', London.

Warren D. H. D. [1983], An Abstract PROLOG Instruction Set, Technical Report 309, Artificial Intelligence Center, Computer Science and Technology Division, SRI International, Menlo Park, CA.

Weidenbach C. [2001], Combining superposition, sorts and splitting, *in* A. Robinson and A. Voronkov, eds, 'Handbook of Automated Reasoning', Vol. II, Elsevier Science, chapter 27, pp. 1965–2013.

Index

Concept index